The European Union and H

The European Union and Human Rights

Analysis, Cases, and Materials

JAN WOUTERS AND MICHAL OVÁDEK

with the editorial assistance of
KATRIEN MARTENS

OXFORD

UNIVERSITY PRESS

OXFORD
UNIVERSITY PRESS

Great Clarendon Street, Oxford, OX2 6DP,
United Kingdom

Oxford University Press is a department of the University of Oxford.
It furthers the University's objective of excellence in research, scholarship,
and education by publishing worldwide. Oxford is a registered trade mark of
Oxford University Press in the UK and in certain other countries

First Edition published in 2021

Impression: 1

Published in the United States of America by Oxford University Press
198 Madison Avenue, New York, NY 10016, United States of America

British Library Cataloguing in Publication Data

Data available

Library of Congress Control Number: 2020948002

ISBN 978-0-19-881417-7 (hbk.)
ISBN 978-0-19-881418-4 (pbk.)

DOI: 10.1093/oso/9780198814177.001.0001

Printed in Great Britain by
Bell & Bain Ltd., Glasgow

Preface

The acts of the European Union (EU) impact profoundly for the wellbeing of people within and beyond the jurisdiction of its Member States. As such, it is an actor that should assiduously integrate in its work the highest levels of human rights protection. This responsibility has, over time, been acknowledged as a matter of law, policy and practice. Today, the EU, while it is not *per se* a human rights entity, has put rights at its constitutional heart. This self-identity is evidenced, for instance by the role played by the EU Charter of Fundamental Rights.

Inevitably, the growth in the EU's acknowledgement of the role of human and fundamental rights has been episodic and diffuse; it has evolved with institutional developments within the Union; and it has, to at least some degree, been overlooked by the specialist literature. As a result, we have lacked authoritative overviews of the entire field, leaving scholars and policy-makers the poorer.

This is the context in which I warmly welcome the publication of *The European Union and Human Rights: Analysis, Cases and Materials*. This is a masterful text that takes on the entire field and delivers a broad, clear overview of the terrain. It does so with a notable degree of reflection and analysis while also presenting foundational texts and academic writings.

The volume is often innovative. This is very much the case with its treatment of the EU's human and fundamental rights systems. As well as addressing the role of such obvious actors as the EU institutions (including the Fundamental Rights Agency), it locates the actual and potential role of the EU Ombudsman and of national human rights institutions. The treatment of "concepts and languages of human rights in the EU" is no less compelling, and all the more commendable for the dearth of cases and materials from which to draw.

Inevitably, the authors had to make choices and not every aspect of the EU's human and fundamental rights practice is reflected. Also, being encyclopaedic in nature, the text deals rather lightly with some issues (though not all – the treatment of migration is an example of a highly detailed examination). This is not a defect – rather it invites and encourages further specialist reflection and research.

I congratulate Jan Wouters and Michal Ovádek for this fine work and I commend it to the attention of EU scholars and practitioners across the disciplines.

Michael O'Flaherty
Director, EU Fundamental Rights Agency

Contents

Table of Cases

COURT OF JUSTICE OF THE EUROPEAN UNION

EUROPEAN COURT OF HUMAN RIGHTS

HUMAN RIGHTS COMMITTEE

INTERNATIONAL COURT OF JUSTICE

NATIONAL JURISDICTIONS

Germany

United States

Table of Legislation

EUROPEAN UNION TREATIES

EUROPEAN UNION
SECONDARY LEGISLATION

Regulations

Decisions

List of Abbreviations

ABER	Agricultures block exemption Regulation
ACP	African, Caribbean, and Pacific
AFET	Foreign Affairs Committee
AFSJ	Area of Freedom, Security and Justice
AG	Advocate General
APA	advance pricing arrangement
AP	action plan
AU	African Union
CAT	Convention against Torture
CBCR	country by country reporting
CDDH	Steering Committee for Human Rights of the Council of Europe
CEAS	Common European Asylum System
CEE	Central and Eastern Europe
CEPOL	European Police College
CETA	Comprehensive Economic and Trade Agreement
CFI	Court of First Instance
CfP	Call for Proposal
CFSP	Common Foreign and Security Policy
CIL	Customary international law
CITES	Convention on International Trade in Endangered Species of Wild Fauna and Flora
CJEU	Court of Justice of the European Union
CODEV	Working Party on Development Cooperation
COHOM	Council Working Party on Human Rights
CoR	Committee of Regions
COREU	EU communications network
COREPER	Committee of Permanent Representatives
CSDP	Common Security and Defence Policy
CSO	Civil society organization
CVM	cooperation and verification mechanism
DAC	Development Assistance Committee
DAG	Domestic Advisory Group
DCI	Development Cooperation Instrument
DCTFA	Deep and Comprehensive Free Trade Area
DEVCO	International Cooperation and Development
DEVE	Committee on Development
DG	Directorate-General
DROI	Subcommittee on Human Rights
EaP	Eastern Partnership
EASO	European Asylum Support Office
EAW	European arrest warrant
EBA	Everything But Arms

ECB	European Central Bank
ECHR	European Convention on Human Rights
ECJ	European Court of Justice
ECN	European Competition Network
ECOSOC	UN Committee on Economic, Social, and Cultural Rights
ECtHR	European Court of Human Rights
EDA	European Defence Agency
EDF	European Development Fund
EDF	European Disability Forum
EDPS	European Data Protection Supervisor
EEA	European Economic Area
EEAS	European Union External Action Service
EEC	European Economic Community
EFSD	European Fund for Sustainable Development
EIDHR	European Instrument for Democracy and Human Rights
EIGE	European Institute for Gender Equality
EIRD	Euro interest rates derivatives
EITI	Extractive Industries Transparency Initiative
ELM	External Lending Mandate
EMCDDA	European Monitoring Centre for Drugs and Drug Addiction
ENI	European Neighbourhood Instrument
ENP	European Neighbourhood Policy
ENNHRI	European Network of National Human Rights Institutions
EOM	election observation mission
EP	European Parliament
EPA	Economic Partnership Agreement
EPC	European Political Community
EPC	European Political Cooperation
EPSR	European Pillar of Social Rights
ESDP	European Security and Defence Policy
ESM	European Stability Mechanism
EU	European Union
eu-LISA	European Agency for the Operational Management of Large-Scale IT Systems in the Area of Freedom, Security and Justice
EUMC	EU Military Committee
EUMC	European Monitoring Centre on Racism and Xenophobia
EUMR	EU Merger Regulation
Eurojust	European Union's Judicial Cooperation Unit
Europol	European Police Office
EUSFTA	EU–Singapore FTA
EUSR	EU Special Representative
FAO	Food and Agricultural Organization
FCC	Federal Constitutional Court of Germany
FDI	foreign direct investment
FEMM	*Committee* on Women's Rights and Gender Equality
FIBER	Fisheries block exemption Regulation
FLEGT	Forest Law Enforcement, Governance and Trade
FRA	Fundamental Rights Agency

FREMP	Working Party on Fundamental Rights, Citizens' Rights, and Free Movement of Persons
Frontex	European Border and Coast Guard Agency
FTA	free trade agreement
FYROM	former Yugoslav Republic of Macedonia
GAMM	Global Approach to Migration and Mobility
GANHRI	Global Alliance of National Human Rights Institutions
GATT	General Agreement on Tariffs and Trade
GBER	General block exemption Regulation
GDPR	General Data Protection Regulation
GFEA	Guarantee Fund for External Actions
GGDC	Good Governance and Development Contracts
GREVIO	Group of experts on action against violence against women and domestic violence
GSP	Generalised Scheme of Preferences
HR	High Representative
HRBA	human rights-based approach
HRC	Human Rights Council
HRD	human rights defender
IA	impact assessment
ICC	International Criminal Court
ICCPR	International Covenant on Civil and Political Rights
ICESCR	International Covenant on Economic, Social and Cultural Rights
ICJ	International Court of Justice
IcSP	Instrument contributing to Stability and Peace
IGC	intergovernmental conference
IGO	intergovernmental organization
IIA	Integrated Impact Assessment
ILO	International Labour Organization
INSC	Instrument for Nuclear Safety Cooperation
IPA	Instrument for Pre-accession Assistance
JHA	Justice and Home Affairs
JOs	joint operations
KPCS	Kimberly Process Certification Scheme
LDCs	Least Developed Countries
LIBE	Committee on Civil Liberties, Justice and Home Affairs
LPP	legal professional privilege
LRA	local and regional authority
MAF	Multi-annual Framework
MEP	Member of the European Parliament
MFA	Macro-Financial Assistance
MFF	Multiannual Financial Framework
MFN	most favoured nation
MoU	memorandum of understanding
NATO	North Atlantic Treaty Organization
NCA	national competition authority
NDAP	national data protection authority

NDICI	Neighbourhood, Development and International Cooperation Instrument
NEB	national equality body
NGEU	Next Generation EU
NGO	non-governmental organization
NHRI	national human rights institution
NPE	normative power Europe
ODA	Official Development Assistance
ODIHR	Office for Democratic Institutions and Human Rights
OECD	Organisation for Economic Co-operation and Development
OSCE	Organization for Security and Co-operation in Europe
PESCO	permanent structured cooperation
PETI	Committee on Petitions
PI	Partnership Instrument
RBA	Rights-based Approach
REIO	regional economic integration organization
RIO	regional integration organization
RUF	Front uni révolutionnaire (Sierra Leone)
SAR	search and rescue
SBC	State Building Contract
SCO	safe country origin
SDGs	Sustainable Development Goals
SEA	Single European Act
SIA	sustainability impact assessment
SMART	Specific Measurable Achievable Relevant and Time-bound
SOFA	Status of Forces Agreement
SOMA	Status of Mission Agreement
SRC	Sector Reform Contracts
TCN	third-country national
TEU	Treaty on European Union
TFEU	Treaty on the Functioning of the European Union
UAM	unaccompanied minor
UDHR	Universal Declaration of Human Rights
UN	United Nations
UNCLOS	UN Convention on the Law of the Sea
UNCRC	UN Convention on the Rights of the Child
UN CRPD	UN Convention on the Rights of Persons with Disabilities
UNCTAD	UN Conference on Trade and Development
UNDG	UN Development Group
UNGA	UN General Assembly
UNHCR	UN High Commissioner for Refugees
UNHRC	UN Human Rights Council
UNICEF	United Nations Children's Fund
UNRWA	UN Relief and Works Agency
UPR	universal periodic review
VAT	value added tax
VCLT	Vienna Convention on the Law of the Treaties

VP	Vice-President
VPA	Voluntary Partnership Agreement
WEU	Western European Union
WIPO	World Intellectual Property Organization
YIRD	Yen interest rates derivatives

1

The Emergence of the EU's Commitment to Human Rights

1.1 Introduction

These days, the European Union (EU) is a recognized human rights actor both globally and in Europe and its neighbourhood. The EU of today has its own legally binding 'bill of rights' in the form of the EU Charter on Fundamental Rights and a dedicated Fundamental Rights Agency (FRA). Its overall commitment to human rights, in addition to being enshrined in the Treaties, is replicated across the Union's many legislative and policy documents. In 2012, the EU received the Nobel Peace Prize for contributing over six decades 'to the advancement of peace and reconciliation, democracy and human rights in Europe'.[1] Nevertheless, like other global political actors, the Union's human rights commitment faces both internal and external pressures from competing objectives and interests, as well as challenges which test the authenticity of its proclaimed human rights identity and aspirations.

Charter of Fundamental Rights of the European Union [2012] OJ C326/391

Preamble

(...) This Charter reaffirms, with due regard for the powers and tasks of the Union and for the principle of subsidiarity, the rights as they result, in particular, from the constitutional traditions and international obligations common to the Member States, the European Convention for the Protection of Human Rights and Fundamental Freedoms, the Social Charters adopted by the Union and by the Council of Europe and the case-law of the Court of Justice of the European Union and of the European Court of Human Rights. In this context the Charter will be interpreted by the courts of the Union and the Member States with due regard to the explanations prepared under the authority of the Praesidium of the Convention which drafted the Charter and updated under the responsibility of the Praesidium of the European Convention. (...)

---

[1] The Nobel Prize Organization, 'The Nobel Peace Prize 2012: European Union (EU)' (*Nobelprize.org*, 12 October 2012) <https://www.nobelprize.org/nobel_prizes/peace/laureates/2012/press.html> accessed 14 August 2020.

The European Union and Human Rights. Jan Wouters and Michal Ovádek, Oxford University Press (2021). © Jan Wouters and Michal Ovádek. DOI: 10.1093/oso/9780198814177.003.0001

Consolidated version of the Treaty on European Union [2012] OJ C326/13

Article 2

The Union is founded on the values of respect for human dignity, freedom, democracy, equality, the rule of law and respect for human rights, including the rights of persons belonging to minorities. These values are common to the Member States in a society in which pluralism, non-discrimination, tolerance, justice, solidarity and equality between women and men prevail.

Article 3

1. The Union's aim is to promote peace, its values and the well-being of its peoples.
5. In its relations with the wider world, the Union shall uphold and promote its values and interests and contribute to the protection of its citizens. It shall contribute to peace, security, the sustainable development of the Earth, solidarity and mutual respect among peoples, free and fair trade, eradication of poverty and the protection of human rights, in particular the rights of the child, as well as to the strict observance and the development of international law, including respect for the principles of the United Nations Charter.

The EU's *de facto* constitution, however, has not always been endowed with human rights provisions. The original founding Treaties contained no mention of human rights—or 'fundamental rights' in EU jargon—and this remained the case until the adoption of the Treaty of Maastricht in 1992. This omission makes sense on the face of it, since the EU had been conceived as an organization with predominantly economic focus and with relatively few competences in non-economic areas.[2] As the pace of integration started to pick up and more policy areas became of EU relevance, human rights have also been gradually brought into the fold.

Nevertheless, pioneering work by Gráinne de Búrca has demonstrated that such a linear understanding of the development of the EU's commitment to human rights is overly simplistic. De Búrca's consultation of the EU's legal-historical records appropriately reveals that the absence of human rights from the founding Treaties of the 1950s was not a foregone conclusion. A tangible alternative whereby the nascent European Community would include a robust human rights component was considered by the drafters of the European Political Community (EPC) treaty in an effort that has ultimately failed on political grounds.[3] The rest is history, but it is notable that the ambition of the draft EPC treaty with respect to placing human rights at the core of the European project would have, according to de Búrca, resolved or at least mitigated a number of issues plaguing the protection of human rights in the EU today.[4]

---

[2] See Article 3 of the 1957 Treaty of Rome for a list of 'activities' of the European Economic Community and compare with competences as they are defined today in Articles 3, 4, and 6 TFEU. Revealingly, no general human rights competence has been created for the EU with the exception of the specific obligation to accede to the ECHR in Article 6(2) TEU.

[3] G de Búrca, 'The Road Not Taken: The European Union as a Global Human Rights Actor' (2011) 105 The American Journal of International Law 649, 664.

[4] Ibid, 652.

G de Búrca, 'The Evolution of EU Human Rights Law' in P Craig and G de Búrca, *The Evolution of EU Law* (2nd edn, Oxford University Press 2011)

The drafters of the EPC Treaty (...) adopted a more restrained approach to the Community, addressing the possibility that the Community institutions themselves could encroach through the exercise of their powers on human rights. The draft EPC Treaty also clearly accorded a key role to the institutions of the ECHR [European Convention on Human Rights] in adjudicating on human rights violations, even while confronting the legal complexities of the fact that the Community could not itself become a party to the Convention on Human Rights.

Ultimately, the draft Treaty on a European Political Community prepared by the Constitutional Committee, which included these provisions on human rights protection, was accepted without difficulty by the Ad Hoc Assembly. However, at the Intergovernmental Conference which followed in 1953, not all of the national delegations were happy with the content of the new draft Treaty. The French delegation in particular raised objections, and argued for a significantly less 'supranational' approach. Eventually, as is well known, the draft European Political Community Treaty was abandoned when the prospects for ratification of the European Defence Community Treaty collapsed. It was at this point that the ambitious early attempts to promote European political integration were abandoned in favour of a significantly more restrained and pragmatic strategy in the shape of the European Economic and Atomic Energy Communities established in 1957. And with the abandonment of these political integration plans, the lively debates and various blueprints for an ambitious European Community human rights system also vanished.

(...)

Human rights protection and promotion have come to represent an important part of the EU's identity today. Values, including the promotion of democracy, human rights, and the rule of law, have been allocated a central place in the constitutional framework and legal discourse of the EU following the Lisbon Treaty. While the claim that the EU can be understood as a human rights organization remains untenable, human rights certainly feature prominently both in the constitutional self-understanding of the EU and in its international self-representation.

The traditional narrative of the evolution of human rights protection within EU law generally begins with the silence of the European Economic Community (EEC) Treaty on the subject and the subsequently dominant economic focus of the Communities, and therefore presents the current situation as a very significant advance, in human rights terms, on those origins. I have suggested, however, that a look back just a few years, prior to the adoption of the EEC Treaty at the efforts of drafting a constitutional framework for the new European Communities, reveals that a robust and comprehensive role for human rights protection within the new European construction was once contemplated. Further, the role envisaged for human rights protection and promotion in the model constitutional framework of the early 1950s was quite different, in several key respects, from that which is outlined in today's EU constitutional framework.

Three key differences have been identified in this chapter. The first is that the early 1950s framework assumed that monitoring and responding to human rights abuses by or within Member States would be a core task of the European Community, while the current constitutional framework resists and seeks to limit any role for the EU in monitoring human rights within the Member States. The second is that the early 1950s framework envisaged a European Community system which would be integrally linked to the regional human rights system, with a formal relationship existing between the Community Court and the European Court of Human Rights. In contrast, the current constitutional framework, even with the prospect of EU accession to the ECHR, emphasizes the autonomy and separateness of the EU's human rights system. It envisions the ECHR as an external system of accountability, and pays little attention to the international human rights regime. The third difference lies in the fact that the 1950s constitutional framework envisaged human rights protection as being equally central to internal and external EU policies and activities, while the role outlined for human rights within today's constitutional framework remains predominantly focused on the external relations of the EU.

As in many other areas of EU law and policy, however, the formal constitutional framework established in the Treaties and in primary legislation represents a particular vision of the EU which is conceived and promulgated by the Member States, but which is often at odds with the evolving practices of European governance. Thus the attempt by the Member States through the Treaties, the Charter, and the mandate of the Fundamental Rights Agency, to restrict or limit any EU monitoring of Member State activities in the field of human rights is at odds with the developing practices of the EU anti-discrimination regime, and more generally with the activities of the network of national human rights bodies and civil society actors which interact with the new Fundamental Rights Agency. Similarly, the official emphasis on the autonomy and distinctiveness of the EU's human rights regime is challenged by the existence of what has been described as a *de facto* 'overlapping consensus' and by the informal mutual monitoring of various national, regional, and international human rights regimes. Thirdly, the official resistance to identifying human rights protection and promotion as a cross-cutting objective of internal EU policy, as compared with external policies, is likely to be undercut by the Commission's moves to develop a genuine practice of impact assessment based on the Charter of Fundamental Rights.

Nevertheless, the 'Masters of the Treaties' continue firmly to resist such a conception of the EU and to deny such a robust role for human rights protection and promotion within EU law and policy. Instead, they seek to define a European Union whose engagement with human rights is deliberately qualified and limited in various ways, with the aim of ensuring that the Member States are as far as possible free from EU monitoring and scrutiny, that the EU's human rights activities are predominantly outwardly and not inwardly focused, and that the autonomy of the EU itself is not excessively constrained by external institutions and norms. In these ways, the formal constitutional framework for human rights in the EU today stands in marked contrast with the overt embrace by the drafters of the early 1950s of the European Community as an organization committed to human rights protection and promotion in all of its spheres of action, both internal and external, which would be properly engaged in monitoring and scrutiny of its Member States, and which would be an integral part of the emerging regional and international network of human rights regimes.

The failed EPC

Preceding the establishment of the EEC, the EPC represented an ambitious European integration attempt of the six founding EEC Member States to create a united Europe based on supranationalism. The EPC was abandoned following the rejection of the related European Defence Community by the French Parliament in 1954, as it became clear that the project was not politically feasible at the time. An early EPC Treaty had, however, been drafted and it was noteworthy for its emphasis on human rights, which was later entirely absent from the text of the EEC-founding Treaty of Rome.

The Draft Treaty embodying the Statute of the European Community, as the full name of the draft EPC Treaty went, for example, stated in Article 2 that the Community was to 'contribute towards the protection of human rights and fundamental freedoms in Member States'. Article 3 made the ECHR an integral part of the draft EPC Treaty. The Treaty even explicitly endowed the Court of the Community with the possibility to adjudicate disputes relating to the ECHR and provided for a referral mechanism that would intertwine the Community with the jurisdiction of the European Court of Human Rights (ECtHR), which at the time of drafting had not yet existed (Article 45). This is glaringly different from the present situation, as the Court of Justice of the European Union (CJEU) recently rejected a proposal that would entail oversight by the ECtHR of the EU system.[5]

1.2 Early Fundamental Rights Case Law in the European Communities

Similarly to other aspects of EU law, judgments of the CJEU have played an important role in establishing the EU's commitment to human rights at the outset of the integration process. This is understandable not only in light of the conspicuous silence of the Treaties regarding human rights but also from the perspective of the Court's desire to secure footing of the embryonic supranational legal order vis-à-vis the EU Member States. At a time when the CJEU started to break the path for the autonomous existence and operation of EU law—as a legal order distinct from both national and international law—in milestone decisions on direct effect and supremacy of EU law,[6] the question of the then Communities' own regard for human rights was a looming threat for the consolidation of EU law. As the Communities had not, unlike the Member States, formally recognized any source of human rights law, there was a genuine concern that national judges and officials in Member States could disregard EU law on the grounds of non-compliance with human rights standards that existed on the national level.[7]

The danger for the autonomy of the EU legal order and supremacy of EU law was not lost on the judges of the CJEU.[8] Although 'fundamental rights' were already unsuccessfully invoked by the Court in 1959 in relation to a decision of the High Authority of the European

---

[5] Opinion of 18 December 2014, *EU accession to the ECHR*, 2/13, ECLI:EU:C:2014:2454.

[6] Judgment of 5 February 1963, *Van Gend en Loos v Nederlandse administratie der* belastingen, 26/62, ECLI:EU:C:1963:1; Judgment of 15 July 1964, *Costa v ENEL*, 6/64, ECLI:EU:C:1964:66.

[7] M Varju, *European Union Human Rights Law: The Dynamics of Interpretation and Context* (Edward Elgar Publishing 2014) 5.

[8] P Pescatore, 'Les droits de l'homme et l'intégration européenne' (1968) 4 Cahiers de droit européen 629.

Coal and Steel Community,[9] the first general definition of the relationship of the European Communities to human rights by the CJEU came in *Stauder*. In this preliminary ruling,[10] a German beneficiary of a welfare scheme for disabled veterans brought an action against the City of Ulm before the administrative court (*Veranwaltungsgericht*) in Stuttgart regarding the requirement of appearance of the name of the beneficiary on a coupon for buying butter at a reduced price. The plaintiff alleged that the requirement violates his fundamental rights guaranteed by the Basic Law (German Constitution), namely the rights to human dignity and equality before law.

Judgment of 12 November 1969, *Stauder v City of Ulm*, 29/69, ECLI:EU:C:1969:57

(...) Can the fact that the Decision of the Commission of the European Communities of 12 February 1969 (69/71/EEC) makes the sale of butter at a reduced price to beneficiaries under certain welfare schemes dependent on revealing the name of the beneficiary to the sellers be considered compatible with the general principles of Community law in force?

(...) According to the order making the reference a strict interpretation of the wording of Article 4 of the Decision of 12 February 1969 makes it impossible to avoid revealing the name of the beneficiary to retailers, who do not normally have a role to play in the provision of social welfare to the underprivileged. The *Verwaltungsgericht* doubts whether such a condition accords with the law, and considers it in any case contrary to the German concept of social welfare and to the German system of protection of fundamental rights which must, at least in part, be guaranteed equally by the Community institutions as part of the protection afforded by the provisions of a Community law which has a superior status.

Grounds of judgment

(...) In a case like the present one, the most liberal interpretation must prevail, provided that it is sufficient to achieve the objectives pursued by the decision in question. It cannot, moreover, be accepted that the authors of the decision intended to impose stricter obligations in some Member States than in others.

(...) It follows that the provision in question must be interpreted as not requiring— although it does not prohibit—the identification of beneficiaries by name. The Commission was thus able to publish on 29 July 1969 an amending decision to this effect. Each of the Member States is accordingly now able to choose from a number of methods by which the coupons may refer to the person concerned.

---

[9] Judgment of 4 February 1959, *Stork & Cie v High Authority of the European Coal and Steel Community*, 1/58, ECLI:EU:C:1959:4. The CJEU remained unfavourable to considering fundamental rights in the subsequent cases of *Geitling* and *Sgarlata* as well. See Judgment of 15 July 1960, *Geitling v High Authority*, 36/59, 37/59, 38/59, and 40/59, ECLI:EU:C:1960:36; Judgment of 1 April 1965, *Sgarlata and others v Commission*, 40/64, ECLI:EU:C:1965:36.

[10] The preliminary ruling procedure is one of the hallmarks of the EU system of judicial protection. Enshrined in Article 267 TFEU, it allows the CJEU to interpret questions of EU law submitted by national courts in the Member States. For a comprehensive overview see eg P Craig and G de Búrca, *EU Law: Text, Cases, and Materials* (6th edn, Oxford University Press 2015) 464–508.

> Interpreted in this way the provision at issue contains nothing capable of prejudicing the fundamental human rights enshrined in the general principles of Community law and protected by the Court.

The case of *Stauder* encapsulated the core issue of Member State courts' wariness regarding the existence of sufficient fundamental rights guarantees under EU law. This was so especially in Germany, where the Basic Law adopted after the end of the Second World War placed fundamental rights indelibly at the centre of the German legal system. In light of the noted lack of formal sources of human rights law in the EU Treaties at the time, the CJEU relied on unwritten general principles of EU law to introduce human rights into the European project. The recognition that 'fundamental human rights [are] enshrined in the general principles of Community law and protected by the Court' has formed the backbone for fundamental rights protection in the EU for decades and is still relevant today.

Although *Stauder* is the first judgment to identify fundamental rights as general principles of EU law, the rise in prominence of this issue is associated with another well-known legal saga from Germany. In 1970, the administrative court in Frankfurt-am-Main put a question to the CJEU for a preliminary ruling regarding the legality of a Council Regulation on agricultural export licences. The administrative court, as well as the plaintiff, a company called Internationale Handelsgesellschaft, raised the concern that the Council Regulation in question infringed disproportionately on the company's freedom to conduct business.

Judgment of 17 December 1970, *Internationale Handelsgesellschaft v Einfuhr- und Vorratsstelle für Getreide und Futtermittel*, 11/70, ECLI:EU:C:1970:114

(...) [according to the *Verwaltungsgericht*] although Community regulations are not German national laws, but legal rules pertaining to the Community, they must respect the elementary, fundamental rights guaranteed by the German Constitution and the essential structural principles of national law. In the event of contradiction with those principles, the primacy of supranational law conflicts with the principles of the German Basic Law. The system of deposits instituted by Regulation No 120/67 is contrary to the principles of freedom of action and disposition, of economic liberty and of proportionality stemming in particular from Articles 2(1) and 14 of the German Basic Law.

Grounds of judgment

3. Recourse to the legal rules or concepts of national law in order to judge the validity of measures adopted by the institutions of the Community would have an adverse effect on **the uniformity and efficacy of Community law.** The validity of such measures can only be judged in the light of Community law. In fact, the law stemming from the Treaty, an independent source of law, cannot because of its very nature be overridden by rules of national law, however framed, without being deprived of its character as Community law and without the legal basis of the Community itself being called in question. Therefore the validity of a Community measure or its effect within a Member State cannot be affected by allegations that it runs counter to either fundamental rights as formulated by the constitution of that State or the principles of a national constitutional structure.

4. However, an examination should be made as to whether or not **any analogous guarantee inherent in Community law has been disregarded**. In fact, **respect for fundamental rights forms an integral part of the general principles of law protected by the Court of Justice. The protection of such rights, whilst inspired by the constitutional traditions common to the Member States, must be ensured within the framework of the structure and objectives of the Community**. It must therefore be ascertained, in the light of the doubts expressed by the Verwaltungsgericht, whether the system of deposits has infringed rights of a fundamental nature, respect for which must be ensured in the Community legal system.

20. (...) the fact that the system of licences involving an undertaking, by those who apply for them, to import or export, guaranteed by a deposit, does not violate any right of a fundamental nature. The machinery of deposits constitutes an appropriate method, for the purposes of Article 40 (3) of the Treaty, for carrying out the common organization of the agricultural markets and also conforms to the requirements of Article 43.

In *Internationale Handelsgesellschaft*, the CJEU reiterated its position from *Stauder* and added that fundamental rights as general principles of EU law are 'inspired by the constitutional traditions common to the Member States'.[11] At the same time, the Court cautioned that the protection of fundamental rights 'must be ensured within the framework of the structure and objectives of the Community' which implied a certain level of reservation in the CJEU's approach to fundamental rights.[12]

The preliminary ruling of the CJEU had not, however, put an end to the case in Frankfurt-am-Main. Faced with a clash of claims to supremacy,[13] the *Verwaltungsgericht* decided to also consult the judicial guardian of the other legal system at stake: the German Constitutional Court (*Bundesverfassungsgericht*).

Bundesverfassungsgericht, Judgment of 29 May 1974, *Solange I*, 2 BvL 52/71

(...) The part of the Basic Law dealing with fundamental rights is an inalienable, essential feature of the valid Basic Law of the Federal Republic of Germany and one which forms part of the constitutional structure of the Basic Law. Article 24 of the Basic Law [on the transfer of sovereign rights to inter-state institutions] does not without reservation allow it to be subjected to qualifications. In this, the present state of integration of the Community

---

[11] The sentence was later codified in the Treaties; see Article 6(3) TEU.

[12] For a discussion of the qualification, see W Weiß, 'The EU Human Rights Regime Post Lisbon: Turning the CJEU into a Human Rights Court?' in S Morano-Foadi and L Vickers (eds), *Fundamental Rights in the EU: A Matter for Two Courts* (Hart Publishing 2015).

[13] The relationship between EU law and national law is not as clear-cut as the CJEU presents it. There is a long-standing constitutional discussion on the primacy of EU law over national law which relates also to who (which court) has the final say in determining the supremacy of one legal order over the other. Therefore, Member States' constitutional courts dispute the assertion of the CJEU that EU law takes precedence under all circumstances over national law and in particular national constitutional law. The complexity of the issue goes beyond purely legal argumentation and requires considering, among others, the extent to which the EU is a sovereign polity. For an overview of the issues at stake see, for example, D Chalmers, G Davies, and G Monti, *European Union Law: Text and Materials* (3rd edn, Cambridge University Press 2014) 199–246.

is of crucial importance. **The Community still lacks a democratically legitimate parliament** directly elected by general suffrage which possesses legislative powers and to which the Community organs empowered to legislate are fully responsible on a political level; **it still lacks, in particular, a codified catalogue of fundamental rights, the substance of which is reliably and unambiguously fixed for the future** in the same way as the substance of the Basic Law and therefore allows a comparison and a decision as to whether, at the time in question, the Community law standard with regard to fundamental rights generally binding in the Community is adequate in the long term measured by the standard of the Basic Law with regard to fundamental rights (without prejudice to possible amendments) in such a way that there is no exceeding the limitation indicated, set by Article 24 of the Basic Law. **As long as this legal certainty, which is not guaranteed merely by the decisions of the European Court of Justice, favourable though these have been to fundamental rights, is not achieved in the course of the further integration of the Community, the reservation derived from Article 24 of the Basic Law applies.** What is involved is, therefore, a legal difficulty arising exclusively from the Community's continuing integration process, which is still in flux and which will end with the present transitional phase.[14]

The judgment of the German Constitutional Court, commonly referred to as *Solange I* for its conditional approach to EU law ('as long as'), attempted to set out a relatively comprehensive framework for the relationship between EU law and national law, especially with respect to fundamental rights. The Constitutional Court, in essence, reserved for itself the right to review EU secondary acts for their compliance with fundamental rights guaranteed under the German constitution until the EU would possess a comparable catalogue of fundamental rights and a democratically elected parliament which would preferably also enact such a catalogue in the EU. The decision was received as a potential threat to European integration, as the idea of national courts conducting judicial review of EU legislation—even in light of national constitutional norms, as made clear in *Internationale Handelsgesellschaft*—ran counter to the goal of ensuring the autonomy, uniformity and effectiveness of EU law.[15] In practice, the German Constitutional Court tried to minimize interference with EU laws and conflicts with the CJEU, as witnessed in the *Solange I* judgment itself where no breach of fundamental rights was found.[16]

The *Solange I* doctrine was revisited by the German Constitutional Court 12 years later in a judgment best known as *Solange II*.[17] The Constitutional Court decided to retract its prerogative to review EU legislation for compliance with fundamental rights guaranteed by the German Basic Law on the condition that their effective protection will continue to be ensured in the EU, not least in the case law of the CJEU. The Court recognized the protection of rights in the EU as 'substantially similar' to that required by the German Basic Law, thus

[14] Foreign Law Translations, 'BVerfGE 37, 271 2 BvL 52/71 Solange I-Beschluß' (*Texas Law*) <https://law.utexas.edu/transnational/foreign-law-translations/german/case.php?id=588> accessed 14 August 2020.

[15] The judgment, among others, prompted the Commission to recommend EU accession to the ECHR as early as 1979. Although this was not immediately taken up, the effort to join the EU was revisited in the 1980s and 1990s, ending with the negative opinion of the CJEU concerning EU competence to accede to the ECHR. The continuance of the accession saga is discussed in more detail in Ch 5.

[16] ER Larnier, 'Solange, Farewell: The Federal German Constitutional Court and the Recognition of the Court of Justice of the European Communities as Lawful Judge' (1988) 11 Boston College International and Comparative Law Review 9, 9–11.

[17] Foreign Law Translations, 'BVerfGE 73, 339 2 BvR 197/83 Solange II-decision' (*Texas Law*) <https://law.utexas.edu/transnational/foreign-law-translations/german/case.php?id=572> accessed 14 August 2020.

establishing the first presumption of equivalent fundamental rights protection relating to the EU.[18] In the process, the German Constitutional Court revised its past expectations of European integration and reflected on some of its achievements.

Bundesverfassungsgericht, Judgment of 22 October 1986, *Solange II*, 2 BvR 197/83

Compared with the standard of fundamental rights under the Basic Law it may be that the guarantees for the protection of such rights established thus far by the decisions of the European Court, since they have naturally been developed case by case, still contain gaps in so far as specific legal principles recognized by the Basic Law or the nature, content or extent of a fundamental right have not individually been the object of a judgment delivered by the Court. **What is decisive, nevertheless, is the attitude of principle which the Court maintains at this stage towards the Community's obligations in respect of fundamental rights** (...).

In the first place, since 1974 all the original member states of the Community (like those which acceded later) have acceded to the European Human Rights Convention, and their respective parliaments have approved their accession; in the second place, the common declaration of 5 April 1977, which was also adopted by the European Parliament, can be judged from the viewpoint of the requirement to be a sufficient parliamentary recognition of a formulated catalogue of effectively operating fundamental rights. Whilst this Chamber in its judgment of 29 May 1974 observed that **the Community lacked a parliament legitimized by direct and democratic means and established by general suffrage which possessed legislative powers and to which the institutions competent to issue legislation were politically fully responsible,** that was an element in the description of the state of integration as it appeared at that time; (...) There was no intention, however, of laying down a constitutional requirement that such a position must have prevailed before there could be any possibility of the withdrawal of the Federal Constitutional Court's jurisdiction over derived Community law (...).

In view of those developments it must be held that, **so long as the European Communities, in particular European Court case law, generally ensure effective protection of fundamental rights as against the sovereign powers of the Communities which is to be regarded as substantially similar to the protection of fundamental rights required unconditionally by the Basic Law, and in so far as they generally safeguard the essential content of fundamental rights, the Federal Constitutional Court will no longer exercise its jurisdiction to decide on the applicability of secondary Community legislation** (...) and **it will no longer review** such legislation by the standard of the fundamental rights contained in the Basic Law (...).[19]

While to an extent backtracking on the conditions for withdrawing jurisdiction promulgated in *Solange I*—there was still no self-standing catalogue of rights[20] and the European Parliament was playing a bit-part role—the judgment in *Solange II* was also grounded in

---

[18] See Ch 5 on the presumption of equivalent protection established by the ECtHR in its case law.
[19] Foreign Law Translations, 'BVerfGE 73, 339 2 BvR 197/83 Solange II-decision' (*Texas Law*) <https://law.utexas.edu/transnational/foreign-law-translations/german/case.php?id=572> accessed 14 August 2020.
[20] The EU institutions started to take steps towards remedying this deficiency in the mid-1970s which eventually culminated into the European Parliament's adoption on 12 April 1989 of a Declaration of Fundamental Rights and Freedoms. The document was not binding but constituted the first elaboration of a list of rights at the EU level.

real developments taking place in the EU. The Constitutional Court took note, in particular, of the growing number of cases and the manner in which arguments based on fundamental rights were appraised by the CJEU,[21] the accession of all EU Member States to the ECHR and the recognition of this source by the CJEU, and a joint declaration of EU institutions on their commitment to human rights.[22] In view of the capacities to protect fundamental rights effectively at the EU level at the time, the most important factor was the case law of the CJEU through which such protection could be most realistically ensured.

In the case of *Nold v Commission*, referenced by the German Constitutional Court in *Solange II* as a breakthrough for fundamental rights in the EU, the CJEU confirmed that compliance with fundamental rights was a condition of validity of EU measures and found that in addition to constitutional traditions common to the Member States, international treaties also represented a vital source of legal inspiration for the promulgation of general principles of EU law.

Judgment of 14 May 1974, *Nold v Commission*, 4/73, ECLI:EU:C:1974:51

13. As the Court has already stated, fundamental rights form an integral part of the general principles of law, the observance of which it ensures.

In safeguarding these rights, the Court is bound to draw inspiration from constitutional traditions common to the Member States, and it **cannot therefore uphold measures which are incompatible with fundamental rights** recognized and protected by the Constitutions of those States.

Similarly, **international treaties for the protection of human rights on which the Member States have collaborated or of which they are signatories, can supply guidelines which should be followed within the framework of Community law.**

The nuanced wording regarding Member States' collaboration on and signatures of human rights treaties might be reflective of the fact that at the time, the ECHR was not ratified by all

---

[21] The German Constitutional Court referred to a number of CJEU cases touching upon fundamental rights protection and the rule of law as testaments of the reliability of the EU court to ensure their protection on a consistent basis. See Judgment of 19 September 1984, *Albert Heijn BV*, 94/83, ECLI:EU:C:1984:285; Judgment of 6 November 1984, *Fearon & Company Limited v Irish Land Commission*, 182/83, ECLI:EU:C:1984:335; Judgment of 16 June 1998, *Racke GmbH & Co. v Hauptzollamt Mainz*, C-162/96, ECLI:EU:C:1998:293; Judgment of 10 July 1984, *Regina v Kent Kirk*, 63/83, ECLI:EU:C:1984:255; Judgment of 14 November 1984, *SA Intermills v Commission of the European Communities*, 323/82, ECLI:EU:C:1984:345; Judgment of 15 May 1986, *Johnston v Chief Constable of the Royal Ulster Constabulary*, 222/84, ECLI:EU:C:1986:206; Judgment of 5 March 1980, *Pecastaing v Belgian State*, 98/79, ECLI:EU:C:1980:69; Judgment of 18 March 1975, *Union syndicale-Service public européen and others v Council of the European Communities*, 72/74, ECLI:EU:C:1975:43; Judgment of 19 October 1977, *Ruckdeschel and Others v Hauptzollamt Hamburg-St. Annen*, 117/76 and 16/77, ECLI:EU:C:1977:160; Judgment of 13 December 1979, *Hauer v Land Rheinland-Pfalz*, 44/79, ECLI:EU:C:1979:290.

[22] Joint Declaration by the European Parliament, the Council and the Commission concerning the protection of fundamental rights and the European Convention for the Protection of Human Rights and Fundamental Freedoms [1977] OJ C103/1. The operative part of the short document read as follows: '1. The European Parliament, the Council and the Commission stress the prime importance they attach to the protection of fundamental rights, as derived in particular from the constitutions of the Member States and the European Convention for the Protection of Human Rights and Fundamental Freedoms. 2. In the exercise of their powers and in pursuance of the aims of the European Communities they respect and will continue to respect these rights.'

EC Member States until 11 days before the publication of the judgment, and the core United Nations treaties—the International Covenant on Civil and Political Rights (ICCPR) and the International Covenant on Economic, Social and Cultural Rights (ICESCR)—were yet to enter into force. Merely a year after the decision in *Nold*, the CJEU referenced articles of the ECHR in support of its reasoning in the case of *Rutili*.[23]

The Court eventually also explicitly tackled the issue of when EC fundamental rights applied to the Member States.[24] In the leading case on the issue, *Wachauf*, the CJEU found that the EC standards are 'binding on the Member States when they implement Community rules'.[25] In the subsequent case, *ERT*, the Court used slightly different wording when it referred to national rules which 'fall within the scope of Community law' as being subject to compliance with EC fundamental rights as interpreted by the CJEU.[26] Both cases later had an impact on the wording of Article 51(1) of the Charter of Fundamental Rights and its interpretation by the Court concerning the scope of applicability of the Charter.[27]

1.3 Development of Social Rights in the Internal Market

While human or fundamental rights were not in the EU's DNA, the situation was different with respect to the internal market which constituted the core of the EU's business. And since the development of the internal market also entailed the movement of workers across the borders of the Member States, some rights of individuals were necessarily implicated in the process. Therefore, in parallel with the evolution of fundamental rights proper in the case law of the CJEU, certain economic and social rights were developed on the basis of the logic of market integration. The most important was the right to non-discrimination on the basis of nationality which covered a range of predominantly market situations relating to the free movement of goods, services, workers, and capital within the EU.[28]

V Kosta, *Fundamental Rights in EU Internal Market Legislation* (Hart Publishing 2015)

(...) the term 'fundamental right' has not been restricted to the range of entitlements which have been traditionally regarded as human rights. The Court has occasionally referred to the so-called 'market freedoms' as 'fundamental rights', implying that they have a similar status and, therefore, in the event of conflict, it is not obvious that they should give way to 'traditional' human rights. This means that not only did the internal market constitute an independent objective of the Community, which was realized through legislative initiatives, but that it was also furthered by recourse to the concept of 'fundamental

---

[23] Judgment of 28 October 1975, *Rutili v Ministre de l'intérieur*, 36/75, ECLI:EU:C:1975:137.

[24] Around this time in the early 1990s it was also asserted by some scholars that the CJEU was using fundamental rights to expand its jurisdiction and assert the supremacy of EU law in new areas without a real concern for the substance of human rights protection within the EU. See J Coppel and A O'Neill, 'The European Court of Justice: Taking Rights Seriously?' (1992) 29 Common Market Law Review 669.

[25] Judgment of 13 July 1989, *Wachauf v Bundesamt für Ernährung und Forstwirtschaft*, 5/88, ECLI:EU:C:1989:321, para 19.

[26] Judgment of 18 June 1991, *Elliniki Radiophonia Tiléorassi AE and Panellinia Omospondia Syllogon Prossopikou v Dimotiki Etairia Pliroforissis and Others*, C-260/89, ECLI:EU:C:1991:254, para 42.

[27] See Ch 4.

[28] See Ch 7.

right' which, until recently, was the only method of protecting human rights in EU law. Arguably, the only 'human right' which has received almost self-standing protection in EU law is the right to non-discrimination on the ground of nationality. Yet, the protection of this right often furthers and rarely clashes with the internal market objective. Thus, enlarging the scope of application of art. 12 EC (now 18 TFEU) was of little danger to the internal market. It follows that the importance attached to art. 12 EC by the Court does not unequivocally prove that the principle of non-discrimination on the ground of nationality per se has equal status with the concern for the functioning of the internal market.

Arguably the most important social right—even though it was not conceived as such— enshrined in the original Treaty of Rome was the requirement for men and women to be paid equally for the same work.[29] The principle of equal pay was included in the Treaty due to fears that some Member States would gain a competitive advantage by allowing women to be paid less than men for the same work. Although the social dimension of equal pay was recognized only at a later stage by the CJEU, the provision represented the first and most significant foray of the EU into the area of social rights and it laid the foundation for the advancement of gender equality in the EU and its eventual incorporation within the EU's identity.[30]

The European social model was more comprehensively affirmed in 1989 by the solemn declaration of the Community Charter of the Fundamental Social Rights of Workers by 11 of the then 12 Member States.[31] While the declaration was non-binding and it did not entail any transfer of competence from the national to the EU level—the Member States remaining primarily responsible for ensuring social rights—it showed that European political leaders were aware even at the time of peak neoliberalism of the need for the EU to have a social dimension. At the same time, the social dimension was also envisaged to have a 'market function', namely avoiding distortion of competition by countries engaging in a 'race to the bottom' in terms of working conditions and social regulation. The Community Charter was an important signal to this effect.

Community Charter of the Fundamental Social Rights of Workers, Declaration of 9 December 1989

Whereas the social consensus contributes to the strengthening of the competitiveness of undertakings, of the economy as a whole and to the creation of employment; whereas in this respect it is an essential condition for ensuring sustained economic development;

Whereas the completion of the internal market must favour the approximation of improvements in living and working conditions, as well as economic and social cohesion within the European Community while avoiding distortions of competition;

Whereas the completion of the internal market must offer improvements in the social field for workers of the European Community, especially in terms of freedom of movement, living and working conditions, health and safety at work, social protection, education and training; (...)

---

[29] Article 119 of the Treaty of Rome; today Article 157 TFEU.
[30] See Article 8 TFEU and Article 23 of the Charter.
[31] The UK initially did not sign the declaration. It only acceded in 1998.

Social protection

10. Every worker of the European Community shall have a right to adequate social protection and shall, whatever his status and whatever the size of the undertaking in which he is employed, enjoy an adequate level of social security benefits.

Persons who have been unable either to enter or re-enter the labour market and have no means of subsistence must be able to receive sufficient resources and social assistance in keeping with their particular situation.

Elderly persons

25. Any person who has reached retirement age but who is not entitled to a pension or who does not have other means of subsistence, must be entitled to sufficient resources and to medical and social assistance specifically suited to his needs.

Disabled persons

26. All disabled persons, whatever the origin and nature of their disablement, must be entitled to additional concrete measures aimed at improving their social and professional integration.

The Community Charter included 30 provisions covering a range of social issues from the right to strike to a minimum employment age of 15 years. The immediate effect of the Community Charter was that it served as the basis of a legislative agenda which led to the enactment of several Directives during the 1990s, such as the Pregnant Workers Directive and the Working Time Directive,[32] concerning minimum working conditions and social protection in the EU. Later on, the list of rights and freedoms in the Community Charter inspired the economic and social rights enshrined in the Charter of Fundamental Rights. The Community Charter of course did not displace the European Social Charter (instead it built on it), a legally binding treaty within the Council of Europe regime with a supervisory quasi-judicial body.[33] The need for the Community Charter was in fact compounded by the absence—which continues to this day—of EU accession to the European Social Charter and to the ECHR. The Community Charter became a precursor; 'a partial step toward the constitutionalization of a bill of individual and collective rights' in the words of Mary Frances Dominick, which was achieved only in 2009 when the Charter of Fundamental Rights entered into force with the same legal value as the EU Treaties.

---

[32] Council Directive 92/85/EEC on the introduction of measures to encourage improvements in the safety and health at work of pregnant workers and workers who have recently given birth or are breastfeeding [1992] OJ L348/1; Council Directive 93/104/EC concerning certain aspects of the organization of working time [1993] OJ L307/18.

[33] European Social Charter (revised) (opened 3 May 1996, entered into force 1 July 1999) 2151 UNTS 277.

> ## MF Dominick, 'Toward a Community Bill of Rights: The European Community Charter of Fundamental Social Rights' (1990) 14 Fordham International Law Journal 639
>
> Giving content to human rights, making them more than mere platitudes or declarations of good intention, is a formidable and often unsuccessful task. The Community has thus far avoided the creation of a bill of rights, even by accession to the European Convention on Human Rights and the European Social Charter. These seemingly apparent steps should be easy as all Member States have already accepted the former and most have accepted, albeit with reservations, the latter. Instead, the protection of individuals vis-à-vis the Community has been left largely to ad hoc, case-by-case determination by the Court of Justice. The result is a common or customary law amalgam of declarations and decisions that should suffice with less comfort for the civil law Member States.
>
> The Community Charter is a partial step toward the constitutionalization of a bill of individual and collective human rights, an effort that would be strengthened by parallel Community accession to the European Convention on Human Rights. One of the less often stated objections to both steps by the British Government is that within the discretion of the Court of Justice is the legal possibility that the rights both instruments contain would have direct effect—i.e., they could be invoked by U.K. citizens in U.K. courts, superseding anterior or posterior U.K. law. These objections are similar to those raised by signatory states, like the United States, which are reluctant to ratify the United Nations Covenants on Civil and Political and Economic and Social Rights.
>
> Civil and political as well as economic and social rights are implicated by the ever-expanding jurisdiction of the Community. To assume benevolently that the Community's conduct will always be such that it will not violate the rights of citizens who empower it is to ignore the constitutional wisdom of its constituent parts. As a federated Europe comes closer to reality, it is essential that its institutional framework contain explicit, invocable, and directly effective fundamental protections for those whom the governments are designed to serve.

More recently, another major initiative was taken to relaunch the policy debate on the social dimension of the EU after a period of euroscepticism. In 2016, the Juncker Commission published a communication laying down the foundation for a new European Pillar of Social Rights (EPSR).[34] This idea was politically endorsed during the Gothenburg Social Summit in November 2017, where 20 key principles were promulgated, structured around three categories. According to the Commission, the Pillar is intended to deliver 'new and more effective rights for citizens'.[35] Several legislative acts have been adopted as part of its implementation, like a new Directive on work–life balance[36] and a Directive on transparent and predictable working conditions.[37] Many other actions are being taken at

---

[34] European Commission, 'Communication from the Commission to the European Parliament, the Council, the European Economic and Social Committee and the Committee of the Regions—Launching a consultation on a European Pillar of Social Rights' COM (2016) 127 final.

[35] European Commission, 'European Pillar of Social Rights, Building a more inclusive and fairer European Union' (ec.europa.eu) <https://ec.europa.eu/commission/priorities/deeper-and-fairer-economic-and-monetary-union/european-pillar-social-rights_en> accessed 14 August 2020.

[36] Directive 2019/1158/EU of the European Parliament and of the Council on work-life balance for parents and carers and repealing Council Directive 2010/18/EU [2019] OJ L188/79.

[37] Directive 2019/1152/EU of the European Parliament and of the Council on transparent and predictable working conditions in the European Union [2019] OJ L186/105.

EU level[38] and progress is being monitored by a renewed Social Scoreboard.[39] Looking at the EPSR's text, it stands out that for a large part the principles featured therein are a restatement of the 1989 Community Charter rights.[40] The commitment to equality of treatment between men and women, the right to healthy and safe working conditions, the right to old age income and to support for people with disabilities are reiterated. The right to vocational training is redefined as and extended to a right to quality and inclusive education, training, and life-long learning, while the right to fair renumeration now includes the right to an adequate minimum wage. New rights include the right to equal employment opportunities for all, to active support to improve employment prospects, to suitable leave for parents and people with caring responsibilities, to protection of personal data of workers, and to healthcare.

European Parliament, Council and Commission Proclamation of the European Pillar of Social Rights, 16 November 2017

Chapter I: Equal opportunities and access to the labour market

1. Education, training and life-long learning
Everyone has the right to quality and inclusive education, training and life-long learning in order to maintain and acquire skills that enable them to participate fully in society and manage successfully transitions in the labour market.

2. Gender equality
Equality of treatment and opportunities between women and men must be ensured and fostered in all areas, including regarding participation in the labour market, terms and conditions of employment and career progression.
  Women and men have the right to equal pay for work of equal value.

3. Equal opportunities
Regardless of gender, racial or ethnic origin, religion or belief, disability, age or sexual orientation, everyone has the right to equal treatment and opportunities regarding employment, social protection, education, and access to goods and services available to the public. Equal opportunities of under-represented groups shall be fostered.

4. Active support to employment
Everyone has the right to timely and tailor-made assistance to improve employment or self-employment prospects. This includes the right to receive support for job search, training and re-qualification. (…)

---

[38] See for an overview: European Commission, 'Factsheet: The European Pillar of Social Rights', 9 April 2019, <https://ec.europa.eu/social/BlobServlet?docId=20980&langId=en> accessed 14 August 2020.

[39] European Commission, 'Social Scoreboard, Supporting the European Pillar of Social Rights' <https://composite-indicators.jrc.ec.europa.eu/social-scoreboard/> accessed 14 August 2020.

[40] S Garben, 'Balancing Fundamental Social and Economic Rights in the EU: In Search of a Better Method' in B Vanhercke and others (eds), *Social Policy in the European Union 1999–2019: The Long and Winding Road* (European Trade Union Institute 2020) 57–58.

Chapter II: Fair working conditions

6. Wages

Workers have the right to fair wages that provide for a decent standard of living.

Adequate minimum wages shall be ensured, in a way that provide for the satisfaction of the needs of the worker and his / her family in the light of national economic and social conditions, whilst safeguarding access to employment and incentives to seek work. In-work poverty shall be prevented. (…)

9. Work-life balance

Parents and people with caring responsibilities have the right to suitable leave, flexible working arrangements and access to care services. Women and men shall have equal access to special leaves of absence in order to fulfil their caring responsibilities and be encouraged to use them in a balanced way.

10. Healthy, safe and well-adapted work environment and data protection

Workers have the right to a high level of protection of their health and safety at work. (…)

Chapter III: Social protection and inclusion

15. Old age income and pensions

Workers and the self-employed in retirement have the right to a pension commensurate to their contributions and ensuring an adequate income. Women and men shall have equal opportunities to acquire pension rights.

Everyone in old age has the right to resources that ensure living in dignity.

16. Health care

Everyone has the right to timely access to affordable, preventive and curative health care of good quality.

17. Inclusion of people with disabilities

People with disabilities have the right to income support that ensures living in dignity, services that enable them to participate in the labour market and in society, and a work environment adapted to their needs.

1.4 Human Rights in Political Cooperation

As a consequence of the abovementioned failure of the European Political Community in 1954, the founding Treaties of the EU offered little in the way of political integration. The difficulty of reaching an agreement on the institutionalization of common political positions of the Member States—particularly in the area of foreign policy—meant that it took until the 1970s to establish a basic framework for political cooperation.

The initially informal European Political Cooperation represented the first agreement of EU Member States on coordinating foreign policy and leveraging their combined political clout internationally.[41] It was based on the Davignon Report which, while emphasizing shared European values and connection to the European Communities (now the EU), founded a cooperation mechanism that was strongly intergovernmental in nature. The adoption of the Davignon Report also confirmed the Member States' view that 'a United Europe should be based on a common heritage of respect for the liberty and rights of man'.

Report by the Foreign Ministers of the Member States on the problems of political unification, 'Davignon Report' (Luxembourg, 27 October 1970)

3. The Heads of State or Government affirmed their 'common conviction that a Europe composed of States which, in spite of their different national characteristics, are united in their essential interests, assured of its internal cohesion, true to its friendly relations with outside countries, conscious of the role it has to play in promoting the relaxation of international tension and the rapprochement among all peoples, and first and foremost among those of the entire European continent, is indispensable if a mainspring of development, progress and culture, world equilibrium and peace is to be preserved'.

4. United Europe, conscious of the responsibilities incumbent on it by reason of its economic development, industrial power and standard of living, intends to step up its endeavours on behalf of the developing countries with a view to setting international relations on a basis of trust.

5. **A united Europe should be based on a common heritage of respect for the liberty and rights of man and bring together democratic States with freely elected parliaments.** This united Europe remains the fundamental aim, to be attained as soon as possible, thanks to the political will of the peoples and the decisions of their Governments.

I. Objectives

This cooperation has two objectives:

(a) To ensure greater mutual understanding with respect to the major issues of international politics, by exchanging information and consulting regularly;

(b) To increase their solidarity by working for a harmonization of views, concertation of attitudes and joint action when it appears feasible and desirable.

The European Political Cooperation was subsequently strengthened and expanded through a series of reports in the 1970s and 1980s. Moreover, the establishment of the European Council in 1974, bringing together the Heads of State and Government and the President of the European Commission, reinforced the emergent political dimension of the European project. In June 1983, at a European Council meeting held

---

[41] See generally S Nutall, *European Political Cooperation* (Oxford University Press 1992).

in Stuttgart, the heads of the then 10 Member States adopted a Solemn Declaration on European Union.

European Council, Solemn Declaration on European Union (Stuttgart, 19 June 1983)

Preamble

The Heads of State or Government of the Member States of the European Communities meeting within the European Council,

resolved to continue the work begun on the basis of the Treaties of Paris and Rome and to create a united Europe, which is more than ever necessary in order to meet the dangers of the world situation, capable of assuming the responsibilities incumbent on it by virtue of its political role, its economic potential and its manifold links with other peoples,

considering that the European idea, the results achieved in the fields of economic integration and political cooperation, and the need for new developments correspond to the wishes of the democratic peoples of Europe, for whom the European Parliament, elected by universal suffrage is an indispensable means of expression,

determined to work together **to promote democracy on the basis of the fundamental rights recognized in the constitutions and laws of the Member States, in the European Convention for the Protection of Human Rights and the European Social Charter**, notably freedom, equality and social justice,

convinced that, in order to resolve the serious economic problems facing the Member States, the Community must strengthen its cohesion, regain its dynamism and intensify its action in areas hitherto insufficiently explored,

resolved to accord a high priority to the Community's social progress and in particular to the problem of employment by the development of a European social policy,

convinced that, by speaking with a single voice in foreign policy, including political aspects of security, Europe can contribute to the preservation of peace,

(…)

determined to achieve a comprehensive and coherent common political approach and reaffirming their will to transform the whole complex of relations between their States into a European Union, have adopted the following:

(…)

   1.2 The Heads of State or Government reaffirm the Declaration on Democracy adopted by the European Council on 8 April 1978 which stated that **respect for and maintenance of representative democracy and human rights in each Member State are essential dements of membership of the European Communities**.

   1.3 In order to achieve ever increasing solidarity and joint action, the construction of Europe must be more clearly oriented towards its general political objectives, more efficient decision-making procedures, greater coherence and close coordination between the different branches of activity, and the search for common policies in all areas of common interest, both within the Community and in relation to third countries.

One of the interesting points of the Solemn Declaration is its reiteration of the principle that democracy and human rights are essential requirements of EU membership. This goes on to show, among others, that the relevance of these values for EU enlargement—a key part of EU foreign policy—runs much deeper than the well-known Copenhagen criteria which came into being in the 1990s.[42]

Building on the Solemn Declaration, European Political Cooperation was finally formalized by the Single European Act, which was signed in 1986 and which also represented the first significant revision of the original Treaty of Rome from 1957. In addition to repeating the commitment of the EU and its Member States to fundamental rights, it placed the principles of democracy, rule of law, and human rights in relation to the Union's international policies. As a side note, the Single European Act revealed the EU's established practice of referring to 'fundamental rights' when it speaks about its internal affairs, whereas preferring the term 'human rights' in non-EU international context.

Single European Act [1987] OJ L169/1

[... the Member States ...]

MOVED by the will to continue the work undertaken on the basis of the Treaties establishing the European Communities and to transform relations as a whole among their States into a European Union, in accordance with the Solemn Declaration of Stuttgart of 19 June 1983,

RESOLVED to implement this European Union on the basis, firstly, of the Communities operating in accordance with their own rules and, secondly, of European Co-operation among the Signatory States in the sphere of foreign policy and to invest this union with the necessary means of action,

DETERMINED to work together **to promote democracy on the basis of the fundamental rights recognized in the constitutions and laws of the Member States, in the Convention for the Protection of Human Rights and Fundamental Freedoms and the European Social Charter**, notably freedom, equality and social justice,

(...)

AWARE of the responsibility incumbent upon Europe to aim at speaking ever increasingly with one voice and to act with consistency and solidarity in order more effectively to protect its common interests and independence, **in particular to display the principles of democracy and compliance with the law and with human rights to which they are attached**, so that together they may make their own contribution to the preservation of international peace and security in accordance with the undertaking entered into by them within the framework of the United Nations Charter,

---

[42] The Copenhagen criteria spelled out the basic requirements of EU membership for countries aspiring to join the Union: stable institutions ensuring democracy, the rule of law, human rights, and protection of minorities; a functioning market economy; and ability to assume responsibilities following from EU membership, including those of the economic and monetary union. The criteria were set at the 1993 European Council meeting in Copenhagen during the Danish Presidency and they responded to the need to present a path to membership for countries of the former eastern bloc after the fall of the Iron Curtain.

1.5 Fundamental Rights in the European Union Era

The European Union as an international actor with legal personality was established by the Treaty of Maastricht in 1993. The Treaty introduced a three-pillar structure which reflected the historical development of EU competencies. Each pillar was regulated by a different set of rules and procedures that determined to which degree the different institutions of the EU were involved. The first pillar comprised the historically core policies of the EU, such as competition, agriculture, and trade, as well as policies where competence was shared between the EU and Member States; these were governed by the so-called community method involving the Commission, the Parliament, and the Council. The second pillar incorporated the former European Political Cooperation under the name Common Foreign and Security Policy (CFSP), while the third pillar concerned police and judicial cooperation in criminal matters. The governance of the second- and third-pillar policies remained largely in the hands of the Member States in the Council of the EU by the virtue of intergovernmental decision-making procedures.

Treaty on European Union ('Maastricht') [1992] OJ C191/1

Article F
1. The Union shall respect the national identities of its Member States, whose systems of government are founded on the principles of democracy.
2. **The Union shall respect fundamental rights**, as guaranteed by the **European Convention for the Protection of Human Rights and Fundamental Freedoms** signed in Rome on 4 November 1950 and as they result from the **constitutional traditions common to the Member States**, as **general principles of Community law**.
3. The Union shall provide itself with the means necessary to attain its objectives and carry through its policies.

Article J.1
1. The Union and its Member States shall define and implement a common foreign and security policy, governed by the provisions of this Title and covering all areas of foreign and security policy.
2. The objectives of the common foreign and security policy shall be:
   - to **safeguard the common values**, fundamental interests and independence of the Union;
   - to strengthen the security of the Union and its Member States in all ways;
   - to preserve peace and strengthen international security, in accordance with the principles of the United Nations Charter as well as the principles of the Helsinki Final Act and the objectives of the Paris Charter;
   - to promote international cooperation;
   - to **develop and consolidate democracy and the rule of law, and respect for human rights and fundamental freedoms**.
3. The Union shall pursue these objectives:

> - by establishing systematic cooperation between Member States in the conduct of policy, in accordance with Article J.2;
> - by gradually implementing, in accordance with Article J.3, joint action in the areas in which the Member States have important interests in common.

Relative to other periods, this was a time of considerable rate of change of the EU Treaties and the wording pertaining to human rights was altered just as often. In addition to modifying provisions on human rights, the Treaty of Amsterdam introduced a sanctioning mechanism—later refined in the Treaty of Nice—for violation of the fundamental principles the EU was founded on. This Article is also known as the 'nuclear option' due to the last resort nature of suspending a Member State's voting rights and the reluctance of other Member States to use it; the Article has so far been only proposed to be invoked once by the Commission (in the case of Poland) despite seemingly appropriate circumstances in a number of other cases as well.[43]

Consolidated version of the Treaty on European Union ('Amsterdam') [1997] OJ C340/145

Article 6 (ex Article F)

1. The Union **is founded on the principles of liberty, democracy, respect for human rights and fundamental freedoms, and the rule of law,** principles which are common to the Member States.
2. The Union shall respect fundamental rights, as guaranteed by the European Convention for the Protection of Human Rights and Fundamental Freedoms signed in Rome on 4 November 1950 and as they result from the constitutional traditions common to the Member States, as general principles of Community law. (...)

Article 7

1. **The Council**, meeting in the composition of the Heads of State or Government and acting by unanimity on a proposal by one third of the Member States or by the Commission and after obtaining the assent of the European Parliament, **may determine the existence of a serious and persistent breach by a Member State of principles mentioned in Article 6(1),** after inviting the government of the Member State in question to submit its observations.
2. **Where such a determination has been made, the Council,** acting by a qualified majority, **may decide to suspend certain of the rights deriving from the application of this Treaty to the Member State in question,** including the voting rights of the representative of the government of that Member State in the Council. In doing

---

[43] See U Sedelmeier, 'Anchoring Democracy from Above? The European Union and Democratic Backsliding in Hungary and Romania after Accession' (2014) 52 Journal of Common Market Studies 105. The mechanism and responses to crises of EU values in the Member States are discussed in more detail in Ch 4.

so, the Council shall take into account the possible consequences of such a suspension on the rights and obligations of natural and legal persons.

The obligations of the Member State in question under this Treaty shall in any case continue to be binding on that State.

Article 11 (ex Article J.1)

1. The Union shall define and implement a common foreign and security policy covering all areas of foreign and security policy, the objectives of which shall be:
   - to safeguard the common values, fundamental interests, independence and integrity of the Union in conformity with the principles of the United Nations Charter;
   - to strengthen the security of the Union in all ways;
   - to preserve peace and strengthen international security, in accordance with the principles of the United Nations Charter, as well as the principles of the Helsinki Final Act and the objectives of the Paris Charter, including those on external borders;
   - to promote international cooperation;
   - to develop and consolidate democracy and the rule of law, and respect for human rights and fundamental freedoms. (...)

At this stage of the EU integration endeavour, it is possible clearly to discern already the different roles fundamental rights play in internal and external policies. Internally, the EU—as pioneered by the Court of Justice in its case law—has recognized the need for respecting fundamental rights in its activities. The protection of fundamental rights at the EU level is principally ensured by the judicial system, commanded by the CJEU, with relatively few other avenues available. As the Treaties indicate, the EU is founded on the presumption that Member States respect fundamental rights themselves and therefore their protection is safeguarded also—or even primarily—on the national level. When that presumption is disrupted, the EU appears ill-equipped (short of the 'nuclear option') to restore fundamental rights guarantees internally, as a number of recent events have suggested.[44]

Externally, the situation is different. Human rights are one of the principles the EU 'seeks to advance in the wider world', in the latest wording of the Treaties (Article 21(1) of the Treaty on European Union (TEU)).[45] To that end, the promotion of human rights is 'mainstreamed' across EU external policies and thus can be found in, CFSP missions, international trade agreements, development cooperation, neighbourhood policy, and others. The EU has even developed a Strategic Framework on Human Rights and Democracy which consolidates the EU's external commitments in this area. The plethora of possibilities related to promoting human rights externally contrasts with the more constrained role of the EU in fundamental rights matters internally. The in-between area of internal fundamental rights checks on EU external action is afflicted by the fact that the CJEU lacks jurisdiction over CFSP activities.[46]

---

[44] See Ch 4.

[45] See Ch 9.

[46] According to Article 24(1) TEU and Article 275 TFEU, the CJEU does not have jurisdiction with regards to Union action under CFSP with the exception of Article 40 TEU on division of competences and when reviewing legality of restrictive measures. For a fuller treatment of this topic, see, for example, C Hillion, 'A Powerless Court? The European Court of Justice and the CFSP' in M Cremona and A Thies (eds), *The European Court of Justice and External Relations Law: Constitutional Challenges* (Hart Publishing 2014). See also Ch 9.

Overall, the difference in the EU's capabilities and willingness regarding fundamental rights at home and abroad can be referred to as the issue of internal/external coherence. Simply put, internal deficiencies in fundamental rights undermine the EU's external credibility as a human rights actor. This lack of coherence compounds the already difficult international environment for the promotion of human rights.

The EU has been largely aware that it needs to make progress on fundamental rights and the process gradually to rectify this has continued after the Treaty of Amsterdam. One of the first steps was to remedy the absence of a catalogue of rights at EU level by adopting the Charter of Fundamental Rights, which is discussed in detail in Chapter 4. The Charter was signed already in 2000, but it was only after the entry into force of the Treaty of Lisbon that it became legally binding primary law on par with the Treaties. However, the scope of application of the Charter can pose significant constraints, as it applies to Member States only when they are implementing EU law.[47]

In addition, the Treaty of Lisbon created an obligation for the EU to accede to the ECHR in order to subject the EU to the same level of fundamental rights oversight as the EU Member States, which have been parties to the ECHR for decades. Although negotiations are still underway, the accession process has been seriously impeded by the CJEU's negative decision in Opinion 2/13.[48]

Consolidated version of the Treaty on European Union [2012]
OJ C326/13

Article 6

1. The Union recognises the rights, freedoms and principles set out in **the Charter of Fundamental Rights of the European Union** of 7 December 2000, as adapted at Strasbourg, on 12 December 2007, **which shall have the same legal value as the Treaties.**

   The provisions of the Charter shall not extend in any way the competences of the Union as defined in the Treaties.
   The rights, freedoms and principles in the Charter shall be interpreted in accordance with the general provisions in Title VII of the Charter governing its interpretation and application and with due regard to the explanations referred to in the Charter, that set out the sources of those provisions.

2. **The Union shall accede to the European Convention for the Protection of Human Rights and Fundamental Freedoms.** Such accession shall not affect the Union's competences as defined in the Treaties.
3. Fundamental rights, as guaranteed by the European Convention for the Protection of Human Rights and Fundamental Freedoms and as they result from the constitutional traditions common to the Member States, shall constitute general principles of the Union's law.

---

[47] Article 51(1) of the Charter.
[48] See Ch 5.

> ### Article 21
>
> 1. The Union's action on the international scene shall be guided by the principles which have inspired its own creation, development and enlargement, and which it seeks to advance in the wider world: democracy, the rule of law, the universality and indivisibility of human rights and fundamental freedoms, respect for human dignity, the principles of equality and solidarity, and respect for the principles of the United Nations Charter and international law.

The EU's commitment to fundamental rights has come a long way since its inception. The legal framework developed over the course of 60 years captures an important part of this evolution, despite the fact that the job is far from done. It is, nevertheless, indicative of the scale of the development that the CJEU, which once initiated with modest formulations the recognition of fundamental rights in the EU, now often advances a rather robust understanding of the rights of individuals. Fundamental rights today form part of the constitutional guarantee of the Union.

Moreover, as the growth of the Union over the years entailed increasing interaction with the international legal order, comparisons of fundamental rights standards under EU law and under international law became of growing relevance. Similarly to the development of the nexus between EU law and national law, the CJEU was called on to clarify the status of international law in the EU legal order in light of fundamental rights. Its judgment in *Kadi* is reminiscent of the German Constitutional Court's decision in *Solange* in that the CJEU refused to abide mechanically by the principle of supremacy of international law, instead requiring that sufficient protection of fundamental rights must be guaranteed. In the absence of such protection in the United Nations system, the CJEU took it upon itself to ensure observance of fundamental rights which sparked a legal controversy of global significance.[49]

> ### Judgment of 3 September 2008, *Yassin Abdullah Kadi and Al Barakaat International Foundation*, C-402/05 P and C-415/05 P, ECLI:EU:C:2008:461
>
> ---
>
> 284. It is also clear from the case-law that respect for human rights is a condition of the lawfulness of Community acts (Opinion 2/94, paragraph 34) and that measures incompatible with respect for human rights are not acceptable in the Community (Case C-112/00 *Schmidberger* [2003] ECR I-5659, paragraph 73 and case-law cited).
> 304. Article 307 EC may in no circumstances permit any challenge to the principles that form part of the very foundations of the Community legal order, one of which

---

[49] The decision has attracted considerable academic attention. See, for example, KS Ziegler, 'Strengthening the Rule of Law, but Fragmenting International Law: The Kadi Decision of the ECJ from the Perspective of Human Rights' (2009) 9 Human Rights Law Review 288; G de Búrca, 'The European Court of Justice and the International Legal Order After Kadi' (2010) 51 Harvard International Law Journal 1; D Halberstam and E Stein, 'The United Nations, the European Union, and the King of Sweden: Economic Sanctions and Individual Rights in Plural World Order' (2009) 46 Common Market Law Review 13.

is the protection of fundamental rights, including the review by the Community judicature of the lawfulness of Community measures as regards their consistency with those fundamental rights.

316. As noted above in paragraphs 281 to 284, **the review by the Court of the validity of any Community measure in the light of fundamental rights must be considered to be the expression**, in a community based on the rule of law, **of a constitutional guarantee stemming from the EC Treaty** as an autonomous legal system which is not to be prejudiced by an international agreement.

326. It follows from the foregoing that the Community judicature must, in accordance with the powers conferred on it by the EC Treaty, ensure the review, in principle the full review, of the lawfulness of all Community acts in the light of the fundamental rights forming an integral part of the general principles of Community law, including review of Community measures which, like the contested regulation, are designed to give effect to the resolutions adopted by the Security Council under Chapter VII of the Charter of the United Nations.

2

Fundamental Rights in the EU Institutional Landscape

2.1 Introduction

The EU's legal and policy documents often present the Union's commitment to human rights as a matter for the EU as a whole or as an aspiration and responsibility shared among the EU institutions and the Member States. Such broad declarations do not tell us, however, how the commitments are implemented and which actors are key to the translation of the commitments into practice in the complex system of multi-level governance in the EU.[1] This chapter introduces the roles of the various institutional actors in the EU fundamental rights architecture (see Figure 2.1).

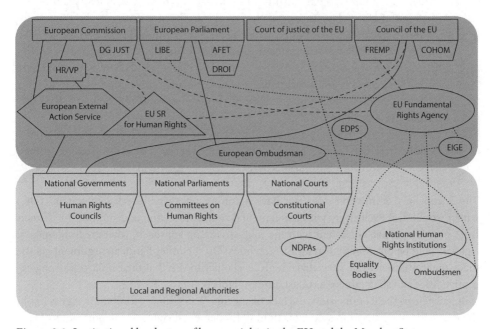

Figure 2.1 Institutional landscape of human rights in the EU and the Member States

---

[1] G Marks, L Hooghe, and K Blank, 'European Integration from the 1980s: State-centric v. Multi-level Governance' (1996) 34 Journal of Common Market Studies 341.

The European Union and Human Rights. Jan Wouters and Michal Ovádek, Oxford University Press (2021). © Jan Wouters and Michal Ovádek. DOI: 10.1093/oso/9780198814177.003.0002

2.2 The European Commission

The European Commission is the most well-known supranational institution of the EU. It acts as the central pillar of the EU system with responsibilities spanning legislative proposals and enforcement of EU law, among others. As such, the Commission has an important role in ensuring that both EU and implementing national law is consistent with fundamental rights. The conduct of the Commission itself is equally subject to fundamental rights requirements which is of additional significance due to its external representation role in which the Commission should also promote human rights. The Commission is, moreover, meant to be completely independent, which raises questions of democratic accountability.[2]

Consolidated version of the Treaty on European Union [2012] OJ C326/13

Article 17

1. The Commission shall promote the general interest of the Union and take appropriate initiatives to that end. **It shall ensure the application of the Treaties**, and of measures adopted by the institutions pursuant to them. It shall **oversee the application of Union law** under the control of the Court of Justice of the European Union. It shall execute the budget and manage programmes. It shall exercise coordinating, executive and management functions, as laid down in the Treaties. With the exception of the common foreign and security policy, and other cases provided for in the Treaties, it shall ensure the **Union's external representation**. It shall initiate the Union's annual and multiannual programming with a view to achieving interinstitutional agreements.
2. Union legislative acts may only be adopted on the basis of a Commission proposal, except where the Treaties provide otherwise. Other acts shall be adopted on the basis of a Commission proposal where the Treaties so provide.

The European Commission does not have a commissioner or directorate-general (DG) which would deal exclusively with fundamental rights protection and promotion.[3] This is from one perspective consistent with the mainstreaming approach, whereby fundamental rights should be omnipresent in all EU activities. On the other hand, an argument can be made that the absence of a specialized high-level office means that the EU lacks a strong executive voice and structure for a robust human rights policy.

In fairness to the Commission, the lack of specific responsibility for human rights has in the past been partially addressed by assigning fundamental rights to the portfolios of several Commissioners. During the second Barroso Commission (2009–2014), the portfolio

---

[2] M Bovens, D Curtin, and P 't Hart, *The Real World of EU Accountability: What Deficit?* (Oxford University Press 2010); B Crum and D Curtin, 'The Challenge of Making European Union Executive Power Accountable' in S Piattoni (ed), *The European Union: Democratic Principles and Institutional Architectures in Times of Crisis* (Oxford University Press 2015).

[3] The Commission's institutional set-up and allocation of responsibilities can change during its term but it is more common for it to be adapted at the beginning of a new mandate which normally coincides with the election of the European Parliament which also elects the President of the Commission (Article 14(1) TEU).

of Commissioner for Justice, Fundamental Rights and Citizenship was created. During the Juncker Commission (2014–2019) the responsibilities with regard to fundamental rights were shared between the Commissioner for Justice, Consumers and Gender Equality Věra Jourová and First Vice-President Frans Timmermans. The latter had been charged specifically with ensuring that every Commission proposal complied with the Charter of Fundamental Rights and with concluding the accession process of the EU to the European Convention on Human Rights (ECHR), but also with better regulation, interinstitutional relations, sustainable development, and others, inevitably diluting his attention to fundamental rights.[4]

Currently, under the von der Leyen Commission (2019–), the fundamental rights responsibilities are divided between three Commissioners. None of their portfolios' titles explicitly mention (human) rights. Jourová is one of seven vice-presidents, and responsible for Values and Transparency. Tasks that fall under her purview include leading the work on the EU's accession to the ECHR, monitoring the application of the Charter of Fundamental Rights, and safeguarding the right of peaceful assembly and the freedom of association. She also bears responsibility for upholding the rule of law, ensuring the transparency of the democratic system, financing and advertising of political parties, and plurality in the media sector.[5] While these tasks seem to be more closely interconnected than Timmermans' portfolio in the Juncker Commission, they still prevent the Commissioner for Values and Transparency from paying full attention to fundamental rights issues. The same holds true for the two Commissioners that are currently steering the work of DG Justice. Didier Reynders as Commissioner for Justice supervises the relationship with the Fundamental Rights Agency and with the Council of Europe, while at the same time he deals with civil, commercial, and criminal justice, the Annual Rule of Law Report, consumer rights, the fight against terrorism, among other areas.[6] Helena Dalli, as Commissioner for Equality, is responsible for anti-discrimination legislation, the implementation of the UN Convention on Rights of Persons with Disabilities, the implementation of the Work–Life Balance Directive, and the EU's response to gender-based violence.[7]

The breadth of the portfolios outlined above requires that scarce resources are distributed across a range of issues of which fundamental rights protection and promotion is only one. The same is evident when it comes to impact assessments which the Commission conducts in preparation of EU actions: the impact of EU laws or international agreements on human rights is only one part of a much broader assessment, and this can raise doubts as to whether the depth of these assessments is sufficient, given that human rights have a wide scope, covering political, civil, economic, social and cultural rights, and freedoms.

Still, the general importance of the Commission in the EU constellation is bound to be evident in the EU's human rights policy, in spite of it not being at the forefront of the Commission's own internal set-up. Indeed, the Commission is listed as one of the responsible institutions for the implementation of 101 out of 113 action points in the Action Plan on Human Rights and Democracy 2015–2019 which, however, only concerns external policies. Among other matters, the Action Plan mentions the enhancement of human rights impact assessments. These represent an important tool at the Commission's disposal in both internal and external law- and policy-making.[8] A new EU Action

---

[4] Mission Letter from Jean-Claude Juncker to Frans Timmermans, 1 November 2014, 4–5.
[5] Mission Letter from Ursula von der Leyen to Věra Jourová, 1 December 2019, 4–6.
[6] Mission Letter from Ursula von der Leyen to Didier Reynders, 1 December 2019, 4–6.
[7] Mission Letter from Ursula von der Leyen to Helena Dalli, 1 December 2019, 4–6.
[8] See Ch 9 for an analysis of impact assessments.

Plan on Human Rights and Democracy for the period of 2020–2024 is currently being drafted.[9]

Commission President Juncker also created the position of Special Envoy for freedom of religion and belief, who worked closely with the Commissioner for International Cooperation and Development and the European Union External Action Service (EEAS) within the policy framework set by the EU Guidelines on the promotion and protection of freedom of religion. The position was not renewed in the von der Leyen Commission.[10]

One of the Commission's flagship internal initiatives on fundamental rights is the Annual report on the application of the Charter, which reports on developments at EU level as well as in the Member States.[11] The report is known for being less critical than a similar annual assessment by the Fundamental Rights Agency (FRA). Nonetheless, the intention behind the drafting exercise is to place fundamental rights—particularly in the context of implementing the EU Charter—on the agenda of the EU institutions. The annual release of the report is normally accompanied by a debate in the European Parliament (EP) and in the Council (followed by a reference in Council conclusions). The ultimate expectation is that the report can lead to improvements in practices of the EU institutions and the Member States.

2.3 The European Parliament

Consolidated version of the Treaty on European Union [2012] OJ C326/13

Article 14

1. The European Parliament shall, jointly with the Council, **exercise legislative and budgetary functions**. It shall exercise functions of **political control and consultation** as laid down in the Treaties. It shall **elect the President of the Commission**.
2. The European Parliament shall be composed of representatives of the Union's citizens. They shall not exceed seven hundred and fifty in number, plus the President. Representation of citizens shall be degressively proportional, with a minimum threshold of six members per Member State. No Member State shall be allocated more than ninety-six seats.

The EP's stature has grown steadily over the years and it is no longer a marginal player in the EU. The EP decides jointly with the Council on most EU laws, international agreements,[12] and the EU budget (including financing instruments relevant for human rights); through these competences, its democratic legitimacy, and serving as a public forum for politicization and awareness raising, it can have a substantial say in EU human (fundamental)

---

[9] See European Commission and Hight Representative for Foreign Affairs and Security Policy, 'Joint Communication to the European Parliament and the Council—EU Action Plan on Human Rights and Democracy 2020–2024' JOIN (2020) 5 final.

[10] The mandate ran from February 2016 to November 2019. The office holder was Ján Figel, a former Slovak deputy prime minister and European Commissioner for education and culture.

[11] Ten annual reports have been drafted to date: European Commission, 'Press Release—European Commission reports on the EU Charter of Fundamental Rights, 10 years on', 5 June 2019.

[12] For example, the European Parliament in 2011 blocked the conclusion of a textile protocol between the EU and Uzbekistan due to concerns over child labour.

rights policy, as is also recognized in the Strategic Framework.[13] The Parliament is cognizant of its human rights potential and tends to portray itself as a major force for human rights, the rule of law, and democracy both inside and outside of the Union. This self-perception is, however, not shared by all in the scholarly literature, at least when it comes to the internal fundamental rights framework of the EU.[14]

As in the case of the Council, and characteristic of the EU as a whole, the rights remit is divided between internal and external aspects, or 'fundamental' and 'human' rights. The former are addressed in the influential Committee on Civil Liberties, Justice and Home Affairs (LIBE), while human rights in EU external relations are dealt with in a subsidiary of the Foreign Affairs Committee (AFET), the Subcommittee on Human Rights (DROI). In their work, both groups engage with a variety of actors beyond EU institutions and bodies, such as civil society organizations, law enforcement agencies, international organizations, national parliaments, and third-country parties. Issues of gender equality and women's rights belong to the purview of the Committee on Women's Rights and Gender Equality (FEMM), which discusses both internal and external dimensions.

The LIBE Committee belongs to the most important committees in the EP due to the growing relevance and sensitivity of the areas it covers (in addition to fundamental rights): the fight against international crime and terrorism, data protection, and discrimination in a number of areas. Much of its work has therefore been recently related to contentious but topical issues of justice and home affairs which have significant fundamental rights implications, such as the reform of the Common European Asylum System and migration more generally, the Passenger Name Record Directive (in connection with counter-terrorism), inquiry on mass surveillance, among other topics. Furthermore, every year LIBE adopts a report on the situation of fundamental rights in the EU in which it evaluates fundamental rights developments in the past year and calls for action.[15] The EP, on the basis of work in LIBE, has also made inroads in enhancing the rule of law framework in the EU with a resolution calling for a reinforcement of monitoring of democracy, the rule of law, and fundamental rights in the EU.[16]

The DROI Subcommittee, consisting of 30 members and 28 substitutes, looks at the state of democracy, human rights, the rule of law, and rights of minorities in countries outside of the EU and strives to ensure the presence of these principles in all areas of the Union's foreign policy. Unlike LIBE, DROI is a subcommittee which in practice means that all matters discussed in DROI are still subject to a final vote of the 'master' AFET Committee. In terms of substance, the DROI Subcommittee is heavily involved in drafting resolutions which comment on the Annual Report on human rights and democracy in the world adopted by the Council.[17] This resolution gives the EP—and therein not only the AFET/DROI (Sub) Committee but also, for example, the Committee on Development (DEVE)—the opportunity to make public its own view on both the assessment of the Annual Report and the

---

[13] Council of the European Union, 'Human Rights and Democracy: EU Strategic Framework and Action Plan', 11855/12, 25 June 2012.

[14] See A Williams, 'Human Rights in the EU' in A Arnull and D Chalmers (eds), *The Oxford Handbook of European Union Law* (Oxford University Press 2015) 249–63, also questioning the significance of the Council for the development of fundamental rights in the EU.

[15] The most recent report available is Committee on Civil Liberties, Justice and Home Affairs, 'Report on the Situation of Fundamental Rights in the European Union in 2017', 201/2103(INI), 13 December 2018.

[16] See Ch 4.

[17] See, for example, European Parliament, 'Resolution on the Annual Report on Human Rights and Democracy in the World and the European Union's policy on the matter 2018', P9_TA(2020)0007, 15 January 2020.

situation of human rights and democracy in the world itself. Another notable annual activity (since 1988) of the Parliament involving the DROI Subcommittee, together with the AFET and DEVE Committees, has been the awarding of the Sakharov Prize for Freedom of Thought to individuals from around the world who have distinguished themselves in the fight for human rights.

In addition, members of the DROI Subcommittee conduct visits to third countries in order to engage in dialogue with relevant stakeholders—different from the official EU human rights dialogues—and assess the human rights situation in the country. These visits are distinct from the EP's election observation missions which send Members of the European Parliament (MEPs) to third countries to monitor and assess the electoral process there, most often as part of a common EU Election Observation Mission organized by the EEAS and the Commission.[18]

The EP also has a secretariat—similarly to the Council—that supports the activities of the MEPs and of the committees. It contains a dedicated Directorate for Impact Assessment and European Added Value which carries out impact assessments (IAs) of legislative amendments, on top of the IAs of legislative proposals prepared by the Commission, which also take into account the potential impact on fundamental rights. There is, however, still room for stronger and more systematic rights-based IAs in the EP.[19]

Finally, as an elected body, the European Parliament is not only an actor with human rights competences but also an institution where EU citizens' fundamental rights are realized. The Charter specifically mentions three rights of EU citizens involving the European Parliament: the right to vote, the right to stand as candidate, and the right to petition the Parliament. With respect to the latter, the EP has a dedicated Committee on Petitions (PETI) which deals with EU citizens' complaints about problems falling within the scope of EU activity.

Charter of Fundamental Rights of the European Union [2012] OJ C326/391

Article 39

Right to vote and to stand as a candidate at elections to the European Parliament

1. Every citizen of the Union has the right to vote and to stand as a candidate at elections to the European Parliament in the Member State in which he or she resides, under the same conditions as nationals of that State.

---

[18] See, for example, A Gawrich, 'The European Parliament in International Election Observation Missions (IEOMs): Division of Labour or Decreased Influence?' in S Stavridis and D Irrera (eds), *The European Parliament and its International Relations* (Routledge 2015) 121–42.

[19] The interinstitutional agreement on better law-making provides that '[t]he European Parliament and the Council will, when they consider this to be appropriate and necessary for the legislative process, carry out impact assessments in relation to their substantial amendments to the Commission's proposal. The European Parliament and the Council will, as a general rule, take the Commission's impact assessment as the starting point for their further work. The definition of a 'substantial' amendment should be for the respective Institution to determine.' See Interinstitutional Agreement between the European Parliament, the Council of the European Union and the European Commission on better law-making [2016] OJ L123/1, para 15.

2. Members of the European Parliament shall be elected by direct universal suffrage in a free and secret ballot.

Article 44

Right to petition

Any citizen of the Union and any natural or legal person residing or having its registered office in a Member State has the right to petition the European Parliament.

2.4 The Council of the European Union

Consolidated version of the Treaty on European Union [2012] OJ C326/13

Article 16

1. The Council shall, jointly with the European Parliament, **exercise legislative and budgetary functions**. It shall carry out policy-making and coordinating functions as laid down in the Treaties.
2. The Council shall consist of a representative of each Member State at ministerial level, who may commit the government of the Member State in question and cast its vote.
3. The Council shall act by a qualified majority except where the Treaties provide otherwise.

The Council of the EU brings together the Member States of the Union. As such, the Treaties vest it with wide-ranging powers, making it arguably the most powerful EU institution. The Council is a co-legislator with the European Parliament but it also decides in non-legislative areas such as the Common Foreign and Security Policy (CFSP). The permanency of this essentially multilateral forum is secured through the General Secretariat of the Council which provides the organizational backbone to the work of the Member States.[20] A continuing feature of the Council is the system of rotating presidencies: every six months a different Member State chairs the meetings of the Council (with the notable exception of the Foreign Affairs Council) which in practice also affects the human rights agenda. That is not to say, however, that the Council would not on the whole subscribe to the EU-wide fundamental rights commitments.

---

[20] D Beach, 'The Facilitator of Efficient Negotiations in the Council: The Impact of the Council Secretariat' in D Naurin and H Wallace (eds), *Unveiling the Council of the European Union: Games Governments Play in Brussels* (Palgrave 2008) 219–37.

Council conclusions on the role of the Council of the European Union in ensuring the effective implementation of the Charter of Fundamental Rights of the European Union, Justice and Home Affairs Council meeting, 24 and 25 February 2011

THE COUNCIL OF THE EUROPEAN UNION,

1. Recalls the Stockholm Programme, which invites the EU institutions and the Member States to ensure that **legislative initiatives are and remain consistent with fundamental rights** throughout the legislative process by way of strengthening the application of the methodology for a **systematic and rigorous monitoring of compliance** with the **European Convention on Human Rights** and the rights, freedoms and principles set out in the **Charter**.

4. Stresses **the role of the Council in ensuring the effective implementation of the Charter** and, being a co-legislator, reaffirms that both its amendments to legislative proposals as well as the acts it adopts by virtue of the Treaty on the initiative of a quarter of Member States must be in conformity with the Charter.

5. Recognizes that respect for **fundamental rights should also be taken into account** when drafting **legal acts which are not subject to a legislative procedure**.

9. Considers it important to make full use of the expertise, knowledge and experience of experts working in the Member States and recalls that **Member States' administrations are the first level where compliance with obligations deriving from the Charter, as well as the constitutional traditions and international obligations common to all Member States, should be guaranteed.**

10. Expects that before proposals for amendments are submitted by Member States to the Council, as well as before legislative initiatives are tabled by a quarter of the Member States, their conformity with the Charter and their impact on fundamental rights have been examined by the Member States involved.

11. Highlights in this regard that the **Council Legal Service**, assisting at all preparatory instances of the Council, is at the Council's disposal and carries out useful and reliable work by providing for **legal opinions and assessing the compliance of legislative and non-legislative proposals**, as well as proposals for amendments, with primary law including **also fundamental rights requirements**.

12. Reiterates that **the interinstitutional agreement 'Common Approach to Impact Assessment' entails the responsibility for each institution to assess the impact of its proposals and amendments.** When making that assessment the Council should give the necessary attention to the impact of its substantive amendments on fundamental rights.

13. Stresses that the **preparatory instances of the Council and the Council itself should**, at an early stage of the legislative procedure, **raise the questions and concerns relating to fundamental rights** in the relevant dossiers on their agenda, **and ensure compatibility with the Charter**.

14. Recalls that in December 2009, immediately after the entry into force of the Lisbon Treaty, which made the Charter legally binding, the Council gave the former ad hoc Working Party on Fundamental Rights and Citizenship a permanent status and

tasked it with all matters relating to fundamental rights, citizens' rights and free movement of persons (hereinafter 'the FREMP Working Party').

15. Emphasizes the need for the fundamental rights dimension to extend to all preparatory instances of the Council and the entire Council structure; for that very reason it considers that the **Council's preparatory instances should benefit from** disposing of short but pragmatic and **methodological guidelines on how to identify and solve problems raised by their own proposals for amendments in relation to their compatibility with fundamental rights.**

17. Encourages the Council's preparatory instances—while recognizing the responsibility of these instances for scrutinizing the compliance with the Charter—to **seek, where necessary, the assistance of the Council Legal Service, and** without prejudice to the responsibility of the Coreper, on a limited case by case basis, **the advice of the FREMP Working Party** with respect to specific fundamental rights issues arising during their work.

18. Recalls the invitation made in the Stockholm Program to all EU institutions to **make full use of the expertise of the European Union Agency for Fundamental Rights (hereinafter: 'Agency') and to consult, where appropriate, with the Fundamental Rights Agency, in line with its mandate, on the development of policies and legislation with implications for fundamental rights.**

19. Reaffirms its intention to take into account the reports and opinions of the Agency on specific thematic topics given in accordance with its mandate.

20. Encourages the **FREMP Working Party to maintain and reinforce the cooperation with the Agency,** inter alia by ensuring follow-up to the reports of the Agency relevant to its work.

21. Underlines the commitment to have an annual exchange of views on the **Commission's annual report** on the application of the Charter.

Although the Council formally convenes governmental officials at the ministerial level, most of its substantive work is done at the level of preparatory bodies of which there are around 150. Two such bodies deal explicitly with human (fundamental) rights, while mirroring the internal–external *summa divisio* present across all EU engagement with human rights: the Working Party on Fundamental Rights, Citizens' Rights, and Free Movement of Persons (FREMP) and the Working Party on Human Rights (COHOM).[21] As a general rule, where agreement is found among Member States at the level of the working parties, the issue is simply rubber-stamped in the appropriate formation of the Council of the Ministers. If agreement is not reached at the working party level, the issue in question travels up for further discussions, first to the Committee of Permanent Representatives (COREPER) and then to the Council.[22]

As a side note, it is worth remarking that the Council and its working parties are notoriously opaque.[23] Much of the work of the preparatory bodies is still shielded from public view,

[21] There are also other working parties dealing with fundamental rights but these usually have a very specific focus, such as the Working Group on Information Exchange and Data Protection.

[22] For more information about the decision-making in the Council, see J Lewis, 'The European Council and the Council of the European Union' in M Cini and N Pérez-Solórzano Borragán (eds), *European Union Politics* (5th edn, Oxford University Press 2016).

[23] See, for example, MZ Hillebrandt, D Curtin, and A Meijer, 'Transparency in the EU Council of Ministers: An Institutional Analysis' (2014) 20 European Law Journal 1.

sometimes so much so that even other EU institutions and bodies can be in the dark with regards to topics of relevance discussed inside Council meetings. As a result, information on Member States' positions regarding issues discussed in the Council, including human rights, is often confined to Brussels insiders.

A. Working Party on Fundamental Rights, Citizens' Rights, and Free Movement of Persons (FREMP)

As is apparent from the title of this working party, FREMP is responsible for the EU's internal fundamental rights agenda. It is chaired by a representative of the government holding the rotating presidency which enables presidencies to some extent to shape the programme of the working party in line with their priorities. This reflects the reality that despite the formal abandonment of the pillar structure by the Treaty of Lisbon, Member States remain the key players—more so than elsewhere—in the area of justice and home affairs (JHA) to which FREMP belongs. Moreover, FREMP was only made permanent in 2009, thus underlining the relative immaturity of the EU's internal fundamental rights regime. In comparison, the externally-minded COHOM was established as early as 1987.

According to a decision of the COREPER, FREMP is tasked with 'all matters relating to fundamental rights and citizens' rights, including free movement of persons, negotiations on accession of the Union to the ECHR, the follow-up of reports from the EU Agency for Fundamental Rights'.[24] Nevertheless, with respect to the FRA, FREMP does not merely follow up reports—it is also the principal forum where FRA's Multi-annual Framework (MAF) is negotiated which gives this working party an important role in the internal architecture of EU fundamental rights. To date, due to the requirement of unanimity, FREMP has failed to agree on extending the scope of the FRA's mandate, even though a majority of the Member States are rumoured to be unopposed to at least including police and judicial cooperation in criminal matters in the MAF. FREMP also continues to support the EU's accession to the ECHR despite the major setback in this process represented by Opinion 2/13 of the Court of Justice of the European Union (CJEU).[25]

Moreover, FREMP has prepared, in collaboration with the Secretariat, methodological guidelines on fundamental rights compatibility of EU laws and policies passing through the Council preparatory bodies.[26] The Council has so far failed properly to put these guidelines into practice and thus live up to its commitment to assess the fundamental rights impact of its policies continually, especially before they take effect (ex-ante). However, it has recently reaffirmed this commitment and expressed 'its readiness to explore ways to make more efficient use of that guidance in Council preparatory bodies, including through training'.[27]

---

[24] Council of the European Union, 'Implications of the Treaty of Lisbon Provisions for the JHA Working Structures', 17653/09, 16 December 2009.

[25] Opinion of 18 December 2014, *EU accession to the ECHR*, 2/13, ECLI:EU:C:2014:2454.

[26] See Council of the European Union, 'Guidelines on Methodological Steps to be Taken to Check Fundamental Rights Compatibility at the Council Preparatory Bodies', 5377/15, 20 January 2015. The guidelines were endorsed by COREPER.

[27] Council of the European Union, 'Council Conclusions on the Charter of Fundamental Rights after 10 Years: State of Play and Future Work', 12357/19, 20 September 2019, 6.

Guidelines on methodological steps to be taken to check fundamental rights compatibility at the Council preparatory bodies, 20 January 2015

PURPOSE

The aim of these guidelines, which should be considered as non-binding advice, is to help the Council preparatory bodies to take the methodological steps necessary to identify and deal with fundamental rights issues arising in connection with the proposals under discussion at the relevant Council preparatory bodies. They provide context and guidance in the process of checking compliance with fundamental rights and, in addition, they also provide a 'fundamental rights check-list' (see Annex V), which is a tool to facilitate the assessment of compatibility with fundamental rights. (...)

ANNEX V

FUNDAMENTAL RIGHTS 'CHECK-LIST'
A tool to facilitate the assessment of compatibility with fundamental rights

1. What fundamental rights are affected?
2. Are the rights in question absolute rights (which may not be subject to limitations, examples being the ban on torture and the prohibition of slavery or servitude)?
3. Would any limitation of/negative impact on fundamental rights be formulated in law, in a clear and predictable (foreseeable) manner?
4. Would any such limitation/negative impact:
   - preserve the essence of the fundamental rights concerned?
   - be necessary to achieve an objective of general interest recognised by the Union or to protect the rights and freedoms of others?
   - be proportionate to the desired aim? That is, would they be appropriate for attaining the objective pursued without going beyond what is necessary to achieve it? Why is no equally effective but less intrusive measure available?
   - If applicable: Consider and identify which safeguards might be necessary to ensure that the negative impact would not amount to a violation of the fundamental right in question (that is, restrict it without justification).

B. Working Party on Human Rights (COHOM)

COHOM covers external aspects of EU human rights policy in the Council since 1987 but it has undergone significant changes during its existence. Prior to the Treaty of Lisbon, it was chaired by rotating presidencies which were faced with the considerable task of coordinating Member States' positions on human rights issues at the UN, in particular the Human Rights Council (HRC). The effectiveness of this arrangement was doubtful, especially as the monthly COHOM sessions could hardly keep up with the pace of diplomacy in New York and Geneva.[28]

---

[28] KE Smith, 'Speaking with One Voice? European Union Coordination on Human Rights Issues at the United Nations' (2006) 44 Journal of Common Market Studies 113, 117. See Ch 9.

Following the institutional innovations of the Lisbon Treaty, COHOM is no longer chaired by the Council presidency. Instead, in a bid to boost the continuity and coherence of EU external action, a representative of the EEAS under the guidance of the High Representative/Vice-President of the Commission (HR/VP) now chairs COHOM, as the HR/VP himself leads the Foreign Affairs Council to which COHOM pertains in the institutional hierarchy of the Council. As a result, EU human rights activity in international fora has become more centralized with COHOM playing a more important role in drafting and making decisions on resolutions presented in the United Nations (UN). COHOM meets nowadays more frequently and in two formations: one is an assembly of Member States' experts based in Brussels, while the other convenes experts from Member States' capitals.[29] Paradoxically, empirical data suggest that the enhanced institutionalisation of COHOM—and EU external action more broadly—has not led to a stronger and more unified EU voice on human rights issues at the UN.[30]

Other notable activity of COHOM is the identification of strategic priorities and their articulation in various policy documents, ranging from the Strategic Framework on Human Rights and Democracy, through EU priorities at the UN human rights fora, to human rights guidelines.[31] In this way, COHOM also aims to contribute to policy coherence and mainstreaming of human rights. In addition, COHOM is an important actor when it comes to human rights dialogues; its decision and assessment is, for example, necessary in order for the EU to even start a human rights dialogue with a third country in the first place. COHOM is also a principal contributor to the EU Annual Report on Human Rights and Democracy in the World where the Council recounts the EU's work and achievements in external action,[32] as well as the forum where EU Human Rights Guidelines are negotiated.[33]

2.5 The Court of Justice

The role of the CJEU in the institutional landscape of the EU is to interpret and apply EU law in a consistent manner and ensure effective judicial protection at the EU level.[34] The CJEU, an EU institution, comprises two judicial instances: the General Court (formerly the Court of First Instance) and, somewhat confusingly, the Court of Justice. The Court of Justice is assisted by Advocates General who provide non-binding legal opinions on cases referred to them by the Court. The historical centrality of the Court to the inclusion of fundamental rights in the integration project has been demonstrated in Chapter 1 on the evolution of the EU's commitment to human rights. The CJEU played an even more

[29] KE Smith, 'EU Member States at the UN: A Case of Europeanization Arrested?' (2017) 55 Journal of Common Market Studies 628, 631.

[30] Ibid, 644–45.

[31] See, for example, Council of the European Union, 'Council Conclusions on EU Priorities in UN Human Rights Fora in 2020', 5982/20, 17 February 2020. In its work, COHOM consults a number of other Council and EU bodies, such as geographical working parties or the Commission, depending on the topic.

[32] The annual report consists of a thematic and country and regional issues part. See, for example, Council of the European Union, 'EU Annual Report on Human Rights and Democracy in the World in 2018', 9024/19, 13 May 2019.

[33] See Ch 9.

[34] See Article 19(1) TEU and Article 47 of the Charter. See also D Leczykiewicz, '"Effective Judicial Protection" of Human Rights after Lisbon: Should National Courts be Empowered to Review EU Secondary Law?' (2010) 35 European Law Review 326.

instrumental part in revolutionizing the EU legal order as a whole by ushering in, in cooperation with national courts, its effectiveness and uniform application across the EU's Member States.[35]

The Judges and Advocates-General of the Court of Justice and the General Court are selected through a rigorous procedure which ensures the integrity of the Court. Article 255 of the Treaty on the Functioning of the European Union (TFEU) provides for the existence of a panel which delivers opinions on the suitability of candidates nominated by the Member States. The opinions of the panel have been always followed by the Member States who decide on appointments by consensus, despite judicial candidates being ruled out on a regular basis by the panel.[36] Appointments at the CJEU are for a period of six years with the possibility of reappointment.[37]

The jurisdiction of the CJEU can be accessed through a variety of actions, yet not all are easily available to individuals.[38] The Court may be asked to give a preliminary ruling on a point of EU law in a case before a Member State court,[39] review acts and establish failures to act of EU institutions,[40] adjudicate failures to fulfil an obligation of a Member State under the Treaties,[41] impose sanctions on Member States for such failures,[42] deliver opinions on compatibility of international agreements with EU law,[43] decide on EU staff disputes,[44] and decide on actions for damages against the EU.[45] In the course of judicial proceedings before the CJEU, the Court can draw on a number of different but often overlapping sources of human rights law: general principles of law,[46] international human rights law,[47] the ECHR,[48] and the EU Charter of Fundamental Rights.[49] Apart from general human rights instruments, the Court also interprets issue-specific secondary EU legislation, such as the ones on anti-discrimination and data protection.[50]

---

[35] See the landmark judgments of 5 February 1963, *Van Gend en Loos v Nederlandse administratie der belastingen*, 26/62, ECLI:EU:C:1963:1 and of 15 July 1964, *Costa v ENEL*, 6/64, ECLI:EU:C:1964:66. On their revolutionary character, see M Rasmussen, 'Revolutionizing European Law: A History of the Van Gend en Loos Judgment' (2014) 12 International Journal of Constitutional Law 136; and the classic treatises on the fundamental impact of judges and the law on the transformation of the EU from an international organization to a federalist-lite polity: E Stein, 'Lawyers, Judges, and the Making of a Transnational Constitution' (1981) 75 The American Journal of International Law 1; JHH Weiler, 'The Transformation of Europe' (1991) 100 Yale Law Journal 2403.

[36] T Dumbrovský, B Petkova, and M van der Sluis, 'Judicial Appointments: The Article 255 TFEU Advisory Panel and Selection Procedures in the Member States' (2014) 51 Common Market Law Review 455.

[37] Articles 253 and 254 TFEU.

[38] Article 19(3) TEU.

[39] Article 267 TFEU. Note that litigants on the national level do not have a right to have their case referred to the CJEU—it is the national court who makes the determination to pose a question to the CJEU. For a comprehensive doctrinal treatment of preliminary references see M Broberg and N Fenger, *Preliminary References to the European Court of Justice* (2nd edn, Oxford University Press 2014).

[40] Articles 263 and 265 TFEU.

[41] Such an action can be brought by the Commission (Article 258 TFEU) or by the Member States (Article 259 TFEU). The latter provision is almost never exercised by the Member States out of fear of reciprocal actions. For a notable exception see Judgment of 16 October 2012, *Hungary v Slovak Republic*, C-364/10, ECLI:EU:C:2012:630.

[42] Article 260 TFEU.

[43] Article 218(11) TFEU.

[44] Article 270 TFEU.

[45] Articles 268 and 340 TFEU.

[46] Judgment of 17 December 1970, *Internationale Handelsgesellschaft mbH v Einfuhr- und Vorratsstelle für Getreide und Futtermittel*, 11/70, ECLI:EU:C:1970:114.

[47] Judgment of 14 May 1974, *Nold v Commission*, 4/73, ECLI:EU:C:1974:51.

[48] Opinion of 28 March 1996, *Community accession to the ECHR*, 2/94, ECLI:EU:C:1996:140, para 33; Article 6 TEU.

[49] Article 6 TEU.

[50] See respectively Chs 7 and 6.

One glaring omission in the jurisdiction of the CJEU is the CFSP.[51] There are two exceptions to this rule. The Court may still adjudicate on the delimitation between the CFSP 'zone'
of competence, governed mainly by the provisions of the Treaty on European Union (TEU),
and the 'standard' Union competences, as defined in Articles 3–6 of the TFEU. Second, and
more importantly from the perspective of fundamental rights, the CJEU also has jurisdiction
in cases where an affected natural or legal person requests a review of the legality of a CFSP
decision providing for restrictive measures (sanctions) against them. In spite of the Court's
general reluctance to annul EU acts on the grounds of fundamental rights,[52] the CJEU has
been more willing to challenge the fundamental rights compliance of targeted sanctions,
famously even when imposed by the UN Security Council.[53] This may be part of a broader
development towards assertiveness of the Court on fundamental rights linked to the post-
Lisbon primary law status of the Charter.[54]

The CJEU is not the only judicial institution, however, responsible for fleshing out
EU law with effective judicial protection.[55] On the contrary, national courts are part and
parcel of the system of remedies designed to make EU rules effective.[56] National courts in
EU Member States are legally bound to apply a multitude of human rights commitments
ranging from those enshrined in their national constitutional law, through the EU Charter
and general principles of EU law (in cases falling within their scope of application), to the
ECHR and international human rights law more generally. National courts can therefore
find themselves in a precarious position when some of the content of these different loyal-
ties clashes.[57]

The overall increase in relevance and salience of fundamental rights in the EU is a trend
that the CJEU is likely to continue to reflect. The number of cases applying fundamental
rights is rising and with it the importance of the Charter in the EU legal order. The growing
reliance on the Charter might, however, push into the background other sources of human
rights law, particularly the ECHR.[58] The CJEU has given some indication that this development might be taking place in its rejection of the draft agreement on the EU's accession to the
ECHR and in its newfound emphasis on the autonomy of the EU legal order.[59]

---

[51] Article 24(1) TEU and Article 275(1) TFEU.

[52] See, however, Judgment of 8 April 2014, *Digital Rights Ireland Ltd v Minister for Communications and Others*,
C-293/12 and C-594/12, ECLI:EU:C:2014:238.

[53] Judgment of 3 September 2008, *Kadi and Al Barakaat International Foundation v Council of the European
Union and Commission of the European Communities*, C-402/05 P and C-415/05 P, ECLI:EU:C:2008:461.

[54] L Ginsborg and others, 'Experiences Regarding Coherence in the European Union Human Rights Context'
(2016) FRAME Deliverable 8.3, 90 <http://www.fp7-frame.eu/wp-content/uploads/2016/09/Deliverable-8.3.pdf>
accessed 14 August 2020.

[55] Article 19(1) TEU.

[56] Judgment of 16 December 1976, *Rewe-Zentralfinanz eG and others v Landwirtschaftskammer für das Saarland*,
33/76, ECLI:EU:C:1976:188.

[57] See, for example, Judgment of 26 February 2013, *Melloni v Ministerio Fiscal*, C-399/11, ECLI:EU:C:2013:107.

[58] For quantitative trends in the CJEU's references to the Charter and the ECHR see G de Búrca, 'After
the EU Charter of Fundamental Rights: The Court of Justice as a Human Rights Adjudicator?' (2013) 20
Maastricht Journal of European and Comparative Law 168, 174–76; M Ovádek, 'External Judicial Review and
Fundamental Rights in the EU: A Place in the Sun for the Court of Justice' (2016) EU Diplomacy Papers
2/2016, 13 <https://www.coleurope.eu/system/files_force/research-paper/edp_2_2016_ovadek_0.pdf> accessed 14 August 2020.

[59] *Opinion 2/13 (EU accession to the ECHR)* (n 25); J Krommendijk, 'The Use of ECtHR Case Law by the Court of
Justice after Lisbon: The View of Luxembourg Insiders' (2015) 22 Maastricht Journal of European and Comparative
Law 812, 831.

> ### G de Búrca, 'After the EU Charter of Fundamental Rights: The Court of Justice as a Human Rights Adjudicator?' (2013) 20 Maastricht Journal of European and Comparative Law 168
>
> (...) the advent of the Charter of Rights and the increase in rights-based arguments being made before the CJEU have—together with other developments—placed increasing pressure on the traditional judicial style and approach of the Court, and have made it more difficult to justify this approach today. The self-referential, formulaic and often minimal style of the single collegiate judgment seems increasingly ill-suited to the changing circumstances and docket of the Court. (...) And yet the three years since the Charter came into force reveals that the CJEU is referring even less now to the ECHR than it did before, and even more rarely to the case law of the Court of Human Rights. More worryingly still, there has been a steady trend towards dispensing with the need for an Advocate General's Opinion in a great many cases, including in 22 of the 124 cases raising human rights claims based on the Charter since 2009.
>
> At present, the CJEU's main focus seems to be on ensuring the acceptability of its judgments to the national courts of the Member States, with less regard for other relevant constituencies including litigants and the public more broadly. Notably, the Court seems largely unconcerned about the external impact and influence of its rulings. The Court appears to have concluded that its existing style and methodology is best suited to maintaining its legitimacy and the acceptability of its rulings to Member State courts. (...) the CJEU, by emphasizing the autonomy of EU law and of its own interpretation, is missing the opportunity of developing informed expertise in the field of human rights adjudication, and of ensuring that its standards of rights protection are at least as developed as the relevant regional and international standards. The Court is also missing the opportunity to improve the quality and fairness of its judgments and to strengthen their legitimacy in the eyes of European citizens and other relevant constituencies. Further, its self-referential and detached style of judgment is also curiously at odds with the internationalist orientation of the EU. The Court's adherence to its conventional style and its avoidance of engagement with the relevant jurisprudence of other bodies and courts in cases involving human rights claims limits the potential influence of its rulings, despite their increasing impact and significance for many actors both within and outside the EU.

2.6 The European External Action Service (EEAS) and EU Special Representative (EUSR) for Human Rights

The EEAS is another obvious actor in EU human rights policy, not least as a consequence of the value orientation of EU foreign policy proclaimed in Article 21 TEU.[60] The EEAS, however, is not an EU institution from the legal perspective of the Treaties.[61] Rather, it is a 'functionally autonomous body' of the EU established by a decision of the Council.[62]

---

[60] See Ch 9.

[61] Article 13 TEU. The Treaty of Lisbon has, nevertheless, foreseen the establishment of the EEAS; see Article 27(3) TEU.

[62] Council Decision (EU) 2010/427 establishing the organisation and functioning of the European External Action Service [2010] OJ L 201/30, Article 1(2).

The composition of the EEAS is hybrid,[63] in the sense that it is filled with both Commission and Member States officials, but in the first place its duties serve to support the High Representative for Foreign Affairs and Security Policy, who is a multifaceted actor.[64]

There are various institutional manifestations of human rights in the EEAS. The Brussels headquarters contains a department responsible for human rights, global and multilateral issues. Most EU Delegations and CSFP missions have a focal point of contact for democracy and human rights who follows relevant developments in the country and organizes calls for proposals related to democracy and human rights. More specifically, a number of Delegations have designated a liaison officer for human rights defenders in line with EU Guidelines on Human Rights Defenders.[65]

Nonetheless, the most important human rights development connected with the EEAS has been the creation of the position of the EUSR for Human Rights.[66] EUSRs are senior diplomats in charge of promoting the EU's interests in specific countries and regions. The EUSR for Human Rights is therefore a thematic exception in a network of territorial specialists, underlining the significance the EU places on projecting the human rights aspects of its foreign policy.[67] Accordingly, the appointment of the EUSR has had the practical consequence of enhancing the EU's international presence with respect to human rights issues.[68]

Council Decision 2012/440/CFSP of 25 July 2012 appointing the European Union Special Representative for Human Rights (OJ L 200/21, 27 July 2012)

Article 2

Policy Objectives

The mandate of the EUSR shall be based on the policy objectives of the Union regarding human rights as set out in the Treaty, the Charter of Fundamental Rights of the European Union as well as the EU Strategic Framework on Human Rights and Democracy and the EU Action Plan on Human Rights and Democracy:

(a) **enhancing the Union's effectiveness, presence and visibility** in protecting and promoting human rights, notably by deepening Union cooperation and political dialogue with third countries, relevant partners, business, civil society and international and regional organisations and through action in relevant international fora;

---

[63] J Bátora, 'The "Mitrailleuse Effect": The EEAS as an Interstitial Organization and the Dynamics of Innovation in Diplomacy' (2013) 51 Journal of Common Market Studies 598, 599–613.

[64] S Keukeleire and T Delreux, *The Foreign Policy of the European Union* (2nd edn, Palgrave 2014) 77–84.

[65] The EU Guidelines on Human Rights Defenders were originally adopted in 2004 and reviewed in 2008. See also Ch 9.

[66] Council Decision (CFSP) 2012/440 appointing the European Union Special Representative for Human Rights [2012] OJ L200/21.

[67] The first EU Special Representative (EUSR) for Human Rights was Stavros Lambrinidis, a former Greek Minister of Foreign Affairs, who held the post from its creation in 2012 to February 2019. Recently, Eamon Gilmore was appointed as the new EUSR for Human Rights. Gilmore had previously served as Irish Minister for Foreign Affairs and Trade, and as EU Special Envoy for the Colombian Peace Process.

[68] W Benedek, 'EU Action on Human and Fundamental Rights in 2012' in M Nowak, KM Januszewski, and T Hofstätter (eds), *All Human Rights for All. Vienna Manual on Human Rights* (Intersentia 2012) 185–89.

(b) enhancing the Union's contribution to the strengthening of democracy and institution building, the rule of law, good governance, respect for human rights and fundamental freedoms worldwide;

(c) **improving the coherence of Union action on human rights** and the integration of human rights in all areas of the Union's external action.

Article 3

Mandate

In order to achieve the policy objectives, the mandate of the EUSR shall be to:

(a) contribute to the implementation of the Union's human rights policy, in particular the EU Strategic Framework on Human Rights and Democracy and the EU Action Plan on Human Rights and Democracy, including by formulating recommendations in this regard;

(b) contribute to the implementation of Union guidelines, toolkits and action plans on human rights and international humanitarian law;

(c) enhance dialogue with governments in third countries and international and regional organisations on human rights as well as with civil society organisations and other relevant actors in order to ensure the effectiveness and the visibility of the Union's human rights policy;

(d) contribute to better coherence and consistency of the Union policies and actions in the area of protection and promotion of human rights notably by providing input to the formulation of relevant policies of the Union.

Article 4

Implementation of the mandate

1. The EUSR shall be responsible for the implementation of the mandate, acting under the authority of the HR.

2. The Political and Security Committee (PSC) shall maintain a privileged link with the EUSR and shall be the EUSR's primary point of contact with the Council. The PSC shall provide the EUSR with strategic guidance and political direction within the framework of the mandate, without prejudice to the powers of the HR.

For all the positive institutional developments, the implementation of human rights actors in the EEAS still leaves much to be desired. EEAS officials involved in the institution's human rights agenda were cited as at times lacking the support of the Head of Delegation and sufficient resources to carry out their activities. The internal organization and logic of the EEAS has also been such as to delegate decisions on human rights in the final instance to geographical units.[69]

---

[69] L Ginsborg and others, 'Experiences Regarding Coherence in the European Union Human Rights Context' (n 54).

2.7 The EU Agency for Fundamental Rights (FRA)

Founded in 2007, the EU FRA is a decentralized agency of the EU dedicated to providing expertise to the institutions and the Member States. It is a successor to the European Monitoring Centre on Racism and Xenophobia (EUMC) but it has a broader mandate which has been intensely negotiated and which is still somewhat contentious today.[70] FRA belongs to a network of agencies working in the area of EU JHA.[71]

The FRA produces a diverse and vast number of reports, opinions, surveys, and data on topics of EU fundamental rights relevance; advises and conducts training of EU and Member States officials; maintains contacts with civil society and networks of human rights institutions; and organizes campaigns and communication activities, among other things. The Agency also achieves visibility and raises its profile in hearings of the EP, most often in the LIBE, through Member State visits at the highest level (FRA Director, currently Michael O'Flaherty) and by ad-hoc participation in the meetings of the preparatory bodies of the Council, chiefly the FREMP.

The legal provisions governing the Agency are mostly contained in Regulation No 168/2007 ('Founding Regulation'). In the absence of a general fundamental rights or a specific FRA-creating competence of the EU, the legal basis of the Regulation establishing the FRA is Article 352 TFEU, also known as the 'flexibility clause', because it is relied upon when no other provision of the Treaties can serve as the legal basis for EU action.

Council Regulation (EC) No 168/2007 establishing a European Union Agency for Fundamental Rights [2007] OJ L53/1

[Preamble]

(9) The Agency should refer in its work to fundamental rights within the meaning of Article 6(2) of the Treaty on European Union, including the European Convention on Human Rights and Fundamental Freedoms, and as reflected in particular in the Charter of Fundamental Rights, bearing in mind its status and the accompanying explanations. The close connection to the Charter should be reflected in the name of the Agency.

---

[70] See GN Toggenburg, 'The Role of the New EU Fundamental Rights Agency: Debating the "Sex of Angels" or Improving Europe's Human Rights Performance?' (2008) 33 European Law Review 385, 386–89. For the origins of the idea of an EU human rights agency, see P Alston and JHH Weiler, 'An "Ever Closer Union" in Need of a Human Rights Policy: The European Union and Human Rights' in P Alston (ed), The EU and Human Rights (Oxford University Press 1999) 3–66, 55–59.

[71] Nine agencies in total form currently part of the JHA network: FRA, European Institute for Gender Equality (EIGE), European Asylum Support Office (EASO), European Police Office (Europol), European Police College (CEPOL), the European Union's Judicial Cooperation Unit (Eurojust), European Monitoring Centre for Drugs and Drug Addiction (EMCDDA), European Agency for the Operational Management of Large-Scale IT Systems in the Area of Freedom, Security and Justice (eu-LISA), and European Border and Coast Guard Agency (Frontex). The JHA agencies are required to report jointly to the Standing Committee on Operational Cooperation on Internal Security (COSI), a preparatory body of the Council. Every year, a different agency chairs the JHA network. In 2020, this was Eurojust.

(10) As the Agency is to be built upon the existing European Monitoring Centre on Racism and Xenophobia, the work of **the Agency should continue to cover the phenomena of racism, xenophobia and anti-Semitism, the protection of rights of persons belonging to minorities, as well as gender equality**, as essential elements for the protection of fundamental rights.

(11) The thematic areas of activity of the Agency should be laid down in the Multiannual Framework, thus defining the limits of the work of the Agency. **Due to the political significance of the Multiannual Framework, it is important that the Council itself should adopt it**, after consulting the European Parliament on the basis of a Commission proposal.

(20) Given the particular functions of the Agency, each Member State should appoint one independent expert to the Management Board. **Having regard to the principles relating to the status and functioning of national institutions for the protection and promotion of human rights (the Paris Principles), the composition of that Board should ensure the Agency's independence from both Community institutions and Member State governments** and assemble the broadest possible expertise in the field of fundamental rights.

Article 2

Objective

The objective of the Agency shall be to provide the relevant institutions, bodies, offices and agencies of the Community and its Member States when implementing Community law with **assistance and expertise relating to fundamental rights in order to support them** when they take measures or formulate courses of action within their respective spheres of competence to fully respect fundamental rights.

Article 3

Scope

3. The Agency shall deal with fundamental-rights issues in the European Union and in its Member States **when implementing Community law**.

Article 4

Tasks

1. To meet the objective set in Article 2 and within its competences laid down in Article 3, the Agency shall:

   (a) **collect, record, analyse and disseminate** relevant, objective, reliable and comparable information and data, including results from research and monitoring communicated to it by Member States, Union institutions as well as bodies, offices and agencies of the Community and the Union, research centres, national bodies, non-governmental organisations, third countries and international organisations and in particular by the competent bodies of the Council of Europe;

(b) develop methods and standards to improve the comparability, objectivity and reliability of data at European level, in cooperation with the Commission and the Member States;

(c) carry out, cooperate with or encourage scientific research and surveys, preparatory studies and feasibility studies, including, where appropriate and compatible with its priorities and its annual work programme, **at the request of the European Parliament, the Council or the Commission;**

(d) formulate and publish conclusions and opinions on specific thematic topics, for the Union institutions and the Member States when implementing Community law, either on its own initiative or at the request of the European Parliament, the Council or the Commission;

(e) **publish an annual report on fundamental-rights issues** covered by the areas of the Agency's activity, also highlighting examples of good practice;

(f) publish thematic reports based on its analysis, research and surveys;

(g) publish an annual report on its activities; and

(h) **develop a communication strategy and promote dialogue with civil society, in order to raise public awareness of fundamental rights and actively disseminate information about its work.**

2. The conclusions, opinions and reports referred to in paragraph 1 may concern proposals from the Commission under Article 250 of the Treaty or positions taken by the institutions in the course of **legislative procedures only where a request by the respective institution has been made in accordance with paragraph 1(d).** They shall not deal with the legality of acts within the meaning of Article 230 of the Treaty or with the question of whether a Member State has failed to fulfil an obligation under the Treaty within the meaning of Article 226 of the Treaty.

Article 5

Areas of activity

1. The Council shall, acting on a proposal from the Commission and after consulting the European Parliament, adopt a Multiannual Framework for the Agency. When preparing its proposal, the Commission shall consult the Management Board.

2. The Framework shall:

(a) cover five years;

(b) **determine the thematic areas of the Agency's activity, which must include the fight against racism, xenophobia and related intolerance;**

(c) be in line with the Union's priorities, taking due account of the orientations resulting from European Parliament resolutions and Council conclusions in the field of fundamental rights;

(d) have due regard to the Agency's financial and human resources; and

(e) include provisions with a view to **ensuring complementarity** with the remit of other Community and Union bodies, offices and agencies, **as well as with the Council of Europe and other international organisations active in the field of fundamental rights.**

3. The Agency shall carry out its tasks within the thematic areas determined by the Multiannual Framework. This shall be without prejudice to the responses of the Agency to requests from the European Parliament, the Council or the Commission under Article 4(1)(c) and (d) outside these thematic areas, provided its financial and human resources so permit.
4. The Agency shall carry out its tasks in the light of its Annual Work Programme and with due regard to the available financial and human resources.

Article 8

Cooperation with organisations at Member State and international level

2. To help it carry out its tasks, the Agency shall cooperate with:
   (a) governmental organisations and public bodies competent in the field of fundamental rights in the Member States, **including national human rights institutions**; and
   (b) the Organisation for Security and Cooperation in Europe (OSCE), especially the Office for Democratic Institutions and Human Rights (ODIHR), **the United Nations** and other international organisations.

Article 9

Cooperation with the Council of Europe

In order to avoid duplication and in order to ensure complementarity and added value, the Agency shall coordinate its activities with those of the Council of Europe, particularly with regard to its Annual Work Programme pursuant to Article 12(6)(a) and cooperation with civil society in accordance with Article 10. To that end, the Community shall, in accordance with the procedure provided for in Article 300 of the Treaty, enter into an agreement with the Council of Europe for the purpose of establishing close cooperation between the latter and the Agency. This agreement shall include the **appointment of an independent person by the Council of Europe, to sit on the Agency's Management Board and on its Executive Board**, in accordance with Articles 12 and 13.

Article 10

Cooperation with civil society; Fundamental Rights Platform

1. **The Agency shall closely cooperate with non-governmental organisations and with institutions of civil society**, active in the field of fundamental rights including the combating of racism and xenophobia at national, European or international level. To that end, the Agency shall establish a cooperation network (**Fundamental Rights Platform**), composed of non-governmental organisations dealing with human rights, trade unions and employer's organisations, relevant social and professional

> organisations, churches, religious, philosophical and non-confessional organisa-
> tions, universities and other qualified experts of European and international bodies
> and organisations.

What the FRA Founding Regulation reveals is, despite the enlarged scope of activity, a clear degree of continuity with its predecessor, the EUMC.[72] Not only are the issues covered previously by the EUMC a mandatory part of the FRA's programming, but the nature of the Agency has remained essentially the same—focusing on information collection and provision of expertise rather than acquiring a real monitoring competence.[73] A seed of a more ambitious vision for FRA was planted in paragraph 20 of the preamble which refers to the UN Paris Principles on national human rights institutions (NHRIs, see below) and the proclaimed independence of the Agency from EU institutions and the Member States.

In reality, the mandate of the FRA is circumscribed in several ways and is more consistent with the model of an EU technocratic agency than the Paris Principles.[74] For one, the Council and the Commission retain significant influence with respect to the work of the Agency. The areas of the FRA's activity are determined through the Multiannual Framework which is adopted unanimously by the Council—with negotiations taking place chiefly in the FREMP—on a proposal of the Commission; the Agency is therefore not fully independent in setting its own agenda.[75] The Commission proposed in June 2020 to scrap the Multiannual Framework, which would give the FRA greater control over its activities.[76]

Second, the Regulation does not envisage a substantial role for the Agency in the EU legislative process by making it dependent on requests by EU institutions. This has been partially offset in practice in recent years through the development of a working relationship between the FRA and the European Parliament, in particular, whereby the Parliament—most often the LIBE—requests the Agency to deliver opinions on compatibility of proposed EU legislation with fundamental rights or specific issues of fundamental rights protection within the EU.

---

[72] Compare the FRA Founding Regulation with Council Regulation (EC) 1035/97 establishing a European Monitoring Centre on racism and xenophobia [1997] OJ L151/1. See also O De Schutter, 'The EU Fundamental Rights Agency: Genesis and Potential' in K Boyle (ed) *New Institutions for Human Rights Protection* (Oxford University Press 2009) 93–135.

[73] Continuity was further ensured by retaining the seat of the institution (Vienna) and a majority of the EUMC staff.

[74] See also J Wouters and M Ovadek, 'Exploring the Political Role of FRA: Mandate, Resources and Opportunities' in R Byrne and H Entzinger (eds), *Human Rights Law and Evidence-Based Policy: The Impact of the EU's Fundamental Rights Agency* (Routledge 2019) 82–102. Apart from the reluctance on the part of certain Member States (and to a lesser degree the Commission) to create a robust mechanism for the monitoring of fundamental rights in the EU, for example in the context of Article 7 TEU, the worries of growing irrelevance of the Council of Europe, which have persisted until today, had an outsized influence on the process of constructing the FRA. See W Hummer, 'The European Fundamental Rights Agency' in A Reinisch and U Kriebaum (eds), *The Law of International Relations: Liber Amicorum Hanspeter Neuhold* (Eleven International Publishing 2007) 117–144.

[75] J Dutheil de la Rochere, 'Challenges for the Protection of Fundamental Rights in the EU at the Time of the Entry into Force of the Lisbon Treaty' (2011) 6 Fordham International Law Journal 1776, 1798. See also M Ovádek, 'The Curious Case of the Fundamental Rights Agency's Mandate: Legal Shrouding and Democratic Politics' (2019) 25 European Public Law 517.

[76] European Commission, 'Proposal for a Council Regulation amending Regulation (EC) No 168/2007 establishing a European Union Agency for Fundamental Rights', COM(2020) 225 final, Brussels, 5 June 2020.

> ## Council Decision (EU) No 2017/2269 establishing a Multiannual Framework for the European Union Agency for Fundamental Rights for 2018–2022 [2017] OJ L326/1
>
> ### Article 2
> ### Thematic areas
> The thematic areas shall be the following:
>
> (a) victims of crime and access to justice;
> (b) equality and discrimination based on any ground such as sex, race, colour, ethnic or social origin, genetic features, language, religion or belief, political or any other opinion, membership of a national minority, property, birth, disability, age or sexual orientation, or on the grounds of nationality;
> (c) information society and, in particular, respect for private life and protection of personal data;
> (d) **judicial cooperation, except in criminal matters;**
> (e) migration, borders, asylum and integration of refugees and migrants;
> (f) racism, xenophobia and related intolerance;
> (g) rights of the child;
> (h) integration and social inclusion of Roma.

Third, the Regulation deliberately excluded police and judicial cooperation in criminal matters ('third pillar' issues) from the remit of FRA's activity by only referring to 'Community law'. Contrary to the expectations of some,[77] the entry into force of the Lisbon Treaty has not changed the status quo as the Member States have so far refused to include third-pillar issues in the MAF, despite reasoned pleas by the Agency.[78] In June 2020, the Commission proposed to replace references to 'Community law' by 'Union law' to remedy this vestige of the pre-Lisbon era. However, the proposal will require unanimous agreement of the Member States to pass. For now, the FRA can only work in third-pillar areas if specifically requested by one of the institutions.

Conscious of the untapped potential in the FRA, a number of actors have called on the institutions to relax the restrictions placed on the Agency's mandate, particularly following an external evaluation reaching the same conclusion.[79] The Management Board of the FRA has recommended in a letter to the European Commission that the Founding Regulation should be revised in a way that would: remove restriction on former third-pillar issues, allow FRA to issue

---

[77] A Von Bogdandy and J von Bernstorff, 'The EU Fundamental Rights Agency within the European and International Human Rights Architecture: The Legal Framework and Some Unsettled Issues in a New Field of Administrative Law' (2009) 46 Common Market Law Review 1035, 1068.

[78] EU Agency for Fundamental Rights, Opinion of the Management Board of the EU Agency for Fundamental Rights on a New Multi-annual Framework (2018–2022) for the Agency, 12 February 2016.

[79] Ramboll, 'External Evaluation of the European Union Agency for Fundamental Rights', Final Report, 19 November 2012 <http://fra.europa.eu/sites/default/files/fra-external_evaluation-final-report.pdf> accessed 14 August 2020. The same conclusion was reached by a second external evaluation in October 2017: 'Optimity, 2nd independent External Evaluation of the European Union Agency for Fundamental Rights', Final Report, 31 October 2017 <https://fra.europa.eu/sites/default/files/fra_uploads/2nd-fra-external-evaluation-october-2017_en.pdf> accessed 14 August 2020.

opinions on draft legislation on its own initiative, and substitute the Council by the Management Board in adopting the MAF.[80] Among the EU institutions, the European Parliament is consistently the most fervent supporter of extending FRA's competences among.[81] Civil society organizations and academics have also backed strengthening the powers of the Agency.[82]

Nevertheless, even when leaving the particular limitations placed on FRA's mandate aside, the design of the Agency is based on a relatively modest template, akin to the institute model of NHRIs.[83] The inability of the FRA to deal with, among other matters, individual complaints regarding human rights abuses ties it to closer cooperation with actual NHRIs in the Member States. While understandably often singled out as a cardinal defect of the institution, the lack of monitoring and enforcement capacities follows fairly evidently from the more general constraint on EU competences in the form of the principle of conferral.[84] Contrary to the narrative of feebleness, it has been argued elsewhere that the FRA derives a kind of disciplinary power from its observation functions.[85] One of the tools where this can be seen in action is the Fundamental Rights Report, an annual report on the state of human rights in the EU which is known to be more critical of the situation than a similar yearly exercise by the Commission.[86]

Moreover, consistent with its constrained mandate, the Agency has fewer resources at its disposal than most other JHA agencies. For most of its existence, the FRA has operated with a budget of around EUR 21 million. In general, the development of JHA agencies' revenue shows that the FRA is getting an increasingly smaller size of the proverbial pie. The revenue trend is revelatory not only with respect to how many resources FRA operates with but also in light of broader narratives about EU concern for fundamental rights. Whereas the budgets of Frontex (European Border and Coast Guard Agency), eu-LISA, and Europol have grown at a considerable rate recently in the wake of terrorist scares and migration crises, there has been no similar increase in the FRA's revenue (see Figure 2.2), despite the extremely significant fundamental rights implications of anti-terrorist and migration policies. It is not only money—the story is the same for allocated personnel.[87] FRA has simply not been a priority for the EU.

---

[80] Letter from Chairperson of the FRA Management Board Maija Sakslin to European Commission Vice-President Viviane Reding, 4 June 2013.

[81] European Parliament, 'Report on the Situation of Fundamental Rights in the European Union in 2012', P7_TA(2014)0173, 27 January 2014.

[82] See, for example, Human Rights and Democracy Network, 'Strengthening the European Union's Response to Human Rights Abuses Inside its Own Borders' (*hrw.org*, 5 August 2013) <http://www.hrw.org/news/2013/08/05/strengthening-european-union-s-response-human-rights-abuses-inside-its-own-borders> accessed 14 August 2020 and GN Toggenburg, 'Fundamental Rights and the European Union: How Does and How Should the EU Agency for Fundamental Rights Relate to the EU Charter of Fundamental Rights?' (2013) EUI Working Papers 2013/13, 1 <http://cadmus.eui.eu/bitstream/handle/1814/28658/LAW_2013_13_Toggenburg.pdf> accessed 14 August 2020.

[83] Office of the High Commissioner for Human Rights, 'National Human Rights Institutions: History, Principles, Roles and Responsibilities' (April 2011) UN Doc HR/P/PT/4/Rev.1, 19.

[84] Toggenburg, 'Role of the New EU Fundamental Rights Agency' (n 70) 387. See Article 5(2) TEU which states that 'the Union shall act only within the limits of the competences conferred upon it by the Member States in the Treaties to attain the objectives set out therein. Competences not conferred upon the Union in the Treaties remain with the Member States'. On the limits of transferring Union powers to agencies, see also Judgment of 13 June 1958, *Meroni and Others v High Authority of the European Coal and Steel Community*, 9/56, ECLI:EU:C:1958:7.

[85] B Sokhi-Bulley, 'The Fundamental Rights Agency of the European Union: A New Panopticism' (2011) 11 Human Rights Law Review 683.

[86] EU Agency for Fundamental Rights, 'Fundamental Rights Report 2019', May 2019 <https://fra.europa.eu/sites/default/files/fra_uploads/fra-2019-fundamental-rights-report-2019_en.pdf> accessed 14 August 2020.

[87] The FRA employs in total less than 120 people, more than only EMCDDA, CEPOL, and EIGE among the JHA agencies.

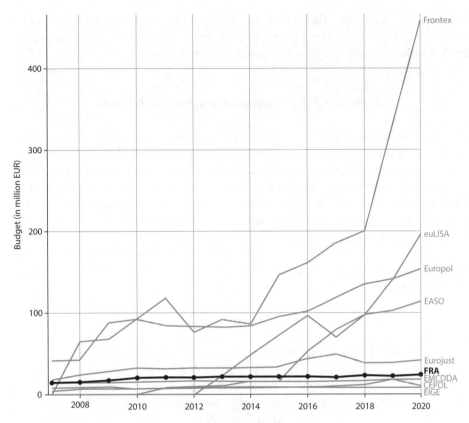

Figure 2.2 Yearly revenue of JHA agencies since 2007[88]

As a final point, the FRA's understated role as an institution responsible for promoting fundamental rights should be highlighted. The Agency has a department dedicated to outreach and awareness raising and, in addition, it liaises with civil society actors, networks of human rights institutions, and equality bodies.[89] Consequently, the FRA fulfils the dual obligation incumbent upon NHRIs in terms of fundamental rights in the EU, as it also loosely appears in the Treaties, facilitating respect for (or protecting) them, as well as their promotion. Diverging from the Treaty text (Article 21 TEU), however, the promotion of fundamental rights by the FRA is for the most part territorially limited to the EU. The Commission's proposal to allow the Agency to be involved in work relating to countries with which the EU has an association agreement, in particular countries participating in the European Neighbourhood Policy, was rejected by the Member States in the drafting process

---

[88] Data from yearly statements of revenue and expenditure. Where available, the data show final revenue after any budgetary amendments. In some cases, the revenue of agencies consists not only of an EU subsidy but also to a lesser extent of Member State and third-country contributions and/or other sources of revenue. The total revenue remains, nonetheless, relevant, as all sources of revenue are taken into account by the EU budgetary authority when drafting the budgets of the agencies and in principle contributions from outside the EU budget can be allocated at a country's discretion to any agency, thus serving as further indication of preference.

[89] The FRA periodically convenes meetings with, for example, the European Network of NHRIs (ENNHRI), European Network of Equality Bodies (Equinet), and ombudsperson institutions.

of the Founding Regulation. The FRA additionally plays a role in the implementation of the UN Convention on the Rights of Persons with Disabilities as part of the EU Framework established to that effect, mainly when it comes to rights promotion and data collection.[90]

2.8 National Human Rights Institutions (NHRIs)

NHRIs are a brainchild of the UN; they have been conceived in recognition of the persistently indispensable role of nation states in human rights protection and therefore as national actors capable of implementing the plethora of international human rights and other commitments taken on by states.[91] The key document setting out the desired characteristics of NHRIs was adopted by the UN General Assembly in 1993 and is best known as the 'Paris Principles'. The extent to which NHRIs comply with these principles is monitored by the Global Alliance of National Human Rights Institutions (GANHRI), previously known as the International Coordinating Committee of National Institutions for the Promotion and Protection of Human Rights, which then makes decisions regarding accreditation of the individual institutions.

Principles relating to the Status of National Institutions (The Paris Principles)

Adopted by General Assembly resolution 48/134 of 20 December 1993

Competence and responsibilities

1. A national institution shall be vested with **competence to promote and protect human rights.**
2. A national institution shall be given **as broad a mandate as possible,** which shall be clearly set forth **in a constitutional or legislative text,** specifying its composition and its sphere of competence.
3. A national institution shall, inter alia, have the following responsibilities:
   (a) **To submit to the Government, Parliament and any other competent body,** on an advisory basis either at the request of the authorities concerned **or through the exercise of its power to hear a matter without higher referral,** opinions, recommendations, proposals and reports on any matters concerning the promotion and protection of human rights; the national institution may decide to publicize them; these opinions, recommendations, proposals and reports, as well as any prerogative of the national institution, shall relate to the following areas:

---

[90] See Ch 5.

[91] The principal idea behind NHRIs is almost as old as the UN itself. See ECOSOC Res 2/9 (21 June 1946) UN Doc E/56/REV.2, para 5. See generally LC Reif, 'Building Democratic Institutions: The Role of National Human Rights Institutions in Good Governance and Human Rights Protection' (2000) 13 Harvard Human Rights Journal 1; A Smith, 'The Unique Position of National Human Rights Institutions: A Mixed Blessing?' (2006) 28 Human Rights Quarterly 904.

(i)   Any legislative or administrative provisions, as well as provisions relating to judicial organizations, **intended to preserve and extend the protection of human rights**; (...)

(ii) Any situation of violation of human rights which it decides to take up;

(iii) The preparation of reports on the national situation with regard to human rights in general, and on more specific matters;

(iv) Drawing the attention of the Government to situations in any part of the country where human rights are violated and making proposals to it for initiatives to put an end to such situations and, where necessary, expressing an opinion on the positions and reactions of the Government;

(b) To **promote and ensure the harmonization of national legislation, regulations and practices with the international human rights instruments to which the State is a party**, and their effective implementation;

(c) To encourage ratification of the above-mentioned instruments or accession to those instruments, and to ensure their implementation;

(d) To **contribute to the reports which States are required to submit to United Nations bodies** and committees, and to regional institutions, pursuant to their treaty obligations and, where necessary, to express an opinion on the subject, with due respect for their independence;

(e) To cooperate with the United Nations and any other organization in the United Nations system, the regional institutions and the national institutions of other countries that are competent in the areas of the protection and promotion of human rights;

(f) To **assist in the formulation of programmes for the teaching** of, and research into, human rights and to take part in their execution in schools, universities and professional circles;

(g) To **publicize human rights and efforts to combat all forms of discrimination**, (...)

Composition and guarantees of independence and pluralism

1. The **composition of the national institution** and the appointment of its members, whether by means of an election or otherwise, shall be established in accordance with a procedure which affords all necessary guarantees to **ensure the pluralist representation of the social forces** (of civilian society) involved in the protection and promotion of human rights (...)

2. The national institution shall have an infrastructure which is suited to the smooth conduct of its activities, in particular **adequate funding**. The purpose of this funding should be to enable it to have its own staff and premises, in order to be independent of the Government and **not be subject to financial control which might affect its independence**.

3. In order to ensure a stable mandate for the members of the national institution, without which there can be no real independence, their **appointment shall be effected by an official act** which shall establish the specific duration of the mandate. This mandate may be renewable, provided that the pluralism of the institution's membership is ensured.

Methods of operation

Within the framework of its operation, the national institution shall:

(a) **Freely consider any questions falling within its competence**, whether they are submitted by the Government or taken up by it **without referral to a higher authority**, on the proposal of its members or of any petitioner,

(b) **Hear any person and obtain any information** and any documents necessary for assessing situations falling within its competence;

(c) **Address public opinion directly** or through any press organ, particularly in order to publicize its opinions and recommendations;

(d) Meet on a regular basis and whenever necessary in the presence of all its members after they have been duly concerned;

(e) Establish working groups from among its members as necessary, and set up local or regional sections to assist it in discharging its functions;

(f) **Maintain consultation** with the other bodies, whether jurisdictional or otherwise, responsible for the promotion and protection of human rights (in particular, ombudsmen, mediators and similar institutions);

(g) In view of the fundamental role played by the non-governmental organizations in expanding the work of the national institutions, **develop relations with the nongovernmental organizations** devoted to promoting and protecting human rights, to economic and social development, to combating racism, to protecting particularly vulnerable groups (especially children, migrant workers, refugees, physically and mentally disabled persons) or to specialized areas.

(...)

A national institution may be authorized to hear and consider complaints and petitions concerning individual situations. Cases may be brought before it by individuals, their representatives, third parties, non-governmental organizations, associations of trade unions or any other representative organizations. (...)

In 2019, there were 80 NHRIs globally that have received full accreditation by the GANHRI, a so-called A-status which signifies full compliance with the Paris Principles. Among EU Member States, there were 16 countries with at least one A-status NHRI and 6 with (only) a B-status NHRI (indicating partial compliance with the Paris Principles). For a variety of reasons, human rights institutions in the Czech Republic, Estonia, Italy, and Malta currently do not possess accreditation from the GANHRI, while Romania has a C-status NHRI (indicating non-compliance with the Paris Principles).[92]

Owing to the fact that the Paris Principles allow NHRIs to have various combinations of competences and responsibilities, NHRIs are diverse not only worldwide but also within the EU.[93] NHRIs therefore share more a commonality of purpose rather than of

---

[92] GANHRI, Chart of the Status of National Institutions, Accreditation Status as of 27 November 2019, <https://nhri.ohchr.org/EN/AboutUs/GANHRIAccreditation/Documents/Status%20Accreditation%20-%20Chart%20%28%2027%20November%202019%29.pdf> accessed 14 August 2020.

[93] For a description of the different models of NHRIs, see Office of the High Commissioner for Human Rights, 'National Human Rights Institutions: History, Principles, Roles and Responsibilities' (April 2011) UN Doc HR/P/PT/4/Rev.1.

modalities. According to the UN High Commissioner for Human Rights, an NHRI is a 'key component of effective national human rights protection systems'.[94] This is also recognized in the EU where the EP, in particular, has been supportive of furthering compliance of European NHRIs with the Paris Principles.[95] As a means of pooling voices and expertise at the European level, NHRIs in Europe have institutionalized their cooperation by setting up the European Network of National Human Rights Institutions (ENNHRI) with a Permanent Secretariat in Brussels which has also been supported by the European Commission.[96]

J Wouters, K Meuwissen, and AS Barros, 'The European Union and National Human Rights Institutions' in J Wouters and K Meuwissen (eds), *National Human Rights Institutions in Europe: Comparative, International and European Perspectives* (Intersentia 2013)

(...) Even if the various EU institutions and bodies working in the field of human rights expressed support for NHRIs and do cooperate to some extent with these institutions, NHRIs are not structurally integrated into the European human rights working culture yet. Especially the non-inclusion of NHRIs in relevant policy documents indicates the lack of their effective integration in the EU's human rights policy.

The entry into force of the Lisbon Treaty created a momentum for the further strengthening of the promotion and protection of human rights in the EU's internal and external policies. At the same time, the increasing establishment and activity of NHRIs all over the globe and in the EU enhances the potential gains of cooperation with NHRIs for the EU.

(...) there is scope for NHRIs to become more important partners of the EU in the implementation of different issue areas relevant to the EU's human rights architecture. NHRIs can help to foster a fundamental rights culture across the EU, through the delivering of human rights expertise in the context of EU policy and law-making initiatives and advising states on the fundamental rights compliance of legislative proposals. Stronger participation policies bring with them greater quality, transparency and legitimacy of policy and law-making processes both within the EU and its Member States when acting within the scope of EU law. NHRIs can report on the national implementation of fundamental rights, or serve as central focal points to inform citizens about their fundamental rights. These examples also point to the significance of NHRIs in ensuring that the fundamental rights contained in the EU Charter become a practical tool for the protection of individuals.

---

[94] UNGA (62th session), 'Report of the United Nations High Commissioner for Human Rights' (2007) UN Doc A/62/36, 5–6 para 15; Office of the High Commissioner for Human Rights, 'National Institutions for the Promotion and Protection of Human Rights' Human Rights Resolution 2005/74.

[95] European Parliament, 'Resolution on the Situation of Fundamental Rights in the European Union 2004–2008', P6_TA(2009)0019, 14 January 2009, para 1.

[96] See G De Beco, 'Networks of European National Human Rights Institutions' (2008) 14 European Law Journal 860.

The main outlet for cooperation of NHRIs with the EU is the Fundamental Rights Agency. The FRA regularly consults the ENNHRI and NHRIs with regards to its programming and opportunities for involvement in projects. NHRIs are obvious partners for the FRA as they often have the specific knowledge of the national context required for FRA output (EU-wide surveys, reports).[97] Conversely, the FRA and its work can serve as an indirect vehicle for NHRIs at the EU level.

As a result of the external human rights commitment of the EU, NHRIs are also a logical 'target' for EU support in third countries. This is explicitly stated in, among others, the Action Plan on Human Rights and Democracy 2015–2019 (Action 1) and in the European Instrument for Democracy and Human Rights (EIDHR), the dedicated EU financing mechanism for democracy and human rights promotion in external contexts.[98] In addition to individual support of NHRIs on a bilateral basis, the EU has, for example, allocated EUR 5 million in 2014 to NHRI assistance as part of a global approach to strengthen the capacities of NHRIs, their regional networks, and of the International Criminal Court (ICC).[99]

The need for capacity building of NHRIs exists not only abroad but also in many EU Member States if NHRIs are to fulfil their important role in the human rights architecture. Although the number of A-status institutions has been increasing, in a survey of NHRIs in EU Member States the FRA pointed out that two main challenges faced by human rights institutions are 'achieving and maintaining a satisfactory level of independence, as well as an adequate mandate and sufficient resources'.[100] The report also warned of duplication of work by different human rights bodies within Member States and noted the better and more comprehensive performance of A-status NHRIs compared to partially and non-accredited institutions;[101] the FRA has accordingly published a Handbook on the accreditation of NHRIs in the EU.[102] Having said that, the conferral of the A-status by the GANHRI does not automatically translate to more effective human rights protection and even the *de facto* independence of A-designated NHRIs can be disconnected from their *de jure* status.[103]

---

[97] J Wouters, K Meuwissen, and AS Barros, 'The European Union and National Human Rights Institutions' in J Wouters and K Meuwissen (eds), *National Human Rights Institutions in Europe: Comparative, International and European Perspectives* (Intersentia 2013) 200.

[98] See Article 2(a)(ii) of Regulation (EU) 235/2014 of the European Parliament and of the Council establishing a financing instrument for democracy and human rights worldwide [2014] OJ L77/85: 'Union assistance should focus on (…) strengthening the rule of law, promoting the independence of the judiciary and of the legislature, supporting and evaluating legal and institutional reforms and their implementation, and promoting access to justice, as well as supporting national human rights institutions.' NHRIs in third countries are also supported by the EU in the context of development cooperation and neighbourhood policies; see Wouters, Meuwissen, and Barros, 'European Union and National Human Rights Institutions' (n 97) 209–03.

[99] See European Instrument for Democracy and Human Rights, Special Measure concerning the Work Programme 2014 for the European Instrument for Democracy and Human Rights (EIDHR) to be financed under budget line 21 04 01 of the general budget of the European Union and European Instrument for Democracy and Human Rights, Annex 5 of the Commission Implementing Decision on the adoption of a special measure for the financing of the Work Programme 2014 for the European Instrument for Democracy and Human Rights (EIDHR).

[100] EU Agency for Fundamental Rights, *National Human Rights Institutions in the EU Member States: Strengthening the Fundamental Rights Architecture in the EU* (Publication Office of the EU 2010) 13.

[101] Ibid, 53–54.

[102] EU Agency for Fundamental Rights, *Handbook on the Establishment and Accreditation of National Human Rights Institutions in the European Union* (Publication Office of the EU 2012).

[103] There are A-status NHRIs in countries such as Morocco where considerable doubt exists as to their independence from the governing class.

2.9 Equality Bodies and Data Protection Authorities

Apart from NHRIs, there are often other institutions at the national level that serve similar—although usually narrower—objectives but do not necessarily fulfil or even aspire to the criteria of the Paris Principles. Two types of such institutions are prominently linked to the EU governance system: national equality bodies (NEBs) and national data protection authorities (NDPAs).[104] Despite the fact that the language of NEBs and NDPAs revolves more around the concepts of equality and data protection respectively rather than human rights in general, the connection of these more specific institutions to the overall EU system of human rights protection is obvious from, among others, the provisions of the EU Charter of Fundamental Rights.[105]

A. National Equality Bodies

NEBs are independent organizations set up at the national level on the basis of EU anti-discrimination Directives concerning race, ethnicity, and gender.[106] Although the legislation specifies some requirements that Member States have had to comply with when designating NEBs, the rules are less elaborate compared to those of the Paris Principles with respect to NHRIs. The discretion afforded to the Member States has resulted in a diverse array of established institutions and therefore also different levels of equality protection across the EU.[107]

Council Directive 2000/43/EC implementing the principle of equal treatment between persons irrespective of racial or ethnic origin [2000] OJ L180/22

Article 13
1. Member States shall designate **a body or bodies** for the promotion of equal treatment of all persons without discrimination on the grounds of racial or ethnic origin. **These bodies may form part of agencies** charged at national level with the defence of human rights or the safeguard of individuals' rights.

---

[104] See generally B De Witte, 'New Institutions for Promoting Equality in Europe: Legal Transfers, National Bricolage and European Governance' (2012) 60 The American Journal of Comparative Law 49; P Hustinx, 'The Role of Data Protection Authorities' in S Gutwirth and others (eds), *Reinventing Data Protection?* (Springer 2009); A Jóri, 'Shaping vs Applying Data Protection Law: Two Core Functions of Data Protection Authorities' (2015) 5 International Data Privacy Law 133.

[105] See Title III (equality) and Article 8 (data protection) of the Charter. See also Article 16 TFEU on right to data protection and Article 19 TFEU on EU competence to adopt non-discrimination measures.

[106] See Council Directive (EC) 2000/43 implementing the principle of equal treatment between persons irrespective of racial or ethnic origin [2000] OJ L180/22 and Gender Equal Treatment Directives (Directive (EU) 2010/41 of the European Parliament and of the Council on the application of the principle of equal treatment between men and women engaged in an activity in a self-employed capacity [2010] OJ L180/1; Directive (EC) 2006/54 of the European Parliament and of the Council on the implementation of the principle of equal opportunities and equal treatment of men and women in matters of employment and occupation (recast) [2006] OJ L204/23; Council Directive (EC) 2004/113 implementing the principle of equal treatment between men and women in the access to and supply of goods and services [2004] OJ L373/37).

[107] European Network of Legal Experts in Gender Equality and Non-discrimination, *A Comparative Analysis of Non-discrimination Law in Europe 2016* (Publication Office of the EU 2016) 108.

> 2. Member States shall ensure that **the competences of these bodies** include:
>   – (...) **providing independent assistance to victims** of discrimination in pursuing their complaints about discrimination,
>   – **conducting independent surveys** concerning discrimination,
>   – **publishing independent reports and making recommendations** on any issue relating to such discrimination.

All Member States have by now designated an NEB in line with Article 13 of the Racial Equality Directive. In many cases, new institutions have been established for this purpose but some countries have opted to consolidate the functions and competences of an NHRI and an NEB into a single institution (eg the Netherlands and Slovakia).[108] In addition to counteracting racial, ethnic, and gender discrimination, which is compulsory under EU law, the mandates of NEBs often cover other grounds, such as religion, age, disability, and sexual orientation.

B de Witte, 'National Equality Institutions and the Domestication of EU Non-discrimination Law' (2011) 18 Maastricht Journal of Comparative and European Law 157

(...) the creation of equality bodies was not an 'invention' of the European Commission when it first proposed a draft of the racial equality Directive, in the final months of 1999. Some European countries had led the way, in particular the United Kingdom and the Netherlands. The practical experience with the operation of the equality bodies in those countries (...) was a source of inspiration for the legal activists and NGOs. That put pressure on the European institutions to include the requirement of having, in every Member State, national equality bodies in charge of helping to enforce the new generation of EU anti-discrimination law.

(...) the EU anti-discrimination regime as a whole constitutes a major change for many national systems of public and private law, due to novel characteristics such as the prohibition of indirect discrimination, the reversal of the burden of proof, and the horizontal effect between private parties. (...) many countries also had to cope with an institutional transplant, namely the creation of public bodies inspired by the Anglo-Dutch model that were to be in charge of promoting the enforcement of the European anti-discrimination norms.

(...) national equality institutions have now become 'semi-autonomous national agencies': they are institutions of national administrative law, and the European Union does not play any direct role in their activity, but some of their functions (namely to promote racial equality and to promote gender equality in the fields covered by the directives) are defined by EU law and can therefore not be removed by the national legislator. Also, EU law requires a minimum degree of independence and effectiveness in the performance of the 'European' functions, in the absence of which the European Commission may bring an infringement action before the Court of Justice against the Member State concerned.

The equality institutions can thus be seen as an example of recourse to new modes of governance by the European Union institutions (...) said to have emerged in EU

---

[108] The Netherlands operates, in addition, a decentralized network of local anti-discrimination offices which also deal with equality protection. For a comprehensive survey of NEBs, see ibid, 107–20.

institutional practice for a variety of reasons including: the need for additional expertise to regulate a complex area of policy-making; the need to take 'some' action even where law-making competences are unavailable or difficult to use; and the wish to improve the implementation of EU law. Of those functional reasons, only the latter seems relevant for the case of the EU-mandated domestic equality agencies: they are meant to help the non-discrimination legal norm become a social reality throughout the European Union.

Similarly to NHRIs, NEBs have also established a European network, called Equinet, to facilitate learning and exchange of best practices and to contribute to European equality policies. Equinet comprises 50 organizations from 37 European countries and, as in the case of ENNHRI, its Secretariat, as well as having a seat in Brussels, has received funding from the European Commission to develop its activities.

At the EU level, Equinet and national equality bodies engage primarily with the FRA in a way comparable to ENNHRI and NHRIs. The FRA's general fundamental rights remit covers all grounds of discrimination and therefore is a suitable platform for all NEBs, irrespective of the peculiarities of their mandate. On the specific issue of gender equality, however, the relevant NEBs also cooperate with the European Institute for Gender Equality (EIGE).[109]

Regulation (EC) No 1922/2006 of the European Parliament and of the Council on establishing a European Institute for Gender Equality [2006] OJ L403/9

Article 2

Objectives
The overall objectives of the Institute shall be **to contribute to and strengthen the promotion of gender equality**, including gender mainstreaming in **all Community policies and the resulting national policies**, and the fight against discrimination based on sex, and to raise EU citizens' awareness of gender equality by **providing technical assistance to the Community institutions**, in particular the Commission, and **the authorities of the Member States**, as set out in Article 3.

Article 3

Tasks
1. To meet the objectives set in Article 2, the Institute shall:
    (a) **collect, analyse and disseminate** relevant objective, comparable and reliable information as regards gender equality, including results from research and best practice communicated to it by Member States, Community institutions, research centres, **national equality bodies**, non-governmental organisations, social partners, relevant third countries and international organisations, and suggest areas for further research;

---

[109] See A Hubert and M Stratigaki, 'The European Institute for Gender Equality: A Window of Opportunity for Gender Equality Policies?' (2011) 18 European Journal of Women's Studies 169.

Article 8

Cooperation with organisations at national and European level, international organisations and third countries

1. To help it carry out its tasks, **the Institute shall cooperate with organisations and experts in the Member States, such as equality bodies**, research centres, universities, non-governmental organisations, social partners as well as with relevant organisations at European or international level and third countries.

B. Data Protection Authorities

Even more specific institutions than the EIGE and NEBs with an increasingly important role to play in the EU system are data protection authorities. Stemming from the EU data protection legislation, the European Data Protection Supervisor (EDPS) and NDPAs are independent institutions responsible for supervising compliance with the EU data protection laws, a role recognized among others by the EU Charter.[110] While the EDPS carries out this function in relation to EU institutions and bodies,[111] the NDPAs were set up under national law in accordance with Article 28 of Directive 95/46/EC.[112] The EU data protection legislation has undergone systemic reform in 2016 and is now consolidated in two legal instruments which also lay down meticulously the conditions NDPAs must conform to, not least as regards their 'complete independence'.[113]

Regulation (EU) 2016/679 of the European Parliament and of the Council on the protection of natural persons with regard to the processing of personal data and on the free movement of such data, and repealing Directive 95/46/EC (General Data Protection Regulation) [2016] OJ L119/1

Article 51

Supervisory authority

1. Each Member State shall provide for one or more independent public authorities to be responsible for monitoring the application of this Regulation, in order to protect

---

[110] See Article 8(3) of the Charter.

[111] Regulation (EU) 2018/1725 of the European Parliament and of the Council on the protection of natural persons with regard to the processing of personal data by the Union institutions, bodies, offices and agencies and on the free movement of such data, and repealing Regulation (EC) No 45/2001 and Decision No 1247/2002/EC [2018] OJ L295/39.

[112] See also Additional Protocol to the Convention for the protection of individuals with regard to automatic processing of personal data, regarding supervisory authorities and transborder data flows (opened 8 November 2001, entered into force 1 July 2004) 2297 UNTS 195, Article 1.

[113] See Regulation (EU) 2016/679 of the European Parliament and of the Council on the protection of natural persons with regard to the processing of personal data and on the free movement of such data, and repealing Directive 95/46/EC (General Data Protection Regulation) [2016] OJ L119/1, Articles 51–59 and Directive (EU) 2016/680 of the European Parliament and of the Council on the protection of natural persons with regard to the processing of personal data by competent authorities for the purposes of the prevention, investigation, detection or prosecution of criminal offences or the execution of criminal penalties, and on the free movement of such data, and repealing Council Framework Decision 2008/977/JHA [2016] OJ L119/89, Articles 41–49.

the fundamental rights and freedoms of natural persons in relation to processing and to facilitate the free flow of personal data within the Union ('supervisory authority').

Article 52

Independence
1. Each supervisory authority shall act with complete independence in performing its tasks and exercising its powers in accordance with this Regulation.

Among the tasks of the EDPS and NDPAs are monitoring, enforcing, and promoting data protection in the EU and the Member States, advising governments and institutions, supervising data controllers and processors, providing information to data subjects, and handling complaints.[114] As the powers of the EDPS and NDPAs can be seen as being equal to the tasks,[115] data protection authorities in the EU possess a comparatively strong and well-defined mandate in contrast to their counterparts in the general domain of fundamental rights.

One of the institutional innovations brought about by the General Data Protection Regulation (GDPR) is the establishment of the European Data Protection Board. The body is not entirely new, as it builds on the pre-existing Article 29 Working Party, but it has now been endowed with a permanent secretariat and legal personality. The Board serves as an operational forum bringing together the heads of all NDPAs and the EDPS to fulfil quite a number of tasks listed in Article 70 of the GDPR. Although it is not a judicial instance, the Board's interpretation of how the GDPR ought to be applied is authoritative for the practice of all relevant stakeholders in the EU data protection ecosystem, from NDPAs to individual data controllers.

Regulation (EU) 2016/679 of the European Parliament and of the Council on the protection of natural persons with regard to the processing of personal data and on the free movement of such data, and repealing Directive 95/46/EC (General Data Protection Regulation) [2016] OJ L119/1

Article 68

European Data Protection Board
1. The European Data Protection Board (the 'Board') is hereby established as a body of the Union and shall have legal personality.
2. The Board shall be represented by its Chair.
3. The Board shall be composed of the head of one supervisory authority of each Member State and of the European Data Protection Supervisor, or their respective representatives.

[114] EU General Data Protection Regulation 2016 (n 113), Article 57; EU Personal Data Protection Regulation 2018 (n 111), Article 57.
[115] EU General Data Protection Regulation 2016 (n 113), Article 58.

4. Where in a Member State more than one supervisory authority is responsible for monitoring the application of the provisions pursuant to this Regulation, a joint representative shall be appointed in accordance with that Member State's law.
5. The Commission shall have the right to participate in the activities and meetings of the Board without voting right. The Commission shall designate a representative. The Chair of the Board shall communicate to the Commission the activities of the Board.

Article 69

Independence

1. The **Board shall act independently** when performing its tasks or exercising its powers pursuant to Articles 70 and 71.
2. Without prejudice to requests by the Commission referred to in point (b) of Article 70(1) and in Article 70(2), **the Board shall**, in the performance of its tasks or the exercise of its powers, **neither seek nor take instructions from anybody**.

Article 70

Tasks of the Board

1. The Board shall ensure the consistent application of this Regulation. To that end, the Board shall, on its own initiative or, where relevant, at the request of the Commission, in particular:
   (a) monitor and ensure the correct application of this Regulation in the cases provided for in Articles 64 and 65 without prejudice to the tasks of national supervisory authorities;
   (b) advise the Commission on any issue related to the protection of personal data in the Union, including on any proposed amendment of this Regulation;
   (c) advise the Commission on the format and procedures for the exchange of information between controllers, processors and supervisory authorities for binding corporate rules;
   (d) issue guidelines, recommendations, and best practices on procedures for erasing links, copies or replications of personal data from publicly available communication services as referred to in Article 17(2);
   (e) examine, on its own initiative, on request of one of its members or on request of the Commission, any question covering the application of this Regulation and issue guidelines, recommendations and best practices in order to encourage consistent application of this Regulation;
   (f) issue guidelines, recommendations and best practices in accordance with point (e) of this paragraph
2. Where the Commission requests advice from the Board, it may indicate a time limit, taking into account the urgency of the matter.
3. The Board shall forward its opinions, guidelines, recommendations, and best practices to the Commission and to the committee referred to in Article 93 and make them public.
4. The Board shall, where appropriate, consult interested parties and give them the opportunity to comment within a reasonable period. The Board shall, without prejudice to Article 76, make the results of the consultation procedure publicly available.

2.10 European Ombudsman

In some countries, the ombudsperson is responsible for attending to human rights complaints relating a wide array of rights or at least those that can be identified as 'core' rights, such as prohibition of torture. In the EU, however, the office of the European Ombudsman has a more administrative character. The European Ombudsman is legally not an EU institution and yet, exceptionally, it has a basis in the Treaties. The Ombudsman has a degree of democratic legitimacy since it is, unusually for the EU, elected by the European Parliament. The body also represents one of the institutionalized checks on accountability of the EU administration.[116]

Consolidated version of the Treaty on the Functioning of the European Union [2012] OJ C326/47

Article 228

1. A European Ombudsman, **elected by the European Parliament, shall be empowered to receive complaints from any citizen of the Union** or any natural or legal person residing or having its registered office in a Member State **concerning instances of maladministration in the activities of the Union institutions,** bodies, offices or agencies, with the exception of the Court of Justice of the European Union acting in its judicial role. He or she shall examine such complaints and report on them.

In accordance with his duties, **the Ombudsman shall conduct inquiries** for which he finds grounds, either on his own initiative or on the basis of complaints submitted to him direct or through a Member of the European Parliament, except where the alleged facts are or have been the subject of legal proceedings. Where the Ombudsman establishes an instance of maladministration, he shall refer the matter to the institution, body, office or agency concerned, which shall have a period of three months in which to inform him of its views. The Ombudsman shall then forward a report to the European Parliament and the institution, body, office or agency concerned. The person lodging the complaint shall be informed of the outcome of such inquiries. (...)

3. The Ombudsman shall be completely independent in the performance of his duties. (...)

That is not to say that the activities of the European Ombudsman would not relate to fundamental rights. In fact, the EU Charter contains a specific provision about the European Ombudsman, as well as a number of other 'administrative human rights' ('citizens' rights in the jargon of the Charter) the compliance of which is monitored by the European Ombudsman, albeit with a strictly circumscribed mandate (no enforcement capacity) and

---

[116] HCH Hofmann and J Ziller, *Accountability in the EU: The Role of the European Ombudsman* (Edward Elgar Publishing 2017).

scope for action (no investigations at national level).[117] Through her powers of inquiry and public profile, the European Ombudsman can expose instances of maladministration at the EU level, raise awareness about complaints, and be an advocate for particular administrative issues, such as greater transparency in the Brexit negotiations. Such activities are consequently important for the effectuation of, in particular, the right to good administration and right of access to documents at the EU level.

Charter of Fundamental Rights of the European Union [2012] OJ C326/391

Article 41

Right to good administration

1. Every person has the right to have his or her affairs handled impartially, fairly and within a reasonable time by the institutions, bodies, offices and agencies of the Union.
2. This right includes:
   (a) the right of every person to be heard, before any individual measure which would affect him or her adversely is taken;
   (b) the right of every person to have access to his or her file, while respecting the legitimate interests of confidentiality and of professional and business secrecy;
   (c) the obligation of the administration to give reasons for its decisions.
3. Every person has the right to have the Union make good any damage caused by its institutions or by its servants in the performance of their duties, in accordance with the general principles common to the laws of the Member States.
4. Every person may write to the institutions of the Union in one of the languages of the Treaties and must have an answer in the same language.

Article 42

Right of access to documents

Any citizen of the Union, and any natural or legal person residing or having its registered office in a Member State, has a right of access to documents of the institutions, bodies, offices and agencies of the Union, whatever their medium.

Article 43

European Ombudsman

Any citizen of the Union and any natural or legal person residing or having its registered office in a Member State has the right to refer to the European Ombudsman cases of maladministration in the activities of the institutions, bodies, offices or agencies of the Union, with the exception of the Court of Justice of the European Union acting in its judicial role.

---

[117] K Kanska, 'Towards Administrative Human Rights in the EU: Impact of the Charter of Fundamental Rights' (2004) 10 European Law Journal 296.

The European Ombudsman also liaises with national ombudspersons, chiefly through the European Network of Ombudsmen. This cooperation mainly allows the European Ombudsman to refer cases that fall outside her mandate to responsible national ombudsmen. National ombudsmen can therefore find themselves in a network with both the European Ombudsman and the FRA.

The European Ombudsman rightly perceives herself as part of the EU fundamental rights ecosystem. More specifically, the body has defended in a thematic paper on the issue the importance of non-judicial and proactive approaches for the realization of human rights. Indeed, the Ombudsman has an unparalleled function which allows her to investigate actions of EU institutions regardless of the policy area. As such, she can point out that the Commission is not sufficiently diligent in conducting impact assessments of trade agreements or highlight the adverse effects of a lack of transparency in the Council on the EU's commitment to democratic decision-making. With few other institutional players capable of scrutinizing EU actions,[118] the Ombudsman's significance exceeds her limited competences.

European Ombudsman, The respect for and pursuit of fundamental rights, Thematic paper, 21 November 2016

Because of their crosscutting nature, fundamental rights issues arise in many EO [European Ombudsman] cases. Naturally, most inquiries concern procedural matters and different aspects of the fundamental right to good administration enshrined in Article 41 of the Charter (e.g. the right to have his/her affairs handled impartially, fairly and within a reasonable time, the right to be heard, the duty to state reasons, the right to have access to the file, the right to receive a reply in his/her own language). Other complaints concern the fundamental right of access to documents (Charter Article 42).

However, many complaints concern, directly or indirectly, other fundamental rights. The EO launches inquiries concerning staff issues, which have a human rights component. The EO has dealt with harassment cases involving human dignity, which constitutes the basis for all human rights (Charter Article 1), women's rights and the protection of persons with disabilities (Article 23 and 26 Charter). Other cases concern unjustified dismissal, fair, and just working conditions (Charter Article 15, 30 and 31). Many cases concern the prohibition of discrimination (Charter Article 21), the fundamental right to health (Charter Article 35) and the fundamental right to the protection of personal data (Charter Article 8). The Ombudsman has also dealt with infringement cases concerning freedom of movement (Charter Article 45), cases concerning the protection of the environment (Charter Article 37) and consumer protection (Charter Article 38).

The EO has therefore intervened in most areas covered by the Charter. The complainants sometimes invoke these rights or the cases focus on an issue which is not framed in fundamental rights terms but which has a fundamental rights dimension. This was most visible in the investigation concerning the Commission's failure to carry out a prior human rights impact assessment of the EU–Vietnam Free Trade Agreement. (...)

Human rights should not and cannot be confined to a strictly legal perspective or adjudicated solely in a court setting. The realisation of human rights depends in the first

---

[118] The Court of Auditors is another institution which scrutinizes EU institutions and occasionally can touch upon fundamental rights issues.

instance on how the Administration deals with them. Ombudsmen can be better placed than the courts to work with the Administration towards human rights compliance, as the service is not alone free and accessible, but also draws on concepts and deals with issues that do not always sit comfortably within the legal framework described above.

Seeing fundamental rights in a broader administrative perspective based on an elementary sense of fairness allows ombudsmen to step outside a binary lawful/unlawful logic and require institutions to do more than courts can. In this way, ombudsmen have a crucial role to play in the human rights arena.

Many human rights violations may go unnoticed because they never reach a court. The restrictive conditions of admissibility before EU or national courts may make a legal action impossible. The victim may not be able, for financial or other reasons, to take legal action. At EU level, the EO may be one remedy available if it involves an action or lack of action by the EU administration.

Unlike courts, the EO also has the power to intervene proactively on her own initiative in situations of systemic human rights issues.

The EO can advance the observance of human rights with respect to the full set of obligations flowing from them (the duty not to interfere, the duty to protect and to prevent human rights violations, the duty to create the institutional machinery and normative framework necessary for the realisation of human rights, the duty to promote fundamental rights and to provide goods and services necessary for their satisfaction).

2.11 EU Member States

Although the Member States are not EU institutions or bodies, their importance in the EU system overall and for the protection of fundamental rights in particular cannot be overlooked. Although this publication focuses on the EU's relationship with human rights, there is no denying that the biggest role in the grand scheme of things still belongs to the Member States. This is simply because most state functions, including all coercive powers, remain at the national level with the EU at best in a coordinating role. Both human rights protection and human rights violations therefore fall largely at the behest of the Member States.

Domestically, national constitutional law of virtually all Member States protects human rights in some way. Often the constitutional law will contain a bill of rights, inspired originally by developments in the seventeenth and eighteenth centuries in England (Habeas Corpus Act 1679, Bill of Rights 1689),[119] France (Declaration of the Rights of Man and of the Citizen 1789), and the United States (Bill of Rights 1789). Judicial review of alleged human rights violations can be either centralized in a single peak court (typically the constitutional court) or dispersed across the court system. In either case, domestic courts are in charge of ensuring that human rights, as following from any applicable legal source, international or domestic, are applied within the legal system. Human rights ordinarily enjoy the highest standing in the domestic legal order and cannot be overridden by legislation.

International human rights law is an indelible part of EU Member States' legal systems.[120] The most important treaty commitment is to the ECHR and its supervisory mechanism led

---

[119] The development can be traced even much further back to the adoption of the Magna Carta in 1215 but it would be a mistake to conflate it with a current day understanding of human rights which to a lesser extent also applies to the other 'original' bills of rights.

[120] See Ch 5.

by the European Court of Human Rights. The ECHR, as interpreted in the case law of the European Court of Human Rights (ECtHR), exerts considerable influence over not only domestic human rights law but legislation, constitutional law and national practices more generally.[121] Much less influential but still present are various international human rights instruments deposited at the UN, some with bodies to monitor compliance at the national level and allowing individual complaints be lodged.[122] Non-treaty obligations notably include customary international law in the human rights domain, difficult as it may be to identify at times.[123]

When it comes to the relation to the EU human rights regime, the most important limitation resides in the requirement that Member States must be implementing EU law for Union standards to apply to the national rule or situation in question.[124] At the same time, Article 2 TEU—and Article 19 TEU with respect to court requirements[125]—binds the Member States to maintain a necessary degree of fundamental rights protection regardless of whether it falls within the scope of EU law. This overarching obligation is consistent with the EU being founded on a set of values which have to be complied with for a country to be eligible to accede to the Union, as stipulated by the Copenhagen criteria.[126] More generally, the Member States must assist, pursuant to the principle of sincere cooperation, the EU in achieving the objectives of the Treaties, including the obligation of Article 3(5) and 21 TEU concerning the promotion of human rights in relations with third countries and organizations.

Consolidated version of the Treaty on European Union [2012] OJ C326/13

Article 4

3. Pursuant to the **principle of sincere cooperation**, the Union and the Member States shall, in full mutual respect, assist each other in carrying out tasks which flow from the Treaties.

The Member States shall take any appropriate measure, general or particular, to ensure fulfilment of the obligations arising out of the Treaties or resulting from the acts of the institutions of the Union.

---

[121] Although its impact varies across time and country, the ECHR's overall influence is indisputable. In the words of Keller and Stone Sweet, 'national officials are, gradually but inexorably, being socialized into a Europe of rights, a unique transnational legal space now developing its own logics of political and juridical legitimacy'. See H Keller and A Stone Sweet (eds), *A Europe of Rights: The Impact of the ECHR on National Legal Systems* (Oxford University Press 2008).

[122] See generally H Keller and G Ulfstein (eds), *UN Human Rights Treaty Bodies: Law and Legitimacy* (Cambridge University Press 2012). See also C McCrudden, 'Why Do National Court Judges Refer to Human Rights Treaties? A Comparative International Law Analysis of CEDAW' (2015) 109 American Journal of International Law 534.

[123] M Wood, 'Customary International Law and Human Rights', EUI Working Papers, AEL 2016/03; H Thirlway, 'Human Rights in Customary Law: An Attempt to Define Some of the Issues' (2015) 28 Leiden Journal of International Law 495; JJ Paust, 'The Complex Nature, Sources and Evidences of Customary Human Rights' (1996) 25 Georgia Journal of International and Comparative Law 147.

[124] See Article 51(1) of the Charter.

[125] Judgment of 27 February 2018, *Associação Sindical dos Juízes Portugueses v Tribunal de Contas*, C-64/16, ECLI:EU:C:2018:117.

[126] See Ch 9.

> The Member States shall facilitate the achievement of the Union's tasks and refrain from any measure which could jeopardise the attainment of the Union's objectives.

From the above it must be clear that Member States can sometimes find themselves in a precarious position if they are to live up to all their domestic, European, and international human rights commitments, in addition to governing their own country well. Take, for instance, national judges, one of the key links in the chain ensuring human rights protection. The judges must apply the domestic constitution, which may or may not take precedence (depending on the country) in boundary cases over international sources, apply international human rights law, which includes being aware of the extremely voluminous case law of the ECtHR, and apply EU fundamental rights but only if the case before the court comes within the material scope of EU law.[127] When, in addition, some of these standards conflict, as they easily can,[128] the national judges are in a bind.

Nevertheless, the realization of human rights is not only about big constitutional questions. The cross-cutting character and mainstreaming of human rights mandates the involvement of both governmental and non-governmental actors across all levels of the state and society. A good example is the role of local and regional authorities (LRAs); far from irrelevant, they can fulfil a significant role in the implementation of human rights, thereby bridging the enforcement gap.[129] Marx and others identified a variety of functions which are exercised in different countries by LRAs to achieve human rights objectives.

A Marx and others, 'Localizing Fundamental Rights in the European Union: What is the Role of Local and Regional Authorities, and How to Strengthen It?' (2015) 7 Journal of Human Rights Practice 246

In order to address this enforcement gap, attention is increasingly turning to the idea of localizing fundamental rights, that is, strengthening local institutions for the protection of fundamental rights. Hence, the role of local and regional authorities (LRAs) in ensuring 'maximum fundamental rights protection at all levels of governance' in the EU has come to the forefront and has been increasingly recognized. The [Committee of Regions] (CoR) has emphasized the role LRAs play in fundamental rights protection, especially as service providers of human rights-related services such as education and health care. This point was reiterated in the Opinion of the CoR on the strategy for the effective implementation by the EU of the Charter of Fundamental Rights. (...)

(...) Besides making rules, LRAs have a second strong policy instrument with which they can influence the protection of fundamental rights. Through budget allocation and service provision they can encourage initiatives and actors to strengthen the protection of fundamental rights. LRAs provide several services which are directly relevant in the context of fundamental rights such as housing, health care, education, and so on. Through

---

[127] With the potential caveat of having or choosing to refer a question for preliminary proceedings to the CJEU under Article 267 TFEU.

[128] Judgment of 26 February 2013, *Melloni v Ministerio Fiscal*, C-399/11, ECLI:EU:C:2013:107.

[129] EM Hafner-Burton, *Making Human Rights a Reality* (Princeton University Press 2013).

service provision, LRAs can promote or inhibit the protection of fundamental rights and promote respect for fundamental rights such as by the promotion of equality. (...)

In respect of LRAs' roles and responsibilities with regard to fundamental rights, central state authorities should make sure to adopt a clear legal, policy and budgetary framework so that LRAs' initiatives can find their place in a coherent pattern of multilevel governance, for example through the allocation of cascading responsibilities and specific mandates, inclusion and participation of LRAs in national plans for protecting fundamental rights and the rule of law, and the adoption of structural budgetary measures allowing LRAs to discharge their role effectively. This will imply the application of the subsidiarity principle to the protection of fundamental rights with a clear recognition of the role of LRAs as the closest authorities to the citizens.

(...) we identified four key roles LRAs can play in this regard: LRAs as rule enforcers through monitoring and complaint handling; LRAs as service providers with attention to fundamental rights issues; LRAs as policy coordinators; and LRAs in a policy supporting role with special attention to awareness-raising.

3

Concepts and Language of Human Rights in the EU

3.1 Introduction

Most human rights research is devoted to how the predominantly legal obligations are implemented in the practice of courts and governments. Nevertheless, the use of the concept of human rights by state institutions cannot only be taken at face value and in isolation from other key constitutional concepts. This chapter therefore looks at the language and concepts surrounding human rights in the EU. First, the dichotomous language of 'human' and 'fundamental' rights—commonplace in the EU—is scrutinized in detail. Second, light is cast on the human rights narratives the EU tells about itself. Finally, the close relationship of human rights with the associated concepts of the rule of law and democracy is posited, both generally and in the EU context.

3.2 Human or Fundamental? On the Language and Concept of Rights

Even a brief look at the EU Treaties makes immediately clear that both 'human' and 'fundamental' rights are mentioned in various parts of the text, most often as part of references to, on the one hand, the European Convention on Human Rights and Fundamental Freedoms and the EU Charter of Fundamental Rights, on the other. What is less obvious from reading the Treaties is whether there is in fact a difference between the two terms or whether they are synonymous.

A. The EU's dichotomous language of rights

Most often it is suggested that when the EU refers to the concept of human rights in connection to its internal affairs, it uses the term 'fundamental rights', while the term 'human rights' is used in the context of external policies. A case could be made that the EU merely replicates the distinction, observable especially in the aftermath of the Second World War in Europe, between domestic 'fundamental' rights enshrined in national constitutions, such as the German *Grundrechte*,[1] and international 'human' rights, as in the 1948 Universal Declaration of Human Rights. The constitutional/international fault line should not be overstated, however, as the former element is very country-specific and not all international instruments use

---

[1] Note, however, that Article 1(2) of the German Basic Law (Constitution), which forms part of the heading 'fundamental rights' (*Grundrechte*), refers also to 'inviolable and inalienable 'human rights' (*Menschenrechte*) as the foundation of every community, of peace and of justice in the world'.

The European Union and Human Rights. Jan Wouters and Michal Ovádek, Oxford University Press (2021). © Jan Wouters and Michal Ovádek. DOI: 10.1093/oso/9780198814177.003.0003

the terminology in the same way. Some countries do not refer to the (substantively similar) rights enshrined in their foundational documents as fundamental or human, while the constitutional traditions of others, such as France, are cognizant of both expressions, not least due to the considerable influence of the international instruments. Lines are further blurred when the two adjectives are combined ('fundamental human rights') or when rights are 'human' but freedoms 'fundamental' (as in the title of the European Convention on Human Rights (ECHR)).

The application of the constitutional/international distinction to the EU's rights language is not without ambiguities either but it is by and large consciously observed by the EU institutions, including when it comes to naming EU agencies (the name of the EU Agency for *Fundamental* Rights corresponds with its internal mandate). The rights protected by the Court of Justice of the European Union (CJEU) as general principles of EU law have been from the outset—albeit after calling them first 'fundamental human' in the 1969 judgment in *Stauder*—'fundamental'.[2] Conversely, international treaties signed by the Member States protected 'human' rights.[3] This created a platform for subsequent codifications of EU fundamental rights in Treaties, in particular the Charter ('of Fundamental Rights'), and legislation to replicate the language first used by the Court in a path-dependent manner.

Furthermore, Article 6(3) of the Treaty on European Union (TEU) stipulates that fundamental rights, as guaranteed by the ECHR, constitute general principles of EU law. This provision makes explicit the linguistic border between the EU and the ECHR: insofar as the EU considers the 'human rights' and 'fundamental freedoms' of the ECHR to be 'fundamental rights', they are part of EU law as general principles. Given that nowhere in the EU Treaties, Charter, or the CJEU case law it is suggested that the ECHR guarantees any rights and freedoms which would not also be 'fundamental rights' in the parlance and purview of the EU, it can be assumed that at the superficial linguistic level the two expressions mean the same thing (they refer to the same abstract concept of rights). This conclusion is further corroborated by the fact that Article 52(3) of the Charter prescribes a legal equivalence of scope and meaning between similar rights contained in the Charter ('of *Fundamental*

---

[2] See Judgment of 17 December 1970, *Internationale Handelsgesellschaft v Einfuhr- und Vorratsstelle für Getreide und Futtermittel*, 11/70, ECLI:EU:C:1970:114, para 4. The reference to 'fundamental human rights' in *Stauder* must be viewed in the context of CJEU translations. The judgment was rendered in 1969, that is prior to the accession of the UK and Ireland in 1973. As a result, the judgment was originally not even available in English—at the time of the decision, it was available in Dutch, French, German, and Italian, with French being the working language of the Court. Three of the four original language versions use the same expression which would translate literally into English as 'fundamental rights of the person' (only the Dutch version would read 'fundamental rights of the human'). The use of the word 'human' in English, as well as the Dutch translation using 'mens', should therefore be understood as referring to the fundamental rights of individuals, rather than referring to the discourse of 'human rights'. By using the word 'person' instead of 'human', the French, German, and Italian versions clearly prevented any ambiguity in this regard. Besides, it can be surmised, at least as far as French (the drafting language) and Italian are concerned, that the choice of words was careful and deliberate, as the more natural expression would have included the word 'human' ('de l'homme/dell'uomo'). This glance across original language versions implies that the break from 'human' rights was present in the case law of the CJEU from the very beginning and the subsequent case law merely simplified the language by dropping 'person'/'human' from 'fundamental rights'. The use of 'fundamental rights' by the Court for internal matters has been consistent since *Stauder* with a few exceptions, such as Judgment of 15 June 1978, *Gabrielle Defrenne v Société anonyme belge de navigation aérienne Sabena*, 149/77, ECLI:EU:C:1978:130, para 26 where the judges somewhat strangely resorted to the four-word phrase 'fundamental personal human rights'. This analysis is of course without prejudice to the intricacies endogenous in the multilingualism of the CJEU and translations of its judgments; see K McAuliffe, 'The Limitations of a Multilingual Legal System' (2013) 26 International Journal for the Semiotics of Law 861.

[3] Judgment of 14 May 1974, *Nold v Commission*, 4/73, ECLI:EU:C:1974:51, para 13.

Rights') and the ECHR—such legal homogeneity would be difficult to achieve if the Charter 'fundamental' rights and the Convention 'human' rights emanated from different first-order concepts.

So why use different expressions to refer to the same concept? There are prosaic as well as political reasons. Prosaically, one can point to the richness of languages and the fact that using synonyms is perfectly legitimate and requires no justification. Moreover, it is inherent in the multilingualism of the EU that expressions with most commonality across languages might be preferred. However, a more political optic would perceive something else in the choice of 'fundamental' over 'human' for the internal purposes of the EU. If we suppose that 'human' rights are primarily associated with international documents agreed upon by sovereign states and 'fundamental' rights connote an internal constitutional (state) setting, it would certainly be commensurate with the CJEU's classification of the EU's legal order as an 'independent source of law' for the Court to also prefer to call the rights it guarantees 'fundamental' rather than 'human'.[4] It is arguably also easier for the CJEU to safeguard its autonomy and define an EU-specific approach to rights when the label does not copy verbatim the language of the ECHR or of other international instruments (despite on substance being heavily inspired by the ECHR and national constitutions). The same arguments hold to an extent for the subsequent codifications and Charter making by political institutions and Member States, although the failed treaty on the European Political Community (EPC) originally contained the exact language of the ECHR with an express incorporation thereof.[5] The prominence of the ECHR even in the early days of European integration, to which the EPC draft treaty was a testament, makes the CJEU's choice of 'fundamental rights', and the EU institutions' subsequent replication of the distinction,[6] appear more intentional than incidental.[7] On the occasion of enacting the Charter, the different names could have conceivably helped to justify, in the eyes of the public, the adoption of another European human rights instrument.[8] On a psychological level, the linguistic distinction cutting along the constitutional/international line might be entrenching the lukewarm reception of international human rights law in the EU, especially when it comes to the CJEU.[9] The foregoing argument also largely coheres with existing knowledge about the nexus of law and multilingualism at the CJEU.[10]

---

[4] Judgment of 15 July 1964, *Costa v ENEL*, 6/64, ECLI:EU:C:1964:66.

[5] See Articles 2, 3, 90, and 116 of the EPC Treaty.

[6] For one of the earliest high-profile examples of the institutions' adoption of the 'fundamental rights' language in EU internal context see Joint Declaration by the European Parliament, the Council and the Commission concerning the protection of fundamental rights and the European Convention for the Protection of Human Rights and Fundamental Freedoms [1977] OJ C103/1.

[7] As was the omission of rights from the EEC Treaty. See MA Dauses, 'The Protection of Fundamental Rights in the Community Legal Order' (1985) 10 European Law Review 398, 399.

[8] In accordance with the constitutional-fundamental/international-human dichotomy, the Charter of *Fundamental* Rights would have been consistent with the EU *Constitutional* Treaty, had it been adopted. See JHH Weiler, 'Does the European Union Truly Need a Charter of Rights?' (2002) 6 European Law Journal 95. Similarly, the EU Agency for Fundamental Rights was originally discussed as a human rights agency. See P Alston and JHH Weiler, 'An "Ever Closer Union" in Need of a Human Rights Policy: The European Union and Human Rights' in P Alston (ed), *The EU and Human Rights* (Oxford University Press 1999).

[9] See Ch 5.

[10] K McAuliffe, 'Language and Law in the European Union: The Multilingual Jurisprudence of the ECJ' in L Solan and P Tiersma (eds), *The Oxford Handbook of Language and Law* (Oxford University Press 2012); K McAuliffe, 'Translating Ambiguity' (2014) 9 The Journal of Comparative Law 65.

K McAuliffe, 'The Limitations of a Multilingual Legal System' (2013) 26 International Journal for the Semiotics of Law 861

The teleological interpretative method employed by the CJEU assumes a normative, platonic notion of 'EU law' which is expressed in one language that exists in many linguistic versions. The Court itself seems to claim that while those linguistic versions may differ from each other on a purely linguistic level, at the legal level they express the same concepts (i.e. each linguistic version of EU law draws from the same EU legal concepts and therefore forms the same, new EU legal language). (...) Similarly, approximation in language and translation in the EU can actually fulfil a positive role in ensuring the effectiveness of the legal order – indeed one could argue that the continued effectiveness of EU law is in fact dependent on its hybrid nature. The EU legal order functions precisely because of the implicit understanding among those who work at the EU level of the indeterminate and imprecise nature of language and law.

(...) The method of teleological interpretation developed by the CJEU and the evolution of the notion of a new EU legal language do ensure the effectiveness of EU law to a large extent. However, the fact remains that different languages offer different accounts of reality. The approximation and imprecision inherent in language and translation do have implications for the case law produced by the CJEU. The concept of a single EU legal language that allows EU law to be uniformly applied throughout the Union is, in fact, necessarily based on a legal fiction. That fiction is a workable one, since EU law does function reasonably effectively. It is nonetheless a fiction, and an awareness of the problems of language and translation should therefore condition our understanding of the multilingual EU legal order.

Beyond such deeper considerations, however, the dual rights language by the EU is nowadays less significant than it may have been in the formative years of EU fundamental rights jurisprudence. For their part, the EU Treaties contain both language which seemingly conforms to the constitutional/international distinction and language which does not. The values listed in Article 2 TEU on which the EU is internally founded include 'respect for human rights'. When it comes to their enforcement through Article 7 TEU and the Commission Rule of Law Framework, the EU institutions often refer to the need for the respect of 'fundamental rights', showing that the two are in practice interchangeable but also perhaps the institutions' preference for linguistic clarity according to the constitutional/international distinction (which need not imply a distinction in terms of substance).[11] Elsewhere, the EU Treaties appear to reflect the constitutional/international (internal/external) distinction: Articles 3(5) and 21 TEU on the EU's external relations mention 'human' rights, whereas Article 67 TFEU on the EU's (internal) area of freedom, security and justice refers to respect for 'fundamental' rights. The various institutions and bodies of the EU tend to follow the internal/external distinction quite methodically in their publications and communications.[12]

The discussion of the EU's language of rights should not be understood as necessarily prejudicing analyses of commonalities and differences between various human/fundamental rights instruments. The legal meaning of rights and the various content given to equally named rights under different instruments does not normally revolve around the

---

[11] See European Commission, 'Communication from the Commission to the European Parliament and the Council—A new EU Framework to strengthen the Rule of Law' COM (2014)158 final 5, 3–6.
[12] EU officials might observe the distinction less strictly in oral communication.

titles of the instruments to which they belong, nor is it usually the constitutional/international distinction between 'fundamental' and 'human' rights as much as acknowledged by courts and practitioners. For example, the legal and judicial application and interpretation of the aforementioned Article 52(3) of the Charter has never considered the linguistic disjunction an obstacle to fulfilling the obligation to align corresponding Charter rights to their ECHR counterparts. In addition, the fact that the two expressions can be treated interchangeably does not in any way preclude differently entitled rights instruments to have different content. Conversely, similarly entitled instruments (and rights) need not necessarily have the same content.

B. A more fundamental distinction?

From a more philosophical perspective, the constitutional/international dichotomy would be likely to be viewed as relatively shallow because a more deep-seated, conceptual distinction has been at times drawn between human and fundamental rights. According to this conceptual distinction, all humans are entitled to enjoy human rights by virtue of their human dignity (their inherent worth as human beings) which is prior to any social structures within which rights might be practically delivered and conditioned. On the other hand, fundamental rights are those rights posited in a legal order (positive law) and tied to the political and social structures and exercise of power in a society. In this stylized account, the former emanate from a natural law source and are in principle ahistorical and universal, whereas the latter are historically contingent and only exist on the basis of and within the political, legal, and social structures kept up by societies. The Italian legal philosopher Gianluigi Palombella supports the maintenance of such a conceptual distinction along similar lines on account of the analytical benefits that this can bring and highlights the problems associated with embedding the two conceptions of rights into a single concept of human rights.

G Palombella, 'From Human Rights to Fundamental Rights: Consequences of a conceptual distinction' (2007) 93 Archiv für Rechts- und Sozialphilosophie 396

Generally speaking proponents of human rights begin with abstract assumptions, which aspire to universal validity. Even when they renounce an absolute foundation, they nonetheless consider human rights to be an essential prerequisite of coexistence, irrespective of the way in which it subsequently orientates its goals. The abstract quality of human rights is the necessary condition of their aspiration to or presumption of 'universality'. In spite of international (or European) treaties and declarations, which aim to manifest themselves in nuclei of 'positivised' rights, the deontological, and therefore Kantian, principled, categorical and pure emphasis of human rights is testament to their 'moral' force. The strength of human rights lies in the fact that they are after all a philosophy. If it is true that they presuppose an ontology, an epistemology, an anthropology, a vision of justice, their persistent abstractness may also function as a kind of permanent critical principle. (...)

   A theory of 'human' rights in itself concludes by bringing a deontological claim, concerning that which we owe to human beings, and which is linked at least to a moral theory and probably also to an anthropology. A theory of 'fundamental' rights by contrast obliges us to focus also on that which is capable of contributing to the existence of a society (or also to recommend them as that which could or should do so): this involves analysis or prescriptions which are not expressed in deontological terms, but in ethical, institutional, political or teleological terms. Fundamental rights must be concretised just as human rights must be considered in the abstract.

(...)

Rights are fundamental if their normative ideals are effectively used as criteria of recognition of the validity of legal norms and of relevant institutional practices. In a certain sense, constituting substantive criteria of public life, fundamental rights also select accepted cultural rights, including the very possibility of affiliation for groups which are right holders within the system to which they appeal and in which they demand protection.

In addition, such a conceptual distinction—but perhaps deviating somewhat from Palombella's dwelling on the abstractness of human rights—can in turn have a bearing on the content of human and fundamental rights, even if in both conceptualizations the rights should at the same time be morally justifiable.[13] Fundamental rights, for example, can be more likely to encompass a more diverse range of rights, including those requiring substantial societal organization and resources, such as the right to receive healthcare and education. Fundamental rights can also be those entitlements which concern the relationship between the governing entity (most often the state) and its subjects (citizens, residents), such as the right to vote in elections, and the relations between subjects, such as the right not to be discriminated against in the workplace. In practice, of course, the implementation of rights blurs the philosophical distinction presented here, as even 'human' rights which would require mere non-interference, such as freedom of speech or assembly, can be put into practice only within the constraints and structures of the real world. Consequently, the tradition of rights, regardless of whether fundamental or human, tends to be strongly entangled with common imaginaries of the known national (the state) and international (Westphalian system of sovereign states) political, legal, social, and economic structures.

Nevertheless, the content of universal and inherent human rights might be limited to a core of inviolable rights that are most closely related to the preservation of human dignity, such as the right to life. What the content of universal and inherent human rights should be is, however, subject to perpetual contestation stemming from different ontological, epistemological, and ethical perspectives on the nature and appropriate aspirations of the social world.[14] The most commonly referenced dividing line is between, on the one hand, universalism, which implies that a single set of human rights (or at least a core thereof) should apply to all human beings, regardless of cultural and other differences, and, on the other hand, particularism, which stresses the importance of diversity and pluralism and thus denies that universality of human rights is normatively desirable or empirically achievable.[15] Nonetheless, this discussion (and

---

[13] As regards the morality and legality of human rights see T Campbell, 'Human Rights: Moral or Legal?' and T Pogge, 'Human Rights as Moral rights' both in D Kinley, W Sadurski, and K Walton (eds), *Human Rights: Old Problems, New Possibilities* (Edward Elgar Publishing 2013).

[14] This is not to say that 'fundamental rights' are never contested—they can of course be contested within their own conceptualization in the same way as 'human rights'.

[15] This is a very general and simplistic description of the debate. For a more learned review of modern arguments in the universalism/particularism discussion see N Walker, 'Universalism and Particularism in Human

others) does not necessarily turn on the conceptual distinction between human rights as a priori inherent and inalienable entitlements and fundamental rights as 'practical' rights protected in a given society and governance system, since in practice the ideals underlying the conceptualization of human rights are implemented through arrangements associated in this stylized distinction with fundamental rights. To exemplify: even if one believes that the right to life is inherent to all human beings and that this right cannot be violated by terminating the life of another, the right to life for everyone in the world as we know it might best be given effect through the enactment and enforcement of legal instruments, such as international human rights treaties prohibiting capital punishment, binding sovereign states and their legal orders which tend to operate on the basis of the logic of positive law.[16]

The above does not mean that it is only practically enforceable 'fundamental' rights which matter: the conceptualization of human rights as naturally given a priori rights can be a powerful source of legitimation and a reason to implement the vision of human rights through practical arrangements and in exceptional cases even possibly derogate from positive legal constraints for that purpose.[17] To give another example: if the context-specific and malleable fundamental rights were made applicable in a particular state only on the condition of holding citizenship, then all those who do not qualify as citizens by the rules of that state could be deprived by the sovereign exercise of state power of even the most basic human rights, such as the right to life. This problem was famously discussed by Hannah Arendt in the context of Nazi Germany's treatment of the Jewish population as the question of who has the right to have rights and the issue of statelessness.[18] As a side note, it is worth noticing how the previously discussed constitutional/international connotation pervades even the philosophical distinction with states as the primary loci of power, including the power to enact, enforce, and justify restrictions to (fundamental) rights. On the contrary, outside the state context the international sphere lacks an appropriately empowered global governance system, and therefore is often symbolically linked to the more idealistic vision of 'human' rights and made more reliant on their moral force emanating from the inherent human dignity of all human beings, which, as a discursive method, may be less potent in international relations than sometimes envisaged.[19]

When it comes to the EU, although it does not philosophize over the conceptual distinction between human and fundamental rights, it is at least rhetorically a proponent of 'the universality and indivisibility of human rights and fundamental freedoms'.[20] Conversely, some of the fundamental rights enshrined in the Charter can only be enjoyed by EU citizens, such as the right to vote, to move freely within the Union, or to receive consular protection abroad,[21] albeit the majority of the Charter provisions can be enjoyed by any person without

---

Rights: Trade-off or Productive Tension?' in Kinley, Sadurski, and Walton (eds), *Human Rights: Old Problems, New Possibilities* (n 8).

[16] For a classical account see HLA Hart, *The Concept of Law* (Oxford University Press 1961). For a different understanding of the concept of law see, for example, R Alexy, 'On the Concept and Nature of Law' (2008) 21 Ratio Juris 281.

[17] For example, in the context of criminal justice—which is, however, also tied to particularly egregious human rights violations—see the legal doctrine formulated by Gustav Radbruch. BH Bix, 'Radbruch's Formula and Conceptual Analysis' (2011) 56 The American Journal of Jurisprudence 45; SL Paulson, 'Radbruch on Unjust Laws: Competing Earlier and Later Views?' (1995) 15 Oxford Journal of Legal Studies 489.

[18] H Arendt, *The Origins of Totalitarianism* (Harcourt 1968).

[19] E Posner, *The Twilight of Human Rights Law* (Oxford University Press 2014). More generally see DP Forsythe, *Human Rights in International Relations* (3rd edn, Cambridge University Press 2012).

[20] Article 21(1) TEU. See also Council of the European Union, 'Human Rights and Democracy: EU Strategic Framework and Action Plan', 11855/12, 25 June 2012.

[21] See Articles 39, 40, 15, 45, and 46 of the Charter.

citizenship limitations, subject to the conditions of applicability and legitimate restrictions of Article 51 and 52 of the Charter. As observed above, Article 2 TEU, as well as the preamble to the TEU, make reference to 'respect for human rights' (rather than fundamental rights as could be expected in the internal context); in line with the conceptual dichotomy portrayed in this sub-section, the term 'human' rights could also speculatively signify that the EU is founded on more than just the 'fundamental' rights accepted within its community of Member States and peoples but instead on the very idea of inalienable rights inherent to all human beings.

3.3 Human Rights Narratives as EU Myths

This book deals mainly with how fundamental/human rights function in the EU and its relations with third countries. As such, the focus is on the modalities of rights, how they operate, and to what results they can lead. Nevertheless, the EU's human rights discourse, broadly construed, is in itself an important statement about the EU. Indeed, as this book documents with respect to the various areas of EU action, human rights are nowadays not incidental or tangential to such action or to the EU's character. On the contrary, human rights have not only been intentionally placed at the core of the EU's policies but have been inserted into essential narratives about what the EU is, what it stands for in the world, and how it was founded. Such narratives are quite literally today embedded in European culture; to paraphrase a famous quip by the anthropologist Clifford Geertz, they form part of 'the stories we tell ourselves about ourselves'.[22] As explored in an original study by Stijn Smismans, the EU's narratives about human rights are in part based on 'non-rational elements' and contain factual errors.[23] They are partly myths, myths with political significance.[24]

Some of the basic elements of the EU's fundamental rights mythology can in fact be easily discerned from the historical overview of the evolution of fundamental rights in the EU covered in Chapter 1. Despite the fact that Articles 2 and 6(1) TEU profess today that the EU is founded upon various values including human rights, it is patently clear from looking at the original Treaty of Rome that the EU made no reference to any values beyond the commitment to European integration and the creation of a common market through which pursuit of economic development was sought.[25] Rather, the EU's claim about its own value-laden foundation is a retrospective assertion from which greater internal legitimation or external credibility can be derived. Even today, the EU continues to lack a proper fundamental rights competence and it leans on the composite character of the EU, whereby Member States' human rights commitments support both internal (as in the mutual trust principle) and external (as in human rights promotion) policies, despite the widespread emphasis on the EU's own role and commitment with respect to human rights in its official communication. Indeed, the gap between rhetoric and action is a recurrent theme in the literature on the EU and its normative discourse.[26] This comes back to haunt the EU when it is, for example, not

---

[22] C Geertz, *The Interpretation of Cultures: Selected Essays by Clifford Geertz* (Basic Books 1973) 448.

[23] S Smismans, 'The European Union's Fundamental Rights Myth' (2010) 48 Journal of Common Market Studies 45.

[24] See also A Williams, *EU Human Rights Policies: A Study in Irony* (Oxford University Press 2004).

[25] Smismans, 'Fundamental Rights Myth' (n 23) 50.

[26] See, for example, H Mayer, 'Is It Still Called 'Chinese Whispers'? The EU's Rhetoric and Action as a Responsible Global Institution' (2008) 4 International Affairs 61.

able to enforce internal compliance with the foundational values, as has been the case in Hungary and Poland in recent years.

S Smismans, 'The European Union's Fundamental Rights Myth' (2010) 48 Journal of Common Market Studies 45

The maximalist myth (...) is based on the idea that fundamental rights have always been at the origin of the EC/EU as a reaction to the war experience and given the particular strong common European heritage of fundamental rights protection. It implies not simply that Community institutions and EC law respect fundamental rights, but also that the EU acts as a guardian on fundamental rights in its Member States and candidate countries, and provides higher fundamental rights standards than other international forums. Moreover, this superior European heritage makes the EU the ideal actor to promote fundamental rights throughout the world. The narrative is told in different settings and does not always imply all the maximalist claims, but there is a common ground of foundational claims which place fundamental rights as inherent to the EC/EU and based on a common heritage.

(...) for a political myth to be propagated it is not always that important whether one truly believes in the myth or only believes in its strategic use, either simply for self-interest, and/or to defend the fundamental values that presumably it favours. There is often an ambiguous tension in political myths between is and ought. One may not believe all the narrative's claims on reality, but believe that the use of the narrative may contribute to how reality ought to be. Hence, one may be critical of the EU's current fundamental rights credentials, but still believe the narrative contributes to the role the EU ought to play in this field. Such a narrative may work as a self-fulfilling prophecy. Moreover, the repetition of the narrative may lead to customization not only to the underlying norms of the narrative, but equally to its selective presentation of facts.

(...) fundamental rights were not part of the initial institutional set-up of the EEC, but several interwoven discourses on fundamental rights developed which assigned, retrospectively, such rights as inherent in the European project and based them on a common European heritage. So while not an ancestral myth, we finally still end up with a foundational myth. The myth makes use of 'concrete universals', arguing that the EU has particularly strong credentials in respecting 'universal' fundamental rights. It does so equally by free-riding on the fundamental rights credentials of its Member States and the CoE. The narrative has been acted upon and led to change, functioning to an extent as a self-fulfilling prophecy.

The strength of the EU's myth-making rhetoric is further underlined by the vast literature on the conception of the EU as a 'normative power'.[27] According to this theorization, which reproduces the language of 'founding principles', the EU's 'constitutional norms represent crucial constitutive factors determining its international identity'.[28] As the story continues,

---

[27] I Manners, 'Normative Power Europe: A Contradiction in Terms?' (2002) 40 Journal of Common Market Studies 235; R Whitman (ed), *Normative Power Europe: Empirical and Theoretical Approaches* (Palgrave Macmillan 2011). For one of the many critiques of 'Normative Power Europe' see A Hyde-Price, '"Normative" Power Europe: A Realist Critique' (2006) 13 Journal of European Public Policy 217.

[28] Manners, 'Normative Power Europe' (n 27) 241.

the EU's normative basis—consisting of the core norms of peace, liberty, democracy, rule of law and human rights, and minor norms of social solidarity, anti-discrimination, sustainable development, and good governance—differentiates the EU from other political actors and predisposes it to act in a distinct way on the international stage, namely as a normative power which diffuses ('normalizes') its own norms in international relations.[29] The partially mythical nature of human rights narratives is congruent with the conscious engagement in international norm entrepreneurship by the EU. No wonder then that the concept of 'normative power' has occasionally been embraced by the official discourse of EU representatives.[30] At the same time, the EU's normative rhetoric and self-construction as a normative international player has often come under fire for not being (sufficiently) acted upon or being misguided in practice.[31]

Nevertheless, as important as the reflexion induced by the mythical perspective on EU human rights narratives and the critiques of 'normative power Europe' is,[32] the EU's commitment to human rights is not all smoke and mirrors. By Smismans' own admission, it is also genuine and has very practical consequences both inside and outside the EU.[33] Moreover, cultivating the narrative despite objective deficiencies in the EU's effectuation of human rights might still be normatively desirable in a way that, for example, perpetuation of xenophobic or other sordid types of discourse would not be. In this book, we look at how fundamental/human rights are put into practice by the EU, including how they, often repeatedly, fail, and the various incoherencies embodied in the EU's approaches. Although we believe that the core human rights ethos of the EU is legitimate and its various manifestations deserve to be studied on their individual merits, we also invite the reader to treat the contents of this book with the necessary critical distance.[34]

3.4 The Rule of Law, Democracy, and Their Relation to Fundamental Rights

Although the focus of this book is squarely on human rights and the EU, this distinction is more borne out of analytical necessity than reflective of how human rights are often spoken about or included in legal and policy documents. As is obvious from Article 2 TEU (but also for example the normative power theory), human rights are often bundled with democracy and the rule of law and variously referred to together as fundamental/foundational values, principles, or ideals. Admittedly, the nature of the interrelations between the various

---

[29] Ibid, 245.

[30] See, for example, European Commission, Speech by President Barroso at Princeton University: 'European Union: An indispensable partner', 27 September 2012, SPEECH/12/650. It should be noted, however, that the statement 'there is no normative power without both soft and hard power' of the former Commission President Barroso is a misinterpretation of Manners' original claim about 'Normative Power Europe', namely because such power is exercised independently of an instrumental threat of force. See Manners, 'Normative Power Europe' (n 27) 242.

[31] See, for example, M Pace, 'The Construction of EU Normative Power' (2007) 45 Journal of Common Market Studies 1039; M Pace, 'Paradoxes and Contradictions in EU Democracy Promotion in the Mediterranean: The Limits of EU Normative Power' (2009) 16 Democratization 39.

[32] T Diez, 'Constructing the Self and Changing Others: Reconsidering "Normative Power Europe"' (2005) 33 Millennium—Journal of International Studies 613.

[33] Smismans, 'Fundamental Rights Myth' (n 23) 56–57.

[34] Indeed, the study of the relationship between the EU and human rights has never been devoid of sharp criticism. For a notable example see A Williams, *EU Human Rights Policies: A Study in Irony* (Oxford University Press 2004).

concepts is blurry not only in the way they are ordinarily employed but also from an academic perspective, not least because all three of the concepts fit well, even on their own, within the moniker 'essentially contested concepts'.[35] Without attempting to cover the topic exhaustively, we review a number of propositions about how the rule of law and democracy relate to fundamental rights, particularly in the context of the EU.

A. The democracy, rule of law, and human rights triumvirate in general

The triumvirate of democracy, the rule of law, and fundamental rights represent the standard core of liberal democratic political systems based on the Western model. From the perspective of rule of law theories, this common sense view of the three concepts as part of one package constitutes a substantive and thick notion of the rule of law.[36] Such a concept of the rule of law is broadly speaking 'substantive'—as opposed to 'formal'—because by comprising fundamental rights it does not merely address the procedural legality of the law (is it sufficiently clear and does it emanate from an authorized source?), which in this case includes democratic legitimacy but also constrains, at least in part, the content of the law (it must comply with rights).[37] The 'thickness' of this conception turns on the extent to which rights circumscribe and prescribe the content of the law: a thinner version would comprise only basic political rights and civil liberties (sometimes referred to as first-generation rights), while a thicker version of the substantive rule of law theory entails also second- and third-generation rights which impose a positive obligation on the state to ensure them, as opposed merely to refraining from interfering with political freedoms. More than one legal theorist has warned against the increased thickening of the concept of the rule of law by adding more and more human rights to international treaties and constitutional documents as it leads, in addition to analytical fuzziness, to the judicialization of politics which has anti-democratic effects.[38] Nevertheless, it is also possible, as has been argued in the case of the EU,[39] that a long list of fundamental rights can contribute to little more than formal legality of the rule of law when rights are seen more as procedural safeguards than moral guarantees of substantive justice.

Universal Declaration of Human Rights (adopted 10 December 1948) UNGA Res 217 A

Preamble

Whereas it is essential, if man is not to be compelled to have recourse, as a last resort, to rebellion against tyranny and oppression, that **human rights should be protected by the rule of law, (...)**

---

[35] WB Gallie, 'Essentially Contested Concepts' (1955) 56 Proceedings of the Aristotelian Society 167.
[36] BZ Tamanaha, *On the Rule of Law: History, Politics, Theory* (Cambridge University Press 2004) 111.
[37] Ibid, 91–92.
[38] Ibid, 113.
[39] See S Douglas-Scott, 'Justice, Injustice and the Rule of Law in the EU' in D Kochenov, G de Búrca, and A Williams (eds), *Europe's Justice Deficit?* (Hart Publishing 2014).

Article 21

(1) **Everyone has the right to take part in the government of his country**, directly or through freely chosen representatives.

(3) **The will of the people shall be the basis of the authority of government**; this will shall be expressed in periodic and genuine elections which shall be by universal and equal suffrage and shall be held by secret vote or by equivalent free voting procedures.

Article 29

(2) In the exercise of his rights and freedoms, everyone shall be subject only to such limitations as are determined by law solely for the purpose of securing due recognition and respect for the rights and freedoms of others and of meeting the just requirements of morality, public order and the general welfare in a **democratic society**.

Human rights and the rule of law have not always been seen as the tight unit they form today in thick conceptions of the latter practiced in liberal-democratic states.[40] Nevertheless, the Universal Declaration of Human Rights (UDHR), very much the original document of the modern international human rights movement, alludes to a normative linkage between democracy, human rights, and the rule of law, albeit the brief reference to the latter doing little to illuminate significantly its role in the triumvirate.[41] The preamble of the UDHR states that human rights should be protected by the rule of law but, without a definition of the rule of law, it may in principle be possible also for the thinnest of rule of law conceptions (a rule *by* law) to satisfy such a requirement. Indeed, by mentioning the two concepts separately, the UDHR implies that the one does not subsume the other, unlike in a thick and substantive notion of the rule of law. Moreover, keeping the notions of human rights and rule of law distinct might in any case be desirable in order to avoid excessive conceptual confusion in light of their essentially contested character and the great heterogeneity in their practical implementation in political systems.

R Peerenboom, 'Human Rights and Rule of Law: What's the Relationship?' (2004) 36 Georgetown Journal of International Law 809

(...) we should not place too high hopes on rule of law as a means of promoting human rights. Rule of law, whether thick, thin or both, provides no guarantee that rights will be taken seriously in practice. Thin theories are normatively thin, and thick conceptions of rule of law may be at odds with international human rights norms and standards, sometimes radically and sometimes to a lesser degree. Non-democratic countries including Islamic theocracies and soft authoritarian socialist states such as Vietnam or China

---

[40] R Peerenboom, 'Human Rights and Rule of Law: What's the Relationship?' (2004) 36 Georgetown Journal of International Law 809, 810.

[41] See also E Katselli, 'The Rule of Law and the Role of Human Rights in Contemporary International Law' in R Dickinson and others (eds), *Examining Critical Perspectives on Human Rights* (Cambridge University Press 2012).

constitute profound challenges to the human rights regime, as do nonliberal states such as Singapore and Malaysia that have well developed legal systems which comply with the requirements of a thin rule of law. But even liberal democracies such as the United States have refused to bring domestic rights policies into compliance with international stand-ards on issues from hate speech to the death penalty.

(...) Appealing to rule of law will do little to resolve the conceptual and normative diffi-culties at the core of the human rights agenda. Rule of law will not settle many of the currently contested issues regarding the proper interpretation and justification of rights. Indeed, rule of law provides little guidance on many of the most controversial issues that currently divide the human rights community and undermine claims of universality. Rule of law is also consistent with a wide range of institutions, the choice and development of which are to a large extent path-dependent. Moreover, rule of law is only one component of a just society. In some cases, the values served by rule of law will need to give way to other values. Invoking rule of law in most cases signals the beginning of normative and political debate, not the end of it.

A similar debate regarding the 'thickness' of the concept has even more profoundly shaken the field of democratic theory. As democracy spread around the world, its various iterations were captured by political scientists through adding adjectives to the concept of democ-racy.[42] Such a practice has proliferated to the point where major academic contestation con-cerned the proper categorization and conceptualization of democratic theories.[43] Both the rule of law and human rights were often at least implicitly caught in the conceptual cross-fire, as scholars grappled with the question whether regimes devoid of or lacking in either or both attributes should still be referred to as democracies, all the while having to tread the line be-tween overstretching the root concept of democracy and conceptual overload whereby too many separate categories are created without sufficiently clear delineation.

A well-known example of drawing a line between the concept of democracy and those of the rule of law and human rights is by employing the adjective 'liberal' and its counterpart 'il-liberal'. The liberal philosophical tradition places at the heart of its ideology the individual and her (human) rights which should not be unduly interfered with through the exercise of public authority. In order to secure such rights vis-à-vis the government, the relationship between the two is governed by certain basic rules and the power of the government must not be unchecked. In the way Fareed Zakaria tells this story, this is the rule of law side of 'constitutional liber-alism' which, as a whole, is traditionally associated with democracy in the West.[44] However, according to Zakaria and others,[45] the fact that constitutional liberalism and democracy have

---

[42] In the EU context, the notion of 'militant democracy' has been invoked to call for the EU to address Member States challenging domestically the values of the Union. See JW Müller, 'The EU as a Militant Democracy, or: Are There Limits to Constitutional Mutations within EU Member States?' (2014) 165 Revista de Estudios Políticos 141; JW Müller, 'Should the EU Protect Democracy and the Rule of Law inside Member States?' (2015) 21 European Law Journal 141.

[43] For a notable example of an attempt to order the academic field see D Collier and S Levitsky, 'Democracy with Adjectives: Conceptual Innovation in Comparative Research' (1997) 49 World Politics 430.

[44] F Zakaria, 'The Rise of Illiberal Democracy' (1997) 76 Foreign Affairs 22, 26. The addition of the concept of 'constitutionalism', similarly contested as all the others, is liable to sow more confusion. It is generally accepted that constitutionalism—broadly the idea that governance takes place in accordance with and on the basis of a particu-larly important, foundational law (not necessarily contained in a single document)—normally entails both indi-vidual rights and checks on government (thus blurring the lines between the various key concepts discussed here) but the erosion of some characteristics of constitutionalism essentially leads to very similar discussions regarding its 'thickness'.

[45] See, for example, SP Huntington, *The Third Wave: Democratization in the Late Twentieth Century* (University of Oklahoma Press 1991).

coincided in the West for a prolonged period of time does not necessarily mean that a country cannot be a democracy without guaranteeing human rights and upholding the rule of law. At the same time, there has been relative consensus among democratic theorists that a certain procedural minimum is necessary for a democracy to exist as distinguishable from mere majoritarian decision-making. Robert Dahl defines seven specific conditions to this end.[46]

**Robert Dahl, *Dilemmas of Pluralist Democracy*
(Yale University Press 1982) 11**

1. Control over government decisions about policy is constitutionally vested in elected officials.
2. Elected officials are chosen in frequent and fairly conducted elections in which coercion is comparatively uncommon.
3. Practically all adults have the right to vote in the election of officials.
4. Practically all adults have the right to run for elective offices in the government.
5. Citizens have a right to express themselves without the danger of severe punishment on political matters broadly defined.
6. Citizens have a right to seek out alternative sources of information. Moreover, alternative sources of information exist and are protected by law.
7. Citizens also have the right to form relatively independent associations or organizations, including independent political parties and interest groups.

The minimum procedural conditions for a democracy by Dahl clearly show that fundamental rights and the rule of law are to some extent necessary for the functioning of a democracy properly so called even in one of its thinnest conceptualizations. In particular, the conditions mention that power is 'constitutionally vested' in elected officials by which it is implied that a basic governing law must be present. Law is also needed for the protection of 'alternative sources of information' or, in other words, a degree of media freedom. A number of political rights constitute further prerequisites for a democracy to function: right to vote, right to run for office, freedom of speech, and freedom of association.

From the brief exposé above it should be evident that there is considerable conceptual intertwinement between democracy, the rule of law, and human rights. This intertwinement is even more pronounced in the way various political-legal systems are organized, as in practice, theoretical considerations about the boundaries between the concepts are less important. Moreover, the triumvirate is typically perceived as mutually reinforcing (if not conditioning) which can incentivize the collective and simultaneous promotion of all three concepts which can be clearly evidenced in the foreign policies of liberal actors such as the EU and the US. Empirical studies on developing countries—which are often targeted with an effort to institute the trio of principles as a bedrock of the political system—show that on the one hand, successfully transitioning to democratic rule based on the rule of law and respect

---

[46] See also PC Schmitter and TL Karl, 'What Democracy Is ... and Is Not' (1991) 2 Journal of Democracy 75 who add two more conditions to Dahl's list: elected officials must be able to exercise their power without being overridden by unelected officials (such as the military) and the polity must be self-governing, independent of outside control (such as colonial governance).

for human rights is extremely difficult, and, on the other, partial and selective implementation of the concepts in developing national settings usually does not suffice to occasion an overall positive change and that certain aspects of the concepts might be more important than others.[47] In addition, any state-building exercise is subject to the caveat that a careful balance between the three concepts must be struck in order to avoid extremes. As explained above, a lack of rule of law checks on democratic power can lead to disregard for individual human rights, while an overly constrained political order can be anti-democratic and excessively judicialized.[48] In between such extremes, however, the precise calibration of any political system founded on the principles of democracy, the rule of law, and human rights rests ultimately on philosophical convictions about which societal values should be promoted and emphasized and how best to achieve them.

B.   Democracy, the rule of law, and fundamental rights in the EU

> ### Consolidated version of the Treaty on European Union [2012] OJ C326/13
>
> ### Article 2
> The Union is founded on the values of respect for human dignity, freedom, **democracy**, equality, **the rule of law and respect for human rights**, including the rights of persons belonging to minorities. These values are common to the Member States in a society in which pluralism, non-discrimination, tolerance, justice, solidarity and equality between women and men prevail.

In the EU, democracy, the rule of law, and human rights belong to the foundational values listed in Article 2 TEU, as well as the preamble. They are also found in the list of 'principles' which should guide the EU's action internationally (Article 21 TEU). However, none of these references contain any definition or elaboration of what these values or principles should entail or how they relate to each other. What we do know is that a serious and persistent breach of Article 2 TEU values by a Member State can lead, according to Article 7 TEU, to the suspension of its rights under the Treaties. In the absence of other possibilities at the EU level to safeguard the EU's foundational values, and in light of the ambiguous and reluctant atmosphere surrounding the application of Article 7 TEU,[49] the Commission established the so-called Rule of Law Framework which in essence adds a preventive step to the triggering

---

[47] See, for example, B Bueno de Mesquita and others, 'Thinking Inside the Box: A Closer Look at Democracy and Human Rights' (2005) 49 International Studies Quarterly 439; C Davenport, 'Liberalizing Event or Lethal Episode: An Empirical Assessment of How National Elections Effect the Suppression of Political and Civil Liberties' (1998) 79 Social Science Quarterly 321.

[48] It has been argued that the tension between democratic decision-making and entrenched constitutional rights has been exacerbated by the internationalization of human rights which, at least to an extent, eroded their democratic legitimacy due to the absence of a global transnational democracy. For a reassessment of this tension see S Besson, 'Human Rights and Democracy in a Global Context: Decoupling and Recoupling' (2011) 4 Ethics and Global Politics 19. See also R Hirschl, *Towards Juristocracy: The Origins and Consequences of the New Constitutionalism* (Harvard University Press 2004).

[49] L Besselink, 'The Bite, the Bark, and the Howl: Article 7 TEU and the Rule of Law Initiatives' in A Jakab and D Kochenov (eds), *The Enforcement of EU Law and Values: Ensuring Member States' Compliance* (Oxford University Press 2017).

of Article 7 TEU and generally attempts to systematize an otherwise barely regulated and controversial area of EU activity. The Communication describing the Framework provides also a rare window into the Commission's understanding of the rule of law and its relation to fundamental rights and democracy in the EU.

European Commission, 'Communication from the Commission to the European Parliament and the Council—A new EU Framework to strengthen the Rule of Law' COM (2014) 158 final 5

The rule of law is the backbone of any modern constitutional democracy. It is one of the founding principles stemming from the common constitutional traditions of all the Member States of the EU and, as such, one of the main values upon which the Union is based. This is recalled by Article 2 of the Treaty on European Union (TEU), as well as by the Preambles to the Treaty and to the Charter of Fundamental Rights of the EU. This is also why, under Article 49 TEU, respect for the rule of law is a precondition for EU membership. Along with democracy and human rights, the rule of law is also one of the three pillars of the Council of Europe and is endorsed in the Preamble to the European Convention for the Protection of Human Rights and Fundamental Freedoms (ECHR).

(...) However, recent events in some Member States have demonstrated that a lack of respect for the rule of law and, as a consequence, also for the **fundamental values which the rule of law aims to protect**, can become a matter of serious concern. (...)

(...) [The rule of law] makes sure that all public powers act within the constraints set out by law, in accordance with the values of democracy and fundamental rights, and under the control of independent and impartial courts.

The precise content of the principles and standards stemming from the rule of law may vary at national level, depending on each Member State's constitutional system. Nevertheless, case law of the Court of Justice of the European Union ('the Court of Justice') and of the European Court of Human Rights, as well as documents drawn up by the Council of Europe, building notably on the expertise of the Venice Commission, provide a non-exhaustive list of these principles and hence define the core meaning of the rule of law as a common value of the EU in accordance with Article 2 TEU.

Those principles include legality, which implies a transparent, accountable, **democratic and pluralistic process for enacting laws**; legal certainty; prohibition of arbitrariness of the executive powers; independent and impartial courts; **effective judicial review including respect for fundamental rights**; and equality before the law.

Both the Court of Justice and the European Court of Human Rights confirmed that **those principles are not purely formal and procedural requirements. They are the vehicle for ensuring compliance with and respect for democracy and human rights. The rule of law is therefore a constitutional principle with both formal and substantive components.**

This means that respect for the rule of law is intrinsically linked to respect for democracy and for fundamental rights: there can be no democracy and respect for fundamental rights without respect for the rule of law and vice versa. Fundamental rights are effective only if they are justiciable. Democracy is protected if the fundamental role of the judiciary, including constitutional courts, can ensure freedom of expression, freedom of assembly and respect of the rules governing the political and electoral process.

The Rule of Law Framework makes clear that in the view of the Commission—basing itself on the case law of the CJEU and European Court of Human Rights and on the work of the Council of Europe—the rule of law is not merely a formal component of legal orders in Europe. Rather, the notion advanced in the document is thick and substantive with a number of principles 'stemming' from the rule of law. In the accompanying Annex to the Rule of Law Framework, the Commission expands on the meaning of those principles and cites case law which partially substantiates the Commission's reading of the principles. The main takeaway from the Rule of Law Framework is that, according to the Commission, the rule of law, democracy and fundamental rights are all 'intrinsically' interconnected and not one of them can effectively function independently of the others.[50] Although the precise contours of the delimitation between the three concepts remain elusive, the Framework emphasizes the importance of the judiciary as ultimately upholding the rule of law and the principles stemming therefrom in the EU and the Member States. The Commission rather categorically asserts that 'fundamental rights are effective only if they are justiciable' and that democracy is protected if courts can ensure a number of essential political freedoms.[51]

The centrality of effective judicial protection in the EU's conception of the rule of law,[52] as well as the legal order as a whole,[53] is indeed well established. Judicial review in the EU also exemplifies the overlap between the concepts of the rule of law and fundamental rights, as, on the one hand, the primary role of the rule of law in the CJEU's doctrine is that no EU or Member State act can escape judicial review for compliance with the Treaties,[54] and, on the other hand, all individuals have the right to an effective remedy in accordance with the requirements of fairness and judicial independence and impartiality.[55] It is more customary for the CJEU to justify judicial review in light of fundamental rights protection than the rule of law but in the manner the latter has been conceptualized by the Court, it cannot be in doubt that the fundamental right to effective judicial protection and exigencies of the rule of law significantly coincide in the EU.[56] In a slightly adjusted take on this conceptual delimitation, the rule of law could also be seen as the other side of the same coin—the side characterized by the principle of separation of powers[57]—as the right to effective judicial protection,

---

[50] It is fair to say that the interconnected view of democracy, the rule of law and fundamental rights is the prevailing one among EU institutions. See European Parliament, 'EU mechanism on democracy, the rule of law and fundamental rights', P8_TA(2016)0409, 25 October 2016.

[51] These statements were made in light of meddling by the Hungarian government in the powers and composition of the Hungarian Constitutional Court in 2013.

[52] Although the case of *Les Verts* is the most well-known when it comes the rule of law in EU law, the concept was cited for the first time by the CJEU already some years prior in the case of *Granaria* as conferring on individuals the right in principle to challenge Community acts. See Judgment of 13 February 1979, *Granaria BV v Hoofdproduktschap voor Akkerbouwprodukten*, 101/78, ECLI:EU:C:1979:38, para 5.

[53] See Art 19(1) TEU. Following the Judgment of 27 February 2018, *Associação Sindical dos Juízes Portugueses v Tribunal de Contas*, C-64/16, ECLI:EU:C:2018:117, the EU requirements (under Article 19 TEU) concerning judicial independence reach deeper into Member State territory than the Charter of Fundamental Rights.

[54] Judgment of 23 April 1986, *Parti écologiste 'Les Verts' v European Parliament*, 294/83, ECLI:EU:C:1986:166, para 23.

[55] Article 47 of the Charter. See also *Associação Sindical dos Juízes Portugueses* (n 53), para 41.

[56] See also Judgment of 28 March 2017, *The Queen, ex parte PJSC Rosneft Oil Company v Her Majesty's Treasury and Others*, C-72/15, ECLI:EU:C:2017:236, para 73.

[57] Judgment of 22 December 2010, *DEB Deutsche Energiehandels- und Beratungsgesellschaft v Bundesrepublik Deutschland*, C-279/09, ECLI:EU:C:2010:811, para 58.

although the principles stemming from the rule of law are broader than actions before a court remedying fundamental rights violations.

Reviewing the case law of the CJEU, Laurent Pech similarly views the rule of law in the EU as being profoundly intertwined with the protection of fundamental rights. In light of cases such as *UPA* and *Kadi* he rejects the notion that the rule of law has or should have a purely formal meaning in the EU legal order;[58] on the contrary, the principle paves the way for the judicial review of both procedural and substantive rights.

L Pech, ' "A Union Founded on the Rule of Law": Meaning and Reality of the Rule of Law as a Constitutional Principle of EU Law' (2010) 6 European Constitutional Law Review 359

It follows that one important, if not the most important, purpose of judicial review, according to the Court, lies in the protection of natural and legal persons' fundamental rights. This means, for instance, that the interpretation and application of the formal components of the rule of law must permanently be guided by this purpose.

In reflecting a broad understanding of the rule of law and suggesting that this constitutional principle, and the legally enforceable 'sub-principles' it encompasses, must serve the primacy and dignity of the individual, the Court of Justice's case-law is not particularly innovative but rather reflects to a great extent national experiences and in particular, the German one. In other words, the Union rule of law is also construed by the Court of Justice as a 'meta-principle' which provides the foundation for an independent and effective judiciary and essentially describes and justifies the subjection of public power to formal and substantive legal constraints with a view to guaranteeing the primacy of the individual and its protection against the arbitrary or unlawful exercise of public power. Although the precise list of principles, standards and values the rule of law entails may naturally vary in each legal system, it is important to emphasise that most if not all European legal systems share in common the use of formal and substantive legal standards and have all known an 'intensification of judicial review', in particular as far as fundamental rights are concerned. Furthermore, most national courts view the formal and substantive components of the rule of law as interdependent. This is the right approach as these formal and procedural components (non-retroactivity, access to courts, etc.), in liberal and democratic European polities, are logically supposed to serve the substantive values (human dignity, social justice, etc.) upon which these societies are founded. Another remarkable shared trait between most national legal systems in Europe is that the strong emphasis on the rule of law as a defining constitutional principle has progressively led to the 'instrumentalisation' of the State, i.e., public authorities are supposed to serve the individual and protect his rights, and the 'subjectivisation' of the law, i.e., individuals must be able to challenge acts that may violate their rights.

---

[58] Joseph Raz has posited, in a typically hard legal-positivist fashion, that the rule of law is in principle compatible with any substantive legal content, regardless of whether the latter complies with human rights or not. See J Raz, 'The Rule of Law and its Virtue' in J Raz (ed), *The Authority of Law: Essays on Law and Morality* (Oxford University Press 1979).

Pech's analysis concurs with the finding that the rule of law is accompanied in the European context by significant judicialization.[59] This is a natural consequence of conceptualizing the rule of law as entailing a substantive review of public power in light of fundamental rights. As discussed above in connection with legal theory in general, such an 'intensification of judicial review' inevitably tests the balance between protection of individuals by independent judiciaries and democratic decision-making.[60] Although the CJEU, especially after the enactment of the Charter, can also be recognized in this account, it can be argued that legalization and judicialization has even deeper roots in the EU than elsewhere. The CJEU, together with national courts, has been instrumental in advancing the integration of the EU,[61] not least through advocating the importance of the principle of effective judicial protection and the principles of effectiveness and equivalence of EU law.[62] The powers of the Union are strictly delimited by the principle of conferral which makes the localization of the correct legal basis, in the absence of general powers, for every EU act an important and recurrent struggle for power, dovetailed by frequent litigation specifying with even more precision the boundaries of EU competences;[63] and the EU Treaties are, according to some, 'over-constitutionalized', because they regulate matters which in a state pertain to ordinary laws.[64] The latter aspect, by placing many areas beyond amendment through ordinary democratic politics, can broadly be seen as constituting a part of the well-known discourse on the 'democratic deficit' of the EU.[65] The EU has been keen on countering such narratives— most notably by successively strengthening the role of the European Parliament (EP) but more symbolically also, for example, by including a Title in the Treaties called 'Provisions on Democratic Principles'—despite academics not always reaching a consensus regarding whether the EU genuinely suffers from a democratic deficit.[66]

---

[59] A concurrent trend identified by scholars in the international sphere has been the legalization of international relations. See J Goldstein, M Kahler, and RO Keohane (eds), *Legalization and World Politics* (MIT Press 2001); KW Abbott, RO Keohane, and A Moravcsik, 'The Concept of Legalization' (2000) 54 International Organization 401. The EU finds itself at the cross-roads between the international and the constitutional level, so arguably both domestic judicialization and international legalization and judicialization are to some extent relevant for it. See AM Burley and W Mattli, 'Europe Before the Court: A Political Theory of Legal Integration' (1993) 47 International Organization 41.

[60] The rise of judicial review and protection of fundamental rights at the expense of representative institutions— a phenomenon stretching far beyond European borders—has been famously, and somewhat provocatively, described as a transition from a democracy to a 'juristocracy' (a rule of judges). See Hirschl, *Towards Juristocracy: The Origins and Consequences of New Constitutionalism* (n 48.

[61] E Stein, 'Lawyers, Judges, and the Making of a Transnational Constitution' (1981) 75 The American Journal of International Law 1; JHH Weiler, 'The Transformation of Europe' (1991) 100 Yale Law Journal 2403; Burley and Mattli, 'Europe Before the Court' (n 59).

[62] See, for example, Judgment of 15 May 1986, *Johnston v Chief Constable of the Royal Ulster Constabulary*, 222/ 84, ECLI:EU:C:1986:206; A Arnull, 'The Principle of Effective Judicial Protection in EU law: An Unruly Horse?' (2011) 36 European Law Review 51.

[63] R Schütze, 'EU Competences: Existence and Exercise' in D Chalmers and A Arnull (eds), *Oxford Handbook of EU Law* (Oxford University Press 2015), 75–103; E Neframi, '"Within the Scope of European Union Law," Beyond the Principle of Conferral?' in J van der Walt and J Ellsworth (eds), *Constitutional Sovereignty and Social Solidarity in Europe* (Nomos 2015) 69–108.

[64] D Grimm, 'The Democratic Costs of Constitutionalisation: The European Case' (2015) 21 European Law Journal 460.

[65] G Majone, 'Europe's 'Democratic Deficit': The Question of Standards' (1998) 4 European Law Journal 5; A Moravcsik, 'In Defence of the 'Democratic Deficit': Reassessing Legitimacy in the European Union' (2002) 40 Journal of Common Market Studies 603; S Hix, *What's Wrong with the Europe Union and How to Fix It* (Polity Press 2008).

[66] Nevertheless, there is agreement to the extent that the answer to the question whether the EU suffers from a democratic deficit turns to a great extent on how the EU is perceived and what normative expectations are attached to it. For example, Andrew Moravcsik and Giandomenico Majone have argued that in view of the principally non-redistributive (regulatory) character of the EU's policies, delegation to the EU can be considered legitimate, as similar tasks would be delegated to executive bodies also within states. See Moravcsik, 'Reassessing Legitimacy'

In an attempt at further democratizing the EU, the Spitzenkandidaten process was introduced and led to the inauguration of the Juncker Commission in 2014. [67] This was undeniably a relevant development from the perspective of the criticism that a basic level of democratic contestation for political leadership is a crucial element of the perceived democratic deficit, especially since EP elections have a second-order quality.[68] However, the democratizing success of the practice has been disputed from the start[69] and many government leaders were displeased, since under the new process, the power to nominate a candidate accorded to the European Council under Article 17(7) TEU was taken out of their hands.[70] In July 2019, Ursula von der Leyen was put forward and elected as President of the European Commission, instead of lead candidate Manfred Weber, who was first advanced by the European People's Party as the largest political grouping in the EP. Since von der Leyen was 'neither a *Spitzenkandidat* nor the focus of political attention during the campaign', her election sits uneasily with a majoritarian idea of democracy within the EU.[71] Surprisingly, von der Leyen herself promised to improve and make more democratic the Spitzenkandidaten system before the next electoral cycle.[72] Other suggestions for boosting European democracy include transnational voting and the institution of a pan-European electoral district.[73]

Consolidated version of the Treaty on European Union [2012] OJ C326/13

Article 10
1. The functioning of the Union shall be **founded on representative democracy**.
2. Citizens are directly represented at Union level in the European Parliament.

(n 65); Majone, 'Democratic Deficit' (n 65). This argument does not fully persuade everyone, however. See A Follesdal and S Hix, 'Why There is a Democratic Deficit in the EU: A Response to Majone and Moravcsik' (2006) 44 Journal of Common Market Studies 533. Moreover, the EU's democratic deficit has, in the eyes of most observers, including Majone, taken a decisive turn for the worse during the Euro crisis. See G Majone, 'From Regulatory State to a Democratic Default' (2014) 52 Journal of Common Market Studies 1216.

[67] The *Spitzenkandidaten* (literally 'top candidates') process underpinning the 2014 EP elections was predicated on the idea that the result of the vote would not only determine the composition of the EP but also who would become the president of the European Commission. For the first time in history, European political parties therefore nominated candidates for the top executive post in the EU, who participated in televised debates exploring the candidates' positions in the public sphere. Following the system's logic, the Member States abided by the result of the elections and nominated Jean-Claude Juncker for the post.

[68] Follesdal and Hix, 'Why There is a Democratic Deficit in the EU: A Response to Majone and Moravcsik' (n 66); H Schmitt, 'The EP Elections of June 2004: Still Second-order?' (2005) 28 West European Politics 650.

[69] SB Hobolt, 'A Vote for the President? The Role of Spitzenkandidaten in the 2014 European Parliament Elections' (2014) 21 Journal of European Public Policy 1528; T Christiansen, 'After the Spitzenkandidaten: Fundamental Change in the EU's Political System?' (2016) 39 West European Politics 992.

[70] But see also Article 14(1) TEU.

[71] M Dawson, 'The Lost Spitzenkandidaten and the Future of European Democracy' (2019) 26 Maastricht Journal of European and Comparative Law 731.

[72] Ursula von der Leyen, Opening Statement in the European Parliament Plenary Session, 16 July 2019.

[73] J Bright and others, 'Europe's Voting Space and the Problem of Second-Order Elections: A Transnational Proposal' (2016) 17 European Union Politics 184; D Bol and others, 'Addressing Europe's Democratic Deficit: An Experimental Evaluation of the Pan-European District Proposal' (2016) 17 European Union Politics 525.

Member States are represented in the European Council by their Heads of State or Government and in the Council by their governments, themselves democratically accountable either to their national Parliaments, or to their citizens.

3. Every citizen shall have the right to participate in the democratic life of the Union. Decisions shall be taken as openly and as closely as possible to the citizen.
4. Political parties at European level contribute to forming European political awareness and to expressing the will of citizens of the Union.

Article 17

7. **Taking into account the elections to the European Parliament** and after having held the appropriate consultations, **the European Council, acting by a qualified majority, shall propose to the European Parliament a candidate for President of the Commission.** This candidate shall be elected by the European Parliament by a majority of its component members. If he does not obtain the required majority, the European Council, acting by a qualified majority, shall within one month propose a new candidate who shall be elected by the European Parliament following the same procedure.

As far as the internal dimension of the EU is concerned, to return to the issue of judicial review and the rule of law, one more complementary critique needs to be made about the CJEU's approach to fundamental rights. Although indeed constituting an examination of the substance of acts of EU institutions and Member States as remarked by Pech and others, the CJEU's judicial review in light of fundamental rights should not be seen as one inevitably pursuing or promoting the ideals embodied by (human) rights.[74] On the contrary, the judicial review and its intensity tend to be firmly embedded in and mindful of the political and legal realities of the EU. The majority of fundamental rights can be limited and balanced against other objectives of the Union,[75] notably those relating to the single market.[76] Higher fundamental rights protection is not the only item on the CJEU's agenda;[77] effectiveness and autonomy of EU law are also taken into account.[78] Moreover, the CJEU works in many instances in tandem with national courts and therefore it is not always able (or willing) to decide singlehandedly on the ultimate outcome of a case.[79] In more normative terms, there

---

[74] A Williams, 'Human Rights in the EU' in A Arnull and D Chalmers (eds), *The Oxford Handbook of European Union Law* (Oxford University Press 2015) 249–63.

[75] Article 52(1) and (2) of the Charter.

[76] Judgment of 12 June 2003, *Schmidberger v Republik Österreich*, C-112/00, ECLI:EU:C:2003:333; Judgment of 11 December 2007, *International Transport Workers' Federation and Finnish Seamen's Union v Viking Line ABP and OÜ Viking Line Eesti*, C-438/05, ECLI:EU:C:2007:772; Judgment of 18 December 2007, *Laval un Partneri Ltd v Svenska Byggnadsarbetareförbundet and Others*, C-341/05, ECLI:EU:C:2007:809.

[77] Judgment of 7 March 2017, *X and X v État belge*, C-638/16 PPU, ECLI:EU:C:2017:173; compare judgment with Opinion of AG Mengozzi in the same case.

[78] Judgment of 26 February 2013, *Melloni v Ministerio Fiscal*, C-399/11, ECLI:EU:C:2013:107; Opinion of 18 December 2014, *EU accession to the ECHR*, 2/13, ECLI:EU:C:2014:2454.

[79] See for example its preliminary ruling on the independence of the Disciplinary Chamber of the Polish Supreme Court: Judgment of 19 November 2019, *A.K. and Others v Sąd Najwyższ*, C-585/18, C-624/18 and C-625/18, ECLI:EU:C:2019:982.

have been calls for the CJEU to become more attentive to whether its interpretation of the law, including fundamental rights, produces just outcomes. In this vein, the rule of law would become more identified with justice, the former incorporating the latter as an essential element.[80]

In general, the same holistic approach to the triumvirate of democracy, the rule of law, and human rights underpins the EU's external promotion efforts, as already hinted at above when discussing 'normative power Europe'. The holistic or interconnected approach has a basis in the Treaties, notably Article 21 TEU which lists the guiding principles of EU external action.[81] To the trio of principles examined here is added another partially overlapping concept, namely that of international law which shall be consolidated and supported by the EU (Article 21(2)(b) TEU) and to whose development the EU shall contribute (Article 3(5) TEU).[82] International law of course itself serves to protect and promote human rights, although the strength and modality of its impact in this regard is subject to some dispute,[83] while at the same time representing the next best thing to a rule of law at international level in the absence of an all-purpose[84] iteration qualitatively comparable to how the rule of law operates domestically in liberal constitutional democracies.[85] A crude way of conceptually understanding the EU's commitment to developing international law alongside democracy, the rule of law, and human rights is to distinguish the latter trio as being primarily addressed to the EU's promotion of values in other countries (where the rule of law can potentially be implemented in its traditional domestic form), whereas the consolidation of international law takes place primarily through the EU's actions in global and multilateral fora. This should not be seen as a clear-cut and mutually exclusive distinction: the EU also often induces (bi- and multilaterally) states to accede to (bi- and multilateral) treaties and comply with international law, and promotes the penetration of international law by thick and substantive notions of democracy, the rule of law, and human rights, hoping that both types of

---

[80] Douglas-Scott, 'Justice, Injustice and the Rule of Law in the EU' in Kochenov, Búrca, and illiams (eds), *Europe's Justice Deficit?* (n 39).

[81] However, it has been noted in the scholarship that human rights and democracy promotion is underpinned by different considerations and their decoupling could boost effectiveness. See S Kahn-Nisser, 'Linkage Leverage Democratization and Liberalization: Is Promoting Democracy the Same as Promoting Human Rights?' (2018) 39 Policy Studies 90.

[82] A special mention along with international law is given to the United Nations Charter which can be said to form the basis of public international law since 1945.

[83] See, from a vast literature, Posner, *The Twilight of Human Rights Law* (n 19); EM Hafner-Burton and K Tsutsui, 'Human Rights in a Globalizing World: The Paradox of Empty Promises' (2005) 110 American Journal of Sociology 1373.

[84] If viewed monolithically, public international law almost certainly does not conform to an even thin notion of the rule of law (as understood in a state setting). However, various 'self-contained regimes' under international law might display greater-than-average adherence to rule of law principles. This has to do with the inherent fragmentation and diversification of international law. See International Law Commission, 'Fragmentation of International Law: Difficulties Arising From the Diversification an Expansion of International Law' (13 April 2006) UN Doc A/CN4/L682, para 486; B Simma and D Pulkowski, 'Of Planets and the Universe: Self-contained Regimes in International Law' (2006) 17 European Journal of International Law 483.

[85] On the conception of the 'international rule of law' see KJ Keith, 'The International Rule of Law' (2015) 28 Leiden Journal of International Law 403; J Waldron, 'Are Sovereigns Entitled to the Benefit of the International Rule of Law?' (2011) 22 European Journal of International Law 315; A Watts, 'The International Rule of Law' (1993) 36 German Yearbook of International Law 15. Considering the insufficiency of international law, in its present form, to live up to the exigencies of the rule of law as conceived domestically—on account of the structural differences between organization of the international sphere and of states—the debate about the rule of law qualities of international law harks back to discussions about whether international law is in fact 'law' (usually, again, in the sense legal theory understood the term 'law' in a domestic setting). See S Chesterman, 'An International Rule of Law?' (2008) 56 The American Journal of Comparative Law 331, 358.

efforts at the same time contribute to the creation and development of an international rule of law.[86] This vision of principled EU external action of course does not entirely stand up to empirical scrutiny—it is rather a conceptually coherent reading of how the EU should act externally on the basis of its constitutional commitments.[87]

Nevertheless, there appears to be less consistency in the domain of external action when it comes to the understanding and use of the three core concepts beyond the references in the EU Treaties. As regards the rule of law, the EU refers to the concept in various ways and seemingly with little regard for conceptual issues.[88] Where the Commission has fleshed out its understanding of the rule of law it has led to a particularly substantive and thick notion of it,[89] to the point of the concept becoming so all-encompassing and stretched so far that a distinction between the rule of law, democracy, and fundamental rights becomes impossible to draw.[90] While the utility and normative desirability of such a lack of conceptual clarity has rightly been questioned,[91] imprecision and inconsistency leave more space for (and are subsequently reproduced as a symptom of) diplomatic manoeuvring in foreign policy. As opposed to domestic politics, foreign policy is, from a traditional realist standpoint, un-encumbered by rules and principles as a result of the generally non-hierarchical/anarchic structure of international relations. According to this line of thinking, constraining oneself in the international environment, as the EU does at least rhetorically, by insisting on the adoption of certain values by third countries, puts one at a competitive disadvantage with respect to other international actors unbridled with rules and principles. If getting rid en-tirely of the principles guiding its external action is not an option, blurry and inconsistent definitions of the concepts the EU wishes to enact externally can be one way of loosening the constraints of principles on its foreign policy. Whatever its rationale, the fact remains that imprecision and inconsistency are widespread in EU external relations. Not only the rule of law but also the manner in which the notion of democracy—and rhetorical innovations such as 'deep democracy'[92]—has been used earned the EU's external value promotion the moniker 'fuzzy liberalism'.[93] The concept of human rights—being often expressed concretely

---

[86] This simplified account discards the effects of the fragmentation of international law to which the EU arguably contributes at least to some extent by concluding a plethora of regional trade agreements and bilateral cooperation agreements. The obligation to 'consolidate' international law (Article 21(2)(b) TEU) could also be read as an obli-gation to reverse the fragmentation of international law. Even if that were the case, however, the current practice of the European Commission pays little attention to its contribution to fragmentation. See, for example, A Kent, 'The EU Commission and the Fragmentation of International Law: Speaking European in a Foreign Land' (2016) 7 Goettingen Journal of International Law 273.

[87] See Ch 9.

[88] L Pech, 'Rule of Law as a Guiding Principle of the European Union's External Action' (2012) CLEER Working Papers 2012/3, 8.

[89] European Commission, 'Communication from the Commission to the European Parliament and the Council—Democratisation, the Rule of Law, Respect for Human Rights and Good Governance: the Challenges of the Partnership between the European Union and the ACP States' COM (1998) 146 final 4.

[90] A Williams, *The Ethos of Europe: Values, Law and Justice in the EU* (Cambridge University Press 2010) 106; A Timmer and others, 'EU Human Rights, Democracy and Rule of Law: From Concepts to Practice' (2014) FRAME Deliverable 3.2, 32 <http://www.fp7-frame.eu/wp-content/uploads/2016/08/10-Deliverable-3.2.pdf> accessed 14 August 2020.

[91] Pech, 'Rule of Law as a Guiding Principle' (n 88) 26.

[92] European Commission, 'Joint Communication to the European Parliament, the Council, the European Economic and Social Committee and the Committee of Regions—A New Response to a Changing Neighbourhood' COM (2011) 303 final. As if to underline the point made here about inconsistency, the term 'deep democracy' has subsequently to its inauguration not been used in the key strategic documents about democracy and human rights promotion. See Council of the European Union, 'Human Rights and Democracy: EU Strategic Framework and Action Plan', 11855/12, 25 June 2012; Council of the European Union, 'Council conclusions on the Action Plan on Human Rights and Democracy 2015–2019', 10897/15, 20 July 2015.

[93] M Kurki, 'Political Economy Perspective: Fuzzy Liberalism and EU Democracy Promotion: Why Concepts Matter' in A Wetzel and J Orbie (eds), *The Substance of EU Democracy Promotion: Concepts and Cases* (Palgrave Macmillan 2015).

in connection with a legal instrument and obligation—has fared somewhat better, but even here the EU's professed commitment to universality and indivisibility has been tested by a *de facto* emphasis on first-generation civil and political rights (implying *divisibility*).[94]

An interesting conceptual middle ground of sorts between the internal and the external sphere of action appears in the area of EU enlargement. Article 49 TEU makes applications for becoming a member of the EU conditional on respect and commitment to promote the values on which the EU is internally founded (Article 2 TEU). The elaboration of Article 2 TEU values takes on a life of its own in the context of the enlargement process which has become many times more demanding and comprehensive since the so-called Copenhagen criteria established 'stability of institutions guaranteeing democracy, the rule of law, human rights and respect for and protection of minorities' as one of the prerequisites of EU membership in 1993.[95] The principles and rules promoted by the EU in its enlargement policy, and to a lesser extent also in the European Neighbourhood Policy (ENP), are drawn from both the EU's internal functioning (such as CJEU interpretations of the Charter) and external sources, among which the ECHR enjoys a privileged position (as it does in the EU itself).

[94] Timmer and others, 'From Concepts to Practice' (n 90) 26–27.
[95] European Council, 'Conclusions of the Presidency', Copenhagen, 21–22 June 1993.

4

The EU Legal Framework for the Protection of Fundamental Rights

4.1 Introduction

The complex history of the EU's commitment to human rights and its multi-level institutional architecture hint at the fact that the corresponding legal framework for the protection of fundamental rights will not be a straightforward affair either. This presumption appears largely correct: human rights law in the EU is made up of a fragmented yet interconnected patchwork of legal instruments comprising overlapping jurisdictions and spanning multiple levels of governance (international, EU, national) (see Figure 4.1). The present chapter offers a global view of this intricate framework and the basic functioning of its key constituents, most notably the Charter of Fundamental Rights.

4.2 Fundamental Rights as General Principles of Law

Prior to the adoption of the EU Charter for Fundamental Rights—which became binding upon the entry into force of the Lisbon Treaty in 2009—the Treaties did not contain any reference to formally binding sources of human rights law.[1] As we have seen in Chapter 1, the CJEU stepped in to fill the void by pronouncing that fundamental rights form part of general principles of law protected by the Court in the EU legal order.

Judgment of 17 December 1970, *Internationale Handelsgesellschaft v Einfuhr- und Vorratsstelle für Getreide und Futtermittel*, 11/70, ECLI:EU:C:1970:114

---

4. (...) In fact, **respect for fundamental rights forms an integral part of the general principles of law protected by the Court of Justice.** The protection of such rights, whilst inspired by the constitutional traditions common to the Member States, must be ensured within the framework of the structure and objectives of the Community.

---

[1] The founding EEC Treaty has, exceptionally, required that Member States observe the principle of equal pay for men and women (now Article 157 TFEU). This provision, however, was linked at the outset more to the internal market logic in the Union rather than any catalogue of fundamental rights. See G More, 'The Principle of Equal Treatment: from Market Unifier to Fundamental Right' in P Craig and G de Búrca (eds), *The Evolution of EU Law* (Oxford University Press 1999) Chapter 14.

The European Union and Human Rights. Jan Wouters and Michal Ovádek, Oxford University Press (2021). © Jan Wouters and Michal Ovádek. DOI: 10.1093/oso/9780198814177.003.0004

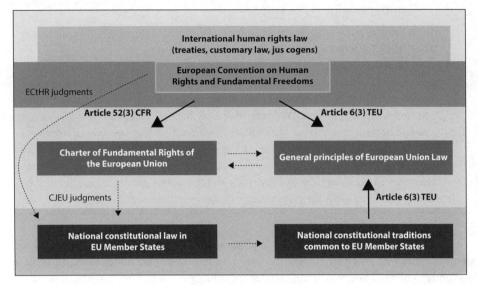

Figure 4.1 Schematic representation of the multi-level, multi-source landscape of human rights law in the EU

General principles of law in the EU signify a set of norms developed by the Court of Justice of the European Union (CJEU) which need not necessarily have an explicit basis in the Treaties.[2] The Court uses these principles for guidance in the interpretation of the Treaties but also as grounds for reviewing EU law and its application.[3] In the promulgation of these principles, the Court can draw 'inspiration' from national constitutional traditions common to the Member States, the European Convention on Human Rights (ECHR)—which is of 'special significance'—and other international human rights treaties.[4]

Judgment of 27 June 2006, *Parliament v Council*, C-540/03, ECLI:EU:C:2006:429

35. Fundamental rights form an integral part of the general principles of law the observance of which the Court ensures. For that purpose, the Court draws inspiration from the **constitutional traditions common to the Member States** and from the guidelines supplied by **international instruments for the protection of human**

---

[2] For the most authoritative and exhaustive treatment of the subject of general principles see T Tridimas, *General Principles of EU Law* (3rd edn, Oxford University Press 2017).

[3] Other principles include, for example: proportionality, legal certainty, legitimate expectations, the precautionary principle, and non-discrimination.

[4] This has been codified in Article 6 TEU, with the exception of international human rights, possibly in recognition of the fact that the CJEU refers to them relatively rarely in its case law, itself a criticized behaviour. See O de Schutter and I de Jesús Butler, 'Binding the EU to International Human Rights Law' (2008) 27 Yearbook of European Law 277; T Ahmed and I de Jesús Butler, 'The European Union and Human Rights: An International Law Perspective' (2006) 17 European Journal of International Law 771.

> **rights** on which the Member States have collaborated or to which they are signa-
> tories. The **ECHR has special significance in that respect.**
>
> 104. In the final analysis, while the Directive leaves the Member States a margin of appreci-
>   ation, it is sufficiently wide to enable them to apply the Directive's rules **in a manner
>   consistent with the requirements flowing from the protection of fundamental rights**
>   (see, to this effect, Case 5/88 *Wachauf* [1989] ECR 2609, paragraph 22).
>
> 105. It should be remembered that, in accordance with settled case-law, the requirements
>   flowing from the protection of general principles recognised in the Community
>   legal order, which include fundamental rights, **are also binding on Member States
>   when they implement Community rules**, and that consequently they are bound, as
>   far as possible, to apply the rules in accordance with those requirements (...)

It is not only the EU which is bound in all its actions by general principles but also the
Member States when they implement EU law.[5] As a result, they are under a duty to apply it
in a fundamental rights-conforming manner, including when a given EU instrument allows
the Member States to exercise discretion. Moreover, the CJEU often finds support for a general principle of law in a number of sources at the same time. The Court also makes explicit
links between general principles and provisions of secondary EU legislation.

> ### Judgment of 15 May 1986, *Johnston v Chief Constable of the Royal Ulster Constabulary*, 222/84, ECLI:EU:C:1986:206
>
> 17. As far as this issue is concerned , it must be borne in mind first of all that Article
>   6 of the Directive [No 76/207] requires Member States to introduce into their in-
>   ternal legal systems such measures as are needed to enable all persons who consider
>   themselves wronged by discrimination 'to pursue their claims by judicial process'.
>   It follows from that provision that the Member States must take measures which are
>   sufficiently effective to achieve the aim of the Directive and that they must ensure
>   that the rights thus conferred may be effectively relied upon before the national
>   courts by the persons concerned.
>
> 18. **The requirement of judicial control stipulated by that article reflects a gen-
>   eral principle of law which underlies the constitutional traditions common to
>   the Member States.** That principle is **also laid down in Articles 6 and 13 of the
>   European Convention for the Protection of Human Rights and Fundamental
>   Freedoms** of 4 November 1950. As the European Parliament, Council and
>   Commission recognized in their Joint Declaration of 5 April 1977 (Official Journal
>   C 103, p. 1) and as the Court has recognized in its decisions, the principles on which
>   that convention is based must be taken into consideration in Community law.
>
> 19. By virtue of Article 6 of Directive No 76/207, interpreted in the light of the general
>   principle stated above, all persons have the right to obtain an effective remedy in a
>   competent court against measures which they consider to be contrary to the prin-
>   ciple of equal treatment for men and women laid down in the Directive. **It is for**

---

[5] Judgment of 13 July 1989, *Wachauf v Bundesamt für Ernährung und Forstwirtschaft*, 5/88, ECLI:EU:C:1989:321,
para 19. See also below the more extensive discussion on the applicability of the Charter.

> **the Member States to ensure effective judicial control** as regards compliance with the applicable provisions of Community law and of national legislation intended to give effect to the rights for which the Directive provides.

Complementary to fundamental rights, the CJEU has also established that equality represents a general principle of law. The roots of equality are in the domain of the internal market which was predicated upon tearing down discriminatory measures hindering, in different ways, the free movement of goods, services, capital, and people (workers).[6] From this line of reasoning the Court has extrapolated the generally applicable principle of equality which requires that 'similar situations shall not be treated differently unless differentiation is objectively justified'.[7] The general principle of equality becomes of relevance not only to the economy of the internal market but also to fundamental rights when it is applied to the treatment of individuals rather than goods.

Judgment of 30 April 1996, *P v S and Cornwall County Council*, C-13/94, ECLI:EU:C:1996:170

17. The principle of equal treatment 'for men and women' to which the directive [76/207] refers in its title, preamble and provisions means, as Articles 2(1) and 3(1) in particular indicate, that there should be 'no discrimination whatsoever on grounds of sex'.
18. Thus, **the directive is simply the expression, in the relevant field, of the principle of equality, which is one of the fundamental principles of Community law.**
19. Moreover, as the Court has repeatedly held, **the right not to be discriminated against on grounds of sex is one of the fundamental human rights whose observance the Court has a duty to ensure.**
20. Accordingly, the scope of the directive cannot be confined simply to discrimination based on the fact that a person is of one or other sex. In view of its purpose and the nature of the rights which it seeks to safeguard, the scope of the directive is also such as to apply to discrimination arising, as in this case, from the gender reassignment of the person concerned.
21. Such discrimination is based, essentially if not exclusively, on the sex of the person concerned. Where a person is dismissed on the ground that he or she intends to undergo, or has undergone, gender reassignment, he or she is treated unfavourably by comparison with persons of the sex to which he or she was deemed to belong before undergoing gender reassignment.
22. To tolerate such discrimination would be tantamount, as regards such a person, to a failure to respect the dignity and freedom to which he or she is entitled, and which the Court has a duty to safeguard.

---

[6] For an argument that not only the past but also the present of anti-discrimination law in the EU is closely tied to the neoliberal ideology underpinning the single market see A Somek, *Engineering Equality: An Essay on European Anti-Discrimination Law* (Oxford University Press 2011). See also S Garben, 'The Constitutional (Im)balance Between "the Market" and "the Social" in the European Union' (2017) 13 European Constitutional Law Review 23.

[7] Judgment of 19 October 1977, *Ruckdeschel and Others v Hauptzollamt Hamburg-St*. Annen, 117/76 and 16/77, ECLI:EU:C:1977:160, para 7.

In *P v S*, the Court can be seen connecting the general principle of equality with a fundamental rights general principle, namely non-discrimination on the grounds of sex, to strengthen its case against a restrictive reading of the directive in question.[8] The Court even brings into play the dignity and freedom of the litigant, as these too form part of fundamental rights protected under general principles of law. The case is a good example of how seamlessly the CJEU is at times able to invoke general principles in support of its argument.

Herein also rests the reason why general principles remain a source of fundamental rights for the CJEU even after the enactment of the Charter. They afford the Court a relatively large margin of discretion to apply rights in a way it sees fit for EU law. The CJEU can look to different written sources of fundamental rights for inspiration but it ultimately ends up creating its own EU-specific version of the right in question which may resemble the original source to a varying degree.[9] While the CJEU typically departs from one of the sources of inspiration—the ECHR or 'common constitutional traditions' of the Member States—the 'translation process' inevitably entails some judicial discretion. The Court's flexibility in this regard is strengthened also by the fact that the notion of common constitutional traditions can be quite ambiguous.[10] Nowadays, the Court has recourse to this method of identifying a fundamental right as a general principle much less often than in the early days of EU integration when few alternative sources were available. With time, the ECHR has proven a more readily operational source embodying the European human rights consensus and not requiring a cumbersome comparative analysis of often very different national constitutional traditions.[11]

Moreover, the elevation of the Charter to primary law has had an impact on fundamental rights protection in the EU, in addition to partial displacement of general principles as a source of fundamental rights. With a written bill of rights (with primary law status) to rely on, the Court has become bolder in applying fundamental rights. Whereas it has in practice been reluctant to annul EU acts on the basis of general principles—even though this would have been permissible under the Court's legal doctrine and hierarchy of EU legal norms—the Charter appears to have bestowed more prominence on fundamental rights protection in EU law. Yet, as the current President of the CJEU usefully pointed out, there is also a noticeable degree of functional continuity between general principles of EU law and the Charter.

---

[8] Elsewhere, the CJEU stated that fundamental rights 'include the general principle of equality and the obligation not to discriminate'. See Judgment of 13 April 2000, *Kjell Karlsson and Others*, C-292/97, ECLI:EU:C:2000:202, para 38.

[9] The CJEU ruled in some cases that EU law provides more extensive protection than the ECHR. See, for example, Judgment of 17 February 2009, *Elgafaji v Staatssecretaris van Justitie*, C-465/07, ECLI:EU:C:2009:94, para 28.

[10] D Blanchard, *La Constitutionnalisation de l'Union Européenne* (Apogée 2001) 166.

[11] Most of the time, however, the CJEU simply declares that a particular right or principle forms part of the common constitutional traditions without including the underlying analysis. Such opacity leaves once again a greater margin of manoeuvre to the Court. See, for example, Judgment of 3 May 2005, *Silvio Berlusconi and Others*, C-387/02, C-391/02, and C-403/02, ECLI:EU:C:2005:270, para 68. An example of the opposite is rare, but can be found in the Judgment of 13 December 1979, *Hauer v Land Rheinland-Pfalz*, 44/79, ECLI:EU:C:1979:290, paras 20–22: see M Graziadei and R de Caria, 'The "Constitutional Traditions Common to the Member States" in the Case-Law of the Court of Justice of the European Union: Judicial Dialogue at its Finest' (2017) 4 Rivista trimestrale di diritto pubblico 949, 960.

> ## K Lenaerts, 'Exploring the Limits of the EU Charter of Fundamental Rights' (2012) 8 European Constitutional Law Review 375
>
> Since from now on the Charter is primary EU law, it fulfils **a triple function**. First, just as general principles of EU law, **the Charter** also **serves as an aid to interpretation**, since both EU secondary law and national law falling within the scope of EU law must be interpreted in light of the Charter. Second, just as general principles, **the Charter may also be relied upon as providing grounds for judicial review**. EU legislation found to be in breach of an Article of the Charter is to be held void and national law falling within the scope of EU law that contravenes the Charter must be set aside. Finally, it continues to operate as **a source of authority for the 'discovery' of general principles of EU law**.

4.3 EU Charter of Fundamental Rights

The EU Charter of Fundamental Rights was originally devised in 2000 by the so-called European Convention consisting of representatives of the European Parliament (EP), national parliaments, the European Commission, and national governments.[12] The document subsequently received approval from the three most important EU institutions—the European Council, Parliament, and the Commission—and was jointly 'solemnly proclaimed' at the Nice summit in December 2000.[13] The process through which the document was drafted differed considerably from the manner in which the EU Treaties are revised at intergovernmental conferences (IGCs).[14] Moreover, it is notable that the points of contestation which arose during the drafting of what was originally a non-binding document (but drafted as if binding), namely the scope of applicability of the Charter, remain one of the central issues nowadays.

> ## G de Búrca, 'The drafting of the European Union Charter of Fundamental Rights' (2001) 26 European Law Review 126
>
> One of the points made here is that although the process of drafting an E.U. Charter of fundamental rights has been a highly ambivalent one in its establishment, its functioning, and its aims, exposing deeply contested political issues at its heart, the unresolved nature of the process and its desired outcome is not an uncommon feature of European constitutional development. The three fundamental points of political contestation which

---

[12] For a full list of the responsible drafters and observers to the process see European Parliament, 'Annex: The Convention responsible for drafting the Charter of Fundamental Rights' (*europarl.europa.eu*) <http://www.europarl.europa.eu/charter/composition_en.htm> accessed 14 August 2020.

[13] The Praesidium of the European Convention also prepared an explanatory document aiding the interpretation of the Charter. See Explanations relating to the Charter of Fundamental Rights [2007] OJ C303/17 and the accompanying discussion below.

[14] See also R Bellamy and J Schönlau, 'The Normality of Constitutional Politics: An Analysis of the Drafting of the EU Charter of Fundamental Rights' (2004) 11 Constellations 412.

were evident in the decision to establish the Charter process, and which also emerged clearly within the process itself, concerned firstly whether the eventual document should be binding or not, secondly the nature and scope of the European Union's policy competence in the field, and thirdly the extent to which it should be applicable to the Member States. Nonetheless, the profound differences of view about its aims, even amongst the central actors within the process, are unlikely to affect the significance of the outcome, given the deliberate emphasis which was placed on the nature of this process. Certainly, for the more immediate future, the high-profile nature of the drafting body's membership effectively guaranteed that the outcome of the process, whatever form it took following the European Council decision at Nice, would be taken seriously. It was established as a novel, experimental, relatively deliberative and open forum for constitutional debate, contrasting quite starkly with the traditional state-dominated I.G.C. processes of tough bargaining and closed diplomacy as the means for Treaty change in the European Union. Clearly there were many limitations to the Charter process, such as the ambiguity of its aims, the suggestion of superficiality implicit in the 'showcasing' idea, the exclusion of civil society representatives from substantive involvement, and the strong position of the drafting group (arguably influenced, at the very least, by the Council's legal advisers in their secretariat). Yet the very act of opening up of a new forum of this kind is suggestive of the potential for newer and more experimental forms of constitutional development in the European Union.

The Charter was not accorded a legally binding status until the entry into force of the Treaty of Lisbon in 2009, as the drafters were originally not able to reach agreement on this point.[15] In the intervening period, the CJEU already started referring to the Charter but the quality and quantity of the references has risen significantly since 2009 in recognition of the legally binding power of the instrument.

The Charter today is the centrepiece of EU fundamental rights law and policy. It is a separate document from the Treaties but holding the same legal value. It consists of a preamble and seven titles, the first six of which contain substantive rights and principles on dignity, freedoms, equality, solidarity, citizens' rights, and justice. The preamble of the Charter references a number of important influences: the ECHR, the Community Charter of the Fundamental Social Rights of Workers,[16] the European Social Charter, and the case law of the CJEU and European Court of Human Rights (ECtHR). The last title covers general provisions on the field of application of the Charter, its scope and interpretation, level of protection, and a prohibition of the abuse of rights. These last provisions merit special attention as they frame the usefulness and impact of all the entitlements and obligations contained in the Charter. Expressed simplistically in view of particularly the limitations in the scope of its applicability, the Charter has not transformed the EU into a human rights organization, or the CJEU into the ECtHR.[17]

---

[15] The legal force of the Charter was already envisaged in the failed Constitutional Treaty which largely served as a template for the Treaty of Lisbon. The fact that the Charter was drafted as potentially binding therefore paid dividends in the end as the process of constitutionalization of the EU progressed even despite the failure of the Constitutional Treaty.

[16] The Community Charter is also mentioned in Article 151 TFEU on social policy.

[17] K Lenaerts, 'Exploring the Limits of the EU Charter of Fundamental Rights' (2012) 8 European Constitutional Law Review 375, 377.

Charter of Fundamental Rights of the European Union [2012] OJ C326/391

TITLE VII

GENERAL PROVISIONS GOVERNING THE INTERPRETATION AND APPLICATION OF THE CHARTER

Article 51

Field of application

1. The provisions of this Charter are addressed to the institutions, bodies, offices and agencies of the Union with due regard for the principle of subsidiarity and to the Member States only when they are implementing Union law. They shall therefore respect the rights, observe the principles and promote the application thereof in accordance with their respective powers and respecting the limits of the powers of the Union as conferred on it in the Treaties.

2. The Charter does not extend the field of application of Union law beyond the powers of the Union or establish any new power or task for the Union, or modify powers and tasks as defined in the Treaties.

Article 52

Scope and interpretation of rights and principles

1. Any limitation on the exercise of the rights and freedoms recognised by this Charter must be provided for by law and respect the essence of those rights and freedoms. Subject to the principle of proportionality, limitations may be made only if they are necessary and genuinely meet objectives of general interest recognised by the Union or the need to protect the rights and freedoms of others.

2. Rights recognised by this Charter for which provision is made in the Treaties shall be exercised under the conditions and within the limits defined by those Treaties.

3. In so far as this Charter contains rights which correspond to rights guaranteed by the Convention for the Protection of Human Rights and Fundamental Freedoms, the meaning and scope of those rights shall be the same as those laid down by the said Convention. This provision shall not prevent Union law providing more extensive protection.

4. In so far as this Charter recognises fundamental rights as they result from the constitutional traditions common to the Member States, those rights shall be interpreted in harmony with those traditions.

5. The provisions of this Charter which contain principles may be implemented by legislative and executive acts taken by institutions, bodies, offices and agencies of the Union, and by acts of Member States when they are implementing Union law, in the exercise of their respective powers. They shall be judicially cognisable only in the interpretation of such acts and in the ruling on their legality.

6. Full account shall be taken of national laws and practices as specified in this Charter.

7. The explanations drawn up as a way of providing guidance in the interpretation of this Charter shall be given due regard by the courts of the Union and of the Member States.

Article 53
Level of protection
Nothing in this Charter shall be interpreted as restricting or adversely affecting human rights and fundamental freedoms as recognised, in their respective fields of application, by Union law and international law and **by international agreements** to which the Union or all the Member States are party, including the European Convention for the Protection of Human Rights and Fundamental Freedoms, and **by the Member States' constitutions.**

Article 54
Prohibition of abuse of rights
Nothing in this Charter shall be interpreted as implying any right to engage in any activity or to perform any act aimed at the destruction of any of the rights and freedoms recognised in this Charter or at their limitation to a greater extent than is provided for herein.

Despite the circumscribed scope of application of the Charter, it would not be correct to say that it does not bring tangible advantages to the EU fundamental rights architecture.[18] It binds as a matter of primary law the EU institutions and sets out a definite—and extensive in comparison to other core human rights treaties—set of rights and freedoms that enjoy this level of protection. It also binds the Member States, even if only 'when implementing EU law'. The Charter, being part of binding EU law as opposed to international human rights law, can be of more practical use by the virtue of long-standing principles which effectuate Union law such as direct effect and supremacy. Finally, the Charter represents an 'anchor' for EU policy-making—a point of reference which helps mainstream fundamental rights throughout the EU, while also adding clarity about their content.

A. The scope of application of the Charter

It is difficult to overstate the importance of Articles 51 and 52 of the Charter on the scope of application of the Charter.[19] Article 51 specifies that all EU institutions and bodies are bound by the Charter which entails a responsibility to 'respect the rights, observe the principles and promotion the application thereof'. Relatively to the Member States, the situation of EU authorities is clear, as the Charter contains no qualifying criterion circumscribing the applicability of the Charter in respect to them.

The Member States are bound by the Charter 'only when implementing EU law'. According to the Explanations, this is merely a restatement of the CJEU's case law.[20] There has, however, been some well-grounded debate regarding the Member States' drafting intention: should the scope of application of the Charter be narrower than that of general principles of EU

---

[18] SA de Vries, 'Balancing Fundamental Rights with Economic Freedoms According to the European Court of Justice' (2013) 9 Utrecht Law Review 169, 186.

[19] An authoritative commentary on the Charter argues that Article 51 should have in fact been made Article 1 of the Charter. See S Peers and others, *The EU Charter of Fundamental Rights: A Commentary* (Hart Publishing 2014) 1454.

[20] In particular *Kjell Karlsson and Others* (n 8) para 37 but in reality, the case law stretches back to at least the *Wachauf* case. See Explanations to the Charter (n 13) 32.

law?[21] Should derogations from the Charter on the national level be justified within the scope of the Charter or beyond it?

The CJEU appears to have decidedly opted for an inclusive reading of the Charter which would mirror its established case law on fundamental rights, not least on the scope of general principles. In so doing, it prevented the inevitable confusion that would arise regarding the distinct applicability of the Charter compared to the general principles. The complexity of the applicability of the Charter was perhaps most straightforwardly simplified by the Court in *Åkerberg Fransson*.

Judgment of 26 February 2013, *Åklagaren v Åkerberg Fransson*, C-617/10, ECLI:EU:C:2013:105

21. Since the fundamental rights guaranteed by the Charter must therefore be complied with where national legislation falls within the scope of European Union law, **situations cannot exist which are covered in that way by European Union law without those fundamental rights being applicable. The applicability of European Union law entails applicability of the fundamental rights guaranteed by the Charter.**

22. Where, on the other hand, a legal situation does not come within the scope of European Union law, the Court does not have jurisdiction to rule on it and **any provisions of the Charter relied upon cannot, of themselves, form the basis for such jurisdiction.**

Therefore, where EU law applies, so does the Charter; the Charter is in other words a necessary corollary of EU law. On the other hand, the CJEU can only apply the provisions of the Charter when they are 'hitched on' to a piece of EU law. Charter rights are not justiciable by themselves with respect to Member State actions. This shows the significance of what counts as Member States 'implementing EU law'. In *Åkerberg Fransson* the legal situation came within the scope of EU law and thus, by extension, the Charter was applicable to the national measures in question. The threshold set by the Court was low—there merely needed to be a part of the subject matter of a case before a national court that has a 'direct link' to EU law.[22] The national measure under fundamental rights review need not even be intended to transpose EU law, even though the CJEU has later backtracked somewhat—*Fransson* having

---

[21] G de Búrca, 'The Drafting of the European Union Charter of Fundamental Rights' (2001) 26 European Law Review 126, 137. See also P Eeckhout, 'The EU Charter of Fundamental Rights and the Federal Question' (2002) 39 Common Market Law Review 945.

[22] Judgment of 26 February 2013, *Åklagaren v Åkerberg Fransson*, C-617/10, ECLI:EU:C:2013:105, paras 24–26. The chain of reasoning of the Court was the following: Mr Åkerberg Fransson received a tax penalty that was, *in part*, linked to his failure to declare value added tax (VAT). Since the collection of VAT has an impact *also* on the financial interests of the EU, and the Member States are under an obligation to combat tax evasion, any national measure, such as the one imposing the tax penalty in question, taken by the Member States for this purpose constitutes an implementation of the relevant EU law (Directive 2006/112) on combatting illicit activities affecting the EU's financial interests. The fact that the national measure in question was not adopted to transpose EU law was immaterial in view of the Court. See also U Bernitz, 'The Scope of the Charter and Its Impact on the Application of the ECHR: The Åkerberg Fransson Case on Ne Bis in Idem in Perspective' in S de Vries, U Bernitz, and S Weatherill (eds), *The EU Charter of Fundamental Rights as a Binding Instrument: Five Years Old and Growing* (Hart Publishing 2015).

been criticized by the German Constitutional Court[23]—and admitted that the intention to transpose is a relevant criterion for assessing the applicability of the Charter.[24]

Due to the 'subject matter approach' of the CJEU,[25] it will be often far from obvious whether a given national implementing measure falls within the scope of EU law and hence also the Charter.[26] In *Siragusa*,[27] the CJEU tempered the mood regarding the applicability of the Charter but also shed some light on the relevant criteria guiding its decisions on this issue.

Judgment of 6 March 2014, *Siragusa v Regione Sicilia*, C-206/13, ECLI:EU:C:2014:126

23. According to the description provided by the referring court, the main proceedings concern an order requiring Mr Siragusa to dismantle work carried out in breach of a law protecting the cultural heritage and the landscape. There is a connection between such proceedings and EU environmental law since protection of the landscape – the aim of the national legislation in question – is an aspect of protection of the environment. In that regard, the referring court refers to various provisions of EU environmental law.

24. However, it should be borne in mind that the concept of 'implementing Union law', as referred to in Article 51 of the Charter, **requires a certain degree of connection above and beyond the matters covered being closely related or one of those matters having an indirect impact on the other** (see, to that effect, Case C-299/95 Kremzow [1997] ECR I-2629, paragraph 16).

25. In order to determine whether national legislation involves the implementation of EU law for the purposes of Article 51 of the Charter, **some of the points to be determined are whether that legislation is intended to implement a provision of EU law; the nature of that legislation and whether it pursues objectives other than those covered by EU law, even if it is capable of indirectly affecting EU law; and also whether there are specific rules of EU law on the matter or capable of affecting it** (...)

26. In particular, **the Court has found that fundamental EU rights could not be applied in relation to national legislation because the provisions of EU law in the subject area concerned did not impose any obligation on Member States** with regard to the situation at issue in the main proceedings (...)

27. As the interested parties which have submitted observations have argued, no specific obligations to protect the landscape, akin to those laid down by Italian law, are imposed on the Member States by the TEU and TFEU provisions referred to by the

---

[23] Bundesverfassungsgericht, Judgment of 24 April 2013, *Counter-Terrorism Database*, 1 BvR 1215/07.

[24] Judgment of 6 March 2014, *Siragusa v Regione Sicilia*, C-206/13, ECLI:EU:C:2014:126, para 25.

[25] Peers and others, *The EU Charter of Fundamental Rights: A Commentary* (n 19) 1452.

[26] M Ovádek, 'Le champ d'application de la Charte des droits fondamentaux de l'Union européenne et les États membres : la malédiction du critère matériel' (2017) 78 Journal de droit européen 386.

[27] *Siragusa* (n 24). Note that *Siragusa* is not a Grand Chamber judgment and thus reflects the work of fewer CJEU judges.

referring court; nor are such obligations imposed by the legislation relating to the Aarhus Convention, nor by Directives 2003/4 and 2011/92.

28. The objectives pursued by that EU legislation are not the same as those pursued by Legislative Decree No 42/04, even though the landscape is one of the factors to be taken into consideration in assessing the impact of a project on the environment in accordance with Directive 2011/92 and among the factors to be taken into consideration as part of the environmental information referred to in the Aarhus Convention, Regulation No 1367/2006 and Directive 2003/4.

29. In Annibaldi, cited in the explanations relating to Article 51 of the Charter, the Court held that the fact that national legislation **is capable of indirectly affecting** the operation of a common organisation of the agricultural markets **cannot in itself constitute a sufficient connection** between that legislation and EU law (Annibaldi, paragraph 22; see also Kremzow, paragraph 16).

30. In that regard, there is nothing to suggest that the provisions of Legislative Decree No 42/04 which are relevant to the case before the referring court fall within the scope of EU law. Those provisions do not implement rules of EU law, a fact which distinguishes the case in which the present request for a preliminary ruling has been made from the case which gave rise to the judgment in Case C-416/10 Križan and Others [2013] ECR, cited by the referring court.

31. It is also important to consider the objective of protecting fundamental rights in EU law, which is to ensure that those rights are not infringed in areas of EU activity, whether through action at EU level or through the implementation of EU law by the Member States.

32. The reason for pursuing that objective is the need to avoid a situation in which the level of protection of fundamental rights varies according to the national law involved in such a way as to undermine the unity, primacy and effectiveness of EU law (see, to that effect, Case 11/70 Internationale Handelsgesellschaft [1970] ECR 1125, paragraph 3, and Case C-399/11 Melloni [2013] ECR, paragraph 60). However, there is nothing in the order for reference to suggest that any such risk is involved in the case before the referring court.

The CJEU lists essentially three non-exhaustive criteria that can help determine whether implementing national legislation falls within the scope of EU law: the intention or the lack thereof to implement EU law; the nature and objectives of the implementing measure (are they different from the objectives of EU legislation?); and whether there are specific EU rules—which ideally impose an obligation on the Member States—on the subject matter or EU rules capable of affecting it. All the while it should be borne in mind that an indirect effect of national law on EU law is in itself not a sufficient connection.

The ruling in *Siragusa* and its criteria were omitted from a more high-profile and controversial case regarding the issuance of a humanitarian visa where the CJEU also found that the Charter, and particularly Articles 4 and 18 thereof on, respectively, the prohibition of torture and right to asylum, are not applicable. However, the case was dissimilar from both *Siragusa* and *Åkerberg Fransson* in that the referring court enquired not about a national implementing measure but rather the interpretation of an EU Regulation (establishing rules on short-term visas in the EU).

Judgment of 7 March 2017, *X and X v État belge*, C-638/16 PPU, ECLI:EU:C:2017:173

---

40. In the present case, it is important to note that the Visa Code was adopted on the basis of Article 62(2)(a) and (b)(ii) of the EC Treaty, pursuant to which the Council of the European Union is to adopt measures concerning visas for intended stays of no more than three months, including the procedures and conditions for issuing visas by Member States.

41. As set out in Article 1 of the Visa Code, the objective thereof is to establish the procedures and conditions for issuing visas for transit through or intended stays on the territory of the Member States not exceeding 90 days in any 180-day period. In Article 2(2)(a) and (b) of the code the concept of 'visa' is defined, for the purpose of the code, as meaning 'an authorisation issued by a Member State' with a view, respectively, to 'transit through or an intended stay on the territory of the Member States for a duration of no more than 90 days in any 180-day period' and to 'transit through the international transit areas of airports of the Member States'.

42. **However, it is apparent from the order for reference and from the material in the file before the Court that the applicants in the main proceedings submitted applications for visas on humanitarian grounds**, based on Article 25 of the Visa Code, at the Belgian embassy in Lebanon, **with a view to applying for asylum in Belgium immediately upon their arrival in that Member State and, thereafter, to being granted a residence permit with a period of validity not limited to 90 days.**

43. In accordance with Article 1 of the Visa Code, **such applications, even if formally submitted on the basis of Article 25 of that code, fall outside the scope of that code**, in particular Article 25(1)(a) thereof, the interpretation of which is sought by the referring court in connection with the concept of 'international obligations' mentioned in that provision.

44. In addition, since, as noted by the Belgian Government and the European Commission in their written observations, no measure has been adopted, to date, by the EU legislature on the basis of Article 79(2)(a) TFEU, with regard to the conditions governing the issue by Member States of long-term visas and residence permits to third-country nationals on humanitarian grounds, the applications at issue in the main proceedings fall solely within the scope of national law.

45. Since the situation at issue in the main proceedings is not, therefore, governed by EU law, the provisions of the Charter, in particular, Articles 4 and 18 thereof, referred to in the questions of the referring court, do not apply to it (see, to that effect, inter alia, judgments of 26 February 2013, Åkerberg Fransson, C-617/10, EU:C:2013:105, paragraph 19, and of 27 March 2014, Torralbo Marcos, C-265/13, EU:C:2014:187, paragraph 29 and the case-law cited).

X and X shows that the inquiry into the subject matter of a referred case for the purpose of ascertaining the applicability of the Charter can be very deep indeed, even where EU law is (seemingly) obviously implicated.[28] The CJEU disregarded the formal connection

---

[28] For a more detailed criticism of the judgment see M Ovádek, ' "Un-Chartered" Territory and Formal Links in EU Law: The Sudden Discovery of the Limits of the EU Charter of Fundamental Rights through Humanitarian Visa' in W Benedek and others (eds), *European Yearbook on Human Rights* (NWV 2017).

between the Visa Code (an EU Regulation) and the visa application based on this piece of EU legislation that was the subject of the proceedings before the national court in Belgium. Instead, the Court looked beyond the formal application and found that the 'true' object of the short-term application was to apply for long-term asylum. Since long-term visas are not covered by EU law (paragraph 44), the 'disguised' visa application cannot be a matter for EU law and consequently the Charter does not apply. It is an unprecedented conclusion that a situation arising directly from EU law—especially a Regulation—can be found to have an ulterior motive which takes it outside the scope of EU law into purely national-legal waters.[29] The judgment can neither be justified—and the Court has not even attempted this—by reference to Belgium's discretion under Article 25 of the Visa Code, as the CJEU held in the past that a 'discretionary power' derived from EU law still falls within its remit.[30]

From the perspective of *Åkerberg Fransson*, the reasoning and outcome of *X and X* appear all the more counterintuitive—as a double standard, even—given that in *Fransson* the Court established a connection with EU law in much less probable circumstances and in the absence of a formal link. However, the Court has signalled a somewhat more restrictive evaluation of the scope of EU law in a number of cases which followed *Fransson*, not least in *Siragusa*.[31] In a way, such judicial behaviour, whereby a wide principle is first established only to be mitigated through subsequent case law, is commonplace at the CJEU. Judicial restraint and a hands-off approach are also more likely to be found in sensitive cases, particularly those relating to the Area of Freedom, Security and Justice (AFSJ), which *X and X* in the context of controversies over EU migration policies certainly was.

Another, very different, situation to which the Charter does not apply is when the Member States decide to cooperate outside the EU legal framework. The issue arose in the context of the establishment of the European Stability Mechanism (ESM), an international organization empowered to provide financial assistance to Eurozone Member States in times of financial crises. The judgment and subsequent case law is problematic from the perspective of fundamental rights protection offered by the Charter, as it opens the door for Member States to escape their obligations under the Charter by taking intergovernmental cooperation outside the framework of the EU Treaties, despite the subject matter of that cooperation being plainly related to EU issues (Eurozone governance in this case).

---

[29] The decision of the CJEU regarding the non-applicability of the Charter runs counter to the Opinion of the Advocate General. See *X and X v État belge* [2017] ECLI:EU:C:2017:93, Opinion of AG Mengozzi, para 88.

[30] Judgment of 21 December 2011, *N. S. v Secretary of State for the Home Department and M. E. and Others v Refugee Applications Commissioner and Minister for Justice, Equality and Law Reform*, C-411/10 and C-493/10, ECLI:EU:C:2011:865, paras 65–68.

[31] See *Siragusa* (n 24); and also Judgment of 27 March 2014, *Torralbo Marcos v Korota SA and Fondo de Garantía Salarial*, C-265/13, ECLI:EU:C:2014:187. There was also a notable reaction to *Åkerberg Fransson* from the German Constitutional Court which warned of expanding the reach of the Charter in such a manner: 'The decision [in *Fransson*] must thus not be understood and applied in such a way that absolutely any connection of a provision's subject-matter to the merely abstract scope of Union law, or merely incidental effects on Union law, would be sufficient for binding the Member States by the Union's fundamental rights set forth in the [EU Charter].' See Bundesverfassungsgericht, Judgment of 24 April 2013, *Counter-Terrorism Database*, 1 BvR 1215/07.

Judgment of 27 November 2012, *Pringle v Government of Ireland and Others*, C-370/12, ECLI:EU:C:2012:756

178. The national court observes, referring to an argument put forward by the applicant in the main proceedings, that the establishment of the ESM outside the European Union legal order may have the consequence that the ESM is removed from the scope of the Charter. The referring court seeks to ascertain whether the establishment of the ESM is thereby in breach of Article 47 of the Charter which guarantees that everyone has the right to effective judicial protection.

179. In that regard, it must be observed that, under Article 51(1) of the Charter, its provisions are addressed to the Member States only when they are implementing Union law. Under Article 51(2), the Charter does not extend the field of application of Union law beyond the powers of the Union, or establish any new power or task for the Union or modify powers and tasks as defined in the Treaties. Accordingly, the Court is called upon to interpret, in the light of the Charter, the law of the European Union within the limits of the powers conferred on it (see Case C-400/10 PPU McB. [2010] ECR I-8965, paragraph 51, and Case C-256/11 Dereci and Others [2011] ECR I-11315, paragraph 71).

180. It must be observed that **the Member States are not implementing Union law,** within the meaning of Article 51(1) of the Charter, **when they establish a stability mechanism such as the ESM where,** as is clear from paragraph 105 of this judgment, **the EU and FEU Treaties do not confer any specific competence on the Union to establish such a mechanism.**

The conclusion that the Member States are not bound by the Charter when acting within the framework of the ESM Treaty was further underlined in cases concerned with the effects of restructuring and austerity policies adopted in the framework of ESM.[32] The CJEU reiterated that when an EU Member State implements the content of a memorandum of understanding (MoU) agreed with the ESM—essentially comprising the rest of the Member States whose currency is the euro—it is not implementing EU law for the purposes of Article 51(1) of the Charter. In *Ledra Advertising*,[33] the complained-about effect of the MoU was that the bank restructuring agreed as part of the deal to provide financial assistance to Cyprus included depositors and shareholders shouldering part of the costs of the recapitalization. The depositors therefore attempted to challenge the MoU before the EU's courts.

Judgment of 20 September 2016, *Ledra Advertising and Others v Commission and European Central Bank*, C-8/15 P to C-10/15 P, ECLI:EU:C:2016:701

53. (...) the duties conferred on the Commission and the ECB within the ESM Treaty, important as they are, do not entail any power to make decisions of their

---

[32] Treaty establishing the European Stability Mechanism [2012] OJ C247E/22.

[33] See also Judgment of 20 September 2016, *Mallis and Others v European Commission and European Central Bank*, C-105/15 P to C-109/15 P, ECLI:EU:C:2016:702 as regards the Cyprus bailout but calling for the judicial review of a statement of the Eurogroup rather than an MoU.

own. Furthermore, the activities pursued by those two institutions within the ESM Treaty commit the ESM alone.

54. In addition, as the Advocate General has observed in point 53 of his Opinion, the fact that one or more institutions of the European Union may play a certain role within the ESM framework does not alter the nature of the acts of the ESM, which fall outside the EU legal order.

55. However, whilst such a finding is liable to have an effect in relation to the conditions governing the admissibility of an action for annulment that may be brought on the basis of Article 263 TFEU, it **cannot prevent unlawful conduct linked**, as the case may be, **to the adoption of a memorandum of understanding on behalf of the ESM from being raised against the Commission and the ECB in an action for compensation under Article 268 TFEU and the second and third paragraphs of Article 340 TFEU.**

57. As regards the Commission in particular, it is stated in Article 17(1) TEU that **the Commission 'shall promote the general interest of the Union' and 'shall oversee the application of Union law'** (...)

58. Furthermore, the tasks allocated to the Commission by the ESM Treaty oblige it, as provided in Article 13(3) and (4) thereof, to ensure that the memoranda of understanding concluded by the ESM are **consistent with EU law** (...)

59. Consequently, **the Commission**, as it itself acknowledged in reply to a question asked at the hearing, retains, within the framework of the ESM Treaty, its role of guardian of the Treaties as resulting from Article 17(1) TEU, so that it **should refrain from signing a memorandum of understanding whose consistency with EU law it doubts.**

64. In accordance with settled case-law, the European Union may incur non-contractual liability under the second paragraph of Article 340 TFEU only if a number of conditions are fulfilled, namely the unlawfulness of the conduct alleged against the EU institution, the fact of damage and the existence of a causal link between the conduct of the institution and the damage complained of (...)

65. As regards the first condition, the Court has already stated on many occasions that a **sufficiently serious breach of a rule of law intended to confer rights on individuals** must be established (...)

66. In the present instance, the rule of law compliance with which the appellants criticise the Commission for not having ensured in the context of the adoption of the Memorandum of Understanding of 26 April 2013 is **Article 17(1) of the Charter.** That provision, which states that everyone has the right to own his or her lawfully acquired possessions, **is a rule of law intended to confer rights on individuals.**

67. Furthermore, **whilst the Member States do not implement EU law in the context of the ESM Treaty, so that the Charter is not addressed to them in that context** (...) on the other hand **the Charter is addressed to the EU institutions, including,** as the Advocate General has noted in point 85 of his Opinion, **when they act outside the EU legal framework**. Moreover, in the context of the adoption of a memorandum of understanding such as that of 26 April 2013, **the Commission is bound**, under both Article 17(1) TEU, which confers upon it the general task of overseeing the application of EU law, and Article 13(3) and (4) of the ESM Treaty, which requires it to ensure that the memoranda of understanding concluded by the ESM

> are consistent with EU law (...), **to ensure that such a memorandum of under-standing is consistent with the fundamental rights guaranteed by the Charter.**
> 68. It should therefore be examined whether the Commission contributed to a suffi-ciently serious breach of the appellants' right to property, within the meaning of Article 17(1) of the Charter, in the context of the adoption of the Memorandum of Understanding of 26 April 2013.
> 69. It must be remembered that **the right to property guaranteed by that provision of the Charter is not absolute and that its exercise may be subject to restrictions jus-tified by objectives of general interest** pursued by the European Union (...)
> 74. In view of the objective of ensuring the stability of the banking system in the euro area, and having regard to the imminent risk of financial losses to which depositors with the two banks concerned would have been exposed if the latter had failed, such measures do not constitute a disproportionate and intolerable interference impairing the very substance of the appellants' right to property. Consequently, **they cannot be regarded as unjustified restrictions on that right** (...)

It follows from *Ledra* and *Mallis* that although the Member States are not bound by the Charter when they implement ESM bailout conditions stipulated in MoUs or Eurogroup statements,[34] the Charter does apply to supranational EU institutions acting outside the EU framework (here in the ESM context), something that was not yet made explicit in *Pringle*.[35] However, the CJEU did not find the involvement of either the Commission or the European Central Bank (ECB) in the disputed acts to be sufficient to warrant their judicial review in accordance with the annulment procedure set out in Article 263 of the Treaty on the Functioning of the European Union (TFEU)—these acts fall outside the scope of EU judicial review, as in the view of the Court the EU institutions do not possess powers to make deci-sions of their own within the ESM framework.

The CJEU nevertheless conceded in *Ledra* that while MoUs cannot be annulled by the Court on the basis of EU law, the role played by the EU institutions in their adoption can be the subject of an action for damages.[36] This follows from the fact that the Commission and the ECB are bound by EU law, including the Charter, even when they act outside the EU legal framework. If EU institutions engage in unlawful conduct from the perspective of EU law which causes damage to someone—such as approving an MoU which would breach the right to property of Cypriot deposit holders—the injured party can bring an action for damages before the EU courts in accordance with Article 268 TFEU in conjunction with Article 340 TFEU, despite not being able to challenge before them the measure at the very origin of the injury. In *Ledra*, the Commission's involvement—in particular the act of signing the MoU—combined with its responsibility under both the EU (Article 17(1) TEU) and ESM Treaties to ensure the correct application of EU law made the Commission potentially liable for the resulting interference with the right to property suffered by the Cypriot applicants.

---

[34] As regards Eurogroup statements, the CJEU added that the Eurogroup itself is not an official configuration of the Council or otherwise an official agency, body, or office of the EU. Its acts and statements therefore fall outside the scope of judicial review under Article 263 TFEU. See *Mallis and Others v European Commission* (n 33) para 61.

[35] See also O De Schutter and P Dermine, 'The Two Constitutions of Europe: Integrating Social Rights in the New Economic Architecture of the Union' (2017) European Journal of Human Rights 108, 129.

[36] See A Poulou, 'The Liability of the EU in the ESM framework' (2017) 24 Maastricht Journal of European and Comparative Law 127.

The applicants' damages claim was assessed by the CJEU in light of its established case law on non-contractual liability of the EU which requires that the Union conduct was unlawful, that damage has occurred, and that it is causally linked to the impugned EU conduct.[37] The first condition mandates more specifically 'a sufficiently serious breach of a rule of law intended to confer rights on individuals'.[38] In other words, not all unlawful conduct of EU institutions will satisfy the first of the three conditions on non-contractual liability but only such that leads to a sufficiently serious violation of rights. In the case at hand, the CJEU found, following a rather limited examination, that although the applicants' right to property under Article 17(1) of the Charter was interfered with as a result of the MoU signed by the Commission, the interference was justified in accordance with Article 52(1) of the Charter (paragraph 74) and the Commission's conduct was therefore lawful.

While *Ledra* can be generally lauded as a positive step towards strengthening the rule of law in EU economic governance and making the EU institutions responsible for ensuring fundamental rights protection outside the EU framework,[39] the CJEU's sole focus on the Commission raises questions about the responsibility of other EU institutions. In its analysis of potential EU liability for fundamental rights infringements, the CJEU emphasized the obligation of the Commission as the 'guardian of the Treaties' under Article 17(1) TEU (and a corresponding provision in the ESM Treaty) which included safeguarding conformity with the Charter of non-EU acts involving the Commission (as a signatory). Article 51(1) of the Charter, however, stipulates that all EU institutions and bodies are to respect and promote the application of the Charter, albeit 'in accordance with their respective powers and respecting the limits of the powers of the Union as conferred on it in the Treaties'. If the latter limitation of Article 51(1) in conjunction with the judgment in *Ledra* were to be interpreted restrictively, the responsibility of other EU institutions to respect and promote the Charter could be viewed as more restricted than the Commission's obligations in this regard or at least as subject to legal contestation (especially in borderline cases), as on the basis of Article 17(1) TEU only the Commission is obliged to ensure general compliance with EU law (including the Charter).

In another case concerning an MoU prescribing austerity measures and concluded between the Commission and a Member State, the CJEU considered the MoU to be an act of an EU institution and reviewed its impact in light of EU fundamental rights standards.[40] The case of *Florescu* was, however, clearly distinguishable from *Ledra*, *Mallis*, and other ESM-related cases, as the MoU, while also imposing austerity conditions in exchange for EU financial assistance, was drafted in the context of Article 143 TFEU and secondary legislation based thereon which enable the EU to provide financial assistance to a Member State whose currency is not the euro, in this case Romania, struggling with a balance of payments crisis.

---

[37] See, for example, Judgment of 14 October 2014, *Giordano v European Commission*, C-611/12 P, ECLI:EU:C:2014:2282, para 35.

[38] Judgment of 4 July 2000, *Laboratoires pharmaceutiques Bergaderm SA and Goupil v Commission of the European Communities*, C-352/98 P, ECLI:EU:C:2000:361, para 42.

[39] See, for example, De Schutter and Dermine, 'The Two Constitutions of Europe' (n 35) 134. On the other hand, in the bigger picture the Commission's complicity in imposing austerity measures, which have appreciably damaged the fundamental rights environment in a number of Member States, have been criticized as embodying a minimalistic approach to fundamental rights characteristic for the EU institutions. See A Williams, 'Human Rights in the EU' in D Chalmers and A Arnull (eds), *Oxford Handbook of EU Law* (Oxford University Press 2015) 266–68.

[40] For a different take in the context of judicial independence, relying instead on Article 19 TEU, see Judgment of 27 February 2018, *Associação Sindical dos Juízes Portugueses v Tribunal de Contas*, C-64/16, ECLI:EU:C:2018:117.

Thus, whereas in *Ledra* the MoU was part of the ESM framework, adjudged by the CJEU to fall outside the scope of EU law including the Charter, in *Florescu* the MoU was interpreted, due to its basis in EU law, as being an EU act with legal force which, moreover, was being implemented for the purposes of Article 52(1) of the Charter by Romania when it introduced austerity measures in national law.[41] As a consequence, in accordance with Article 52(1) and the 'hitching-on' doctrine of *Fransson* the Charter was applicable to the implementing Romanian austerity law which restricted the pension rights of the claimants (former judges) for having concurrent public sector income as university lecturers. The claimants alleged in the domestic proceedings, which were stayed to refer a question to the CJEU for a preliminary ruling, a violation of Article 17(1) of the Charter on the right to property and Article 2(2)(b) of the Equal Treatment Directive on indirect discrimination. In its answer to the referring Romanian court, the CJEU in essence rejected both pleas, the former as being justified as a proportionate and necessary restriction on the right to property in line with Article 52(1) of the Charter and the latter as being inapplicable due to raising a discriminatory ground not covered by the Equal Treatment Directive.

Judgment of 13 June 2017, *Florescu v Casa Judeţeană de Pensii Sibiu*, C-258/14, ECLI:EU:C:2017:448

---

31. In the present case, it should be noted that the Memorandum of Understanding was concluded between the European Community, represented by the Commission, and Romania. The memorandum is based in law on Article 143 TFEU, which gives the Union the power to grant mutual assistance to a Member State whose currency is not the euro and which faces difficulties or is seriously threatened with difficulties as regards its balance of payments. Pursuant to that provision, the Commission is to recommend to the Council, under certain conditions, the granting of such mutual assistance and the appropriate methods in that regard. It is for the Council to grant such mutual assistance and to lay down the terms and conditions for that assistance by the adoption of directives or decisions.

32. Regulation No 332/2002 establishes the procedures applicable to the mutual assistance facility provided for in Article 143 TFEU. Article 1(2) of that regulation states that the Commission, in accordance with a decision adopted by the Council pursuant to Article 3 of that regulation and after consulting the Economic and Financial Committee, is to be empowered on behalf of the European Union to contract borrowings on the capital markets or with financial institutions.

33. The first sentence of Article 3a of Regulation No 332/2002 provides that the Commission and the Member State concerned are to conclude a Memorandum of Understanding setting out in detail the conditions laid down by the Council, pursuant to Article 3 of that regulation. The Memorandum of Understanding concluded between the European Union and Romania, whose interpretation is sought by the referring court in the present case, was adopted in accordance with that procedure, the Council having successively adopted two decisions, namely Decision

---

[41] See also M Menelaos and P Dermine, 'Bailouts, the Legal Status of Memoranda of Understanding, and the Scope of Application of the EU Charter: Florescu' (2018) 55 Common Market Law Review 643.

2009/458 granting mutual assistance for Romania pursuant to Article 143 TFEU and Decision 2009/459, which makes available to Romania a medium-term loan amounting to a maximum of EUR 5 billion, Article 2(2) of which provides that the **economic policy conditions attached to the financial assistance granted by the Union shall be laid down in a Memorandum of Understanding.**

34. Accordingly, as noted by the Advocate General in point 52 of his Opinion, **the Memorandum of Understanding gives concrete form to an agreement between the EU and a Member State on an economic programme,** negotiated by those parties, whereby that Member State undertakes to comply with predefined economic objectives in order to be able, subject to fulfilling that agreement, to benefit from financial assistance from the EU.

35. **As an act whose legal basis lies in the provisions of EU law** mentioned in paragraphs 31 to 33 of the present judgment and concluded, in particular, by the European Union, represented by the Commission, the Memorandum of Understanding **constitutes an act of an EU institution within the meaning of Article 267(b) TFEU.**

41. That being said, **the Memorandum of Understanding, although mandatory, contains no specific provision requiring the adoption of the national legislation at issue** in the main proceedings.

45. In the present case, as stated by the referring court, Law No 329/2009, on the 're-organisation of certain public authorities and institutions, on streamlining public spending, on supporting businesses and on complying with the framework agreements with the [Commission] and the [IMF]', was adopted in order for **Romania to be able to comply with the commitments it made to the European Union, which are set out in the Memorandum of Understanding.** (...)

46. **Among the conditions attached to the financial assistance,** set out in the Memorandum of Understanding, point 5(a) thereof requires **a reduction of the public sector wage bill,** while the fourth subparagraph of point 5(b) states that, in order to improve the long-term sustainability of the public finances, the **key parameters of the pension system are to be reformed.**

47. **It must therefore be held that the purpose of the measure at issue in the main proceedings,** which simultaneously pursues the two objectives referred to in the previous paragraph of the present judgment, **is to implement the undertakings given by Romania in the Memorandum of Understanding, which is part of EU law.**

48. It is true that the Memorandum of Understanding leaves Romania some discretion in deciding what measures are most likely to lead to performance of those undertakings. However, on the one hand, where a Member State adopts measures in the exercise of the discretion conferred upon it by an act of EU law, it must be regarded as implementing that law, within the meaning of Article 51(1) of the Charter (...) On the other hand, **the objectives set out in Article 3(5) of Decision 2009/459, as well as those set out in the Memorandum of Understanding, are sufficiently detailed and precise** to permit the inference that the purpose of the prohibition on combining a public-sector retirement pension with income from activities carried out in public institutions, stemming from Law No 329/2009, is to implement both the memorandum and that decision, and thus EU law, within the meaning of Article 51(1) of **the Charter.** Consequently, the latter **is applicable to the dispute in the main proceedings.**

49. In those circumstances, it is necessary to examine whether Article 17 of the Charter, in particular paragraph 1 thereof, precludes national legislation such as that at issue in the case in the main proceedings. In order to determine the scope of the fundamental right to peaceful enjoyment of property, it is necessary, having regard to Article 52(3) of the Charter, to take account of Article 1 of Protocol No 1 to the European Convention for the Protection of Human Rights and Fundamental Freedoms (...)

50. In that regard, where legislation provides for the automatic payment of a social benefit, it generates a proprietary interest for persons meeting the requirements thereof falling within the ambit of Article 1 of Protocol No 1 to that convention (...) **The rights resulting from the payment of contributions to a social security scheme thus constitute rights of property** for the purposes of that article (...)

51. With regard to Article 17 of the Charter, it is clear from the settled case-law of the Court that the right of property enshrined in that article is not absolute and that its exercise may be subject to restrictions justified by objectives of general interest pursued by the European Union (...)

52. In the case in the main proceedings, the national measure at issue does not, admittedly, entail an outright deprivation of the right to a pension of the persons in the situation of the applicants in the main proceedings in so far as they may continue to receive their pension if they relinquish the parallel pursuit of a paid professional activity with a public institution. However, **such a measure restricts the use and enjoyment of the pension entitlement** of the persons concerned, in that it entails a suspension of the payment of their pension when they have opted, instead, to pursue such an activity.

54. It is (...) necessary to determine whether the restriction of the right to property, resulting from the prohibition laid down by Law No 329/2009 on the combining of a net public-sector retirement pension with income from an activity carried out in a public institution, **is consistent with the essential content of the right to property, whether it fulfils an objective of general interest, and whether it is necessary for that purpose.**

59. (...) the national legislation at issue in the main proceedings is capable of attaining the general interest objective pursued and is necessary to attain that objective.

More recently, another line of argument was developed by the CJEU to get around the limited scope of application of the Charter in defence of certain essential characteristics of effective judicial protection—most importantly, judicial independence. In the *Associação Sindical dos Juízes Portugueses (ASJP)* case[42] concerning austerity measures in Portugal reducing the salaries of public sector workers including national judges, the Court based its upholding of judicial independence on Article 19(1) TEU read in light of Article 2 TEU instead of Article 47 of the Charter.[43] Seemingly, the reason was that the material criterion of Article 51(1) of the Charter would have prevented EU law from playing any role in what was an overtly domestic dispute, despite the facts of the case being similar to those in *Florescu*. In an

---

[42] *Associação Sindical dos Juízes Portugueses* (n 40).
[43] See excerpt in Section 4.6. See also, but less explicitly in *Achmea*, which concerned an arbitration clause in an agreement between the Netherlands and Slovakia: Judgment of 6 March 2018, *Slovak Republic v Achmea*, C-284/16, ECLI:EU:C:2018:158, para 55.

unprecedented move most likely directed at Poland where judicial independence is severely threatened, the CJEU distinguished the broader scope of Article 19(1) TEU from the scope of the Charter.[44] The Court seemed to suggest that the working of all national courts and tribunals could come under scrutiny, since the fact that they will potentially apply or interpret EU law suffices to bring them into the 'fields covered by EU law', constituting the scope of application of Article 19(1) TEU.[45]

The finding in *ASJP* has been consolidated in two infringement cases denouncing the forced retirement of senior judges of both the Polish Supreme Court[46] and the ordinary Polish Courts.[47] The CJEU has explicitly confirmed that the material scope of Article 19(1) TEU extends to 'the fields covered by Union law', 'irrespective of whether the Member States are implementing Union law within the meaning of Article 51(1) of the Charter'.[48] Finally, in a recent preliminary ruling, the CJEU has examined the concerns of the Labour Chamber of the Polish Supreme Court about the independence and impartiality of the newly established Disciplinary Chamber.[49] The CJEU found that it had jurisdiction over the case on the basis of both Article 19(1) TEU[50] and Article 47 of the Charter.[51] Since the actions in the main proceedings concerned the alleged infringement of a rule of EU law—namely the prohibition against discrimination on grounds of age as protected by Directive 2000/78—the case evidently fell within the scope of application of Article 19(1) TEU.[52] To conclude, the scope of the EU law obligation on Member States to ensure effective judicial protection at the national level, which includes that courts and judges are independent, is larger than the scope of the Charter.[53]

Judgment of 24 June 2019, *Commission v Poland*, C-619/18, ECLI:EU:C:2019:531

49. The **principle of the effective judicial protection** of individuals' rights under EU law, referred to in the **second subparagraph of Article 19(1) TEU**, is a general

---

[44] It can be contended that the Court's reasoning concerning the admissibility of the case was not sufficient; the CJEU was much more thorough in the assessment of the relationship between EU and national measures in *Florescu*: M Ovádek, 'Has the CJEU Just Reconfigured the EU Constitutional Order?' (*Verfassungsblog*, 28 February 2018) <https://verfassungsblog.de/has-the-cjeu-just-reconfigured-the-eu-constitutional-order/> accessed 14 August 2020.

[45] *Associação Sindical dos Juízes Portugueses* (n 40) paras 39–40; L Pech and S Platon, 'Judicial Independence under Threat: The Court of Justice to the Rescue in the ASJP Case' (2018) 55 Common Market Law Review 1827, 1839–1841.

[46] Judgment of 24 June 2019, *Commission v Poland*, C-619/18, ECLI:EU:C:2019:531.

[47] Judgment of 5 November 2019, *Commission v Poland*, C-192/18, ECLI:EU:C:2019:924.

[48] Judgment of 24 June 2019, *Commission v Poland*, C-619/18, ECLI:EU:C:2019:531, para 50; Judgment of 5 November 2019, *Commission v Poland*, C-192/18, ECLI:EU:C:2019:924, para 101; A Torres Pérez, 'From Portugal to Poland: The Court of Justice of the European Union as Watchdog of Judicial Independence' (2020) 27 Maastricht Journal of European and Comparative Law 105, 112–18.

[49] Judgment of 19 November 2019, *A.K. and Others v Sąd Najwyższy*, C-585/18, C-624/18, and C-625/18, ECLI:EU:C:2019:982.

[50] Ibid, paras 82–84.

[51] Ibid, paras 78–81.

[52] *A.K. and Others v Sąd Najwyższy* [2019] ECLI:EU:C:2019:551, Opinion of AG Tanchev, paras 86–88; M Leloup, 'An Uncertain First Step in the Field of Judicial Self-government' (2020) 16 European Constitutional Law Review 145.

[53] For the material rule of law component of the case law mentioned, see below under Section 4.6.

principle of EU law stemming from the constitutional traditions common to the Member States, which has been enshrined in Articles 6 and 13 of the European Convention for the Protection of Human Rights and Fundamental Freedoms, signed in Rome on 4 November 1950, and which is **now reaffirmed by Article 47 of the Charter** (…)

50. As regards the **material scope of the second subparagraph of Article 19(1) TEU**, that provision moreover refers to '**the fields covered by Union law**', **irrespective of whether the Member States are implementing Union law within the meaning of Article 51(1) of the Charter** (judgment of 27 February 2018, *Associação Sindical dos Juízes Portugueses*, C-64/16, EU:C:2018:117, paragraph 29).

51. Contrary to what has been claimed by the Republic of Poland and Hungary in this respect, the fact that the national salary reduction measures at issue in the case which gave rise to the judgment of 27 February 2018, *Associação Sindical dos Juízes Portugueses* (…) were adopted due to requirements linked to the elimination of the excessive budget deficit of the Member State concerned and in the context of an EU financial assistance programme for that Member State did not, as is apparent from paragraphs 29 to 40 of that judgment, play any role in the interpretation which led the Court to conclude that the second subparagraph of Article 19(1) TEU was applicable in the case in question. That conclusion was reached on the basis of the fact that **the national body** which that case concerned (…) **could**, subject to verification to be carried out by the referring court in that case, **rule, as a court or tribunal, on questions concerning the application or interpretation of EU law and which therefore fell within the fields covered by EU law** (…)

52. Furthermore, although, as the Republic of Poland and Hungary point out, the organisation of justice in the Member States falls **within the competence of those Member States**, the fact remains that, when exercising that competence, the Member States are **required to comply with their obligations deriving from EU law** (…) and, in particular, from the second subparagraph of Article 19(1) TEU (…) Moreover, by requiring the Member States thus to comply with those obligations, the **European Union is not** in any way claiming to exercise that competence itself nor is it, therefore, contrary to what is alleged by the Republic of Poland, **arrogating that competence**.

53. Lastly, in respect of Protocol (No 30), it must be observed that it does not concern the second subparagraph of Article 19(1) TEU and it should also be recalled that it does not call into question the applicability of the Charter in Poland, nor is it intended to exempt the Republic of Poland from the obligation to comply with the provisions of the Charter (…)

54. It follows from all of the foregoing that **the second subparagraph of Article 19(1) TEU requires Member States to provide remedies that are sufficient to ensure effective legal protection, within the meaning in particular of Article 47 of the Charter, in the fields covered by EU law** (…)

Still, the CJEU's jurisdiction is not unlimited. Recently, the Grand Chamber[54] has clarified the procedural rule that the Court cannot issue advisory opinions on general or hypothetical

---

[54] Judgment of 26 March 2020, *Miasto Łowicz and Prokurator Generalny*, C-558/18 and C-563/18, ECLI:EU:C:2020:234.

questions, meaning where these are not of relevance to the case before the national judge.[55] *In casu*, two Polish judges asked whether the new Polish legislation relating to a disciplinary regime for judges was compatible with Article 19(1) TEU. The Court distinguished infringement actions, where it must rule whether a national measure is compliant with general EU law, from preliminary ruling procedures, where it provides the national courts with an interpretation of EU law that is needed in order to resolve the disputes before them. In the latter situation, it is not sufficient that the courts in question could rule on issues concerning the application or interpretation of EU law in other cases.[56]

Judgment of 26 March 2020, *Miasto Łowicz and Prokurator Generalny*, C-558/18 and C-563/18, ECLI:EU:C:2020:234

---

44. (...) it has (...) been consistently held that the procedure provided for in **Article 267 TFEU** is an **instrument of cooperation** between the Court of Justice and the national courts, by means of which **the Court provides the national courts with the points of interpretation of EU law which they need in order to decide the disputes before them** (...) The justification for a reference for a preliminary ruling is **not that it enables advisory opinions on general or hypothetical questions** to be delivered **but rather that it is necessary for the effective resolution of a dispute** (...)

47. In that context, the task of the Court must be distinguished according to whether it is requested to give a preliminary ruling or to rule on an action for failure to fulfil obligations. Whereas, in an **action for failure to fulfil obligations**, the Court must ascertain whether the **national measure** or practice challenged by the Commission or another Member State, **contravenes EU law in general**, without there being any need for there to be a relevant dispute before the national courts, the Court's function in proceedings for a **preliminary ruling** is, by contrast, to help the referring court to **resolve the specific dispute** pending before that court (...)

49. In the present case, it must be held, **first**, that the **disputes in the main proceedings are not substantively connected to EU law, in particular to the second subparagraph of Article 19(1) TEU** to which the questions referred relate, and that the referring courts are not therefore required to apply that law, or that provision, in order to determine the substantive solution to be given to those disputes. In that respect, the present joined cases can be **distinguished**, in particular, **from** the case which gave rise to the judgment of 27 February 2018, *Associação Sindical dos Juízes Portugueses* (C-64/16, EU:C:2018:117), in which the referring court had to rule on an action seeking annulment of administrative decisions reducing the remuneration of the members of the Tribunal de Contas (Court of Auditors, Portugal)

---

[55] See, for example Judgment of 15 December 1995, *Union royale belge des sociétés de football association and Others v Bosman and Others*, C-415/93, ECLI:EU:C:1995:463, para 61; Judgment of 7 June 2007, *van der Weerd and Others*, C-222/05 to C-225/05, ECLI:EU:C:2007:318, para 22.

[56] After reaching this conclusion, the Court did include an important warning towards the Polish authorities, namely that '(p)rovisions of national law which expose national judges to disciplinary proceedings as a result of the fact that they submitted a reference to the Court for a preliminary ruling cannot (...) be permitted'. See *Miasto Łowicz and Prokurator Generalny* (n 54) paras 54–59.

pursuant to national legislation which provided for such a reduction and whose compatibility with the second subparagraph of Article 19(1) TEU was challenged before that referring court.

50. **Secondly**, although the Court has already held to be admissible questions referred for a preliminary ruling on the interpretation of procedural provisions of EU law which the referring court is required to apply in order to deliver its judgment (...), that is **not the scope of the questions** raised in the present joined cases.

51. **Thirdly**, an answer by the Court to those questions does **not appear capable of providing the referring courts with an interpretation of EU law which would allow them to resolve procedural questions of national law** before being able to rule on the substance of the disputes before them. In that regard, the present cases also **differ**, for example, from the cases giving rise to the judgment of 19 November 2019, *A. K. and Others (Independence of the Disciplinary Chamber of the Supreme Court)* (C-585/18, C-624/18 and C-625/18, EU:C:2019:982), in which the interpretation sought from the Court was such as to have a bearing on the issue of determining which court had jurisdiction for the purposes of settling disputes relating to EU law, as is clear specifically from paragraphs 100, 112 and 113 of that judgment.

52. In those circumstances, it is **not apparent** from the orders for reference that there is a **connecting factor** between the provision of EU law to which the questions referred for a preliminary ruling relate and the disputes in the main proceedings, and which makes it necessary to have the interpretation sought so that the referring courts may, by applying the guidance provided by such an interpretation, make the decisions needed to rule on those disputes.

53. **Those questions do not therefore concern an interpretation of EU law which meets an objective need for the resolution of those disputes, but are of a general nature.**

B. Limitations on the rights in the Charter

Most fundamental rights and freedoms are not absolute and therefore can be lawfully limited when certain conditions are met.[57] As a result, they can be balanced against other principles, rights, and obligations or derogated from in the pursuit of specific objectives. The CJEU has operated in its case law with a general rule regarding limitations on fundamental rights and freedoms, which was inspired by the ECHR,[58] long before the Charter codified the limitation clause in Article 52(1).

---

[57] The rights enshrined in Title I of the Charter (human dignity, right to life and integrity of the person, prohibition of torture and of slavery) can for the most part be considered to constitute 'absolute' rights which cannot be limited. See Explanations to the Charter (n 13) Title I. See also Judgment of 12 June 2003, *Schmidberger v Republik Österreich*, C-112/00, ECLI:EU:C:2003:333, para 80.

[58] See, for example, *Fogarty v United Kingdom*, App no 37112/97, 21 November 2001.

Judgment of 13 July 1989, *Wachauf v Bundesamt für Ernährung und Forstwirtschaft*, 5/88, ECLI:EU:C:1989:321

---

18. The fundamental rights recognized by the Court are not absolute, however, but must be considered in relation to their social function. Consequently, restrictions may be imposed on the exercise of those rights, in particular in the context of a common organization of a market, provided that those restrictions in fact correspond to objectives of general interest pursued by the Community and do not constitute, with regard to the aim pursued, a disproportionate and intolerable interference, impairing the very substance of those rights.

Wachauf is notable for mentioning the social function of the fundamental rights as a relevant criterion for their limitation, with the rules of the single market representing a particular point of reference in that regard.[59] Cases subsequent to *Wachauf*—and ultimately also Article 52(1) of the Charter—have used a slightly different wording.

Charter of Fundamental Rights of the European Union [2012] OJ C326/391

Article 52

Scope and interpretation of rights and principles

1. Any **limitation** on the exercise of the rights and freedoms recognised by this Charter must be **provided for by law** and **respect the essence of those rights and freedoms**. Subject to the principle of proportionality, limitations may be made only **if they are necessary** and genuinely meet **objectives of general interest** recognised by the Union **or the need to protect the rights and freedoms of others.**

The Charter provision contains several conditions applicable to restrictions on rights and freedoms guaranteed by the Charter: they need to be 'provided for by law'; respect the 'essence' of the restricted rights and freedoms; be necessary; and justified by either an 'objective of general interest recognised by the Union' or a 'need to protect the rights and freedoms of others'. The necessity and legitimacy of the objectives pursued are part of the general principle of proportionality.[60] When it comes to the judicial review of EU laws setting out limitations on fundamental rights and freedoms, it is justified on the grounds that the EU legislature's discretion is limited with respect to interferences with fundamental rights. The precise extent of the lawmakers' discretion depends on the area concerned, the nature of the right at stake, the nature and seriousness of the restriction, and the object pursued.[61]

---

[59] The social function of fundamental rights, namely the right to property, is also mentioned in one of the earliest cases concerning limitations on fundamental rights, *Hauer v Land Rheinland-Pfalz* (n 11). It is also one of the cases which compared the constitutional traditions of the Member States in promulgating a general principle of EU law regarding the right to property (see also n 11).

[60] See generally TI Harbo, 'The Function of the Proportionality Principle in EU Law' (2010) 16 European Law Journal 158.

[61] Judgment of 8 April 2014, *Digital Rights Ireland Ltd v Minister for Communications and Others*, C-293/12 and C-594/12, ECLI:EU:C:2014:238, para 47.

First, the requirement for the limitation to be 'provided for by law' entails that there is a specific legal basis for the restriction in question.[62] The legal basis must also be sufficiently clear and precise and must 'afford a measure of legal protection against any arbitrary interference' by defining the scope of the limitation.[63]

Second, the respect for the 'essence' of rights and freedoms is a rewording of the 'substance' of rights previously used by the Court. Nevertheless, the CJEU does not provide any definition of 'essence' or break it down into more specific conditions.[64] Rather, the Court evaluates whether the 'essence' of rights was compromised without reference to any other criteria. This element of Article 52(1) of the Charter therefore does not appear to represent an important hurdle for fundamental rights restrictions; the CJEU has to date never ascertained that a given limitation violated the essence of any rights or freedoms, even when it found 'a particularly serious interference',[65] and in at least one case it skipped the assessment of the criterion completely.[66]

Third, when it comes to the principle of necessity, the CJEU looks closely at whether a lesser interference with the rights in question was not sufficient to achieve the aims pursued.[67] With respect to the right to protection of personal data, the CJEU stated that any derogations or limitations must be 'strictly necessary'.[68] In addition to necessity but still as part of the general principle of proportionality, the CJEU can also examine whether the restriction is appropriate for attaining the objective pursued.[69]

Fourth, the CJEU considers the legitimacy of the objectives pursued by the limitation on fundamental rights. In its case law, the Court has recognized a relatively wide array of objectives as satisfying this criterion: common organization of the market;[70] protection of public health;[71] fish stock conservation;[72] transparency;[73] fight against serious crime (in particular organized crime and terrorism);[74] and international security.[75] These can be understood as vertical limitations on fundamental rights of individuals due to the public policy character of the competing objective.

Alternatively, limitations on fundamental rights can be justified in view of protecting rights and freedoms of others. This part of Article 52(1) of the Charter represents the horizontal dimension of the limitation clause as it concerns the balancing of individuals' rights against each other. According to the CJEU's settled case law, rights and freedoms stemming from human rights law can be balanced not only against other rights of the same character

---

[62] Judgment of 1 July 2010, *Knauf Gips KG v European Commission*, C-407/08 P, ECLI:EU:C:2010:389, para 91.

[63] Judgment of 17 December 2015, *WebMindLicenses kft v Nemzeti Adó*, C-419/14, ECLI:EU:C:2015:832, para 81.

[64] In one case, the CJEU interpreted 'essence' as meaning that 'the limitation does not call into question that right as such'. See Judgment of 6 October 2015, *Delvigne v Commune de Lesparre Médoc and Préfet de la Gironde*, C-650/13, ECLI:EU:C:2015:648, para 48.

[65] *Digital Rights Ireland* (n 61) para 39.

[66] Judgment of 9 November 2010, *Volker und Markus Schecke GbR and Hartmut Eifert v Land Hessen*, C-92/09 and C-93/09, ECLI:EU:C:2010:662.

[67] Ibid, para 74.

[68] Ibid, para 77; *Digital Rights Ireland* (n 61) para 52.

[69] *Digital Rights Ireland* (n 61) para 49.

[70] *Wachauf* (n 5) para 18.

[71] Judgment of 29 April 1999, *The Queen v Secretary of State for the Environment and Ministry of Agriculture, Fisheries and Food, ex parte H.A. Standley and Others and D.G.D. Metson and Others*, C-293/97, ECLI:EU:C:1999:215, para 56.

[72] *Giordano v European Commission* (n 37) para 50.

[73] *Volker und Markus Schecke* (n 66) para 71.

[74] *Digital Rights Ireland* (n 61) para 51.

[75] Judgment of 3 September 2008, *Yassin Abdullah Kadi and Al Barakaat International Foundation v Council and Commission*, C-402/05 P and C-415/05 P, ECLI:EU:C:2008:461, para 86.

but also, for example, the free movement rights guaranteed under the Treaties, and vice versa.[76] The distinction between the two has, however, become less precise after the adoption of the Charter which incorporates some of the EU economic freedoms in its catalogue of rights.[77]

SA de Vries, 'Balancing Fundamental Rights with Economic Freedoms According to the European Court of Justice' (2013) 9 Utrecht Law Review 169

(...) the fact that the restriction on free movement within the internal market was a result of the exercise of a fundamental right in cases such as *Schmidberger* or *Viking* does not influence the finding that the Treaty rules on free movement – the fundamental economic freedoms – are applicable in the first place. In this sense, the exercise of fundamental rights does not escape the scope of application of the Treaty provisions. (...)

Yet the Court immediately admits the necessity to reconcile in this context fundamental rights with the Treaty freedoms. The important consequence of this approach is a shift in the burden of proof. Where in Strasbourg [ECtHR] the proponents of economic rights might have to justify a restriction on human rights, in Luxembourg [CJEU] the fundamental, human rights proponents will have to justify their actions and establish that the restriction on free movement is justified on the basis of protecting fundamental rights. (...) After all, the very fact that the protection of fundamental rights in cases where a conflict with fundamental freedoms arises must be justified in the light of the economic freedoms, could jeopardise the equality or indivisibility of fundamental rights and economic freedoms. Viewed from this perspective the EU may indeed not yet have been fully transformed into a Human Rights Organization. At the same time, though, the Court has managed to find ways to incorporate fundamental rights in its free movement case law and has thus provided for a 'human rights dimension' of the internal market. (...)

In balancing fundamental rights and fundamental freedoms the Court draws inspiration from its case law on fundamental freedoms and public interests. Furthermore, the balancing exercise by the ECJ through the application of the proportionality test appears to be—at least in some cases—rather similar to the 'margin of appreciation test' applied

---

[76] See, for example, *Schmidberger v Republik Österreich* (n 57) where a public demonstration restricting the free movement of goods was deemed legitimate on the grounds of fundamental rights protection, namely freedom of expression and freedom of assembly. Other important 'balancing' cases include Judgment of 14 October 2004, *Omega Spielhallen- und Automatenaufstellungs v Oberbürgermeisterin der Bundesstadt Bonn*, C-36/02, ECLI:EU:C:2004:614; Judgment of 22 December 2010, *Sayn-Wittgenstein v Landeshauptmann von Wien*, C-208/09, ECLI:EU:C:2010:806; Judgment of 11 December 2007, *International Transport Workers' Federation and Finnish Seamen's Union v Viking Line ABP and OÜ Viking Line Eesti*, C-438/05, ECLI:EU:C:2007:772; and Judgment of 18 December 2007, *Laval un Partneri Ltd v Svenska Byggnadsarbetareförbundet and Others*, C-341/05, ECLI:EU:C:2007:809.

[77] See, especially, Article 15 of the Charter on the right to provide services and establish oneself in any Member State. The incorporation under the Charter does not seem to have seriously affected the Court, as it does not conduct separate examination on the basis of Article 15 of the Charter where it has already conducted review in light of the applicable free movement Treaty articles: Judgment of 30 April 2014, *Pfleger and Others*, C-390/12, ECLI:EU:C:2014:281, para 60. See also Judgment of 4 July 2013, *Gardella v Istituto nazionale della previdenza sociale (INPS)*, C-233/12, ECLI:EU:C:2013:449, para 39 regarding the connection of Article 15 to Article 45 TFEU on free movement of workers. Article 16 of the Charter has also been found by the Court to be linked to Article 49 TFEU on the freedom of establishment: Judgment of 30 June 2016, *Sokoll-Seebacher and Naderhirn v Hemetsberger and Others*, C-634/15, ECLI:EU:C:2016:510, para 22.

by the ECtHR. Where typically national or sensitive interests and values are involved, like 'gambling' or public health, Member States have a greater margin of discretion than in cases where more 'holistic' or universal values, like the protection of consumers, are at issue. The 'good old principle' of proportionality here serves as an instrument to balance the different public interests with the fundamental freedoms.

The case of *Philip Morris* provides a recent example of how the CJEU approaches limitations on fundamental rights. The tobacco company challenged an EU Directive imposing certain restrictions on the labelling of tobacco products on the ground that the law infringed Philip Morris' freedom of expression and information protected under Article 11 of the Charter (which corresponds to Article 10 ECHR). Although the CJEU recognized that Philip Morris' freedom of expression was indeed restricted by virtue of Article 13(1) of Directive 2014/40,[78] the Court found the restriction to comply with the requirements of Article 52(1) of the Charter. The Court weighed freedom of expression against a host of countervailing provisions of EU primary law, including Article 35 of the Charter which provides in the relevant passage that '[a] high level of human health protection shall be ensured in the definition and implementation of all the Union's policies and activities'.

Judgment of 4 May 2016, *Philip Morris Brands SARL and Others v Secretary of State for Health*, C-547/14, ECLI:EU:C:2016:325

146. The referring court asks the Court to examine the validity of Article 13(1) of Directive 2014/40 in the light of **Article 11 of the Charter** and the principle of proportionality.

147. **Article 11 of the Charter affirms the freedom of expression and information.** That freedom is also protected under Article 10 of the European Convention for the Protection of Human Rights and Fundamental Freedoms (...) which applies, in particular, as is clear from the case-law of the European Court of Human Rights, to the dissemination by a business of commercial information, including in the form of advertising. Given that the freedom of expression and information laid down in Article 11 of the Charter has—as is clear from Article 52(3) thereof and the Explanations Relating to the Charter as regards Article 11—the same meaning and scope as the freedom guaranteed by the Convention, it must be held that that freedom covers the use by a business, on the packaging and labelling of tobacco products, of indications such as those covered by Article 13(1) of Directive 2014/40 (...)

148. **The prohibition on including on the labelling of unit packets and on outside packaging, as well as on the tobacco product itself,** the elements and features referred to in Article 13(1) of Directive 2014/40 **constitutes**, it is true, **an interference with a business's freedom of expression and information.**

---

[78] Directive 2014/40/EU of the European Parliament and of the Council on the approximation of the laws, regulations and administrative provisions of the Member States concerning the manufacture, presentation and sale of tobacco and related products and repealing Directive 2001/37/EC [2014] OJ L127/1.

149. In accordance with **Article 52(1) of the Charter,** any limitation on the exercise of the rights and freedoms laid down by the Charter must be provided for by law and respect the essence of those rights and freedoms and, in compliance with the principle of proportionality, is permissible only if it is necessary and actually meets objectives of general interest recognised by the European Union or the need to protect the rights and freedoms of others.

150. In that regard, the Court finds, first, that the interference identified in paragraph 148 of this judgment must be regarded as being **provided for by law** given that it results from a provision adopted by the EU legislature.

151. Secondly, **the essence of a business's freedom of expression** and information is not affected by Article 13(1) of Directive 2014/40 inasmuch as that provision, far from prohibiting the communication of all information about the product, merely controls, in a very clearly defined area, the labelling of those products by prohibiting only the inclusion of certain elements and features (...)

152. Thirdly, the interference with the freedom of expression and information that has been found to exist meets an **objective of general interest recognised by the European Union, namely, the protection of health.** Given that it is undisputed that tobacco consumption and exposure to tobacco smoke are causes of death, disease and disability, the prohibition laid down in Article 13(1) of Directive 2014/40 contributes to the achievement of that objective in that it is intended to prevent the promotion of tobacco products and incitements to use them.

153. Fourthly, as regards the **proportionality of the interference** found, it is important to point out that the second sentence of **Article 35 of the Charter** and Articles 9 TFEU, 114(3) TFEU and 168(1) TFEU require that a high level of human health protection be ensured in the definition and implementation of all the Union's policies and activities.

154. In those circumstances, the determination of the validity of Article 13(1) of Directive 2014/40 must be carried out in accordance with the **need to reconcile the requirements of the protection of those various fundamental rights and legitimate general interest objectives, protected by the EU legal order, and striking a fair balance between them** (...)

155. It should be stated in that regard that **the discretion enjoyed by the EU legislature, in determining the balance to be struck, varies for each of the goals justifying restrictions on that freedom** and depends on the nature of the activities in question. In the present case, the claimants in the main proceedings rely, in essence, under Article 11 of the Charter, on the freedom to disseminate information in pursuit of their commercial interests.

156. It must, however, be stated that **human health protection**—in an area characterised by the proven harmfulness of tobacco consumption, by the addictive effects of tobacco and by the incidence of serious diseases caused by the compounds those products contain that are pharmacologically active, toxic, mutagenic and carcinogenic—**outweighs the interests put forward by the claimants** in the main proceedings.

157. Indeed, as is apparent from the second sentence of Article 35 of the Charter and Articles 9 TFEU, 114(3) TFEU and 168(1) TFEU, a high level of human health

protection must be ensured in the definition and implementation of all the European Union's policies and activities.

158. The Court finds, in the light of the foregoing, (i) that **the prohibition laid down in Article 13(1) of Directive 2014/40 is such as to protect consumers against the risks associated with tobacco use**, as follows from paragraph 152 of this judgment, and (ii) that that **prohibition does not go beyond what is necessary** in order to achieve the objective pursued.

159. On this point, the Court cannot accept the argument that the prohibition concerned is not necessary because consumer protection is already adequately ensured by the mandatory health warnings mentioning the risks associated with tobacco use. In fact, awareness of those risks may, on the contrary, be diminished by information that might suggest that the product concerned is less harmful or is beneficial in some respects.

160. Nor can the Court accept the argument that the objective pursued could be achieved by other, less restrictive measures, such as regulating the use of the elements and features referred to in Article 13 of Directive 2014/40, instead of prohibiting them, or adding certain supplementary health warnings. Such measures would not be as effective for ensuring the protection of consumers' health, since the elements and features referred to in Article 13 are, by their very nature, likely to encourage smoking (…). It cannot be accepted that those elements and features may be included for the purpose of giving consumers clear and precise information, inasmuch as they are **intended more to exploit the vulnerability of consumers of tobacco products who, because of their nicotine dependence, are particularly receptive to any element suggesting there may be some kind of benefit linked to tobacco consumption**, in order to vindicate or reduce the risks associated with their habits.

161. In those circumstances, it must be held that, in prohibiting the placing, on the labelling of unit packets and on the outside packaging, as well as on the tobacco product itself, of the elements and features referred to in Article 13(1) of Directive 2014/40, even when they include factually accurate information, the EU legislature did not fail to strike a fair balance between the requirements of the protection of the freedom of expression and information and those of human health protection.

C. Relation of the Charter to the ECHR and national constitutions

Although the enactment of the Charter has created a focal point in the EU fundamental rights framework, it has not removed the links to other sources, mainly the ECHR and national constitutional traditions, which had been originally acknowledged by the CJEU in its case law on general principles of EU law (see Figure 4.2). The third paragraph of Article 52 of the Charter prescribes a convergence of meaning and scope between equivalent provisions of the ECHR and the Charter, while the fourth paragraph insists on a 'harmonious interpretation' of the Charter with national constitutional traditions.

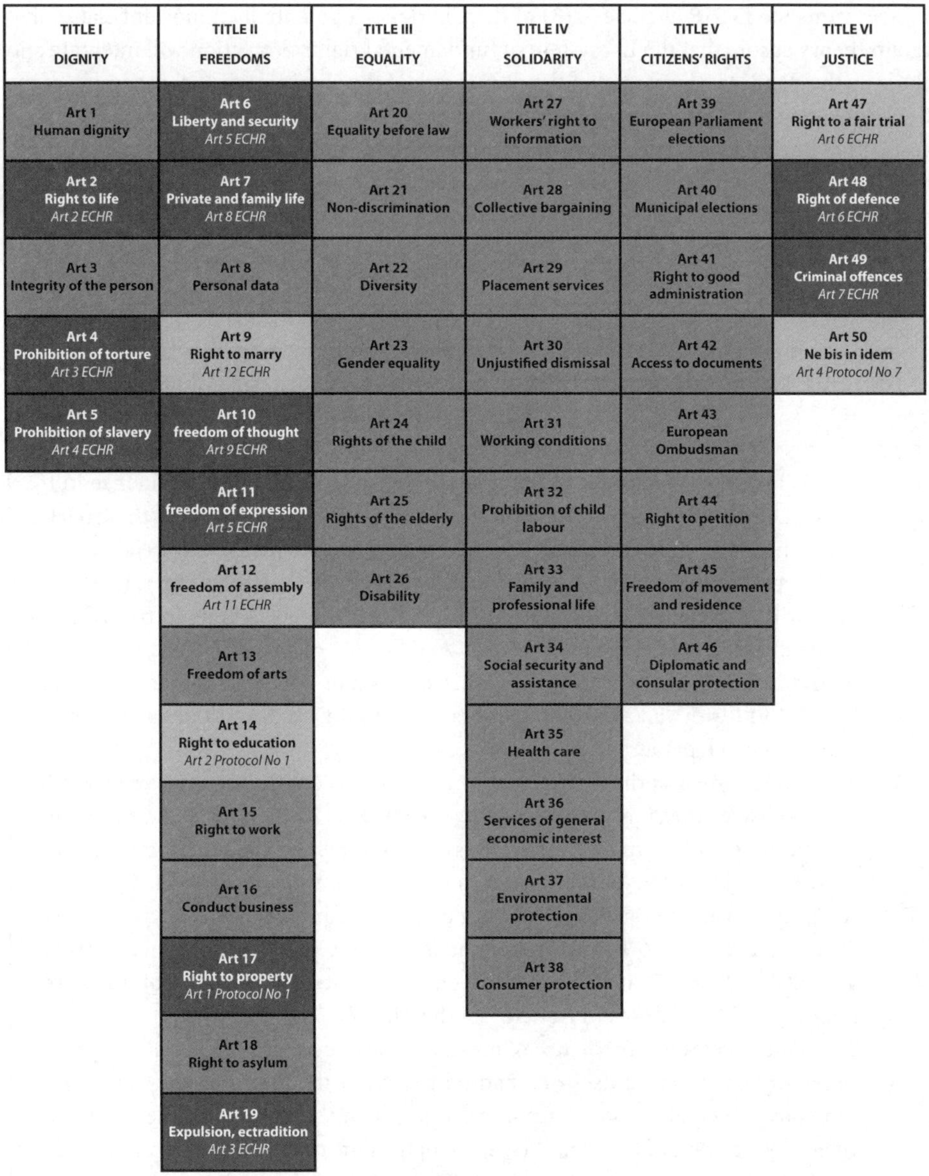

TITLE I DIGNITY	TITLE II FREEDOMS	TITLE III EQUALITY	TITLE IV SOLIDARITY	TITLE V CITIZENS' RIGHTS	TITLE VI JUSTICE
Art 1 Human dignity	Art 6 Liberty and security *Art 5 ECHR*	Art 20 Equality before law	Art 27 Workers' right to information	Art 39 European Parliament elections	Art 47 Right to a fair trial *Art 6 ECHR*
Art 2 Right to life *Art 2 ECHR*	Art 7 Private and family life *Art 8 ECHR*	Art 21 Non-discrimination	Art 28 Collective bargaining	Art 40 Municipal elections	Art 48 Right of defence *Art 6 ECHR*
Art 3 Integrity of the person	Art 8 Personal data	Art 22 Diversity	Art 29 Placement services	Art 41 Right to good administration	Art 49 Criminal offences *Art 7 ECHR*
Art 4 Prohibition of torture *Art 3 ECHR*	Art 9 Right to marry *Art 12 ECHR*	Art 23 Gender equality	Art 30 Unjustified dismissal	Art 42 Access to documents	Art 50 Ne bis in idem *Art 4 Protocol No 7*
Art 5 Prohibition of slavery *Art 4 ECHR*	Art 10 freedom of thought *Art 9 ECHR*	Art 24 Rights of the child	Art 31 Working conditions	Art 43 European Ombudsman	
	Art 11 freedom of expression *Art 5 ECHR*	Art 25 Rights of the elderly	Art 32 Prohibition of child labour	Art 44 Right to petition	
	Art 12 freedom of assembly *Art 11 ECHR*	Art 26 Disability	Art 33 Family and professional life	Art 45 Freedom of movement and residence	
	Art 13 Freedom of arts		Art 34 Social security and assistance	Art 46 Diplomatic and consular protection	
	Art 14 Right to education *Art 2 Protocol No 1*		Art 35 Health care		
	Art 15 Right to work		Art 36 Services of general economic interest		
	Art 16 Conduct business		Art 37 Environmental protection		
	Art 17 Right to property *Art 1 Protocol No 1*		Art 38 Consumer protection		
	Art 18 Right to asylum				
	Art 19 Expulsion, ectradition *Art 3 ECHR*				

Figure 4.2 Corresponding rights between the Charter and the ECHR according to the Explanations[79]

[79] According to the Explanations to the Charter (part on Article 52), blue-shaded provisions have no equivalent in the ECHR, red should have the same meaning and scope as a corresponding ECHR provision, and yellow should have the same meaning but have a wider scope than the corresponding ECHR provision. Note, however, that the figure merely replicates the guidance in the Explanations—in reality, more Charter rights have a corresponding provision in the ECHR and Protocols thereto (eg Article 14 ECHR is not too dissimilar from Article 21 of the Charter) which are sometimes even mentioned as inspiration in other parts of the Explanations. Nevertheless, in the absence of the Explanations explicitly recognizing such a correspondence between provisions of the two instruments, it is entirely up to the CJEU to decide whether Article 52(3) of the Charter must be applied in the application of a given provision of the Charter.

As regards the ECHR, Article 52(3) of the Charter is a potentially important clause that can in theory ensure that the EU system of fundamental rights protection will integrate and abide by the standards developed in the framework of the Convention.[80] An example of the CJEU invoking this provision can be found in *WebMindLicenses*, a case involving a tax investigation during which telecommunications were intercepted and e-mails seized without judicial authorization. Other recent examples include *A.K.* with regard to the rights to a fair trial and an effective remedy[81] and *Rayonna prokuratura Lom* with regard to the right to liberty and security.[82]

Judgment of 17 December 2015, *WebMindLicenses kft v Nemzeti Adó*, C-419/14, ECLI:EU:C:2015:832

70. In this instance, as regards, in the first place, the obtaining of the evidence in the context of the criminal procedure, it should be noted that **Article 7 of the Charter, concerning the right to respect for private and family life,** contains rights which correspond to those guaranteed by Article 8(1) of the ECHR and that, **in accordance with Article 52(3) of the Charter, Article 7 thereof is thus to be given the same meaning and the same scope as Article 8(1) of the ECHR, as interpreted by the case-law of the European Court of Human Rights** (judgments in McB., C-400/10 PPU, EU:C:2010:582, paragraph 53, and Dereci and Others, C-256/11, EU:C:2011:734, paragraph 70).

71. Thus, **since interception of telecommunications constitutes interference with the exercise of the right guaranteed by Article 8(1) of the ECHR** (see, inter alia, European Court of Human Rights, Klass and Others v. Germany, 6 September 1978, § 41, Series A no. 28; Malone v. the United Kingdom, 2 August 1984, § 64, Series A no. 82; Kruslin v. France and Huvig v. France, 24 April 1990, § 26 and § 25, Series A nos. 176-A and 176-B; and Weber and Saravia v. Germany (dec.), no. 54934/00, § 79, ECHR 2006-XI), **it also constitutes a limitation on the exercise of the corresponding right laid down in Article 7 of the Charter.**

72. **The same applies to the seizure of emails in the course of searches at the professional or business premises** of a natural person or the premises of a commercial company, which also constitutes interference with the exercise of the right guaranteed by Article 8 of the ECHR (see, inter alia, European Court of Human Rights, **Niemietz v. Germany**, 16 December 1992, §§ 29 to 31, Series A no. 251-B; Société Colas Est and Others v. France, no. 37971/97, §§ 40 and 41, ECHR 2002-III; and Vinci Construction and GTM Génie Civil et Services v. France, nos. 63629/10 and 60567/10, § 63, 2 April 2015).

---

[80] P Eeckhout, 'Human Rights and the Autonomy of EU Law: Pluralism or Integration?' (2013) 66 Current Legal Problems 169.

[81] Article 47 of the Charter cf Articles 6 and 13 of the ECHR: *A.K. and Others v Sąd Najwyższy* (n 49) paras 116–118.

[82] Article 6 of the Charter cf. Article 5 of the ECHR: Judgment of 19 September 2019, *Rayonna prokuratura Lom*, C-467/18, ECLI:EU:C:2019:765, paras 42–45.

73. Such limitations are accordingly possible only if they are provided for by law and if, in observance of the principle of proportionality, they are necessary and genuinely meet objectives of general interest recognised by the European Union.

However, and particularly in the absence of the EU's accession to the ECHR, it is only the EU courts who decide when and how to put Article 52(3) into effect. This can lead the CJEU to at times interpret Charter rights (purposely or otherwise) in a distinct manner from the ECHR even where it ought not to do so. In the sour post-Opinion 2/13 atmosphere between the Luxembourg and Strasbourg courts, the CJEU began referring to a passage in the Explanations that conditions the convergence clause of Article 52(3) of the Charter.

Judgment of 15 February 2016, *J. N. v Staatssecretaris voor Veiligheid en Justitie*, C-601/15 PPU, ECLI:EU:C:2016:84

47. (...) However, the explanations relating to Article 52 of the Charter indicate that paragraph 3 of that article is intended to ensure the necessary consistency between the Charter and the ECHR, 'without thereby adversely affecting the autonomy of Union law and (...) that of the Court of Justice of the European Union'.

The relationship between the Charter and the ECHR with respect to corresponding rights is also of relevance to the Member States, especially when they are implementing EU law for the purposes of Article 51(1) of the Charter. In *Dereci*, the CJEU has given guidance to an Austrian court regarding which legal framework is applicable when. It could be argued, however, that it is not for the CJEU to tell national courts whether another international obligation (Article 8 ECHR) should be applied if a given case falls outwith the scope of EU law.

Judgment of 15 November 2011, *Dereci and Others v Bundesministerium für Inneres*, C-256/11, ECLI:EU:C:2011:734

70. As a preliminary point, it must be observed that in so far as Article 7 of the Charter of Fundamental Rights of the European Union ('the Charter'), concerning respect for private and family life, contains rights which correspond to rights guaranteed by Article 8(1) of the ECHR, the meaning and scope of Article 7 of the Charter are to be the same as those laid down by Article 8(1) of the ECHR, as interpreted by the case-law of the European Court of Human Rights (...)

71. However, it must be borne in mind that the provisions of the Charter are, according to Article 51(1) thereof, addressed to the Member States only when they are implementing European Union law. Under Article 51(2), the Charter does not extend the field of application of European Union law beyond the powers of the Union, and it does not establish any new power or task for the Union, or modify powers and tasks as defined in the Treaties. Accordingly, the Court is called upon

to interpret, in the light of the Charter, the law of the European Union within the limits of the powers conferred on it (...)

72. Thus, in the present case, **if the referring court considers**, in the light of the circumstances of the disputes in the main proceedings, **that the situation of the applicants in the main proceedings is covered by European Union law, it must examine whether the refusal of their right of residence undermines the right to respect for private and family life provided for in Article 7 of the Charter**. On the other hand, if it takes the view that that situation is not covered by European Union law, it must undertake that examination in the light of Article 8(1) of the ECHR.

73. All the Member States are, after all, parties to the ECHR which enshrines the right to respect for private and family life in Article 8.

The CJEU established that in cases before national courts where rights protected under the Charter correspond to rights guaranteed by the ECHR, in this case respect for private and family life, the determination of the applicable fundamental rights instrument is contingent upon the assessment of the subject matter. If the legal situation is covered by EU law, the seized national court should examine the case in light of the Charter; if not, it should work with the ECHR. This is consistent with the basic principle underlying the applicability of the Charter for the purposes of Article 51(1) ('Member States implementing EU law') mentioned previously: where a subject matter falls within the scope of EU law, the Charter applies. When this is not the case, fundamental rights protection should be ensured through the closest proxy: the ECHR. At the same time, as the Court emphasized in *Fransson*, the ECHR is formally not part of EU law and therefore the relationship between the Convention and national law is not governed by it.

Judgment of 26 February 2013, *Åklagaren v Åkerberg Fransson*, C-617/10, ECLI:EU:C:2013:105

---

44. As regards, first, the conclusions to be drawn by a national court from a conflict between national law and the ECHR, it is to be remembered that whilst, as Article 6(3) TEU confirms, fundamental rights recognised by the ECHR constitute general principles of the European Union's law and whilst Article 52(3) of the Charter requires rights contained in the Charter which correspond to rights guaranteed by the ECHR to be given the same meaning and scope as those laid down by **the ECHR, the latter does not constitute, as long as the European Union has not acceded to it,** a legal instrument which has been formally incorporated into European Union law. Consequently, European Union law does not govern the relations between the ECHR and the legal systems of the Member States, nor does it determine the conclusions to be drawn by a national court in the event of conflict between the rights guaranteed by that convention and a rule of national law (...)

Nevertheless, the potential conundrums resulting from the application of Article 52(3) of the Charter from the perspective of national courts were discussed by AG Kokott in *Puškár*.

In particular, the Advocate General entertained the possibility that the application of the derogation from Article 52(3) of the Charter which enables the EU legal order to offer a higher standard of fundamental rights protection than that available under the ECHR (read inclusively with the case law of the Strasbourg Court) could lead to a violation of Article 52(3), namely when the higher EU protection of one right could come at the expense of another covered by the scope of Article 52(3). In such a situation, AG Kokott advises national courts to refer a question for a preliminary ruling to the CJEU—subject to the requirements of Article 267 TFEU—potentially to allow the Luxembourg Court to bring the differing EU and ECHR standards in line with Article 52(3) of the Charter.[83]

Puškár v Finančné riaditeľstvo Slovenskej republiky and Kriminálny úrad finančnej správy [2017] ECLI:EU:C:2017:253, Opinion of AG Kokott

123. (…) EU law permits the Court of Justice to deviate from the case-law of the ECtHR only to the extent that the former ascribes more extensive protection to specific fundamental rights than the latter. **This deviation in turn is only permitted provided that it does not also cause another fundamental right in the Charter corresponding to a right in the ECHR to be accorded less protection than in the case-law of the ECtHR.** One thinks, for example, of cases in which a trade-off must be made between specific fundamental rights.

124. If a permissible, more extensive, protection for a fundamental right is provided for in the case-law of the Court of Justice, the primacy of EU law obliges national courts to follow the case-law of the Court of Justice in the application of EU law and to grant this protection.

125. However if the national court comes to the conclusion that the case-law of the Court of Justice provides less protection than the case-law of the ECtHR in respect of a specific fundamental right provided for in both the Charter and in the ECHR, this inevitably leads to a question of the interpretation of EU law with regard to the fundamental right in question and Article 52(3) of the Charter. **That conclusion by the national court would amount to the view that the interpretation of the fundamental right in question by the Court of Justice is not compatible with Article 52(3).**

In order also to give due credit to the national constitutional traditions in the Member States and not only the ECHR, the CJEU has created the possibility for national courts to substitute the Charter by national standards even where the legal situation falls within the scope of EU law (but is not 'entirely determined' by it).[84] The caveat, echoing Article 53 of the Charter, is that the application of the national standard must not undermine the level of protection provided for by the Charter and the primacy, unity, and effectiveness of EU law. In paragraph 45 of *Fransson* (but also in other cases) the CJEU furthermore recalls the

---

[83] *Puškár v Finančné riaditeľstvo Slovenskej republiky and Kriminálny úrad finančnej správy* [2017] ECLI:EU:C:2017:253, Opinion of AG Kokott, para 126.

[84] Applied also in Judgment of 30 May 2013, *Jeremy F v Premier minister*, C-168/13 PPU, ECLI:EU:C:2013:358.

obligation of the national court to 'give full effect' to provisions of EU law, including those of the Charter. In line with its established case law, the CJEU demands that any conflicting provisions of national law are set aside by national courts, irrespective of their constitutional status.[85]

Judgment of 26 February 2013, *Åklagaren v Åkerberg Fransson*, C-617/10, ECLI:EU:C:2013:105

---

29. That said, **where a court of a Member State is called upon to review whether fundamental rights are complied with by a national provision or measure** which, in a situation where action of the Member States is not entirely determined by European Union law, implements the latter for the purposes of Article 51(1) of the Charter, **national authorities and courts remain free to apply national standards of protection of fundamental rights, provided that the level of protection provided for by the Charter,** as interpreted by the Court, **and the primacy, unity and effectiveness of European Union law are not thereby compromised.**

45. As regards, next, the conclusions to be drawn by a national court from a conflict between provisions of domestic law and rights guaranteed by the Charter, it is settled case-law that a national court which is called upon, within the exercise of its jurisdiction, to apply provisions of European Union law is under a duty to give full effect to those provisions, if necessary refusing of its own motion to apply any conflicting provision of national legislation, even if adopted subsequently, and it is not necessary for the court to request or await the prior setting aside of such a provision by legislative or other constitutional means (Case 106/77 **Simmenthal** [1978] ECR 629, paragraphs 21 and 24; Case C-314/08 Filipiak [2009] ECR I-11049, paragraph 81; and Joined Cases C-188/10 and C-189/10 Melki and Abdeli [2010] ECR I-5667, paragraph 43).

There is an inherent tension in the provisions of the Charter and the CJEU's case law in their relation to fundamental rights protection at the national level. On the one hand, Article 53 protects the standards of national constitutions against retrogression by the Charter. On the other hand, national standards may not undercut the primacy, unity, and effectiveness of EU law, including the Charter. In an ideal world, the two (three with the ECHR) sets of standards will be always in sync and even where rights protection at national level is higher than that of the Charter, it will be so in way sympathetic to EU law. The case of *Melloni*, which was decided on the same day as *Fransson*, exemplifies interactions between EU and national law, and their respective fundamental rights standards, in the real world.

---

[85] See Judgment of 9 March 1978, *Amministrazione delle Finanze dello Stato v Simmenthal SpA*, 106/77, ECLI:EU:C:1978:49.

Judgment of 26 February 2013, *Melloni v Ministerio Fiscal*, C-399/11, ECLI:EU:C:2013:107

49. Regarding the scope of the right to an effective judicial remedy and to a fair trial provided for in Article 47 of the Charter, and the rights of the defence guaranteed by Article 48(2) thereof, **it should be observed that, although the right of the accused to appear in person at his trial is an essential component of the right to a fair trial, that right is not absolute** (...) The accused may waive that right of his own free will, either expressly or tacitly, provided that the waiver is established in an unequivocal manner, is attended by minimum safeguards commensurate to its importance and does not run counter to any important public interest. In particular, violation of the right to a fair trial has not been established, even where the accused did not appear in person, if he was informed of the date and place of the trial or was defended by a legal counsellor to whom he had given a mandate to do so.

55. By its third question, the national court asks, in essence, whether Article 53 of the Charter must be interpreted as allowing the executing Member State to make the surrender of a person convicted in absentia conditional upon the conviction being open to review in the issuing Member State, **in order to avoid an adverse effect on the right to a fair trial and the rights of the defence guaranteed by its constitution.**

56. **The interpretation envisaged by the national court** at the outset **is that Article 53 of the Charter gives general authorisation to a Member State to apply the standard of protection of fundamental rights guaranteed by its constitution when that standard is higher than that deriving from the Charter and,** where necessary, **to give it priority over the application of provisions of EU law.** Such an interpretation would, in particular, allow a Member State to make the execution of a European arrest warrant issued for the purposes of executing a sentence rendered in absentia subject to conditions intended to avoid an interpretation which restricts or adversely affects fundamental rights recognised by its constitution, even though the application of such conditions is not allowed under Article 4a(1) of Framework Decision 2002/584.

57. Such an interpretation of Article 53 of the Charter cannot be accepted.

58. **That interpretation of Article 53 of the Charter would undermine the principle of the primacy of EU law** inasmuch as it would allow a Member State to disapply EU legal rules which are fully in compliance with the Charter where they infringe the fundamental rights guaranteed by that State's constitution.

59. It is settled case-law that, by virtue of the principle of primacy of EU law, which is an essential feature of the EU legal order (see Opinion 1/91 [1991] ECR I-6079, paragraph 21, and Opinion 1/09 [2011] ECR I-1137, paragraph 65), **rules of national law, even of a constitutional order, cannot be allowed to undermine the effectiveness of EU law on the territory of that State** (see, to that effect, inter alia, Case 11/70 Internationale Handelsgesellschaft [1970] ECR 1125, paragraph 3, and Case C-409/06 Winner Wetten [2010] ECR I-8015, paragraph 61).

60. It is true that Article 53 of the Charter confirms that, where an EU legal act calls for national implementing measures, **national authorities and courts remain free to apply national standards of protection of fundamental rights, provided that the level of protection provided for by the Charter, as interpreted by the Court, and the primacy, unity and effectiveness of EU law are not thereby compromised.**

63. Consequently, allowing a Member State to avail itself of Article 53 of the Charter to make the surrender of a person convicted in absentia conditional upon the conviction being open to review in the issuing Member State, a possibility not provided for under Framework Decision 2009/299, in order to avoid an adverse effect on the right to a fair trial and the rights of the defence guaranteed by the constitution of the executing Member State, by casting doubt on the uniformity of the standard of protection of fundamental rights as defined in that framework decision, would undermine the principles of mutual trust and recognition which that decision purports to uphold and would, therefore, compromise the efficacy of that framework decision.

Melloni demonstrates that in practice, a higher level of fundamental rights protection in the Member States can run counter to some constitutional objectives of the Union legal order, such as the principle of mutual trust between Member States.[86] The argument of the Court proceeds in two steps. First, the Court ascertains that the right to a fair trial does not exclude the possibility of *in absentia* trials. This provides the justificatory ground for the level of protection offered by the Charter—in the interpretation of the CJEU—which was lower than that afforded to the applicant by the Spanish constitution. Second, and more importantly, the Court reads a condition into Article 53 of the Charter which is not present in the text, namely that (higher) national standards can be applied only if they do not undermine essential features of EU law (primacy, unity, and effectiveness).

In a sense, by making the application of fundamental rights derived from national constitutions conditional upon observance of the basic principles of EU law, the Court is merely restating its long-held view on the primacy and unity of EU law that dates back to cases such as *Costa v ENEL* and *Internationale Handelsgesellschaft*.[87]

Judgment of 17 December 1970, *Internationale Handelsgesellschaft v Einfuhr- und Vorratsstelle für Getreide und Futtermittel*, 11/70, ECLI:EU:C:1970:114

---

3. Recourse to the legal rules or concepts of national law in order to judge the validity of measures adopted by the institutions of the Community would have an adverse effect on the uniformity and efficacy of Community law. The validity of such measures can only be judged in the light of Community law. In fact, the law stemming from the Treaty, an independent source of law, cannot because of its very nature be overridden by rules of national law, however framed, without being deprived of its character as Community law and without the legal basis of the Community itself being called in question. **Therefore the validity of a Community measure or its effect within a Member State cannot be affected by allegations that it runs counter**

---

[86] See also below Section 4.5.

[87] In *Costa*, one of the most revered cases in the legal history of the EU, the CJEU established the principle that EU law must take precedence over national law, as otherwise the 'executive force' of EU law would vary from one Member State to another. In *Internationale Handelsgesellschaft*, recounted in Ch 1, the Court asserted the presence of fundamental rights in EU law formally independent from national legal sources. See Judgment of 17 December 1970, *Internationale Handelsgesellschaft mbH v Einfuhr- und Vorratsstelle für Getreide und Futtermittel*, 11/70, ECLI:EU:C:1970:114.

> to either fundamental rights as formulated by the constitution of that State or the principles of a national constitutional structure.

The question posed by the entry into force of the Charter, and therefore of Article 53, is whether it ought to have changed anything about the fundamental principles of EU law, especially as they relate to national constitutions.[88] The Court's answer in *Melloni* was a resounding 'no'. It should not come as too much of a surprise; the CJEU had been willing to read the principle of primacy of EU law into the founding Treaties, so why not do so again with the Charter?

Although the principle of primacy, as well as that of direct effect, have never been codified by the Treaties, they are generally accepted by all relevant stakeholders in the EU legal order as essential characteristics of the latter. As shown in Chapter 1, while constitutional courts of Member States may not necessarily buy into the view that ultimate interpretative authority lies with the Court of Justice, or that national constitutional provisions are always to be set aside for the benefit of Union law, they will by and large accept the authority of EU laws and the CJEU's decisions in practice. As long as deference to the CJEU remains the norm and defiance the exception, the Union legal system can continue operating.[89] The fundamental rights upshot of the Court's case law is the recognition that EU-wide standards can to an extent, contrary to the wording of Article 53 of the Charter, legally undermine national human rights standards in the Member States.

The judgment in *Melloni* also contradicted the aspiration of Article 52(4) of the Charter which speaks of harmonious interpretation of the Charter with national constitutions. Indeed, the Explanations to the Charter state that the rights contained therein should seek to offer a high level of protection rather than identify the lowest common denominator among the constitutions of the Member States.

Explanations relating to the Charter of Fundamental Rights [2007] OJ C303/17

Explanation on Article 52—Scope and interpretation of rights and principles
(...)
The rule of interpretation contained in paragraph 4 has been based on the wording of Article 6(3) of the Treaty on European Union and takes due account of the approach to common constitutional traditions followed by the Court of Justice (e.g., judgment of 13 December 1979, Case 44/79 *Hauer* [1979] ECR 3727; judgment of 18 May 1982, Case 155/79 *AM&S* [1982] ECR 1575). Under that rule, **rather than following a rigid approach of 'a lowest common denominator'**, the Charter rights concerned should be interpreted in a way **offering a high standard of protection which is adequate for the law of the Union** and in harmony with the common constitutional traditions.

Yet, when faced with a conflict between a higher (Spanish Constitution) and a lower standard (Italian Constitution), the Court in *Melloni* opted for the latter as the common EU

---

[88] The Explanation relating to Article 53 provides no more guidance as to its interpretation.

[89] For a recent example of domestic defiance of the CJEU see MA Madsen, HP Olsen, and U Sadl, 'Competing Supremacies and Clashing Institutional Rationalities: The Danish Supreme Court's Decision in the Ajos Case and the National Limits of Judicial Cooperation' (2017) 23 European Law Journal 140.

level of protection, which conveniently provided fewer obstacles to the implementation of the Framework Decision on the European Arrest Warrant. It should be at the same time acknowledged that the text of the Explanations regarding Article 52(4) of the Charter technically allows for such an interpretation, as the 'high standard' of fundamental rights protection should also be 'adequate for the law of the Union'.

In this connection it is, nevertheless, worth recalling that in the past, the CJEU has recognized a higher than average level of national fundamental rights protection as a legitimate ground for restricting the free movement of services within the EU. The Court held that a prohibition on a laser-tag game in Germany was compatible with EU internal market law, recognizing the high importance accorded to the right to human dignity—to which the seized German courts considered the laser game an affront—in the German constitutional system. This finding was supported by the assertion that human dignity represented a general principle of EU law, so the German justification was in principle in concordance with EU fundamental rights aspirations (now enshrined in Article 1 of the Charter).

Judgment of 14 October 2004, *Omega Spielhallen- und Automatenaufstellungs v Oberbürgermeisterin der Bundesstadt Bonn*, C-36/02, ECLI:EU:C:2004:614

12. The referring court states that human dignity is a constitutional principle which may be infringed either by the degrading treatment of an adversary, which is not the case here, or by the awakening or strengthening in the player of an attitude denying the fundamental right of each person to be acknowledged and respected, such as the representation, as in this case, of fictitious acts of violence for the purposes of a game. It states that a cardinal constitutional principle such as human dignity cannot be waived in the context of an entertainment (...)

23. By its question, the referring court asks, first, whether the prohibition of an economic activity for reasons arising from the protection of fundamental values laid down by the national constitution, such as, in this case, human dignity, is compatible with Community law (...)

34. (...) the Community legal order undeniably strives to ensure respect for human dignity as a general principle of law. There can therefore be no doubt that the objective of **protecting human dignity is compatible with Community law**, it being immaterial in that respect that, in Germany, the principle of respect for human dignity has a particular status as an independent fundamental right.

35. Since both the Community and its Member States are required to respect fundamental rights, **the protection of those rights is a legitimate interest which, in principle, justifies a restriction of the obligations imposed by Community law, even under a fundamental freedom guaranteed by the Treaty such as the freedom to provide services** (...)

39. In this case, it should be noted, first, that, according to the referring court, the prohibition on the commercial exploitation of games involving the simulation of acts of violence against persons, in particular the representation of acts of homicide, **corresponds to the level of protection of human dignity which the national constitution seeks to guarantee in the territory of the Federal Republic of Germany.**

> It should also be noted that, by prohibiting only the variant of the laser game the object of which is to fire on human targets and thus 'play at killing' people, the contested order **did not go beyond what is necessary** in order to attain the objective pursued by the competent national authorities.
>
> 40. In those circumstances, the order of 14 September 1994 cannot be regarded as a measure unjustifiably undermining the freedom to provide services.

Therefore, the question whether a higher national standard is compatible with EU law should not be answered in the abstract—the application of common EU human rights standards is always tied to a concrete area and exercise of EU competence. Where, like in *Melloni*, the legal question in the case is regulated by harmonized EU rules, the Member States' margin of discretion to apply higher than EU-wide human rights standards will be constrained. On the contrary, the Member States should enjoy more latitude on questions which are only tangentially affected by EU legislation or in areas where the EU has not exercised its competences.

That the setting aside of national constitutional law in *Melloni* does not mean that the same outcome will be achieved in all cases concerning conflicts between various provisions of EU and national law was recently confirmed in the case known as *Taricco II*. The case was a follow-up to a previous judgment of the CJEU, *Taricco I*, in which the Court asked Italian courts to disapply statutory limitations of the Italian Criminal Code on the ground that they led to impunity for tax fraud which also affected the financial interests of the EU (Article 325 TFEU).[90] The Italian Constitutional Court pushed back against this interpretation in light of constitutional guarantees—namely the principle of legality—applicable in criminal proceedings in Italy. Unlike in *Melloni*, however, the CJEU did not insist on the application of the previous ruling if the result were to violate the fundamental rights of the prosecuted persons. The case is also a prime example of judicial dialogues between peak national courts and the CJEU touching upon the issue of which court should have the final say in the determination of a dispute when rules and legal orders collide.

Judgment of 5 December 2017, *M.A.S. and M.B. (Taricco II)*, C-42/17, ECLI:EU:C:2017:936

46. The competent **national courts**, for their part, when they have to decide in proceedings before them to disapply the provision of the Criminal Code at issue, **are required to ensure that the fundamental rights of persons accused of committing criminal offences are observed** (see, to that effect, judgment in Taricco, paragraph 53).

47. In that respect, the national authorities and courts remain free to apply national standards of protection of fundamental rights, provided that the level of protection provided for by the Charter, as interpreted by the Court, and the primacy, unity and effectiveness of EU law are not thereby compromised (...)

---

[90] Judgment of 8 September 2015, *Taricco and Others*, C-105/14, ECLI:EU:C:2015:555.

48. In particular, where the imposition of criminal penalties is concerned, the competent national courts must ensure that the rights of defendants flowing from the **principle that offences and penalties must be defined by law are guaranteed.**

49. **According to the referring court, those rights would not be observed if the provisions of the Criminal Code at issue were disapplied in the proceedings pending before it,** in so far as, first, the persons concerned could not reasonably foresee before the delivery of the Taricco judgment that that Article 325 TFEU requires the national court to disapply those provisions in the circumstances set out in that judgment.

50. Second, according to the referring court, the national court would not be able to define the particular circumstances in which it would have to disapply those provisions, namely where they prevent the imposition of effective and deterrent penalties in a significant number of cases of serious fraud, without exceeding the limits imposed on its discretion by the principle that offences and penalties must be defined by law.

51. In this respect, the importance given, **both in the EU legal order and in national legal systems,** to the principle that offences and penalties must be defined by law, as to its requirements concerning the **foreseeability, precision and non-retroactivity of the criminal law** applicable, must be recalled.

52. That principle, as enshrined in **Article 49 of the Charter,** must be observed by the Member States when they implement EU law, in accordance with Article 51(1) of the Charter, which is the case where, in the context of their obligations under Article 325 TFEU, they provide for the application of criminal penalties for infringements relating to VAT. **The obligation to ensure the effective collection of the Union's resources cannot therefore run counter to that principle (...)**

53. Moreover, the principle that offences and penalties must be defined by law forms part of the **constitutional traditions common to the Member States (...)**

54. It may be seen from the Explanations relating to the Charter of Fundamental Rights (OJ 2007 C 303, p. 17) that, in accordance with Article 52(3) of the Charter, the right guaranteed in Article 49 has the same meaning and scope as the right guaranteed by the ECHR.

58. (...) the requirements of foreseeability, precision and non-retroactivity inherent in the principle that offences and penalties must be defined by law apply also, in the Italian legal system, to the limitation rules for criminal offences relating to VAT.

59. It follows, first, that **it is for the national court to ascertain whether the finding, required by** paragraph 58 of **the Taricco judgment,** that the provisions of the Criminal Code at issue prevent the imposition of effective and deterrent criminal penalties in a significant number of cases of serious fraud affecting the financial interests of the Union **leads to a situation of uncertainty in the Italian legal system as regards the determination of the applicable limitation rules, which would be in breach of the principle that the applicable law must be precise. If that is indeed the case, the national court is not obliged to disapply the provisions of the Criminal Code at issue.**

60. Second, the requirements mentioned in paragraph 58 above preclude the national court, in proceedings concerning persons accused of committing VAT

infringements before the delivery of the Taricco judgment, from disapplying the provisions of the Criminal Code at issue. The Court has already pointed out in paragraph 53 of that judgment that, if those provisions were disapplied, penalties might be imposed on those persons which, in all likelihood, would not have been imposed if those provisions had been applied. **Those persons could thus be made subject, retroactively, to conditions of criminal liability that were stricter than those in force at the time the infringement was committed.**

61. **If the national court were thus to come to the view that the obligation to disapply the provisions of the Criminal Code at issue conflicts with the principle that offences and penalties must be defined by law, it would not be obliged to comply with that obligation**, even if compliance with the obligation allowed a national situation incompatible with EU law to be remedied (...). It will then be for the national legislature to take the necessary measures (...)

D. Difference between rights and principles in Article 52(5) of the Charter

Another contested general provision of the Charter is found in Article 52(5) which was added to the post-Lisbon binding version of the text.[91] It postulates that the Charter contains, in addition to rights and freedoms, 'principles', the justiciability of which should be more circumscribed.

Charter of Fundamental Rights of the European Union [2012] OJ C326/391

Article 52

Scope and interpretation of rights and principles

5. **The provisions of this Charter which contain principles** may be implemented by legislative and executive acts taken by institutions, bodies, offices and agencies of the Union, and by acts of Member States when they are implementing Union law, in the exercise of their respective powers. They shall be **judicially cognisable only in the interpretation of such acts and in the ruling on their legality**.

The Explanations to the Charter provide more detail about the difference between rights and principles. They specify that principles should be invoked before courts only insofar as they become part of implementing acts. The subsequent sentence also indicates the unwillingness of the EU institutions and the Member States to be held to obligations following from Charter principles. Finally, the examples of principles given by the Charter show that they are to be found primarily among economic and social rights.

---

[91] P Craig and G de Búrca, *EU Law: Text, Cases, and Materials* (6th edn, Oxford University Press 2015) 398.

Explanations relating to the Charter of Fundamental Rights [2007] OJ C303/17

Explanation on Article 52—Scope and interpretation of rights and principles

Paragraph 5 clarifies the distinction between 'rights' and 'principles' set out in the Charter. According to that distinction, subjective rights shall be respected, whereas principles shall be observed (Article 51(1)). Principles may be implemented through legislative or executive acts (adopted by the Union in accordance with its powers, and by the Member States only when they implement Union law); accordingly, **they become significant for the Courts only when such acts are interpreted or reviewed. They do not however give rise to direct claims for positive action by the Union's institutions or Member States authorities.** (...) For illustration, examples for principles, recognised in the Charter include e.g. Articles 25, 26 and 37. In some cases, an Article of the Charter may contain both elements of a right and of a principle, e.g. Articles 23, 33 and 34.

The CJEU has so far avoided interpreting Article 52(5) of the Charter. Its foremost opportunity to tackle the distinction between principles and rights arose in the case of *Association de Mediation Sociale*.[92] The case called for the interpretation of Article 27 of the Charter on the right to information and consultation of workers. While the CJEU handed down its judgment—Article 27 could not be applied to a dispute between private parties against a conflicting norm of national law—without clarifying Article 52(5) of the Charter, the preceding Opinion of the responsible Advocate General had engaged with this issue at length.[93] While recognizing that the distinction between rights and principles exists in a number of Member States and was also present in the drafting of the Charter, Advocate General Cruz Villalón was concerned about preserving the force of social and employment rights when it comes to judicial review.

Association de médiation sociale v Union locale des syndicats and Others [2013] ECLI:EU:C:2013:491, Opinion of AG Cruz Villalón

---

45. Both in the actual Charter and in the constitutional traditions of the Member States, it is common to regard as 'rights' or 'social rights' that substantive content relating to social policy which, because it cannot create legal situations directly enforceable by individuals, operates only following action or implementation by the public authorities. They are (social) 'rights' by virtue of their subject-matter, or even their identity, and 'principles' by virtue of their operation.

47. (...) The authors of the Charter relied on the experience of some Member States, where a similar distinction had allowed full justiciability of 'rights' and a reduced, or in some cases no, justiciability of 'principles'.

49. In summary, the Member States which draw a distinction similar to that provided for in Article 52(5) of the Charter have established a category complementary to that of 'rights', a category incapable of giving rise to individual rights which can be directly relied on before the courts, but which is endowed with normative force at

---

[92] Judgment of 15 January 2014, *Association de médiation sociale v Union locale des syndicats CGT and Others*, C-176/12, ECLI:EU:C:2014:2.

[93] Although the CJEU has not followed either the conclusion or the reasoning of the Advocate General, the Opinion might still prove a useful reference point should the Court attempt to interpret Article 52(5) of the Charter in the future.

the constitutional level allowing the review of acts, primarily those of a legislative nature. That idea also reflects the concern within the Convention entrusted with drafting the Charter and within the Convention on the Future of Europe. **Several Member States feared that the recognition of particular economic and social rights would result in the judicialisation of public policy, particularly in areas of significant budgetary importance**. In fact, what would ultimately be called 'principles' were described in the initial drafts as 'social principles'. Although that adjective would later be removed, it is clear that the main concern of the authors of the Charter concerned rights to social benefits and social and employment rights.

66. (…) Article 3(1) of Directive 2002/14 provides the content of the 'principle' with substantive and direct expression: the personal scope of the right to information and consultation. Needless to say, establishing of the status of the holder of a right is an essential precondition for its exercise, from which it is possible to identify the special protection provided for by the Charter. (…)

74. Although the abovementioned article of the Charter requires the cooperation of the European Union legislature, this does not mean that **such cooperation entails unlimited delegation in favour of the legislature, in particular where such delegation may lead to undermining the meaning of the second sentence of Article 52(5) of the Charter**. That would be the result if, by choosing to legislate by means of a directive, the legislature were able to deprive individuals, *in disputes inter privatos*, of the judicial review of validity which the Charter guarantees them.

The concerns about the practical relevance of Charter provisions marked as principles in the meaning of Article 52(5) have been borne out in the eyes of at least some observers. The CJEU has interpreted EU social legislation broadly already prior to the Charter and this practice seems to have been largely unaffected by its enactment. Analysing the case law of the Court, Niall O'Connor found few notable effects of the Charter in the area of social and employment law. The provisions may, nevertheless, act as a barrier against EU legislation being used to disrupt social standards.[94] The point is that ultimately it is about the willingness of the CJEU to hand down bold judgments in a sensitive area for the Member States.

N O'Connor, 'Interpreting employment legislation through a fundamental rights lens: What's the purpose?' (2017) 8 European Labour Law Journal 193

From a brief analysis of the use of the Charter as an interpretative tool, we can see that it is both evolutionary and revolutionary. It is evolutionary in that the social rights derive largely from pre-existing legislation which has long been given a purposive and usually employee-friendly reading. It is revolutionary in that the economic freedoms, although similarly steeped in long-standing jurisprudence, have emboldened the CJEU to disrupt existing approaches to the interpretation of legislation. What the case law does show is that there is a glimmer of hope that the Charter's social provisions may have bite but only if the CJEU choses to engage with them in any meaningful way. Even if the social provisions lack any real force as tools of

---

[94] For a similar but somewhat more optimistic reading of Article 27 of the Charter concerning workers' rights to information and consultation see P Herzfeld Olsson, 'Possible Shielding Effects of Article 27 on Workers' Rights to Information and Consultation in the EU Charter of Fundamental Rights' (2016) 32 International Journal of Comparative Labour Law and Industrial Relations 251.

interpretation that is not to deny the other uses to which they may be put. One might wonder whether the Charter's social rights may act as a constraint on the EU legislature's ability to amend existing employment legislation if that legislation, whether or not that legislation has been explicitly tied to the Charter through the Explanations. As the CJEU's pick and choose approach demonstrates, however, such an outcome is far from guaranteed. Of course, the present paper may be open to similar criticisms of being overly selective, having engaged only with Articles 31 and 16 of the Charter. Having said that, it has long been accepted that Article 31 is the strongest of the social rights contained in the Charter, being free from any constraints of 'EU law or national laws and practices'. If such a provision has proven incapable of influencing the CJEU's approach to interpretation, then it is unlikely that any social provision can. It can only be hoped that the CJEU will abandon its formalistic approach to the Charter by embracing a more holistic analysis of all of its provisions.

Moreover, it should be noted that the Charter also contains a provision which counterbalances social and economic rights of workers. Article 16 of the Charter provides that the 'freedom to conduct a business in accordance with Union law and national laws and practices is recognised'. While this provision resembles more a principle than a right, it is not included as one of the examples of the former in Article 52(5) of the Charter. In any case, the CJEU has invoked Article 16 in support of business freedom, notably in the cases of *Alemo-Herron* and *AGET Iraklis*.

Judgment of 21 December 2016, *Anonymi Geniki Etairia Tsimenton Iraklis (AGET Iraklis) v Ypourgos Ergasias, Koinonikis Asfalisis kai Koinonikis Allilengyis*, C-201/15, ECLI:EU:C:2016:972

---

66. In the present instance, as the referring court has pointed out, national legislation such as that at issue in the main proceedings entails a limitation on exercise of the freedom to conduct a business enshrined in Article 16 of the Charter.

67. The Court has indeed already held that the protection afforded by that provision covers the freedom to exercise an economic or commercial activity, freedom of contract and free competition (judgment of 22 January 2013, Sky Österreich, C-283/11, EU:C:2013:28, paragraph 42).

69. It cannot (…) be contested that the establishment of **a regime imposing a framework for collective redundancies such as the regime at issue in the main proceedings constitutes an interference in the exercise of the freedom to conduct a business** and, in particular, the freedom of contract which undertakings in principle have, inter alia in respect of the workers which they employ, since it is not in dispute that under that regime the national authority's opposition to certain plans for collective redundancies may result in the employer being prevented from putting those plans into effect.

86. (…) in the light of the wording of Article 16 of the Charter, which differs from the wording of the other fundamental freedoms enshrined in Title II thereof, yet is similar to that of certain provisions of Title IV of the Charter, **the freedom to conduct a business may be subject to a broad range of interventions on the part of public authorities that may limit the exercise of economic activity in the public interest** (…)

103. (…) such legislation also fails to comply with the principle of proportionality laid down in Article 52(1) of the Charter and, therefore, with Article 16 thereof.

Judgment of 18 July 2013, *Alemo-Herron and Others v Parkwood Leisure*, C-426/11, ECLI:EU:C:2013:521

31. (...) the referring court does indeed indicate that the right not to join an association is not at issue in the main proceedings. However, the interpretation of Article 3 of Directive 2001/23 [on transfers of undertakings] must in any event **comply with Article 16 of the Charter, laying down the freedom to conduct a business.**

32. That fundamental right covers, inter alia, freedom of contract, as is apparent from the explanations provided as guidance to the interpretation of the Charter (OJ 2007 C 303, p. 17) and which, in accordance with the third subparagraph of Article 6(1) TEU and Article 52(7) of the Charter, have to be taken into account for the interpretation of the Charter (Case C-283/11 Sky Österreich [2013] ECR, paragraph 42).

33. In the light of Article 3 of Directive 2001/23, it is apparent that, by reason of the freedom to conduct a business, the transferee must be able to assert its interests effectively in a contractual process to which it is party and to negotiate the aspects determining changes in the working conditions of its employees with a view to its future economic activity.

34. However, the transferee in the main proceedings is **unable to participate in the collective bargaining body** at issue. In those circumstances, the transferee can neither assert its interests effectively in a contractual process nor negotiate the aspects determining changes in working conditions for its employees with a view to its future economic activity.

35. In those circumstances, **the transferee's contractual freedom is seriously reduced to the point that such a limitation is liable to adversely affect the very essence of its freedom to conduct a business.**

36. Article 3 of Directive 2001/23, read in conjunction with Article 8 of that directive, **cannot be interpreted as entitling the Member States to take measures which, while being more favourable to employees, are liable to adversely affect the very essence of the transferee's freedom to conduct a business** (...)

E. Horizontal effect of the Charter

The abovementioned examples of disputes concerning the interpretation of economic and social rights, such as the *AMS* case, represent a class of actions which raise questions about the so-called horizontal direct effect of the Charter. The key question, put simply, is whether the rights enshrined in the Charter can be invoked in disputes between two private parties. If interpreted strictly, it could be argued that Article 51(1) of the Charter only allows the Charter to be invoked vertically, that is when one of the parties to a dispute is a public law institution of the EU or the Member State ('when implementing Union law').

Nevertheless, at least some provisions of the Charter are likely to have horizontal direct effect, an issue which ultimately depends on the determination of the CJEU. One reason for such a conclusion is that the doctrine of horizontal direct effect has been successfully established for other provisions of EU primary law, notably on equal pay.[95] Another reason is the wording of the Charter which in many instances refers to individuals, businesses, and other private parties, suggesting that some of the rights are intended to protect interests in horizontal judicial

---

[95] See Ch 7.

disputes. Indeed, the CJEU conceived of horizontal direct effect of Article 27 of the Charter in *AMS* as a possibility; the issue with that provision was in the view of the Court not its potential horizontality but the fact that it was not sufficiently elaborated and required further implementation by the means of EU legislation.[96] As the Court explicitly stated, the situation differed from the case of *Kücükdeveci* where the invoked Article 21(1) of the Charter concerning non-discrimination was in itself sufficiently precise in order to have horizontal direct effect.[97] In *Egenberger*, the Court established that the prohibition of discrimination on grounds of religion or belief, laid down in Article 21(1) of the Charter, is applicable in horizontal relations. It equally made a significant opening towards the possibility of recognizing the horizontal direct effect of Article 21 with regard to other discrimination grounds.[98] Still, the conferral of horizontal direct effect remains a vexed question not only due to legal-technical reasons (does it overstep the scope of the Charter?) but also for broader reasons relating to the role of law and in particular fundamental rights in private relations. The EU is yet to hold a deep discussion on this issue.

E Frantziou, 'The Horizontal Effect of the Charter of Fundamental Rights of the EU: Rediscovering the Reasons for Horizontality' (2015) 21 European Law Journal 657

It does not suffice merely to acknowledge that a degree of horizontality is needed in order to accommodate fundamental rights in a modern social setting. Important choices will also need to be made as to what standards we apply to penalize private breaches of fundamental rights and what kind of private actions give rise to such breaches in the first place. This exercise goes to the heart of a renewed commitment to horizontal effect, especially in the EU, where the imposition of obligations has not, so far, followed clear standards as regards the attribution of responsibility. Should all private relations be considered as potentially subject to a horizontality formula and, if so, what limits could be drawn to define it? For instance, are we to understand, per Brysk, the 'private authority relationship' as the external normative standard? Or is it more appropriate to utilize principles such as dignity as the conceptual foundation of horizontality in the field of fundamental rights, delineating the relevant obligations based on the nature of what is protected rather than the degree of power that the potential obligor might hold?

There is no denying that establishing a fully fledged and well-functioning horizontal rights system at the EU level will be challenging. However, embarking on an analysis of horizontal effect is necessary in the EU today. Questions regarding the horizontal effect of Charter provisions continue to reach the Court, despite its unwillingness openly to discuss them in its case law. Further, national courts are already being faced with cases regarding the horizontal effect of the Charter's provisions, so that settling this issue at the Court of Justice level is required in order to avoid different interpretations of the Charter across the EU. Ultimately though, developing horizontal effect in respect of the Charter

---

[96] For a legal provision to have direct effect, it is well-established in the CJEU's case law that it must be clear, unconditional, sufficiently precise, and not requiring implementing measures. See Judgment of 5 February 1963, *Van Gend en Loos v Nederlandse administratie der belastingen*, 26/62, ECLI:EU:C:1963:1.

[97] *Association de médiation sociale v Union locale des syndicats* (n 92) para 47.

[98] See Ch 7; Judgment of 17 April 2018, *Egenberger v Evangelisches Werk für Diakonie und Entwicklung e.V.*, C-414/16, ECLI:EU:C:2018:257, paras 76–77.

also likely to contribute to the setting in motion of a long-overdue, broader debate, regarding the social and political framework in which this new fundamental rights list is intended to operate. As Leczykiewicz puts it, this relates 'not only to the appropriate reach of EU law in national legal orders, but also to the appropriate balance between liberalism and public intervention, free market and social justice'.

F. Use of the Charter at national level

Although it is indeed the CJEU that is responsible for the final interpretation of the Charter, this does not mean that it would be alone in that effort. The Charter is nowadays a routine part of the work of all EU institutions, in line with the objective of mainstreaming fundamental rights across EU policies, and also of the Member States. Within the perspective of judicial protection, the manner and frequency with which the Charter is used by national courts is particularly important. An analysis of the Fundamental Rights Agency has shown that the use of the Charter varies from court to court even within the same country.[99] Moreover, the Charter is often invoked by national courts in combination with another source of human rights, most often the ECHR or the national constitution. The research has also shown that the difficult issue of scope of the Charter (Article 51) is often neglected; nonetheless, this does not prevent courts or national authorities to refer to the Charter as a source of inspiration or as an instrument guiding interpretation in situations falling outside the scope of EU law (where the Charter applies). In practice, however, the Charter has been referred to only very sparingly in the course of national legislative procedures and parliamentary debates.[100] The main obstacles to a more comprehensive use of the Charter, next to the complicated Article 51 test, have been identified as the distinction in the Charter's language between rights and principles, the lack of experience and training of legal practitioners and the fact that the legal standing of the Charter—as an instrument of primary EU law—is not made explicit in national law.[101]

EU Agency for Fundamental Rights, 'Fundamental Rights Report 2017', May 2017

More needs to be known about the Charter's 'life' at national level—the level at which the document, like EU law in general, is mainly implemented and applied. National parliaments incorporate EU legislation into national law. National governments, regional and local authorities, as well as national judiciaries apply EU law provisions and the Charter when delivering on their tasks and dealings with citizens. Whenever they act within the scope of an EU law provision, national authorities and judges are

---

[99] EU Agency for Fundamental Rights, 'Fundamental Rights Report 2017', May 2017 <http://fra.europa.eu/sites/default/files/fra_uploads/fra-2017-fundamental-rights-report-2017_en.pdf> accessed 14 August 2020, 38.

[100] Ibid, 46–50; EU Agency for Fundamental Rights, 'Fundamental Rights Report 2019', May 2019 <https://fra.europa.eu/sites/default/files/fra_uploads/fra-2019-fundamental-rights-report-2019_en.pdf> accessed 14 August 2020, 49–53.

[101] EU Agency for Fundamental Rights, 'Fundamental Rights Report 2020', June 2020, <https://fra.europa.eu/sites/default/files/fra_uploads/fra-2020-fundamental-rights-report-2020_en.pdf> accessed 14 August 2020, 20.

bound by the Charter. Against this backdrop, it is recognised that national authorities are key actors in—to borrow the words of the European Parliament—giving 'concrete effect to the rights and freedoms enshrined in the Charter'. In 2016, the parliament reiterated its call not to forget 'the importance of raising awareness about the Charter'. Moreover, on 19 February 2016, the Dutch Presidency of the EU convened a conference to exchange ideas about the challenges of applying the Charter at national level. Finally, in June 2016, the Council of the EU agreed on Conclusions on the application of the Charter, placing the national application of the Charter at the centre of attention.

Judges use the Charter for different purposes. Often national law—mostly, but not exclusively, when falling within the scope of EU law—is interpreted in light of the Charter. Sometimes domestic constitutional reviews even include checking whether a national law is consistent with the Charter. In rare cases, the Charter forms the basis for directly granting individuals a specific right. Just as in past years, it appears that the most frequent use of the Charter before national courts takes place when interpreting national or even EU secondary law. (...)

The Charter's added value as part of EU law becomes most obvious where the substantial scope of its provisions goes beyond that of comparable national norms and, in addition, these provide individuals directly with individual rights. National courts rather seldom explicitly interpret Charter provisions as granting individual rights. (...)

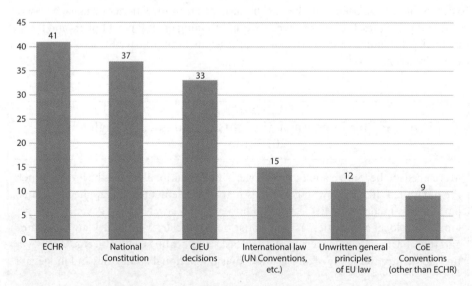

Figure 4.3 Number of references to other legal sources alongside the Charter in court decisions analysed by legal source referred to

Notes: Based on 70 court decisions analysed by FRA. There were issued in 27 EU Member States in 2016. Up to four decisions were reported per Member State, no decision was reported for Malta. More than one legal source can be referred to in one court decision

Source: FRA, 2016

FRA opinion 1.3

EU Member States should ensure that relevant legislative files and policies are checked for Charter compliance and increase efforts to ensure that Charter obligations are mainstreamed whenever states act within the scope of EU law. This could include dedicated policymaking to promote awareness of the Charter rights and targeted training modules in the relevant curricula for national judges and other legal practitioners. As FRA has stressed in previous years, it is advisable for the Member States to embed training on the Charter in the wider human rights framework, including the European Convention on Human Rights (ECHR) and the case law of the European Court of Human Rights (ECtHR).

G. Explanations relating to the Charter

Additionally to the Charter, and unlike in the case of the Treaties, the drafters prepared so-called 'Explanations'. Although they do not possess the status of law, the Explanations shed light, article by article of the Charter, on some of the rationale behind the enacted provisions. The preamble to the Charter reaffirms that the Explanations are to be taken into account in the interpretation of the Charter by courts.

Charter of Fundamental Rights of the European Union [2012] OJ C326/391

Preamble

(...) **the Charter will be interpreted by the courts of the Union and the Member States with due regard to the explanations** prepared under the authority of the Praesidium of the Convention which drafted the Charter and updated under the responsibility of the Praesidium of the European Convention.

Explanations relating to the Charter of Fundamental Rights [2007] OJ C303/17

These explanations were originally prepared under the authority of the Praesidium of the Convention which drafted the Charter of Fundamental Rights of the European Union. (...) **Although they do not as such have the status of law, they are a valuable tool of interpretation intended to clarify the provisions of the Charter.**

Explanation on Article 1—Human dignity

The dignity of the human person is not only a fundamental right in itself but constitutes the real basis of fundamental rights. The 1948 Universal Declaration of Human Rights enshrined human dignity in its preamble: 'Whereas recognition of the inherent dignity and of the equal and inalienable rights of all members of the human family is the foundation of freedom, justice and peace in the world. 'In its judgment of 9 October 2001 in Case C-377/98 *Netherlands v European Parliament and Council* [2001] ECR I-7079, at grounds

70-77, the Court of Justice confirmed that a fundamental right to human dignity is part of Union law.

It results that none of the rights laid down in this Charter may be used to harm the dignity of another person, and that the dignity of the human person is part of the substance of the rights laid down in this Charter. It must therefore be respected, even where a right is restricted.

The Explanations resemble *travaux préparatoires* in that the legislator intended them—as is clear from Article 52(7) of the Charter and Article 6(1) TEU—to serve as supplementary means of interpretation of the Charter, in line with the logic of Article 32 of the Vienna Convention on the Law of Treaties (VCLT).[102] On the other hand, the Explanations do not strictly document the preparatory work of the drafters or the progress of negotiations, as is customary for *travaux préparatoires* in international treaty-making, but rather reveal pertinent sources, as well as directions for interpretation, for the individual articles of the Charter that the drafters would like the interpreting judicial bodies to take into account.

Consolidated version of the Treaty on European Union [2012] OJ C326/13

Article 6

1. (...) The rights, freedoms and principles in the Charter **shall be interpreted** in accordance with the general provisions in Title VII of the Charter governing its interpretation and application and **with due regard to the explanations referred to in the Charter**, that set out the sources of those provisions.

4.4 EU Secondary Law

EU secondary law consists, as per Article 288 TFEU, of Directives, Decisions and Regulations. These are the three main legally binding acts which can be adopted under different procedures by EU institutions in the exercise of Union competences. In general, the difference between the three types of secondary law is that Regulations are directly applicable (require no transposition by Member States) and binding *erga omnes*. Directives are not directly applicable—they first require transposition into domestic law by Member States which must take place within the transposition period (typically two years). Decisions are, like Regulations, directly applicable but they have a more specific remit; in particular, when they are addressed to a specific natural and legal person, Decisions are only binding upon the addressee and not generally.

Although it is true that fundamental rights are on the whole primarily regulated in the realm of constitutional law—which in the case of the EU is represented by the Charter— secondary legislation can be of vital use as well, not least due to its understandably greater

---

[102] Vienna Convention on the Law of the Treaties (adopted 23 May 1969, entered into force 27 January 1980) 1155 UNTS 331.

malleability. There are a number of ways EU secondary law can be of relevance to fundamental rights. For example, it can be used to codify the case law of the CJEU;[103] define new
rights and specify the content and scope of individual rights;[104] or create an institutional
framework for the protection and promotion of individual rights.[105]

In the absence of a general fundamental rights competence,[106] the EU must rely on specific
legal bases that confer on it the possibility to create secondary legislation relevant to fundamental rights. The strength and character of the link of such legislation to fundamental rights
varies from detailed and robust regimes for the protection of a particular right (data protection) through areas where multiple rights are inherently affected or intentionally developed
by much of the legislation (criminal law, migration) to laws which on the surface have only
a minimal connection to fundamental rights (free movement of goods). Due to the cross-
cutting nature of fundamental rights protection, however, even in the latter case rights will
play some kind of a—no matter how peripheral—role. This omnipresence of fundamental
rights, especially in view of the material scope of the Charter and the legalistic character of the
EU, unsettles the constitutional principle of conferred powers, according to Elise Muir.

E Muir, 'Fundamental Rights: An Unsettling Competence' (2014) 15 Human Rights Review 25

In this contribution, it is submitted that the increased importance of fundamental rights
on the legal agenda of the European Union may question the 'constitutional' foundations of the European legal order. This is particularly the case of the doctrine of attributed
competences that governs the allocation of competences and exercise thereof in the relationship between the European Union and its Member States. The expansion of EU fundamental rights law stretches to the limits the doctrine that carefully circumscribes the
process of European integration. (...)

For example, what is remarkable from the CJEU fundamental rights case law is the
extension of the protection of certain fundamental rights from the realm of vertical relationships (individual v. public authority) to that of interpersonal relationships such as
business related activities with an EU dimension (e.g., employment situations or sale of
goods and services). EU equality Directives can thereby be directly invoked against non-
state actors. This is particularly important since EU equality legislation and EU equality

---

[103] See, for example, the 'right to be forgotten' established by the CJEU in Judgment of 13 May 2014, *Google Spain SL and Google Inc. v Agencia Española de Protección de Datos (AEPD) and Mario Costeja González*, C-131/12, ECLI:EU:C:2014:317 and subsequently codified in Article 17 of the General Data Protection Regulation. Note, however, that the right to be forgotten was already part of the proposal of the Regulation which was made public prior to the CJEU's judgment in *Google v Spain*. Nonetheless, the fact that the Court put the right into practice before the adoption of the Regulation certainly influenced its drafting.

[104] This can be of particular importance when it comes to the distinction between principles and rights in the Charter. Secondary legislation is capable of implementing provisions of the Charter which contain principles. See *Association de médiation sociale v Union locale des syndicats CGT and Others* [2013] ECLI:EU:C:2013:491, Opinion of AG Cruz Villalón, para 66. In any case, constitutional catalogues of rights, such as the Charter, are often deliberately vague and in need of further specification. This task is regularly fulfilled by courts but the legislature may also—where its competences allow—decide to enact laws fleshing out constitutional rights.

[105] See in this connection the setting up of national equality bodies under the Equality Directives; national data protection authorities and the European Data Protection Supervisor; or the Founding Regulation of the Fundamental Rights Agency, discussed in Ch 2.

[106] Opinion of 28 March 1996, *Community accession to the ECHR*, 2/94, ECLI:EU:C:1996:140, para 27.

case law apply not only to cross-border disputes but also to litigation located within a single Member State (Stone Sweet and Stranz 2012). This exemplifies the intense intrusion of EU fundamental rights law in domestic law and policy in so far as practices within a Member State fall within the scope of EU law as soon as they infringe upon the principle of equality covered in one of the EU Directives prohibiting discrimination (de Mol 2011).

(...)

The debate on the scope of application of the various EU instruments for the protection of fundamental rights reflects the difficulty of containing an individual rights-based European integration process within the boundaries established by the doctrine of attributed competences. The claims to universalism that are inherent to the very existence of fundamental rights protection enhance the pressure placed on the constitutional principle; the scope of application of EU law is likely to be interpreted ever more generously by the EU judiciary so as to enhance individual protection. Such pressure has reached its apex in proposals by academics and advocate generals to expand the scope of EU law to new types of fundamental rights violations. Most recent and advanced proposals, by von Bogdandy and his colleagues from Heidelberg on the one hand (Von Bogdandy et al. 2012) and Advocate General Sharpston on the other, suggest anchoring the expansion of the scope of EU law in the provisions on EU citizenship.

(...) Yet, particularly interesting situations occur when EU political institutions are called upon to make positive choices concerning standards for fundamental rights protection in the EU. Interestingly, European institutions may set such standards in a variety of settings that may or not be the expression of a fundamental right competence of the European Union. In other words, the EU may establish levels of protection in policy fields that are not identified in the catalog of EU competences (the EU Treaties) as directly concerned with fundamental right protection, thus at times making it difficult for those affected to understand the dynamics of EU intervention on matters of fundamental right protection. Three main types of settings may be distinguished.

The first of them is when fundamental rights are indirectly addressed in EU legislation. Such legislation may indeed primarily focus on other EU objectives such as market integration but meanwhile set standards for the protection of specific fundamental rights (De Witte 2006). The EU legislator may for example decide to harmonize certain aspects of national provisions on data protection or media freedom in order to eliminate obstacles to the internal market in services (Kosta 2013). This is illustrated by the Audiovisual Media Services Directive (2010) that contains specific provisions on human dignity and discrimination (Article 9(1)c) or reflections on the adoption of a European Disability Act (European Commission 2011) for the protection of disabled persons in access to goods and services. The dynamics of the internal market may thus be used to incidentally advance a fundamental rights agenda.

Such an instrumental use of internal market legal bases may serve for the protection of individuals but it also allows for circumvention of a direct and open political debate on the appropriateness of EU intervention to define certain core values. In this context, the difficulty lies in the fact that the competence of EU institutions to address fundamental rights matters is not explicit and is thus unclear. Both the existence of a competence to address the matter and the level of protection to be chosen are difficult to anticipate on the basis of explicit EU Treaty provisions. This blurs the constitutional framework for EU intervention in fundamental rights matters.

The second type of active intervention by EU political institutions in fundamental rights matters relates to explicit and self-standing fundamental rights legal bases. With the Amsterdam and the Lisbon Treaty, two particularly interesting legal bases have been created for the adoption of fundamental rights legislation, Articles 19 and 16 TFEU, respectively. These legal bases illustrate the difficulty for the treaty-makers to allocate institutional powers to define the content and scope of EU fundamental rights protection, as will now be illustrated.

Article 19(1) was introduced into the TFEU by the Amsterdam Treaty and enables the adoption of legislation to combat discrimination based on sex, racial or ethnic origin, religion or belief, disability, age, or sexual orientation. Following the entry into force of the Amsterdam Treaty, two Directives were promptly adopted on this basis: the 'Race' Equality Directive and the Framework Equality Directive (2000). Soon after, their adoption followed another antidiscrimination instrument on equal treatment between men and women concerning access to goods and services (2004). Despite the success of the new antidiscrimination legal base, it possesses characteristics that illustrate the discomfort of the Treaty makers with this unique competence. In the Amsterdam Treaty, the powers to legislate in this field had been granted to the Council, who were to adopt legislation by a unanimous vote upon a proposal from the Commission, and after consultation of the European Parliament.

The three directives adopted on the basis of Article 19 TFEU have thus been adopted with mere consultation of the European Parliament. The choice of such a legislative procedure may appear surprising since the European Parliament is the EU institution that carries the most democratic legitimacy and is also often seen as an institution that is favorable towards the protection of minorities. The Lisbon Treaty subsequently amended Article 19(1) TFEU to the effect that the European Parliament ought now to grant its consent to the adoption of antidiscrimination legislation. This 'take it or leave it' option in relation to antidiscrimination, as well as the maintenance of the unanimity requirement for voting in the Council have however been severely criticized (Bell 2004). This allocation of competences to legislate on the reach of EU antidiscrimination among EU institutions thus reveals the discomfort of the authors of the Treaty with this new type of competence.

Another example of a fundamental rights legal base is Article 16(2) TFEU, which is concerned with the right to the protection of personal data and was introduced by the Lisbon Treaty. EU legislation for data protection already existed (and still exists) before these proposals but it was adopted on the basis of Article 114 TFEU and was an example of an internal market instrument incidentally addressing fundamental rights concerns. In contrast, the new legal base is to be found in the Title of the Treaty entitled 'provisions having general application' and in principle stands independently from the provisions on market integration. According to the new provision, the EU legislator 'shall lay down the rules relating to the protection of individuals with regard to the processing of personal data by Union institutions, bodies, offices and agencies, and by the Member States when carrying out activities which fall within the scope of Union law, and the rules relating to the free movement of such data.' In contrast with EU antidiscrimination law the authors of the Treaty have opted for the ordinary legislative procedure. This time however, the discomfort of the Treaty makers with this fundamental rights legislative competence can be seen from their attempts to circumscribe the scope of the protection to EU activities, and that of Member States which fall within the scope of EU law and relate to the free movement of data. Although this new legal base has been given a self-standing position in the TFEU (distinct from internal market legal bases), its exact wording is unquestionably ambiguous and seems designed precisely to avoid an unlimited expansion of the scope of EU law through data protection legislation.

A third point of tension between EU and domestic competences on matters of fundamental rights protection relates to EU competences that although not directly or explicitly shaped in terms of fundamental rights protection are inherently intermingled with such rights; as is the case with EU migration and criminal law. These areas of EU law are much more inherently connected with fundamental rights protection than EU internal market law for instance. When the EU legislator regulates these sensitive fields, it makes clear and unavoidable choices on the adequate level of fundamental rights protection. This may be seen for example in the wording of the Family Reunification Directive (2003) as well as the Return Directive (2008). The Court of Justice has confirmed the fundamental rights dimension of these instruments and strengthened it by imposing fundamental rights compliant interpretations on these types of EU instruments (CJEU Parliament v. Council 2006; El Dridi 2006).

The most salient feature of the tension between EU criminal and migration competences and the scope of EU fundamental rights protection lies in the increased reliance of these emerging fields of EU law on the application of the principle of mutual recognition. Mutual recognition, originally shaped in the context of EU economic law, is transposed to areas of law of a much more delicate nature for individual freedoms. The system for the allocation of responsibilities towards asylum seekers among the Member States as well as the European Arrest Warrant, for example, have both been established by EU legislation based on the assumption that Member States provided equivalent levels of fundamental rights protection.

This has raised tremendous concerns that individuals may be transferred from one Member State to another without due regard for their fundamental rights. As a result, and on an invitation to do so by the European Court of Human Rights, the CJEU has recently ruled in relation to the functioning of the European Common Asylum System that EU law 'precludes the application of a conclusive presumption that [another] Member State (...) observes the fundamental rights of the European Union' (N.S. 2011). This approach imposes a duty to ensure that individuals would not face a real risk of being subjected to inhuman or degrading treatment if transferred to another Member State when the national authorities cannot be unaware of systemic deficiencies in that other Member State.

Although the Court's concern for fundamental rights is most welcome from the perspective of individual rights' protection, the approach chosen makes it difficult for observers to grasp the reach of EU law on fundamental rights matters. What is indeed remarkable about these developments is the way the combined use of EU legislation in sensitive fields and case law on fundamental rights results in an obligation on the Member States—flowing from EU law—to exercise a form of fundamental rights scrutiny of the practices of their peers (Canor 2013); and so, in relation to practices for which EU law standards do not necessarily exist. In other words, the principle of mutual recognition on which procedural coordination is based comes together with a form of peer review duty on fundamental rights matters in other Member States beyond the scope of EU legislative competences. One may regret that fundamental right standards are not subject to a clearer and more transparent political debate upstream the legislative process.

There is thus an inherent tension between the doctrine of allocation of competences and the dynamics of fundamental rights protection. While the doctrine of allocation of competences is thought to be the umbilical cord feeding the existence and growth of EU competences, fundamental rights protection constantly questions this one-sided feeding process in the context of both the EU passive and active protection systems. The logic of fundamental rights protection relies on a universalized and supreme vision of mankind that is designed and destined to test the limits of public control. An ever stronger fundamental rights discourse at EU level is thus hard to reconcile with the traditional doctrine of attributed competences seeking to circumscribe EU constraints on domestic policies.

It is therefore clear that in order to provide even a cursory overview of the EU secondary legislation that develops or concretises fundamental rights and freedoms, it is necessary to look at a number of EU competences provided for in the Treaties. Perhaps the most straightforward starting points are the two legal bases which specifically enable the adoption of EU legislation in the areas of data protection and anti-discrimination. As will be shown below, however, secondary legislation on anti-discrimination is not based only on Article 19 TFEU; nor is all legislation relevant to data protection based on Article 16 TFEU, as illustrated by the example of the Audiovisual Media Services Directive given above by Muir.

Consolidated version of the Treaty on the Functioning of the European Union [2012] OJ C326/47

Article 16

1. Everyone has the right to the protection of personal data concerning them.
2. The European Parliament and the Council, acting in accordance with the ordinary legislative procedure, shall lay down the rules relating to the protection of individuals with regard to the processing of personal data by Union institutions, bodies, offices and agencies, and by the Member States when carrying out activities which fall within the scope of Union law, and the rules relating to the free movement of such data. Compliance with these rules shall be subject to the control of independent authorities.

The rules adopted on the basis of this Article shall be without prejudice to the specific rules laid down in Article 39 of the Treaty on European Union.

Article 19

1. Without prejudice to the other provisions of the Treaties and within the limits of the powers conferred by them upon the Union, the Council, acting unanimously in accordance with a special legislative procedure and after obtaining the consent of the European Parliament, may take appropriate action to combat discrimination based on sex, racial or ethnic origin, religion or belief, disability, age or sexual orientation.
2. By way of derogation from paragraph 1, the European Parliament and the Council, acting in accordance with the ordinary legislative procedure, may adopt the basic

> principles of Union incentive measures, excluding any harmonisation of the laws and regulations of the Member States, to support action taken by the Member States in order to contribute to the achievement of the objectives referred to in paragraph 1.

It is worth pointing out that the number of grounds of discrimination covered by Article 19 TFEU and in relation to which the EU may decide to enact secondary legislation is dwarfed by the broad range of non-exhaustive grounds mentioned in Article 21 of the Charter. These do not, however, represent legal bases for EU legislative action.

Charter of Fundamental Rights of the European Union [2012] OJ C326/391

Article 21

Non-discrimination

1. Any discrimination based on any ground such as **sex, race, colour, ethnic or social origin, genetic features, language, religion or belief, political or any other opinion, membership of a national minority, property, birth, disability, age or sexual orientation** shall be prohibited.
2. Within the scope of application of the Treaties and without prejudice to any of their specific provisions, any discrimination on **grounds of nationality** shall be prohibited.

A. General Data Protection Regulation

The right to the protection of personal data is one of the more innovative aspects of EU fundamental rights protection, in particular as it enjoys constitutional protection as a matter of Article 8 of the Charter. Data protection has emerged as one of the mainstays in the EU's agenda in the 1990s, first not explicitly recognized as a fundamental right but later in tandem with and under the additional aegis of the Charter, especially after the Charter became legally binding following the entry into force of the Treaty of Lisbon.

G González Fuster, *The Emergence of Personal Data Protection as a Fundamental Right of the EU* (Springer 2014)

A number of elements which could be considered well-established principles applicable to the processing of personal data are not mentioned in Article 8 of the Charter: for instance, the right to receive information, the idea of control articulated through a right to erasure or cancellation, or security and confidentiality obligations.

Article 8 of the Charter has been described as an innovative fundamental right that was, however, not really new. It is certainly rooted in previously existing instruments. It innovates to the extent that it establishes that the elements mentioned deserve to be protected as elements of a fundamental right deserving protection per se, and that the protection is not exclusively granted to data in a way or another related to the right to respect for private life, but to personal data in general. In this sense, it goes beyond the scope of the protection granted on the basis of the ECHR, and of the common constitutional traditions of the Member States.

The right's name echoes the significance of previous instruments on personal data protection, but nevertheless brings forward a new notion: the 'protection of personal data', a phrase that could not be found as such in Directive 95/46/EC, and only incidentally in Convention 108 (which was overtly devoted to 'data protection'). (...)

Article 16 TFEU—the first paragraph of which reproduces Article 8(1) of the Charter—has served as the legal basis for the General Data Protection Regulation (GDPR) and an accompanying Directive on data protection in criminal matters—together one of the most significant legislative reforms at the EU level in recent times.[107] The Regulation replaces and builds on Directive 95/46/EC which has yielded a rich body of case law, including hallmarks such as the right to be forgotten,[108] and established data protection as one of the key policy areas of concern for the EU.[109] The crux of the GDPR—a complex statute otherwise—is captured in seven main principles governing processing of personal data.

Regulation (EU) 2016/679 of the European Parliament and of the Council of 27 April 2016 on the protection of natural persons with regard to the processing of personal data and on the free movement of such data, and repealing Directive 95/46/EC (General Data Protection Regulation) [2016] OJ L119/1

Article 5

Principles relating to processing of personal data

1. Personal data shall be:
   (a) processed **lawfully, fairly and in a transparent** manner in relation to the data subject ('lawfulness, fairness and transparency');
   (b) collected for **specified, explicit and legitimate purposes** and not further processed in a manner that is incompatible with those purposes; further processing for archiving purposes in the public interest, scientific or historical research purposes or statistical purposes shall, in accordance with Article

---

[107] Regulation (EU) 2016/679 of the European Parliament and of the Council on the protection of natural persons with regard to the processing of personal data and on the free movement of such data, and repealing Directive 95/46/EC (General Data Protection Regulation) [2016] OJ L119/1; Directive 2016/680/EU of the European Parliament and of the Council on the protection of natural persons with regard to the processing of personal data by competent authorities for the purposes of the prevention, investigation, detection or prosecution of criminal offences or the execution of criminal penalties, and on the free movement of such data, and repealing Council Framework Decision 2008/977/JHA [2016] OJ L119/89.

[108] *Google v Spain* (n 103).

[109] Directive 95/46/EC of the European Parliament and of the Council on the protection of individuals with regard to the processing of personal data and on the free movement of such data [1995] OJ L281/31.

89(1), not be considered to be incompatible with the initial purposes ('purpose limitation');

(c) adequate, relevant and **limited to what is necessary** in relation to the purposes for which they are processed ('data minimisation');

(d) **accurate** and, **where necessary, kept up to date**; every reasonable step must be taken to ensure that personal data that are inaccurate, having regard to the purposes for which they are processed, are erased or rectified without delay ('accuracy');

(e) kept in a form **which permits identification of data subjects for no longer than is necessary** for the purposes for which the personal data are processed; personal data may be stored for longer periods insofar as the personal data will be processed solely for archiving purposes in the public interest, scientific or historical research purposes or statistical purposes in accordance with Article 89(1) subject to implementation of the appropriate technical and organisational measures required by this Regulation in order to safeguard the rights and freedoms of the data subject ('storage limitation');

(f) processed in a manner that ensures **appropriate security of the personal data**, including protection against unauthorised or unlawful processing and against accidental loss, destruction or damage, using appropriate technical or organisational measures ('integrity and confidentiality').

2. **The controller shall be responsible for, and be able to demonstrate compliance** with, paragraph 1 ('accountability').

The principles contained in Article 5 of the GDPR expand on and clarify the much less refined Article 8(2) of the Charter. They occupy a central place in the EU data protection regime as a result of the difficulties of more traditional law-making techniques to regulate an area exceptionally complex in nature and one which is in 'constant flux'.[110] Nevertheless, the principles also set the ground for the rest of the Regulation which focuses on their translation into concrete rights for data subjects, such as rights to information, access, rectification, and erasure,[111] and obligations for data controllers who, in accordance with the principle of accountability of Article 5(2) GDPR, are charged with ensuring that data processing abides by the provisions of the GDPR.

In addition, the Regulation comprises rules on the institutional framework for the enforcement of data protection, the backbone of which was already set up under Directive 95/46/EC. The GDPR notably requires the continued operation of independent supervisory authorities (national data protection authorities) with specific duties, such as the imposition of fines at the national level, and creates the European Data Protection Board which is an institutionalised form of the former Article 29 Working Party, responsible for monitoring of the application of the Regulation and for drawing up authoritative guidelines and opinions.[112]

---

[110] P de Hert and others, 'The Proposed Regulation and the Construction of a Principles-driven System for Individual Data Protection' (2013) 26 Innovation: The European Journal of Social Science Research 133, 142.

[111] See Articles 12–22 GDPR.

[112] See Articles 58 and 70 GDPR; see also Ch 2 on institutions.

A higher degree of institutionalization and responsibility also calls for individual safeguards and complaint mechanisms to ensure that the rights of, in particular, data subjects are not trampled on or overlooked. For this reason the Regulation contains specific provisions on the right to file a complaint with a supervisory authority, the right to an effective judicial remedy against the same and against a controller or processor, the right to representation by non-profit organization, and the right to compensation and liability.[113] This set of rights, which in less robust versions exists also in other EU laws,[114] shows that secondary legislation often explicitly engages with fundamental rights other than those narrowly associated with the subject area (right to data protection). In particular, access to justice rights elaborating on the general provision of Article 47 of the Charter in the specific context of the secondary legislation, in addition to being essential components of the rule of law, are an expression of a long and deeply held concern for judicial control and remedies in EU law.[115] Although in theory such rights could also be derived by the CJEU from the Charter or the general principle of effective judicial control, their inclusion in the law (the GDPR) removes ambiguity and strengthens legal certainty of fundamental rights.

As with most rights, there are also limits to privacy and data protection posed by other fundamental rights, notably freedom of expression but also the freedom to conduct business. For example, the media disseminates publicly information about individuals who might have an interest in keeping that information private. The introduction of the right to be forgotten creates obligations and burdens which constrain search engines' freedom to conduct business. Privacy and data protection are therefore not exempt from the hard choices inherent in balancing different rights and freedoms, even though the often-conflicting right to privacy and freedom of expression can also at times be complementary. At the same time, there are intrinsic differences between the right to privacy and the right to data protection, the latter representing in part a modern take on privacy fit for the digital age.

C Docksey, 'Four fundamental rights: finding the balance' (2016) 6 International Data Privacy Law 195

The fundamental rights to freedom of expression and public access to documents on the one hand, and privacy and data protection on the other hand, are closely related and indeed partly overlapping. With regard to the latter, the roots of data protection lie in the right to privacy, and indeed the right to data protection has been developed specifically to protect privacy in the information society.

However, the two fundamental rights in each pair are not the same. On the one hand, there are the classic first-generation rights to privacy and freedom of expression, enshrined respectively in Articles 8 ECHR and 7 of the Charter and Articles 10 ECHR and 11 of the Charter. Each right consists of a general prohibition coupled with criteria justifying interference with the right.

---

[113] Articles 77–82 GDPR.

[114] See, for example, 'defence of rights' provisions in equal treatment Directives.

[115] See, for example, Judgment of 15 May 1986, *Johnston v Chief Constable of the Royal Ulster Constabulary*, 222/84, ECLI:EU:C:1986:206, para 18.

On the other hand, there are the two more modern 'active' rights, which consist of a number of specific elements, including actions to be taken and specific safeguards. The essential elements of the right to data protection are enshrined in Article 8 of the Charter and Article 16 of the Treaty and enumerated in more detail in the Data Protection Directive 95/46/EC, the Data Protection Regulation 45/2001, and the ePrivacy Directive 2002/58/EC. Similarly the basic elements of the right to access to documents are enshrined in Article 42 of the Charter and Article 15 TFEU and enumerated in more detail in the Access to Documents Regulation 1049/2001.

In consequence data protection and public access to documents are quite different to the rights to privacy and freedom of expression because they lay down positive actions to be taken rather than a general interdiction, and thus not only set forth the right but also the specific elements of the right.

(...) in some contexts, such as mass surveillance and independent regulation, the rights of privacy and data protection and freedom of expression function in a wholly complementary fashion, each reinforcing the other. As the UN Special Rapporteur has pointed out, 'the right to privacy is often understood as an essential requirement for the realization of the right to freedom of expression'.

B. Directives on equality and anti-discrimination

In the field of equality and anti-discrimination, the EU has been traditionally active in safeguarding the principle of equal pay for men and women, long before the two have become associated with the language of fundamental rights.[116] Part of the rationale behind this particular area of equality has been its link to the operation of the internal market—there are significant efficiency gains to be reaped from wage parity based on gender, and discriminatory obstacles to be taken down for the sake of the single market. The other part is the social 'face' of the Union—the idea that social objectives represent legitimate goals in the EU's policies. A provision on equal pay for men and women has been included in the Treaties from the very beginning and can today be found in Article 157 TFEU.

Consolidated version of the Treaty on the Functioning of the European Union [2012] OJ C326/47

Article 157

1. Each Member State shall ensure that the principle of equal pay for male and female workers for equal work or work of equal value is applied.
2. For the purpose of this Article, 'pay' means the ordinary basic or minimum wage or salary and any other consideration, whether in cash or in kind, which the worker receives directly or indirectly, in respect of his employment, from his employer.

---

[116] See Judgment of 8 April 1976, *Defrenne v Société anonyme belge de navigation aérienne Sabena*, 43/75, ECLI:EU:C:1976:56. See Ch 7 for a more detailed discussion of equality and anti-discrimination law.

Equal pay without discrimination based on sex means:
  (a) that pay for the same work at piece rates shall be calculated on the basis of the same unit of measurement;
  (b) that pay for work at time rates shall be the same for the same job.

3. The European Parliament and the Council, acting in accordance with the ordinary legislative procedure, and after consulting the Economic and Social Committee, shall adopt measures to ensure the application of the principle of equal opportunities and equal treatment of men and women in matters of employment and occupation, including the principle of equal pay for equal work or work of equal value.

4. With a view to ensuring full equality in practice between men and women in working life, the principle of equal treatment shall not prevent any Member State from maintaining or adopting measures providing for specific advantages in order to make it easier for the underrepresented sex to pursue a vocational activity or to prevent or compensate for disadvantages in professional careers.

The first equality and non-discrimination legislation, some of which is still in force today,[117] was adopted by the European Economic Community in the 1970s.[118] The legislation has always taken the form of Directives, as social policy remains a comparatively sensitive area for the Member States, and Directives allow, within limits, the accommodation of peculiar national attitudes in the transposition of EU laws into the domestic system. Unlike in the past, when equal treatment Directives could be based only on the predecessor of Article 157 TFEU or the internal market clause providing for approximation of laws,[119] Article 19 TFEU now contains ,a specific legal basis for the enactment of secondary legislation on the combatting of discrimination on the grounds of sex, racial or ethnic origin, religion or belief, disability, age or sexual orientation.

The consequence of having multiple legal bases has been that the EU legal order developed a plethora of Directives that serve the purpose of equality and anti-discrimination. Most of them are, nevertheless, still connected with the single market rationale by relating to employment and provision of goods and services.[120] Thus the Recast Directive prohibits direct or indirect discrimination on grounds of sex in relation to access to employment, working conditions (including pay), and occupational schemes for social security.[121] Similar ends are sought in relation to self-employed

---

[117] Council Directive 79/7/EEC on the progressive implementation of the principle of equal treatment for men and women in matters of social security [1978] OJ L6/24.

[118] Council Directive 75/117/EEC on the approximation of the laws of the Member States relating to the application of the principle of equal pay for men and women [1975] OJ L45/19; Council Directive 76/207/EEC on the implementation of the principle of equal treatment for men' and women as regards access to employment, vocational training and promotion, and working conditions [1976] OJ L39/40.

[119] Today Article 114 and 115 TFEU.

[120] Nevertheless, the Directive on access to and supply of goods and services is based on Article 19 TFEU.

[121] Directive 2006/54/EC of the European Parliament and of the Council on the implementation of the principle of equal opportunities and equal treatment of men and women in matters of employment and occupation (recast) [2006] OJ L204/23. Importantly, the Recast Directive, as well as most other equality legislation, provides for the reversal of the burden of proof (Article 19) whereby it is for the respondent (usually an employer) to prove that the principle of equal treatment has been observed when an allegation to the contrary is brought before a court.

persons,[122] general social security schemes,[123] and access to goods and services.[124] The latter includes the prohibition of unequal treatment as a result of using gender 'as a factor in the calculation of premiums and benefits for the purpose of insurance and related financial services'.[125] A part of this provision was annulled by the Court in *Test Achats* due to the fact that the Directive had not stipulated a time limit on derogations from the requirement of equal treatment in actuarial matters.[126]

Gender equality for specific groups of workers is furthermore promoted by the Directive on the safety and health of pregnant workers and the Directive on work–life balance.[127] They lay down a minimum level of requirements that must be observed throughout the EU and which entail among others, the right to maternity leave of at least 14 weeks;[128] prohibition of dismissal during pregnancy and maternity leave;[129] and an individual right to parental leave for men and women.[130] The predecessor Directive on parental leave[131] provided the legally binding foundation in EU law for the implementation of a framework agreement agreed between social partners—European employers and trade union organizations—during social dialogues at the EU level.[132] Similar Directives still exist on part-time work and fixed-term contracts.[133]

Thanks to the predecessor of Article 19 TFEU—Article 13 introduced by the Amsterdam Treaty—two Directives targeting grounds for discrimination other than gender have also become part of the *acquis communautaire*.[134] The Racial Equality Directive combats discrimination on the basis of race or ethnic origin in the contexts of access to employment, including self-employment; access to vocational training; working conditions, including dismissal and pay; membership of professional organizations; social security and healthcare; education; and access to supply of goods and services.[135] The second Directive

---

[122] Directive 2010/41/EU of the European Parliament and of the Council on the application of the principle of equal treatment between men and women engaged in an activity in a self-employed capacity [2010] OJ L180/1.

[123] Council Directive on progressive implementation of equal treatment for men and women in matters of social security 1978 (n 117)

[124] Council Directive 2004/113/EC implementing the principle of equal treatment between men and women in the access to and supply of goods and services [2004] OJ L373/37.

[125] Ibid, Article 5.

[126] Judgment of 1 March 2011, *Association Belge des Consommateurs Test-Achats ASBL and Others v Conseil des ministres*, C-236/09, ECLI:EU:C:2011:100.

[127] Council Directive 92/85/EEC on the introduction of measures to encourage improvements in the safety and health at work of pregnant workers and workers who have recently given birth or are breastfeeding (Pregnancy Directive) [1992] OJ L348/1; Directive 2019/1158/EU of the European Parliament and of the Council on work–life balance for parents and carers and repealing Council Directive 2010/18/EU [2019] OJ L188/79.

[128] Article 8 EEC Pregnancy Directive 1992 (n 127).

[129] Ibid, Article 10.

[130] Article 5(1) EU Work–Life Balance Directive (n 127).

[131] Council Directive 2010/18/EU implementing the revised Framework Agreement on parental leave concluded by BUSINESSEUROPE, UEAPME, CEEP and ETUC and repealing Directive 96/34/EC [2010] OJ L68/13.

[132] See Articles 154 and 155 TFEU. The social partners may also opt for a so-called autonomous agreement which leaves the responsibility for their implementation solely to them without involving Union law and institutions.

[133] See Council Directive 97/81/EC concerning the Framework Agreement on part-time work concluded by UNICE, CEEP and the ETUC [1997] OJ L14/9; Council Directive 1999/70/EC concerning the Framework Agreement on fixed-term work concluded by ETUC, UNICE and CEEP [1999] OJ L175/43.

[134] The third Directive adopted on the basis of Article 19 TFEU was the EC Directive implementing the principle of equal treatment between men and women in the access to and supply of goods and services (n 124).

[135] Article 3 of Council Directive 2000/43/EC implementing the principle of equal treatment between persons irrespective of racial or ethnic origin [2000] OJ L180/22.

on employment equality targets discrimination on the grounds of belief, disability, age, and sexual orientation in matters relating to employment and occupation.[136] As already mentioned, the non-discrimination legislation remains rather fragmented at present, since most discrimination grounds are only covered in the area of employment. Already in 2008, the Commission has presented a Proposal for a Council Directive on implementing the principle of equal treatment also outside the labour market.[137] The legal basis for this draft directive is Article 19 TFEU, and the required unanimity in the Council has not yet been reached.

Council Directive 2000/78/EC establishing a general framework for equal treatment in employment and occupation [2000] OJ L303/16

Article 5

Reasonable accommodation for disabled persons

In order to guarantee compliance with the principle of equal treatment in relation to persons with disabilities, reasonable accommodation shall be provided. This means that employers shall take appropriate measures, where needed in a particular case, to enable a person with a disability to have access to, participate in, or advance in employment, or to undergo training, unless such measures would impose a disproportionate burden on the employer. This burden shall not be disproportionate when it is sufficiently remedied by measures existing within the framework of the disability policy of the Member State concerned.

Directive 2000/78 also contains a short provision on the 'reasonable accommodation for disabled persons'. Rights and obligations related to issues of disability furthermore stem from the Member States' and from the EU's accession to the United Nations Convention on the Rights of Persons with Disabilities (UN CRPD).[138] Moreover, after years of discussions and delays, a self-standing European Accessibility Act was adopted in 2019.[139] This directive covers the unhindered access to certain products and services for persons with disabilities and contains extensive obligations for manufacturers, importers, distributors, and service providers.

---

[136] Council Directive 2000/78/EC establishing a general framework for equal treatment in employment and occupation [2000] OJ L303/16.

[137] European Commission, Proposal for a Council Directive on implementing the principle of equal treatment between persons irrespective of religion or belief, disability, age or sexual orientation, COM(2008) 426 final, Brussels, 2 July 2008.

[138] See Ch 5.

[139] Directive 2019/882/EU of the European Parliament and of the Council on accessibility requirements for products and services [2019] OJ L151/70. Note that the directive is based not on Article 19 TFEU, but on Article 114 TFEU on harmonization of laws in the internal market.

Directive 2019/882/EU of the European Parliament and of the Council on accessibility requirements for products and services [2019] OJ L151/70

Article 1

Subject matter

The purpose of this Directive is to contribute to the proper functioning of the internal market by approximating the laws, regulations and administrative provisions of the Member States as regards accessibility requirements for certain products and services by, in particular, eliminating and preventing barriers to the free movement of products and services covered by this Directive arising from divergent accessibility requirements in the Member States.

As a final point, it is worth mentioning that the EU equality regime allows Member States to take positive action—also known as affirmative action or positive discrimination—to tackle existing discriminatory imbalances. Positive action is legitimised by Article 157(4) TFEU as regards gender equality and by similar clauses included in all the individual Directives on anti-discrimination. Article 5 of the Racial Equality Directive provides an example as good as any other.

Council Directive 2000/43/EC implementing the principle of equal treatment between persons irrespective of racial or ethnic origin [2000] OJ L180/22

Article 5

Positive action

With a view to ensuring full equality in practice, the principle of equal treatment shall not prevent any Member State from maintaining or adopting specific measures to prevent or compensate for disadvantages linked to racial or ethnic origin.

C. Directives on rights of victims and rights of suspects and accused persons

The enactment and application of common European instruments in the area of criminal justice, such as the European Arrest Warrant and the Framework Decision on mutual recognition of judgments,[140] has led to the need to create legislation providing for minimal standards of rights across the EU. With criminal law traditionally being a national domain of action, the criminal justice systems tend to vary significantly from one Member State to the

---

[140] Council Framework Decision 2002/584/JHA on the European arrest warrant and the surrender procedures between Member States [2002] OJ L190/1; Council Framework Decision 2008/978/JHA on the European evidence warrant for the purpose of obtaining objects, documents and data for use in proceedings in criminal matters [2008] OJ L350/72; Council Framework Decision 2008/909/JHA on the application of the principle of mutual recognition to judgments in criminal matters imposing custodial sentences or measures involving deprivation of liberty for the purpose of their enforcement in the European Union [2008] OJ L327/27.

other. The EU has used this fact, along with the gradual deepening of European integration, as an argument to agree on a number of Directives laying down common standards in particular as regards the rights of victims of crimes and the rights of suspects and accused persons. The competence to legislate in these areas is explicitly indicated in Article 82(2) TFEU.

Consolidated version of the Treaty on the Functioning of the European Union [2012] OJ C326/47

Article 82

2. To the extent necessary to facilitate mutual recognition of judgments and judicial decisions and police and judicial cooperation in criminal matters having a cross-border dimension, the European Parliament and the Council may, by means of directives adopted in accordance with the ordinary legislative procedure, establish minimum rules. Such rules shall take into account the differences between the legal traditions and systems of the Member States.

They shall concern:
   (a) mutual admissibility of evidence between Member States;
   (b) the rights of individuals in criminal procedure;
   (c) the rights of victims of crime;
   (d) any other specific aspects of criminal procedure which the Council has identified in advance by a decision; for the adoption of such a decision, the Council shall act unanimously after obtaining the consent of the European Parliament.

Adoption of the minimum rules referred to in this paragraph shall not prevent Member States from maintaining or introducing a higher level of protection for individuals.

When it comes to the rights of victims, several Directives have been adopted to ensure a minimum level of protection across the EU. Central to this area of legislation is Directive 2012/29/EU which establishes in general the minimum standards on the rights, support and protection of victims of crime.[141] The Directive specifies rights in three clusters: rights relating to provision of information and support, such as right to receive information about their case and right to support services;[142] rights relating to participation in the criminal proceedings, such as right to be heard;[143] and rights relating to the protection of victims, such as right to protection from repeat victimization, intimidation and retaliation.[144] The Directive also requires that officials who come into contact with victims receive specialist training for that purpose.[145]

---

[141] Directive 2012/29/EU of the European Parliament and of the Council establishing minimum standards on the rights, support and protection of victims of crime, and replacing Council Framework Decision 2001/220/JHA [2012] OJ L315/57.
[142] Ibid, Chapter 2.
[143] Ibid, Chapter 3.
[144] Ibid, Chapter 4.
[145] Ibid, Article 25.

Other Directives provide for more detailed rules on rights of specific groups of victims. The rights of victims of humans trafficking are protected by Directive 2011/36/EU which includes the protection of child victims.[146] Children are also specifically protected under Directive 2011/93/EU in the context of combatting sexual abuse and child pornography.[147] Moreover, three instruments focus on particular cross-border elements of victim protection. The European Protection Order and the Regulation on mutual recognition of protection measures in civil matters created the possibility to transfer protection measures of both the criminal and civil kind to other Member States.[148] The third mechanism allows victims of 'violent intentional crimes' to file a claim for compensation in the Member State of residence even where these were committed in a different Member State.[149]

As regards the rights of suspects and accused persons, the EU has published a 'Roadmap on procedural rights' in 2009 which set out the legislative agenda for the step-by-step adoption of five Directives on: the right to interpretation and translation; the right to information and about rights; the right to legal advice and aid; the right for detainees to communicate with family members, employers, and consular authorities; and the right to protection for vulnerable suspects.[150]

The legislative efforts based on the roadmap have yielded six different Directives, each fleshing out a particular set of criminal procedural rights. For the moment, the roadmap appears to be legislatively exhausted with focus shifting towards effective implementation of the rights and obligations in the Directives, which is a key challenge for fundamental rights more generally. The transposition deadline for four of the adopted Directives expired in 2018 or prior (in 2013, 2014, 2016, and April 2018 respectively). First, the Directive on the right to interpretation and translation in criminal proceedings entails, among others, that suspects or accused persons receive, if needed, interpretation and translation of essential documents without incurring any costs.[151] Second, the Directive on the right to information requires that suspects or accused persons be informed—in a simple and accessible language—about their minimum procedural rights relating to: access to a lawyer, entitlement to free legal advice, information about the accusation, interpretation, and translation, and right to remain silent.[152] The Directive on the right to information furthermore states that any suspect or accused person must be provided with a so-called letter of rights. A model letter of rights is included in the Annex to the Directive.

---

[146] Directive 2011/36/EU of the European Parliament and of the Council on preventing and combating trafficking in human beings and protecting its victims, and replacing Council Framework Decision 2002/629/JHA [2011] OJ L101/1.

[147] See Articles 19 and 20 of Directive 2011/93/EU of the European Parliament and of the Council on combating the sexual abuse and sexual exploitation of children and child pornography, and replacing Council Framework Decision 2004/68/JHA [2011] OJ L335/1.

[148] Directive 2011/99/EU of the European Parliament and of the Council on the European protection order [2011] OJ L338/2; Regulation (EU) 606/2013 of the European Parliament and of the Council on mutual recognition of protection measures in civil matters [2013] OJ L181/4.

[149] Article 1 of Council Directive 2004/80/EC relating to compensation to crime victims [2004] OJ L261/15.

[150] Resolution of the Council on a Roadmap for strengthening procedural rights of suspected or accused persons in criminal proceedings [2007] OJ C295/1.

[151] Directive 2010/64/EU of the European Parliament and of the Council on the right to interpretation and translation in criminal proceedings [2010] OJ L280/1.

[152] Directive 2012/13/EU of the European Parliament and of the Council on the right to information in criminal proceedings [2012] OJ L142/1.

Directive 2012/13/EU of the European Parliament and of the Council on the right to information in criminal proceedings [2012] OJ L142/1

Annex I

Indicative model Letter of Rights

The sole purpose of this model is to assist national authorities in drawing up their Letter of Rights at national level. Member States are not bound to use this model. When preparing their Letter of Rights, Member States may amend this model in order to align it with their national rules and add further useful information. The Member State's Letter of Rights must be given upon arrest or detention. This however does not prevent Member States from providing suspects or accused persons with written information in other situations during criminal proceedings.

You have the following rights when you are arrested or detained:

A. ASSISTANCE OF A LAWYER/ENTITLEMENT TO LEGAL AID

You have the right to speak confidentially to a lawyer. A lawyer is independent from the police. Ask the police if you need help to get in contact with a lawyer, the police shall help you. In certain cases the assistance may be free of charge. Ask the police for more information.

B. INFORMATION ABOUT THE ACCUSATION

You have the right to know why you have been arrested or detained and what you are suspected or accused of having done.

C. INTERPRETATION AND TRANSLATION

If you do not speak or understand the language spoken by the police or other competent authorities, you have the right to be assisted by an interpreter, free of charge. The interpreter may help you to talk to your lawyer and must keep the content of that communication confidential. You have the right to translation of at least the relevant passages of essential documents, including any order by a judge allowing your arrest or keeping you in custody, any charge or indictment and any judgment. You may in some circumstances be provided with an oral translation or summary.

D. RIGHT TO REMAIN SILENT

While questioned by the police or other competent authorities, you do not have to answer questions about the alleged offence. Your lawyer can help you to decide on that.

E. ACCESS TO DOCUMENTS

When you are arrested and detained, you (or your lawyer) have the right to access essential documents you need to challenge the arrest or detention. If your case goes to court, you (or your lawyer) have the right to access the material evidence for or against you.

F. INFORMING SOMEONE ELSE ABOUT YOUR ARREST OR DETENTION/ INFORMING YOUR CONSULATE OR EMBASSY

When you are arrested or detained, you should tell the police if you want someone to be informed of your detention, for example a family member or your employer. In certain cases the right to inform another person of your detention may be temporarily restricted. In such cases the police will inform you of this.

If you are a foreigner, tell the police if you want your consular authority or embassy to be informed of your detention. Please also tell the police if you want to contact an official of your consular authority or embassy.

G. URGENT MEDICAL ASSISTANCE

When you are arrested or detained, you have the right to urgent medical assistance. Please let the police know if you are in need of such assistance.

H. PERIOD OF DEPRIVATION OF LIBERTY

After your arrest you may be deprived of liberty or detained for a maximum period of ... [fill in applicable number of hours/days]. At the end of that period you must either be released or be heard by a judge who will decide on your further detention. Ask your lawyer or the judge for information about the possibility to challenge your arrest, to review the detention or to ask for provisional release.

The third Directive concerns the right of access to a lawyer and the right to communicate with third persons.[153] It stipulates that the right of access to a lawyer applies from the outset of police questioning and includes the right to confidential meetings between the suspect and their lawyer.[154] The right to communicate with a third person means that suspects or accused persons are entitled to communicate without undue delay with at least one third person, designated by them.[155] Fourth, the Directive on strengthening the presumption of innocence provides for, among others, a prohibition on public authorities to make public statements about the guilt of the suspect before proven guilty.[156]

The fifth and sixth Directive were due to be transposed in 2019 and concern the rights of children and the right to legal aid.[157] The former provides additional child-specific rights to the general fundamental rights protection of suspects, such as more extensive assistance by a lawyer, informing of parents, or audiovisual recording of questioning.[158] Finally, the Directive on the right to legal aid requires that suspects and accused persons without sufficient resources have the right to legal aid 'when the interests of justice so require'. The Directive then lays down the criteria according to which Member States can make the assessment of the material and legal situation of the defendant.[159] In line with the objectives of the

---

[153] Directive 2013/48/EU of the European Parliament and of the Council on the right of access to a lawyer in criminal proceedings and in European arrest warrant proceedings, and on the right to have a third party informed upon deprivation of liberty and to communicate with third persons and with consular authorities while deprived of liberty [2013] OJ L294/1.

[154] Ibid, Articles 3 and 4.

[155] Ibid, Article 6.

[156] Article 4 of Directive 2016/343/EU of the European Parliament and of the Council on the strengthening of certain aspects of the presumption of innocence and of the right to be present at the trial in criminal proceedings [2016] OJ L65/1.

[157] Directive 2016/800/EU of the European Parliament and of the Council on procedural safeguards for children who are suspects or accused persons in criminal proceedings [2016] OJ L132/1; Directive 2016/1919/EU of the European Parliament and of the Council on legal aid for suspects and accused persons in criminal proceedings and for requested persons in European arrest warrant proceedings [2016] OJ L297/1.

[158] See Articles 6, 7, and 9 of EU Directive on procedural safeguards for accused children 2016 (n 157).

[159] See Article 4 of EU Directive on legal aid for suspects and accused persons in criminal proceedings 2016 (n 157).

roadmap, all the procedural rights Directives contain a clause on the specific treatment of vulnerable persons.

Most of the legislation on criminal law enacted in the EU—and especially those Directives that focus on rights of individuals—is not invented out of thin air by European legislators but often follows and reproduces, to a varying degree, the already well-developed case law of the ECtHR, while at the same time striving to find the right balance for the purposes of EU law. The secondary legislation in turn contributes to the definition and realization of rights relevant to criminal procedure found mainly in Title VI of the Charter or rights protected as a matter of general principles of EU law.[160] Regardless, implementation of the Directives in the Member States is not always straightforward and in some instances it can require substantial modifications to the domestic criminal justice systems. For example, a number of Member States had to introduce in their legal orders from scratch the concept of 'victim' and its standing in the criminal proceedings. Research shows that even though the transposition phases for all six Directives have expired, their provisions are still far from implemented by all Member States.[161]

The foregoing overview of secondary legislation on rights in criminal procedure in the EU provides merely a glimpse of the impact of EU-level legal instruments in this area. Almost all criminal law is very closely tied up with issues of fundamental rights, and EU legislation is no exception in this regard. Crimes almost inherently impinge upon fundamental rights of others, while criminal proceedings and penal sanctions restrict fundamental rights of suspects and perpetrators. It is the role of fundamental rights law and adjudication to ensure that the application of criminal law does not result in illegitimate infringements of fundamental rights of any of the parties concerned, be they victims, suspects, or convicted persons.[162] At the same time, the legislators and courts are faced with the perpetual difficulty of striking the right balance between, on the one hand, the effectiveness of the criminal procedure, and, on the other hand, guaranteeing a level of fundamental rights protection which complies with international, European, and domestic standards.[163] It has been argued that the more recent pattern of legislative activity at the EU level has served to correct an imbalance in the nexus between security and human rights prior to the Treaty of Lisbon.

C Harding, 'EU Criminal Law under the Area of Freedom, Security, and Justice' in D Chalmers and A Arnull (eds), *The Oxford Handbook of European Union Law* (Oxford University Press 2015)

(...) as the concept of the AFSJ became fleshed out, concerns began to emerge regarding a bias towards security, and the overall coherence of the AFSJ package of policy and activity. The question remains concerning the interrelation between and the precise interpretation and role of the elements of freedom, security, and justice.

---

[160] Another right that tends to be critically affected by the regulation of criminal justice systems is the prohibition of torture and inhuman or degrading treatment or punishment (Article 4 of the Charter).

[161] C Riehle and A Clozel, '10 Years after the Roadmap: Procedural Rights in Criminal Proceedings in the EU Today' (2020) 20 ERA Forum 321.

[162] See generally S Trechsel and S Summers, *Human Rights in Criminal Proceedings* (Oxford University Press 2005).

[163] At the EU level, fundamental rights tensions are most clearly manifested in the application of the principle of mutual trust and in the effectiveness of European criminal law instruments, such as the European Arrest Warrant.

It may be plausibly argued that, insofar as the AFSJ is a matter of crime control, then the balancing of individual freedom and collective or public security reflects a natural tension within the field of criminal law, as articulated in Packer's classic analysis and then mediated through a legal balancing exercise within the framework of human rights protection. The discussion excited by the flurry of anti-terrorist activity, which resulted in a number of EU measures in the early years of this century, provides a characteristic example of such freedom v security critical debate. The 'justice' element of the AFSJ may then be seen as that mediating process which seeks to reconcile and accommodate these competing objectives, and in the European context signals the significant relevance of both the European Human Rights Convention (ECHR) and the EU Charter of Fundamental Rights for developing EU criminal law. It is significant also in this connection to note the emphasis placed on human rights arguments in the 2009 Stockholm Programme. In its opening statement for the Programme, the European Council refers first to the need to focus on the interests and needs of citizens and to ensure respect for fundamental freedoms and integrity while guaranteeing security, and that the AFSJ must 'above all be a single area in which fundamental rights are protected'. The stronger commitment to the 'rights agenda' that has emerged post-Lisbon, evident for instance in the revitalized legislative programme in relation to defence rights, may be seen as a move towards rebalancing the freedom/security tension within the AFSJ.

The evolution of the AFSJ as a legal concept is now best encapsulated in Article 67 of the TFEU, located at the beginning of Title V of the Treaty. Article 67 represents some reconfiguration and different emphasizing of the previous Treaty provisions relating to the AFSJ (Articles 29 EU and 67 EC). In particular, the present Article 67 emphasizes in its first paragraph the respect for fundamental rights and the diversity of national legal systems and traditions, so giving rights protection and legal diversity a sure place and guiding role in the whole AFSJ project. This tenor is maintained in the following paragraphs, with references to fairness towards third-country nationals in paragraph 2 and the role of the Union in facilitating access to justice in paragraph 4. Moreover, the role of mutual recognition as the 'cornerstone' of legal development in this field of action is recognized in both the third and fourth paragraphs of Article 67. Meanwhile, the substance of the AFSJ is summarized in two main objectives: internal freedom of movement, secured through a common position on external borders, immigration and asylum; and internal security secured through a common position and effective cooperation on crime, racism, and xenophobia. It is also significant that the latter are grouped together as threats to security, justifying common EU action.

D. Free movement, immigration, and asylum

Similarly to the area of criminal law, the legislative regulation of migration has severe repercussions for the rights and freedoms of individuals. The most critical intersections of migration law and policy with fundamental rights are examined in depth in Chapter 8. The present section has the more modest goal of looking at some of the provisions of EU secondary legislation which flesh out the rights of various groups of migrants (EU citizens and workers, third country nationals, asylum seekers). The types of legislative measures vary in their legal bases and context from those originating in internal market and citizenship legislation, such as the Regulation on free movement of workers and Directive on free movement of EU citizens, to those belonging to the Area of Freedom, Security and Justice, such as rules on immigration and asylum.

When it comes to, first, the free movement rights of EU citizens, these represent one of the cornerstones of the EU's identity. As such, they are protected under both the TFEU and the Charter.

Consolidated version of the Treaty on the Functioning of the European Union [2012] OJ C326/47

Article 20

1. Citizenship of the Union is hereby established. **Every person holding the nationality of a Member State shall be a citizen of the Union.** Citizenship of the Union shall be additional to and not replace national citizenship.
2. Citizens of the Union shall enjoy the rights and be subject to the duties provided for in the Treaties. They shall have, inter alia:
   (a) the right to move and reside freely within the territory of the Member States;

Article 21

1. Every citizen of the Union shall have **the right to move and reside freely within the territory of the Member States**, subject to the limitations and conditions laid down in the Treaties and by the measures adopted to give them effect.
2. If action by the Union should prove necessary to attain this objective and the Treaties have not provided the necessary powers, the European Parliament and the Council, acting in accordance with the ordinary legislative procedure, may adopt provisions with a view to facilitating the exercise of the rights referred to in paragraph 1.
3. For the same purposes as those referred to in paragraph 1 and if the Treaties have not provided the necessary powers, the Council, acting in accordance with a special legislative procedure, may adopt measures concerning social security or social protection. The Council shall act unanimously after consulting the European Parliament.

Charter of Fundamental Rights of the European Union [2012] OJ C326/391

Freedom of movement and of residence

1. Every citizen of the Union has the right to move and reside freely within the territory of the Member States.
2. Freedom of movement and residence may be granted, in accordance with the Treaties, to nationals of third countries legally resident in the territory of a Member State.

The most important piece of secondary law relating to the free movement of EU citizens is Directive 2004/38/EC.[164] It applies to all EU citizens and sets out the legal framework for the enjoyment of rights of movement and residence, as well as of their family members under specific circumstances. The Directive specifies, among others, that EU citizens: can enter and exit other Member States without visa or similar formalities;[165] have the right of residence in another Member State for up to three months without any conditions other than holding a valid identity card or passport;[166] have the right of residence beyond three months as long as they are (self-)employed, studying, or have sufficient resources in order not to become a burden on the host Member State;[167] and have the right to permanent residence after a continuous period of legal residence of five years.[168]

N Nic Shuibhne, 'The Developing Legal Dimensions of Union Citizenship' in D Chalmers and A Arnull (eds), *The Oxford Handbook of European Union Law* (Oxford University Press 2015)

(...) citizenship has both enriched pre-existing EU rights and established novel dimensions of the scope of EU law more autonomously beyond the threshold of economic activity—and even, in exceptional circumstances, beyond the conventional free movement law threshold of cross-border connections. Its intersection with questions of a constitutional nature about sovereignty, rights, and the boundaries between EU and state competences means that the development of citizenship law represents, in several respects, a microcosm of the development of EU law more generally. In addition, its acute resonance with broader debates on identity, migration, and social priorities underscores its critical role, both actual and potential, in current disputes about the role and even the future of the EU.

(...) Directive 2004/38 was intended to have both simplifying or consolidating and rights-strengthening purposes. Examples of the latter objective include the enhanced protection established for the family members of Union citizens in situations of the death of the citizen or his/her departure from a host state (Article 12) as well as in cases of divorce, annulment of marriage, or termination of a registered partnership (Article 13). The rights-strengthening impulse of the Directive reflected a dynamic that was clearly evident in case law on the free movement of persons more generally. For example, reflecting the Union's incrementally deepening concern for the protection of fundamental rights, respect for the family life of Union citizens had become a powerful source of material rights in the case law—whether the applicant was engaged in economic activity or not. More generally, the Court has consistently stressed that the provisions of the Directive should not be interpreted restrictively. It has also continued to require that qualitative,

---

[164] Directive 2004/38/EC of the European Parliament and of the Council on the right of citizens of the Union and their family members to move and reside freely within the territory of the Member States amending Regulation (EEC) No 1612/68 and repealing Directives 64/221/EEC, 68/360/EEC, 72/194/EEC, 73/148/EEC, 75/34/EEC, 75/35/EEC, 90/364/EEC, 90/365/EEC, and 93/96/EEC [2004] OJ L158/77.
[165] Ibid, Article 4(1) and Article 5(1).
[166] Ibid, Article 6.
[167] Ibid, Article 7(1).
[168] Ibid, Article 16, but see Article 17 for exemptions from the general rule.

case-by-case assessments of individual situations must be made when the determination of eligibility for EU rights protection is at stake.

(...) Permanent residence is one of the most important innovations of the Directive. Recital 17 of the preamble asserts that the status 'would strengthen the feeling of Union citizenship and is a key element in promoting social cohesion'. Article 16(1) confers a right of permanent residence on Union citizens 'who have resided legally for a con-tinuous period of five years in the host Member State'. Article 16(2) extends the right to third-country national family members who meet the same criteria—in effect, shifting their situation at this point from derived towards more autonomous rights. Conditions regarding permitted interruptions to continuity of residence are outlined in Article 16(3), and, according to Article 16(4), the right will be lost only through absence from the host state for a period exceeding two consecutive years. Articles 17 and 18 set out a series of exemptions and other conditions, for example on the acquisition of the right before five years in certain cases, and Articles 19–21 outline relevant administrative formalities.

(...) The legal basis on which a Member State national resides in a host state can be linked to Union law where the individual meets the conditions of Directive 2004/38, including the requirement of either economic activity or financial self-sufficiency in ac-cordance with Article 7. Conversely, where a condition required by the Directive is not fulfilled, an EU basis for lawful residence cannot normally be claimed. However, as the Court emphasized in *Martínez Sala*, Member State nationals might be lawfully resident in a host state on the basis of national law. In such cases, they fall within the personal scope of Articles 20 and 21 TFEU and the host state is, in consequence, bound by the require-ments of non-discrimination on the grounds of nationality for any related claims that fall within the material scope of EU law.

(...) The Court has consistently confirmed that the material scope of the Treaty cannot be extended to 'internal situations which have no link with [Union] law'. This does not mean that situations that are purely internal to one state can never come within the scope of the Treaty. But it does mean that a 'link' with Union law must be established. For citi-zenship law, a cross-border connection normally provides the relevant link—usually, but not necessarily, through the exercise of movement.

Markedly, the adjudication concerning the rights of EU citizens protected by, among others, Directive 2004/38/EC has in recent years undergone an adverse shift which saw the CJEU become more reluctant to interpret the free movement rights of EU citizenship expan-sively.[169] In light of the overlapping and multi-instrument fundamental rights architecture in the EU, such a more restrictive approach is liable to also negatively affect rights guaranteed by the EU Charter of Fundamental Rights and/or international human rights law. The CJEU has demonstrably prevaricated in some instances when it came to the application of dedi-cated human rights instruments in cases about EU citizenship, not least in the *Alimanovic* case.[170]

---

[169] D Thym, 'When Union Citizens Turn into Illegal Migrants: The Dano Case' (2015) 40 European Law Review 249, 252.

[170] Judgment of 15 September 2015, *Jobcenter Berlin Neukölln v Alimanovic and Others*, C-67/14, ECLI:EU:C:2015:597.

K Hamenstädt, 'The impact of the duration of lawful residence
on the rights of European Union citizens and their third-country
family members' (2017) 24 Maastricht Journal of European and
Comparative Law 63

In the so-called 'constituent phase' of the case law on European Union citizenship, the CJEU held in its often quoted *Grzelczyk* judgment that 'Union citizenship is destined to be the fundamental status of nationals of the Member States, enabling those who find themselves in the same situation to enjoy the same treatment in law irrespective of their nationality, subject to such exceptions as are expressly provided for.' This judgment is embedded in a series of other judgments such as *Martinez Sala*, *D'Hoop*, *MRAX*, and *Baumbast* and *R* (...) The equal treatment component of the *Grzelczyk* formula seems to have governed the development of Union citizenship also in the following so-called consolidation phase, in which the CJEU refined its case law and which is marked by the codification of the Court's case law in Directive 2004/38/EC.

Over the last couple of years we have witnessed a conceptual shift in the CJEU's approach to Union citizenship. This shift is said to be 'characterised by an apparent retreat from the Court's original vision of citizenship in favour of a minimalist interpretation' (...)

As to the applicability of the Charter, the *Alimanovic* case differs from the *Dano* case in one significant respect. While the Court held in *Dano* that the conditions for the granting of these benefits that were in dispute were not regulated by secondary legislation with the consequence that the Member State was not implementing Union law within the meaning of Article 51(1) of the Charter, Ms Alimanovic and her daughter were able to rely on Article 14(4)(b) of the Citizenship Directive and consequently they had a right of residence on the basis of this provision or rather its German implementing law. By applying the German provision that implemented Article14(4)(b) of the Citizenship Directive, national authorities implemented Union law in terms of Article 51(1) of the Charter and were consequently bound by the Charter. The Charter in turn requires that an individual assessment and balancing process are conducted when it concerns the right to private and family life (Article 7 of the Charter). Given that Ms Alimanovic gave birth to her three children in Germany, it is startling that the CJEU did not address Article 7 of the Charter. Moreover, an application of the Charter would have given the Court the chance to elaborate on Article 34 of the Charter (which pertains to social security and social assistance).

Nevertheless, until recently the rise of EU fundamental rights and citizenship was concomitant. Judgments such as *Ruiz Zambrano* and *Rottman* gave hope to many an observer that the two concepts would become inextricably linked at a fundamental level.[171] Instead, cases such as *Alimanovic* brought thinking about rights and citizenship back to planet EU where fundamental rights guarantees are linked to the exercise of Union citizenship which

---

[171] Judgment of 8 March 2011, *Ruiz Zambrano v Office national de l'emploi*, C-34/09, ECLI:EU:C:2011:124; Judgment of 2 March 2010, *Rottmann v Freistaat Bayern*, C-135/08, ECLI:EU:C:2010:104.

has the side-effect of reverse discrimination—those EU citizens who 'stay put' and do not exercise their free movement rights enjoy lesser protection under EU law than those who move across Member States' borders (which for Schengen members are not even physically in place).[172] EU citizens are as a result not all equal and EU citizenship does not function properly as a basic federal status.[173] This choice has been consciously embedded in the Treaties and it is difficult to expect the judiciary or the legislature to overturn it without a Treaty amendment.

S Iglesias Sánchez, 'Fundamental Rights and Citizenship of the Union at a Crossroads: A Promising Alliance or a Dangerous Liaison?' (2014) 20 European Law Journal 464

The intersection between European citizenship and fundamental rights is extremely complex to articulate without pushing the contours of one of them beyond the carefully built-up constitutional balances, since their underlying rationales give rise to significant tensions and difficulties when assessing the possible ways forward. The inter-state dimension of integration being still far from completed, the emphasis has traditionally been put on the reassurance of the protection and enjoyment of rights of Union citizens against Member States other than the one of nationality. Nonetheless, such an approach widens the gap between the status of movers and non-movers aggravating the phenomenon of reverse discrimination, even in the field of fundamental rights, and therefore, undermining the aspirations towards equal rights, enshrined in the ideal of citizenship. On the other hand, a competence-based approach, even if desirable for its suitability to create areas of uniform protection matching the fields of political responsibility of the Union, is controversial. In this regard, the difficulties lie with the overlapping of powers and with the complexity of the system of allocation of competences. These solutions are potentially pervasive and would need, in any case, a wide institutional backing and a revision of the Treaties.

Returning to EU secondary law, related to the Directive on citizenship is the codified Regulation on the free movement of workers.[174] The Regulation is based on the primary right to work in any Member State of the EU protected by the Treaties from the very beginning of European integration and which has been subject to extensive interpretation by the CJEU throughout the decades. More recently, however, this foundational principle has come under sustained fire in the political discourse in a number of Member States,[175] most visibly in the run-up to the British referendum on leaving the EU of 23 June 2016 which resulted in the 'Brexit' of the United Kingdom.

---

[172] See, for example, A Tryfonidou, 'Reverse Discrimination in Purely Internal Situations: An Incongruity in a Citizens' Europe' (2008) 23 Legal Issues of Economic Integration 43.
[173] D Kochenov (ed), *EU Citizenship and Federalism: The Role of Rights* (Cambridge University Press 2017).
[174] Regulation (EU) 492/2011 of the European Parliament and of the Council on freedom of movement for workers within the Union [2011] OJ L141/1.
[175] E Spaventa, 'The Free Movement of Workers in the Twenty-first Century' in A Arnull and D Chalmers (eds), *The Oxford Handbook of European Union Law* (Oxford University Press 2015).

> ## Consolidated version of the Treaty on the Functioning of the European Union [2012] OJ C326/47
>
> ### Article 45
> 1. **Freedom of movement for workers shall be secured within the Union.**
> 2. Such freedom of movement shall **entail the abolition of any discrimination based on nationality** between workers of the Member States as regards employment, remuneration and other conditions of work and employment.
> 3. It shall entail the right, subject to limitations justified on grounds of public policy, public security or public health:
>   (a) to accept offers of employment actually made;
>   (b) to move freely within the territory of Member States for this purpose;
>   (c) to stay in a Member State for the purpose of employment in accordance with the provisions governing the employment of nationals of that State laid down by law, regulation or administrative action;
>   (d) to remain in the territory of a Member State after having been employed in that State, subject to conditions which shall be embodied in regulations to be drawn up by the Commission.
> 4. The provisions of this Article shall not apply to employment in the public service.

The essential rationale of the Regulation on free movement of workers within the EU is the elimination of discrimination against EU workers on the ground of nationality. This entails in particular that national laws in Member States may not prescribe requirements that would lead to either direct or indirect exclusion of nationals of other Member States from employment opportunities, or to the restriction of the number of EU workers from other Member States.[176] Furthermore, the Regulation covers some employment and social rights of migrating EU workers. The terms of employment, especially regarding pay, dismissal, social and tax advantages, and even membership of trade unions, must be the same for all EU workers in a given Member State.[177] Workers from other Member States are also entitled to the same rights and benefits in relation to housing,[178] while their children have the right to access the educational system under the same conditions as the children of the host Member State.[179]

As opposed to EU citizens—workers or otherwise—the legislation on immigration of non-EU nationals is governed by the Treaties under the heading of the Area of Freedom, Security and Justice.[180] More specifically, a number of EU secondary laws on immigration have been adopted on the basis of Article 79(2) TFEU. Notably, however, EU Member States have been so far reluctant to exercise the legislative powers when it comes to defining the legal conditions of entry and residence, including long-term visas, for third country

---

[176] Articles 1–4 of EU Regulation on free movement of workers within the EU 2011 (n 174).
[177] Ibid, Articles 7 and 8.
[178] Ibid, Article 9.
[179] Ibid, Article 10.
[180] Note, however, that insofar as third-country nationals are also family members of EU citizens, many of the pertinent legal situations are covered by EC Directive on the rights of EU citizens and their family members 2004 (n 164).

nationals under point (a) of Article 79(2) TFEU. The absence of a general framework on legal routes to the EU—with the narrow exceptions of Directive 2016/801 and Directive 2009/50[181]—is an important part of the broader debate on EU migration policies discussed in depth in Chapter 8.

Consolidated version of the Treaty on the Functioning of the European Union [2012] OJ C326/47

Article 79

1. The Union shall develop a common immigration policy aimed at ensuring, at all stages, the efficient management of migration flows, fair treatment of third-country nationals residing legally in Member States, and the prevention of, and enhanced measures to combat, illegal immigration and trafficking in human beings.
2. For the purposes of paragraph 1, the European Parliament and the Council, acting in accordance with the ordinary legislative procedure, shall adopt measures in the following areas:
   (a) the conditions of entry and residence, and standards on the issue by Member States of long-term visas and residence permits, including those for the purpose of family reunification;
   (b) the definition of the rights of third-country nationals residing legally in a Member State, including the conditions governing freedom of movement and of residence in other Member States;
   (c) illegal immigration and unauthorised residence, including removal and repatriation of persons residing without authorisation;
   (d) combating trafficking in persons, in particular women and children.
3. The Union may conclude agreements with third countries for the readmission to their countries of origin or provenance of third-country nationals who do not or who no longer fulfil the conditions for entry, presence or residence in the territory of one of the Member States.
4. The European Parliament and the Council, acting in accordance with the ordinary legislative procedure, may establish measures to provide incentives and support for the action of Member States with a view to promoting the integration of third-country nationals residing legally in their territories, excluding any harmonisation of the laws and regulations of the Member States.
5. This Article shall not affect the right of Member States to determine volumes of admission of third-country nationals coming from third countries to their territory in order to seek work, whether employed or self-employed.

---

[181] See Directive 2016/801/EU of the European Parliament and of the Council on the conditions of entry and residence of third-country nationals for the purposes of research, studies, training, voluntary service, pupil exchange schemes or educational projects and au pairing [2016] OJ L132/21 and Council Directive 2009/50/EC on the conditions of entry and residence of third-country nationals for the purposes of highly qualified employment [2009] OJ L155/17.

Where the EU has adopted common rules on immigration, these have taken almost always the form of directives rather than regulations. As a result, implementation of EU rules varies significantly from one Member State to another, but, in general, the Member States have tended to restrict the rights of migrants in their domestic application of the relevant EU legislation. Two EU directives adopted in 2003, in particular, have had significant implications for the rights of third-country nationals in the EU.

First, Directive 2003/109/EC on the status of long-term residents in the EU from third countries harmonizes to an extent the conditions under which non-EU citizens should be accorded long-term resident status in a Member State and the conditions under which such long-term residents may move between Member States.[182] Importantly, the Directive also specifies that long-term resident status entails the right to equal treatment with nationals of the Member State in question but only with respect to areas explicitly enumerated in Article 11(1) of the Directive.[183] At the same time, however, a series of exceptions built into the Directive afford the Member States considerable discretion to derogate from the principle of equal treatment of third-country nationals who are long-term residents.[184] The same is true, *mutatis mutandi*, about the equal treatment of third-country workers who are not long-term residents in Directive 2011/98/EU.[185]

Second, Directive 2003/86/EC on the right to family reunifications sets out the conditions for the reunification of the so-called sponsors—third-country nationals holding a valid residence permit for at least one year with reasonable prospects of obtaining permanent residence rights—with their family members (chiefly spouses and minor children) from outside the EU.[186] The Directive, which also applies to refugees, was challenged before the CJEU by the EP on the ground that several of its provisions permitting derogations from granting the right to family reunification ran counter to fundamental rights requirements, especially as following from Article 8 ECHR on the right to respect for family life.[187] The Court, however, dismissed the action by finding that the Directive does not authorize fundamental rights violations and that in any case it leaves the Member States sufficiently wide discretion to implement the EU rules in a manner consistent with fundamental rights requirements.[188] In a number of other cases, the Court has taken a keener interest in protecting the fundamental right of family reunification with nationals of non-EU countries.[189]

---

[182] See Article 5 and Article 14 of Council Directive 2003/109/EC concerning the status of third-country nationals who are long-term residents [2003] OJ L16/44.

[183] The areas of equal treatment include: access to and conditions of employment; education and training; recognition of professional diplomas; social security; tax benefits; access to goods and services made available to the public; freedom of association and membership of trade unions; and free access to the entire territory of the Member State concerned.

[184] See Article 11(2) and (3) EC Directive on status of third-country nationals who are long-term residents 2003 (n 182). See also L Halleskov, 'The Long-term Residents Directive: A Fulfilment of the Tampere Objective of Near-equality?' (2005) 7 European Journal of Migration and Law 181, 183.

[185] See Article 12 of Directive 2011/98/EU of the European Parliament and of the Council on a single application procedure for a single permit for third-country nationals to reside and work in the territory of a Member State and on a common set of rights for third-country workers legally residing in a Member State [2011] OJ L343/1.

[186] Council Directive 2003/86/EC on the right to family reunification [2003] OJ L251/12.

[187] Judgment of 27 June 2006, *Parliament v Council*, C-540/03, ECLI:EU:C:2006:429.

[188] Ibid, para 104.

[189] See Judgment of 4 March 2010, *Chakroun v Minister van Buitenlandse Zaken*, C-578/08, ECLI:EU:C:2010:117; Judgment of 16 January 2014, *Reyes v Migrationsverket*, C-423/12, ECLI:EU:C:2014:16; J Hardy, 'The Objective of Directive 2003/86 Is to Promote the Family Reunification of Third Country Nationals' (2012) 14 European Journal of Migration and Law 439, 441.

R Schweitzer, 'A Stratified Right to Family Life? On the Logic(s) and
Legitimacy of Granting Differential Access to Family Reunification
for Third-country Nationals Living within the EU' (2015) 41 Journal
of Ethnic and Migration Studies 2130

The EU directive defines family reunification as 'the entry into and residence in a Member
State by family members of a third country national residing lawfully in that Member
State in order to preserve the family unit' (Art. 2 (d)). Put differently, it means the admission of a foreigner (who would otherwise have no particular claim to be admitted) to a
state, based on that person's specific relationship (which is seen as inherently valuable and
thus worth preserving) with another foreigner, who has already been admitted to reside
in that state. What is at stake, therefore, are two rather different kinds of claims: Firstly,
that of the lawful resident (A) to have his or her family life respected by the state in which
he or she lives; and secondly, that of a family member residing abroad (B) to enter that
state, in order to make this family life possible. Here, Carens reminds us that 'family reunification is primarily about the moral claims of insiders, not outsiders', and thus a question of 'the responsibilities of liberal democratic states toward those whom they govern'.
While the European Court of Human Rights (ECtHR) has acknowledged this interpretation, the interests of insider spouses play only a marginal role in its jurisprudence on
family reunification cases, which 'are still predominantly seen as immigration cases'. The
central puzzle, then, is that the state in question has a moral obligation to meet A's claim
(by not interfering with his or her family life), but also has the sovereign right to refuse
B's claim (to enter its territory), wherever deemed necessary in order to preserve public
order, national security, the economic well-being, or even the particular character, culture or identity of the nation. (...) In practice, the 'right to family reunification' is the
point where these claims effectively converge, and where the state's obligation to (equally)
protect the liberal rights of all its subjects intersects with its commonly presumed right or
even obligation to (selectively) control immigration. It is this contradiction that underpins what I call a stratified right to family life, and which can be traced (...) from normative debates around membership and national belonging to the current legal-political
reality of family reunification within the EU.

Other EU legislation on immigration tends to focus more on the procedural and technical aspects of granting residence permits and managing expulsion of irregular migrants.
Directive 2011/98/EU attempts to simplify and harmonize the issuance of residence and
work permits by establishing a single permit for both, obtainable through a single application procedure in each Member State.[190] The format of the single permits follows the
uniform template specified in Regulation (EC) 1030/2002.[191] When it comes to exiting the
EU, Directive 2008/115/EC provides for common rules on returning illegally staying third-
country nationals, including a generic set of procedural rights for the affected migrants.[192]
This Directive operates where possible in connection with readmission agreements between

[190] EU Directive on a single permit for third-country nationals 2011 (n 185).
[191] Council Regulation (EC) 1030/2002 laying down a uniform format for residence permits for third-
country nationals [2002] OJ L157/1.
[192] Directive 2008/115/EC of the European Parliament and of the Council on common standards and procedures in Member States for returning illegally staying third-country nationals [2008] OJ L348/98. Article 1 of the
Directive states that returns of illegal migrants must take place in accordance with fundamental rights, including
refugee protection obligations.

the EU and third countries. The purpose of such agreements is the facilitation of returns of migrants who are no longer in a legal position to stay in the EU. In addition, third-country nationals who are victims of human trafficking are subject to a special residence permit regime when cooperating with national authorities.[193] The Directive (2004/81/EC) also complements the more general legislative framework on the rights of victims of trafficking in human beings.[194]

The final group of third-country nationals whose rights can be severely impacted by EU secondary legislation are refugees and asylum seekers. The Treaty roots of the so-called Common European Asylum System (CEAS) are in Article 78 TFEU which also explicitly references the obligation on the CEAS to be in compliance with international refugee protection law.

Consolidated version of the Treaty on the Functioning of the European Union [2012] OJ C326/47

Article 78

1. The Union shall develop **a common policy on asylum**, subsidiary protection and temporary protection with a view to offering appropriate status to any third-country national requiring international protection and **ensuring compliance with the principle of non-refoulement. This policy must be in accordance with the Geneva Convention** of 28 July 1951 and the Protocol of 31 January 1967 relating to the status of refugees, and other relevant treaties.

2. For the purposes of paragraph 1, the European Parliament and the Council, acting in accordance with the ordinary legislative procedure, shall adopt measures for a common European asylum system comprising:
   (a) a uniform status of asylum for nationals of third countries, valid throughout the Union;
   (b) a uniform status of subsidiary protection for nationals of third countries who, without obtaining European asylum, are in need of international protection;
   (c) a common system of temporary protection for displaced persons in the event of a massive inflow;
   (d) common procedures for the granting and withdrawing of uniform asylum or subsidiary protection status;
   (e) criteria and mechanisms for determining which Member State is responsible for considering an application for asylum or subsidiary protection;
   (f) standards concerning the conditions for the reception of applicants for asylum or subsidiary protection;
   (g) partnership and cooperation with third countries for the purpose of managing inflows of people applying for asylum or subsidiary or temporary protection.

---

[193] Council Directive 2004/81/EC on the residence permit issued to third-country nationals who are victims of trafficking in human beings or who have been the subject of an action to facilitate illegal immigration, who co-operate with the competent authorities [2004] OJ L261/19.

[194] EU Directive on preventing and combating trafficking in human beings and protecting its victims 2011 (n 146).

> 3. In the event of one or more Member States being confronted by an emergency situation characterised by a sudden inflow of nationals of third countries, the Council, on a proposal from the Commission, may adopt provisional measures for the benefit of the Member State(s) concerned. It shall act after consulting the European Parliament.

The EU has adopted a number of laws on the basis of the various subparagraphs of Article 78(2) TFEU. In most cases, the EU asylum legislation has been already revised, sometimes more than once, and even at the moment it is in the process of being renegotiated to align it more effectively to the preferences of the Member States in the wake of the migrant and refugee crisis of 2014 and 2015. These preferences, however, on the whole put the limitation of migratory inflows and externalization of migration governance ahead of fundamental rights considerations and refugee protection obligations.[195]

M Den Heijer, J Rijpma, and T Spijkerboer, 'Coercion, prohibition, and great expectations: The continuing failure of the Common European Asylum System' (2016) 53 Common Market Law Review 607

The European response to the refugee policy crisis is premised on an intensification of the prohibition of the cross-border movement of refugees, combined with neglect of the position of refugees in the region. It is unlikely that even the number of resettlements proposed by the Commission (which are entirely inadequate) will be realized. The prohibition approach to refugee movement is both unrealistic (refugees are bound to seek safety, whether we like it or not), and it is illegitimate morally (Art. 14 of the Universal Declaration of Human Rights grants everyone the right to seek asylum) as well as legally (the principle of *non-refoulement*). At the external borders, the European response does not do away with the unrealistic expectations of what borders can achieve, because it is assumed that border controls can bring down the number of migrants, and because policy makers still dream on about push-backs without meaningful individual assessment. In the Common European Asylum System, the uneven sharing of the burden among Member States and the drastic divergence in the protection afforded by Member States to refugees remain to be addressed.

It has to be emphasized that the present European crisis is a crisis of refugee policy, not a refugee crisis. The numbers in themselves are not the problem; the way in which the European Union deals with them is. The direction in which the European Union is now taking asylum law and policy mainly reproduces, and in important ways intensifies, those elements of EU law and policy which have caused the crisis. Therefore, the EU response is likely to make the crisis worse. This is tragic, all the more so because it is not necessary. A less disastrous approach would require doing away with the tunnel vision in which EU policy makers are presently caught – would require doing away with the idea that if

---

[195] See, for example, N El-Enany, 'The EU Asylum, Immigration and Border Control Regimes: Including and Excluding: The "Deserving Migrant"' (2013) 15 European Journal of Social Security 171; T Gammeltoft-Hansen, *Access to Asylum: International Refugee Law and the Globalisation of Migration Control* (Cambridge University Press 2011).

> policy doesn't work, more of the same policy is the appropriate response. It would require a reconsideration of the very foundations of the Common European Asylum System: coercion, prohibition, unrealistic expectations of what borders can do, and a confederate approach without addressing legitimate concerns of Member States, third States and refugees.

At the heart of EU asylum legislation is the Dublin III Regulation.[196] The main function of the Regulation—currently in its third iteration—is to lay down rules guiding the determination of the responsible Member State for a given asylum application. In principle, Member States at the external borders of the EU are obliged to process asylum claims or begin return procedures in cases where the persons entering the Member State do not fulfil the requirements for legal entry.[197] When third-country nationals (or stateless persons) reach another Member State anyway, as was habitually the case especially during the refugee crisis, the Dublin Regulation provides for 'take charge' and 'take back' requests and procedures which aim to channel such persons back into the Member State responsible.[198] The basic principle of the Dublin Regulation—that asylum applications are to be limited to a single claim in one responsible Member State which usually lies at the external border of the EU—is accompanied by a number of exceptions relating to minors and family members. More importantly, the overall functioning of the Regulation has been at times de facto suspended and in any case marked by an implementation failure on the part of the Member States.[199] The execution of the Dublin Regulation in practice has been aided—with mixed success—by the creation of a large-scale IT system (managed by a dedicated EU agency, EU-LISA) for the comparison of fingerprints of third-country nationals, also known as Eurodac.[200] The Regulation has been a source of deep divisions between the Member States, chiefly following the Syrian refugee crisis and the associated mismanagement of refugee flows into the EU. Therefore, the Commission has put forward a proposal to reform the current system and make it more transparent and effective. This Dublin IV Regulation would include a corrective allocation mechanism to deal with situations of disproportionate pressure on the asylum systems of certain Member States.[201]

---

[196] Regulation (EU) 604/2013 of the European Parliament and of the Council establishing the criteria and mechanisms for determining the Member State responsible for examining an application for international protection lodged in one of the Member States by a third-country national or a stateless person [2013] OJ L180/31.

[197] D Thym, 'The "Refugee Crisis" as a Challenge of Legal Design and Institutional Legitimacy' (2016) 53 Common Market Law Review 1545, 1547–48.

[198] See Article 18 of EU Regulation establishing the criteria and mechanisms for determining the Member State responsible for examining an application for international protection 2013 (n 196). The CJEU has explicitly stated that the Regulation 'seeks to prevent' secondary movements of third-country nationals in the EU. See Judgment of 17 March 2016, *Mirza v Bevándorlási és Állampolgársági Hivatal*, C-695/15 PPU, ECLI:EU:C:2016:188, para 52.

[199] Thym, 'The "Refugee Crisis" as a Challenge of Legal Design and Institutional Legitimacy' (n 197).

[200] Regulation (EU) No 603/2013 of the European Parliament and of the Council on the establishment of 'Eurodac' for the comparison of fingerprints for the effective application of Regulation (EU) No 604/2013 establishing the criteria and mechanisms for determining the Member State responsible for examining an application for international protection lodged in one of the Member States by a third-country national or a stateless person and on requests for the comparison with Eurodac data by Member States' law enforcement authorities and Europol for law enforcement purposes, and amending Regulation (EU) No 1077/2011 establishing a European Agency for the operational management of large-scale IT systems in the area of freedom, security and justice [2013] OJ L180/1.

[201] European Commission, 'Proposal for a Regulation of the European Parliament and of the Council establishing the criteria and mechanisms for determining the Member State responsible for examining an application for international protection lodged in one of the Member States by a third-country national or a stateless person (recast)', COM(2016) 270 final, Brussels, 4 May 2016.

The CEAS is, furthermore, underpinned by three key Directives which aim to approximate national laws on asylum to a common standard. First, the Qualifications Directive sets out the criteria according to which applications for refugee status or subsidiary protection are to be assessed, the substantive requirements of qualification for refugee or subsidiary protection, and the content of the protection granted.[202] The Directive only establishes the minimum conditions to be observed by the Member States—they are free to apply standards which are more favourable to refugees.[203] The Qualifications Directive—as the CEAS more generally—is inherently linked to international law, namely the Geneva Convention of 28 July 1951 relating to the Status of Refugees, as supplemented by the New York Protocol of 31 January 1967.

Second, Directive 2013/32/EU establishes common procedures for granting and withdrawing international protection.[204] The procedures are intended to act both as a harmonizing force for Member States' asylum laws and as a bulwark against arbitrary decisions and the undermining of basic obligations. The Directive, therefore, prescribes minimum guarantees and rights of asylum seekers which must be observed by the Member States in the course of asylum procedures. For example, the Member States are obliged to give information to asylum seekers regarding the possibility of applying for refugee status and register applications within three or, exceptionally, ten days;[205] the decisions on asylum applications must be taken individually, objectively, and impartially, and following a personal interview (save for exceptional circumstances) which complies with requirements specified in the Directive;[206] and, among others, asylum seekers have the right to stay pending a decision on the asylum claim, right to free legal assistance and representation in appeals procedures, and the right to an effective remedy before a court or tribunal against decisions concerning their asylum claims.[207]

An important concept included in the Asylum Procedures Directive (2013/32/EU) is that of a 'safe third country'. In essence, the Directive allows Member States to designate third countries as 'safe' and apply this concept when evaluating asylum applications, provided that certain principles and rules, such as that the asylum seeker will face no risk of serious harm, and the principle of *non-refoulement* as laid down in the Geneva Convention, are observed.[208] The designation of third countries as safe for the purposes of asylum procedures harbours potential for controversy as the Member States have an incentive to designate countries with dubious security and human rights conditions as safe in order to materialize their interest in decreasing the number of refugees and migrants admitted to the EU.

[202] Directive 2011/95/EU of the European Parliament and of the Council on standards for the qualification of third-country nationals or stateless persons as beneficiaries of international protection, for a uniform status for refugees or for persons eligible for subsidiary protection, and for the content of the protection granted [2011] OJ L337/9.
[203] Ibid, Article 3.
[204] Directive 2013/32/EU of the European Parliament and of the Council on common procedures for granting and withdrawing international protection [2013] OJ L180/60.
[205] Ibid, Article 8 and Article 6.
[206] Ibid, Article 10(3)(a) and Articles 14–17.
[207] Ibid, Article 9, Article 20, and Article 46.
[208] Ibid, Article 38.

M Hunt, 'The Safe Country of Origin Concept in European Asylum
Law: Past, Present and Future' (2014) 26 International Journal
of Refugee Law 500

Can any country truly be considered safe for the purpose of asylum? Is it correct that
some asylum seekers should be presumed 'bogus' simply on the basis of nationality? As
nationals of almost all European Union (EU) member states are currently recognized as
refugees abroad, it has been suggested that 'the presumed "safety" of a country is never
absolute'. However, the idea that asylum applications can be treated as 'unfounded' if
they originate from a certain country has nevertheless become a staple practice amongst
policy makers in Europe. (...)

While concerns remain regarding effective remedies and the generalised assessment
structure that is embodied by the SCO [safe country of origin] notion, Directive 2013/
32/EU nevertheless represents a significant improvement on current measures. As
Annex I remains unchanged and would serve as the non derogable minimum standard
of assessment, the transposition of this Directive will require a significant real terms improvement in procedural standards in many member states. The Directive also addresses
key concerns raised by human rights groups in relation to the procedural deterioration
associated with safe country practices. While an SCO application may still be subject
to accelerated procedures, or even rejected as manifestly unfounded, these procedural
short cuts would not prevent the right to a personal interview in which an applicant can
present their case for protection before a decision is made. Depending on national legislation, an applicant may either be granted suspensive effect during the outcome of first
instance appeals, or have the right to review by a court or tribunal. Problems would of
course persist in relation to what evidence an applicant can present that a determining
authority would consider as sufficient and reliable. (...)

Third, Directive 2013/33/EU provides for common minimum standards of reception
of asylum seekers.[209] Applicants for international protection have in principle the right to
move freely within the territory of the host Member State or a within a designated area.[210] In
practice, however, a number of Member States have had widespread recourse to the detention of asylum seekers, despite the fact that Article 8 of Directive 2013/33/EU lists detention
as the exception to the norm. The Directive specifies, furthermore, not only the guarantees
and conditions of detention but also the general material conditions for reception of asylum
seekers.[211] The Member States are also obliged to provide a minimum level of healthcare,
education to minors, and a limited access to the labour market.[212]

What has for the most part not been heeded during the migration and refugee crisis is
the obligation on the Member States to conduct the AFSJ policies in light of the principle
of solidarity and fair sharing of responsibility. This could be witnessed also in the Member
States' refusal to make use of the Temporary Protection Directive which was enacted in

---

[209] Directive 2013/33/EU of the European Parliament and of the Council of 26 June 2013 laying down standards for the reception of applicants for international protection [2013] OJ L180/96.
[210] Ibid, Article 7.
[211] Ibid, Articles 9–11 and Articles 17 and 18. Derogations from the standards of material conditions are possible, however; see Article 20 of the Directive.
[212] Ibid, Articles 14, 15, and 19.

2001 specifically for the purpose of dealing with mass influxes of displaced persons.[213] The Directive was eminently suited to alleviate both the additional burden on Member States at the external borders of the EU and the distress of the asylum seekers during the Syrian refugee crisis by providing immediate and temporary protection to asylum seekers and obliging Member States to cooperate. The worry is that the ongoing reform of EU asylum and immigration law will again fail to operationalize the principle of solidarity between the Member States.[214]

Consolidated version of the Treaty on the Functioning of the European Union [2012] OJ C326/47

Article 80

The policies of the Union set out in this Chapter and their implementation shall be governed by the **principle of solidarity and fair sharing of responsibility**, including its financial implications, **between the Member States**. Whenever necessary, the Union acts adopted pursuant to this Chapter shall contain appropriate measures to give effect to this principle.

4.5 The Principle of Mutual Trust

Underpinning a number of legal mechanisms inside the EU is the principle of mutual trust. Although not explicitly mentioned as such in the Treaties, the principle of mutual trust requires according to the CJEU each Member State 'to consider all the other Member States to be complying with EU law and particularly with the fundamental rights recognised by EU law'.[215] This entails that ordinarily a Member State, including its courts, cannot even check whether in a specific case another Member State observed fundamental rights prescribed by EU law.[216] In other words, the principle of mutual trust represents another instance of a presumption of equivalent protection of fundamental rights, similar to those established by the German Constitutional Court with its *Solange* doctrine (Chapter 1) and European Court of Human Rights with the *Bosphorus* doctrine (Chapter 5), only in this case the presumption applies horizontally between EU Member States. The horizontality of mutual trust is associated with the principle of equality of Member States: 'it is because Member States, and particularly their national courts, are deemed equal before the Treaties that they are able to trust each other to protect fundamental rights adequately and it is because they trust each other that judicial cooperation in civil and criminal matters is feasible'.[217]

---

[213] Council Directive 2001/55/EC on minimum standards for giving temporary protection in the event of a mass influx of displaced persons and on measures promoting a balance of efforts between Member States in receiving such persons and bearing the consequences thereof [2001] OJ L212/12.

[214] The CJEU offered a degree of support to the principle of solidarity as expressed in Article 80 TFEU in a case concerning a temporary asylum relocation scheme. See Judgment of 6 September 2017, *Slovak Republic and Hungary v Council*, C-643/15 and C-647/15, ECLI:EU:C:2017:631.

[215] Opinion of 18 December 2014, *EU accession to the ECHR*, 2/13, ECLI:EU:C:2014:2454, para 191.

[216] Ibid, para 192.

[217] K Lenaerts, 'La vie après l'avis: Exploring the Principle of Mutual (yet not Blind) Trust' (2017) 54 Common Market Law Review 805, 812.

As already hinted at earlier, mutual trust is of particular importance for legal instruments enabled by expansions of EU competences in the 1990s and 2000s. The so-called Area of Freedom, Security and Justice (AFSJ) comprises laws and policies on migration, asylum, borders, police and judicial cooperation in criminal matters, and judicial cooperation in civil matters. The construction of the AFSJ therefore obviously touches upon many issues which are sensitive from a fundamental rights perspective. The drafters of the Treaties were aware of this—Article 67(1) TFEU clearly stipulates that the AFSJ comes 'with respect for fundamental rights'. Although mutual trust predominantly forms the foundation for the operation of AFSJ instruments, it can be found in other areas of EU law as well. For example, Regulation 1/2003 presupposes that the rights of defence are sufficiently equivalent across EU Member States so as to enable cross-border cooperation in the enforcement of EU competition law.[218]

Despite Article 2 TEU, which obliges EU Member States to observe fundamental rights, forming the deep foundation for the existence of mutual trust in the EU, the principle is only operational through specific legal instruments laid down in EU legislation, as well as the principle of mutual recognition of judicial decisions which is also enshrined in the Treaties. Mutual recognition of judgments is a process by which decisions from one Member State are recognized and enforced in another and it has been recognized as 'the cornerstone of judicial co-operation in both civil and criminal matters within the Union'.[219] This has led to the enactment of numerous secondary laws facilitating the mutual recognition of enforcement orders,[220] judgments in civil and commercial matters,[221] protection measures for victims,[222] financial penalties,[223] and many others. The idea behind expanding the scope of mutual recognition through legislation is to enable a free circulation of judicial decisions as a sort of corollary to the free movement of persons within the EU.

Mutual recognition does not exhaust the concept of mutual trust; rather, it is a specific manifestation of it. The principle of mutual trust—elevated to a constitutional role by the CJEU in Opinion 2/13[224]—is of a more general nature and underpins all cooperative behaviour of Member States within the AFSJ. This has been clearly demonstrated in some of the most sensitive cases, such as when asylum seekers or prisoners are sent from one Member State to another pursuant to the relevant EU laws. As the CJEU explained in the *N.S.* case, the obligation on Member States to comply with the Dublin Regulation and, as the case may be, send an asylum seeker to the country of first entry despite inadequate reception conditions is not vitiated by

---

[218] Recital 16 of Council Regulation (EC) No 1/2003 on the implementation of the rules on competition laid down in Articles 81 and 82 of the Treaty [2003] OJ L1/1.

[219] European Council, Presidency conclusions, Tampere, 15 and 16 October 1999, point 33. It should not be confused with mutual recognition of goods in the single market, a principle famously expounded in Judgment of 20 February 1979, *Rewe-Zentral AG v Bundesmonopolverwaltung für Branntwein (Cassis de Dijon)*, 120/78, ECLI:EU:C:1979:42. The two are similar but for reasons of clarity the single market version of the principle is not discussed here.

[220] Regulation (EC) No 805/2004 of the European Parliament and of the Council creating a European Enforcement Order for uncontested claims [2004] OJ L143/15.

[221] Regulation (EU) No 1215/2012 of the European Parliament and of the Council on jurisdiction and the recognition and enforcement of judgments in civil and commercial matters [2012] OJ L351/1.

[222] Regulation (EU) No 606/2013 of the European Parliament and of the Council on mutual recognition of protection measures in civil matters [2013] OJ L181/4.

[223] Council Framework Decision 2005/214/JHA on the application of the principle of mutual recognition to financial penalties [2005] OJ L76/16.

[224] D Halberstam, ' "It's the Autonomy, Stupid!" A Modest Defense of Opinion 2/13 on EU Accession to the ECHR, and the Way Forward' (2015) 16 German Law Journal 105.

any infringement of fundamental rights.[225] The mutual confidence on which the EU asylum system is predicated ordinarily prevents Member States to scrutinize each other in terms of fundamental rights protection.[226] In the area of asylum, the mutual confidence is also bolstered by Member States' commitment to the Geneva Convention and the 1967 Protocol which serve to safeguard certain rights of asylum seekers.[227] As regards both asylum and criminal law cooperation, the EU moreover enacts 'trust-enhancing' legislation:[228] minimum standards of fundamental rights protection which must be available to all victims, suspects,[229] asylum seekers,[230] and other groups in all EU Member States. Such legislative instruments must of course always comply as well with the Charter of Fundamental Rights.

The CJEU has always been at pains to stress that mutual trust and the cooperation based thereon can only be suspended in exceptional circumstances. Nevertheless, in recent judgments, such exceptional circumstances have taken on more concrete contours after criticism, in particular following Opinion 2/13, highlighting that the Court promoted mutual trust (and therefore also European integration) at the expense of fundamental rights.[231] Some of the problems with the operation of mutual trust also surfaced in the context of human rights supervision by the ECtHR which has had its own dilemmas regarding whether the EU can at all times be presumed to offer an equivalent level of fundamental rights protection, especially when it comes to mechanisms based on mutual trust.[232]

The case law on derogations from mutual trust has emerged in two core and most sensitive areas of the AFSJ: criminal law and asylum. In *Aranyosi and Căldăraru*, the CJEU stated that in the execution of European arrest warrants, consideration had to be given to prison conditions in the requesting countries on account of the fugitives' fundamental rights.[233] More specifically, the cases concerned two European arrest warrants, issued by Hungarian and Romanian courts respectively pursuant to the Framework Decision on the European arrest warrant (EAW),[234] seeking the surrender of Mr Aranyosi and Mr Căldăraru by German authorities where both were arrested in 2015. In a request for a preliminary ruling, the seized German court (the *Hanseatisches Oberlandesgericht* in Bremen) raised the issue of the surrender's compatibility with fundamental rights guaranteed under the ECHR and EU law in light of evidence of prison overcrowding in both Hungary and Romania. The German court pointed to numerous judgments of the ECtHR finding violation of Article 3 ECHR on the prohibition of torture and inhuman or degrading treatment or punishment, which also covers inadequate prison conditions.[235]

---

[225] Judgment of 21 December 2011, *N.S. v Secretary of State for the Home Department and M. E. and Others v Refugee Applications Commissioner and Minister for Justice, Equality and Law Reform*, C-411/10 and C-493/10, ECLI:EU:C:2011:865, para 82.

[226] Ibid, para 83.

[227] Ibid, paras 75, 78.

[228] Lenaerts, 'La vie après l'avis' (n 217) 838.

[229] See Section 4.4.C above.

[230] See, for example, Directive 2013/33/EU of the European Parliament and of the Council of 26 June 2013 laying down standards for the reception of applicants for international protection [2013] OJ L180/96.

[231] S Peers, 'The EU's Accession to the ECHR: The Dream Becomes a Nightmare' (2015) 16 German Law Journal 213; E Spaventa, 'A Very Fearful Court? The Protection of Fundamental Rights in the European Union After Opinion 2/13' (2015) 22 Maastricht Journal of European and Comparative Law 35.

[232] See discussion of the case law on the *Bosphorus* doctrine in Ch 5.

[233] Judgment of 5 April 2016, *Aranyosi and Căldăraru v Generalstaatsanwaltschaft Bremen*, C-404/15 and C-659/15 PPU, ECLI:EU:C:2016:198.

[234] Council Framework Decision on the European arrest warrant 2002 (n 140).

[235] See, for example, *Burlacu v Romania*, App no 51318/12, 10 June 2014; *Varga and Others v Hungary*, App nos 14097/12, 45135/12, 73712/12, 34001/13, 44055/13, and 64586/13, 10 March 2015.

> ## Judgment of 5 April 2016, *Aranyosi and Căldăraru v Generalstaatsanwaltschaft Bremen*, C-404/15 and C-659/15 PPU, ECLI:EU:C:2016:198
>
> 43. The ECtHR has found Hungary to be in violation by reason of the overcrowding in its prisons (...). The ECtHR held that it was established that Hungary was in violation of Article 3 ECHR by imprisoning the applicants in cells that were **too small and that were overcrowded**. The ECtHR treated those proceedings as a pilot case after **450 similar cases against Hungary were brought** before it with respect to inhuman conditions of detention.
> 60. In a number of judgments issued on 10 June 2014, the ECtHR found Romania to be in violation by reason of the overcrowding in its prisons (...). The ECtHR held it to be established that Romania was in violation of Article 3 ECHR by imprisoning the applicants in cells that were **too small and overcrowded, that lacked adequate heating, that were dirty and lacking in hot water for showers**.
> 75. It should be recalled, as a preliminary point, that the purpose of the Framework Decision (...) is to replace the multilateral system of extradition based on the European Convention on Extradition of 13 December 1957 **with a system of surrender between judicial authorities of convicted or suspected persons for the purpose of enforcing judgments or of conducting prosecutions**, that system of surrender being **based on the principle of mutual recognition (...)**
> 76. The Framework Decision thus seeks, by the establishment of a new simplified and more effective system for the surrender of persons convicted or suspected of having infringed criminal law, to facilitate and accelerate judicial cooperation with a view to contributing to the objective set for the European Union to become **an area of freedom, security and justice, founded on the high level of confidence which should exist between the Member States (...)**
> 77. **The principle of mutual recognition on which the European arrest warrant system is based is itself founded on the mutual confidence between the Member States that their national legal systems are capable of providing equivalent and effective protection of the fundamental rights recognised at EU level**, particularly in the Charter (...)
> 78. **Both the principle of mutual trust between the Member States and the principle of mutual recognition are, in EU law, of fundamental importance** given that they allow an area without internal borders to be created and maintained. More specifically, **the principle of mutual trust requires**, particularly with regard to the area of freedom, security and justice, **each of those States, save in exceptional circumstances, to consider all the other Member States to be complying with EU law and particularly with the fundamental rights recognised by EU law (...)**
> 79. In the area governed by the Framework Decision, the principle of mutual recognition, which constitutes, as is stated notably in recital (6) of that Framework Decision, the 'cornerstone' of judicial cooperation in criminal matters, is given effect in Article 1(2) of the Framework Decision, pursuant to which **Member States are in principle obliged to give effect to a European arrest warrant (...)**
> 80. It follows that **the executing judicial authority may refuse to execute such a warrant only in the cases, exhaustively listed, of obligatory non-execution**, laid down in Article 3 of the Framework Decision, **or of optional non-execution**, laid down

in Articles 4 and 4a of the Framework Decision. Moreover, the execution of the European arrest warrant may be made subject only to one of the conditions exhaustively laid down in Article 5 of that Framework Decision (...)

81. It must, in that context, be noted that recital 10 of the Framework Decision states that **the implementation of the mechanism of the European arrest warrant as such may be suspended only in the event of serious and persistent breach by one of the Member States of the principles referred to in Article 2 TEU, and in accordance with the procedure provided for in Article 7 TEU.**

82. However, first, the Court has recognised that **limitations of the principles of mutual recognition and mutual trust between Member States can be made 'in exceptional circumstances'** (...)

83. Second, as is stated in Article 1(3) thereof, **the Framework Decision is not to have the effect of modifying the obligation to respect fundamental rights** as enshrined in, inter alia, the Charter.

84. In that regard, it must be stated that compliance with **Article 4 of the Charter, concerning the prohibition of inhuman or degrading treatment or punishment, is binding,** as is stated in Article 51(1) of the Charter, **on the Member States and, consequently, on their courts, where they are implementing EU law,** which is the case when the issuing judicial authority and the executing judicial authority are applying the provisions of national law adopted to transpose the Framework Decision (...)

85. As regards the prohibition of inhuman or degrading treatment or punishment, laid down in Article 4 of the Charter, **that prohibition is absolute in that it is closely linked to respect for human dignity,** the subject of Article 1 of the Charter (...)

86. That the right guaranteed by Article 4 of the Charter is absolute is confirmed by Article 3 ECHR, to which Article 4 of the Charter corresponds. As is stated in Article 15(2) ECHR, no derogation is possible from Article 3 ECHR.

87. Articles 1 and 4 of the Charter and Article 3 ECHR enshrine one of the fundamental values of the Union and its Member States. (...)

88. It follows that, **where the judicial authority of the executing Member State is in possession of evidence of a real risk of inhuman or degrading treatment of individuals detained in the issuing Member State,** having regard to the standard of protection of fundamental rights guaranteed by EU law and, in particular, by Article 4 of the Charter (...), **that judicial authority is bound to assess the existence of that risk when it is called upon to decide on the surrender to the authorities of the issuing Member State** of the individual sought by a European arrest warrant. **The consequence of the execution of such a warrant must not be that that individual suffers inhuman or degrading treatment.**

89. To that end, the executing judicial authority must, initially, rely on **information that is objective, reliable, specific and properly updated on the detention conditions prevailing in the issuing Member State and that demonstrates that there are deficiencies, which may be systemic or generalised, or which may affect certain groups of people, or which may affect certain places of detention.** That information may be obtained from, inter alia, judgments of international courts, such as judgments of the ECtHR, judgments of courts of the issuing Member State, and also decisions, reports and other documents produced by bodies of the Council of Europe or under the aegis of the UN.

91. Nonetheless, **a finding that there is a real risk of inhuman or degrading treatment by virtue of general conditions of detention in the issuing Member State cannot lead, in itself, to the refusal to execute a European arrest warrant.**
92. Whenever the existence of such a risk is identified, **it is then necessary that the executing judicial authority make a further assessment, specific and precise,** of whether there are substantial grounds to believe that the individual concerned will be exposed to that risk because of the conditions for his detention envisaged in the issuing Member State.
93. The mere existence of **evidence that there are deficiencies**, which may be systemic or generalised, or which may affect certain groups of people, or which may affect certain places of detention, with respect to detention conditions in the issuing Member State **does not necessarily imply that, in a specific case, the individual concerned will be subject to inhuman or degrading treatment** in the event that he is surrendered to the authorities of that Member State.

As one could expect based on Opinion 2/13, the CJEU began its examination by talking up the importance of mutual trust and the exceptionality of derogating from it, which was furthermore confirmed in the context of the case by the EAW Framework Decision. The Court even cited an interesting point in the recital of the EAW Framework Decision which states that the execution of an EAW can be suspended only when a serious and persistent breach of the values listed in Article 2 TEU has been established through the procedure set out in Article 7 TEU (see below). Nevertheless, the CJEU thereafter recognized the primacy of fundamental rights obligations which cannot be altered by the application of the EAW Framework Decision—an argument previously undermined to some extent by the *Melloni* decision of 2013. The human rights angle in the case at hand was strengthened by the fact that the right at stake (prohibition against inhumane and degrading treatment) is an absolute right from which no derogation is possible under the ECHR or the Charter. The CJEU consequently allowed an exception from the principle of mutual trust—for which no provision is in fact made in the EAW Framework Decision—while at the same time trying to make sure that it would only be applied in exceptional circumstances dictated by serious human rights concerns.

Indeed, the CJEU went as far as to say that evidence of human rights deficiencies—which in any case must be drawn from objective, reliable, specific, and properly updated sources[236]—is not in itself sufficient to suspend the presumption of equivalent protection of fundamental rights derived from the principle of mutual trust. It must be established in the particular circumstances of each case whether an individual will run a 'real' risk of being subject to conditions in breach of fundamental rights guaranteed under EU law. To that extent, a judicial authority executing an EAW can request information from the Member State that issued the warrant regarding the conditions

---

[236] It should be noted that information about human rights situations in the Member States, for the purpose of mutual trust but not only that, could be facilitated by the EU itself if it undertook to create a database compiling all the relevant assessments conducted by various international organizations. However, a number of Member States are opposed to the EU becoming more involved in anything approaching a general monitoring of human rights in the Member States, citing lack of competence. The EU Fundamental Rights Information System, developed by the Fundamental Rights Agency, is so far the most concrete foray in this area.

to which the prosecuted individual will be exposed.[237] Although such requests must be handled as a matter of urgency, any additional time needed to establish the state of the fundamental rights situation in the issuing Member State cannot lead to a breach of the individual's rights, especially those potentially resulting from an excessive length of detention.

The findings of the CJEU on poor detention conditions amounting to inhuman or degrading treatment in *Aranyosi* were confirmed and further specified in the Court's ruling on the EAW against Hungarian national *ML*,[238] prompted by a request of the same Higher Regional Court of Bremen. The Court reiterated its two-step requirement of proving both the existence of systemic and generalized deficiencies as well as the real risk the surrendered person will run to be subject to inhuman or degrading treatment in the particular circumstances of his future detention, in order to refuse the surrender.[239] The CJEU added to its previous decision that the existence of a legal remedy in Hungary to review the legality of detention conditions was not sufficient to replace in any way the individual assessment to be carried out by the executing judicial authorities.[240] Only the conditions in the prison where the person concerned is intended to be detained have to be assessed, and the supposed ill-treatment has to attain a minimum level of severity in order to constitute a violation of Article 4 of the Charter.[241]

On the same day, the CJEU issued a ruling in the case of *LM (Minister for Justice and Equality)*.[242] In the aforementioned case law, the refusal to carry out an EAW was based on the absolute right prohibiting torture in Article 4 of the Charter (and Article 3 of the ECHR), backed by a substantial number of ECtHR decisions that indeed found violations with regard to the detention system of the Member States concerned. Now for the first time, the CJEU was confronted with the question (posed by the High Court of Ireland) whether the risk of a breach of the fundamental right to an independent tribunal was also sufficient to deviate from the principle of mutual recognition and refrain from giving effect to the arrest warrant issued by the Polish authorities. In another landmark ruling, the Court replied in the affirmative, referring to the case of *Associação Sindical dos Juízes Portugueses*[243] to identify the access to an independent judge as a core element of the right to a fair trial under Article 19 TEU and Article 47 of the Charter.[244] It then upheld its two-step test, and held that it was for the referring executing judicial authority to determine whether there exist systemic or generalized deficiencies so far as concerns the independence of the issuing Member State's judiciary and whether, in the individual circumstances of the case at hand, the person to be surrendered will run the risk of breach of his right to a fair trial.[245]

---

[237] *Aranyosi and Căldăraru* (n 233) paras 94–95.

[238] Judgment of 25 July 2018, *ML (Conditions of detention in Hungary)*, C-220/18 PPU, ECLI:EU:C:2018:589.

[239] Ibid, paras 60–62.

[240] Ibid, para 75.

[241] With special importance to be attached to the personal space available to a detainee, see *ML* (n 238) paras 87, 91–92.

[242] Judgment of 25 July 2018, *LM (Minister for Justice and Equality)*, C-216/18 PPU, ECLI:EU:C:2018:586.

[243] *Associação Sindical dos Juízes Portugueses* (n 40).

[244] See above, under Section 4.3.A, and below, under Section 4.6, for an excerpt of the *ASJP* case.

[245] C Rizcallah, 'Arrêt "LM": un risque de violation du droit fondamental à un tribunal indépendant s'oppose-t-il à l'exécution d'un mandate d'arrêt européen?' (2018) 9 Journal de droit européen 348.

**Judgment of 25 July 2018, *LM (Minister for Justice and Equality)*,
C-216/18 PPU, ECLI:EU:C:2018:586**

43. (…) the Court has recognised that **limitations may be placed on the principles of mutual recognition and mutual trust between Member States** 'in exceptional circumstances' (see, to that effect, judgment of 5 April 2016, *Aranyosi and Căldăraru*, C-404/15 and C-659/15 PPU, EU:C:2016:198, paragraph 82 and the case-law cited).

44. In that context, the Court has acknowledged that, subject to certain conditions, the executing judicial authority has the power to bring the surrender procedure established by Framework Decision 2002/584 to an end where surrender may result in the requested person being subject to inhuman or degrading treatment within the meaning of Article 4 of the Charter (…)

46. In the present instance, the person concerned, relying upon the reasoned proposal and the documents to which it refers, has opposed **his surrender to the Polish judicial authorities**, submitting, in particular, that his surrender **would expose him to a real risk of a flagrant denial of justice on account of the lack of independence of the courts of the issuing Member State resulting from implementation of the recent legislative reforms of the system of justice in that Member State.**

47. It should thus, first of all, be determined whether, like a real risk of breach of Article 4 of the Charter, a **real risk of breach of the fundamental right of the individual concerned to an independent tribunal and, therefore, of his fundamental right to a fair trial as laid down in the second paragraph of Article 47 of the Charter** is capable of permitting the executing judicial authority to refrain, by way of exception, from giving effect to a European arrest warrant, on the basis of Article 1(3) of Framework Decision 2002/584.

48. In that regard, it must be pointed out that the requirement of judicial independence forms part of the **essence of the fundamental right to a fair trial**, a right which is of cardinal importance as a guarantee that all the rights which individuals derive from EU law will be protected and that the values common to the Member States set out in Article 2 TEU, in particular the value of the rule of law, will be safeguarded.

50. In accordance with **Article 19 TEU**, which gives concrete expression to the value of the rule of law affirmed in Article 2 TEU, it is for the national courts and tribunals and the Court of Justice to ensure the full application of EU law in all Member States and judicial protection of the rights of individuals under that law (…)

53. In order for that protection to be ensured, maintaining the independence of those bodies is essential, as confirmed by the **second paragraph of Article 47 of the Charter, which refers to access to an 'independent' tribunal as one of the requirements linked to the fundamental right to an effective remedy** (judgment of 27 February 2018, *Associação Sindical dos Juízes Portugueses*, C-64/16, EU:C:2018:117, paragraph 41).

58. The **high level of trust between Member States on which the European arrest warrant mechanism is based** is thus founded on the **premiss that the criminal courts of the other Member States**—which, following execution of a European arrest warrant, will have to conduct the criminal procedure for the purpose of prosecution, or of enforcement of a custodial sentence or detention order, and the substantive criminal proceedings—**meet the requirements of effective judicial protection**, which include, in particular, the independence and impartiality of those courts.

59. It must, accordingly, be held that the existence of a **real risk** that the person in respect of whom a European arrest warrant has been issued will, if surrendered to the issuing judicial authority, suffer a **breach of his fundamental right to an independent tribunal** and, therefore, of the essence of his fundamental right to a fair trial, a right guaranteed by the second paragraph of Article 47 of the Charter, is **capable of permitting the executing judicial authority to refrain, by way of exception, from giving effect to that European arrest warrant**, on the basis of Article 1(3) of Framework Decision 2002/584.

61. (…) the executing judicial authority must, as a **first step, assess,** on the basis of material that is objective, reliable, specific and properly updated concerning the operation of the system of justice in the issuing Member State (…), **whether there is a real risk, connected with a lack of independence of the courts of that Member State on account of systemic or generalised deficiencies there, of the fundamental right to a fair trial being breached.** Information in a reasoned proposal recently addressed by the Commission to the Council on the basis of Article 7(1) TEU is particularly relevant for the purposes of that assessment.

68. If, having regard to the requirements noted in paragraphs 62 to 67 of the present judgment, the executing judicial authority finds that there is, in the issuing Member State, a real risk of breach of the essence of the fundamental right to a fair trial on account of systemic or generalised deficiencies concerning the judiciary of that Member State, such as to compromise the independence of that State's courts, that authority must, as a **second step, assess specifically and precisely whether, in the particular circumstances of the case, there are substantial grounds for believing that, following his surrender to the issuing Member State, the requested person will run that risk.** (…)

78. If the information which the issuing judicial authority, after having, if need be, sought assistance from the central authority or one of the central authorities of the issuing Member State, as referred to in Article 7 of Framework Decision 2002/584 (…), has sent to the executing judicial authority does not lead the latter to discount the **existence of a real risk** that the individual concerned will suffer in the issuing Member State a breach of his fundamental right to an independent tribunal and, therefore, of the essence of his fundamental right to a fair trial, **the executing judicial authority must refrain from giving effect to the European arrest warrant relating to him.**

Another area where the appearance of significant cracks in fundamental rights protection in the EU forced the CJEU to consider derogations from the principle of mutual trust is asylum law. The original intransigence of the Court when it came to blocking transfers of asylum seekers under the Dublin Regulation expressed in *Abdullahi*[246] has been somewhat relaxed in more recent case law. As in the case of prison overcrowding, asylum conditions in a number of Member States have been condemned in the rulings of the ECtHR and with it the associated EU transfer procedures based on mutual trust.[247] In *C. K. and Others*,[248] the CJEU partially responded to such criticism, contrary to the Opinion

---

[246] Judgment of 10 December 2013, *Abdullahi v Bundesasylamt*, C-394/12, ECLI:EU:C:2013:813.

[247] See, most notably, *M.S.S. v Belgium and Greece*, App no 30696/09, 21 January 2011; *Tarakhel v Switzerland*, App no 29217/12, 4 November 2014, discussed in light of the *Bosphorus* doctrine in Ch 5.

[248] Judgment of 16 February 2017, *C. K. and Others v Republika Slovenija*, C-578/16 PPU, ECLI:EU:C:2017:127.

of the Advocate General who argued in favour of respecting the principle of mutual trust.[249] The case concerned a couple who entered Croatia on short-term visa and subsequently crossed with falsified Greek identification to Slovenia where they applied for asylum (and later gave birth to a child). Croatia being the country of first entry and therefore responsible for examining the asylum applications under Article 12 of the Dublin Regulation,[250] Slovenian authorities requested Croatia to take charge of the applications. Following Croatia's acceptance of the responsibility to examine the asylum applications which entailed the transfer of the asylum seekers from Slovenia to Croatia, the asylum seekers challenged the Slovenian refusal to examine their applications and the decision to transfer them to Croatia in the Slovenian court system. The asylum seekers alleged, among other matters, that the mother was suffering from depression and suicidal tendencies which would be aggravated by occasioning their movement to Croatia. In response, Slovenia sought confirmation that asylum conditions in Croatia were not deficient and that the asylum seekers would receive the proper medical care. The Constitutional Court in Slovenia remained, nonetheless, concerned about whether the transfer of asylum seekers would comply with the prohibition on inhuman and degrading treatment and the principle of non-refoulement.

Judgment of 16 February 2017, *C. K. and Others v Republika Slovenija*, C-578/16 PPU, ECLI:EU:C:2017:127

59. (…) the rules of secondary EU law, including the provisions of the Dublin III Regulation, must be interpreted and applied in a manner consistent with the fundamental rights guaranteed by the Charter (…). The prohibition of inhuman or degrading treatment or punishment, laid down in Article 4 of the Charter, is, in that regard, of fundamental importance, to the extent that it is absolute in that it is closely linked to respect for human dignity, which is the subject of Article 1 of the Charter (see, to that effect, judgment of 5 April 2016, Aranyosi and Căldăraru, C-404/15 and C-659/15 PPU, EU:C:2016:198, paragraphs 85 and 86).

60. In its judgment of 21 December 2011, N. S. and Others (…), the Court stressed that **the transfer of asylum seekers within the framework of the Dublin system may, in certain circumstances, be incompatible with the prohibition laid down in Article 4 of the Charter**. It thus held that an asylum seeker would run a real risk of being subjected to inhuman or degrading treatment, within the meaning of that article, in the event of a transfer to a Member State in which there are substantial grounds for believing that **there are systemic flaws** in the asylum procedure and in the conditions for the reception of applicants. Consequently, in accordance with the prohibition laid down in that article, the Member States may not carry out transfers within the framework of the Dublin system to a Member State in the case where they cannot be unaware that such flaws exist in that Member State.

---

[249] *C. K. and Others v Republika Slovenija* [2017] ECLI:EU:C:2017:108, Opinion of AG Tanchev.
[250] Regulation (EU) No 604/2013 of the European Parliament and of the Council establishing the criteria and mechanisms for determining the Member State responsible for examining an application for international protection lodged in one of the Member States by a third-country national or a stateless person [2013] OJ L180/31.

65. (...) the transfer of an asylum seeker within the framework of the Dublin III Regulation can take place **only in conditions which preclude that transfer from resulting in a real risk of the person concerned suffering inhuman or degrading treatment**, within the meaning of Article 4 of the Charter.

66. In that regard, it is not possible to exclude from the outset the possibility that, given the **particularly serious state of health of an asylum seeker**, his transfer pursuant to the Dublin III Regulation may result in such a risk for him.

75. Consequently, where an asylum seeker provides, particularly in the context of an effective remedy guaranteed to him by Article 27 of the Dublin III Regulation, **objective evidence**, such as medical certificates concerning his person, **capable of showing the particular seriousness of his state of health and the significant and irreversible consequences to which his transfer might lead, the authorities of the Member State concerned, including its courts, cannot ignore that evidence. They are, on the contrary, under an obligation to assess the risk** that such consequences could occur when they decide to transfer the person concerned or, in the case of a court, the legality of a decision to transfer, since the execution of that decision may lead to inhuman or degrading treatment of that person (...)

76. It is, therefore, for those authorities to **eliminate any serious doubts concerning the impact of the transfer on the state of health of the person concerned**. In this regard, in particular in the case of a serious psychiatric illness, it is not sufficient to consider only the consequences of physically transporting the person concerned from one Member State to another, but **all the significant and permanent consequences that might arise from the transfer must be taken into consideration**.

89. In any event, **if the state of health of the asylum seeker concerned does not enable the requesting Member State to carry out the transfer before the expiry of the six-month period** provided for in Article 29(1) of the Dublin III Regulation, **the Member State responsible would be relieved of its obligation to take charge of the person concerned** and responsibility would then be transferred to the first Member State, in accordance with paragraph 2 of that article.

94. (...) the interpretation of Article 4 of the Charter in the present judgment is not invalidated by the judgment of 10 December 2013, Abdullahi (C-394/12, EU:C:2013:813, paragraph 60), in which the Court held, with regard to the Dublin II Regulation, in essence, that, in circumstances such as those of the case giving rise to that judgment, the only way in which an asylum seeker could call his transfer into question was by pleading systemic flaws in the Member State responsible. Apart from the fact that the Court has held (...) that, with regard to the rights enjoyed by an asylum seeker, the Dublin III Regulation differs in essential respects from the Dublin II Regulation, it must be recalled that that judgment was delivered in a case involving a national who had not claimed, before the Court of Justice, any particular circumstances indicating that his transfer would, in itself, be contrary to Article 4 of the Charter. (...)

95. Finally, **that interpretation fully respects the principle of mutual trust** since, far from affecting the existence of a presumption that fundamental rights are respected in each Member State, it ensures that the exceptional situations referred to in the present judgment are duly taken into account by the Member States. Moreover, if a Member State were to proceed with the transfer of an asylum seeker in such situations, the resulting inhuman and degrading treatment would not be attributable,

> directly or indirectly, to the authorities of the Member State responsible, but to the first Member State alone.

That *C. K. and Others* belongs to the same line of case law relaxing the strain on the principle of mutual trust caused by the potential of EU law in the AFSJ to infringe fundamental rights as *Aranyosi and Căldăraru* was made clear by the Court from the beginning. The CJEU proceeded to recognize the obligation on Member States to ensure—in the presence of evidence of health problems—that the impact of a Dublin transfer on the asylum seeker does not violate the prohibition on inhuman and degrading treatment (Article 4 of the Charter). This can ultimately lead to the Dublin transfer being cancelled altogether if it cannot be executed within six months, in which case the originally responsible Member State would be relieved of its responsibility which would then be incurred by the Member State requesting the transfer of the asylum seekers. Finally, the CJEU proclaimed that this new interpretation was in line with the principle of mutual trust and it distinguished the case of *C. K. and Others* from *Abdullahi* by pointing out that the legislator improved the fundamental rights quality of the Dublin Regulation during the revision in 2013 and that in *Abdullahi* the applicant did not allege a violation of Article 4 of the Charter.

In *Jawo*,[251] finally, the CJEU was asked whether the German courts could refuse to transfer the applicant to Italy on the basis of his future living conditions, expected to constitute the risk to amount to inhuman or degrading treatment under Article 4 of the Charter. For the first time, the Court analysed the individual circumstances of an asylum seeker, not only during the asylum procedures in the requesting country but also thereafter, when international protection has been granted. Because of the importance of the principle of mutual trust, systemic deficiencies have to reach a particularly high level of severity in order to constitute a breach of Article 4 of the Charter. Nevertheless, the CJEU did leave open the possibility to refrain from transferring an asylum seeker if this would result in the person ending up in a situation of extreme material poverty, not allowing him to meet his most basic needs.

Judgment of 19 March 2019, *Abubacarr Jawo v Bundesrepublik Deutschland*, C-163/17, ECLI:EU:C:2019:218

91. (...) it must be noted that, in order to fall within the **scope of Article 4 of the Charter**, which corresponds to Article 3 ECHR, and of which the meaning and scope are therefore, in accordance with Article 52(3) of the Charter, the same as those laid down by the ECHR, the **deficiencies** referred to in the preceding paragraph of the present judgment **must attain a particularly high level of severity**, which depends on all the circumstances of the case (...)

92. That particularly high level of severity is attained where the indifference of the authorities of a Member State would result in a person wholly dependent on State support finding himself, irrespective of his wishes and personal choices, **in a situation of extreme material poverty that does not allow him to meet his most basic needs,**

---

[251] Judgment of 19 March 2019, *Abubacarr Jawo v Bundesrepublik Deutschland*, C-163/17, ECLI:EU:C: 2019:218.

such as, inter alia, food, personal hygiene and a place to live, and that undermines his physical or mental health or puts him in a state of degradation incompatible with human dignity (…)

94. A circumstance such as that mentioned by the referring court, according to which, as stated in the report referred to in paragraph 47 of the present judgment, the forms of support in family structures, available to the nationals of the Member State normally responsible for examining the application for international protection to deal with the inadequacies of that Member State's social system, are generally lacking for the beneficiaries of international protection in that Member State, is not sufficient ground for a finding that an applicant for international protection would, in the event of transfer to that Member State, be faced with such a situation of extreme material poverty.

95. Nonetheless, it cannot be entirely ruled out that an applicant for international protection may be able to demonstrate the existence of **exceptional circumstances that are unique to him** and mean that, in the event of transfer to the Member State normally responsible for processing his application for international protection, he would find himself, because of his particular vulnerability, irrespective of his wishes and personal choices, in a situation of extreme material poverty meeting the criteria set out in paragraphs 91 to 93 of the present judgment after having been granted international protection.

Overall, the tension between mutual trust and fundamental rights on display in the above cases can be more generally characterized as one between effectiveness and efficiency of EU law, on the one hand, and protection of individual fundamental rights, on the other. The judgments in *Aranyosi* and *C. K.* are aimed to appease those critics of the Court, including the institution which often acts as a check on EU judicial developments, the German Constitutional Court,[252] which found the CJEU's treatment of mutual trust and mechanisms based thereon damaging to basic constitutional values (individual human rights) for the sake of shielding progress of European integration. The problem can be at least partially traced to the lack of EU human rights competences: the conferral of competences concerning the creation of mutual recognition instruments on the EU has not been matched by a corresponding growth in EU oversight of compliance with fundamental rights in the Member States. As some scholars have pointed out,[253] the most sustainable way forward for internal EU cooperation on AFSJ issues—one consistent with neofunctionalist theory of European integration[254]—might involve at least a partial supranationalization of fundamental rights in the EU which could ensure through effective monitoring and compliance mechanisms that all Member States observe the values and standards on which mutual trust is founded to a sufficient extent. The likely lack of competence increase might on the contrary lead to further derogations from mutual trust and a resulting diminution of effectiveness of the EU laws relying on it.

[252] Bundesverfassungsgericht, Judgment of 15 December 2015, *European Arrest Warrant Extradition*, 2 BvR 2735/14.

[253] See, for example, C Eckes, 'Protecting Fundamental Rights in the EU's Compound Legal Order: Mutual Trust Against Better Judgment?' (2016) Amsterdam Centre for European Law and Governance Research Paper No 2016-06.

[254] For an example of how the logic of spill-overs might have influenced the creation of the European Border and Coast Guard, see A Niemann and J Speyer, 'A Neofunctionalist Perspective on the "European Refugee Crisis": The Case of the European Border and Coast Guard' (2018) 56 Journal of Common Market Studies 23.

E Gill-Pedro and X Groussot, 'The Duty of Mutual Trust in EU Law and the Duty to Secure Human Rights: Can the EU's Accession to the ECHR Ease the Tension?' (2017) 35 Nordic Journal of Human Rights 258

(...) a true 'symbiotic relationship' between the principle of mutual trust and human rights may be emerging. This 'principled approach' has been confirmed in the AFSJ case law concerning not only the EAW and the Dublin Regulation but also civil matters such as child abduction and asylum law. This 'principled approach 'establishes a move from a logic of presumption (of the foreign decision/standard) to a logic of conditionality (of the foreign decision/standard). (...) The general consequence of this move results in a requalification of the effectiveness of EU law and an increased reliance on human rights. Its practical consequence, particularly in the area of the AFSJ, is an increased role of national judicial authorities in not only issuing authorities but also executing authorities. The national executing authorities have a greater authority and become 'bouche de la loi étrangère'.

(...) the relationship between harmonisation and mutual trust has been very problematic. It has undermined the ability of member states to uphold the fundamental rights they are committed to upholding; harmed the legitimacy and acceptability of the rulings of both the CJEU and the EU measures giving effect to the AFSJ; and resulted in a crisis of trust. The CJEU has not been insensitive to these concerns. As Wischmeyer points out, the CJEU had recognised that too extensive an interpretation of the principle of mutual trust 'would ultimately destroy the confidence on which the system of mutual recognition [...] rests'. While the deification of mutual trust was very much in evidence in Opinion 2/13— and even recent case-law of the CJEU continues to reflect a top-down approach to mutual trust and harmonisation set out in the previous section–there have been developments in the case law of the CJEU that point towards a change of approach to one that will not seek to impose trust from above, but that will instead support systems through which trust can be generated and developed—trust through systemic harmonisation. However, the recent case law of the CJEU post-Opinion 2/13 has shown a clear shift in the mutual trust case law with a move, resulting in a requalification of the effectiveness of EU law and an increased reliance on human rights. The CJEU has created the conditions for limiting the principle of effectiveness of EU law and enhancing the protection of individual human rights. This has been done by framing a fully fledged constitutional principle of mutual trust. (...)

4.6 Protection of EU Values through Articles 2 and 7 TEU

At the most basic level, mutual trust between Member States rests on Article 2 TEU which enshrines the core EU values. Part of the reason why derogations from the principle of mutual trust caused a stir was that the idea of Member States not being able to live up to their commitments to EU values—of which fundamental rights are a central part—was relatively foreign. That idea is no longer foreign and not only when it comes to fundamental rights. Despite being for years readied, unsuccessfully according to some,[255] for joining the European club—an admittedly elitist notion of European integration—a number of acceding

---

[255] D Kochenov, *EU Enlargement and the Failure of Conditionality: Pre-accession Conditionality in the Fields of Democracy and the Rule of Law* (Kluwer Law International 2008).

Member States have failed on more than an occasion to live up to, and in at least two cases consciously undermined, the common EU values.

Consolidated version of the Treaty on European Union [2012] OJ C326/13

Article 2

The Union is founded on the values of respect for human dignity, freedom, **democracy**, equality, **the rule of law** and **respect for human rights**, including the rights of persons belonging to **minorities**. These values are common to the Member States in a society in which pluralism, non-discrimination, tolerance, justice, solidarity and equality between women and men prevail.

The casual observer could be excused if Article 2 TEU appears trivial or redundant, at least when it comes to fundamental rights protection. After all, the Charter of Fundamental Rights and the general principles of EU law appear to provide much more concrete and developed guarantees than the declaratory wording of Article 2 TEU. Despite the vague, programmatic and slightly inaccurate[256] wording of the provision, it carries considerable significance and potential which becomes more visible after consulting Article 7 TEU.

Consolidated version of the Treaty on European Union [2012] OJ C326/13

Article 7

1. On a reasoned proposal by one third of the Member States, by the European Parliament or by the European Commission, the Council, acting by a majority of four fifths of its members after obtaining the consent of the European Parliament, may determine that there is **a clear risk of a serious breach by a Member State of the values referred to in Article 2**. Before making such a determination, the Council shall hear the Member State in question and may address recommendations to it, acting in accordance with the same procedure.

The Council shall regularly verify that the grounds on which such a determination was made continue to apply.

2. The European Council, acting by unanimity on a proposal by one third of the Member States or by the Commission and after obtaining the consent of the European Parliament, may **determine the existence of a serious and persistent breach** by a Member State of the values referred to in Article 2, after inviting the Member State in question to submit its observations.

---

[256] As discussed in Ch 1 and Ch 3, the EU was founded as an economic integration project with values playing at best an implicit role (through commitments at national level) which has grown in stature and become formalized only gradually over the decades.

3. Where a determination under paragraph 2 has been made, the Council, acting by a qualified majority, may decide to **suspend certain of the rights deriving from the application of the Treaties to the Member State in question, including the voting rights of the representative of the government of that Member State in the Council.** In doing so, the Council shall take into account the possible consequences of such a suspension on the rights and obligations of natural and legal persons.

The obligations of the Member State in question under the Treaties shall in any case continue to be binding on that State.

4. The Council, acting by a qualified majority, may decide subsequently to vary or revoke measures taken under paragraph 3 in response to changes in the situation which led to their being imposed.
5. The voting arrangements applying to the European Parliament, the European Council and the Council for the purposes of this Article are laid down in Article 354 of the Treaty on the Functioning of the European Union.

Article 7 TEU represents the primary mechanism of enforcing the common EU values vis-à-vis the Member States. It can be invoked by the Council and the EP in case there is a 'clear risk of a serious breach' in any Member State of the values contained in Article 2 TEU. This is the preventive limb of the mechanism aimed at dissuading a Member State leaning in some way towards infringing EU values to reverse course. More serious consequences are attached to a determination which can be made, unanimously (without the offending Member State), by the European Council with the consent of the Parliament in case of a 'serious and persistent breach' of Article 2 TEU values. Following such a decision, the Council can suspend Member State rights under the Treaties,[257] including voting rights in the Council which constitutes the gravest sanction available in the EU system.

Until December 2017, however, and despite clear evidence of rule of law 'backsliding' in a number of Member States, the Article 7 TEU procedure had never been triggered. Explications for this can be found in the high voting majorities required, and the palpable political sensitivity of these types of decisions. When in 2000 EU Member States imposed sanctions on Austria for forming a coalition with the far-right populist party FPÖ, they have done so through concerted diplomatic action rather than invoking Article 7 TEU.[258] The first time a proposal to trigger the mechanism was put forward was in December 2017, by the Commission, after two years of discussions as part of the Rule of Law Framework,[259] during which Poland successfully undermined its Constitutional Court and was about similarly to undermine the Supreme Court.[260] A number of observers have criticized the Commission for dithering when resolute action was needed, while recognizing the shortcomings of the overall

---

[257] It is unclear what is meant by Member State rights (short of voting rights) and the scholarly literature is for the most part silent on this point. See L Besselink, 'The Bite, the Bark, and the Howl: Article 7 TEU and the Rule of Law Initiatives' in A Jakab and D Kochenov (eds), *The Enforcement of EU Law and Values: Ensuring Member States' Compliance* (Oxford University Press 2017).

[258] See K Lachmayer, 'Questioning the Basic Values—Austria and Jörg Haider' in Jakab and Kochenov (eds), *Enforcement of EU Law* (n 257).

[259] European Commission, 'Communication from the Commission to the European Parliament and the Council—A new EU Framework to strengthen the Rule of Law', COM(2014) 158 final, 5.

[260] L Pech and KL Scheppele, 'Illiberalism Within: Rule of Law Backsliding in the EU' (2017) 19 Cambridge Yearbook of European Legal Studies 3.

institutional design of the EU which circumscribes the possibilities for meaningful EU intervention in Member States 'backsliding' from rule of law, fundamental rights, and democratic
commitments.[261] As a result, scholars also attempted to suggest improvements, from 'reverse
Solange' to a 'Copenhagen Commission',[262] few of which have so far gained much traction
in practice, however.[263] Pech and Scheppele are among those who have tracked the developments in Poland and Hungary since the beginning of their constitutional downturn and
suggested the EU must act faster and more decisively, including when it comes to triggering
Article 7 TEU, if it wants to prevent the spread of illiberalism within the Union.[264]

L Pech and KL Scheppele, 'Illiberalism Within: Rule of Law Backsliding in the EU' (2017) 19 Cambridge Yearbook of European Legal Studies 3

To summarise our argument: the Commission invoked a new Rule of Law Framework
to cope with a rapidly deteriorating situation in Poland, after the government bluntly
attacked the Constitutional Tribunal, but we believe that this effort was bound to fail given
that the new framework was based on the questionable presumption that a discursive
approach could produce positive results. This presumption reflected the Commission's
failure to learn the right lessons from the Hungarian case, which strongly suggested that a
discursive approach would be ineffective in a situation where there was a concerted plan
to evade Article 2 values. The presumption of a discursive resolution further reflected the
Commission's failure to appreciate that would-be-authoritarians always seek to consolidate power as soon as possible and regrettably, the Rule of Law Framework simply delays
the time when Article 7 TEU might be invoked until after the critical consolidation of
power has already occurred. The Commission's activation of the Rule of Law Framework
against Poland has revealed further shortcomings, including the Commission's failure to
treat like situations alike by invoking the Rule of Law Framework only against Poland
and not against Hungary, as well as by the Commission's reluctance to move to the next
logical stage—Article 7 TEU—when confronted with belligerent rhetoric and complete
non-compliance with its recommendations. In the Commission's defence, however, it is

---

[261] See the contributions to C Closa and D Kochenov (eds), *Reinforcing Rule of Law Oversight in the European Union* (Cambridge University Press 2016). The perceived inability of the EU to deal with its own crises of values underlines the problem of incoherence between external promotion of these values and the lack of capacity to en-force them internally. This can be most starkly seen in the enlargement process where applicant countries are faced with strict conditionality to comply with set requirements relating to a range of areas, including EU values. The contrast with the EU's internal workings is sometimes referred to as the 'Copenhagen dilemma', named after the Copenhagen criteria.

[262] A Von Bogdandy and others, 'Reverse Solange—Protecting the Essence of Fundamental Rights against EU Member States' (2012) 49 Common Market Law Review 489; JW Müller, 'A Democracy Commission of One's Own, or: What it would take for the EU to safeguard Liberal Democracy in its Member States' in Jakab and Kochenov (eds), *Enforcement of EU Law* (n 257).

[263] For an overview, see M Ovádek, 'The Rule of Law in the EU: Many Ways Forward but Only One Way to Stand Still?' (2018) 40 Journal of European Integration 495.

[264] Some scholars have introduced a distinction between illiberal 'turns' and 'swerves' to allow for more nu-anced assessments of the values situation in EU Member States. Whereas most Central European Member States have 'merely' taken some illiberal swerves here and there—the overall institution of liberal democracy recovering and remaining in place—Hungary has in recent times come to the brink of an illiberal, autocratic turn which on the contrary signals a more permanent change to the political structure of the Hungarian state. See L Bustikova and P Guasti, 'The Illiberal Turn or Swerve in Central Europe?' (2017) 5 Politics and Governance 166.

difficult to be bold and firm when you have to work with intergovernmental institutions such as the European Council, which has been reluctant to engage in any criticism of Member States.

Looking beyond the Hungarian and Polish cases, our key argument is that the only way to prevent the occurrence of a consolidated autocracy in violation of EU values is to act fast as soon as the danger signals are clear. A recommendation for speed, however, goes against the general tendency of EU institutions to assume that stalling for time solves most problems. The Rule of Law Framework appears to be designed for normal times when simply slowing a process down cools heads and makes friendly resolution of disputes more likely. But in the abnormal times of a budding autocracy inside the EU, the Rule of Law Framework simply adds a de facto compulsory step before the activation of one of the two arms of Article 7. While this may enable the Commission to accumulate incriminating evidence and help create a political environment in which the rogue government may progressively lose the support of its peers before the eventual triggering of Article 7, the Framework has also arguably made the situation worse by enabling rogue governments, who did not care about their international reputations, to consolidate power in plain sight while the EU dithered over what to do.

If this problem of rogue Member States within the EU is to be solved, we believe that all EU institutions must use all of the tools at their disposal. The Commission must revive and reframe its use of the infringement procedure. We also call on the Commission to vigorously press the European Council and the Council to unequivocally support its efforts in establishing unambiguous deadlines and instructions when the Rule of Law Framework has been invoked. The European Parliament could have triggered Article 7 if it had worked toward establishing the two-thirds vote it would take to do so. But that could only be done if partisan politics were put aside so that powerful parties such as the European People's Party did not shield their member governments from the consequences of violating EU basic values. Even the Court of Justice must recognise that the EU faces new challenges that call for adjustment of existing doctrine created in better times. For instance, where any EU Member State ceases to comply with the most basic understanding of the rule of law and the EU institutions have otherwise failed to effectively correct the situation, the principle of mutual trust ought to be adjusted.

Europe has been juggling multiple crises in recent years, so the internal affairs of a rogue government or two may seem less critical to Europe's well-being than crises that affect multiple states at the same time, like the Euro-crisis, refugee crisis or the fallout from Brexit. But the proliferation inside the EU of governments that no longer share basic European values undermines the reason for existence of the EU in the first place. It also threatens the functioning of a legal framework which 'is based on the fundamental premiss that each Member State shares with all the other Member States, and recognizes that they share with it, a set of common values on which the EU is founded'. The 'values crisis' may not seem as urgent as the other crises on European plates, but it has the most far-reaching implications for the European project because without common values, there are fewer reasons for the EU to exist. Europe therefore fails to act at its peril. And it needs to act before rogue governments bent on establishing authoritarian regimes become ever more entrenched.

Under the first paragraph of Article 7 TEU, outlining the preventive mechanism, the Council is obliged to organize one or more hearings ('shall hear') whenever the procedure is triggered by the Member States, the EP, or the Commission. There is no legal obligation to subsequently determine the existence of 'a clear risk of a serious breach' of the Article 2 values, and this can only be decided by a majority of four-fifths of the Council's members. Over the past few years, the procedure was triggered with regard to two Member States (only), Poland and Hungary, respectively by the Commission in December 2017[265] and by the Parliament in September 2018.[266] The issue in Poland relates specifically to the 'reform' of the judicial system through several legislative interventions, threatening the independence of the judiciary, and therewith the rule of law in general (see below). Up to now, the Polish authorities have been able to put forward their views during three separate hearings before the General Affairs Council, between June and December 2018. The resolution of the Parliament that triggered the Article 7(1) mechanism in relation to Hungary addressed not only the rule of law backsliding in the country, it also raised concerns relating to corruption, freedom of expression, academic freedom, freedom of religion, migrant rights, and rights of minorities.[267] Two hearings took place in September and December 2019.[268]

The unstructured organization of the Article 7(1) hearings has attracted much criticism: hardly any transparency exists with regard to the choice of topics, conduct, role of the Parliament, and outcome of the hearings.[269] Most alarmingly, they have not achieved any tangible results. The EP has referred to reports and statements of several international bodies indicating that the situation in both countries has only deteriorated since the initiation of the Article 7 procedures.[270] Several explanations have been given for the current stand-still and the reluctance of the Council to make any determination on the clear risk of a serious breach of the Union values. These include the 'compliance dilemma', counting on voluntary compliance via amicable solutions, and the important role of party politics ('partisanship') within the Parliament.[271] In an attempt to streamline the hearing process and to 'create a level playing field for all Member States involved', the Council has adopted a set of 'standard modalities' in July 2019.[272] Recently, the EP adopted an interim report on the 2017 Commission Proposal with regard to Poland. The Parliament urges the Council and Commission to act swiftly with regard to the Polish situation, including by taking budgetary measures, as well as to extend the scope of the current Article 7(1) TEU proceedings to include democracy and human rights issues.[273]

For all the difficulties of enforcing values within the EU, Article 7 TEU makes clear that compliance with the values represents a legal obligation, the infringement of which can be

---

[265] European Commission, 'Reasoned Proposal in accordance with Article 7(1) of the Treaty on European Union regarding the Rule of Law in Poland', COM(2017) 835 final, Brussels, 20 December 2017.

[266] European Parliament, 'Resolution on a proposal calling on the Council to determine, pursuant to Article 7(1) of the Treaty on European Union, the existence of a clear risk of a serious breach by Hungary of the values on which the Union is founded', P8_TA(2018)0340, 12 September 2018.

[267] In total, 12 areas of concern are mentioned in paragraph 1 of the Resolution.

[268] L Pech, 'The Rule of Law in the EU: The Evolution of the Treaty Framework and Rule of Law Toolbox' (2020) Reconnect Working Paper no 7, March 2020, 25.

[269] L Pech, 'From "Nuclear Option" to Damp Squib? A Critical Assessment of the Four Article 7(1) TEU Hearings to Date' (*Verfassungsblog*, 13 November 2019) <https://verfassungsblog.de/from-nuclear-option-to-damp-squib/> accessed 14 August 2020.

[270] European Parliament, 'Resolution on ongoing hearings under Article 7(1) of the TEU regarding Poland and Hungary', P9_TA(2020)0014, 16 January 2020, para 3.

[271] C Closa, 'Institutional Logics and the EU's Limited Sanctioning Capacity under Article 7 TEU' (2020) International Political Science Review, Special Issue Article, 1.

[272] Council of the European Union, Standard modalities for hearings referred to in Article 7(1) TEU, 10641/2/19, 9 July 2019.

[273] European Parliament, LIBE Interim Report on the proposal for a Council decision on the determination of a clear risk of a serious breach by the Republic of Poland of the rule of law, A9-0138/2020, 20 July 2020.

sanctioned through the procedures provided for by Article 7 TEU. What distinguishes this legal obligation from those incumbent on the Member States by virtue of the Charter and other EU laws is that unlike the latter, compliance with Article 2 TEU is required in a general manner without any material or other limitations. This is a critical distinction of constitutional importance—which has been validated even in a reluctant Opinion of the Council Legal Service on the Commission's Rule of Law Framework[274]—and it strikes at the core of how the relationship between the EU and its Member States has always operated.

Traditionally (generalizing somewhat), EU law, including all associated obligations and principles, apply to Member States only when the latter act within the material scope of EU law. In other words, the subject matter of a certain action must be covered (sufficiently) by EU law. With respect to fundamental rights, this cardinal rule of application of EU law is evidenced most clearly in Article 51(1) of the Charter which states that the Charter only applies to Member States when they are implementing EU law (see above). On the contrary, compliance with Article 2 TEU is required from the Member States at all times, regardless of whether their actions relate to areas governed by EU law or not. This means that there is a general, sanctionable obligation on Member States to respect fundamental rights by virtue of their EU membership.

More debatable are other effects of Articles 2 and 7 TEU, namely whether infringements of the values can be sanctioned also through other means than the procedures provided for by Article 7 TEU. Some scholars have argued that Article 2 TEU can serve as the basis for, among others, 'systemic infringement actions' whereby the Commission by virtue of Article 258 TFEU,[275] or Member States through Article 259 TFEU,[276] would bundle Member State infringements and then hit the recalcitrant Member State with a more serious legal action, or the abolition of the material requirement of Article 51(1) of the Charter.[277] The consensus in the academic world seems to be, however, that albeit being a legal obligation, Article 2 TEU can only be sanctioned through the designated procedures in Article 7 TEU.[278] This apparent consensus also showed in the first infringement cases where the Commission attempted to address rule of law deficiencies in Poland and Hungary. It sought to rely on a convoluted variety of provisions in a bid to find EU law competences that would apply to the situations at hand. In a case concerning the politicization and undermining of independence of the judiciary in Hungary (by lowering the compulsory retirement age of judges and public prosecutors from 70 to 62) the Commission relied on the ground of age discrimination prohibited by the Employment Equality Directive.[279] As a result, the Commission did not address the crux of the matter, because it had no general competence allowing that. With regard to the introduction of a different retirement age for female judges (60 years) and male judges (65 years) in Poland, the alleged infringement related to Directive 2006/54 on Gender Equality in Employment.[280] In this case however, and as was in the meantime determined in

---

[274] Opinion of the Council Legal Service, 10296/14, 27 May 2014.

[275] KL Scheppele, 'Enforcing the Basic Principles of EU Law through Systemic Infringement Actions' in Closa and Kochenov (eds), *Reinforcing Rule of Law Oversight* (n 261).

[276] D Kochenov, 'Biting Intergovernmentalism: The Case for the Reinvention of Article 259 TFEU to Make it a Viable Rule of Law Enforcement Tool' (2016) 15 Hague Journal on the Rule of Law 153.

[277] A Jakab, 'Application of the EU CFR by National Courts in Purely Domestic Cases' in Jakab and Kochenov (eds), *Enforcement of EU Law* (n 257).

[278] For a more expansive and optimistic reading of Article 2 TEU see C Hillion, 'Overseeing the Rule of Law in the EU: Legal Mandate and Means' in Closa and Kochenov (eds), *Reinforcing Rule of Law Oversight* (n 261).

[279] Judgment of 6 November 2012, *Commission v Hungary*, C-286/12, ECLI:EU:C:2012:687.

[280] Judgment of 5 November 2019, *Commission v Poland*, C-192/18, ECLI:EU:C:2019:924, paras 47–84.

the *ASJP* preliminary ruling[281] (see below), also Article 19(1) was accepted as a justiciable expression of the value of the rule of law.[282]

Stronger monitoring and enforcement of (other) EU values in the Member States likely necessitates amendments to the Treaties which are difficult to achieve in the current political environment in Europe.[283] The fact that the EU's competences are limited when it comes to enforcing Article 2 TEU values in the Member States does not detract from the normative desirability of increased EU involvement in this area. Carlos Closa succinctly summarized the key arguments in support of EU engagement with respect to the rule of law, but they apply by analogy to other values as well, including the commitment to fundamental rights.

C Closa, 'Reinforcing EU Monitoring of the Rule of Law: Normative Arguments, Institutional Proposals and the Procedural Limitations' in C Closa and D Kochenov, *Reinforcing Rule of Law Oversight in the European Union* (Cambridge University Press 2016)

Three normative arguments justify the involvement of the European Union in a re-inforced monitoring of compliance of the Rule of Law requirement by its Member States. The first argument derives from the model of community that the EU stands for: the EU is a *community of law* which depends on mutual recognition and mutual trust. Secondly, the breach of the principle of the Rule of Law affects all the members of this community. This principle can be labelled the *all affected principle*. The third argument refers to the consistency between the EU's own proclaimed values and policies. Consistency demands that the same requirements apply through time and across policies (unless there are over-riding normative arguments which cancel this requirement).

EU institutions have attempted to address the values enforcement lacuna, but the success of these initiatives has been limited at best. The abovementioned Rule of Law Framework developed by the Commission was meant to systematize the process preceding the triggering of Article 7 TEU (see Figure 4.4). The Framework is a soft law instrument that allows the Commission to start a structured dialogue with Member States on addressing and redressing 'systemic threats' to the rule of law in order to prevent the emergence of a 'clear risk of a serious breach' under Article 7 TEU.[284] From the outset it has been criticized for offering little more than political dialogue and adding nothing to the Commission's ability to deal with infringements of EU values beyond what is already available in the Treaties. Even this limited initiative has been undermined by the Council Legal Service, in the opinion of which the Framework is essentially illegal.[285] The use of the Framework until now has shown few signs of success and has only been applied to Poland.[286] As Pech and Scheppele point out, the

---

[281] *Associação Sindical dos Juízes Portugueses* (n 40).

[282] Judgment of 5 November 2019, *Commission v Poland*, C-192/18, ECLI:EU:C:2019:924, paras 85–135.

[283] O Garner, 'Reinforcing Rule of Law Oversight in the European Union' (2017) 15 International Journal of Constitutional Law 866, 872.

[284] European Commission, 'Communication from the Commission to the European Parliament and the Council—A new EU Framework to strengthen the Rule of Law', COM(2014) 158 final, 3.

[285] Opinion of the Council Legal Service, 10296/14, 27 May 2014.

[286] A choice which seems rather arbitrary: P Bárd and S Carrera, 'The Commission's Decision on "Less EU" in Safeguarding the Rule of Law: A Play in Four Acts' (2017) CEPS Policy Insights 2017/08, 5.

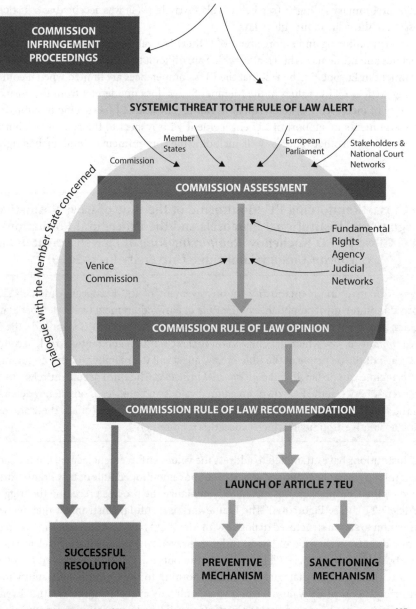

Figure 4.4 The EU Rule of Law Framework developed by the European Commission[287]

slow political dialogue and hesitance to trigger even the preventive stage of Article 7 TEU have in fact allowed the nascent autocrats in Hungary and Poland the time to consolidate their power.

[287] European Commission, 'Annexes to the Communication from the Commission to the European Parliament and the Council—A new EU Framework to strengthen the Rule of Law' COM(2014) 158 final.

For its part, at the suggestion of the Council Legal Service after it attacked the Commission's Framework,[288] the Council has attempted to join the rule of law discourse with its own initiative, an annual rule of law dialogue.[289] Although the Member States have committed 'themselves to establishing a dialogue among all Member States within the Council to promote and safeguard the rule of law in the framework of the Treaties', the Council conclusions from which this dialogue sprung up is revealing as to the light-heartedness of the Member States' conviction to take the issue of the rule of law (and values more generally) seriously. The whole organization of the annual rule of law dialogue is set out on a single page, containing only seven points, half of which are concerned more with Member State sovereign prerogatives and the EU's limited competence in this area than with actually addressing rule of law deficiencies. It is therefore no surprise that the Council rule of law dialogue has been criticized in strong terms in the literature: Pech and Scheppele called the dialogue 'tragically ineffective'[290] and Closa 'very vague and imprecise' and 'deprived of any coercive power'.[291] Although subsequent Council Presidencies have signalled intention to give greater weight to the annual rule of law dialogue, it is difficult to discern a tangible positive impact of the entire exercise other than as a putative display of commitment to EU values. Even the latter, however, is difficult to regard as important and genuine given that the European Council (which brings together highest representatives of Member State governments) refrained from criticizing fellow members, Hungary and Poland, when they ostentatiously pursued an agenda undermining common EU values.

The ambition of the European Parliament has always been somewhat higher when it comes to EU values than what the Commission and the Council came up with. However, the Parliament has been met with reluctance from other institutions and consequently not had the means to implement its proposals in an admittedly challenging legal environment where EU competences are sparse and contested. The EP has been nonetheless present in the debate at least since 2013 when the Tavares report comprehensively criticized developments in Hungary.[292] Since then, the EP has called for the creation of mechanisms and institutions to increase protection of EU values. In October 2016, it called on the Commission to table a proposal for an interinstitutional agreement establishing an EU mechanism on democracy, the rule of law and fundamental rights which would consolidate and enhance the Commission Framework and Council dialogue, include a wider range of actors and create an expert panel.[293] As with all previous efforts, this one, too, was rejected by the other EU

---

[288] Opinion of the Council Legal Service, 10296/14, 27 May 2014. It should be noted that it was a group of Member States' foreign affairs ministers (and later the Council itself) who originally called on the Commission and the Parliament to become engaged in a debate on how to safeguard fundamental EU values. See Council of the European Union, 'Council conclusions on fundamental rights and rule of law and on the Commission 2012 Report on the Application of the Charter of Fundamental Rights of the European Union', 10168/13, 6, and 7 June 2013.

[289] Council of the European Union, 'Conclusions of the Council of the EU and the Member States meeting within the Council on ensuring respect for the rule of law', 17014/14, 16 December 2014.

[290] Pech and Scheppele, 'Illiberalism Within' (n 260) 29.

[291] C Closa, 'Reinforcing EU Monitoring of the Rule of Law: Normative Arguments, Institutional Proposals and the Procedural Limitations' in Closa and Kochenov (eds) *Reinforcing Rule of Law Oversight* (n 261) 33.

[292] European Parliament, 'Report on the situation of fundamental rights: standards and practices in Hungary', P7_TA(2013)0315, 25 June 2013.

[293] European Parliament, 'EU mechanism on democracy, the rule of law and fundamental rights', P8_TA(2016)0409, 25 October 2016. The proposal to create an expert group is not unlike the suggestions of the academic Jan-Werner Müller to create a 'Copenhagen Commission'. See, for example, JW Müller, 'Protecting the Rule of Law and (Democracy!) in the EU: The Idea of a Copenhagen Commission' in Closa and Kochenov (eds), *Reinforcing Rule of Law Oversight* (n 261).

institutions; the Commission refused to propose the requested legislation, citing sufficiency of existing mechanisms.[294]

DRAFT INTERINSTITUTIONAL AGREEMENT
EUROPEAN UNION PACT ON DEMOCRACY, THE RULE OF LAW AND FUNDAMENTAL RIGHTS

Article 1

The core values and founding principles of the Union, namely democracy, the rule of law and fundamental rights, shall be upheld throughout the Union in a Union Pact on Democracy, the Rule of Law and Fundamental Rights (EU Pact for DRF), which provides for the definition, elaboration, monitoring and enforcement of those values and principles, and shall address both the Member States and the Union institutions.

Article 2

The EU Pact for DRF shall consist of:

- an annual Report on democracy, the rule of law and fundamental rights (European DRF Report) with country-specific recommendations incorporating the reporting done by the FRA, the Council of Europe, and other relevant authorities in the field;
- an annual inter-parliamentary debate on the basis of the European DRF Report,
- arrangements for remedying possible risks and breaches, as provided for by the Treaties, including the activation of the preventative or corrective arms of Article 7 TEU,
- a policy cycle for democracy, the rule of law and fundamental rights (DRF Policy Cycle) within the Union institutions.

Article 3

The EU Pact for DRF shall be expanded to incorporate the Commission's Rule of Law Framework and the Council's Rule of Law Dialogue into a single Union instrument.

The Parliament did not abandon its efforts and in November 2018 put forward a new proposal for a 'comprehensive, permanent and objective EU mechanism for the protection of democracy, the rule of law and fundamental rights', underlining that 'such a mechanism is more urgently needed now than ever before'.[295] Once again, the Commission was not fully convinced of the EP's proposal, but it did open a wide debate on the possible ways to reinforce its rule of law toolbox. It launched a Rule of Law Review Cycle, which will monitor rule of law related developments in all 27 Member States and culminate in an Annual Rule

---

[294] European Commission, 'Follow up to the European Parliament resolution on with recommendations to the Commission on the establishment of an EU mechanism on democracy, the rule of law and fundamental rights', SP(2017) 16, Brussels, 17 February 2017.

[295] European Parliament, 'Resolution on the need for a comprehensive EU mechanism for the protection of democracy, the rule of law and fundamental rights', P8_TA(2018)0456, 7 November 2018.

of Law Report.[296] In a subsequent communication, the Commission set out a number of proposals in three areas: promotion, prevention and enforcement.[297] The Council reacted to the Commission's plans during a re-evaluation of its rule of law dialogue in November 2019. It wants to undertake a yearly stocktaking exercise concerning the 'state of play and key developments as regards the rule of law' based on the future Commission's Annual Rule of Law Reports.[298] The enforcement of Article 2 values is meanwhile still being debated in the Parliament. In October 2020, the EP adopted a new proposal on the establishment of an EU Mechanism on Democracy, the Rule of Law and Fundamental Rights through an interinstitutional agreement, which would consolidate and supersede the existing instruments.[299] While building on the 2016 resolution, the EP no longer calls on the Commission to table a proposal but rather sees itself as having the competence to propose an interinstitutional agreement under Article 295 TFEU. Important is the Parliament's critique of the fact that the current initiatives by the Commission fail to encompass the areas of democracy and fundamental rights.[300] It has been argued that the Commission's new set of actions is focused too much on prevention, and does not fully accept the reality of the deliberate dismantling of the rule of law by autocrats in at least two Member States.[301]

D Kochenov, 'Elephants in the Room: The European Commission's 2019 Communication on the Rule of Law' (2019) 11 Hague Journal on the Rule of Law 423

The Commission admitted that part of the challenges that the Rule of Law is now facing is an outcome of deliberate policy choices. It does not seem that the Communication has provided any new approach to such 'hard cases', however, besides promising that the Commission will try to do its job. Most importantly, the literature on Rule of Law backsliding—in radical contrast with the Commission's Communication—clearly advocates one essential point: it is necessary to be crystal clear on the nature of the problem at hand and to act accordingly. Once constitutional capture and systemic backsliding in the Member States where opposition to the Rule of Law is a systemic political choice has been clearly outlined as the core problem, this is bound to alter the remedies required to deal with it. (...)

Failing to answer the question 'what is the problem?' clearly undermines the clarity of the Commission's view of the remedies proposed. This fundamental mistake could very easily be avoided. Inspired by the need for more dialogue with the likes of Hungary and Poland and advocating the view that nobody is perfect, the Communication is thus

---

[296] European Commission, 'Communication from the Commission to the European Parliament, the European Council and the Council on Further strengthening the Rule of Law within the Union' COM(2019) 163 final, Brussels, 3 April 2019. A first Annual Report is currently being prepared.

[297] European Commission, 'Communication from the Commission, Strengthening the Rule of Law within the Union—A blueprint for action' COM(2019) 343 final, Brussels, 17 July 2019.

[298] Council of the European Union, 'Presidency conclusions—Evaluation of the annual rule of law dialogue', 14173/19, 19 November 2019.

[299] European Parliament, 'The establishment of an EU Mechanism on Democracy, the Rule of Law and Fundamental Rights', P9_TA(2020)0251, 7 October 2020.

[300] Ibid, para 4.

[301] L Pech and others, 'The Commission's Rule of Law Blueprint for Action: A Missed Opportunity to Fully Confront Legal Hooliganism' (*reconnect-europe.eu/blog*, 4 September 2019) <https://reconnect-europe.eu/blog/commission-rule-of-law-blueprint/> accessed 14 August 2020.

obviously not the most effective roadmap—with respect—to deal with constitutional capture, which is the only Rule of Law problem hollowing EU's Article 2 TEU promises and worthy of urgent attention. Even the feast of literature on the topic in the context of what Ronald Janse called the ongoing 'renaissance van de Rechtsstaat' apparently had little effect on the Commission. In the Rule of Law Communication, however welcome, it is the Rule of Law, precisely, that remained, most regrettably, the elephant in the room.

The mandate of the Fundamental Rights Agency (FRA) further illustrates the difficulties the EU has faced in institutionalizing some form of oversight over Member States' compliance with common values. When following the Haider affair the EU Network of Independent Experts on Fundamental Rights was set up by the European Commission, upon request of the European Parliament, it was given the mandate to monitor the fundamental rights situation in the Member States and the EU. After it ceased activity in 2006, however, the monitoring role has not been passed over to the FRA, illustrating the scale of Member State concerns about EU meddling in domestic affairs. As a result, the EU does not have a formally designated body monitoring fundamental rights in the Member States, something that would appear as an implied necessity for the purposes of Article 7 TEU or the principle of mutual trust. The FRA, as well as the Commission and the Parliament, nonetheless, report on fundamental rights developments in the Member States but they are not necessarily vested with all the means necessary to exercise this role fully and might occasionally withhold criticism (in particular naming and shaming), knowing that it can spark allegations of lack of competence.

Since the early years of the Union's—then the European Economic Community's—existence, trust was put in national courts to act as 'gatekeepers' of the rule of law and other values within the EU. These courts may trigger the preliminary ruling mechanism to ensure the uniform application of EU legislation and they are competent to protect the rights that individuals derive from EU law directly.[302] In this way, they play a major role in safeguarding the principle of effective judicial protection enshrined in Article 19 TEU and Article 47 of the Charter. In recent years, doubts have been cast on the independence and impartiality of national courts and judges, constituting an essential requirement of effective judicial protection and consequently of the principle of the rule of law,[303] in a number of EU Member States. This worrying trend has translated into several infringement cases and preliminary rulings by the CJEU.[304]

In a case concerning an alleged threat to the independence of Portuguese judges stemming from salary cuts, the CJEU found that the principle of effective judicial protection enshrined in Article 19 TEU requires, among others, that judicial independence at national level is secured. In a ground-breaking move, the Court arrived at this conclusion after identifying the scope of application of Article 19 TEU to be broader than that contained in Article 51(1) of the Charter which requires Member States to be implementing EU law.[305] In this way, the CJEU gave concrete expression to the rule of law obligation of

---

[302] *Van Gend en Loos* (n 96).

[303] See among others *LM (Minister for Justice and Equality)* (n 242) paras 48, 63; Judgment of 24 June 2019, *Commission v Poland*, C-619/18, ECLI:EU:C:2019:531, para 58; Judgment of 5 November 2019, *Commission v Poland*, C-192/18, ECLI:EU:C:2019:924, para 106.

[304] K Lenaerts, 'New Horizons for the Rule of Law Within the EU' (2020) 21 German Law Journal 29.

[305] See Section 4.3.A above.

Article 2 TEU for the first time, albeit at the expense of relaxing the traditional material requirement that normally governs the relationship between EU and national law (as we know it, for example, from the applicability of the Charter). As a result, the obligation to ensure judicial independence of judges at national level can be used as a tool in the EU's fight against rule of law backsliding. This has been partially confirmed in a preliminary ruling on the request of an Irish court wishing to suspend the execution of an EAW due to concerns about the rule of law in Poland. The CJEU agreed that defective judicial independence in a Member State can constitute a legitimate factor in considering the suspension of execution of an EAW.[306]

Judgment of 27 February 2018, *Associação Sindical dos Juízes Portugueses v Tribunal de Contas*, C-64/16, ECLI:EU:C:2018:117.

29. First of all, the Court of Justice points out that as regards the material scope of the second subparagraph of **Article 19(1) TEU**, that provision **relates to 'the fields covered by Union law', irrespective of whether the Member States are implementing Union law, within the meaning of Article 51(1) of the Charter.**

30. According to Article 2 TEU, the European Union is founded on values, such as the rule of law, which are common to the Member States in a society in which, inter alia, justice prevails. In that regard, it should be noted that **mutual trust between the Member States and, in particular, their courts and tribunals is based on the fundamental premiss that Member States share a set of common values on which the European Union is founded**, as stated in Article 2 TEU (...)

31. The European Union is a union based on the rule of law in which individual parties have the right to challenge before the courts the legality of any decision or other national measure relating to the application to them of an EU act (...)

32. **Article 19 TEU, which gives concrete expression to the value of the rule of law stated in Article 2 TEU, entrusts the responsibility for ensuring judicial review in the EU legal order not only to the Court of Justice but also to national courts and tribunals (...)**

33. Consequently, national courts and tribunals, in collaboration with the Court of Justice, fulfil a duty entrusted to them jointly of ensuring that in the interpretation and application of the Treaties the law is observed (...)

34. The Member States are therefore obliged, by reason, inter alia, of the **principle of sincere cooperation**, set out in the first subparagraph of Article 4(3) TEU, to ensure, in their respective territories, the application of and respect for EU law (...). In that regard, as provided for by the second subparagraph of Article 19(1) TEU, Member States are to provide remedies sufficient to ensure effective judicial protection for individual parties in the fields covered by EU law. It is, therefore, for the Member States to establish a system of legal remedies and procedures ensuring effective judicial review in those fields (...)

---

[306] *LM (Minister for Justice and Equality)* (n 242). See Section 4.5 above.

35. **The principle of the effective judicial protection of individuals' rights under EU law, referred to in the second subparagraph of Article 19(1) TEU, is a general principle of EU law** stemming from the constitutional traditions common to the Member States, which has been enshrined in Articles 6 and 13 of the European Convention for the Protection of Human Rights and Fundamental Freedoms, signed in Rome on 4 November 1950, and which is now reaffirmed by Article 47 of the Charter (...)

36. The very existence of effective judicial review designed to ensure compliance with EU law is of the essence of the rule of law (see, to that effect, judgment of 28 March 2017, Rosneft, C-72/15, EU:C:2017:236, paragraph 73 and the case-law cited).

37. It follows that every **Member State must ensure that the bodies which, as 'courts or tribunals' within the meaning of EU law, come within its judicial system in the fields covered by that law, meet the requirements of effective judicial protection.**

38. In that regard, the Court notes that the factors to be taken into account in assessing whether a body is a 'court or tribunal' include, inter alia, whether the body is established by law, whether it is permanent, whether its jurisdiction is compulsory, whether its procedure is inter partes, whether it applies rules of law **and whether it is independent** (...)

The many legislative interventions in Poland affecting the status of judges have been a cause for serious concern for both the judges themselves, as evidenced by preliminary questions referred to the CJEU by several Polish courts, and for the European Commission, which has to this date launched four infringement procedures relating to effective judicial protection in Poland. In the first two of those cases—and the only ones where the CJEU has up to now delivered the final judgments—both the Polish Law on the Supreme Court[307] and the Polish Law on Ordinary Courts[308] have been deemed incompatible with Article 19(1) TEU, by introducing a compulsory retirement age for judges and at the same time granting the Polish president and the Minister of Justice the discretionary power to extend the period of judicial activity of the otherwise forcefully retired judges.[309] The independence of the judiciary was further undermined by the institution of a Disciplinary Chamber to be part of the Polish Supreme Court and by the reform of the law on the National Council of the Judiciary in late 2017, expanding the influence of the current regime on the election of the members. The situation has resulted in both a preliminary question from the Labour Chamber of the Polish Supreme Court and an infringement action instituted by the Commission. With regard to the first, the CJEU has provided the Polish Chamber with several guiding factors to take into account when deciding on the independence and impartiality of the Disciplinary Chamber, while leaving the final decision to the national judge.[310] In the infringement case, however, the CJEU has already granted an order for interim measures suspending the application of certain rules that constitute the Disciplinary Chamber's competence with regard to disciplinary cases against judges.[311]

---

[307] Judgment of 24 June 2019, *Commission v Poland*, C-619/18, ECLI:EU:C:2019:531.

[308] Judgment of 5 November 2019, *Commission v Poland*, C-192/18, ECLI:EU:C:2019:924.

[309] M Coli, 'The Judgment of the CJEU in Commission v. Poland II (C-192/18): The Resurgence of Infringement Procedures as a Tool to Enforce the Rule of Law?' (*Diritti Comparati*, 21 November 2019) <www. diritticomparati.it/judgment-cjeu-commission-v-poland-ii-c-192-18-resurgence-infringement-procedures-tool-enforce-rule-law/> accessed 14 August 2020.

[310] *A.K. and Others v Sąd Najwyższy* (n 49); E Zelazna, 'The Rule of Law Crisis Deepens in Poland after A.K. v. Krajowa Rada Sadownictwa and CP, DO v. Sad Najwyzszy' (2019) 4 European Papers 907.

[311] Order of 8 April 2020, *Commission v Poland*, C-791/19 R, ECLI:EU:C:2020:277.

Judgment of 19 November 2019, *A.K. and Others v Sąd Najwyższy*, C-585/18, C-624/18 and C-625/18, ECLI:EU:C:2019:982

120. That **requirement that courts be independent**, which is inherent in the task of adjudication, forms **part of the essence of the right to effective judicial protection and the fundamental right to a fair trial, which is of cardinal importance as a guarantee that all the rights which individuals derive from EU law will be protected and that the values common to the Member States set out in Article 2 TEU, in particular the value of the rule of law, will be safeguarded** (...)

121. According to settled case-law, the requirement that courts be independent has two aspects to it. The **first aspect**, which is **external** in nature, requires that the court concerned exercise its functions wholly autonomously, without being subject to any hierarchical constraint or subordinated to any other body and without taking orders or instructions from any source whatsoever, thus **being protected against external interventions or pressure liable to impair the independent judgment** of its members and to influence their decisions (...)

122 The **second aspect**, which is internal in nature, is linked to impartiality and seeks to ensure that an equal distance is maintained from the parties to the proceedings and their respective interests with regard to the subject matter of those proceedings. That aspect requires **objectivity and the absence of any interest in the outcome of the proceedings** apart from the strict application of the rule of law (...)

132. It is ultimately for the referring court to rule on that matter having made the relevant findings in that regard. (...) According to settled case-law, the Court may, however, in the framework of the judicial cooperation provided for by that article and on the basis of the material presented to it, provide the national court with an interpretation of EU law which may be useful to it in assessing the effects of one or other of its provisions (...)

171. (...) **Article 47 of the Charter** (...) **must be interpreted as precluding cases concerning the application of EU law from falling within the exclusive jurisdiction of a court which is not an independent and impartial tribunal, within the meaning of the former provision**. That is the case where the objective circumstances in which that court was formed, its characteristics and the means by which its members have been appointed are capable of giving rise to legitimate doubts, in the minds of subjects of the law, as to the imperviousness of that court to external factors, in particular, as to the direct or indirect influence of the legislature and the executive and its neutrality with respect to the interests before it and, thus, may lead to that court not being seen to be independent or impartial with the consequence of prejudicing the trust which justice in a democratic society must inspire in subjects of the law. It is for the referring court to determine, in the light of all the **relevant factors** established before it, whether that applies to a court such as the Disciplinary Chamber of the Sąd Najwyższy (Supreme Court).

The most recent continuance of the Polish rule of law backsliding saga relates to the entry into force of the so-called Muzzle Law effectuating the complete dismantling of the principle of judicial independence in Poland. This law prevents judges from controlling the validity of judicial appointments and making references for preliminary rulings on such questions to the CJEU. It makes it much easier to institute disciplinary actions against judges in relation to the content of their judicial decisions. Following an open letter of rule of law specialists to the President of the European Commission von der Leyen,[312] the Commission has recently started an infringement procedure against the new law.[313] The radical reforms of the Polish judicial system have also led to several cases before the European Court of Human Rights, all related to either appointments or premature terminations of mandates of judges (and one public prosecutor).[314]

Up to now, the case law on the right to an effective legal remedy under both Article 19(1) TEU and Article 47 of the Charter—as an expression of the general principle of the rule of law—has only focused on the conditions of independence and impartiality of the court or tribunal in question. Recently, in a staff case where the CJEU's Grand Chamber has over-turned a decision of the EU Civil Service Tribunal, the right to be judged by a tribunal 'previously established by law' was discussed.[315] Pech has contended that the same argumentation can be used as a precedent to deal with 'fake judges' appointed unlawfully by the Polish National Council of the Judiciary or by the President. The 'Muzzle Law' cannot be a lawful obstacle for judges when assessing the legality of individual appointments, since, according to the Grand Chamber, 'the Courts of the European Union must be able to check whether an irregularity vitiating the appointment procedure at issue could lead to an infringement' of the fundamental right to an effective remedy.[316]

Poland is by no means the only EU Member State where serious violations of the rule of law, democratic principles, and fundamental rights are taking place at the hands of the governing authorities. Even only with regard to judicial independence issues under Article 19(1) TEU, preliminary references are also pending before the CJEU with regard to Hungary, Malta, and Romania. While the debate on appropriate institutional responses to rule of law and democracy backsliding has been progressing, the offenders have lost little time in continuing the project of liberal-democratic dismantlement. In Hungary, also sub-ject to an Article 7 TEU procedure, fundamental principles such as democracy, equality, and pluralism are under constant attack. Cases relating to specific infringements have been brought before the CJEU; examples include the lack of independence of the data protection authority,[317] the registration duty for civil society organizations receiving foreign funding,[318]

---

[312] L Pech, W Sadurski, and KL Scheppele, 'Open Letter to the President of the European Commission re-garding Poland's "Muzzle Law"' (*Verfassungsblog*, 9 March 2020) <https://verfassungsblog.de/open-letter-to-the-president-of-the-european-commission-regarding-polands-muzzle-law/> accessed 14 August 2020.

[313] European Commission, 'Rule of Law: European Commission launches infringement procedure to safe-guard the independence of judges in Poland', Press Release, 29 April 2020.

[314] These five cases are still pending before the ECtHR: *Grzęda v Poland*, App no 43572/18; *Xero Flor v Poland*, App no 4907/18; *Broda and Bojara v Poland*, App nos 26691/18 and 27367/18; *Żurek v Poland*, App no 39650/18; *Sobczyńska and Others v Poland*, App nos 62765/14, 62769/14, 62772/14, and 11708/18. One case in relation to the status of the Disciplinary Chamber and the Chamber of Extraordinary Control and Public Affairs of the Supreme Court is pending as well: *Reczkowicz and Others v Poland*, App nos 43447/19, 49868/19 and 57511/19. See A Bodnar, 'Strasbourg Steps in' (*Verfassungsblog*, 7 July 2020) <https://verfassungsblog.de/strasbourg-steps-in/> accessed 14 August 2020.

[315] The Court of Justice concluded that the sole disregard for a new public call for applications to fill the post of a judge of the EU civil service tribunal did not amount to an infringement of the appointment procedure of such gravity as to vitiate the right of the parties to a hearing by a tribunal previously established by law: Judgment of 26 March 2020, *Review of Simpson v Council*, C-542/18 RX-II and C-543/18 RX-II, ECLI:EU:C:2020:232, para 79.

[316] Ibid, para 55; L Pech, 'Dealing with "fake judges" under EU Law: Poland as a Case Study in light of the Court of Justice's ruling of 26 March 2020 in Simpson and HG' (2020) Reconnect Working Paper no 8, May 2020.

[317] Found to be contrary to Article 28(1) of the Data Protection Directive 95/46/EC: Judgment of 8 April 2014, *Commission v Hungary*, C-288/12, ECLI:EU:C:2014:237.

[318] Found to be contrary to Article 63 TFEU and Articles 7, 8, and 12 of the Charter: Judgment of 18 June 2020, *Commission v Hungary*, C-78/18, ECLI:EU:C:2020:476.

and the requirement of an international treaty between Hungary and the State of origin for the continuance of activities of foreign universities.[319]

European Parliament, Opinion of the Committee on Constitutional Affairs for the Committee on Civil Liberties, Justice and Home Affairs on the situation in Hungary (pursuant to the European Parliament resolution of 17 May 2017) (2017/2131(INL)), 26 March 2018

---

10. Notes that the Venice Commission stated that the limitation of the role of the Hungarian Constitutional Court leads to a risk that it may negatively affect the separation of powers, the protection of human rights and the rule of law; is particularly concerned about the **reintroduction, at the constitutional level, of provisions that should fall within the scope of ordinary law, and which have already been found to be unconstitutional**, with the aim to avoid constitutional review; recommends a review of the functioning and powers of the National Judicial Council in order to ensure that it can fulfil its role as Hungary's independent body of judicial self-government, and calls for the jurisdiction of the Constitutional Court to be restored in full;

11. Is worried about the **shrinking space for civil society organisations and the attempts to control NGOs and to restrict their ability to carry out their legitimate work**, such as the adoption of the so-called 'Stop Soros' legislative package; recalls that the Venice Commission stated in its 'opinion on the draft law on the transparency of organisations receiving support from abroad' (endorsed on 17 June 2017) that such a law would cause a **disproportionate and unnecessary interference with the freedoms of association and expression, the right to privacy, and the prohibition of discrimination**;

12. Deeply regrets the antagonistic and misleading rhetoric sometimes used by the Hungarian institutions when referring to the European Union; and the deliberate choice of the authorities to adopt legislation directly breaching Union values; recalls the objectives set out in Article 3(1) and (2) TEU that Hungary agreed to attain when joining the Union in 2004; reminds that joining the European Union was a voluntary act based on the national sovereignty, with a broad consensus across the Hungarian political spectrum;

13. Emphasises that the **infringement procedure has shown its limits** in addressing systematic violations of Union values because of its main focus on technical matters which allow governments to propose formal remedies while keeping the laws breaching Union law in force

---

[319] Pending, found to be contrary to, among other EU and World Trade Organization rules, Articles 13 and 14(3) of the Charter by AG Kokott: *Commission v Hungary* [2020] ECLI:EU:C:2020:172, Opinion of AG Kokott.

5

International Law, the ECHR, and the EU

5.1 Introduction

With respect to the EU, international law features both as an object of the EU's internal fundamental rights regime and as a source of human rights obligations. Whereas the latter reflects
the original conception of international human rights law, the former is capable of generating
unease due to the scope for contravening the principle of supremacy of international law.[1]
Moreover, although the European Convention on Human Rights (ECHR) can, in principle,
be regarded as international law, it is of special importance to the legal order of the EU and its
Member States, in addition to representing the most developed regional regime of human rights
protection in the world. The specific character of the EU as neither a typical international (intergovernmental) organization nor a state often complicates the relationship with international law
further. Nonetheless, Article 3(5) of the Treaty on European Union (TEU) requires the EU to
contribute, in its international relations, 'to the protection of human rights (…) as well as the
strict observance and the development of international law, including the respect for the principles of the United Nations Charter'. The EU has often struggled to live up to the latter part of
the treaty commitment, occasionally due to difficulties with squaring respect for human rights
and for the authority of the UN Charter.

5.2 Application of EU Fundamental Rights to International Law

By far the most authoritative statement on the nexus between the protection of fundamental
rights in the EU and the reception of international law therein can be found in the four cases
comprising the *Kadi* saga. Although the legal arguments advanced, accepted, and rejected
throughout the judicial proceedings have been comprehensively discussed in the literature,[2]

---

[1] See, for example, A Nollkaemper, 'Rethinking the Supremacy of International Law' (2010) 65 Zeitschrift für
öffentliches Recht 65.

[2] See J Kokott and C Sobotta, 'The Kadi Case—Constitutional Core Values and International Law—Finding
the Balance?' (2012) 23 European Journal of International Law 1015; KS Ziegler, 'Strengthening the Rule of Law,
but Fragmenting International Law: The Kadi Decision of the ECJ from the Perspective of Human Rights' (2009)
9 Human Rights Law Review 288; C Tomuschat, 'Case T-306/01, Ahmed Ali Yusuf and Al Barakaat International
Foundation v. Council and Commission; Case T-315/01, Yassin Abdullah Kadi v. Council and Commission' (2006)
43 Common Market Law Review 537, 545–51; E Defeis, 'Targeted Sanctions, Human Rights, and the Court of First
Instance of the European Community' (2007) 30 Fordham International Law Journal 1449; M Avbelj, F Fontanelli,
and G Martinico, *Kadi on Trial: A Multifaceted Analysis of the Kadi Trial* (Routledge 2014); B Kunoy and A Dawes,
'Plate Tectonics in Luxembourg: The Ménage a Trois Between EC Law, International Law and the European
Convention on Human Rights Following the UN Sanctions Cases' (2009) 46 Common Market Law Review 73; D
Halberstam and E Stein, 'The United Nations, the European Union, and the King of Sweden: Economic Sanctions
and Individual Rights in a Plural World Order' (2009) 46 Common Market Law Review 13; E de Wet, 'From Kadi
to Nada: Judicial Techniques Favouring Human Rights over United Nations Security Council Sanctions' (2013)
12 Chinese Journal of International Law 787; J Wouters, 'The Tormented Relationship Between International

The European Union and Human Rights. Jan Wouters and Michal Ovádek, Oxford University Press (2021). © Jan Wouters and
Michal Ovádek. DOI: 10.1093/oso/9780198814177.003.0005

no analysis of the EU's commitment to human rights would be complete without recounting the key aspects and outcomes of *Kadi I* and *II*.

In 1999, the UN Security Council adopted Resolution 1267 on the situation in Afghanistan.[3] The Resolution demanded that the Taliban ceases to support terrorism and that it surrenders Usama bin Laden to appropriate authorities. In order to enforce the Resolution, the Security Council instituted a sanctions regime on the Taliban which consisted of a flight ban on Taliban-associated aircraft and an asset freeze on funds controlled by the Taliban, as well as any other financial resources made available for the benefit of the Taliban by associated designated persons. The responsibility to designate aircraft and funds for sanctioning in the implementation of the Resolution by UN Member States was given to the newly created Sanctions Committee, composed of members of the Security Council. The Security Council tightened the sanctions regime a year later in Resolution 1333 and extended its scope to cover, among others, the Al-Qaeda organization and all individuals associated with bin Laden.[4] The Sanctions Committee was tasked with maintaining an updated list of such individuals and entities.

Both Resolutions were implemented at EU level by EU Member States through the Common Foreign and Security Policy (CFSP) Common Positions and Council Regulations which were successively amended in accordance with developments in the UN Security Council and the Sanctions Committee.[5] The *Kadi* saga starts with Regulation (EC) No 467/2001 which prescribed the freezing of assets of all persons and entities designated by the Sanctions Committee and listed in Annex I to the Regulation. Article 10(1) of the Regulation empowered the Commission to update the list in Annex I on the basis of determinations made by the UN Security Council or the Sanctions Committee. Shortly after the 11 September terrorist attacks, on 19 October 2001, the Sanctions Committee published a new list of individuals whose assets were to be immediately frozen. On the same day, the European Commission added the names of these individuals, which included Mr Yassin Abdullah Kadi, to the sanction list in Annex I of Regulation 467/2001.[6]

Mr Kadi challenged the Regulations implementing the UN Security Council Resolutions, principally on the grounds that the EU measures violated his fundamental rights. More specifically, he alleged a breach of his right to a fair hearing, the right to property and the principle of proportionality, and the right to effective judicial review.[7] The Court of First Instance (nowadays known as the General Court) was faced with a dilemma: on the one hand, it was already well-established that the EU legal order is based on the rule of law and respecting

---

Law and EU Law' in P Dekker, R Dolzer, and M Waibel (eds), *Making Transnational Law Work in the Global Economy: Essays in Honour of Detlev Vagts* (Cambridge University Press 2010).

[3] UNSC Res 1267 (15 October 1999) UN Doc S/RES/1267.

[4] UNSC Res 1333 (19 December 2000) UN Doc S/RES/1333.

[5] See Council Common Position concerning restrictive measures against the Taliban [1999] OJ L294/1; Regulation (EC) 337/2000 concerning a flight ban and a freeze of funds and other financial resources in respect of the Taliban of Afghanistan [2000] OJ L43/1; Commission Regulation (EC) 2062/2001 amending, for the third time, Council Regulation (EC) No 467/2001 prohibiting the export of certain goods and services to Afghanistan, strengthening the flight ban and extending the freeze of funds and other financial resources in respect of the Taliban of Afghanistan and repealing Regulation (EC) No 337/2000 [2001] OJ L277/25; Regulation (EC) 467/2001 prohibiting the export of certain goods and services to Afghanistan, strengthening the flight ban and extending the freeze of funds and other financial resources in respect of the Taliban of Afghanistan, and repealing Regulation No 337/2000 [2001] OJ L67/1.

[6] See Commission Regulation (EC) 2062/2001 amending, for the third time, Council Regulation (EC) No 467/2001 (n 5) 25.

[7] Judgment of 21 September 2005, *Kadi v Council of the European Union and Commission of the European Communities*, T-315/01, ECLI:EU:T:2005:332, para 59.

fundamental rights is a condition of legality of EU acts such as the Regulations imposing the freezing of Mr Kadi's assets in the case at hand. On the other hand, the Court of First Instance felt compelled to observe the principle of supremacy of international law—and in particular of obligations following from the UN Charter—as expressed in Article 27 of the Vienna Convention on the Law of the Treaties (VCLT) and Article 103 of the UN Charter, relevant especially in light of the binding nature of Chapter VII decisions of the Security Council.

Judgment of 21 September 2005, *Kadi v Council and Commission*, T-315/01, ECLI:EU:T:2005:332

178. The Court considers it appropriate to consider, in the first place, **the relationship between the international legal order under the United Nations and the domestic or Community legal order**, and also the extent to which the exercise by the Community and its Member States of their powers is bound by resolutions of the Security Council adopted under Chapter VII of the Charter of the United Nations.

179. **This consideration will effectively determine the scope of the review of lawfulness, particularly having regard to fundamental rights (...)**

182. As regards, first, the relationship between the Charter of the United Nations and the domestic law of the Member States of the United Nations, that rule of primacy is derived from the principles of customary international law. Under Article 27 of the Vienna Convention on the Law of Treaties of 23 May 1969 (...) a party may not invoke the provisions of its internal law as justification for its failure to perform a treaty.

183. As regards, second, the relationship between the Charter of the United Nations and international treaty law, that rule of primacy is expressly laid down in Article 103 of the Charter which provides that, '[i]n the event of a conflict between the obligations of the Members of the United Nations under the present Charter and their obligations under any other international agreement, their obligations under the present Charter shall prevail'. In accordance with Article 30 of the Vienna Convention on the Law of Treaties, and contrary to the rules usually applicable to successive treaties, that rule holds good in respect of Treaties made earlier as well as later than the Charter of the United Nations. According to the International Court of Justice, all regional, bilateral, and even multilateral, arrangements that the parties may have made must be made always subject to the provisions of Article 103 of the Charter of the United Nations (judgment of 26 November 1984, delivered in the case concerning military and paramilitary activities in and against Nicaragua (*Nicaragua v. United States of America*), ICJ Reports, 1984, p. 392, paragraph 107).

184. That primacy extends to decisions contained in a resolution of the Security Council, in accordance with Article 25 of the Charter of the United Nations, under which the Members of the United Nations agree to accept and carry out the decisions of the Security Council. According to the International Court of Justice, in accordance with Article 103 of the Charter, the obligations of the Parties in that respect prevail over their obligations under any other international agreement (Order of 14 April 1992 (provisional measures), Questions of Interpretation and Application of the 1971 Montreal Convention arising from the Aerial Incident

at Lockerbie (*Libyan Arab Jamahiriya v United States of America*), ICJ Reports, 1992, p. 16, paragraph 42 (...)

199. In this context it is to be borne in mind, first, that in accordance with Article 48(2) of the Charter of the United Nations, the decisions of the Security Council 'shall be carried out by the Members of the United Nations directly and through their action in the appropriate international agencies of which they are members' and, second, that according to the case-law (*Poulsen and Diva Navigation*, paragraph 158 above, paragraph 9, and *Racke*, paragraph 158 above, paragraph 45, and Case 41/74 *Van Duyn* [1974] ECR 1337, paragraph 22), the Community must respect international law in the exercise of its powers and, consequently, Community law must be interpreted, and its scope limited, in the light of the relevant rules of international law.

200. By conferring those powers on the Community, the Member States demonstrated their will to bind it by the obligations entered into by them under the Charter of the United Nations (...)

205. Following that reasoning, it must be held, first, that the Community may not infringe the obligations imposed on its Member States by the Charter of the United Nations or impede their performance and, second, that in the exercise of its powers it is bound, by the very Treaty by which it was established, to adopt all the measures necessary to enable its Member States to fulfil those obligations.

215. Any review of the internal lawfulness of the contested regulation, especially having regard to the provisions or general principles of Community law relating to the protection of fundamental rights, would therefore imply that the Court is to consider, indirectly, the lawfulness of those resolutions. In that hypothetical situation, in fact, the origin of the illegality alleged by the applicant would have to be sought, not in the adoption of the contested regulation but in the resolutions of the Security Council which imposed the sanctions (...).

225. It must therefore be considered that the resolutions of the Security Council at issue fall, in principle, outside the ambit of the Court's judicial review and that the Court has no authority to call in question, even indirectly, their lawfulness in the light of Community law. On the contrary, the Court is bound, so far as possible, to interpret and apply that law in a manner compatible with the obligations of the Member States under the Charter of the United Nations.

226. None the less, the Court is empowered to check, indirectly, the lawfulness of the resolutions of the Security Council in question with regard to jus cogens, understood as a body of higher rules of public international law binding on all subjects of international law, including the bodies of the United Nations, and from which no derogation is possible.

292. None of the applicant's pleas in law or arguments having been successful, the action must be dismissed.

The Court of First Instance ruled in favour of the latter consideration—judicial review of the EU Regulations in question would have amounted to an impermissible challenge to the supremacy of the UN Charter. As the Court of First Instance was aware that its refusal to review the sanctions *de facto* deprived Mr Kadi of any opportunity to dispute his inclusion on the list of suspected terrorist financiers—due to the lack of any review at UN level—in violation of his human rights, the Court made a somewhat half-hearted attempt at checking whether the Security Council Resolutions in question comply with *jus cogens*, the peremptory norms of international law from which no derogation is possible. The Court of First Instance found no breaches of *jus cogens* but the Court's treatment of peremptory norms was condemned by scholars,[8] governmental submissions in the second instance,[9] and in any case set aside on appeal, as the whole judgment, by the Court of Justice.[10]

In essence, the appeal judgment of the Court of Justice (CJEU) reversed the interpretation given to the relationship between EU law and international law. The CJEU held that the constitutional characteristics of the EU legal order—especially the rule of law and respect for fundamental rights—cannot be suspended as a result of obligations following from international agreements.[11] By treating the UN Charter merely as an international agreement, the CJEU irked a significant portion of the scholarly punditry who regard the UN Charter as the founding constitution of the modern international legal order.[12] Nor did the CJEU's statement that the primacy of international law is not threatened,[13] as the measure under its review was the implementing EU Regulation and not the Security Council Resolution, convince many.[14]

Judgment of 3 September 2008, *Kadi and Al Barakaat International Foundation v Council and Commission*, C-402/05 P and C-415/05 P, ECLI:EU:C:2008:461

281. In this connection it is to be borne in mind that **the Community is based on the rule of law, inasmuch as neither its Member States nor its institutions can avoid review of the conformity of their acts with the basic constitutional charter, the EC Treaty**, which established a complete system of legal remedies and procedures designed to enable the Court of Justice to review the legality of acts of the institutions (Case 294/83 Les Verts v Parliament [1986] ECR 1339, paragraph 23).

282. It is also to be recalled that **an international agreement cannot affect** the allocation of powers fixed by the Treaties or, consequently, **the autonomy of the Community legal system**, observance of which is ensured by the Court by virtue of the exclusive jurisdiction conferred on it by Article 220 EC, jurisdiction that the Court has, moreover, already held to form part of the very foundations of the Community (see, to that effect, Opinion 1/91 [1991] ECR I-6079, paragraphs 35

---

[8] Wouters, 'Tormented Relationship Between International Law and EU Law' (n 2) 215; Tomuschat, 'Case T-306/01, Ahmed Ali Yusuf and Al Barakaat International Foundation v. Council and Commission' (n 2) 545–551; Defeis, 'Targeted Sanctions, Human Rights, and the Court of First Instance of the European Community' (n 2) 1454.

[9] Judgment of 3 September 2008, *Kadi and Al Barakaat International Foundation v Council of the European Union and Commission of the European Communities*, C-402/05 P and C-415/05 P, ECLI:EU:C:2008:461, paras 264–268.

[10] Ibid, para 287.

[11] The CJEU referred to the Treaties as the 'constitutional charter' of the EU—repeating its language from the case of *Les Verts*—and also to 'constitutional principles' of the Treaties, notably fundamental rights. Such constitutional language reappeared in an even more forceful manner later in Opinion of 18 December 2014, *EU accession to the ECHR*, 2/13, ECLI:EU:C:2014:2454 but, paradoxically, with the leitmotif of securing the autonomy of EU law rather than enhancing the protection of fundamental rights.

[12] See, for example, Wouters, 'Tormented Relationship Between International Law and EU Law' (n 2).

[13] See *Kadi and Al Barakaat International Foundation v Council of the European Union and Commission of the European Communities* (n 9) para 288.

[14] See, for example: A Tzanakopoulos, 'The Solange Argument as a Justification for Disobeying the Security Council in the Kadi Judgments' in Avbelj, Fontanelli, and Martinico (eds), *Kadi on Trial: A Multifaceted Analysis of the Kadi Judgment* (n 2).

and 71, and Case C-459/03 Commission v Ireland [2006] ECR I-4635, paragraph 123 and case-law cited).

283. In addition, according to settled case-law, **fundamental rights form an integral part of the general principles of law whose observance the Court ensures.** For that purpose, the Court draws inspiration from the constitutional traditions common to the Member States and from the guidelines supplied by international instruments for the protection of human rights on which the Member States have collaborated or to which they are signatories. In that regard, the ECHR has special significance (see, inter alia, Case C-305/05 Ordre des barreaux francophones et germanophone and Others [2007] ECR I-5305, paragraph 29 and case-law cited).

284. **It is also clear from the case-law that respect for human rights is a condition of the lawfulness of Community acts** (Opinion 2/94, paragraph 34) **and that measures incompatible with respect for human rights are not acceptable in the Community** (Case C-112/00 Schmidberger [2003] ECR I-5659, paragraph 73 and case-law cited).

285. **It follows from all those considerations that the obligations imposed by an international agreement cannot have the effect of prejudicing the constitutional principles of the EC Treaty, which include the principle that all Community acts must respect fundamental rights, that respect constituting a condition of their lawfulness which it is for the Court to review in the framework of the complete system of legal remedies established by the Treaty.**

286. In this regard it must be emphasised that, in circumstances such as those of these cases, **the review of lawfulness** thus to be ensured by the Community judicature **applies to the Community act intended to give effect to the international agreement at issue, and not to the latter as such.**

287. With more particular regard to a Community act which, like the contested regulation, is intended to give effect to a resolution adopted by the Security Council under Chapter VII of the Charter of the United Nations, **it is not, therefore, for the Community judicature,** under the exclusive jurisdiction provided for by Article 220 EC, **to review the lawfulness of such a resolution adopted by an international body, even if that review were to be limited to examination of the compatibility of that resolution with jus cogens.**

288. However, **any judgment given by the Community judicature deciding that a Community measure intended to give effect to such a resolution is contrary to a higher rule of law in the Community legal order would not entail any challenge to the primacy of that resolution in international law.**

290. It must therefore be considered whether, as the Court of First Instance held, as a result of the principles governing the relationship between the international legal order under the United Nations and the Community legal order, any judicial review of the internal lawfulness of the contested regulation in the light of fundamental freedoms is in principle excluded, notwithstanding the fact that, as is clear from the decisions referred to in paragraphs 281 to 284 above, **such review is a constitutional guarantee forming part of the very foundations of the Community.**

291. In this respect it is first to be borne in mind that **the European Community must respect international law in the exercise of its powers** (Poulsen and Diva Navigation, paragraph 9, and Racke, paragraph 45), the Court having in addition stated, in the same paragraph of the first of those judgments, that a measure adopted by virtue of

those powers must be interpreted, and its scope limited, in the light of the relevant rules of international law.

298. It must however be noted **that the Charter of the United Nations does not impose the choice of a particular model for the implementation of resolutions** adopted by the Security Council under Chapter VII of the Charter, since they are to be given effect in accordance with the procedure applicable in that respect in the domestic legal order of each Member of the United Nations. **The Charter of the United Nations leaves the Members of the United Nations a free choice among the various possible models for transposition of those resolutions into their domestic legal order.**

299. **It follows from all those considerations that it is not a consequence of the principles governing the international legal order under the United Nations that any judicial review of the internal lawfulness of the contested regulation in the light of fundamental freedoms is excluded** by virtue of the fact that that measure is intended to give effect to a resolution of the Security Council adopted under Chapter VII of the Charter of the United Nations.

300. What is more, **such immunity from jurisdiction for a Community measure like the contested regulation, as a corollary of the principle of the primacy at the level of international law of obligations under the Charter of the United Nations,** especially those relating to the implementation of resolutions of the Security Council adopted under Chapter VII of the Charter, **cannot find a basis in the EC Treaty.**

301. Admittedly, the Court has previously recognised that Article 234 of the EC Treaty (now, after amendment, Article 307 EC) could, if the conditions for application have been satisfied, allow derogations even from primary law, for example from Article 113 of the EC Treaty on the common commercial policy (see, to that effect, Centro-Com, paragraphs 56 to 61).

302. It is true also that Article 297 EC implicitly permits obstacles to the operation of the common market when they are caused by measures taken by a Member State to carry out the international obligations it has accepted for the purpose of maintaining international peace and security.

303. **Those provisions cannot, however, be understood to authorise any derogation from the principles of liberty, democracy and respect for human rights and fundamental freedoms enshrined in Article 6(1) EU as a foundation of the Union.**

304. **Article 307 EC [Article 351 TFEU] may in no circumstances permit any challenge to the principles that form part of the very foundations of the Community legal order,** one of which is the protection of fundamental rights, including the review by the Community judicature of the lawfulness of Community measures as regards their consistency with those fundamental rights.

305. Nor **can an immunity from jurisdiction for the contested regulation** with regard to the review of its compatibility with fundamental rights, arising from the alleged absolute primacy of the resolutions of the Security Council to which that measure is designed to give effect, **find any basis in the place that obligations under the Charter of the United Nations would occupy in the hierarchy of norms within the Community legal order if those obligations were to be classified in that hierarchy.**

306. Article 300(7) EC provides that agreements concluded under the conditions set out in that article are to be binding on the institutions of the Community and on Member States.

307. Thus, by virtue of that provision, supposing it to be applicable to the Charter of the United Nations, the latter would have **primacy over acts of secondary Community law** (see, to that effect, Case C-308/06 Intertanko and Others [2008] ECR I-0000, paragraph 42 and case-law cited).

308. **That primacy at the level of Community law would not, however, extend to primary law, in particular to the general principles of which fundamental rights form part.**

309. That interpretation is supported by Article 300(6) EC, which provides that an international agreement may not enter into force if the Court has delivered an adverse opinion on its compatibility with the EC Treaty, unless the latter has previously been amended.

316. As noted above in paragraphs 281 to 284, **the review by the Court of the validity of any Community measure in the light of fundamental rights must be considered to be the expression, in a community based on the rule of law, of a constitutional guarantee stemming from the EC Treaty as an autonomous legal system which is not to be prejudiced by an international agreement.**

317. The question of the Court's jurisdiction arises in the context of the internal and autonomous legal order of the Community, within whose ambit the contested regulation falls and in which the Court has jurisdiction to review the validity of Community measures in the light of fundamental rights.

326. It follows from the foregoing that **the Community judicature must**, in accordance with the powers conferred on it by the EC Treaty, **ensure the review, in principle the full review**, of the lawfulness of all Community acts in the light of the fundamental rights forming an integral part of the general principles of Community law, including review of Community measures which, like the contested regulation, are designed to give effect to the resolutions adopted by the Security Council under Chapter VII of the Charter of the United Nations.

Kadi is one of the most important cases ever decided by the CJEU. A key reason for that is the explicitly constitutional language the Court employed when speaking about the EU legal order and the sanctity of the internal constitutional principles thereof. In fact, there are few judgments in the whole edifice of CJEU case law which mounted such a strong defence of the rule of law and fundamental rights in the EU in face of competing interests (supremacy of international law, counter-terrorism). Whereas the approach of the Court of First Instance can be termed 'monist' for respecting the primacy of hierarchically higher rules of law (the Chapter VII Security Council Resolutions) within a single integrated conception of municipal and international law, the approach of the CJEU was referred to as 'dualist' or 'pluralist' for marking out the territory of EU law against international law.[15] Although the CJEU's strongly dualist stance exacerbates the ongoing fragmentation of international law, some have praised the judgment's contribution to the international rule of law and fundamental rights protection.[16]

---

[15] See Wouters, 'The Tormented Relationship Between International Law and EU Law' (n 2) 212; G de Búrca, 'The European Court of Justice and the International Legal Order After Kadi' (2010) 51 Harvard International Law Journal 1, 2. See also the judgment in *Nada v Switzerland*, App no 10593/08, 12 September 2012.

[16] Ziegler, 'Strengthening the Rule of Law' (n 2) 288–305.

The conclusion that the CJEU is bound to review the implementing EU Regulations, regardless of the supremacy of the Security Council Resolutions which they closely transpose,[17] led the Court also to re-examine the actual fundamental rights complaints of Mr Kadi. The CJEU found an infringement of Mr Kadi's rights of defence and the right to property. The Court was particularly unimpressed by the absence of a possibility to review the sanctions instituted against the applicant at UN level. In such circumstances, the CJEU was emboldened to conduct its own judicial review and dismiss the option of deferring to the 'in essence diplomatic' procedures before the Sanctions Committee. This issue would later return in the second legal challenge brought by Mr Kadi before the EU courts.

Judgment of 3 September 2008, *Kadi and Al Barakaat International Foundation v Council and Commission*, C-402/05 P and C-415/05 P, ECLI:EU:C:2008:461

---

318. It has in addition been maintained that, having regard to the deference required of the Community institutions vis-à-vis the institutions of the United Nations, the Court must forgo the exercise of any review (…) **given that, under the system of sanctions set up by the United Nations, having particular regard to the re-examination procedure which has recently been significantly improved by various resolutions of the Security Council, fundamental rights are adequately protected.**

319. According to the Commission, so long as under that system of sanctions the individuals or entities concerned have an acceptable opportunity to be heard through a mechanism of administrative review forming part of the United Nations legal system, the Court must not intervene in any way whatsoever.

320. In this connection it may be observed, first of all, that if in fact, as a result of the Security Council's adoption of various resolutions, amendments have been made to the system of restrictive measures set up by the United Nations with regard both to entry in the summary list and to removal from it [see, in particular, Resolutions 1730 (2006) of 19 December 2006, and 1735 (2006) of 22 December 2006], **those amendments were made after the contested regulation had been adopted so that, in principle, they cannot be taken into consideration in these appeals.**

321. In any event, the existence, within that United Nations system, of the re-examination procedure before the Sanctions Committee, even having regard to the amendments recently made to it, cannot give rise to generalised immunity from jurisdiction within the internal legal order of the Community.

322. Indeed, **such immunity, constituting a significant derogation from the scheme of judicial protection of fundamental rights laid down by the EC Treaty, appears unjustified, for clearly that re-examination procedure does not offer the guarantees of judicial protection.**

323. In that regard, although it is now open to any person or entity to approach the Sanctions Committee directly, submitting a request to be removed from the

---

[17] Antonios Tzanakopoulos argued that the lack of discretion on the part of the EU—especially insofar as the Commission's measure to include Mr Kadi on the list is concerned, as it merely copied over the list of the Sanctions Committee—should have been taken into account by the EU judiciary. See Tzanakopoulos, 'The Solange Argument as a Justification for Disobeying the Security Council in the Kadi Judgments' (n 14) 142.

summary list at what is called the 'focal' point, **the fact remains that the procedure before that Committee is still in essence diplomatic and intergovernmental, the persons or entities concerned having no real opportunity of asserting their rights and that committee taking its decisions by consensus, each of its members having a right of veto.**

324. The Guidelines of the Sanctions Committee, as last amended on 12 February 2007, make it plain **that an applicant submitting a request for removal from the list may in no way assert his rights himself during the procedure before the Sanctions Committee or be represented for that purpose,** the Government of his State of residence or of citizenship alone having the right to submit observations on that request.

325. Moreover, **those Guidelines do not require the Sanctions Committee to communicate to the applicant the reasons and evidence justifying his appearance in the summary list or to give him access, even restricted, to that information.** Last, if that Committee rejects the request for removal from the list, it is under no obligation to give reasons.

334. (…) in the light of the actual circumstances surrounding the inclusion of the appellants' names in the list of persons and entities covered by the restrictive measures contained in Annex I to the contested regulation, it must be held that the rights of the defence, in particular **the right to be heard, and the right to effective judicial review of those rights, were patently not respected.**

335. According to settled case-law, the principle of effective judicial protection is a general principle of Community law stemming from the constitutional traditions common to the Member States, which has been enshrined in Articles 6 and 13 of the ECHR, this principle having furthermore been reaffirmed by Article 47 of the Charter of fundamental rights of the European Union (…)

348. Because the Council **neither communicated to the appellants the evidence used against them** to justify the restrictive measures imposed on them **nor afforded them the right to be informed of that evidence within a reasonable period after those measures were enacted,** the appellants were not in a position to make their point of view in that respect known to advantage. Therefore, the appellants' rights of defence, in particular the right to be heard, were not respected.

352. It must, therefore, be held that **the contested regulation,** in so far as it concerns the appellants, **was adopted without any guarantee being given as to the communication of the inculpatory evidence against them or as to their being heard in that connection,** so that it must be found that that regulation was adopted according to a procedure in which the appellants' **rights of defence were not observed,** which has had the further consequence that the **principle of effective judicial protection has been infringed.**

369. The contested regulation, in so far as it concerns Mr Kadi, was adopted without furnishing any guarantee enabling him to put his case to the competent authorities, in a situation in which the restriction of his property rights must be regarded as significant, having regard to the general application and actual continuation of the freezing measures affecting him.

370. It must therefore be held that, in the circumstances of the case, the imposition of the restrictive measures laid down by the contested regulation in respect of Mr Kadi, by including him in the list contained in Annex I to that regulation, constitutes an unjustified restriction of his right to property.

The violations of Mr Kadi's rights of defence, right to an effective judicial remedy, and his right to property were found by the CJEU ultimately to boil down to the lack of reasons and information provided to him by the sanctioning EU authorities (as it was the EU implementing measure under review, not the Security Council Resolution). Without the necessary information, Mr Kadi was unable to mount a meaningful legal challenge against his inclusion on the list of suspected terrorist associates. The fact that such information was also not provided by the Sanctions Committee, the procedures of which in any event had not allowed Mr Kadi to obtain the necessary judicial protection, only underlined for the CJEU the fundamental rights deficiencies of the sanctions regime.

In the aftermath of *Kadi*, EU Member States and the Commission scrambled to remedy the procedural lacunae singled out by the CJEU in its judgment—all the more so as the CJEU, realizing the adverse potential of its ruling for international security, permitted the annulled sanctions to remain in place for another three months after the publication of the decision.[18] During this time, the French Permanent Representative of France to the UN requested the Sanctions Committee, on behalf of the EU, to make public a summary of reasons for Mr Kadi's inclusion on the sanctions list.[19] This summary of reasons was subsequently communicated to Mr Kadi by the Commission. The Commission also evaluated Mr Kadi's reply to the summary but ultimately considered the maintenance of sanctions against him justified.[20] Mr Kadi therefore brought another action for annulment under Article 263 TFEU before the General Court.

The General Court was careful to follow closely the precedent laid down by the CJEU in *Kadi I* which led the former Court of First Instance to the conclusion that the applicant's rights of defence were observed 'only in the most formal and superficial sense', as the European Commission never truly considered second-guessing the findings of the Sanctions Committee.[21] Moreover, the summary of reasons published by the Sanctions Committee and communicated to Mr Kadi by the Commission was, in the General Court's view, 'clearly insufficient to enable the applicant to launch an effective challenge to the allegations against him', especially as no further evidence was adduced by the UN or EU bodies.[22] A re-examination procedure introduced by the Sanctions Committee which gave Mr Kadi the opportunity to present his case for delisting (unsuccessfully) was found equally inadequate to safeguard the applicant's rights.[23] The General Court hence decided to annul (again) the disputed Regulation on the account that the rights of defence, the right to an effective remedy and the right to property were breached in the case.

On appeal, the CJEU upheld the operative conclusion that the Regulation providing for the freezing of funds of Mr Kadi shall be annulled. The Court changed, nevertheless, much of the underlying reasoning. As opposed to the General Court, which found that the lack of evidence and access to information in itself constituted a violation of fundamental rights, the CJEU found it necessary to balance carefully the fundamental rights of Mr Kadi against the legitimate security interests of the international community. The Court has remarked that in some instances, such interests can justify not disclosing evidence to the person affected by the restrictive measures. In the event of judicial proceedings, however, the absence

---

[18] *Kadi and Al Barakaat International Foundation v Council of the European Union and Commission of the European Communities* (n 9) para 376.
[19] Judgment of 30 September 2010, *Kadi v Commission*, T-85/09, ECLI:EU:T:2010:418, para 49.
[20] Ibid, para 61.
[21] Ibid, para 171.
[22] Ibid, para 174.
[23] Ibid, para 180.

of supplementary evidence would make it more difficult to substantiate the statement of reasons on which the listing of terrorist suspects rests.

Judgment of 18 July 2013, *Commission and Others v Kadi*, C-584/10 P, C-593/10 P and C-595/10 P, ECLI:EU:C:2013:518

103. In this case, it is necessary to determine whether, **in the light of the requirements** (...) relating to the maintenance **of international peace and security while respecting international law,** and specifically the principles of the Charter of the United Nations, **the fact that Mr Kadi and the Courts of the European Union did not have access to the information and evidence relied on against him** (...) **constitutes an infringement of the rights of the defence and the right to effective judicial protection.**

104. (...) **it is the task of the Security Council to determine what constitutes a threat to international peace and security and to take the measures necessary,** by means of the adoption of resolutions under Chapter VII of that Charter, to maintain or restore international peace and security, in accordance with the purposes and principles of the United Nations, including respect for human rights.

107. Consequently, where, under the relevant Security Council resolutions, the Sanctions Committee has decided to list the name of an organisation, entity or individual on its Consolidated List, the competent European Union authority must, in order to give effect to that decision on behalf of the Member States, take the decision to list the name of that organisation, entity or individual, or to maintain such listing, in Annex I to Regulation No 881/2002 on the basis of the summary of reasons provided by the Sanctions Committee. On the other hand, **there is no provision in those resolutions to the effect that the Sanctions Committee is automatically to make available** to, in particular, the European Union authority responsible for the adoption by the European Union of its decision to list or maintain a listing, **any material other than that summary of reasons.**

122. (...) there is no requirement that that authority produce before the Courts of the European Union all the information and evidence underlying the reasons alleged in the summary provided by the Sanctions Committee. It is however necessary that the information or evidence produced should support the reasons relied on against the person concerned.

130. Having regard to the preventive nature of the restrictive measures at issue, if, in the course of its review of the lawfulness of the contested decision (...) the Courts of the European Union consider that, at the very least, **one of the reasons mentioned in the summary provided by the Sanctions Committee is sufficiently detailed and specific, that it is substantiated and that it constitutes in itself sufficient basis to support that decision,** the fact that the same cannot be said of other such reasons cannot justify the annulment of that decision. In the absence of one such reason, the Courts of the European Union will annul the contested decision.

131. **Such a judicial review is indispensable to ensure a fair balance between the maintenance of international peace and security and the protection of the fundamental rights and freedoms of the person concerned** (...), **those being shared values of the UN and the European Union.**

133. Such a review is all the more essential since, despite the improvements added, in particular after the adoption of the contested regulation, the procedure for delisting and ex officio re-examination at UN level **they do not provide to the person** whose name is listed on the Sanctions Committee Consolidated List and, subsequently, in Annex I to Regulation No 881/2002, **the guarantee of effective judicial protection**, as the European Court of Human Rights, endorsing the assessment of the Federal Supreme Court of Switzerland, has recently stated in paragraph 211 of its judgment of 12 September 2012, *Nada v. Switzerland* (...)

134. **The essence of effective judicial protection must be that it should enable the person concerned to obtain a declaration from a court**, by means of a judgment ordering annulment whereby the contested measure is retroactively erased from the legal order and is deemed never to have existed, that the listing of his name, or the continued listing of his name, on the list concerned was vitiated by illegality, the recognition of which may re-establish the reputation of that person or constitute for him a form of reparation for the non-material harm he has suffered (...)

135. It follows from the criteria analysed above that, **for the rights of the defence and the right to effective judicial protection to be respected first, the competent European Union authority must (i) disclose to the person concerned the summary of reasons** provided by the Sanctions Committee which is the basis for listing or maintaining the listing of that person's name in Annex I to Regulation No 881/ 2002, (ii) **enable him effectively to make known his observations** on that subject and (iii) **examine, carefully and impartially, whether the reasons alleged are well founded**, in the light of the observations presented by that person and any exculpatory evidence that may be produced by him.

136. Second, respect for those rights implies that, in the event of a legal challenge, **the Courts of the European Union are to review**, in the light of the information and evidence which have been disclosed inter alia **whether the reasons relied on in the summary provided by the Sanctions Committee are sufficiently detailed and specific and, where appropriate, whether the accuracy of the facts relating to the reason concerned has been established.**

137. On the other hand, **the fact that the competent European Union authority does not make accessible to the person concerned and, subsequently, to the Courts of the European Union information or evidence** which is in the sole possession of the Sanctions Committee or the Member of the UN concerned and which relates to the summary of reasons underpinning the decision at issue, **cannot, as such, justify a finding that those rights have been infringed.** However, in such a situation, the Courts of the European Union, which are called upon **to review whether the reasons contained in the summary provided by the Sanctions Committee are well founded in fact**, taking into consideration any observations and exculpatory evidence produced by the person concerned and the response of the competent European Union authority to those observations, **will not have available to it supplementary information or evidence. Consequently, if it is impossible for the Courts to find that those reasons are well founded, those reasons cannot be relied on as the basis for the contested listing decision.**

138. Hence (...) the General Court erred in law by basing its finding that the rights of the defence and the right to effective judicial protection and, consequently, the principle of proportionality had been infringed, on the failure of the Commission

to disclose to Mr Kadi and to the General Court itself the information and evidence underlying the reasons for maintaining the listing of Mr Kadi's name in Annex I to Regulation No 881/2002, when (...) the Commission was not in possession of that information and evidence.

139. (...) the fact that the party concerned and the Courts of the European Union do not have access to information or evidence which the competent Union authority does not have in its possession constitutes, as such, an infringement of the rights of the defence or the right to effective judicial protection.

140. (...) the General Court erred in law by basing (...) its finding that there had been such an infringement on the fact that, in its opinion, **the allegations made in the summary of reasons provided by the Sanctions Committee were vague and lacking in detail, even though such a general conclusion cannot be drawn if each of those reasons is examined separately**.

163. (...) **none of the allegations** presented against Mr Kadi in the summary provided by the Sanctions Committee **are such as to justify the adoption**, at European Union level, **of restrictive measures** against him, either because the statement of reasons is insufficient, or because information or evidence which might substantiate the reason concerned, in the face of detailed rebuttals submitted by the party concerned, is lacking.

By providing detailed guidelines on balancing fundamental rights with counter-terrorism measures, the necessity to review the precision of reasons provided by the Sanctions Committee, and the implications for judicial proceedings of non-disclosure of supporting evidence, the CJEU has concluded the *Kadi* saga. Indeed, the overall guidance provided by the CJEU for the future was perhaps the most important outcome of the case, as Mr Kadi was by the time of the Court's appeal decision in *Kadi II* already delisted from both the UN and EU sanctions list.

Despite the milder tone of *Kadi II*, the CJEU points again to the insufficiency of the human rights safeguards existing at the UN level. The Court has repeated this criticism and uses it to strengthen the rationale for carrying out judicial review itself (paragraph 133) despite the fact that following the reproach in *Kadi I*, the UN improved procedures for delisting and created the Office of the Ombudsperson who assisted the Sanctions Committee with delisting requests. The Court's reasoning was aimed at those who wished to see more deference from a regional organization and its legal order towards international law and the UN. What the CJEU implicitly stated was that, in essence, as long as the UN Security Council does not develop sufficient human rights guarantees for the sanctions regime, the EU judiciary has an obligation to review cases challenging EU implementation measures of the UN sanctions. Such 'as long as' (*Solange*) logic is well-known from the CJEU's own relationship to the constitutional courts of EU Member States who have granted a presumption of equivalent fundamental rights protection to the EU (as has the European Court of Human Rights (ECtHR) in its *Bosphorus* doctrine).[24] The expectation of Member States' constitutional courts that the CJEU must protect fundamental rights in the domain of EU law has even been touted as a reason for the CJEU's reluctance in *Kadi* to adhere strictly to the principle of supremacy of international law in the absence of sufficient fundamental rights safeguards at the UN level.[25]

---

[24] See Ch 1 as regards the *Solange* judgment of the German Constitutional Court and see Section 5.4.A below as regards the *Bosphorus* judgment.

[25] See Kokott and Sobotta, 'The Kadi Case—Constitutional Core Values and International Law—Finding the Balance?' (n 2) 1019.

Nevertheless, the CJEU has set the threshold for a potential *Solange*-type presumption high by maintaining that the satisfaction of the right to effective judicial protection entails that a person concerned can obtain 'a declaration from a court'.[26] While relatively uncontroversial in domestic settings, in the circumstances of the UN Security Council, where even the International Court of Justice has only minimal jurisdiction, the establishment of a court for the sanctions regime represents a tall order for the UN system. The possibility of the CJEU refraining from judicial review of EU implementing measures of UN Security Council Resolutions is therefore likely to remain in the realm of the purely theoretical in the foreseeable future.

The underlying complex interrelationships between the legal orders of EU Member States, the EU itself, and the UN/international system reveals that the CJEU's concern for Mr Kadi's fundamental rights does not necessarily stem from an altruistic belief in universal human rights protection. Rather, the CJEU was more than mindful of protecting the autonomy of EU law and of its own judicial prerogatives within the EU legal order, both vis-à-vis EU Member States by fulfilling the conditions of the *Solange* presumption of equivalent rights protection, as well as from international law and institutions by insulating the EU system from an unconditional binding effect of UN Security Council Resolutions.

The fact that the principle of autonomy embodies a key motive in the CJEU's restrained approach to external sources of law is clearly brought to light when juxtaposing *Kadi* with another long-running legal saga: the EU accession to the ECHR.[27] In connection with the latter, the CJEU has produced two negative binding Opinions and in particular in the more recent *Opinion 2/13*, the Court has stressed the importance of preserving the autonomy of EU law despite the obvious contribution the EU's accession to the ECHR would make to the rule of law and human rights protection in Europe. Thus, whereas in *Kadi* the CJEU indirectly reviewed legal measures created by the UN in the international legal order on the basis of fundamental rights, in *Opinion 2/13* the Court rejected the proposal for precisely such fundamental rights oversight of its own legal system by the ECtHR. Such an EU-centric approach to human rights protection does little to aid the EU's purported image as a global human rights actor.

While the area of sanctions is the most litigated domain connected to international law, the application of EU fundamental rights crops up in other international issues as well. A good example is the increasingly global reach of EU data protection law which includes the rights to privacy and data protection enshrined in Articles 7 and 8 of the Charter. In the case of *Schrems*, the CJEU struck down an adequacy decision concerning data transfers to the US due to lack of compatibility with EU data protection principles and the Charter.[28] Similarly, in *Opinion 1/15* the CJEU found a proposed agreement on passenger name records between the EU and Canada incompatible with EU law.[29] The fundamental rights protection related to personal data guaranteed within the EU can travel in this way beyond the Union's borders. *Opinion 1/15* is at the same time a major landmark for fundamental rights review of international agreements negotiated by the EU, showing that the Charter is now firmly part

---

[26] Judgment of 18 July 2013, *Commission and Others v Kadi*, C-584/10 P, C-593/10 P, and C-595/10 P, ECLI:EU:C:2013:518, para 134.

[27] M Ovádek, 'External Judicial Review and Fundamental Rights in the EU: A Place in the Sun for the Court of Justice' (2016) EU Diplomacy Papers 2/2016, 13 <https://www.coleurope.eu/system/files_force/research-paper/edp_2_2016_ovadek_0.pdf> accessed 14 August 2020.

[28] Judgment of 6 October 2015, *Schrems v Data Protection Commissioner*, C-362/14, ECLI:EU:C:2015:650.

[29] The opinion was requested by the European Parliament.

of the constitutional framework against which all EU legal acts, including treaties, can be measured.[30]

> ### Opinion of 26 July 2017, *Canada–EU Passenger Name Record Agreement*, 1/15, ECLI:EU:C:2017:592
>
> 35. The Parliament submits that, having regard to the serious doubts expressed by the EDPS, in particular, in his opinion of 30 September 2013, and to the case-law resulting from the judgment of 8 April 2014, *Digital Rights Ireland and Others* (C-293/12 and C-594/12, EU:C:2014:238), there is legal uncertainty as to whether the envisaged agreement is compatible with Article 16 TFEU and with Article 7, Article 8 and Article 52(1) of the Charter (...).
>
> 36. According to the Parliament, the transfer of PNR data from the European Union to Canada for the purposes of the Canadian authorities possibly accessing that data, as provided for in the envisaged agreement, falls within the scope of Articles 7 and 8 of the Charter. That data, taken as a whole, may allow very precise conclusions to be drawn concerning the private lives of the persons whose PNR data is processed, such as their permanent or temporary places of residence, their movements and their activities. That agreement therefore entails wide-ranging and particularly serious interferences with the fundamental rights guaranteed in Articles 7 and 8 of the Charter.
>
> 122. Since the PNR data (...) includes information on identified individuals, namely air passengers flying between the European Union and Canada, the various forms of processing to which, under the envisaged agreement, that data may be subject, namely its transfer from the European Union to Canada, access to that data with a view to its use or indeed its retention, **affect the fundamental right to respect for private life, guaranteed in Article 7 of the Charter**.
>
> 123. Furthermore, the processing of the PNR data covered by the envisaged agreement **also falls within the scope of Article 8 of the Charter** because it constitutes the processing of personal data within the meaning of that article and, accordingly, must necessarily satisfy the data protection requirements laid down in that article (...).
>
> 124. As the Court has held, **the communication of personal data to a third party, such as a public authority, constitutes an interference with the fundamental right enshrined in Article 7 of the Charter, whatever the subsequent use of the information communicated**. The same is true of the retention of personal data and access to that data with a view to its use by public authorities. In this connection, it does not matter whether the information in question relating to private life is sensitive or whether the persons concerned have been inconvenienced in any way on account of that interference (...).
>
> 125. Consequently, both the transfer of PNR data from the European Union to the Canadian Competent Authority and the framework negotiated by the European Union with Canada of the conditions concerning the retention of that data, its use and its subsequent transfer to other Canadian authorities, Europol, Eurojust,

---

[30] For comment, see C Docksey, 'Opinion 1/15: Privacy and Security, Finding the Balance' (2017) 24 Maastricht Journal of European and Comparative Law 768.

judicial or police authorities of the Member States or indeed to authorities of third countries, which are permitted, inter alia, by Articles 3, 4, 6, 8, 12, 15, 16, 18 and 19 of the envisaged agreement, **constitute interferences with the right guaranteed in Article 7 of the Charter.**

126. Those operations **also constitute an interference with** the fundamental right to the protection of personal data guaranteed in **Article 8 of the Charter since they constitute the processing of personal data** (...).

136. However, the rights enshrined in Articles 7 and 8 of the Charter **are not absolute rights,** but must be considered in relation to their function in society (...).

163. (...) as regards the PNR data to be transferred to Canada, headings 5, 7 and 17 of the Annex to the envisaged agreement **do not delimit in a sufficiently clear and precise manner the scope of the interference** with the fundamental rights enshrined in Articles 7 and 8 of the Charter.

204 Air passengers who have left Canada have, as a general rule, been subject to checks on entry to and on departure from Canada. Similarly, their PNR data has been verified before their arrival in Canada and, as the case may be, during their stay and on their departure from that non-member country. In those circumstances, those passengers should be regarded as not presenting, in principle, a risk as regards terrorism or serious transnational crime, in so far as neither those checks and verifications, nor any other circumstance, have revealed the existence of objective evidence to that effect. In any event, it is not apparent that all air passengers who have travelled to Canada would present, after their departure from that country, a higher risk than other persons who have not travelled to that country during the previous five years and in respect of whom Canada does not therefore hold PNR data.

205 Consequently, as regards air passengers in respect of whom no such risk has been identified on their arrival in Canada and up to their departure from that non-member country, there would not appear to be, once they have left, a connection— even a merely indirect connection—between their PNR data and the objective pursued by the envisaged agreement which would justify that data being retained. The considerations put forward before the Court, inter alia, by the Council and the Commission regarding the average lifespan of international serious crime networks and the duration and complexity of investigations relating to those networks, **do not justify the continued storage of the PNR data of all air passengers after their departure from Canada** for the purposes of possibly accessing that data, regardless of whether there is any link with combating terrorism and serious transnational crime (...).

206 The continued storage of the PNR data of all air passengers after their departure from Canada is **not** therefore **limited to what is strictly necessary.**

228. Under Article 8(3) of the Charter, compliance with the requirements stemming from Article 8(1) and (2) thereof is subject to control by an independent authority.

231. Article 10 of the envisaged agreement **does not guarantee in a sufficiently clear and precise manner** that **the oversight of compliance** with the rules laid down in that agreement relating to the protection of individuals with regard to the processing of PNR data **will be carried out by an independent authority** (...)

5.3 International Human Rights Law and the EU

To date, the EU has signed only two international human rights treaties[31]—the Convention on the Rights of Persons with Disabilities (CRPD) and the Istanbul Convention on preventing and combating violence against women and domestic violence.[32] Only the CRPD has also been ratified and consequently has become an 'integral part' of EU law. Therefore, it is binding on the Member States, as a matter of EU law, to implement the international obligations contained therein.[33] The EU also has a special and complicated relationship with the ECHR which technically qualifies as international but has the distinct qualities of an advanced regional human rights system. Both of these are discussed in more detail in sections 5.5 and 5.6 below. There is, however, a plethora of human rights obligations in general public international law by which EU Member States are bound but whose status in the EU is somewhat ambiguous due to the lack of formal accession and non-state character of the EU.

By ratifying human rights treaties, Member States assume human rights obligations contained therein, normally coupled with some kind of a monitoring mechanism (see Table 5.1). The territorial scope of applicability of the treaties is as a general rule limited to the territory of the contracting party. In a situation where all EU Member States have become a party to a given agreement, the whole territory of the EU is technically covered by the treaty. This does not mean, however, that a protection gap cannot arise. Are the Member States still bound by the human rights agreements when they confer powers on the EU to act instead?

The answer is clear from both the perspective of EU law and of international law insofar as rights and obligations arising from treaties concluded by EU Member States before they joined the EU. Article 351 TFEU explicitly states that accession to the EU does not release Member States from their prior international legal commitments.[34] The CJEU had recognized the validity of this provision in its case law—even stating that it is in accordance with principles of international law—before later conditioning its application in *Kadi*.[35]

Consolidated version of the Treaty on the Functioning of the European Union [2012] OJ C326/47

Article 351

The rights and obligations arising from agreements concluded before 1 January 1958 or, for acceding States, **before the date of their accession**, between one or more Member

---

[31] As opposed to many international conventions in areas that are more closely connected to its economic objectives, such as (free) trade agreements, see in general: A Mohay, 'The Status of International Agreements Concluded by the European Union in the EU Legal Order' (2017) 33, 3/4 Pravni Vjesnik 151. For the human rights implications of FTAs, see Ch 10.

[32] Convention on the Rights of Persons with Disabilities (adopted 13 December 2006, entered into force 3 May 2008) 2515 UNTS 3; Council of Europe Convention on preventing and combating violence against women and domestic violence (adopted 11 May 2011, entered into force 1 August 2014) CETS No 210.

[33] Article 216(2) TFEU; Judgment of 30 April 1974, *Haegeman v Belgian State*, 181/73, ECLI:EU:C:1974:41, para 5; Judgment of 7 October 2004, *Commission of the European Communities v French Republic*, C-239/03, ECLI:EU:C:2004:598.

[34] See also Judgment of 4 July 2000, *Commission of the European Communities v Portuguese Republic*, C-62/98, ECLI:EU:C:2000:358, para 44.

[35] See Judgment of 14 January 1997, *The Queen, ex parte Centro-Com Srl v HM Treasury and Bank of England*, C-124/95, ECLI:EU:C:1997:8, para 56.

Table 5.1 Acceptance of UN Human Rights Conventions by EU Member States

Human rights instrument	Austria	Belgium	Bulgaria	Croatia	Cyprus	Czech Republic	Denmark	Estonia	Finland	France	Germany	Gree...
Convention on the Prevention and Punishment of the Crime of Genocide (1948)	A 1958	R 1951	A 1950	R(S) 1992	A 1982	R(S) 1993	R 1951	A 1991	A 1959	R 1950	A 1954	R 1954
Convention relating to the Status of Refugees (1951)	R 1954	R 1953	A 1993	R(S) 1992	R(S) 1963	A(S) 1993	R 1952	A 1997	A 1968	R 1954	R 1953	R 1960
International Convention on the Elimination of All Forms of Racial Discrimination (1966)	R 1972	R 1975	R 1966	R(S) 1992	R 1967	R(S) 1993	R 1971	A 1991	R 1970	A 1971	R 1969	R 1970
International Covenant on Civil and Political Rights (1966)	R 1978	R 1983	R 1970	R(S) 1992	R 1969	R(S) 1993	R 1972	A 1991	R 1975	A 1980	R 1973	A 1997
Optional Protocol to the International Covenant on Civil and Political Rights (1966)	R 1987	A 1994	A 1992	A 1995	R 1992	A(S) 1993	R 1972	A 1991	R 1975	A 1984	A 1993	A 1997
International Covenant on Economic, Social and Cultural Rights (1966)	R 1978	R 1983	R 1970	R(S) 1992	R 1969	R(S) 1993	R 1972	A 1991	R 1975	A 1980	R 1973	A 1985
Protocol relating to the Status of Refugees (1967)	A 1973	A 1969	A 1993	A(S) 1992	A 1968	A(S) 1993	A 1968	A 1997	A 1968	A 1971	A 1969	A 1968
International Convention on the Suppression and Punishment of the Crime of Apartheid (1973)	-	-	R 1974	R(S) 1992	-	R(S) 1993	-	A 1991	-	-	-	-
Convention on the Elimination of All Forms of Discrimination against Women (1979)	R 1982	R 1985	R 1982	R(S) 1992	A 1985	R(S) 1993	R 1983	A 1991	R 1986	R 1983	R 1985	R 1983
Convention against Torture and Other Cruel, Inhuman or Degrading Treatment or Punishment (1984)	R 1987	R 1999	R 1986	R(S) 1992	R 1991	R(S) 1993	R 1987	A 1991	R 1989	R 1986	R 1990	R 1988
Convention on the Rights of the Child (1989)	R 1992	R 1991	R 1991	R(S) 1992	R 1991	R(S) 1993	R 1991	A 1991	R 1991	R 1990	R 1992	R 1993
Second Optional Protocol to the International Covenant on Civil and Political Rights, aiming at the Abolition of the Death Penalty (1989)	R 1993	R 1998	R 1999	A 1995	A 1999	A 2004	R 1994	A 2004	R 1991	A 2007	R 1992	A 1997
Optional Protocol to the Convention on the Elimination of All Forms of Discrimination against Women (1999)	R 2000	R 2004	R 2006	R 2001	R 2002	R 2001	R 2000	-	R 2000	R 2000	R 2002	R 2002

Hungary	Ireland	Italy	Latvia	Lithuania	Luxembourg	Malta	Netherlands	Poland	Portugal	Romania	Slovakia	Slovenia	Spain	Sweden
A ?2	A 1976	A 1952	A 1992	A 1996	A 1981	A 2014	A 1966	A 1950	A 1999	A 1950	R(S) 1993	R(S) 1992	A 1968	R 1952
A ?9	A 1956	R 1954	A 1997	A 1997	R 1953	A 1971	R 1956	A 1991	A 1960	A 1991	A(S) 1993	R(S) 1992	A 1978	R 1954
R ?7	R 2000	R 1976	A 1992	R 1998	R 1978	R 1971	R 1971	R 1968	A 1982	A 1970	R(S) 1993	R(S) 1992	A 1968	R 1971
R ?4	R 1989	R 1978	A 1992	A 1991	R 1983	A 1990	R 1978	R 1977	R 1978	R 1974	R(S) 1993	R(S) 1992	R 1977	R 1971
A ?88	A 1989	R 1978	A 1994	A 1991	A 1983	A 1990	R 1978	A 1991	R 1983	A 1993	A(S) 1993	A 1993	A 1985	R 1971
R ?74	R 1989	R 1978	A 1992	A 1991	R 1983	R 1990	R 1978	R 1977	R 1978	R 1974	R(S) 1993	R(S) 1992	R 1977	R 1971
A ?89	A 1968	A 1972	A 1997	A 1997	A 1971	A 1971	A 1968	A 1991	A 1976	A 1991	A(S) 1993	A(S) 1992	A 1978	A 1967
?74	–	-	A 1992	-	-	-	-	R 1976	-	R 1978	R(S) 1993	R(S) 1992	-	-
R ?980	A 1985	R 1985	A 1992	A 1994	R 1989	A 1991	R 1991	R 1980	R 1980	R 1982	R(S) 1993	R(S) 1992	R 1984	R 1980
R ?987	R 2002	R 1989	A 1992	A 1996	R 1987	A 1990	R 1988	R 1989	R 1989	A 1990	R(S) 1993	A 1993	R 1987	R 1986
R ?991	R 1992	R 1991	A 1992	A 1992	R 1994	R 1990	R 1995	R 1991	R 1990	R 1990	R(S) 1993	R(S) 1992	R 1990	R 1990
A ?994	A 1993	R 1995	A 2013	R 2002	R 1992	A 1994	R 1991	R 2014	R 1990	R 1991	R 1999	R 1994	R 1991	R 1990
A 2000	R 2000	R 2000	-	R 2004	R 2003	A 2019	R 2002	A 2003	R 2002	R 2003	R 2000	R 2004	R 2001	R 2003

Continued

Table 5.1 Continued

Human rights instrument	Austria	Belgium	Bulgaria	Croatia	Cyprus	Czech Republic	Denmark	Estonia	Finland	France	Germany	Greec
Optional Protocol to the Convention on the Rights of the Child on the Sale of Children, Child Prostitution and Child Pornography (2000)	R 2004	R 2006	R 2002	R 2002	R 2006	R 2013	R 2003	R 2004	R 2012	R 2003	R 2009	R 2008
Optional Protocol to the Convention on the Rights of the Child on the Involvement of Children in Armed Conflicts (2000)	R 2002	R 2002	R 2002	R 2002	R 2010	R 2001	R 2002	R 2014	R 2002	R 2003	R 2004	R 2003
Optional Protocol to the Convention against Torture and Other Cruel, Inhuman or Degrading Treatment or Punishment (2002)	R 2012	S 2005	R 2011	R 2005	R 2009	R 2006	R 2004	R 2006	R 2014	R 2008	R 2008	R 2014
Convention on the Rights of Persons with Disabilities (2006)	R 2008	R 2009	R 2012	R 2007	R 2011	R 2009	R 2009	R 2012	R 2016	R 2010	R 2009	R 2012
Optional Protocol to the Convention on the Rights of Persons with Disabilities (2006)	R 2008	R 2009	S 2008	R 2007	R 2011	S 2007	A 2014	A 2012	R 2016	R 2010	R 2009	R 2012
International Convention for the Protection of All Persons from Enforced Disappearance (2006)	R 2012	R 2011	S 2008	S 2007	S 2007	R 2017	S 2007	-	S 2007	R 2008	R 2009	R 2015
Optional Protocol to the International Covenant on Economic, Social and Cultural Rights (2008)	-	R 2014	-	-	-	-	-		R 2014	R 2015	-	-
Optional Protocol to the Convention on the Rights of the Child on a Communications Procedure (2011)	S 2012	R 2014	-	R 2017	R 2017	R 2015	A 2015	-	R 2015	R 2016	R 2013	-

R: Ratification (Approval/Acceptance/Signature without reservation as to ratification)
A: Accession (S): Succession S: Signature

Hungary	Ireland	Italy	Latvia	Lithuania	Luxembourg	Malta	Netherlands	Poland	Portugal	Romania	Slovakia	Slovenia	Spain	Sweden
10	S 2000	R 2002	R 2006	A 2004	R 2011	R 2010	R 2005	R 2005	R 2003	R 2001	R 2004	R 2004	R 2001	R 2007
10	R 2002	R 2002	R 2005	R 2003	R 2004	R 2002	R 2009	R 2005	R 2003	R 2001	R 2006	R 2004	R 2002	R 2003
12	S 2007	R 2013	-	A 2014	R 2010	R 2003	R 2010	R 2005	R 2013	R 2009	S 2018	A 2007	R 2006	R 2005
07	R 2018	R 2009	R 2010	R 2010	R 2011	R 2012	R 2016	R 2012	R 2009	R 2011	R 2010	R 2008	R 2007	R 2008
07	-	R 2009	R 2010	R 2010	R 2011	R 2012	-	-	R 2009	S 2008	R 2010	R 2008	R 2007	R 2008
07	S 2007	R 2015	-	R 2013	S 2007	R 2015	R 2011	S 2013	R 2014	S 2008	R 2014	S 2007	R 2009	S 2007
12	S 2012	R 2015	-	-	R 2015	-	S 2009	-	R 2013	-	R 2012	S 2009	R 2010	-
-	R 2014	R 2016	-	S 2015	R 2016	S 2012	-	S 2013	R 2013	S 2012	R 2013	R 2018	R 2013	-

States on the one hand, and one or more third countries on the other, **shall not be affected by the provisions of the Treaties.**

To the extent that such agreements are not compatible with the Treaties, the Member State or States concerned shall take all appropriate steps to eliminate the incompatibilities established. Member States shall, where necessary, assist each other to this end and shall, where appropriate, adopt a common attitude.

In applying the agreements referred to in the first paragraph, Member States shall take into account the fact that the advantages accorded under the Treaties by each Member State form an integral part of the establishment of the Union and are thereby inseparably linked with the creation of common institutions, the conferring of powers upon them and the granting of the same advantages by all the other Member States.

The same principle can be found in the case law of the ECtHR which stated that a contracting party to the ECHR 'is considered to retain Convention liability in respect of treaty commitments subsequent to the entry into force of the Convention'.[36] Ultimately, such liability remains in place even where a presumption of equivalent protection of fundamental rights is granted by the ECtHR, as is the case with the EU.[37] In addition, Article 30 of the Vienna Convention on the Law of Treaties (VCLT) contains the foundation of a similar principle, albeit worded more narrowly as concerning same-subject treaties.

The issue is that there are only two major treaties containing human rights obligations that were concluded before the entry into force of the Treaty of Rome in 1958. These are the UN Charter (in force since 24 October 1945) and the ECHR (in force since 3 September 1953). Whereas the human rights credentials of the ECHR are, as one of the most influential human rights treaties in history, self-explanatory, the UN Charter only contains a few provisions on human rights. The UN Charter mentions that among the purposes of the UN is 'to achieve international cooperation (…) in promoting and encouraging respect for human rights and for fundamental freedoms for all without distinction as to race, sex, language, or religion'.[38] It is further specified that the respect for rights and freedoms is 'universal', and that UN Member States pledged to 'take joint or separate action' in cooperation with the UN for their achievement.[39]

J Klabbers, 'Straddling the Fence: The EU and International Law' in D Chalmers and A Arnull (eds), *The Oxford Handbook of European Union Law* (Oxford University Press 2015)

(…) the CJEU has been decidedly stingy in allowing 'anterior' treaties to continue to be applied. In many cases, any conflict between an international agreement and EU law has been 'defined away', with the Court in one case even going so far as to ascribe binding force to a later treaty that was still under negotiation. In other cases it gratefully used the circumstance that an agreement had been amended at some point in time to disqualify

---

[36] *Bosphorus Hava Yollari Turizm ve Ticaret Anonim Şiketi v Ireland*, App no 45036/98, 30 June 2005, para 154.
[37] See below for a more comprehensive account of the *Bosphorus* presumption.
[38] Article 1 of the UN Charter.
[39] Articles 55(c) and 56 of the UN Charter.

it as anterior for purposes of the application of Article 351 TFEU, and in yet other cases it left ultimate findings to the domestic courts that submitted the preliminary reference involving Article 351.

Moreover, the Court has been very strict in applying the second paragraph of Article 351 TFEU, which holds that Member States shall terminate all incompatibilities between the agreement in question and EU law. This involves at the very least a duty to seek re-negotiation, and the practical feasibility of doing so is not considered much of an argument; in cases involving Portugal, the fact that treaty partners included states in serious disarray (Yugoslavia, Angola) did not soften the Court's stance.

However, even with respect to the UN Charter and the ECHR, to which all EU Member States acceded prior to joining the EU, the application of Article 351 TFEU could entail certain caveats. In *Kadi I*, the CJEU found that Article 351 TFEU 'may in no circumstances permit any challenge to the principles that form part of the very foundations of the Community legal order'.[40] As a result, contrary to the General Court's reading of the same case, the CJEU stated that in the event of a conflict, EU primary law, especially insofar as it concerns fundamental rights protection, would take precedence over international agreements, including the UN Charter.[41] Such a conflict should not occur in the exercise of international human rights responsibilities under the ECHR or the UN Charter but it is nonetheless notable that the CJEU does not explicitly address the underlying issue of EU Member States being concurrently bound in the exercise of their roles within the EU by the CJEU's interpretation (which establishes supremacy of EU primary law over the UN Charter in matters affecting EU constitutional principles) and by Article 103 of the UN Charter which in essence prescribes the exact opposite.[42] The interpretation put forward by the Court in *Kadi* also points to the necessity of looking at international human rights obligations in the EU not only as a collection of 27 Member States' international law commitments but also at the obligations of the EU as a self-standing actor under international law with legal personality and international responsibility.

Before exploring more in-depth how the EU as a self-standing entity could be bound by international human rights law, one more issue concerning Article 351 TFEU needs to be addressed. Article 351 TFEU speaks of treaties concluded prior to the creation of the European Economic Community or prior to accession to the EU. As the current composition of the EU has been moulded through successive rounds of enlargements, what counts as prior international commitments varies within the EU with respect to almost all human rights treaties (ECHR being the exception). For example, for the vast majority of the Member

---

[40] *Kadi and Al Barakaat International Foundation v Council of the European Union and Commission of the European Communities* (n 9) para 304.

[41] Ibid, para 308. The CJEU held that international law takes precedence over EU secondary law and in some instances over primary law but not when the EU's constitutional foundations would be endangered.

[42] While conflict may not arise when Member States are exercising their human rights duties under any of the three treaties (UN Charter, ECHR, EU)—for now notwithstanding the differing breadth and depth given to specific rights in the three regimes—it can occur when other constitutional principles of the EU legal order are at stake and which cannot be, according to the CJEU, dislodged, with reference to Article 351 TFEU, by prior international legal commitments of EU Member States. A concrete example of occasional conflict can be found between the EU Member States' human rights obligations under the ECHR and the principle of mutual trust between Member States, especially in cases concerning the functioning of the Common European Asylum System. In such cases, the doctrine of the CJEU might still accord primacy to EU constitutional principles over the ECHR but this can be easily at odds with the international perspective on the responsibility of ECHR contracting parties to, in the first place, respect their obligations under that treaty.

States, the International Covenant on Civil and Political Rights (ICCPR) will count as a prior international agreement. Does this mean that their obligations under the ICCPR are more 'immune' from the EU Treaties by virtue of Article 351 TFEU than the obligations of the remaining eight Member States who acceded to the ICCPR after joining the EU? It is likely that if faced with a case on this issue, the CJEU would, in light of *Kadi*, again favour an interpretation stressing the unique character of the Treaties for all Member States in contrast to other international agreements. Another international court could of course see the issue differently.

Related to the subject of diversity in prior commitments is the question whether the EU has succeeded to the human rights obligations of the Member States. Succession can occur when members of an international organization transfer competences to it, which were already governed by an international agreement. It is important for the functioning of the international legal system that international organizations assume responsibility for transferred competences, as otherwise states could delegate powers in an attempt to escape international obligations. At the same time, given that sovereign states remain the central units in the modern international order, member states of international organizations cannot easily shed their obligations under international law, as seen at the example of the ECtHR which, while willing to adopt a presumption that an international organization on the whole complies with the ECHR, treats states as ultimately liable for failures to perform human rights obligations even when state competences are in some form delegated to an international organization.[43] This is also related to the fact that without formal membership, international organizations, including the EU, fall outside the reach of treaty monitoring bodies and courts.

The CJEU has accepted succession in areas where the EU was vested with exclusive competences, such as trade.[44] According to one international law perspective, which is not shared by all, however,[45] succession can be viewed more broadly as occurring whenever powers are transferred from member states to an international organization, irrespective of the internal designation of the delimitations.[46] In any event, succession in the view of the CJEU can only relate to treaty obligations entered into prior to acceding to the EU. This raises again the issue of Member States acceding at different points in time and with different prior human rights

---

[43] *Bosphorus v Ireland* (n 36) para 154. See also UN Human Rights Committee (94th session) *Sayadi v Belgium*, Communication no 1472/2006 (29 December 2008) UN Doc CCPR/C/94/D/1472/2006, where the HRC faced a similar issue as the CJEU did in *Kadi*. The HRC found Belgium liable for its complicity in the EU implementation of the UN sanctions regime. The decision was severely criticized: see M Milanovic, 'The Human Rights Committee's Views in Sayadi v. Belgium: A Missed Opportunity' (2009) 1 Goettingen Journal of International Law 519. For counterexamples where international monitoring and judicial bodies refused to attribute acts of an international organization to its member states see UN Human Rights Committee (29th session) *H.v.d.P. v The Netherlands*, Communication no 217/1986 (8 April 1987) UN Doc CCPR/C/OP/2.

[44] Judgment of 12 December 1972, *International Fruit Company NV and Others v Produktschap voor Groenten en Fruit*, 21/72 to 24/72, ECLI:EU:C:1972:115, para 18. In Judgment of 21 December 2011, *Air Transport Association of America and Others v Secretary of State for Energy and Climate Change*, C-366/10, ECLI:EU:C:2011:864 the CJEU went even further when it de facto stated that succession only occurs where 'a full transfer of powers' from national to EU level had taken place (para 63). Most recently this line of reasoning concerning exclusive competence has been reaffirmed in Opinion of 16 May 2017, *Singapore* FTA, 2/15, ECLI:EU:C:2017:376, para 248.

[45] For an argument that only treaties to which the EU is a formal party are binding upon it see R Schütze, '"The Succession Doctrine" and the European Union' in A Hull and others (eds), *A Constitutional Order of States? Essays in EU Law in Honour of Alan Dashwood* (Hart Publishing 2011) 475. Similarly, opposition to the argument that EU succeeded to Member States' obligations under human rights treaties was expressed by L Bartels, 'The EU's Human Rights Obligations in Relation to Policies with Extraterritorial Effects' (2014) 25 European Journal of International Law 1071.

[46] T Ahmed and I de Jesús Butler, 'The European Union and Human Rights: An International Law Perspective' (2006) 17 European Journal of International Law 771, 790.

commitments (with the exception of the ECHR). Therefore, while a reasonably convincing case can be made for the EU's succession to Member States' obligations following from the ECHR,[47] the situation is less clear with respect to other treaties to which some but not all EU Member States were already a party before joining the EU. It would probably be unworkable in practice for the EU to be only responsible within its sphere of competences to uphold human rights as following from prior human rights treaties vis-à-vis some Member States but not others, as in the majority of cases the EU is presenting a common policy or action that involves all the Member States.[48] The need for a practical solution to this conundrum could require the EU in its observance of human rights to set aside the distinction between prior and eventual commitments, as long as some (a majority, perhaps) of Member States brought with them prior human rights obligations, while others have subscribed to these after joining the EU.[49]

Succession of the EU to international obligations of the Member States does not, however, enjoy universal consensus. The CJEU holds a rather restrictive view regarding the conditions under which the EU succeeds to obligations following from treaties to which all the Member States are a party but not the EU.[50] The CJEU has been also explicit about Article 351 TFEU not binding the EU to prior agreements concluded by the Member States.[51] Similarly, when the Court of First Instance declared de facto EU succession to obligations of the UN Charter in *Kadi I*,[52] the argument was not picked up by the overturning appeal judgment of the CJEU and it received criticism in the literature.[53] Others have argued that succession is a misleading term when it comes to international organizations, as the constituting member states retain their sovereignty even after transferring powers,[54] while still other scholars found international law unfit to define succession for international organizations, advising the EU to instead create a consistent succession doctrine in its own legal order.[55]

Although succession to Member States' human rights obligations has not been so far recognised by the CJEU, the distinction between the ECHR—as a treaty to which all Member States have acceded before joining the EU—and other (mainly UN) human rights treaties is underscored in the way the CJEU has treated these different sources in the internal EU framework of fundamental rights protection. Whereas the ECHR is of 'special significance' and referred to—along with the case law of the ECtHR—relatively often by the CJEU, other

---

[47] G Schermers, 'The European Communities Bound by Fundamental Human Rights' (1990) 27 Common Market Law Review 249, 251–52.

[48] See and compare with Ahmed and de Jesús Butler, 'The European Union and Human Rights' (n 46) 791.

[49] It is important not to confuse succession to Member States' human rights obligations with a transferral of Member States' competences in the area of human rights. The EU has only limited explicit human rights competence (see above); the succession to obligations would require the EU to respect these obligations in the exercise of its existing competences.

[50] J Wouters, J Odermatt, and T Ramopoulos, 'Worlds Apart? Comparing the Approaches of the European Court of Justice and the EU Legislature to International Law' in M Cremona and A Thies (eds), *The European Court of Justice and External Relations Law: Constitutional Challenges* (Hart Publishing 2014).

[51] Judgment of 14 October 1980, *Attorney General v Burgoa*, 812/79, ECLI:EU:C:1980:231, para 9.

[52] *Kadi v Council of the European Union and Commission of the European Communities* (n 7) para 200.

[53] F Naert, 'Binding International Organisations to Member State Treaties or Responsibility of Member States for Their own Actions in the Framework of International Organisations' in J Wouters and others (eds), *Accountability for Human Rights Violations by International Organisations* (Intersentia 2010) 150.

[54] O De Schutter, 'Human Rights and the Rise of International Organisations: The Logic of Sliding Scales in the Law of International Responsibility' in Wouters and others (eds), *Accountability for Human Rights Violations by International Organisations* (n 53) 63.

[55] Wouters, Odermatt, and Ramopoulos, 'Worlds Apart? Comparing the Approaches of the European Court of Justice and the EU Legislature to International Law' (n 50).

sources of international human rights law have been rarely present in CJEU's interpret-ations,[56] despite recognizing that 'international treaties for the protection of human rights on which the Member States have collaborated or of which they are signatories, can supply guidelines which should be followed within the framework of Community law'.[57] Other EU institutions are faring substantially better when it comes to referring to international human rights law;[58] even EU statutory law displays more receptiveness to international norms than the case law of the CJEU, as demonstrated, for example, by Article 78 TFEU and EU sec-ondary law on the Common European Asylum System. Still, fundamental rights guaranteed by the ECHR are acknowledged in Article 6 TEU as constituting general principles of EU law without any mention of other international human rights sources. The same holds true for Article 52(3) of the EU Charter of Fundamental Rights regarding the equivalence of scope and meaning of Charter and ECHR rights.

Treaties are not the only source of international human rights that has been neglected by the CJEU and which from the perspective of international law is capable of binding the EU. More directly than by succession to Member States' responsibilities, the EU is bound by rules of customary international law and *jus cogens* norms which comprise also human rights standards. As a matter of EU law, in addition to the discarded application of *jus cogens* by the Court of First Instance in *Kadi*, the CJEU has recognized in its case law that the EU is bound by customary international law,[59] as it is by international law more generally,[60] which is also emphasized by Article 3(5) TEU.[61] Equally importantly, the EU is subject to the rules of cus-tomary international law and *jus cogens* also as a matter of international law. In either case, however, rights aspiring to the status of customary international law, and embodied in even the most well-known international human rights instruments, such as the International Covenant on Economic, Social and Cultural Rights (ICESCR), will often not, however, fulfil the requisite standards of uniform practice and *opinio juris* to represent binding obligations under international law.[62]

---

[56] When the CJEU does refer to international human rights law, it does so typically in an ornamental and supplemental fashion, that is without the reference being decisive for the outcome of a case. See, for example, Judgment of 20 October 1994, *Scaramuzza v Commission*, C-76/93 P, ECLI:EU:C:1994:371 and Judgment of 2 March 2010, *Rottmann v Freistaat Bayern*, C-135/08, ECLI:EU:C:2010:104 (Universal Declaration of Human Rights); Judgment of 27 June 2006, *Parliament v Council*, C-540/03, ECLI:EU:C:2006:429 (International Covenant on Civil and Political Rights); Judgment of 13 April 2010, *Bressol and Others v Gouvernement de la Communauté française*, C-73/08, ECLI:EU:C:2010:181 (International Covenant on Economic, Social and Cultural Rights); Judgment of 14 February 2008, *Dynamic Medien Vertriebs v Avides Media*, C-244/06, ECLI:EU:C:2008:85 (Convention on the Rights of the Child); Judgment of 11 December 2007, *International Transport Workers' Federation and Finnish Seamen's Union v Viking Line ABP and OÜ Viking Line Eesti*, C-438/05, ECLI:EU:C:2007:772 (ILO Convention No 87).

[57] Judgment of 14 May 1974, *Nold v Commission*, 4/73, ECLI:EU:C:1974:51, para 13.

[58] For a study on the use of international law generally see Wouters, Odermatt, and Ramopoulos, 'Worlds Apart? Comparing the Approaches of the European Court of Justice and the EU Legislature to International Law' (n 50).

[59] Judgment of 16 June 1998, *Racke GmbH & Co. v Hauptzollamt Mainz*, C-162/96, ECLI:EU:C:1998:293, paras 45 and 46.

[60] Judgment of 24 November 1992, *Anklagemyndigheden v Poulsen and Diva Navigation Corp*, C-286/90, ECLI:EU:C:1992:453, paras 9 and 10.

[61] Article 3(5) TEU states that 'In its relations with the wider world, the Union shall (...) contribute (...) to the strict observance and the development of international law, including respect for the principles of the United Nations Charter'.

[62] L Bartels, 'The EU's Human Rights Obligations in Relation to Policies with Extraterritorial Effects' (2015) 25 European Journal of International Law 1071, 1087.

T Ahmed and I de Jesús Butler, 'The European Union and Human Rights: An International Law Perspective' (2006) 17 European Journal of International Law 771

While the question whether the EU is bound by the provisions of international human rights law directly has received consideration, most scholarship tends to focus on the extent to which the EU is bound to respect human rights by virtue of its internal rules. Where international law is discussed it is largely confined to the ECHR and the extent to which its provisions form part of the EU's internal legal order (via 'general principles of law' and Article 6 TEU) and the legal weight of the Charter of Fundamental Rights, rather than by virtue of any obligations which might be incumbent on the EU directly under international law.

An intergovernmental organization (IGO) may derive obligations both from its internal constitution and international law more generally. Despite the ECJ's [European Court of Justice's] lack of reliance on international human rights law as a source of human right obligations, from the perspective of international law, the EU, as an IGO, is subject to international law. (...)

Customary international law (CIL) is the body of international law binding on all States which derives from the practice and legal opinion (*opinio juris*) of states themselves. Unlike legal obligations deriving from treaties, which states must accede to or ratify in order to be bound by their terms, CIL may emerge without the express consent of every state to a particular rule. (...) The ECJ has itself expressly acknowledged the applicability of CIL to the actions of the EC and EU in their internal and external relations. However, the ECJ has yet to pronounce on the applicability of international human rights law to the EC and EU insofar as they form part of CIL.

Much of the debate over the status of human rights in CIL has centred on the status of the United Nations Universal Declaration of Human Rights, 1948. Despite the uncertainties, there are at least some rights whose existence as part of CIL has been recognized by the International Court of Justice (ICJ): the right to self-determination; the prohibition on genocide; freedom from racial discrimination including apartheid, and the prohibition on slavery; freedom from arbitrary detention and the right to physical integrity; protection against denial of justice.

The ICJ has further found that the 'rules concerning the basic rights of the human person' in international law are *erga omnes* in nature. That is, they are considered to be 'the concern of all States. In view of the importance of the rights involved, all States can be held to have a legal interest in their protection.' Thus, where EU law conflicts with CIL on human rights, even where these EU rules are meant to apply only as between the Member States, it will violate obligations towards all other (non-Member) States. Put otherwise, any breach by the EU of human rights in CIL, even if it does not necessarily disclose a violation of international law as between the Member States, will amount to a violation of international obligations owed to all other states.

Within CIL there also exists a category of rules that have achieved the status of *jus cogens* (or peremptory norms) which have the effect of invalidating conflicting rules of international law created by treaties, including rules derived from those treaties such as the acts of IGOs. Article 53 of the Vienna Convention on the Law of Treaties (1969) defines a rule of *jus cogens* as 'a norm accepted and recognized by the international community of States as a whole as a norm from which no derogation is permitted'. However, as might be expected, that body of human rights law which might be said to have attained the status of *jus cogens* is narrower still than that which has entered into CIL. Certain international judicial bodies have had occasion expressly to recognize that particular rights have achieved this status: the prohibition on torture; the right to life; the right to equality before the law and non-discrimination; and the prohibition on slavery.

Perhaps over-generously, the Court of First Instance (CFI) recently appeared to consider all human rights to have attained the status of *jus cogens* in international law. In its Kadi and Yusuf judgments, the CFI considered the legality of several regulations adopted by the EC in execution of measures mandated by the United Nations Security Council over the course of several resolutions adopted under Chapter VII of the UN Charter. (...) The CFI considered that the obligation to protect human rights (with no more precision) formed a rule of *jus cogens* in international law, and any Security Council resolution and consequently any EU action taken to implement such resolution that violated human rights would be void in international law. This of course raises the question of which human rights should be considered to fall within this category. The approach of the CFI in this regard was to resort to the UDHR [Universal Declaration of Human Rights] and the ICCPR rather than the ECHR. In doing so, the CFI did not engage in any analysis of CIL to assess whether the relevant rights were in fact 'accepted and recognized by the international community of States' as peremptory norms. Rather, it seemed to assume that the rights in question were *jus cogens* in nature by virtue of their presence in these instruments. While such an assessment may be tantalizing for some human rights lawyers, the lack of any analysis does undermine the integrity of the finding that all human rights as featured in the UDHR or ICCPR can be classed as rules of *jus cogens*.

Regardless of the perspectives of EU judicial bodies, it is clear from the above that, in international law, the EU as an IGO is bound to respect rules of CIL. Any EU treaty provision or treaty-based secondary legislation that conflicts with CIL on human rights, while not automatically void, will violate obligations towards all third states because human rights are considered to be *erga omnes* in nature. Further, any rule created through the EU which conflicts with rules that are *jus cogens* in nature will be void. (...)

Presuming that the EU is bound by customary international law and that a given human rights norm within this source is identified, what legal effects will such an international obligation have in the EU system? The answer can be extracted by analogy from the CJEU decision in *ATAA*.[63] In this case the Court held that customary international law can in some circumstances be relied upon in order to enable the review of validity of an EU measure, provided that (i) the EU competence to adopt the measure is called into question and that (ii) the EU measure is liable to affect rights which an individual derives from EU law or create obligations under EU law.[64] Even if these two conditions are satisfied, the Court will only conduct light judicial review, in essence verifying whether the EU 'made manifest errors of assessment concerning the conditions for applying [customary international law]'.[65] The legal effects and their assessment by the CJEU differ from the effects and more common tests for establishing whether a given legal act has direct effect or is directly applicable;[66] the Court motivated this in *ATAA* by stating that 'a principle of customary international law does not

[63] *Air Transport Association of America* (n 44).
[64] Ibid, para 107.
[65] Ibid, para 110.
[66] K Lenaerts, 'Direct Applicability and Direct Effect of International Law in the EU Legal Order' in I Govaere and others (eds), *The European Union in the World Essays in Honour of Marc Maresceau* (Brill 2013).

have the same degree of precision as a provision of an international agreement'.[67] It should be added, however, that even international—in particular of the multilateral kind, which would apply to human rights treaties—agreements are often held not to have direct effect.[68]

In spite of the variety of ways by which the EU can be bound by international human rights law—succession, customary international law, *jus cogens*—clearly the most preferable one from the point of view of legal certainty and the international rule of law is fully fledged accession of the EU to the relevant human rights treaties. Short of formal accession, it would be possible for the EU to declare unilaterally its acceptance of human rights treaties as binding upon it.[69] Such declarations have not yet taken place but in fairness to EU institutions and bodies, international human rights law is regularly referred to and taken into account in their practice, policies, and legislation.

One reason why the EU itself has not formally acceded to many international human rights treaties is that they are typically oriented towards states, in keeping with the state-centric nature of the Westphalian system of international relations and law. The EU is, on the contrary and despite a high degree of integration, not a state even by the admission of its own 'supreme court'.[70] Accommodating organizations like the EU therefore often requires specific amendments to the human rights treaties. These normally take the form of so-called REIO (regional economic integration organizations) or RIO (regional integration organizations) clauses which allow for the possibility of such organizations to accede to a treaty. Most human rights treaties still do not contain a RIO clause; the first treaty which included one has subsequently seen the EU accede to it.

Convention on the Rights of Persons with Disabilities (adopted 13 December 2006, entered into force 3 May 2008) 2515 UNTS 3

Article 44

Regional integration organizations

1. 'Regional integration organization' shall mean an organization constituted by sovereign States of a given region, **to which its member States have transferred competence in respect of matters governed by the present Convention.** Such organizations shall declare, in their instruments of formal confirmation or accession, the extent of their competence with respect to matters governed by the present Convention. Subsequently, they shall inform the depositary of any substantial modification in the extent of their competence.

---

[67] *Air Transport Association of America* (n 44) para 110.

[68] The core of the direct effect test consists of looking at the overall purpose and context of an international agreement and whether the invoked provision is unconditional and sufficiently clear and precise. See, for example, Judgment of 15 July 2004, *Syndicat professionnel coordination des pêcheurs de l'étang de Berre et de la région v Électricité de France (EDF)*, C-213/03, ECLI:EU:C:2004:464. The direct effect test is more stringent than in the case of EU law proper. See F Martines, 'Direct Effect of International Agreements of the European Union' (2014) 25 European Journal of International Law 129; S Gáspár-Szilágyi, 'The "Primacy" and "Direct Effect" of EU International Agreements' (2015) 21 European Public Law 343.

[69] Office of the High Commissioner for Human Rights, Europe Regional Office, 'The European Union and International Human Rights Law' (2011) 22. Voluntary declarations are a recognized form of creating legal obligations in international law. See ICJ, Judgment of 20 December 1974, *Nuclear Tests (Australia v France)*, 1974 ICJ Reports 253, para 43.

[70] *Opinion 2/13 (EU accession to the ECHR)* (n 11) para 156.

> 2. References to 'States Parties' in the present Convention shall apply to such organizations **within the limits of their competence.**
>
> 4. Regional integration organizations, **in matters within their competence,** may exercise their right to vote in the Conference of States Parties, **with a number of votes equal to the number of their member States that are Parties to the present Convention.** Such an organization shall not exercise its right to vote if any of its member States exercises its right, and vice versa.

A second contributing reason for the formal absence of the EU from human rights treaties is the lack of clarity regarding the EU's competences. Article 216(1) TFEU states that the EU may conclude international agreements where: the Treaties or EU secondary law explicitly provide for such a competence; the conclusion of a treaty is necessary to achieve an objective contained in the Treaties; or where a treaty is 'likely to affect common rules or alter their scope'. In *Opinion 2/94*, the CJEU clarified that the EU possessed no explicit or implicit competence to conclude treaties in the field of human rights.[71] The Court also indicated that when the modifications resulting from the conclusion of a treaty would be of 'constitutional significance' for the EU's internal system of human rights protection, such an international agreement cannot be concluded on the basis of the lacuna-filling competence of Article 352 TFEU.[72] As a consequence of *Opinion 2/94*, the EU amended the Treaties with an explicit competence authorizing accession to the ECHR.[73]

No such amendment has, however, taken place for the purposes of the EU becoming a party to the CRPD. The EU found the legal basis for the conclusion of the Convention in Article 19 TFEU (anti-discrimination competence) and Article 114 TFEU (approximation of laws in the internal market).[74] While invoking Article 19 TFEU is self-evident, the reference to Article 114 TFEU has to do with the myriad internal market areas on which disability rights and obligations touch upon.[75] The case of the EU accession to the CRPD can be distinguished from the negative conclusion of *Opinion 2/94* regarding accession to the ECHR, as it could be argued that an issue-specific treaty with a less robust institutional backbone, such as the CRPD, is of lesser 'constitutional significance' than the ECHR regime. In addition, the general anti-discrimination competence of Article 19 TFEU did not exist at the time of *Opinion 2/94* and would in any event be less sufficient for the purposes of the much wider substantive scope of the ECHR. The EU accession to the CRPD therefore sent a cautiously positive signal as regards the possibility of the EU joining other human rights conventions without the need to amend the provisions of the EU Treaties. This has been confirmed by the EU's signing of the Council of Europe Istanbul Convention on violence against women which was also occasioned without treaty reform and even without relying on Article 19 TFEU for legal basis (see section 5.5).

All in all, international law and EU law contain a number of avenues for binding the EU to international human rights obligations. In practice, there is, however, also considerable uncertainty as regards the various international sources of human rights law which is not

---

[71] Opinion of 28 March 1996, *Community accession to the ECHR*, 2/94, ECLI:EU:C:1996:140, paras 27–28.

[72] Ibid, para 35.

[73] See Article 6(2) TEU.

[74] Council Decision 2010/48/EC concerning the conclusion, by the European Community, of the United Nations Convention on the Rights of Persons with Disabilities [2009] OJ L23/35.

[75] R Forastiero, 'Article 44' in V Della Fina and others (eds), *The United Nations Convention on the Rights of Persons with Disabilities* (Springer 2017) 683.

helped by the inward-looking attitude of the CJEU. The CJEU has, among others, failed to clarify whether the EU is bound by the UN Charter (which includes human rights provisions) as a matter of succession to Member States' prior obligations after setting aside the judgment of the CFI in *Kadi*. The overall lack of engagement with international human rights in EU law sits uncomfortably with the requirement of Article 3(5) TEU for the EU to contribute to 'strict observance and development of international law'.

I de Jesús Butler and O De Schutter, 'Binding the EU to International Human Rights Law' (2008) 27 Yearbook of European Law 277

While the ECJ ensures that the Union does not violate human rights through its actions, its approach has several shortcomings. The focus has been almost exclusively on the European Convention on Human Rights, ignoring the range of other human rights treaties to which all or some of the Member States are party. This has led the Union to be estranged from the universal human rights regimes established under the UN as well as other regional instruments. In consequence, the Union recognizes neither the range of rights nor the interpretation of rights accepted by its Member States (as well as significant numbers of third States) under these treaties. This has also led to a failure to understand the true nature of human rights as imposing positive as well as negative obligations. The reluctance of the EU to commit to international human rights standards may result in several negative consequences. First, where Member States attempt to implement their human rights obligations this may conflict with Union law. Permitting Member States human rights exceptions threatens the uniformity of EU law, which is more pronounced in relation to those treaties to which only some of the Member States are party. Second, Article 307 of the EC Treaty requires Member States to eliminate inconsistencies between pre-existing treaties with third States and EU law, which includes the denunciation of such treaties. This is not only politically embarrassing, but potentially illegal under international law. In this dysfunctional relationship between the EU and human rights, it is the individual that will suffer as human rights standards are lowered and legal uncertainty prevails.

A continued lack of integration of the EU into international legal structures in the area of human rights would have the consequence of creating space for divergence between fundamental rights protection within the EU and internationally. This undermines the universality of human rights, as recognized by not only the foundational documents in the field, such as the Universal Declaration of Human Rights and the UN Charter, but also—conscious of the adverse impact of double standards on its international image—by the EU itself.[76] Moreover, by avoiding international human rights law, the EU risks offering narrower and shallower fundamental rights protection, as the combined scope and depth of rights contained in international treaties is at least theoretically greater than that of the EU Charter of Fundamental Rights or even of the ECHR alone.[77] The ideal solution

---

[76] See Council of the European Union, 'Human Rights and Democracy: EU Strategic Framework and Action Plan', 11855/12, 25 June 2012.

[77] Notwithstanding the higher general effectiveness of the EU legal order. See C Tomuschat, 'The Relationship Between EU Law and International Law in the Field of Human Rights' (2016) 35 Yearbook of European Law 604, who goes as far as to argue that: 'The legal regime of human rights is well consolidated in the EU. No observer can

for making EU fundamental rights protection international in scope is direct Union accession to human rights treaties, as this would also subject the EU to the oversight of monitoring bodies.[78] Although some progress has been made in this regard, both the EU and the international community can do more to advance human rights protection in Europe and beyond.

5.4 The EU and the ECHR

As mentioned previously, the ECHR—although also representing a form of international law—is of special significance to the EU legal order. While in the past the relationship between the two has been developed primarily by the CJEU by referring to the ECHR and the interpretations of the ECtHR in its case law on fundamental rights as general principles of EU law, the importance of the ECHR, underlined by the desire of the EU to accede to it, has been more recently codified in EU primary law. The status of other Council of Europe treaties with a human rights remit, notably the European Social Charter, enjoy a somewhat less privileged—but still distinct in comparison to general international law—status in EU law. This, however, mirrors the relative significance of the respective treaties in the national legal systems of the EU Member States where the ECHR also ranks as the most influential overall. The most important reason behind the ECHR's success, in addition to its longevity (it pre-dates all UN human rights treaties), is undoubtedly the robustness of judicial oversight provided by the ECtHR and its related ability to interpret the Convention as a 'living instrument'.[79]

Consolidated version of the Treaty on European Union [2012] OJ C326/13

Article 6

2. The Union shall accede to the European Convention for the Protection of Human Rights and Fundamental Freedoms. Such accession shall not affect the Union's competences as defined in the Treaties.
3. Fundamental rights, as guaranteed by the European Convention for the Protection of Human Rights and Fundamental Freedoms and as they result from the constitutional traditions common to the Member States, shall constitute general principles of the Union's law.

---

currently identify serious lacunae that would negatively affect their effectiveness. (...) Human rights within the EU are intimately connected with the European Convention on Human Rights but they exceed by far, on account of their level of perfection, the standards applicable at universal level.'

[78] I de Jesús Butler and O De Schutter, 'Binding the EU to International Human Rights Law' (2008) 27 Yearbook of European Law 277.

[79] See, for example, G Letsas, 'The ECHR as a Living Instrument: Its Meaning and Legitimacy' in A Follesdal, B Peters, and G Ulfstein (eds), *Constituting Europe: The European Court of Human Rights in a National, European and Global Context* (Cambridge University Press 2013).

Consolidated version of the Treaty on the Functioning of the European Union [2012] OJ C326/47

Article 151

The Union and the Member States, **having in mind fundamental social rights such as those set out in the European Social Charter signed at Turin on 18 October 1961** and in the 1989 Community Charter of the Fundamental Social Rights of Workers, shall have as their objectives the promotion of employment, improved living and working conditions, so as to make possible their harmonisation while the improvement is being maintained, proper social protection, dialogue between management and labour, the development of human resources with a view to lasting high employment and the combating of exclusion.

Charter of Fundamental Rights of the European Union [2012] OJ C326/391

Preamble

This Charter reaffirms, with due regard for the powers and tasks of the Union and for the principle of subsidiarity, the rights as they result, in particular, from the constitutional traditions and international obligations common to the Member States, the **European Convention for the Protection of Human Rights and Fundamental Freedoms**, the **Social Charters** adopted by the Union and **by the Council of Europe** and **the case-law** of the Court of Justice of the European Union and **of the European Court of Human Rights**. (...)

Article 52
Scope and interpretation of rights and principles

3. In so far as this Charter contains **rights which correspond to rights guaranteed by the Convention for the Protection of Human Rights and Fundamental Freedoms, the meaning and scope of those rights shall be the same as those laid down by the said Convention.** This provision shall not prevent Union law providing more extensive protection.

Article 53
Level of protection

Nothing in this Charter shall be interpreted as restricting or adversely affecting human rights and fundamental freedoms as recognised, in their respective fields of application, by Union law and international law and by international agreements to which the Union or all the Member States are party, including the **European Convention for the Protection of Human Rights and Fundamental Freedoms**, and by the Member States' constitutions.

Article 6 TEU and the EU Charter of Fundamental Rights affirm the established status of the ECHR in EU law built up over decades of EU integration. The first time the CJEU referred to the ECHR in its case law was in *Rutili* in 1975 and if it was not for France's delaying of the ratification of the Convention, the CJEU may have already mentioned the ECHR explicitly a year earlier in *Nold*.[80] By 1989, the CJEU spoke of the 'particular significance' (later

---

[80] See Judgment of 28 October 1975, *Rutili v Ministre de l'intérieur*, 36/75, ECLI:EU:C:1975:137 and *Nold v Commission* (n 57).

'special') of the ECHR and since 1996 the Court has been also citing individual judgments of the ECtHR.[81] The case law developments were codified for the first time by the Treaty of Maastricht and accession to the ECHR began to be explored without so far successfully materializing—for a variety of reasons—more than 25 years ago.

In the continued absence of formal accession of the EU to the Convention, and thus subjecting the Union to the jurisdiction of the ECtHR, there remains room for divergence and double standards between fundamental rights protection in the EU, as guaranteed by the CJEU, and the ECHR, as guaranteed by the ECtHR. This is so despite the efforts of the drafters of the EU Treaties to ensure that the legal regime of the EU does not appreciably diverge from, and in particular fall below, the human rights standards of the ECHR regime, as witnessed in the explicit convergence requirement of Article 52(3) of the Charter and Article 6(3) TEU transposing the ECHR into general principles of EU law. Although with subtle semantic shift, the CJEU has visibly inserted itself in between the ECHR and the EU legal order by tempering the automatic execution of the two provisions of EU primary law. Whereas Article 6(3) TEU openly states that fundamental rights guaranteed by the ECHR 'shall constitute general principles of the Union's law', the CJEU sometimes interprets the same relationship as one which allows it to 'draw inspiration' from the ECHR in promulgating general principles.[82] As regards Article 52(3) of the Charter, the CJEU has reserved itself the right to derogate from the obligation to align the meaning and scope of Charter rights to corresponding ECHR standards where this could adversely affect the autonomy of EU law and the CJEU.[83] The CJEU also occasionally reminds its interlocutors that the ECHR is formally not part of EU law, which is true but usually mentioned in the context of a judgment that in some way contests the ECHR.[84] Overall, the CJEU has resisted being bypassed in the integration of ECHR law into the EU legal framework and the Court stands ready to take steps to preserve its latitude in the realm of EU law vis-à-vis the ECHR. The downside of the CJEU's preservation of autonomy is that it also broadens the potential for divergence which was meant to be contained by Article 52(3) of the Charter and Article 6(3) TEU.

A. The view from Strasbourg

From the perspective of the ECtHR, the EU has equally represented a special case requiring adjustments to the Court's ordinary mode of operation. It was clear from the outset to the ECHR regime that the EU could not represent an area somehow 'beyond' human rights oversight. Yet direct monitoring was not an option due to non-existence of EU accession to the ECHR. The evident solution was for the ECtHR to look closely at how the commitments of EU Member States under the ECHR—Member States who were assuredly within the reach of the Strasbourg Court's jurisdiction—could be construed in relation to their concurrent membership of the Union. The approach developed by the ECtHR, which has eventually

---

[81] Judgment of 21 September 1989, *Hoechst v Commission*, 46/87 and 227/88, ECLI:EU:C:1989:337; and Judgment of 30 April 1996, *P v S and Cornwall County Council*, C-13/94, ECLI:EU:C:1996:170. The CJEU has subsequently also acknowledged that its older case law may require changes in light of standards developed by the Strasbourg Court. See Judgment of 22 October 2002, *Roquette Frères SA v Directeur général de la concurrence, de la consommation et de la répression des fraudes, and Commission of the European Communities*, C-94/00, ECLI:EU:C:2002:603, para 29.

[82] *Parliament v Council* (n 56) para 35.

[83] Judgment of 15 February 2016, *J. N. v Staatssecretaris voor Veiligheid en Justitie*, C-601/15 PPU, ECLI:EU:C:2016:84, para 47.

[84] See, for example, *Opinion 2/13 (EU accession to the ECHR)* (n 11) para 179.

crystallized into the *Bosphorus* doctrine, was initially prompted by applications of individuals whose rights were somehow impacted upon by actions of the EU and who sought redress against the only accountable actors under the ECHR—the EU Member States.

Thus in *Senator Lines*, a case which was struck out of the registry of the ECtHR without a judgment having been delivered,[85] a maritime transport company brought an action against all (then 15) EU Member States on the basis of alleging an infringement of Article 6 ECHR (right to a fair trial) in proceedings before the European Commission and the EU judiciary.[86] The company complained about a Commission decision imposing a fine for an infringement of EU competition law which was payable before the former Court of First Instance could render its decision on the maritime company's appeal against the fine. The ECtHR did not rule on the application as in the meanwhile the Court of First Instance annulled the fine imposed by the Commission which was central to the grounds for the application. The judgment of the ECtHR would have been all the more interesting given that the case concerned an exclusive competence of the EU (competition) and a decision of the most supranational actor thereof (the Commission), neither of which could have been brought directly before the ECtHR. The EU Member States would rightly have protested as having no role to play in the Commission's enforcement of competition rules but the ECtHR could have retorted that the Member States can be held ultimately responsible under the Convention for the EU's failings to comply with human rights, as the EU is the Member States' creation and their obligations under the ECHR already existed at the time of EU accession/establishment.

In fact, by the time *Senator Lines* was struck out, the ECtHR had already established a relevant precedent on state responsibility in cases involving the transfer of powers to an international organization. In *Matthews v the UK*, the Strasbourg Court held that the right to vote of Ms Matthews was violated by the UK when Gibraltar was excluded from electing Members of the European Parliament.

Matthews v United Kingdom, App no 24833/94, 18 February 1999

7. On 12 April 1994 the applicant applied to the Electoral Registration Officer for Gibraltar to be registered as a voter at the elections to the European Parliament. The Electoral Registration Officer replied on 25 April 1994:

'The provisions of Annex II of the EC Act on Direct Elections of 1976 limit the franchise for European parliamentary elections to the United Kingdom. This Act was agreed by all member States and has treaty status. This means that Gibraltar will not be included in the franchise for the European parliamentary elections.'

---

[85] ECHR, Press release issued by the Registrar, 'Cancellation of hearing in the case *Senator Lines GmbH v the 15 Member States of the European Union*, App no 56672/00', 16 October 2003.

[86] Another case brought against all the then 15 EU Member States but declared inadmissible was *Société Guérin Automobiles v the 15 States of the European Union*, App no 51717/99, 4 July 2000. In this case a car importing company complained about the lack of precision as to the character of and applicable time limits in a Commission decision refusing to investigate a competition complaint submitted by the company. An appeal against the decision before the Court of First Instance was subsequently declared inadmissible due to it being brought after the expiry of the time limit. The ECtHR found the complaint inadmissible on the ground that it fell outside the material scope of the Convention which leaves a certain margin of appreciation to contracting parties in organizing their procedural matters. Consequently, it was not necessary for the Court to assess whether the application was admissible *ratione personae*.

24. The applicant alleged a breach of Article 3 of Protocol No. 1, which provides:

'The High Contracting Parties undertake to hold free elections at reasonable intervals by secret ballot, under conditions which will ensure the free expression of the opinion of the people in the choice of the legislature.'

29. Article 1 of the Convention requires the High Contracting Parties to 'secure to everyone within their jurisdiction the rights and freedoms defined in ... [the] Convention' (...)

31. The Court must nevertheless consider whether, notwithstanding the nature of the elections to the European Parliament as an organ of the EC, the United Kingdom can be held responsible under Article 1 of the Convention for the absence of elections to the European Parliament in Gibraltar, that is, whether the United Kingdom is required to 'secure' elections to the European Parliament notwithstanding the Community character of those elections.

32. The Court observes that acts of the EC as such cannot be challenged before the Court because the EC is not a Contracting Party. **The Convention does not exclude the transfer of competences to international organisations provided that Convention rights continue to be 'secured'. Member States' responsibility therefore continues even after such a transfer.**

33. In the present case, the alleged violation of the Convention flows from an annex to the 1976 Act, entered into by the United Kingdom, together with the extension to the European Parliament's competences brought about by the Maastricht Treaty. The Council Decision and the 1976 Act (see paragraph 18 above), and the Maastricht Treaty, with its changes to the EEC Treaty, all **constituted international instruments which were freely entered into by the United Kingdom.** Indeed, the 1976 Act cannot be challenged before the European Court of Justice for the very reason that it is not a 'normal' act of the Community, but is a treaty within the Community legal order. The Maastricht Treaty, too, is not an act of the Community, but a treaty by which a revision of the EEC Treaty was brought about. **The United Kingdom, together with all the other parties to the Maastricht Treaty, is responsible *ratione materiae* under Article 1 of the Convention and, in particular, under Article 3 of Protocol No. 1, for the consequences of that Treaty.**

34. In determining to what extent the United Kingdom is responsible for 'securing' the rights in Article 3 of Protocol No. 1 in respect of elections to the European Parliament in Gibraltar, the Court recalls that the Convention is intended to guarantee rights that are not theoretical or illusory, but practical and effective (...) It is uncontested that **legislation emanating from the legislative process of the European Community affects the population of Gibraltar in the same way as legislation which enters the domestic legal order exclusively via the House of Assembly.** To this extent, there is no difference between European and domestic legislation, and no reason why the United Kingdom should not be required to 'secure' the rights in Article 3 of Protocol No. 1 in respect of European legislation, in the same way as those rights are required to be 'secured' in respect of purely domestic legislation. In particular, **the suggestion that the United Kingdom may not have effective control over the state of affairs complained of cannot affect the position, as the United Kingdom's responsibility derives from its having entered into**

> treaty commitments subsequent to the applicability of Article 3 of Protocol No.
> 1 to Gibraltar, namely the Maastricht Treaty taken together with its obligations
> under the Council Decision and the 1976 Act. Further, the Court notes that on
> acceding to the EC Treaty, the United Kingdom chose, by virtue of Article 227(4) of
> the Treaty, to have substantial areas of EC legislation applied to Gibraltar (see para-
> graphs 11 to 14 above).
>
> 35. It follows that the United Kingdom is responsible under Article 1 of the Convention
>   for securing the rights guaranteed by Article 3 of Protocol No. 1 in Gibraltar regard-
>   less of whether the elections were purely domestic or European.
>
> 52. As to the context in which the European Parliament operates, the Court is of the view
>   that **the European Parliament represents the principal form of democratic, pol-
>   itical accountability in the Community system**. The Court considers that whatever
>   its limitations, the European Parliament, which derives democratic legitimation from
>   the direct elections by universal suffrage, must be seen as that part of the European
>   Community structure which best reflects concerns as to 'effective political democracy'.
>
> 53. Even when due allowance is made for the fact that Gibraltar is excluded from cer-
>   tain areas of Community activity (see paragraph 12 above), there remain signifi-
>   cant areas where Community activity has a direct impact in Gibraltar. Further, as
>   the applicant points out, measures taken under Article 189b of the EC Treaty and
>   which affect Gibraltar relate to important matters such as road safety, unfair con-
>   tract terms and air pollution by emissions from motor vehicles and to all measures
>   in relation to the completion of the internal market.
>
> 54. The Court thus finds that the European Parliament is sufficiently involved in the
>   specific legislative processes leading to the passage of legislation under Articles
>   189b and 189c of the EC Treaty, and is sufficiently involved in the general demo-
>   cratic supervision of the activities of the European Community, to constitute part of
>   the 'legislature' of Gibraltar for the purposes of Article 3 of Protocol No. 1.

The *Matthews* judgment was a clear signal to EU Member States regarding their ongoing responsibility under the Convention regardless of their engagement in constructing 'an ever-closer Union'. Although contracting parties are free to transfer their competences to international organizations, the obligation resulting from Article 1 ECHR to 'secure' rights and freedoms provided for by the Convention continued to rest with the states. Unlike in the succeeding *Bosphorus* decision, in *Matthews* the ECtHR only ever considered the responsibility of states for ensuring that the provisions of the ECHR are observed, without discussing the standard of fundamental rights protection offered at the level of the EU. In the specific, but to an extent generalizable circumstances of *Matthews*, the responsibility of the UK could not be removed or mitigated by reference to the multilateral character of the EU arrangements which gave rise to the infringement of Ms Matthews's right to vote. The ECtHR pointed in particular to two factors: the essentially intergovernmental and voluntary nature of the Maastricht Treaty expanding the competences of the European Parliament in conjunction with the existing exclusion of Gibraltarian representation therefrom; and the posterior character of the Maastricht Treaty with respect to the applicability of the ECHR and Protocol No 1 to Gibraltar.

The ECtHR's reasoning in *Matthews* was mindful of two pitfalls present more generally in conceptualizations of the relationship between EU Member States and international human rights obligations. First, the situation in *Matthews* allowed the Court to sidestep the issue of exclusive competence that arose in *Senator Lines*—it would be slightly more contentious to attribute the whole responsibility to a contracting party if the infringing actions were taken solely by supranational EU institutions. The corollary of the intergovernmental nature of the relevant EU treaties and Council Decision is voluntariness of the UK's involvement in their making. The infringement of Ms Matthews's right to vote was for the most part not a result of a delegated action on the part of an independent EU institution; rather, the violation was directly traceable to the UK's agreements to first subject the territory of Gibraltar to certain EU laws, then exclude Gibraltar from being able to vote in European Parliament elections when these were established and finally—and equally importantly for the outcome of the case—extend the competences of the EP through the Maastricht Treaty without changing any of the previous arrangements applicable to Gibraltar. One issue the ECtHR could afford to gloss over was that the Council of Ministers, which adopted one of the disputed decisions, represented an institution of the Community in its own right despite serving *de facto* as a forum for intergovernmental deliberation of the Member States.

The second pitfall the ECtHR avoided without drawing too much attention to it was making sure that the infringement of rights is connected to a treaty concluded after the right to vote in Article 3 of Protocol No 1 to the Convention was made applicable in Gibraltar. This way the Court could avoid the debate on whether ECHR and Protocol No 1 provisions take precedence over contracting parties' commitments under other treaties concluded earlier. That is also why the Maastricht Treaty was instrumental to the ECtHR's reasoning—at the time of the application it was the only EU treaty concluded after (1992) the UK filed a declaration in 1988 by which Protocol No 1 to the Convention became applicable to Gibraltar. As a result, the UK could not claim that the right to vote for Gibraltarians under Article 3 of Protocol No 1 did not yet exist when it extended the competences of the European Parliament, as was in fact the case with the Single European Act (SEA), a major treaty revision signed in 1986 which also conferred more powers on the elected EP. In *Matthews*, the ECtHR scarcely mentioned the SEA, as doing so could raise the question whether the UK intended to limit the application of the ECHR regime (in Gibraltar) only to those of its state functions not yet transferred to the EU (or other international organization); or, alternatively, whether contracting parties can incur responsibility under the ECHR and Protocol No 1 also with respect to prior treaty obligations. In practice, the ECtHR made greater use of the Maastricht Treaty also because it made the task of establishing that the EP constituted a part of 'legislature' for the purposes of Article 3 of Protocol No 1 easier. The latter point was disputed in a dissenting opinion of Judges Freeland and Jungwiert but on the whole the judgment was adopted by a clear majority of fifteen votes to two. Subsequent treaty revisions, not least the Treaty of Lisbon, have further reinforced the role of the EP.

Nevertheless, the most significant ECtHR judgment regarding the relationship between the EU and the ECHR came in *Bosphorus* where the Court discernibly parted with the approach espoused in *Matthews*. The case of *Bosphorus* concerned the impounding of an aircraft leased from the former Yugoslavia by a Turkish airline operator on the basis of UN Security Council sanctions against Yugoslavia implemented in the EU via a Council Regulation. The aircraft was impounded in Ireland against whom the applicant company ('Bosphorus') brought an action before the ECtHR after a series of unsuccessful legal challenges before Irish courts which also included a preliminary ruling by the CJEU[87] (finding that the restriction on the applicant's right to property was proportionate in light of realizing the objective of international security).[88] The situation was analogous to *Kadi* in that

---

[87] Judgment of 30 July 1996, *Bosphorus Hava Yollari Turizm ve Ticaret AS v Minister for Transport, Energy and Communications and others*, C-84/95, ECLI:EU:C:1996:312.
[88] *Bosphorus v Ireland* (n 36).

it emanated from an EU implementation of a UN sanctions regime; the Strasbourg Court, however, was called upon to evaluate the fundamental rights credentials of the EU system and give guidance to EU Member States on reconciling their obligations under the ECHR, on the one hand, and EU law, on the other.

Bosphorus Hava Yollari Turizm ve Ticaret Anonim Şirketi v Ireland, App no 45036/98, 30 June 2005

---

148. (...) the Court finds that the impugned interference was not the result of an exercise of discretion by the Irish authorities, either under Community or Irish law, but rather **amounted to compliance by the Irish State with its legal obligations flowing from Community law** and, in particular, Article 8 of Regulation (EEC) no. 990/93.

150. (...) the general interest pursued by the impugned measure was compliance with legal obligations flowing from the Irish State's membership of the European Community.

    It is, moreover, a legitimate interest of considerable weight. **The Convention has to be interpreted in the light of any relevant rules and principles of international law applicable in relations between the Contracting Parties** (...) which principles include that of *pacta sunt servanda*. The Court has also long recognised the growing importance of international cooperation and of the consequent **need to secure the proper functioning of international organisations** (...) Such considerations are critical for a supranational organisation such as the European Community. This Court has accordingly accepted that **compliance with Community law by a Contracting Party constitutes a legitimate general-interest objective** within the meaning of Article 1 of Protocol No. 1 (...)

151. The question is therefore whether, and if so to what extent, that important general interest of compliance with Community obligations can justify the impugned interference by the Irish State with the applicant company's property rights.

152. The Convention does not, on the one hand, prohibit Contracting Parties from transferring sovereign power to an international (including a supranational) organisation in order to pursue cooperation in certain fields of activity (...) Moreover, even as the holder of such transferred sovereign power, that organisation is not itself held responsible under the Convention for proceedings before, or decisions of, its organs as long as it is not a Contracting Party (...)

153. On the other hand, it has also been accepted that a Contracting Party is responsible under Article 1 of the Convention for all acts and omissions of its organs regardless of whether the act or omission in question was a consequence of domestic law or of the necessity to comply with international legal obligations. Article 1 makes no distinction as to the type of rule or measure concerned and does not exclude any part of a Contracting Party's 'jurisdiction' from scrutiny under the Convention (...)

154. In reconciling both these positions and thereby establishing the extent to which a State's action can be justified by its compliance with obligations flowing from its membership of an international organisation to which it has transferred part of its sovereignty, **the Court has recognised that absolving Contracting States completely from their Convention responsibility in the areas covered by such a transfer**

would be incompatible with the purpose and object of the Convention; the guarantees of the Convention could be limited or excluded at will, thereby depriving it of its peremptory character and undermining the practical and effective nature of its safeguards (...) **The State is considered to retain Convention liability in respect of treaty commitments subsequent to the entry into force of the Convention** (...)

155. In the Court's view, State action taken in compliance with such legal obligations is justified **as long as the relevant organisation is considered to protect fundamental rights, as regards both the substantive guarantees offered and the mechanisms controlling their observance, in a manner which can be considered at least equivalent to that for which the Convention provides** (see M. & Co., cited above, p. 145, an approach with which the parties and the European Commission agreed). **By 'equivalent' the Court means 'comparable'; any requirement that the organisation's protection be 'identical' could run counter to the interest of international cooperation pursued** (see paragraph 150 above). However, any such finding of equivalence could not be final and would be susceptible to review in the light of any relevant change in fundamental rights protection.

156. **If such equivalent protection is considered to be provided by the organisation, the presumption will be that a State has not departed from the requirements of the Convention when it does no more than implement legal obligations flowing from its membership of the organisation.**

   However, **any such presumption can be rebutted if, in the circumstances of a particular case, it is considered that the protection of Convention rights was manifestly deficient.** In such cases, the interest of international cooperation would be outweighed by the Convention's role as a 'constitutional instrument of European public order' in the field of human rights (...)

157. It remains the case that a State would be fully responsible under the Convention for all acts falling outside its strict international legal obligations. (...) *Matthews* can also be distinguished [from *Bosphorus*]: the acts for which the United Kingdom was found responsible were 'international instruments which were freely entered into' by it (...)

159. (...) While the founding treaties of the European Communities did not initially contain express provisions for the protection of fundamental rights, the ECJ subsequently recognised that such rights were enshrined in the general principles of Community law protected by it, and that the Convention had a 'special significance' as a source of such rights. Respect for fundamental rights has become 'a condition of the legality of Community acts' (...) and in carrying out this assessment the ECJ refers extensively to Convention provisions and to this Court's jurisprudence. At the relevant time, these jurisprudential developments had been reflected in certain treaty amendments (...).

160. However, **the effectiveness of such substantive guarantees of fundamental rights depends on the mechanisms of control** in place to ensure their observance.

162. It is true that access of individuals to the ECJ under these provisions is limited: they have no locus standi under Articles 169 and 170; their right to initiate actions under Articles 173 and 175 is restricted as is, consequently, their right under Article 184; and they have no right to bring an action against another individual.

163. It nevertheless remains the case that **actions initiated before the ECJ by the Community institutions or a member State constitute important control of**

compliance with Community norms to the indirect benefit of individuals. Individuals can also bring an action for damages before the ECJ in respect of the non-contractual liability of the institutions (…)

164. Moreover, **it is essentially through the national courts that the Community system provides a remedy to individuals** against a member State or another individual for a breach of Community law (…) It was the development by the ECJ of important notions such as the supremacy of Community law, direct effect, indirect effect and State liability (…) which greatly enlarged the role of the domestic courts in the enforcement of Community law and its fundamental rights guarantees.

(…) While the ECJ's role is limited to replying to the interpretative or validity question referred by the domestic court, the reply will often be determinative of the domestic proceedings (as, indeed, it was in the present case (…) and detailed guidelines on the timing and content of a preliminary reference have been laid down by the EC Treaty provision and developed by the ECJ in its case-law. The parties to the domestic proceedings have the right to put their case to the ECJ during the Article 177 process. It is further noted that national courts operate in legal systems into which the Convention has been incorporated, albeit to differing degrees.

165. In such circumstances, **the Court finds that the protection of fundamental rights by Community law can be considered to be, and to have been at the relevant time, 'equivalent' (within the meaning of paragraph 155 above) to that of the Convention system. Consequently, the presumption arises that Ireland did not depart from the requirements of the Convention when it implemented legal obligations flowing from its membership of the European Community** (see paragraph 156 above).

166. The Court has had regard to the nature of the interference, to the general interest pursued by the impoundment and by the sanctions regime and to the ruling of the ECJ (in the light of the opinion of the Advocate General), a ruling with which the Supreme Court was obliged to and did comply. It considers it clear that there was no dysfunction of the mechanisms of control of the observance of Convention rights.

In the Court's view, therefore, **it cannot be said that the protection of the applicant company's Convention rights was manifestly deficient, with the consequence that the relevant presumption of Convention compliance by the respondent State has not been rebutted.**

The ECtHR has almost entirely agreed with the submission of Ireland and intervention by the European Commission which, in essence, distinguished the *Bosphorus* case from *Matthews* as following from the fact that neither the government nor the courts of Ireland had discretion in their implementation of the Regulation instituting an embargo against the former Yugoslavia and the subsequent preliminary ruling handed down in the case by the CJEU. Moreover, the Court recognized that compliance with EU law of contracting parties to the ECHR represents a legitimate general interest 'of considerable weight' which can justify interference with human rights if the EU itself offers sufficient rights protection. Based on this reasoning of strict international obligations and legitimate interest in international cooperation, the ECtHR moved to examine whether the source of the obligations—the EU legal order—contained guarantees of fundamental rights protection equivalent to those incumbent on contracting parties under the Convention.

The short answer of the Strasbourg Court was 'yes'. The ECtHR closely scrutinized the substantive rights recognized in the EU and the functioning of the system of EU judicial protection and, while finding individual access to the CJEU unsatisfactory,[89] concluded that the fundamental rights protection offered by the EU can be considered equivalent (meaning comparable). In light of the presumption, the Court limited the judicial review to establishing whether in the individual case at hand, the 'protection of Convention rights was manifestly deficient'. As this was not the case, Ireland was presumed to have complied with its obligations under the ECHR by virtue of equivalent protection of rights in the EU.

The presumption of equivalent protection of fundamental rights granted to the EU by the ECtHR is in essence the same as the one put in place by the Federal Constitutional Court of Germany (FCC) in *Solange II*.[90] This kind of a presumption is about the ECtHR (and the FCC) refraining from individual judicial review in light of ECHR or German law in cases alleging fundamental rights violations by the EU or the Member States strictly implementing EU obligations.[91] The presumptions safeguard the authority of EU institutions, in particular the CJEU, to preside more autonomously over the EU legal order which is an essential component of the functioning of supranational institutions (such as the CJEU).

Despite the establishment of the presumption, the ECtHR was quick to point out that contracting parties are not absolved of their obligations under the Convention. States retain liability for infringements of the ECHR with respect to subsequent treaty commitments (paragraph 154), among which are the EU Treaties. The presumption of equivalent protection merely adds an intermediary step to this state liability in cases where the contracting party in question had no margin of discretion with respect to an international legal obligation. On the contrary, the exercise of any discretion on the part of the contracting party renders the presumption of equivalent protection, and indeed the connection of the national action to international obligations, irrelevant for the purposes of the ECtHR's examination of human rights violations. Thus, for example, in *Cantoni v France* the Strasbourg Court found that the fact that a national law transposes an EU directive almost word for word does not remove France's responsibility to promulgate laws which comply with Article 7 ECHR.[92]

As illustrated by the case of *M.S.S v Belgium and Greece*,[93] the notion of strict international obligations can be construed rather narrowly. In this case concerning intra-EU transfers of asylum seekers in accordance with the Dublin Regulation, the ECtHR held that because the Dublin Regulation gave Belgium the possibility to derogate from the general rule and examine an asylum application instead of transferring the asylum seeker to the responsible state (Greece), Belgium's decision not to exercise this discretion under the Regulation, while being aware of systemic violations of asylum seekers' rights in Greece, did not emanate from

---

[89] The lack of individual access concerns Article 263(4) TFEU, as famously interpreted by the *Plaumann* decision. See Judgment of 15 July 1963, *Plaumann and Others v Commission of the European Economic Community*, 25/62, ECLI:EU:C:1963:17. Over the years, some attempts have been made at easing the criteria for access of individuals to the EU courts but the standard remains rather restrictive.

[90] It is interesting to note that in the context of the ECHR, the presumption was already outlined by the European Commission of Human Rights—an oversight body abolished in 1998—in the case of *M & Co v the Federal Republic of Germany*, App no 13258/87, 9 February 1990. The ECtHR referred to this case repeatedly in *Bosphorus*. The *Solange II* presumption of the FCC had of course been already in place at that time (since 1986).

[91] The ECtHR is technically not refraining entirely from conducting judicial review but the standard of review is severely circumscribed to only checking whether a manifest deficiency occurred in the individual case.

[92] *Cantoni v France*, App no 17862/91, 11 November 1996.

[93] *M.S.S. v Belgium and Greece*, App no 30696/09, 21 January 2011.

a strict legal obligation under EU law.[94] Consequently, the transfer of the asylum seeker to Greece by Belgium was not covered by the presumption of equivalent protection; Belgium's liability was reviewed in full by the Court, finding a violation of Article 13 ECHR on the right to an effective remedy in conjunction with Article 3 ECHR on the prohibition of torture and inhuman or degrading treatment or punishment.[95]

Similarly, the ECtHR found the presumption of equivalent protection inapplicable in *Michaud v France*.[96] The case concerned a French law implementing an EU directive requiring lawyers to report suspicions of money laundering or terrorist financing. Before reaching out to Strasbourg, a French lawyer tried unsuccessfully to challenge the law at the Conseil d'État, alleging a lack of precision of the measure and an infringement of the lawyer's right to privacy. Although the ECtHR found no violation of the Convention, it distinguished the case from *Bosphorus* by pointing to two features. First, unlike in *Bosphorus*, the disputed measure was implementing an EU directive (not a regulation) which gave France a margin of appreciation when transposing the Directive into domestic law.[97] Second and more importantly, and as opposed to the Irish Supreme Court in *Bosphorus*, the Conseil d'État did not refer a question for a preliminary ruling to the CJEU before deciding the case in France.[98] As a result, the presumption that the EU offers equivalent rights protection did not apply.

Michaud v France, App no 12323/11, 6 December 2012

115. The Court is therefore obliged to note that because of the decision of the *Conseil d'État* not to refer the question before it to the Court of Justice for a preliminary ruling, even though that court had never examined the Convention rights in issue, the *Conseil d'État* ruled **without the full potential of the relevant international machinery for supervising fundamental rights—in principle equivalent to that of the Convention—having been deployed**. In the light of that choice and the importance of what was at stake, the presumption of equivalent protection does not apply.

The case of *Michaud* shows that the ECtHR does not grant the presumption to EU Member States on theoretical grounds; on the contrary, the judicial protection necessary for effective enjoyment of human rights must be present as well. In the circumstances of the case, the ECtHR was of the view that the absence of a preliminary reference vitiated the presumption of equivalent protection. Such a decision speaks to the worries of the CJEU about its exclusive role (autonomy) in the interpretation of EU law, as the ECtHR's requirement for the Conseil

---

[94] Ibid, para 340.
[95] The case of *M.S.S. v Belgium and Greece* had important implications not only for EU refugee laws but also more broadly for the notion of mutual trust between Member States which is founded upon the presumption that each Member State observes fundamental rights. The decision prompted the CJEU to subsequently accept that systemic deficiencies represent a legitimate ground for the suspension of mutual trust. See Judgment of 21 December 2011, *N.S. and Others*, C-411/10 and C-493/10, ECLI:EU:C:2011:865 and Ch 4.
[96] *Michaud v France*, App no 12323/11, 6 December 2012.
[97] Ibid, para 113.
[98] Ibid, para 115.

d'État to make a preliminary reference potentially disrupts the CJEU's case law on the issue.[99] The Strasbourg Court had already stated previously that an arbitrary refusal by a national court to engage with the CJEU on the basis of Article 267 TFEU can amount to an infringement of Article 6 ECHR on the right to a fair trial.[100]

An example of successful application of the *Bosphorus* presumption can be found in *Povse v Austria*.[101] In this case the ECtHR held that Austrian courts who ordered the return of a child to its father in Italy after he was given sole custody by Italian courts did no more than abide by strict obligations flowing from EU law,[102] namely the Brussels IIa Regulation on mutual recognition and enforcement of judgments in matters of parental responsibility.[103] The presumption was applicable not only because it concerned an EU regulation but also—and mainly—because the Austrian courts sought a preliminary ruling by the CJEU which prohibited them from reviewing the merits of the case. The lack of discretion to examine the merits of the return decision distinguished *Povse* from *M.S.S.* and the recourse to the CJEU fulfilled the role of a control mechanism which was absent in *Michaud*.[104]

More dramatic and damaging for the relationship between the Strasbourg and the Luxembourg courts was the ECtHR's judgment in *Tarakhel v Switzerland*.[105] The case revolved around another human rights challenge of transfers of asylum seekers under the Dublin Regulation from a country reached through secondary movement (Switzerland) back to the country of first entry (Italy). Switzerland, notwithstanding its lack of EU membership, participated in the Dublin system through an international agreement with the EU. For the same reasons as in *M.S.S.*—Switzerland could have exercised discretion under the Dublin Regulation—the ECtHR found the presumption of equivalent protection inapplicable.[106] However, the Strasbourg Court put the (other) presumption of human rights protection as between EU Member States (mutual trust) under more scrutiny than in *M.S.S.* Whereas in that judgment the Court considered transfers unacceptable in light of the near-complete breakdown of the Greek asylum system, in *Tarakhel* the deficiencies of the Italian asylum system were not of the same scale or gravity. Nonetheless, the ECtHR held that in the individual case it was 'incumbent on Swiss authorities to obtain assurances from their Italian counterparts that on their arrival in Italy the applicants will be received in facilities and in conditions adapted to the age of the children, and that the family will be kept together'.[107] At the time, this ran contrary to the case law of the CJEU which accepted the existence of 'systemic deficiencies in the asylum procedure and in the conditions for the reception of asylum applicants' in the receiving Member State to constitute the only valid ground for contesting a transfer decision under the Dublin Regulation.[108] The CJEU's approach to human rights based challenges to the principle of mutual trust has later softened

---

[99] Under the *CILFIT* doctrine, highest national courts may in specific circumstances refrain from referring a question for a preliminary ruling in accordance with Article 267 TFEU. See Judgment of 6 October 1982, *Srl CILFIT and Lanificio di Gavardo SpA v Ministry of Health*, 283/81, ECLI:EU:C:1982:335, para 21.

[100] See *Lutz John v Germany*, App no 15073/03, 13 February 2007. See also *Dhahbi v Italy*, App no 17120/09, 8 April 2014 and *Sanofi Pasteur v France*, App no 25137/16, 13 February 2020.

[101] *Povse v Austria*, App no 3890/11, 18 June 2013.

[102] Ibid, para 87.

[103] Council Regulation (EC) 2201/2003 concerning jurisdiction and the recognition and enforcement of judgments in matrimonial matters and the matters of parental responsibility, repealing Regulation (EC) No 1347/2000 [2003] OJ L338/1.

[104] *Povse v Austria* (n 101).

[105] *Tarakhel v Switzerland*, App no 29217/12, 4 November 2014.

[106] Ibid, para 90.

[107] Ibid, para 120

[108] See Judgment of 10 December 2013, *Abdullahi v Bundesasylamt*, C-394/12, ECLI:EU:C:2013:813, para 60. Previously, see *N.S. and Others* (n 95).

in cases such as *Aranyosi and Căldăraru* and *C.K. and Others*,[109] despite strengthening the principle in *Opinion 2/13*.[110]

Avotiņš v Latvia[111] was the first judgment concerning the *Bosphorus* presumption after the CJEU vehemently rejected a draft agreement on the EU's accession to the ECHR, including oversight by the ECtHR. As a result, there had been expectations as to the Strasbourg Court's reaction to the CJEU's adversarial posturing prior to the publication of the judgment in *Avotiņš*. The case originated from a debt repayment dispute related to the EU regime for mutual recognition and enforcement of foreign judgments in civil and commercial matters.[112]

Avotiņš v Latvia, App no 17502/07, 23 May 2016

105. The Court reiterates that the application of the *Bosphorus* presumption [presumption of equivalent protection] in the legal system of the European Union is subject to two conditions (...) These are the absence of any margin of manoeuvre on the part of the domestic authorities and the deployment of the full potential of the supervisory mechanism provided for by European Union law (...)

106. With regard to the first condition, the Court notes at the outset that the provision to which the Senate of the Supreme Court gave effect was contained in a Regulation, which was directly applicable in the Member States in its entirety, and not in a Directive, which would have been binding on the State with regard to the result to be achieved but would have left it to the State to choose the means and manner of achieving it (see, conversely, Michaud, cited above, § 113). As to the precise provision applied in the instant case, namely Article 34(2) of the Brussels I Regulation, the Court notes that it allowed the refusal of recognition or enforcement of a foreign judgment only within very precise limits and subject to certain preconditions, namely that 'the defendant [had] not [been] served with the document which instituted the proceedings or with an equivalent document in sufficient time and in such a way as to enable him to arrange for his defence, unless the defendant [had] failed to commence proceedings to challenge the judgment when it [had been] possible for him to do so'. It is clear from the interpretation given by the CJEU (...) that **this provision did not confer any discretion on the court** from which the declaration of enforceability was sought. The Court therefore concludes that the Senate of the Latvian Supreme Court did not enjoy any margin of manoeuvre in this case.

---

[109] Although the Judgment of 5 April 2016, *Aranyosi and Căldăraru v Generalstaatsanwaltschaft Bremen*, C-404/15 and C-659/15 PPU, ECLI:EU:C:2016:198 concerned mutual trust in the area of EU criminal law, the CJEU's greater openness to taking into account detention conditions in another Member State could be extended, *mutatis mutandis*, to asylum matters. Evidence of greater mindfulness of human rights considerations in the functioning of mutual trust as regards EU asylum law was borne out to some extent by the Judgment of 16 February 2017, *C.K. and Others v Republika Slovenija*, C-578/16 PPU, ECLI:EU:C:2017:127, where the CJEU conditioned transfers of asylum seekers upon there being no possibility of 'a real and proven risk of the person concerned suffering inhuman or degrading treatment' within the meaning of Article 4 of the Charter (EU equivalent of Article 3 ECHR). However, in Judgment of 19 March 2019, *Abubacarr Jawo v Bundesrepublik Deutschland*, C-163/17, ECLI:EU:C:2019:218 the CJEU set this criterion in stone and required that in order to justify the refusal to transfer an asylum applicant, his living conditions after the transfer have to be such that he would live in a situation of extreme material poverty that does not allow him to meet his most basic needs (see Ch 4).

[110] *Opinion 2/13 (EU accession to the ECHR)* (n 11).

[111] *Avotiņš v Latvia*, App no 17502/07, 23 May 2016.

[112] Council Regulation (EC) No 44/2001 of 22 December 2000 on jurisdiction and the recognition and enforcement of judgments in civil and commercial matters ('Brussels I Regulation') was the Regulation applicable in the proceedings. It was replaced in 2015 by Regulation (EU) No 1215/2012 ('Brussels I *bis*').

107. The present case is therefore distinguishable from that of M.S.S., cited above. In that case, in examining the issue of Belgium's responsibility under the Convention, the Court noted that, under the terms of the applicable Regulation (the Dublin II Regulation), the Belgian State authorities retained the discretionary power to decide whether or not to make use of the 'sovereignty' clause which allowed them to examine the asylum application and to refrain from sending the applicant back to Greece if they considered that the Greek authorities were likely not to fulfil their obligations under the Convention (§§ 339–40). By contrast, **Article 34(2) of the Brussels I Regulation did not grant States any such discretionary powers of assessment.**

108. In its third-party submissions the AIRE Centre argued that the Senate of the Latvian Supreme Court could and should have had recourse to Article 34(1) of the Brussels I Regulation, according to which the request for a declaration of enforceability had to be refused if 'recognition [was] manifestly contrary to public policy in the Member State in which recognition [was] sought'. According to the AIRE Centre this provision allowed the Latvian court a degree of discretion (see paragraph 94 above). However, the arguments raised by the applicant before the Supreme Court were confined to the application of paragraph 2 of Article 34. The Court will therefore confine its analysis to the applicant's complaints as raised before the Supreme Court and in the context of the present proceedings. **It considers that it is not its task to determine whether another provision of the Brussels I Regulation should have been applied.**

109. As regards the second condition, namely the deployment of the full potential of the supervisory mechanism provided for by European Union law, the Court observes at the outset that in the Bosphorus judgment, cited above, it recognised that, taken overall, the supervisory mechanisms put in place within the European Union afforded a level of protection equivalent to that for which the Convention mechanism provided (ibid., §§ 160–64). Turning to the specific circumstances of the present case, it notes that the **Senate of the Supreme Court did not request a preliminary ruling from the CJEU** regarding the interpretation and application of Article 34(2) of the Regulation. However, it considers that this second condition should be applied without excessive formalism and taking into account the specific features of the supervisory mechanism in question. **It considers that it would serve no useful purpose to make the implementation of the Bosphorus presumption subject to a requirement for the domestic court to request a ruling from the CJEU in all cases without exception**, including those cases where no genuine and serious issue arises with regard to the protection of fundamental rights by EU law, or those in which the CJEU has already stated precisely how the applicable provisions of EU law should be interpreted in a manner compatible with fundamental rights.

110. The Court observes that, in a different context, it has held that national courts against whose decisions no judicial remedy exists in national law are obliged to give reasons for refusing to refer a question to the CJEU for a preliminary ruling, in the light of the exceptions provided for by the case-law of the CJEU. The national courts must therefore state the reasons why they consider it unnecessary to seek a preliminary ruling (see Ullens de Schooten and Rezabek v. Belgium, nos. 3989/07 and 38353/07, § 62, 20 September 2011, and Dhahbi v. Italy, no. 17120/09, §§ 31–34, 8 April 2014). The Court emphasises that the purpose of the review it conducts in this regard is to ascertain whether the refusal to refer a question for a preliminary ruling constituted in itself a violation of Article 6 § 1 of the Convention; in so doing,

it takes into account the approach already established by the case-law of the CJEU. **This review therefore differs from that which it conducts when, as in the present case, it examines the decision not to request a preliminary ruling as part of its overall assessment of the degree of protection of fundamental rights afforded by European Union law.** The Court carries out this assessment, in line with the case-law established in Michaud, in order to determine whether it can apply the presumption of equivalent protection to the decision complained of, a presumption which the Court applies in accordance with conditions which it has itself laid down.

111. The Court thus considers that the question **whether the full potential of the supervisory mechanisms provided for by European Union law was deployed**—and, more specifically, whether the fact that the domestic court hearing the case did not request a preliminary ruling from the CJEU is apt to preclude the application of the presumption of equivalent protection—**should be assessed in the light of the specific circumstances of each case.** In the present case it notes that **the applicant did not advance any specific argument concerning the interpretation of Article 34(2) of the Brussels I Regulation and its compatibility with fundamental rights** such as to warrant a finding that a preliminary ruling should have been requested from the CJEU. This position is confirmed by the fact that the applicant did not submit any request to that effect to the Senate of the Latvian Supreme Court. **The present case is thus clearly distinguishable from Michaud, cited above, in which the national supreme court refused the applicant's request to seek a preliminary ruling from the CJEU even though the issue of the Convention compatibility of the impugned provision of European Union law had never previously been examined by the CJEU** (ibid., § 114). Hence, the fact that the matter was not referred for a preliminary ruling is not a decisive factor in the present case. The second condition for application of the Bosphorus presumption should therefore be considered to be satisfied.

112. In view of the foregoing considerations, **the Court concludes that the presumption of equivalent protection is applicable in the present case**, as the Senate of the Supreme Court did no more than implement Latvia's legal obligations arising out of its membership of the European Union (see, mutatis mutandis, Povse, cited above, § 78). Accordingly, **the Court's task is confined to ascertaining whether the protection of the rights guaranteed by the Convention was manifestly deficient** in the present case such that this presumption is rebutted. (…) In examining this issue the Court must have regard both to Article 34(2) of the Brussels I Regulation as such and to the specific circumstances in which it was implemented in the present case.

113. In general terms, the Court observes that the Brussels I Regulation is based in part on mutual recognition mechanisms which themselves are founded on the principle of mutual trust between the Member States of the European Union. The Preamble to the Brussels I Regulation states that the approach underpinning the Regulation is one of 'mutual trust in the administration of justice' within the EU, which implies that **'the declaration that a judgment is enforceable should be issued virtually automatically** after purely formal checks of the documents supplied, without there being any possibility for the court to raise of its own motion any of the grounds for non-enforcement provided for by this Regulation' (see paragraph 54 above). **The Court is mindful of the importance of the mutual recognition mechanisms for the construction of the area of freedom, security and justice** referred to in Article 67 of the TFEU, **and of the mutual trust which they require.** (…) Hence, it

considers the creation of an area of freedom, security and justice in Europe, and the adoption of the means necessary to achieve it, to be wholly legitimate in principle from the standpoint of the Convention.

114. Nevertheless, the methods used to create that area must not infringe the fundamental rights of the persons affected by the resulting mechanisms, as indeed confirmed by Article 67(1) of the TFEU. However, **it is apparent that the aim of effectiveness pursued by some of the methods used results in the review of the observance of fundamental rights being tightly regulated or even limited.** (...) Limiting to exceptional cases the power of the State in which recognition is sought to review the observance of fundamental rights by the State of origin of the judgment could, in practice, run counter to the requirement imposed by the Convention according to which **the court in the State addressed must at least be empowered to conduct a review commensurate with the gravity of any serious allegation of a violation of fundamental rights** in the State of origin, in order to ensure that the protection of those rights is not manifestly deficient.

115. Moreover, the Court observes that where the domestic authorities give effect to European Union law and have no discretion in that regard, the presumption of equivalent protection set forth in the Bosphorus judgment is applicable. This is the case where the mutual recognition mechanisms require the court to presume that the observance of fundamental rights by another Member State has been sufficient. The domestic court is thus deprived of its discretion in the matter, leading to automatic application of the Bosphorus presumption of equivalence. The Court emphasises that this results, paradoxically, in a **twofold limitation of the domestic court's review of the observance of fundamental rights, due to the combined effect of the presumption on which mutual recognition is founded and the Bosphorus presumption of equivalent protection.**

116. In the Bosphorus judgment the Court reiterated that the Convention is a 'constitutional instrument of European public order' (ibid., § 156). Accordingly, the Court must satisfy itself, where the conditions for application of the presumption of equivalent protection are met (see paragraphs 105–106 above), that the mutual recognition mechanisms do not leave any gap or particular situation which would render the protection of the human rights guaranteed by the Convention manifestly deficient. In doing so it takes into account, in **a spirit of complementarity**, the manner in which these mechanisms operate and in particular the aim of effectiveness which they pursue. Nevertheless, **it must verify that the principle of mutual recognition is not applied automatically and mechanically (...) to the detriment of fundamental rights** (...) In this spirit, where the courts of a State which is both a Contracting Party to the Convention and a Member State of the European Union are called upon to apply a mutual recognition mechanism established by EU law, they must give full effect to that mechanism where the protection of Convention rights cannot be considered manifestly deficient. However, **if a serious and substantiated complaint is raised before them to the effect that the protection of a Convention right has been manifestly deficient and that this situation cannot be remedied by European Union law, they cannot refrain from examining that complaint on the sole ground that they are applying EU law.**

117. The Court must now seek to ascertain whether the protection of fundamental rights afforded by the Senate of the Latvian Supreme Court was manifestly deficient in the

present case such that the presumption of equivalent protection is rebutted, as regards both the provision of European Union law that was applied and its implementation in the specific case of the applicant.

118. The Court considers that the requirement to exhaust remedies arising from the mechanism provided for by Article 34(2) of the Brussels I Regulation as interpreted by the CJEU (the defendant must have made use of any remedies available in the State of origin in order to be able to complain of a failure to serve him with the document instituting the proceedings), is not in itself problematic in terms of the guarantees of Article 6 § 1 of the Convention. **This is a precondition** which pursues the aim of ensuring the proper administration of justice in a spirit of procedural economy and which is based on an approach **similar to that underpinning the rule of exhaustion of domestic remedies set forth in Article 35 § 1 of the Convention.** This approach comprises two strands. Firstly, **States are dispensed from answering before an international body for their acts before they have had an opportunity to put matters right through their own legal system** and, secondly, it is presumed that there is an effective remedy available in the domestic system in respect of the alleged breach (...) Hence, **the Court sees no indication that the protection afforded was manifestly deficient in this regard.**

120. (...) the applicant maintained, in particular, before the Latvian courts that he had not been duly notified in good time of the summons to appear before the Limassol District Court and the request by the company F.H. Ltd., with the result that he had been unable to arrange for his defence. He therefore argued that recognition of the impugned judgment should have been refused under Article 34(2) of the Brussels I Regulation. The applicant contended that the summons had been sent to an address where it had been physically impossible to reach him, even though the Cypriot and Latvian lawyers representing the claimant company had been perfectly aware of his business address in Riga and could easily have obtained his private address (see paragraph 30 above). He therefore raised cogent arguments in the Latvian courts alleging the existence of a procedural defect which, a priori, was contrary to Article 6 § 1 of the Convention and precluded the enforcement of the Cypriot judgment in Latvia.

121. In the light of the general principles reiterated above, the Court notes that, in the proceedings before the Senate of the Supreme Court, the applicant complained that he had not received any summons or been notified of the Cypriot judgment. In so doing he relied on the grounds for non-recognition provided for by Article 34(2) of the Brussels I Regulation. **That provision states expressly that such grounds may be invoked only on condition that proceedings have previously been commenced to challenge the judgment in question, in so far as it was possible to do so.** The fact that the applicant relied on that Article without having challenged the judgment as required necessarily raised the question of the availability of that legal remedy in Cyprus in the circumstances of the present case. In such a situation the Senate was not entitled simply to criticise the applicant, as it did in its judgment of 31 January 2007, for not appealing against the judgment concerned, and to remain silent on the issue of the burden of proof with regard to the existence and availability of a remedy in the State of origin; Article 6 § 1 of the Convention, like Article 34(2) in fine of the Brussels I Regulation, required it to verify that this condition was satisfied, in the absence of which it could not refuse to examine the applicant's complaint. The Court considers that the determination of the burden of proof, which,

as the European Commission stressed (see paragraph 92 above), is not governed by European Union law, was therefore decisive in the present case. Hence, that point should have been examined in adversarial proceedings leading to reasoned findings. However, the Supreme Court tacitly presumed either that the burden of proof lay with the defendant or that such a remedy had in fact been available to the applicant. **This approach, which reflects a literal and automatic application of Article 34(2) of the Brussels I Regulation, could in theory lead to a finding that the protection afforded was manifestly deficient such that the presumption of equivalent protection of the rights of the defence guaranteed by Article 6 § 1 is rebutted.** Nevertheless, **in the specific circumstances of the present application the Court does not consider this to be the case, although this shortcoming is regrettable.**

122. It is clear, in fact, from the information provided by the Cypriot Government at the Grand Chamber's request, and not disputed by the parties, that Cypriot law afforded the applicant, after he had learned of the existence of the judgment, a perfectly realistic opportunity of appealing despite the length of time that had elapsed since the judgment had been given. In accordance with Cypriot legislation and case-law, where a defendant against whom a judgment has been given in default applies to have that judgment set aside and alleges, on arguable grounds, that he or she was not duly summoned before the court which gave judgment, the court hearing the application is required—and not merely empowered—to set aside the judgment given in default (…) In the instant case the Court considers that, in the period between 16 June 2006 (the date on which he was given access to the entire case file at the premises of the first-instance court and was able to acquaint himself with the content of the Cypriot judgment) and 31 January 2007 (the date of the hearing of the Senate of the Supreme Court), **the applicant had sufficient time to pursue a remedy in the Cypriot courts.** However, for reasons known only to himself, he made no attempt to do so.

123. The fact that the Cypriot judgment made no reference to the available remedies does not affect the Court's findings. (…) **It was therefore up to the applicant himself, if need be with appropriate advice, to enquire as to the remedies available in Cyprus after he became aware of the judgment in question.**

125. Hence, in the specific circumstances of the present case, **the Court does not consider that the protection of fundamental rights was manifestly deficient such that the presumption of equivalent protection is rebutted.**

Avotiņš v Latvia represents so far the most in-depth treatment of not only the presumption of equivalent protection of the EU, including the criterion of manifest deficiency, but also of the Convention requirements applicable to mutual recognition processes between EU Member States.[113] The ECtHR started the relevant part of the judgment with magnanimity towards the CJEU—it recounted and consolidated the case law regarding the existence of the *Bosphorus* presumption and confirmed that it is indeed applicable to the case at hand. By upholding the presumption despite the non-use of the preliminary reference procedure, the Strasbourg Court even went on to alleviate some of the concerns of the CJEU with respect

---

[113] It has been argued that the ECtHR applied a somewhat light touch to the *Bosphorus* doctrine in some previous cases. See C Ryngaert, 'Oscillating between Embracing and Avoiding Bosphorus: The European Court of Human Rights on Member State Responsibility for Acts of International Organisations and the Case of the European Union' (2014) 39 European Law Review 176.

to setting requirements for when requests for preliminary rulings under Article 267 TFEU are necessary. The CJEU must have been relieved to see that recourse to Article 267 TFEU has not become a *conditio sine qua non* for the applicability of the *Bosphorus* presumption in the assessment of the ECtHR. As opposed to Mr Michaud, Mr Avotiņš did not request the Latvian Supreme Court to ask the CJEU for interpretive guidance and, in such circumstances, the ECtHR found that the absence of a preliminary ruling by the CJEU should not prejudice the presumption of equivalent protection of the EU.

Similarly, the Strasbourg Court's assessment of the other criterion underlying the *Bosphorus* presumption—the existence of a strict international (EU) legal obligation—exhibited a constructive understanding of EU law. The Court stated that the Brussels I Regulation imposed a strict obligation of mutual recognition on the Latvian Supreme Court, leaving no room for discretion for either the Supreme Court or the Latvian government. This was adjudged so despite the fact that another provision of the Brussels I Regulation would allow the Supreme Court to derogate from mutual recognition on public policy grounds; the provision was not, however, invoked by the complainant or applied by the Supreme Court. In these circumstances, the ECtHR refrained from evaluating whether EU law was to be applied differently, especially when that would require an *ex officio* intervention by the Latvian Supreme Court, and for good reasons. First, the role of the ECtHR is to assess compatibility with the Convention and not to serve as a 'Court of fourth instance' even though the line between the two can be at times blurry.[114] Second, the Court adheres to the adversarial principle and therefore must rule on the facts and the law of the case as demarcated during the domestic proceedings. Third and related, the fact that the dispute concerned principally the application of a provision of EU law rather than national law does not entitle the ECtHR to enlarge the scope of its review, bearing in mind that the courts of EU Member States are also part of the decentralized system of judicial protection in the EU and are bound by the interpretation of the CJEU.

However, as reasonable as the decision not to second guess what the applicable EU law was in the dispute before the Latvian Supreme Court appears in hindsight, the Strasbourg Court could have gone down a more intrusive path. It should be recalled that in *M.S.S.* the interpretation of the strict legal obligation requirement also concerned the application of an EU Regulation by an EU Member State. Nevertheless, in that case the ECtHR found that by not applying the provision of the Dublin Regulation allowing for discretion ('the sovereignty clause'), Belgium's actions were not covered by the concept of strict legal obligation which is a condition for the applicability of the *Bosphorus* presumption. This contrasts with the more deferential approach to the non-exercise of the discretionary provision (Article 34(1) of the Brussels I Regulation) in *Avotiņš*. In fairness to the ECtHR, there are distinguishing factors that justify the opposing approaches. The gravity of human rights violations involved in a transfer of an asylum seeker to a country with a dysfunctional asylum system and the risk of persecution in his country of origin where he could be subsequently returned are undoubtedly greater and warrant closer ECtHR involvement than a violation of fair trial rights in a debt repayment case.[115] Moreover, whereas the onus of mutual recognition in Latvia fell on the Supreme Court, in *M.S.S.* the reliance on mutual trust was primarily driven by the Belgian

---

[114] See, for example, *Pelipenko v Russia*, App no 69037/10, 1 October 2012, para 65: 'the Court reiterates that it is in the first place for the national authorities, notably the courts, to interpret and apply domestic law (…)'. See also M Dahlberg, '"It is not Its Task to Act as a Court of Fourth Instance": The Case of the ECtHR' (2014) 7 European Journal of Legal Studies 84.

[115] This factor would most likely not be openly acknowledged by the ECtHR with a view to give equal consideration to all violations of the Convention.

executive branch. Finally and perhaps most importantly, unlike Mr Avotiņš's pleading before the Latvian Supreme Court with respect to the Brussels I Regulation, the applicant's request in *M.S.S.*, supported by the United Nations High Commissioner for Refugees, to be allowed to stay in Belgium in light of the dire situation in Greece required Belgium to exercise their discretion under the Dublin Regulation.

Once the ECtHR established the applicability of the presumption of equivalent protection, it delved with rigour into whether the presumption was rebutted as a result of human rights protection being manifestly deficient in the case at hand. A close reading of *Avotiņš* shows that the ECtHR was not willing to be as deferential to the EU on this point compared to the question of the applicability of the presumption as a whole. The Court explained that the obligation to comply with EU law cannot serve as the sole justification for denying judicial review in cases where 'a serious and substantiated complaint is raised (...) to the effect that the protection of a Convention right has been manifestly deficient and that this situation cannot be remedied by European Union law' (paragraph 116). While this does not amount to a dismantling of the *Bosphorus* presumption, the ECtHR has raised its expectations of contracting parties' national courts when it comes to protecting Convention rights vis-à-vis the application of EU law. The unprecedented depth of the Strasbourg Court's examination of whether rights protection was manifestly deficient in the case at hand similarly indicates a greater readiness of the Court to intervene into the application of EU law by EU Member States. *Avotiņš* may therefore have consequences for the EU legal order which the CJEU might not find welcome: in most mutual trust/recognition cases, the only judicial remedy at EU level for human rights complaints is an Article 267 TFEU reference to the CJEU. Although more questions for preliminary rulings could represent a way of placating the ECtHR, the resulting increase in caseload is not desired by the CJEU. This approach would in any case constrain the role of national judges in the decentralized scheme of EU judicial protection and make the operation of mutual trust/recognition less smooth, again to the detriment of the CJEU's vision of the system.[116] The alternative to greater resort to Article 267 TFEU by Member States' courts is ignoring the warning of the ECtHR and maintaining deference towards all EU obligations without checking for human rights compliance. Following *Avotiņš*, however, it is clear that the finding of manifestly deficient human rights protection—and thus a rebuttal of the *Bosphorus* presumption by the ECtHR—could be around the corner.[117]

For the time being, however, the most recent ECtHR judgments are not moving in that direction. The case of *Pirozzi v Belgium*[118] concerned the execution by the Belgian authorities of a European arrest warrant issued by Italy. The applicant argued that his right to a fair trial under Article 6 of the ECHR had been violated, since he had been convicted *in absentia* by the Italian courts (allegedly obliging the competent court in Belgium to disregard the warrant). In a slightly less substantiated reasoning than was the case in *Avotiņš*, the ECtHR found the presumption of equivalent protection to be applicable in the context of the Framework Decision on the European arrest warrant,[119] apprehensive of its reliance on the

---

[116] A useful analogy is with that of a federal country. In most federations, it is possible for the courts of one state to review or refuse the execution of a decision originating from another state in only very exceptional circumstances.

[117] The only dissenting judge in *Avotiņš*, András Sajó, argued against upholding the *Bosphorus* presumption in the circumstances of the case.

[118] *Pirozzi v Belgium*, App no 21055/11, 17 April 2018.

[119] Council Framework Decision 2002/584/JHA on the European arrest warrant and the surrender procedures between Member States [2002] OJ L190/1.

principle of mutual trust between EU Member States.[120] Looking at the specific facts at hand, the Italian applicant had both been officially informed of the date and place of his trial and had been effectively defended by a lawyer which led to a reduction of his sentence on appeal. These elements were sufficient for the ECtHR to conclude that there had not been a manifestly insufficient protection of the applicant's right to a fair trial that would lead to a rebuttal of the *Bosphorus* presumption.[121]

In *Romeo Castaño v Belgium*, the ECtHR seems to have gone one step further in honouring the principle of mutual trust as developed by the CJEU. The relevant facts were slightly different from those in earlier case law on European arrest warrants in the sense that the alleged infringement of an ECHR right concerned the non-execution of the Belgian authorities of a Spanish extradition request. The applicants complained that their right to an effective investigation—as the procedural aspect of Article 2 ECHR—had been breached since the suspected killer of their father could not be brought to justice in Spain. Belgium's refusal to extradite was motivated by the real risk that the accused would run of being subjected to inhuman or degrading treatment during her incarceration in Spain. Following its case law in *Avotiņš* and *Pirozzi*, the ECtHR first determined that a risk of a violation of Article 3 ECHR is a legitimate concern that may cause Belgium to disregard the Spanish request for cooperation. The Court, however, went on to investigate whether this refusal was based on legitimate reasons and found that the Belgian authorities did not conduct a sufficiently detailed and thorough investigation as to the future detention circumstances in this individual case. Hence, the ECtHR ordered Belgium to either re-examine the factual basis for its refusal to extradite, or to honour the arrest warrant after all. Admittedly, it based its conclusion on the high standards of protection under Article 2 ECHR and reiterated that its findings do not release Belgium or other states from their obligation not to extradite a person when he or she would run a real risk of being subjected to treatment contrary to Article 3 ECHR in the requesting country (paragraph 92). While the *Romeo Castaño* case does not deal directly with the *Bosphorus* presumption, it shows that the ECtHR, at least to a certain extent, respects the fundamental importance accorded to the duty to cooperate and the principle of mutual trust within the EU legislative framework. This has been one of the major obstacles to EU accession to the ECHR identified by the CJEU.

Romeo Castaño v Belgium, App no 8351/17, 9 July 2019

80. The Court observes that the applicants' complaint under Article 2 of the Convention stemmed from the **refusal of the Belgian courts to execute the European arrest warrants issued by the Spanish authorities** in respect of N.J.E. They complained that the Belgian authorities' refusal to execute the European arrest warrants **deprived them of the enjoyment of their right to an effective official investigation by Spain.** (...)

82. In the present case the mechanism under which Spain sought Belgium's cooperation was the system put in place within the EU by the **Framework Decision on the European arrest warrant** (...) Applying the principles set out above, **the Court must therefore first examine whether, in this context, the Belgian authorities**

---

[120] *Pirozzi v Belgium* (n 118), paras 59–62.
[121] Ibid, paras 70–71.

responded properly to the request for cooperation. It must then verify whether the refusal to cooperate was based on legitimate grounds.

83. As regards the **first** question, the Court observes that the Belgian authorities provided their Spanish counterparts with a **properly reasoned response**. As the Belgian Court of Cassation pointed out in its judgment of 19 November 2013, the mechanism in question is based on a high degree of trust between member States which entails a presumption of observance of fundamental rights by the issuing State. In view of this principle, any refusal to surrender an individual must be supported by detailed evidence of a clear threat to his or her fundamental rights capable of rebutting the presumption in question. In the present case the Court of Cassation found that the Indictments Division (…) had provided legal justification (…) for its decision to **refuse execution of the European arrest warrants issued by the Spanish investigating judge, on account of the risk of an infringement of N.J.E.'s fundamental rights in the event of her surrender to Spain, and in particular the risk that she would be detained there in conditions contrary to Article 3 of the Convention** (…)

84. The Court notes that the approach taken by the Belgian courts is compatible with the principles it has set out in its case-law (see **Pirozzi**, cited above, §§ 57-64, which echoes the methodology advocated in **Avotiņš** v. Latvia [GC], no. 17502/07, §§ 105–27, 23 May 2016). According to that case-law, in the context of execution of a European arrest warrant by an EU member State, **the mutual recognition mechanism should not be applied automatically and mechanically to the detriment of fundamental rights.**

85. As to the **second** question the Court emphasises that, from the standpoint of the Convention, a risk to the person whose surrender is sought of being subjected to inhuman and degrading treatment on account of the conditions of detention in Spain may constitute a legitimate ground for refusing execution of the European arrest warrant and thus for refusing cooperation with Spain. Nevertheless, **given the presence of third-party rights, the finding that such a risk exists must have a sufficient factual basis.**

86. In this connection the Court notes that the Indictments Division based its decision mainly on international reports and on the context of 'Spain's contemporary political history' (…) It is true that the Indictments Division referred to observations published in 2015 by the Human Rights Committee concerning the existence of incommunicado detention (…), but **it did not conduct a detailed, updated examination of the situation prevailing in 2016 and did not seek to identify a real and individualised risk of a violation of N.J.E.'s Convention rights or any structural shortcomings with regard to conditions of detention in Spain.**

87. The Court also notes that, according to the Spanish Government's observations concerning the legislative framework governing incommunicado detention, that regime would not be applicable in a situation such as that in the present case. As this issue was not discussed before the Belgian courts, the Court does not consider it necessary to determine it.

88. The Court further takes note of the applicants' argument, not disputed by the Government, to the effect that numerous European arrest warrants had been issued and executed in respect of suspected members of ETA without the executing States identifying any risk of a violation of the fundamental rights of the persons being surrendered, and that Belgium had been among the executing States (…)

89. Lastly, the Court is of the view that the circumstances of the case and the interests at stake should have prompted the Belgian authorities, making use of the possibility afforded by Belgian law (...), to request additional information concerning the application of the detention regime in N.J.E.'s case, and in particular concerning the place and conditions of detention, in order to ascertain whether there was a real and concrete risk of a violation of the Convention in the event of her surrender.

90. In view of the foregoing, the Court considers that the **examination conducted by the Belgian courts during the surrender proceedings was not sufficiently thorough for it to find that the ground they relied on in refusing to surrender N.J.E., to the detriment of the applicants' rights, had a sufficient factual basis.**

91. The Court therefore concludes that Belgium failed in its obligation to cooperate arising under the procedural limb of Article 2 of the Convention, and that there has been a violation of that provision.

92. The Court would emphasise that this finding of a violation of Article 2 of the Convention does not necessarily entail a requirement for Belgium to surrender N.J.E. to the Spanish authorities. The reason which has prompted the Court to find a violation of Article 2 is the lack of sufficient factual basis for the refusal to surrender her. This in no way releases the Belgian authorities from their obligation to ensure that in the event of her surrender to the Spanish authorities N.J.E. would not run a risk of treatment contrary to Article 3 of the Convention. More generally, **this judgment cannot be construed as lessening the obligation for States not to extradite a person to a requesting country where there are serious grounds to believe that if the person is extradited to that country he or she will run a real risk of being subjected to treatment contrary to Article 3** (see, in particular, Soering v. the United Kingdom, 7 July 1989, § 88, Series A no. 161; Mamatkulov and Askarov v. Turkey [GC], nos. 46827/99 and 46951/99, § 67, ECHR 2005-I; and Trabelsi v. Belgium, no. 140/10, § 116, ECHR 2014 (extracts)), and hence to verify that no such risk exists.

B. EU accession to the ECHR

As mentioned previously, *Avotiņš* was partially a reaction to the CJEU rejecting a draft agreement on EU accession to the ECHR in *Opinion 2/13*. The accession saga has much deeper roots, however: it has been explored by the European Commission since the late-1970s and supported by a multitude of actors, not least the EU Member States and the Council of Europe.[122] For all the success of judicially driven development of fundamental rights protection in the EU, unlike the domestic legal orders of the Member States the EU system lacked external oversight and, also at the time, a bill of rights which would be directly binding on the EU. Moreover, individuals whose rights under the Convention are harmed exclusively by the EU institutions without the involvement of EU Member States have currently no certain way of accessing the jurisdiction of the ECtHR against the EU, or at least bringing such a case

---

[122] P Gragl, *The Accession of the European Union to the European Convention on Human Rights* (Hart Publishing 2013); F Korenica, *The EU Accession to the ECHR: Between Luxembourg's Search for Autonomy and Strasbourg's Credibility on Human Rights Protection* (Springer 2015); G Di Federico, 'Fundamental Rights in the EU: Legal Pluralism and Multi-Level Protection after the Lisbon Treaty' in G Di Federico (ed), *The EU Charter of Fundamental Rights: From Declaration to Binding Instrument* (Springer 2011) 18–19.

against the Member States would face the legal uncertainty of attributing responsibility to states for exclusive EU competences. Accession of the EU to the ECHR could resolve these issues, as well as simplify the cumbersome arrangements of the *Bosphorus* presumption for determining the margin of discretion enjoyed by Member States in executing EU law obligations.[123] Another important facet of accession would be the shrinking of opportunity for divergence and double standards between the ECHR and the EU regime for human rights protection. In strict legal terms, the consequence of accession to the ECHR would be that the Convention would become also formally 'an integral part' of EU law.[124]

From one side, the EU Member States have therefore been interested in bringing the oversight and formal obligations of the EU in line with those applicable to them, at least insofar as the ECHR is concerned. On the other side, the Council of Europe's interest lies in preserving its relevance which has, contrary to the EU's, diminished in previous decades. As without doubt the most important institution under the auspices of the Council of Europe is the ECHR and the associated Court in Strasbourg, binding the EU to this regime would showcase the ongoing significance of the Council and its instruments. Accession would also formally subject the CJEU to the jurisdiction of the ECtHR which would prove a much more difficult issue to address than anyone could have anticipated when accession was put in front of the CJEU for the first time in 1994. At that point the prospect of binding the EU to the ECHR was picked up by some Member States who deemed it warranted requesting an opinion from the CJEU on whether accession was possible under the EU treaty framework applicable at the time. In a succinct judgment, the CJEU replied in the negative.

Opinion of 28 March 1996, *Community accession to the ECHR*, 2/94, ECLI:EU:C:1996:140

(...) the Treaty has established the special procedure of a prior reference to the Court of Justice for the purpose of ascertaining, **before the conclusion of the agreement, whether the latter is compatible with the Treaty.**

6. That procedure is a special procedure of collaboration between the Court of Justice on the one hand and the other Community institutions and the Member States on the other whereby, at a stage prior to conclusion of an agreement which is capable of giving rise to a dispute concerning the legality of a Community act which concludes, implements or applies it, the Court is called upon to ensure (...) that in the interpretation and application of the Treaty the law is observed.

23. It follows from Article 3b of the Treaty, which states that **the Community** is to act within the limits of the powers conferred upon it by the Treaty and of the objectives assigned to it therein, that it **has only those powers which have been conferred upon it.**

---

[123] This includes the EU being able to defend itself directly as a party to proceedings before the ECtHR. Currently, the European Commission sends its submissions to the Strasbourg Court in cases involving EU actions but this is only an improvised solution. The separate issue of whether the *Bosphorus* presumption of equivalent protection would continue to apply even after EU accession is a contested one.

[124] Judgment of 30 April 1974, *Haegeman v Belgian State*, 181/73, ECLI:EU:C:1974:41, para 5.

24. That principle of conferred powers must be respected in both the internal action and the international action of the Community.

25. The Community acts ordinarily on the basis of specific powers which, as the Court has held, are not necessarily the express consequence of specific provisions of the Treaty but may also be implied from them.

26. Thus, in the field of international relations, at issue in this request for an Opinion, it is settled case-law that the competence of the Community to enter into international commitments may not only flow from express provisions of the Treaty but also be implied from those provisions. The Court has held, in particular, that, whenever Community law has created for the institutions of the Community powers within its internal system for the purpose of attaining a specific objective, the Community is empowered to enter into the international commitments necessary for attainment of that objective even in the absence of an express provision to that effect (see Opinion 2/91 of 19 March 1993 [1993] ECR I-1061, paragraph 7).

27. **No Treaty provision confers on the Community institutions any general power to enact rules on human rights or to conclude international conventions in this field.**

28. In the absence of express or implied powers for this purpose, it is necessary to consider whether Article 235 of the Treaty [Article 352 TFEU] may constitute a legal basis for accession.

29. Article 235 is designed to **fill the gap where no specific provisions of the Treaty confer on the Community institutions express or implied powers to act**, if such powers appear none the less to be necessary to enable the Community to carry out its functions with a view to attaining one of the objectives laid down by the Treaty.

30. **That provision, being an integral part of an institutional system based on the principle of conferred powers, cannot serve as a basis for widening the scope of Community powers beyond the general framework created by the provisions of the Treaty** as a whole and, in particular, by those that define the tasks and the activities of the Community. On any view, Article 235 cannot be used as a basis for the adoption of provisions whose effect would, in substance, be to amend the Treaty without following the procedure which it provides for that purpose.

31. It is in the light of those considerations that the question whether accession by the Community to the Convention may be based on Article 235 must be examined.

33. (...) it is well settled that fundamental rights form an integral part of the general principles of law whose observance the Court ensures. For that purpose, the Court draws inspiration from the constitutional traditions common to the Member States and from the guidelines supplied by international treaties for the protection of human rights on which the Member States have collaborated or of which they arc signatories. In that regard, the Court has stated that the Convention has special significance (see, in particular, the judgment in Case C-260/89 ERT [1991] ECR I-2925, paragraph 41).

34. Respect for human rights is therefore a condition of the lawfulness of Community acts. **Accession to the Convention would, however, entail a substantial change in the present Community system for the protection of human rights** in that it would entail the entry of the Community into a distinct international institutional system as well as integration of all the provisions of the Convention into the Community legal order.

35. **Such a modification** of the system for the protection of human rights in the Community, with equally fundamental institutional implications for the Community and for the Member States, **would be of constitutional significance and would therefore be such as to go beyond the scope of Article 235. It could be brought about only by way of Treaty amendment.**
36. It must therefore be held that, as Community law now stands, the Community has no competence to accede to the Convention.

Opinion 2/94 was praised for giving due weight to the foundational principle of conferral which underpins all EU action.[125] The CJEU identified no competence of the EU, express or implied, to enact rules or conclude international agreements in the field of human rights. It furthermore held that the gap-filling Article 352 TFEU cannot serve as the basis for acceding to the ECHR in light of the 'constitutional significance' of the changes resulting from the EU's accession;[126] doing so would in essence amount to modifying the Treaties without following the mandatory procedures for their amendment. As a result, the CJEU clearly stated that EU accession to the ECHR would require an amendment to the Treaties.

It took the Member States more than ten years but the Treaty of Lisbon amended Article 6 TEU, including a provision stating that 'the Union shall accede' to the ECHR but without affecting the EU's competences.[127] The same was restated and developed in a protocol and a declaration attached to the Treaties—the CJEU would later make multiple references to these safeguards of EU specificity and autonomy when rejecting a draft accession agreement in *Opinion 2/13*. Moreover, the procedural arrangements for the adoption of the international agreement on the accession of the EU to the ECHR were inserted into Article 218 TFEU: an accession agreement will require the consent of the European Parliament, unanimity in the Council of the EU and ratification by the Member States.

Consolidated version of the Treaty on European Union [2012] OJ C326/13

Protocol (No 8) relating to Article 6(2) of the Treaty on European Union on the Accession of the Union to the European Convention on the Protection of Human Rights and Fundamental Freedoms

Article 1

The agreement relating to the accession of the Union to the European Convention on the Protection of Human Rights and Fundamental Freedoms (hereinafter referred to as the 'European Convention') provided for in Article 6(2) of the Treaty on European Union shall make provision for preserving the specific characteristics of the Union and Union law, in particular with regard to:

---

[125] J Kokott and F Hoffmeister, 'Opinion 2/94, Accession of the Community to the European Convention for the Protection of Human Rights and Fundamental Freedoms' (1996) 90 The American Journal of International Law 664.
[126] It should be noted that Article 352 TFEU serves as the legal basis of the Regulation establishing the EU Agency for Fundamental Rights. The creation of an EU agency does not, however, carry constitutional significance for the EU as a whole, unlike accession to the ECHR.
[127] Article 6(2) TEU.

(a) the specific arrangements for the Union's possible participation in the control bodies of the European Convention;

(b) the mechanisms necessary to ensure that proceedings by non-Member States and individual applications are correctly addressed to Member States and/or the Union as appropriate.

Article 2

The agreement referred to in Article 1 shall ensure that accession of the Union shall not affect the competences of the Union or the powers of its institutions. It shall ensure that **nothing therein affects the situation of Member States in relation to the European Convention**, in particular in relation to the Protocols thereto, measures taken by Member States derogating from the European Convention in accordance with Article 15 thereof and reservations to the European Convention made by Member States in accordance with Article 57 thereof.

Article 3

Nothing in the agreement referred to in Article 1 **shall affect Article 344** of the Treaty on the Functioning of the European Union.

Declarations annexed to the Final Act of the Intergovernmental Conference which adopted the Treaty of Lisbon, signed on 13 December 2007

A. Declarations concerning provisions of the Treaties

2. Declaration on Article 6(2) of the Treaty on European Union

The Conference agrees that the Union's accession to the European Convention for the Protection of Human Rights and Fundamental Freedoms should be arranged in such a way as to preserve the specific features of Union law. In this connection, the Conference notes the existence of a regular dialogue between the Court of Justice of the European Union and the European Court of Human Rights; such dialogue could be reinforced when the Union accedes to that Convention.

Consolidated version of the Treaty on the Functioning of the European Union [2012] OJ C326/47

Article 218

6. The Council, on a proposal by the negotiator, shall adopt a decision concluding the agreement.

Except where agreements relate exclusively to the common foreign and security policy, **the Council shall adopt the decision concluding the agreement**:

(a) **after obtaining the consent of the European Parliament** in the following cases:

(ii) **agreement on Union accession to the European Convention for the Protection of Human Rights and Fundamental Freedoms**;

8. The Council shall act by a qualified majority throughout the procedure.

> However, it shall act unanimously when the agreement covers a field for which unanimity is required for the adoption of a Union act as well as for association agreements and the agreements referred to in Article 212 with the States which are candidates for accession. **The Council shall also act unanimously for the agreement on accession of the Union to the European Convention for the Protection of Human Rights and Fundamental Freedoms**; the decision concluding this agreement shall enter into force after it has been approved by the Member States in accordance with their respective constitutional requirements.

It was not only the EU Treaties which needed to be amended to allow for EU accession to the ECHR. The Council of Europe adopted Protocol No 14 amending the ECHR, Article 59(2) of which now states that 'the European Union may accede to this Convention'. With these modifications in place, the negotiations regarding an accession agreement could finally begin in 2010. They were concluded in less than three years after being characterized as 'very intense' and EU accession to the ECHR as being of 'key importance'.[128] The negotiations took place first between a working group of 14 European states established by the Steering Committee for Human Rights of the Council of Europe (CDDH), on the one hand, and the European Commission as the official EU negotiator, on the other. In the second phase, the Commission negotiated the draft agreement in an ad hoc group with all the 47 member countries of the Council of Europe. The courts in Strasbourg and Luxembourg were not entirely on the sidelines either: the presidents of the two courts issued a joint statement, in the context of regular meetings between them, which underlined the importance of coordination mechanisms post-accession.[129] Exceptionally, the CJEU had even drawn up a discussion document outlining the Court's views on safeguarding the specific characteristics of the Union legal order and its judicial system.[130]

The Draft Agreement on the Accession of the European Union to the Convention for the Protection of Human Rights and Fundamental Freedoms was agreed in principle between the EU and the Council of Europe on 5 April 2013. The draft agreement consisted of 12 Articles but was further to be accompanied by declarations and amendments on various technical points necessary for the accommodation of the EU into the whole ECHR regime. The package of instruments facilitating the accession included an explanatory report which shed light on the rationale behind the provisions of the draft agreement and could be used as an interpretive tool.[131]

---

[128] Gragl (n 122) 6–7.

[129] Joint communication from Presidents Costa and Skouris, Strasbourg and Luxembourg, 24 January 2011, published on the websites of both courts.

[130] Discussion document of the Court of Justice of the European Union on certain aspects of the accession of the European Union to the European Convention for the Protection of Human Rights and Fundamental Freedoms, Luxembourg, 5 May 2010.

[131] See Fifth negotiation meeting between the CDDH ad hoc negotiation group and the European Commission on the accession of the European Union to the European Convention on Human Rights, Final Report to the CDDH, Strasbourg, 10 June 2013, 47+1(2013)008.

Draft revised agreement on the accession of the European Union to the Convention for the Protection of Human Rights and Fundamental Freedoms, Strasbourg, 5 April 2013

Preamble

Considering that the accession of the European Union to the Convention will enhance coherence in human rights protection in Europe;

Considering, in particular, that any person, non-governmental organisation or group of individuals should have the right to submit the acts, measures or omissions of the European Union to the external control of the European Court of Human Rights (...);

Considering that, having regard to the specific legal order of the European Union, which is not a State, its accession requires certain adjustments to the Convention system to be made by common agreement,

(...)

Article 1—Scope of the accession and amendments to Article 59 of the Convention

3. Accession to the Convention and the protocols thereto shall impose on the European Union obligations with regard only to acts, measures or omissions of its institutions, bodies, offices or agencies, or of persons acting on their behalf. Nothing in the Convention or the protocols thereto shall require the European Union to perform an act or adopt a measure for which it has no competence under European Union law.

4. For the purposes of the Convention, of the protocols thereto and of this Agreement, an act, measure or omission of organs of a member State of the European Union or of persons acting on its behalf shall be attributed to that State, even if such act, measure or omission occurs when the State implements the law of the European Union, including decisions taken under the Treaty on European Union and under the Treaty on the Functioning of the European Union. This shall not preclude the European Union from being responsible as a co-respondent for a violation resulting from such an act, measure or omission, in accordance with Article 36, paragraph 4, of the Convention and Article 3 of this Agreement.

Article 3—Co-respondent mechanism

1. Article 36 of the Convention shall be amended as follows:
   a. the heading of Article 36 of the Convention shall be amended to read as follows: 'Third party intervention and co-respondent';
   b. a new paragraph 4 shall be added at the end of Article 36 of the Convention, which shall read as follows:

   '4. The European Union or a member State of the European Union may become a co-respondent to proceedings by decision of the Court in the circumstances set out in the Agreement on the Accession of the European Union to the Convention for the Protection of Human Rights and Fundamental Freedoms. A co-respondent is a party to the case. The admissibility of an application shall be assessed without regard to the participation of a co-respondent in the proceedings.'

2. Where an application is directed against one or more member States of the European Union, the European Union may become a co-respondent to the proceedings in respect of an alleged violation notified by the Court if it appears that such allegation calls into question the compatibility with the rights at issue defined in the Convention or in the protocols to which the European Union has acceded of a provision of European Union law, including decisions taken under the Treaty on European Union and under the Treaty on the Functioning of the European Union, notably where that violation could have been avoided only by disregarding an obligation under European Union law.

3. Where an application is directed against the European Union, the European Union member States may become co-respondents to the proceedings in respect of an alleged violation notified by the Court if it appears that such allegation calls into question the compatibility with the rights at issue defined in the Convention or in the protocols to which the European Union has acceded of a provision of the Treaty on European Union, the Treaty on the Functioning of the European Union or any other provision having the same legal value pursuant to those instruments, notably where that violation could have been avoided only by disregarding an obligation under those instruments.

4. Where an application is directed against and notified to both the European Union and one or more of its member States, the status of any respondent may be changed to that of a co-respondent if the conditions in paragraph 2 or paragraph 3 of this article are met.

5. A High Contracting Party shall become a co-respondent either by accepting an invitation from the Court or by decision of the Court upon the request of that High Contracting Party. When inviting a High Contracting Party to become co-respondent, and when deciding upon a request to that effect, the Court shall seek the views of all parties to the proceedings. When deciding upon such a request, the Court shall assess whether, in the light of the reasons given by the High Contracting Party concerned, it is plausible that the conditions in paragraph 2 or paragraph 3 of this article are met.

6. In proceedings to which the European Union is a co-respondent, if the Court of Justice of the European Union has not yet assessed the compatibility with the rights at issue defined in the Convention or in the protocols to which the European Union has acceded of the provision of European Union law as under paragraph 2 of this article, sufficient time shall be afforded for the Court of Justice of the European Union to make such an assessment, and thereafter for the parties to make observations to the Court. The European Union shall ensure that such assessment is made quickly so that the proceedings before the Court are not unduly delayed. The provisions of this paragraph shall not affect the powers of the Court.

7. If the violation in respect of which a High Contracting Party is a co-respondent to the proceedings is established, the respondent and the co-respondent shall be jointly responsible for that violation, unless the Court, on the basis of the reasons given by the respondent and the co-respondent, and having sought the views of the applicant, decides that only one of them be held responsible.

Article 6—Election of judges

1. A delegation of the European Parliament shall be entitled to participate, with the right to vote, in the sittings of the Parliamentary Assembly of the Council of Europe whenever the Assembly exercises its functions related to the election of judges in accordance with Article 22 of the Convention. The delegation of the European

Parliament shall have the same number of representatives as the delegation of the State which is entitled to the highest number of representatives under Article 26 of the Statute of the Council of Europe.

Article 7—Participation of the European Union in the meetings of the Committee of Ministers of the Council of Europe

2. The European Union shall be entitled to participate in the meetings of the Committee of Ministers, with the right to vote, (...)

The draft agreement makes clear from the outset that its scope is limited, as far as the EU is concerned, to the competences that the EU already has, and actions or omissions associated therewith (Article 1). The agreement also states that EU Member States retain their liability under the Convention even when they are implementing EU law, although the EU can become a co-respondent in such a situation. The co-respondent mechanism is the most important feature of the draft agreement. It both allows the EU, the Member States, or other ECHR parties to become party to the proceedings before the ECtHR and it makes possible to hold the EU and its Member States jointly liable for acts or omissions in breach of the ECHR (Article 3(7)). Moreover, in cases concerning the compatibility of the ECHR with EU law, the CJEU would be invited to make a determination on the same point prior to the decision of the ECtHR, if the question of law had not been previously settled by the CJEU (Article 3(6)). The co-respondent mechanism, as well as the procedure for prior involvement of the CJEU, was predicted to prove controversial from the perspective of autonomy of EU law and the prerogatives of the CJEU in that relation,[132] and this turned out to be the case in *Opinion 2/13*. The overall balancing exercise between autonomy and accession faced by the drafters of the agreement was likened to 'walking on a tightrope'.[133]

The explanatory report describes the motivation for establishing the co-respondent mechanism. The principal reason is the accommodation of the EU's specific features, chiefly its composite nature and the autonomy of its legal order, without treating it as a state.[134] The report also explicitly acknowledges that the co-respondent mechanism was devised to avoid gaps in protection of human rights in the ECHR system and that the obligations to remedy violations of the Convention would be the same for co-respondents as they are in normal ECtHR proceedings.[135] The introduction of the mechanism would not spell the end for third-party intervention of the EU in ECtHR cases—the EU (or an EU Member State if the action was directed against the EU) would only become a co-respondent if specific conditions were met. These conditions reflect the various situations encountered by the ECtHR in its case law.[136] For example, EU Member States could become co-respondents if the infringement of ECHR rights at stake relates to EU primary law, as was in essence the case in *Matthews v the*

---

[132] See, for example, G Gaja, 'The "Co-respondent Mechanisms" According to the Draft Agreement for the Accession of the EU to the ECHR' in V Kosta, N Skoutaris, and V Tzevelekos (eds), *The EU Accession to the ECHR* (Hart Publishing 2014); Gragl (n 122) 234–37.

[133] T Lock, 'Walking on a Tightrope: The Draft ECHR Accession Agreement and the Autonomy of the EU Legal Order' (2011) 48 Common Market Law Review 1025. The same tension was thoroughly explored in two monographs on the subject: Gragl (n 122) and Korenica (n 122).

[134] Fifth negotiation meeting between the CDDH ad hoc negotiation group and the European Commission on the accession of the European Union to the European Convention on Human Rights, Final Report to the CDDH, Strasbourg, 10 June 2013, 47+1(2013)008rev2, para 38.

[135] Ibid, para 39.

[136] Ibid, paras 47–50.

UK. Another scenario would touch upon the requirement of strict international legal obligation of the *Bosphorus* presumption: the EU would become a co-respondent in cases, such as *Bosphorus,* where the Member State violating the ECHR was implementing EU law without any discretion.

The agreement in principle on the draft accession agreement was subject to the EU requesting an opinion from the CJEU on its compatibility with the Treaties pursuant to Article 218(11) TFEU. First to impart her view on the draft agreement was Advocate General (AG) Kokott who identified a number of deficiencies from the perspective of EU law.[137] Nevertheless, the AG advised the CJEU to give a conditional 'yes' to EU accession to the ECHR, provided certain amendments are made to the draft agreement. The CJEU, however, adopted a staunchly different, almost combative, approach to the document put in front of it. The Court listed all the possible reasons why the agreement was incompatible with EU law and instead of a conditional green light, accession under the conditions agreed after three years of negotiating was emphatically rejected.

Opinion of 18 December 2014, *EU accession to the ECHR*, 2/13, ECLI:EU:C:2014:2454

154. That accession would, however, still be characterised by significant distinctive features.

155. Ever since the adoption of the ECHR, it has only been possible for State entities to be parties to it, which explains why, to date, it has been binding only on States. This is also confirmed by the fact that, to enable the accession of the EU to proceed, not only has Article 59 of the ECHR been amended, but the agreement envisaged itself contains a series of amendments of the ECHR that are to make accession operational within the system established by the ECHR itself.

156. Those amendments are warranted precisely because, unlike any other Contracting Party, **the EU is, under international law, precluded by its very nature from being considered a State**.

157. As the Court of Justice has repeatedly held, **the founding treaties of the EU, unlike ordinary international treaties, established a new legal order**, possessing its own institutions, for the benefit of which the Member States thereof have limited their sovereign rights, in ever wider fields, and **the subjects of which comprise not only those States but also their nationals** (see, in particular, judgments in van Gend & Loos, 26/62, EU:C:1963:1, p. 12, and Costa, 6/64, EU:C:1964:66, p. 593, and Opinion 1/09, EU:C:2011:123, paragraph 65).

158. The fact that the EU has a new kind of legal order, the nature of which is peculiar to the EU, its own constitutional framework and founding principles, a particularly sophisticated institutional structure and a full set of legal rules to ensure its operation, has consequences as regards the procedure for and conditions of accession to the ECHR.

159. It is precisely in order to ensure that that situation is taken into account that the Treaties make accession subject to compliance with various conditions.

---

[137] *Opinion 2/13 (EU accession to the ECHR)* [2014] ECLI:EU:C:2014:2475, Opinion of AG Kokott.

164. (...) the conditions to which accession is subject under the Treaties are intended, particularly, to ensure that accession **does not affect the specific characteristics of the EU and EU law.**

165. It should be borne in mind that these characteristics include those relating to the **constitutional structure of the EU**, which is seen in the principle of conferral of powers referred to in Articles 4(1) TEU and 5(1) and (2) TEU, and in the institutional framework established in Articles 13 TEU to 19 TEU.

167. These essential characteristics of EU law have given rise to **a structured network of principles, rules and mutually interdependent legal relations linking the EU and its Member States, and its Member States with each other, which are now engaged**, as is recalled in the second paragraph of Article 1 TEU, **in a 'process of creating an ever closer union among the peoples of Europe'.**

168. This legal structure is based on the fundamental premiss that each Member State shares with all the other Member States, and recognises that they share with it, **a set of common values on which the EU is founded**, as stated in Article 2 TEU. **That premiss implies and justifies the existence of mutual trust between the Member States** that those values will be recognised and, therefore, that the law of the EU that implements them will be respected.

174. In order to ensure that the specific characteristics and the autonomy of that legal order are preserved, the Treaties have established a judicial system intended to ensure consistency and uniformity in the interpretation of EU law.

175. In that context, it is for the national courts and tribunals and for the Court of Justice to ensure the full application of EU law in all Member States and to ensure judicial protection of an individual's rights under that law (...)

176. In particular, the judicial system as thus conceived has as its **keystone the preliminary ruling procedure provided for in Article 267 TFEU**, which, by setting up a dialogue between one court and another, specifically between the Court of Justice and the courts and tribunals of the Member States, has the object of securing **uniform interpretation of EU law** (see, to that effect, judgment in van Gend & Loos, EU:C:1963:1, p. 12), thereby serving **to ensure its consistency, its full effect and its autonomy** as well as, ultimately, the particular nature of the law established by the Treaties (see, to that effect, Opinion 1/09, EU:C:2011:123, paragraphs 67 and 83).

177. **Fundamental rights, as recognised in particular by the Charter, must therefore be interpreted and applied within the EU in accordance with the constitutional framework** referred to in paragraphs 155 to 176 above.

179. It must be borne in mind that, in accordance with Article 6(3) TEU, fundamental rights, as guaranteed by the ECHR, constitute general principles of the EU's law. However, as the EU has not acceded to the ECHR, the latter **does not constitute a legal instrument which has been formally incorporated into the legal order of the EU** (...)

180. By contrast, **as a result of the EU's accession the ECHR**, like any other international agreement concluded by the EU, would, by virtue of Article 216(2) TFEU, be binding upon the institutions of the EU and on its Member States, and **would** therefore **form an integral part of EU law** (...)

181. Accordingly, the EU, like any other Contracting Party, would be subject to external control to ensure the observance of the rights and freedoms the EU would undertake to respect in accordance with Article 1 of the ECHR. In that context, the EU and its institutions, including the Court of Justice, would be **subject to the control**

mechanisms provided for by the ECHR and, in particular, to the decisions and the judgments of the ECtHR.

182. The Court of Justice has admittedly already stated in that regard that an international agreement providing for the creation of a court responsible for the interpretation of its provisions and whose decisions are binding on the institutions, including the Court of Justice, is not, in principle, incompatible with EU law; that is particularly the case where, as in this instance, the conclusion of such an agreement is provided for by the Treaties themselves. **The competence of the EU in the field of international relations and its capacity to conclude international agreements necessarily entail the power to submit to the decisions of a court which is created or designated by such agreements as regards the interpretation and application of their provisions** (see Opinions 1/91, EU:C:1991:490, paragraphs 40 and 70, and 1/09, EU:C:2011:123, paragraph 74).

183. Nevertheless, the Court of Justice has also declared that an international agreement may affect its own powers only if the indispensable conditions for safeguarding the essential character of those powers are satisfied and, consequently, there is **no adverse effect on the autonomy of the EU legal order** (...)

184. In particular, any action by the bodies given decision-making powers by the ECHR, as provided for in the agreement envisaged, **must not have the effect of binding the EU and its institutions**, in the exercise of their internal powers, **to a particular interpretation of the rules of EU law** (...)

185. It is admittedly inherent in the very concept of external control that, on the one hand, the interpretation of the ECHR provided by the ECtHR would, under international law, be binding on the EU and its institutions, including the Court of Justice, and that, on the other, the interpretation by the Court of Justice of a right recognised by the ECHR would not be binding on the control mechanisms provided for by the ECHR, particularly the ECtHR (...)

186. The same would not apply, however, with regard to the interpretation by the Court of Justice of EU law, including the Charter. In particular, **it should not be possible for the ECtHR to call into question the Court's findings in relation to the scope *ratione materiae* of EU law**, for the purposes, in particular, of determining whether a Member State is bound by fundamental rights of the EU.

189. In so far as **Article 53 of the ECHR** essentially reserves the power of the Contracting Parties to lay down higher standards of protection of fundamental rights than those guaranteed by the ECHR, that provision **should be coordinated with Article 53 of the Charter**, as interpreted by the Court of Justice, so that the power granted to Member States by Article 53 of the ECHR is limited—with respect to the rights recognised by the Charter that correspond to those guaranteed by the ECHR—to that which is necessary to ensure that the level of protection provided for by the Charter and the primacy, unity and effectiveness of EU law are not compromised.

191. In the second place, it should be noted that the **principle of mutual trust between the Member States is of fundamental importance in EU law, given that it allows an area without internal borders to be created and maintained. That principle requires, particularly with regard to the area of freedom, security and justice, each of those States, save in exceptional circumstances, to consider all the other Member States to be complying with EU law and particularly with the fundamental rights recognised by EU law** (...)

192. Thus, when implementing EU law, the Member States may, under EU law, be required to presume that fundamental rights have been observed by the other Member States, so that not only may they not demand a higher level of national protection of fundamental rights from another Member State than that provided by EU law, but, save in exceptional cases, **they may not check whether that other Member State has actually, in a specific case, observed the fundamental rights guaranteed by the EU.**

193. The approach adopted in the agreement envisaged, which is to treat the EU as a State and to give it a role identical in every respect to that of any other Contracting Party, specifically disregards the intrinsic nature of the EU and, in particular, fails to take into consideration the fact that the Member States have, by reason of their membership of the EU, accepted that relations between them as regards **the matters covered by the transfer of powers from the Member States to the EU are governed by EU law to the exclusion, if EU law so requires, of any other law.**

194. In so far as the **ECHR would**, in requiring the EU and the Member States to be considered Contracting Parties not only in their relations with Contracting Parties which are not Member States of the EU but also in their relations with each other, including where such relations are governed by EU law, **require a Member State to check that another Member State has observed fundamental rights, even though EU law imposes an obligation of mutual trust between those Member States, accession is liable to upset the underlying balance of the EU and undermine the autonomy of EU law.**

196. In the third place, it must be pointed out that **Protocol No 16 permits the highest courts and tribunals of the Member States to request the ECtHR to give advisory opinions** on questions of principle relating to the interpretation or application of the rights and freedoms guaranteed by the ECHR or the protocols thereto, **even though EU law requires those same courts or tribunals to submit a request to that end to the Court of Justice for a preliminary ruling under Article 267 TFEU.**

197. It is indeed the case that the agreement envisaged does not provide for the accession of the EU as such to Protocol No 16 and that the latter was signed on 2 October 2013, that is to say, after the agreement reached by the negotiators in relation to the draft accession instruments, namely on 5 April 2013; nevertheless, since the ECHR would form an integral part of EU law, the mechanism established by that protocol could—notably where the issue concerns rights guaranteed by the Charter corresponding to those secured by the ECHR—**affect the autonomy and effectiveness of the preliminary ruling procedure provided for in Article 267 TFEU.**

198. In particular, it cannot be ruled out that a request for an advisory opinion made pursuant to Protocol No 16 by a court or tribunal of a Member State that has acceded to that protocol could trigger the procedure for the prior involvement of the Court of Justice, thus **creating a risk that the preliminary ruling procedure provided for in Article 267 TFEU might be circumvented**, a procedure which, as has been noted in paragraph 176 of this Opinion, is the keystone of the judicial system established by the Treaties.

201. The Court has consistently held that **an international agreement cannot affect the allocation of powers fixed by the Treaties or, consequently, the autonomy of the EU legal system, observance of which is ensured by the Court.** That principle is notably enshrined in **Article 344 TFEU**, according to which Member States

undertake not to submit a dispute concerning the interpretation or application of the Treaties to any method of settlement other than those provided for therein (see, to that effect, Opinions 1/91, EU:C:1991:490, paragraph 35, …)

202. Furthermore, **the obligation of Member States to have recourse to the procedures for settling disputes established by EU law—and, in particular, to respect the jurisdiction of the Court of Justice**, which is a fundamental feature of the EU system—**must be understood as a specific expression of Member States' more general duty of loyalty resulting from Article 4(3) TEU** (see, to that effect, judgment in Commission v Ireland, EU:C:2006:345, paragraph 169), it being understood that, under that provision, the obligation is equally applicable to relations between Member States and the EU.

203. It is precisely in view of these considerations that Article 3 of Protocol No 8 EU expressly provides that the accession agreement must not affect Article 344 TFEU.

204. However, as explained in paragraph 180 of this Opinion, as a result of accession, the ECHR would form an integral part of EU law. Consequently, **where EU law is at issue, the Court of Justice has exclusive jurisdiction in any dispute between the Member States and between those Member States and the EU regarding compliance with the ECHR.**

205. Unlike the international convention at issue in the case giving rise to the judgment in Commission v Ireland (EU:C:2006:345, paragraphs 124 and 125), which expressly provided that the system for the resolution of disputes set out in EU law must in principle take precedence over that established by that convention, **the procedure for the resolution of disputes provided for in Article 33 of the ECHR could apply to any Contracting Party and, therefore, also to disputes between the Member States, or between those Member States and the EU, even though it is EU law that is in issue.**

206. In that regard, contrary to what is maintained in some of the observations submitted to the Court of Justice in the present procedure, the fact that Article 5 of the draft agreement provides that proceedings before the Court of Justice are not to be regarded as a means of dispute settlement which the Contracting Parties have agreed to forgo in accordance with Article 55 of the ECHR is not sufficient to preserve the exclusive jurisdiction of the Court of Justice.

207. **Article 5 of the draft agreement** merely reduces the scope of the obligation laid down by Article 55 of the ECHR, but **still allows for the possibility that the EU or Member States might submit an application to the ECtHR**, under Article 33 of the ECHR, concerning an alleged violation thereof by a Member State or the EU, respectively, in conjunction with EU law.

208. The very existence of such a possibility undermines the requirement set out in Article 344 TFEU.

209. This is particularly so since, if the EU or Member States did in fact have to bring a dispute between them before **the ECtHR, the latter would**, pursuant to Article 33 of the ECHR, **find itself seised of such a dispute.**

210. Contrary to the provisions of the Treaties governing the EU's various internal judicial procedures, which have objectives peculiar to them, **Article 344 TFEU is specifically intended to preserve the exclusive nature of the procedure for settling those disputes within the EU**, and in particular of the jurisdiction of the Court of Justice in that respect, and thus precludes any prior or subsequent external control.

211. Moreover, Article 1(b) of Protocol No 8 EU itself refers only to the mechanisms necessary to ensure that proceedings brought before the ECtHR by non-Member States are correctly addressed to Member States and/or to the EU as appropriate.

212. Consequently, **the fact that Member States or the EU are able to submit an application to the ECtHR is liable in itself to undermine the objective of Article 344 TFEU and, moreover, goes against the very nature of EU law, which, as noted in paragraph 193 of this Opinion, requires that relations between the Member States be governed by EU law to the exclusion, if EU law so requires, of any other law.**

213. In those circumstances, **only the express exclusion of the ECtHR's jurisdiction under Article 33 of the ECHR over disputes between Member States or between Member States and the EU** in relation to the application of the ECHR within the scope *ratione materiae* of EU law **would be compatible with Article 344 TFEU.**

223. As Article 3(5) of the draft agreement provides, if the EU or Member States **request leave to intervene as co-respondents** in a case before the ECtHR, they **must give reasons** from which it can be established that the conditions for their participation in the procedure are met, and the ECtHR is to decide on that request in the light of the plausibility of those reasons.

224. Admittedly, in carrying out such a review, the ECtHR is to ascertain whether, in the light of those reasons, it is plausible that the conditions set out in paragraphs 2 and 3 of Article 3 are met, and that review does not relate to the merits of those reasons. However, the fact remains that, in carrying out that review, **the ECtHR would be required to assess the rules of EU law governing the division of powers between the EU and its Member States** as well as the criteria for the attribution of their acts or omissions, in order to adopt a final decision in that regard which would be binding both on the Member States and on the EU.

226. Secondly, Article 3(7) of the draft agreement provides that if the violation in respect of which a Contracting Party is a co-respondent to the proceedings is established, **the respondent and the co-respondent are to be jointly responsible for that violation.**

227. That **provision does not preclude a Member State from being held responsible,** together with the EU, **for the violation of a provision of the ECHR in respect of which that Member State may have made a reservation** in accordance with Article 57 of the ECHR.

228. Such a consequence of Article 3(7) of the draft agreement is at odds with Article 2 of Protocol No 8 EU, according to which the accession agreement is to ensure that nothing therein affects the situation of Member States in relation to the ECHR, in particular in relation to reservations thereto.

229. Thirdly, there is provision at the end of Article 3(7) of the draft agreement for an exception to the general rule that the respondent and co-respondent are to be jointly responsible for a violation established. **The ECtHR may decide, on the basis of the reasons given by the respondent and the co-respondent,** and having sought the views of the applicant, **that only one of them is to be held responsible for that violation.**

230. **A decision on the apportionment as between the EU and its Member States of responsibility** for an act or omission constituting a violation of the ECHR established by the ECtHR **is also one that is based on an assessment of the rules of EU law governing the division of powers between** the EU and its Member States and the attributability of that act or omission.

231. Accordingly, to permit the ECtHR to adopt such a decision would also risk adversely affecting the division of powers between the EU and its Member States.

241. (…) **the prior involvement procedure should be set up in such a way as to ensure that, in any case pending before the ECtHR, the EU is fully and systematically informed,** so that the competent EU institution is able to assess whether the Court of Justice has already given a ruling on the question at issue in that case and, if it has not, to arrange for the prior involvement procedure to be initiated.

245. The interpretation of a provision of EU law, including of secondary law, requires, in principle, a decision of the Court of Justice **where that provision is open to more than one plausible interpretation.**

246. **If the Court of Justice were not allowed to provide the definitive interpretation of secondary law**, and if the ECtHR, in considering whether that law is consistent with the ECHR, had itself to provide a particular interpretation from among the plausible options, **there would most certainly be a breach of the principle that the Court of Justice has exclusive jurisdiction over the definitive interpretation of EU law.**

247. Accordingly, **limiting the scope of the prior involvement procedure, in the case of secondary law, solely to questions of validity adversely affects the competences of the EU and the powers of the Court of Justice** in that it does not allow the Court to provide a definitive interpretation of secondary law in the light of the rights guaranteed by the ECHR.

249. It is evident from the second subparagraph of Article 24(1) TEU that, as regards the provisions of the Treaties that govern the **CFSP, the Court of Justice has jurisdiction only to monitor compliance with Article 40 TEU and to review the legality of certain decisions as provided for by the second paragraph of Article 275 TFEU.**

250. According to the latter provision, the Court of Justice is to have jurisdiction, in particular, to rule on proceedings, brought in accordance with the conditions laid down in the fourth paragraph of Article 263 TFEU, reviewing the legality of decisions providing for restrictive measures against natural or legal persons adopted by the Council on the basis of Chapter 2 of Title V of the EU Treaty.

251. Notwithstanding the Commission's systematic interpretation of those provisions in its request for an Opinion—with which some of the Member States that submitted observations to the Court have taken issue—essentially seeking to define the scope of the Court's judicial review in this area as being sufficiently broad to encompass any situation that could be covered by an application to the ECtHR, it must be noted that the Court has not yet had the opportunity to define the extent to which its jurisdiction is limited in CFSP matters as a result of those provisions.

252. However, for the purpose of adopting a position on the present request for an Opinion, it is sufficient to declare that, as EU law now stands, **certain acts adopted in the context of the CFSP fall outside the ambit of judicial review by the Court of Justice.**

253. That situation is **inherent to the way in which the Court's powers are structured by the Treaties,** and, as such, can only be explained by reference to EU law alone.

254. Nevertheless, on the basis of accession as provided for by the agreement envisaged, **the ECtHR would be empowered to rule on the compatibility with the ECHR of certain acts, actions or omissions performed in the context of the CFSP, and notably of those whose legality the Court of Justice cannot, for want of jurisdiction, review in the light of fundamental rights.**

255. Such a situation would effectively **entrust the judicial review of those acts, actions or omissions on the part of the EU exclusively to a non-EU body**, albeit that any such review would be limited to compliance with the rights guaranteed by the ECHR.

256. The Court has already had occasion to find that **jurisdiction to carry out a judicial review of acts, actions or omissions on the part of the EU**, including in the light of fundamental rights, **cannot be conferred exclusively on an international court which is outside the institutional and judicial framework of the EU** (see, to that effect, Opinion 1/09, EU:C:2011:123, paragraphs 78, 80 and 89).

257. Therefore, although that is a consequence of the way in which the Court's powers are structured at present, the fact remains that the agreement envisaged fails to have regard to the specific characteristics of EU law with regard to the judicial review of acts, actions or omissions on the part of the EU in CFSP matters.

Opinion 2/13 belongs to one of the most controversial and criticized cases ever decided by the CJEU. Most commentators were stunned upon the release of the Opinion and reacted negatively to the decision for its failure to properly account for the benefits the accession would have on human rights protection in Europe and the role the EU should play in that regard.[138] Far fewer scholars attempted to mount a defence of the Opinion but even these did not agree entirely with the Court.[139]

In general, the CJEU put tremendous emphasis on the specificity and novelty of EU law which, in its view, have not received sufficient attention by the drafters of the accession agreement. The overriding concern centred on the preservation of autonomy of the EU legal order and the CJEU's exclusive position within it. This is understandable from one perspective—the CJEU is more guarded than Member States' highest courts because the EU is not a state and does not possess the sovereign grounding or a thick constitutional authority capable of mobilizing resources as the Member States do.[140] It is noteworthy that in protecting its autonomy and that of the EU legal system, however, the CJEU uses explicitly constitutional vocabulary in order to strengthen the position of EU law vis-à-vis the international legal environment (specifically the ECHR). In the first part of the merits, the CJEU recounted what it considered the main elements of the self-proclaimed constitutional framework of the EU liable to be affected by accession to the ECHR: the principle of mutual trust between the Member States supported by common values (Article 2 TEU) and the uniform interpretation, autonomy and full effectiveness of EU law—applicable not only to states but also individuals—as ensured by the CJEU and Member State courts especially through the preliminary reference procedure of Article 267 TFEU. The Court underlined its message of constitutionalism and uniqueness of the EU legal order by referring to such classic judgments as *Costa v ENEL*,[141] *van Gend en Loos*,[142] *Internationale Handelsgesellschaft*,[143] *Kadi*,[144] and others.

[138] See, for example, S Peers, 'The EU's Accession to the ECHR: The Dream Becomes a Nightmare' (2015) 16 German Law Journal 213.

[139] See, in particular, D Halberstam, '"It's the Autonomy, Stupid!" A Modest Defense of Opinion 2/13 on EU Accession to the ECHR, and the Way Forward' (2015) 16 German Law Journal 105.

[140] P Lindseth, *Power and Legitimacy: Reconciling Europe and the Nation-State* (Oxford University Press 2010).

[141] Judgment of 15 July 1964, *Costa v ENEL*, 6/64, ECLI:EU:C:1964:66.

[142] Judgment of 5 February 1963, *Van Gend en Loos v Nederlandse administratie der belastingen*, 26/62, ECLI:EU:C:1963:1.

[143] Judgment of 17 December 1970, *Internationale Handelsgesellschaft mbH v Einfuhr- und Vorratsstelle für Getreide und Futtermittel*, 11/70, ECLI:EU:C:1970:114.

[144] *Kadi and Al Barakaat International Foundation v Council of the European Union and Commission of the European Communities* (n 9).

It should be also borne in mind that Article 6(2) TEU has placed the EU under an obligation ('shall') to accede to the ECHR, albeit one subject to the conditions specified in particular in Protocol No 8. The Court's Opinion picked apart the draft agreement in a way that stresses the conditionality of Article 6(2) TEU and especially Protocol No 8 but gives little weight to the mandatory character of EU accession to the ECHR.[145] When seen from the perspective of guiding meta principles of the EU legal order, there is no a priori reason why the CJEU should be meticulously insulating EU law from external oversight at the expense of promoting fundamental rights protection and the rule of law. If anything, the EU Treaties, not least Article 2 TEU, should induce the CJEU to promote the latter two as values the EU is professedly founded upon. There is little doubt that EU accession to the ECHR would benefit both human rights and the rule of law in Europe, but *Opinion 2/13* gave the negotiators a mountain to climb.

The objections of the CJEU rendering the draft accession agreement incompatible with EU treaties can be divided into seven main points. In comparison, AG Kokott, who advised the Court to conditionally accept the draft agreement, identified only three issues that required the attention of the negotiators. In any case, the issues highlighted by the CJEU were: (i) conflict between Article 53 of the Charter and Article 53 ECHR; (ii) effect on mutual trust and recognition; (iii) preliminary rulings according to Protocol No 16 to the ECHR and Article 267 TFEU; (iv) incompatibility with Article 344 TFEU; (v) the co-respondent mechanism and (vi) the prior involvement procedure of the CJEU therein; and (vii) judicial oversight of the CFSP.

The first substantive objection of the CJEU related to the concurrent application of Article 53 ECHR and Article 53 of the Charter. Both provisions preclude the human rights instruments from serving as a basis for lowering existing protection under national or international law.[146] As we know from *Melloni*, however, in the EU legal order the CJEU may rule national human rights standards incompatible with Article 53 of the Charter if they undermine the unity, primacy, or effectiveness of EU law, despite offering a higher level of protection than the Charter.[147] The CJEU's worry with respect to Article 53 ECHR is, in essence, that Member States could use it as a basis for circumventing its *Melloni* interpretation of Article 53 of the Charter.

One of the problems with relying on the *Melloni* argument in order to block the entire accession to the ECHR is that, as explained previously in Chapter 4, the doctrine of preventing Member States from adopting higher human rights protection is linked to specific instances of exercising EU competences. In *Melloni*, the higher protection available in Spain consisted of the possibility to review convictions rendered *in absentia* prior to executing a European Arrest Warrant (EAW). The CJEU ruled against the possibility to offer this level of protection, as the grounds for refusing the execution of an EAW were exhaustively regulated by the relevant Framework Decision and did not include this possibility. On the contrary, in areas not or only marginally governed by EU law, Member States should retain the ability to offer higher fundamental rights protection in accordance with the wording of Article 53 of the Charter, the ECHR or any other equivalent provision in other human rights treaties.[148] Although only wishing (entitled) to prevent the relatively

---

[145] The word 'autonomy' appears in the Court's assessment 12 times, while the obligation to accede is acknowledged once and that in connection with the conditions attached to it.

[146] The Charter copied this provision from the ECHR, hence the identical numbering.

[147] Judgment of 26 February 2013, *Melloni v Ministerio Fiscal*, C-399/11, ECLI:EU:C:2013:107, para 60.

[148] See, for example, Article 73 of the Istanbul Convention on Preventing and Combating Violence Against Women and Domestic Violence on completion of the accession by the EU.

rare *Melloni* scenario, the CJEU's very specific objection contributed to the blanket rejection of the draft agreement.

In any case, the Court's concern regarding the effect of Article 53 ECHR is more hypothetical than real. Given that the Member States are already bound by both, situations where the concurrent compliance with both Articles 53 would create problems could already arise, albeit not as part of one integrated legal system. The fact that such conflicts do not abound highlights the theoretical nature of the CJEU's objection which, nevertheless, will now need to be overcome in the next draft agreement. Moreover, in the event of accession (and as is the case now) the ECtHR would have no mandate or interest to force Member States to apply higher than Convention standards which would infringe on essential characteristics of EU law.[149] The Court's broad understanding of conflict between obligations under EU primary law and other international sources is exclusionary towards international law and grounded in the overall constitutional approach of *Opinion 2/13* which intends to place Member States' responsibilities related to the EU above all their other international commitments, even when the exercise of the latter is only hypothetical.[150]

Second, the CJEU objected to the potential disruption to the principle of mutual trust. The principle requires Member States to 'trust' that each one of them complies with fundamental rights in the exercise of EU tasks such as transferring asylum seekers, recognizing judgments from other Member States, relocating detainees, and others. The CJEU raising this issue is somewhat puzzling, as mutual trust is already currently challenged in ECtHR judgments, as seen in the *Bosphorus* line of case law. Accession could on the contrary facilitate the EU's ability to defend its policies directly before the ECtHR thanks to the co-respondent mechanism. One possible explanation for why the CJEU brought up mutual trust is that the draft accession agreement does not mention the *Bosphorus* presumption—the Court could have inferred, not completely without reason, that EU accession to the ECHR would spell the end of this special treatment of EU law by the ECtHR.[151] In other words, while, on the one hand, the quasi-federal constellation—unchanged after accession—inside the EU would demand continued restraint when it comes to checking fundamental rights observance between Member States, one of the rationales for accession is the 'normalization' of oversight of the EU by the ECtHR which would, on the other hand, mandate putting the EU on equal footing with other contracting parties in the eyes of the ECHR regime.[152] Nevertheless, even though the CJEU's constitutional self-interest in blocking accession on this ground can be understood, it is the ECtHR in whose hands the fate of the *Bosphorus* presumption ultimately resides, both pre- and post-accession. The deference displayed by the Strasbourg Court in the subsequent *Avotiņš*, *Pirozzi*, and *Romeo Castaño* decisions shows that the CJEU could have placed more trust in the ECtHR's respect for European integration. The foregoing is without prejudice to the contention that the CJEU should in any case be concerned in the first place about respect for fundamental rights, enshrined also specifically in Article 67(1)

---

[149] P Eeckhout, 'Opinion 2/13 on EU Accession to the ECHR and Judicial Dialogue: Autonomy or Autarky?' (2015) 38 Fordham International Law Journal 955, 967.

[150] Ibid, 967–68.

[151] O De Schutter, 'La jurisprudence Bosphorus Survivra-t-elle à l'Adhésion?' (2012) Journal des Tribunaux 598 and O De Schutter, 'Bosphorus Post-Accession: Redefining the Relationship Between the European Court of Human Rights and the Parties to the Convention' in V Kosta, N Skoutaris, and V Tzevelekos (eds), *The EU Accession to the ECHR* (Hart Publishing 2014) arguing that there are good reasons to think that accession would spell the end for the *Bosphorus* presumption.

[152] The demand of the CJEU for 'EU exceptionalism' with respect to the ECHR was criticized in the literature. See E Spaventa, 'A Very Fearful Court? The Protection of Fundamental Rights in the European Union

TFEU with regards to the Area of Freedom Security and Justice, rather than the smoothness of the operation of mutual trust.[153]

The third issue raised by the CJEU ventured again into the realm of the hypothetical.[154] The Court pointed to Protocol No 16 to the ECHR,[155] which allows the highest courts to submit questions for 'advisory opinions' to the ECtHR, as interfering with the autonomy of EU law, namely the EU's own preliminary ruling procedure under Article 267 TFEU. However, not only did the draft accession agreement not provide for EU accession to Protocol No 16 but only a minority of EU Member States have thus far ratified the Protocol.[156] The hypothetical nature of the objection aside, there is no compelling reason why the courts of EU Member States should not have the option to refer questions regarding the interpretation of another international agreement to the relevant international court, especially when the advisory opinions provided are non-binding.[157] Should the Member States violate their EU law obligations as a result of Protocol No 16—or any other treaty—such an infringement can be addressed through established procedures within the EU; this is a distinct issue from accession to the ECHR, however. The CJEU was, in addition, concerned about becoming involved through the prior involvement procedure in the advisory opinions of the ECtHR, as this could prevent the application of its own Article 267 TFEU preliminary ruling procedure. Again, setting aside the rarity of such a hypothetical scenario, accession would make possible at least some CJEU involvement in EU-relevant interpretation of the ECHR, as opposed to the non-accession situation.[158] The Court's worry is possibly more that the ultimate—yet paradoxically non-binding—authority lies in this scenario with the Strasbourg Court and not with itself as in the Article 267 TFEU procedure.

Fourth, the CJEU challenged the compatibility of the draft accession agreement with Article 344 TFEU which safeguards its exclusive adjudicative role with regards to the EU Treaties. The provision requires Member States to bring proceedings against each other in matters of EU law only before the CJEU and not any other international court. On the basis of Article 344 TFEU, the CJEU complained about the potential effect of a parallel provision in the ECHR, Article 33, which allows the contracting parties to the Convention to bring a case against one another before the ECtHR. If such a dispute were to involve points of EU law, this would infringe upon Article 344 TFEU. The CJEU went even further, however, when it stated that the mere possibility of Member States submitting a dispute to the ECtHR pursuant to Article 33 ECHR is sufficient to 'undermine the requirement set out in Article 344 TFEU' (paragraph 208).

After Opinion 2/13' (2015) 22 Maastricht Journal of European and Comparative Law 35; T Isiksel, 'European Exceptionalism and the EU's Accession to the ECHR' (2016) 27 European Journal of International Law 565.

[153] Peers, 'The Dream Becomes a Nightmare' (n 138) 221.
[154] Eeckhout, 'Opinion 2/13 on EU Accession to the ECHR and Judicial Dialogue' (n 149) 972.
[155] Council of Europe, 'Protocol No 16 to the Convention on the Protection of Human Rights and Fundamental Freedoms', Strasbourg, 2 October 2013.
[156] As of writing, the eight Member States that have done so are Estonia, Finland, France, Greece, Lithuania, Netherlands, Slovakia, and Slovenia.
[157] See Article 5 of Protocol No. 16 (n 155).
[158] Since indeed, the current situation is equally complex, see K Lemmens, 'Protocol No 16 to the ECHR: Managing Backlog through Complex Judicial Dialogue?' (2019) 15 European Constitutional Law Review 691, 705–08.

Convention for the Protection of Human Rights and Fundamental Freedoms (adopted 4 November 1950, entered into force 3 September 1953) 213 UNTS 221

Article 33
Inter-State cases

Any High Contracting Party may refer to the Court any alleged breach of the provisions of the Convention and the Protocols thereto by another High Contracting Party.

Consolidated version of the Treaty on the Functioning of the European Union [2012] OJ C326/47

Article 344

Member States undertake not to submit a dispute concerning the interpretation or application of the Treaties to any method of settlement other than those provided for therein.

Unlike the previous three objections, the one concerning Article 344 TFEU and Article 33 ECHR was also identified by AG Kokott. Her reading of the problem was, however, considerably more restrained than that of the Court. The AG considered that the EU has internal tools at its disposal which make it capable to enforce compliance with Article 344 TFEU, in particular infringement proceedings which could be directed against Member States bringing an EU law relevant case to the ECtHR. If the CJEU were not to satisfy itself with this solution alone, the AG suggested that it could demand a declaration from the Member States to the effect that they will refrain from using Article 33 ECHR in a way which would not comply with Article 344 TFEU.[159] The AG also warned that a more exclusionary interpretation of Article 344 TFEU could be inconsistent with a number of existing international agreements providing for a dispute resolution mechanism entered into by both the EU and Member States.[160] As on most points, however, the CJEU did not follow—without disproving—the reasoning of the AG and instead adopted a strict interpretation of the compatibility of the draft agreement with Article 344 TFEU.

Moreover, according to the Court's previous case law on the issue, it was sufficient for the 'competing' international agreement to make compliance with Article 344 TFEU possible for EU Member States.[161] The CJEU distinguished that precedent, the case of *MOX Plant*, which concerned a dispute between Ireland and the UK under the UN Convention on the Law of the Sea (UNCLOS), on the ground that Article 282 thereof includes a clause according to which dispute resolution is to be deferred to a different forum (such as the CJEU)

---

[159] *Opinion 2/13 (EU accession to the ECHR)*, Opinion of AG Kokott (n 137) paras 118–120.

[160] Ibid, para 117. Johansen gives the following examples of dispute resolution provisions in mixed agreements potentially incompatible with Article 344 TFEU: Article 32 of the Convention for the Protection of the Marine Environment of the North-East Atlantic (adopted 22 September 1992) 32 ILM 1069; Article 16 of the Convention on Access to Information, Public Participation in Decision-Making and Access to Justice in Environmental Matters (adopted 25 June 1998) 2162 UNTS 447; Article 21 of the Convention on the Transboundary Effects of Industrial Accidents (adopted 17 March 1992) 2105 UNTS 457; Article 57 of the Customs Convention on the International Transport of Goods Under Cover of TIR Carnets (adopted 14 November 1975) 1079 UNTS 89; and Article 35 of the United Nations Convention against Transnational Organized Crime (adopted 29 September 2003) 2225 UNTS 209. See S Johansen, 'The Reinterpretation of TFEU Article 344 in Opinion 2/13 and Its Potential Consequences' (2015) 16 German Law Journal 169, 176.

[161] Judgment of 30 May 2006, *Commission of the European Communities v Ireland*, C-459/03, ECLI:EU:C:2006:345, paras 124–125; Johansen, 'The Reinterpretation of TFEU Article 344' (n 160) 173–74.

if so required by another treaty (such as Article 344 TFEU) to which the disputing states are a party. However, this distinction appears superficial as even under Article 282 UNCLOS it is possible for Member States to bring an interstate action that would infringe upon Article 344 TFEU.[162] Thus it is difficult to justify the CJEU's reinterpretation of Article 344 TFEU which departs from previous case law, ignores the opinion of the AG, raises questions over compatibility of existing agreements, and generally displays considerable distrust towards the Member States and the EU's internal ability to enforce compliance with the Treaties.

Fifth, and perhaps most legitimately, the CJEU scrutinized the proposed functioning of the co-respondent mechanism. In particular, the Court took issue with the ECtHR assessing the EU's and the Member States' requests for leave for becoming a co-respondent, as well as with the Strasbourg Court apportioning responsibility for Convention violations as between them even when the latter decision merely confirms an agreement regarding liability made by the respondent and the co-respondent. In both instances, the review conducted by the ECtHR could affect the division of powers between the EU and its Member States and the exclusive jurisdiction of the CJEU to establish whether the apportionment of responsibility reflects EU rules. Furthermore, the CJEU noted that the wording of the draft agreement as regards the joint responsibility of a respondent and a co-respondent does not take into account that the Member States have filed reservations under international law with respect to certain provisions of the ECHR. According to the Court, disregarding the Member States' reservations would represent a breach of Article 2 of Protocol No 8 EU which states that the accession agreement shall not affect the situation of the Member States vis-à-vis the ECHR.

As regards the co-respondent mechanism, the CJEU was on common ground with the preceding view of the AG. In the opinion of both, the draft agreement was required to exclude ECtHR assessments of requests for leave to become a co-respondent and of responsibility apportionment. The draft agreement also needed to be amended in order to guarantee that the reservations of the Member States will be respected when it comes to joint liability with the EU. The key difference was of course that on the whole, Advocate General Kokott proposed to rule the draft agreement compatible with the EU Treaties, provided the necessary amendments are introduced, while the Court rejected the agreement. In any case, commentators disagreed also on this issue, one seeing the CJEU as conflating international responsibility and internal division of powers, another concurring with the objections expressed by the CJEU.[163]

Sixth, and related to the previous ground, both the AG and the CJEU found deficiencies in the set-up of the prior involvement procedure of the CJEU in proceedings before the Strasbourg Court. The Luxembourg judiciary held that EU institutions must be systematically informed about pending cases before the ECtHR in order to be able to make the determination regarding whether the prior involvement procedure should be triggered. The CJEU must, in its own view, be involved where a provision of EU law is 'open to more than one plausible interpretation' (paragraph 245). Moreover, the CJEU construed Article 3(6) of the draft agreement as precluding it from ruling on the interpretation, allowing rulings only on validity, of provisions of EU secondary law. This, in turn, was found impermissible in light of the adverse effect such limited scope of the prior involvement procedure could have

---

[162] Ibid, 173–76. Article 282 UNCLOS reads: 'If the States Parties which are parties to a dispute concerning the interpretation or application of this Convention have agreed, through a general, regional or bilateral agreement or otherwise, that such dispute shall, at the request of any party to the dispute, be submitted to a procedure that entails a binding decision, that procedure shall apply in lieu of the procedures provided for in this Part, unless the parties to the dispute otherwise agree.'

[163] Eeckhout, 'Opinion 2/13 on EU Accession to the ECHR and Judicial Dialogue' (n 149).

on the powers of the CJEU.[164] A future agreement on EU accession to the ECHR will there-fore also have to improve this technical point regarding the cooperation between the ECtHR and the CJEU. It should be borne in mind that, as the AG pointed out, the Statute of the Court of Justice will equally need to be amended, pursuant to Article 281 TFEU, to allow for the new procedure involving the CJEU in proceedings before another international court.[165]

The final seventh point flagged by the CJEU possibly caused the most exasperation among the critics. The CJEU found that the ECtHR cannot be the sole body with powers to rule on matters falling within the EU's CFSP in view of its own effective exclusion from judicial review of CFSP measures. The Court alleged that this arrangement failed to take into account the 'specific characteristics of EU law' (paragraph 257) without considering that a treaty provision (Article 24(1) TEU) explicitly excluding the CJEU's jurisdiction over CFSP matters could also represent a 'specific' feature of EU law, one moreover expressly included by the Member States in the constitutional framework of the EU. Although the rejection of ECtHR jurisdiction over CFSP matters is quite possibly consistent with the CJEU's previous case law,[166] the 'selfish Court' attitude shines through this final objection of the CJEU the most.[167] The CJEU ap-pears to lack appreciation for the possibility that the treaty-makers intended to exclude con-currently CJEU jurisdiction over CFSP and at the same time require the EU to accede to the ECHR, thus subjecting CFSP to the oversight of the ECtHR but not the CJEU.[168]

Opinion 2/13 (EU accession to the ECHR) [2014] ECLI:EU:C:2014:2475, Opinion of AG Kokott

---

193. By contrast, conflicting case-law and threats to the supranational structure of the EU are precluded altogether in so far as the authors of the founding Treaties of the EU consciously refrained from setting up a supranational structure and renounced the uniform and autonomous interpretation of EU law by a judicial institution of the EU itself in a particular area—in this case, in the field of the CFSP. **The absence of sufficient arrangements within the EU, by which the autonomy of EU law alone can be protected, can hardly be used as an argument against recognition of the jurisdiction of the judicial body of an international organisation.** Furthermore, **the effectiveness of legal protection for individuals is strengthened, rather than weakened,** in such a situation by the recognition of an international jurisdiction.

194. This applies a fortiori with regard to the EU's proposed accession to the ECHR, because, by Article 6(2) TEU, **the authors of the Treaty of Lisbon consciously con-ferred on the EU institutions the power to implement that accession,** and the task of doing so, **without first configuring the CFSP along supranational lines or, in**

---

[164] The Advocate General also requested the drafters to clarify that not only rulings on validity but also inter-pretation, as regards EU secondary law, can be provided by the CJEU in the course of the prior involvement pro-cedure. See *Opinion 2/13 (EU accession to the ECHR)*, Opinion of AG Kokott (n 137).

[165] Ibid, paras 74–76.

[166] Opinion of 8 March 2011, *Creation of a unified patent litigation system*, 1/09, ECLI:EU:C:2011:123, paras 78, 80, and 89.

[167] B De Witte, 'A Selfish Court? The Court of Justice and the Design of International Dispute Settlement Beyond the European Union' in Cremona and Thies (eds), *The European Court of Justice and External Relations Law: Constitutional Challenges* (n 50) 33–46.

[168] 'The EU's Accession to the ECHR—a "NO" from the ECJ!' (2015) 52 Common Market Law Review 1, 13, Editorial comments.

particular, giving the Courts of the EU comprehensive jurisdiction with regard to the CFSP. It would appear, therefore, that the authors of the Treaty of Lisbon did not themselves see any contradiction between the very limited jurisdiction of the Courts of the EU in relation to the CFSP, on the one hand, and recognition of the jurisdiction of the ECtHR in consequence of the EU's accession to the ECHR, on the other.

The CFSP ground for rejecting the draft agreement also makes very conspicuous the more general point about the underlying principles which were guiding the CJEU in *Opinion 2/13*. As opposed to AG Kokott, the Court failed to mention the crucial fact that accession of the EU to the ECHR would strengthen legal protection of individuals, both on the whole and in the particular circumstances of the CFSP. The EU's declared commitment to the rule of law and fundamental rights was set aside in favour of preserving the autonomy of the EU legal order and the powers of the CJEU. A number of observers have detected in this approach a high degree of concern for legal formalization of every imaginable aspect of the post-accession relationship between the EU and the ECHR.[169] In *Opinion 2/13*, the Court can be seen attempting to legally pre-empt as many adverse—from its constitutional perspective—scenarios as possible so as to safeguard the theoretical purity of the Union legal order even when similar results could be achieved through less onerous means (such as EU internal instruments). This shows a lack of trust not only towards the ECtHR but also towards the Member States, the EU institutions, and their corresponding ability to ensure compliance with the EU Treaties through existing formal (eg through infringement proceedings under Article 258 TFEU) and informal (eg through peer pressure in the Council) mechanisms.

Despite the negative conclusion of *Opinion 2/13*, accession to the ECHR remains a treaty obligation for the EU. The EU is therefore looking for ways to overcome the seven obstacles identified by the CJEU, some of which might be relatively easy to address (Article 33 ECHR), while others considerably less so (CFSP). Taken together, some commentators have questioned whether accession under the circumstances demanded by the CJEU would still represent a beneficial step for human rights protection in Europe in light of the carve outs potentially required in the ECHR regime.[170] While accession remains in the work programme of the European Commission and solutions are concomitantly sought by the European Parliament[171] and the Council,[172] for the time being the status of the ECHR does not amount to that of an 'integral part of EU law', nor can individuals bring actions directly against the Union before the ECtHR. If and when accession of the EU to the ECHR will happen is currently unknown.

In the midst of the controversy over EU accession, however, it is easy to forget about the continued importance of the ECHR not only for the EU—still recognized as general principles of EU law—but also, and perhaps more importantly, for the Member States' national

---

[169] J Odermatt, 'A Giant Step Backwards? Opinion 2/13 on the EU's Accession to the European Convention on Human Rights' (2015) 47 New York University Journal of International Law & Politics 783, 791; 'The EU's Accession to the ECHR—a "NO" from the ECJ!' (n 168).

[170] Peers, 'The Dream Becomes a Nightmare' (n 138). On the contrary, Łazowski and Wessel, for example, think that overcoming the situation is still desirable. See A Łazowski and RA Wessel, 'When Caveats Turn into Locks: Opinion 2/13 on Accession of the European Union to the ECHR' (2015) 16 German Law Journal 179, 211.

[171] See, for example, European Parliament, 'Resolution on the implementation of the Charter of Fundamental Rights of the European Union in the EU institutional framework', P8_TA(2019)0079, 12 February 2019, para 29.

[172] See, for example, Council of the European Union, 'Outcome of the 3717th Council Meeting Justice and Home Affairs', 12837/19, 7 and 8 October 2019, 11.

legal systems. The ECHR has served as the main reference framework for human rights protection in Europe for almost 70 years and along the way it had a profound impact on the way human rights developed in the territories of the various contracting parties, including those of EU Member States.[173] Even though the way the Convention is incorporated in Member States tends to differ, it has almost universally empowered national judges to evaluate domestic developments in the light of their compatibility with the ECHR and the case law of the ECtHR.[174] The effects of the ECHR on national legal systems, including the less obvious ones such as impact on legal culture, are numerous, wide-ranging, and dynamic.[175] Suffice to say that the boastful claim of the ECtHR that the ECHR represents a 'constitutional instrument of European public order' is not baseless.[176]

5.5 Other Council of Europe Instruments

Although the ECHR is the defining Council of Europe treaty, there are other instruments in the human rights domain which have been touted as suitable for EU accession. Most recently, the EU has signed the Convention on preventing and combating violence against women and domestic violence ('Istanbul Convention').[177] In addition to laying down a framework for combating violence against women through prevention, protection, and support, the Convention also includes general clauses on preventing all forms of discrimination against women and promotes a gender-conscious approach to law and policy. Moreover, it provides for the establishment of an expert body, the Group of experts on action against violence against women and domestic violence (GREVIO), which is tasked with monitoring the implementation of the Convention. GREVIO prepares reports and recommendations on the basis of information submitted to it, which can originate also from national non-governmental organizations; it does not, however, have enforcement capacities and it cannot entertain individual complaints concerning violations of the Istanbul Convention.

Council of Europe Convention on preventing and combating violence against women and domestic violence (adopted 11 May 2011, entered into force 1 August 2014) CETS No 210

Article 1—Purposes of the Convention
  1 The purposes of this Convention are to:
  a   protect women against all forms of violence, and prevent, prosecute and eliminate violence against women and domestic violence;

---

[173] In the 1990s, accession to the ECHR has even become a prerequisite for countries aspiring to join the EU.

[174] A Stone Sweet and H Keller, 'The Reception of the ECHR in National Legal Orders' in H Keller and A Stone Sweet (eds), *A Europe of Rights: The Impact of the ECHR on National Legal Systems* (Oxford University Press 2008) 28–29.

[175] See generally Keller and Stone Sweet (eds), *A Europe of Rights: The Impact of the ECHR on National Legal Systems* (n 174).

[176] *Loizidou v Turkey*, App no 15318/89, 23 March 1995, Grand Chamber, Judgment of 23 March 1995.

[177] The treaty was signed by Ambassador Joseph Filletti of the Permanent Representative of Malta to the Council of Europe—Malta being the holder of the rotating Presidency of the Council of the EU at the time—and Věra Jourová, then EU Commissioner for Justice, Consumers and Gender Equality on 13 June 2017.

> b   contribute to the elimination of all forms of discrimination against women
>   and promote substantive equality between women and men, including by
>   empowering women;
> c   design a comprehensive framework, policies and measures for the protection of
>   and assistance to all victims of violence against women and domestic violence;
> d   promote international co-operation with a view to eliminating violence against
>   women and domestic violence;
> e   provide support and assistance to organisations and law enforcement agencies
>   to effectively cooperate in order to adopt an integrated approach to eliminating
>   violence against women and domestic violence.
> 2 In order to ensure effective implementation of its provisions by the Parties, this
>   Convention establishes a specific monitoring mechanism.
>
> ### Article 4—Fundamental rights, equality and non-discrimination
> 1 Parties shall take the necessary legislative and other measures to promote and pro-
>   tect the right for everyone, particularly women, to live free from violence in both
>   the public and the private sphere.
> 2 Parties condemn all forms of discrimination against women and take, without
>   delay, the necessary legislative and other measures to prevent it, in particular by:
>   –   embodying in their national constitutions or other appropriate legislation the prin-
>   ciple of equality between women and men and ensuring the practical realisation of this
>   principle;
>   –   prohibiting discrimination against women, including through the use of sanctions,
>   where appropriate;
>   –   abolishing laws and practices which discriminate against women.
>
> ### Article 75—Signature and entry into force
> 1 This Convention shall be open for signature by the member States of the Council of
>   Europe, the non-member States which have participated in its elaboration and **the
>   European Union.**

From the perspective of the values and rights protected and promoted by the EU, its accession to the Istanbul Convention is logical.[178] EU ratification of the Convention was also
recommended by the UN Committee on the rights of persons with disabilities in view of
the EU's obligations under the CRPD.[179] The EU has signed the Convention alongside its
Member States—the legal scenario is one of a mixed agreement,[180] whereby the EU is competent for some but not all parts of the Convention. Insofar as the EU adopted common rules
in areas affected by the Convention—and there are multiple—it is exclusively competent according to Article 3(2) TFEU which codified the *ERTA* line of case law despite lacking an
explicit exclusive competence in most of the areas covered by the Convention.[181] Still, the

---

[178] See, in particular, Article 8 TFEU, Articles 2 and 3 TEU, Article 23 of the Charter, and objective 14 of the
Action Plan on Human Rights and Democracy (2015–2019). See also Council of the European Union, Council
Conclusions on the Gender Action Plan 2016–2020, 13201/15, 26 October 2015.

[179] Committee on the Rights of Persons with Disabilities, Concluding observations on the initial report of the
European Union, CRPD/C/EU/CO/1, 2 October 2015, para 21.

[180] See generally C Hillion and P Koutrakos (eds), *Mixed Agreements Revisited: The EU and its Member States
in the World* (Hart Publishing 2010).

[181] Judgment of 31 March 1971, *Commission v Council (ERTA)*, 22/70, ECLI:EU:C:1971:32.

Member States possess relevant competences for the Istanbul Convention, such as criminal sanctioning, and therefore the EU cannot ratify the Convention alone. In light of domestic political developments in a number of Member States,[182] it remains a real possibility that the EU will ultimately not be able ratify the Istanbul Convention, despite having already signed it.[183] Most domestic pressure on governments coalesced around misplaced concerns over the definition of gender provided by the Convention as meaning 'the socially constructed roles, behaviours, activities and attributes that a given society considers appropriate for women and men'. In July 2018, the Constitutional Court of Bulgaria declared the ratification of the Istanbul Convention unconstitutional, taking issue with the 'wide' definition of gender and undoubtedly further complicating the possible accession of the Union as well.[184]

The different issue areas affected by the Istanbul Convention have also complicated the answer to the question of which provision of the EU Treaties should serve as the legal basis for the signing of the Convention by the EU. The case law of the CJEU requires that the choice of legal basis 'must rest on objective factors amenable to judicial review, which include the aim and content' and where more than one purpose or component are present, the EU measure concluding the treaty (a Council decision) should be based on a single predominant legal basis unless the multiple objectives carry equal weight.[185] In its proposal, the Commission suggested Article 82(2) TFEU on police and judicial cooperation in criminal matters and Article 84 TFEU on promoting and supporting crime prevention to constitute the main legal bases for the Council decisions on the signing and conclusion of the Istanbul Convention. The Legal Service of the Council of the EU disagreed with the combination of the legal bases in one act, however, which led the Council to adopt two separate decisions regarding the signing of the Convention.[186] One decision related to the EU's competence in judicial cooperation in criminal matters (the legal basis proposed by the Commission), while the other covered the Union's competence in asylum and the principle of non-refoulement. The split legal bases were necessary in view of the different compositions of the Council, as the UK and Ireland have opted into the relevant EU criminal law legislation but not into asylum matters. This intervention has however not completely resolved the legal uncertainty with regard to the compatibility of the choice of the legal bases with the Treaties. Therefore, the European Parliament has requested an opinion from the CJEU on the matter.[187]

---

[182] As of August 2020, six Member States have not ratified the Istanbul Convention: Bulgaria, Czechia, Hungary, Latvia, Lithuania, and Slovakia. On 25 July 2020, Poland announced that it would withdraw from the Convention, as its government claims that the text is 'harmful' because it 'contains elements of an ideological nature' requiring schools to teach children about gender: Nils Muiznieks, Amnesty International, 'While Tackling COVID-19 Europe is Being Stalked by a Shadow Pandemic: Domestic Violence' (*amnesty.org*, 31 July 2020) <http://www.amnesty.org/en/latest/news/2020/07/while-tackling-covid-19-europe-is-being-stalked-by-a-shadow-pandemic-domestic-violence/> accessed 14 August 2020.

[183] For arguments in support of EU ratification, see S De Vido, 'The ratification of the Council of Europe Istanbul Convention by the EU : A Step Forward in the Protection of Women from Violence in the European Legal System' (2017) 9 European Journal of Legal Studies 69.

[184] See C Burke and A Molitorisová, 'Reservations/Declarations under the Council of Europe Convention on Preventing and Combating Violence against Women and Domestic Violence (Istanbul Convention) and Convention on the Elimination of All Forms of Discrimination against Women (CEDAW) in Light of Sex/Gender Constitutional Debates' (2019) 8 International Human Rights Law Review 188.

[185] Judgment of 11 June 2014, *Commission v Council*, C-377/12, ECLI:EU:C:2014:1903, para 34.

[186] Council Decision (EU) 2017/865 on the signing, on behalf of the European Union, of the Council of Europe Convention on preventing and combating violence against women and domestic violence with regard to matters related to judicial cooperation in criminal matters [2017] OJ L131/11; Council Decision (EU) 2017/866 on the signing, on behalf of the European Union, of the Council of Europe Convention on preventing and combating violence against women and domestic violence with regard to asylum and non-refoulement [2017] OJ L131/13.

[187] European Parliament, Resolution seeking an opinion from the Court of Justice on the compatibility with the Treaties of the proposals for the accession by the European Union to the Council of Europe Convention on

A more consequential step for the integration of the EU into existing Council of Europe rights instruments (other than the ECHR) would entail the Union's accession to the European Social Charter.[188] Such a development is merely hypothetical at the moment, as the Charter does not contain an REIO clause that would allow the EU to accede. Moreover, potential EU accession would have to face obstacles similar to those listed in *Opinion 2/ 13* by the CJEU, especially concerning the principle of autonomy of the EU legal order, as was already presciently observed in a 2004 in-depth study of the possibility of EU accession to the European Social Charter by Olivier De Schutter.[189] The variable geometry of shared competences in the area of social policy and the fragmented landscape of Member States commitments under the Social Charter make any agreement on the EU's accession to the Charter difficult. It would require a convergence of social policy perspectives among the Member States, as well as a willingness to strengthen cooperation and ensure compliance on the EU level. Despite the presently hypothetical nature of the EU's accession, the monitoring body of the European Social Charter—the European Committee of Social Rights—drew up a working document detailing the relationship between EU law and the Charter and recommended measures which could be taken in lieu of accession to reinforce the relationship between the two systems. The document also notes that unlike under the ECHR, the EU enjoys no presumption of equivalent protection of social rights under the European Social Charter (paragraph 66).

European Committee of Social Rights, 'The relationship between European Union law and the European Social Charter', Working Document, 15 July 2014

7. The Charter is a Council of Europe treaty, which was adopted in 1961 and revised in 1996 and which safeguards social and economic rights, that is human rights affecting people's everyday lives. These rights are additional to the civil and political rights enshrined in the Convention for the Protection of Human Rights and Fundamental Freedoms of 1950 ('the Convention'). Like the Convention rights, those recognised under the Charter have their origin in the Universal Declaration of Human Rights.

8. The 1961 Charter sets out to establish **binding international legal guarantees in the same way as the Convention but without going so far as to set up a dedicated court**. The Revised Charter updates and adds to the rights enshrined in the 1961 instrument. One of its sources of inspiration was EU law.

9. The Charter guarantees a wide range of fundamental rights, mainly relating to working conditions, freedom to organise, health, housing and social protection. Specific emphasis is laid on the protection of vulnerable persons such as elderly

---

preventing and combating violence against women and domestic violence and on the procedure for that accession, P8_TA(2019)0357, 4 April 2019. At the time of writing, the case (Opinion 1/19) is still pending.

[188] European Social Charter (adopted 18 October 1961, entered into force 26 February 1965) 529 UNTS 89. See generally N Bruun and others (eds), *The European Social Charter and Employment Relation* (Hart Publishing 2017).

[189] O De Schutter, 'L'adhésion de l'Union européenne à la Charte sociale européenne révisée', EUI Working Paper LAW 2004/11, 37.

people, children, people with disabilities and migrants. The Charter requires that enjoyment of the rights it lays down should be guaranteed without discrimination.

10. In view of this diversity, the Charter is based on what is termed an *à la carte* ratification system, enabling states, under certain circumstances (...), to choose the provisions they are willing to accept as binding international legal obligations. This means that while signatory states are encouraged to make progress in accepting the Charter's provisions, they are also allowed to adapt the commitments they enter into at the time of ratification to the level of legal protection of social rights attained by their own system.

11. According to the Charter, states' compliance with their commitments under the Charter is subject to the international supervision of the Committee. Its fifteen members, who are independent and impartial, are elected by the Committee of Ministers of the Council of Europe for a six-year term of office, which is renewable once. The Committee verifies compliance with the Charter under two separate procedures: the reporting procedure, whereby member states submit regular national reports, and the collective complaints procedure, based on the filing of complaints by employer and employee organisations and non-governmental organisations.

19. In general, the rights established by the Charter are guaranteed in a more or less explicit and detailed manner by EU law. (...) the 98 paragraphs of the Revised Charter can be matched to binding provisions of primary or secondary EU law, albeit with some differences of both form and substance.

22. At present the 28 EU member states are part of the 'system' of the Charter treaties (the 1961 Charter, the Additional Protocol of 1988, the Additional Protocol of 1995 and the Revised Charter), albeit with differences regarding the commitments they have entered into: nine states are bound by the 1961 Charter (five of which are also bound by the Protocol of 1988) and nineteen by the Revised Charter. With the exception of two states, France and Portugal—which have accepted all the paragraphs of the Revised Charter—the others have ratified a greater or lesser number of provisions of either version of the Charter. Only fourteen EU member states have accepted the 1995 Protocol establishing a system of collective complaints. This results in a variety of situations and contracted obligations. The table in Appendix I provides detailed information on the undertakings made by each EU member state with regard to the provisions of the Charter.

23. There is a clear lack of uniformity in the acceptance of Charter provisions by the EU member states. This is the result of the choices made by each State Party when expressing its sovereign will on the basis of the Charter acceptance system described above (...). While not amounting to an anomaly in itself, this lack of uniformity sometimes reveals a lack of consistency. Where the protection of some fundamental social rights is concerned, some states have chosen not to enter any undertaking under the Charter; yet, pursuant to EU law, they have adopted legal instruments or measures providing equal or greater protection than that guaranteed in the Charter provision(s) they have not accepted. In other words, while applying the EU's binding standards in an area covered by the Charter, some states have not accepted the Charter provisions establishing legally equivalent guarantees.

24. Given this situation, it would be expedient to identify the Charter provisions which EU member states should accept because they belong to the EU. Greater consistency as regards EU member states' social rights commitments under the two

standard-setting systems may contribute in future to the realisation of the European Parliament's proposal that the EU should accede to the Charter (...)

65. (...) European Union law can play a positive role in the Charter's implementation; nonetheless, **there is no presumption of conformity with the Charter when a state is in compliance with the directives**, even if their subject matter comes within the scope of the Charter.

66. **The fact that provisions of national law draw on an EU directive does not exempt them from conforming to the requirements of the Charter**. It is true that the Committee is not competent for assessing the conformity of national situations with a European Union directive, nor the conformity of such a directive with the Charter. However, when the EU member states agree on binding measures that they apply to themselves by means of a directive, affecting the way in which they implement Charter rights, they should take account of the commitments they made when they ratified the European Social Charter both in drawing up that directive and in transposing it into their national law. **It is ultimately for the Committee to assess compliance of a national situation with the Charter, including in the event of transposition of a European Union directive into national law.**

67. The Committee considers that **neither the situation of social rights in the EU's legal order nor the procedures for establishing secondary legislation in these matters would justify a similar presumption, even rebuttable, as to the conformity of legal texts of the EU with the European Social Charter.**

68. Whenever it has to assess situations where the states take into account or are bound by EU legal instruments, the Committee examines on a **case-by-case basis** whether the States Parties implement the rights guaranteed by the Charter in their national law.

82. In the meantime, other practical arrangements which could lead to greater convergence between the two legal orders do seem feasible.

83. For instance, **the EU could encourage its member states to harmonise their commitments, in particular by all ratifying the revised Charter and all accepting all the provisions in the Charter which are most directly related in terms of substance to the provisions of EU law and the competences of the EU.** For example, these include Articles 4§3 (equal pay for women and men) and 2§1 (reasonable working hours).

84. It would be useful for a definition of a kind of 'Community core' within the Charter to be drawn up so as to give EU member states clear indications in this respect.

85. **A commitment of all EU member states concerning the collective complaints procedure** would also help to ensure greater balance between EU members in terms of taking the Charter on board, as the current difference between those which have accepted the procedure and those which have not would disappear.

86. In addition, **if the Charter was taken into account by EU lawmakers** (Commission, Council and Parliament), this would ensure that any new EU legislation **increased the convergence** between the two legal orders.

87. Lastly, **the links between the Committee and the Fundamental Rights Agency could be extended** with a view to enabling the Committee to make still greater use than at present of the Agency's research in finding out more about and better understanding the actual situation of social rights in states.

5.6 Convention on the Rights of Persons with Disabilities (CRPD)

The first international human rights treaty to which the EU has become a party is the UN CRPD.[190] The Convention, which represents the first international legally binding framework specifically designed to improve the rights of people with disabilities, was adopted in December 2006 together with its Optional Protocol at the UN Headquarters in New York. It has been so far ratified by 181 parties, including the EU, while 9 more countries have signed but not ratified the treaty, including the US. The Optional Protocol to the CRPD establishes jurisdiction of the monitoring body, the Committee on the Rights of Persons with Disabilities, over individual complaints against the parties to the Convention.[191] The Optional Protocol has been to date ratified by 96 state parties but not the EU.[192]

Convention on the Rights of Persons with Disabilities (adopted 13 December 2006, entered into force 3 May 2008) 2515 UNTS 3

Article 1
Purpose

The purpose of the present Convention is **to promote, protect and ensure the full and equal enjoyment of all human rights and fundamental freedoms by all persons with disabilities**, and to promote respect for their inherent **dignity**.

Persons with disabilities include those who have long-term physical, mental, intellectual or sensory impairments which in interaction with various barriers may hinder their full and effective participation in society on an equal basis with others.

Article 3
General principles

The principles of the present Convention shall be:

(a) respect for inherent dignity, individual autonomy including the freedom to make one's own choices, and independence of persons;
(b) non-discrimination;
(c) full and effective participation and inclusion in society;
(d) respect for difference and acceptance of persons with disabilities as part of human diversity and humanity;
(e) equality of opportunity;
(f) accessibility;
(g) equality between men and women;

---

[190] Convention on the Rights of Persons with Disabilities (adopted 13 December 2006, entered into force 3 May 2008) 2515 UNTS 3.

[191] Optional Protocol to the Convention on the Rights of Persons with Disabilities (adopted 13 December 2006, entered into force 3 May 2008) 2518 UNTS 283.

[192] The Optional Protocol also includes a RIO clause enabling the EU to accede to it. See Article 11 of the Optional Protocol.

(h) respect for the evolving capacities of children with disabilities and respect for the right of children with disabilities to preserve their identities.

Article 9
Accessibility

1. To enable persons with disabilities to live independently and participate fully in all aspects of life, States Parties shall take appropriate measures to ensure to persons with disabilities access, on an equal basis with others, to the physical environment, to transportation, to information and communications, including information and communications technologies and systems, and to other facilities and services open or provided to the public, both in urban and in rural areas. (…)

Article 33
National implementation and monitoring

1. States Parties, in accordance with their system of organisation, shall designate one or more focal points within government for matters relating to the implementation of the present Convention, and shall give due consideration to the establishment or designation of a coordination mechanism within government to facilitate related action in different sectors and at different levels.
2. **States Parties shall**, in accordance with their legal and administrative systems, maintain, strengthen, designate or **establish** within the State Party, **a framework**, including one or more independent mechanisms, as appropriate, **to promote, protect and monitor implementation of the present Convention. When designating or establishing such a mechanism, States Parties shall take into account the principles relating to the status and functioning of national institutions for protection and promotion of human rights.**
3. **Civil society**, in particular persons with disabilities and their representative organisations, **shall be involved** and participate fully **in the monitoring process.**

Article 34
Committee on the Rights of Persons with Disabilities

1. There shall be established a Committee on the Rights of Persons with Disabilities (hereafter referred to as the Committee), which shall carry out the functions hereinafter provided.
2. The Committee shall consist, at the time of entry into force of the present Convention, of 12 experts. After an additional sixty ratifications or accessions to the Convention, the membership of the Committee shall increase by six members, attaining a maximum number of 18 members.

Article 35
Reports by States Parties

1. Each State Party shall submit to the Committee, through the Secretary-General of the United Nations, **a comprehensive report on measures taken to give effect to**

> its obligations under the present Convention and on the progress made in that regard, within two years after the entry into force of the present Convention for the State Party concerned.
> 2. Thereafter, States Parties shall submit subsequent reports at least every four years and further whenever the Committee so requests.

With respect to the EU, the CRPD entered into force on 22 January 2011, thus becoming the first international human rights agreement concluded by the EU. The EU entered into the Convention next to its Member States in the so-called mixed agreement situation, whereby neither the EU nor the Member States have exclusive competence to accede to an international agreement by themselves.[193] The legal basis for the Council Decision on the conclusion of the Convention were Article 19 TFEU (EU legislative powers in anti-discrimination matters) and Article 114 TFEU (legislative harmonization in the internal market).[194] Thus, as opposed to EU accession to the ECHR, an amendment to the EU Treaties was not necessary. The EU's accession to the CRPD was on the part of international law enabled by an RIO clause contained in Article 44 of the Convention which further stipulates that the EU is obliged—upon accession and following substantial modifications to its competences—to declare 'the extent of their competence with respect to matters governed by the present Convention'. While the EU deposited such a declaration when it concluded the CRPD, it has not submitted a revised account of its competences relating to the Convention following the significant amendments effected by the Treaty of Lisbon which entered into force in 2009. These have partially expanded the extent of the EU's competences pertinent to the CRPD beyond the original declaration which, nevertheless, remains for the most part still relevant today. Internally, the overarching division of competences, in particular as regards EU external representation with respect to the Convention, is governed by a specific agreement on the 'code of conduct' of the various EU institutions and the Member States which mirrors the distinctions between areas of exclusive and shared competences as provided for in the EU Treaties.[195]

Council Decision of 26 November 2009 concerning the conclusion, by the European Community, of the United Nations Convention on the Rights of Persons with Disabilities [2009] OJ L23/35

Annex II

Declaration concerning the competence of the European Community with regard to matters governed by the United Nations Convention on the Rights of Persons with Disabilities

(…)

---

[193] L Waddington 'The European Union and the United Nations Convention on the Rights of Persons with Disabilities: A Story of Exclusive and Shared Competences' (2011) 18 Maastricht Journal of European and Comparative Law 431.

[194] See also below the debate over competence and legal bases in the conclusion of the Marrakesh Treaty.

[195] Code of Conduct 2010/C 340/08 between the Council, the Member States and the Commission setting out internal arrangements for the implementation by and representation of the European Union relating to the United Nations Convention on the Rights of Persons with Disabilities [2010] OJ C340/11.

Article 44(1) of the United Nations Convention on the Rights of Persons with Disabilities (hereinafter referred to as the Convention) provides that a regional integration organisation in its instrument of formal confirmation or accession is to declare the extent of its competence with respect to matters governed by the Convention.

(...)

In accordance with Article 44(1) of the Convention, **this Declaration indicates the competences transferred to the Community by the Member States** under the Treaty establishing the European Community, **in the areas covered by the Convention**.

The scope and the exercise of Community competence are, by their nature, subject to continuous development and the Community will complete or amend this Declaration, if necessary, in accordance with Article 44(1) of the Convention.

In some matters the European Community has exclusive competence and in other matters competence is shared between the European Community and the Member States. The Member States remain competent for all matters in respect of which no competence has been transferred to the European Community.

At present:

1. The Community has **exclusive competence** as regards the compatibility of State aid with the common market and the Common Custom Tariff.

To the extent that provisions of Community law are affected by the provision of the Convention, the European Community has an exclusive competence to accept such obligations **with respect to its own public administration**. In this regard, **the Community declares that it has power to deal with regulating the recruitment, conditions of service, remuneration, training etc. of non-elected officials under the Staff Regulations** and the implementing rules to those Regulations.

2. The **Community shares competence with Member States** as regards action to combat discrimination on the ground of disability, free movement of goods, persons, services and capital agriculture, transport by rail, road, sea and air transport, taxation, internal market, equal pay for male and female workers, trans-European network policy and statistics.

The **European Community has exclusive competence to enter into this Convention in respect of those matters only to the extent that provisions of the Convention or legal instruments adopted in implementation thereof affect common rules previously established by the European Community**. When Community rules exist but are not affected, in particular in cases of Community provisions establishing only minimum standards, the Member States have competence, without prejudice to the competence of the European Community to act in this field. Otherwise competence rests with the Member States. A list of relevant acts adopted by the European Community appears in the Appendix hereto. **The extent of the European Community's competence ensuing from these acts must be assessed by reference to the precise provisions of each measure**, and in particular, the extent to which these provisions establish common rules.

3. The following EC policies may also be relevant to the UN Convention: Member States and the Community shall work towards developing a coordinated strategy

for employment. The Community shall contribute to the development of quality of education by encouraging cooperation between Member States and, if necessary, by supporting and supplementing their action. The Community shall implement a vocational training policy which shall support and supplement the action of the Member States. In order to promote its overall harmonious development, the Community shall develop and pursue its actions leading to the strengthening of its economic and social cohesion. The Community conducts a development cooperation policy and economic, financial and technical cooperation with third countries without prejudice to the respective competences of the Member States.

Annex III

Reservation by the European Community to Article 27(1) of the UN Convention on the Rights of Persons with Disabilities

The European Community states that pursuant to Community law (notably Council Directive 2000/78/EC of 27 November 2000 establishing a general framework for equal treatment in employment and occupation), the Member States may, if appropriate, enter their own reservations to Article 27(1) of the Disabilities Convention to the extent that Article 3(4) of the said Council Directive provides them with the **right to exclude non-discrimination on the grounds of disability with respect to employment in the armed forces from the scope of the Directive. Therefore, the Community states that it concludes the Convention without prejudice to the above right, conferred on its Member States by virtue of Community law.**

The declaration of the EU regarding its competences relevant to the CRPD includes a long appendix listing EU legislation (in total, 48 acts) which in some way relates to the matters covered by the Convention. The various EU acts are categorized in six groups: accessibility (eg Directive 95/16/EC on harmonization of laws relating to lifts); independent living and social inclusion, work, and employment (eg Directive 2006/54/EC on equal treatment of men and women in employment); personal mobility (eg Regulation (EC) No 1107/2006 on the rights of disabled persons when travelling by air); access to information (eg Directive 2007/65/EC on coordination of provisions concerning television broadcasting activities); statistics and data collection (eg Regulation (EC) No 458/2007 on the European system of integrated social protection statistics); and international cooperation (eg Regulation (EC) No 1905/2006 establishing a financing instrument for development cooperation).

The list of relevant EU legislation is particularly significant, as the EU possesses very few explicit exclusive competences in the issue areas most pertinent to the CRPD. Most of these competences—for example social policy, internal market, or non-discrimination—are rather shared with the Member States in the division established by the Treaties.[196] Therefore, it has been consistently held by the CJEU that the EU attains exclusive responsibility (competence) for parts of a treaty only when it had already previously exercised its shared competence as regards a given matter covered by the international agreement.[197] Not only that but also the legislation created by the EU in such an area must be *affected* by the treaty which in practice means that EU legislation laying down only minimum common standards—a regular

---

[196] See Article 4 TFEU which lists competences shared between the EU and Member States.
[197] See notably *Commission v Council (ERTA)* (n 181) para 22.

EU legislative practice in areas of shared competences—can be unaffected by the treaty in question (here the CRPD). If common EU rules are indeed unaffected, the Member States retain their competences and responsibility with respect to that part of the treaty. As a result, in order to determine for which parts of the CRPD the EU is exclusively responsible, it would be necessary to look at the individual provisions of existing EU secondary law—listed by the EU in its declaration but since extended and amended—to understand whether they can be affected by the Convention. Owing to the many shared competences at stake, the case of EU accession to and responsibility under the CRPD is a good example of why mixed agreements continue to represent such a contentious subject in both the study and practice of EU law.

At the same time as lodging its declaration and concluding the CRPD, the EU entered into a reservation with respect to the obligation of non-discrimination in employment on the grounds of disability required by Article 27(1) of the Convention.[198] More specifically, the EU's reservation safeguards the right of EU Member States under EU law (Article 3(4) of the Council Directive 2000/78/EC on equal treatment in employment and occupation) to exclude the application of non-discrimination on the grounds of disability to employment in the armed forces. Since such a reservation does not undermine the general 'object and purpose' of the CRPD, it is permissible under the Convention.[199]

One of the most important obligations imposed on the parties to the Convention, including the EU, is the general requirement to promote, protect, and monitor the implementation of the CRPD (Article 33). To this end, the CRPD obliges the contracting parties to create a framework containing at least one independent monitoring mechanism modelled upon the principles which provide for the independence and pluralism of national human rights institutions (NHRIs), also known as the Paris Principles.[200] The CRPD therefore also prescribes that civil society must be fully part of the monitoring mechanism. The Committee on the Rights of Persons with Disabilities elaborated in more detail its expectations of the frameworks in the 'Guidelines on independent monitoring frameworks and their participation in the work of the Committee'.[201]

The EU Framework for UN CRPD was enacted in 2013 and its operation was comprehensively reviewed by the FRA in an Opinion in 2016.[202] In accordance with the requirements set out in Article 33(2) of the CRPD, the Framework covers the fulfilment of the three tasks of promoting, protecting, and monitoring the implementation of the CRPD in matters of EU competence. As such, it is complementary to the EU Member States' national frameworks and monitoring mechanisms which in many cases have been entrusted to one of the established national human rights actors discussed in Chapter 2 such as NHRIs or ombudspersons. The three tasks are carried out in the context of two pillars of EU responsibilities: the first relates to the EU's legislative and policy competences transferred to the EU level by the Member States (as described in the EU's declaration to the CRPD), while the second

---

[198] The Vienna Convention on the Law of the Treaties defines reservations as 'a unilateral statement, however phrased or named, made by a State, when signing, ratifying, accepting, approving or acceding to a treaty, whereby it purports to exclude or to modify the legal effect of certain provisions of the treaty in their application to that State'. See Article 19 of the Vienna Convention on the Law of Treaties, 23 May 1969, 1155 UN Treaty Series 331.

[199] Pursuant to Article 46 of the CRPD, reservations which are incompatible with the object and purpose of the Convention are not permitted.

[200] See Ch 2 for a discussion of the Paris Principles in connection with NHRIs.

[201] Committee on the Rights of Persons with Disabilities, Guidelines on independent monitoring frameworks and their participation in the work of the Committee, adopted 2 September 2016 at 16th session.

[202] Opinion of the European Union Agency for Fundamental Rights concerning requirements under Article 33 (2) of the UN Convention on the Rights of Persons with Disabilities within the EU context, FRA Opinion 3/2016, Vienna, 13 May 2016.

covers the implementation of the CRPD in the EU's internal administration and exercise of Union public authority by its organs and personnel. Membership of the EU Framework is composed of the European Parliament, more specifically its Petitions Committee (PETI), the European Ombudsman, the European Commission (until 2015), the EU Agency for Fundamental Rights (FRA), and the European Disability Forum (EDF). All the members of the EU Framework are tasked with promoting, protecting, and monitoring the CRPD in their respective capacities. Especially as regards the latter two tasks, the competences to carry them out effectively vary considerably among the Framework members.

Council of the EU, Note on the set up of the EU-level Framework required by Art. 33.2 of the UN Convention on the Rights of Persons with Disabilities, 2012

(...)

The EU framework's mandate covers areas of EU competence, and it is a complement to **the national frameworks and independent mechanisms which bear the main responsibility** for the promotion, protection and monitoring of the UNCPRD in the Member States.

(...)

4.2.1 Compliance of the Member States with the Convention when implementing EU law

The protection of individuals against breaches of the Convention by the Member States when implementing EU law is **primarily a matter for the national frameworks and courts.** The EU framework's role in the protection of individuals' rights is complementary to the national frameworks.

The European Parliament's Petitions Committee (PETI) also contributes to the protection against Member States breaches of the Convention when implementing EU law as it can hear all **petitions from any EU citizen** on matters that come within the Union's field of activity and directly affect them (Art. 227 TFEU). The Committee is independent from the Member States and the Commission when carrying out this task.

The Commission can deal with citizens' complaints (as provided for in Art. 20 para 2.d TFEU), **monitor Member States' compliance with the Convention when implementing EU law** and start infringement proceedings in case of non-compliance within areas of EU competence (Art. 258 TFEU). In performing this task the Commission is independent from the Member States as defined in the Treaties.

4.2.2 Compliance of the EU institutions with the Convention

The monitoring of alleged **breaches of the Convention in the form of maladministration** in the activities of the EU institutions is primarily the task of the **European Ombudsman.** He can hear and investigate complaints raising issues of law and good administration as well as undertake ex officio investigations and produce reports (Article 228 TFEU). The European Ombudsman can investigate and report on possible maladministration by the Commission in the administrative phases of its complaints-handling and monitoring activity. The Ombudsman is independent from all the other EU institutions as well as from any Government, institution, body or office.

The European Parliament's Petitions Committee plays a broad protection role as regards compliance with the Convention by the EU **institutions in their policy-making and legislative actions, including when the EU institutions act in their public administration functions** (e.g. in staff cases). It hears petitions concerning EU legislation and policies and can table oral questions to the Council and the Commission for debate in the plenary, or issue reports and/or resolutions.

EDF receives information and complaints from persons with disabilities about their individual experiences, and brings these to the attention of the responsible administrations as well as the general public. EDF can write third party interventions to a number of national and European Courts.

4.3.1 Monitoring the implementation of the Convention by the EU institutions through EU law and policies

EDF independently performs systematic monitoring of the implementation of the Convention by the EU through law and policies, including by examining new legislative proposals, and receives complaints relating to their implementation. It can therefore assess progress, stagnation or retrogression in the enjoyment of rights over a certain period of time. The European Ombudsman complements the monitoring of the institutions' implementation of the Convention, as he can open own initiative inquiries and issue reports on instances of maladministration in the EU institutions and bodies, offices and agencies. **The implementation of the Convention by the EU through its law and policies is to some extent monitored in ex ante impact assessments prepared by Commission departments and examined by the Impact Assessment Board (IAB), a central quality control and support body operating independently of the Commission's policy making departments.** In particular, the Operational Guidance on taking account of fundamental rights in Commission Impact Assessments requires the verification of compliance with the UN Convention. Progress in this area could also be reported on in the Annual Report on the application of the Charter of Fundamental Rights.

4.3.2 Monitoring Member States' compliance with the Convention when implementing EU law

As a complement to the national frameworks and in accordance with the EU founding treaties, the Commission independently monitors how Member States implement and apply EU legislation falling within the scope of the Convention. This is done for instance in **Commission reports on the application of directives and regulations.** The Commission also addresses related matters in communications and staff working papers. Ultimately, the Commission can start infringement proceedings to ensure that EU legislation which puts the Convention into effect is correctly implemented.

4.3.3 Provision of data and development of indicators

The **FRA independently collects and analyses data within the limits of its mandate.** Providing such data in an independent manner will be its **main task in the framework.** In this context and in cooperation with the Commission, the FRA shall also develop indicators and benchmarks to support the monitoring process.

When it comes to the obligation to promote the CRPD, the members of the Framework use a variety of means to raise awareness of the Convention and encourage its broad implementation.

The Commission, which withdrew from the Framework in late 2015 following the publication of observations on the EU by the Committee on the Rights of Persons with Disabilities,[203] has supported mutual learning and exchange of good practices by organizing trainings for legal practitioners and policy-makers, information sessions for staff, an annual forum on the implementation of the CRPD for stakeholders and civil society, as well as an annual conference on the occasion of the European Day of Persons with Disabilities which is celebrated on 3 December. The European Ombudsman disseminates information regarding the CRPD through the European Network of Ombudsmen which comprises ombudsperson offices in 36 European countries. In addition, the annual activity report of the European Ombudsman contains a section dedicated to the CRPD.[204] Raising awareness of fundamental rights is also one of the general responsibilities of FRA according to its mandate;[205] this includes the rights of persons with disabilities and the CRPD specifically on which the FRA, among others, regularly reports and publishes other materials.[206] As the only civil society stakeholder in the Framework, the outreach of the EDF covers independent awareness-raising campaigns and media activities, as well as capacity-building of disability organizations and networks.

The EU Framework has also its own work programme and a secretariat and a chair who are chosen among the four members of the Framework and appointed for two years (currently the position of chair is held by the European Ombudsman, while the FRA is responsible for the Framework's secretariat). The role of the secretariat is to coordinate the organization of the Framework and prepare meetings which are led by the chair in the spirit of collegiality. The work programme for 2019–2020 contains 11 joint activities ranging from collecting promising practices to analysing draft legislation for compliance with the CRPD.[207] Although all four members of the Framework have responsibilities under the work programme, the crux of the workload falls to FRA and EDF. The EU Framework works towards developing synergies with the national frameworks and monitoring mechanisms which, as the EU consistently claims, bear the primary responsibility for the promotion, protection and monitoring of the implementation of the CRPD. The monitoring work is supplemented by a number of networks, some of which are organized at the European level, such as the CRPD Working Group of the European Network of National Human Rights Institutions (ENNHRI), the European Network of Equality Bodies (Equinet), and the European Network of Ombudsmen.

The international monitoring of the CRPD takes place at the level of the UN and belongs to the purview of the Committee on the Rights of Persons with Disabilities, set up under the Convention. The EU was subject to the periodical review process in 2015 following the European Commission's submission of the initial report on the implementation of the Convention in the EU in 2014, which the Committee subsequently considered and followed up with its concluding observations. The concluding observations of the Committee

---

[203] See Committee on the Rights of Persons with Disabilities, Concluding observations on the initial report of the European Union, CRPD/C/EU/CO/1, 2 October 2015, para 77.

[204] European Ombudsman, 'Annual Activity Report of the Principal Authorising Officer by Delegation, year 2018', 21–22.

[205] See Article 4(1)(h) of Council Regulation (EC) No 168/2007 establishing a European Union Agency for Fundamental Rights [2007] OJ L53/1.

[206] See, for example, EU Agency for Fundamental Rights, 'Fundamental Rights Report 2019', 227–37. Discrimination on the basis of disability is part of the thematic areas of FRA according to its Multiannual Framework. See Article 2(b) of Council Decision (EU) 2017/2269 establishing a Multiannual Framework for the European Union Agency for Fundamental Rights for 2018–2022 [2017] OJ L326/1.

[207] EU Framework to promote, protect and monitor the implementation of the CRPD: Work Programme 2019–2020, January 2019.

contained 94 paragraphs of which the vast majority were dedicated to criticism and recommendations as regards both general obligations and specific rights.

Committee on the Rights of Persons with Disabilities, Concluding observations on the initial report of the European Union, CRPD/C/EU/CO/1, 2 October 2015

4. The **Committee notes with appreciation** that the European Union is **the first regional organization to ratify a human rights treaty concluded under the auspices of the United Nations, thus setting a positive precedent in public international law.** The Committee notes the provisions of articles 21 and 26 of the Charter of Fundamental Rights of the European Union, which explicitly prohibit discrimination on the grounds of disability, and provides for equal participation of persons with disabilities in society. The Committee notes the positive trend to include the rights of persons with disabilities in the financing of its external actions, the inclusion of disability in priority areas of the European Union communication on the post-2015 Sustainable Development Goals, the adoption by the Council of the European Union of conclusions regarding the inclusion of persons with disabilities in disaster management and its commitment to the Sendai Framework for Disaster Risk Reduction 2015-2030

5. The Committee notes that for the 2014-2020 programming period, **the European Structural and Investment Funds Regulations contain provisions that reflect the entry into force of the Convention** and enhance the promotion of equality, non-discrimination, inclusion and accessibility for persons with disabilities through actions under the Funds.

7. The Committee calls upon the European Union to ratify the **Optional Protocol** to the Convention.

8. The Committee is concerned that **the European Union has failed to conduct a cross-cutting, comprehensive review of its legislation** aimed at harmonizing it with the Convention, and that no strategy on the implementation of the Convention across all its institutions exists.

12. The Committee is concerned that the **impact assessment guidelines only include one reference** relating to compliance with the Convention.

16. The Committee is concerned that **the declaration of competence further to article 44 of the Convention has not been updated and does not comprehensively refer to legislation** applicable to or affecting persons with disabilities.

28. The Committee is concerned that the **European Accessibility Act** has not yet been adopted by the European Union and that existing European policies, legislation, regulations and programmes have not been sufficiently assessed in respect of accessibility for persons with disabilities.

34. The Committee notes with deep concern the precarious situation of **persons with disabilities in the current migrant crisis in the European Union**. It is also concerned that refugees, migrants and asylum seekers with disabilities continue to be detained within the European Union in conditions which do not provide appropriate support and reasonable accommodation. The Committee is concerned that the migration decision-making procedure is not accessible for all persons with

disabilities and that information and communication are not provided in accessible formats.

46. The Committee is concerned that persons with disabilities are exposed to **involuntary treatment, including forced sterilization and abortion**, in European Union **member States**.

56. The Committee is concerned that **austerity measures have resulted in cuts in social services and support to families and community-based services**, among others, which restrict the right of persons with disabilities to family life, and the right of children with disabilities to live in family settings.

71. The Committee encourages the European Union to take all appropriate measures to ratify and implement the **Marrakesh Treaty** as soon as possible.

72. The Committee is concerned at the **lack of consistent and comparable data** on persons with disabilities in the European Union, and the lack of human rights indicators.

74. The Committee notes with concern the **lack of a systematic and institutionalized approach to mainstream the rights of persons with disabilities across all European Union international cooperation policies and programmes**. The Committee also notes the lack of coordination and coherence among European Union institutions and the lack of disability focal points. It is also concerned that **European Union international development funding is used to create or renovate institutional settings for the placement of persons with disabilities, segregated special education schools and sheltered workshops**, contrary to the principles and provisions of the Convention.

77. The Committee recommends that the European Union take measures to **decouple the roles of the European Commission in the implementation and monitoring of the Convention**, by removing it from the independent monitoring framework, so as to ensure **full compliance with the Paris Principles**, and ensure that the framework has **adequate resources** to perform its functions. The Committee also recommends that the European Union consider the establishment of an inter-institutional co-ordination mechanism and the designation of focal points in each European Union institution, agency and body.

88. The Committee is concerned that **European Union institutions are not role models** with regard to employment of persons with disabilities.

The types of concerns and recommendations expressed by the Committee were multifarious. Some were more general in nature (eg comprehensive review of legislation), others very specific and concrete (eg ratification of the Marrakesh Treaty) but on the whole the observations of the Committee are clearly comprehensive. Some concerns, such as the one on forced sterilization and abortion (paragraph 46), relate to an issue existing at the level of some EU Member States and it is not obvious whether the EU is in a position to effectively address them within the boundaries of its competences. It should be borne in mind that the Member States' implementation of the CRPD is subject to an independent individual review by the Committee.

As mentioned previously, one of the consequential recommendations of the Committee was to remove the Commission from the EU Framework in light of the Paris Principles and the requirement of independence. The Committee took issue with the Commission being both an EU focal point for the implementation of the CRPD pursuant to Article 33(1) of the Convention and a member of the independent monitoring framework prescribed by

Article 33(2). As a consequence, the Commission withdrew from the EU Framework in late 2015. The Commission's responsiveness to this point is laudable, especially as the status of FRA with respect to fundamental rights in general remains non-compliant with the Paris Principles.[208] However, as the FRA itself points out, the EU Framework should be further strengthened by basing it on a legally binding Union act which should, among others, empower its members, especially the European Ombudsman and the FRA, to issue opinions on relevant draft EU legislation on their own initiative.[209] This would represent a more serious reform of the EU Framework than the mere withdrawal of one of its members and there is little evidence in view of the circumscribed mandates of both the European Ombudsman and the FRA that political appetite for a change towards more independent human rights oversight exists in the EU.

The overall result of EU accession to the CRPD is multilevel implementation and monitoring of the Convention involving governmental and civil society actors across all levels. National frameworks are complemented by the EU Framework and both are kept in check by the UN Committee through periodic review. The combined institutional and legal structures in the area of disability—which lest it be forgotten requires constant political, economic, and societal backing to translate into concrete progress on the ground—represent the standard expected of the EU in other thematic areas of fundamental rights as well.

Another international agreement—the ratification of which was also recommended by the CRPD Committee—capable of bolstering the legal framework for the benefit of persons with disabilities is the Marrakesh Treaty to Facilitate Access to Published Works for Persons Who Are Blind, Visually Impaired or Otherwise Print Disabled. The impetus to adopt this treaty was linked to the previously agreed CRPD which requires its contracting parties to take measures reducing barriers to access by persons with disabilities to copyrighted materials.[210] Although such enabling measures have already existed in the domestic legal orders of a number of countries—in the EU in accordance with discretion available under Directive 2001/29[211]—there was no commonly agreed international framework on exceptions and limitations to copyright and the cross-border transfer of accessible works, which in particular disadvantaged visually impaired persons in developing countries who have for a long time been experiencing a 'book famine'.[212] After years of negotiations, which have seen a variety of proposals for a non-binding international framework (including from the EU) rejected,[213] a binding treaty was adopted in Marrakesh in 2013 under the auspices of the

[208] See Ch 2.
[209] Opinion of the European Union Agency for Fundamental Rights concerning requirements under Article 33 (2) of the UN Convention on the Rights of Persons with Disabilities within the EU context, FRA Opinion 3/2016, Vienna, 13 May 2016, 4.
[210] Article 30(3) of the CRPD states that 'States Parties shall take all appropriate steps, in accordance with international law, to ensure that laws protecting intellectual property rights do not constitute an unreasonable or discriminatory barrier to access by persons with disabilities to cultural materials'. The right to take part in cultural life enshrined in Article 15(1)(a) of the International Covenant on Economic, Social and Cultural Rights (ICESCR) also played an important part in the pursuit of the Marrakesh Treaty. See C Sganga, 'Disability, Right to Culture and Copyright: Which Regulatory Option?' (2015) 29 International Review of Law, Computers and Technology 88.
[211] See Article 5(3)(b) of Directive 2001/29/EC of the European Parliament and of the Council on the harmonisation of certain aspects of copyright and related rights in the information society [2001] OJ L167/10.
[212] K Köklü, 'The Marrakesh Treaty—Time to End the Book Famine for Visually Impaired Persons Worldwide' (2014) 45 International Review of Intellectual Property and Competition Law 737.
[213] See World Intellectual Property Organization, 'Draft Joint Recommendation Concerning the Improved Access to Works Protected by Copyright for Persons with a Print Disability, Proposal by the Delegation of the European Union', SCCR/20/12, 17 June 2010; S Vezzoso, 'The Marrakesh Spirit—A Ghost in Three Steps?' (2014) 45 International Review of Intellectual Property and Competition Law 796; Sganga, 'Disability, Right to Culture and Copyright: Which Regulatory Option?' (n 210) 99.

World Intellectual Property Organization (WIPO), a self-funding UN agency. The Treaty, representing a rare achievement by enmeshing intellectual property and human rights,[214] entered into force on 30 June 2016 and has been to date ratified or acceded to by 64 states not counting the EU. With the ratification of the Treaty by the Union in October 2018, its provisions became binding on all 27 (then 28) EU Member States as well.

After signing the Marrakesh Treaty in 2014, the EU has taken over four years to ratify it and introduce amending legislation which aims to bring EU and Member States intellectual property rules in line with the mandatory exceptions and limitations on copyright required by the Marrakesh Treaty.[215] The ratification was delayed because of a legal dispute concerning the proper legal basis for EU action and the nature of the competence (shared or exclusive). The dispute was ultimately resolved by the CJEU in *Opinion 3/15* where the Court found the EU to possess exclusive competence to conclude the Marrakesh Treaty, despite rejecting the argument of, among others, the Commission and of the AG that common commercial policy (Article 207 TFEU) should be part of the legal basis for the EU's conclusion of the agreement.[216]

Opinion of 14 February 2017, *Marrakesh Treaty to Facilitate Access to Published Works*, 3/15, ECLI:EU:C:2017:114

---

61. According to the Court's settled case-law, **the mere fact that an EU act is liable to have implications for international trade is not enough for it to be concluded that the act must be classified as falling within the common commercial policy.** On the other hand, an EU act falls within that policy if it relates specifically to international trade in that it is essentially intended to promote, facilitate or govern trade and has direct and immediate effects on trade (...)

62. In order to determine **whether the Marrakesh Treaty falls within the common commercial policy**, it is necessary to examine both the **purpose of that treaty and its content.**

82. (...) **the purpose of the Marrakesh Treaty** is to improve the position of beneficiary persons by facilitating, through various means, the access of such persons to published works; it **is not to promote, facilitate or govern international trade in accessible format copies.**

85. Moreover, the Commission's argument that, of the rules governing intellectual property, only those relating to moral rights are not encompassed by the concept of 'commercial aspects of intellectual property', as referred to in Article 207 TFEU, cannot be accepted, as **it would lead to an excessive extension of the field covered**

---

[214] L Helfer, 'Human Rights and Intellectual Property: Mapping an Evolving and Contested Relationship' in RC Dreyfuss and J Pila (eds), *The Oxford Handbook of Intellectual Property Law* (Oxford University Press 2018).

[215] Directive (EU) 2017/1564 of the European Parliament and of the Council on certain permitted uses of certain works and other subject matter protected by copyright and related rights for the benefit of persons who are blind, visually impaired or otherwise print-disabled and amending Directive 2001/29/EC on the harmonisation of certain aspects of copyright and related rights in the information society [2017] OJ L242/6; Regulation (EU) 2017/1563 of the European Parliament and of the Council on the cross-border exchange between the Union and third countries of accessible format copies of certain works and other subject matter protected by copyright and related rights for the benefit of persons who are blind, visually impaired or otherwise print-disabled [2017] OJ L242/1.

[216] *Opinion 3/15 (Marrakesh Treaty to Facilitate Access to Published Works)* [2016] ECLI:EU:C:2016:657, Opinion of AG Wahl.

by the common commercial policy by bringing within that policy rules that have no specific link with international trade.

97. It is thus apparent not only that **the cross-border exchange promoted by the Marrakesh Treaty is outside the normal framework of international trade** but also that the international trade in accessible format copies which might be engaged in by ordinary operators for commercial purposes, or simply outside the framework of exceptions or limitations for beneficiary persons, is not included in the special scheme established by that treaty.

100. (...) **the mere fact that the scheme** introduced by the Marrakesh Treaty may possibly apply to works which are, or may be, commercially exploited and that it **may,** in that event, **indirectly affect international trade** in such works **does not mean that it is within the ambit of the common commercial policy** (...)

101. It must therefore be held that the conclusion of **the Marrakesh Treaty does not fall within the common commercial policy** defined in Article 207 TFEU and, consequently, that the European Union **does not have exclusive competence under Article 3(1)(e) TFEU** to conclude that treaty.

102. Pursuant to Article 3(2) TFEU, **the European Union has exclusive competence for the conclusion of an international agreement when** its conclusion is provided for in a legislative act of the Union or is necessary to enable the Union to exercise its internal competence, or in so far as **its conclusion may affect common rules or alter their scope.**

105. (...) the Court has held that **there is a risk that common EU rules may be adversely affected by international commitments undertaken by the Member States,** or that the scope of those rules may be altered, which is such as to **justify an exclusive external competence of the European Union,** where those commitments fall within the scope of those rules (...)

107. In particular, such international commitments may affect EU rules or alter their scope when the commitments fall within **an area which is already covered to a large extent by such rules** (...)

108. That said, since the EU is vested only with conferred powers, any competence, especially where it is exclusive, must have its basis in conclusions drawn from a **comprehensive and detailed analysis of the relationship between the international agreement envisaged and the EU law in force.** That analysis must take into account the areas covered, respectively, by the rules of EU law and by the provisions of the agreement envisaged, their foreseeable future development and the nature and content of those rules and those provisions, in order to determine **whether the agreement is capable of undermining the uniform and consistent application of the EU rules** and the proper functioning of the system which they establish (...)

110. Articles 2 to 4 of Directive 2001/29 confer on authors the exclusive right to authorise or prohibit the reproduction, communication to the public and distribution of works.

111. Furthermore, **Article 5(3)(b) of Directive 2001/29 specifies that Member States may opt to provide for an exception or limitation to the rights of reproduction and communication** to the public in respect of 'uses, for the benefit of people with a disability, which are directly related to the disability and of a non-commercial nature, to the extent required by the specific disability'. It follows from Article 5(4) of the directive that Member States may also provide for an exception or limitation to the right of

distribution to the extent that such an exception or limitation is justified by the purpose of the act of reproduction authorised under Article 5(3)(b) of the directive.

112. It follows that **the exception or limitation provided for by the Marrakesh Treaty will have to be implemented within the field harmonised by Directive 2001/29. The same is true of the import and export arrangements** prescribed by that treaty, inasmuch as they are ultimately intended to permit the communication to the public or the distribution, in the territory of a Contracting Party, of accessible format copies published in another Contracting Party, without the consent of the rightholders being obtained.

113. Although a number of the governments that have submitted observations to the Court have maintained in this connection that the obligations laid down by the Marrakesh Treaty could be implemented in a manner that is compatible with Directive 2001/29, it should be observed that, according to the Court's settled case-law, **Member States may not enter, outside the framework of the EU institutions, into international commitments falling within an area that is already covered to a large extent by common EU rules, even if there is no possible contradiction between those commitments and the common EU rules** (...)

126. (...) it is apparent that whilst the Member States have the option of implementing, for the benefit of persons with a disability, an exception or limitation to the harmonised rules set out in Articles 2 to 4 of Directive 2001/29, **that option is granted by the EU legislature and is highly circumscribed by the requirements of EU law** (...)

127. It is important to point out in this regard that, whilst **Article 5(3)(b) of Directive 2001/29 provides only for an option** allowing the Member States to introduce an exception or limitation for beneficiary persons, **Article 4 of the Marrakesh Treaty lays down an obligation** to introduce such an exception or limitation.

128. Consequently, the conclusion of the Marrakesh Treaty would mean that **the various constraints and requirements imposed by EU law (...) will apply to all the Member States**, which would henceforth be required to provide for such an exception or limitation under Article 4 of that treaty.

129. Accordingly, **the body of obligations laid down by the Marrakesh Treaty falls within an area that is already covered to a large extent by common EU rules and the conclusion of that treaty may thus affect those rules or alter their scope.**

130. It follows from the foregoing considerations that the conclusion of the Marrakesh Treaty falls within the **exclusive competence of the European Union.**

The CJEU first disposed of the notion that the common commercial policy covered intellectual property rules when these are principally of a non-commercial nature, such as exceptions and limitations on intellectual property and its cross-border exchange for the benefit of persons with disabilities. The fact that indirectly some international trade in commercial works could be affected was not in itself sufficient to justify the extension of the common commercial policy to the Marrakesh Treaty and its rules and exceptions on intellectual property rights. The EU therefore did not have exclusive competence pursuant to Article 3(1)(e) TFEU to conclude the Marrakesh Treaty.

In the second place, the CJEU examined the EU's competence to conclude the Marrakesh Treaty under Article 3(2) TFEU which is a codification of the *ERTA* doctrine regarding implied powers.[217] More specifically in the case at hand, the third alternative espoused by Article

---

[217] *Commission v Council (ERTA)* (n 181).

3(2) TFEU—that the EU has exclusive competence to conclude a treaty when it may 'affect common rules or alter their scope'—had to be considered due to the existence of Directive 2001/29 which regulated in EU law the matters covered by the Marrakesh Treaty. In line with its established case law,[218] the CJEU conducted a 'comprehensive analysis' of the relationship between the Marrakesh Treaty and the relevant provisions of Directive 2001/29. In the analysis, the Court essentially looks at two aspects: the extent to which the international and EU rules overlap, and the risk of EU rules being affected by the treaty in question. In the case of the Marrakesh Treaty, the CJEU found that the provisions of the international agreement would be implemented within the field harmonized by Directive 2001/29 (overlap) and that the EU rules would probably be affected by the Marrakesh Treaty, especially as the optional copyright exception permitted by Article 5(3)(b) of the Directive would turn into a mandatory obligation for the Member States post-accession.[219] The CJEU hence established that the conclusion of the Marrakesh Treaty falls within the exclusive competence of the EU in accordance with the third limb of Article 3(2) TFEU. The effect of such exclusivity is that the Member States 'no longer have the right, acting individually or even collectively, to undertake obligations with third countries which affect those rules'.[220]

While *Opinion 3/15* settled the question of whether the EU's competence to conclude the agreement is shared or exclusive, the CJEU was not asked to engage with the question of the correct legal basis for the Council Decision on the conclusion of the Marrakesh Treaty. The choice of legal basis remained still important notwithstanding the exclusive competence of the EU to enter into the Treaty, as the internal EU procedure for the conclusion of the Treaty varies as per different provisions of the EU Treaties. Whereas, for example, Article 19 TFEU on the EU's legislative competence in the area of non-discrimination (including on the grounds of disability) follows the special legislative procedure requiring unanimity in the Council, Article 114 TFEU on the approximation of laws in the internal market follows the ordinary legislative procedure with qualified majority voting in the Council and greater involvement of the European Parliament. In the end, the Marrakesh Treaty was concluded solely on the basis of Article 114 TFEU,[221] which entailed the consent of the Parliament, and the implementing Directive and Regulation too were based on this provision, thus granting the Parliament a full role in the legislative process.

---

[218] See, for example, Opinion of 14 October 2014, *Accession of third states to the 1980 Hague Convention*, 1/13, ECLI:EU:C:2014:2303.

[219] The Court rejected the argument of a number of Member States who claimed that because the obligation laid down by the Marrakesh Treaty to provide copyright exceptions could be accommodated by virtue of Article 5(3)(b) of Directive 2001/29 they should be allowed to enter into the Treaty themselves. The CJEU held that the competence is exclusively the Union's, as the optional copyright exception is granted by EU law and its exercise is in any case circumscribed by other paragraphs of Article 5 of the Directive. In addition, the mandatory character of the copyright exception under the Marrakesh Treaty would alter the legal status quo under EU law whereby not all Member States decided to implement the optional copyright exception pursuant to Article 5(3)(b) of the Directive for the benefit of persons with disabilities.

[220] *Commission v Council (ERTA)* (n 181) para 17.

[221] Council Decision EU/2018/254 on the conclusion on behalf of the European Union of the Marrakesh Treaty to Facilitate Access to Published Works for Persons who are Blind, Visually Impaired, or otherwise Print Disabled [2018] OJ L48/1.

6

Fundamental Rights in EU Competition Enforcement

6.1 Introduction

Competition policy belongs to the most traditional and strongest exclusive internal policies of the EU.[1] Article 3(1)(g) of the E(E)C Treaty prohibited the distortion of competition in the internal market (originally the 'common market'). That provision remained in the same place in the Treaties until the revision by the Treaty of Lisbon, when France negotiated its removal from the main body of the EU's constitutional charter; the commitment to undistorted competition was instead moved to Protocol No 27.

PROTOCOL (No 27) ON THE INTERNAL MARKET AND COMPETITION

THE HIGH CONTRACTING PARTIES,

CONSIDERING that **the internal market as set out in Article 3 of the Treaty on European Union includes a system ensuring that competition is not distorted,**

HAVE AGREED that:

To this end, the Union shall, if necessary, take action under the provisions of the Treaties, including under Article 352 of the Treaty on the Functioning of the European Union.

This protocol shall be annexed to the Treaty on European Union and to the Treaty on the Functioning of the European Union.

In a development telling of the significance of competition law for the EU as an entity, the Court of Justice of the European Union (CJEU) found opportunity to comment on the Treaty change inspired by long-standing French suspicions towards competition law as primarily an import of German economic thinking known as ordoliberalism which constrains the margin of manoeuvre of government economic interventions.[2] In the Court's view, as well as in the Commission's,[3] the relegation of the competition provision to Protocol No 27

---

[1] The EU's exclusive competence in competition matters is provided for by Article 3(1)(b) TFEU.

[2] The influence of ordoliberal ideology on the development and practice of EU competition law is an often cited but misunderstood point. See KK Patel and H Schweitzer (eds), *The Historical Foundations of EU Competition Law* (Oxford University Press 2013); PJ Cardwell and H Snaith, '"There's a Brand New Talk, but it's Not Very Clear": Can the Contemporary EU Really be Characterized as Ordoliberal?' (2018) 56 Journal of Common Market Studies 1053; M Vatiero, 'The Ordoliberal Notion of Market Power' (2010) 6 European Competition Journal 689.

[3] Statement by European Commissioner for Competition Neelie Kroes on results of June 21–22 European Council—Protocol on Internal Market and Competition, MEMO 07/250, 23 June 2007, Commission: 'An Internal Market without competition rules would be an empty shell—nice words, but no concrete results. The Protocol on Internal Market and Competition agreed at the European Council clearly repeats that competition policy is

The European Union and Human Rights. Jan Wouters and Michal Ovádek, Oxford University Press (2021). © Jan Wouters and Michal Ovádek. DOI: 10.1093/oso/9780198814177.003.0006

changed nothing about the fundamental character of the competence and the rules in the Union legal order.

Judgment of 17 November 2011, *Commission v Italy*, C-496/09, ECLI:EU:C:2011:740

60. As to the seriousness of the infringement, **the vital nature of the Treaty rules on competition must be recalled,** in particular those on State aid, **which are the expression of one of the essential tasks with which the European Union is entrusted.** At the time of the Court's assessment of the appropriateness and the amount of the present penalty payment, that vital nature is apparent from Article 3(3) TEU, namely the establishment of an internal market, **and from Protocol No 27 on the internal market and competition, which forms an integral part of the Treaties in accordance with Article 51 TEU, and states that the internal market includes a system ensuring that competition is not distorted.**

Having been used to reinforce the market integration objective of the EU,[4] among other things, the rationale of competition policy today is linked predominantly to the notion of consumer welfare, despite the fact that the latter does not feature as the sole standard against which anticompetitive practices are judged in the CJEU's case law.[5] The lack of complete consensus on applying the consumer welfare standard has to do with potentially contending objectives of competition law, such as protecting 'the structure of the market and, in so doing, competition as such'.[6] This is in turn based on the belief that the long-term benefits of safeguarding the structure of the market through the 'maintenance of effective competition' may outweigh potential gains which can be achieved in a given case by looking at the immediate effects on consumer welfare, however broadly construed.[7]

EU competition policy comprises a number of limbs, each with its own peculiarities and rules but together contributing to the objective of protecting (relatively) undistorted competition in the Union's internal market. The first and most orthodox aspect of competition law is the prohibition of agreements and concerted practices restricting competition, mostly known in the form of cartel agreements.[8] Second, the Treaty on the Functioning of the

---

fundamental to the Internal Market. It retains the existing competition rules which have served us so well for 50 years. It re-confirms the European Commission's duties as the independent competition enforcement authority for Europe.'

[4] See Judgment of 13 July 1966, *Établissements Consten S.à.R.L. and Grundig-Verkaufs-GmbH v Commission*, 56/64 and 58/64, ECLI:EU:C:1966:41.

[5] A Jones and B Sufrin, *EU Competition Law: Text, Cases, and Materials* (6th edn, Oxford University Press 2016) 42.

[6] Judgment of 6 October 2009, *GlaxoSmithKline Services and Others v Commission and Others*, C-501/06 P, C-513/06 P, C-515/06 P, and C-519/06 P, ECLI:EU:C:2009:610, para 63. See also L Lovdahl Gormesen, 'The Conflict between Economic Freedom and Consumer Welfare in the Modernisation of Article 82' (2007) 3 European Competition Journal 329.

[7] Judgment of 21 February 1973, *Europemballage Corporation and Continental Can Company*, 6/72, ECLI:EU:C:1973:22, para 25. In EU competition law, the term 'consumer' should be understood as subsuming both intermediate and ultimate consumers; it does not (only) refer to private end-users and their welfare. See Article 2(1)(b) of the Council Regulation (EC) No 139/2004 on the control of concentrations between undertakings [2004] OJ L24/1 ('Merger Regulation').

[8] Article 101 TFEU.

European Union (TFEU) forbids the abuse of dominant position in cases where undertakings (EU jargon for companies, broadly defined)[9] possess too much market power.[10] Third, EU law guards the internal market against distortion of competition owing to mergers of large companies.[11] Fourth, EU rules on State aid ensure that Member States do not distort competition by providing financial or other distorting support to companies.[12] Fifth, the EU promotes liberalization of services of general economic interest, such as telecommunications, energy, and transport, which are often in the hands of the Member States' governments, by enacting EU legislation and enforcing common rules.[13]

Nevertheless, the key reason why EU competition policy is an interesting and important case study from the point of view of fundamental rights application is enforcement.[14] Unlike in other areas, the EU, in particular the European Commission, wields considerable powers when it comes to the protection of undistorted competition in the internal market. Although the extent of the enforcement powers and their potential impact on fundamental rights differ between the various aspects of competition policy, the field as a whole embodies supranational authority as almost none other does.[15] This is so despite the fact that in enforcing competition law the Commission cooperates closely with national competition authorities (NCAs) as part of the European Competition Network (ECN) and that the majority of decisions applying EU antitrust rules are taken by the NCAs.[16]

6.2 Competition Enforcement in the EU

The impact of EU competition enforcement is felt directly, and often very significantly,[17] by individual legal persons. This increases both the demands placed on the responsible EU enforcement actor (the Commission) to ensure fundamental rights are observed in all

---

[9] See Judgment of 23 April 1991, *Klaus Höfner and Fritz Elser v Macrotron*, C-41/90, ECLI:EU:C:1991:161, para 21: 'the concept of an undertaking encompasses every entity engaged in an economic activity, regardless of the legal status of the entity'.

[10] Article 102 TFEU.

[11] Most importantly by applying the Merger Regulation.

[12] Articles 107–109 TFEU. State aid law is often treated separately from the first three issues which are at the core of competition law proper—in the US commonly known as antitrust law—with similar enforcement procedures (especially Articles 101 and 102 TFEU). Although it relates to governmental actions rather than those of private entities, the ultimate objective of EU State aid regulation is largely the same: to ensure undistorted competition in the internal market. At the international level, EU State aid law finds an analogy in the anti-subsidies framework of the World Trade Organization (WTO).

[13] See, for example, Directive 2009/72/EC of the European Parliament and of the Council concerning common rules for the internal market in electricity and repealing Directive 2003/54/EC [2009] OJ L211/55.

[14] See A Andreangeli, *EU Competition Enforcement and Human Rights* (Edward Elgar Publishing 2008) for a still-relevant monograph on this issue; see also T Bombois, *La protection des droits fondamentaux des entreprises en droit européen répressif de la concurrence* (Larcier 2012).

[15] Despite being an exclusive competence, competition laws and policies also exist at national level in EU Member States. The CJEU has consistently held that EU and national competition laws apply in parallel without their areas of application coinciding. See Judgment of 14 February 2012, *Toshiba Corporation and Others v Úřad pro ochranu hospodářské soutěže*, C-17/10, ECLI:EU:C:2012:72, para 81 and the case law cited.

[16] The consistency of EU competition enforcement is strengthened not only through cooperation and coordination but also by virtue of the fact that basic competition (particularly antitrust) rules are very similar, sometimes to the letter, at both the EU and national levels. That is not to say, however, that national laws may not introduce additional rules—within the limits set by relevant EU laws, especially as regards the internal market—such as on the criminalization of certain anticompetitive behaviours.

[17] See, for example, the EUR 2.42 billion fine imposed on Google for abusing dominance by giving advantage to its comparison shopping service. Commission Decision of 27 June 2017 relating to proceedings under Article 102 of the Treaty on the Functioning of the European Union and Article 54 of the Agreement on the European Economic Area (Case AT.39740, *Google Search (Shopping)*).

stages of the enforcement procedures and the overall risk of fundamental rights infringe-ments occurring. As a rare instance of direct EU enforcement against individuals,[18] com-petition enforcement can be—and often is—challenged before the EU courts which are equally charged with ensuring the protection of fundamental rights. Competition law cases represent a significant strain on the EU courts, especially the General Court which has first-instance jurisdiction in direct actions pursuant to Article 256 TFEU, due to their exceptional complexity requiring considerable judicial resources.[19] When at one point the length of pre-dominantly competition cases started to amount to a breach of individuals' right to a trial without undue delay resulting in potentially costly damages for the EU (see section 6.6), the Member States decided to double the number of General Court judges.[20] As competition law is in the first place enforced through administrative action, the European Ombudsman is also entitled to entertain complaints directed against the Commission's conduct in competi-tion proceedings.

Enforcement of each of the different limbs of competition policy follows a specific pro-cedure with some shared features especially in antitrust matters (cartels, abuse of dominant position, and, to a lesser degree, mergers). The key common denominator in all of them is the central and multifarious role of the Commission. One of the particular features of the Commission's regulatory and enforcement role in the area of competition is recourse to soft law instruments—the Commission has issued a considerable number of guidelines and no-tices which are per se not legally binding but nonetheless have the objective of increasing predictability and transparency of the Commission's activities, be it the setting of fines,[21] defining the relevant market,[22] or many others. Despite their 'soft' character, these instru-ments have very real impacts on the behaviour of undertakings and enforcers alike and raise a number of thought-provoking and practical questions in the field.[23]

The following paragraphs briefly introduce the relevant EU competition provisions and sketch out the most important elements of enforcement of four domains of competi-tion policy where enforcement can lead directly to fundamental rights complaints. The first subsection on Article 101 TFEU covers a number of general issues of competition law and

---

[18] As opposed to, for example, general enforcement of EU law compliance against Member States through in-fringement proceedings.

[19] See the length of, for example, Judgment of 17 September 2007, *Microsoft v Commission*, T-201/04, ECLI:EU:T:2007:289 running to almost 1,400 paragraphs.

[20] See Regulation 2015/2422 of the European Parliament and of the Council amending Protocol No 3 on the Statute of the Court of Justice of the European Union [2015] OJ L341/14. See also recital (3) of the Regulation: 'The situation in which the General Court finds itself has causes relating, inter alia, to the increase in the number and variety of legal acts of the institutions, bodies, offices and agencies of the Union, as well as to the volume and complexity of the cases brought before the General Court, particularly in the areas of competition, State aid and intellectual property.' For a critical appraisal of the judicial reform see A Alemanno and L Pech, 'Thinking Justice Outside the Docket: A Critical Assessment of the Reform of the EU's Court System' (2017) 54 Common Market Law Review 129. It should be noted that proposals calling for the setting up of a specialist competition tribunal in line with Article 257 TFEU were not followed by the EU legislators. For one such proposal see D Hadroušek and M Smolek, 'Solving the EU's General Court' (2015) 40 European Law Review 188.

[21] Guidelines on the method of setting fines imposed pursuant to Article 23(2)(a) of Regulation No 1/2003 [2006] OJ C210/02.

[22] Commission Notice on the Definition of the Relevant Market for the Purposes of Community Competition Law [1997] OJ C372/5.

[23] See, for example, M Cini, 'The Soft Law Approach: Commission Rule-Making in the EU's State Aid Regime' (2001) 8 Journal of European Public Policy 192; N Petit and M Rato, *From Hard to Soft Enforcement of EC Competition Law* (Bruylant 2008); O Stefan, *Soft Law in Court: Competition Law, State Aid and the Court of Justice of the European Union* (Kluwer Law International 2012); Z Georgieva, 'Soft Law in EU Competition Law and Its Judicial Reception in Member States: A Theoretical Perspective' (2015) 16 German Law Journal 223.

enforcement by the Commission which are also applicable to provisions on the abuse of a dominant position and merger control. Enforcement of market liberalizing measures (the fifth limb of competition policy in the abovementioned overview) is omitted, as it relies primarily on tools of a general character such as infringement proceedings under Article 258 TFEU which are in any case concerned in the first place with the duties of the Member States. It should be borne in mind that the following is little more than a taste of a vast and dynamic field of EU law.

A. Agreements restricting competition (Article 101 TFEU) and antitrust enforcement in general

---

Consolidated version of the Treaty on the Functioning of the European Union [2012] OJ C326/47

Article 101

1. The following shall be **prohibited as incompatible with the internal market**: all **agreements between undertakings**, decisions by associations of undertakings and **concerted practices which may affect trade between Member States and which have as their object or effect the prevention, restriction or distortion of competition within the internal market**, and in particular those which:
   (a) directly or indirectly fix purchase or selling prices or any other trading conditions;
   (b) limit or control production, markets, technical development, or investment;
   (c) share markets or sources of supply;
   (d) apply dissimilar conditions to equivalent transactions with other trading parties, thereby placing them at a competitive disadvantage;
   (e) make the conclusion of contracts subject to acceptance by the other parties of supplementary obligations which, by their nature or according to commercial usage, have no connection with the subject of such contracts.
2. Any agreements or decisions prohibited pursuant to this Article shall be automatically void.
3. The provisions of paragraph 1 may, however, be declared inapplicable in the case of:
   — any agreement or category of agreements between undertakings,
   — any decision or category of decisions by associations of undertakings,
   — any concerted practice or category of concerted practices,

which contributes to improving the production or distribution of goods or to promoting technical or economic progress, while allowing consumers a fair share of the resulting benefit, and which does not:

(a) impose on the undertakings concerned restrictions which are not indispensable to the attainment of these objectives;
(b) afford such undertakings the possibility of eliminating competition in respect of a substantial part of the products in question.

Article 101 TFEU covers the most traditional forms of competition distortion which take place through express or tacit agreements or concerted practices between undertakings. The first paragraph includes a list of the most notoriously damaging practices for competition, sometimes also referred to as 'hard-core' restrictions, which almost invariably lead to a finding of breach of Article 101 TFEU by the competent authorities if these represent the 'object' of the agreement.[24] In such cases, the enforcing authorities may forego an analysis of the actual effects of the competition-restricting agreement because of the harmfulness, by their very nature, to the 'proper functioning of normal competition'.[25] Other anticompetitive practices can be justified provided that they comply with the criteria listed in the third paragraph of Article 101 TFEU or in case they fall under one of the block exemptions.[26] In general, vertical agreements (between companies on different levels of the supply chain) are more likely to satisfy the exemption criteria than horizontal agreements (between competitors).[27] Moreover, in the view of the Commission, the scope of Article 101(1) TFEU does not cover agreements of minor importance which do not restrict competition by effect to an appreciable extent. The Commission therefore does not pursue investigations into such agreements, in accordance with the thresholds and conditions set out in its 'De Minimis Notice'.[28]

Establishing the existence of an anticompetitive agreement or concerted practice can be fiendishly difficult. Nearly every aspect of the provisions laid down by Article 101 TFEU has been heavily litigated and disputed by affected undertakings and enforcers alike which is not surprising in view of the often enormous stakes involved. The litigation has among others prompted the CJEU to lay down a robust definition of what constitutes an agreement and concerted practice. The basic idea is that unilateral conduct of undertakings is not covered by Article 101 TFEU,[29] but coordination in any form can be.

---

[24] In the words of the CJEU, 'where the anti-competitive object of the agreement is established it is not necessary to examine its effects on competition'. See Judgment of 26 November 2015, *Maxima Latvija*, C-345/14, ECLI:EU:C:2015:784, para 17.

[25] Judgment of 11 September 2014, *Groupement des cartes bancaires (CB) v Commission*, C-67/13 P, ECLI:EU:C:2014:2204, para 50. However, 'object' restrictions of competition 'must be interpreted restrictively and can be applied only to certain types of coordination between undertakings which reveal a sufficient degree of harm to competition that it may be found that there is no need to examine their effects'. See *Maxima Latvija* (n 24) para 18.

[26] Commission Regulation (EU) No 330/2010 on the application of Article 101(3) of the Treaty on the Functioning of the European Union to categories of vertical agreements and concerted practices [2010] OJ L102/1; Commission Regulation (EU) No 316/2014 on the application of Article 101(3) of the Treaty on the Functioning of the European Union to categories of technology transfer agreements [2014] OJ L93/17; Commission Regulation (EU) No 1217/2010 on the application of Article 101(3) of the Treaty on the Functioning of the European Union to certain categories of research and development agreements [2010] OJ L335/36.

[27] There are recognized circumstances in which horizontal agreements can be permitted, such as cooperation on research and development. See Commission Regulation (EU) No 1217/2010 (n 26).

[28] Notice on agreements of minor importance which do not appreciably restrict competition under Article 101(1) of the Treaty on the Functioning of the European Union (De Minimis Notice) [2014] OJ C291/1.

[29] The line between unilateral measures and agreements can be at times very difficult to discern and the EU courts are aware of that: 'a distinction should be drawn between cases in which an undertaking has adopted a genuinely unilateral measure, and thus without the express or implied participation of another undertaking, and those in which the unilateral character of the measure is merely apparent. Whilst the former do not fall within Article 85(1) of the Treaty, the latter must be regarded as revealing an agreement between undertakings and may therefore fall within the scope of that article. That is the case, in particular, with practices and measures in restraint of competition which, though apparently adopted unilaterally by the manufacturer in the context of its contractual relations with its dealers, nevertheless receive at least the tacit acquiescence of those dealers.' See Judgment of 26 October 2000, *Bayer AG v Commission*, T-41/96, ECLI:EU:T:2000:242, para 71.

> ### Judgment of 26 October 2000, *Bayer AG v Commission*, T-41/96, ECLI:EU:T:2000:242
>
> 66. (...) where a decision on the part of a manufacturer constitutes unilateral conduct of the undertaking, that decision escapes the prohibition in Article 85(1) of the Treaty (...)
> 67. (...) in order for there to be an agreement within the meaning of Article 85(1) of the Treaty it is sufficient that the undertakings in question should have expressed their joint intention to conduct themselves on the market in a specific way (...)
> 68. As regards the form in which that common intention is expressed, it is sufficient for a stipulation to be the expression of the parties' intention to behave on the market in accordance with its terms (...) without its having to constitute a valid and binding contract under national law (...)
> 69. It follows that the concept of an agreement within the meaning of Article 85(1) of the Treaty, as interpreted by the case-law, centres around **the existence of a concurrence of wills between at least two parties, the form in which it is manifested being unimportant so long as it constitutes the faithful expression of the parties' intention.**

The evidentiary burden is on the Commission to prove that an agreement, in some form, exists between undertakings and the case of *Bayer* illustrates the difficulties entailed in that endeavour, particularly in the context of distribution and supply agreements which are vertical in character and require as a matter of fact a degree of contact between the companies operating at the various levels of the chain.[30] In *Bayer*, as well as in *Volkswagen*,[31] the General Court annulled the Commission's fine on the basis of the finding that the conduct in question, albeit anticompetitive, was unilateral in nature, regardless of a vertical contractual relationship existing between the parties. What was missing in the cases according to the General Court was proof of at least a tacit approval of the anticompetitive policy on the part of the pharmaceutical wholesalers and car dealers contracted by Bayer and Volkswagen respectively.

As companies tend to be smart and inventive when engaging in illegal activities, the scope of Article 101 TFEU extends to 'concerted practices'. The CJEU explicitly recognized that the object of the provision is to 'bring within the prohibition of that Article a form of coordination between undertakings which, without having reached the stage where an agreement properly so-called has been concluded, knowingly substitutes practical cooperation between them for the risks of competition'.[32] Such coordination can be inferred from the behaviour of the participants,[33] but must also be actually implemented on the market in a manner causally linked to the collusion.[34] However, as regards the latter point, once the existence of concerted action is established by the authorities, the finding creates a presumption that the collusion was put into effect on the market by the undertakings.[35] It is then up to the undertakings

---

[30] But the standard of proof when proving the existence of an anticompetitive agreement is the same with respect to both vertical and horizontal agreements. See Judgment of 10 February 2011, *Activision Blizzard Germany v Commission*, C-260/09 P, ECLI:EU:C:2011:62, paras 71–72.

[31] Judgment of 3 December 2003, *Volkswagen v Commission*, T-208/01, ECLI:EU:T:2003:326.

[32] Judgment of 14 July 1972, *ICI v Commission (Dyestuffs)*, 48/69, ECLI:EU:C:1972:70, para 64.

[33] Ibid, para 65.

[34] Judgment of 8 July 1999, *Hüls AG v Commission (Polypropylene)*, C-199/92 P, ECLI:EU:C:1999:358, para 161.

[35] Ibid, para 162.

concerned to adduce evidence to the contrary,[36] namely that the market has followed the conditions of competition despite there being direct or indirect contact between economic operators with the object or effect of influencing the conduct of a competitor or disclosing their own course of conduct.[37] The conclusion that undertakings have engaged in concerted practices can be based on direct exchanges of information through meetings (frequent or not),[38] phone calls, e-mails, or letters, and, considerably less likely, on indirect contact and sharing of information through intermediaries.

Before moving on to the modalities of enforcing Article 101 TFEU, one more basic aspect of competition law should be concisely introduced. Market definition is a rudimentary analytical element of 'essential significance',[39] and of relevance not only to the application of Article 101 TFEU but also Article 102 TFEU and the Merger Regulation.[40] Defining the market is necessary, among other things, in order to determine whether an anticompetitive agreement must be examined in light of EU and/or national rules,[41] the degree of market power for the purposes of Article 102 TFEU, and whether a merger would create a dominant position. In essence, markets are delineated on the basis of product interchangeability and geography. Market definition, especially with respect to the criterion of product interchangeability, is often a complex problem involving sophisticated economic assessments trying to answer the question, for example, whether bananas are competing in the same market with other fruits.[42]

The legal basis of contemporary antitrust enforcement in the EU is Regulation 1/2003 which applies to infringements under both Article 101 and 102 TFEU. It reformed the existing competition enforcement regime by allowing NCAs and national courts to apply and enforce Articles 101 and 102 TFEU including through cross-border cooperation (decentralization),[43] while at the same time strengthening the enforcement powers of the Commission.[44] The Commission may, in particular: investigate specific sectors or types of

---

[36] Ibid.

[37] Judgment of 16 December 1975, *Coöperatieve Vereniging 'Suiker Unie' UA and others v Commission*, 40–48, 50, 54–56, 111, 113, and 114/73, ECLI:EU:C:1975:174, para 174.

[38] See, for example, Judgment of 4 June 2009, *T-Mobile Netherlands BV v Raad van bestuur van de Nederlandse Mededingingsautoriteit*, C-8/08, ECLI:EU:C:2009:343.

[39] *Continental Can* (n 7) para 32.

[40] See A Fletcher and B Lyons, *Geographic Market Definition in European Commission Merger Control*, Centre For Competition Policy, January 2016.

[41] In applying national competition rules, national courts and NCAs are obliged to also apply the provisions of the TFEU if the competition infringements fall within their scope. In case of anticompetitive agreements, Article 101 TFEU must be applied when trade between EU Member States may be affected (as opposed to merely intra-Member State commerce). See Article 3 of Council Regulation (EC) No 1/2003 on the implementation of the rules on competition laid down in Articles 81 and 82 of the Treaty [2003] OJ L1/1 (Regulation 1/2003).

[42] According to one judgment of the CJEU from 1978, bananas are in a market of their own: '(...) a very large number of consumers having a constant need for bananas are not noticeably or even appreciably enticed away from the consumption of this product by the arrival of other fresh fruit on the market and that even the personal peak periods only affect it for a limited period of time and to a very limited extent from the point of view of substitutability'. See Judgment of 14 February 1978, *United Brands Company and United Brands Continentaal BV v Commission*, 27/76, ECLI:EU:C:1978:22, paras 34–35. For detailed guidance regarding the Commission's approach to market definition see Commission Notice on the Definition of the Relevant Market for the Purposes of Community Competition Law [1997] OJ C372/5.

[43] See also Directive 2014/104/EU of the European Parliament and of the Council on certain rules governing actions for damages under national law for infringements of the competition law provisions of the Member States and of the European Union [2014] OJ L349/1 which was introduced to facilitate private litigation of infringements of EU competition law.

[44] A number of procedural aspects pertaining to the Commission's conduct of antitrust proceedings is further elaborated in an implementing Commission Regulation. See Commission Regulation (EC) No 773/2004 relating to the conduct of proceedings by the Commission pursuant to Articles 81 and 82 of the EC Treaty [2004] OJ L123/18, as amended by later acts.

agreements;[45] request all necessary information from undertakings;[46] interview any natural or legal person with their consent;[47] conduct inspections in business and exceptionally other premises, land, or means of transport;[48] examine records, make copies, seal premises and records (up to 72 hours), and request explanations from staff;[49] impose sanctions up to 1 per cent of total turnover in case the undertaking supplies incorrect or misleading information or otherwise fails to comply or refuses to cooperate with the investigation as specified in the Regulation;[50] require an infringement to stop and impose behavioural or, as last resort, structural remedies on the undertaking, as well as fines up to 10 per cent of total turnover;[51] enter into commitment decisions;[52] and impose interim measures.[53] It goes without saying that all actions must be carried out in a manner compliant with fundamental rights, in particular the Charter as regards EU law,[54] as well as national rules with respect to matters not regulated by EU law (eg implementation of coercive measures). The Regulation also presumes that the rights of defence in all Member States are 'sufficiently equivalent' for cross-border enforcement purposes,[55] thus representing a manifestation of the mutual trust presumption outside the context of the provisions of the EU Treaties pertaining to the Area of Freedom, Security and Justice.[56]

Council Regulation (EC) No 1/2003 on the implementation of the rules on competition laid down in Articles 81 and 82 of the Treaty [2003] OJ L1/1

Article 23

Fines

2. **The Commission may by decision impose fines on undertakings** and associations of undertakings where, **either intentionally or negligently:**
   (a) they infringe **Article 81 or Article 82 of the Treaty**; or
   (b) they contravene a decision ordering interim measures under Article 8; or
   (c) they fail to comply with a commitment made binding by a decision pursuant to Article 9.

For each undertaking and association of undertakings participating in the infringement, the fine **shall not exceed 10% of its total turnover** in the preceding business year. (…)

3. In fixing the amount of the fine, regard shall be had both to the **gravity and to the duration of the infringement.**

---

[45] Article 17 of Regulation 1/2003.
[46] Ibid, Article 18(1).
[47] Ibid, Article 19.
[48] Ibid, Articles 20 and 21.
[49] Ibid, Article 20(2).
[50] Ibid, Article 23(1).
[51] Ibid, Articles 7(1) and 23. The same provision permits the Commission to find that an infringement has been committed in the past. This has the potential of allowing affected private parties to claim damages before national courts.
[52] Ibid, Article 7.
[53] Ibid, Article 8.
[54] See recital 37 of Regulation 1/2003.
[55] See recital 16 of Regulation 1/2003.
[56] See Ch 4.

Article 27

Hearing of the parties, complainants and others

1. Before taking decisions as provided for in Articles 7, 8, 23 and Article 24(2), the Commission shall give the undertakings or associations of undertakings which are the subject of the proceedings conducted by the Commission **the opportunity of being heard** on the matters to which the Commission has taken objection. The Commission shall base its decisions only on objections on which the parties concerned have been able to comment. (...)

2. **The rights of defence of the parties concerned shall be fully respected in the proceedings**. They shall be entitled to have **access to the Commission's file**, subject to the legitimate interest of undertakings in the **protection of their business secrets**. The right of access to the file shall not extend to confidential information and internal documents of the Commission or the competition authorities of the Member States. In particular, the right of access shall not extend to correspondence between the Commission and the competition authorities of the Member States, or between the latter, including documents drawn up pursuant to Articles 11 and 14. Nothing in this paragraph shall prevent the Commission from disclosing and using information necessary to prove an infringement. (...)

Article 101 TFEU investigations can originate in a number of sources. The Commission is entitled to open an investigation on its own motion or it can act on the basis of a complaint which in most cases would come from a competitor. Nevertheless, the most particular source of enforcement action relating to anticompetitive agreements is the Commission's leniency programme which incentivizes cartel members to betray one another and report the infringement to the Commission in exchange for immunity from or reduction of fines otherwise imposed under Article 23(2) of Regulation (EC) 1/2003.[57] Immunity is granted only to the first undertaking to submit evidence on the secret cartel—if the Commission already possesses substantial evidence of its own, a potential fine can only be reduced (thus second and third comers can only obtain a fine reduction). The leniency programme, the use of which has recently seen manifold increases around the world,[58] is therefore capable of triggering a race among cartel members in order to secure immunity. However, it is a pragmatic instrument borne out of difficulties with proving the existence of cartels and concerted foul play, and as such raises not only questions of fairness[59] but also whether overall compliance might be undermined as a result.[60]

---

[57] See Article 1 Commission Regulation (EU) 2015/1348 of 3 August 2015 amending Regulation (EC) No 773/2004 relating to the conduct of proceedings by the Commission pursuant to Articles 81 and 82 of the EC Treaty [2015] OJ L208 which inserts, among others, Article 4a concerning the Commission's leniency programme into Regulation (EC) No 773/2004.

[58] Thus inspiring the title of a dedicated edited volume. See C Beaton-Wells and C Tran (eds), *Anti-Cartel Enforcement in a Contemporary Age: Leniency Religion* (Bloomsbury 2015).

[59] The Commission sees the moral compromise as one worth having: 'By their very nature, secret cartels are often difficult to detect and investigate without the cooperation of undertakings or individuals implicated in them. Therefore, the Commission considers that it is in the Community interest to reward undertakings involved in this type of illegal practices which are willing to put an end to their participation and co-operate in the Commission's investigation, independently of the rest of the undertakings involved in the cartel. The interests of consumers and citizens in ensuring that secret cartels are detected and punished outweigh the interest in fining those undertakings that enable the Commission to detect and prohibit such practices.' See the recital of the Commission Notice on Immunity from fines and reduction of fines in cartel cases [2006] OJ C298/11.

[60] See J Murphy, 'Combining Leniency Policies and Compliance Programmes to Prevent Cartels' in C Beaton-Wells and C Tran (eds), *Anti-Cartel Enforcement in a Contemporary Age: Leniency Religion* (Bloomsbury 2015) 322–23.

Once an investigation into a potential infringement of EU antitrust law is underway, the Commission is free to make use of the abovementioned powers to obtain the necessary information. The one method most dreaded by undertakings is the so-called dawn raid whereby the Commission, usually in cooperation with officials of the relevant NCA and sometimes accompanied by the police, conducts a surprise inspection of an undertaking's premises. In the context of inspections, the Commission is allowed to obtain information through a variety of means and the undertaking is obliged to cooperate, even if not directly incriminate itself in its answers to the inspectors' questions.[61] If an undertaking takes issue with the conduct of the investigation, it can contact the Hearing Officer, an independent arbiter who is in charge of, among others, ensuring that the various rights of the parties—such as legal professional privilege or right to information—are respected in competition procedures. The Hearing Officer is responsible for safeguarding the exercise of procedural rights not only in Article 101 TFEU proceedings before the Commission but also Article 102 TFEU and the Merger Regulation. During and at the end of each procedure, he or she drafts a report regarding the observance of rights and time limits. The powers and functions of the Hearing Officer are governed by a Commission Decision.

Decision of the President of the European Commission of 13 October 2011 on the function and terms of reference of the hearing officer in certain competition proceedings [2011] OJ L275/29

Article 3

Method of Operation

1. In exercising his or her functions, the hearing officer shall act **independently**.
2. In exercising his or her functions, the hearing officer shall take account of the need for effective application of the competition rules in accordance with Union legislation in force and the principles laid down by the Court of Justice.

Article 14

Interim report and observations

1. The hearing officer shall submit an interim report to the competent member of the Commission on the hearing and the conclusions he or she draws with regard to the respect for the effective exercise of procedural rights. The **observations in this report shall concern procedural issues** including the following:
   (a) disclosure of documents and access to the file;
   (b) time limits for replying to the statement of objections;
   (c) the observance of the right to be heard;
   (d) the proper conduct of the oral hearing.

---

[61] The Commission has drafted a non-binding note detailing some of the aspects of its inspections. See Explanatory note on Commission inspections pursuant to Article 20(4) of Council Regulation No 1/2003, Revised on 11 September 2015.

If an investigation substantiates the Commission's suspicions, it sends a statement of objections containing the anticompetitive charges to the undertakings concerned. The undertakings have the right to mount their defence in writing but also orally before the Hearing Officer, including with the aid of non-confidential information in the Commission's file (right of access to the file). After taking account of the objections raised by the undertakings and following a consultation with representatives of NCAs known as the Advisory Committee,[62] the Commission adopts a decision to either stop the proceedings, impose a sanction,[63] or propose a commitment.[64] A non-confidential version excluding information for example about the company's business secrets or the Commission's investigative practices is then made public.[65]

The most attention-grabbing outcomes of competition cases are fines which can amount to a maximum of 10 per cent of total annual turnover (see Table 6.1 for the ten highest cartel fines per case levied in September 2019). Fines have the dual purpose of punishment and deterrence, the latter especially in cases involving cartels, and they are calculated on the basis of a methodology made broadly public by the Commission which takes into account both aggravating (eg repeat offender) and mitigating (eg negligence rather than intent) circumstances.[66] Fines can be lowered by up to 10 per cent if the wrongdoers accept the Commission's offer to settle a case (which is not always proposed), as this saves the Commission time and resources. The Commission may also impose periodic penalty payments (up to 5 per cent of average daily turnover) in order to compel undertakings to comply with its decisions and requests.[67] The imposition of fines is subject to the principle of equal treatment, as nowadays laid down in Articles 20 and 21 of the Charter, which requires that comparable situations may not be treated differently and that different situations may not be treated in the same way without proper justification.[68]

Table 6.1 Ten highest cartel fines per case as of September 2019[69]

Year	Case	Final amount in EUR
2016/2017	Trucks	3,807,022,000
2012	TV and computer monitor tubes	1,409,588,000
2013/2016	Euro interest rates derivatives (EIRD)	1,276,433,000
2008	Carglass	1,185,500,000
2019	Forex	1,068,879,000
2014	Automotive bearings	953,306,000
2007	Elevators and escalators	832,422,250
2001	Vitamins	790,515,000
2010/2017	Airfreight (including re-adoption)	785,345,000
2013/2015	Yen interest rates derivatives (YIRD)	669,719,000

---

[62] See Article 14 of Regulation 1/2003.

[63] Ibid, Article 7.

[64] Ibid, Article 9. A commitment decision does not need to find an infringement of competition and does not impose fines; instead it requires undertakings to adapt their practices in a competition-friendly manner.

[65] See Article 30 of Regulation 1/2003.

[66] Guidelines on the method of setting fines imposed pursuant to Article 23(2)(a) of Regulation No 1/2003 [2006] OJ C210/02.

[67] Article 24 of Regulation 1/2003.

[68] Judgment of 12 November 2014, *Guardian Industries v Commission*, C-580/12 P, ECLI:EU:C:2014:2363.

[69] Includes fines to all fined undertakings in the case; final amounts after litigation before EU courts and amendments, see <http://ec.europa.eu/competition/cartels/statistics/statistics.pdf> accessed 14 August 2020.

When a decision by the Commission is taken, regardless of whether it imposes a fine, the addressee(s) and other parties able to prove standing under the restrictive Article 263(4) TFEU have the right to appeal the Commission decision to the EU courts.[70] The court of first instance in such cases is as per Article 256 TFEU in conjunction with Article 263(4) TFEU the General Court and the applicants are able to dispute any aspect of the decision, procedural or substantive, factual, or legal, including the amount of the fine.[71] However, one of the most challenging aspects of judicial review of competition cases is assessing economic analyses underlying the Commission decision and the arguments of the applicants. The issue of standard of review catches the General Court in two minds: on the one hand, it is charged with reviewing in-depth the decisions of the Commission as a fundamental check on executive power (ensuring effective judicial protection), while on the other, the Court is not well placed to be reassessing the complex economic determinations made by the Commission, at least not systematically.

Judgment of 17 September 2007, *Microsoft v Commission*, T-201/04, ECLI:EU:T:2007:289

87. (…) although as a general rule the Community Courts undertake a comprehensive review of the question as to whether or not the conditions for the application of the competition rules are met, their **review of complex economic appraisals made by the Commission is necessarily limited** to checking whether the relevant rules on procedure and on stating reasons have been complied with, whether the facts have been accurately stated and **whether there has been any manifest error of assessment** or a misuse of powers (…)

88. Likewise, in so far as the Commission's decision is the result of complex technical appraisals, those appraisals are in principle subject to only limited review by the Court, which means that **the Community Courts cannot substitute their own assessment of matters of fact for the Commission's** (…)

89. However, while the Community Courts recognise that the Commission has a margin of appreciation in economic or technical matters, that **does not mean that they must decline to review the Commission's interpretation of economic or technical data**. The Community Courts must not only establish whether the evidence put forward is factually **accurate, reliable and consistent** but must also determine whether that evidence contains all the relevant data that must be taken into consideration in appraising a complex situation and whether it is capable of substantiating the conclusions drawn from it (…)

In practice, the General Court's review of the facts grants a certain margin of appreciation to the Commission, especially in complex economic matters, while being at the same

---

[70] Settlement decisions can also be challenged and exceptionally are set aside by the General Court. See, for example, Judgment of 13 December 2016, *Printeos v Commission*, T-95/15, ECLI:EU:T:2016:722. Settlement decisions can raise issues in connection with the right against self-incrimination but the Commission approach is probably broadly compatible with the fundamental rights standards of the ECHR. See the criteria espoused by the ECtHR in *Natvlishvili v Georgia*, App no 9043/05, 29 April 2014, paras 91–92.

[71] See Judgment of 15 March 2000, *Cimenteries CBR and Others v Commission*, T-25 to 26/95, T-30 to 32/95, T-34 to 39/95, T-42 to 46/95, T-48/95, T-50 to 65/95, T-68 to 71/95, T-87 to 88/95, T-103 to 104/95, ECLI:EU:T:2000:77, para 719 and Article 31 of Regulation 1/2003.

time mandated to prod the accuracy and completeness of the Commission's assessments.[72] Most often, the judicial review has consisted of determining whether a manifest error of assessment occurred on the part of the Commission.[73] The same applies to the review of fines where the EU courts can additionally take into account whether the fine was calculated on the basis of the Commission's own guidelines on fines.[74] It should be recognized, however, that the case law of both EU courts is not entirely consistent on the depth of judicial review, and the manifest error test can be often found missing with the courts instead conducting an examination of varying depth without specific reference to which standard of review is being applied.[75] Nevertheless, and somewhat predictably, the CJEU ruled that in general the standard of review applied by EU courts in competition cases is satisfactory from the perspective of Article 47 of the Charter on the right to effective judicial protection.[76]

Judgments of the General Court can be appealed in the final instance by either or both parties to the Court of Justice. Such appeals can be made, however, only on points of law—the facts remain as they were established by the Commission and the General Court. In addition, the CJEU is also empowered to review the amount of fines imposed by the Commission. Although its jurisdiction in this regard is according to Article 31 of Regulation 1/2003 'unlimited', the CJEU ordinarily refrains from reassessing the already limited review of fines by the General Court. Notwithstanding the considerable margin of discretion attributed to executive power in the EU competition regime, appeals to the CJEU in competition cases are increasingly accompanied by allegations concerning infringements of fundamental rights, especially as the fairness or celerity of the first-instance proceedings before the General Court can also be cast in doubt on appeal to the CJEU.[77]

The final and increasingly important piece in the antitrust enforcement jigsaw is private enforcement through damages litigation. Comparisons have been often drawn between the enforcement of competition rules in the EU where the Commission and the NCAs are responsible for the vast majority of enforcement action and the US where most of competition enforcement comes from private action. The EU has therefore been attempting to pave the way for more private enforcement in Europe, as evident already in Regulation 1/2003.[78] More recently these efforts have culminated in the adoption of Directive 2014/104/EU which has harmonized certain rules governing actions for damages in the national law of the Member States for competition infringements.

---

[72] See Judgment of 8 December 2011, *KME Germany and Others v Commission*, C-272/09 P, ECLI:EU:C:2011:810, para 94. See also M Botta and A Svetlicinii, 'The Standard of Judicial Review in EU Competition Law Enforcement and Its Compatibility with the Right to a Fair Trial Under the EU Charter of Fundamental Rights' in T Kerikmäe (ed), *Protecting Human Rights in the EU: Controversies and Challenges of the Charter of Fundamental Rights* (Springer 2013) 122. However, see F C de la Torre and E Gippini Fournier, *Evidence, Proof and Judicial Review in EU Competition Law* (Edward Elgar Publishing 2017), para 6.075 arguing that 'complex economic assessments' can also be just matters of law.

[73] The General Court has found manifest errors of assessment in the Commission's decisions on a number of occasions. See, for an example in the context of mergers, Judgment of 25 October 2002, *Tetra Laval v Commission*, T-5/02, ECLI:EU:T:2002:264.

[74] See Judgment of 16 June 2011, *Heineken v Commission*, T-240/07, ECLI:EU:T:2011:284, paras 308–309. See also Guidelines on the method of setting fines imposed pursuant to Article 23(2)(a) of Regulation No 1/2003 [2006] OJ C210/02.

[75] See de la Torre and Gippini Fournier, *Evidence, Proof and Judicial Review in EU Competition Law* (n 72), paras 6.024–6.085.

[76] *KME Germany* (n 72) para 106. For a comprehensive and authoritative analysis of the issue of judicial review in EU competition law, see C de la Torre and Gippini Fournier, *Evidence, Proof and Judicial Review in EU Competition Law* (n 72) chapter 6.

[77] A number of cases concerning fundamental rights issues in proceedings before the General Court, such as the right to a fair trial without undue delay, is discussed in section 6.6.

[78] See recital 7 and Articles 6 and 15 of Regulation 1/2003.

Private enforcement comprises two types of actions which can relate to infringements of both Article 101 and 102 TFEU. First, stand-alone actions alleging the infringement of competition rules and damages resulting therefrom without any prior decision of competition authorities. The complexity and evidentiary burden of these actions means they are rarely brought and even more rarely successful, at least in Europe. Second and more typical in the EU context, follow-on actions claim damages on the basis of a competition infringement established prior by a competition authority (the Commission or NCAs). The debate in the EU on enhancing private enforcement, including the contribution of Directive 2014/104/EU, is mainly focused on how to facilitate this second type of action for damages.

There have been and remain a number of important obstacles in the facilitation of private enforcement which takes place in the national courts of the Member States, as the CJEU has no jurisdiction over such actions for damages.[79] Some of the obstacles identified in the literature are the passing-on defence which allows guilty undertakings to argue that overcharges suffered by purchasers were passed on, at least in part, to consumers; the rules on court standing (*locus standi*) for competitors, purchasers (direct and indirect), consumers and their ability to effectively bring collective actions; the right and ability to access the file detailing the competition infringement of a competition authority and the subsequent balancing between access and protection of business secrets of guilty undertakings; the quantification of loss, direct and indirect; and cross-border recognition of decisions and cooperation between NCAs and national courts.[80] Although the CJEU has clarified certain aspects of private enforcement in its case law and the EU legislature harmonized certain rules on damages actions through Directive 2014/104/EU, the private enforcement record remains overall patchy and varies considerably between Member States.

Directive 2014/104/EU of the European Parliament and of the Council on certain rules governing actions for damages under national law for infringements of the competition law provisions of the Member States and of the European Union [2014] OJ L349/1

Article 1

Subject matter and scope

1. This Directive sets out certain rules necessary to ensure that **anyone who has suffered harm caused by an infringement of competition law** by an undertaking or by an association of undertakings **can effectively exercise the right to claim full compensation** for that harm from that undertaking or association. It sets out rules fostering undistorted competition in the internal market and removing obstacles to its proper functioning, by ensuring **equivalent protection** throughout the Union for anyone who has suffered such harm.

---

[79] Pursuant to Articles 268 and 340 TFEU the General Court has jurisdiction over actions for damages directed against the EU on the basis of non-contractual liability. This does not extend to jurisdiction over disputes between two private parties with the exception of preliminary rulings referred to the CJEU by national courts.

[80] See CH Bovis and CM Clarke, 'Private Enforcement of EU Competition Law' (2015) 36 Liverpool Law Review 49; D Ashton, *Competition Damages Actions in the EU: Law and Practice* (2nd edn, Edward Elgar Publishing 2018).

2. This Directive sets out rules coordinating the enforcement of the competition rules by competition authorities and the enforcement of those rules in **damages actions** before national courts.

Article 3

Right to full compensation

1. Member States shall ensure that **any natural or legal person who has suffered harm caused by an infringement of competition law is able to claim and to obtain full compensation** for that harm.
2. Full compensation shall place a person who has suffered harm in the position in which that person would have been had the infringement of competition law not been committed. It shall therefore cover the right to compensation for actual loss and for loss of profit, plus the payment of interest.

Article 5

Disclosure of evidence

1. Member States shall ensure that in proceedings relating to an action for damages in the Union, upon request of a claimant who has presented a reasoned justification containing reasonably available facts and evidence sufficient to support the plausibility of its claim for damages, **national courts are able to order the defendant or a third party to disclose relevant evidence which lies in their control**, subject to the conditions set out in this Chapter. Member States shall ensure that national courts are able, upon request of the defendant, to order the claimant or a third party to disclose relevant evidence.

Article 11

Joint and several liability

1. Member States shall ensure that undertakings which have infringed competition law through joint behaviour **are jointly and severally liable for the harm caused** by the infringement of competition law; with the effect that each of those undertakings is bound to compensate for the harm in full, and the injured party has the right to require full compensation from any of them until he has been fully compensated.

Article 13

Passing-on defence

Member States shall ensure that the defendant in an action for damages can invoke as a defence against a claim for damages the fact that **the claimant passed on the whole or part of the overcharge resulting from the infringement of competition law**. The **burden of proving** that the overcharge was passed on shall be **on the defendant**, who may reasonably require disclosure from the claimant or from third parties.

B. Abuse of a dominant position (Article 102 TFEU)

Consolidated version of the Treaty on the Functioning of the European Union [2012] OJ C326/47

Article 102

Any **abuse** by one or more undertakings of a **dominant position** within the internal market or in a substantial part of it shall be prohibited as **incompatible with the internal market** in so far as it may affect trade between Member States.

Such abuse may, in particular, consist in:

(a) directly or indirectly imposing **unfair purchase or selling prices** or other unfair trading conditions;

(b) **limiting production, markets or technical development** to the prejudice of consumers;

(c) applying **dissimilar conditions** to equivalent transactions with other trading parties, thereby placing them at a competitive disadvantage;

(d) making the conclusion of contracts **subject to** acceptance by the other parties of **supplementary obligations** which, by their nature or according to commercial usage, have no connection with the subject of such contracts.

Whereas Article 101 TFEU requires the competition-harming conduct to involve at least two undertakings, Article 102 TFEU covers in the first place unilateral conduct which amounts to an abuse of a dominant position and potentially affects trade between Member States.[81] The word abuse must be emphasized—the provision does not prohibit dominant positions ('dominance') as such. The classic statement on what 'dominant position' and 'abuse' mean for the purposes of Article 102 TFEU has been given by the CJEU in the case of *Hoffmann-La Roche*.

Judgment of 13 February 1979, *Hoffmann-La Roche & Co. AG v Commission*, 85/76, ECLI:EU:C:1979:36

---

38. (...) Article 86 prohibits any abuse by an undertaking of a dominant position in a substantial part of the common market in so far as it may affect trade between Member States.

The dominant position thus referred to relates to **a position of economic strength enjoyed by an undertaking which enables it to prevent effective competition being maintained on the relevant market by affording it the power to behave to an appreciable extent independently of its competitors, its customers and ultimately of the consumers.**

---

[81] The application of one does not exclude the application of the other. Moreover, Article 102 TFEU covers also 'collective dominance' but the findings thereof are, compared to unilateral abuses, rare.

> 91. (...) the concept of abuse is an objective concept relating to the behaviour of an undertaking in a dominant position which is such **as to influence the structure of a market** where, as a result of the very presence of the undertaking in question, the degree of competition is weakened and **which, through recourse to methods different from those which condition normal competition** in products or services on the basis of the transactions of commercial operators, **has the effect of hindering the maintenance of the degree of competition still existing in the market or the growth of that competition.**

Nevertheless, the notion of both abuse and dominance has been notoriously difficult to define in an uncontroversial manner. The overall application of Article 102 TFEU continues to attract more than a fair share of criticism, not least from the United States where most of the global technological giants heavily fined by the EU in recent years are based.[82] The controversy surrounding Article 102 TFEU has, however, been traditionally more profound than allegations of bias; in simplified terms the central question has been whether punishment of abuses of dominant position has served to protect the competitors for their own sake or the structure of competition in the interest of consumer welfare.[83] Such debates have been fuelled by lack of analysis of negative market effects in some cases, thus echoing in a more contested way the divide between restrictions by object and by effect present in the case law on Article 101 TFEU.[84]

The first step in the Commission's or an NCA's assessment of potential Article 102 TFEU infringements is to determine whether an undertaking holds a dominant position in a particular market. As mentioned previously and expounded in more detail in a Commission notice (which reflects CJEU case law),[85] the relevant market is defined by reference to the product and geographic market followed by a more detailed analysis of both demand- and supply-side substitutability. Once the relevant market is defined, the competition authority is able to identify the undertakings involved in servicing the market and their respective market shares. Market share and its durability are usually a crucial aspect of the inquiry into dominance but as consistently held by the CJEU and reflected in the Commission's guidance on its enforcement priorities relating to Article 102 TFEU,[86] it must be viewed in conjunction

---

[82] See, for example, fines of EUR 497.2 million and EUR 561 million imposed on Microsoft for two separate 'tying' infringements in 2004 (Windows Media Player) and 2013 (Internet Explorer, breach of commitment) respectively (COMP/C-3/37.792 [2007] OJ L32/23; COMP/39.530 [2013] OJ C120/15); a fine of EUR 1.06 billion imposed on Intel for conditional rebates in the x86 CPU market (COMP/C-3/37.990 [2009] OJ C227/13); fines of EUR 2.42 billion, EUR 4.34 billion, and EUR 1.49 billion imposed on Google LLC and Alphabet Inc. (Google's parent company) for giving advantage to their own comparison shopping service, for illegal practices regarding Android mobile devices and for abusive practices in online advertising (IP/17/1784, 27 June 2017; IP/18/4581, 18 July 2018; IP/19/1770, 20 March 2019).

[83] Jones and Sufrin, *EU Competition Law: Text, Cases, and Materials* (n 5) 257.

[84] P Ibáñez Colomo, 'Beyond the "More Economics-Based Approach": A Legal Perspective on Article 102 TFEU Case Law' (2016) 53 Common Market Law Review 709, 712. See also L Lovdahl Gormsen, *A Principled Approach to Abuse of Dominance in European Competition Law* (Cambridge University Press 2010); F Etro and I Kokkoris (eds), *Competition Law and the Enforcement of Article 102* (Oxford University Press 2010).

[85] Commission Notice on the Definition of the Relevant Market for the Purposes of Community Competition Law [1997] OJ C372/5. It should be added that the existence of the Notice prompted the General Court to remind the Commission that it must abide by the rules stipulated therein in view of the legitimate expectations it creates, as is the case with other similar soft law instruments. See Judgment of 28 April 2010, *Amann & Söhne GmbH & Co KG v Commission*, T-446/05, ECLI:EU:T:2010:165, paras 136–137.

[86] Guidance on the Commission's enforcement priorities in applying Article 82 of the EC Treaty to abusive exclusionary conduct by dominant undertakings [2009] OJ C45/7.

with other factors and in light of the overall structure and dynamics of the market.[87] As a general rule, the Commission does not pursue investigations into dominance where the market share of an undertaking is below 40 per cent, unless the specific circumstances of the case warrant an exception.[88]

While not per se illegal, undertakings in a dominant position incur special duties of care not to distort or restrict competition on the market. The scope of such duties is not fixed but rather determined on a case-by-case basis which can prove problematic from the point of view of legal certainty, as undertakings may not be aware that their activities are crossing the line.[89] This is not to say that dominant undertakings' actions having adverse effects on less efficient competitors inevitably amount to a breach of Article 102 TFEU, as made clear by the CJEU in *Post Danmark*.[90]

Judgment of 27 March 2012, *Post Danmark A/S v Konkurrencerådet*, C-209/10, ECLI:EU:C:2012:172

---

21. It is settled case-law that a finding that an undertaking has such a **dominant position is not in itself a ground of criticism** of the undertaking concerned. (...) It is in no way the purpose of Article 82 EC to prevent an undertaking from acquiring, on its own merits, the dominant position on a market (...) Nor does that provision seek to ensure that competitors less efficient than the undertaking with the dominant position should remain on the market.

22. Thus, **not every exclusionary effect is necessarily detrimental to competition** (...). Competition on the merits may, by definition, lead to the departure from the market or the marginalisation of competitors that are less efficient and so less attractive to consumers from the point of view of, among other things, price, choice, quality or innovation.

Abuse is found, as per the definition in *Hoffmann-La Roche* cited above, when a dominant undertaking takes measures which are different from those available in the conditions of normal competition—stemming from the very fact of dominance and the resulting weakened competition—and which distort or preclude the growth of the residual competition in the market. In reality, establishing the existence of abuse of a dominant position is

---

[87] Judgment of 13 February 1979, *Hoffmann-La Roche & Co. AG v Commission*, 85/76, ECLI:EU:C:1979:36, paras 39–40. According to the Guidance on the Commission's enforcement priorities (n 86) para 12, the assessment of dominance takes into account market position (shares) of the dominant undertaking and its competitors; the possibility or otherwise of expansion or entry of competitors; and the countervailing buyer power of the undertaking's customers.

[88] See Guidance on the Commission's enforcement priorities (n 86) para 14. Most findings of abuse of dominant position concern undertakings with very high market shares in the relevant market. The lowest market share in a case where abuse was found amounted to 39.7% in the last year under assessment by the Commission. The finding of dominance was influenced by the fact that all the other competitors in the market held market shares almost four or more times smaller. See Judgment of 17 December 2003, *British Airways v Commission*, T-219/99, ECLI:EU:T:2003:343, para 211.

[89] The point of EU competition law is, however, that they should at the very least tread carefully when in a dominant position and potentially seek guidance from competition authorities if in doubt.

[90] Conversely, not all competition on price is necessarily legitimate. See Judgment of 3 July 1991, *AKZO Chemie BV v Commission*, C-62/86, ECLI:EU:C:1991:286, para 70.

very sensitive to the facts of the case and the concrete measures taken by the undertaking concerned in the specific conditions of competition in the relevant market. Nevertheless, certain behaviours of dominant undertakings are more often associated with exclusionary effects on the competition than others to the point when a pattern of exclusionary practices by 'object'—the treatment of which may differ, however, when evaluated under Article 101 TFEU or the Merger Control Regulation—can be identified in the case law of the CJEU.[91] Such practices, which correspond to a large extent to those found in the non-exhaustive list in Article 102 TFEU, are first in the cross-hairs of the Commission, as elaborated in the Guidance on enforcement priorities, and their enforcement is more likely to pass judicial review without requiring a fully fledged analysis of effects of the practices on the market. The Commission Guidance also elaborates the conditions under which dominant undertakings can justify otherwise abusive behaviour (necessity or efficiency), similarly to exemptions available under Article 101(3) TFEU in the case of anticompetitive agreements.

Guidance on the Commission's enforcement priorities in applying Article 82 of the EC Treaty to abusive exclusionary conduct by dominant undertakings [2009] OJ C45/7

---

5. In applying Article 82 to exclusionary conduct by dominant undertakings, the Commission will focus on those **types of conduct** that are **most harmful to consumers**. Consumers benefit from competition through lower prices, better quality and a wider choice of new or improved goods and services. The Commission, therefore, will direct its enforcement to ensuring that markets function properly and that consumers benefit from the efficiency and productivity which result from effective competition between undertakings.

D. Objective necessity and efficiencies

28. In the enforcement of Article 82, the Commission will also examine claims put forward by a dominant undertaking that its conduct is **justified**. A dominant undertaking may do so either by demonstrating that its conduct is **objectively necessary** or by demonstrating that its conduct **produces substantial efficiencies which outweigh any anti-competitive effects** on consumers. In this context, the Commission will assess whether the conduct in question is indispensable and proportionate to the goal allegedly pursued by the dominant undertaking.

IV. SPECIFIC FORMS OF ABUSE

A. Exclusive dealing

32. A dominant undertaking may try to **foreclose its competitors** by hindering them from selling to customers through use of **exclusive purchasing** obligations or **rebates**, together referred to as exclusive dealing. (...)

---

[91] Ibáñez Colomo (n 84) 709.

33. **An exclusive purchasing obligation** requires a customer on a particular market to purchase exclusively or to a large extent only from the dominant undertaking. Certain other obligations, such as stocking requirements, which appear to fall short of requiring exclusive purchasing, may in practice lead to the same effect.

37. **Conditional rebates** are rebates granted to customers to reward them for a particular form of purchasing behaviour. The usual nature of a conditional rebate is that the customer is given a rebate if its purchases over a defined reference period exceed a certain threshold, the rebate being granted either on all purchases (retroactive rebates) or only on those made in excess of those required to achieve the threshold (incremental rebates). (...) such rebates—when granted by a dominant undertaking—can also have actual or potential foreclosure effects similar to exclusive purchasing obligations. (...)

B. Tying and bundling

47. A dominant undertaking may try to foreclose its competitors by **tying or bundling**. (...)

48. 'Tying' usually refers to situations where customers that purchase one product (the tying product) are required also to purchase another product from the dominant undertaking (the tied product). (...) '**Bundling**' usually refers to the way products are offered and priced by the dominant undertaking. In the case of pure bundling the products are only sold jointly in fixed proportions. In the case of mixed bundling, often referred to as a multi-product rebate, the products are also made available separately, but the sum of the prices when sold separately is higher than the bundled price.

C. Predation

63. In line with its enforcement priorities, the Commission will generally intervene where there is evidence showing that a **dominant undertaking engages in predatory conduct by deliberately incurring losses or foregoing profits in the short term** (referred to hereafter as 'sacrifice'), so as to foreclose or be likely to foreclose one or more of its actual or potential competitors with a view to strengthening or maintaining its market power, thereby causing consumer harm.

Enforcement powers and procedures, including those for judicial review, are in other respects similar or identical to those applicable to infringements of Article 101 TFEU, as a result of being largely governed by the same legal instrument (Regulation 1/2003) (see previous Section 6.2.B).

C. Mergers (Regulation No 139/2004)

Council Regulation (EC) No 139/2004 on the control of concentrations between undertakings [2004] OJ L24/1

Article 3

Definition of concentration

1. A **concentration** shall be deemed to arise where a **change of control on a lasting basis** results from:
   (a) the **merger** of two or more previously independent undertakings or parts of undertakings, or
   (b) the **acquisition,** by one or more persons already controlling at least one undertaking, or by one or more undertakings, whether by purchase of securities or assets, by contract or by any other means, of direct or indirect control of the whole or parts of one or more other undertakings.
2. Control shall be constituted by rights, contracts or any other means which, either separately or in combination and having regard to the considerations of fact or law involved, confer the **possibility of exercising decisive influence on an undertaking** (...)
4. The creation of **a joint venture** performing on a lasting basis **all the functions of an autonomous economic entity** shall constitute a concentration within the meaning of paragraph 1(b).

Article 4

Prior notification of concentrations and pre-notification referral at the request of the notifying parties

1. **Concentrations with a Community dimension** defined in this Regulation **shall be notified to the Commission prior to their implementation** and following the conclusion of the agreement, the announcement of the public bid, or the acquisition of a controlling interest.

Notification may also be made where the undertakings concerned demonstrate to the Commission a good faith intention to conclude an agreement or, in the case of a public bid, where they have publicly announced an intention to make such a bid, provided that the intended agreement or bid would result in a concentration with a Community dimension. (...)

EU competition law in the area of concentrations departs from the starting point that corporate mergers can increase consumer welfare through increased efficiency, innovation and other benefits. Mergers by nature also reduce the number of undertakings operating in markets and therefore may reduce effective competition, in particular (but not only) if they lead to the creation or strengthening of dominant positions. As a result, it has been found opportune by the EU to enact legislation which regulates 'concentrations with a [Union] dimension' with the aim of preventing distortion of competition in the internal market, or parts of it, of the EU. At heart, the law obliges undertakings to request approval from the

Commission of mergers, acquisitions, and joint ventures. The current Merger Regulation 139/2004 came into being in 2004 and superseded the previous merger control regime which was in existence since 1989.[92] In 2014, the Commission presented a White Paper which assessed the functioning of the system and found that it generally fulfils its purpose well, albeit with some room for improvement.[93] As opposed to the other components of EU competition policy, there is no specific Treaty provision for merger control; the Regulation is therefore based on Article 103 TFEU (for its connection to Articles 101 and 102 TFEU) and the flexibility clause (Article 352 TFEU).

There are two key elements which must be fulfilled to render the Merger Regulation applicable to undertakings. First, the venture in question must satisfy the relatively broad definition of a 'concentration' given in Article 2 of the Merger Regulation. Second, it must have an EU dimension. This criterion is satisfied when certain thresholds concerning the global and EU turnover of the undertakings concerned are met, in accordance with Article 1 of the Regulation and with the method of calculating turnovers outlined in Article 5. If both criteria are fulfilled, the concentration in question must be notified to the Commission prior to its implementation, with the possibility of being referred to a Member State NCA if the concentration may significantly affect competition in the Member State's market.[94] Conversely, the Merger Regulation also allows concentrations below the 'EU dimension' threshold to be handled by the Commission upon referral of NCAs or request of undertakings.[95] EU merger law therefore emphasizes ex ante enforcement, unlike Articles 101 and 102 TFEU which are primarily enforced ex post facto of the competition infringement. The notification procedure is often preceded by informal discussions between the undertakings concerned and the Commission (specifically DG Competition) regarding the proposed concentration. Notification is then carried out through forms which are contained in the Commission Implementing Regulation.[96]

Council Regulation (EC) No 139/2004 on the control of concentrations between undertakings [2004] OJ L24/1

Article 2

Appraisal of concentrations

1. (…) the Commission shall take into account:
   (a) **the need to maintain and develop effective competition** within the common market in view of, among other things, the structure of all the markets concerned and the actual or potential competition from undertakings located either within or outwith the Community;

---

[92] Council Regulation (EEC) No 4064/89 on the control of concentrations between undertakings [1989] OJ L395/1.

[93] European Commission, White Paper—Towards more effective EU merger control, COM(2014) 449 final, 9 July 2014, paras 78–79.

[94] Article 4(4) of the Merger Regulation.

[95] See Article 22 and Article 4(5) of the Merger Regulation.

[96] Commission Regulation (EC) No 802/2004 implementing Council Regulation (EC) No 139/2004 on the control of concentrations between undertakings [2004] OJ L133/1, as amended.

> (b) **the market position of the undertakings** concerned and their economic and financial power, the **alternatives** available to suppliers and users, their **access** to supplies or markets, any legal or other barriers to entry, supply and demand **trends** for the relevant goods and services, the **interests of** the intermediate and ultimate **consumers**, and the **development of technical and economic progress** provided that it is to consumers' advantage and does not form an obstacle to competition.

Following notification, the Commission has initially 25 days to investigate and respond to the request (Phase I). At this stage, the Commission can already issue clearance that the merger does not raise doubts about its compatibility with the internal market, either immediately or subject to specified conditions. If, however, there are 'serious doubts' as to the concentration's compatibility with the internal market, the Commission may launch a more in-depth investigation (Phase II) involving a formal statement of objections and the convening of an oral hearing at the request of the undertakings, similarly to the procedure for investigations of infringements of Articles 101 and 102 TFEU. During the whole investigative process, the Commission has at its disposal powers corresponding to those available under Regulation 1/2003.[97] Phase II concludes with a decision of the Commission on the compatibility of the concentration with the internal market, possibly subject to commitments. When making the assessment, the Commission must take into account a number of considerations such as the market position of the undertakings concerned, their economic and financial power, whether they operate in the same market (horizontal) or at different levels of the value chain (vertical), and other points.[98] Decisions of the Commission can in any case be appealed to the General Court and later to the Court of Justice.

The Commission may also impose fines for lack of compliance with the merger control procedures. Failure to cooperate with the Commission's investigation of the concentration in accordance with the Merger Regulation can cost undertakings up to 1 per cent of global turnover.[99] If a concentration is implemented without prior clearance (so-called gun-jumping) or in breach of a commitment, the Commission can impose a fine up to 10 per cent of global turnover and dissolve the illegally implemented concentration in order to restore effective competition in the market.[100] One of the most high-profile sanctions imposed in the area of merger control concerned Facebook's acquisition of WhatsApp in 2014. Although the takeover was cleared by the Commission in October 2014 following a Phase I inquiry, it was found out in 2016 that Facebook supplied misleading information during the investigation. The company was fined EUR 110 million as a result, in accordance with Article 14(1) of the Merger Regulation, regardless of the fact that the misleading information had no impact on the authorization of the concentration granted in 2014.[101]

---

[97] See Articles 11 to 15 of the Merger Regulation.
[98] Ibid, Article 2.
[99] Ibid, Article 14(1).
[100] Ibid, Articles 14(2) and 8(4).
[101] Summary of Commission Decision of 18 May 2017 imposing fines under Article 14(1) of Council Regulation (EC) No 139/2004 for the supply by an undertaking of incorrect or misleading information (Case M.8228—Facebook/WhatsApp (Art. 14(1) proc.)) [2017] OJ C286/6.

D. State aid (Article 107 TFEU)

Consolidated version of the Treaty on the Functioning of the European Union [2012] OJ C326/47

Article 107

1. Save as otherwise provided in the Treaties, any aid granted by a Member State or through State resources in any form whatsoever which distorts or threatens to distort competition by favouring certain undertakings or the production of certain goods **shall**, in so far as it affects trade between Member States, **be incompatible with the internal market.**

2. The **following shall be compatible with the internal market:**
   (a) aid having a social character, granted to individual consumers, provided that such aid is granted without discrimination related to the origin of the products concerned;
   (b) aid to make good the damage caused by natural disasters or exceptional occurrences;
   (c) aid granted to the economy of certain areas of the Federal Republic of Germany affected by the division of Germany, in so far as such aid is required in order to compensate for the economic disadvantages caused by that division. Five years after the entry into force of the Treaty of Lisbon, the Council, acting on a proposal from the Commission, may adopt a decision repealing this point.

3. The following may be considered to be compatible with the internal market:
   (a) aid to promote the economic development of areas where the standard of living is abnormally low or where there is serious underemployment, and of the regions referred to in Article 349, in view of their structural, economic and social situation;
   (b) aid to promote the execution of an important project of common European interest or to remedy a serious disturbance in the economy of a Member State;
   (c) aid to facilitate the development of certain economic activities or of certain economic areas, where such aid does not adversely affect trading conditions to an extent contrary to the common interest;
   (d) aid to promote culture and heritage conservation where such aid does not affect trading conditions and competition in the Union to an extent that is contrary to the common interest;
   (e) such other categories of aid as may be specified by decision of the Council on a proposal from the Commission.

Article 108

1. The **Commission** shall, in cooperation with Member States, keep under **constant review all systems of aid** existing in those States. It shall propose to the latter any appropriate measures required by the progressive development or by the functioning of the internal market.

2. If, **after giving notice** to the parties concerned to submit their comments, the Commission finds that aid granted by a State or through State resources is not compatible with the internal market having regard to Article 107, or that such aid is

> being misused, **it shall decide that the State concerned shall abolish or alter such aid** within a period of time to be determined by the Commission.
>
> If the State concerned does not comply with this decision within the prescribed time, the Commission or any other interested State may, in derogation from the provisions of Articles 258 and 259, **refer the matter to the Court of Justice of the European Union direct.** (…)
>
> 4. The Commission may adopt regulations relating to the categories of State aid that the Council has, pursuant to Article 109, determined may be exempted from the procedure provided for by paragraph 3 of this Article.

The purpose of State aid control is the same as the general objective of other EU competition rules—ensuring that the internal market is not unduly distorted and that exemptions are applied in a consistent manner across the Union. The part of the independent supervisor is again played by the European Commission which verifies notified State aid measures, similarly to its role in merger control. The specificity of State aid, nevertheless, lies in the presence of national public authority—whereas in other areas the Commission enforces competition law primarily as between private entities, State aid directly implicates Member State governments exercising public power.[102] In addition, decisions on granting support to sectors and undertakings often receive domestic media attention and touch upon national sensitivities, thus being liable to prompt national backlash against interference from 'outside' when the Commission becomes involved. Enforcement of EU State aid rules therefore represents possibly the most delicate competition task for the Commission.

The comparatively greater sensitivity of State aid is reflected in the multiple exemptions from the general prohibition on State aid provided for by the TFEU and EU secondary law. According to Article 107(2) TFEU, three types of aid 'shall' be compatible with the internal market: aid of a social character, as long as there is no discrimination relating to the origin of products concerned; aid addressing the damage caused by natural disasters and other 'exceptional occurrences'; and aid granted to certain areas of Germany with the intention of mitigating disparities between the West and East.[103] Even more types of aid 'may' be considered compatible with the internal market according to Article 107(3) TFEU: aid for underdeveloped regions, projects of common European interest, culture and heritage protection, and any other areas established in EU legislation. Most of such legislative provisions, for example relating to sport and infrastructure support, are included in the General block exemption Regulation (GBER),[104] the content of which is regularly updated by the Commission

---

[102] Here the Member States are referred to in their role as benefactors not beneficiaries. Public entities exercising official authority which are recipients of state funding, such as the army or the police, do not qualify as 'undertakings' for the purposes of Article 107(1) TFEU, unless they engage in an economic activity which can be separated from public powers. See Judgment of 18 March 1997, *Diego Calì & Figli*, C-343/95, ECLI:EU:C:1997:160, para 16. The delineation between an 'undertaking' and public authorities falling outside the scope of competition law can also be found in other limbs of EU competition rules. See, for example, Judgment of 12 July 2012, *Compass-Datenbank GmbH*, C-138/11, ECLI:EU:C:2012:449.

[103] The CJEU stated this exemption should be construed narrowly. See Judgment of 19 September 2000, *Germany v Commission*, C-156/98, ECLI:EU:C:2000:467. Moreover, the provision (Article 107(2)(c) TFEU) provides for the possibility to repeal the exemption by a decision of the Council but this option has not been so far taken up.

[104] Commission Regulation (EU) No 651/2014 declaring certain categories of aid compatible with the internal market in application of Articles 107 and 108 of the Treaty [2014] OJ L187/1.

(belonging to the purview of DG Competition).[105] Furthermore, sector-specific exemptions from EU State aid law can be found in the Fisheries (FIBER) and Agricultures (ABER) block exemption Regulations.[106] Finally, a general *de minimis* exemption applies to aid not exceeding EUR 200,000 (EUR 100,000 in the road transport sector) per undertaking over a period of three years.[107] The proliferation of exemptions has been part of the State aid modernization agenda whereby pro-growth/investment/employment aid initiatives of Member States are subject to fewer EU hurdles, while the Commission's capacities to look more carefully into potentially competition-distorting measures, including entire sectors,[108] have been consolidated. This approach was meant to be in line with the Juncker Commission credo of being 'big on big things and small on small things'.[109]

Paragraph 1 of Article 107 TFEU provides the basis of the Union definition of State aid. A sizeable body of case law has, however, emerged with respect to every element of the Treaty definition which adds considerable detail to questions of EU State aid law applicability. In order to facilitate compliance, the Commission has issued, as elsewhere in competition policy, an exhaustive notice summarizing the case law and practice relating to the notion of State aid.[110] The main elements of the definition covered in the Notice are: 'the existence of an undertaking, the imputability of the measure to the State, its financing through State resources, the granting of an advantage, the selectivity of the measure and its effect on competition and trade between Member States'.[111] It is worth highlighting that the definition of State aid is constructed broadly, covering subsidies and economic benefits granted in any form and with any objective or cause by the State.[112] What matters are the effects of the measure.[113]

Where a prospective Member State measure satisfies the definition of aid, and it is not covered by an exemption, the plans to grant such aid must be notified by the Member State concerned to the Commission. The applicable procedure is set out in Article 108 TFEU and a related Council Regulation.[114] The notifying Member State is required to submit all necessary information in order to enable the Commission to assess the compatibility of the proposed aid with the internal market—until that decision is made, the aid shall not be put into effect (the so-called standstill clause).[115] In the first stage lasting up to two months, the

---

[105] See, recently, Commission Regulation (EU) 2017/1084 of 14 June 2017 amending Regulation (EU) No 651/2014 as regards aid for port and airport infrastructure, notification thresholds for aid for culture and heritage conservation and for aid for sport and multifunctional recreational infrastructures, and regional operating aid schemes for outermost regions and amending Regulation (EU) No 702/2014 as regards the calculation of eligible costs [2017] OJ L156/1.

[106] Commission Regulation (EU) No 1388/2014 declaring certain categories of aid to undertakings active in the production, processing and marketing of fishery and aquaculture products compatible with the internal market in application of Articles 107 and 108 of the Treaty on the Functioning of the European Union [2014] OJ L369/37; Commission Regulation (EU) No 702/2014 declaring certain categories of aid in the agricultural and forestry sectors and in rural areas compatible with the internal market in application of Articles 107 and 108 of the Treaty on the Functioning of the European Union [2014] OJ L193/1.

[107] Commission Regulation (EU) No 1407/2013 on the application of Articles 107 and 108 of the Treaty on the Functioning of the European Union to de minimis aid [2013] OJ L352/1.

[108] See Article 25 Council Regulation (EU) 2015/1589 laying down detailed rules for the application of Article 108 of the Treaty on the Functioning of the European Union [2015] OJ L248/9.

[109] European Commission, 'The Juncker Commission: The Right Team to Deliver Change', SPEECH/14/585, 10 September 2014.

[110] Commission Notice on the notion of State aid as referred to in Article 107(1) of the Treaty on the Functioning of the European Union, C/2016/2946 [2016] OJ C262/1.

[111] Ibid, para 5.

[112] Judgment of 24 July 2003, *Altmark Trans and Regierungspräsidium Magdeburg*, C-280/00, ECLI:EU:C:2003:415, para 84; Judgment of 2 July 1974, *Italy v Commission*, 173/73, ECLI:EU:C:1974:71, para 13.

[113] Ibid.

[114] Council Regulation (EU) 2015/1589 (n 108).

[115] Ibid, Articles 2 and 3.

Commission makes a preliminary examination of the notification which can lead to one of three findings: that the planned measure does not constitute aid under EU law; that it is compatible with the internal market; or that doubts regarding its compatibility necessitate a formal investigation.[116] In the latter case, the Member State and undertakings concerned can respond to the doubts raised by the Commission.[117] The final decision—which can, however, be revoked if it comes to light that it was based on incorrect information—should be taken by the Commission within 18 months and can be made subject to conditions.[118]

The presence of Member States and national sensibilities also means that the Commission's powers are slightly curtailed in State aid compared to antitrust matters. For example, the Commission can only request information from aid beneficiaries if the Member State concerned agrees to the request.[119] The Commission is also required to inform the Member State concerned in advance if it wishes to conduct an on-site monitoring visit regarding compliance with decisions on individual aid.[120] Nevertheless, complaints alleging the existence of unlawful aid—that is, aid not exempted by the Commission or an applicable provision—can be submitted by interested parties to the Commission which can subsequently open a formal investigation (which it can do also on its own motion).[121] The Commission can also issue an information injunction—and have it enforced by the CJEU—if a Member State refuses to supply information pertaining to unlawful aid.[122] More recently, the Commission has been given the power to investigate State aid measures in a particular sector of the economy across several Member States.[123] Exceptionally, but again underlining the specificity of State aid law, the Council is able to pronounce particular measures as being compatible with the internal market in derogation from the Commission's investigations and oversight.[124]

Council Regulation (EU) 2015/1589 laying down detailed rules for the application of Article 108 of the Treaty on the Functioning of the European Union [2015] OJ L248/9

Article 2

Notification of new aid

1. Save as otherwise provided in regulations made pursuant to Article 109 TFEU or to other relevant provisions thereof, **any plans to grant new aid shall be notified to the Commission** in sufficient time by the Member State concerned. The Commission shall inform the Member State concerned without delay of the receipt of a notification.

---

[116] Ibid, Article 4.
[117] Ibid, Article 6.
[118] Ibid, Article 9.
[119] Ibid, Article 7(2)(b).
[120] Ibid, Article 27.
[121] Ibid, Article 24.
[122] Ibid, Article 12.
[123] Ibid, Article 25. The first such inquiry, into electricity capacity mechanisms, was launched in 2015 and concluded a year later.
[124] Article 108(2) TFEU.

> ## Article 3
>
> ### Standstill clause
>
> Aid notifiable pursuant to Article 2(1) **shall not be put into effect before the Commission has taken,** or is deemed to have taken, **a decision authorising such aid.**

Unlawful aid incompatible with the internal market must be recovered in order to restore effective competition. If necessary, the Commission may impose interim measures—such as a suspension injunction to halt the aid measure or a recovery injunction—before it reaches a final decision on the compatibility of unlawful aid with the internal market. Recovery of aid, which must include interest rates, can only be ordered for unlawful or misused aid subject to a ten-year statutory limitation.[125] In case of non-compliance with a recovery or injunction decision, the Commission can directly request a declaration from the CJEU recognizing the failure of the Member State concerned to comply with the Commission's decisions without having to follow the procedures for infringement proceedings (Articles 258 and 259 TFEU).[126] Where such a declaration does still not lead to Member State compliance, the Commission may request the CJEU, in accordance with Article 260(2) TFEU, to impose financial sanctions on the Member State. No fines can be imposed on Member States at an earlier stage of the enforcement of EU State aid rules.[127]

One of the publicly most salient State aid decisions of the Commission related to the recovery of unlawful aid provided by Ireland to Apple.[128] Following an investigation launched in 2013, the Commission came to the conclusion in August 2016 that Ireland granted Apple illegal State aid worth an unprecedented EUR 13 billion in the period between 2003 and 2014. The amount of unlawful aid was in fact much higher, as the first advantageous tax ruling originated from 1991 (the second was issued in 2007) but under the limitation statute aid granted more than ten years prior to Commission's initial probe (in 2013) is not eligible for recovery; all State aid granted prior to 2003 was classified as 'existing' aid which is non-recoverable. The key objection of the Commission related to the fact that the illegal Irish tax rulings enabled transfer pricing arrangements (methods for pricing transactions between enterprises under common control) within Apple's corporate structures which did not respect the arm's length principle (transactions should be priced as if they are made between independent companies in regular market conditions). As a result, the tax paid by Apple in the surveyed period was considerably lower than what it would have been if the arm's length principle was respected. While Ireland was not the only Member State whose tax rulings have been found deficient in light of EU State aid law,[129] the sheer amount of aid ordered for

---

[125] Article 17 of Regulation 2015/1589.

[126] Article 108(2) TFEU.

[127] Undertakings concerned can be fined for supplying incorrect information or lack of compliance with information requests and the like. See Article 8 of Regulation 2015/1589. The Regulation explains the impossibility of fining Member States in paragraph 16 of the recital: 'Fines and periodic penalty payments are not applicable to Member States, since they are under a duty to cooperate sincerely with the Commission in accordance with Article 4(3) TEU, and to provide the Commission with all information required to allow it to carry out its duties under this Regulation.'

[128] Commission Decision (EU) 2017/1283 on State aid SA.38373 (2014/C) (ex 2014/NN) (ex 2014/CP) implemented by Ireland to Apple (notified under document C(2017) 5605) [2017] OJ L187/1.

[129] See Commission Decision (EU) 2016/1699 on the excess profit exemption State aid scheme SA.37667 (2015/C) (ex 2015/NN) implemented by Belgium (notified under document C(2015) 9837) [2016] OJ L260/61; Commission Decision (EU) 2017/502 on State aid SA.38374 (2014/C ex 2014/NN) implemented by the Netherlands to Starbucks (notified under document C(2015) 7143) [2017] OJ L83/38; Commission Decision (EU) 2016/2326 on State aid SA.38375 (2014/C ex 2014/NN) which Luxembourg granted to Fiat (notified under document C(2015) 7152) [2016] OJ L351/1.

recovery makes the case particularly contentious. This becomes clear from the two appeals filed by Ireland and Apple—both were disputing the Commission's decision on altogether 23 grounds, including, among others, misunderstanding of Irish tax law, abuse of the Commission's State aid competence, and a breach of procedural rights, such as the obligation to state reasons required by Article 41(2)(c) of the Charter protecting the right to good administration. On 15 July 2020 the General Court stunningly annulled the decision.[130]

The application of State aid rules, especially in cases such as that of Apple which introduce a novel interpretation of the law, is in inherent tension with the principles of legitimate expectations and legal certainty.[131] The crux of the issue is that the decisions of the Commissions on State aid—be they recovery or authorizing decisions—cannot always be foreseen by beneficiaries, which is liable to hamper their business. However, the principle of legitimate expectations is interpreted restrictively in State aid by the CJEU.[132] The principle has been in some instances connected to the right to property (Article 1 of Protocol No 1 to the European Convention on Human Rights (ECHR)) by the European Court of Human Rights (ECtHR);[133] in the case law of the CJEU, legitimate expectations are examined separately from the scope of Article 17 of the Charter on the right to property (which is analogous to the ECHR guarantee).[134]

L Lovdahl Gormsen and C Mifsud-Bonnici, 'Legitimate Expectation of Consistent Interpretation of EU State Aid Law: Recovery in State Aid Cases Involving Advanced Pricing Agreements on Tax' (2017) 8 Journal of European Competition Law and Practice 423

This paper argues the Commission's order of recovery in the recent tax cases is highly questionable due to the Commission's novel legal analysis of EU State aid law. While the Commission is in its good right to change the way in which it thinks about State aid, it has to change its thinking in a manner that is foreseeable. Otherwise it runs counter to the general EU law principle on legal certainty and breaches the legitimate expectations of multinational companies, which make use of tax rulings issued by national tax authorities to manage their tax liability efficiently. The very objective of an advance pricing arrangement ('APAs') is the achievement of legal certainty to a multinational's tax liability. While multinationals cannot entertain legitimate expectations merely on the basis that such an

---

[130] Judgment of 15 July 2020, *Ireland and Others v Commission*, T-778/16 and T-892/16, ECLI:EU:T:2020:338. The Court upheld the pleas in law alleging that, in its alternative line of reasoning, the Commission had not succeeded in showing that there was a selective advantage for the purposes of Article 107(1) TFEU and did not see the need to examine the complaints alleging breaches of essential procedural requirements and of the right to be heard. The United States has tried to intervene in Case T-892/16 without success: Order of 17 May 2018, *United States of America v Apple Sales International and Others*, C-12/18 P(I), ECLI:EU:C:2018:330.

[131] In addition to the excerpt below see R Fadiga, 'Of Apples, Cars, and Coffee—Against the Commission's Remedy to Unlawful Tax Rulings' (2018) 10 European Journal of Legal Studies 209.

[132] See, for example, Judgment of 24 March 2011, *ISD Polska and Others v Commission*, C-369/09 P, ECLI:EU:C:2011:175.

[133] *Pine Valley Developments Ltd and Others v Ireland*, App no 12742/87, 29 November 1991. However, note that generally the ECtHR grants considerable discretion to states when it comes to enforcement of tax laws and presumably the intersection between the State aid inquiries into tax rulings and the right to property would be viewed in this light as well. See *Impar Ltd v Lithuania*, App no 13102/04, Judgment of 5 January 2010, para 34.

[134] In the context of State aid, the principle of legitimate expectations and the right to property were discussed by the Grand Chamber of the CJEU in Judgment of 19 July 2016, *Kotnik and Others v Državni zbor Republike Slovenije*, ECLI:EU:C:2016:570, para 61. In the context of free movement of services, see Judgment of 11 June 2015, *Berlington Hungary v Magyar Állam*, C-98/14, ECLI:EU:C:2015:386, para 75.

arrangement was concluded with a national tax authority, these widely used practices give an important context to this paper. The EU bloc, as a whole, attempts to attract and stimulate investment, thus it is important that multinationals have legal certainty. It is a general principle of EU law, which is shared by the national legal orders of all EU Member States, and one which puts investors at ease that their rights and property are protected. Therefore, within the context of the widespread use of tax rulings and also the significant amount of tax liability shouldered by multinationals, a defence of legitimate expectations should not be discounted hastily.

(...) While recovery is a mechanism, which attempts to restore the situation before the granting of aid, and is not equivalent to imposing a fine for anticompetitive behaviour, it may also be punitive in nature if the recovery runs well above the multi-million euro mark, goes back up to 10 years and more importantly is applied retroactively. The Commission should have engaged with its Member States, their tax and accounting bodies and multi-national groups affected by its change in State aid analysis to afford those affected the opportunity to amend their arrangements with national tax authorities. It could also have proposed to the Council a new regulation on the basis of Article 109 TFEU.

6.3 Undertakings as Beneficiaries of Fundamental Rights

Before moving to the specific rights protection issues arising in the context of EU competition law, it is pertinent to clarify the obvious fact that in virtually all cases in this area, the beneficiaries of fundamental rights are not natural but legal persons, more specifically business entities (broadly construed as 'undertakings' in the EU competition parlance). The issue comes naturally into sharper focus if the term 'fundamental rights' used in the internal EU context is replaced by the more internationally used 'human rights'. The question to what extent corporate entities possess such rights is of some significance not only in competition law but also in other traditional areas of EU activity, such as the internal market, which often directly affect business entities more than they do natural persons.

Fortunately, the question is to a large extent settled, at least for the purposes of EU competition law. The Charter specifically protects the freedom to conduct a business (Article 16), as well as mentioning that business secrecy is a legitimate balancing interest when it comes to the right of persons to have access to their files (Article 41(2)(b)). In addition, Articles 42 to 44 of the Charter explicitly refer to legal persons as beneficiaries of the right of access to documents, the right to refer cases of maladministration to the European Ombudsman, and the right to petition the European Parliament, respectively. Elsewhere, the Charter tends to refer to beneficiaries of rights and freedoms as 'every person' or 'everyone'. That these words include in many cases—there are some, such as the right to life, where this would be nonsensical—legal persons is supported by most European human rights traditions, not least the ECHR and the interpretation given to it by the ECtHR,[135] as demonstrated in a

---

[135] Article 1 of the ECHR states: 'The High Contracting Parties shall secure to everyone within their jurisdiction the rights and freedoms defined in Section I of this Convention.' The more contentious cases have concerned the extent of protection accorded to commercial expression under Article 10 ECHR on freedom of expression. In a leading case on the matter, the ECtHR found that in principle Article 10 ECHR protects also the imparting of information of a commercial nature. See *Markt Intern Verlag GmbH and Beermann v Germany, Merits*, App no 10572/83, 20 November 1989. See also *Niemietz v Germany*, App no 13710/88, 16 December 1992 where the ECtHR held that the right to respect for private life protected by Article 8 ECHR encompasses 'activities of a professional or business nature'.

landmark study on the human rights of companies in the ECHR system.[136] Especially insofar as due process rights are concerned,[137] which are of main interest in competition law, there are few reasons to think that business entities should generally benefit from less extensive fundamental rights protection than natural persons.[138] The same holds true, subject to differences emanating from the lawful regulation of economic activities, for the right to property protected by Article 1 of Protocol 1 to the ECHR and Article 17 of the Charter.

Moreover, due to the economic orientation of the European project, business entities are richly represented in the history of EU-level litigation and the CJEU has not questioned their general predisposition to benefit from fundamental rights—especially those relating to access to justice and fairness of administrative proceedings—protected by the Court.[139] The crucial procedural rights of undertakings investigated for competition infringements, such as the right to be heard, were recognized by the CJEU in the formative era of fundamental rights protection in the EU as general principles of law,[140] as well as included in some form in the first laws regulating competition enforcement.[141]

Outside the strict confines of competition law, the CJEU has had the opportunity to give a preliminary ruling on the question whether a national rule precluding the granting of legal aid to legal persons is compatible with the principle of effectiveness of EU law.[142] For the purposes of answering this question, the CJEU had to examine whether Article 47(3) of the Charter which states that legal aid 'shall be made available to those who lack sufficient resources in so far as such aid is necessary to ensure effective access to justice' excludes legal persons from its scope. The Court looked at both linguistic and legal arguments when settling the question.

Judgment of 22 December 2010, *DEB Deutsche Energiehandels- und Beratungsgesellschaft mbH v Bundesrepublik Deutschland*, C-279/09, ECLI:EU:C:2010:811

---

35. As regards the Charter, Article 52(3) thereof states that, in so far as the Charter contains rights which correspond to those guaranteed by the ECHR, their meaning and scope are to be the same as those laid down by the ECHR. (...)
36. As regards in particular Article 47(3) of the Charter, the last paragraph of the Explanation relating to Article 47 mentions the judgment in *Airey v. Ireland* of 9

---

[136] M Emberland, *The Human Rights of Companies: Exploring the Structure of ECHR Protection* (Oxford University Press 2006).

[137] Under the ECHR chiefly protected by Articles 6 and 13 ECHR.

[138] There are exceptions and grey areas. For example, the privilege against self-incrimination, recognized as forming part of Article 6 ECHR for the purposes of criminal law in *Saunders v United Kingdom*, App no 19187/91, 17 December 1996 has not been as yet expressly extended by the ECtHR to legal persons. In the US, the Supreme Court has held that legal persons may not benefit from the right not to incriminate themselves. See *Hale v Henkel* 201 US 43 (1906), 69 and 70, *United States v White* 322 US 694 (1944). The CJEU's view of this issue is discussed below.

[139] See Judgment of 17 December 1970, *Internationale Handelsgesellschaft*, 11/70, ECLI:EU:C:1970:114.

[140] *Hoffmann-La Roche* (n 87) para 9.

[141] See, for example, Article 20 of Regulation No 17 First Regulation implementing Articles 85 and 86 of the Treaty [1962] OJ 13/204.

[142] Judgment of 22 December 2010, *DEB Deutsche Energiehandels- und Beratungsgesellschaft mbH v Bundesrepublik Deutschland*, C-279/09, ECLI:EU:C:2010:811.

October 1979 (Eur. Court H.R., Series A, No 32, p. 11), according to which provision should be made for legal aid where the absence of such aid would make it impossible to ensure an effective remedy. No indication is given as to whether such aid must be granted to a legal person or of the nature of the costs covered by that aid.

37. That provision must be interpreted in its context, in the light of other provisions of EU law, the law of the Member States and the case-law of the European Court of Human Rights.

38. As the Commission of the European Communities observed in its written submissions, the word 'person' used in the first two paragraphs of Article 47 of the Charter may cover individuals, but, **from a purely linguistic point of view, it does not exclude legal persons.**

39. It should be noted in that connection that, although the explanations relating to the Charter do not provide any clarification in this regard, **the use of the word 'Person', in the German language version of Article 47, as opposed to the word 'Mensch'**, which is used in numerous other provisions—for example, in Articles 1, 2, 3, 6, 29, 34 and 35 of the Charter—**may be an indication that legal persons are not excluded from the scope of that article.**

40. Moreover, the right to an effective remedy before a court, enshrined in Article 47 of the Charter, is to be found under **Title VI of that Charter**, relating to justice, **in which other procedural principles are established which apply to both natural and legal persons.**

41. The fact that the right to receive legal aid is not to be found in Title IV of the Charter, relating to solidarity, **indicates that that right is not conceived primarily as social assistance**, whereas in German law it does appear to be conceived as such, a factor on which the German Government has relied in support of its argument that that assistance must be reserved to natural persons.

44. As the Advocate General pointed out in points 76 to 80 of his Opinion, examination of the law of the Member States brings to light the absence of a truly common principle which is shared by all those States as regards the award of legal aid to legal persons. However, in point 80 of that Opinion, the Advocate General also pointed out that, in the practice of the Member States which allow legal aid to be granted to legal persons, there is a relatively **widespread distinction between profit-making and non-profitmaking legal persons.**

52. It is apparent from (…) examination of the case-law of the European Court of Human Rights that the **grant of legal aid to legal persons is not in principle impossible**, but must be assessed in the light of the applicable rules and the situation of the company concerned.

The CJEU concluded that Article 47(3) of the Charter in principle allows legal persons to benefit from legal aid in the interest of effective access to justice. However, when formulating or interpreting rules on legal aid—at least in areas where EU law is applicable—Member States may take into account the situation of the legal person requesting legal aid. The ensuing limitations on the right to legal aid of legal persons must comply with the standard proportionality test spelled out in Article 52 of the Charter. The non-exhaustive factors to be taken into consideration in this regard are 'the form of the legal person in question and whether it is profit-making or non-profit-making; the financial capacity of the partners or shareholders; and the ability of those partners or shareholders to obtain the sums necessary to institute legal proceedings.[143] As an aside relevant for this chapter, the judgment in *DEB* also confirms that 'other procedural principles' protected under Title VI of the Charter apply to both natural and legal person (paragraph 40).

6.4 Rights of Defence in EU Competition Proceedings

Competition law and its enforcement can be intrusive, disruptive, and punishing. As such, the undertakings affected by it need to have the opportunity to mount an effective defence of the legality of their conduct when they become accused of foul play. Legal principles protecting private parties from arbitrary governmental actions in administrative proceedings and ensuring equality in private litigation are universally recognized as foundational for most if not all legal orders. EU competition law is not different in this regard.[144] As a specificity of State aid control, the Member States, as the addressees of Commission decisions, are also entitled to virtually the same standard of rights of defence as private persons subject to other aspects of EU competition law. Conversely, the beneficiaries of State aid who tend to be the most affected by the interventions of the Commission possess only limited procedural rights, equal to those of affected competitors (rights of interested parties).[145]

Judgment of 15 March 2000, *Cimenteries CBR and Others v Commission*, T-25 to 26/95, T-30 to 32/95, T-34 to 39/95, T-42 to 46/ 95, T-48/95, T-50 to 65/95, T-68 to 71/95, T-87 to 88/95, T-103 to 104/ 95, ECLI:EU:T:2000:77

---

106. The Court points out that the provisions to which the applicants refer, which lay down an obligation on the Commission to notify the undertakings and associations of undertakings in writing of the objections raised against them, enshrine **the fundamental principle of Community law that the rights of the defence must be respected in all proceedings in which sanctions may be imposed**. The proper observance of that general principle requires that the undertakings and associations of undertakings concerned be afforded the opportunity during the administrative procedure to make known their views on the truth and relevance of the facts, charges and circumstances relied on by the Commission (...)

Rights of defence, recognized among others in Article 48(2) of the Charter, is an umbrella term comprising a number of legal principles and entitlements which serve to protect the interests of private parties in the course of competition proceedings. Most of the rights represent essential procedural requirements which must be observed lest the decisions adopted

---

[143] Ibid, para 62.
[144] See also Article 27(2) of Regulation 1/2003.
[145] Judgment of 6 March 2003, *Westdeutsche Landesbank Girozentrale v Commission*, T-228/99 and T-233/99, ECLI:EU:T:2003:57, paras 120–125; and recital 18, Articles 6 and 24 of Regulation 2015/1589 (n 125).

be vitiated by defect. The following paragraphs look at the most important elements of this fundamental rights protection in EU competition law, in particular antitrust proceedings concerning infringements of Articles 101 and 102 TFEU where the finding of liability carries the most serious implications.[146]

A. Right to be heard and access to file

The most rudimentary component of the rights of defence is the right to be heard, today also enshrined in Article 41(2)(a) of the Charter.[147] The right to be heard in antitrust proceedings conducted by the Commission has been recognized in the relevant legislation from the very beginning of Community competition law.[148] It has been established early in the practice of the Commission and the case law of the CJEU that the first step in the proceedings, the statement of objections outlining the Commission's complaints as to the undertaking's conduct, including the factual basis supporting the allegations, is indispensable to enable the exercise of the right to be heard.[149] This allows the undertakings concerned to formulate their views with regard to the complaints and defend themselves against the accusations, including in an oral hearing conducted by the Hearing Officer at the request of the undertaking concerned.[150] The essential procedural character of the hearings is underlined by the fact that a failure to organize a hearing in accordance with Articles 12 and 14 of Commission Regulation 773/2004 automatically vitiates the administrative procedure by defect without the need for the undertaking concerned to demonstrate the existence of detrimental effects on its defence.[151]

In order to facilitate the undertakings' right to be heard, the Commission must furthermore supply, in the course of the administrative procedure, 'the details necessary to the defence'.[152] Effective enjoyment of the right to be heard therefore requires the consultation of information and evidence which often may only exist on file with the Commission. In other words, the right to be heard is closely bound up with the right of access to the file.[153] Both are protected as part of the right to good administration of Article 41 of the Charter.[154]

---

[146] Note that the principles covered in the following section regarding the question of criminality of competition proceedings can be broadly seen as also forming part of the rights of the defence.

[147] For an early application of the principle that parties must be able to formulate opinions in relation to the relevant facts and documents see Judgment of 22 March 1961, *Société nouvelle des usines de Pontlieue— Aciéries du Temple (S.N.U.P.A.T.) v High Authority of the European Coal and Steel Community*, 42/59 and 49/59, ECLI:EU:C:1961:5.

[148] See Article 19 of Council Regulation No 17.

[149] Judgment of 15 July 1970, *Boehringer Mannheim GmbH v Commission*, 45/69, ECLI:EU:C:1970:73, para 9.

[150] See Articles 12 and 14 of Commission Regulation 773/2004 (n 44).

[151] Judgment of 21 September 2017, *Ferriere Nord SpA v Commission*, C-88/15 P, ECLI:EU:C:2017:716, para 55.

[152] *Boehringer* (n 149) para 9.

[153] See Judgment of 18 December 1992, *Cimenteries CBR and Others v Commission*, T-10/92, T-11/92, T-12/92 and T-15/92, ECLI:EU:T:1992:123, para 38.

[154] The right to be heard is found in paragraph (2)(a) and the right to have access to one's own file in (2)(b). For a recent reference to both Charter provisions see Judgment of 14 September 2017, *LG Electronics v European Commission*, C-588/15 P and C-622/15 P, ECLI:EU:C:2017:679, para 43.

Judgment of 13 February 1979, *Hoffmann-La Roche & Co. AG v Commission*, 85/76, ECLI:EU:C:1979:36

11. Thus it emerges from the provisions quoted above and also from the general principle to which they give effect that in order to respect the principle of the right to be heard the undertakings concerned must have been afforded the opportunity during the administrative procedure to **make known their views on the truth and relevance of the facts and circumstances alleged and on the documents used by the Commission to support its claim that there has been an infringement** of Article 86 of the Treaty.

12. The Commission does not deny that, since it took the view that it was bound to observe professional secrecy, it refused to pass on the data that it had obtained from competitors or customers of Roche which formed the basis, together with other data, of its assessment of the market shares and of the view that the disputed contracts restrict competition.

13. Although Article 20(2) of Regulation No 17 provides that 'Without prejudice to the provisions of Articles 19 and 21, the Commission and the competent authorities of the Member States, their **officials and other servants shall not disclose information** acquired by them as a result of the application of this regulation and of the kind covered by professional secrecy', **this rule must**, as the express reference to Article 19 confirms, **be reconciled with the right to be heard**.

14. The said **Article 20** by providing undertakings from whom information has been obtained with a guarantee that their interests which are closely connected with observance of professional secrecy, are not jeopardized, enables the Commission to collect on the widest possible scale the requisite data for the fulfilment of the task conferred upon it by Articles 85 and 86 of the Treaty without the undertakings being able to prevent it from doing so, but it **does not nevertheless allow it to use**, to the detriment of the undertakings involved in a proceeding referred to in Regulation No 17, **facts, circumstances or documents which it cannot in its view disclose if such a refusal of disclosure adversely affects that undertaking's opportunity to make known effectively its views on the truth or implications of those circumstances, on those documents** or again on the conclusions drawn by the Commission from them.

Similarly important for Articles 101, 102 TFEU, and merger cases,[155] the right of access to the file, however, is in inherent tension and must be balanced with the confidentiality of information collected by the Commission during investigation and protected by professional secrecy.[156] Such information may include business secrets of competitors or other undertakings, other information covered by professional secrecy, confidential information and internal reports of the Commission and the NCAs, as well as correspondence between the

---

[155] Although it has been argued that the rights of defence and the right to be heard should be protected more extensively in Articles 101 and 102 TFEU proceedings (in light of their gravity) than in merger cases, the General Court has recently reaffirmed the centrality of these rights across competition law, including merger notification proceedings. See Judgment of 7 March 2017, *United Parcel Service v Commission*, T-194/13, ECLI:EU:T:2017:144; see also A Andreangeli, 'Competition Law and Fundamental Rights' (2017) Survey, Journal of European Competition Law and Practice 10.

[156] Article 28 of Regulation 1/2003. See also Article 339 TFEU.

competition authorities.[157] The rationale behind safeguarding the secrecy of information is to allow the Commission to collect evidence corroborating competition infringements as widely as possible, thus gaining access to data which would not otherwise be shared with the investigators.

However, where the frustration of the right to access the file stemming from confidentiality of the sensitive information sought prejudices the ability of the accused undertaking to express its views on that information, the Commission may not rely on that evidence to find an infringement of EU competition law.[158] The extent of the obligation to grant access to documents and of the obligation to protect the confidentiality of third party or internal information, and their reconciliation in case of conflict, is therefore frequently litigated.

It is not enough for parties to have a right to be heard, the hearings also need to be fair (as required by Articles 41(1) and 47(2) of the Charter). Before the EU courts, the exercise of the right to be heard of undertakings charged with competition infringements must therefore take place under conditions which are not substantially less advantageous than those under which the Commission pleads its case. This is a widely accepted principle of law known as 'equality of arms', the observance of which the CJEU dwells on as well in competition proceedings.

Judgment of 12 November 2014, *Guardian Industries v Commission*, C-580/12 P, ECLI:EU:C:2014:2363

---

30. **The principle of respect for the rights of the defence is a fundamental principle of EU law.** That principle would be infringed if a judicial decision were to be based on facts and documents of which the parties themselves, or one of them, have not been able to take cognisance and in relation to which they have not therefore been able to formulate an opinion (…)

31. **The principle of equality of arms**, which is a corollary of the very concept of a fair hearing and the aim of which is to ensure a balance between the parties to proceedings, guaranteeing that any document submitted to the court may be examined and challenged by any party to the proceedings, **implies that each party must be afforded a reasonable opportunity to present his case**, including his evidence, **under conditions that do not place him at a substantial disadvantage vis-à-vis his opponent** (…)

B. Right to good administration and duty to give reasons

In addition to the right to be heard and access to file, Article 41(1) of the Charter confers on individuals the right to have their administrative file 'handled impartially, fairly and within a reasonable time' by the institutions of the EU. It also obliges the administration to

---

[157] Articles 27(2) and 28 of Regulation 1/2003 and Article 18(3) of the Merger Regulation codify to a large extent the preceding case law on this issue.

[158] *Hoffmann-La Roche* (n 87) para 14; Judgment of 7 June 1983, *Musique Diffusion française and Others v Commission*, 100 to 103/80, ECLI:EU:C:1983:158, para 29.

give reasons for its decisions.[159] Article 41(1) essentially replicates the basic requirements of Article 47 of the Charter relating to the fairness of trials in court for the purpose of administrative proceedings, both of which are to an extent modelled upon Articles 6 and 13 ECHR.[160]

The principle of sound administration and the duty of care, as the substance of Article 41 of the Charter has been often referred to in the past, have been acknowledged as imposing an obligation on the competent institution to examine carefully and impartially all the relevant aspects of each case.[161] It follows for the Commission that 'evidence must be assessed in its entirety, taking into account all relevant circumstances' and explanations provided when evidence is excluded from the appraisal.[162] In addition, sound administration necessitates the Commission not to overburden the undertaking concerned with requests for information after the delivery of the statement of objections, as this can have a negative effect on the company's ability to formulate its defence.[163]

A more frequently litigated element of Article 41(1) of the Charter is the length of the Commission competition proceedings. Building on ECtHR case law, the EU judiciary has held that the reasonableness of the duration must be determined in light of the particular circumstances of the case, taking account of the context, the various procedural stages followed by the Commission, the conduct of the parties during the proceedings, the complexity of the case, and its importance for the parties.[164] Findings of breach of the reasonable time requirement are rare and even if established, the chance that they would result in an annulment of the delayed Commission decision is low. These principles echo the judiciary's approach to court delays (see Section 6.6).

Judgment of 17 December 2015, *Société nationale des chemins de fer français v Commission*, T-242/12, ECLI:EU:T:2015:1003

393. However, infringement of the principle that the Commission must act within a reasonable time, if established, **would justify the annulment of a decision** taken at the end of an administrative procedure in competition proceedings **only in so far as it also constituted an infringement of the rights of defence** of the undertaking concerned. Where it has not been established that the undue delay has adversely affected the ability of the undertakings concerned to defend themselves effectively, failure to comply with the principle that the Commission must act within a reasonable time **cannot affect the validity of the administrative procedure** and can therefore be **regarded only as a cause of damage** capable of being relied on before the EU judicature. In any event, it must also be borne in mind that, during the investigation

---

[159] Article 41(2)(c) of the Charter. See also Article 296 TFEU which requires all legal acts to state reasons on which they are based.

[160] As regards the requirement of impartiality see Judgment of 11 July 2013, *Ziegler v Commission*, C-439/11 P, ECLI:EU:C:2013:513, para 155.

[161] Judgment of 24 January 1992, *La Cinq v Commission*, T-44/90, ECLI:EU:T:1992:5, para 86.

[162] Judgment of 9 December 2014, *SP SpA v Commission*, T-472/09 and T-55/10, ECLI:EU:T:2014:1040, para 187.

[163] Judgment of 30 September 2003, *Atlantic Container Line and Others v Commission*, T-191/98, T-212/98 to T-214/98, ECLI:EU:T:2003:245, para 418.

[164] Judgment of 22 October 1997, *SCK and FNK v Commission*, T-213/95 and T-18/96, ECLI:EU:T:1997:157, para 57.

> phase referred to in Article 108(2) TFEU, **interested parties such as the applicant in the present case, far from enjoying the same rights of defence** as those which individuals against whom a procedure has been instituted are recognised as having, the parties concerned have only the right to be involved in the administrative procedure to the extent appropriate in the light of the circumstances of the case (…)

The determination of Commission compliance with the reasonable time requirement furthermore takes into account whether the complained-about proceedings were directed against the applicants or whether the latter constitute 'merely' interested parties who qualified for standing under Article 263(4) TFEU. The General Court has implied that interested parties, such as undertakings that benefited from illegal State aid subject to a Commission recovery decision, do not enjoy the same level of rights protection as the parties against whom competition action is taken. In fact, this is true more generally with respect to the rights of the defence: they are less extensive for interested parties when compared to—to continue with the State aid example—Member States in Article 108(2) TFEU proceedings.[165]

As per Article 41(2)(c) of the Charter (and Article 296 TFEU), the right to good administration also entails a duty on the part of the Commission to justify its decisions in the course of competition proceedings. The obligation to state reasons is relatively broad as it plays an important enabling role in allowing both the undertakings concerned and the EU courts to appraise the factual nature and legality of the decision.

Judgment of 27 March 2014, *Saint-Gobain Glass France SA and Others v Commission*, T-56/09 and T-73/09, ECLI:EU:T:2014:160

144. **The purpose of the obligation to state reasons is to enable the Courts of the EU to review the legality** of the decision and to provide the person concerned with sufficient information to make it possible to ascertain whether the decision is well founded or whether it is vitiated by a defect which may permit its legality to be contested (…)

145. The statement of reasons must therefore in principle be notified to the person concerned **at the same time as the act adversely affecting him** and a failure to state the reasons cannot be remedied by the fact that the person concerned learns the reasons for the decision during the proceedings before the Court (…)

146. The requirement to state reasons must be assessed according to the circumstances of the case. It is not necessary for the reasoning to go into all the relevant facts and points of law, since the question whether the statement of reasons meets the requirements of Article 253 EC must be assessed with regard not only to the **wording of the measure** in question **but also to the context** in which the measure was adopted (…)

147. As regards the indication of figures relating to the calculation of the fines, it should be observed that the Commission did not in fact provide details in the contested decision of the specific Saint-Gobain sales figures which it took into account in order to calculate the fine imposed on that undertaking.

[165] Judgment of 17 December 2015, *Société nationale des chemins de fer français v Commission*, T-242/12, ECLI:EU:T:2015:1003, para 361.

> 148. As regards the determination of fines for infringements of competition law, how-
> ever, the **Commission fulfils its obligation to state reasons where it indicates**, in
> its decision, **the factors on the basis of which the gravity and duration of the in-
> fringement were assessed**, without being required to include in it a more detailed
> account or the figures relating to the method of calculating the fines (…)

The Commission is not required to publish specific figures with respect to the calculation of fines in order to comply with the duty to give reasons. The rationale behind this is that if investigated undertakings could precisely calculate the fine to be imposed, they could perform a simple cost-benefit analysis of the profits derived from the competition infringement and the costs resulting from the fine, which would weaken the deterrent effect of fines.[166]

The duty to state reasons extends to all decisions of the Commission and it can play a particularly critical role when it comes to inspections, as the documents collected thereby are only admissible insofar as they relate to the purpose or subject matter of the inspection.[167] Therefore the reasons listed by the Commission in an inspection decision—which represents a basic guarantee of the rights of defence—subsequently circumscribe its search and seizure powers during the inspection.[168]

> **Judgment of 6 September 2013, *Deutsche Bahn AG and Others v Commission*, T-289/11, T-290/11, and T-521/11, ECLI:EU:T:2013:404**
>
> 77. (…) **in order to ensure that the undertaking is able to exercise its right of op-
> position, the inspection decision must contain**, apart from the formal particulars
> listed in Article 20(4) of Regulation No 1/2003, a **description of the features of the
> suspected infringement**, by indicating the market thought to be affected and the
> nature of the suspected competition restrictions, as well as the sectors covered by
> the alleged infringement, **the supposed degree of involvement** of the undertaking
> concerned, **the evidence sought** and **the matters to which the investigation must
> relate** (…)

C. Right to legal assistance

Undertakings have the right to be assisted by lawyers throughout any stage of competition enforcement.[169] Crucially, this right applies also when the Commission is executing an inspection of the premises on the basis of Article 20(4) of Regulation 1/2003,[170] despite the fact

---

[166] Judgment of 27 March 2014, *Saint-Gobain Glass France SA and Others v Commission*, T-56/09 and T-73/09, ECLI:EU:T:2014:160, para 151.

[167] See Article 20(4) of Regulation 1/2003; Judgment of 17 October 1989, *Dow Benelux v Commission*, 85/87, ECLI:EU:C:1989:379, para 18.

[168] Judgment of 18 June 2015, *Deutsche Bahn AG and Others v Commission*, C-583/13 P, ECLI:EU:C:2015:404, para 60.

[169] Judgment of 18 May 1982, *AM & S v Commission*, 155/79, ECLI:EU:C:1982:157, para 18.

[170] Judgment of 6 September 2013, *Deutsche Bahn AG and Others v Commission*, T-289/11, T-290/11 and T-521/11, ECLI:EU:T:2013:404, para 81.

that in practice the Commission is not going to wait for a long time for the arrival of a legal counsel during a 'dawn raid'.[171]

One of the key issues relating to the right to legal assistance is the extent of the legal professional privilege (LPP). LPP protects the confidentiality of written communication between the client and the attorney and it is 'of great importance (...) for the proper administration of justice (...) in a democratic society' both from the perspective of the rights of the defence and the maintenance of the rule of law.[172] In the landmark judgment *AM & S v Commission*, the CJEU made reliance on LPP by undertakings in competition proceedings subject to two conditions: the client–attorney communication must be made 'for the purposes and in the interests of the client's rights of defence' and the lawyers consulted must be independent lawyers, that is not in an employment relationship with the undertaking (in-house lawyers).[173]

Judgment of 18 May 1982, *AM & S v Commission*, 155/79, ECLI:EU:C:1982:157

24. As regards the second condition, it should be stated that the requirement as to the position and status as an independent lawyer, which must be fulfilled by the legal adviser from whom the written communications which may be protected emanate, is based on a **conception of the lawyer's role as collaborating in the administration of justice by the courts and as being required to provide, in full independence,** and in the overriding interests of that cause, such **legal assistance** as the client needs. The counterpart of that protection lies in the rules of professional ethics and discipline which are laid down and enforced in the general interest by institutions endowed with the requisite powers for that purpose. (...)

The same conceptualization of LPP was upheld almost 30 years later in *Akzo Nobel*.[174] The CJEU (and before, the General Court) found on the basis of a comparative examination of Member States' legal systems that no uniform tendency regarding the extension of LPP to in-house lawyers could be observed. The CJEU therefore saw no justification for changing its own case law on the issue.[175] The Court was equally unmoved by arguments alleging that a difference between the scope of LPP as guaranteed in EU law and national law infringes upon the principle of legal certainty. The CJEU stated that the applicable notion of LPP can be determined by undertakings according to whether it is the Commission or the NCA carrying out the investigation and in particular the seizure of documents without legal certainty thereby being affected.[176] This conclusion is not, in the Court's view, prejudiced by the fact that the Commission is regularly assisted by NCAs during inspections—the rights of defence, including LPP, in such circumstances are derived from EU law, not national law.[177]

---

[171] European Commission, Explanatory note on Commission inspections pursuant to Article 20(4) of Council Regulation No 1/2003, Revised on 11 September 2015, para 6. For an extensive overview of the compatibility of the Commission's 'dawn raids' with the undertakings' rights of defence see H Andersson, *Dawn Raids Under Challenge: Due Process Aspects on the European Commission's Dawn Raid Practices* (Hart Publishing 2018).

[172] *Michaud v France*, App no 12323/11, 6 December 2012, para 123; *AM & S* (n 169) para 20.

[173] *AM & S* (n 169) para 21.

[174] Judgment of 14 September 2010, *Akzo Nobel Chemicals Ltd and Akcros Chemicals Ltd v Commission*, C-550/07 P, ECLI:EU:C:2010:512.

[175] Ibid, para 76.

[176] Ibid, para 105.

[177] Ibid, para 119.

There are circumstances in which the conditions attached to LPP might be slightly relaxed. The General Court has recognized that internal notes confined to reporting the text or content of communications with independent lawyers are also covered by LPP.[178] Likewise, internal preparatory documents gathering information for the exclusive purpose of seeking legal assistance from an independent lawyer can be withheld from the Commission on the basis of LPP.[179] However, the onus to prove that a disputed preparatory document qualifies for LPP is on the undertaking concerned and the possibility to invoke this defence is construed restrictively: it must be 'unambiguously clear' from the content or context of the document that it was prepared solely for consulting an external lawyer.[180]

D. Privilege against self-incrimination

The privilege against self-incrimination is another element of the rights of the defence[181] which to an extent circumscribes and must be balanced against the inquiry powers of the Commission and the effectiveness of competition enforcement. However, the principle is not explicitly included in any EU statutory instrument as far as competition law is concerned,[182] nor is it mentioned in the Charter of Fundamental Rights. Privilege against self-incrimination has thus been recognized by the CJEU as a corollary of the rights of the defence that undertakings may rely on in competition proceedings, while at the same time distinguishing this right from those available under international human rights instruments and Member State laws to natural persons in the context of criminal law.[183] The Court stated that the Commission 'may not compel an undertaking to provide it with answers which might involve an admission of (...) an infringement'.[184]

The undertakings' right not to incriminate themselves is not absolute, however.[185] Although the privilege applies to all stages of Commission inquiries, undertakings remain under an obligation to answer factual questions and surrender documents relating to the facts, even if those may enable the Commission to find an infringement of competition law.[186] Moreover, the CJEU demands that undertakings invoking the privilege against self-incrimination prove that coercion was used to obtain the incriminating information and that there was 'actual interference' with the right of the undertakings not to be compelled by the Commission to admit participation in a competition infringement.[187] The CJEU also

---

[178] Order of 4 April 1990, *Hilti Aktiengesellschaft v Commission*, T-30/89, ECLI:EU:T:1990:27, para 18.

[179] Judgment of 17 September 2007, *Akzo Nobel Chemicals Ltd and Akcros Chemicals Ltd v Commission*, T-125/03 and T-253/03, ECLI:EU:T:2007:287, paras 122–123.

[180] Ibid, para 124.

[181] Although in the interpretation of the ECtHR in the context of criminal procedure the right not to incriminate oneself is also connected to the preservation of personal autonomy and privacy. See *Saunders* (n 138); Andreangeli, *EU Competition Enforcement and Human Rights* (n 14) 126. See also the discussion in the following section as regards the criminality of EU competition enforcement.

[182] It can be found in criminal law instruments. See Article 7 of Directive (EU) 2016/343 of the European Parliament and of the Council on the strengthening of certain aspects of the presumption of innocence and of the right to be present at the trial in criminal proceedings [2016] OJ L65/1.

[183] Judgment of 18 October 1989, *Orkem v Commission*, 374/87, ECLI:EU:C:1989:387, paras 29–35.

[184] Ibid, para 35.

[185] Judgment of 20 February 2001, *Mannesmannröhren-Werke v Commission*, T-112/98, ECLI:EU:T:2001:61, para 66.

[186] Ibid, para 65 and case law cited.

[187] Judgment of 15 October 2002, *Limburgse Vinyl Maatschappij NV (LVM) v Commission*, C-238/99 P, C-244/99 P, C-245/99 P, C-247/99 P, C-250/99 P to C-252/99 P and C-254/99 P, ECLI:EU:C:2002:582, para 275.

views its approach to the privilege as being consistent with developments in the case law of the ECtHR which recognized the privilege in cases subsequent to the CJEU's landmark *Orkem* judgment.[188] Not all commentators have shared that sentiment.[189]

E. Respect for private and family life

Charter of Fundamental Rights of the European Union [2012] OJ C326/391

Article 7

Respect for private and family life

Everyone has the right to respect for his or her private and family life, home and communications.

Although representing a separate fundamental rights guarantee from the rights of the defence, respect for private and family life plays an important role in Commission inspections. The right represents a basic safeguard against arbitrary or disproportionate intervention by public authorities—such as the Commission—in the private sphere of both natural and legal persons.[190] The Charter provision corresponds for the purposes of Article 52(3) thereof to Article 8 ECHR.[191]

Originally, the CJEU did not recognize the applicability of Article 8 ECHR as covering the business premises of undertakings investigated by the Commission, as these are not explicitly mentioned in the provision.[192] However, following the landmark ECtHR judgment in the case of *Niemietz v Germany*,[193] the CJEU admitted that the right to respect for private life can extend to business premises.[194] Since then, the CJEU has consistently argued that the safeguards placed on the exercise of the Commission's enforcement powers, in particular insofar as they concern search and seizure at undertakings' premises, comply with the standards developed by the ECtHR. The most contentious aspect of this alleged equivalence concerns the requirement of prior judicial authorization for inspections of premises.

---

[188] Judgment of 29 June 2006, *Commission v SGL Carbon*, C-301/04 P, ECLI:EU:C:2006:432, paras 43–44. Two landmark judgments were handed down by the ECtHR during the 1990s: *Funke v France*, App no 10828/84, 25 February 1993; and *Saunders* (n 138).

[189] W van Overbeek, 'The Right to Remain Silent in Competition Investigations: The Funke Decision of the Court of Human Rights Makes Revision of the ECJ's Case Law Necessary' (1994) 15 European Competition Law Review 127; M Veenbrink, 'The Privilege against Self-Incrimination in EU Competition Law: A Deafening Silence?' (2015) 42 Legal Issues of Economic Integration 119.

[190] Judgment of 14 November 2012, *Nexans v Commission*, T-135/09, ECLI:EU:T:2012:596, para 40.

[191] See Explanations relating to the Charter of Fundamental Rights [2007] OJ C303/17, Article 52.

[192] Judgment of 21 September 1989, *Hoechst v Commission*, 46/87 and 227/88, ECLI:EU:C:1989:337, para 18.

[193] *Niemietz v Germany* (n 135).

[194] Judgment of 22 October 2002, *Roquette Frères SA v Directeur général de la concurrence, de la consommation et de la répression des fraudes and Commission*, C-94/00, ECLI:EU:C:2002:603, para 29.

> ## Judgment of 6 September 2013, *Deutsche Bahn AG and Others v Commission*, T-289/11, T-290/11, and T-521/11, ECLI:EU:T:2013:404
>
> 65. It must be noted that the exercise of the powers of **inspection** conferred on the Commission by Article 20(4) of Regulation No 1/2003 vis-à-vis an undertaking **constitutes a clear interference with the latter's right to respect for its privacy, private premises and correspondence.** That is not disputed by the Commission or by the interveners in these proceedings. The question at issue in this instance is therefore whether the lack of a prior judicial warrant automatically renders the administrative interference illegal and, as the case may be, whether the system established by Regulation No 1/2003 offers sufficient safeguards in the absence of prior judicial authorisation.
> 66. In its recent decisions (Harju v. Finland, no. 56716/09, §§ 40 and 44, 15 February 2011, and Heino v. Finland, no. 56715/09, §§ 40 and 44, 15 February 2011), the ECtHR drew attention to the importance of **conducting a particularly rigorous review in cases where inspections can take place without prior judicial authorisation.** It also clearly laid down the principle that **the absence of prior judicial authorisation may be counterbalanced by a comprehensive post-inspection review.**
> 67. Therefore, the inevitable conclusion to be drawn from the recent case-law of the ECtHR is that the lack of a prior judicial warrant is not capable, in itself, of rendering an interference within the meaning of Article 8 ECHR illegal.

The EU courts have relied heavily on the possibility allowed by the ECtHR whereby prior judicial authorization of inspections can be counterbalanced by a more stringent *ex post* judicial review.[195] In addition to claiming that such in-depth review of the inspections is a reality in the EU,[196] the EU courts have pointed to five categories of safeguards that circumscribe the Commission's powers of inspection and which serve as a benchmark for subsequent review of legality (see Table 6.2).

Table 6.2 Safeguards restricting Commission inspection powers

Safeguards restricting Commission inspection powers under Regulation 1/2003, in particular Article 20(4), as outlined in Judgment of 6 September 2013, *Deutsche Bahn AG and Others v Commission*, T-289/11, T-290/11, and T-521/11, ECLI:EU:T:2013:404, paras 74–100	
Statement of reasons	• Specify the subject matter and purpose of inspection, date, penalties for non-compliance, right of review by CJEU, and presumptions as to the suspected competition infringement, including its nature, markets and sectors affected, degree of involvement, and evidence sought[197]

---

[195] Jones and Sufrin, *EU Competition Law: Text, Cases, and Materials* (n 5) 914.

[196] See *Deutsche Bahn* [2015] (n 168) where the CJEU first upheld the general conclusion that judicial protection before the EU courts complies with the ECHR standards but then, as if to corroborate that finding, looked closely at the statement of reasons in the Commission inspection decision and found that the actual scope of the inspection carried out went beyond the limits stemming from the decision, thus holding that the General Court's first-instance review was in this case partly deficient.

[197] However, the Commission 'must not set out the exact legal nature of the alleged infringements, communicate to the undertaking all the information at its disposal, or indicate the period during which the suspected infringement was committed' in the statement of reasons appended to the inspection decision: *Deutsche Bahn*, [2013] (n 170) para 76.

Safeguards restricting Commission inspection powers under Regulation 1/2003, in particular Article 20(4), as outlined in Judgment of 6 September 2013, *Deutsche Bahn AG and Others v Commission*, **T-289/11, T-290/11, and T-521/11, ECLI:EU:T:2013:404, paras 74–100**

Limits imposed on the Commission during inspection	• Documents not relating to the activities of the undertaking on the market are excluded from the Commission's reach
	• Right to legal assistance and legal professional privilege
	• Privilege against self-incrimination
	• Explanatory notes on the methodology of Commission inspections
Lack of force	• The Commission may not access premises or furniture by force
	• Right to oppose at any time moment during the inspection and to examine the inspection decision with the assistance of lawyers
	• The Commission may not use the threat of penalty under Article 23 of Regulation 1/2003 to obtain concessions from undertakings beyond their duty to cooperate
National authorities	• In case the undertaking concerned opposes the Commission inspection, the assistance of national authorities—which may involve judicial authorizations—must be requested
	• If national authorities are assisting, the Member State concerned must ensure that the inspection is not arbitrary or disproportionate and that coercive measures are carried out in compliance with national laws[198]
Ex post facto remedies	• EU courts have the competence to review comprehensively, *ex post facto*, the validity of inspection decisions
	• Undertakings concerned can obtain a stay of the implementation of the inspection decision through an application for interim relief pursuant to Article 278 TFEU, including under an expedited procedure in accordance with Article 105(2) of the Rules of Procedure of the Court of Justice
	• On the basis of Article 340 TFEU, the EU can be sued for non-contractual liability in case of damages arising from its actions

6.5 Antitrust Fines as Criminal Sanctions? Requisite Level of Protection in EU Competition Law

One of the allegations often made against the EU competition regime is that the sanctions it imposes on undertakings infringing EU antitrust rules are *de facto* of a criminal nature,[199] contrary to what Regulation 1/2003 explicitly self-proclaims.[200] From a fundamental rights perspective, the distinction between criminal and 'administrative' sanctioning connotes a difference in, on the one hand, the level of protection afforded to individuals subject to EU antitrust enforcement, in particular their rights of defence, and, on the other, the scope

---

[198] However, where judicial authorization is required under national law, the domestic court is not entitled to question the necessity of the Commission inspection decision and its validity can only be reviewed by EU courts. See Article 20(8) of Regulation No 1/2003, and *Roquette Frères* (n 194) paras 67–68.

[199] As of recently, the polemic could be feasibly extended to certain fines imposed in the context of merger control and decisions ordering recovery of illegally granted State aid. See, for example, Commission Decision (EU) 2017/1283 of 30 August 2016 on State aid SA.38373 (2014/C) (ex 2014/NN) (ex 2014/CP) implemented by Ireland to Apple (notified under document C(2017) 5605) [2017] OJ L187/1.

[200] Article 23(5) of Regulation 1/2003: 'Decisions taken pursuant to paragraphs 1 and 2 [on the Commission's ability to impose fines] shall not be of a criminal law nature.'

of obligations due on the part of the investigation and enforcement authorities. Generally speaking, if fines levied by the Commission represent 'merely' administrative sanctions, requirements following from European human rights standards are less stringent than if the sanctions are criminal.

The EU and the CJEU have been traditionally loath to accept that competition proceedings at Union level might constitute in fact criminal prosecution. As early as 1970 the CJEU rejected the arguments of a company requesting a higher standard of rights of defence in light of the nature of competition enforcement.[201] The Court essentially held that the application of the Treaty provision on prohibition of anticompetitive agreements by the Commission, 'even where it may lead to fines', is an administrative procedure.[202] As a result, some fundamental rights seen as core requirements of modern criminal procedure were recognized by the CJEU in the context of EU competition law only relatively recently.[203] For example, in somewhat of a breakthrough, the CJEU admitted that presumption of innocence forms part of the general principles of law applicable to competition proceedings.

Judgment of 8 July 1999, *Hüls AG v Commission (Polypropylene)*, C-199/92 P, ECLI:EU:C:1999:358

65. It follows that, inasmuch as they relate to the assessment by the Court of First Instance of the evidence adduced, the appellant's complaints cannot be examined in an appeal. However, it is incumbent on the Court to verify whether, in making that assessment, the Court of First Instance committed an error of law by **infringing the general principles of law, such as the presumption of innocence** and the applicable rules of evidence, such as those concerning the burden of proof (…)

150. It must also be accepted that, given the nature of the infringements in question and the nature and degree of severity of the ensuing penalties, the principle of the **presumption of innocence applies to the procedures relating to infringements of the competition rules applicable to undertakings that may result in the imposition of fines or periodic penalty payments** (see, to that effect, in particular the judgments of the European Court of Human Rights of 21 February 1984, *Öztürk*, Series A No 73, and of 25 August 1987 Lutz, Series A No 123-A).

Hüls is significant not only because it recognized the relevance of the principle of presumption of innocence for EU competition law but also because the CJEU accepted that this was warranted on account of the nature of the infringement and the nature and degree of severity of the sanctions. Although not referring to the nature of the infringement and the fines as 'criminal', the CJEU may have implicitly conceded as much by citing two judgments

---

[201] *Boehringer* (n 149). This was not even the first time the CJEU called the application of the predecessor of Article 101 TFEU 'administrative proceedings', while rejecting the undertakings' pleas for more extensive rights of defence, in particular as regards their access to file. See *Consten and Grundig* (n 4). See also F Graupner, 'Commission Decision-Making on Competition Questions' (1973) 10 Common Market Law Review 291 for one of the first academic articles doubting the compatibility of early EU competition law enforcement with fundamental rights.

[202] *Boehringer* (n 149) para 23.

[203] HP Nehl, 'Article 48—Presumption of Innocence and Right of Defence (Administrative Law)' in S Peers and others (eds), *The EU Charter of Fundamental Rights: A Commentary* (Hart Publishing 2014) 1281.

of the ECtHR in cases revolving around the distinction between 'regulatory' and 'criminal' offences.[204] In *Özturk*, the ECtHR found that prosecution for a road traffic incident leading to a fine designated as regulatory under German law could nevertheless qualify as a criminal charge for the purposes of Article 6(3) ECHR, which endows individuals with a minimum level of fundamental rights protection in criminal procedures.[205] The same was held to be true with respect to the applicability of Article 6(2) ECHR on presumption of innocence in *Lutz v Germany*.[206]

Convention for the Protection of Human Rights and Fundamental Freedoms (adopted 4 November 1950, entered into force 3 September 1953) 213 UNTS 221

Article 6

(1) In the **determination of his civil rights and obligations or of any criminal charge** against him, everyone is entitled to a **fair and public hearing within a reasonable time** by an **independent** and **impartial tribunal** established by law. Judgment shall be pronounced publicly but the press and public may be excluded from all or part of the trial in the interests of morals, public order or national security in a democratic society, where the interests of juveniles or the protection of the private life of the parties so require, or to the extent strictly necessary in the opinion of the court in special circumstances where publicity would prejudice the interests of justice.

(2) Everyone charged with a criminal offence shall be **presumed innocent until proved guilty** according to law.

(3) Everyone charged with a criminal offence has the following minimum rights:

   (a) to be **informed promptly**, in a language which he understands and in detail, of the nature and cause of the accusation against him;

   (b) to have adequate time and facilities for the **preparation of his defence**;

   (c) to defend himself in person or through legal assistance of his own choosing or, if he has not sufficient means to pay for legal assistance, to be given it free when the interests of justice so require;

   (d) to examine or have examined witnesses against him and to obtain the attendance and examination of witnesses on his behalf under the same conditions as witnesses against him;

   (e) to have the **free assistance of an interpreter** if he cannot understand or speak the language used in court.

Article 7

(1) No one shall be held guilty of any criminal offence on account of any **act or omission which did not constitute a criminal offence under national or international law at the time when it was committed. Nor** shall **a heavier penalty** be imposed than the one that was applicable at the time the criminal offence was committed.

---

[204] The CJEU was already implored to give more weight to fundamental rights considerations in light of the *Öztürk* case by AG Vesterdorf in *Rhône-Poulenc v Commission* [1991] ECLI:EU:T:1991:38, 884–86.

[205] *Öztürk v Germany*, App no 8544/79, 12 May 1982.

[206] *Lutz v Germany*, App no 9912/82, 25 August 1987.

It is more generally the realm of the ECHR on which much of the fundamental rights criticism of the EU antitrust regime has been based. The question whether Article 6 ECHR, in particular the additional safeguards provided for by paragraphs 2 and 3 thereof (and also Article 7(1)), applies in the case of EU competition proceedings turns on the examination of whether competition infringements can be classified as criminal offences in the autonomous meaning of Articles 6 and 7 ECHR.[207] As confirmed in the Özturk and Lutz judgments, the relevant test is contained in another decision of the ECtHR, *Engel and Others v the Netherlands*.[208] While the interpretation in *Engel* concerned the term 'criminal charge' in Article 6(1) ECHR, the two aforementioned judgments made clear that the same test also guides the interpretation of 'criminal offence' for the purposes of Article 6(2) and (3) ECHR.

Engel and Others v the Netherlands, App nos 5100/71; 5101/71; 5102/71; 5354/72; 5370/72, 8 June 1976

82. In this connection, it is first necessary to know **whether the provision(s) defining the offence charged belong, according to the legal system of the respondent State, to criminal law, disciplinary law or both concurrently. This however provides no more than a starting point.** The indications so afforded have only a formal and relative value and must be examined in the light of the common denominator of the respective legislation of the various Contracting States.
The very nature of the offence is a factor of greater import. When a serviceman finds himself accused of an act or omission allegedly contravening a legal rule governing the operation of the armed forces, the State may in principle employ against him disciplinary law rather than criminal law. In this respect, the Court expresses its agreement with the Government.
However, supervision by the Court does not stop there. Such supervision would generally prove to be illusory if it did not also take into consideration **the degree of severity of the penalty that the person concerned risks incurring.** In a society subscribing to the rule of law, there belong to the 'criminal' sphere deprivations of liberty liable to be imposed as a punishment, except those which by their nature, duration or manner of execution cannot be appreciably detrimental. The seriousness of what is at stake, the traditions of the Contracting States and the importance attached by the Convention to respect for the physical liberty of the person all require that this should be so.

According to the ECtHR, three cumulative criteria underpin the determination of a criminal charge under the Convention: the classification of the offence as criminal or otherwise in national law (without this having a conclusive effect on the autonomous interpretation of 'criminal' under the ECHR); the nature of the offence; and the degree of severity of the potential sanction. Applying these criteria to national competition proceedings, the ECtHR

---

[207] Without going into a detailed discussion of the binding effect of the ECHR on the exercise of EU exclusive competences. See Ch 5 in that regard. It is sufficient to remark here that fundamental rights guaranteed by the ECHR constitute general principles of EU law by virtue of Article 6(3) TEU and they are also of relevance to the interpretation of corresponding Charter rights and freedoms in accordance with Article 52(3) of the Charter.

[208] *Engel and Others v the Netherlands*, App nos 5100/71; 5101/71; 5102/71; 5354/72; 5370/72, 8 June 1976.

indeed found, albeit not in particularly strong terms,[209] Article 6 ECHR applicable. A fourth criterion of sorts has been additionally identified in the field of tax law, which could be also of relevance to competition fines, namely that for a financial penalty to have a criminal connotation, it should be 'very substantial'.[210] In light of the serious consequences of competition proceedings at EU level, in particular the severity of available financial penalties which have a punitive and deterrent function typical for criminal law,[211] the highly plausible conjecture, supported in part by a decision of the European Commission of Human Rights in *M. & Co.* and a more recent judgment of the ECtHR in an Italian cartel case,[212] can be made that in general Article 6 ECHR should be deemed as applicable to the enforcement of EU competition law. This is less controversial than the volume of the surrounding discussion might suggest—the CJEU recognized (again without mentioning the word criminal) that the right to a fair trial as a general principle of EU law was inspired by Article 6 ECHR and must be observed in EU competition procedures.[213] The more contentious question concerns the extent of fundamental rights protection which must be ensured in the course of competition proceedings as a result.

The ECtHR made clear in *Jussila* that not all infringements of the law caught by the Convention definition of 'criminal offence' are necessarily subject to the most stringent requirements of Article 6 ECHR.[214] As some criminal cases 'do not carry any significant degree of stigma'—and competition infringements would readily fit into this category—not all charges considered 'criminal' for the purpose of Article 6 ECHR are of the same weight, especially as over the years the application of the *Engel* criteria led to a broadening of the scope of the provision beyond what is traditionally considered as criminal law (the 'hard core of criminal law').[215] As a result, 'the criminal-head guarantees will not necessarily apply with their full stringency' to areas such as competition law, despite the fact that Article 6 ECHR might be applicable in general. Moreover, even very substantial financial penalties being imposed by the means of an administrative decision have been in principle found compatible

---

[209] In *Société Stenuit v France*, App no 11598/85, 27 February 1992, the application was withdrawn following an examination by the Commission (human rights) which found the case admissible within the criminal remit of Article 6 ECHR. The Commission also found a violation of Article 6(1) ECHR but it should be pointed out that the disputed French competition proceedings were not up to the same standard as EU competition proceedings and the French system was reformed soon after (leading to the withdrawal of the case from the ECtHR). The ECtHR held in *Jussila v Finland*, App no 73053/01, 23 November 2006 that the decision of the Commission represented a recognition of the fact that prosecution of competition infringements is in principle covered by Article 6 ECHR, although not as part of the hard core of criminal law. See para 43 of *Jussila*.

[210] *Bendenoun v France*, App no 12547/86, 24 February 1994, para 47. There is clearly some overlap with the third criterion of *Engel* but the ECtHR in this case attempted to fine-tune its analysis to offences typically associated with administrative governance and not (hard-core) criminal prosecution. See also Joint Partly Dissenting Opinion of Judges Costa, Cabral Barreto, and Mularoni, joined by Judge Caflisch in *Jussila*.

[211] Although the ECtHR has stated that administrative penalties can also have these functions. See *Öztürk* (n 205) para 53; *Janosevic v Sweden*, App no 34619/97, 23 July 2002, para 68.

[212] See *A. Menarini Diagnostics S.R.L. v Italy*, App no 43509/08, 27 September 2011, para 62; and *M. & Co. v Federal Republic of Germany*, App no 13258/87, decision of 9 February 1990 as to the admissibility. The *M. & Co.* case concerned the enforcement of a European Commission competition fine in German courts. The European Commission for Human Rights found the case inadmissible on the basis of an early application of the doctrine of equivalent protection of fundamental rights known today chiefly from the *Bosphorus* judgment. For the purpose of analysing the equivalence of rights protection in Germany and the EU, it was assumed, without going into detail why or touching upon the question of criminality (but citing the *Öztürk* judgment), that the antitrust proceedings in question would be covered by Article 6 ECHR if they were conducted by Germany, a Party to the Convention.

[213] Judgment of 17 December 1998, *Baustahlgewebe v Commission*, C-185/95 P, ECLI:EU:C:1998:608, para 21.

[214] *Jussila* (n 209) para 43.

[215] Ibid.

with Article 6 ECHR by the ECtHR,[216] as long as the sanction can be appealed to a court with jurisdiction to examine all aspects of the decision.[217] This was also confirmed in the specific circumstances of antitrust violations which, among other things, implies that the often criticized multi-hatted role of the Commission as investigator, prosecutor, and adjudicator is not incompatible with Article 6 ECHR, as long as its decisions can be appealed to a court with full jurisdiction.[218]

The preceding view from Strasbourg implying that in general no major incompatibility exists between the way EU competition law is applied and the requirements of Article 6 ECHR is shared in the EU. This was expressly articulated by AG Kokott in the context of the opinion procedure regarding the EU's possible accession to the ECHR,[219] which is not to say, however, that all elements of the putative compliance with Article 6 ECHR are uncontroversial.

For one, the concept of 'full jurisdiction' required by the ECtHR to be available for review of competition law sanctions has received scrutiny in the EU system of judicial protection. On the surface, everything appears in order. As per Article 31 of Regulation 1/2003, adopted on the basis of Article 261 TFEU, the CJEU has 'unlimited jurisdiction' with respect to fines imposed by the Commission on undertakings for infringements of Articles 101 and 102 TFEU.[220] Although on appeal the CJEU no longer reappraises the facts, the General Court has the power to scrutinize in the first instance any aspect of the Commission decision and the procedure leading up to its adoption.[221] The CJEU has consistently held that the EU system of judicial review complies with the requirements of Article 47 of the Charter which enshrines the principle of effective judicial protection and corresponds to a large extent to (and therefore also satisfies) Articles 6 and 13 ECHR.

Judgment of 10 July 2014, *Telefónica and Telefónica de España v Commission*, C-295/12 P, ECLI:EU:C:2014:2062

42. According to established case-law, EU law provides for a system of judicial review of Commission decisions relating to proceedings under Article 102 TFEU which affords all the safeguards required by Article 47 of the Charter (see, to that effect, Chalkor v Commission EU:C:2011:815, paragraph 67, and Otis and Others EU:C:2012:684, paragraphs 56 and 63). That system of judicial review consists in a review of the legality of the acts of the institutions for which provision is made in Article 263 TFEU, which may be supplemented, pursuant to Article 261 TFEU,

---

[216] Administrative penalties in the area of tax law have been furthermore found compatible with the right to property of Article 1 of Protocol No 1 to the ECHR. See *Impar Ltd v Lithuania*, App no 13102/04, 5 January 2010, para 34.

[217] See, for example, *Janosevic* (n 210) para 81; *Bendenoun* (n 210) para 46.

[218] *Menarini* (n 212) para 62. For criticism of the institutional inadequacy of the Commission, see IS Forrester, 'Due Process in EC Competition Cases: A Distinguished Institution with Flawed Procedures' (2009) 34 European Law Review 817. See also D Slater, S Thomas, and D Waelbroeck, 'Competition Law Proceedings before the European Commission and the Right to a Fair Trial: No Need for Reform?' (2009) 5 European Competition Journal 97; W Wils, 'The Compatibility with Fundamental Rights of the EU Antitrust Enforcement System in Which the European Commission Acts Both as Investigator and as First-Instance Decision Maker' (2014) 37 World Competition 5.

[219] *Opinion 2/13 (EU accession to the ECHR)* [2014] ECLI:EU:C:2014:2475, View of AG Kokott, para 151.

[220] For the equivalent in the context of merger control, see Article 16 of the Merger Regulation (n 7).

[221] *Cimenteries CBR and Others v Commission* (n 71) para 719.

> by the Court's unlimited jurisdiction with regard to the penalties provided for in regulations.
>
> 57. (…) **the review of legality provided for by Article 263 TFEU satisfies the requirements of the principle of effective judicial protection enshrined in Article 6(1) of the ECHR,** which corresponds in EU law to Article 47 of the Charter (…)

The problem with the 'fullness' of the EU judiciary's jurisdiction stems, however, from its application in practice. As described previously,[222] the General Court might be often reluctant to reassess complex econometric assessments conducted by the Commission to establish the existence of a competition infringement. The standard of review is as a consequence frequently limited to identifying 'manifest errors' of assessment on the part of the Commission or similarly diluted judicial analyses. The CJEU, too, tends to defer to the General Court and the Commission when it comes to the calculations of appropriate fines. Such shortcomings, while justifiable to some extent on account of expediency, highlight that the concept of 'full jurisdiction' should not be taken overly literally. It is notable that in the very case used by AG Kokott to support the conclusion that the EU competition enforcement system complies with the requirements of Article 6 ECHR, a lone dissenting opinion of one of the ECtHR judges takes serious issue precisely with the deficient standard of review applied in his view in that case.[223]

Nevertheless, in other respects the high confidence in EU compliance with the ECHR rests on the existence of extensive procedural safeguards developed over the decades of competition litigation and now also enshrined in the Charter. These cover both the general objective of Articles 6 and 13 ECHR—a fair trial and the availability of an effective remedy—as well as the particulars of ECHR protection relating to the length of the proceedings, presumption of innocence, double jeopardy rule (*ne bis in idem*), and others. While these rights can be made applicable in the EU by virtue of general principles of EU law—taking cue from ECHR law and/or national constitutional traditions—they are nowadays most obviously consolidated in the Charter which has equal value as the EU Treaties.

Charter of Fundamental Rights of the European Union [2012] OJ C326/391

Article 47

Right to an effective remedy and to a fair trial

Everyone whose rights and freedoms guaranteed by the law of the Union are violated has the **right to an effective remedy** before a tribunal in compliance with the conditions laid down in this Article.

Everyone is entitled to a **fair and public hearing within a reasonable time by an independent and impartial tribunal previously established by law.** Everyone shall have the **possibility of being advised, defended and represented.**

Legal aid shall be made available to those **who lack sufficient resources** in so far as such aid is necessary to ensure effective access to justice.

---

[222] See Section 6.2.A above.
[223] See dissenting opinion of Judge Pinto de Albuquerque in *Menarini* (n 212).

Article 47 of the Charter covers most of the procedural guarantees existing under Articles 6(1) and 13 ECHR. Notwithstanding the more extensive protection offered by Article 47,[224] the Charter provisions correspond to those of the ECHR and thus should be given the same scope and meaning on the basis of Article 52(3) of the Charter. As far as administrative conduct is concerned, which in the EU means the conduct of the Commission during competition proceedings as well,[225] similar guarantees to those of Article 47 are provided by Article 41 of the Charter. Articles 48 and 49 of the Charter concern rights of defence in criminal proceedings which correspond, for the purposes of Article 52(3), to those of Articles 6(2), 6(3), and 7 ECHR. In light of the foregoing discussion, however, competition law can be subjected to less stringent procedural requirements in comparison to the 'hard-core' of criminal law and thus not all aspects of the rich ECtHR case law interpreting Article 6 ECHR must be applied in the EU. Nevertheless, three essential general principles traditionally associated with criminal law do also apply to EU competition proceedings: presumption of innocence, the principle of legality and *ne bis in idem*.[226] As all of them find their expression in the Charter (as well as in the ECHR) in the context of criminal law (implicitly in the case of Article 48 of the Charter), the CJEU has been at times hesitant to refer explicitly to the Charter provision when applying the principles to competition proceedings. In any case, the dynamic interpretation of the provisions of the Convention by the ECtHR mandates vigilance in the EU if it is to ensure continually that competition law does not fall short of the moving frontiers of fundamental rights protection, regardless of the blurred nature of EU antitrust enforcement.

A. Presumption of innocence

Charter of Fundamental Rights of the European Union [2012] OJ C326/391

Article 48

Presumption of innocence and right of defence

1. Everyone who has been charged shall be **presumed innocent until proved guilty** according to law.
2. Respect for the rights of the defence of anyone who has been charged shall be guaranteed.

As mentioned above, the CJEU recognized in *Hüls* that presumption of innocence is a general principle of law relevant to competition proceedings. While during *Hüls* the Charter was not yet in existence, the explicit application of Article 48 of the Charter has remained the exception rather than the rule in the Court's case law on presumption of innocence in competition proceedings.[227] This is not problematic as long as the substance of the principle

---

[224] Explanations relating to the Charter of Fundamental Rights [2007] OJ C303/17, Article 47.

[225] *Ziegler* (n 160) para 154.

[226] Other fundamental rights and the specific issues they raise in EU competition proceedings are tackled in subsequent sections of this chapter.

[227] This is also a consequence of parties not mentioning the Charter in their pleas. For a short exception see Judgment of 19 June 2014, *FLS Plast v Commission*, C-243/12 P, ECLI:EU:C:2014:2006, paras 23–33.

is consistently applied. Nevertheless, individuals would arguably benefit from greater legal certainty if the Court systematically developed the principle within the framework of the Charter, including in accordance with Article 52(3) regarding homogenous meaning and scope with the ECHR (bearing in mind the caveat concerning the 'hard core' of criminal law). Article 48 of the Charter is in fact drafted in a broader way than the corresponding provisions of the ECHR (Article 6(2) and (3)), as it omits the word 'criminal' and is therefore well-suited to being invoked in competition proceedings and other mixed administrative procedures concerning EU law.

The main issue in EU competition law concerning the presumption of innocence relates to the concept of single economic entity. Where a subsidiary is entirely or almost entirely owned by the parent company, there is a rebuttable presumption that the parent company exercises decisive influence over the subsidiary, as a result of which competition infringements can be imputed to it.[228] This presumption is in direct tension with the presumption of innocence, as the parent company and the subsidiary are normally established as distinct legal persons in national law. For the purposes of EU competition law, the term 'undertaking' can comprise several legal and natural persons if these form a single economic unit.[229] If the entire capital of a subsidiary is not held only by one parent company, the Commission must establish that decisive influence of the latter over the former has in fact been exercised in order to impute liability (and resulting sanctions) to the parent company.[230]

What makes the presumption of liability of the parent company compliant with fundamental rights is, in the opinion of the CJEU, the fact that it can be rebutted by showing that the subsidiary acted independently on the market.[231] On the contrary, parent companies have alleged on a number of occasions that in practice the presumption is *de facto* irrefutable due to the excessively restrictive threshold required to establish the absence of 'decisive influence'.[232] The CJEU rejects that notion: the difficulty of disproving the presumption does not in itself mean that it is in fact irrefutable.[233] Proving negative facts is notoriously difficult, however, in particular where the evidentiary standard requires proof of universal propositions.[234] Evidence to be adduced in order to rebut the presumption of decisive influence can relate to organizational, economic, and legal links between the parent and subsidiary, while the EU judicature is obliged to examine all relevant factors when determining the success of the rebuttal. However, the fact that a single instruction from the parent company has not been followed by its subsidiary is not in itself sufficient to refute the presumption: the failure to carry out instructions must be established to represent the norm in the parent–subsidiary

---

[228] See, for example, Judgment of 26 September 2013, *The Dow Chemical Company v Commission*, C-179/12 P, ECLI:EU:C:2013:605, para 56.

[229] Judgment of 12 July 1984, *Hydrotherm Gerätebau GmbH v Compact del Dott. Ing. Mario Andreoli & C. Sas*, 170/83, ECLI:EU:C:1984:271, para 11. Interestingly, the current doctrine contradicts the Court's early view of the question whether more than one legal person can form an undertaking. See *Société nouvelle des usines de Pontlieue—Aciéries du Temple (S.N.U.P.A.T.)* (n 147).

[230] Judgment of 25 October 1983, *Allgemeine Elektrizitäts-Gesellschaft AEG-Telefunken AG v Commission*, 107/82, ECLI:EU:C:1983:293, para 50.

[231] Judgment of 8 May 2013, *Eni v Commission*, C-508/11 P, ECLI:EU:C:2013:289, para 50.

[232] See, for example, Judgment of 16 June 2016, *Evonik Degussa and AlzChem AG v Commission*, C-155/14 P, ECLI:EU:C:2016:446, para 43.

[233] Judgment of 5 March 2015, *Commission and Others v Versalis and Others*, C-93/13 P and C-123/13 P, ECLI:EU:C:2015:150, para 46.

[234] See KW Saunders, 'The Mythic Difficulty in Proving a Negative' (1985) 15 Seton Hall Law Review 276, 288 who firmly argues, using examples from US law, that the difficulty lies in proving universal statements rather than negative facts.

relationship.[235] Overall, the Court views the presumption as respecting the balance that needs to be struck between the effectiveness of antitrust enforcement and the rights and principles safeguarding affected individuals.[236]

B. Principle of legality (*nulla poena sine lege*) and proportionality

---

Charter of Fundamental Rights of the European Union [2012] OJ C326/391

Article 49

Principles of legality and proportionality of criminal offences and penalties

1. **No one shall be held guilty of any criminal offence** on account of any act or omission **which did not constitute a criminal offence under national law or international law at the time when it was committed. Nor shall a heavier penalty be imposed than the one that was applicable at the time** the criminal offence was committed. If, subsequent to the commission of a criminal offence, the law provides for a lighter penalty, that penalty shall be applicable.

2. This Article shall not prejudice the trial and punishment of any person for any act or omission which, at the time when it was committed, was criminal according to the general principles recognised by the community of nations.

3. The severity of penalties must **not be disproportionate** to the criminal offence.

Article 49 of the Charter houses three basic principles of law. First, it contains the legal guarantee against arbitrary criminalization and punishments (in Latin known as *nullum crimen, nulla poena sine lege*). This also implies that a heavier penalty cannot be imposed on the basis of a law subsequent to the criminal offence. Thus far paragraph 1 corresponds to Article 7(1) ECHR. The Charter provision, however, contains a second widely accepted principle of criminal law, namely that where a subsequent law allows for a lighter penalty, it should be applied to a past criminal offence (also known as *lex mitior*).[237] Third, the Charter prescribes that penalties be proportionate to criminal offence. The second paragraph of Article 49 which mirrors Article 7(2) ECHR is not relevant here.

The legal principles, in the Charter explicitly linked to criminal law, have been invoked numerous times before the EU judiciary in both the guise of the Charter provision and as general principles of EU law.[238] In *Koninklijke Philips Electronics NV v Commission*, the General Court confirmed that the first legal principle of Article 49 of the Charter regarding the non-retroactivity of laws must be observed in administrative procedures capable of leading to fines, despite Article 23(5) of Regulation 1/2003 defining competition fines as not

---

[235] *Evonik Degussa* (n 232) paras 32, 33, 41.

[236] *Eni v Commission* (n 231) para 50.

[237] The Explanations to the Charter make reference to Article 15 of the Covenant on Civil and Political Rights with respect to the rule on more lenient penal law.

[238] For an early application of the Charter provision, see Judgment of 29 March 2011, *ThyssenKrupp Nirosta GmbH v Commission*, C-352/09 P, ECLI:EU:C:2011:191, para 80.

being of a criminal nature.[239] Non-retroactivity is judged through the prism of foreseeability and the principle is invoked in relation to not only strictly statutory law but also established competition enforcement practices of the Commission which apply particular interpretations of the law. A change in such interpretations should be reasonably foreseeable to satisfy the principle of non-retroactivity.[240] The Commission, however, enjoys a wide margin of discretion in pursuing competition infringements and the circumstances under which an undertaking can harbour legitimate expectations with respect to future Commission practice are limited. Undertakings must take special care when assessing the risks associated with their professional activities.[241] As a consequence, pleas alleging a breach of the *nulla poena sine lege* principle are usually unsuccessful. This has held true even when the application of soft law subsequent to the competition infringement led to the imposition of a higher penalty than that resulting from the guidance on fining applicable during the period of the infringement. The General Court explicitly held, without any reference to the Charter, that the Commission is entitled to 'apply retroactively, to the detriment of those concerned, rules of conduct designed to produce external effects' and that it is 'under no obligation to apply the *lex mitior*'.[242]

The EU courts similarly recognize the applicability of the principle of proportionality provided for by Article 49(3) of the Charter to EU competition fines. The principle is usually read in conjunction with Article 23(3) of Regulation 1/2003 which sets out gravity and duration of the competition infringement as key for determining the amount of the fine. Further specifications of these requirements are found in the case law and in the Commission Guidelines on the method of setting fines.[243]

Judgment of 29 February 2016, *Schenker Ltd v Commission*, T-265/12, ECLI:EU:T:2016:111

245. As regards the principle of proportionality and the principle that the punishment must fit the offence, those principles require that **fines must not be disproportionate to the objectives pursued**, that is to say, to **compliance** [sic] **with the European Union competition rules**, and that the amount of the fine imposed on an undertaking for an infringement in competition matters should be proportionate to the infringement, seen as a whole, having regard, in particular, to its **gravity**. In particular, the principle of proportionality obliges the Commission to set the fine proportionately to the **factors taken into account for the purposes of assessing the gravity** of the infringement and also to apply those factors in a **way** which is **consistent and objectively justified** (...)

---

[239] Judgment of 9 September 2015, *Koninklijke Philips Electronics NV v Commission*, T-92/13, ECLI:EU:T:2015:605, paras 136–137. Reference to the non-criminal nature of competition fines is not always made in the application of Article 49 of the Charter. See, for example, Judgment of 8 September 2016, *Lundbeck v Commission*, T-472/13, ECLI:EU:T:2016:449, para 763.

[240] Judgment of 2 February 2012, *Denki Kagaku Kogyo and Denka Chemicals v Commission*, T-83/08, ECLI:EU:T:2012:48, para 120.

[241] Judgment of 28 June 2005, *Dansk Rørindustri and Others v Commission*, C-189/02 P, C-202/02 P, C-205/02 P to C-208/02 P and C-213/02 P, ECLI:EU:C:2005:408, para 219.

[242] *Denki and Denka* (n 240) para 126.

[243] Guidelines on the method of setting fines imposed pursuant to Article 23(2)(a) of Regulation No 1/2003 [2006] OJ C210/2.

> 246. Further, it must be recalled that, in order to **assess** the **gravity** of an infringement of European Union competition law, the Commission must take account of a **large number of factors**, the nature and importance of which vary according to the type of infringement in question and the particular circumstances of the case. Those factors may, depending on the circumstances, include the **volume and value of the goods** in respect of which the infringement was committed and the size and **economic power** of the undertaking and, consequently, the **influence which the undertaking was able to exert on the market** (...)

As in the case of arguments regarding the presumption of innocence, the principle of proportionality is rarely invoked successfully by litigants. This has to do also with the CJEU's view that the upper limit for competition fines, set at 10 per cent of total turnover in accordance with Article 23(2) of Regulation 1/2003, 'is already a guarantee that the fine is not disproportionate to the size of the undertaking, determined by reference to its worldwide turnover'.[244]

C. *Ne bis in idem*

> ### Charter of Fundamental Rights of the European Union [2012] OJ C326/391
>
> ---
>
> ### *Article 50*
>
> ### Right not to be tried or punished twice in criminal proceedings for the same criminal offence
>
> No one shall be liable to be tried or punished again in criminal proceedings for an offence for which he or she has already been finally acquitted or convicted within the Union in accordance with the law.

Article 50 of the Charter gives expression to the well-established principle often referred to as *ne* (or *non*) *bis in idem*, also known as the double jeopardy clause in the US. Although the principle is not found in the ECHR itself but rather in Article 4 of Protocol No 7 to the Convention (which is not expressly mentioned by the convergence clause in Article 52(3) of the Charter), the Charter provision should be given the same meaning and scope insofar as the jurisdiction of a single Member State is concerned.[245] The key difference of Article 50 of the Charter from ECHR law stems from its cross-border application in the EU: in principle the scope of the Charter right covers any proceedings initiated in the same matter against the same individual in any EU Member State.[246]

While once again the wording of the Charter Article refers clearly to criminal proceedings, in line with the ECHR and the history of the legal principle, a wider-than-criminal-law use

---

[244] Judgment of 26 January 2017, *Villeroy & Boch SAS v Commission*, C-644/13 P, ECLI:EU:C:2017:59, para 81.

[245] Explanations relating to the Charter of Fundamental Rights [2007] OJ C303/17, Article 50.

[246] See more generally B van Bockel (ed), *Ne Bis in Idem in EU Law* (Cambridge University Press 2016).

of the provision appears inherent from a systemic point of view of EU law. The Explanations to the Charter give three examples from the case law of the EU judicature of the application of *ne bis in idem* but only one of them concerns criminal proceedings.[247] The other two cases mentioned relate to disciplinary proceedings in an EU staff case (one of the first ever applications of the principle at EU level) and competition law, namely the case of *Limburgse Vinyl Maatschappij v Commission*.[248] Indeed, EU competition law is by nature not a stranger to the double jeopardy rule—the scope of multiplicity of proceedings and punishments is considerable, as undertakings infringing competition rules can be subject to both EU- and national-level enforcement both within and outside the EU territory. The issue of concurrent competition enforcement in the EU and the US was tackled in a CJEU judgment dating back to 1972.

Judgment of 14 December 1972, *Boehringer v Commission*, 7/72, ECLI:EU:C:1972:125

---

2. The applicant complains that the Commission thereby violated a general principle of law prohibiting double penalties for the same action.
3. In fixing the amount of a fine the **Commission must take account of penalties which have already been borne by the same undertaking for the same action**, where penalties have been imposed for infringements of the cartel law of a Member State and, consequently, have been **committed on Community territory**. It is only necessary to decide the question whether the Commission may also be under a duty to set a penalty imposed by the authorities of a third State against another penalty if in the case in question **the actions of the applicant complained of by the Commission, on the one hand, and by the American authorities, on the other, are identical.**
4. Although **the actions on which the two convictions in question are based arise out of the same set of agreements they nevertheless differ essentially as regards both their object and their geographical emphasis.**

In *Boehringer*, the applicant based their argument on, among others, the concept of 'same offence' in German criminal law. The CJEU rejected the argument without defining what the elements of the principle should be in EU law. Similarly to the previously discussed fundamental rights, the *ne bis in idem* principle does not enjoy an expansive interpretation in the context of EU competition law, certainly not to the point where it would severely restrict the ability of European competition authorities to prosecute competition infringements.[249] This conclusion has also not been altered by the introduction of a more structured test for defining identical legal circumstances for the purposes of applying the principle in *Aalborg Portland*.[250] The threefold condition of identity/unity established therein by the CJEU remains in use today.

---

[247] Judgment of 11 February 2003, *Gözütok and Brügge*, C-187/01 and C-385/01, ECLI:EU:C:2003:87.
[248] Judgment of 20 April 1999, *Limburgse Vinyl Maatschappij NV and Others v Commission*, T-305/94, T-306/94, T-307/94, T-313/94 to T-316/94, T-318/94, T-325/94, T-328/94, T-329/94, and T-335/94, ECLI:EU:T:1999:80.
[249] *Limburgse Vinyl Maatschappij* [2002] (n 187); *Toshiba Corporation* (n 15).
[250] Judgment of 7 January 2004, *Aalborg Portland and Others v Commission*, C-204/00 P, C-205/00 P, C-211/00 P, C-213/00 P, C-217/00 P, and C-219/00 P, ECLI:EU:C:2004:6. See also Judgment of 29 June 2006, *Showa Denko v Commission*, C-289/04 P, ECLI:EU:C:2006:431, para 50.

> ### Judgment of 7 January 2004, *Aalborg Portland and Others v Commission*, C-204/00 P, C-205/00 P, C-211/00 P, C-213/00 P, C-217/00 P, and C-219/00 P, ECLI:EU:C:2004:6
>
> 338. As regards observance of the principle ne bis in idem, the application of that principle is subject to the **threefold condition of identity** of the facts, unity of **offender** and unity of the **legal interest** protected. Under that principle, therefore, **the same person cannot be sanctioned more than once for a single unlawful course of conduct designed to protect the same legal asset.**

The most complete discussion of *ne bis in idem* in EU competition law to date occurred in the procedure concerning a preliminary reference made by a Czech court regarding the competence of NCAs to apply national law on cartels when the Commission opens proceedings against the same cartel members. The situation was rendered more complicated by virtue of the facts of the case dating before the Czech Republic's accession to the EU. Advocate General (AG) Kokott, in particular, addressed the issues raised by this case in a comprehensive manner, paying attention among others to the questions of criminality of EU competition proceedings and the applicability of the Charter and of corresponding ECHR standards, which were largely omitted from the Court's answer to the regional court in Brno.

> ### *Toshiba Corporation and Others v Commission* [2011] ECLI:EU:C:2011:552, Opinion of AG Kokott
>
> 101. **It is in fact common ground that the ne bis in idem principle must be observed in proceedings for the imposition of a fine under antitrust law because of their similarity to proceedings at criminal law.** The Commission none the less casts doubt on the applicability of the ne bis in idem principle in this case, at least as far as Article 50 of the Charter of Fundamental Rights is concerned.
> 102. The Commission submits that the Charter of Fundamental Rights is applicable only in relation to the implementation of EU law. Since the Czech competition authority relied only on national competition law in its contested decision in this case, it was not bound by the Charter.
> 103. That objection does not hold water. It is indeed true that Article 51(1) of the Charter of Fundamental Rights states that the Charter applies 'to the Member States only when they are implementing Union law'. The mere fact that national competition law is applicable ratione materiae in the present case does not mean, however, that there are no requirements of EU law as to how the case should be dealt with.
> 104. As I have already said, the procedural rules of Regulation No 1/2003—unlike its substantive rules—have been applicable in the Czech Republic since the date of its accession to the European Union. They include not least the rules and principles governing the delimitation of competences within the network of European competition authorities which was established by Regulation No 1/2003. **Those rules and principles must be interpreted and applied in accordance with EU primary law, including the fundamental rights of the EU.**

106. Those fundamental rights, which must be respected in determining the margin for manoeuvre left to the Czech authority, include in particular the ne bis in idem principle, as codified in Article 50 of the Charter of Fundamental Rights. For the ne bis in idem principle affects not only matters of substance but also matters of procedure. For example, as well as protecting the defendant, the ne bis in idem principle also serves to prevent conflicts of jurisdiction (so-called positive conflicts of jurisdiction) between the different authorities, which may be dealing with the matter as a criminal case or an administrative offence.

115. Of the aforementioned three conditions, the application of the first two (identity of the facts and unity of offender) is not in issue. What is in dispute, however, is the applicability of the third condition, that is to say the criterion of unity of the legal interest protected. (...)

116. In areas of law other than competition law, however, the Court has not applied that third condition. For the purposes of disciplinary proceedings under civil service law, it has thus been guided only by the factual situation (whether the facts were 'different'). Indeed, in the context of the rules governing the area of freedom, security and justice (...) the Court has expressly considered the criterion of unity of the legal interest protected to be irrelevant. In such circumstances, it has consistently held that the only relevant criterion is identity of the material acts, understood as the existence of a set of concrete circumstances which are inextricably linked together.

117. To interpret and apply the ne bis in idem principle so differently depending on the area of law concerned is detrimental to the unity of the EU legal order. The crucial importance of the ne bis in idem principle as a founding principle of EU law which enjoys the status of a fundamental right means that its content must not be substantially different depending on which area of law is concerned. For the purposes of determining the scope of the guarantee provided by the ne bis in idem principle, as now codified in Article 50 of the Charter of Fundamental Rights, the same criteria should apply in all areas of EU law. (...)

119. For the purposes of identifying the relevant criteria for defining idem, it must be borne in mind that the ne bis in idem principle is based largely on a fundamental right enshrined in the ECHR, more specifically, Article 4(1) of Protocol No 7 to the ECHR, although that protocol has not yet been ratified by all the EU Member States. That close proximity to the ECHR is indicated not only by the Explanations on Article 50 of the Charter of Fundamental Rights, which must be duly taken into account by the courts of the European Union and of the Member States, but also by the previous case-law of the Court of Justice concerning the general EU-law principle of ne bis in idem.

120. The requirement of homogeneity is therefore applicable. It follows from that requirement that rights contained in the Charter which correspond to rights guaranteed by the ECHR are to have the same meaning and scope as those laid down by the ECHR. In other words, Article 4(1) of Protocol No 7 to the ECHR, as interpreted by the European Court of Human Rights (ECtHR), describes the minimum standard that must be guaranteed in the interpretation and application of the ne bis in idem principle in EU law.

121. Whereas the case-law of the ECtHR on the meaning of idem had lacked uniformity for a long time, the ECtHR held, in a landmark judgment in 2009, that Article 4 of Protocol No 7 to the ECHR prohibits the prosecution or trial of a second offence in so far as it arises from identical facts or facts which are substantially the same. This means that the ECtHR has regard only to whether or not the facts are identical and expressly not to the legal classification of the offence. (…) There is nothing to indicate that the ECtHR might be inclined to the view that the scope of the guarantee provided by the ne bis in idem principle is less extensive specifically in the area of competition law. (…)

122. It follows that, for the purposes of interpreting and applying idem in the context of the prohibition against prosecution and punishment for the same cause of action under EU law also, account should henceforth be taken only of the identity of the facts (which necessarily includes the unity of the offender).

123. Retaining the criterion of unity of the legal interest protected would have the effect, ultimately, of narrowing the scope of the prohibition against prosecution and punishment for the same cause of action under EU law and causing the guarantee which it provides to fall short of the minimum standard laid down in Article 4(1) of Protocol No 7 to the ECHR. This would not be compatible with the requirement of homogeneity. (…)

124. It must there be concluded that, for the purposes of determining idem within the meaning of the ne bis in idem principle, account is to be taken only of the material acts, understood as the existence of a set of concrete circumstances which are inextricably linked together. In other words, the two cases must concern identical facts or facts which are substantially the same.

In this ambitious Opinion, AG Kokott advanced a reinterpretation of the CJEU's case law on the elements of the *ne bis in idem* principle. She argued for a unified approach across all EU law which would abolish the more restrictive interpretation used by the Court for the purposes of competition proceedings. In addition to safeguarding the unity of the EU legal order and strengthening the fundamental rights of individuals implicated in competition proceedings, the AG viewed the reinterpretation as mandatory from the perspective of the requirement of homogeneity with the ECHR prescribed by Article 52(3) of the Charter, citing in particular the leading judgment of the ECtHR on this issue, *Zolotukhin v Russia*.[251] The CJEU has, however, decided not to follow the advice of AG Kokott and instead affirmed the threefold condition of identity set out in *Aalborg Portland*.[252] Regardless, the operative conclusion of the Court's judgment was the same as that of the AG, as both found that Toshiba could not rely on the principle of *ne bis in idem* due to the facts of the cases not being identical.[253] Subsequent cases show that the ambiguity as to the scope of the principle in competition proceedings persists, but the Court has thus far not deviated from its previous decisions.[254]

---

[251] *Zolotukhin v Russia*, App no 14939/03, 10 February 2009. The ECtHR confirmed that the same approach applies in case of legal persons. See *Grande Stevens v Italy*, App no 18640/10, 4 March 2014. See also P Oliver and T Bombois, 'Competition and Fundamental Rights' (2015) 6 Journal of European Competition Law and Practice 598, 607.

[252] *Toshiba Corporation* (n 15) para 97.

[253] Ibid, paras 98, 102.

[254] See Judgment of 3 April 2019, *Powszechny Zakład Ubezpieczeń na Życie S.A. v Prezes Urzędu Ochrony Konkurencji i Konsumentów*, C-617/17, ECLI:EU:C:2019:283.

6.6 Court Delays and the Remedial Conundrum

Competition law is notorious for its complexity and high stakes both of which increase the time it takes for the Commission to investigate and for the EU courts to adjudicate the cases. The Commission's investigations vary widely but usually take no less than a year before the desired decision is reached and it is not rare for the Commission to be collecting evidence and pondering its moves for years before it makes a decision.[255]

Commission decisions can be appealed to the General Court where delays have proliferated in recent years prompting the EU institutions to double the number of judges at the General Court. Even before the effects of the increase of judges could kick in,[256] the General Court started to become more efficient in case handling: whereas the average competition case decided between 2012 and 2015 took around 47 months, this was down to 38 months in 2016 and 2018 (with an exceptionally low average of 22 months in 2017). Similarly, the average length of State aid cases (which are counted separately in the Court's statistical records) decreased from 32 months to 27 months between 2012 and 2016. A further appeal before the CJEU took on average another 13 months in 2016.[257] The European Court of Auditors verified the statistics on judicial activity and conducted a comprehensive study of the internal procedures of both EU courts and found room for improvement in the way cases are managed.

European Court of Auditors, 'Performance review of case management at the Court of Justice of the European Union', Special report No 14 pursuant to Article 287(4) TFEU, 2017

91. Currently the CJEU's approach to setting an indicative time-frame anticipates that the timelines set are to be respected on average. Lengthy cases are expected to be compensated by those requiring less time. Cases are still monitored individually and reminders issued when indicative deadlines are not met to **ensure that focus is maintained on cases that have overrun those limits** (...)

92. Our review of the first part of the case management process, which is known as the **written procedure**, revealed that there is only **limited scope to reduce the duration of this stage**. It is mainly the responsibility of the Registries; it includes the reception of the case and the preparation of the case documents. (...)

96. There are both advantages and disadvantages to the current regime whereby French is the language of deliberation and the de facto working language of the institution. Consideration has been given within the CJEU to performing a cost-benefit analysis on the **possibility to extend the language of deliberation to languages other than French in the General Court** and this could help to assess the situation and to provide support to any future decision (...)

---

[255] For example, the first fine imposed by the Commission in the *Google Search (Shopping)* case emanated from nearly seven years of investigation and proceedings before the Commission, see <https://ec.europa.eu/competition/elojade/isef/case_details.cfm?proc_code=1_39740> accessed 14 August 2020. The appeals against all three Google cases to the General Court are still ongoing and it will take multiple years before the final judgments will be rendered with the possibility of further prolongation by appeal to the CJEU. See ongoing cases T-612/17 *(Shopping)*, T-604/18 *(Android)*, and T-334/19 *(AdSense)*.
[256] European Court of Auditors, 'Performance review of case management at the Court of Justice of the European Union', Special report No 14 pursuant to Article 287(4) TFEU, 2017, para 90.
[257] Court of Justice of the European Union, Annual Reports on Judicial Activity, 2016 and 2018.

The duration of proceedings is significant for a number of interrelated reasons. First, competition proceedings have a considerable impact on the legal certainty of the undertakings concerned. For example, it may be more difficult to raise investments when a company faces the threat of an antitrust fine, a negative merger decision or a decision on the recovery of state aid. As fines can in some cases even *de facto* end a company's existence, undertakings usually have an interest in proceedings being concluded swiftly to regain certainty regarding their situation. Second, competition proceedings represent a considerable and unique strain on the Union's resources as there are virtually no other areas of competence where the Commission would have similar powers of enforcement and due to the aforementioned complexity of the cases. Third, and most significantly from a legal perspective, all persons (legal and natural) have a right to have their affairs handled without delay in both administrative proceedings and court cases.[258] Fourth, when court proceedings are found to be in violation of the right to a fair trial without undue delay on account of their excessive duration, the EU can be sued—so far, the damages resulting from excessively lengthy competition cases are counted in the hundreds of thousands of euros.[259] The rationale of the prohibition on undue delays is best summarized by the adage 'justice delayed is justice denied'. In this connection it should be recalled that actions brought before EU courts do not have a suspensory effect on the execution of EU acts unless the courts provide for it.[260] As a result, fines imposed by the Commission are in principle payable straightaway; in practice, the Commission allows undertakings to deposit a bank guarantee (which incurs interest, however) instead of immediately paying the full fine while the decisions are under judicial review. Such an approach is consistent with ECtHR case law which recommends cautiousness when it comes to enforcing administrative sanctions prior to judicial review.[261]

A. The reasonable time requirement

The first time the CJEU found a breach of the reasonable time requirement, as protected as a general principle of law embodying Article 6(1) ECHR, in the case of *Baustahlgewebe*.[262] Drawing on the case law of the ECtHR, the CJEU judged the reasonableness of the first-instance trial in light of the specific circumstances of the case, in particular its importance to the person concerned, its complexity and the conduct of the applicant and of the competent authorities (the Commission).[263] The Court concluded that the complaint of the undertaking against the length of the first-instance proceedings, which lasted in total five years and six months, was well founded, and on that basis it reduced the amount of the fine imposed by the Commission. The CJEU also engaged in reflection as regards the EU judicial architecture and its impact on length of proceedings.

---

[258] See Articles 41(1), 47 of the Charter, and 6(1) ECHR.
[259] European Court of Auditors, 'Performance review' (n 256) para 6.
[260] Article 278 TFEU.
[261] *Janosevic* (n 211) para 106: 'The [ECtHR] notes that neither Article 6 nor, indeed, any other provision of the Convention can be seen as excluding, in principle, enforcement measures being taken before decisions on tax surcharges have become final. (…) However, considering that the early enforcement of tax surcharges may have serious implications for the person concerned and may adversely affect his or her defence in the subsequent court proceedings, (…) the States are required to confine such enforcement within reasonable limits that strike a fair balance between the interests involved. This is especially important in cases like the present one in which enforcement measures were taken on the basis of decisions by an administrative authority, that is, before there had been a court determination of the liability to pay the surcharges in question.'
[262] *Baustahlgewebe* (n 213).
[263] Ibid, para 29.

Judgment of 17 December 1998, *Baustahlgewebe v Commission*, C-185/95 P, ECLI:EU:C:1998:608

41. As regards the conduct of the competent authorities, it must be borne in mind that the purpose of attaching the Court of First Instance to the Court of Justice and of introducing two levels of jurisdiction was, first, to improve the judicial protection of individual interests, in particular in proceedings necessitating close examination of complex facts, and, second, to maintain the quality and effectiveness of judicial review in the Community legal order, by enabling the Court of Justice to concentrate on its essential task, namely to ensure that in the interpretation and application of Community law the law is observed.

42. That is why **the structure of the Community judicial system justifies**, in certain respects, the **Court of First Instance**, which is responsible for establishing the facts and undertaking a substantive examination of the dispute, **being allowed a relatively longer period to investigate actions** calling for a close examination of complex facts. However, **that task does not relieve the Community court established especially for that purpose from the obligation of observing reasonable time-limits** in dealing with cases before it.

43. Account must also be taken of the **constraints inherent in proceedings before the Community judicature**, associated in particular with the use of **languages** provided for in Article 35 of the Rules of Procedure of the Court of First Instance, and of the obligation, laid down in Article 36(2) of those rules, to publish judgments in the languages referred to in Article 1 of Regulation No 1 of the Council of 15 April 1958 determining the languages to be used by the European Economic Community (...)

In a later case the CJEU refused to seriously address the argument that the length of competition proceedings should take into account both the administrative and judicial proceedings.[264] These days complaints about the former are normally addressed under Article 41(1) of the Charter,[265] while the latter as part of an examination of Article 47 of the Charter.

Opportunities for the CJEU to expand on its approach to the reasonable time requirement had been relatively few and far between until the General Court's docket became earnestly clogged up at the end of the first decade of the twenty-first century. The first taste of things to come was the finding of a violation of the reasonable time requirement in *Der Grüne Punkt—Duales System Deutschland*.[266] Although departing from the remedy for delays used in *Baustahlgewebe*, the CJEU confirmed the case-specific test of what constitutes reasonable time. The Court shied away from taking over the more detailed guidelines existing in the well-developed case law of the ECtHR relating to the issue of delays,[267] as well as laying down any objective and specific time limits incumbent on EU judicial procedures. On the

---

[264] *Limburgse Vinyl Maatschappij* [2002] (n 187) para 229. See, however, Opinion of AG Kokott in *Solvay v Commission* [2011] ECLI:EU:C:2011:256, para 345 who addressed this issue in a different case.

[265] *Ziegler* (n 160) para 154.

[266] Judgment of 16 July 2009, *Der Grüne Punkt—Duales System Deutschland GmbH v Commission*, C-385/07 P, ECLI:EU:C:2009:456.

[267] Court delays are persistently ranked as some of the most frequent violations of fundamental rights in Europe, as a result of which the ECtHR has had thousands of opportunities to examine cases of delay.

contrary, the CJEU affirmed that the list of criteria for assessing delays is not exhaustive and thus could be even more case-specific if necessary.

Judgment of 16 July 2009, *Der Grüne Punkt—Duales System Deutschland GmbH v Commission*, C-385/07 P, ECLI:EU:C:2009:456

181. It must also be borne in mind that the reasonableness of the period for delivering judgment is to be appraised in the light of the **circumstances specific to each case**, such as the complexity of the case and the conduct of the parties (...)

182. The Court has held in that regard that the list of relevant criteria **is not exhaustive** and that the assessment of the reasonableness of a period does not require a systematic examination of the circumstances of the case in the light of each of them, where the duration of the proceedings appears justified in the light of one of them. Thus, the **complexity of the case** or the **dilatory conduct** of the applicant may be deemed to justify a duration which is prima facie too long (...)

183. In the present case, it must be stated that the length of the proceedings before the Court of First Instance, which amounted to **approximately 5 years and 10 months**, cannot be justified by any of the particular circumstances of the case.

184. It appears, in particular, that the period between the notification, in September 2002, of the end of the written procedure and the opening, in June 2006, of the oral procedure lasted for **3 years and 9 months**. The length of that period cannot be explained by the circumstances of the case, whether it be the complexity of the dispute, the conduct of the parties or by supervening procedural matters.

Since then, the finding that the reasonable time requirement was breached was made by the CJEU on several occasions, despite the fact that the appropriate remedy was an action for damages which needed to be brought before the General Court. In these recent cases, the CJEU found the length of judicial proceedings ranging from four years and seven months to five years and nine months as incompatible with Article 47 of the Charter.[268] In other cases, it was the General Court examining the reasonableness of its own conduct in the course of actions for damages.[269] As will be demonstrated in the next sub-section, this is not unproblematic.

---

[268] *Guardian Industries* [2014] (n 68); Judgment of 12 June 2014, *Deltafina SpA v Commission*, C-578/11 P, ECLI:EU:C:2014:1742; Judgment of 26 November 2013, *Kendrion NV v Commission*, C-50/12 P, ECLI:EU:C:2013:771; Judgment of 26 November 2013, *Gascogne Sack Deutschland v Commission*, C-40/12 P, ECLI:EU:C:2013:768; Judgment of 26 November 2013, *Groupe Gascogne v Commission*, C-58/12 P, ECLI:EU:C:2013:770.

[269] Judgment of 17 February 2017, *Plásticos Españoles, SA (ASPLA) and Armando Álvarez, SA v European Union*, T-40/15, ECLI:EU:T:2017:105. However, see Judgment of 1 February 2017, *Aalberts Industries NV v European Union*, T-725/14, ECLI:EU:T:2017:47 where the General Court held that, having regard to the circumstances of the case, proceedings lasting four years and three months did not violate the undertaking's rights under Article 47 of the Charter.

B. Remedies for delay

Although the examination of the reasonableness of the duration of proceedings in EU law could do with firmer commitments and clearer guidelines as to what constitutes 'unreasonable' time, it is the realm of remedies for delay that raises deeper fundamental rights issues. Article 47 of the Charter, as well as Article 13 ECHR, require that individuals have the right to an effective remedy when their rights and freedoms are violated.

In the first EU case where a remedy for delay was ordered, *Baustahlgewebe*, the CJEU decided to immediately apply the redress itself for reasons of economy of procedure—the Court reduced the antitrust fine by ECU 50,000. In order procedurally to do that, the Court had to annul the entire fine and subsequently reimpose the new reduced fine. The CJEU also established that, despite representing a procedural irregularity, the dilatory proceedings before the General Court (then Court of First Instance) do not lead to the annulment of the judgment in entirety unless the delay is such as to prejudice the outcome of the case (which has so far never happened). This is consistent with the CJEU's approach to delay in administrative proceedings.[270]

Judgment of 17 December 1998, *Baustahlgewebe v Commission*, C-185/95 P, ECLI:EU:C:1998:608

---

48. For reasons of economy of procedure and in order to ensure an **immediate and effective remedy** regarding a procedural irregularity of that kind, it must be held that the plea alleging excessive duration of the proceedings is well founded for the purposes of setting aside the contested judgment in so far as it set the amount of the fine imposed on the appellant at ECU 3 million.

49. However, **in the absence of any indication that the length of the proceedings affected their outcome in any way, that plea cannot result in the contested judgment being set aside in its entirety.**

141. Having regard to all the circumstances of the case, **the Court considers that a sum of ECU 50 000 constitutes reasonable satisfaction for the excessive duration of the proceedings.**

142. Consequently, since the contested judgment is to be annulled to the extent to which it determined the fine (see paragraph 48 of this judgment), the Court of Justice, giving final judgment, in accordance with Article 54 of its Statute, sets that fine at ECU 2 950 000.

Ten years later, the CJEU was faced with a situation when a fine reduction was not available to amend the violation of the reasonable time requirement, as the Commission imposed in the first place a behavioural obligation rather than a fine on the undertaking in question for its abuse of dominant position. Concurring with the AG, the CJEU directed the undertaking towards an action for damages in accordance with what are today Articles 268 and 340 TFEU.

---

[270] See, for example, *Société nationale des chemins de fer français v Commission* (n 165) para 393.

> **Judgment of 16 July 2009, *Der Grüne Punkt—Duales System Deutschland GmbH v Commission*, C-385/07 P, ECLI:EU:C:2009:456**
>
> 194. In addition, as the Advocate General stated at points 305 and 306 of his Opinion, having regard to the need to ensure that Community competition law is complied with, the Court of Justice cannot allow an appellant to reopen the question of the existence of an infringement, on the sole ground that there was a failure to adjudicate within a reasonable time, where all of its pleas directed against the findings made by the Court of First Instance concerning that infringement and the administrative procedure relating to it have been rejected as unfounded.
> 195. Conversely, as the Advocate General stated at point 307 et seq. of his Opinion, the failure on the part of the Court of First Instance to adjudicate within a reasonable time can give rise to a claim for damages brought against the Community under Article 235 EC and the second paragraph of Article 288 EC.

A trio of cases decided in 2013 appears to have settled for now the CJEU's doctrine regarding the appropriate remedy for undue delay.[271] Choosing between the precedent in *Baustahlgewebe* and *Der Grüne Punkt*, the CJEU opted for the latter and renounced fine reductions for not representing a generally applicable remedy, as opposed to actions for damages. The Court made clear that the failure of the General Court to adjudicate the case in the first instance within a reasonable time, as required by Article 47 of the Charter, 'constitutes a sufficiently serious breach of a rule of law that is intended to confer rights on individuals'. This is one of the requirements for establishing liability of the EU under the *Bergaderm* line of case law.[272] The explicit recognition that a sufficiently serious breach occurred was meant to act as an invitation for the parties to seek damages, and so it did, with all three undertakings winning partially their claims in 2017.[273] The undertakings could not, however, obtain damages as part of the appeal to the CJEU but must have had recourse to the appropriate procedure (Articles 256(1), 268, and 340(2) TFEU) which confer jurisdiction for actions for damages on the General Court.

> **Judgment of 26 November 2013, *Kendrion NV v Commission*, C-50/12 P, ECLI:EU:C:2013:771**
>
> 93. Admittedly, the present case concerns a situation analogous to that giving rise to the judgment in *Baustahlgewebe v Commission*. However, a claim for damages brought against the European Union pursuant to Article 268 TFEU and the second paragraph of Article 340 TFEU constitutes an effective remedy of general application for asserting and penalising such a breach, since such a claim can cover all the situations where a reasonable period of time has been exceeded in proceedings.

[271] *Kendrion* [2013] (n 268); *Gascogne Sack Deutschland* [2013] (n 268); *Groupe Gascogne* [2013] (n 268).
[272] Judgment of 4 July 2000, *Laboratoires pharmaceutiques Bergaderm SA and Goupil v Commission of the European Communities*, C-352/98 P, ECLI:EU:C:2000:361, para 42.
[273] Judgment of 10 January 2017, *Gascogne Sack Deutschland and Gascogne v European Union*, T-577/14, ECLI:EU:T:2017:1; Judgment of 1 February 2017, *Kendrion NV v European Union*, T-479/14, ECLI:EU:T:2017:48.

95. It follows that **a claim for compensation for the damage caused by the failure by the General Court to adjudicate within a reasonable time may not be made directly to the Court of Justice in the context of an appeal, but must be brought before the General Court** itself.

99. It will also be **for the General Court to assess both the actual existence of the harm alleged and the causal connection between that harm and the excessive length of the legal proceedings** in dispute by examining the evidence submitted for that purpose.

100. (...) the General Court must, in accordance with the second paragraph of Article 340 TFEU, take into consideration the general principles applicable in the legal systems of the Member States for actions based on similar breaches. In that context, the General Court must, in particular, ascertain whether it is possible to identify, **in addition to any material loss, any other type of harm sustained by the party affected by the excessive period**, which should, where appropriate, be suitably compensated.

101. It is therefore for the **General Court**, which has jurisdiction under Article 256(1) TFEU, to determine such claims for damages, **sitting in a different composition from that which heard the dispute giving rise to the procedure whose duration** is criticised and applying the criteria set out in paragraphs 96 to 100 above.

106. In the light of the foregoing, it must be found that the procedure in the General Court breached the second paragraph of Article 47 of the Charter in that it failed to comply with the requirement that it adjudicate within a reasonable time, which constitutes a sufficiently serious breach of a rule of law that is intended to confer rights on individuals (Case C-352/98 P Bergaderm and Goupil v Commission [2000] ECR I-5291, paragraph 42).

In deciding that only an action for damages constitutes an effective remedy for the purpose of Article 47 of the Charter, the CJEU disregarded the Opinion of AG Kokott who pleaded in another case for the *Baustahlgewebe* approach of reducing fines which represents 'an immediate and effective remedy' and is fully in line with the Court's unlimited jurisdiction with respect to fines (Article 261 TFEU).[274] The same sentiment has been expressed by AG Wathelet in *Guardian Industries*. The CJEU has gone on to reiterate its position anyway.[275]

Guardian Industries v Commission [2014] ECLI:EU:C:2014:272, Opinion of AG Wathelet

110. In my opinion, the appropriate mechanism for remedying a breach by the General Court of the reasonable time principle in a case such as the present, would, for reasons of economy of procedure and also to ensure an immediate and effective remedy, be to reduce the fine rather than to leave it to the parties to bring an action for damages before

[274] Opinion of AG Kokott in *Solvay v Commission* [2011] ECLI:EU:C:2011:256, para 331. The Advocate General also called for a higher level of fine reduction than the one adopted in *Baustahlgewebe*.
[275] *Guardian Industries* [2014] (n 68). See also *Deltafina SpA* (n 268).

the General Court which, necessarily, will have been found to have failed to observe that principle by being unable to deliver its judgment within a reasonable time.

111. Indeed, **it would be paradoxical if the only way to obtain redress for excessively lengthy legal proceedings were to bring another legal action, which would necessarily entail additional costs** (both for the parties and for the company) and **further delay.**

Apart from the obvious issue of having to initiate another legal action in order to obtain redress for a violation of their rights, undertakings can be rightly made uneasy by the fact that the action for damages takes place before the same court who caused the injury in the first place. Already AG Léger in his Opinion to *Baustahlgewebe* identified this as problematic, especially from the point of view of the guarantee of judicial impartiality as interpreted by the ECtHR.[276] The problem comes into sharp focus in particular in cases where the CJEU did not preliminarily establish the existence of undue delay so as to make the subsequent action for damages appear more impartial.[277] Overall, the CJEU has satisfied itself with the General Court sitting in a different composition when ruling on claims relating to violations for which it itself has been at fault but the sufficiency of this measure in light of the requirements of the ECHR—which should have a decisive effect in line with Article 52(3) of the Charter—is questionable. Similar questions can be posed regarding the effectiveness of the remedy. Damages have been awarded in 2017 in a handful of cases and they have related to the material cost of the bank guarantees lodged by the undertakings concerned.[278] The saga has further been continued by the CJEU, denouncing the General Court's approach to the awarded compensations. In three key judgments delivered on 13 December 2018 the Court ruled that the EU cannot be held liable for the costs the undertakings incurred as a result of maintaining, of their own choosing, bank guarantees in favour of the Commission for the payment of fines at a time when it was obvious to them that the proceedings before the General Court in relation to those fines would be excessively long.[279] Non-material damage awarded has been minimal.

---

[276] Opinion of AG Léger in *Baustahlgewebe GmbH v Commission* [1998] ECLI:EU:C:1998:37, para 67.

[277] For such 'un-prejudged' actions for damages see *Plásticos Españoles, SA (ASPLA)* (n 269); *Aalberts Industries* (n 269). The CJEU is not consistent when it comes to this prejudging of the existence of delay on appeal, although in most cases it appears to still make the finding, 'where it is clear', that the General Court breached the reasonable time requirement in first-instance proceedings. But see, for a recent example, Judgment of 21 September 2017, *Riva Fire SpA v Commission*, C-89/15 P, ECLI:EU:C:2017:713, para 54.

[278] The awards have ranged from EUR 57,000 in *Gascogne Sack and Gascogne* to EUR 655,000 in *Guardian Industries*. See *Gascogne Sack Deutschland and Gascogne v European Union* [2017] (n 273); and Judgment of 7 June 2017, *Guardian Europe v European Union*, T-673/15, ECLI:EU:T:2017:377.

[279] Judgment of 13 December 2018, *European Union v Gascogne Sack Deutschland and Gascogne*, C-138/17 P and C-146/17 P, ECLI:EU:C:2018:1013; Judgment of 13 December 2018, *European Union v Kendrion*, C-150/17 P, ECLI:EU:C:2018:1014; Judgment of 13 December 2018, *European Union v ASPLA and Armando Álvarez*, C-174/17 P and C-222/17 P, ECLI:EU:C:2018:1015.

M Ovádek, 'At Last! Reaching the Remedy for Delay after a Long Ride through the EU Judicial System' (2017) 24 Maastricht Journal of European and Comparative Law 438

In order to regain a bird's-eye view of the interlinked parts of the remedies-for-delay saga, it is perhaps appropriate to pause for a moment and reconstruct the scenario once again. After discernibly delayed first instance proceedings, usually concerning a competition in-fringement, litigants normally appeal the case to the CJEU for a breach of rights (Article 47 of the Charter). In *Gascogne*, *Gascogne Sack Deutschland* and *Kendrion*, the CJEU told the appellants that it could not remedy the violation of their right by the General Court in the course of the appeal; rather, the *only* effective remedy in such a case is for the liti-gants to initiate an action for damages before the General Court. The CJEU, nonetheless, took the opportunity to take the heat off the General Court by establishing the violation of the reasonable time requirement. This had a positive impact on the impartiality of the remedial proceedings, although (...) the General Court thoroughly reanalysed the exist-ence and extent of delay.

The issue with this litigation sequence is that it does not necessarily follow from a strict reading of the CJEU's case law which can prove contradictory for a party seeking relief for a breach of its right to a hearing within a reasonable time. If such a hypothet-ical litigant sticks to the established interpretation of the case law and decides to skip appealing the first-instance decision to the CJEU on its way to the action for damages, which according to the CJEU constitutes the only effective remedy but which does not require a previous appeal judgment, the General Court will be judging its own conduct in entirety without any previous pre-determination by the CJEU, in comparison to the situation in *Gascogne* and others. In fact, a similar scenario has recently transpired in *Aalberts*, whereby the litigant did not complain about the length of the first-instance proceedings in the appeal case before the CJEU, which subsequently led to the General Court, without the prior involvement of the CJEU, finding no violation of the reasonable time requirement. Moreover, as the breach of the reasonable time requirement is nor-mally, in itself, an insufficient reason to set aside the delayed decision, it is in principle impossible to even bring an appeal case before the CJEU on the ground of delay in the absence of other grounds for appeal. The CJEU will declare such appeals inadmissible, as it has done so in the past.

In the hypothetical, but wholly realistic scenario, as demonstrated by the *Aalberts* case, where the action for damages before the General Court has not been prejudged by the CJEU, it is difficult to see how this could comply with the requirements of judicial independence and impartiality pursuant to Article 6(1) ECHR. The ECtHR has con-sistently held that impartiality must be assessed through a subjective and an objective test. Subjective impartiality is not particularly problematic in view of the present legal problem, as the action for damages is not adjudicated by the same judges responsible for the delay. In addition, the personal integrity of the judges of the General Court would be largely unquestioned; the only accusation would concern potential personal bias re-sulting from professional affiliation (solidarity) with colleagues in charge of the dilatory case. This would be, however, difficult to establish, since the ECtHR recognizes a pre-sumption of judges' compliance with the subjective test, while impartiality is considered in the circumstances of each case.

When it comes to the objective test, the hurdle is more difficult to overcome. The question to be answered is whether 'there is legitimate reason to fear that a particular body lacks impartiality' and whether this is objectively justifiable. In the leading ECtHR case on impartiality of proceedings against affiliated courts, *Mihalkov v. Bulgaria*, the Strasbourg court considered objective impartiality in conjunction with the criterion of independence, and consequently found a violation of Article 6(1) ECHR. The ECtHR reasoned that the professional attachment between a district and a city court in Sofia, which both featured as defendants in the case, was in itself capable of eliciting doubts as to the impartiality and independence of the seized court. In addition, the doubts were strengthened by the fact that, similarly to *Gascogne Sack Deutschland and Gascogne*, the indemnity awarded to the applicant was to be paid from the court's budget. The CJEU did in fact cite *Mihalkov* in support of its plea to be replaced by the Commission as the defendant, but this was rejected by the General Court which pointed to differences between the factual situation in *Mihalkov* and in the General Court's own case, since *Mihalkov* did not concern damages for undue delay.

The foregoing analysis leads to a complex picture of the General Court's impartiality in the remedial proceedings. The action for damages initiated by Gascogne could *just* clear the objective test, for the sole reason that the litigants themselves did not question the impartiality of the General Court in the application. It could then be deduced, for example in the course of a potential appeal before the CJEU, that the applicants did not perceive the General Court as breaching their right to an independent and impartial tribunal. However, had Gascogne raised the issue of the General Court's impartiality, and provided the standards set by the ECtHR in *Mihalkov* were not to be relaxed before the EU courts in the circumstances of remedies for unreasonable delay, the EU courts in *Gascogne Sack Deutschland and Gascogne* would have trouble meeting them: the General Court thoroughly re-examined its own conduct; the defendant and the adjudicator were professionally affiliated (part of the same institution) and the damages were paid out of the CJEU's institutional budget.

As a final point, it should be recalled that, generally speaking, ECHR standards flow directly into EU law by virtue of Article 52(3) of the Charter, which prescribes convergence of scope and meaning between identical rights protected by the Charter and by the ECHR. The Explanations to the Charter do not confirm verbatim that the right to an independent and impartial tribunal contained in Article 47 of the Charter is identical to the same right under Article 6(1) ECHR—as the scope of protection is more extensive under the Charter—but they do state that 'in all respects other than their scope, the guarantees afforded by the ECHR apply in a similar way to the Union'. The CJEU, however, has recently (in keeping with Opinion 2/13) protested against unrestrained application of Article 52(3) of the Charter on the ground that transposition of ECHR standards must take due account of the EU courts' autonomy.

(…)

The ECtHR requires that any remedy designated to alleviate undue delay must be effective in both law and practice and the remedy must also be sufficient and accessible. When it comes to remedies of a general nature, such as an action for damages under Articles 268 and 340 TFEU, the ECtHR in particular stresses the need to point to concrete examples in the case law whereby it was possible for an aggrieved party to obtain relief through the remedy in question. In addition, the ECtHR has a preference for preventive as opposed to compensatory remedies, although both are capable of being effective in principle. The ECtHR, nevertheless, also acknowledges the necessity of compensating for proceedings that have already been excessively delayed.

It was also noted by the ECtHR that a follow-up action for damages may be rendered inadequate where it, too, takes an excessively long period of time. This period also comprises the enforcement stage of the proceedings, meaning the payment of any awarded compensation. In order to meet the reasonable time requirement with respect to an action for compensation resulting from undue delay, the ECtHR has observed that a state may need to apply different procedural rules from those generally applicable in actions for damages, without prejudice to the guarantee of fairness as enshrined in Article 6 ECHR. Similarly, the rules governing legal costs may also necessitate diverging from those that would normally be applicable, as the aggrieved party is forced to initiate such proceedings in the interest of obtaining relief.

6.7 Competition Law and Data Protection

The objective of EU competition law is relatively singular: ensuring that competition in the internal market is undistorted, potentially with the caveat of maximizing consumer welfare. However, this relative clear-mindedness as to the goals of competition law has emanated from a long-standing discussion regarding the importance of other public policy objectives and how these should be dealt with in the context of competition law, if at all. The debate is still alive today.[280]

The CJEU has recognized that competition can in some cases be legitimately restricted on grounds which differ from those listed under Article 101(3) TFEU in case of agreements. In the seminal case of *Wouters*, the CJEU found a restriction of competition to escape the prohibition of Article 101 TFEU on the ground that it was inherent in the regulation imposing requirements on members of the Dutch bar for the sake of the proper practice of the legal profession.[281] The restrictions must still be necessary and proportionate in order to qualify for this exception from competition rules.[282] Other cases such as *Albany*,[283] *FFAD*,[284] or more recently *OTOC*[285] support the existence of a general (albeit limited) judicial doctrine on non-economic policy considerations *de facto* justifying otherwise illegal restrictions of competition in the EU. In this connection, Costa-Cabral and Lynskey have highlighted the

---

[280] C Townley, *Article 81 EC and Public Policy* (Hart Publishing 2009); S Kingston, *Greening EU Competition Law and Policy* (Cambridge University Press 2012). For a defence of a narrower conception of competition law and an illuminating review of the former book see O Odudu, 'The Wider Concerns of Competition Law' (2010) 30 Oxford Journal of Legal Studies 599. See also A Jones and J Davies, 'Merger Control and the Public Interest: Balancing EU and National Law in the Protectionist Debate' (2014) 10 European Competition Journal 453.

[281] Judgment of 19 February 2002, *Wouters and Others v Algemene Raad van de Nederlandse Orde van Advocaten*, C-309/99, ECLI:EU:C:2002:98, para 97.

[282] Judgment of 18 July 2006, *Meca-Medina and Majcen v Commission*, C-519/04 P, ECLI:EU:C:2006:492, para 45.

[283] Judgment of 21 September 1999, *Albany International BV v Stichting Bedrijfspensioenfonds Textielindustrie*, C-67/96, ECLI:EU:C:1999:430.

[284] Judgment of 23 May 2000, *Entreprenørforeningens Affalds/Miljøsektion (FFAD) v Københavns Kommune*, C-209/98, ECLI:EU:C:2000:279.

[285] Judgment of 28 February 2013, *Ordem dos Técnicos Oficiais de Contas v Autoridade da Concorrência*, C-1/12, ECLI:EU:C:2013:127.

increasing relevance of another area of law where the EU's presence is very substantial: data protection.[286]

Data protection concerns tend, however, to be more ubiquitous (and rising) than other public policy objectives. Data protection's pervasiveness in the EU is further underlined by it being a fundamental right protected under the Charter; the legislative significance and judicial activity is equally considerable at the EU level in this area.

Charter of Fundamental Rights of the European Union [2012] OJ C326/391

Article 8

Protection of personal data

1. Everyone has the **right to the protection of personal data** concerning him or her.
2. Such data must be processed fairly for specified purposes and on the basis of the consent of the person concerned or some other legitimate basis laid down by law. Everyone has the right of access to data which has been collected concerning him or her, and the right to have it rectified.
3. Compliance with these rules shall be subject to control by an **independent authority**.

The status of protection of personal data as a fundamental right in the EU legal order means that compliance with it represents a condition of legality of any EU act and hence measures incompatible with human rights are not acceptable in the EU.[287] Competition decisions of the Commission form no exception in this regard. Moreover, on the basis of Article 51(1) of the Charter, the Commission is under an obligation to promote the application of fundamental rights enshrined in the Charter in accordance with its powers. Although the extent of this obligation is not entirely settled,[288] Costa-Cabral and Lynskey have outlined how in practice the Commission could consider the impact of its competition decisions on data protection in the case of merger control.

F Costa-Cabral and O Lynskey, 'Family Ties: The Intersection between Data Protection and Competition in EU Law' (2017) 54 Common Market Law Review 11

This 'mainstreaming' of fundamental rights indicates that the Commission is required to consider how its decisions—including competition law decisions—impact upon fundamental rights. This could be done ex ante or ex post, or both.

---

[286] F Costa-Cabral and O Lynskey, 'Family Ties: The Intersection between Data Protection and Competition in EU Law' (2017) 54 Common Market Law Review 11.

[287] Judgment of 3 September 2008, *Kadi and Al Barakaat International Foundation v Council and Commission*, C-402/05 P and C-415/05 P, ECLI:EU:C:2008:461, para 284.

[288] Judgment of 20 September 2016, *Ledra Advertising Ltd and Others v European Commission and European Central Bank*, C-8/15 P to C-10/15 P, ECLI:EU:C:2016:701, para 75.

In its Facebook/Whatsapp merger decision, the Commission held that the merging entities were not direct competitors on any relevant markets and therefore the transaction would not lead to a significant impediment of effective competition and could be cleared without remedies. The shortcomings of this decision, in particular its failure to examine whether a market for the acquisition of personal data exists and whether competition on data protection on this market would suffer post-merger, were outlined in section 3 above. However, in addition to internalizing data protection's normative concerns in this way, the Commission could also consider whether data protection law could have an external influence on competition law. Again, precedent for such external influence exists in the context of merger control.

While the Commission has sole jurisdiction to assess mergers within the EUMR, Article 21(4) EUMR provides for a limited exception to this. It allows Member States 'to take appropriate measures to protect legitimate interests other than those taken into consideration by this Regulation', provided they are compatible with the general principles and provisions of EU law. Media plurality is included amongst these legitimate interests. Thus although the Commission is obliged to respect the pluralism of the media pursuant to Article 11(2) of the Charter, it fulfils this obligation by allowing Member States to examine the potential impact of a merger on plurality. According to Jones and Davies, this does not confer new rights on Member States: rather, it 'articulates their inherent power to impose, subject to EU law, obstacles to investment or make it subject to additional conditions and requirements, on the basis of public interest grounds'. Mergers in media markets are therefore examined in parallel by competition agencies and sector-specific regulatory bodies, with these two agencies assessing the merger according to different substantive standards. Underpinning this intervention is the idea that democracy will be undermined if media power is concentrated in the hands of a limited number of media barons with the potential power to jeopardize the free flow of ideas. The Commission could fulfil its obligation to respect the right to data protection in competition law decisions by applying an analogous procedure and allowing a competent body (for instance, the EDPS) to assess the implications of a concentration on data protection. It is important to note that in circumstances such as these, media plurality, or data protection, acts as an external constraint on competition law: the assessment which is removed from the hands of DG Competition is a non-competition assessment. Moreover, should the EDPS [European Data Protection Supervisor] (or national data protection authorities) undertake such a non-competition assessment of a competition law transaction to guarantee its compatibility with the data protection rules, this assessment would be in compliance with their institutional 'independence'. This independence merely prohibits data protection authorities from seeking or taking instructions from third parties; it does not, and should not, prevent data protection authorities from cooperating with one another, or with other regulators and agencies.

Alternatively (or in addition) the Commission could require an ex post assessment of the impact of concentrations on fundamental rights. Such ex post checks are carried out in the context of EU legislative instruments, and there is no legal obstacle to their use to evaluate the effects of a competition decision on fundamental rights. In this way, empirical evidence could be gathered to inform Commission decision-making in areas such as mergers in data-driven markets. Indeed, precedent for such ex-post assessment of mergers by the Commission already exists. Many mergers are passed subject to economic conditions that are verified ex post and, pursuant to the EUMR [EU Merger Regulation], the validity of these merger clearance decisions is contingent upon respect for these economic conditions. The Commission could therefore also render the validity of its merger decisions contingent on respect for data protection conditions stipulated in advance of the merger.

7
Equality and Non-discrimination Law in the EU

7.1 Introduction

Equality and non-discrimination are established among constitutional principles of modern liberal democracies.[1] They are explicitly acknowledged as foundational values in the EU context in Article 2 of the Treaty on European Union (TEU). Similarly, the right to non-discrimination enjoys wide recognition in international human rights law—it is contained in the Universal Declaration of Human Rights (Article 7), the International Covenants on Civil and Political Rights (Article 26) and Economic, Social and Cultural Rights (Article 2(2)), the European Convention on Human Rights and Fundamental Freedoms (Article 14), the International Convention on the Elimination of All Forms of Racial Discrimination, the International Labour Organization Convention No 111, and others.

In the EU, non-discrimination had a specific role to play from the outset of European integration. Despite being founded without explicit reference to human rights, the original Treaty of Rome nonetheless prohibited discrimination on the basis of nationality (now Article 18 of the Treaty on the Functioning of the European Union (TFEU)), as well as discrimination regarding pay between men and women (now Article 157 TFEU). These and other internal market non-discrimination provisions were not drafted in pursuit of social ideals but were simply deemed necessary for bringing down trade barriers and achieving economic integration across Europe. In the Western Europe of 1957, operating a business across borders was much more difficult than it is today because national governments protected domestic enterprises from foreign competition through discriminatory measures. As for pay discrimination between men and women, the economic rationale was somewhat different: France, having already enacted equal pay laws nationally, demanded the inclusion of the provision on equal pay in the Treaty of Rome, as it feared the absence of similar standards in other Member States would otherwise place it at a competitive disadvantage.[2]

The non-discrimination and equality landscape is substantially different today. The originally purely economic justification attached to the abovementioned Treaty provisions was, in particular as regards equal pay, supplemented by a social justification by the Court of

---

[1] Although an argument about the existence of a distinction between 'equality' and 'non-discrimination' could be made, the terms are used interchangeably in this chapter, more or less in line with their general use in EU law. In the words of the CJEU, '(…) it matters little whether the principle (…) is described as the "principle of equal treatment" or the "principle of non-discrimination". They are simply two labels for a single general principle of Community law, which prohibits both treating similar situations differently and treating different situations in the same way unless there are objective reasons for such treatment.' Judgment of 27 January 2005, *Europe Chemi-Con (Deutschland) GmbH v Council*, C-422/02 P, ECLI:EU:C:2005:56, para 33. For a more nuanced application of the two concepts see, for example, C McCrudden and S Prechal, 'The Concepts of Equality and Non-Discrimination in Europe: A Practical Approach', European Network of Legal Experts in the field of Gender Equality, 2009.

[2] C Hoskyns, ' "Give Us Equal Pay and We'll Open Our Own Doors": A Study of the Impact in the Federal Republic of Germany and the Republic of Ireland of the European Community's Policy on Women's Rights' in M Buckley and M Anderson (eds), *Women, Equality and Europe* (Macmillan 1988) 33–55.

The European Union and Human Rights. Jan Wouters and Michal Ovádek, Oxford University Press (2021). © Jan Wouters and Michal Ovádek. DOI: 10.1093/oso/9780198814177.003.0007

Justice of the European Union (CJEU).[3] Article 3(3) TEU today lists combating social exclusion and discrimination among the Union's objectives. Secondary laws making concrete
the requirements of equality were enacted.[4] Crucially, the scope of non-discrimination was
enlarged, paving the way for Directives on racial equality and non-discrimination in the field
of employment on the grounds of religion, disability, age, and sexual orientation (the so-
called protected grounds).[5] Article 19 TFEU enables the EU to adopt legislation combatting discrimination based on any of these grounds, while Article 10 TFEU obliges the EU
to place anti-discrimination at the heart of its policies and activities. Finally, the CJEU identified the principle of equality as a general principle of EU law,[6] which has moreover been
given a broad constitutional expression in Article 21 of the Charter. Overall, the application
of these rules has led to a considerable body of case law developed by the CJEU with respect
to various forms of discrimination. Since the early years of CJEU case law on discrimination,
the concept is consistently held to consist of treating similar situations differently or different
situations identically.[7]

Consolidated version of the Treaty on European Union [2012] OJ C326/13

Article 3

3. The Union shall establish an internal market. It shall work for the sustainable development of Europe based on balanced economic growth and price stability, a highly
competitive social market economy, aiming at **full employment and social progress**, and a high level of protection and improvement of the quality of the environment. It shall promote scientific and technological advance.

It shall **combat social exclusion and discrimination, and shall promote social justice
and protection, equality between women and men, solidarity between generations** and
protection of the rights of the child.

It shall promote economic, social and territorial **cohesion**, and solidarity among
Member States.

It shall respect its rich cultural and linguistic **diversity**, and shall ensure that Europe's
cultural heritage is safeguarded and enhanced.

---

[3] Judgment of 8 April 1976, *Defrenne v Société anonyme belge de navigation aérienne Sabena (Defrenne II)*, 43/
75, ECLI:EU:C:1976:56, paras 7–12. The prohibition of discrimination based on nationality even played a part
in rationalizing the precedence of EU law over national law, on the ground that 'the executive force of [Union]
law cannot vary from one State to another in deference to subsequent domestic laws, without (...) giving rise
to the discrimination prohibited by Article [18 TFEU]'. See Judgment of 15 July 1964, *Costa v E.N.E.L.*, 6/64,
ECLI:EU:C:1964:66.

[4] Starting with, as regards equal pay, Council Directive 75/117/EEC on the approximation of the laws of the
Member States relating to the application of the principle of equal pay for men and women [1975] OJ L45/19; as
regards non-discrimination of workers, Regulation (EEC) No 1612/68 of the Council on freedom of movement for
workers within the Community [1968] OJ L257/2.

[5] Council Directive 2000/43/EC implementing the principle of equal treatment between persons irrespective
of racial or ethnic origin [2000] OJ L180/22; Council Directive 2000/78/EC establishing a general framework for
equal treatment in employment and occupation [2000] OJ L303/16.

[6] Judgment of 19 October 1977, *Ruckdeschel and Others v Hauptzollamt Hamburg-St. Annen*, 117/76 and 16/77,
ECLI:EU:C:1977:160, para 7.

[7] Judgment of 17 July 1963, *Italy v Commission*, 13/63, ECLI:EU:C:1963:20, para 4.

Consolidated version of the Treaty on the Functioning of the European Union [2012] OJ C326/47

Article 10

In defining and implementing its policies and activities, the Union shall aim to combat **discrimination** based on sex, racial or ethnic origin, religion or belief, disability, age or sexual orientation.

Charter of Fundamental Rights of the European Union [2012] OJ C326/391

Non-discrimination

Article 21

1. Any **discrimination** based on any ground such as sex, race, colour, ethnic or social origin, genetic features, language, religion or belief, political or any other opinion, membership of a national minority, property, birth, disability, age or sexual orientation **shall be prohibited**.
2. Within the scope of application of the Treaties and without prejudice to any of their specific provisions, any discrimination **on grounds of nationality shall be prohibited**.

What the following sections will also reveal, however, is that despite the considerable evolution and extension of EU anti-discrimination law in the period since the turn of the millennium, the landscape of equal treatment remains considerably fragmented. The variety of legal instruments which co-exist in this area often have different scope, status, and effects. The underlying legal-philosophical move from economic rationalization to protection of fundamental rights has not been fully realized either. Overall, the sometimes very specific legal ambiguities presented in this chapter and the often granular case law of the CJEU feed into the overarching narrative about the nature of the relationship between the EU and human rights.

R Xenidis, 'Shaking the normative foundations of EU equality law: Evolution and hierarchy between market integration and human rights rationales', EUI Working Papers LAW 2017/04

Despite a new rationale promoting a genuine protection of equality as a fundamental right, few references to the Charter as a primary source of law have been made. It seems that the CJEU is privileging a pragmatic approach in order to avoid a controversy similar to what happened in Germany after *Mangold*. While non-discrimination law has lately been vested with the dimension of a fundamental right, and its underlying narrative has changed, this has affected the actual content of non-discrimination rights in a minor way. In fact, in the hands of the EU, non-discrimination law remains obviously anchored in the market, guaranteeing market access rights as the core of its equality protection. This ensures that non-discrimination law remains within the scope of EU law, and at the same time covers important parts of the typical subset of social relationships—work and consumption—especially in the case of race and gender, protected both within the labour market and in the access to goods and services. (...) uncertainties remain as regards the place of the Charter and its wide range of protected categories under the developing general principle of non-discrimination. The reach and boundaries of non-discrimination law are therefore blurry, and the non-discrimination battle seems to have lost priority. This is problematic in light of the uneven nature of the present protection, which privileges certain identity traits over others. At the current stage, the EU is a more legally protected place for women and people of colour than for gays or persons with disabilities. The tacit nature of hierarchies in equality protection—result of political backlash, and not of an explicit political and societal debate—gives wrong signals in terms of prioritisation of values. One necessary next step for the EU to take, within its competence, is therefore to extend market access rights to level off the protection of all grounds. However, the pushback has led to different make up solutions, such as a more bottom-up and horizontal enforcement through the national equality bodies, or the interpretation of the binding Charter in the hands of the CJEU. (...) However, the latest signals given by the Court of Justice show more restraint than bravery, confirming the dissonance between a bold discourse depicting the EU as a human rights promoter and the very functional nature of the EU legal order.

7.2 Discrimination on Grounds of Nationality

Consolidated version of the Treaty on the Functioning of the European Union [2012] OJ C326/47

Article 18
Within the scope of application of the Treaties, and without prejudice to any special provisions contained therein, **any discrimination on grounds of nationality shall be prohibited**.

The European Parliament and the Council, acting in accordance with the ordinary legislative procedure, may adopt **rules designed to prohibit such discrimination**.

Article 18 TFEU contains the general prohibition of discrimination on the grounds of nationality. According to the CJEU, the provision requires plainly that 'persons in a situation governed by Community law be placed on a completely equal footing with nationals of the Member State'.[8] However, the person wishing to rely on Article 18 TFEU must be a national of a Member State (an EU citizen)—it does not apply to third-country nationals seeking equal treatment on par with EU citizens.[9] Moreover, as is customary for EU law, the application of Article 18 TFEU is circumscribed by the scope of application of the Treaties. The CJEU usually determines whether a situation falls within the scope of the Treaties by looking not only at other substantive provisions of the Treaties but also EU legislation in the area concerned. The Court tends to interpret this criterion rather broadly. For example, the

[8] Judgment of 2 February 1989, *Cowan v Trésor public*, 186/87, ECLI:EU:C:1989:47, para 10.
[9] Judgment of 4 June 2009, *Vatsouras v Arbeitsgemeinschaft (ARGE) Nürnberg 900*, C-22/08 and C-23/08, ECLI:EU:C:2009:344, para 52.

fact that the EU legislature has not enacted any rules in a given area (air transport to third countries) and that a provision of the Treaty (Article 58(1) TFEU) derogates from the application of the general provisions on free movement of services has not stopped the Court from finding that such a situation falls within the scope of application of the Treaties for the purposes of Article 18 TFEU. The CJEU relied on legislation in the adjacent area of air transport *within* the EU (Regulation 1008/2008), which is covered by the freedom to provide services (Article 56 TFEU), to extend the principle of non-discrimination to the area of air transport services concerning routes *outside* the EU.[10] A similarly expansive interpretation of the scope of application of EU law grants the protection of Article 18 TFEU to individuals receiving services in another Member State.[11]

The application of Article 18 TFEU is furthermore subject to a *lex specialis* limitation. The CJEU has consistently held that the general prohibition on non-discrimination applies independently 'only to situations governed by EU law in respect of which the Treaty lays down no specific prohibition of discrimination'.[12] As a result, it is more habitual for cases to be dealt with under other provisions of the Treaties, in particular the provisions governing the free movement of goods, persons, services, and capital, all of which have an extensive scope of application.

Importantly, Article 18 TFEU has direct effect. This means that it can be invoked immediately by individuals before courts which must apply and enforce it. EU law typically distinguishes between two types of direct effect: vertical and horizontal. Whereas the former concerns the invocation of EU law against the Member States, the latter is of relevance in relationships between two private parties. Although vertical direct effect is more common and less controversial, as Member States co-create and are explicitly committed through the Treaties to EU law, due to its more pervasively regulatory character horizontal direct effect is more contested and found applicable with respect to fewer provisions of EU law. When it comes to non-discrimination, horizontal direct effect is eminently pertinent, as private parties are often found relying on discriminatory practices without the involvement of the Member State.

The vertical direct effect of Article 18 TFEU is well established and has never really been in question.[13] Legal and natural persons have been relying on the provision with varying degrees of success and in various types of legal situations since the inception of the European Economic Community but their arguments were never dismissed by the CJEU on the ground that Article 18 TFEU (previously Articles 12, 6, and 7) could not be invoked against a Member State. It is true that direct effect requires the provision of EU law concerned to be 'clear and unconditional' in order to confer rights on individuals but this was never deemed problematic in the case of Article 18 TFEU, especially as the historic judgment establishing the legal concept of direct effect, *Van Gend en Loos*, unmistakeably stipulated that a clearly defined negative Treaty obligation on the Member States, that is a prohibition of certain conduct, is 'ideally adapted to produce direct effects in the legal relationship between Member States and their subjects'.[14]

---

[10] Judgment of 18 March 2014, *International Jet Management GmbH*, C-628/11, ECLI:EU:C:2014:171, paras 34–62. See also Judgment of 25 January 2011, *Neukirchinger v Bezirkshauptmannschaft Grieskirchen*, C-328/08, ECLI:EU:C:2011:27, para 29.

[11] *Cowan* (n 8); Judgment of 24 November 1998, *Bickel and Franz*, C-274/96, ECLI:EU:C:1998:563.

[12] See, for example, Judgment of 18 July 2017, *Erzberger v TUI AG*, C-566/15, ECLI:EU:C:2017:562, para 25.

[13] For early application, see *Italy v Commission* (n 7).

[14] Judgment of 5 February 1963, *Van Gend en Loos v Nederlandse administratie der belastingen*, 26/62, ECLI:EU:C:1963:1.

Perhaps surprisingly, the CJEU has also recognized early on the horizontal direct effect of Article 18 TFEU, even before accepting the same for Article 157 TFEU on equal pay.[15] In *Walrave*, the predecessor of Article 18 TFEU has been applied together with provisions on free movement of workers and services to the rules of the International Cycling Union requiring the pacemaker and the stayer in world cycling championships to be of the same nationality.

Judgment of 12 December 1974, *Walrave and Koch v Association Union Cycliste Internationale and Others*, 36/74, ECLI:EU:C:1974:140

---

15. It has been alleged that the prohibitions in these **Articles refer only to restrictions which have their origin in acts of an authority and not to those resulting from legal acts of persons or associations who do not come under public law.**

16. Articles 7, 48, 59 have in common the prohibition, in their respective spheres of application, of any discrimination on grounds of nationality.

17. **Prohibition of such discrimination** does not only apply to the action of public authorities but **extends likewise to rules of any other nature aimed at regulating in a collective manner gainful employment and the provision of services.**

18. The **abolition** as between Member States **of obstacles to freedom of movement** for persons and to freedom to provide services, which are fundamental objectives of the Community (...), **would be compromised** if the abolition of barriers of national origin could be neutralized by obstacles resulting from the exercise of their legal autonomy by associations or organizations which do not come under public law.

19. Since, **moreover, working conditions** in the various Member States **are governed sometimes by means of provisions laid down by law or regulation and sometimes by agreements and other acts concluded or adopted by private persons,** to limit the prohibitions in question to acts of a public authority would risk creating inequality in their application.

The CJEU thus recognized the horizontal direct effect of Article 18 TFEU. Nevertheless, this was made easier in the circumstances of the case by the joint application of the general prohibition of discrimination with its specific emanations in the context of free movement of workers and services.[16] In addition, the judgment raised the question whether such horizontal effect is limited to collective agreements. There was reason to think that, at least as regards the employment conditions of workers, the prohibition of discrimination on the grounds of nationality also concerned conditions embedded in individual agreements, as this was explicitly provided for in Article 7(4) of Regulation 1612/68.[17] Indeed, the CJEU later confirmed that all measures treating a national of a different Member State more

---

[15] *Defrenne v SABENA (Defrenne II)* (n 3) para 39.

[16] The horizontal direct effect of the provisions on free movement of workers and services is well established and its application is more straightforward than in the case of Article 18 TFEU. See, for example, Judgment of 6 June 2000, *Angonese v Cassa di Risparmio di Bolzano SpA*, C-281/98, ECLI:EU:C:2000:296, para 36.

[17] Regulation (EEC) No 1612/68 of the Council on freedom of movement for workers within the Community [1968] OJ L257/2. Although not applying Article 18 TFEU, a relevant interpretation of Article 7(4) of Regulation 1612/68 can be found in Judgment of 12 February 1974, *Sotgiu v Deutsche Bundespost*, 152/73, ECLI:EU:C:1974:13.

severely or placing them in a less advantageous situation are caught by the Treaty prohibition in the fields of free movement of workers and freedom to provide services.[18] The Court also upheld the horizontal direct effect of Article 18 TFEU where other non-discrimination provisions were not applicable.[19] The situation was, nonetheless, one where an organization imposed conditions on the individual concerned which adversely affected 'the exercise of the fundamental freedoms guaranteed under the Treaty', namely the applicant's freedom to move and work in a Member State different from the one of his origin. In other words, although the situation—which concerned the payment of higher medical fees than those paid by nationals of the country in question (Luxembourg)—was not caught by the remit of Article 45 TFEU on the free movement of workers, the application of Article 18 TFEU in its stead was still connected to Mr Ferlini's exercise of his freedom to move and work anywhere in the EU.[20]

Such a connection can also be made explicit by the CJEU applying, usually in vertical situations, Article 18 TFEU in conjunction with Article 21 TFEU on the freedom to move and reside within the territory of the host Member State,[21] or applying Article 21 TFEU alone if the case at hand falls entirely within the scope of the latter.[22] The bottom line is that when applying, both horizontally and vertically, Article 18 TFEU, the Court looks for a material link to EU law, which can be more or less tenuous, similarly to the way the provisions of the Charter and general principles, including non-discrimination (of which Article 18 is an expression) and fundamental rights, are applied.[23] In any case, Article 18 TFEU has a gap-filling nature: it only comes into play if there is no more specific prohibition of discrimination on the grounds of nationality,[24] or in addition to them. Although Article 21(2) of the Charter reproduced verbatim the wording of Article 18 TFEU, it offers only symbolic added value and is rarely invoked or interpreted.

The judgment in *Ferlini* also exemplifies another general aspect of the principle of non-discrimination in the EU. The discrimination against Mr Ferlini was not overt: the relevant decision of the group of healthcare providers did not explicitly state that nationals of other Member States are subject to higher hospital fees. Rather, Mr Ferlini was discriminated against because the criterion applied by the healthcare providers when determining the amount of medical fees due turned on one's affiliation to the national social security system.

---

[18] Judgment of 13 December 1984, *Eberhard Haug-Adrion v Frankfurter Versicherungs-AG*, 251/83, ECLI:EU:C:1984:397.

[19] Judgment of 3 October 2000, *Ferlini v Centre hospitalier de Luxembourg*, C-411/98, ECLI:EU:C:2000:530.

[20] Ibid, para 50. See also M de Mol, 'The Novel Approach of the CJEU on the Horizontal Direct Effect of the EU Principle of Non-discrimination: (Unbridled) Expansionism of EU Law?' (2011) 18 Maastricht Journal of European and Comparative Law 109, 116.

[21] See, for example, Judgment of 2 June 2016, *Commission v the Netherlands*, C-233/14, ECLI:EU:C:2016:396.

[22] Judgment of 8 June 2017, *Mircea Florian Freitag*, C-541/15, ECLI:EU:C:2017:432, para 31. Note that where the situation concerns employment, Article 45 TFEU on free movement of workers is applied as a more specific expression of the principle of free movement of persons (Article 21 TFEU). Both of these provisions have a non-discrimination component (as regards nationality) which allows them to be applied independently from the general principle enshrined in Article 18 TFEU. Nevertheless, in practice, all three provisions might play a role in determining the outcome of a case. See, for example, Judgment of 25 October 2012, *Déborah Prete v Office national de l'emploi*, C-367/11, ECLI:EU:C:2012:668.

[23] See Ch 4.

[24] The most important specific Treaty provisions requiring non-discrimination are those relating to the free movement of persons and the single market: Article 21 TFEU (persons); Articles 34, 36, 37 TFEU (goods); Article 45(2) TFEU (workers); Articles 49, 54, 55, 56, and 61 TFEU (establishment and services); Articles 63 and 65(3) TFEU (capital). Most of these provisions do not explicitly refer to non-discrimination but they have been extensively interpreted by the CJEU in line with the overarching objective of establishing and safeguarding equal treatment of persons, goods, workers, service providers and recipients, and capital as far as their intra-EU origin and movement is concerned.

Whereas this was almost universally the case for the nationals of Luxembourg, it was not so for nationals of other Member States.[25] The *de facto* result of applying the criterion was therefore discrimination on the grounds of nationality. The CJEU calls it 'indirect' or 'covert' discrimination and it has formed the basis of many findings of discriminatory practices.

Judgment of 27 October 2009, *Land Oberösterreich v ČEZ as*, C-115/08, ECLI:EU:C:2009:660

92. (...) it is settled case-law that the rules regarding equality of treatment between nationals and non-nationals forbid not only overt discrimination by reason of nationality or, in the case of a company, its seat, but also all **covert forms of discrimination** which, by the application of other distinguishing criteria, lead to the same result (...)

Unlike direct discrimination, indirect discrimination can be justified by reference to 'objective factors unrelated to the nationality of the persons concerned' and provided that such a *de facto* discriminatory measure is proportionate to the aim legitimately pursued.[26] There are also limited and specific exceptions permitting direct discrimination: Article 45(3) and (4) TFEU enable Member States overtly to treat similar situations differently on the grounds of public policy, public security, public health, and when it comes to employment in public service. Limitations of the principle of non-discrimination between nationals of EU Member States can furthermore have basis in secondary law. A prominent example of such a limitation is Article 24(2) of Directive 2004/38/EC which allows Member States to curb social assistance in a discriminatory manner under the given conditions.

Directive 2004/38/EC of the European Parliament and of the Council on the right of citizens of the Union and their family members to move and reside freely within the territory of the Member States [2004] OJ L158/77

Article 24

Equal treatment

1. Subject to such specific provisions as are expressly provided for in the Treaty and secondary law, all Union citizens residing on the basis of this Directive in the territory of the host Member State shall enjoy equal treatment with the nationals of that Member State within the scope of the Treaty. The benefit of this right shall be extended to family members who are not nationals of a Member State and who have the right of residence or permanent residence.
2. By way of derogation from paragraph 1, **the host Member State shall not be obliged to confer entitlement to social assistance during the first three months of residence or,** where appropriate, the longer period provided for in Article 14(4)(b),

---

[25] *Ferlini* (n 19) para 58.
[26] *Angonese* (n 16) para 42.

> nor shall it be obliged, **prior to acquisition of the right of permanent residence, to grant maintenance aid for studies**, including vocational training, consisting in student grants or student loans to persons other than workers, self-employed persons, persons who retain such status and members of their families.

The requirement to treat EU citizens equally in comparable situations is frequently at the centre of media attention in the context of 'welfare tourism' and allegations relating to the abuse by nationals of other Member States of the host Member State's social system. Indeed, as Article 24(2) of Directive 2004/38/EC demonstrates, Member States have themselves been keen to attach various caveats to the principle of non-discrimination on the basis of nationality. It is not difficult to understand why such limitations are imposed: governments are under constant political and economic pressure to balance budgets and curbing access to social benefits is one way of reducing otherwise spiralling welfare expenses.

In the Court's case law, the tension between restrictions on access to social assistance and equal treatment of EU citizens regardless of nationality has notably manifested itself in the development of the 'real link' doctrine in EU citizenship.[27] The doctrine concerns the conditions under which differential treatment of EU nationals can be justified in the context of accessing social assistance. The CJEU in principle recognizes—subject to the principle of proportionality—that host Member States may require nationals of other Member States to have a 'real' or 'genuine' link to the host Member State in order to qualify for social assistance measures available to the nationals of the host Member State.[28] Such a link is most obviously established when migrating EU citizens are economically active in the host Member State, including by genuinely seeking employment.[29] The family circumstances of jobseekers are also of relevance to the determination of the real link with the labour market of the host Member State.[30] In general, the requirements concerning the proof of a real link between the claimant and the benefit in question 'must not be too exclusive in nature or unduly favour an element which is not necessarily representative of the real and effective degree of connection'.[31]

Economically inactive EU citizens are in a more difficult position with respect to the real link test. Although students studying in a different Member State might not be obliged to establish a link with the host Member State's employment market in order to qualify for maintenance assistance,[32] they may be required to demonstrate to that effect the existence of a genuine link through other means,[33] notably a prolonged (five years) period of prior residence intended to ensure a certain degree of integration into the society of the host Member State.[34] No less important a rationale than integration for allowing *de facto* differential treatment of EU students is the requirement that they do not become an unreasonable burden on the social assistance system of the host Member State.[35] This requirement is better known

---

[27] PJ Neuvonen, *Equal Citizenship and Its Limits in EU Law: We The Burden?* (Hart Publishing 2016) 66.

[28] See Judgment of 23 March 2004, *Collins v Secretary of State for Work and Pensions*, C-138/02, ECLI:EU:C:2004:172, para 67. For a case concerning the requirement of a real link of a Member State national to her own country of origin after exercising her free movement rights see Judgment of 11 July 2002, *D'Hoop and Office national de l'emploi*, C-224/98, ECLI:EU:C:2002:432, para 38.

[29] *Collins* (n 28) para 70; *Vatsouras* (n 9) para 37. Note that the right to equal treatment is not subject to the real link test once the migrating EU national attains the status of a worker.

[30] *Prete* (n 22) para 48.

[31] Judgment of 4 October 2012, *Commission v Austria*, C-75/11, ECLI:EU:C:2012:605, para 62.

[32] Judgment of 15 March 2005, *Bidar*, C-209/03, ECLI:EU:C:2005:169, para 58.

[33] Ibid, para 62.

[34] Judgment of 18 November 2008, *Förster v Hoofddirectie van de Informatie Beheer Groep*, C-158/07, ECLI:EU:C:2008:630, paras 52, 58.

[35] *Commission v Austria* (n 31) para 60.

from the 'welfare tourism' cases where it has played a central role in justifying Member State restrictions on social assistance.[36] On the whole, the case law confirms the ongoing significance of economic considerations for the enjoyment of EU citizenship and the related right to equal treatment,[37] despite the commonplace narrative often pointing to the decoupling of individuals' rights under EU law from the paradigm of economic integration.[38]

NN Shuibhne, 'The Resilience of EU Market Citizenship' (2010) 47 Common Market Law Review 1597

Almost every substantive judgment on EU citizenship to date has related (to borrow from the free movement of goods) actually or potentially, directly or indirectly to free movement and residence rights. In the breakthrough citizenship case of *Martínez Sala*, the Court of Justice adapted the case law on service recipients (...) to apply rights developed originally for the economically active (material) to the situation of EU citizens (personal) who were accepted as being lawfully resident (through Community or national means) in a host State irrespective of the extent to which they currently met the economic self-sufficiency and/or medical insurance conditions of the Residence Directives. In that case, non discriminatory access to a child-raising allowance was extracted from the material Treaty scope of social advantages—bestowed normally on migrant workers—and transposed to the personal scope of a lawfully resident, non-working migrant EU citizen.

Building on these foundations, citizenship is often used as an additional plank in economic free movement cases. It has also been used to justify 'pure' rights to movement and residence. But the legal contribution of EU citizenship has enabled much more than this too, in summary: (1) softening the impact of the legislative self-sufficiency/medical insurance limitations, especially through the invocation of proportionality; (2) bringing substantive policy issues within the scope of the Treaty; (3) revisiting case law which had more restrictive outcomes because of reliance on the economic freedoms, often to enable more comprehensive protection of fundamental rights; and even (4) guarding against potential inconveniences that might affect the (as yet indeterminate) exercise of free movement rights. Increasingly, the humanity of the person and the added value of citizenship are engaged to rationalise these expansionist trends in case law on personal movement. The concept of citizenship is thus seen as bringing a—legitimate—material dimension to the interpretative process. (...)

But all of this still fits readily with the idea of market citizenship, especially given the overwhelming emphasis in citizenship case law on the potency of cross-border movement. So, yes, the case law on EU citizenship pushes the boundaries of EU free movement law, but not further than can be explained through a constitutionalised understanding of the primary driver: facilitating (advocating?) the exercise of movement and residence rights. Creeping towards the fringes of free movement law, however, there are interesting questions that stretch the market framework in more difficult and intriguing ways. (...)

---

[36] Judgment of 11 November 2014, *Dano v Jobcenter Leipzig*, C-333/13, ECLI:EU:C:2014:2358; Judgment of 15 September 2015, *Jobcenter Berlin Neukölln v Alimanovic*, C-67/14, ECLI:EU:C:2015:597.
[37] Neuvonen, *Equal Citizenship* (n 27) 71.
[38] See, for example, *Förster v Hoofddirectie van de Informatie Beheer Groep* [2008] ECLI:EU:C:2008:399, Opinion of AG Mazák, para 54.

7.3 Gender Discrimination

As mentioned above, the prohibition of gender or sex discrimination,[39] is as old as the EU itself, insofar as discrimination in pay is concerned. A plethora of legislative activity, CJEU case law, and even Treaty amendments has cemented the importance of gender equality in the EU legal edifice since its inception. As far as principles and values are concerned, few other ideas now enjoy such explicit recognition of their centrality to the EU.

Consolidated version of the Treaty on the Functioning of the European Union [2012] OJ C326/47

Article 8

In all its activities, the Union shall aim to eliminate inequalities, and to promote equality, between men and women.

Although the role of EU law is still most pronounced when it comes to equalization of working conditions, its reach is both deeper and wider.[40] Whereas the original provision, Article 119 of the Treaty of Rome, only referred to the equality of 'pay' between men and women, subsequent interpretation and application of this provision and the related Directive overcame arguments to confine the scope of the non-discrimination requirement to only wage in the strict sense, and instead construed equal pay as encompassing various supplements and compensations to basic pay. The prohibition of gender discrimination (and promotion of gender equality) at EU level has also become explicitly wider, indeed horizontal, as Articles 8 and 10 TFEU and Articles 21 and 23 of the Charter testify.

Charter of Fundamental Rights of the European Union [2012] OJ C326/391

Article 23

Equality between women and men

Equality between women and men must be ensured **in all areas**, including employment, work and pay.

The principle of equality shall **not prevent** the maintenance or adoption of **measures providing for specific advantages in favour of the under-represented sex.**

---

[39] The two terms are used here for the most part interchangeably, although in reality they denote somewhat different concepts. 'Gender' is a more inclusive term than 'sex', encompassing the socially constructed aspects attached to sexes (gender roles) and the individual understanding of one's sex (gender identity). The EU Treaties and the Charter only refer to 'sex' and 'sexual orientation'. We discuss the latter in this section as a ground of discrimination conceptually related to gender, while recognizing that the two grounds are legally separate. See Article 19 TFEU.

[40] Which is not to say that, for example, wage disparities have completely disappeared as the situation improved. Moreover, solutions outside the strictures of 'hard' law play a part as well. See, for example, Commission Recommendation 2014/124/EU on strengthening the principle of equal pay between men and women through transparency [2014] OJ L69/112.

EU legislation today expressly covers specific subjects such as equal treatment in self-employment,[41] access to and supply of goods and services,[42] parental leave,[43] and pregnant workers.[44] The Union is also vested with a supportive competence in the area of social policy, allowing it to adopt measures concerning the equal treatment of men and women in the labour market and at work.

Consolidated version of the Treaty on the Functioning of the European Union [2012] OJ C326/47

Article 153

1. With a view to achieving the objectives of Article 151, the Union shall support and complement the activities of the Member States in the following fields:
   (i) **equality between men and women** with regard to **labour market opportunities** and **treatment** at work;

A. Equal pay, employment, and social security

Consolidated version of the Treaty on the Functioning of the European Union [2012] OJ C326/47

Article 157

1. Each Member State **shall ensure** that **the principle of equal pay for male and female workers for equal work or work of equal value** is applied.
2. For the purpose of this Article, 'pay' means the ordinary basic or minimum wage or salary and any other consideration, whether in cash or in kind, which the worker receives directly or indirectly, in respect of his employment, from his employer.
   Equal pay without discrimination based on sex means:
   (a) that pay for the same work at piece rates shall be calculated on the basis of the same unit of measurement;
   (b) that pay for work at time rates shall be the same for the same job.
3. The European Parliament and the Council, acting in accordance with the ordinary legislative procedure, and after consulting the Economic and Social Committee, shall adopt measures to ensure the application of the principle of equal opportunities and equal treatment of men and women in matters of employment and occupation, including the principle of equal pay for equal work or work of equal value.

---

[41] Directive 2010/41/EU of the European Parliament and of the Council on the application of the principle of equal treatment between men and women engaged in an activity in a self-employed capacity and repealing Council Directive 86/613/EEC [2010] OJ L180/1.

[42] Council Directive 2004/113/EC implementing the principle of equal treatment between men and women in the access to and supply of goods and services [2004] OJ L373/37.

[43] Directive 2019/1158/EU of the European Parliament and of the Council of 20 June 2019 on work-life balance for parents and carers and repealing Council Directive 2010/18/EU [2019] OJ L188/79..

[44] Council Directive 92/85/EEC on the introduction of measures to encourage improvements in the safety and health at work of pregnant workers and workers who have recently given birth or are breastfeeding (tenth individual Directive within the meaning of Article 16 (1) of Directive 89/391/EEC) [1992] OJ L348/1.

4. With a view to ensuring full equality in practice between men and women in working life, the **principle of equal treatment shall not prevent any Member State from maintaining or adopting measures providing for specific advantages in order to make it easier for the underrepresented sex** to pursue a vocational activity or to prevent or compensate for disadvantages in professional careers.

One of the most foundational legal sagas in all of EU law concerns the application of Article 157 TFEU's predecessor, Article 119 of the Treaty of Rome. In the 1950s and 1960s, Ms Defrenne worked as a stewardess for the then Belgian national airline, Sabena. To Ms Defrenne's disadvantage, the company operated a policy under which female flight attendants were paid less than their male colleagues and, in addition, were forced to retire 15 years earlier (at age 40) in accordance with applicable Belgian legislation. In three *Defrenne* cases adjudicated in the 1970s, the second of which led to the most ground-breaking pronouncement, the CJEU was called upon by Belgian national courts to interpret EU law relating to the principle of equal treatment between men and women in matters of pay and employment.

In *Defrenne I*, the CJEU decided that social security benefits, namely retirement pensions, do not come within the ambit of the term 'pay' in the meaning of what is now Article 157(2) TFEU (despite not being in principle 'alien' to the concept) when the social security schemes from which such benefits are derived are established by legislation 'without any element of agreement within the undertaking or the occupational branch concerned'. The judgment in *Defrenne I* later served as a foundation for a step in the opposite direction when the CJEU somewhat controversially recognized that occupational pensions, even when *de facto* replacing state social security schemes, do fall within the scope of 'pay' for the purposes of equal treatment between men and women,[45] obliterating in the process the Occupational Social Security Directive enacted partially on the basis of *Defrenne I*.[46]

Judgment of 25 May 1971, *Defrenne v Belgian State (Defrenne I)*, 80/70, ECLI:EU:C:1971:55

7. Although consideration in the nature of social security benefits is not therefore in principle alien to the concept of pay, **there cannot be brought within this concept, as defined in Article 119, social security schemes or benefits, in particular retirement pensions, directly governed by legislation without any element of agreement** within the undertaking or the occupational branch concerned, which are **obligatorily applicable to general categories of workers.**

8. These schemes assure for the workers the benefit of a legal scheme, the financing of which workers, employers and possibly the public authorities contribute in a measure **determined less by the employment relationship between the employer and the worker than by considerations of social policy.**

---

[45] Judgment of 17 May 1990, *Barber v Guardian Royal Exchange Assurance Group*, C-262/88, ECLI:EU:C:1990:209.

[46] Council Directive 86/378/EEC on the implementation of the principle of equal treatment for men and women in occupational social security schemes [1986] OJ L225/40.

9. Accordingly, the part due from the employers in the financing of such schemes does not constitute a direct or indirect payment to the worker.

10. Moreover the worker will normally receive the benefits legally prescribed not by reason of the employer's contribution but solely because the worker fulfils the legal conditions for the grant of benefits.

It was, however, in the second bout between Ms Defrenne and Sabena that the CJEU delivered a truly game-changing decision which resonated in EU law beyond the principle of equal treatment. In *Defrenne II*, the main subject of the dispute was the lower pay received by Ms Defrenne in comparison to her male colleagues. The Court established that (now) Article 157 TFEU has horizontal direct effect, meaning that the principle of equal pay for men and women must be observed not only by Member States (vertical direct effect) but also private parties, notably employers. This conclusion was all the more remarkable given that the original wording of Article 119 of the Rome Treaty interpreted at the time was more unambiguously addressed to the Member States, not to private parties. The context in which *Defrenne II* was rendered helps explain the relatively radical, unprecedented, and rare step of recognizing horizontal direct effect of a given Treaty provision: some Member States have at the time largely failed to implement the equal pay provision (despite a deadline having been stipulated) which had negative economic and social consequences. The latter were also recognized by the CJEU as a rationale for the protection of the principle of equal pay in the EU in one of the early moves aimed at breaking out of the confines of the perception that the Community was no more than a purely economic integration endeavour.

Judgment of 8 April 1976, *Defrenne v SABENA (Defrenne II)*, 43/75, ECLI:EU:C:1976:56

7. The question of the direct effect of Article 119 must be considered in the light of the nature of the principle of equal pay, the aim of this provision and its place in the scheme of the Treaty.

8. Article 119 pursues **a double aim**.

9. First, in the light of the different stages of the development of social legislation in the various Member States , the aim of Article 119 is to **avoid a situation in which undertakings established in states which have actually implemented the principle of equal pay suffer a competitive disadvantage** in intra-Community competition as compared with undertakings established in states which have not yet eliminated discrimination against women workers as regards pay.

10. Secondly, this provision forms part of the social objectives of the community, **which is not merely an economic union,** but is at the same time intended, by common action, **to ensure social progress and seek the constant improvement of the living and working conditions of their peoples,** as is emphasized by the preamble to the Treaty.

11. This aim is accentuated by the insertion of Article 119 into the body of a chapter devoted to social policy whose preliminary provision, Article 117, marks 'the need to promote improved working conditions and an improved standard of living for workers, so as to make possible their harmonization while the improvement is being maintained'.

12. This double aim, which is at once economic and social, shows that the **principle of equal pay forms part of the foundations of the Community**.

18. For the purposes of the implementation of these provisions a distinction must be drawn within the whole area of application of Article 119 between, first, **direct** and overt **discrimination which may be identified solely with the aid of the criteria based on equal work and equal pay** referred to by the Article in question and, secondly, **indirect** and disguised **discrimination which can only be identified by reference to more explicit implementing provisions** of a Community or national character.

19. It is impossible not to recognize that the complete implementation of the aim pursued by Article 119, by means of the elimination of all discrimination, direct or indirect, between men and women workers, not only as regards individual undertakings but also entire branches of industry and even of the economic system as a whole, **may in certain cases involve the elaboration of criteria** whose implementation necessitates the taking of appropriate measures at Community and national level.

20. This view is all the more essential in the light of the fact that the Community measures on this question, to which reference will be made in answer to the second question, implement Article 119 from the point of view of extending the narrow criterion of 'equal work', in accordance in particular with the provisions of Convention No 100 on equal pay concluded by the International Labour Organization in 1951, Article 2 of which establishes the principle of equal pay for work 'of equal value'.

21. Among the **forms of direct discrimination which may be identified solely by reference to the criteria laid down by Article 119** must be included in particular those which have their origin in legislative provisions or in collective labour agreements and which may be detected on the basis of a purely legal analysis of the situation.

22. This applies even more in cases where men and women receive unequal pay for equal work carried out in the same establishment or service, whether public or private.

24. **In such situation, at least, Article 119 is directly applicable** and may thus give rise to individual rights which the courts must protect.

30. It is also impossible to put forward arguments based on the fact that Article 119 **only refers expressly to 'Member States'**.

31. Indeed, as the Court has already found in other contexts, the fact that certain provisions of the Treaty are formally addressed to the Member States **does not prevent rights from being conferred at the same time on any individual** who has an interest in the performance of the duties thus laid down.

32. The very wording of Article 119 shows that it imposes on states a duty to **bring about a specific result** to be mandatorily achieved within a fixed period.

33. The effectiveness of this provision cannot be affected by the fact that the duty imposed by the Treaty has not been discharged by certain Member States and that the joint institutions have not reacted sufficiently energetically against this failure to act.

35. Finally, in its reference to 'Member States', Article 119 is alluding to those states in the exercise of **all those of their functions** which may usefully contribute to the implementation of the principle of equal pay.

36. Thus, contrary to the statements made in the course of the proceedings this provision is **far from merely referring the matter to the powers of the national legislative authorities**.

37. Therefore, **the reference to 'Member States'** in Article 119 **cannot be interpreted as excluding the intervention of the courts in direct application of the treaty.**

38. Furthermore it is not possible to sustain any objection that the application by national courts of the principle of equal pay would amount to modifying independent agreements concluded privately or in the sphere of industrial relations such as individual contracts and collective labour agreements.

39. In fact, since Article 119 is mandatory in nature, **the prohibition on discrimination between men and women applies not only to the action of public authorities, but also extends to all agreements which are intended to regulate paid labour collectively, as well as to contracts between individuals.**

65. (…) the application of Article 119 was to have been fully secured by the **original Member States as from 1 January 1962,** the beginning of the second stage of the transitional period, and by the new Member States as from 1 January 1973, the date of entry into force of the accession treaty.

67. (…) **Council Directive No 75/117 does not prejudice the direct effect of Article 119** and the period fixed by that directive for compliance therewith does not affect the time-limits laid down by Article 119 of the EEC Treaty and the accession treaty.

68. Even in the areas in which Article 119 has no direct effect, that provision cannot be interpreted as reserving to the national legislature exclusive power to implement the principle of equal pay since, to the extent to which such implementation is necessary, it may be relieved by a combination of Community and national measures.

69. The governments of Ireland and the United Kingdom have drawn the Court's attention to the **possible economic consequences** of attributing direct effect to the provisions of Article 119, on the ground that such a decision might, in many branches of economic life, result in the introduction of claims dating back to the time at which such effect came into existence.

70. **In view of the large number of people concerned** such claims, which undertakings could not have foreseen, might **seriously affect the financial situation** of such undertakings and even drive some of them to bankruptcy.

75. Therefore, **the direct effect of Article 119 cannot be relied on in order to support claims concerning pay periods prior to the date of this judgment,** except as regards **those workers who have already brought legal proceedings** or made an equivalent claim.

The first aspect of the principle of equal pay addressed by the CJEU in *Defrenne II* relates to its rationale. The transformation of the EU into something more—without clarity on what exactly—than an economic integration project has been a source of perennial fascination and debate for observers. The Court's pronouncement about the 'dual objective' of equal pay represented a significant contribution to this debate by explicitly recognizing the social function of the EU. The CJEU's reference to the preamble, which identifies a role for the EU when it comes to 'social progress' and the advancement of working conditions, carried an integrationist undertone consistent with the significance ascribed to the Court in taking supranational integration forward at a challenging period of time in Europe.[47] A similar point

---

[47] See, for example, ML Volcansek, 'The European Court of Justice: Supranational Policy-making' (1992) 15 West European Politics 109–121; A Stone Sweet, *The Judicial Construction of Europe* (Oxford University Press 2004).

about the non-economic purpose of the equal pay principle was later made by AG Cosmas in *Deutsche Telekom v Schröder*, linking the principle to human dignity.[48] In the subsequent judgment, the Court held that the social aim of Article 157 TFEU takes precedence over the economic rationale.[49]

Deutsche Telekom v Schröder [1998] ECLI:EU:C:1998:467, Opinion of AG Cosmas

80. Nonetheless, regardless of whether that 'economic' objective truly reflected the intentions of the historical Community legislature, it no longer corresponds to present-day thinking. In a community governed by the rule of law, which respects and safeguards human rights, **the requirement of equal pay for men and women is founded mainly on the principles of human dignity and equality between men and women and on the precept of improving working conditions**, not on objectives which are economic in the narrow sense set out above.

In the second place, and most importantly, the CJEU recognized the direct effect of the Treaty provision on equal pay. The Court did so by pointing to the fact that direct discrimination, which was at stake in the proceedings brought by Ms Defrenne, was identifiable on the basis of Article 119 (now Article 157 TFEU) alone without a need for implementing provisions providing further detail. Crucially, the direct effect (also called confusingly 'direct applicability' by the Court) was horizontal as well as vertical—both public authorities and private parties were liable to be sued by individuals affected by a breach of the principle of equal pay for men and women. The Court made explicit, however, that when it comes to indirect discrimination, implementing measures, which can also be adopted by the EU, might be necessary to implement the principle enshrined in Article 157 TFEU. The implication hinted at by the Court was that in such circumstances individuals might not be able to rely on the direct effect of the Treaty provision. In a later judgment the CJEU clarified that indirect discrimination does fall within Article 157 TFEU but the latter is only directly effective in such circumstances when the (indirect) discrimination can be established using exclusively the criteria contained in Article 157 TFEU (equal pay for equal work) without relying on any laws, EU or national, implementing the principle of equal pay.[50]

Ten years after *Defrenne II* the *Marshall* case shed light on the issue of direct effect of the principle of equal treatment as implemented by EU legislation.[51] The case concerned the interpretation of Council Directive 76/207/EEC which, despite not being legally based on provisions relating to social policy (such as Article 157 TFEU), was closely connected to the issue of gender discrimination at the workplace.[52] The CJEU interpreted the term

---

[48] The Advocate General even included a footnote to exemplify the morality of the justifications at play: 'Nowadays, to rely on such an objective would be tantamount to asserting, for example, that child labour must be prohibited not because it shames the civilized world but mainly because undertakings which exploit children are more competitive than those which use adult workers.' See footnote 25 in his Opinion.

[49] Judgment of 10 February 2000, *Deutsche Telekom v Schröder*, C-50/96, ECLI:EU:C:2000:72, para 57.

[50] Judgment of 31 March 1981, *J.P. Jenkins v Kingsgate (Clothing Productions) Ltd*, 96/80, ECLI:EU:C:1981:80.

[51] Judgment of 26 February 1986, *Marshall v Southampton and South-West Hampshire Area Health Authority (Teaching)*, 152/84, ECLI:EU:C:1986:84.

[52] Council Directive 76/207/EEC on the implementation of the principle of equal treatment for men and women as regards access to employment, vocational training and promotion, and working conditions [1976] OJ L39/40.

'dismissal' contained in Article 5(1) of Directive 76/207 as covering situations in which workers are compulsorily dismissed for having reached pensionable age.[53] The issue was that the retirement age under national legislation in the UK was different for men and women, thus constituting discrimination on the grounds of sex which was prohibited by Directive 76/207. Nevertheless, in order for Ms Marshall to be able to invoke Article 5(1) of Directive 76/207 in a national court, the provision needed to be directly effective. Consistent with its previous findings on the question,[54] the CJEU indeed recognized that Article 5(1) had vertical direct effect on account of the fact that the provision was sufficiently clear and precise and the Member State has failed to implement the Directive in the prescribed transposition period. However, the direct effect did not extend to horizontal situations, with the CJEU arguing that the wording of now Article 288 TFEU only refers to Member States as regards the binding nature of Directives, and therefore obligations contained in Directives could not bind private parties. It is worth recalling that the CJEU rejected the same argument in the *Defrenne II* case when interpreting Article 157 TFEU (see paragraph 30 of the decision).[55] In the end, Ms Marshall was still able to rely on Article 5(1) of Directive 76/207 by virtue of vertical direct effect as she was employed by a public authority. The Court stated that the vertical effect was applicable to Member States regardless of whether they were exercising their public powers or merely acting as employers. Overall, *Marshall* entrenched the fragmented effects of the principle of non-discrimination on the grounds of sex: whereas Article 157 TFEU on equal pay was given horizontal direct effect, other aspects of gender equality—being expounded in Directives such as 76/207 rather than Treaty provisions—could not be relied on could not be relied on in cases against private parties.[56]

Judgment of 26 February 1986, *Marshall v Southampton and South-West Hampshire Area Health Authority (Teaching)*, 152/84, ECLI:EU:C:1986:84

46. It is necessary to recall that, according to a long line of decisions of the Court (…), wherever the provisions of a directive appear, as far as their subject-matter is concerned, to be **unconditional and sufficiently precise, those provisions may be relied upon by an individual against the state where that state fails to implement the directive in national law** by the end of the period prescribed or where it fails to implement the directive correctly.

47. That view is based on the consideration that it would be incompatible with the binding nature which Article 189 confers on the directive to hold as a matter of

---

[53] *Marshall* (n 51) para 38. There was a competing provision, Article 7(1)(a) of Council Directive 79/7/EEC on the progressive implementation of the principle of equal treatment for men and women in matters of social security [1979] OJ L6/24 (still in force), which permitted Member States to derogate from the principle of equal treatment as regards the determination of pensionable age. The Court interpreted this exception narrowly in light of the 'fundamental importance' of the principle of equality. See *Marshall* (n 51) para 36.

[54] Judgment of 4 December 1974, *van Duyn v Home Office*, 41/74, ECLI:EU:C:1974:133; Judgment of 5 April 1979, *Ratti*, 148/78, ECLI:EU:C:1979:110; Judgment of 19 January 1982, *Becker v Finanzamt Münster-Innenstadt*, 8/81, ECLI:EU:C:1982:7.

[55] The same observation can be found in P Craig and G de Búrca (eds), *The Evolution of EU Law* (5th edn, Oxford University Press 2011) 195.

[56] de Mol, 'Horizontal Direct Effect' (n 20) 117.

principle that the obligation imposed thereby cannot be relied on by those concerned. From that the Court deduced that a Member State which has not adopted the implementing measures required by the directive within the prescribed period may not plead, as against individuals, its own failure to perform the obligations which the directive entails.

48. With regard to the argument that a directive may not be relied upon against an individual, it must be emphasized that according to Article 189 of the EEC Treaty the binding nature of a directive, which constitutes the basis for the possibility of relying on the directive before a national court, exists only in relation to 'each Member State to which it is addressed'. It follows that **a directive may not of itself impose obligations on an individual and that a provision of a directive may not be relied upon as such against such a person.** (...)

49. In that respect it must be pointed out that where a person involved in legal proceedings is able to rely on a directive as against the state he may do so **regardless of the capacity in which the latter is acting**, whether employer or public authority. In either case it is necessary to prevent the state from taking advantage of its own failure to comply with Community law.

Returning for the final time to *Defrenne II*, another remarkable aspect of the judgment was the Court's imposition of a temporal limitation as to its effect.[57] The potential economic consequences of the recognition of the horizontal direct effect of the principle of equal pay for men and women were at the time enormous. Millions of women were paid less than men for the same work between 1 January 1962, the date by which the original six Member States were obliged to implement the provision, and 8 April 1976, the date the judgment in *Defrenne II* was handed down. In principle, by virtue of the judgment compensation should have been payable to all of those women. The CJEU, however, limited the effects of its decision, so that Article 157 TFEU could only be invoked before national courts (where compensation claims would have been sought) with respect to discriminatory practices occurring after the date of the publication of *Defrenne II*. The only exception were claims which were already pending before national courts at the time—these could also benefit from the ground-breaking interpretation of the CJEU.

The *Defrenne* saga came to a close in its third iteration. *Defrenne III* concerned the breadth of Article 157 TFEU and the general principle of non-discrimination between men and women as regards employment and working conditions beyond the scope of equal pay. The CJEU put brakes on the former but acknowledged the fundamental rights status of elimination of discrimination based on sex at a time when fundamental rights parlance in the EU was still in its infancy.

---

[57] The CJEU mentioned that taking into account the fact that some Member States persisted with practices which were contrary to Article 119 EEC Treaty (now 157 TFEU) was exceptional. It also ascribed part of the blame to the Commission which, despite issuing warnings, did not initiate infringement proceedings against the offending Member States. See paras 51 and 73 of *Defrenne II*.

Judgment of 15 June 1978, *Defrenne v Société anonyme belge de navigation aérienne Sabena (Defrenne III)*, 149/77, ECLI:EU:C:1978:130

15. The field of application of Article 119 must be determined within the context of the system of the social provisions of the Treaty, which are set out in the chapter formed by Article 117 et seq.

16. The general features of the conditions of employment and working conditions are considered in Articles 117 and 118 from the point of view of the harmonization of the social systems of the Member States and of the approximation of their laws in that field.

19. In contrast to the provisions of Articles 117 and 118, **which are essentially in the nature of a programme, Article 119, which is limited to the question of pay discrimination between men and women workers, constitutes a special rule, whose application is linked to precise factors.**

20. In these circumstances it is **impossible to extend the scope of that Article** to elements of the employment relationship other than those expressly referred to.

21. In particular, the fact that the fixing of certain conditions of employment – such as a special age-limit – may have pecuniary consequences is not sufficient to bring such conditions within the field of application of Article 119, which is based on the **close connexion which exists between the nature of the services provided and the amount of remuneration.**

23. It is, therefore, impossible to widen the terms of Article 119 to the point, first, of jeopardizing the direct applicability which that provision must be acknowledged to have in its own sphere and, secondly, of intervening in an area reserved by Articles 117 and 118 to the discretion of the authorities referred to therein.

26. The Court has repeatedly stated that respect for fundamental personal human rights is one of the general principles of Community law, the observance of which it has a duty to ensure.

27. **There can be no doubt that the elimination of discrimination based on sex forms part of those fundamental rights.**

28. Moreover, the same concepts are recognized by the European Social Charter of 18 November 1961 and by Convention No 111 of the International Labour Organization of 25 June 1958 concerning discrimination in respect of employment and occupation.

The CJEU refused to extend the principle of equal pay for men and women to cover general equality in working conditions too, as sought by Ms Defrenne. The Court expressly stated that Article 157 TFEU is a special rule which stipulates the factors that allow courts to assess directly whether pay discrimination is occurring or not. Conversely, equality in working conditions was not regulated with the same level of detail in the Treaties. Instead, harmonization of access to employment and working conditions formed part of the EU's social policy objectives which were of a programmatic nature and thus requiring implementing measures to be implemented. Such EU legislation was already enacted at the time of the CJEU's reply to the preliminary reference,[58] but it was not applicable to the facts of the case which occurred prior to the adoption of that legislation.

---

[58] Council Directive 76/207/EEC on the implementation of the principle of equal treatment for men and women as regards access to employment, vocational training and promotion, and working conditions [1976] OJ L39/40. Of

The restrictive approach to the concept of 'pay' adopted in *Defrenne III* contrasts with other developments in the case law. Various benefits and compensations have been adjudged to constitute 'pay' for the purposes of Article 157 TFEU, ranging from travel facilities to severance benefits and statutory sick pay.[59] As explained above, due to the horizontal direct effect being only recognized with respect to Article 157 TFEU, the decision about where to draw the line between the principle of equal pay and other facets of the general principle of equal treatment (such as access to employment) was of considerable practical importance. Moreover, certain aspects of the legislative implementation of gender equality further heightened the divide, in particular as regards exceptions from the requirement of equal treatment in matters of social security, notably contained in Article 7 of Council Directive 79/7/EEC.

Council Directive 79/7/EEC on the progressive implementation of the principle of equal treatment for men and women in matters of social security [1979] OJ L6/24

Article 7

1. This Directive shall be without prejudice to the right of Member States to exclude from its scope:

   (a) the **determination of pensionable age for the purposes of granting old-age and retirement pensions** and the possible consequences thereof for other benefits;
   (c) the granting of old-age or invalidity benefit entitlements by virtue of the derived entitlements of a wife;
   (d) the granting of increases of long-term invalidity, old-age, accidents at work and occupational disease benefits for a dependent wife;

The line between pay, governed by Article 157 TFEU, and social security benefits, governed primarily by Council Directive 79/7/EEC, was most dramatically transformed by the *Barber* judgment which demonstrated the Court's courage to interpret an impactful Treaty provision in contravention of EU secondary law. Already in the preceding *Bilka* case, the CJEU ruled that supplementary occupational social security benefits financed by the employer fell within the scope of the equal pay requirement of Article 157 TFEU.[60] In *Barber* and subsequently *Coloroll*, the Court brought within the purview of the concept of 'pay' all benefits following

---

particular relevance would have been Article 5 which subjected all working conditions to the principle of equal treatment on the grounds of sex. The Directive is no longer in force nowadays, as it has been replaced by Directive 2006/54/EC of the European Parliament and of the Council on the implementation of the principle of equal opportunities and equal treatment of men and women in matters of employment and occupation (recast) [2006] OJ L204/23.

[59] See Judgment of 9 February 1982, *Garland v British Rail Engineering Limited*, 12/81, ECLI:EU:C:1982:44; Judgment of 13 July 1989, *Rinner-Kühn v FWW Spezial-Gebäudereinigung*, 171/88, ECLI:EU:C:1989:328; *Barber* (n 45). See also <<<REFO:BK>>>P Craig and G de Búrca, *EU Law: Text, Cases, and Materials* (5th edn, Oxford University Press 2011) 861<<<REFC>>>.

[60] Judgment of 13 May 1986, *Bilka—Kaufhaus GmbH v Karin Weber von Hartz*, 170/84, ECLI:EU:C:1986:204.

from an occupational pension scheme.[61] This was significant, because occupational pension schemes, which were regulated by private law agreements between employees and employers rather than by statutory law, were widespread in some EU Member States (in particular the UK) and the rules relating to the payment of the benefits were often different for men and women, among others reasons on the basis of different life expectancies of men and women. The pensionable age for women was typically lower, something Mr Barber and subsequently hundreds of thousands of others complained about before national courts.

Judgment of 17 May 1990, *Barber v Guardian Royal Exchange Assurance Group*, C-262/88, ECLI:EU:C:1990:209

6. Mr Barber was made redundant with effect from 31 December 1980 when he was aged 52. (…) He would have been entitled to a retirement pension as from the date of his 62nd birthday. **It is undisputed that a woman in the same position as Mr Barber would have received an immediate retirement pension** as well as the statutory redundancy payment and that the total value of those benefits would have been greater than the amount paid to Mr Barber.

28. It must therefore be concluded that, unlike the benefits awarded by national statutory social security schemes, a pension paid under a contracted-out scheme constitutes consideration paid by the employer to the worker in respect of his employment and consequently **falls within the scope of Article 119 of the Treaty.**

32. In the case of the first of those two questions thus formulated, it is sufficient to point out that Article 119 prohibits any discrimination with regard to pay as between men and women, whatever the system which gives rise to such inequality. Accordingly, **it is contrary to Article 119 to impose an age condition which differs according to sex in respect of pensions paid under a contracted-out scheme,** even if the difference between the pensionable age for men and that for women is based on the one provided for by the national statutory scheme.

It is worth recalling that the core issue in *Barber* harks back to the first *Defrenne* judgment. In the latter, the CJEU decided that social security schemes governed by statutory legislation without any agreement between the individual and the employer are *not* covered by Article 157 TFEU. The Court distinguished the circumstances in *Barber* by pointing to three criteria: the pension scheme was set up by an agreement between the worker and the employer;[62] it was financed entirely by the employer without any contribution from the public authorities; and the applicable rules, including those on retirement age, were laid down in the agreement and not in national legislation.[63] This is not to say that the private occupational arrangements were more insidious than statutory social security—the age difference was in fact the same

---

[61] *Barber* (n 45); Judgment of 28 September 1994, *Coloroll Pension Trustees Ltd v Russell and Others*, C-200/91, ECLI:EU:C:1994:348. On this case and the post-Barber cases, see *inter alia* W van Gerven, W Devroe and J Wouters, 'Current Issues of Community Law concerning Equality of Treatment between Women and Men in Social Security Matters' in C McCrudden (ed), *Equality of Treatment between Women and Men in Social Security* (Butterworths 1994) 7–44

[62] The fact that the pension fund was set up in the form of a trust and managed by trustees did not affect the conclusion reached by the CJEU. See *Barber* (n 45) para 29.

[63] *Barber* (n 45) paras 25–27.

in the circumstances of *Barber* in both statutory and occupational pension schemes. The age difference in statutory social security schemes was, however, exempted from the principle of equal treatment on the grounds of sex in accordance with Article 7 of Council Directive 79/7/EEC. Moreover, as argued unsuccessfully by the Member States in their submissions to the Court, the fact that the occupational pension schemes were contracted out did not mean that their purpose was different from their statutory counterparts. Similarly to *Defrenne II*, the CJEU decided to limit the temporal effects of *Barber* in light of the contrary legal positions enshrined in secondary law and the potential economic fallout from the judgment.[64] The Member States even took the extra step to entrench the temporal limitation in Treaty law.[65]

Predictably, the *Barber* decision sparked a fresh wave of fine-grained litigation relating to pension schemes.[66] The judgment made the boundary between occupational and statutory pension schemes an important one and it was logical that it was tested by enterprising individuals. Most of the complex post-*Barber* case law was codified in a new Directive in 2006 which has remained in force since. The Directive also consolidated and recast previously disparate Directives relating to the principle of equal treatment in employment matters, pay, burden of proof, and occupational social security schemes. The Directive has as its legal basis in what is now Article 157(3) TFEU.

Directive 2006/54/EC of the European Parliament and of the Council on the implementation of the principle of equal opportunities and equal treatment of men and women in matters of employment and occupation (recast) [2006] OJ L204/23

CHAPTER 1

Equal pay
Article 4

For the same work or for work to which equal value is attributed, direct and indirect discrimination on grounds of sex with regard to **all aspects and conditions of remuneration** shall be eliminated.

In particular, where a job classification system is used for determining pay, it shall be based on the same criteria for both men and women and so drawn up as to exclude any discrimination on grounds of sex.

CHAPTER 2

Equal treatment in occupational social security schemes
Article 5

Without prejudice to Article 4, there shall be **no direct or indirect discrimination on grounds of sex in occupational social security schemes**, in particular as regards:

---

[64] Ibid, paras 41–45.

[65] It can still be found there. See Protocol No 33 concerning Article 157 of the Treaty on the Functioning of the European Union. Note, however, that the CJEU softened the application of the Protocol. See, for example, Judgment of 28 September 1994, *Fisscher v Voorhuis Hengelo BV and Stichting Bedrijfspensioenfonds voor de Detailhandel*, C-128/93, ECLI:EU:C:1994:353.

[66] For an overview of this case law see Craig and de Búrca, *EU Law: Text, Cases, and Materials*, (n 59) 864–67.

(a) the scope of such schemes and the conditions of access to them;
(b) the obligation to contribute and the calculation of contributions;
(c) the calculation of benefits, including supplementary benefits due in respect of a spouse or dependants, and the conditions governing the duration and retention of entitlement to benefits.

Article 8

Exclusions from the material scope

1. This Chapter **does not apply to**:

(a) individual contracts for self-employed persons;
(c) **insurance contracts to which the employer is not a party**, in the case of workers;
(d) **optional provisions** of occupational social security schemes offered to participants individually to guarantee them:
(i) either additional benefits,
(ii)   or a choice of date on which the normal benefits for self-employed persons will start, or a choice between several benefits;
(e) occupational social security schemes in so far as benefits are financed by contributions **paid by workers on a voluntary basis**.

Article 9

Examples of discrimination

1. Provisions contrary to the principle of equal treatment shall include those based on sex, either directly or indirectly, for:

(a) determining the persons who may participate in an occupational social security scheme;
(c) laying down different rules as regards the age of entry into the scheme or the minimum period of employment or membership of the scheme required to obtain the benefits thereof;
(e) setting different conditions for the granting of benefits or restricting such benefits to workers of one or other of the sexes;
(f) fixing different retirement ages;
(h) setting different levels of benefit, except in so far as may be necessary to take account of actuarial calculation factors which differ according to sex in the case of defined-contribution schemes; in the case of funded defined-benefit schemes, certain elements may be unequal where the inequality of the amounts results from the effects of the use of actuarial factors differing according to sex at the time when the scheme's funding is implemented;
(i) setting different levels for workers' contributions;

CHAPTER 3

Equal treatment as regards access to employment, vocational training and promotion and working conditions

Article 14

Prohibition of discrimination

1. There shall be no direct or indirect discrimination on grounds of sex in the public or private sectors, including public bodies, in relation to:

   (a) **conditions for access to employment, to self-employment or to occupation**, including selection criteria and recruitment conditions, whatever the branch of activity and at all levels of the professional hierarchy, including promotion;
   (b) **access to all types and to all levels of vocational guidance**, vocational **training**, advanced vocational training and retraining, including practical work experience;
   (c) **employment and working conditions**, including dismissals, as well as pay as provided for in Article 141 of the Treaty;
   (d) **membership of, and involvement in, an organisation of workers or employers**, or any organisation whose members carry on a particular profession, including the benefits provided for by such organisations.

Other legislative acts were enacted to strengthen various aspects of the principle of equality between men and women. Directive 2010/41/EU governs the application of equal treatment as regards self-employed persons who are subjects of a number of exceptions under the 2006 Equal Treatment Directive in employment-related matters.[67] The aforementioned Council Directive 79/7 on the 'progressive implementation' of the principle of equal treatment in matters of social security provides for equal treatment but the social security at stake must be connected to employment and at least one category of risk stipulated in the Directive.[68] In the interpretation of this instrument, the CJEU drew a distinction between (employment-related) social security and social assistance, thereby excluding from its scope, for example, certain housing benefits.[69] The Pregnancy Directive 92/85 is associated with gender equality in the EU but it was created on the premise of strengthening health and safety at work.[70] Nonetheless, in addition to health and safety protection, the Directive ensures certain employment rights for pregnant workers, workers who recently gave birth, and breastfeeding workers, such as paid time off for antenatal examinations (Article 9), prohibition

---

[67] Directive 2010/41/EU of the European Parliament and of the Council on the application of the principle of equal treatment between men and women engaged in an activity in a self-employed capacity and repealing Council Directive 86/613/EEC [2010] OJ L180/1.

[68] The statutory social security scheme must protect against one of the following risks: sickness, invalidity, old age, accidents at work and occupational diseases, and unemployment. See Article 3(1)(a) of Directive 79/7/EEC.

[69] Judgment of 4 February 1992, *The Queen v Secretary of State for Social Security, ex parte Smithson*, C-243/90, ECLI:EU:C:1992:54. Social assistance can fall within the scope of the Directive if it intends to replace social security. See Article 3(1)(b) of Directive 79/7/EEC.

[70] Council Directive 92/85/EEC on the introduction of measures to encourage improvements in the safety and health at work of pregnant workers and workers who have recently given birth or are breastfeeding [1992] OJ L348/1, as amended in 2007, 2014, and 2019.

of dismissal (Article 10), and, notably, at least 14 weeks of paid maternity leave (Article 8). These rights are complemented by the provisions of the 2006 Equal Treatment Directive, especially Article 15 thereof which guarantees that female workers can return to their job after maternity leave on no less favourable terms.[71] The Parental Leave Directive 2010/18 implemented a framework agreement concluded between social partner organizations at EU level. The agreement laid down the minimum requirements for the regulation of parental leave, chiefly a minimum leave period of four months, but on the whole a large margin of discretion is left to Member States. Recently, the Parental Leave Directive was replaced by a more comprehensive Directive 2019/1158 on work–life balance for parents and carers.[72] The Directive obliges Member States to ensure the right to paternity leave for fathers for at least ten days on the occasion of the birth of their child. It extends the period of non-transferable parental leave and introduces the possibility to take up carers' leave outside of parental leave. The Directive is still being implemented in Member States' national legislation. A framework agreement concluded between social partners still exists on part-time work and it prohibits discrimination between part-time and full-time workers.[73] This has *de facto* significance for gender equality, as the majority of part-time workers are women.

The final Directive from the legislative edifice of gender equality not mentioned yet is Council Directive 2004/113/EC on equal access to and supply of goods and services.[74] In addition to giving effect to the prohibition of discrimination based on sex—as is customary for equality legislation in general—in the area specified, the Directive was designed with a particular sector in mind, namely insurance services (Article 5). Nevertheless, the scope of the Directive is general: it applies to all goods and services providers, private and public, and requires that an individual's choice of contractual partner is not based on the person's sex (Article 3).[75]

Article 5 of Directive 2004/113/EC, which provides that the use of sex as a factor in insurance (actuarial) calculations shall not translate into differences in individuals' premiums and benefits, was at the heart of one of the more recent weighty forays of the CJEU into gender equality law. In *Test-Achats*, the Court invalidated—in itself an exceptional action—paragraph 2 of Article 5 of Directive 2004/113/EC which permitted Member States to derogate from the obligation to eradicate insurance disparities stemming from the use of sex as a risk factor.[76] In a relatively short judgment, the CJEU took a strong position on the importance of the principle of equality between men and women and emphasises its fundamental rights status.

---

[71] A specific provision is made for paternity and adoption leave in Article 16 of the 2006 Equal Treatment Directive.

[72] Directive 2019/1158/EU of the European Parliament and of the Council on work–life balance for parents and carers and repealing Council Directive 2010/18/EU [2019] OJ L188/79.

[73] Council Directive 97/81/EC concerning the Framework Agreement on part-time work concluded by UNICE, CEEP and the ETUC [1998] OJ L14/9.

[74] Council Directive 2004/113/EC implementing the principle of equal treatment between men and women in the access to and supply of goods and services [2004] OJ L373/37.

[75] Pursuant to Article 3(3), the Directive does not apply to media, advertisements, and education. It also does not apply to employment and self-employment but these areas are covered to an extent by the 2006 Equal Treatment Directive and Directive 2010/41/EU as regards self-employed persons.

[76] The date by which the CJEU's judgment had to be implemented was set at 21 December 2012 to allow insurance providers to adjust their actuarial calculations.

Judgment of 1 March 2011, *Association belge des Consommateurs Test-Achats ASBL*, C-236/09, ECLI:EU:C:2011:100

17. **Articles 21 and 23 of the Charter** state, respectively, that any discrimination based on sex is prohibited and that equality between men and women must be ensured in all areas. Since recital 4 to Directive 2004/113 expressly refers to Articles 21 and 23 of the Charter, **the validity of Article 5(2) of that directive must be assessed in the light of those provisions** (...)

18. The right to equal treatment for men and women is the subject of provisions in the FEU Treaty. First, under Article 157(1) TFEU, each Member State must ensure that the principle of equal pay for men and women for equal work or work of equal value is applied. Secondly, Article 19(1) TFEU provides that, after obtaining the consent of the European Parliament, the Council may take appropriate action to combat discrimination based on sex, racial or ethnic origin, religion or belief, disability, age or sexual orientation.

19. While Article 157(1) TFEU establishes the principle of equal treatment for men and women in a specific area, Article 19(1) TFEU confers on the Council competence which it must exercise in accordance, inter alia, with the second subparagraph of Article 3(3) TEU, which provides that the European Union is to combat social exclusion and discrimination and to promote social justice and protection, equality between men and women, solidarity between generations and protection of the rights of the child, and with Article 8 TFEU, under which, in all its activities, the European Union is to aim to eliminate inequalities, and to promote equality, between men and women.

20. In the **progressive achievement of that equality**, it is the **EU legislature** which, in the light of the task conferred on the European Union by the second subparagraph of Article 3(3) TEU and Article 8 TFEU, determines when it will take action, having regard to the development of economic and social conditions within the European Union.

21. However, when such action is decided upon, it must contribute, in a coherent manner, to the achievement of the intended objective, without prejudice to the possibility of providing for **transitional periods or derogations of limited scope**.

22. As is stated in recital 18 to Directive 2004/113, **the use of actuarial factors related to sex was widespread** in the provision of insurance services at the time when the directive was adopted.

23. Consequently, **it was permissible for the EU legislature to implement the principle of equality for men and women**—more specifically, the application of the rule of unisex premiums and benefits—**gradually, with appropriate transitional periods**.

26. (...) given that Directive 2004/113 is silent as to the length of time during which those differences may continue to be applied, Member States which have made use of the option [to derogate from the unisex obligation] are permitted to allow insurers to apply the unequal treatment **without any temporal limitation**.

27. The Council expresses its doubts as to whether, in the context of certain branches of private insurance, the respective situations of men and women policyholders may be regarded as comparable, given that, from the point of view of the modus operandi of insurers, in accordance with which risks are placed in categories on the basis of statistics, the levels of insured risk may be different for men and for women. **The Council argues that the option provided for in Article 5(2) of Directive 2004/**

> 113 is intended merely to make it possible not to treat different situations in the same way.
>
> 29. (...) it should be pointed out that the **comparability of situations must be assessed in the light of the subject-matter and purpose of the EU measure** which makes the distinction in question (...). In the present case, that distinction is made by Article 5(2) of Directive 2004/113.
>
> 30. (...) **Directive 2004/113 is based on the premiss that,** for the purposes of applying the principle of equal treatment for men and women, enshrined in Articles 21 and 23 of the Charter, **the respective situations of men and women with regard to insurance premiums and benefits contracted by them are comparable.**
>
> 31. Accordingly, there is a risk that EU law may **permit the derogation** from the equal treatment of men and women, provided for in Article 5(2) of Directive 2004/113, **to persist indefinitely.**
>
> 32. **Such a provision**, which enables the Member States in question to maintain without temporal limitation an exemption from the rule of unisex premiums and benefits, **works against the achievement of the objective of equal treatment between men and women**, which is the purpose of Directive 2004/113, and is incompatible with Articles 21 and 23 of the Charter.
>
> 33. That provision must therefore be considered to be **invalid** upon the expiry of an appropriate transitional period.

The judgment was heavily criticized by some commentators.[77] It was alleged that the CJEU's invalidation of Article 5(2) misplaced the Court's concern for fundamental rights and paradoxically left the insured worse off after premium and benefits adjustments. The resulting legal situation also still did not address indirect discrimination, so insurers were able simply to rewrite the actuarial factors to capture sex differences by other (indirect) means. To give an example: whereas prior to the judgment some insurers may have priced car insurance differently on the basis of whether the insured is male or female, after *Test-Achats* went into effect the same or similar disparity could be achieved by differential pricing of insurance for large and powerful cars as opposed to insurance for smaller vehicles (reflecting empirically observable and statistically significant differences in consumer behaviour).

Even if it were true that total welfare of service recipients declined as a consequence of the ruling—a claim that would require more solid empirical evidence—the legal circumstances of the case should mitigate some of the critique levied against the CJEU. It was not the judges but the EU legislator who decided in the first place to remove gender discrimination from insurance premiums and benefits by virtue of Article 5(1) of Directive 2004/113. The Court did not base its conclusion on a separate appraisal of the state of the insurance sector—it merely followed the logic inherent in the Directive, namely that the situation of men and women with respect to insurance premiums and benefits is comparable but treated differently by insurers, *ipso facto* constituting discrimination under EU law. As this was the basic premise of the Directive, as is clear from the recitals quoted by the Court, the possibility of an indefinite derogation from Article 5(1) indeed permitted the discriminatory treatment in many Member States to continue without a set deadline. If the intervention in the insurance markets, although led by the well-meaning goal of gender equality, was misguided

---

[77] See, for example, E Schanze, 'Injustice by Generalization: Notes on the Test-Achats Decision of the European Court of Justice' (2013) 14 German Law Journal 423.

from the outset, then the fault should lie primarily with the actors who designed and justi-fied the policy on grounds of gender equality, that is the EU political institutions. In view of the rationale of the Directive, the indefinite derogation from prohibiting sex discrimination in insurance premiums represented an in-built inconsistency which the CJEU 'merely' re-moved. Such a judicial approach might be criticized for being insufficiently concerned with the ultimate outcomes of judgments but that is a discussion which goes well beyond debating the merits of the *Test-Achats* case.[78] The fact remains that such 'process-oriented review' is an established part of the CJEU's methodological repertoire.[79] Finally, what also escalated the Court's response was that in the context of the Directive, variation in insurance premiums and benefits on the basis of gender actuarial factors was essentially framed, through the prin-ciple of equality between men and women, as a fundamental rights issue.

Indirectly, the *Test-Achats* judgment raised questions also in relation to the 2006 Equal Treatment Directive. Article 9(1)(h) thereof mentions as an example of sex discrimination the setting of different levels of benefits in occupational security schemes, *except* when a dif-ference in benefits results from actuarial calculations factoring in the sex of the beneficiary. This exception was originally promulgated in the post-*Barber* cases *Neath* and *Coloroll*.[80] Although it goes against the general thrust of Article 5(1) of Directive 2004/113 and *Test-Achats*, it must be remembered that the CJEU's invalidation of the derogation in Article 5(2) of that Directive was based chiefly on a practical argument against the way that particular piece of legislation was drafted. The judgment should therefore not be read as modifying Article 9(1)(h), as highlighted in even stronger terms by the Commission. Similarly, there is as of yet no discernible evidence indicating that the CJEU intends to dismantle all actuarial calculations which directly use sex as a risk factor.

Guidelines on the application of Council Directive 2004/113/EC to insurance, in the light of the judgment of the Court of Justice of the European Union in Case C-236/09 (Test-Achats) [2012] OJ C11/1

---

23. Article 9(1)(h) of Directive 2006/54/EC allows for the setting of different levels of benefits between men and women when justified by actuarial calculation factors. **The Commission considers that the Test-Achats ruling has no legal implications for this provision**, which applies in the different and clearly separable context of occupational pensions and which is also drafted in a very different way from Article 5(2) of the Directive. Indeed, under Article 9(1)(h) of Directive 2006/54/EC, the setting of different benefits for men and women is not considered discriminatory when justified by actuarial data.

---

[78] Van Gestel and de Poorter wrote that such judicial review 'cannot capture the substantive truth-value or val-idity of the empirical basis on which laws and regulations rest'. See R van Gestel and J de Poorter, 'Putting Evidence-based Law Making to the Test: Judicial Review of Legislative Rationality' (2016) 4 The Theory and Practice of Legislation 155, 157.

[79] K Lenaerts, 'The European Court of Justice and Process-Oriented Review' (2012) 31 Yearbook of European Law 3.

[80] Judgment of 22 December 1993, *Neath v Hugh Steeper Ltd*, C-152/91, ECLI:EU:C:1993:949; *Coloroll* (n 61).

B. Horizontal provisions and examples of sex discrimination

As in other areas of EU non-discrimination, there is a number of common features in the legislation on sex discrimination. The most important of them relate to whether and how the finding of discrimination can be justified and the ability to take positive action aimed at ensuring equality between men and women in practice. Although not framed as such in EU law, the latter can be conceptually connected to the former, as the reversal or balancing of a discriminatory situation through positive or 'affirmative' action entails conferring advantage on (positively 'discriminating') the group which is *de facto* discriminated against. Such action is, within limits, exempted from the prohibition of gender discrimination.

As already mentioned in the context of discrimination on the grounds of nationality, direct discrimination is more difficult to justify than indirect discrimination. There must be a specific exception or justification in the law permitting any form of direct discrimination.[81] With the exception of age discrimination,[82] 'objective justification' is only available for indirect discrimination. On the whole, direct discrimination of the kind witnessed in the *Defrenne* saga is much less common nowadays and most cases instead concern indirect discrimination. Nonetheless, as some of the examples already cited show, notably Article 7 of Council Directive 79/7/EEC on (non-occupational) social security, direct discrimination between men and women is still permitted in certain contexts. The most common justificatory ground for direct discrimination, present across all equality legislation, is occupational requirement. Paragraph 2 of Article 14 of the 2006 Equal Treatment Directives provides a representative example.

Directive 2006/54/EC of the European Parliament and of the Council on the implementation of the principle of equal opportunities and equal treatment of men and women in matters of employment and occupation (recast) [2006] OJ L204/23

Article 14

2. Member States may provide, as regards access to employment including the training leading thereto, **that a difference of treatment which is based on a characteristic related to sex shall not constitute discrimination where,** by reason of the nature of the particular occupational activities concerned or of the context in which they are carried out, **such a characteristic constitutes a genuine and determining occupational requirement,** provided that its **objective is legitimate** and the **requirement is proportionate.**

Typically, the occupational requirement justification is invoked in relation to professions in the security sector (police, military).[83] In the case of *Johnston*—better known for its procedural implications—the CJEU ruled that sex can be a 'determining factor' when it comes to hiring police officers, partially on account of the dangerous security context

---

[81] This applies *mutatis mutandis* across the whole gamut of EU anti-discrimination law.
[82] See Article 6(1) of Directive 2000/78.
[83] Not only, however. See, for a different example, Judgment of 8 November 1983, *Commission v United Kingdom*, 165/82, ECLI:EU:C:1983:311.

which prevailed in Northern Ireland at the time.[84] Sex has also been accepted as a legitimate determining factor for the hiring of prison wards and head prison wards.[85] Other cases addressed sex-based occupational requirements in the military.[86] In *Sirdar*, the Court recognized that the Royal Marines constitute a special force with operational demands capable of justifying sex to constitute a determining factor.[87] In *Kreil*, a German law excluding women from all military posts involving the use of arms was found to be incompatible with the occupational requirement exception provided for in Article 2(2) of Directive 76/207 (now in an amended form Article 14(2) of Directive 2006/54/EC).[88] The CJEU viewed the exclusionary provisions as violating the principle of proportionality, because it led to women being barred from nearly all posts in the army.[89] Ms Kreil's desire to join the Bundeswehr and her willingness to mount a judicial challenge against the rejection proved to be a turning point for military service in Germany. The CJEU judgment opened access for women to army posts with almost immediate effect and today there are more than 21,000 women serving across the various corps of the Bundeswehr. Not long after *Kreil* and partially as a consequence thereof, the CJEU set a limit to the intrusion of EU gender equality law into Member States' military affairs in *Dory*.[90] The Court held that EU law 'does not preclude compulsory military service being reserved to men', despite the situation at hand clearly constituting sex discrimination against men whose entry into the labour market was, unlike that of women, delayed as a result of compulsory military service. The finding was made on the ground that EU law should not encroach on a traditional sphere of Member State competence—organization of the armed forces—but the CJEU did not furnish it with much legal argumentation. It was certainly not made clear in legal terms why the effects of EU prohibitions on sex discrimination were present in *Kreil* but not *Dory*, as both cases essentially concerned the organization of the German armed forces.[91] Nevertheless, the original discriminatory situation no longer exists as Germany stopped compulsory military service altogether in 2011.

Sex discrimination concerning access to security-related occupations is not only direct—working in the police or the military is frequently conditioned by various criteria relating to the physical condition and constitution of the applicants which may give a *de facto* advantage to one sex, usually men. Such indirect discrimination can in principle be justified on objective grounds, including under the legislative exception available in Article 14(2) of Directive 2006/54/EC, but it must in any case comply with the principle of proportionality. The recent case of *Kalliri* provides an apposite example of indirect discrimination in access to the Greek police academy.

---

[84] Judgment of 15 May 1986, *Johnston v Chief Constable of the Royal Ulster Constabulary*, 222/84, ECLI:EU:C:1986:206, para 37. The now superseded Directive 76/207 only used the term 'determining factor', as opposed to the more complex wording of Article 14(2) of the 2006 Equality Treatment Directive in force today, without this affecting the interpretation of the provisions.

[85] Judgment of 30 June 1988, *Commission v France*, 318/86, ECLI:EU:C:1988:352, para 17.

[86] See more generally on the subject of female army service I Eulriet, *Women and the Military in Europe: Comparing Public Cultures* (Palgrave Macmillan 2012).

[87] Judgment of 26 October 1999, *Sirdar v The Army Board and Secretary of State for Defence*, C-273/97, ECLI:EU:C:1999:523, para 31.

[88] Judgment of 11 January 2000, *Kreil v Bundesrepublik Deutschland*, C-285/98, ECLI:EU:C:2000:2, para 29.

[89] Women were at the time only allowed to join medical and military music services.

[90] Judgment of 11 March 2003, *Dory v Bundesrepublik Deutschland*, C-186/01, ECLI:EU:C:2003:146.

[91] Craig and de Búrca, *EU Law: Text, Cases, and Materials* (n 59) 902

Judgment of 18 October 2017, *Ypourgos Esoterikon, Ypourgos Ethnikis Pedias kai Thriskevmaton v Maria-Eleni Kalliri*, C-409/16, ECLI:EU:C:2017:767

10. Ms Kalliri made an application to participate in the competition (...) [the] police station returned those documents to her on the ground that **she was not of the minimum height of 1.70m** required under Article 2(1)(f) of Presidential Decree 4/1995, as amended by Article 1(1) of Presidential Decree 90/2003, since she was only 1.68m tall.

23. It follows that Directive 76/207 applies to a person seeking employment, and also in regard to the selection criteria and **recruitment conditions of that employment** (...)

28. In that regard, it must be noted that the law treats persons submitting applications to the competition for entry to the police school identically, whatever their sex.

29. Consequently, that law does not constitute direct discrimination, within the meaning of the first indent of Article 2(2) of Directive 76/207.

30. Nevertheless, such a law may constitute indirect discrimination within the meaning of the second indent of Article 2(2).

31. The Court has consistently held that **indirect discrimination arises where a national measure, albeit formulated in neutral terms, works to the disadvantage of far more women than men** (...)

32. In the present case, the referring court itself found in its decision that **a much larger number of women than men are of a height of less than 1.70m**, such that, by the application of that law, **women are very clearly at a disadvantage compared with men** as regards admission to the competition for entry to the Greek Officers' School and School for Policemen. It follows that the law at issue in the main proceedings **constitutes indirect discrimination**.

33. However the second indent of Article 2(2) of Directive 76/207 provides that such a law does not constitute indirect discrimination prohibited by that directive **if it is objectively justified by a legitimate aim, and the means of achieving that aim are appropriate and necessary.**

35. In the present case, the Greek Government submits that the aim of the law at issue in the main proceedings is to enable the effective accomplishment of the task of the Greek police and that possession of certain particular physical attributes, such as being of a minimum height, is a necessary and appropriate condition for achieving that aim.

36. It should be recalled that the Court has already held that the **concern to ensure the operational capacity and proper functioning of the police services constitutes a legitimate objective** (...)

37. It must, however, be ascertained **whether a minimum height requirement**, such as provided for in the law at issue in the main proceedings, **is suitable for securing the attainment of the objective** pursued by that law **and does not go beyond what is necessary** in order to attain it.

38. In that regard, while it is true that the exercise of police functions involving the protection of persons and goods, the arrest and custody of offenders and the conduct of crime prevention patrols may require the use of physical force requiring a particular physical aptitude, **the fact remains that certain police functions, such as providing assistance to citizens or traffic control, do not clearly require the use of significant physical force** (...)

39. Furthermore, even if all the functions carried out by the Greek police required a particular physical aptitude, it would not appear that such an aptitude is necessarily connected with being of a certain minimum height and that shorter persons naturally lack that aptitude.

40. In that context, it may be taken into account that until 2003 the Greek law required, for the purposes of admission to the competition for entry to the Greek School for Police Officers and Policemen, different minimum heights for men and for women, since, regarding the latter, the minimum height was fixed at 1.65m, compared with 1.70m for men.

42. In any event, the aim pursued by the law at issue in the main proceedings could be achieved by measures that are less disadvantageous to women, such as a preselection of candidates to the competition for entry into Schools for Police Officers and Policemen based on specific tests allowing their physical ability to be assessed.

43. It follows that, subject to the assessments that it is for the national court to carry out, the law in question is not justified.

Although the CJEU recognized the legitimate aim—operational capacity of the police— pursued by the Greek authorities in maintaining the minimum height requirement for enrolment in the police academy, the measure did not pass the rest of the proportionality test. The Court pointed out that not all functions of the police entail physical force and even if they did, the discriminating criterion (minimum height) would not be the ideal determinant of physical aptitude. Passing a test of physical ability would, for example, represent a requirement less prejudicial to women. In addition, the Court noted that in the past Greek law appeared to be aware of the potentially discriminating character of a general minimum height requirement for both men and women by setting different thresholds for each.

A different type of exception from the constraints of anti-discrimination law is embodied in the positive action clauses. These can be found not only in virtually all secondary equality law but also in Article 23(2) of the Charter and Article 157(4) TFEU. The clause typically states that the principle of equal treatment does not prevent Member States from adopting measures which through specific advantages support the underrepresented group (sex). The CJEU controversially placed limits on the positive action exception in the *Kalanke* case. The Court complained, among others, that the quota system at stake in the proceedings substituted equality of opportunity for equality of result by virtue of guaranteeing equally qualified female candidates an appointment or promotion. The Court also pointed out that positive action, similarly to other exceptions, is still a derogation from the principle of equal treatment and must therefore be interpreted strictly.[92]

Judgment of 17 October 1995, *Kalanke v Freie Hansestadt Bremen*, C-450/93, ECLI:EU:C:1995:322

22. National rules which guarantee women absolute and unconditional priority for appointment or promotion go beyond promoting equal opportunities and overstep the limits of the exception in Article 2(4) of the Directive.

[92] Judgment of 17 October 1995, *Kalanke v Freie Hansestadt Bremen*, C-450/93, ECLI:EU:C:1995:322, para 21.

> 23. Furthermore, in so far as it seeks to achieve equal representation of men and women in all grades and levels within a department, **such a system substitutes for equality of opportunity** as envisaged in Article 2(4) **the result** which is only to be arrived at by providing such equality of opportunity.

In *Roca Álvarez*, the CJEU struck down a national measure which was argued by the Spanish government to constitute positive action for the benefit of women. The Court held that the disputed national measure in fact perpetuated stereotypes about male/female division of parental responsibility and as such could not be exempted under any of the positive action clauses. In its reasoning, the Court shared its view of the rationale of positive action. In the words of the CJEU, the positive action clauses strive to achieve 'substantive, rather than formal equality'.

Judgment of 30 September 2010, *Roca Álvarez v Sesa Start España ETT SA*, C-104/09, ECLI:EU:C:2010:561

---

32. (...) as regards the promotion of equal opportunities for men and women and the reduction of the factual inequalities that affect women's opportunities in the area of working conditions, the Spanish Government submitted in its observations that the objective pursued in reserving for mothers entitlement to the leave at issue in the main proceedings is to compensate for the genuine disadvantages suffered by women, in comparison to men, in keeping their jobs following the birth of a child. (...)

33. As the Court has consistently held, Article 2(4) of Directive 76/207 is **specifically and exclusively designed to authorise measures which, although discriminatory in appearance, are in fact intended to eliminate or reduce actual instances of inequality which may exist in society.** That provision thus authorises national measures relating to access to employment, including promotion, which give a specific advantage to women with a view to improving their ability to compete on the labour market and to pursue a career on an equal footing with men (...)

34. The aim of Article 2(4) is to achieve **substantive, rather than formal, equality** by reducing de facto inequalities which may arise in society and, thus, in accordance with Article 157(4) TFEU, to prevent or compensate for disadvantages in the professional career of the relevant persons (...)

35. (...) the leave at issue in the main proceedings takes the form of permission to be absent during the working day or a reduction of its duration. Certainly, such a measure could have the effect of putting women at an advantage by allowing mothers whose status is that of an employed person to keep their job and to devote time to their child. That effect is reinforced by the fact that if the father of the child is himself an employed person, he is entitled to take this leave in the place of the mother, who would not suffer adverse consequences for her job as a result of care and attention devoted to the child.

36. However, to hold, as the Spanish Government submits, that only a mother whose status is that of an employed person is the holder of the right to qualify for the leave at issue in the main proceedings, whereas a father with the same status can only enjoy this right but not be the holder of it, is **liable to perpetuate a traditional**

distribution of the roles of men and women by keeping men in a role subsidiary to that of women in relation to the exercise of their parental duties (...)

Waddington and Bell warn against the conflation of the various types of anti-discrimination measures and subjecting all of them to the proportionality test which applies to positive action under EU law, as this could unduly restrict Member States' latitude in righting discrimination. The scholars distinguish positive action from 'reasonable accommodation' which entails that individuals with particular characteristics are treated differently from individuals who lack this characteristic. As it currently stands, EU law only provides for a reasonable accommodation obligation with respect to disability.[93] Positive duties, such as mainstreaming and data collection, aimed at combatting discrimination are another category distinguished from positive action, as are general measures promoting social exclusion. Article 8 TFEU puts the EU under a positive duty to 'eliminate inequalities and promote equality between men and women'.

L Waddington and M Bell, 'Exploring the Boundaries of Positive Action under EU Law: A Search for Conceptual Clarity' (2011) 48 Common Market Law Review 1503

(...) under EU law, positive action measures must comply with the principle of proportionality in order to be lawful, and not amount to discrimination against individuals who are not members of the favoured group. It is therefore vital to determine whether any particular measure amounts to positive action, and consequently should be subject to the proportionality test, or whether it falls within the range of other tools that have been developed to combat discrimination and promote equality. If instruments such as reasonable accommodation, mainstreaming linked to positive duties, data collection, and policies to promote social inclusion are conflated with positive action, there is not only a risk of terminological and conceptual confusion, but also that such measures are tested against, and even fail to comply with, the proportionality principle.

(...) there is a tendency to identify some of these concepts with positive action, even within the Court of Justice. This is particularly worrying, given that courts play a key role in applying the proportionality test, which essentially has been developed through case law within the EU. However, measures that are not positive action should be subject to less judicial scrutiny under EU law. Applying such scrutiny, and especially the proportionality requirement, to these measures can result in their being undermined, and hamper Member State action to combat discrimination and promote equality. For example, the proportionality principle might call into question positive action measures that do not have a time limit, or are not subject to periodic review. While we have argued that it could be proportionate to adopt open-ended forms of positive action in some circumstances, the question of time-limits illustrates the importance of distinguishing measures to promote equality that fall outside the category of positive action. It is clear, for example, that many social welfare benefits are intended to be indefinite in nature, such as benefits linked to older age. Similarly, equality data collection is an activity with no

---

[93] L Waddington and M Bell, 'Exploring the Boundaries of Positive Action under EU Law: A Search for Conceptual Clarity' (2011) 48 Common Market Law Review 1503, 1517.

essential end-point; ongoing data gathering will be needed to establish not only if equality is attained, but also that it is maintained. In addition, EU law requires Member States to ensure a reasonable accommodation duty on a permanent basis. Establishing the boundaries of positive action, and distinguishing it from other instruments in the arsenal of equality measures, is therefore vital to ensure the integrity of EU anti-discrimination law.

C. Sexual orientation

Judgment of 30 April 1996, *P v S and Cornwall County Council*, C-13/94, ECLI:EU:C:1996:170

20. Accordingly, the scope of the directive cannot be confined simply to discrimination based on the fact that a person is of one or other sex. In view of its purpose and the nature of the rights which it seeks to safeguard, **the scope of the directive is also such as to apply to discrimination arising**, as in this case, from the **gender reassignment of the person** concerned.

21. **Such discrimination is based, essentially if not exclusively, on the sex of the person** concerned. Where a person is dismissed on the ground that he or she intends to undergo, or has undergone, gender reassignment, he or she is treated unfavourably by comparison with persons of the sex to which he or she was deemed to belong before undergoing gender reassignment.

22. To tolerate such discrimination would be tantamount, as regards such a person, to **a failure to respect the dignity and freedom to which he or she is entitled**, and which the Court has a duty to safeguard.

Although in the 1990s the CJEU explicitly extended the protection of EU equality legislation to transsexuals[94]—rejecting a textual argument about 'men and women' in the process—the Court did not contest discrimination against same-sex couples prior to the conclusion of the Amsterdam Treaty which rendered sexual orientation one of the grounds which could be protected in EU secondary law. In other words, while discrimination due to gender reassignment was an issue essentially falling within the scope of discrimination based on 'sex', sexual orientation was recognized as a separate ground of discrimination which the Court was unwilling to include in the notion of sex discrimination. The CJEU was not swayed by the fact that the Human Rights Committee, the body in charge of monitoring the International Covenant on Civil and Political Rights (ICCPR), held that sexual orientation was included in references to 'sex' in Articles 2(1) and 26 of the Covenant.[95] *Grant* therefore belongs, at least to some extent, to the line of case law where the CJEU showed its limited openness to aligning itself with international law.

---

[94] Other cases have also addressed transgender discrimination. See Judgment of 7 January 2004, *K.B. v National Health Service Pensions Agency and Secretary of State for Health*, C-117/01, ECLI:EU:C:2004:7; Judgment of 27 April 2006, *Richards v Secretary of State for Work and Pensions*, C-423/04, ECLI:EU:C:2006:256.
[95] *Toonen v Australia*, views adopted on 31 March 1994, 50th session, point 8.7.

Judgment of 17 February 1998, *Grant v South-West Trains Ltd*, C-249/96, ECLI:EU:C:1998:63

7. (…) Ms Grant applied on 9 January 1995 for travel concessions for her female partner, with whom she declared she had had a 'meaningful relationship' for over two years.

8. SWT refused to allow the benefit sought, on the ground that for unmarried persons **travel concessions could be granted only for a partner of the opposite sex.**

43. Ms Grant submits (…) that, like certain provisions of national law or of international conventions, **the Community provisions on equal treatment of men and women should be interpreted as covering discrimination based on sexual orientation.** She refers in particular to the International Covenant on Civil and Political Rights of 19 December 1966 (…), in which, **in the view of the Human Rights Committee** established under Article 28 of the Covenant, **the term 'sex' is to be taken as including sexual orientation** (…)

44. The Covenant is one of the international instruments relating to the protection of human rights of which the Court takes account in applying the fundamental principles of Community law (…)

45. However, although respect for the fundamental rights which form an integral part of those general principles of law is a condition of the legality of Community acts, **those rights cannot in themselves have the effect of extending the scope of the Treaty provisions beyond the competences of the Community** (…)

46. Furthermore, in the communication referred to by Ms Grant, the Human Rights Committee, which is not a judicial institution and whose findings have no binding force in law, confined itself, as it stated itself without giving specific reasons, to 'noting … that in its view the reference to "sex" in Articles 2, paragraph 1, and 26 is to be taken as including sexual orientation'.

47. Such an observation, which does not in any event appear to reflect the interpretation so far generally accepted of the concept of discrimination based on sex which appears in various international instruments concerning the protection of fundamental rights, cannot in any case constitute a basis for the Court to extend the scope of Article 119 of the Treaty. That being so, the scope of that article, as of any provision of Community law, is to be determined only by having regard to its wording and purpose, its place in the scheme of the Treaty and its legal context. **It follows from the considerations set out above that Community law as it stands at present does not cover discrimination based on sexual orientation**, such as that in issue in the main proceedings.

Nevertheless, the Court did take note of the fact that the Amsterdam Treaty was about to enter into force and it would introduce a legislative competence permitting the EU to take action against discrimination based on sexual orientation.[96] The Amsterdam Treaty became the first international instrument to list sexual orientation explicitly as a protected ground for anti-discrimination purposes. Significantly, the legislative competence, now enshrined in Article 19 TFEU, gave rise to Directive 2000/78/EC which prohibits discrimination on the

---

[96] Judgment of 17 February 1998, *Grant v South-West Trains Ltd*, C-249/96, ECLI:EU:C:1998:63, para 48.

grounds of religion or belief, disability, age, or sexual orientation as regards employment and occupation.[97]

In *Maruko*, the CJEU was called upon to adjudicate whether a survivor's benefit granted under an occupational pension scheme comes within the auspices of Directive 2000/78/EC and if so, whether same-sex partners are entitled to equal treatment.[98] When it came to the first question, the CJEU applied the criteria developed in the *Defrenne I* and *Barber* line of case law in order to determine whether the pension scheme at issue qualifies as 'pay' for the purposes of Article 157 TFEU. This was relevant because the interpretation of Article 157 TFEU is referred to in recital 13 of Directive 2000/78/EC as a source of interpretive guidance with regards to pension schemes. The picture was further complicated by another recital, number 22, which states that the Directive is 'without prejudice to national laws on marital status and the benefits dependent thereon'. The CJEU held that not only in the case at hand the survivor's benefit granted under an occupational pension scheme came within the scope of Directive 2000/78/EC by virtue of constituting 'pay' in the meaning of Article 157 TFEU but the Directive also prohibited the discrimination based on sexual orientation. The latter finding turned on the modalities of German national law, as the survivor needed to be in a comparable situation to married couples and EU law does not govern the legal arrangements between partners of the same sex. The second part of recital 22 was therefore given little weight by the Court, as benefits dependent on marital status were adjudged to fall within the remit of Directive 2000/78/EC. Ultimately, the question whether the situation of married and same-sex couples was comparable was left to the referring national court to decide, although both the national court and the CJEU clearly favoured an affirmative answer.[99]

The decision in *Maruko* was subsequently reaffirmed by the Court in *Römer* and *Hay* which concerned other types of benefits.[100] *Hay*, in particular, enriched EU anti-discrimination law, as the case concerned a dispute between two private parties, thereby opening questions of horizontal direct effect. Although the CJEU did not analyse the direct effect of Directive 2000/78/EC (as it was not asked by the national court), the almost routine application of the Directive in a quasi-horizontal court case is in itself important due to the generally recognized sentiment that Directives do not have horizontal direct effect.[101] This orthodoxy has a number of caveats, however, notably the *Mangold/Kücükdeveci* cases,[102] and *Hay* has been dubbed as standing 'midway between horizontal direct effect and indirect effect (the consistent interpretation doctrine)'.[103]

Somewhat curiously, none of the three cases on discrimination grounded in sexual orientation cited above (*Maruko, Römer, Hay*) mention the Charter of Fundamental Rights.

---

[97] Regarding national implementation of Directive 2000/78/EC with respect to sexual orientation, see C Waaldijk and MT Bonini-Baraldi, *Sexual Orientation Discrimination in the European Union: National Laws and the Employment Equality Directive* (TMC Asser Press 2006).

[98] Judgment of 1 April 2008, *Maruko v Versorgungsanstalt der deutschen Bühnen*, C-267/06, ECLI:EU:C:2008:179.

[99] Ibid, paras 67–69.

[100] Judgment of 10 May 2011, *Römer v Freie und Hansestadt Hamburg*, C-147/08, ECLI:EU:C:2011:286; Judgment of 12 December 2013, *Hay v Crédit agricole mutuel de Charente-Maritime et des Deux-Sèvres*, C-267/12, ECLI:EU:C:2013:823.

[101] See the discussion of *Marshall* above.

[102] See section on age discrimination below. See also the most recent judgment concerning religious discrimination (*Egenberger*) below.

[103] G Zaccaroni, 'Differentiating Equality? The Different Advancements in the Protected Grounds in the Case Law of the European Court of Justice' in LS Rossi and F Casolari (eds), *The Principle of Equality in EU Law* (Springer 2017) 183. Indirect effect is a doctrine developed by the CJEU which requires national courts to interpret national law in conformity with EU law insofar as it can. See Judgment of 10 April 1984, *von Colson and Kamann v Land Nordrhein-Westfalen*, 14/83, ECLI:EU:C:1984:153, para 28.

Article 9 thereof provides that the right to marry and the right to found a family is regulated in national law. At first sight, it might seem strange that the provision essentially marks out the territory of national competence. Nevertheless, there is significance in the wording (or its absence) of Article 9 of the Charter—it does not mention either right (to marry or found a family) as belonging to the provenance of opposite sex couples. While the provision has so far received minimal attention in the EU courts,[104] it played a part in a case before the ECtHR. In *Schalk and Kopf v Austria*, the ECtHR relied on a comparison of Article 12 ECHR with Article 9 of the Charter in order to relax the notion of 'men and women' contained in the former.[105] The Charter was implicitly cast as a progressive human rights instrument which dropped the mention of opposite sexes in relation to marriage and right to found a family, which is not to say, however, that same-sex couples gained a right to marry—the ECtHR was explicit in leaving a large margin of discretion to the contracting parties regarding same-sex marriages.

Schalk and Kopf v Austria, App no 30141/04, 24 June 2010

61. **Regard being had to Article 9 of the Charter, therefore, the Court would no longer consider that the right to marry enshrined in Article 12 must in all circumstances be limited to marriage between two persons of the opposite sex.** Consequently, it cannot be said that Article 12 is inapplicable to the applicants' complaint. However, as matters stand, the question whether or not to allow same-sex marriage **is left to regulation by the national law** of the Contracting State.
62. In that connection the Court observes that marriage has deep-rooted social and cultural connotations which may differ largely from one society to another. **The Court reiterates that it must not rush to substitute its own judgment in place of that of the national authorities,** who are best placed to assess and respond to the needs of society (see B. and L. v. the United Kingdom, cited above, § 36).
63. In conclusion, the Court finds that Article 12 of the Convention does not impose an obligation on the respondent Government to grant a same-sex couple like the applicants access to marriage.

To date, the CJEU's possibly most significant foray into same-sex couples law came in *Coman*.[106] Mr Coman got married to Mr Hamilton, a US citizen, in Brussels. The case reached the CJEU through a preliminary reference from the Romanian Constitutional Court after the couple appealed the national authorities' refusal to grant a residence permit to Mr Hamilton. Mr Coman, a Romanian national, sought the residence permit on the basis of provisions of Directive 2004/38/EC concerning family reunification. The Court ruled that the term 'spouse' in Article 2(2) of Directive 2004/38/EC extends to same-sex marriages

[104] To date only one staff case dealt with an allegation partially concerning Article 9 of the Charter. The action was dismissed as unfounded. See Judgment of 18 June 2015, *EG v European Parliament*, F-79/14, ECLI:EU:F:2015:63.

[105] Article 12 ECHR, entitled 'Right to marry', reads: 'Men and women of marriageable age have the right to marry and to found a family, according to the national laws governing the exercise of this right.'

[106] Judgment of 5 June 2018, *Coman et al v Inspectoratul General pentru Imigrări*, C-673/16, ECLI:EU:C:2018:385.

for the purposes of free movement rights within the Union. The Court's interpretation precludes Member States in which gay marriage is not recognized from restricting the derived right of residence of same-sex couples. While seeing important positives for the lives of same-sex couples in the EU, most commentators agree that the CJEU was careful to steer away from suggesting that EU law might require Member States to enable same-sex marriage as such.[107]

Judgment of 5 June 2018, *Coman et al v Inspectoratul General pentru Imigrări*, C-673/16, ECLI:EU:C:2018:385

35. (…) it should be pointed out, first of all, that **the term 'spouse' within the meaning of Directive 2004/38 is gender-neutral** and may therefore cover the same-sex spouse of the Union citizen concerned.

37. Admittedly, a person's status, which is relevant to the rules on marriage, is a matter that falls within the competence of the Member States and EU law does not detract from that competence (…) **The Member States are thus free to decide whether or not to allow marriage for persons of the same sex.**

40. (…) the refusal by the authorities of a Member State to recognise, for the sole purpose of granting a derived right of residence to a third-country national, the marriage of that national to a Union citizen of the same sex, concluded, during the period of their genuine residence in another Member State, in accordance with the law of that State, may interfere with the exercise of the right conferred on that citizen by Article 21(1) TFEU to move and reside freely in the territory of the Member States.

7.4 Racial Discrimination

Soon after the entry into force of the Amsterdam Treaty, the EU exercised its new legislative competences in anti-discrimination by adopting two Directives: the abovementioned Directive 2000/78/EC on non-discrimination in employment matters and Directive 2000/43/EC on race equality ('Race Equality Directive'). Whereas the scope of Directive 2000/78/EC is self-evidently limited in material terms, the Race Equality Directive has a broad scope, as a result of which race and ethnicity are not one of the protected grounds in Directive 2000/78/EC on non-discrimination in employment.[108]

---

[107] U Belavusau and D Kochenov, 'Same-Sex Spouses: More Free Movement, but What about Marriage?' (2020) 57 Common Market Law Review 227; J Rijpma, 'You Gotta Let Love Move' (2019) 15 European Constitutional Law Review 324.

[108] The same applies as well to the separate and generally more robust equality laws applicable to discrimination on the grounds of sex and nationality.

Council Directive 2000/43/EC of 29 June 2000 implementing the principle of equal treatment between persons irrespective of racial or ethnic origin [2000] OJ L180/22

Article 3

Scope

1. Within the limits of the powers conferred upon the Community, this Directive shall apply to all persons, **as regards both the public and private sectors**, including public bodies, in relation to:
   (a) conditions for access to employment, to self-employment and to occupation, including selection criteria and recruitment conditions, whatever the branch of activity and at all levels of the professional hierarchy, including promotion;
   (b) access to all types and to all levels of vocational guidance, vocational training, advanced vocational training and retraining, including practical work experience;
   (c) employment and working conditions, including dismissals and pay;
   (d) membership of and involvement in an organisation of workers or employers, or any organisation whose members carry on a particular profession, including the benefits provided for by such organisations;
   (e) social protection, including social security and healthcare;
   (f) social advantages;
   (g) education;
   (h) access to and supply of goods and services which are available to the public, including housing.
2. **This Directive does not cover difference of treatment based on nationality and is without prejudice to provisions and conditions relating to the entry into and residence of third-country nationals and stateless persons on the territory of Member States,** and to any treatment which arises from the legal status of the third-country nationals and stateless persons concerned.

It is worth noting the broader context in which the Racial Equality Directive was adopted. On the one hand, the EU was in the process of preparing itself and Central and Eastern European candidate countries for future accession. On the other hand, the EU was at the time going through the 'Haider affair' in which the then 14 EU Member States imposed diplomatic sanctions against the other Member State, Austria, for creating a ruling coalition with the openly xenophobic FPÖ, a populist political party led by Jörg Haider.[109] Both developments, external and internal, were propitious to the signalling of the EU's commitment to fundamental rights and anti-discrimination. In addition, the entry into force of the Amsterdam Treaty made it possible to express that commitment in legislative terms.[110] As observed by Case and Givens, however, these contextual factors do not inherently explain the adoption of the Race Equality Directive. Rather, the Directive was to a significant extent driven politically by a coalition of societal interests led by activist lawyers seeking the

---

[109] For more information see, for example, K Lachmayer, 'Questioning the Basic Values—Austria and Jörg Haider' in A Jakab and D Kochenov (eds), *The Enforcement of EU Law and Values* (Oxford University Press 2017).
[110] Furthermore, the EU became equipped with the sanctioning mechanism enshrined in Article 7 TEU, even though it did not make use of it in the Austrian situation. Further on this, see Ch 4.

judicialization of race and ethnic equality, as happened previously in, notably, the area of gender equality.

R Evans Case and TE Givens, 'Re-engineering Legal Opportunity Structures in the European Union? The Starting Line Group and the Politics of the Racial Equality Directive' (2010) 48 Journal of Common Market Studies 221

(...) We conclude that the RED [Racial Equality Directive] was not, as some theories would predict, the product of national politicians seeking either to avoid electorally unpopular issues by channelling them into the courts or to standardize racial discrimination policy in order to reduce a comparative disadvantage. Further, although policy borrowing from earlier sex discrimination explains some of the RED's provisions, it fails to explain the key provisions concerning legal standing and national enforcement bodies, neither of which are provided for in the EU gender equality policy domain. We conclude that the RED was driven by a coalition of societal interests that straddled the divide between transnational society and European institutions. Led by activist lawyers, this coalition sought to constitutionalize its policy preferences and obtain a set of reforms intended to create opportunities for interest groups to shift policy-making into the courts. It skilfully exploited EU institutions and operated as a powerful and persuasive constituency for reforms intended to have these effects.

Our conclusion rests upon three main findings. First, the SLG's focus on obtaining a new set of legal resources, most especially a Treaty article that would have had direct effect; on developing institutional resources for litigation; and on liberalizing the rules regarding legal standing, reflect its overarching objective of using strategic litigation in order to advance its egalitarian and pluralistic goals through the courts. Second, interviews with SLG figures confirm that the SLG recognized that its preferred reforms would facilitate strategic litigation and an expansion of the judicial role in policy-making. Finally, post-RED efforts to train strategic litigators reinforce our finding that the SLG sought to liberalize legal opportunity structures in order to pursue this sort of activity.

Despite the advocacy efforts behind the Race Equality Directive, Article 19 TFEU clearly does not have direct effect—it only provides for a legislative competence.[111] Moreover, unlike in the area of gender discrimination, strategic litigation has so far yielded few successes. Few cases invoking the provisions of the Directive have reached the CJEU and even then most of the arguments were rejected or found inadmissible by the Court.[112] The remaining cases have provided some limited guidance as to the application of the Directive.

---

[111] The coalition of societal interests did manage, however, to induce the EU institutions to introduce a provision on equality bodies. See Article 13 of the Racial Equality Directive. See also Ch 2 on the fundamental rights institutional environment of which equality bodies are part.

[112] See Judgment of 6 October 2005, *Vajnai*, C-328/04, ECLI:EU:C:2005:596; Judgment of 12 May 2011, *Runevič-Vardyn and Wardyn v Vilniaus miesto savivaldybės administracija and Others*, C-391/09, ECLI:EU:C:2011:291; Judgment of 7 July 2011, *Ministerul Justiției și Libertăților Cetățenești v Ștefan Agafiței and Others*, C-310/10, ECLI:EU:C:2011:467; Judgment of 24 April 2012, *Kamberaj v Istituto per l'Edilizia sociale della Provincia autonoma di Bolzano (IPES) and Others*, C-571/10, ECLI:EU:C:2012:233; Judgment of 19 April 2012, *Meister v Speech Design Carrier Systems GmbH*, C-415/10, ECLI:EU:C:2012:217; Judgment of 31 January 2013, *Belov v CHEZ Elektro Balgaria AD and Others*, C-394/11, ECLI:EU:C:2013:48; Judgment of 6 April 2017, *Jyske Finans A/S v Ligebehandlingsnævnet*, C-668/15, ECLI:EU:C:2017:278.

In *Feryn*, the Belgian equality body sued—without representing any particular victim—a garage and sectional door manufacturer, alleging that the latter applied a discriminatory recruitment policy in breach of the Race Equality Directive. The company argued before a national court that its publicly anti-immigrant recruitment policy merely catered to the demands of the customers who were supposedly reluctant to let door fitters of immigrant origin into their homes.[113] Without addressing this defence, the CJEU held that public statements by an employer to the effect that employees of a certain ethnic or racial origin will not be hired constitute direct discrimination within the meaning of Article 2(2)(a) of Directive 2000/43, because such statements are likely 'strongly to dissuade certain candidates from submitting their candidature and, accordingly, to hinder their access to the labour market'.[114] It is notable that the CJEU interpreted the reference to 'immigrants' in the public notice of the employer in light of racial and ethnic origin rather than nationality, an obviously contending ground of discrimination.[115] In any case, the Court strengthened the position of race equality advocates by allowing the action despite the fact that it was brought without there being an identifiable victim of the discriminatory practice. The Court rationalized this finding by stating that '[t]he objective of fostering conditions for a socially inclusive labour market would be hard to achieve if the scope of Directive 2000/43 were to be limited to only those cases in which an unsuccessful candidate for a post, considering himself to be the victim of direct discrimination, brought legal proceedings against the employer'.[116] Moreover, the CJEU found that sanctions adopted in accordance with Article 15 of the Directive—which must be effective, proportionate and dissuasive—were applicable regardless of there being no identifiable victim of the discrimination.[117]

The case of *Deckmyn* touched upon the Race Equality Directive only tangentially but this does not necessarily detract from its potential significance.[118] The core of the case concerned a drawing made by Mr Deckmyn, himself a member, for the Belgian far-right party Vlaams Belang, which depicted the mayor of Gent dropping coins from the sky to veiled persons with coloured skin as white-skinned onlookers watch with unease. The drawing clearly resembled one of the covers of the popular comic book 'Suske en Wiske' and, as a consequence, the owners of the copyright to the original work brought an action against Mr Deckmyn for a copyright infringement. Mr Deckmyn's defence turned on the concept of 'parody' referred to in Article 5(3)(k) of Directive 2001/29,[119] which was held to constitute an autonomous concept in EU law, the characteristics of which were given as 'first, to evoke an existing work, while being noticeably different from it, and secondly, to constitute an expression of humour or mockery'.[120] However, a fair balance between the interests of the copyright holders and the

[113] Judgment of 10 July 2008, *Centrum voor gelijkheid van kansen en voor racismebestrijding v Firma Feryn NV*, C-54/07, ECLI:EU:C:2008:397, para 18.
[114] Ibid, para 28.
[115] Although it is true that it was in the first place the referring national court which legally framed the question in terms of the Racial Equality Directive.
[116] *Feryn* (n 113) para 24.
[117] Ibid, paras 36–40. The CJEU added that: '[i]f it appears appropriate to the situation at issue in the main proceedings, those sanctions may, where necessary, include a finding of discrimination by the court or the competent administrative authority in conjunction with an adequate level of publicity, the cost of which is to be borne by the defendant. They may also take the form of a prohibitory injunction, in accordance with the rules of national law, ordering the employer to cease the discriminatory practice, and, where appropriate, a fine. They may, moreover, take the form of the award of damages to the body bringing the proceedings.'
[118] Judgment of 3 September 2014, *Deckmyn and Vrijheidsfonds VZW v Vandersteen and Others*, C-201/13, ECLI:EU:C:2014:2132.
[119] Directive 2001/29/EC of the European Parliament and of the Council of 22 May 2001 on the harmonisation of certain aspects of copyright and related rights in the information society [2001] OJ L167/10.
[120] *Deckmyn* (n 118) paras 17 and 33.

freedom of expression of the user of the work had to be struck at the same time.[121] The CJEU added—with reference to the Race Equality Directive—that the reluctance to see a work protected by one's copyright be associated with discriminatory messages, such as the one conveyed by the disputed drawing, represents a legitimate interest of the copyright holder.[122] As the dispute was taking place between two private parties, the CJEU *de facto* cautiously hinted at the need to apply horizontally the principle of equal treatment between persons irrespective of racial or ethnic origin in line with the Race Equality Directive and Article 21(1) of the Charter.[123]

A much lengthier ruling in *CHEZ Razpredelenie Bulgaria AD* established that a claim of discrimination on the grounds of race and ethnicity can also be brought by someone who is not a member of the disadvantaged ethnicity.[124] Ms Nikolova, a Romanian operating a grocery shop in Bulgaria, was impacted by a measure taken by a Bulgarian electricity company purported to tackle tempering with electricity meters in an area inhabited predominantly by persons of Roma origin. Although Ms Nikolova herself was not of Roma origin, the CJEU extended the scope of protection from discrimination to persons in her situation, termed 'discrimination by association' by AG Kokott.[125]

Judgment of 16 July 2015, *CHEZ Razpredelenie Bulgaria AD v Komisia za zashtita ot diskriminatsia*, C-83/14, ECLI:EU:C:2015:480

---

22. In 1999 and 2000, CHEZ RB installed the electricity meters for all the consumers of that district on the concrete pylons forming part of the overhead electricity supply network, at a height of between six and seven metres, whereas in the other districts the meters installed by CHEZ RB are placed at a height of 1.70 metres, usually in the consumer's property, on the façade or on the wall around the property ('the practice at issue').

56. (...) the scope of Directive 2000/43 cannot, in the light of its objective and the nature of the rights which it seeks to safeguard, be defined restrictively (...) in this instance, such as to justify the interpretation that the principle of equal treatment to which that directive refers applies not to a particular category of person but by reference to the grounds mentioned in Article 1 thereof, so that **that principle is intended to benefit also persons who, although not themselves a member of the race or ethnic group concerned, nevertheless suffer less favourable treatment or a particular disadvantage on one of those grounds** (...)

59. As regards the situation at issue in the main proceedings, while accepting that, as Ms Nikolova asserts before the Court, she is not of Roma origin, the fact remains that it is indeed Roma origin, in this instance that of most of the other inhabitants

---

[121] Ibid, para 27.

[122] Ibid, paras 29–31.

[123] Ibid, para 30.

[124] Judgment of 16 July 2015, *CHEZ Razpredelenie Bulgaria AD v Komisia za zashtita ot diskriminatsia*, C-83/14, ECLI:EU:C:2015:480. The referring court cited the judgments in *Feryn* (no need for an identifiable victim) and the Judgment of 17 July 2008, *Coleman v Attridge Law*, C-303/06, ECLI:EU:C:2008:415 where the Court held that 'application of the principle of equal treatment is not limited solely to persons possessing the protected characteristic'. See *CHEZ*, para 32.

[125] *CHEZ Razpredelenie Bulgaria AD v Komisia za zashtita ot diskriminatsia* [2015] ECLI:EU:C:2015:170, Opinion of AG Kokott, para 55.

of the district in which she carries on her business, which constitutes the factor on the basis of which she considers that she has suffered less favourable treatment or a particular disadvantage.

81. The matters which may be taken into consideration in this connection include, in particular, the fact, noted by the referring court, that it is common ground and not disputed by CHEZ RB that the latter has established the practice at issue only in urban districts which, like the 'Gizdova mahala' district, are known to have Bulgarian nationals of Roma origin as the majority of their population.

82. The same applies to the fact relied on by the KZD in its observations submitted to the Court that, in various cases that were brought before the KZD, CHEZ RB asserted that in its view the damage and unlawful connections are perpetrated mainly by Bulgarian nationals of Roma origin. Such assertions could in fact suggest that the practice at issue is based on ethnic stereotypes or prejudices, the racial grounds thus combining with other grounds.

127. **Although it seems that it necessarily follows from the taking into account of all the foregoing criteria that the practice at issue cannot be justified within the meaning of Article 2(2)(b) of Directive 2000/43 since the disadvantages caused by the practice appear disproportionate to the objectives pursued**, in the context of proceedings concerning a preliminary reference made on the basis of Article 267 TFEU it is for the referring court to carry out the final assessments which are necessary in that regard.

It remained for the national court to establish whether the practice of placing electricity meters at abnormal height in areas with a large Roma population constituted discrimination and if so, whether it could be objectively justified. It can be inferred from the judgment that the CJEU and the Advocate General considered the practice discriminatory and disproportional (therefore also not justifiable on objective grounds).

A more recent case clarified the notion of ethnic origin within the meaning of Article 1 of the Racial Equality Directive.[126] A Danish national who was born in Bosnia and Herzegovina but later obtained Danish citizenship was asked to provide additional proof of identity when acquiring a loan for the purchase of a motor vehicle in Denmark on account of his driving licence stating that he was born in Bosnia and Herzegovina (it did not state his nationality). The credit institution requesting the additional information argued that it was required to do so under Directive 2005/60/EC on prevention of money laundering and terrorist financing.[127]

Judgment of 6 April 2017, *Jyske Finans A/S v Ligebehandlingsnævnet*, C-668/15, ECLI:EU:C:2017:278.

16. With regard, in the first place, to whether the practice at issue in the main proceedings constitutes **different treatment directly based on ethnic origin** within the

126 *Jyske Finans* (n 112).
127 Directive 2005/60/EC of the European Parliament and of the Council of 26 October 2005 on the prevention of the use of the financial system for the purpose of money laundering and terrorist financing [2005] OJ L309/15 (now replaced by Directive 2015/849/EU).

meaning of Article 1 of Directive 2000/43, it is necessary to examine **whether,** in a case such as that in the main proceedings, **a person's country of birth is to be regarded as directly or inextricably linked to his specific ethnic origin.**

17. It should be noted in that regard that **the concept of 'ethnicity' has its origin in the idea of societal groups marked in particular by common nationality, religious faith, language, cultural and traditional origins and backgrounds (…)**

18. While a person's country of birth does not appear on that list of criteria, it should be noted that, as the list begins with the words 'in particular', it is not exhaustive and it cannot therefore be ruled out that a **person's country of birth** might be included among those criteria. However, even if that were the case, it is clear that it is only one of the specific factors which may justify the conclusion that a person is a member of an ethnic group and **is not decisive in that regard.**

19. **Ethnic origin cannot be determined on the basis of a single criterion but, on the contrary, is based on a whole number of factors,** some objective and others subjective. Moreover, it is not disputed that a country of birth cannot, in general and absolute terms, act as a substitute for all the criteria set out in paragraph 17 above.

20. As a consequence, **a person's country of birth cannot, in itself, justify a general presumption that that person is a member of a given ethnic group such as to establish the existence of a direct or inextricable link between those two concepts.**

21. Furthermore, **it cannot be presumed that each sovereign State has one, and only one, ethnic origin.**

24. Moreover, as is apparent from recital 13 and Article 3(3) of Directive 2000/43, **the directive does not cover different treatment on grounds of nationality.**

25. It follows that a practice such as that at issue in the main proceedings, which requires a customer whose driving licence indicates a country of birth other than a Member State of the European Union or the EFTA to produce additional identification in the form of a copy of the customer's passport or residence permit, **does not mean that the person concerned is subject to different treatment that is directly based on his ethnic origin.**

27. The words 'particular disadvantage' used in that provision must be understood as meaning that it is particularly persons of a given ethnic origin who are at a disadvantage because of the measure at issue (…)

33. (…) the argument that the use of the neutral criterion at issue in the main proceedings, namely a person's country of birth, is generally more likely to affect persons of a 'given ethnicity' than 'other persons' cannot be accepted.

The CJEU held that a number of factors can bear on the definition of what constitutes a given 'ethnicity'. While the country of birth can also be of relevance in this regard, it cannot be a decisive criterion. Moreover, it cannot be presumed that there is only one ethnicity in the territory of a sovereign state.[128] A differential treatment purely based on the country of origin does not therefore represent direct discrimination within the meaning of the Racial Equality Directive. Neither could the Court find indirect discrimination. Because all persons born outside the territory of the EU/EFTA are treated equally (unfavourably), there was no

---

[128] Although not mentioned by the Court, this holds particularly true for Bosnia and Herzegovina where the roles of the three constituent 'peoples'—Bosniak, Croatian, and Serbian—are strongly entrenched in the provisional (but persisting) constitutional solution created by the 1995 Dayton Agreement.

particular disadvantage attributable to the claimant's ethnicity compared to 'other persons'. The measure could instead hypothetically qualify as discrimination based on nationality but, as the CJEU pointed out in paragraph 24 of the judgment, such discrimination is explicitly excluded from within the scope of the Directive.

Overall, the Race Equality Directive has been falling short of its promise in the eyes of most commentators, chiefly due to the limited litigation it has given rise to, and some have consequently called for its amendment.[129] One strong advantage of the Directive is its broad material scope which covers areas such as education which is for example excluded from the scope of EU gender equality law.[130] On the other hand, the restriction on the personal scope of the Race Equality Directive on the grounds of nationality represents a significant lacuna in fundamental rights protection. The most challenging aspects might, however, reside not in the doctrinal operation of the law but its practical application on the ground. In 2012, the EU Fundamental Rights Agency (FRA) pointed to some of the steps that should be taken in that direction, including positive action and promotion of equality, and they remain valid today.

European Union Agency for Fundamental Rights, *The Racial Equality Directive: application and challenges* (Publications Office of the European Union 2012)

Awareness of the national legislative and procedural framework giving effect to the prohibition on discrimination appears to be low among racial minorities as well as the social partners in some EU Member States more generally. This, in turn, affects the degree to which victims pursue their rights. In itself this may reduce the frequency with which the prohibition of discrimination is enforced and remedies are obtained. This will also then have an impact on the overall deterrent effect of the equality regime.

(...)

A preventive, rather than reactive, approach to indirect discrimination and the adoption of positive action measures can be noted across the Member States. This not only allows complicated socio-economic problems to be addressed but also pre-empts breaches of non-discrimination law. Measures that reflect the interlocking nature of disadvantage suffered by minority groups across areas such as employment, housing and education should be encouraged and broadened so that they are applied systematically across policy areas and throughout the Member States, rather than on a more limited ad hoc or project-driven basis.

As repeatedly underlined by the EUMC and FRA, without collection of ethnically disaggregated data it is difficult to develop policies to prevent discrimination and promote equality. This renders it difficult to identify where problems exist, and also to measure the success or otherwise of measures to combat the latter. In this sense, the realisation of the EU obligation under Article 10 TFEU to combat discrimination when 'defining and implementing its policies and activities' would be greatly facilitated by the systematic collection of data at Member State level, as well as the establishment of common EU-wide indicators. Such data is often also needed in order to prove claims of indirect

---

[129] E Howard, 'The EU Race Directive: Time for Change?' (2007) 8 International Journal of Discrimination and the Law 237.

[130] See Article 3(3) of Directive 2004/113/EC implementing the principle of equal treatment between men and women in the access to and supply of goods and services.

discrimination. Parties to the International Convention on the Elimination of All Forms of Racial Discrimination should be mindful of their obligations in this regard.

7.5 Religious Discrimination

Charter of Fundamental Rights of the European Union [2012] OJ C326/391

Article 10

Freedom of thought, conscience and religion
1. **Everyone has the right to freedom of thought, conscience and religion.** This right includes freedom to change religion or belief and freedom, either alone or in community with others and in public or in private, to manifest religion or belief, in worship, teaching, practice and observance.
2. **The right to conscientious objection is recognised**, in accordance with the national laws governing the exercise of this right.

Article 14

Right to education
3. The freedom to found educational establishments with due respect for democratic principles and the right of parents to ensure the education and teaching of their children **in conformity with their religious**, philosophical and pedagogical **convictions** shall be respected, in accordance with the national laws governing the exercise of such freedom and right.

Article 22

Cultural, religious and linguistic diversity
The Union shall respect cultural, religious and linguistic diversity.

Consolidated version of the Treaty on the Functioning of the European Union [2012] OJ C326/47

Article 17
1. **The Union respects and does not prejudice the status under national law of churches and religious associations** or communities in the Member States.
2. The Union equally respects the status under national law of philosophical and non-confessional organisations.
3. Recognising their identity and their specific contribution, the Union shall maintain an open, transparent and regular dialogue with these churches and organisations.

Compared to some other grounds of discrimination, religion shows up in a number of provisions of EU primary law. Most of these provisions have a different purpose than combatting discrimination, however: they implicitly convey concerns of the Member States— especially those where religion retains an important place in society—as to possible encroachment by the EU into the religious domain which is emphasized as belonging rather strictly to the exclusive purview of the Member States.[131] EU primary law therefore not only protects religious freedom (Article 10 of the Charter) but religious diversity is also to be respected by the EU (Article 22), children free to be educated in line with parents' religious convictions (Article 14), and churches and religious associations' status in national law not prejudiced by the EU.

Nevertheless, in terms of anti-discrimination, there is only one secondary law instrument with a substantive scope limited to occupation matters: the Employment Equality Directive which summarily covers discrimination on the grounds of religion, age, disability, and sexual orientation.[132] In addition to direct and indirect discrimination, the Directive—and the same goes for the Racial Equality Directive and Directive 2006/54/EC on gender equality in employment—prohibits harassment and instruction to discriminate.

Council Directive 2000/78/EC establishing a general framework for equal treatment in employment and occupation [2000] OJ L303/16

Article 3

Scope

3. Harassment shall be deemed to be a form of discrimination within the meaning of paragraph 1, when unwanted conduct related to any of the grounds referred to in Article 1 takes place with the purpose or effect of violating the dignity of a person and of creating an intimidating, hostile, degrading, humiliating or offensive environment. In this context, the concept of harassment may be defined in accordance with the national laws and practice of the Member States.

4. An instruction to discriminate against persons on any of the grounds referred to in Article 1 shall be deemed to be discrimination within the meaning of paragraph 1.

Prior to the existence of the abovementioned legal framework for the protection against religious discrimination in the EU, the CJEU was to a limited extent faced with questions relating to the reasonable accommodation of religious beliefs in EU law on three occasions. However, these cases did not leave a substantial imprint on EU law as far as religious equality is concerned.[133]

---

[131] Even if not mentioned in EU primary law as often, most grounds of discrimination represent sensitive topics for the Member States which retain a firm grip on key issues such as same-sex marriage.

[132] Council Directive 2000/78/EC establishing a general framework for equal treatment in employment and occupation [2000] OJ L303/16.

[133] Judgment of 27 October 1976, *Prais v Council of the European Communities*, 130/75, ECLI:EU:C:1976:142 concerned the recruitment of EU staff; Judgment of 5 October 1988, *Steymann v Staatssecretaris van Justitie*, 196/ 87, ECLI:EU:C:1988:475 concerned the question whether activities preformed in a religious community come within the scope of internal market law; and Judgment of 12 November 1996, *United Kingdom of Great Britain and Northern Ireland v Council*, C-84/94, ECLI:EU:C:1996:431 concerned a legal challenge of the Working Time Directive.

> ### E Relaño Pastor, 'Towards Substantive Equality for Religious Believers in the Workplace? Two Supranational European Courts, Two Different Approaches' 5 (2016) Oxford Journal of Law and Religion 255
>
> The CJEU has only once pronounced on reasonable discrimination on grounds of religion in 1976, quite long before the EU Equality Directives. In *Prais*, the plaintiff complained about scheduling a written test for recruitment on a Jewish holiday in which she was not permitted to travel or write according her religion. The Court carried out a balancing exercise weighing the interest of the candidate's religious practices and the principle of equality according to which all written test should be administered under the same conditions and the same dates for all candidates. The Court admitted that 'if a candidate informs the appointing authority that religious reasons make certain dates impossible for him the appointing authority should take this into account in fixing the date for written tests, and endeavour to avoid such dates', but 'if the candidate does not inform the appointing authority in good time of his difficulties, the appointing authority would be justified in refusing to afford an alternative date, particularly if there are other candidates who have been convoked for the test.' The logic of a reasonable accommodation is already included in an embryonic stage in the legal reasoning of *Prais*.
>
> A decade after *Prais*, the Luxembourg Court ruled on another religious issue, the *Steymann* case relating to economic activities carried out by members of a religious community or spiritual inspiration. And in *United Kingdom of Great Britain and Northern Ireland v Council of the European Union* regarding the annulment of Council Directive 93/104/EC of 23 November 1993, concerning certain aspects of the organization of working time, the Court showed some sensibility towards the religious and cultural diversity and upheld that 'whilst the question whether to include Sunday in the weekly rest period is ultimately left to the assessment of Member States, having regard, in particular, to the diversity of cultural, ethnic and religious factors in those States (second sentence of Article 5, read in conjunction with the tenth recital), the fact remains that the Council has failed to explain why Sunday, as a weekly rest day, is more closely connected with the health and safety of workers than any other day of the week.'

Nowadays, the most important point of reference for non-discrimination of religious beliefs is the Employment Equality Directive in conjunction with the provisions on religious diversity and freedom enshrined in EU primary law. Nevertheless, owing at least in part to its substantive limitation,[134] the Employment Equality Directive has not yet led to the emergence of a consolidated body of case law, with the exception of age discrimination.[135] The ground of religious discrimination has in fact been the least litigated of all the discrimination grounds—although it has been gaining momentum in recent years—but the few decisions handed down by the CJEU have still sparked considerable debate. The two first decisions touch upon an issue of relevance to millions of European citizens and immigrants: the wearing of Islamic headscarves in the workplace.

Although both cases relate to similar legal questions, there are also important differences between them. In *Bougnaoui*, the aggrieved individual complained of being dismissed from

---

[134] Although the Racial Equality Directive does not suffer from the material limitation of its scope, it has led to a similarly small number of cases.

[135] The volume of litigation, with the exception of age discrimination, contrasts unfavourably with that spurred by sex discrimination legislation adopted in the 1970s.

a company because of her refusal to remove her Islamic headscarf when sent on assignment to customers. The company justified the dismissal by referring to the wishes of their customers and therefore the connection between appearing 'neutral' and the company's business interest. Ms Bougnaoui was eventually dismissed as a consequence of refusing to comply with the company's demands to stop wearing the headscarf at work. The question referred for a preliminary ruling to the CJEU was, in essence, whether the rationale of the dismissal qualified as a 'genuine and determining occupational requirement' in the meaning of Article 4(1) of the Employment Equality Directive, thereby justifying the difference in treatment accorded to Ms Bougnaoui.

Judgment of 14 March 2017, *Bougnaoui and Association de défense des droits de l'homme (ADDH) v Micropole SA*, C-188/15, ECLI:EU:C:2017:204

---

30. In so far as the ECHR and, subsequently, the Charter use the term 'religion' in a broad sense, in that they include in it the freedom of persons to manifest their religion, the EU legislature must be considered to have intended to take the same approach when adopting Directive 2000/78, and therefore the concept of 'religion' in Article 1 of that directive should be interpreted as covering **both the *forum internum*, that is the fact of having a belief, and the *forum externum*, that is the manifestation of religious faith in public.**

37. (...) it should be borne in mind that the Court has repeatedly held that it is clear from Article 4(1) of Directive 2000/78 that it is not the ground on which the difference of treatment is based but a **characteristic related to that ground** which must constitute a genuine and determining occupational requirement (...)

38. It should, moreover, be pointed out that, in accordance with recital 23 of Directive 2000/78, **it is only in very limited circumstances that a characteristic related, in particular, to religion may constitute a genuine and determining occupational requirement.**

39. It must also be pointed out that, according to the actual wording of Article 4(1) of Directive 2000/78, **such a characteristic may constitute such a requirement only 'by reason of the nature of the particular occupational activities concerned or of the context in which they are carried out'.**

40. It follows from the information set out above that the concept of a 'genuine and determining occupational requirement', within the meaning of that provision, refers to a requirement that is objectively dictated by the nature of the occupational activities concerned or of the context in which they are carried out. **It cannot, however, cover subjective considerations, such as the willingness of the employer to take account of the particular wishes of the customer.**

In the first place, the CJEU pointed out the corresponding character of Article 10(1) of the Charter and Article 9 ECHR which meant that the obligation of homogenous interpretation of Article 52(3) of the Charter was applicable. The term 'religion' used in Article 1 of the Employment Equality Directive was subsequently interpreted as covering both religious belief and manifestation of the belief in public, in line with the ECHR and the Charter.

Second, it was not entirely clear from the facts as presented to the Court whether the dismissal was based on a *prima facie* neutral measure (indirect discrimination) or whether it was directly discriminatory (probably the case). The CJEU left this question to the national court to assess, limiting itself to stating that if the measure was deemed only indirectly discriminatory—meaning there was a general policy prohibiting all religious symbols at the workplace regardless of religion—there was the possibility of objective justification subject to the principle of proportionality, as a policy of neutrality would have represented a legitimate aim of the company (the point was addressed in *Achbita*).

Nevertheless, the genuine occupational requirement exception constituted the only avenue through which direct discrimination—which by all accounts was at stake—could have been in theory justified. The CJEU firmly rejected this option. The exception is qualified by the occupational requirement being objectively 'dictated' by the nature of the occupational activities or their context. Particular (discriminatory) wishes of a customer are, on the contrary, subjective considerations which fall outside the scope of the occupational requirement exception from the prohibition of discrimination.

The second case, decided by the CJEU on the same day as *Bougnaoui*, involved more fundamental and controversial choices for the EU judicature. Ms Achbita worked as a receptionist for the security company G4S. She came to the company when it already operated an unwritten rule that employees could not wear visible signs of their political, philosophical, or religious beliefs in the workplace. Soon after announcing that she would like to wear the Islamic headscarf at work, the company formalized the unwritten prohibition. Ms Achbita was subsequently dismissed upon insisting to wear a headscarf to work despite the company's policy. Although the national court's preliminary reference asked about direct discrimination, this case obviously raised the issue of indirect discrimination, as G4S' policy applied to manifestations of all beliefs equally (it was 'apparently neutral').

Judgment of 14 March 2017, *Achbita and Centrum voor gelijkheid van kansen en voor racismebestrijding v G4S Secure Solutions NV*, C-157/15, ECLI:EU:C:2017:203

34. In the present case, it is not inconceivable that the referring court might conclude that the internal rule at issue in the main proceedings introduces a difference of treatment that is indirectly based on religion or belief, for the purposes of Article 2(2)(b) of Directive 2000/78, if it is established—which it is for the referring court to ascertain—that **the apparently neutral obligation it encompasses results, in fact, in persons adhering to a particular religion or belief being put at a particular disadvantage.**

35. Under Article 2(2)(b)(i) of Directive 2000/78, such a difference of treatment does not, however, amount to indirect discrimination within the meaning of Article 2(2)(b) of the directive **if it is objectively justified by a legitimate aim and if the means of achieving that aim are appropriate and necessary.**

37. As regards, in the first place, the condition relating to the existence of a legitimate aim, it should be stated that the desire to display, in relations with both public and private sector customers, **a policy of political, philosophical or religious neutrality must be considered legitimate.**

38. An employer's wish to project an image of neutrality towards customers relates to **the freedom to conduct a business that is recognised in Article 16 of the Charter** and is, in principle, legitimate, notably where the employer involves in its pursuit of that aim only those workers who are required to come into contact with the employer's customers.

39. An interpretation to the effect that the pursuit of that aim allows, within certain limits, a restriction to be imposed on the freedom of religion is moreover, borne out by the case-law of the European Court of Human Rights in relation to Article 9 of the ECHR (judgment of the ECtHR of 15 January 2013, Eweida and Others v. United Kingdom, CE:ECHR:2013:0115JUD004842010, paragraph 94).

40. As regards, in the second place, the appropriateness of **an internal rule such as that at issue in the main proceedings**, it must be held that the fact that workers are prohibited from visibly wearing signs of political, philosophical or religious beliefs **is appropriate for the purpose of ensuring that a policy of neutrality is properly applied,** provided that that policy is genuinely pursued in a consistent and systematic manner (...)

41. In that respect, **it is for the referring court to ascertain whether G4S had, prior to Ms Achbita's dismissal, established a general and undifferentiated policy of prohibiting the visible wearing of signs** of political, philosophical or religious beliefs in respect of members of its staff who come into contact with its customers.

42. As regards, in the third place, the question whether the prohibition at issue in the main proceedings was necessary, it must be determined whether **the prohibition is limited to what is strictly necessary.** In the present case, what must be ascertained is whether the prohibition on the visible wearing of any sign or clothing capable of being associated with a religious faith or a political or philosophical belief **covers only G4S workers who interact with customers. If that is the case, the prohibition must be considered strictly necessary for the purpose of achieving the aim pursued.**

43. In the present case, so far as concerns the refusal of a worker such as Ms Achbita to give up wearing an Islamic headscarf when carrying out her professional duties for G4S customers, it is for the referring court to ascertain whether, taking into account the inherent constraints to which the undertaking is subject, and without G4S being required to take on an additional burden, **it would have been possible for G4S, faced with such a refusal, to offer her a post not involving any visual contact with those customers, instead of dismissing her.** It is for the referring court, having regard to all the material in the file, to take into account the interests involved in the case and to **limit the restrictions on the freedoms concerned to what is strictly necessary.**

The CJEU held that as long as neutrality and proportionality requirements were observed, the internal ban on religious and other symbols of G4S should be considered legal. The national court was obliged to verify whether indeed the policy was generally applied against all employees and not only Muslims. Moreover, it could not go beyond what is strictly necessary to ensure that the company appears neutral in its business with customers. This is a compromise solution that only permits a company to maintain the appearance of neutrality externally but cannot apply a similar measure for purely internal purposes.

The Court derived the justification for business neutrality from the vague 'business right' of Article 16 of the Charter which stipulates that '[t]he freedom to conduct a business in accordance with Union law and national laws and practices is recognised'. However, this reference further aggravated the conspicuous absence of counterbalancing fundamental rights on the side of the individual. The CJEU did not have recourse to any of the provisions safeguarding religious diversity and freedom of religion in the EU (listed at the start of the section) in order to carry out a balancing exercise between the competing interests and rights of the company and the individual. This is all the more surprising because in terms of fundamental rights, religion is, as mentioned above, significantly represented (certainly more so than the right to do business) in EU law and, moreover, the CJEU conveniently quoted the part of *Eweida and Others v UK* which suited its argument but not the fact that the ECtHR in that judgment conducted a balancing test of competing fundamental rights and found in favour of the individual.[136] In light of the obligation of Article 52(3) of the Charter to interpret corresponding rights between the Charter and the ECHR similarly and the *Eweida* judgment,[137] the CJEU's omission of freedom of religion (Article 10 of the Charter) from the discussion of the merits of the allegations means *Achbita* is unsatisfactorily reasoned.

The CJEU may have consciously diluted references to provisions on fundamental rights protection of religious belief in EU law because the judgment in *Achbita* is clearly problematic from the perspective of religious freedom and discrimination.[138] By accepting indirectly discriminatory behaviour of private enterprises with respect to its own employees on account of the public's discriminatory attitudes towards religious diversity, the CJEU is implicitly affirming that businesses have the right—bolstered legally by Article 16 of the Charter—to cater to public discrimination, insofar as they do not do so through directly discriminatory measures as was the case in *Bougnaoui*. The combined pronouncement in the two cases therefore contains the recipe for justified discrimination by businesses: instead of discriminating directly against some employees wearing religious clothing (as in *Bougnaoui*), companies can promulgate a general rule prohibiting religious symbols in the workplace which can achieve *de facto* the same result but legal under the terms of the Employment Equality Directive (as in *Achbita*). Although the latter policy must also affect non-Muslims to be legal, the solution on the whole largely defers the problem of religious discrimination to the market and the behaviour of private entities and citizens. Some commentators predicted the CJEU will have greater concern for discrimination against Muslim women in the workplace.[139]

---

[136] *Eweida and Others v UK*, App no 48420/10, 15 January 2013. The ECtHR, unlike the CJEU, transparently juxtaposed the clash between freedom of religion and the interests of the company: '(...) the Court has reached the conclusion in the present case that a fair balance was not struck. On one side of the scales was Ms Eweida's desire to manifest her religious belief. As previously noted, this is a fundamental right: because a healthy democratic society needs to tolerate and sustain pluralism and diversity; but also because of the value to an individual who has made religion a central tenet of his or her life to be able to communicate that belief to others. On the other side of the scales was the employer's wish to project a certain corporate image. The Court considers that, while this aim was undoubtedly legitimate, the domestic courts accorded it too much weight. Ms Eweida's cross was discreet and cannot have detracted from her professional appearance. There was no evidence that the wearing of other, previously authorised, items of religious clothing, such as turbans and hijabs, by other employees, had any negative impact on British Airways' brand or image' [94]. See also R McCrea, 'Religion in the Workplace: Eweida and Others v United Kingdom' (2014) 77 The Modern Law Review 277.

[137] Although admittedly the ECtHR has been less accommodating towards manifestations of religious beliefs in other cases. See E Relaño Pastor, 'Towards Substantive Equality for Religious Believers in the Workplace? Two Supranational European Courts, Two Different Approaches' (2016) 5 Oxford Journal of Law and Religion 255, 276.

[138] See also E Howard, 'Islamic Headscarves and the CJEU: Achbita and Bougnaoui' (2017) 24 Maastricht Journal of European and Comparative Law 348.

[139] Relaño Pastor (n 137) 279.

One of the most recent cases concerns the right of religious organizations to select applicants based on faith. In the circumstances of the case, Ms Egenberger's application was rejected on the basis of her not being of any religious denomination. That this represented a difference in treatment was not disputed—the issue was more whether religious organizations were entitled to discriminate in light of Directive 2000/78. The CJEU held that although the special status of religious organization is to be taken into account, in no circumstances can criteria for employment be placed beyond the reach of judicial review. It is for the national courts to establish whether in a given case religion constitutes a 'legitimate, genuine and justified' occupational requirement (having regard to the organization's ethos) that would sanction differential treatment, in accordance with Article 4(2) of Directive 2000/78. The CJEU also reaffirmed that if necessary, provisions of national law must make way in order to safeguard compliance with EU law, including rights deriving from the Charter (here Articles 21 and 47). The judgment thus amounts, in essence, to a recognition that Article 21 of the Charter—and specifically the ground of religion mentioned therein—has horizontal direct effect, subject to the proviso on the scope of EU law of Article 51 of the Charter.[140] The CJEU subsequently extensively cited the *Egenberger* ruling as precedent in the case of *IR v JQ* where it cast doubt on the requirement of a Catholic hospital that doctors in managerial positions respect the Catholic Church's notion of marriage in light of the criteria contained in Article 4(2) of Directive 2000/78.[141]

Judgment of 17 April 2018, *Egenberger v Evangelisches Werk für Diakonie und Entwicklung e. V.*, **C-414/16, ECLI:EU:C:2018:257**

43. It should be noted, as a preliminary point, that **it is not disputed** between the parties to the main proceedings **that the rejection of Ms Egenberger's application on the ground that she was of no denomination constitutes a difference of treatment on grounds of religion** within the meaning of Article 4(2) of Directive 2000/78.

51. The objective of Article 4(2) of Directive 2000/78 is (…) to ensure a **fair balance between the right of autonomy of churches** and other organisations whose ethos is based on religion or belief, on the one hand, **and**, on the other hand, **the right of workers**, inter alia when they are being recruited, not to be **discriminated against on grounds of religion or belief**, in situations where those rights may clash.

53. In the event of a dispute, however, it must be possible for the balancing exercise to be the subject if need be of **review by an independent authority, and ultimately by a national court.**

55. (…) where a church or other organisation whose ethos is based on religion or belief asserts, in support of an act or decision such as the rejection of an application for employment by it, that by reason of the nature of the activities concerned or the context in which the activities are to be carried out, religion constitutes a genuine, legitimate and justified occupational requirement, having regard to the ethos of the

---

[140] Seen in light of previous cases concerning age discrimination (see below), the *Egenberger* case is important for explicitly extending horizontal direct effect to another ground of discrimination. The legal situation appears to therefore slowly edge towards a recognition that all the grounds listed in Article 21 of the Charter can be invoked before a court in disputes between private parties.

[141] Judgment of 11 September 2018, *IR v JQ*, C-68/17, ECLI:EU:C:2018:696.

church or organisation, **it must be possible for such an assertion to be the subject, if need be, of effective judicial review** by which it can be ensured that the criteria set out in Article 4(2) of Directive 2000/78 are satisfied in the particular case.

56. Article 17 TFEU cannot invalidate that conclusion.

58. (...) Article 17 TFEU expresses the neutrality of the European Union towards the organisation by the Member States of their relations with churches and religious associations and communities. On the other hand, **that article is not such as to exempt compliance with the criteria set out in Article 4(2)** of Directive 2000/78 from effective judicial review.

61. (...) in the balancing exercise provided for in Article 4(2) of Directive 2000/78 (...) **the Member States** and their authorities, including judicial authorities, **must**, except in very exceptional cases, **refrain from assessing whether the actual ethos of the church or organisation concerned is legitimate** (see, to that effect, ECtHR, 12 June 2014, Fernández Martínez v. Spain, CE:ECHR:2014:0612JUD005603007, § 129). They must nonetheless ensure that there is no infringement of the right of workers not to be discriminated against on grounds inter alia of religion or belief. Thus, by virtue of Article 4(2), **the purpose of the examination is to ascertain whether the occupational requirement imposed by the church** or organisation, by reason of the nature of the activities concerned or the context in which they are carried out, **is genuine, legitimate and justified, having regard to that ethos.**

62. As regards the interpretation of the concept of 'genuine, legitimate and justified occupational requirement' in Article 4(2) of Directive 2000/78, it follows expressly from that provision that it is by reference to the **'nature' of the activities** concerned or the **'context' in which they are carried out** that religion or belief may constitute such an occupational requirement.

63. Thus **the lawfulness** from the point of view of that provision of a difference of treatment on grounds of religion or belief **depends on the objectively verifiable existence of a direct link between the occupational requirement imposed by the employer and the activity concerned.** Such a link may follow either from the nature of the activity, **for example** where it involves taking part in the **determination of the ethos of the church** or organisation in question or **contributing to its mission of proclamation,** or else from the circumstances in which the activity is to be carried out, such as the need to ensure a credible **presentation of the church** or organisation to the outside world.

65. (...) first, as regards the **'genuine'** nature of the requirement, that the use of that adjective **means** that, in the mind of the EU legislature, **professing the religion** or belief on which the ethos of the church or organisation is founded **must appear necessary** because of the importance of the occupational activity in question for the manifestation of that ethos or the exercise by the church or organisation of its right of autonomy.

66. Secondly, as regards the **'legitimate'** nature of the requirement, the use of that term shows that the EU legislature wished to ensure that the requirement of professing the religion or belief on which the ethos of the church or organisation is founded is **not used to pursue an aim that has no connection with that ethos or with the exercise by the church or organisation of its right of autonomy.**

67. Thirdly, as regards the **'justified'** nature of the requirement, that term implies not only that compliance with the criteria in Article 4(2) of Directive 2000/78 can be reviewed by a national court, but also that **the church or organisation imposing the requirement is obliged to show, in the light of the factual circumstances of the case, that the supposed risk of causing harm to its ethos or to its right of autonomy is probable and substantial**, so that imposing such a requirement is indeed necessary.

76. **The prohibition of all discrimination on grounds of religion or belief is mandatory as a general principle of EU law.** That prohibition, which is laid down in **Article 21(1) of the Charter, is sufficient in itself to confer on individuals a right which they may rely on as such in disputes between them in a field covered by EU law** (…)

77. As regards its mandatory effect, **Article 21 of the Charter is no different, in principle, from the various provisions of the founding Treaties prohibiting discrimination on various grounds, even where the discrimination derives from contracts between individuals** (…)

81. Further, where the **national court** is called on to ensure that Articles 21 and 47 of the Charter are observed, while possibly balancing the various interests involved, such as respect for the status of churches as laid down in Article 17 TFEU, it **will have to take into consideration the balance struck between those interests by the EU legislature in Directive 2000/78**, in order to determine the obligations deriving from the Charter in circumstances such as those at issue in the main proceedings (…)

A final case worth mentioning concerns a preliminary ruling where the CJEU needed to consider the compatibility with Articles 1 and 2(2) of Directive 2000/78 of a German rule reserving certain employment (and renumeration) privileges on the occasion of Good Friday for members of specific religious denominations.[142] The applicant, Mr Achatzi, not belonging to such a religious group, complained about not being able to rely on public holiday pay for the work he did on Good Friday. The Court quickly came to the conclusion that this situation amounted to direct discrimination, since the differential treatment relied directly on the membership of certain churches. The difference in treatment was not necessary for the protection of freedom of religion of third parties (Article 2(5) Dir 2000/78) or for compensation for disadvantages linked to religion (Article 7(1) Dir 2000/78).[143] Very importantly, the Court reaffirmed the horizontal direct effect of Article 21 of the Charter. In order to restore equal treatment, even a private employer was consequently obliged also to grant other employees a public holiday on Good Friday.[144] The ground of religious discrimination, but mostly the confirmation of horizontal direct effect with regard to the other discrimination grounds in Article 21 of the Charter are bound to be further refined in future case law

---

[142] Judgment of 22 January 2019, *Cresco Investigation GmbH v Markus Achatzi*, C-193/17, ECLI:EU:C:2019:43.
[143] Ibid, paras 51, 61, 66.
[144] Ibid, para 89.

7.6 Age Discrimination

Charter of Fundamental Rights of the European Union [2012] OJ C326/391

Article 25

The rights of the elderly

The Union recognises and respects the rights of the elderly to lead a life of dignity and independence and to participate in social and cultural life.

Article 32

Prohibition of child labour and protection of young people at work

The **employment of children is prohibited.** The **minimum age of admission to employment may not be lower than the minimum school-leaving age,** without prejudice to such rules as may be more favourable to young people and except for limited derogations.

Young people admitted to work must have working conditions appropriate to their age and be protected against economic exploitation and any work likely to harm their safety, health or physical, mental, moral or social development or to interfere with their education.

Age constitutes another of the grounds of discrimination prohibited by Article 21(1) of the Charter and the Employment Equality Directive. Furthermore, in accordance with Article 32 of the Charter, age represents the determining condition when it comes to the prohibition of child labour. This provision also *de facto* provides for a positive action derogation on the grounds of age from the principle of non-discrimination as it allows young people to receive specific protective treatment against economic exploitation and 'working conditions appropriate to their age'. Although a similar argument could be made about Article 25 of the Charter on the rights of the elderly, the provision is noticeably vaguer.

Age as a ground of discrimination has not only been the most litigated among the grounds protected by the Employment Equality Directive, it has also been at the centre of disputes which have shaken the fundamentals of EU law at large. In the first ground-breaking case, *Mangold*, the CJEU established that the general principle of non-discrimination on the grounds of age could be invoked in disputes between private parties (horizontal direct effect) despite the fact that the deadline for the transposition of the Employment Equality Directive had not yet expired at that point in time.[145] The dispute in the main proceedings concerned a fixed-term contract by which Mr Helm employed Mr Mangold. The contract was concluded for a fixed period for the sole reason that German statutory law made it expressly easier to offer fixed-term contracts to workers who were over 52 years old. Mr Mangold alleged that the limitation of the term of his contract, despite being based on a provision of German law, is incompatible with the Employment Equality Directive. Although the referring national court recognized that the contract was concluded before the transposition period of the Directive ended, it was also cognizant of the obligation on Member States to

---

[145] Judgment of 22 November 2005, *Mangold v Helm*, C-144/04, ECLI:EU:C:2005:709.

refrain from adopting measures in the intervening period which would seriously undermine the objectives of the Directive.[146] Moreover, due to the contract being fixed term, the Framework Agreement on fixed-term contracts, which was agreed at EU level, was relevant to the dispute.[147]

Judgment of 22 November 2005, *Mangold v Helm*, C-144/04, ECLI:EU:C:2005:709

57. Paragraph 14(3) of the TzBfG, however, by permitting employers to conclude without restriction fixed-term contracts of employment with workers over the age of 52, **introduces a difference of treatment on the grounds directly of age.**

59. As is clear from the documents sent to the Court by the national court, the purpose of that legislation is plainly to **promote the vocational integration of unemployed older workers**, in so far as they encounter considerable difficulties in finding work.

60. **The legitimacy of such a public-interest objective cannot reasonably be thrown in doubt**, as indeed the Commission itself has admitted.

61. An objective of that kind must as a rule, therefore, be regarded as justifying, 'objectively and reasonably', as provided for by the first subparagraph of Article 6(1) of Directive 2000/78, a difference of treatment on grounds of age laid down by Member States.

62. It still remains to be established whether, according to the actual wording of that provision, the means used to achieve that legitimate objective are 'appropriate and necessary'.

63. In this respect the Member States unarguably enjoy broad discretion in their choice of the measures capable of attaining their objectives in the field of social and employment policy.

64. However, as the national court has pointed out, application of national legislation such as that at issue in the main proceedings leads to a situation in which **all workers** who have reached the age of 52, without distinction, whether or not they were unemployed before the contract was concluded and whatever the duration of any period of unemployment, may lawfully, until the age at which they may claim their entitlement to a retirement pension, be offered fixed-term contracts of employment which may be renewed an indefinite number of times. **This significant body of workers, determined solely on the basis of age, is thus in danger**, during a substantial part of its members' working life, **of being excluded from the benefit of stable employment** which, however, as the Framework Agreement makes clear, constitutes a major element in the protection of workers.

65. In so far as such legislation takes the age of the worker concerned as the only criterion for the application of a fixed-term contract of employment, when it has not been shown that fixing an age threshold, as such, **regardless of any other consideration linked to the structure of the labour market** in question or the personal

---

[146] Judgment of 18 December 1997, *Inter-Environnement Wallonie ASBL v Région wallonne*, C-129/96, ECLI:EU:C:1997:628.

[147] Council Directive 1999/70/EC concerning the framework agreement on fixed-term work concluded by ETUC, UNICE and CEEP [1999] OJ L175/43.

situation of the person concerned, is objectively necessary to the attainment of the objective which is the vocational integration of unemployed older workers, **it must be considered to go beyond what is appropriate and necessary in order to attain the objective pursued.** (...)

66. The fact that, when the contract was concluded, **the period prescribed for the transposition into domestic law of Directive 2000/78 had not yet expired** cannot call that finding into question.

74. (...) **Directive 2000/78 does not itself lay down the principle of equal treatment in the field of employment and occupation**. Indeed, in accordance with Article 1 thereof, the sole purpose of the directive is 'to lay down a general framework for combating discrimination on the grounds of religion or belief, disability, age or sexual orientation', the source of the actual principle underlying the prohibition of those forms of discrimination being found, as is clear from the third and fourth recitals in the preamble to the directive, in various international instruments and in the constitutional traditions common to the Member States.

75. **The principle of non-discrimination on grounds of age must thus be regarded as a general principle of Community law. Where national rules fall within the scope of Community law**, which is the case with Paragraph 14(3) of the TzBfG, as amended by the Law of 2002, as being a measure implementing Directive 1999/70 (...), and reference is made to the Court for a preliminary ruling, **the Court must provide all the criteria of interpretation** needed by the national court to determine whether those rules are compatible with such a principle (...)

76. **Consequently, observance of the general principle of equal treatment, in particular in respect of age, cannot as such be conditional upon the expiry of the period allowed the Member States for the transposition of a directive** intended to lay down a general framework for combating discrimination on the grounds of age, in particular so far as the organisation of appropriate legal remedies, the burden of proof, protection against victimisation, social dialogue, affirmative action and other specific measures to implement such a directive are concerned.

77. In those circumstances it is the responsibility of the national court, hearing a dispute involving the principle of non-discrimination in respect of age, to provide, in a case within its jurisdiction, the legal protection which individuals derive from the rules of Community law and to ensure that those rules are fully effective, **setting aside any provision of national law which may conflict with that law** (...)

The CJEU adjudged the German statutory law at issue, albeit pursuing a legitimate aim, to have disproportionately interfered with the prohibition on age discrimination of Article 6(1) of the Employment Equality Directive. Part of the problem was that the law affected all workers above 52, not only those who were unemployed and thus in line with the objective of the law to reduce unemployment among older persons.

Mangold's challenge to the then established order of EU law was considerable. The *Marshall* line of case law excluded the horizontal direct effect of Directives. To reduce the contradiction the CJEU was at pains to stress that the general principle requiring the national court to set aside domestic legislation was not subsumed by the Directive.[148] Although

---

[148] The same reasoning—focusing on Article 21 of the Charter as containing the general principle—was present, *mutatis mutandi*, in *Egenberger* and the subsequent case law on religious discrimination (see previous section above).

the general principle of non-discrimination on the grounds of age has self-standing legal value apart from the Employment Equality Directive, the latter is of obvious relevance as a specific expression (albeit not a source) of the general principle in matters of employment. Therefore the fact that the transposition deadline for the Directive had not yet passed was significant.

It should also be recognized, however, that *Mangold* did not feature a purely national or horizontal situation. The CJEU took care to underline that the challenged German rules fell within the scope of EU law by virtue of implementing Directive 1999/70 on fixed-term contracts. This is reminiscent of the way Article 51(1) of the Charter operates with respect to Member States today when the applicability of the Charter hinges on whether the Member States are implementing EU law.[149] In addition, the important role played by statutory law in the dispute, though taking place between two private parties, and the obligation on Germany not to undermine the objectives of the Employment Equality Directive even before its transposition deadline meant that there was a vertical element to the horizontal direct effect of the general principle of non-discrimination on the grounds of age. Nevertheless, a number of commentators found the Court's judgment insufficiently reasoned. The German Constitutional Court also had a say. It pointed to the impact of the CJEU's decision on legitimate expectations of private parties vis-à-vis national law, suggested that the Member States mis-transposing EU law should bear the costs, and reiterated that it reserves itself the power to review EU acts if they are manifestly ultra vires and result in a specific violation of the principle of conferral.[150] This was held not to be the case in *Mangold*.

A Eriksson, 'European Court of Justice: Broadening the scope of European nondiscrimination law' (2009) 7 International Journal of Constitutional Law 731

It is true that the general principle of equality implies, potentially, a prohibition of any discrimination on specific grounds. It is also true that any specific prohibition is an expression of that general principle. However, neither article 13 EC nor the implementing directives necessarily reflect a preexisting prohibition of all possible forms of discrimination. Rather, it is envisaged that the Community legislature and the member states may take appropriate action in this regard if they consider it necessary. For the Court to devise such a general principle without a conclusive legal basis severely restricts the legislature's prerogative and discretion to shape the scope and the limits of European nondiscrimination law. Now that the period for implementation has elapsed and all member states are bound by the Framework Directive, there is no question that the principle of nondiscrimination on the grounds of age is a general one. However, at the time of the Mangold decision, this was not the case. To base its finding, legally, on the existence of a general principle of prohibiting age discrimination, the Court should have shown in detail that such a principle actually existed at that time. Be that as it may, it merely made a reference to the general principle of equality, which exists, obviously, though it is not identical to the specific prohibition of age discrimination.

---

[149] See Ch 4 as regards the applicability of the Charter.
[150] Bundesverfassungsgericht, Order of 6 July 2010, 2 BvR 2661/06, para 61.

The Court's position would have been strengthened if it had taken into account articles 21 and 25 of the European Charter of Fundamental Rights as proof of the member states' general wish to prohibit age discrimination. However, the charter was not (...) binding law. Moreover, merely because the Framework Directive was concluded unanimously does not, in itself, prove the existence of a general principle in that sense; by adopting the directive, the member states wished to be bound by its provisions after the implementation period has elapsed. There is no indication that they wished merely to affirm an already binding principle. Even though age discrimination sometimes is considered in international law to fall under the rubric of discrimination on grounds of 'other status', this does not raise the specific prohibition of age discrimination to the level of a general principle of Community law; the international jurisprudence to that effect is 'too recent and uneven'. In view of these considerations, the ECJ was rightly reproached for having exceeded its competence by contriving a general principle of Community law prohibiting the discrimination on the basis of age.

Nonetheless, the Court, once again, affirmed the existence of such a general principle in its recent decision in Bartsch, even though it denied its applicability to the instant case. It held that the general principle must be applied where there is a link with Community law. While it is true that, in several other decisions in the field of nondiscrimination law, the Court did not mention the existence of a general principle of nondiscrimination on specific grounds, this was because such a reference was not necessary. In those cases, the Court could rely directly on article 141 EC or on the respective directives themselves, as the period for transposition of the directives had expired. (...)

The core idea behind *Mangold*—that the general principle of non-discrimination on the grounds of age has horizontal direct effect—was confirmed although not applied in the case of *Bartsch*.[151] The CJEU made clear, following the Opinion of the Advocate General,[152] that the scope of EU law remains an important criterion in determining whether the general principle of EU law is applicable in the case at hand. What, according to the Court, distinguished the case of *Bartsch* from *Mangold* was that the national measures in the former case did not transpose any EU legislation and therefore there was no link between national and EU law that would trigger the operation of the general principle of non-discrimination on the grounds of age. In addition, the alleged infringement occurred before the transposition deadline for the Employment Equality Directive expired. The case was as a consequence addressed purely in accordance with provisions of national law.

Another breakthrough in the case law came in *Kücükdeveci*.[153] Ms Kücükdeveci sued her former employer on the grounds that the notice period applicable to her dismissal was calculated as if she worked at the company for merely three years when in fact she did so for ten. The employer based their calculation of the notice period on German statutory law which stated that 'periods prior to the completion of the employee's 25th year of age are not taken into account'. As Ms Kücükdeveci started working at the company when she was 18, 7 years of her work were discounted from the notice period calculation. She alleged that the difference of treatment on the basis of age was contrary to EU law.

---

[151] Judgment of 23 September 2008, *Bartsch v Bosch und Siemens Hausgeräte (BSH) Altersfürsorge*, C-427/06, ECLI:EU:C:2008:517.

[152] *Bartsch v Bosch und Siemens Hausgeräte (BSH) Altersfürsorge* [2008] ECLI:EU:C:2008:297, Opinion of AG Sharpston.

[153] Judgment of 19 January 2010, *Kücükdeveci v Swedex GmbH & Co. KG*, C-555/07, ECLI:EU:C:2010:21.

Judgment of 19 January 2010, *Kücükdeveci v Swedex GmbH & Co. KG*, C-555/07, ECLI:EU:C:2010:21

21. (...) the Court has acknowledged the existence of a principle of non-discrimination on grounds of age which must be regarded as a general principle of European Union law (see, to that effect, Mangold, paragraph 75). Directive 2000/78 gives specific expression to that principle (...)

22. It should also be noted that Article 6(1) TEU provides that **the Charter of Fundamental Rights** of the European Union is to have the same legal value as the Treaties. Under **Article 21(1)** of the charter, '[a]ny discrimination based on ... age ... shall be prohibited'.

24. **In contrast** to the situation concerned in Case C-427/06 *Bartsch* [2008] ECR I-7245, the allegedly discriminatory conduct adopted in the present case on the basis of the national legislation at issue occurred **after the expiry of the period** prescribed for the Member State concerned for the **transposition** of **Directive 2000/78**, which, for the Federal Republic of Germany, ended on 2 December 2006.

25. **On that date, that directive had the effect of bringing within the scope of European Union law the national legislation at issue in the main proceedings, which concerns a matter governed by that directive, in this case the conditions of dismissal.**

27. It follows that it is **the general principle of European Union law prohibiting all discrimination on grounds of age, as given expression in Directive 2000/78**, which **must be the basis of the examination** of whether European Union law precludes national legislation such as that at issue in the main proceedings.

39. The referring court indicates that **the aim of the national legislation** at issue in the main proceedings **is to afford employers greater flexibility in personnel management** by alleviating the burden on them in respect of the dismissal of young workers, from whom it is reasonable to expect a greater degree of personal or occupational mobility.

40. However, **the legislation is not appropriate for achieving that aim, since it applies to all employees who joined the undertaking before the age of 25, whatever their age at the time of dismissal.**

42. It should be added that, as the referring court points out, **the national legislation at issue in the main proceedings affects young employees unequally**, in that it affects young people who enter active life early after little or no vocational training, but not those who start work later after a long period of training.

48. (...) in applying national law, the national court called on to interpret it is required to do so, as far as possible, **in the light of the wording and the purpose of the directive** in question, in order to achieve the result pursued by the directive and thereby comply with the third paragraph of Article 288 TFEU (...). The requirement for national law to be interpreted in conformity with European Union law is inherent in the system of the Treaty, since it permits the national court, within the limits of its jurisdiction, to **ensure the full effectiveness of European Union law** when it determines the dispute before it (...)

49. According to the national court, however, because of its clarity and precision, the second sentence of Paragraph 622(2) of the BGB **is not open to an interpretation in conformity with Directive 2000/78.**

50. (...) Directive 2000/78 merely gives expression to, but does not lay down, the principle of equal treatment in employment and occupation, and that the principle of non-discrimination on grounds of age is a general principle of European Union law in that it constitutes a specific application of the general principle of equal treatment (...)

51. In those circumstances, **it is for the national court**, hearing a dispute involving the principle of non-discrimination on grounds of age as given expression in Directive 2000/78, **to provide**, within the limits of its jurisdiction, **the legal protection which individuals derive from European Union law** and to ensure the full effectiveness of that law, **disapplying if need be any provision of national legislation contrary to that principle** (...)

53. The need to ensure the full effectiveness of the principle of non-discrimination on grounds of age, as given expression in Directive 2000/78, means that the national court, faced with a national provision falling within the scope of European Union law which it considers to be incompatible with that principle, and which cannot be interpreted in conformity with that principle, must decline to apply that provision, without being either compelled to make or prevented from making a reference to the Court for a preliminary ruling before doing so.

54. (...) **By reason of the principle of the primacy of European Union law, which extends also to the principle of non-discrimination on grounds of age**, contrary national legislation which falls within the scope of European Union law must be disapplied (...)

Kücükdeveci confirmed and bolstered the interpretation espoused in *Mangold* and *Bartsch*. The horizontal direct effect of the general principle of non-discrimination on grounds of age applies within the scope of EU law, the latter being the case even when national law contradicts or does not implement an EU Directive, and moreover benefits from the principle of primacy which may require a national court to set aside incompatible national legislation. The Court also clearly spelled out the distinction between the direct effect of general principles of EU law, in this case of non-discrimination on grounds of age, which can be horizontal and EU Directives which cannot have horizontal direct effect. Nonetheless, the two are closely linked as regards age discrimination in the sense that Directive 2000/78 gives expression to the general principle of non-discrimination on grounds of age which itself is a specific application of the general principle of equal treatment. In combination with the requirement for the legal action to fall within the scope of EU law, including the Employment Equality Directive, the CJEU had in essence devised a way of circumventing the lack of horizontal direct effect of Directives, albeit incompletely at first, given that other grounds of discrimination prohibited under the Employment Equality Directive had not yet received express recognition as general principles of EU law in the case law, despite this being implied in the judgments and Article 21(1) of the Charter.[154]

A shift can be discerned in *Egenberger*, where—at least—the discrimination ground of 'religion or belief' was given horizontal direct effect. First, the Court confirmed that also the prohibition of all discrimination on grounds of religion (but only this ground is mentioned) is mandatory as a general principle of EU law, merely laid down in the field of employment

---

[154] By referring to the latter in *Kücükdeveci*, the CJEU has strengthened the legal basis for its anti-discrimination doctrine and addressed one of the criticisms levied against its reasoning in *Mangold*. The difference

in Directive 2000/78.[155] It goes on to state that as 'regards its mandatory effect, Article 21 of the Charter is no different, in principle, from the various provisions of the founding Treaties prohibiting discrimination on various grounds, even where the discrimination de-rives from contracts between individuals'.[156] This statement opens up the possibility to rec-ognize the horizontal direct effect with regard to the other discrimination grounds under Directive 2000/87, but also with regard to those grounds that were not given expression in the Founding Treaties or in secondary EU legislation. It remains to be seen how the CJEU's case law will develop in this respect, but there is indeed scarce reason to think that, in light of the criteria for applicability of the Charter and their interpretation by the CJEU,[157] there should be any distinction between general principles relating to grounds of discrimination promulgated by the CJEU and the prohibition of discrimination on all the grounds provided for by Article 21(1) of the Charter.

One of the more recent and controversial cases addressing the issue of direct effect of non-discrimination on grounds of age is *Dansk Industri* (also known as *Ajos* for the company on whose behalf the action was brought).[158] The facts of the case were not too different from *Mangold* and *Kücükdeveci*: the dispute featured again an employer and a former employee (two private parties) and statutory law alleged to be in breach of the Employment Equality Directive, namely Danish law which excluded retiring workers from receiving a severance allowance. The employer complained about the impact the application of the general prin-ciple of non-discrimination on grounds of age would have on the principles of protection of legitimate expectations and legal certainty attached to the Danish national law according to which the employer determined their legal situation. As a clear precedent already existed in CJEU case law concerning the disputed provision of Danish law,[159] it was straightforward for the Court to affirm that the statute indeed breached the prohibition of age discrimination re-quired by the general principle of EU law and the Employment Equality Directive. The more difficult issue resided in addressing the concerns of the sceptical Danish Supreme Court re-garding the role of legitimate expectations and legal certainty that private parties derive from national law.

Judgment of 19 April 2016, *Dansk Industri v Estate of Karsten Eigil Rasmussen*, C-441/14, ECLI:EU:C:2016:278

---

26. (...) in the light of the fact that the Court has previously held that Articles 2 and 6(1) of **Directive 2000/78** are to be interpreted as **precluding national legislation**, such as the legislation that is the subject of the present request for a preliminary ruling, pursuant to which workers who are eligible for an old-age pension from

---

between mentioning the Charter in one case but not the other could have stemmed from the Charter only be-coming legally binding after the entry into force of the Treaty of Lisbon which was after the *Mangold* decision.

[155] Judgment of 17 April 2018, *Egenberger v Evangelisches Werk für Diakonie und Entwicklung e. V.*, C-414/16, ECLI:EU:C:2018:257, paras 75–76.
[156] Ibid, para 77.
[157] Most famously in Judgment of 26 February 2013, *Åklagaren v Åkerberg Fransson*, C-617/10, ECLI:EU:C:2013:105. See Ch 4 for a more in-depth explanation.
[158] Judgment of 19 April 2016, *Dansk Industri v Estate of Karsten Eigil Rasmussen*, C-441/14, ECLI:EU:C:2016:278.
[159] Judgment of 12 October 2010, *Ingeniørforeningen i Danmark*, C-499/08, ECLI:EU:C:2010:600.

their employer under a pension scheme which they joined before attaining the age of 50 cannot, on that ground alone, claim a severance allowance aimed at assisting workers with more than 12 years of service in the undertaking in finding new employment, **the same applies with regard to the fundamental principle of equal treatment**, the general principle prohibiting discrimination on grounds of age being merely a specific expression of that principle.

31. It follows that, in applying national law, national courts called upon to interpret that law are required to consider the whole body of rules of law and to apply methods of interpretation that are recognised by those rules in order to **interpret it, so far as possible, in the light of the wording and the purpose of the directive concerned in order to achieve the result sought by the directive and consequently comply with the third paragraph of Article 288 TFEU** (...)

32. It is true that the Court has stated that **this principle of interpreting national law in conformity with EU law has certain limits**. Thus, the obligation for a national court to refer to EU law when interpreting and applying the relevant rules of domestic law is limited by general principles of law and **cannot serve as the basis for an interpretation of national law *contra legem*** (...)

33. It should be noted in that connection that **the requirement to interpret national law in conformity with EU law entails the obligation for national courts to change its established case-law**, where necessary, if it is based on an interpretation of national law that is incompatible with the objectives of a directive (...)

34. Accordingly, the national court cannot validly claim in the main proceedings that it is impossible for it to interpret the national provision at issue in a manner that is consistent with EU law by mere reason of the fact that it has consistently interpreted that provision in a manner that is incompatible with EU law.

37. (...) in the present case, if it considers that it is impossible for it to interpret the national provision at issue in a manner that is consistent with EU law, **the national court must disapply that provision**.

38. (...) with regard to identifying the obligations deriving from the principle of the protection of legitimate expectations for a national court adjudicating in a dispute between private persons, it should be noted that **a national court cannot rely on that principle in order to continue to apply a rule of national law that is at odds with the general principle prohibiting discrimination on grounds of age**, as laid down by Directive 2000/78.

39. Indeed, the application of the principle of the protection of legitimate expectations as contemplated by the referring court would, in practice, have the **effect of limiting the temporal effects of the Court's interpretation** because, as a result of that application, such an interpretation would not be applicable in the main proceedings.

40. (...) the interpretation which the Court, in the exercise of the jurisdiction conferred upon it by Article 267 TFEU, gives to EU law clarifies and, where necessary, **defines the meaning and scope of that law as it must be, or ought to have been, understood and applied from the time of its coming into force**. It follows that, unless there are **truly exceptional circumstances**, which is not claimed to be the case here, EU law as thus interpreted must be applied by the courts even to legal relationships which arose and were established before the judgment ruling on the request for interpretation, provided that in other respects the conditions for bringing a dispute relating to the application of that law before the courts having jurisdiction are satisfied (...)

41. Moreover, the **protection of legitimate expectations cannot**, in any event, **be relied on for the purpose of denying an individual** who has brought proceedings culminating in the Court interpreting EU law as precluding the rule of national law at issue **the benefit of that interpretation** (...)

In *Dansk Industri*, the CJEU can be seen sticking to its proverbial guns. The Danish Supreme Court cast doubt on the effects of the general principle of non-discrimination on grounds of age when conflicting with national law but the CJEU would have none of it. It reiterated its doctrine regarding the principle of consistent interpretation (sometimes also called indirect effect) as requiring, if necessary, for national courts to change their established interpretation of national law or, should that not be possible (because national law clearly contradicts EU law), the national court is under an obligation, in accordance with the principle of primacy of EU law, to disapply the contravening provision of national law. Invoking the principles of protection of legitimate expectations and legal certainty did not change anything about the outcome. The CJEU would only allow a derogation in the form of a temporal limitation—of the kind provided in *Defrenne II* and *Barber*—on the effects of its decision in exceptional circumstances which was not the case in *Dansk Industri*.

Although normally when the Court lays down an interpretation of EU law in a preliminary ruling the matter is considered settled, in *Dansk Industri/Ajos* the Danish Supreme Court did not take kindly to the CJEU's judgment. In a rare act of overt defiance, the Danish Supreme Court refused to follow the preliminary ruling of the CJEU and consequently denied the principle of non-discrimination horizontal direct effect in the case at hand. The Danish Supreme Court has cited concerns over national sovereignty in its defiance of the CJEU.

MA Madsen, HP Olsen, and U Sadl, 'Competing Supremacies and Clashing Institutional Rationalities: The Danish Supreme Court's Decision in the Ajos Case and the National Limits of Judicial Cooperation' (2017) 23 European Law Journal 140

In its decision in the Ajos case, the SCDK [Supreme Court of Denmark] disregarded the guidelines of the Court of Justice of the European Union (CJEU) (...). More notably still, the SCDK used the occasion to set new boundaries to the applicability of the CJEU's rulings in Denmark. It did so in two steps: first, the SCDK delimited the competences of the European Union (EU) through the lens of its interpretation of the Danish Accession Act. Second, the SCDK delimited its own power within the Danish Constitution. In regard to the first point, it concluded that the judge-made principles of EU law developed after the latest amendments to the Accession Act, such as the general principle of non-discrimination on the grounds of age, were not binding. (...)

(...) The result of the approach is effectively a domestication of the question of the effect of EU law—now essentially a question of the limits of the Danish Accession Act. (...)

Using this approach, the legal status of the contested principle of non-discrimination is that of an unwritten principle without a clear legal basis in the Treaty. As such, it is not deemed to be covered by the Accession Act. Instead, the SCDK views it as judge-made and thus belonging to a quasi-legal realm outside the constitutionally binding sphere of EU law in Denmark. This reconstruction of the 'method' of the CJEU is obviously deeply troubling when seen from a supranational perspective. The consequence is that every single national constitution of Member States creates its own variation of EU law. That transforms EU law from an autonomous order into a residual order, the latter contingent on national legal practice and specific constitutional provisions. (…)

(…) The approach of supposedly avoiding politics, the formal Leitmotiv of the decision and its formalism, comes across as political. The main reason for this is that EU law cannot simply be reduced to an exterior phenomenon. Rather, it is part and parcel of the Danish law. It follows that switching it off, as is done in the Ajos case, even when justified under an interpretation of national law, necessarily entails applying one law by breaking another. That is not a viable path for any legal system taking supranational obligations seriously.

7.7 Discrimination on Grounds of Disability

Charter of Fundamental Rights of the European Union [2012] OJ C326/391

Article 26

Integration of persons with disabilities

The Union recognises and respects the right of persons with disabilities to benefit from measures designed to ensure their independence, social and occupational integration and participation in the life of the community.

In addition to race, religion, sexual orientation, and age, disability is another prohibited ground of discrimination under the Employment Equality Directive. Specific to the ground of disability, however, the protection from discrimination is set in the broader context of the EU's accession to the Convention on the Rights of Persons with Disabilities (CRPD) (discussed in Chapter 5), which provides additional impetus and guidance for EU action in this area, and recently further enhanced by the European Accessibility Act (see below). National implementation of anti-discrimination in the area of disability is nevertheless subject to horizontal EU law requirements, such as the compliance with the general principle of equal treatment even when increasing protection for workers with disability.[160]

As mentioned previously, the case law on the application of the Employment Equality Directive is, with the exception of age limited. Therefore there is only a handful of cases (but growing) interpreting the Directive in relation to discrimination on the ground of disability. One of the key issues raised in this line of case law has been the definition of 'disability' for the purposes of identifying those persons or groups of persons who can avail themselves of

---

[160] In Judgment of 9 March 2017 *Milkova v Izpalnitelen direktor na Agentsiata za privatizatsia i sledprivatizatsionen control*, C-406/15, ECLI:EU:C:2017:198 a Bulgarian law increased the protection from dismissal of workers with disabilities but the benefits were not available to civil servants with disabilities. This was incompatible with EU law.

the protection from discrimination guaranteed by the Employment Equality Directive, although it should be noted that discrimination by association is also covered.[161] In one of the first cases, *Chacón Navas*, the CJEU was asked whether sickness came within the remit of the term 'disability' within the meaning of the Employment Equality Directive.[162] The Court replied in the negative.

Judgment of 11 July 2006, *Chacón Navas v Eurest Colectividades SA*, C-13/05, ECLI:EU:C:2006:456

43. Directive 2000/78 aims to combat certain types of discrimination as regards employment and occupation. In that context, the concept of '**disability' must be understood as referring to a limitation which results in particular from physical, mental or psychological impairments and which hinders the participation of the person concerned in professional life**.

44. However, by using the concept of 'disability' in Article 1 of that directive, **the legislature deliberately chose a term which differs from 'sickness'**. The two concepts cannot therefore simply be treated as being the same.

45. Recital 16 in the preamble to Directive 2000/78 states that the 'provision of measures to accommodate the needs of disabled people at the workplace plays an important role in combating discrimination on grounds of disability'. The importance which the Community legislature attaches to measures for adapting the workplace to the disability demonstrates that it envisaged situations in which participation in professional life is hindered over a long period of time. **In order for the limitation to fall within the concept of 'disability', it must therefore be probable that it will last for a long time**.

46. There is nothing in Directive 2000/78 to suggest that workers are protected by the prohibition of discrimination on grounds of disability as soon as they develop any type of sickness.

Moreover, the CJEU stated, in line with Recital 17 of the Directive, that the Directive does not require the recruitment or preclude the dismissal of individuals 'who are not competent, capable and available to perform the essential functions of the post concerned, without prejudice to the obligation to provide reasonable accommodation for people with disabilities'.[163] According to Article 5 of the Directive, reasonable accommodation requires employers to take appropriate measures to enable a person with a disability to 'have access to, participate in, or advance in employment', unless such measures imposed a disproportionate burden on the employer.[164]

---

[161] *Coleman* (n 124) para 51.

[162] Judgment of 11 July 2006, *Chacón Navas v Eurest Colectividades SA*, C-13/05, ECLI:EU:C:2006:456. For criticism that the CJEU defined disability in a constrained manner associated with the outdated 'medical' model of disability see DL Hosking, 'A High Bar for EU Disability Rights' (2007) 36 Industrial Law Journal 228.

[163] *Chacón Navas* (n 162) para 49.

[164] In 2013, Italy was condemned in infringement proceedings for failing to implement Article 5 of the Employment Equality Directive properly into its national law. More specifically, the transposition was deficient because Italy did not impose an obligation on employers to provide reasonable accommodation to persons with disabilities. See Judgment of 4 July 2013, *Commission v Italy*, C-312/11, ECLI:EU:C:2013:446.

Taking account of the EU's accession to the CRPD, the Court refined its definition of disability in *HK Danmark*.[165] Notably, the CJEU recognized that illness can in some circumstances be covered by the concept of 'disability' for the purposes of the Employment Equality Directive. In addition, the Court found a reduction in working time an eligible measure of reasonable accommodation in the meaning of Article 5 of the Directive.

Judgment of 11 April 2013, *HK Danmark v Dansk almennyttigt Boligselskab and Dansk Arbejdsgiverforening*, C-335/11 and C-337/11, ECLI:EU:C:2013:222

28. It should be noted, as a preliminary point, that, by virtue of Article 216(2) TFEU, **where international agreements are concluded by the European Union they are binding on its institutions, and consequently they prevail over acts of the European Union** (...)

29. It should also be recalled that **the primacy of international agreements concluded by the European Union over instruments of secondary law means that those instruments must as far as possible be interpreted in a manner that is consistent with those agreements** (...)

30. It follows from Decision 2010/48 that the European Union has approved the UN Convention. The provisions of that convention are thus, from the time of its entry into force, **an integral part of the European Union legal order** (...)

32. It follows that **Directive 2000/78 must, as far as possible, be interpreted in a manner consistent with that convention**.

37. The UN Convention, which was ratified by the European Union by decision of 26 November 2009, in other words after the judgment in *Chacón Navas* had been delivered, acknowledges in recital (e) that 'disability is an evolving concept and that disability results from the interaction between persons with impairments and attitudinal and environmental barriers that hinders their full and effective participation in society on an equal basis with others'. Thus the second paragraph of Article 1 of the convention states that persons with disabilities include 'those who have long-term physical, mental, intellectual or sensory impairments which in interaction with various barriers may hinder their full and effective participation in society on an equal basis with others'.

38. Having regard to the considerations set out in paragraphs 28 to 32 above, **the concept of 'disability' must be understood as referring to a limitation which results in particular from physical, mental or psychological impairments which in interaction with various barriers may hinder the full and effective participation of the person concerned in professional life on an equal basis with other workers**.

39. In addition, it follows from the second paragraph of Article 1 of the UN Convention that the physical, mental or psychological **impairments must be 'long-term'**.

40. (...) it does not appear that Directive 2000/78 is intended to cover only disabilities that are congenital or result from accidents, to the exclusion of those caused

---

[165] Judgment of 11 April 2013, *HK Danmark v Dansk almennyttigt Boligselskab and Dansk Arbejdsgiverforening*, C-335/11 and C-337/11, ECLI:EU:C:2013:222.

by illness. **It would run counter to the very aim of the directive, which is to implement equal treatment, to define its scope by reference to the origin of the disability.**

41. It must therefore be concluded that if **a curable or incurable illness entails a limitation** which results in particular from physical, mental or psychological impairments which in interaction with various barriers may hinder the full and effective participation of the person concerned in professional life on an equal basis with other workers, and the limitation is a long-term one, **such an illness can be covered by the concept of 'disability' within the meaning of Directive 2000/78.**

42. On the other hand, an illness not entailing such a limitation is not covered by the concept of 'discrimination' within the meaning of Directive 2000/78. **Illness as such cannot be regarded as a ground in addition to those in relation to which Directive 2000/78 prohibits discrimination** (…)

54. (…) with respect to Directive 2000/78, [reasonable accommodation] must be understood as referring to the elimination of the various barriers that hinder the full and effective participation of persons with disabilities in professional life on an equal basis with other workers.

55. As recital 20 in the preamble to Directive 2000/78 and the second paragraph of Article 2 of the UN Convention envisage not only material but also organisational measures, and the term 'pattern' of working time must be understood as the rhythm or speed at which the work is done, it cannot be ruled out that **a reduction in working hours may constitute one of the accommodation measures** referred to in Article 5 of that directive.

The definition laid down in *HK Danmark* by the CJEU in light of the EU's accession to the CRPD was subsequently upheld in *Z*.[166] In this case the Court ruled out that the fact that a woman was missing a uterus and could therefore not give birth would constitute disability for the purposes of the Employment Equality Directive, as the condition in itself did not hinder or make it impossible for the woman to carry out her work. Moreover, the Court established that the CRPD did not have direct effect in EU law and could therefore not be relied upon to invalidate EU legislation such as the Employment Equality Directive. This had to do with the 'programmatic' nature of the CRPD which contained provisions that were not unconditional and sufficiently precise in order to have direct effect.[167]

In *Glatzel*, the applicant did not rely on the Employment Equality Directive (because it was not relevant to the dispute) but on his right to non-discrimination on the ground of disability as provided for in Article 21(1) of the Charter.[168] The dispute related to the validity of physical requirements for the granting of certain motor vehicle licences under EU law.[169] Mr Glatzel was visually impaired in one of his eyes to the extent that he was not able to pass the necessary medical examination prescribed by EU rules. He challenged the validity of those requirements on the ground that they discriminate against persons with a visual disability

---

[166] Judgment of 18 March 2014, *Z. v A Government department, The Board of management of a community school*, C-363/12, ECLI:EU:C:2014:159.

[167] Ibid, para 90.

[168] Judgment of 22 May 2014, *Glatzel v Freistaat Bayern*, C-356/12, ECLI:EU:C:2014:350.

[169] Directive 2006/126/EC of the European Parliament and of the Council on driving licences (Recast) [2006] OJ L403/18.

for whom it was more difficult to obtain a driving licence as a result. The CJEU replied that
even if the rules were discriminatory against Mr Glatzel, such indirect discrimination would
be justified in view of the objective to ensure road safety. The Court held that in laying down
the disputed requirements, the EU legislature did not impose disproportionate burdens on
persons with a visual disability.[170] The situation was not changed by reference to Article 26
of the Charter which mandates the integration of persons with disabilities but which, as a result of its wording and legal status as a principle, does not entail any specific measures being
taken and the provision does not as such have direct effect.

Judgment of 22 May 2014, *Glatzel v Freistaat Bayern*, C-356/12, ECLI:EU:C:2014:350

74. It must be recalled, as is clear from Article 52(5) and (7) of the Charter and the
Explanations relating to the Charter of Fundamental Rights (OJ 2007 C 303, p. 17)
concerning Articles 26 and 52(5) of the Charter, **that reliance on Article 26 thereof
before the court is allowed for the interpretation and review of the legality of legislative acts of the European Union which implement the principle** laid down in
that article, namely the integration of persons with disabilities.

75. As regards the implementation of that principle by Directive 2006/126, it is clear
in particular from the wording of recital 14 in the preamble thereto that '[s]pecific
provisions should be adopted to make it easier for physically disabled persons to
drive vehicles'. Likewise, Article 5(2) of that directive refers to the conditions for the
issue of driving licences to drivers with disabilities, in particular as regards the authorisation to drive adapted vehicles.

76. Thus, in so far as Directive 2006/126 is a legislative act of the European Union
implementing the principle contained in Article 26 of the Charter, the latter provision is intended to be applied to the case in the main proceedings.

77. Furthermore, **by virtue of the second sentence of Article 51(1) of the Charter, the
EU legislature is to observe and promote the application of the principles laid
down in it**. As regards the principle of the integration of persons with disabilities,
Article 26 of the Charter states that the Union is to recognise and respect the right
of persons with disabilities to benefit from measures designed to ensure their independence, social and occupational integration and participation in the life of the
community.

78. Therefore, although Article 26 of the Charter requires the European Union to respect and recognise the right of persons with disabilities to benefit from integration measures, **the principle enshrined by that article does not require the EU
legislature to adopt any specific measure. In order for that article to be fully effective, it must be given more specific expression in European Union or national
law. Accordingly, that article cannot by itself confer on individuals a subjective
right which they may invoke as such** (see, to that effect, as regards Article 27 of the
Charter, Case C-176/12 Association de mediation sociale EU:C:2014:2, paragraphs
45 and 47).

---

[170] *Glatzel* (n 168) para 72.

Finally, in *FOA* the CJEU was faced with the question of whether obesity falls within the scope of 'disability'.[171] The case concerned a public sector employee who was allegedly dismissed on the ground of being obese. The aggrieved employee claimed that the dismissal constituted discrimination against people with obesity and that the protection of the Employment Equality Directive for disabled persons should cover also this condition. The CJEU refused to recognize that obesity could represent a separate ground of discrimination but it entertained the possibility that under certain conditions, it could fall within the definition of 'disability' for the purposes of the Employment Equality Directive.

Judgment of 18 December 2014, *Fag og Arbejde (FOA) v Kommunernes Landsforening (KL)*, C-354/13, ECLI:EU:C:2014:2463

33. In that connection, it should be stated that no provision of the TEU or TFEU prohibits discrimination on grounds of obesity as such. In particular, neither Article 10 TFEU nor Article 19 TFEU makes reference to obesity.

34. As regards more specifically Article 19 TFEU, it follows from the case-law of the Court that that article contains only the rules governing the competencies of the EU and that, since it does not refer to discrimination on grounds of obesity as such, it cannot constitute a legal basis for measures of the Council of the European Union to combat such discrimination (...)

35. Nor does European Union secondary legislation lay down a general principle of non-discrimination on grounds of obesity as regards employment and occupation. In particular, Directive 2000/78 does not mention obesity as a ground for discrimination.

36. According to the case-law of the Court, **the scope of Directive 2000/78 should not be extended by analogy beyond the discrimination based on the grounds listed exhaustively in Article 1** thereof (...)

54. (...) concept of 'disability' must be understood as referring **not only to the impossibility** of exercising a professional activity, **but also to a hindrance** to the exercise of such an activity. Any other interpretation would be incompatible with the objective of that directive (...)

55. Moreover, it would run counter to the very aim of the directive, which is to implement equal treatment, to define its scope by reference to the origin of the disability (...)

58. It should be noted that obesity does not in itself constitute a 'disability' within the meaning of Directive 2000/78, on the ground that, by its nature, **it does not necessarily entail the existence of a limitation** (...)

59. However, in the event that, under given circumstances, **the obesity of the worker concerned entails a limitation** which results in particular from physical, mental or psychological impairments that in interaction with various barriers may hinder the full and effective participation of that person in professional life on an equal basis with other workers, and the limitation is a long-term one, **obesity can**

---

[171] Judgment of 18 December 2014, *Fag og Arbejde (FOA) v Kommunernes Landsforening (KL)*, C-354/13, ECLI:EU:C:2014:2463.

> **be covered by the concept of 'disability'** within the meaning of Directive 2000/78
> (see, to that effect, judgment in HK Danmark, EU:C:2013:222, paragraph 41).
> 60. Such would be the case, in particular, **if the obesity of the worker hindered his
> full and effective participation in professional life on an equal basis with other
> workers** on account of reduced mobility or the onset, in that person, of medical
> conditions preventing him from carrying out his work or causing discomfort when
> carrying out his professional activity.

The CJEU confirmed its earlier case law when it held that not only the impossibility of a professional activity but also its hindrance falls within the concept of 'disability', regardless of the origin of the disability. This in principle allows the treatment of obesity as a disability, provided that it complies with the criteria of the definition of disability established by the Court previously.[172] Since the finding of disability for the purposes of the Employment Equality Directive for a given condition is not affected by the kind of accommodating measures taken by employers, it was irrelevant in the case that the public authority employing the alleging individual did not accommodate his obesity when he was employed.

Another important piece of EU legislation was adopted in 2019, namely Directive 2019/882/EU on the accessibility requirements for products and services[173]—in short, the European Accessibility Act. This Directive harmonizes the accessibility requirements for products and services and therewith vastly improved the previously unsatisfactory state of European law on disability. The proposal for the act was motivated by the obligation the EU and its Member States had incurred under the United Nations CRPD. Article 3 thereof refers to accessibility as one of the core principles of the CRPD that should be considered in relation to the enjoyment of the rights and freedoms included in the Convention. Article 9 CRPD obliges the EU and the Member States, each to the extent of their competences, as parties to the Convention, to take appropriate measures to ensure accessibility in a wide range of areas. Despite the clear link with the prohibition of discrimination based on disability as well as the social policy dimension of the subject matter, the Accessibility Act is not based on Article 19 TFEU, but on Article 114 TFEU on harmonization of laws in the internal market. The emphasis on the functioning of the internal market can unambiguously be discovered in the first article, and while the accession to the CRPD is referred to multiple times in the recital,[174] no reference to 'discrimination' or 'equal treatment' is made. The purpose was to present the Act as not only beneficial to persons with disabilities, but also to businesses, which can reduce costs of regulatory compliance thanks to a convergence of accessibility standards.

A wide range of products and services comes within the scope of the Act, including for example self-service terminals, computer hardware systems, passenger transport services, and e-commerce services (Article 2). The definition of 'person with disability' has been copied

---

[172] The precedent was upheld in the Judgment of 18 January 2018, *Ruiz Conejero v Ferroser Servicios Auxiliares SA and Ministerio Fiscal*, C-270/16, ECLI:EU:C:2018:17, para 30. In this case, the aggrieved individual's obesity was recognized as disability under Spanish national law, a fact that, however, was not prejudicial to the question whether the EU law definition of 'disability' similarly covered the situation of the person in the domestic proceedings. In its reply to the preliminary question, the CJEU told the national court to apply the EU law definition of disability based on the judgment in *FOA* to establish whether the case falls within the scope of Directive 2000/78.

[173] Directive 2019/882/EU of the European Parliament and of the Council on the accessibility requirements for products and services [2019] OJ L151/70.

[174] See Recitals 3, 5, 12, 13, 14, 15, 16, 17, and 50.

from the CJEU's case law (Article 3(1)). The content of the Act itself is very technical and contains detailed instructions and obligations for manufacturers, importers, distributors and service providers in several Annexes. Given the nature of the imposed requirements, the transposition period proceeds in stages, with Member States having to adopt the appropriate measures by June 2022 and having to apply them by June 2025. Logically, no case law has emerged on the Accessibility Act as of yet.

Directive 2019/882/EU of the European Parliament and of the Council on the accessibility requirements for products and services [2019] OJ L151/70

(2) The demand for accessible products and services is high and the number of persons with disabilities is projected to increase significantly. An environment where products and services are more accessible allows for a more inclusive society and facilitates independent living for persons with disabilities. In this context, it should be borne in mind that the prevalence of disability in the Union is higher among women than among men.

(3) This Directive defines persons with disabilities in line with the United Nations Convention on the Rights of Persons with Disabilities, adopted on 13 December 2006 (UN CRPD), to which the Union has been a Party since 21 January 2011 and which all Member States have ratified. The UN CRPD states that persons with disabilities 'include those who have long-term physical, mental, intellectual or sensory impairments which in interaction with various barriers may hinder their full and effective participation in society on an equal basis with others'. This Directive promotes full and effective equal participation by improving access to mainstream products and services that, through their initial design or subsequent adaptation, address the particular needs of persons with disabilities.

Article 1

Subject matter

The purpose of this Directive is to **contribute to the proper functioning of the internal market** by approximating the laws, regulations and administrative provisions of the Member States as regards accessibility requirements for certain products and services by, in particular, **eliminating and preventing barriers to the free movement of products and services covered by this Directive arising from divergent accessibility requirements** in the Member States.

Article 6

Free movement

Member States shall not impede, for reasons related to accessibility requirements, the making available on the market in their territory of products or the provision of services in their territory that comply with this Directive.

Article 28

Working Group

The Commission shall establish a **working group** consisting of representatives of market surveillance authorities, authorities responsible for compliance of services and relevant stakeholders, including **representatives of persons with disabilities organisations**.

8

Human Rights in EU Migration Laws and Policies

8.1 Introduction

Migration governance, just as many other policy areas nowadays, is multi-layered and consists of a patchwork of national, EU, and international laws and policies. The present chapter looks at the EU level of migration governance in Europe and its borders. It analyses the tools used as part of EU migration policy and argues that these are very much focused on control which has negative implications for the human rights of migrants. While the notion of migration covers both immigration and emigration, this chapter focuses on the laws and policies regulating immigration into the EU and briefly touches upon third-country nationals' (TCNs) rights of residence and movement within the EU.

8.2 Fundamentals of EU Migration and Asylum Policy

The EU's current status as a major international player in migration governance has become possible only after the development of the relevant competences on migration and asylum. The original Treaty of Rome included no provisions on migration other than those ushering in the free movement of workers among EU Member States. TCNs were for a long time a domestic matter for the Member States. This was not only due to the economic focus of the EU project; it was a positive choice to exclude TCNs from internal free movement that is enjoyed by all EU nationals and their family members (which can include TCNs).[1] Today the free movement of EU Member State nationals has been incorporated into the notion of EU citizenship which—contrary to what the name might suggest—does not create a new and separate bond of nationality between the EU and the citizen but refers to a collection of rights, duties, and political participation stemming from EU law.[2] When a core group of Member States teamed up to abolish internal border controls under the Schengen agreements, drawing in immigration and asylum policies regarding TCNs was considered a necessary implication. In the words of Costello, the view that internal free movement requires protection from outside(rs) 'provided the institutional rationalisation for much of the activity in the admissions field under the Schengen arrangements and continues to be a feature of EU policy discourse on asylum and migration today'.[3]

---

[1] E Guild, 'The Europeanisation of Europe's Asylum Policy' (2006) 18 International Journal of Refugee Law 630, 633.
[2] C Costello, *The Human Rights of Migrants and Refugees in European Law* (Oxford University Press 2016) 14.
[3] Ibid, 15.

The European Union and Human Rights. Jan Wouters and Michal Ovádek, Oxford University Press (2021). © Jan Wouters and Michal Ovádek. DOI: 10.1093/oso/9780198814177.003.0008

> ## G Malmersjo and M Remáč, 'Schengen and the management of the EU's external borders', European Parliamentary Research Service Briefing, April 2016
>
> The 'Schengen acquis' was originally created outside the European legal framework. The Schengen acquis is built on the 1985 Agreement on the gradual abolition of checks at their common borders (Schengen Agreement). This international agreement was signed outside the EU framework and proposed a gradual abolition of border checks at the common borders between the five contracting parties. The Agreement proposed harmonisation in various areas such as visa policies or strengthening cooperation in police or judicial matters. In 1990, the Agreement was amended by the Convention implementing the Schengen Agreement. The Convention entered into force in 1995, abolishing the internal borders among the contracting countries and creating a single external border with a single set of applicable rules. (…)

The first step towards developing a migration and asylum policy at the EU level was taken with the Maastricht Treaty when the so-called third pillar was created, including a commitment that the policies shall comply with the European Convention on Human Rights (ECHR). Yet, the workings of this pillar were highly disputable, as they lacked parliamentary oversight, judicial control, and transparency. The link between internal free movement and asylum and migration policies came to the fore with the Treaty of Amsterdam. Persistent criticism against the incoherence of the policies at the time resulted in the insertion of migration and asylum into the EU realm, via the elegant solution 'to maintain and develop the Union as an Area of Freedom, Security and Justice (AFSJ), in which the free movement of persons is assured in conjunction with appropriate measures with respect to external border controls, asylum, immigration and the prevention and combating of crime'. The AFSJ was further developed in the programmes of the European Council Summits in Tampere (1999–2004), The Hague (2004–2009), and Stockholm (2010–2014). Today, the core of the AFSJ is set out in Article 3 of the Treaty on European Union (TEU) and Article 67 of the Treaty on the Functioning of the European Union (TFEU).

> ## Consolidated version of the Treaty on European Union [2012] OJ C326/13
>
> ### Article 3
> 2. The Union shall offer its citizens **an area of freedom, security and justice without internal frontiers**, in which the free movement of persons is ensured in conjunction with **appropriate measures with respect to external border controls, asylum, immigration** and the prevention and combating of crime.

> ## Consolidated version of the Treaty on the Functioning of the European Union [2012] OJ C326/47
>
> ### *Article 67*
>
> 1. The Union shall constitute an area of freedom, security and justice **with respect for fundamental rights** and the different legal systems and traditions of the Member States.
> 2. It shall ensure the absence of internal border controls for persons and shall frame a **common policy on asylum, immigration and external border control**, based on **solidarity between Member States**, which is **fair towards third-country nationals**. For the purpose of this Title, stateless persons shall be treated as third-country nationals.
> 3. The Union shall endeavour to ensure a high level of security through measures to prevent and combat crime, racism and xenophobia, and through measures for coordination and cooperation between police and judicial authorities and other competent authorities, as well as through the mutual recognition of judgments in criminal matters and, if necessary, through the approximation of criminal laws.
> 4. The Union shall facilitate access to justice, in particular through the principle of mutual recognition of judicial and extrajudicial decisions in civil matters.

The Treaty of Lisbon introduced a number of important changes to the EU landscape which generated an environment considerably more favourable for the defence of the rights of migrants. With the entry into force of the Treaty, the European Parliament (EP) became a co-legislator for a number of matters which were originally part of the third pillar, such as legal migration, visa lists, and most criminal law and policing measures. In addition, Member States now lack a 'veto power', as the Council is no longer required to act unanimously in this field (except for a few cases such as social security for migrants) [4]. Most importantly, the Treaty enabled Court of Justice of the European Union (CJEU) jurisdiction in the AFSJ, as a result of which the Court may give preliminary rulings to any national court or tribunal on the validity of EU measures in the AFSJ,[5] and made the EU Charter legally binding on the EU. The impact of these preliminary references to the CJEU in asylum and migration matters will become clear throughout the chapter.

8.3 Migrants' Rights

According to the Universal Declaration of Human Rights (UDHR), all individuals are entitled to respect for their human rights, regardless of their legal or residency status.[6] The following overview also relates in principle to all migrants travelling to the EU, although some variation in applicable rights stems from the different status of migrants (asylum seekers, refugees, irregular migrants, and so on). In all cases, Member States are entitled to offer more protection than EU law. In addition, it should be pointed out that in theory, the rights enshrined in the Charter contain no territorial delimitation and could be exercised also outside the territory of

---

[4] Article 48 TFEU.
[5] Article 19 TEU and Article 267 TFEU.
[6] Universal Declaration Human Rights (adopted 10 December 1948) GA Res 217 A, Article 1 and 2.

the EU.[7] In practice, 'a sufficiently close link' with the EU might need to be established,[8] and it has been asserted that the Charter's extraterritorial application will need to be examined on a case-by-case basis, as the EU legal system might pose 'autonomous requirements' independent of the concept of jurisdiction in general international law or human rights law.[9]

A. Right to life and human dignity

> ### Charter of Fundamental Rights of the European Union [2012] OJ C326/391
>
> ---
>
> #### Article 2
>
> #### Right to life
> 1. Everyone has the right to life.
> 2. No one shall be condemned to the death penalty, or executed.

At first sight, the right to life may seem somewhat redundant when it comes to the EU, as all the Member States have abolished the death penalty (which is prohibited) and the use of lethal force in law enforcement is severely circumscribed. Nonetheless, the right to life, as enshrined in Article 2(1) of the Charter and Article 2 ECHR, also entails the prohibition to use unreasonable force which can affect how the entry of migrants is restricted by authorities. It may also translate into a duty to render assistance to persons in distress (in particular at sea), a point debated by international law scholars.[10]

> ### I Papanicolopulu, 'The Duty to Rescue at Sea, in Peacetime and in War: A General Overview' (2016) 98 International Review of the Red Cross 491
>
> ---
>
> (...) the duty to rescue people in distress at sea can be considered as another side of the right to life, which every individual enjoys under human rights law. The right to life is codified in various human rights treaties – for example, Article 6 of the International

---

[7] Responsibility for extraterritorial human rights violations is also possible under the ECHR. The leading case, *Al Skeini v United Kingdom*, App no 55721/07, 7 July 2011, established as one of the decisive criteria 'the exercise of physical power and control over the person in question' (para 136) which is of particular relevance to migration situations where EU Member States might be acting outside their own territory to control or prevent migration (for example naval missions in international waters or the territorial waters of a third country such as Libya).

[8] Judgment of 30 April 1996, *Boukhalfa v Federal Republic of Germany*, C-214/94, ECLI:EU:C:1996:174.

[9] V Moreno-Lax and C Costello, 'The Extraterritorial Application of the EU Charter of Fundamental Rights: From Territoriality to Facticity, the Effectiveness Model' in S Peers and others (eds), *The EU Charter of Fundamental Rights: A Commentary* (Hart Publishing 2014), 1660 and 1678. Although for other reasons, the extraterritoriality of the Charter has not been supported in a case whose factual situation created an opportunity in this regard. See Judgment of 7 March 2017, *X and X v État belge*, C-638/16 PPU, ECLI:EU:C:2017:173.

[10] S Trevisanut, 'Is There a Right to be Rescued at Sea? A Constructive View' (2014) 4 Questions of International Law 3.

Covenant on Civil and Political Rights (ICCPR) and Article 2 of the European Convention for the Protection of Human Rights and Fundamental Freedoms (ECHR).

(...) Negative obligations require the State to abstain from taking human life. Positive obligations include both substantial obligations and procedural obligations. (...)

Positive duties, both substantial and procedural, are particularly relevant in the case of people at risk of losing their lives at sea. In the case of people taking to sea, in fact, loss of life is a real risk. States should take measures to at least minimize the phenomenon, if not avoid it. (...)

(...) [in litigation, there is also a] need to establish that the individuals whose right to life was at issue were under the jurisdiction of the defendant State. While the concept of jurisdiction has been progressively expanded to include both de jure and de facto exercise of power over individuals, there is still the need to prove that individuals were, somehow, either under the de jure jurisdiction of a State or under the de facto control of State organs. In a case in which a vessel navigating on the high seas is not rescued by other passing vessels, it would be difficult to establish a sufficiently strong link between the vessel in need and the potentially rescuing vessel that would reach the threshold of jurisdiction under human rights law. Furthermore, if the vessel were a private vessel, it would still be necessary to establish the requisite jurisdictional link between it and the flag State. (...)

Another foundational human right which has been more clearly identified as applying in the context of EU migration governance is human dignity. Article 1 of the Charter states that '[h]uman dignity is inviolable. It must be respected and protected.' The provision has been invoked in the context of a dispute concerning whether national authorities can examine the sexual orientation of asylum seekers.[11] Human dignity in conjunction with the prohibition on inhuman and degrading treatment (Article 4 of the Charter) applies also more generally throughout migration law, requiring that at all times migrants are treated in accordance with these minimum guarantees from which no derogation is possible (they are absolute).

Judgment of 16 February 2017, *C. K. and Others v Republika Slovenija*, C-578/16 PPU, ECLI:EU:C:2017:127

59. (...) in accordance with the settled case-law of the Court, the rules of secondary EU law, including the provisions of the Dublin III Regulation, must be interpreted and applied in a manner consistent with the fundamental rights guaranteed by the Charter (...). **The prohibition of inhuman or degrading treatment or punishment**, laid down in Article 4 of the Charter, is, in that regard, of fundamental importance, to the extent that it is absolute in that it is closely linked to respect for human dignity, which is the subject of Article 1 of the Charter (...)

---

[11] Judgment of 25 January 2018, *F v Bevándorlási és Állampolgársági Hivatal*, C-473/16, ECLI:EU:C:2018:36, para 35.

Recently, the issue of human dignity surfaced in the context of refugees having been denied their 'most basic needs'. In *Jawo*,[12] the CJEU acknowledged that a situation of extreme material poverty that does not allow the asylum seeker to meet his most basic needs puts that person 'in a state of degradation incompatible with human dignity'.[13] In another seminal case, the Grand Chamber ruled on a preliminary question on the interpretation of Article 20 of Directive 2013/33/EU (on standards for the reception of applicants for international protection, see below under Section 8.3.B) that provides circumstances under which Member States may reduce or withdraw certain material reception conditions. The applicant, Mr Haqbin, had been temporarily excluded from such conditions by the Belgian Federal agency for reception of asylum seekers by way of sanction for breaching rules of the accommodation centre and exhibiting seriously violent behaviour. The Court replied that Member States are required to guarantee continuously and without interruption a dignified standard of living and that the authorities responsible for the reception of asylum seekers must provide the material reception conditions guaranteeing that standard of living, in compliance with the respect for human dignity. Sanctions that have the effect of depriving asylum seekers from the possibility to meet their most basic needs are incompatible with Article 1 of the Charter of Fundamental rights.

Judgment of 12 November 2019, *Zubair Haqbin v Federaal Agentschap voor de opvang van asielzoekers*, C-233/18, ECLI:EU:C:2019:956

45. (...) in accordance with Article 20(5) of Directive 2013/33, any sanction within the meaning of Article 20(4) thereof must be objective, impartial, reasoned and proportionate to the particular situation of the applicant and must, **under all circumstances, ensure access to health care and a dignified standard of living** for the applicant.

46. With regard specifically to the requirement to ensure a dignified standard of living, it is apparent from recital 35 of Directive 2013/33 that the directive seeks to **ensure full respect for human dignity** and to promote the application, inter alia, of **Article 1 of the Charter of Fundamental Rights** and has to be implemented accordingly. In that regard, respect for human dignity within the meaning of that article **requires the person concerned not finding himself or herself in a situation of extreme material poverty that does not allow that person to meet his or her most basic needs such as a place to live, food, clothing and personal hygiene, and that undermines his or her physical or mental health or puts that person in a state of degradation incompatible with human dignity** (see, to that effect, judgment of 19 March 2019, Jawo, C-163/17, EU:C:2019:218, paragraph 92 and the case-law cited).

47. A **sanction** that is imposed exclusively on the basis of one of the reasons mentioned in Article 20(4) of Directive 2013/33 and consists in the **withdrawal, even if only a temporary one, of the full set of material reception conditions or of material reception conditions relating to housing, food or clothing would be irreconcilable**

---

[12] Judgment of 19 March 2019, *Abubacarr Jawo v Bundesrepublik Deutschland*, C-163/17, ECLI:EU:C:2019:218. For the analysis of this judgment with regard to the principle of mutual trust, see Ch 4.

[13] Ibid, para 92.

> with the requirement, arising from the third sentence of Article 20(5) of the directive, to ensure a dignified standard of living for the applicant, since it would preclude the applicant from being allowed to meet his or her most basic needs such as those mentioned in the previous paragraph.
>
> 48. Such a sanction would also amount to a failure to comply with the proportionality requirement under the second sentence of Article 20(5) of Directive 2013/33, in so far as even the most stringent sanctions, whose objective is to punish, in criminal law, the breaches or behaviour referred to in Article 20(4) of the directive, cannot deprive the applicant of the possibility of meeting his or her most basic needs.
>
> 49. That consideration is not called into question by the fact, mentioned by the referring court, that an applicant excluded by way of sanction from an accommodation centre in Belgium is said to be provided, upon the imposition of that sanction, with a list of private centres for the homeless likely to host him or her. (…)

B. Prohibition on arbitrary detention

One of the areas of migration law and policy of the EU and especially its Member States which continues to spark controversy is the detention of migrants: individuals convicted of no criminal offence but who may be detained during their asylum application or pending their removal from the host country. The relevant EU law governing the subject can be found in Directive 2008/115/EC ('Returns Directive'),[14] Directive 2013/33/EU ('Reception Directive'),[15] and Regulation (EU) No 604/2013 ('Dublin III Regulation').[16] In general, these instruments can be said to attempt to limit the use of detention as an instrument of migration governance by Member States. At the same time, they do not make detention unlawful as a matter of principle, and a number of Member States make use of the possibility to detain migrants, including asylum seekers. As also demonstrated by the *Haqbin* case,[17] EU law guarantees detained asylum seekers and TCNs earmarked for removal from the country a minimum standard of conditions which must in any case respect human dignity and the prohibition on inhuman and degrading treatment. At the same time, EU rules on detention also typically contain exceptions allowing for stricter treatment of detained migrants, as exemplified by Article 10 of the Reception Directive.

---

[14] Directive 2008/115/EC of the European Parliament and of the Council on common standards and procedures in Member States for returning illegally staying third-country nationals [2008] OJ L348/98.

[15] Directive 2013/33/EU of the European Parliament and of the Council laying down standards for the reception of applicants for international protection [2013] OJ L180/96.

[16] Regulation (EU) No 604/2013 of the European Parliament and of the Council establishing the criteria and mechanisms for determining the Member State responsible for examining an application for international protection lodged in one of the Member States by a third-country national or a stateless person [2013] OJ L180/31.

[17] Judgment of 12 November 2019, *Zubair Haqbin v Federaal Agentschap voor de opvang van asielzoekers*, C-233/18, ECLI:EU:C:2019:956.

Regulation (EU) No 604/2013 of the European Parliament and of the Council establishing the criteria and mechanisms for determining the Member State responsible for examining an application for international protection lodged in one of the Member States by a third-country national or a stateless person [2013] OJ L180/31

Article 28

Detention

1. Member States **shall not hold a person in detention for the sole reason** that he or she is subject to the procedure established by this Regulation.
2. **When there is a significant risk of absconding, Member States may detain** the person concerned in order to secure transfer procedures in accordance with this Regulation, on the basis of an individual assessment and only in so far as detention is proportional and other less coercive alternative measures cannot be applied effectively.
3. **Detention shall be for as short a period as possible** and shall be for no longer than the time reasonably necessary to fulfil the required administrative procedures with due diligence until the transfer under this Regulation is carried out.

Directive 2013/33/EU of the European Parliament and of the Council laying down standards for the reception of applicants for international protection [2013] OJ L180/96

Article 10

Conditions of detention

1. Detention of applicants shall take place, as a rule, in **specialised detention facilities**. Where a Member State cannot provide accommodation in a specialised detention facility and is obliged to resort to prison accommodation, the detained applicant shall be kept **separately from ordinary prisoners** and the detention conditions provided for in this Directive shall apply.

   As far as possible, detained applicants shall be kept separately from other third-country nationals who have not lodged an application for international protection.

   When applicants cannot be detained separately from other third-country nationals, the Member State concerned shall ensure that the detention conditions provided for in this Directive are applied.

2. Detained applicants shall have **access to open-air spaces**.
3. Member States shall ensure that persons representing the United Nations High Commissioner for Refugees (UNHCR) **have the possibility to communicate with and visit applicants** in conditions that respect privacy. That possibility shall also apply to an organisation which is working on the territory of the Member State concerned on behalf of UNHCR pursuant to an agreement with that Member State.

4. Member States shall ensure that family members, legal advisers or counsellors and persons representing relevant non-governmental organisations recognised by the Member State concerned have the possibility to communicate with and visit applicants in conditions that respect privacy. **Limits to access to the detention facility may be imposed only where, by virtue of national law, they are objectively necessary for the security, public order or administrative management of the detention facility,** provided that access is not thereby severely restricted or rendered impossible.

5. Member States shall ensure that applicants in detention are systematically **provided with information** which explains the rules applied in the facility and sets out their rights and obligations in a language which they understand or are reasonably supposed to understand. Member States may derogate from this obligation in duly justified cases and for a reasonable period which shall be as short as possible, in the event that the applicant is detained at a border post or in a transit zone. (...)

All EU legislation in essence conveys that detention should be used as a measure of last resort. Some EU Member States, such as Hungary or the Czech Republic, have, however, aroused suspicion that detention is used even where other, less intrusive measures were available. The CJEU has had the opportunity to comment on the use of detention in the context of transfers of asylum seekers (on account of a serious risk of absconding) between Member States under the Dublin Regulation. The Court held that it is not sufficient for Member States' authorities to detain asylum seekers on the basis of administrative practice or national case law—due to the high protection entailed in the relevant EU law provisions, and having regard to the conditions for limiting fundamental rights enshrined in Article 52(1) of the Charter, detention requires a basis in statutory law of general application which specifies the objective criteria determining the risk of absconding justifying detention under Article 28(2) of the Dublin III Regulation.

Judgment of 15 March 2017, *Policie ČR, Krajské ředitelství policie Ústeckého kraje, odbor cizinecké policie v Al Chodor*, C-528/15, ECLI:EU:C:2017:213

24. **The referring court asks**, in essence, whether Article 2(n) and Article 28(2) of the Dublin III Regulation, read in conjunction, must be interpreted as requiring Member States to **establish, in a national law, objective criteria underlying the reasons for believing that an applicant** for international protection ('the applicant') who is subject to a transfer procedure **may abscond**, and whether the absence of those criteria in a national law leads to the inapplicability of Article 28(2) of that regulation.

36. As regards the objective pursued by Article 2(n) of the Dublin III Regulation, read in conjunction with Article 28(2) thereof, it must be recalled that, by authorising the detention of an applicant in order to secure transfer procedures pursuant to that regulation where there is a significant risk of absconding, **those provisions provide for a limitation on the exercise of the fundamental right to liberty enshrined in Article 6 of the Charter** (...).

37. In that regard, it is clear from **Article 52(1) of the Charter that any limitation on the exercise of that right must be provided for by law and must respect the essence of that**

right and be subject to the principle of proportionality. In so far as the Charter contains rights which correspond to rights guaranteed by the ECHR, Article 52(3) of the Charter provides that the meaning and scope of those rights must be the same as those laid down by that convention, while specifying that EU law may provide more extensive protection. For the purpose of interpreting Article 6 of the Charter, **account must therefore be taken of Article 5 of the ECHR as the minimum threshold of protection**.

38. According to the European Court of Human Rights, any deprivation of liberty must be lawful not only in the sense that it must have a legal basis in national law, but also that lawfulness concerns the quality of the law and **implies that a national law authorising the deprivation of liberty must be sufficiently accessible, precise and foreseeable** in its application in order **to avoid all risk of arbitrariness** (see, to that effect, judgment of the European Court of Human Rights of 21 October 2013, Del Río Prada v Spain, CE:ECHR:2013:1021JUD004275009, §125).

40. It follows from the foregoing that the **detention of applicants**, constituting a serious interference with those applicants' right to liberty, **is subject to compliance with strict safeguards**, namely the presence of a legal basis, clarity, predictability, accessibility and protection against arbitrariness.

43. Taking account of the purpose of the provisions concerned, and in the light of the high level of protection which follows from their context, **only a provision of general application could meet the requirements of clarity, predictability, accessibility and, in particular, protection against arbitrariness**.

44. The adoption of **rules of general application provides the necessary guarantees in so far as such wording sets out the limits of the flexibility of those authorities** in the assessment of the circumstances of each specific case in a manner that is binding and known in advance. Furthermore, (...) criteria established by a binding provision are best placed for the external direction of the discretion of those authorities for the purposes of protecting applicants against arbitrary deprivations of liberty.

45. It follows that Article 2(n) and Article 28(2) of the Dublin III Regulation, read in conjunction, must be interpreted as requiring that the **objective criteria underlying the reasons for believing that an applicant may abscond must be established in a binding provision of general application**. In any event, **settled case-law confirming a consistent administrative practice** on the part of the Foreigners Police Section, such as in the main proceedings in the present case, **cannot suffice**.

46. **In the absence of those criteria in such a provision**, as in the main proceedings in the present case, **the detention must be declared unlawful**, which leads to the inapplicability of Article 28(2) of the Dublin III Regulation.

Following a recent study, the Council of Europe has decided to carry out a codifying exercise to draft a detailed set of immigration detention rules based on current international and regional human rights standards. The study found that existing international instruments dealing with administrative detention of immigrants are 'scattered, inadequate, inconsistent and not effective' insofar as they concern this question. As a consequence, there is uncertainty as to what extent instruments are applicable to certain situations involving immigrants or can be applied by analogy.[18] For instance, whether the restriction of movement of

---

[18] This area is studied notably by the Committee of experts on administrative detention of migrants which is part of the Council of Europe European Committee on Legal Co-operation. See <http://www.coe.int/en/web/cdcj/activities/administrative-detention-migrants> accessed 14 August 2020.

asylum seekers can be qualified as detention has been contested in the past particularly in the context of transit zones at airports[19] and currently in the context of transit zones at external borders,[20] in addition to the practice of some EU Member States to restrict the movement of asylum seekers to a specific part in their territory or district. The restriction of movement in the context of initial reception gains particular importance in the context of 'hotspots' established in Greece and Italy (see below).

The risk of arbitrary detention is particularly high when countries face a sudden massive influx of asylum seekers, as was the case in the EU in 2015. The human rights community has therefore tried to identify and encourage alternatives to detention in view of the fact that it should represent a measure of last resort. The EU Agency for Fundamental Rights (FRA) drafted a short brief outlining such possibilities. The Agency argued that alternatives to detention are not only less detrimental to the human rights of migrants (in particular vulnerable persons) but also that they are more cost-effective for states to implement. As alternatives to detention also restrict migrants' rights, regard must still be had to their compliance with the conditions governing limitations on fundamental rights within the EU.

EU Agency for Fundamental Rights, 'Alternatives to detention for asylum seekers and people in return procedures', 9 October 2015

(...) According to EU law, as well as Article 5 of the European Convention of Human Rights, deprivation of liberty for immigration-related reasons can only be used as a measure of last resort. An assessment needs to be made in each individual case to determine whether all the preconditions required to prevent arbitrary detention are fulfilled. Under Article 8 of the Reception Conditions Directive 2013/33/EU and Article 15 of the Return Directive 2008/115/EC, detention must not be used when less intrusive measures are sufficient to achieve the legitimate objective pursued. Most of the wide array of alternatives to detention imply some restrictions on freedom of movement and/or other fundamental rights. Any restrictions to these rights must be in conformity with Article 52(1) of the EU Charter of Fundamental Rights. This means that limitations must be provided for by law, must genuinely meet objectives of general interest recognised by the Union or the need to protect the rights and freedoms of others, respect the essence of the right, and be proportionate. Alternatives to detention must, therefore, be distinguished from unconditional release from detention or unrestricted placement in open facilities. (...)

Obligation to surrender passports or travel documents
This obligation may be imposed alone or together with other alternatives, such as the duty to stay in a particular location or area. It is a soft measure that essentially serves to

---

[19] *Amuur v France*, App no 19776/92, 25 June 1996.

[20] With regard to the Röszke transit zone at the Serbian-Hungarian border, see ongoing Joined Cases C-924/19 PPU and C-925/19 PPU, *FMS and Others v Országos Idegenrendészeti Főigazgatóság Dél-alföldi Regionális Igazgatóság*. Advocate General Pikamäe already classified the transit zone as 'detention' in his Opinion (ECLI:EU:C:2020:294), see below.

ensure that valid identity and travel documents are not lost or destroyed during the time required to prepare the return and removal process.

Residence restrictions

Such restrictions impose the duty of remaining at a particular address or residing within a specific geographical area, often combined with regular reporting requirements. The designated places can be open or semi-open facilities run by the government or non-governmental organizations (NGOs), as well as hotels, hostels or private addresses. The regime imposed can vary, but people generally have to be present at the designated location at certain times, while absences are usually only allowed with a well-founded justification.

Release on bail and provision of sureties by third parties

In the context of criminal law, it is not uncommon to allow the release of a detained person on condition of bail, which will be forfeited if the person does not report to the authorities. Release based on financial guarantees is infrequently used in asylum and pre-removal proceedings, partly because it is assumed that many asylum seekers or third-country nationals in return procedures would not have the necessary means to put up bail.

Regular reporting to the authorities

This alternative obliges people to report to the police or immigration authorities at regular intervals, and is one of the more frequent alternatives to detention found in national legislation. Reporting duties on a daily, bi-weekly, weekly or even less frequent basis may also be imposed as an additional requirement to the obligation to reside in a specified area or location.

Placement in open facilities with caseworker support

This is an innovative alternative to detention that combines classical social work with time spent at designated places. Asylum seekers or people in return procedures are placed in open facilities and provided with individual coaches or counsellors to inform and advise them about their situation and options. This form of alternative was established following evidence that compliance with a return decision depends on the level of trust the person affected by the decision has in the authorities of the host country. Such trust is created through individual counselling and contacts with external actors, such as NGOs.

Electronic monitoring

Electronic monitoring or tagging is primarily used in the context of criminal law. Its use as a substitute for immigration detention is limited. Electronic monitoring is the most intrusive of the various alternatives to detention, as it substantially interferes with a person's right to privacy, restricts freedom of movement and can have a negative impact on their dignity. It can also lead to discrimination through the potential association of people wearing an electronic device with criminals.

C. Right to asylum

Charter of Fundamental Rights of the European Union [2012] OJ C326/391

Article 18

Right to asylum

The **right to asylum** shall be guaranteed **with due respect for** the rules of the **Geneva Convention** of 28 July 1951 and the Protocol of 31 January 1967 relating to the status of refugees **and in accordance with the Treaty** on European Union and the Treaty on the Functioning of the European Union (hereinafter referred to as 'the Treaties').

The Refugee Convention and Protocol are one of the few international instruments explicitly mentioned in the Charter and the EU Treaties. These references helpfully reaffirm the importance of the commitment to the right to non-refoulement (see below). Nevertheless, the references are to some extent puzzling in the context of the right to asylum as the Refugee Convention does not in fact confer explicitly such an individual right on asylum seekers. On the other hand, there is precedent for a right to asylum in Article 14 of the Universal Declaration of Human Rights.[21] Despite lacking an addressee (who has the right to asylum?), it has been argued that Article 18 of the Charter constitutes a subjective and enforceable right of individuals under EU law.

MT Gil-Bazo, 'The Charter of Fundamental Rights of the European Union and the Right to be Granted Asylum in the Union's Law' (2008) 27 Refugee Survey Quarterly 33

(...) The provision also raises issues insofar as it makes reference to the United Nations Convention relating to the Status of Refugees (...) and its Protocol as the standards that need to be complied with in the application of this right, despite the fact that neither one of these instruments explicitly recognizes asylum as one of the rights to which refugees are entitled.

While article 18 imposes an obligation to guarantee the right to asylum, it does not say who is entitled to it. The question therefore arises as to whether this is a right of States, or a right of individuals. This question is far from a purely intellectual exercise. While the right of States to grant asylum to individuals is well established as a matter of international law, the right of individuals to be granted asylum is not explicitly enshrined in any international instruments of universal scope, although it is recognized in international treaties of regional scope. (...)

(...) despite its unclear wording and lack of explicit subject, the right to asylum / droit d'asile in article 18 of the Charter is to be construed as a subjective and enforceable right

---

[21] Article 14 UDHR states: '1. Everyone has the right to seek and to enjoy in other countries asylum from persecution. 2. This right may not be invoked in the case of prosecutions genuinely arising from non-political crimes or from acts contrary to the purposes and principles of the United Nations.'

of individuals to be granted asylum under the Union's law. An interpretation of the provision in the light of the intention of the drafters and the overall context of the Charter, further supported by the travaux préparatoires, shows that the right to be granted asylum, despite not being of treaty nature in international law, constitutes legally binding primary law in the Union.

The foregoing analysis of article 18 by reference to the Union's own interpretative criteria and the legally binding force of human rights in the Union's legal order has demonstrated that the content of this provision is to be determined by reference to international human rights treaties and to the constitutional traditions of Member States.

In particular, it has been argued here that the beneficiaries of this provision are all those individuals whose international protection grounds are established under any instrument of international human rights law, including the Refugee Convention and the European Convention on Human Rights. Since asylum is a shared competence between the Union and its Member States, the protection of article 18 applies in all areas of activity of the Union and its Member States that fall within the scope of application of the Union's law.

However, once established, asylum is an autonomous concept in the Union's legal order and therefore its scope of application needs to be determined by application of the Union's own rules.

The force of Article 18 of the Charter has proven more limited in practice. Unsurprisingly from a political perspective, the many secondary rules on asylum procedures and standards are of primary concern to the EU and its Member States (which create and mould them in the first place).[22] When called upon to recognize the right of asylum of certain Syrian applicants in a politically charged case, the CJEU ducked the issue.[23] On the contrary, when a reference to the right to asylum was politically expedient in light of the majority view of the Council, the CJEU included a reference to Article 18 of the Charter in its judgment concerning a challenge to temporary relocation measures. Even then, however, the reference was of a purely supportive nature and not part of the core reasoning of the Court. This modest function of Article 18 of the Charter is likely to be the most realistic interpretation of the provision and the one which is most likely to prevail in what is an overall migration-sceptic environment.

Judgment of 6 September 2017, *Slovak Republic and Hungary v Council*, C-643/15 and C-647/15, ECLI:EU:C:2017:631

343. [The relocation scheme] is on the contrary a crisis-management measure, taken at EU level, whose purpose is to ensure that the **fundamental right to asylum**, laid down in Article 18 of the Charter, can be exercised properly, in accordance with the Geneva Convention.

---

[22] Such an interpretation is also supported by the reference to the EU Treaties in Article 18 of the Charter; the EU Treaties constitute the basis of all EU asylum legislation.

[23] *X and X v État belge* (n 9).

D. Right to *non-refoulement*

Charter of Fundamental Rights of the European Union [2012] OJ C326/391

Article 19

Protection in the event of removal, expulsion or extradition

1. Collective expulsions are prohibited.
2. No one may be removed, expelled or extradited to a State where there is a serious risk that he or she would be subjected to the death penalty, torture or other inhuman or degrading treatment or punishment.

One of the cardinal rights in the context of migration is the principle of *non-refoulement*. It is enshrined in various international Conventions,[24] most notably Article 33(1) of the 1951 Refugee Convention, as well as the EU Charter and the TFEU.[25] Interestingly, the right was not included in the ECHR but it has been read into Article 3 ECHR in the landmark case of *Soering*.[26] This obligation not to return migrants to territories where their rights or freedoms would be threatened has also reached international customary status[27] and as such also binds the EU and its Member States.

***Soering v United Kingdom*, App no 14038/88, 7 July 1989**

---

91. (...) the decision by a Contracting State to extradite a fugitive may give rise to an issue under Article 3, and hence engage the responsibility of that State under the Convention, **where substantial grounds have been shown for believing that the person** concerned, if extradited, **faces a real risk of being subjected to torture or to inhuman or degrading treatment or punishment in the requesting country.** (...)

This obligation may also be triggered when national border guards try to prevent migrants from reaching the territory of a state—sometimes by returning them to their point of departure. In *Hirsi Jamaa and Others v Italy*, the European Court of Human Rights (ECtHR) ruled that Italy was supposed to know that the Somali and Eritrean migrants whom they had intercepted and forced to return to Libya risked being subjected to serious human rights violations upon return. Italy was therefore found in violation of Article 3

---

[24] Article 3(1) of the Convention against Torture (CAT); Article 7 of the International Convention on Civil and Political Rights, as interpreted by UN Human Rights Committee, 'CCPR General Comment No 20: Article 7' (10 March 1992) UN Doc HRI/GEN/1/Rev 1, para 9. See also UN Committee on the Rights of the Child, 'General Comment No 6: Treatment of unaccompanied and separated children outside their country of origin' (1 September 2005) UN Doc CRC/GC/2005/6, para 27 interpreting the prohibition of torture as containing an implicit obligation not to return children to a country where there are substantial grounds for believing that there is a real risk of irreparable harm.

[25] Article 19(2) of the Charter; Article 78(1) TFEU.

[26] *Soering v United Kingdom*, App no 14038/88, 7 July 1989, para 91.

[27] UN High Commissioner for Refugees, 'Note on international protection' (13 September 2001) UN Doc A/AC 96/951, para 16.

ECHR, as well as Articles 4 (prohibition of slavery and forced labour) and 14 (prohibition of discrimination) ECHR.[28] In *ND and NT v Spain*, where the two applicants formed part of a large group that stormed the border crossing between Morocco and Spain, a violation of the prohibition of collective expulsion (Article 4 of Protocol no 4 to the ECHR) was found.[29] This judgment was however overturned by the ECtHR's Grand Chamber stating that the applicants did not make use of the existing legal procedures for gaining lawful entry to Spanish territory and hence did not enjoy the protection of Protocol no 4.[30] As such, the Grand Chamber seems to have established serious limits to the principle of non-refoulement in the context of 'hot returns',[31] and the effect on so-called push-back policies remains to be seen.

European Union Agency for Fundamental Rights, *Scope of the principle of non-refoulement in contemporary border management: evolving areas of law* **(Publications Office of the European Union 2016)**

Although a number of areas call for more legal clarity, there is a solid basis for concluding that jurisdiction may vest, and non-refoulement may apply, in many of the presented scenarios. Especially since the ECtHR ruling in the Hirsi case, the extension of the effective control doctrine to encompass control over an individual has been widely accepted and broadly applied.

The grey areas that remain concern EU Member State operations in third countries, especially when EU Member States, EU institutions, or EU agencies 'assist' third countries in their efforts to manage migration flows. It is debated whether non-refoulement applies in such situations, which involve activities carried out under the umbrella of cooperation or external relations but, in some cases, with the ultimate aim of preventing migration flows from heading towards the EU. Hathaway and Gammeltoft-Hansen have argued that donor states cannot avoid their obligations under international human rights and refugee law in all instances in such situations. They take the debate a step further by arguing that, based on the exercise of public powers, jurisdiction is triggered. The logic behind this reasoning is that a state cannot be allowed to perpetrate, on the territory of another state, human rights violations that are not permitted on its own territory. Therefore, jurisdiction for human rights obligations follows the state's exercise of powers.

The principle of *non-refoulement*, often with reference to the 1951 Refugee Convention, is replicated across most EU secondary law on migration. Article 21 of Directive 2011/95/EU ('Qualification Directive') stipulates that 'Member States shall respect the principle of *non-refoulement* in accordance with their international obligations'.[32] This protection from

---

[28] *Hirsi Jamaa and Others v Italy*, App no 27765/09, 23 February 2012, paras 125–126.

[29] *ND and NT v Spain*, App no 8675/15 and 8697/15, 3 October 2017, paras 102–108.

[30] *ND and NT v Spain*, App no 8675/15 and 8697/15, Grand Chamber, 13 February 2020, para 231.

[31] For which the ECtHR has received some serious criticism, see among others A Lübbe, 'The Elephant in the Room: Effective Guarantee of Non-Refoulement after ECtHR N.D. and N.T.?' (*Verfassungsblog*, 19 February 2020) <https://verfassungsblog.de/the-elephant-in-the-room/> accessed 14 August 2020.

[32] Directive 2011/95/EU of the European Parliament and of the Council on standards for the qualification of third-country nationals or stateless persons as beneficiaries of international protection, for a uniform status for refugees or for persons eligible for subsidiary protection, and for the content of the protection granted [2011] OJ L337/9.

refoulement covers both refugees and persons eligible for subsidiary protection (protection of persons not qualifying as refugees).[33] The principle of *non-refoulement* is, however, not limited to refugees and persons with subsidiary protection status: under other EU instruments it extends to asylum seekers (ie persons seeking refugee or subsidiary protection status), irregular migrants, and persons in return procedures, including those refused at the border.[34]

Directive 2013/32/EU of the European Parliament and of the Council on common procedures for granting and withdrawing international protection [2013] OJ L180/60

Article 9

Right to remain in the Member State pending the examination of the application

1. Applicants shall be allowed to remain in the Member State, for the sole purpose of the procedure, until the determining authority has made a decision (...). That right to remain shall not constitute an entitlement to a residence permit.

2. Member States may make an exception only where (...) they will surrender or extradite, as appropriate, a person either to another Member State pursuant to obligations in accordance with a European arrest warrant or otherwise, or to a third country or to international criminal courts or tribunals.

3. A Member State **may extradite** an applicant to a third country pursuant to paragraph 2 **only where the competent authorities are satisfied that an extradition decision will not result in direct or indirect refoulement in violation of the international and Union obligations of that Member State.**

Moreover, the CJEU has interpreted the obligation of *non-refoulement* as subsuming situations in which a TCN suffering from a serious illness would be removed to a country where appropriate treatment is not available.[35] After earlier reluctance stemming from concern over the system of mutual trust,[36] the Court recognized that this situation must also be prevented in the context of transfers of asylum seekers to the competent Member States under the Dublin Regulation, as has been held by the ECtHR.[37] This is at the same time an implicit admission of the fact that not all EU Member States have been able to ensure minimum human rights guarantees for migrants at all times.

---

[33] Ibid, Article 20(2).

[34] See Articles 4(4) and 5 of the Returns Directive; Articles 35 and 38 of Directive 2013/32/EU of the European Parliament and of the Council on common procedures for granting and withdrawing international protection [2013] OJ L180/60 ('Asylum Procedures Directive').

[35] Judgment of 18 December 2014, *Centre public d'action sociale d'Ottignies-Louvain-la-Neuve v Abdida*, C-562/13, ECLI:EU:C:2014:2453, para 48.

[36] See Ch 4.

[37] *M.S.S. v Belgium and Greece*, App no 30696/09, 21 January 2011.

Judgment of 16 February 2017, *C. K. and Others v Republika Slovenija*, C-578/16 PPU, ECLI:EU:C:2017:127

44. (...) there is an obligation on the competent authorities and the national court to examine all the circumstances of significance for observance of the **principle of non-refoulement**, including the state of health of the person concerned, in the case where an asylum seeker claims that the Member State responsible for his application is not a 'safe State' for him. In that context, those authorities must take into account the applicant's personal situation in Slovenia and **assess whether the mere fact of transferring that person might in itself be contrary to the principle of non-refoulement.**

E. Right to private and family life

Another barrier to removal of migrants from the territory of the EU, recognized both in EU law (Article 7 of the Charter) and the ECHR (Article 8), is the right to private and family life. This right is, unlike the prohibition on torture, not absolute and can therefore be subject to limitations in accordance with Article 52(1) of the Charter. The right to private and family life is often invoked in the context of migration disputes with the aim of protecting migrants against expulsion. Consistent with the primary legal protection of the Charter and the ECHR, EU secondary law prescribes family unity and life as one of the factors which must be taken into account in the implementation of migration policy. In this regard, the 'best interests of the child' play a particularly important role, in line with the 1989 UN Convention on the Rights of the Child.[38]

These concepts related to the right to family life also confer concrete entitlements on TCNs. TCNs, including refugees (but not persons with subsidiary protection), have the right to family reunification under conditions specified in Council Directive 2003/86/EC ('Family Reunification Directive').[39] Moreover, family members of persons granted international protection (persons with both refugee and subsidiary protection status) are able to benefit from the same protection status in the interest of family unity. This mechanism is therefore capable of protecting migrants who are not eligible for international protection from extradition by virtue of being family members of eligible persons. The rationale behind such protection—in addition to the inherent value of family unity itself—relates to the risk of family members of persecuted persons becoming targets themselves upon return.

---

[38] For example, recital 18 of the Qualifications Directive states: 'The "best interests of the child" should be a primary consideration of Member States when implementing this Directive, in line with the 1989 United Nations Convention on the Rights of the Child. In assessing the best interests of the child, Member States should in particular take due account of the principle of family unity, the minor's well-being and social development, safety and security considerations and the views of the minor in accordance with his or her age and maturity.'

[39] Council Directive 2003/86/EC on the right to family reunification [2003] OJ L251/12.

Directive 2011/95/EU of the European Parliament and of the Council on standards for the qualification of third-country nationals or stateless persons as beneficiaries of international protection, for a uniform status for refugees or for persons eligible for subsidiary protection, and for the content of the protection granted [2011] OJ L337/9

Article 23

Maintaining family unity

1. Member States shall **ensure that family unity can be maintained.**
2. Member States shall **ensure that family members of the beneficiary of international protection who do not individually qualify for such protection are entitled to claim the benefits** referred to in Articles 24 to 35, in accordance with national procedures and as far as is compatible with the personal legal status of the family member.
4. Notwithstanding paragraphs 1 and 2, Member States may refuse, reduce or withdraw the benefits referred to therein for reasons of **national security or public order.**
5. Member States may decide that this Article also applies to other close relatives who lived together as part of the family at the time of leaving the country of origin, and who were wholly or mainly dependent on the beneficiary of international protection at that time.

F. Right to leave/enter

On the one hand, under international human rights law, individuals have a right to leave their country.[40] On the other hand, it does not accord them the right to enter another country, different from their own. In *Abdulaziz,* the ECtHR pointed out the tension that exists between the sovereign right of states to organize their immigration policies and the right to reunification mandating the entry of family members to the UK.

Abdulaziz, Cabales and Balkandali v the United Kingdom, App no 9214/80; 9473/81; 9474/81, 28 May 1985

67. (…) the extent of a State's **obligation to admit** to its territory relatives of settled immigrants will vary according to the particular circumstances of the persons involved. Moreover, the Court cannot ignore that the present case is concerned not only with family life but also with immigration and that, as a matter of well-established

---

[40] Article 13 UDHR; Article 12 ICCPR; Article 2 of Protocol No 4 to the ECHR; UN Human Rights Committee, 'General Comment No 27: Article 12' (2 November 1999) UN Doc CCPR/C/21/Rev.1/Add.9, para 9. See also, UN Human Rights Committee (15th session) *Vidal Martins v Uruguay,* Communication no 57/1979 (23 March 1982) UN Doc CCPR/C/15/D/57/1979.

> international law and subject to its treaty obligations, a State has the **right to control the entry of non-nationals** into its territory.

By reason of obligations taken on in bilateral or multilateral treaties—such as the T(F)EU or the ECHR—a state may be therefore obliged to allow entry of non-nationals. Within the EU, of course, the presumption is reversed with respect to EU citizens—they have the right in principle to both enter and exit any EU Member State; the rub of that is Member States severely restricting their own sovereign prerogative to regulate entry of (EU) migrants to the country (an issue which has animated numerous Brexit discussions). The right to reunification of TCNs under EU law or the ECHR and the possibility to seek asylum are examples of *de facto* rights to enter Member States from outside the EU.

8.4 Migration Channels to the EU

The EU measures on legal immigration for TCNs cover the conditions of entry and residence for certain categories of migrants, such as students and researchers, highly qualified workers under the EU Blue Card Directive, as well as family members of EU residents via family reunification. Former Article 63 TEC introduced by the Treaty of Amsterdam required the adoption of measures as part of a common migration policy. However, to date there is no single policy on labour migration but rather several dispersed initiatives for specific EU immigration policies where Member States have a shared interest.

Consolidated version of the Treaty on the Functioning of the European Union [2012] OJ C326/47

Article 79

1. The Union shall develop **a common immigration policy aimed at ensuring, at all stages, the efficient management of migration flows, fair treatment of third-country nationals residing legally in Member States, and the prevention of, and enhanced measures to combat, illegal immigration and trafficking in human beings.**

2. For the purposes of paragraph 1, the European Parliament and the Council, acting in accordance with the ordinary legislative procedure, shall adopt measures in the following areas:

   (a) the **conditions of entry and residence**, and standards on the issue by Member States of **long-term visas and residence permits**, including those for the purpose of family reunification;

   (b) the definition of the **rights of third-country nationals** residing legally in a Member State, including the conditions governing freedom of movement and of residence in other Member States;

   (c) **illegal immigration** and unauthorised residence, including removal and repatriation of persons residing without authorisation;

   (d) combating **trafficking** in persons, in particular women and children.

3. The Union may conclude **agreements with third countries** for the readmission to their countries of origin or provenance of third-country nationals who do not or who no longer fulfil the conditions for entry, presence or residence in the territory of one of the Member States.

4. The European Parliament and the Council, acting in accordance with the ordinary legislative procedure, may establish measures to provide incentives and support for the action of Member States with a view to promoting the integration of third-country nationals residing legally in their territories, excluding any harmonisation of the laws and regulations of the Member States.

5. This Article **shall not affect the right of Member States to determine volumes of admission of third-country nationals** coming from third countries to their territory in order to seek work, whether employed or self-employed.

It has been argued that the overall restrictiveness of EU migration policies negatively impacts fundamental rights of migrants and in particular the protection enshrined in the asylum framework. Limited access for regular migration by default directs migrants to irregular entry and more dangerous journeys. This structural state of EU migration policy has only been aggravated by the migration surges of 2015–2016 and the accompanying heightened focus on migration and border control.

N El-Enany, 'EU Asylum and Immigration Law under the Area of Freedom, Security, and Justice' in D Chalmers and A Arnull (eds), *The Oxford Handbook of European Union Law* (Oxford University Press 2015)

(...) the quality and effectiveness of the CEAS legislation is questionable in that the asylum Directives contain broad scope for discretion in application and suffer from incomplete or mal-implementation, resulting in vast differences in practice across the EU in the level of protection afforded to asylum seekers, as well as diverse rates of recognition of refugees. Despite the CJEU's willingness to interpret EU asylum provisions in a manner that protects refugees, uniformity and complete application of the asylum Directives have not been achieved through the Court's exercise of its jurisdiction. (...)

With respect to EU immigration law, Member States' muted enthusiasm for harmonization of rules on regular migration into the Union has meant that a coherent and comprehensive EU immigration law remains elusive. Instead, common rules on the entry and residence of specific categories of individuals have been adopted. Where such legislation does exist, the Court of Justice has played an important role in placing a brake on Member States' narrow and seemingly contrived interpretations of the rights granted to third-country nationals.

Despite Member States' reluctance to adopt measures on regular migration into the EU, they have in general been eager to adopt legislative and operational measures in the interests of curbing irregular migration. (...) the EU's highly restrictive wider migration and border control policy subverts protective elements that might be observed in its asylum legislation. Access to EU territory is severely limited for all migrants, irrespective of their motives for moving. Migrants' departure points are being pushed further afield and their journeys to the EU are becoming more dangerous. With these effects in mind, (…) reform of substantive internal protection standards is insufficient in the absence of comprehensively addressing the relationship between migration policy and asylum, in particular the effects of border control measures in restricting access to protection.

A. Highly skilled workers

In 2009, the EU has enacted Directive 2009/50/EC ('Blue Card Directive') which aimed to foster the entry of high-skilled TCNs to the EU. Applicants for an EU Blue Card must present a work contract in the EU of at least 1 year providing a salary of at least 1.5 times the average gross annual salary in the destination Member State. The proof of work must be supported by additional documents proving qualifications, travel arrangements, and health insurance. Blue Card holders are treated on par with nationals in matters of working conditions and other basic rights but do not have the freedom to seek employment which is not highly qualified. The Blue Card Directive also softens the requirements for family reunification laid down in the Family Reunification Directive. Under Article 6 of the Directive, Member States retain discretion in how many highly qualified TCNs they want to admit in their territories.

Council Directive 2009/50/EC on the conditions of entry and residence of third-country nationals for the purposes of highly qualified employment [2009] OJ L155/17

Article 5

Criteria for admission

1. (…) a third-country national who applies for an **EU Blue Card** under the terms of this Directive shall:
   (a) present a **valid work contract** or, as provided for in national law, a binding job offer for highly qualified employment, of at least one year in the Member State concerned;
   (b) present a document attesting **fulfilment of the conditions** set out under national law for the exercise by Union citizens of the regulated profession specified in the work contract or binding job offer as provided for in national law;
   (c) for unregulated professions, present the documents attesting the **relevant higher professional qualifications** in the occupation or sector specified in the work contract or in the binding job offer as provided for in national law;
   (d) present a **valid travel document**, as determined by national law, an application for a visa or a visa, if required, and evidence of a valid residence permit or of a national long-term visa, if appropriate. Member States may require the period of validity of the travel document to cover at least the initial duration of the residence permit;
   (e) present evidence of having or, if provided for by national law, having applied for a **sickness insurance** for all the risks normally covered for nationals of the Member State concerned for periods where no such insurance coverage and

> corresponding entitlement to benefits are provided in connection with, or resulting from, the work contract;
> (f) **not be considered to pose a threat to public policy, public security or public health.**

The EU Blue Card system has not been found to be effective in practice.[41] A review of the Directive has shown that Member States are applying the Directive inconsistently, while also offering parallel domestic structures for the admission of highly skilled workers. This makes the system fragmented and inefficient. In addition, the Commission found the criteria for granting an EU Blue Card to be 'quite high'. The overall assessment is that the Directive provided for inadequate harmonization and has resulted in a low number of Blue Card holders. The statistics show that the system has basically only taken off in Germany which grants more than 70 per cent of Blue Cards issued in the EU.[42] The 2016 Commission's Impact Assessment was accompanied by a proposal that aimed to overhaul the Blue Card Directive in order to make the EU a more competitive destination for highly skilled workers. Despite several calls to resume and finalize work on a revised directive,[43] the interest of Member States seems to have waned and shifted in favour of making the current Directive more effective.

More generally, EU-level harmonization of migration rules pertaining to TCNs with the goal of streamlining procedures has been undertaken as part of Directive 2011/98/EU ('Single Permit Directive').[44] While not setting out grounds for admission, the Single Permit Directive enables TCNs to obtain work and residence permits via a single procedure, rather than requiring separate applications for these two permits. The objective is to simplify the procedures for their admission and to facilitate the control of their status in the Member States. The Directive also lays down a common set of rights to third-country workers legally residing in a Member State, irrespective of the purposes for which they were initially admitted to the territory of that Member State, based on equal treatment with nationals of that Member State.

B. Students and researchers

Another channel of legal migration supported by the EU concerns students and researchers. In 2016, the EU adopted a new framework in this area, replacing Directives 2004/114/EC and 2005/71/EC which regulated studies and research separately.[45] The scope of the Directive is

---

[41] European Commission, 'Impact Assessment accompanying Proposal for a Directive of the European Parliament and the Council on the conditions of entry and residence of third-country nationals for the purposes of highly skilled employment and repealing Directive 2009/50/EC', SWD(2016) 193 final, Strasbourg, 7 June 2016.

[42] Due to overlap and fragmentation of national permit schemes, the data on Blue Cards is not entirely accurate. According to Eurostat numbers, 13,869 Blue Cards were issued in the EU-25 in 2014. Numbers have risen to 32,678 issued Blue cards in 2018. The UK, Ireland, and Denmark have continuously applied their opt-outs.

[43] See, for example, European Commission, 'Communication from the Commission to the European Parliament and the Council, Enhancing legal pathways to Europe: an indispensable part of a balanced and comprehensive migration policy' COM(2018) 635 final, Brussels, 12 September 2018.

[44] Directive 2011/98/EU of the European Parliament and of the Council on a single application procedure for a single permit for third-country nationals to reside and work in the territory of a Member State and on a common set of rights for third-country workers legally residing in a Member State [2011] OJ L343/1.

[45] Council Directive 2004/114/EC on the conditions of admission of third-country nationals for the purposes of studies, pupil exchange, unremunerated training or voluntary service [2004] OJ L375/12; Council Directive 2005/71/EC on a specific procedure for admitting third-country nationals for the purposes of scientific research [2005] OJ L289/15.

in fact broader than studies and research as it covers also training and voluntary service (extension to pupil exchanges and au pair placements is optional). The Directive includes both general and group-specific conditions of eligibility.

Directive (EU) 2016/801 of the European Parliament and of the Council on the conditions of entry and residence of third-country nationals for the purposes of research, studies, training, voluntary service, pupil exchange schemes or educational projects and au pairing [2016] OJ L132/21

Article 7

General conditions

1. As regards the admission of a third-country national under this Directive, the applicant shall:
   (a) present a **valid travel document**, as determined by national law, and, if required, an application for a visa or a valid visa or, where applicable, a valid residence permit or a valid long-stay visa; Member States may require the period of validity of the travel document to cover at least the duration of the planned stay;
   (b) if the third-country national is a minor under the national law of the Member State concerned, present a **parental authorisation** or an equivalent document for the planned stay;
   (c) present evidence that the third-country national has or, if provided for in national law, has applied for **sickness insurance** for all risks normally covered for nationals of the Member State concerned; the insurance shall be valid for the duration of the planned stay;
   (e) provide the evidence requested by the Member State concerned that during the planned stay the third-country national will have **sufficient resources to cover subsistence costs without having recourse to the Member State's social assistance system, and return travel costs**. The assessment of the sufficient resources shall be based on an individual examination of the case and shall take into account resources that derive, inter alia, from a grant, a scholarship or a fellowship, a valid work contract or a binding job offer or a financial undertaking by a pupil exchange scheme organisation, an entity hosting trainees, a voluntary service scheme organisation, a host family or an organisation mediating au pairs.

In *Ben Alaya* the CJEU ruled that the Students Directive 2004/114 effectively harmonizes the rules of admission for students from third countries and that the fulfilment of the exhaustive criteria listed in the Directive effectively confers a right of entry on the applicants. This reasoning can be extended by analogy to the present Directive 2016/801 which lays down similar conditions for admission. In the circumstances of the *Ben Alaya* case, a Tunisian student was accepted at a German university but was refused entry and residence for alleged inadequacy of his grades (which the educational institution, however, found sufficient), his weak knowledge of German, and the lack of connection between his course of study and his chosen career (a condition not provided for by the Directive). The CJEU held that Member States cannot impose additional requirements to those listed in the Directive.

Judgment of 10 September 2014, *Ben Alaya v Bundesrepublik Deutschland*, C-491/13, ECLI:EU:C:2014:2187

15. After obtaining his baccalaureate in Tunisia in 2010 and enrolling at university there to study information technology, Mr Ben Alaya took steps to be able to begin higher education (bachelor's degree) in Germany. On several occasions, he was **accepted by the Technische Universität Dortmund** to study mathematics. Mr Ben Alaya made **a number of applications to the competent German authorities for a student visa** in order to attend that course or to undergo the language training organised by the university for foreign nationals seeking access to higher education. All those applications were refused.

16. The most recent decision refusing to grant Mr Ben Alaya a visa, adopted on 23 September 2011, was based on **doubts as to his motivation for wishing to study in Germany**, particularly in the light of the inadequacy of the grades previously obtained, his weak knowledge of German and the fact that there was no connection between his proposed course of study and his intended career.

21. By its question, the referring court asks, in essence, whether Article 12 of Directive 2004/114 must be interpreted as meaning that the Member State concerned is **obliged to admit to its territory a third-country national** who wishes to stay more than three months in that territory for study purposes, **where that person meets the conditions for admission** laid down in Articles 6 and 7 of the directive.

29. (...) the Court has held that, according to recitals 6 and 7 to Directive 2004/114, that directive is intended to promote the mobility of students who are third-country nationals to the European Union for the purpose of education, that mobility being intended to **promote Europe as a world centre of excellence for studies and vocational training** (Sommer, C-15/11, EU:C:2012:371, paragraph 39). In particular, recital 6 to the directive states that the approximation of the national legislation of the Member States relating to the conditions of entry and residence is part of that objective.

30. **To allow a Member State to introduce**, in relation to the admission of third-country nationals for study purposes, **conditions additional to those laid down in Articles 6 and 7** of Directive 2004/114 **would be contrary to the objective pursued by that directive** of promoting the mobility of such nationals.

31. It follows, therefore, from the general structure and objectives of Directive 2004/114 that, pursuant to Article 12 of that directive, Member States are required to issue a residence permit for study purposes to an applicant who meets the conditions laid down in Articles 6 and 7 of that directive, since those provisions **exhaustively list both the general and the specific conditions** that must be met by an applicant for a student residence permit, **as well as the possible grounds for refusing to admit such an applicant.**

The judgments in *Ben Alaya* and earlier cases, such as *Koushkaki* and *Air Baltic*,[46] have contributed to the strengthening of the rule of law in migration procedures and the confirmation of harmonisation as the aim of EU rules on migration law. As regards EU migration

---

[46] Judgment of 19 December 2013, *Koushkaki*, C-84/12, ECLI:EU:C:2013:862 on the exhaustiveness of the grounds for refusal in the EU Visa Code; Judgment of 4 September 2014, *Air Baltic*, C-575/12, ECLI:EU:C:2014:2155 on the exhaustiveness of entry conditions in the Schengen Border Code.

policy more generally, it has led scholars to conclude that when an EU law instrument sets out exhaustive requirements for admission, stay, or visa applications, a right to migration can be claimed. Member States would then only have discretion in the assessment of the facts.[47]

C. Family reunification

As one of the main channels for legal migration to the EU, family reunification has accounted for approximately a third of all TCN arrivals until recently. This avenue is predominantly[48] regulated by the Family Reunification Directive, which applies to all EU Member States except Denmark, Ireland, and, previously, the UK. The Directive does not apply to family members of EU citizens who exercised their right to free movement, as they can benefit from more favourable rules under Directive 2004/38.[49] The Family Reunification Directive is the first specialized international instrument to establish a distinct right to family reunification,[50] which was confirmed in CJEU case law.[51] It is based on the consideration that it promotes the integration of TCNs and their family members.

Council Directive 2003/86/EC on the right to family reunification [2003] OJ L251/12

Article 1

The purpose of this Directive is to determine the conditions for the exercise of the right to family reunification by third country nationals residing lawfully in the territory of the Member States.

The Directive provides a list of conditions which Member States may impose on the sponsor[52] or the spouse. If these conditions are met, Member States are obliged to admit

---

[47] S Peers, 'Back to School: The CJEU Confirms that Third-Country National Students Have a Right of Entry' (*EU Law Analysis*, 10 September 2014) <http://eulawanalysis.blogspot.com/2014/09/back-to-school-cjeu-confirms-that-third.html> accessed 14 August 2020.

[48] There are other instruments of EU migration legislation with references to family reunification, such as the Blue Card Directive (see above). They rely on the Directive but often provide for more favourable rules and include some sponsors who do not fall under the latter Directive.

[49] Directive 2004/38/EC of the European Parliament and of the Council on the right of citizens of the Union and their family members to move and reside freely within the territory of the Member States amending Regulation (EEC) No 1612/68 and repealing Directives 64/221/EEC, 68/360/EEC, 72/194/EEC, 73/148/EEC, 75/34/EEC, 75/35/EEC, 90/364/EEC, 90/365/EEC, and 93/96/EEC [2004] OJ L158/77.

[50] Recitals 2, 4, 15, and Article 1 of Council Directive 2003/86/EC on the right to family reunification [2003] OJ L251/12.

[51] Judgment of 27 June 2006, *European Parliament v Council*, C-540/03, ECLI:EU:C:2006:429; Judgment of 4 March 2010, *Rhimou Chakroun*, C-578/08, ECLI:EU:C:2010:117; Judgment of 6 December 2012, *O, S v Maahanmuuttovirasto and Maahanmuuttovirasto v L*, C-356/11 and C-357/11, ECLI:EU:C:2012:776.

[52] A sponsor to an application for family reunification in most Member States is a third-country national (TCN) who is in possession of a valid continuous or permanent residence permit, including beneficiaries of international protection. Students and/or workers may act as sponsors in many Member States, provided that they fulfil the general requirements for family reunification. Furthermore, most national laws allow beneficiaries of subsidiary protection to apply for family reunification often under the same conditions as refugees. All but one Member State allow unaccompanied minors (UAMs) who have obtained refugee status or subsidiary protection to become sponsors of family reunification.

the nuclear family[53] of the sponsor. The Member States have some discretion in verifying whether the (non-exhaustive) conditions are met. However, this should not lead to undermining the objective of the Family Reunification Directive, which is the promotion of family unity.[54] On the other hand, granting the right to family reunification may not impair the effectiveness of the Directive either. Therefore, national legislation under which, in the absence of a decision being adopted within six months, the competent authorities must automatically issue a residence permit without first establishing the existence of the relevant family links, is not allowed.[55]

Crucially, once in the EU, family members have access to rights on an equal footing with the sponsor, depending on the latter's status. This includes access to education, vocational training, and guidance, and employment and self-employment. The Directive also prescribes an individual assessment of each application,[56] which should be carried out in accordance with the general principles of EU law, in particular the principles of effectiveness and proportionality, as well as in light of the EU Charter, the ECHR, and the UN Convention on the Rights of the Child.[57]

Family members may also enjoy access to healthcare, social benefits, long-term residency, and citizenship. However, the conditions of such access are not regulated by the Family Reunification Directive beyond the general obligation to afford family members the same treatment as the sponsor as regards access to education, employment, and training.[58] In most cases family members are subject to more stringent conditions than native citizens or even other legally residing TCNs. By way of illustration, most Member States provide access to social benefits only after a number of years of residence or consider it as an obstacle on the path to reunification, as sponsors are subject to an income requirement.

A number of Member States have recently made changes to their policies and practices on family reunification. For example, in Belgium, an income requirement was introduced for exercising the right to family reunification in 2011. In addition, an application fee was introduced[59] and processing time for the application was prolonged from six to nine months. Belgium has also increasingly invested in the fight against marriages of convenience and other abuses.[60] Amidst increasing arrivals of asylum-seekers in Europe, countries have adopted (far-reaching) restrictions on the right of family reunification of persons with a subsidiary protection and even refugee status.[61]

Fundamental rights guide the interpretation given to the Family Reunification Directive by the Court of Justice. For instance, Article 8 ECHR—which corresponds to Article 7 of the Charter—has been interpreted in a manner requiring the application procedure for family

---

[53] Member States usually extend the scope of family reunification beyond the nuclear family, which consists of core members such as the mother, father, and their minor unmarried children. Depending on the national law, the scope of family reunification can include parents, adult children, same-sex partners, non-married partners, and/or foster children.

[54] *European Parliament v Council* (n 51) paras 54, 59 and 61–62; *Chakroun* (n 51) paras 43 and 47.

[55] Judgment of 20 November 2019, *X v Belgische Staat*, C-706/18, ECLI:EU:C:2019:993.

[56] Article 17 of the Family Reunification Directive.

[57] *European Parliament v Council* (n 51) paras 37 and 105.

[58] Article 14 of the Family Reunification Directive.

[59] In Belgium, family members of refugees and beneficiaries of subsidiary protection are exempted from the payment of a retribution for the introduction of the application for family reunification (which is EUR 160–215 for other applicants) yet they are not exempted from the fees which are imposed by the consulate or local authority where the application is submitted.

[60] European Migration Network, 'Family Reunification of Third-Country Nationals in the EU plus Norway: national practices' (April 2017) 12.

[61] M Wagner and others, 'The Implementation of the Common European Asylum System', European Parliament Study, May 2016, 40–41.

reunification to be flexible, prompt, and effective. Along those lines, most Member States take a more accommodating stance on applications by beneficiaries of international protection than in relation to TCNs generally, and often accept alternative methods to prove identity and family ties.[62]

Tanda-Muzinga v France, App no 2260/10, 10 July 2014

73. (...) the Court considers that, in view of the decision taken some months previously to grant the applicant refugee status, and the subsequent recognition of the principle that he was entitled to family reunification, **it was of crucial importance that the visa applications be examined promptly, attentively and with particular diligence**. It is not the Court's task to take the place of the competent authorities in examining whether or not the civil-status certificates submitted in support of the request for family reunification were fraudulent (...). However, the Court is competent to ascertain whether the domestic courts, in applying and interpreting the provisions of that provision, secured the guarantees set forth in Article 8 of the Convention, taking into account the applicant's refugee status and the protection of his interests protected by it. In this connection, it considers that, in the circumstances of the present case, **the respondent State was under an obligation**, in order to respond to the applicant's request, **to institute a procedure that took into account the events that had disrupted and disturbed his family life and had led to his being granted refugee status**. The Court will therefore concentrate its assessment on the quality of this procedure and focus its attention on the 'procedural requirements' of Article 8 of the Convention (...).

74. In this connection, the Court observes that the applicant's family life had been discontinued purely as a result of his **decision to flee** his country of origin, **out of a genuine fear of persecution** within the meaning of the 1951 Geneva Convention (...). Accordingly, and contrary to what was consistently asserted by the relevant ministry throughout the interlocutory proceedings and the proceedings on the merits (...), and until the communication of the application to the respondent Government, **the applicant could not be held responsible for the separation from his family**. The arrival of his wife and children, who were aged three, six and thirteen at the time of the request for family reunification and were themselves refugees in a third country, was thus **the only means by which family life could resume**.

75. The Court reiterates that the **family unity is an essential right of refugees** and that family reunion is an essential element in enabling persons who have fled persecution to resume a normal life (...). It further reiterates that it has held that obtaining such international protection constitutes evidence of the vulnerability of the parties concerned (...). In this connection, it notes that there exists a consensus at international and European level on the **need for refugees to benefit from a family reunification procedure that is more favourable than that foreseen for other aliens**, as evidenced by the remit and the activities of the UNHCR and the standards set out in Directive 2003/86 EC of the European Union (...) In this context, the Court considers that it was essential for the national authorities to take account of the

---

[62] European Migration Network (n 60) 33.

> applicant's vulnerability and his particularly difficult personal history, to pay close attention to his arguments of relevance to the outcome of the dispute, to inform him of the reasons preventing family reunification, and, lastly, to take a rapid decision on the visa applications.

In addition, even when a situation is not explicitly covered by the Family Reunification Directive, the right to family life is upheld in both EU primary law,[63] and international human rights law.[64] In particular, Article 14 ECHR requires a reasonable and objective justification or substantiated reasons for any difference in treatment of persons in a similar situation.[65] Furthermore, Article 8 ECHR may also serve as a stepping stone for sponsors excluded from the scope of the Directive, but falling within the scope of national law. It must be noted, however, that, contrary to the Directive, Article 8 ECHR does not offer a direct right to family reunification, meaning it does not entail an absolute obligation to respect people's choice of residence as a family.[66] The admission of the relatives to the territory of a state will depend on the particular circumstances of the persons involved, as well as the general interest of the state.

Biao v Denmark, App no 38590/10, 24 May 2016

117. The Court reiterates that **where immigration is concerned, Article 8, taken alone, cannot be considered to impose on a State a general obligation to respect a married couple's choice of country for their matrimonial residence or to authorise family reunification on its territory.** Nevertheless, in a case which concerns family life as well as immigration, the extent of a State's obligations to admit to its territory relatives of persons residing there will vary according to the particular circumstances of the persons involved and the general interest (...). Moreover, the Court has, on many occasions, accepted that **immigration control**, which serves the general interests of the economic well-being of the country, **pursued a legitimate aim** within the meaning of Article 8 of the Convention (...).

118. That being said, the present case concerns compliance with Article 14 of the Convention read in conjunction with Article 8, with the result that **immigration control measures**, which may be found to be compatible with Article 8 § 2, including with the legitimate aim requirement, **may** nevertheless **amount to unjustified discrimination** in breach of Article 14 read in conjunction with Article 8. It appears that case-law on these matters is rather sparse. In *Hode and Abdi*, (...) the Court accepted that offering incentives to certain groups of immigrants may amount to a legitimate aim for the purposes of Article 14 of the Convention. Furthermore, in *Abdulaziz, Cabales and Balkandali* (...), the Court found legitimate the aim cited

---

[63] Articles 7, 9, and 33 of the Charter.

[64] Articles 12 and 16 UDHR; Articles 17, 23, and 24 of the International Covenant on Civil and Political Rights; Articles 10, 16, and 22 of the Convention on the Rights of the Child and Article 8 ECHR.

[65] See *Hode and Abdi v United Kingdom*, App no 22341/09, 6 Nov 2012, paras 54–55; *Pajić v Croatia*, App no 68453/13, 23 Feb 2016, paras 81–83; *Taddeuci v Italy*, App no 51362/09, 30 June 2016, paras 94–98; *Biao v Denmark*, App no 38590/10, 24 May 2016, paras 122–137.

[66] *Hode and Abdi v United Kingdom* (n 65).

by the Government for the differential treatment on the ground of birth, namely 'to avoid the hardship which women having close ties to the United Kingdom would encounter if, on marriage, they were obliged to move abroad in order to remain with their husbands' or, in other words, to distinguish a group of nationals who, seen from a general perspective, had lasting and strong ties with the country.

D. Asylum

As alluded to earlier, the Treaty of Amsterdam provided the EU with law-making powers in the field of asylum and migration and established the legal basis for the development of a common EU asylum and migration policy as called for in the Tampere Council conclusions and as part of the broader aspiration of transforming the EU into an AFSJ (see Figure 8.1). Interestingly, the first instrument adopted under the Tampere programme set up a scheme to deal with mass arrivals— in particular due to war, violence, or human rights violations—but it has never been triggered.[67] Since then the EU has been working towards establishing and tweaking the Common European Asylum System (CEAS) which includes common rules on the determination of the responsibility for asylum applications (the Dublin system), rules on asylum procedures, the qualification of applicants for international protection and related rights, and reception conditions.

European Council, Presidency conclusions, Tampere, 15 and 16 October 1999, conclusion 13.

The European Council reaffirms the importance the Union and Member States attach to absolute respect of the right to seek asylum. It has agreed to work towards establishing a Common European Asylum System, based on the full and inclusive application of the Geneva Convention, thus ensuring that nobody is sent back to persecution, i.e. maintaining the principle of non-refoulement.

The creation of the CEAS took place in two phases. During the first phase, between 1999 and 2005, measures harmonizing minimum asylum standards were laid down in EU law. These minimum standards included five key components: the 'Asylum Procedures Directive' (2005),[68] the 'Reception Conditions Directive',[69] the 'Qualification Directive' (2004),[70] the

---

[67] Council Directive 2001/55/EC on minimum standards for giving temporary protection in the event of a mass influx of displaced persons and on measures promoting a balance of efforts between Member States in receiving such persons and bearing the consequences thereof [2001] OJ L212/12.

[68] Council Directive 2005/85/EC on minimum standards on procedures in Member States for granting and withdrawing refugee status [2005] OJ L326/13; superseded by Directive 2013/32/EU of the European Parliament and of the Council on common procedures for granting and withdrawing international protection [2013] OJ L180/60.

[69] Council Directive 2003/9/EC laying down minimum standards for the reception of asylum seekers [2003] OJ L31/18; superseded by Directive 2013/33/EU of the European Parliament and of the Council laying down standards for the reception of applicants for international protection (recast) [2013] OJ L180/96.

[70] Council Directive 2004/83/EC on minimum standards for the qualification and status of third country nationals or stateless persons as refugees or as persons who otherwise need international protection and the content of the protection granted [2004] OJ L304/12; superseded by Directive 2011/95/EU of the European Parliament and

'Dublin Regulation' (2003),[71] and the 'Eurodac Regulation' (2000).[72] In the second phase, these minimum standards were built upon to develop the CEAS with a focus on improving the effectiveness and fairness of the system. As in other parts of EU law, the legislative landscape has been visibly impacted over the years by landmark rulings of the CJEU and the ECtHR.

The updated Reception Conditions Directive lays out common standards for the reception of applications for international protection across the Member States.[73] On the basis of the Directive, Member States are obliged to ensure material reception conditions from the moment of application to international protection.[74] This also entails access to 'the necessary' healthcare (medical and psychological),[75] employment,[76] and education for minors.[77]

Directive 2013/33/EU laying down standards for the reception of applicants for international protection (recast) [2013] OJ L180/96

Article 2

Definitions

For the purposes of this Directive:

g) '**material reception conditions**': means the reception conditions that include housing, food and clothing provided in kind, or as financial allowances or in vouchers, or a combination of the three, and a daily expenses allowance;

---

of the Council on standards for the qualification of third-country nationals or stateless persons as beneficiaries of international protection, for a uniform status for refugees or for persons eligible for subsidiary protection, and for the content of the protection granted [2011] OJ L337/9.

[71] Council Regulation (EC) No 343/2003 establishing the criteria and mechanisms for determining the Member State responsible for examining an asylum application lodged in one of the Member States by a third-country national [2003] OJ L50/1; superseded by Regulation (EU) No 604/2013 of the European Parliament and of the Council establishing the criteria and mechanisms for determining the Member State responsible for examining an application for international protection lodged in one of the Member States by a third-country national or a stateless person [2013] OJ L180/31.

[72] Council Regulation (EC) No 2725/2000 of 11 December 2000 concerning the establishment of 'Eurodac' for the comparison of fingerprints for the effective application of the Dublin Convention [2000] OJ L316/1; superseded by Regulation (EU) No 603/2013 of the European Parliament and of the Council on the establishment of 'Eurodac' for the comparison of fingerprints for the effective application of Regulation (EU) No 604/2013 establishing the criteria and mechanisms for determining the Member State responsible for examining an application for international protection lodged in one of the Member States by a third-country national or a stateless person and on requests for the comparison with Eurodac data by Member States' law enforcement authorities and Europol for law enforcement purposes, and amending Regulation (EU) No 1077/2011 establishing a European Agency for the operational management of large-scale IT systems in the area of freedom, security and justice [2013] OJ L180/1.

[73] Directive 2013/33/EU laying down standards for the reception of applicants for international protection (recast) [2013] OJ L 180/96.

[74] Ibid, Article 3(1).

[75] Ibid, Article 19.

[76] Ibid, Article 15.

[77] Ibid, Article 14.

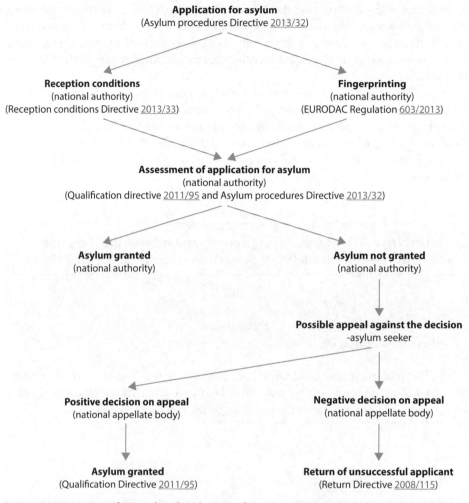

Figure 8.1 Overview of EU asylum legislation in force

The standards also restrict the detention of vulnerable persons, particularly minors.[78] With regard to detention in general the Reception Directive provides that 'Member States shall not hold a person in detention for the sole reason' that the person is an asylum-seeker. Member States may only resort to detention for one of the reasons set out in the Directive, 'when it proves necessary and on the basis of an individual assessment (…)'.[79] The Directive thereby formally meets the requirements set out in the case law. However, the discretion left to the Member States due to a number of open-ended grounds and vague formulations undermines these safeguards. It is up to the CJEU to rein in derogations from the general rule prohibiting detention.

---

[78] Ibid, Article 8.
[79] Ibid.

Judgment of 15 February 2016, *J. N. v Staatssecretaris van Veiligheid en Justitie*, C-601/15 PPU, ECLI:EU:C:2016:84

---

55. (...) the detention of an applicant where the protection of **national security or public order** so requires is, by its very nature, an appropriate measure for protecting the public from the threat which the conduct of such a person represents and is thus suitable for attaining the objective pursued by point (e) of the first subparagraph of Article 8(3) of Directive 2013/33.

56. As to whether the power which that provision confers on Member States to detain an applicant on grounds related to the protection of national security or public order is necessary, the Court stresses that, in view of the importance of the **right to liberty** enshrined in Article 6 of the Charter and the gravity of the interference with that right which detention represents, **limitations on the exercise of the right must apply only in so far as is strictly necessary** (...).

66. So far as the concept of 'public security' is concerned (...) this concept covers both the internal security of a Member State and its external security and that, consequently, a threat to the functioning of institutions and essential public services and the survival of the population, as well as the risk of a serious disturbance to foreign relations or to peaceful coexistence of nations, or a risk to military interests, may affect public security (...).

67. Thus, placing or keeping an applicant in detention under point (e) of the first subparagraph of Article 8(3) of Directive 2013/33 is, in view of the requirement of necessity, justified on the ground of a threat to national security or public order **only if the applicant's individual conduct represents a genuine, present and sufficiently serious threat, affecting a fundamental interest of society or the internal or external security of the Member State concerned** (...).

68. Point (e) of the first subparagraph of Article 8(3) of Directive 2013/33 is also not disproportionate in relation to the objectives sought. The Court notes in this regard that **that provision results from a fair balance** between the general interest objective pursued, namely the protection of national security and public order, and the interference with the right to liberty to which detention gives rise (...).

Reception conditions have proven to constitute a rather difficult field of harmonization and continue to vary significantly between the EU Member States.[80] The differences in reception conditions might[81] trigger secondary movement or, more importantly, bring courts to suspend transfers of asylum-seekers to the responsible Member State, and thereby obstruct distribution mechanisms.[82] In addition, challenges remain in terms of capacity. During periods of decrease in arrivals, reception capacities come under the scrutiny of austerity measures or are slimmed down out of belief they would constitute 'a pull factor'.[83] This

---

[80] European Commission, 'Report to the Council and to the European Parliament on the application of Directive 2003/9/EC of 27 January 2003 laying down minimum standards for the reception of asylum seekers', COM(2007) 745 final, Brussels, 26 November 2007.

[81] The level of material reception conditions during the asylum procedure may have variable impact on secondary movements of asylum seekers because other pull factors such as social ties (including family reunification), reputation of other countries, or job opportunities may be regarded as more important by asylum seekers.

[82] Wagner and others, 'The Implementation of the Common European Asylum System' (n 61) 82.

[83] Ibid, 42, 82. A widely reported amendment to Danish law, for example, provided for the possibility to search and seize asylum-seekers' valuable assets to offset the costs of hosting them.

is linked to a significant degree to poor contingency planning by the Member States in question and a failure to adapt to increased reception needs readily.

Another continuous difficulty seems to be the provision of an adequate standard of living in reception facilities, in particular appropriate to applicants' (special) reception needs.[84] To this effect, the Reception Conditions Directive leaves it to the Member States to determine how the identification of vulnerable persons should be carried out.[85] Few Member States, however, have included detailed vulnerability assessment procedures into their national legislation, resulting in a degree of arbitrariness.[86] In addition, it has been reported that many refugees face difficulties in finding adequate housing in the private housing market after receiving a positive decision regarding their claim, and thus are subjected to living in reception facilities and conditions for a longer period of time.[87]

Neither the Treaties nor the Charter provide a definition of the terms 'asylum' and 'refugee'. Instead they refer to the Refugee Convention and its Protocol.[88] The lack of EU-level harmonization of the definitions contributes to significant discrepancies in recognition rates, while disparities in the use of different levels of protection status also persist. In 2016, the overall protection rate was 77.4 per cent for Sweden, 35.2 per cent for the neighbouring Finland, and 8.5 per cent for Hungary. In its 2016 Proposal for a Qualification Regulation,[89] the Commission would like to remedy this by reforming the criteria for granting international protection. More specifically, the proposal aims to oblige Member States to assess the possibility of alternative protection in the country of origin of the individual so as to refuse protection status to those who should be able to find safety in other parts of the country in question. Some Member States have already actively applied this concept, resulting in lower recognition rates for countries of origin such as Iraq and Afghanistan in 2016.[90] The chances of obtaining international protection still vary dramatically from one country to the other; for Iraqis, for example, recognition rates in 2018 ranged from 94.2 per cent in Italy to 12 per cent in Bulgaria.[91]

In any case, the recast Qualification Directive has been quite successful in aligning most rights and benefits granted to persons with an international protection status, except for the contentious topics of residence permits and access to social welfare. Beneficiaries of subsidiary protection shall receive a residence permit which must be valid for at least one year while refugee status holders shall receive a residence permit which shall be valid for at least three years.[92] Likewise, Member States may limit the social benefits granted to beneficiaries

---

[84] EU Agency for Fundamental Rights, 'Current migration situation in the EU: Oversight of reception facilities', September 2017, 4–5; Wagner and others, 'The Implementation of the Common European Asylum System' (n 61) 85.

[85] S Peers, 'The EU Directive on Reception Conditions: A Weak Compromise', Statewatch Analysis, July 2012, 6.

[86] Wagner and others, 'The Implementation of the Common European Asylum System' (n 61) 87.

[87] Ibid, 86.

[88] Article 2 of Directive 2011/95/EU of the European Parliament and of the Council on standards for the qualification of third-country nationals or stateless persons as beneficiaries of international protection, for a uniform status for refugees or for persons eligible for subsidiary protection, and for the content of the protection granted [2011] OJ L337/9 (hereafter 'recast Qualification Directive').

[89] European Commission, 'Proposal for a Regulation on standards for the qualification of third-country nationals or stateless persons as beneficiaries of international protection, for a uniform status for refugees or for persons eligible for subsidiary protection and for the content of the protection granted and amending Council Directive 2003/109/EC of 25 November 2003 concerning the status of third-country nationals who are long-term residents', COM(2016) 466 final, Brussels, 13 July 2016; not yet adopted as of April 2020.

[90] European Council on Refugees and Exiles, 'Asylum Statistics 2016: sharper inequalities and persisting asylum lottery', 17 January 2017.

[91] European Council on Refugees and Exiles, 'Asylum Statistics 2018: changing arrivals, same concerns', 25 January 2019.

[92] Article 24 of the recast Qualification Directive.

of subsidiary protection to 'core benefits'.[93] Some countries have reduced the duration of the international protection status altogether with possible consequences for family reunification.

The discretion to introduce restrictions on the duration of residence permits for beneficiaries of international protection, as well as on waiting periods for family reunification, has proven useful to Member States in their quest to reduce their 'appeal' to asylum-seekers.[94] The Commission initiated a number of infringement proceedings against several Member States for their failure to implement *inter alia* the recast Qualification Directive and the recast Asylum Procedures Directive. The possibly most divergent national practices relate to the implementation of Article 15 of the Qualification Directive. Most Member States do not have a set of guidelines for the interpretation of the notions of 'real risk', 'serious harm', 'armed conflict', or the individualization of the serious threat, which are key to granting international protection. As a result, asylum-seekers fleeing a given third country at the same moment can frequently receive different protection statuses in different Member States. For example, whereas most eligible asylum-seekers from Syria in 2016 received refugee status in Austria, Belgium, or Italy, in the same year Syrian asylum-seekers received mostly subsidiary protection in Spain, Sweden, or Hungary.[95] These inconsistencies have been sometimes referred to as the 'asylum lottery'.[96]

Similarly, a number of observers have voiced criticism about the recast Asylum Procedures Directive's failure to minimize derogations and reduce complexity.[97] Discrepancies in procedural guarantees between Member States, especially the use of accelerated procedures, safe country lists, and access to legal aid and information, are not only problematic in terms of (lack of) harmonization but also from a human rights perspective. Asylum-seekers' claims for international protection might significantly depend on which Member State examines their application, while Member States wishing to curb immigration have an incentive to introduce additional legal hurdles in national asylum procedures in order to deter asylum-seekers and thus deflect responsibility. The use of the concept of 'safe country of origin' in conjunction with accelerated rejection procedures is a case in point.

M Wagner and others, 'The Implementation of the Common European Asylum System', European Parliament Study, May 2016

The increased application of the safe country of origin and safe third country of origin concepts in the context of accelerated and border procedures increases risks of asylum seekers being subjected to expedited procedures that do not ensure a proper examination of their protection needs in practice, in particular where effective access to legal assistance and representation is not guaranteed. The increasing trend at EU level towards a

---

[93] Ibid, Article 29.

[94] Wagner and others, 'The Implementation of the Common European Asylum System' (n 61) 11.

[95] Asylum Information Database, 'Refugee rights subsiding? Europe's two-tier protection regime and its effect on the rights of beneficiaries', 30 March 2017.

[96] Ibid; European Council on Refugees and Exiles, 'Asylum Statistics 2016' (n 90).

[97] C Costello and E Honcox, 'The Recast Asylum Procedures Directive 2013/32/EU: Caught between the Stereotypes of the Abusive Asylum Seeker and the Vulnerable Refugee' in V Chetail, P De Bruycker, and F Maiani (eds), *Reforming the Common European Asylum System: The New European Refugee Law* (Martinus Nijhoff 2015); European Council on Refugees and Exiles, 'Information Note on Directive 2013/32/EU of the European Parliament and of the Council of 26 June 2013 on common procedures for granting and withdrawing international protection (recast)', December 2014.

purely nationality-driven approach whereby all resources are mainly invested in expedited procedures dealing with the manifestly well-founded and unfounded applications is worrying as it is based on simplified assumptions that ignore the complexity of asylum and mixed migration and may lead to increased risks of *refoulement*.

Due to the intended harmonization of Member States' asylum procedures and qualification requirements, the EU has also decided to lay down rules governing the concepts of safe countries (without so far harmonizing the lists of safe countries). The application of these concepts essentially allows Member States to afford asylum-seekers less than full examination of their applications for international protection. Article 35 of the Asylum Procedures Directive introduces the concept of 'first country of asylum' which essentially enables Member States to declare asylum claims inadmissible (Article 33(2)(b) of the Directive) if the applicant already received refugee status in another country or he or she can receive sufficient protection there, including the guarantee of *non-refoulement*, provided that the applicant will be readmitted to that 'first country of asylum'. As with the following concepts, asylum-seekers should be given the possibility to rebut the presumption that a certain country offers sufficient protection.

Directive 2013/32/EU of the European Parliament and of the Council on common procedures for granting and withdrawing international protection [2013] OJ L180/60

Article 35

The concept of first country of asylum

A country can be considered to be a **first country of asylum** for a particular applicant if:

(a) he or she has been **recognised** in that country **as a refugee** and he or she can still avail himself/herself of that protection; or
(b) he or she otherwise **enjoys sufficient protection** in that country, including benefiting from the principle of **non-refoulement**,
     provided that he or she will be readmitted to that country.

(...)

Article 36

The concept of safe country of origin

1. A third country designated as a **safe country of origin** in accordance with this Directive may, after an individual examination of the application, be considered as a safe country of origin for a particular applicant only if:
    (a) he or she has the nationality of that country; or
    (b) he or she is a stateless person and was formerly habitually resident in that country, and he or she **has not submitted any serious grounds for considering**

the country not to be a safe country of origin in his or her particular circumstances and in terms of his or her qualification as a beneficiary of international protection in accordance with Directive 2011/95/EU.

2. Member States shall lay down in **national legislation** further rules and modalities for the application of the safe country of origin concept.

Article 37

National designation of third countries as safe countries of origin

1. Member States may retain or introduce legislation that allows, in accordance with Annex I, for the **national designation of safe countries of origin** for the purposes of examining applications for international protection.
2. Member States shall **regularly review the situation** in third countries designated as safe countries of origin in accordance with this Article.
3. The assessment of whether a country is a safe country of origin in accordance with this Article shall be based on a **range of sources of information**, including in particular information from other Member States, EASO, UNHCR, the Council of Europe and other relevant international organisations.
4. Member States shall notify to the Commission the countries that are designated as safe countries of origin in accordance with this Article.

Article 38

The concept of safe third country

1. Member States may apply the **safe third country concept** only where the competent authorities are satisfied that a person seeking international protection will be treated in accordance with the following principles in the third country concerned:
   (a) **life and liberty are not threatened** on account of race, religion, nationality, membership of a particular social group or political opinion;
   (b) there is **no risk of serious harm** as defined in Directive 2011/95/EU;
   (c) the **principle of non-refoulement** in accordance with the Geneva Convention is respected;
   (d) the prohibition of removal, in violation of the **right to freedom from torture and cruel, inhuman or degrading treatment** as laid down in international law, is respected; and
   (e) the **possibility exists to request refugee status** and, if found to be a refugee, to receive protection in accordance with the Geneva Convention.
2. The application of the safe third country concept shall be subject to rules laid down in national law, including:
   (a) rules requiring **a connection between the applicant and the third country** concerned on the basis of which it would be reasonable for that person to go to that country;
   (b) **rules on the methodology** by which the competent authorities satisfy themselves that the safe third country concept may be applied to a particular country or to a particular applicant. Such methodology shall include case-by-case

consideration of the safety of the country for a particular applicant and/or national designation of countries considered to be generally safe;

(c) rules in accordance with international law, **allowing an individual examination of whether the third country concerned is safe for a particular applicant** which, as a minimum, shall permit the applicant to challenge the application of the safe third country concept on the grounds that the third country is not safe in his or her particular circumstances. The applicant shall also be allowed to challenge the existence of a connection between him or her and the third country in accordance with point (a).

(...)

Article 39

The concept of European safe third country

1. Member States may provide that **no, or no full, examination of the application for international protection** and of the safety of the applicant in his or her particular circumstances (...) shall take place in cases where a competent authority has established, on the basis of the facts, that the applicant is seeking to enter or has entered illegally into its territory from a safe third country according to paragraph 2.

2. A third country can only be considered as a safe third country for the purposes of paragraph 1 where:

    (a) it has ratified and observes the provisions of the **Geneva Convention** without any geographical limitations;

    (b) it has in place an **asylum procedure prescribed by law;** and

    (c) it has ratified the **European Convention for the Protection of Human Rights and Fundamental Freedoms** and observes its provisions, including the standards relating to effective remedies.

3. The applicant shall be **allowed to challenge the application of the concept** of European safe third country on the grounds that the third country concerned is not safe in his or her particular circumstances.

4. The Member States concerned shall lay down in national law the modalities for implementing the provisions of paragraph 1 and the consequences of decisions pursuant to those provisions in accordance with the principle of non-refoulement, including providing for exceptions from the application of this Article for humanitarian or political reasons or for reasons of public international law.

(...)

The Asylum Procedures Directive provides for three additional 'safe country' concepts on top of the 'first country of asylum'. The concept of safe country of origin applies to nationals or habitually resident stateless persons of third countries which are designated in national law as 'safe' in accordance with the criteria laid down in Annex I and Article 37 of the Asylum Procedures Directive which require it being shown that there is 'generally and consistently no persecution, (...) no torture or inhuman or degrading treatment or punishment and no threat by reason of indiscriminate violence in situations of international or internal armed conflict' in the third country. The second concept is that of 'safe third country' which, subject to the conditions of Article 38 of the Directive, can be applied to asylum-seekers with a connection (such as the presence of family members) to a particular third country.[98] The third concept is that of 'European safe third country' which is similar to the general safe third country concept; a key difference is the requirement that a European safe third country has ratified the ECHR which should constitute a guarantee of sufficient human rights protection warranting the return of asylum-seekers there.

There is significant divergence in the use of the safe country concepts by Member States.[99] Such divergence is partially inherent in the design of the EU law in question: Directives are not directly applicable but must be transposed into national law, and in the process of transposition, a degree of divergence among national rules inevitably creeps in. Second, the use of the safe country concepts is not obligatory for Member States and, as a result, countries pick and choose which concepts shall be part of their legal orders. Nevertheless, the general incidence of safe country concepts has proliferated following the 2015 refugee crisis with more and more Member States introducing these concepts as grounds for inadmissibility for asylum applications or as warranting the application of an expedited procedure.[100] Granting protection to asylum-seekers coming from a safe country of origin, a safe third country or a first country of asylum, as defined in the Asylum Procedures Directive, remains a possibility mandated by the Directive but applicants are faced with the need of rebutting presumptions concerning the safety of the country designated as safe under one of the concepts.

As part of the European Agenda on Migration, the Commission proposed a Regulation on 9 September 2015[101] to establish a common EU list of safe countries of origin for the purposes of the recast Asylum Procedures Directive. The proposed list comprised Albania, Bosnia and Herzegovina, the former Yugoslav Republic of Macedonia, Kosovo, Montenegro, Serbia, and Turkey. However, it soon came under criticism, in particular due to the inclusion of Turkey, thus stalling the initiative as a result.[102] Some organizations also raise concerns from the viewpoint of the principle of non-discrimination, claiming it will contribute to the stereotyping of application on the basis of nationality and 'a race to the bottom' in terms of countries adhering to standards.[103] The idea has fed into proposals for the reform of the CEAS. The new proposed Asylum Procedures Regulation would centralize the assessment of 'safety' by leaving the review of the situation in third countries to

---

[98] In Greece—a key state in the EU asylum architecture—two decisions by the Greek Appeals Committees clarified that transit through a country in geographical proximity to the country of origin does not in itself represent a sufficient connection. See 9th Appeals Committee, Decision 15602/2017; 11th Appeals Committee, Decision 14011/2017.

[99] The procedural divergence manifests itself, more generally, in disparities in processing times and celerity of expedited asylum procedures. Article 31(9) of the Asylum Procedures Directive requires Member States to set 'reasonable' time limits for the first instance decision to be reached and Article 39(2) leaves Member States discretion to set time limits for applicants to exercise their right to an effective remedy. Although data on the use of accelerated procedures in Member States are not collected systematically, making it difficult to evaluate current practices, the time frames for accelerated procedures appear to vary significantly. See A Orav and J Apap, 'Safe countries of origin: Proposed common EU list', European Parliamentary Research Service Briefing, February 2017.

[100] Asylum Information Database, 'Admissibility, responsibility and safety in European asylum procedures', 7 September 2016.

[101] European Commission, 'Proposal for a Regulation of the European Parliament and of the Council establishing an EU common list of safe countries of origin for the purposes of Directive 2013/32/EU of the European Parliament and of the Council on common procedures for granting and withdrawing international protection, and amending Directive 2013/32/EU', COM(2015) 452 final, Brussels, 9 September 2015.

[102] Orav and Apap, 'Safe countries of origin: Proposed common EU list' (n 99).

[103] European Council on Refugees and Exiles, 'ECRE argues against a common EU list of "safe countries of origin"', 23 October 2015.

the Commission, assisted by the European Union Agency for Asylum, which has been proposed to be created through extending the mandate of the European Asylum Support Office (EASO). The concept of safe third country has been similarly reinvigorated after 2015 with the purpose of confining asylum-seekers to countries at the EU's external borders. Notably, Hungary introduced a list of safe third countries in July 2015, which included, among others, Serbia, the former Yugoslav Republic of Macedonia (FYROM), and Kosovo, and has since resorted to a blanket application of the concept in respect of Serbia, which has been heavily criticized for disregarding fundamental rights and crucial protection guarantees in the asylum process. The Hungarian list of safe third countries was subsequently amended to include Turkey.

Ilias and Ahmed v Hungary, App no 47287/15, 14 March 2017

124. (…) **the Government's list of safe third countries (…), disregarded the country reports and other evidence submitted by the applicants and imposed an unfair and excessive burden of proof on them.** Moreover, the Court observes that, owing to a mistake, the first applicant was interviewed with the assistance of an interpreter in Dari, a language he does not speak, and the asylum authority provided him with an information leaflet on asylum proceedings that was also in Dari (see paragraph 13 above). As a consequence, his chances of actively participating in the proceedings and explaining the details of his flight from his country of origin were extremely limited. (…) the applicants [therefore] did not have the benefit of effective guarantees which would have protected them from exposure to a real risk of being subjected to inhuman or degrading treatment in breach of Article 3 of the Convention.

Following the implementation of the EU–Turkey deal of 18 March 2016, the Greek Asylum Service had to rely upon safe country concepts for the first time. Various stakeholders raised serious concerns against the presumption of Turkey constituting a safe third country with a view to declaring inadmissible the applications of migrants crossing the Aegean Sea to Greece. Although Greek law has not set out a list of safe third countries—contrary to Hungary or Serbia—applications have been declared inadmissible at first instance on the basis that Turkey satisfied the safety criteria. On appeal, these inadmissibility decisions were deemed incompatible with the asylum *acquis*. In June 2016, the composition of these Appeals Committees was modified, and more inadmissibility decisions were upheld. On 22 September 2017, the Greek Council of State delivered two long-awaited judgments regarding two Syrian nationals whose claims were rejected as inadmissible. It confirmed the legality of the fast-tracking of all applications from all new migrants arriving via the Aegean by examining the safe third country concept in relation to Turkey. Most importantly, the judgments upheld the dismissal of asylum claims on the basis of Turkey being a safe third country. The dissenting judge pointed out the problematic nature of the putative Turkish human rights guarantees on which the EU–Turkey 'statement' was alleged to have been founded.

> **European Council on Refugees and Exiles, 'Greek Council of State dismisses all complaints on fast track border procedure and declares Turkey "safe third country" based on doubtful documentation', 6 October 2017**
>
> (...)   It is a fact known to all that in the past years and particularly in 2016 in Turkey, both before and after the failed coup of 15 July 2016, prevails a regime, in which fundamental rights and liberties are openly violated, judicial independence has been dismantled, where freedom of speech and press are not applied and guarantees of rule of law are not applied to those opposing the regime; the assurances of the diplomatic authorities of this country, forming part of the hierarchy of said regime, have no credibility. This is valid when both the Directive and Greek law do not refer to any protection status, but require the highest possible protection status ('in accordance with the Geneva Convention') to be guaranteed, as seen below. What matters is not the protective legislation of a country, but whether and how that is implemented in practice (...)

In any case, even before the merits of international protection are assessed, the question is asked where protection within the EU should be provided. The Dublin system establishes the principle that only one Member State is responsible for examining an asylum application. The objective is to avoid overlapping applications in different Member States and in particular abuse of the asylum system by applicants. The criteria for establishing responsibility range, in hierarchical order, from family considerations (especially as regards minors), to possession of a visa or residence permit in a Member State, to whether the applicant has entered the EU irregularly or regularly.[104] Dublin is supported by the Eurodac Regulation[105] which contributes evidence for the application of some of the criteria under the hierarchy. In practice, the responsible Member State is often the one entered irregularly by asylum-seekers, despite this criterion being the lowest in the hierarchy. Where such asylum-seekers manage to nonetheless cross into another Member State (also known as secondary movement), the Dublin Regulation provides for a legal mechanism by which asylum-seekers can be transferred back to the responsible Member State. As a result, Member States lying at the borders of the EU—in particular the southern borders, by virtue of the geopolitical and economic situation in the Middle East and Africa—are determined as responsible for most asylum applications filed in the EU.[106]

---

[104] Article 7 of Regulation (EU) No 604/2013 establishing the criteria and mechanisms for determining the Member State responsible for examining an application for international protection lodged in one of the Member States by a third-country national or a stateless person [2013] OJ L180/31.

[105] Regulation (EU) No 603/2013 on the establishment of 'Eurodac' for the comparison of fingerprints for the effective application of Regulation (EU) No 604/2013 establishing the criteria and mechanisms for determining the Member State responsible for examining an application for international protection lodged in one of the Member States by a third-country national or a stateless person and on requests for the comparison with Eurodac data by Member States' law enforcement authorities and Europol for law enforcement purposes, and amending Regulation (EU) No 1077/2011 establishing a European Agency for the operational management of large-scale IT systems in the area of freedom, security and justice [2013] OJ L180/1.

[106] See also Ch 4 on EU secondary law on migration.

Regulation (EU) No 604/2013 of the European Parliament and of the Council of 26 June 2013 establishing the criteria and mechanisms for determining the Member State responsible for examining an application for international protection lodged in one of the Member States by a third-country national or a stateless person [2013] OJ L180/31

Article 13

Entry and/or stay

1. Where it is established, on the basis of proof or circumstantial evidence (...) that an applicant has irregularly crossed the border into a Member State by land, sea or air having come from a third country, **the Member State thus entered shall be responsible for examining the application for international protection.** That responsibility shall cease 12 months after the date on which the irregular border crossing took place.

2. When a Member State cannot or can no longer be held responsible in accordance with paragraph 1 of this Article and where it is established (...) that the applicant— who has entered the territories of the Member States irregularly or whose circumstances of entry cannot be established—has been **living for a continuous period of at least five months in a Member State before lodging the application for international protection, that Member State shall be responsible** for examining the application for international protection.

If the applicant has been living for periods of time of at least five months in several Member States, the Member State where he or she has been living most recently shall be responsible for examining the application for international protection.

The Dublin system was brought into existence roughly 30 years ago as a flanking measure to maintain control after the abolition of border control by a small group of Western European countries and was not part of the EU until 1999. Today it includes 31 countries which are rather different from each other in terms of not only economic and social conditions but also effective human rights protection. Although the system was revised several times, its central tenets remain untouched and there is an obvious reluctance on the part of Member States to rethink the principles which underpin it.[107] The ECtHR[108] and the CJEU[109] have contributed important interpretations of the successive Dublin Regulations and their implementation. At the practical level, statistics on the application of the Dublin procedure remain highly scarce, despite clear obligations on Member States to provide data

---

[107] S Peers, 'Reconciling the Dublin System with European Fundamental Rights and the Charter' (2014) 15 ERA Forum 485.

[108] According to the ECtHR in *M.S.S. v Belgium and Greece*, App no 30696/09, 21 January 2011, the Dublin system 'does not exempt [national authorities] from carrying out a thorough and individualized examination of the situation of the person concerned and from suspending enforcement of the removal order should the risk of inhuman and degrading treatment be established'.

[109] Judgment of 21 December 2011, *N.S. v Secretary of State for the Home Department and M. E. and Others v Refugee Applications Commissioner and Minister for Justice, Equality and Law Reform*, C-411/10 and C-493/10, ECLI:EU:C:2011:865; Judgment of 16 February 2017, *C.K. and Others v Republika Slovenija*, C-578/16 PPU, ECLI:EU:C:2017:127.

to Eurostat under the Migration Statistics Regulation.[110] For illustration, the EASO Annual Report 2016 skipped an account of the Dublin system altogether as 'at the time of writing comprehensive data on Dublin indicators in 2016 was not available from Eurostat'.[111] It should be noted that although the little available data seem to indicate a more efficient use of the Dublin procedures in 2016, the overall number of effected transfers compared to the number of procedures initiated and the costs entailed remains low.[112] Overall, the Dublin system and the responsibility principle it enshrines have been seen as deeply problematic for quite some time already; the recent refugee influx has only aggravated the problems and made them stand out more.

A Ripoll Servent, 'A New Form of Delegation in EU Asylum: Agencies as Proxies of Strong Regulators' (2018) 56 Journal of Common Market Studies 83

The increase in asylum seekers in 2015 has underlined the malfunctioning of the Common European Asylum System (CEAS). With this increase in the number of asylum-seekers, the core of the system—the Dublin III Regulation—has shown its limitations and led Member States to find alternative answers (...)

(...) the potential free movement of asylum-seekers generated concerns among Member States, who believed that refugees might abuse the system and lodge applications in several countries (...). These concerns grew during the 1990s, when the fall of the Soviet Union and the conflicts in the former Yugoslavia led to a steep increase in the number of asylum-seekers—affecting mostly northern Member States and Germany in particular. (...)

From the start, discussions focused on two potential mechanisms to distribute asylum-seekers: Back in 1994, the German presidency proposed a system based on a 'capacity principle' to redistribute people seeking temporary protection, which clearly imitated the scheme used in the German Länder (...). The idea behind the German proposal was to share the number of asylum-seekers in proportion to population, territory and GDP (...). While receiving countries like Germany and the Netherlands were clearly in favour, other Member States, like France and the UK, resisted the idea, since they received much fewer applications (...). Instead, the distribution of the asylum 'burden' followed (...) a 'responsibility system': whoever let asylum-seekers into the Schengen territory should be made responsible for them. This logic naturally translated into the 'first country of entry principle': if a Member State was not able to control its border or provided a visa that allowed an asylum-seeker to enter the territory, then it should also bear the 'burden' of the application (...)

The 'responsibility principle' does not lead to the typical free-riding situation where there is an 'exploitation of the great by the small' (...); rather, we witness an inverse

---

[110] Regulation (EC) No 862/2007 of the European Parliament and of the Council on Community statistics on migration and international protection and repealing Council Regulation (EEC) No 311/76 on the compilation of statistics on foreign workers [2007] OJ L199/23.

[111] European Asylum Support Office, 'Annual Report on the situation of asylum in the European Union 2016', 5 July 2017, 30.

[112] Wagner and others, 'The Implementation of the Common European Asylum System' (n 61); Asylum Information Database, 'Admissibility, responsibility and safety' (n 100) 13–14.

relationship of 'exploitation of the small by the great'. The origin of this relationship lies in Schengen, which establishes that free movement across a common area without internal borders can only work as long as all external borders are equally well protected. This means that Schengen is only as good as its 'weakest link' and this implies a very different distribution of costs and benefits. This logic also explains why Member States at the border accepted the Dublin Convention—taking responsibility for the borders was seen as a trade-off for the benefits they would enjoy as members of the Schengen area. (...)

In the course of 2015 the strict application of the Dublin Regulation would have resulted in Italy being responsible for the digestion of approximately 170,000 applications and Greece for roughly 860,000 claims. Due to the structural flaws of the Dublin system and the lack of an immediate joint EU response, Member States with the highest influx started to ignore Dublin rules widely by waiving through persons who did not explicitly request asylum on their territory. Member States could moreover avoid taking fingerprints to prevent responsibility. After it was revealed at the end of 2015 that Greece and Italy failed or neglected to register all newcomers, the Commission stepped up pressures on frontline countries, launched infringement proceedings, and advised the use of coercion if necessary.[113] In line with this, the system created a culture of fear of bumping into authorities which has, among other things, contributed to the disappearances of unaccompanied children from care.[114]

As mentioned above, these deficiencies, which became all the more visible and critical due to the high migratory pressures experienced in 2015/2016, have been subject of judicial disputes before European and national courts, in particular with regard to the right to seek asylum and the provision and quality of reception facilities in the Member States. As a consequence of some of these judicial developments,[115] Member States have been suspending Dublin transfers to some other Member States, notably Greece but also Hungary and Italy. Nevertheless, the intersection of the Dublin system and human rights guarantees came to the attention of the ECtHR at its inception and it has featured frequently in the Convention case law ever since. It has been consistently held by the ECtHR that the Dublin system cannot entirely and automatically release contracting parties from their responsibilities under the ECHR.[116]

T.I. v United Kingdom, App no 43844/98, 7 March 2000

(...) the indirect removal in this case to an intermediary country, which is also a Contracting State, **does not affect the responsibility of the United Kingdom** to ensure that the applicant is not, as a result of its decision to expel, exposed to treatment contrary to Article 3 of the Convention. Nor can the United Kingdom rely automatically in that context on the arrangements made in the Dublin Convention concerning the attribution of responsibility between European countries for deciding asylum claims. **Where States**

---

[113] European Commission, 'Progress Report on the Implementation of the Hotspots in Italy', COM(2015) 678 final, Brussels, 15 December 2015.
[114] Asylum Information Database, 'Admissibility, responsibility and safety' (n 100) 48.
[115] See Ch 4 on mutual trust and Ch 5 on the response of the ECtHR to the problem of human rights guarantees within the Dublin system.
[116] See the discussion of the *Bosphorus* doctrine in Ch 5.

> **establish international organisations,** or *mutatis mutandis* international agreements, to pursue co-operation in certain fields of activities, **there may be implications for the protection of fundamental rights.** It would be incompatible with the purpose and object of the Convention if Contracting States were thereby absolved from their responsibility under the Convention in relation to the field of activity covered by such attribution (…).

In an attempt to reanimate Dublin, an emergency relocation scheme was introduced in the midst of the refugee crisis. The European Commission proposed to use the emergency response mechanism under Article 78(3) of the TFEU for the first time in order to set up a temporary relocation scheme applying to a total of 40,000 persons (from states with an average asylum recognition rate of above 75 per cent) in need of international protection who arrived in either Italy (24,000) or Greece (16,000) after 15 April 2015. In his speech on the 2015 State of the Union from 9 September 2015, President of the European Commission Jean-Claude Juncker announced a proposal for a second emergency mechanism aimed to relocate a further 120,000 people seeking international protection from Italy, Greece, and Hungary. At the same time, the Commission proposed a permanent crisis relocation mechanism which would be triggered in crisis situations to help relieve pressure on border Member States that are most exposed to migratory pressures (and with whom responsibility often lies under the Dublin system). While the permanent relocation mechanism has so far not been adopted[117]—facing considerable political opposition in a number of Member States—the temporary relocation scheme was adopted by the Council[118] but had to contend with insufficient implementation. The application for annulment brought by Slovakia and Hungary against the relocation scheme was thoroughly rejected by the CJEU which underlined, among others, the importance of the principle of solidarity and fair sharing of responsibility in EU asylum governance, laid down in Article 80 TFEU.

Judgment of 6 September 2017, *Slovak Republic and Hungary v Council of the European Union*, C-643/15 and C-647/15, ECLI:EU:C:2017:631

291. When one or more Member States are faced with an emergency situation within the meaning of Article 78(3) TFEU, **the burdens entailed by the provisional measures adopted under that provision for the benefit of that or those Member States must, as a rule, be divided between all the other Member States, in accordance with the principle of solidarity and fair sharing of responsibility** between the Member States, since, in accordance with Article 80 TFEU, that principle governs EU asylum policy.

292. Accordingly, in the present case the Commission and the Council rightly considered, at the time of adoption of the contested decision, that the **distribution of the relocated applicants among all the Member States,** in keeping with the

---

[117] N Zaun, 'States as Gatekeepers in EU Asylum Politics: Explaining the Non-adoption of a Refugee Quota System' (2018) 56 Journal of Common Market Studies 44; E Thielemann, 'Why Refugee Burden-Sharing Initiatives Fail: Public Goods, Free-Riding and Symbolic Solidarity in the EU' (2018) 56 Journal of Common Market Studies 63.

[118] Council Decision (EU) 2015/1601 establishing provisional measures in the area of international protection for the benefit of Italy and Greece [2015] OJ L248/80; Council Decision (EU) 2016/1754 amending Decision (EU) 2015/1601 establishing provisional measures in the area of international protection for the benefit of Italy and Greece [2016] OJ L268/82.

> principle laid down in Article 80 TFEU, was **a fundamental element** of the contested decision. That is clear from the many references which the contested decision makes to that principle, in particular in recitals 2, 16, 26 and 30.
>
> 293. Faced with Hungary's refusal to benefit from the relocation mechanism as the Commission had proposed, **the Council cannot be criticised, from the point of view of the principle of proportionality,** for having concluded on the basis of the principle of solidarity and fair sharing of responsibility laid down in Article 80 TFEU that Hungary had to be allocated relocation quotas in the same way as all the other Member States that were not beneficiaries of the relocation mechanism.

The Commission initiated infringement proceedings against the Member States least compliant with the temporary relocation mechanism: Poland, Hungary, and the Czech Republic. The CJEU upheld the Commission's actions for failure to fulfil obligations under Decisions 2015/1523 and 2015/1601. The three Member States in question could not rely on Article 72 TFEU, preserving for Member States the ability to exercise responsibilities with regard to the maintenance of law and order and the safeguarding of internal security in AFSJ matters, to avoid their responsibility to contribute to the relocation of applicants for international protection.[119] This conclusion could not be changed by the alleged ineffectiveness of the relocation mechanism.[120]

8.5 Migration Control and Border Policies

The previous section gave an overview of the main legal channels for accessing the EU. It may be concluded that, as it stands, the EU migration governance includes very few regular migration opportunities. In addition, it is aimed at certain profiles of migrants: the family in the strict sense, the student, the—preferably highly skilled—worker. Due to limited legal avenues, people increasingly resort to irregular migration.[121] This was highlighted by AG Mengozzi in the case of *X and X* as part of his argument that Member States should grant humanitarian visas to asylum-seekers applying extraterritorially for short-term visas with the intention to request asylum.

X and X v État belge [2017] ECLI:EU:C:2017:93, Opinion AG Mengozzi

157. Frankly, **what alternatives did the applicants** in the main proceedings **have?** Stay in Syria? Out of the question. Put themselves at the mercy of unscrupulous smugglers, risking their lives in doing so, in order to attempt to reach Italy or Greece? Intolerable. Resign themselves to becoming illegal refugees in Lebanon, with no prospect of international protection, even running the risk of being returned to Syria? Unacceptable.

---

[119] Judgment of 2 April 2020, *European Commission v Republic of Poland and Others*, C-715/17, C-718/17, and C-719/17, ECLI:EU:C:2020:257, paras 171–172.

[120] Ibid, paras 180–185.

[121] Yet recent proposals to reform the asylum system still do not address this critical factor in migration.

> 158. To paraphrase the European Court of Human Rights, the purpose of the Charter is to protect rights which are not theoretical or illusory, but real and effective. (...)

The CJEU did not side with the Opinion of AG Mengozzi and instead rejected the suggestion that EU law would require Member States to accept applications for short-term visas filed for the purpose of obtaining international protection in one of the Member States.[122] This judgment of the CJEU is in line with established thinking in the EU about a need for migration control whereby the Member States can tightly regulate migration and enforce restrictions not only internally but also at the borders, and, increasingly, beyond them (extraterritorially). What the recent refugee crisis—and the ongoing high number of displaced persons around the world—contributed to this paradigm is that the conferral of international protection is now *de facto* included in migration control. It has been argued that the increasing 'securitization' of migration has recently extended to human rights which have become co-opted in the EU's and Member States' migration control activities.

V Moreno-Lax, 'The EU Humanitarian Border and the Securitization of Human Rights: The 'Rescue-Through-Interdiction/Rescue-Without-Protection' Paradigm' (2018) 56 Journal of Common Market Studies 119

The securitization of migration engenders continuous anxiety, calling for continuous vigilance to anticipate and minimize risks, legitimizing policies of permanent exceptionality. Under this optic, EU border policing, as facilitated/co-ordinated by Frontex, has been framed as a set of 'securitizing practices' pertaining to this process (...)

In the Mediterranean, against a backdrop of spiralling fatalities (...), the narratives of 'tragedy', 'emergency' and 'crisis' intersect with the securitization discourse (...), articulating demands for 'urgent action' that reinforce the security response (...)—helping also to re-frame it as merciful and key to guarantee migrant survival (...). Security, in this context, is permeated by 'humanitarianism' construed as life-saving conduct predicated on principles of humanity (...). By turning border crossing into a humanitarian issue, border interventions can be substantiated on compassionate grounds.

This is how human rights become securitized. The process constitutes a securitization (that of human rights) within a larger (already 'normalized') securitization (that of migration). (...) It is the defence of (a certain facet of) human rights that 'border integrity' symbolizes that justifies the attack on (one of the other dimensions of) human rights. Proximate and more distant notions of the same clash and discord, justifying the annihilation of (some) human rights so that (other) human rights can prevail. This omnifarious nature of human rights serves to downplay the real-world impact of maritime action on the concrete (human) rights of 'boat migrants'. Human rights become both the means and the end of the securitizing process; hijacked as the tool and artefact of securitization (...).

Conversely, a rule-of-law-abiding understanding of human rights would embrace the whole gamut of legal entitlements (...), such as to leave any country, to asylum, or to non-refoulement, allowing access to the full protection they entail (...).

---

[122] *X and X v État belge* (n 9).

The desperate situation of irregular Mediterranean crossers attests to the urgency of a change of paradigm. One that abolishes the 'rescue-through-interdiction'/'rescue-without-protection' model and lives up to the full dignity of 'boat migrants', recognizing that they may have good reasons (if not rights) that 'lead them justifiably to seek access to our territory' (...). Such an alternative model of 'accessible-protection-in-practice' needs investment in genuine SAR [search and rescue] and the opening of channels for safe and legal arrival (...). It requires an inversion of priorities: a return to de-securitized borderlands and the integral re-subjectification of 'boat migrants'—in line with rule of law standards.

Needless to say, the EU offers a different picture of its border policies. The official position of the Union—as it developed during the heightened migratory inflows of 2015 and 2016—is neatly summarized in the preamble of the newly enacted European Border and Coast Guard Agency, which emphasizes the connection between ensuring continued free movement of persons within the EU and the need to improve the 'management' of external borders. This entails, among other things, 'integrated border management' in which borders are approached holistically, bringing together different agencies and authorities to ensure not only security but also passage of legitimate trade and persons. The concept has been used and promoted in some shape or form by the EU since 2002.

Regulation (EU) 2016/1624 of the European Parliament and of the Council on the European Border and Coast Guard and amending Regulation (EU) 2016/399 of the European Parliament and of the Council and repealing Regulation (EC) No 863/2007 of the European Parliament and of the Council, Council Regulation (EC) No 2007/2004 and Council Decision 2005/267/EC [2016] OJ L251/1

---

(1) At its meeting on 25 and 26 June 2015, the European Council called for wider efforts in resolving unprecedented migratory flows towards Union territory in a comprehensive manner, including by **reinforcing border management** to better manage growing mixed migratory flows. Furthermore, at their informal meeting on migration on 23 September 2015, the Heads of State or Government stressed the need to **tackle the dramatic situation** at the external borders and to **strengthen the controls at those borders** (...)

(2) The objective of Union policy in the field of external border management is to develop and implement European **integrated border management** at national and Union level, which is **a necessary corollary to the free movement of persons within the Union** and is a fundamental component of an area of freedom, security and justice. European integrated border management is central to improving migration management. The aim is to **manage the crossing of the external borders efficiently and address migratory challenges and potential future threats at those borders**, thereby contributing to addressing serious crime with a cross-border dimension and ensuring a high level of internal security within the Union. At the same time, it is necessary to **act in full respect for fundamental rights** and in a manner that safeguards the free movement of persons within the Union.

A. Hotspots

An important—initially temporary—measure taken in response to the heightened influx of migrants in 2015 was the establishment of so-called hotspots in conjunction with an increased presence on the ground of EU agencies, namely Frontex (most significantly), Europol, and EASO. The 'hotspot approach' was presented as the emergency deployment of operational EU capacities in the 'screening' of TCNs (identification, fingerprinting, and registration), provision of information and assistance, and the preparation and removal of irregular immigrants in countries under pressure due to the number of people arriving—notably Greece and Italy—and the other Member States wanting to contain them at the borders.[123]

While the policy documents clearly envisage a multi-agency approach, the staff numbers on the ground show an overly present Frontex and substantially less represented EASO, Europol, and the EU Agency for Fundamental Rights (FRA), revealing a focus on Frontex-related tasks, in particular border control.[124] It is illustrative that the FRA had only temporary and minimal presence in the hotspots; despite the enormous impact on human rights of hotspots and more generally the processing of large numbers of migrants, the FRA was not, on account of its mandate and capacity,[125] in a position to monitor the human rights situation on the ground properly. It is similarly illustrative that whereas Frontex and EASO have received substantially increased funding for their work in recent years, no similar uptick in resources occurred at the FRA.

The focus on border control and effective returns as part of the hotspots approach became even more explicit after the 'conclusion' of the EU–Turkey statement, when the Commission announced the Greek hotspots 'will need to be adapted' to the 'objective of implementing returns to Turkey'.[126] Since then, the boundary between detention, reception, and increased control and punishment has been increasingly blurred in European migration and asylum policy. In Italy, 2015–2016 was marked with reports on arbitrary detention with a view to identification and coercion to give fingerprints.[127] In Greece, asylum-seekers could not travel to the mainland or other islands during the treatment of their request at the hotspots, with the exception of vulnerable migrants and people in a procedure of family reunification.[128] With respect to fingerprinting, it should be borne in mind that the Eurodac Regulation is at the core of identification of migrants, establishing a central system into which the fingerprints of all arriving migrants should be logged for the purpose of assessing international protection claims (and responsibility for them).[129]

---

[123] European Commission, 'Communication from the Commission to the European Parliament, the Council, the European Economic and Social Committee and the Committee of the Regions: A European Agenda on Migration' (13 May 2015) COM(2015) 240 final.

[124] European Commission, 'Hotspots State of Play', 18 December 2017 <https://ec.europa.eu/home-affairs/sites/homeaffairs/files/what-we-do/policies/european-agenda-migration/press-material/docs/state_of_play_-_hotspots_en.pdf> accessed 14 August 2020.

[125] See Ch 2.

[126] European Commission, 'Next operational steps in EU–Turkey cooperation in the field of migration', COM(2016) 166, 16 March 2016.

[127] Danish Refugee Council, 'Fundamental Rights and the EU Hotspot Approach', 1 October 2017, 18.

[128] Ibid, 19.

[129] Regulation (EU) No 603/2013 of the European Parliament and of the Council on the establishment of 'Eurodac' for the comparison of fingerprints for the effective application of Regulation (EU) No 604/2013 establishing the criteria and mechanisms for determining the Member State responsible for examining an application for international protection lodged in one of the Member States by a third-country national or a stateless person and on requests for the comparison with Eurodac data by Member States' law enforcement authorities and Europol for law enforcement purposes, and amending Regulation (EU) No 1077/2011 establishing a European Agency for the operational management of large-scale IT systems in the area of freedom, security and justice

That Member States and EU institutions do not regard hotspots as constituting deten-tion does not mean that it is not in fact the case. The ECtHR has recently reiterated that not the classification but concrete circumstances determine the applicability of Article 5 ECHR prohibiting arbitrary restriction of physical liberty. Although the facts of the case pre-date hotspots—the migrants in the case crossed to Italy following the Arab Spring events in Tunisia—the findings of the ECtHR are relevant in this regard. States are obliged to adopt laws which clearly and precisely govern the requirements and procedural guarantees of measures restricting liberty regardless of whether they are formally classified as detention in domestic law.[130] This applies 'even in the context of a migration crisis'. Advocate General Pikamaë has very recently advised the CJEU to determine that the forced stay of asylum-seekers in the transit zone of Röszke on the Serbian–Hungarian border, also not a designated hotspot, constitutes 'detention' within the meaning of Article 2(h) of Directive 2013/33/EU. Since the preconditions for such a detention, namely (among others) a motivated decision preceded by an individual assessment of each case and provision of information and legal as-sistance, have not been met, the detention should also be declared illegal.[131]

Khlaifia and Others v Italy, App no 16483/12, 15 December 2016

58. **The Government argued** in the first place that Article 5 was inapplicable in the present case as the applicants had not been deprived of their liberty. They had been received in a CSPA [Early Reception and Aid Centre], **a centre not designed for detention but to provide first aid and assistance** (in terms of health and hygiene in particular) **to all the migrants** who arrived in Italy in 2011 for the time necessary to identify them, in accordance with the relevant Italian and European rules, and to proceed with their return. (...)

64. The Court reiterates that, in proclaiming the right to liberty, the first paragraph of Article 5 is concerned with a person's physical liberty and its aim is to ensure that **no one should be dispossessed of such liberty in an arbitrary fashion** (...) In order to determine whether a person has been deprived of liberty, the starting-point must be his or her concrete situation, and account must be taken of a whole range of criteria such as the type, duration, effects and manner of implementation of the measure in question (...).

71. In the light of the foregoing, the Court finds that **the classification of the appli-cants' confinement in domestic law cannot alter the nature of the constraining measures** imposed on them (...). Moreover, **the applicability of Article 5 of the Convention cannot be excluded by the fact, relied on by the Government, that the authorities' aim had been to assist the applicants and ensure their safety** (...). Even measures intended for protection or taken in the interest of the person con-cerned may be regarded as a deprivation of liberty. (...)

[2013] OJ L180/1. It should also be noted that the Eurodac fingerprint database has by now transcended its original asylum-only related purpose and it can be accessed, under special criteria, for security and criminal reasons.

[130] A similar doctrine regarding domestic law classification of criminal offences is well-established in the *Engel* line of ECtHR case law. See Ch 6.

[131] *FMS and Others v Országos Idegenrendészeti Főigazgatóság Dél-alföldi Regionális Igazgatóság* [2020] ECLI:EU:C:2020:294, Opinion AG Pikamäe, paras 170, 178, and 186.

106. (...) the Court finds that **the provisions applying to the detention of irregular migrants were lacking in precision**. That legislative ambiguity has given rise to numerous situations of de facto deprivation of liberty and the fact that placement in a CSPA is not subject to judicial supervision cannot, even in the context of a migration crisis, be compatible with the aim of Article 5 of the Convention: to ensure that no one should be deprived of his or her liberty in an arbitrary fashion

Despite government denial, the laws in both Italy and Greece have enabled a degree of arbitrariness in the detention of migrants in hotspots and similar facilities.[132] According to an opinion of FRA on the hotspots, the risk of absconding—which represents a legitimate ground for detention—is simply automatically presumed in the case of migrants arriving to Greek islands; this obviously defies the case-by-case approach underlying most fundamental rights of migrants, including the prohibition on arbitrary detention. The FRA opinion is more generally one of the best-informed resources analysing the impact of hotspots on fundamental rights and it is therefore worth quoting at length. While coated in diplomatic language (the FRA is after all part of the EU institutional landscape), the opinion has highlighted a number of significant fundamental rights deficiencies in the hotspot approach, including the complicity of Frontex in participating in enforcement measures which may have breached the fundamental rights of migrants.[133] In an update of its 2016 Opinion, the FRA observes that only 3 out of the 21 formulated shortcomings were properly addressed in recent years.[134]

European Union Agency for Fundamental Rights, 'Opinion of the European Union Agency for Fundamental Rights on fundamental rights in the "hotspots" set up in Greece and Italy', FRA Opinion 5/2016, 29 November 2016

The European Union's 'hotspot' approach is a building block of its response to asylum seekers and migrants arriving at its territory by sea, often traumatised or in distress. It enables the European Union (EU) to assist in a more targeted manner frontline Member States in handling the arising challenges. (...)

However, despite a number of important initiatives the EU and national bodies undertake serious fundamental rights gaps persist, affecting the work of all actors in the hotspots, including EU bodies. While some of these can be addressed at the level of

---

[132] An Italian national judge is quoted admitting that 'the interpretation of the conditions concerning the grounds for and duration of the confinement of migrants in a CSPA was sometimes vague' in the *Khlaifia* judgment (para 25). In both countries the hotspots as such also originally lacked a legal basis, despite being partially operational since October 2015. References to hotspots in the legislation of both countries were introduced in 2016 and 2017.

[133] It has been argued that the role and responsibility of Frontex in relation to hotspots should be more clearly defined in EU law. The changes introduced in the formal transformation of Frontex into a European Border and Coast Guard Agency fall short of such a legal framework. See E Wauters and S Cogolati, 'Crossing the Mediterranean Sea: EU Migration Policies and Human Rights', Leuven Centre for Global Governance Studies Working Paper No 180, November 2016.

[134] These are 'Excessive use of force to take fingerprints', 'Experience of escorts deployed through Frontex for readmissions', and 'Effective monitoring of forced returns by independent entities': European Union Agency for Fundamental Rights, 'Update of the 2016 Opinion of the European Union Agency for Fundamental Rights on fundamental rights in the 'hotspots' set up in Greece and Italy', FRA Opinion 3/2019, 4 March 2019, see Table 1.

individual hotspots, others are directly linked to the overall mode of operation of the hotspots. Many of the protection challenges experienced in the Greek hotspots, which this opinion outlines, are the consequence of new arrivals' prolonged stay there. The possibility of swift onward movement of new arrivals to other locations avoids overcrowding and is an essential pre-condition for their dignified treatment in line with the requirements of the Charter of Fundamental Rights of the European Union (Charter). Other challenges with a similarly profound impact encountered in both Greece and Italy relate to unaccompanied children, including the operation of national guardianship systems. The hotspot approach is deemed to fail in respecting the Charter rights if these systemic issues are not addressed through concerted legislative, policy and operational response at both the EU and national level.

Delays in processing applications for international protection are a key bottleneck. This is especially the case in Greece, where, contrary to Italy, asylum claims are examined in the hotspots. Such delays have particular fundamental rights implications for unaccompanied children. The availability of lawyers who can provide support during first instance asylum proceedings is limited in the hotspots. (...)

Given the specific vulnerability of unaccompanied children and their protection needs, which cannot adequately be met in the hotspots, their asylum claims should be treated as a matter of priority, regardless of their nationality. In practice, significant delays often occur in registering and/or examining asylum claims by unaccompanied children.

Many persons arriving at the hotspots belong to vulnerable groups, for example children or persons who suffer trauma because they escaped an armed conflict or lost family members at sea. Identifying vulnerabilities beyond those that are visible prima facie or self-declared poses a challenge in most hotspots, notably as regards victims of trafficking in human beings. In the Greek hotspots, the absence of standard operating procedures contributes to an overall fragmentation of responsibilities for identification and referral. The important role of female staff is not always fully reflected. (...)

In the Greek hotspots, several factors lead to tensions putting at risk the safety of people hosted in the camps as well as the staff working there, such as limited community outreach activities about the persons staying in the hotspots, combined with overcrowding, lack of information (in spite of considerable efforts to improve the situation involving also EU actors) and protracted stay. Instances of violence, riots and demonstrations reported from the hotspots in Greece almost on a weekly basis signal frustration, communication gaps and a high level of distrust by asylum seekers. Many of them have stayed in a situation of legal limbo for too long with uncertainty on whether they would be given asylum or returned to Turkey. The infrastructure, operation and staffing of the hotspots is not adapted to the need to guarantee the safety of persons facing heightened risks, particularly women and children.

The role of the hotspots in supporting effective returns has become particularly prominent in Greece as a result of the EU–Turkey statement. Return decisions issued to new arrivals are systematically, without an individual assessment, accompanied by a detention decision, which allows to impose pre-removal detention also on persons who have agreed to return to Turkey. Although the readmissions take place under national law, challenges in respecting fundamental rights safeguards by the national authorities have implications for Frontex which provides escort staff for these operations.

To enable a possible removal to Turkey under the EU–Turkey statement, upon arrival all migrants in the Greek islands are systematically issued a return decision indicating that they will be readmitted to Turkey. This decision also contains a detention order based on a presumed risk of absconding, a ground considered as legitimate by national legislation (as well as by Article 15 of the Return Directive). This risk is, however, assumed automatically and is not supported by any specific arguments.

In practice, the migrants, virtually all of whom apply for asylum, are generally released from the hotspot (…) after a period necessary to complete the first registration procedures and are free to move around the island. The suspended return decision, however, remains valid and the person can be detained at any point. In particular, if a person agrees to be readmitted to Turkey and withdraws the asylum application, a practice that has been observed in some hotspots entails the deprivation of liberty of such persons (for example in a dedicated part of the hotspot) until the removal operation is prepared and executed with significant support of Frontex. This can take days or even weeks. As set out above, such coercive measure may be considered disproportionate given that the original detention decision was not based on an individualised assessment, and that the person actually agreed to return voluntarily which seems to be in contradiction with the notion of risk of absconding. Furthermore, being detained upon withdrawing an asylum application may have negative effects on the willingness of persons with even low prospects of obtaining international protection to return voluntarily.

While it must be admitted that the hotspots have substantially increased registration and fingerprinting rates,[135] they may not be called a great success from the viewpoint of swift processing of requests and providing access to protection. The hotspots have served as a filtering mechanism, sorting out the 'likely refugees' and the 'likely migrants', which has on more than one occasion been based on simplistic reasoning.[136] In Italy, forcible fingerprinting and disinformation of migrants, particularly in the first stages of the procedure, has been reported.[137] Currently, the situation has improved drastically and three of the designated hotspots (Lampedusa, Pozzallo, and Messina) are almost empty. In Greece on the other hand, a great number of asylum-seekers have sometimes for years been stuck on the mainland and islands, waiting to have their cases processed. According to reports, they have been living in deplorable conditions and some have been arbitrarily detained when protesting against these conditions.[138] On some of the Aegean Islands, the situation has further deteriorated, with increased numbers of arrivals in late 2019,[139] and especially after recent political tensions in EU–Turkey relations and Turkey lifting strict border controls with Greece.[140] Although the hotspots went from a measure of crisis management to a core element of the EU's asylum system, the corresponding legal framework, which would also set out concretely how compliance with fundamental rights is to be ensured, is yet to be established.[141]

[135] D Neville, S Sy, and A Rigon, 'On the Frontline: The Hotspot Approach yo Managing Migration', European Parliament Study, May 2016.

[136] Asylum Information Database, 'Admissibility, responsibility and safety' (n 100) 10.

[137] Asylum Information Database, 'Country Report—Italy: 2016 Update', February 2017, 21–22 and 36.

[138] Asylum Information Database, 'Country Report—Greece: 2017 Update', March 2018.

[139] European Commission, 'Communication from the Commission to the European Parliament, the European Council and the Council, Progress report on the Implementation of the European Agenda on Migration' COM(2019) 481 final, Brussels, 16 October 2019.

[140] B Mandiraci, 'Sharing the Burden: Revisiting the EU–Turkey Migration Deal' (*International Crisis Group*, 13 March 2020) <http://www.crisisgroup.org/europe-central-asia/western-europemediterranean/turkey/sharing-burden-revisiting-eu-turkey-migration-deal> accessed 14 August 2020.

[141] In the words of the European Commission: 'The hotspot approach has shown itself to be a flexible and useful EU instrument that can be adapted to any Member State in the same situation. Based on the lessons learned in Greece and Italy, the Commission will present later in the autumn guidelines, including a template for standard operating procedures on how to set up and use hotspots in case of disproportionate migratory pressure at the

B. European Border and Coast Guard Agency (Frontex)

The establishment of Frontex in 2004 occurred in an environment which was highly politicized and in which migration and asylum matters were already treated largely in a securitized manner.[142] It is little surprise therefore that Frontex would be developed along similar lines. Moreover, Member State sensitivities over national prerogatives, which typically accompany the establishment of agencies dealing with justice and home affairs issues, contributed to Frontex being shielded from oversight by the EP. At the same time, reluctance to transfer core national powers (border control) to the EU level was palpable.

S Leonard, 'The Creation of FRONTEX and the Politics of Institutionalisation in the EU External Borders Policy' (2009) 5 Journal of Contemporary European Research 371

The establishment of FRONTEX came as a response to the perceived need for an increase in cooperation amongst EU Member States with regard to external border controls. This was prompted by three main factors. First of all, as explained in the introduction to this article, migration has generally become an increasingly contentious issue in Europe since the 1990s, which has led European states to examine ways of reinforcing border controls to restrict the access of migrants and asylum-seekers to their territory (...). Secondly, as the date of the enlargement of the EU to ten new Member States in 2004 drew closer, there were specific concerns that these new Member States would not be able to effectively control the new external borders of the EU. (...)

When it was consulted on the Commission proposal, the European Parliament put forward several amendments aiming to reinforce its own control powers and those of the European Commission over the Agency. However, in a context where the European Parliament was weak because of the consultation procedure, they were not accepted by the Council and were not included in the Council Regulation in the end. As a result, the various mechanisms of control over FRONTEX are firmly in the hands of the main stakeholders (i.e. the Member States), with the important exception of budgetary control, where the European Parliament can play (and has already played) a crucial role.

(...) The isolation of the European Parliament—the traditional human rights champion in the EU—in the negotiations also contributes to explaining the relative low priority given to human rights issues in the activities of the Agency.

Increased migration into the EU along a continuing securitized perception of it resulted in an incremental expansion of Frontex' legal mandate. The founding Regulation[143] was amended twice[144] before the relaunch of Frontex as European Border and Coast Guard

---

external border of any Member State.' European Commission, 'Communication on the Delivery of the European Agenda on Migration', COM(2017) 558 final, Brussels, 27 September 2017, 12.

[142] S Leonard, 'The Creation of FRONTEX and the Politics of Institutionalisation in the EU External Borders Policy' (2009) 5 Journal of Contemporary European Research 371; J Huysmans, 'The European Union and the Securitization of Migration' (2000) 38 Journal of Common Market Studies 751.

[143] Council Regulation (EC) No 2007/2004 establishing a European Agency for the Management of Operational Cooperation at the External Borders of the Member States of the European Union [2004] OJ L349/1.

[144] Regulation (EU) No 1168/2011 of the European Parliament and of the Council amending Council Regulation (EC) No 2007/2004 establishing a European Agency for the Management of Operational Cooperation

Agency in 2016,[145] although the Agency remains commonly known as Frontex. The expansion of the mandate crystallized into a set of core tasks which comprise strategy, operations, coordination, assistance and urgent action.

Regulation (EU) 2016/1624 of the European Parliament and of the Council on the European Border and Coast Guard and amending Regulation (EU) 2016/399 of the European Parliament and of the Council and repealing Regulation (EC) No 863/2007 of the European Parliament and of the Council, Council Regulation (EC) No 2007/2004 and Council Decision 2005/267/EC [2016] OJ L251/1

(11)   (...) The key role of the Agency should be to establish a technical and operational strategy for implementation of **integrated border management at Union level**; to oversee the effective functioning of **border control at the external borders**; to provide increased technical and operational assistance to Member States through joint operations and rapid border interventions; to ensure the practical execution of measures in a situation requiring urgent action at the external borders; to provide technical and operational assistance in the support of search and rescue operations for persons in distress at sea; and to organise, coordinate and conduct return operations and return interventions.

Frontex has been involved in border and migration control in particular through so-called joint operations (JOs). In JOs, Frontex essentially blends its own capacity with that of participating Member State in the joint pursuit of pre-defined objectives in accordance with an operational plan. As regular border control is in the exclusive purview of the Member States, Frontex has traditionally had more of a coordinating and gap-filling role in the grand scheme of border management (but its own resources have expanded considerably in recent years). As part of JOs, Frontex has been notably active in the Mediterranean, executing and assisting interception and diversion operations (JO Hera 2006–7, JO Nautilus/Chronos 2006–2011) and apprehending, transferring, and interviewing migrants (JO Poseidon, JO Triton). Search and rescue activities were added to the Frontex portfolio in 2014. Overall, all these JOs have attempted to shut down or at least disrupt migration routes to the EU from Africa and the Middle East.[146]

Nevertheless, Frontex, even following its latest update, remains an organization with an essentially subsidiary nature to national authorities insofar as border and migration control is concerned, with, in particular, the role of the host Member State in JOs being recognized

at the External Borders of the Member States of the European Union [2011] OJ L304/1; Regulation (EU) No 656/2014 of the European Parliament and of the Council establishing rules for the surveillance of the external sea borders in the context of operational cooperation coordinated by the European Agency for the Management of Operational Cooperation at the External Borders of the Member States of the European Union [2014] OJ L189/93.

[145] Regulation (EU) 2016/1624 of the European Parliament and of the Council on the European Border and Coast Guard and amending Regulation (EU) 2016/399 of the European Parliament and of the Council and repealing Regulation (EC) No 863/2007 of the European Parliament and of the Council, Council Regulation (EC) No 2007/2004 and Council Decision 2005/267/EC [2016] OJ L251/1.

[146] M Lemberg-Pedersen, 'Losing the Right to Have Rights: EU Externalization of Border Control' in EA Andersen and EM Lassen (eds), *Europe and the Americas: Transatlantic Approaches to Human Rights* (Brilll Nijhoff 2015) 408.

as crucial from the perspective of responsibility. At the same time, the powers and scope for autonomous action of Frontex have never been wider. This mixed nature of the agency can lead to uncertainty in the demarcation of responsibilities between Member States and Frontex, including the delimitation of accountability for human rights violations.[147] Frontex can, of course, be challenged in line with the general procedures of the EU before the CJEU. Under Article 263 TFEU, its acts producing legal effects vis-à-vis third parties can be reviewed by the CJEU;[148] similarly, under Article 340 TFEU in conjunction with Article 268 TFEU, Frontex—as an agency of the Union—can be held liable for any non-contractual damage in accordance with the *Bergaderm* criteria.[149] In practice, both judicial avenues are rather restrictive for individuals who would like to complain about human rights abuse,[150] albeit additionally jurisdiction of national courts in actions against the EU is not per se excluded.[151] Frontex has also been endowed, following criticism, with a fundamental rights officer in charge of a complaints mechanism and with a consultative forum comprising other institutions.

Regulation (EU) 2016/1624 of the European Parliament and of the Council on the European Border and Coast Guard and amending Regulation (EU) 2016/399 of the European Parliament and of the Council and repealing Regulation (EC) No 863/2007 of the European Parliament and of the Council, Council Regulation (EC) No 2007/2004 and Council Decision 2005/267/EC [2016] OJ L251/1

Article 70

Consultative forum

1. A consultative forum shall be established by the Agency to assist the executive director and the management board **with independent advice in fundamental rights matters.**

2. The Agency shall invite EASO, the **European Union Agency for Fundamental Rights**, the United Nations High Commissioner for Refugees and other relevant organisations to participate in the consultative forum. (...)

5. Without prejudice to the tasks of the fundamental rights officer, **the consultative forum shall have effective access to all information concerning the respect for fundamental rights**, including by **carrying out on-the-spot visits to joint**

---

[147] S Carrera, L Den Hertog, and J Parkina, 'The Peculiar Nature of EU Home Affairs Agencies in Migration Control: Beyond Accountability versus Autonomy?' (2013) 15 European Journal of Migration and Law 337, 342.

[148] There is also the possibility under Article 265 TFEU to bring a case on the basis that Frontex failed to act.

[149] Judgment of 4 July 2000, *Laboratoires pharmaceutiques Bergaderm SA and Goupil v Commission of the European Communities*, C-352/98 P, ECLI:EU:C:2000:361, para 42: '(...) Community law confers a right to reparation where three conditions are met: the rule of law infringed must be intended to confer rights on individuals; the breach must be sufficiently serious; and there must be a direct causal link between the breach of the obligation resting on the State and the damage sustained by the injured parties.'

[150] S Wolff and A Schout, 'Frontex as Agency: More of the Same?' in C Kaunert, S Leonard, and JD Occhipint (eds), *Justice and Home Affairs Agencies in the European Union* (Routledge 2015) 45.

[151] Article 274 TFEU states: 'Save where jurisdiction is conferred on the Court of Justice of the European Union by the Treaties, disputes to which the Union is a party shall not on that ground be excluded from the jurisdiction of the courts or tribunals of the Member States.'

operations or rapid border interventions subject to the agreement of the host Member State, and to hotspot areas, return operations and return interventions.

Article 71

Fundamental rights officer

1. A fundamental rights officer shall be **appointed by the management board**. He or she shall have the tasks of contributing to the Agency's fundamental rights strategy, of monitoring its compliance with fundamental rights and of promoting its respect of fundamental rights. The fundamental rights officer shall have the necessary qualifications and experience in the field of fundamental rights.
2. The fundamental rights officer **shall be independent** in the performance of his or her duties. He or she shall report directly to the management board and cooperate with the consultative forum. The fundamental rights officer shall so report on a regular basis and as such contribute to the mechanism for monitoring fundamental rights.

Article 72

Complaints mechanism

1. The Agency shall, in cooperation with the fundamental rights officer, take the necessary measures to set up a complaints mechanism in accordance with this Article to **monitor and ensure the respect for fundamental rights in all the activities** of the Agency.
2. **Any person who is directly affected by the actions of staff** involved in a joint operation, pilot project, rapid border intervention, migration management support team deployment, return operation or return intervention and who considers him or herself to have been the subject of a breach of his or her fundamental rights due to those actions, or any party representing such a person, **may submit a complaint in writing** to the Agency.
3. Only substantiated complaints involving concrete fundamental rights violations shall be admissible.
4. The fundamental rights officer shall be responsible for handling complaints received by the Agency in accordance with the right to good administration. For this purpose, the fundamental rights officer shall **review the admissibility** of a complaint, register admissible complaints, forward all registered complaints to the executive director, forward complaints concerning members of the teams to the home Member State, inform the relevant authority or body competent for fundamental rights in a Member State, and register **and ensure the follow-up** by the Agency or that Member State.
6. In the case of a registered complaint concerning a staff member of the Agency, **the executive director shall ensure appropriate follow-up**, in consultation with the fundamental rights officer, **including disciplinary measures as necessary**. The executive director shall report back within a determined timeframe to the fundamental rights officer as to the findings and follow-up made by the Agency in response to a complaint, including disciplinary measures as necessary.

Although none of these measures can be seen as substitutes for effective judicial protection—in relation to which the absence of EU accession to the ECHR is notably detrimental—they at least show a basic recognition of the need to take fundamental rights seriously in border management and migration control, especially in light of Frontex's expanded role in the sensitive area of returning migrants.[152] The fact that the members of the consultative forum are expressly given the power to carry out checks in Frontex operations, including hotspots, is certainly a positive step for fundamental rights oversight,[153] in particular as the mandate of, for example, the FRA does not explicitly comprise such operational activities.

Nevertheless, it remains to be seen how effective the fundamental rights checks on Frontex put in place by the EU legislator will be. For instance, as of June 2017, only two complaints had been declared admissible under the new complaints mechanism, and only a dozen had been received in total.[154] Moreover, while the fundamental rights officer is responsible for monitoring it, it is not clear what suffices as 'appropriate follow-up' to complaints by the executive director of Frontex.[155] The 2017 report of the consultative forum sheds light on further causes for concern over fundamental rights protection at Frontex.

Frontex Consultative Forum on Fundamental Rights, Fifth Annual Report, 2017

(...) against the repeated recommendations made by the Forum, the European Commission and the European Parliament, Frontex maintained its reluctance to adequately capacitate the Fundamental Rights Office with the provision of sufficiently qualified staff to carry out its increased responsibilities. As already highlighted in last year's report, and despite the remarkable commitment and efforts of the Fundamental Rights Officer, the lack of adequate staffing seriously hinders the Agency's ability to deliver on its fundamental rights obligations including on key areas such as Frontex operational activities, the newly established complaints mechanism or the protection of children. (...)

[152] See Article 28 and subsequent provisions of Regulation 2016/1624. In 2017, Frontex coordinated and co-financed 341 forced return operations at EU level (47 per cent more than in 2016). See Frontex Consultative Forum on Fundamental Rights, Fifth Annual Report, 2017, 35.
[153] As of 2019, the members of the consultative forum were the following international organizations, EU agencies, and non-governmental organizations: The AIRE Centre (Advice on Individual Rights in Europe); Amnesty International European Institutions Office; Churches' Commission for Migrants in Europe; Council of Europe; European Asylum Support Office; European Council on Refugees and Exiles; European Union Agency for Fundamental Rights; International Commission of Jurists; International Organization for Migration; Jesuit Refugee Service Europe; Organisation for Security and Co-operation in Europe, Office for Democratic Institutions and Human Rights; Platform for International Cooperation on Undocumented Migrants; Red Cross EU Office; Save the Children; United Nations High Commissioner for Refugees.
[154] European Commission, Fourth report from the Commission to the European Parliament, the European Council and the Council on the operationalisation of the European Border and Coast Guard, COM(2017) 201 final, Brussels, 2 March 2017, 11.
[155] Article 25(4) of the new Frontex Regulation provides explicitly for the obligation to suspend or terminate activities in response to serious or persistent rights violations: 'The executive director shall, after consulting the fundamental rights officer and informing the Member State concerned, withdraw the financing of a joint operation, rapid border intervention, pilot project, migration management support team deployment, return operation, return intervention or working arrangement or suspend or terminate, in whole or in part such activities, if he or she considers that there are violations of fundamental rights or international protection obligations that are of a serious nature or are likely to persist. The executive director shall inform the management board of such a decision.'

In the context of Frontex operations, focus was maintained on the central Mediterranean with relevant exchanges on Joint Operation Triton and the adoption of a code of conduct for NGOs engaged in search and rescue (…). At the same time, the Forum reiterated its concern about Frontex activities in Hungary as the developments in Hungarian law and practice have further exacerbated the risks of Frontex being involved in serious fundamental rights violations (…)

In 2016 and in the first quarter of 2017, NGO vessels rescued an increasingly large number of people in the Mediterranean Sea. They joined Frontex assets deployed as part of Operation Triton, Italian national maritime assets and navy vessels as part of EUNAVFOR Med (as well as merchant vessels) in being called upon to contribute to search and rescue (SAR) operations at sea, in compliance with international law obligations.

The intensity of the flow of migrants (some 180 000 arriving by sea in 2017) in increasingly shoddy vessels, with ever more unsafe conditions aboard, led NGOs to strengthen SAR capacities in closer proximity to Libya, which in turn sparked a debate about their role, including accusations of encouraging more dangerous sea crossings and of links with human smugglers. With the reactivation of patrolling by the Libyan coastguard in the second half of 2017 (with consequent concerns about Libyan Coast Guard practices and for the human rights of migrants transferred back to Libyan detention facilities and the introduction by Italian authorities of a mandatory Code of Conduct for NGO vessels operating in the SAR area near Libyan waters, the controversy came to a head. This raised concerns with a number of Forum members about the direction of Frontex operations and the impact of measures taken against NGOs on their ability to continue life-saving operations at sea.

(…) Members of the Forum stressed the importance of conducting SAR operations, whilst clarifying roles and responsibilities of the different actors involved, emphasising the need to establish clear channels of communication. Frontex clarified in the meeting that it appreciates the role which NGOs play with regard to SAR and called for joint ideas for strengthening efforts to efficiently save lives at sea.

Overall, some observers have pointed out Frontex's place at the heart of the securitized and humanitarian approach to migration. Before Moreno-Lax (cited above) identified the co-option of human rights in the 'humanitarian-ized' justification for EU and Member State border policies, Aas and Gundhus observed the incoherence between Frontex's relatively recent adoption of a human rights discourse and the practice of its border policing. The incongruity between commitments to rights protection and security veiled as humanitarianism—stemming from the securitized perspective of migration—is fundamental to the entire enterprise of migration control at the EU's borders and it is heightened by the sense that the policed southern borderlands of the EU mark a dividing line between the global 'haves' a 'have-nots'.

KF Aas and HOI Gundhus, 'Policing Humanitarian Borderlands: Frontex, Human Rights and the Precariousness of Life' (2015) 55 The British Journal of Criminology 1

We have shown (…) the somewhat paradoxical and incongruous discursive prominence of humanitarian narratives and sentiments employed in the practices of border policing by Frontex officers and the agency as a whole. We have pointed out that the latter may be employing and promoting the discourse as a mode of governance and as a way of legitimating its own existence. In terms of analysis, Fassin (...) suggests that the increasing relevance of humanitarian reason and governance has taken place at the expense of the language of rights, which may in fact be gradually becoming outdated. The mobilization of emotional responses of compassion and the urge to assist practically thereby takes precedence over formal structures of rights and legal obligations. This may certainly seem the case considering the persisting structural obstacles facing those wishing to claim the right to asylum in Europe, as well as the conspicuous absence of the right to life in Frontex' internal organizational discourse.

However, our findings also partly contradict this predicament and reveal that the language of humanitarian assistance has grown alongside an intensified organizational focus on human rights. Frontex is increasingly and actively employing the language of human rights in its training courses for border guards and in its organizational structure. Exemplified by its Fundamental Rights Strategy and its Code of Conduct, it aims to raise the standards of police professionalism, including a lower threshold for reprimanding incorrect conduct of its officers. The development is partly a result of political struggles and pressure by other EU actors, such as the Council of Europe, PACE and the Committee on Migration, Refugees and Displaced Persons (2013). It is also an example of a more general trend within modern policing (...) and penal governance, where human rights have become, as Whitty (...) observes, a significant organizational risk (legal and reputational), which needs to be managed alongside other organizationally defined forms of risk.

Interestingly, the emotive narratives of compassion and humanitarian assistance are more prominent in the interviews with border guard officers who at the same time seldom explicitly mention human rights. Most of our interviewees nevertheless consider humane treatment of migrants as an important part of their professional identity, which also distinguishes them from other, less humane, police cultures. On the other hand, Frontex seems to have appropriated the language of fundamental rights as a standard item of its self-presentation. We are in a limited position to judge the impact of these developments on practice. As pointed out by previous research, human rights principles per se provide no firm base for police practice and can be subject to considerable flexibility of interpretation and enacting (...). The fact remains though that migrants' lives remain imperilled and their deaths are not systematically counted nor analyzed as organizationally defined forms of risk. Nor is there a systematic evaluation of the consequences of Frontex operations and diversion practices for migrant security, for the right to life and for the principle of non-refoulement. There is therefore a persisting and fundamental incoherence and discrepancy between the discursive attentions paid to human rights and humanitarian ideals and the practical focus on minimizing risk as defined by the objectives of state security.

This incoherence and duality characterizes the nature of policing of what might be termed humanitarian borderlands. The notion of a borderland is employed not only to denote the geographical proximity to the border, but also alludes to an uncertain, intermediate space or a region which is neither lawless nor marked by a well-functioning rule of law. In such a context, policing is conducted in a shifting terrain between conditions which are at the same time regulated and unregulated, humane and inhumane. This type of policing is, paradoxically, often conducted simultaneously with, against and through humanity. The mission is framed and legitimized through the language of humanitarianism and human rights, officers are partly required to perform their tasks as humanitarian agents, at the same time as they find themselves complicit and practically involved in deeply inhumane conditions.

Moreover, policing in humanitarian borderlands is marked by the challenges of working in multi-jurisdictional spaces with unclear lines of responsibility and frequent blame shifting between EU bodies, national authorities of member states and third countries. Officers are exposed to situations which, naturally and professionally, require of them certain emotional responses and sentiments, but which may also lead them to become emotionally distant or have difficulties processing the experiences in the aftermath of the operations (...). And while the persistent absence of official recording of border-related deaths might be seen as a sign of political indifference, the tragedies can have a great impact on the individual level—a situation for which officers often feel unprepared. As one officer put it, 'You get thrown to the wolves. Suddenly you are at the frontline. You see the fates of those coming over. You find people in cars who are dehydrated, who are about to die. You can in fact risk finding people who are dead already' (...). These challenging tasks are often invisible to the national public and are poorly acknowledged by national police and justice authorities.

While such conditions may be relatively common in international policing operations in the Global South, such as UN peace keeping operations (...), what is peculiar about Frontex is that it is operating in the humanitarian borderlands of Europe. Consequently, its operations are exposed to a greater level of scrutiny and demands for transparency, but at the same time also vested with a greater sense of political urgency. While the police are, colloquially, often described as 'the thin blue line' between order and disorder, the good and evil, in the case of border police the line gets an additional meaning of being a boundary marked by global inequality. Frontex is fending off migration pressures at Europe's doorstep, which is a crucial insight into the realpolitik behind its controversial yet persistent organizational growth.

C. Operation Sophia

As if EU action at the borders was not complex enough—with Frontex and Member States' coast guards jointly and individually taking action to control migration—the EU has added, at the peak of the migration inflows, a naval operation in the Mediterranean called EUNAVFOR MED Operation Sophia.[156] The Operation was part of a comprehensive approach to tackle immigration to the EU from Africa and the Middle East and its main stated objective has been to disrupt the business model of migrant smugglers and human traffickers who foster migration via the Mediterranean. Operation Sophia has been established under the rules of the Common Security and Defence Policy (CSDP) in May 2015,[157] and its mandate ended permanently on 31 March 2020. A new naval operation called EUNAVFOR MED Operation Irini has been launched. The main focus of this new operation has shifted from migration to the enforcement of the Libya arms embargo, in accordance with United Nations Security Council Resolution 2292[158].[159] As a secondary task, it also continues the efforts of Operation Sophia with regard to detection and monitoring of human smuggling

---

[156] Institutions of the EU have given considerable publicity to the fact that the Operation was named 'Sophia' after a child born on one of the frigates operating in the Mediterranean as part of EUNAVFOR MED. This illustrates how the EU has attempted to put into fore the life-saving aspect of its border and migration control.

[157] See Ch 9.

[158] United Nations Security Council, Resolution 2292 (2016), 14 June 2016.

[159] Article 2(1) Council Decision (CFSP) 6414/20 on a European Union military operation in the Mediterranean (EUNAVFOR MED IRINI) [2020] OJ L101/4.

and trafficking networks.[160] Since the chapter deals specifically with migration issues, and the workings of the entirely new Operation Irini remain to be discovered, the following part will focus on Operation Sophia.

Given that Operation Sophia entailed the proactive use of force in international waters, it arguably required UN Security Council approval to be in compliance with international law.[161] The UN Security Council has issued such an approval in October 2015 when it adopted Resolution 2240 which has been renewed four times, the mandate lasting each time 12 months. The wording of the Resolution made clear that any counter-trafficking action could be taken 'on the high seas off the coast of Libya'.

United Nations Security Council, Resolution 2240 (2015), 9 October 2015

The Security Council,
(...)

7. *Decides*, with a view to saving the threatened lives of migrants or of victims of human trafficking on board such vessels as mentioned above, to **authorise**, in these exceptional and specific circumstances, for a period of one year from the date of the adoption of this resolution, **Member States, acting nationally or through regional organisations** that are engaged in the fight against migrant smuggling and human trafficking, **to inspect on the high seas off the coast of Libya vessels** that they have reasonable grounds to suspect are being used for migrant smuggling or human trafficking from Libya, provided that such Member States and regional organisations make good faith efforts to obtain the consent of the vessel's flag State prior to using the authority outlined in this paragraph;

8. *Decides* to authorise for a period of one year from the date of the adoption of this resolution, Member States acting nationally or through regional organisations to **seize vessels inspected** under the authority of paragraph 7 that are **confirmed as being used for migrant smuggling or human trafficking from Libya** (...)

10. *Decides* to authorise Member States acting nationally or through regional organisations to use **all measures commensurate to the specific circumstances in confronting migrant smugglers** or human traffickers in carrying out activities under paragraphs 7 and 8 (...)

The original mandate of Operation Sophia has been amended in 2016 and 2017 to include among the tasks of the mission training of the Libyan Coast Guard and Navy; contributing to enforcing a UN-imposed arms embargo on the high seas off the coast of Libya; surveillance of trafficking of oil exports from Libya. The cooperation with Libyan enforcement authorities has raised human rights concerns in light of the destabilized situation in the country

---

[160] Ibid, Article 5.

[161] It could also be argued alternatively that Article 110 of the United Nations Convention on the Law of the Sea and Article 8 of the Protocol against the Smuggling of Migrants by Land, Sea and Air, Supplementing the United Nations Convention against Transnational Organized Crime provide sufficient legal basis for the activities carried out under Operation Sophia. See G Bevilacqua 'Exploring the Ambiguity of Operation Sophia Between Military and Search and Rescue Activities' in G Andreone (ed), *The Future of the Law of the Sea* (Springer 2017).

and associated rampant human rights abuses of, in particular, migrants.[162] Although not formally part of the mandate, the creation of Operation Sophia was spurred on by reports of hundreds of deaths in the Mediterranean, of migrants trying to reach Europe on inadequate vessels. This is acknowledged in the preamble to the establishing Council Decision.

Council Decision (CFSP) 2015/778 of 18 May 2015 on a European Union military operation in the Southern Central Mediterranean (EUNAVFOR MED) [2015] OJ L122/31

(2)   On 23 April 2015, the European Council expressed its **indignation about the situation** in the Mediterranean and underlined that the Union will mobilise all efforts at its disposal to **prevent further loss of life at sea** and to tackle the root causes of this human emergency, in cooperation with the countries of origin and transit, and that the immediate priority is to prevent more people from dying at sea. The European Council committed to strengthening the Union's presence at sea, to preventing illegal migration flows and to reinforcing internal solidarity and responsibility.

Search and rescue has also become the area where Operation Sophia had the most impact (despite its stated focus on tackling smugglers and traffickers). It has been reported that the Operation helped rescue around 40,000 people and 'neutralized' around 470 vessels in its first two years of operation.[163] However, as the objectives of the Operation were less concerned with search and rescue and more with disrupting trafficking and smuggling, there was considerable scepticism regarding what can realistically be achieved on the migration front by the deployment of military assets in the Mediterranean. A report by a UK House of Lords committee deemed the challenge of perpetual migration across the Mediterranean to be too big for Operation Sophia or similar military endeavour.

House of Lords, European Union Committee, 'Operation Sophia, the EU's naval mission in the Mediterranean: an impossible challenge', 13 May 2016

1. The current migration crisis is exacerbated by conflicts in the Middle East and the security vacuum in Libya, but it is also part of a wider phenomenon of mass migration from the developing to the developed world. This will remain a challenge for the developed world in the long term.

---

[162] Reports described particularly serious human rights abuses such as torture and enslavement. See UN Support Mission in Libya and Office of the United Nations High Commissioner for Human Rights, '"Detained and Dehumanised": Report on Human Rights Abuses against Migrants in Libya' (*ohchr.org*, 13 December 2016) <http://www.ohchr.org/Documents/Countries/LY/DetainedAndDehumanised_en.pdf> accessed 14 August 2020; Human Rights Watch, 'Italy: Navy Support for Libya May Endanger Migrants' (*hrw.org*, 2 August 2017) <http://www.hrw.org/news/2017/08/02/italy-navy-support-libya-may-endanger-migrants> accessed 14 August 2020.

[163] Council of the European Union, 'EUNAVFOR MED Operation Sophia: mandate extended until 31 December 2018', Press Release, 25 July 2017.

2. Current policies to deal with economic migration and refugees are unable to cope with the numbers in question. The international legal architecture, political acceptance and financial resources to manage an era of mass migration are not in place. This must be addressed urgently at the European level.
5. The intentions and objectives set out for Operation Sophia exceed what can realistically be achieved. A mission acting only on the high seas is not able to disrupt smuggling networks, which thrive on the political and security vacuum in Libya, and extend through Africa.
9. Libya has become a springboard for irregular migration to Europe. Libyan state weakness has been a key factor underlying the exceptional rate of irregular migration on the central Mediterranean route in recent years.
18. We conclude that a military response can never, in itself, solve the problem of irregular migration. As long as there is need for asylum from refugees and demand from economic migrants, the business of people smuggling will continue to exist and the networks will adapt to changing circumstances.
19. Nor is policing the EU's external border a feasible long term solution. Measures to tackle the problem must be taken before the migrants journey to Europe. The EU needs governments in the Middle East and North Africa that it can work with on migration. Therefore, building the resilience of these countries is critical.

It should also be pointed out that unlike Frontex, Operation Sophia had no internal complaints mechanism or a fundamental rights officer to address human rights abuses which might conceivably occur in the context of the activities carried out by the Operation. One such concrete concern related to precluding migrants from leaving a country (Libya) or the prohibition of *refoulement* in cases where the Operation might cooperate with Libyan authorities to take back migrants who have embarked on the sea. The principle of *non-refoulement* and international human rights law were recognized as binding on Operation Sophia in the preamble (recital 6) of its founding Decision.

G Butler and M Ratcovich, 'Operation Sophia in Uncharted Waters: European and International Law Challenges for the EU Naval Mission in the Mediterranean Sea' (2016) 85 Nordic Journal of International Law 235

In order to ensure the efficiency of the obligations under international refugee law, and perform them in good faith without having to risk breaches, states need to treat presumptive refugees, that is, asylum seekers, as refugees for the purpose of the application of the non-refoulement obligation until their refugee status has been determined. Accordingly, in the case of mixed migration flows, as are the prevalent conditions for Operation Sophia, a state needs to treat both refugees and asylum-seekers as refugees for the purpose of the application of the non-refoulement obligation under the Refugee Convention. Refugees and asylum-seekers intercepted or rescued by naval vessels engaged in Operation Sophia must thus not be returned to states where they would be at risk of persecution.

(...) Naturally, Operation Sophia does not prevent anyone from leaving the territory of an EU Member State. Nor does it prevent any person subject to the jurisdiction of an EU Member State to leave any territory. However, it may, at least indirectly, prevent people from leaving Libya. It is not clear if, and if so where, the legal ground for this limitation of the freedom of movement exists.

International human rights law places important restraints on the authority of Member States to take measures under Operation Sophia. While some of these restraints, including the rights to liberty and property, require Member States to create additional legal regulation, others, such as the right to life and the non-refoulement obligation, prevent them from acting in certain ways. This is, however, not to say that international human rights law hinders the performance of Operation Sophia. Importantly, UNSC Resolution 2240 (2015) repeatedly refers to the protection of migrants. The explicit intention of the resolution is to disrupt the organised criminal enterprises engaged in migrant smuggling and human trafficking and prevent loss of lives. The resolution does not intend to undermine the human rights of individuals or prevent them from seeking protection under international human rights and international refugee law. All migrants shall be treated with humanity and dignity and their rights shall be fully respected. Member States carrying out activities through Operation Sophia shall thus provide for the safety of persons on board vessels subject to inspection or seizure, 'as an utmost priority'.

D. Externalization and the EU–Turkey statement

The creation of the EU common asylum and migration policy has entailed involving governments of neighbouring and other third countries in control, detention, and—to a lesser extent—protection functions of EU migration management. The belief in relying on third countries to assist in carrying out certain policies could already be witnessed in the European Council's Tampere conclusions of 1999 when a bulk of EU justice and home affairs agenda was launched. More recently, the external dimension of migration governance has started to feature prominently in proposals for the reform of the Common European Asylum System and has been seized by some individual states as a way out of the political impasse on the European level.

European Council, Presidency conclusions, Tampere, 15 and 16 October 1999

11. The European Union needs a comprehensive approach to migration addressing political, human rights and development issues in countries and regions of origin and transit. This requires combating poverty, improving living conditions and job opportunities, preventing conflicts and consolidating democratic states and ensuring respect for human rights, in particular rights of minorities, women and children. To that end, the Union as well as Member States are invited to contribute, within their respective competence under the Treaties, to a greater **coherence of internal and external policies** of the Union. Partnership with third countries concerned will also be a key element for the success of such a policy, with a view to promoting co-development.

The actions of the EU and its Member States related or motivated by migration governance outside their territory have been variously termed as simply external relations[164] or foreign policy,[165] or more specifically as juxtaposed control,[166] remote control,[167] and ext raterritorialization.[168] There are various forms and degrees of involvement with neighbouring or other third countries in migration management. In 2005, a framework for the external dimension of the common migration and asylum policy was introduced under the name 'Global Approach to Migration', since 2012 supplemented by 'and Mobility' (GAMM). The GAMM defines the policy relationship between migration and (other) external action objectives, in particular those relating to development (often discussed as the 'migration-development nexus'). The area of migration is thus of prime interest to broader concerns about the coherence of external and internal policies of the EU. The initial, yet continuously relevant, focus of the GAMM was on the southern Mediterranean and Sub-Saharan Africa, and especially 'the fight against illegal immigration' in those regions.

Multiple legal and soft law instruments were developed to implement the objectives of GAMM.[169] The EU incentivized relevant third countries, in particular those participating in the European Neighbourhood Policy,[170] to agree so-called Mobility Partnerships and Common Agendas for Migration and Mobility. While not agreements in the legal sense, these political statements provide a framework for dialogue and cooperation on migration issues. The most important purpose of these instruments to the EU is to facilitate the return and readmission of irregular migrants. In return, the EU might be willing to relax visa requirements for the citizens of the third country concerned. Financial (development) aid from the EU is frequently part of the package as well.

The Mobility Partnerships entail the negotiation of legally binding visa facilitation and readmission agreements. The main purpose of readmission agreements, as stated by the European Commission, is 'to agree with the administration of the partner country on a swift and efficient readmission procedure'.[171] This focus on efficiency is liable to be in conflict with procedural rigour guaranteeing that rights of migrants—and particularly those eligible for international protection—are ensured in return procedures. In an evaluation of EU readmission agreements, the Commission warned, however, that the swiftness and efficiency which these agreements aim to foster 'must not be compromised by including measures which could give grounds to a revision of previous final return decisions or final refusals of

---

[164] S Peers, *EU Justice and Home Affairs Law* (Oxford University Press 2011) 127.

[165] S Lavenex, 'Shifting Up and Out: The Foreign Policy of European Immigration Control' (2006) 29 West European Politics 329.

[166] G Clayton, 'The UK and Extraterritorial Immigration Control: Entry Clearance and Juxtaposed Control' in B Ryan and V Mitsilegas (eds), *Extraterritorial Immigration Control* (Martinus Nijhoff 2010); M Cremona and J Rijpma 'The Extra Territorialisation of EU Migration Policy and the Rule of Law', EUI Working Paper LAW 2007/01.

[167] V Guiraudon, 'Before the EU Border: Remote Control of the "Huddled Masses"' in K Groenendijk, E Guild, and P Minderhoud (eds), *In Search of Europe's Borders* (Brill 2003) 41.

[168] B Ryan and V Mitsilegas, *Extraterritorial Immigration Control* (Martinus Nijhoff 2010).

[169] In addition to those discussed below, see Council Directive 2001/51/EC supplementing the provisions of Article 26 of the Convention implementing the Schengen Agreement [2001] OJ L187/45; and Council Regulation (EC) No 377/2004 on the creation of an immigration liaison officers network [2004] OJ L64/1, now superseded by Regulation (EU) No 2019/1240 of the European Parliament and of the Council on the creation of a European network of immigration liaison officers [2019] OJ L198/88.

[170] See Ch 9.

[171] European Commission, 'Evaluation of EU Readmission Agreements', COM(2011) 76 final, Brussels, 23 February 2011, 11. The absence of readmission agreements does not prevent Member States from requesting third countries to take back irregular migrants.

asylum applications, unless the relevant EU acquis so allows'.[172] This is an explicit acknowledgement that readmission agreements should not raise fundamental rights 'barriers' to expelling migrants from EU territory beyond existing international human rights obligations and the relevant standards existing within the EU.[173] Nevertheless, the most recent readmission agreements concluded by the EU at least include provisions broadly recognizing the application of international human rights law, as in the example of the EU–Armenia agreement below. As a further potential safeguard, the Commission has also suggested to monitor whether the treatment of returnees 'post-return' complies with human rights obligations.[174]

Agreement between the European Union and the Republic of Armenia on the readmission of persons residing without authorisation [2013] OJ L289/13

Article 2

Fundamental principles

While strengthening cooperation on preventing and combating irregular migration, the Requested and Requesting State shall, in the application of this Agreement to persons falling within its scope, **ensure respect for human rights and for the obligations and responsibilities** following from relevant international instruments applicable to them, in particular:

— the Universal Declaration of the Human Rights of 10 December 1948,
— the Convention of 4 November 1950 for the Protection of Human Rights and Fundamental Freedoms,
— the International Covenant of 16 December 1966 on Civil and Political Rights,
— the UN Convention of 10 December 1984 against Torture and Other Cruel, Inhuman or Degrading Treatment or Punishment,
— the Convention of 28 July 1951 relating to the Status of Refugees and the Protocol of 31 January 1967 relating to the Status of Refugees.

The Requested State shall in particular ensure, in compliance with its obligations under the international instruments listed above, the protection of the rights of persons readmitted to its territory.

The Requesting State should give preference to voluntary return over forced return where there are no reasons to believe that this would undermine the return of a person to the Requested State.

The GAMM, the European Agenda for Migration, and proposed migration compacts all emphasize the link between development and migration. Development cooperation—and

---

[172] Ibid.
[173] Under the readmission agreements, the EU can also, of course, be requested to readmit migrants. The agreements are only discussed from the perspective of the EU due to being overwhelmingly instruments of EU migration governance—they are of only marginal use to the third countries concerned due to the predominant direction of migration flows.
[174] European Commission, Evaluation of EU Readmission Agreements (n 171) 13–14.

notably funding—is considered the main leverage in discussions on return, readmission, and migration control. The mechanism is essentially one of conditionality—if countries agree to repatriate irregular migrants swiftly or prevent migration to Europe, the EU will reward them with development aid or other types of concessions such as market access ('migration-trade nexus'). The underlying reasoning relates to the idea of 'addressing root causes of migration', which can be anything from conflict and disasters to simply poverty (absolute or relative to European living standards).[175] Additionally, transit countries—states such as Morocco or Libya through which migrants from source countries travel to reach the EU—are engaged in this externalized response to migration by implementing 'stumbling blocks' en route from, most notably, Sub-Saharan Africa to the Mediterranean shores of EU Member States. However, studies have shown that improving living standards are accompanied by more migration in the earlier stages of the migration process.[176] NGOs and the EP have warned that development cooperation should stick to its primary aim and exclude any form of conditionality based on migration indicators in the allocation of EU development aid, while addressing the root causes of displacement by focusing on crisis management and prevention.[177]

It is important to note that not all externalization initiatives are per se problematic from a human rights perspective. The value and necessity of cooperation between states in managing cross-boundary phenomena is self-evident. An external dimension as part of a common approach to migration and asylum protection and management is thus certainly justifiable to a certain extent. Nonetheless, issues may arise where the engagement with third countries obscures the responsibility of the actors involved or where cooperation on migration control creates or aggravates human rights abuses. These two pitfalls can go hand in hand if various unorthodox arrangements are put in place to manage migration in dubious human rights circumstances. 'Novel' governance instruments—which frequently circumvent traditional fundamental rights and rule of law safeguards—are in part also a result of the fragmented and incomplete constellation of competences among the EU and the Member States.[178] The most prominent of these unorthodox instruments is doubtless the so-called 'EU–Turkey statement', the conclusion of which represented a watershed moment during the 2015–2016 peak migration influx.

The EU–Turkey statement, announced on 18 March 2016, put essentially in place an exchange of migrants arriving from Turkey to Greece. Under the terms of the statement, '[a]ll new irregular migrants crossing from Turkey into Greek islands as from 20 March 2016 will be returned to Turkey', while '[f]or every Syrian being returned to Turkey from Greek islands, another Syrian will be resettled from Turkey to the EU taking into account the UN

---

[175] Note that in cases where the root cause of migration is a humanitarian crisis, such as a conflict, there is a danger that not only development aid (employed putatively to prevent crises by investing in stability or 'resilience') but also humanitarian aid is misused for migration control instead of humanitarian purposes (responding to life-threatening needs). A parallel may be drawn with the problem of asylum-seekers eligible for international protection (on account of fleeing a conflict) being treated as 'merely' economic migrants. In times of large-scale crises (or when conflicts are numerous and perpetual), there might be a temptation to blur the lines between humanitarian aid and refugees, on the one hand, and development aid—which itself should be used for development rather than migration control but where more discretion and some overlapping objectives might usually exist—and voluntary migration, on the other hand.

[176] JC Berthélemy, M Beuran, and M Maurel, 'Aid and Migration: Substitutes or Complements' (2009) 37 World Development 1589, 1599; P Collier, *Exodus: Immigration and Multiculturalism in the 21st Century* (Allen Lane 2013).

[177] M Latek, 'Growing impact of EU migration policy on development cooperation', European Parliamentary Research Service Briefing, October 2016.

[178] S Carrera, R Radescu, and N Reslow, 'EU External Migration Policies: A Preliminary Mapping of the Instruments, the Actors and their Priorities', EURA-net project, 2015, 7.

Vulnerability Criteria' (these refugees should have been resettled within the EU in accordance with a proportional relocation scheme).[179] To get Turkey to agree to this deal, the EU promised to disburse EUR 3 billion on projects supporting refugees and host communities in Turkey, and another EUR 3 billion by the end of 2018, once the previous sum was depleted. Moreover, it promised progress on Turkey's accession to the EU, visa liberalization, and a modernization of the EU–Turkey customs union. The size of the concessions on the side of the EU illustrates how desperate the EU was to stem the migration flows in 2016.

EU–Turkey statement, Press release, 18 March 2016

In order to break the business model of the smugglers and to offer migrants an alternative to putting their lives at risk, the EU and Turkey today decided to end the irregular migration from Turkey to the EU. In order to achieve this goal, they agreed on the following additional action points:

1) All new irregular migrants crossing from Turkey into Greek islands as from 20 March 2016 will be returned to Turkey. This will take place in full accordance with EU and international law, thus excluding any kind of collective expulsion. All migrants will be protected in accordance with the relevant international standards and in respect of the principle of non-refoulement. It will be a temporary and extraordinary measure which is necessary to end the human suffering and restore public order. Migrants arriving in the Greek islands will be duly registered and any application for asylum will be processed individually by the Greek authorities in accordance with the Asylum Procedures Directive, in cooperation with UNHCR. Migrants not applying for asylum or whose application has been found unfounded or inadmissible in accordance with the said directive will be returned to Turkey. Turkey and Greece, assisted by EU institutions and agencies, will take the necessary steps and agree any necessary bilateral arrangements, including the presence of Turkish officials on Greek islands and Greek officials in Turkey as from 20 March 2016, to ensure liaison and thereby facilitate the smooth functioning of these arrangements. The costs of the return operations of irregular migrants will be covered by the EU.
2) For every Syrian being returned to Turkey from Greek islands, another Syrian will be resettled from Turkey to the EU taking into account the UN Vulnerability Criteria. A mechanism will be established, with the assistance of the Commission, EU agencies and other Member States, as well as the UNHCR, to ensure that this principle will be implemented as from the same day the returns start. Priority will be given to migrants who have not previously entered or tried to enter the EU irregularly.

---

[179] The statement was being negotiated since October 2015 and preceded by a joint action plan under which Turkey was to 'step up' readmission of irregularly crossing migrants from Turkey to Greece. Interestingly, a regular readmission agreement had already been signed in 2013 and was due to enter into force in 2017. The gravity of the situation in 2015, however, required urgent and more specific commitments in the perspective of the EU.

In the classification of McConnachie, the EU–Turkey statement constitutes a prime example of protection bargaining and quid pro quo replacing a principle-centred asylum policy.[180] At the same time, according to Cherubini, the conclusion of the EU–Turkey statement was hardly a rare or unexpected event; rather it fit well within the overall EU pursuit of externalization (or 'outsourcing') of migration to third countries.[181] What does make the statement stand out in any case, however, is its legal nature (or the lack thereof). Indeed, the EU–Turkey statement (or 'EU–Turkey deal') consciously evades the traditional terminology of international agreements. The extent of how legally dubious the statement is has fully surfaced in judicial proceedings brought by persons directly affected by it.

Order of 28 February 2017, *NG v European Council*, T-193/16, ECLI:EU:T:2017:129

8. On 18 March 2016, **a statement was published on the Council's website in the form of Press Release** No 144/16, designed to give an account of the results of 'the third meeting since November 2015 dedicated to deepening Turkey-EU relations as well as addressing the migration crisis' ('the meeting of 18 March 2016') between 'the Members of the European Council' and 'their Turkish counterpart' ('the EU–Turkey statement').

27. (...) institutions were asked, in particular, to inform the Court **whether the meeting of 18 March 2016 had led to a written agreement** and, if so, to send it any documents enabling the **identification of the parties that had agreed** the 'additional action points' referred to in the EU–Turkey statement.

28. In its replies of 18 November 2016 to the Court's questions, the European Council explained, inter alia, that, **to the best of its knowledge, no agreement or treaty** in the sense of Article 218 TFEU or Article 2(1)(a) of the Vienna Convention on the law of treaties of 23 May 1969 **had been concluded between the European Union and the Republic of Turkey. The EU–Turkey statement**, as published by means of Press Release No 144/16, **was**, it submitted, merely **'the fruit of an international dialogue between the Member States and [the Republic of] Turkey** and—in the light of its content and of the intention of its authors—[was] **not intended to produce legally binding effects** nor constitute an agreement or a treaty'.

29. The European Council also provided a number of documents relating to the **meeting of 18 March 2016 which constituted, according to that institution, a meeting of the Heads of State or Government of the Member States of the European Union with the representative of the Republic of Turkey, and not a meeting of the European Council** in which that third country had participated.

30. (...) the Commission informed the Court, inter alia, that it was clear from the vocabulary used in the EU–Turkey statement, in particular the use of the word 'will' in the English version, that **it was not a legally binding agreement but a political**

---

[180] K McConnachie, 'Refugee Protection and the Art of the Deal' (2017) 9 Journal of Human Rights Practice 190.
[181] F Cherubini, 'The "EU–Turkey Statement" of 18 March 2016: A (Umpteenth?) Celebration of Migration Outsourcing' in S Baldin and M Zago (eds), *Europe of Migrations: Policies, Legal Issues and Experiences* (Edizioni Università di Trieste 2017) 36.

arrangement reached by the 'Members of the European Council, [that is to say,] the Heads of State or Government of the Member States, the President of the European Council and the President of the Commission', which had been recounted in its entirety in the body of Press Release No 144/16 relating to the meeting of 18 March 2016 and setting out the EU–Turkey statement.

48. (...) it is for the Court to assess whether the EU–Turkey statement, as published by means of that press release, reveals the existence of a measure attributable to the institution concerned in the present case, namely, the European Council, and whether, by that measure, that institution concluded an international agreement, which the applicant describes as the 'challenged agreement', adopted in disregard of Article 218 TFEU and corresponding to the contested measure.

55. Press Release No 144/16 relating to the meeting of 18 March 2016 states, first, that **the EU–Turkey statement is the result of a meeting between the 'Members of the European Council'** and their 'Turkish counterpart'; secondly, that it was the 'Members of the European Council' who met with their Turkish counterpart and, thirdly, **that it was 'the EU and [the Republic of] Turkey' which agreed** on the additional action points set out in that statement. **It is therefore necessary to determine whether the use of those terms implies, as the applicant submits, that the representatives of the Member States participated in the meeting of 18 March 2016 in their capacity as members of the 'European Council' institution or that they participated in that meeting in their capacity as Heads of State or Government of the Member States of the European Union.**

56. In this regard, the Court notes that, although Press Release No 144/16, by which the EU–Turkey statement was published, includes, in its **online version** provided by the applicant as an annex to the application, the indication '**Foreign affairs and international relations**', which relates in principle to the work of the European Council, the **PDF version** of that press release provided by the European Council, for its part, bears the heading '**International Summit**', which relates in principle to the meetings of the Heads of State or Government of the Member States of the European Union with the representatives of third countries. Consequently, no conclusion can be drawn regarding the presence of those indications.

57. Next, with regard to the content of the EU–Turkey statement, **the use of the expression 'Members of the European Council' and the indication that it was the European Union** which agreed on the additional action points with the Republic of Turkey **could, admittedly, imply that the representatives of the Member States of the European Union had acted, during the meeting of 18 March 2016, in their capacity as members of the 'European Council' institution and had, notwithstanding that institution's lack of legislative competence, as expressly mentioned in Article 15(1) TEU, decided to conclude legally an agreement with that third country** outside of the procedure laid down in Article 218 TFEU.

58. **However**, in its reply of 18 November 2016, the European Council explained that the expression 'Members of the European Council' contained in the EU–Turkey statement must be understood as a reference to the Heads of State or Government of the Member States of the European Union, since they make up the European Council. Furthermore, the reference in that statement to the fact that 'the EU and [the Republic of] Turkey' had agreed on certain additional action points is

explained by the emphasis on simplification of the words used for the general public in the context of a press release.

59. According to that institution, **the term 'EU' must be understood in this journalistic context as referring to the Heads of State or Government of the Member States of the European Union**. In this regard, the European Council insisted on the form in which the EU–Turkey statement at issue in the present case was published, namely, that of a **press release which, by its nature, serves only an informative purpose and has no legal value.** (...)

60. On account of the target audience of such informative support, the press release in which the EU–Turkey statement had been set out intentionally used simplified wording, plain language and shorthand. However, **this popularisation of words cannot be used to proceed with legal and regulatory assessments and, in particular, cannot alter the content or the legal nature** of the procedure to which it relates, namely, an international summit, as the PDF version of the press release relating to the EU–Turkey statement indicates.

63. In this regard, the Court finds that the official documents relating to the meeting of 18 March 2016, provided by the European Council at the Court's request, show that **two separate events,** that is to say, **the meeting of that institution and an international summit, were organised in parallel** in distinct ways from a legal, formal and organisational perspective, confirming **the distinct legal nature of those two events.**

67. (...) **notwithstanding the regrettably ambiguous terms of the EU–Turkey statement, as published by means of Press Release No 144/16, it was in their capacity as Heads of State or Government of the Member States that the representatives of those Member States met with the Turkish Prime Minister on 18 March 2016 in the premises shared by the European Council and the Council,** namely, the Justus Lipsius building.

68. In this regard, the fact that the President of the European Council and the President of the Commission, not formally invited, had also been present during that meeting cannot allow the conclusion that, because of the presence of all those Members of the European Council, the meeting of 18 March 2016 took place between the European Council and the Turkish Prime Minister.

69. Referring to several documents produced by its **President, the European Council indicated** that, in practice, the Heads of State or Government of the Member States of the European Union **conferred upon him a task of representation and coordination of negotiations with the Republic of Turkey in their name,** which explains his presence during the meeting of 18 March 2016. (...)

72. It follows from all of the foregoing considerations that, independently of whether it constitutes, as maintained by the European Council, the Council and the Commission, a political statement or, on the contrary, as the applicant submits, a measure capable of producing binding legal effects, the EU–Turkey statement, as published by means of Press Release No 144/16, **cannot be regarded as a measure adopted by the European Council, or, moreover, by any other institution, body, office or agency of the European Union,** or as revealing the existence of such a measure that corresponds to the contested measure.

Two similar actions were brought before the General Court and decided on the same day, using the same argumentation.[182] These actions reveal in detail the extraordinary nature of the EU–Turkey statement; the confusion surrounding the statement on account of its questionable character is considerable. The entire statement was alleged to have been published in a press release, without any other prior legal procedure taking place. In other words, the EU committed multiple billion euros and established a readmission mechanism on the basis of a press release. It therefore goes without saying that, although the General Court avoided addressing this point, the statement strongly resembles an international agreement, given how tangible, concrete, and consequential it has been for both migrants and EU finances. It is, moreover, pertinent to point out that both the readmission of migrants and financial commitments are normally underwritten by an international agreement (a treaty) within the meaning of the Vienna Convention on the Law of the Treaties or the vocabulary of the EU Treaties (such as the one used in Article 218 TFEU). This is borne out and compounded by the fact that EU law provides for EU competences—albeit shared with the Member States— as regards both migration (return and readmission) and development/humanitarian aid. The exercise of these competences entails the use of the appropriate procedures, notably specified in Article 218 TFEU which would necessitate the involvement of the EP. In addition to sidestepping the question of whether the statement is an agreement in the legal meaning, the General Court did not engage with the potential problem of whether the EU prerogatives in the area of returns and aid have been potentially encroached upon if, as was held by the Court, it was the Member States, acting in their own capacity, and not the EU that 'agreed' to the statement.

This was indeed the critical point on which the General Court let the application fail. The circumstances raise some doubts with respect to this conclusion, however. The meeting at which the statement was agreed took place in the building belonging jointly to the European Council and the Commission. Both the President of the European Council and the President of the European Commission—both of whom are formally part of the European Council, the institution[183]—with the President of the European Council even being designated as representing the Member States. The General Court rejected these seemingly logical signs indicating that it was the European Council meeting with the Turkish counterparts. It found that on the same date and at the same venue, both a European Council meeting and an 'international summit' between Turkey and the Member States (with the participation of the Presidents of the European Council and Commission) were taking place.

An appeal was brought against all three orders of the General Court, and the Court was again asked to rule on the validity of the EU–Turkey statement. Rather disappointingly, the appeals were dismissed as manifestly unfounded. The Court deemed the arguments of the appellants not sufficiently clear and precise; it held that the appeal lacked a coherent structure and did not bring forward any clear legal contentions of the General Court's decisions. Furthermore, the Court is on appeal not able to review the General Court's assessment of the relevant facts and evidence.[184]

---

[182] Order of 28 February 2017, *NF v European Council*, T-192/16, ECLI:EU:T:2017:128; Order of 28 February 2017, *NM v European Council*, T-257/16, ECLI:EU:T:2017:130.

[183] Article 15(2) TEU states: 'The European Council shall consist of the Heads of State or Government of the Member States, together with its President and the President of the Commission. The High Representative of the Union for Foreign Affairs and Security Policy shall take part in its work.'

[184] Order of 12 September 2018, *NF and Others v European Council*, C-208/17 P to C-210/17 P, ECLI:EU:C:2018:705.

It is scarcely necessary to emphasize how undignified the entire situation appears from the outside. The press release at the centre of the dispute is simultaneously said to contain the entire written record of a hugely consequential intergovernmental deal and only use simplified, journalistic language whereby references to the 'EU' actually mean the Member States and 'agree[ing]' does not create agreements. Overall, the judicial proceedings have revealed that the EU–Turkey statement is a prime example of how semi-formal arrangements for the externalization of migration governance can muddle responsibility for crucial decisions, contribute to opacity and legal grey areas, and avoid established procedures ensuring democratic legitimacy.[185] This debacle for EU law is only offset to some extent by the existence of international law and, in particular, the ECHR regime which should act as a backstop against the complete undermining of human rights and rule of law standards by the EU Member States and Turkey.[186]

While the statement has contributed to decreasing migration flows on the Eastern Mediterranean route, it has not lived up to its principal commitments in practice. In 2017, there were still more people arriving to Greece than were being returned to Turkey. According to the European Commission, as of March 2020, almost 27,000 Syrian refugees have been resettled from Turkey in the EU. However, only 2,735 refugees have been returned from Greece to Turkey since March 2016.[187] The promised 1:1 ratio between returns and resettlements has therefore overwhelmingly not transpired in practice, which is consider to be a 'major obstacle to progress.'[188] Meanwhile, around 40,000 migrants remain stuck in squalid conditions on Greek islands, as relocation within the EU has also failed to meet targets.[189]

The implementation of returns to Turkey was to a large extent hindered—on legitimate grounds—by the Greek asylum system. While the Greek Asylum Service has been implementing the EU–Turkey deal, rejecting asylum applications on the ground that Turkey is a 'safe third country' and offers sufficient protection,[190] the Appeals Committees initially overturned 70 out of 72 first-instance decisions by rebutting the safe third-country presumption. Subsequently, following pressure of the European Commission[191] and the European Council the Greek Parliament approved an amendment to its asylum law which increased

---

[185] In an action brought by NGO Access Info Europe, the General Court has decided that access to Commission documents with regard to (the legal analysis of) the EU–Turkey Statement could be refused on the basis of the legal advice exception in the Transparency Regulation No 1049/2001: Judgment of 7 February 2018, *Access Info Europe v Commission*, T-852/16, ECLI:EU:T:2018:71.

[186] However, in a recent judgment concerning detention and conditions in a hotspot on the Greek islands following 'entry into force' of the EU–Turkey statement the ECtHR held that there was no violation of Article 3 ECHR on inhumane and degrading treatment in relation to the conditions in the hotspot, nor a violation of Article 5(1) ECHR, with detention for the purposes of returns under the statement not being arbitrary or unlawful, according to the Court. See *J.R. and Others v Greece*, App no 22696/16, 25 January 2018.

[187] European Commission, 'EU–Turkey Statement, Four years on', March 2020, <https://ec.europa.eu/home-affairs/sites/homeaffairs/files/what-we-do/policies/european-agenda-migration/20200318_managing-migration-eu-turkey-statement-4-years-on_en.pdf> accessed 14 August 2020.

[188] European Commission, 'Communication from the Commission to the European Parliament, the European Council and the Council, Progress report on the Implementation of the European Agenda on Migration' COM(2019) 481 final, Brussels, 16 October 2019, 6.

[189] The now-expired relocation measures were Council Decision (EU) 2015/1601 establishing provisional measures in the area of international protection for the benefit of Italy and Greece [2015] OJ L248/80; and Council Decision (EU) 2016/1754 amending Decision (EU) 2015/1601 establishing provisional measures in the area of international protection for the benefit of Italy and Greece [2016] OJ L268/82.

[190] European Council on Refugees and Exiles, 'Greece Amends its Asylum Law after Multiple Appeals Board Decisions Overturn the Presumption of Turkey as a "Safe Third Country"' (*ECRE*, 24 June 2016) <http://www.ecre.org/greece-amends-its-asylum-law-after-multiple-appeals-board-decisions-overturn-the-presumption-of-turkey-as-a-safe-third-country/> accessed 14 August 2020.

[191] E Zalan, 'EU Pushes Greece to Set Up New Asylum Committees' (*EU Observer*, 15 June 2016) <https://euobserver.com/migration/133841> accessed 14 August 2020.

the number of government representatives sitting on the Appeals Committees, removed the possibility for asylum seekers to request a personal hearing before the Committees, and enabled the European Asylum Office to conduct interviews of applicants in the context of the exceptional procedure applied at the border.[192] The context and timing gave rise to serious concerns as regards the constitutionality of the amendment and the impartiality and independence of the Appeals Committees, in particular in view of the right to an effective remedy protected by Article 47 of the Charter and Article 13 ECHR. Nevertheless, the Greek Council of State decided the new composition was constitutional and that Turkey could be considered a safe third country.[193]

To carry out the EU–Turkey deal, Greek authorities have also instituted a policy of containment, keeping asylum-seekers confined to the islands in order to process most asylum-seekers under an accelerated procedure designed to assess whether the asylum-seeker in question may be sent back to Turkey. However, continued (and in the autumn of 2019 even increased) arrivals, mismanagement of aid, continued slow pace of decision-making in asylum procedures, and initial rejections of returns to Turkey by Greek Appeals Committees have stranded asylum-seekers in overcrowded camps and abysmal conditions for months or even years, while they awaited the processing of their asylum applications. This, together with the authorities' failure to identify vulnerable people who are exempt from the above procedure, has resulted in deteriorating security and mental health of the asylum-seekers on the islands.[194] Conditions are particularly worrying and extremely dire in Moria on Lesbos, where a refugee camp set up for 3,500 people has been inhabited by some 20,000 asylum seekers before being destroyed by a fire during a coronavirus outbreak in September 2020.[195]

Despite financial and technical assistance to Greece, various organizations have highlighted the serious shortcomings in the access to asylum for people arriving to Greece. Greek legislation adopted following the EU–Turkey statement established a fast-track procedure for examining the eligibility and admissibility for international protection claims within 15 days, including appeal. There is no guaranteed free legal assistance during the initial procedure and oral hearings during the appeal are limited. In practice, the procedure takes far longer and considerable discrepancies in waiting periods exist, depending on the nationality of the asylum-seeker, due to presumptions about eligibility for international protection. Other issues include poor or no translation during interviews in some cases, as well as a lack of access to information and legal assistance.[196] The EU–Turkey statement has therefore not only failed to address the untenable migration situation in Greece effectively, it has also failed to maintain the same level of respect for human rights of migrants. Returns to Turkey could in some cases constitute a breach of the EU's or Greece's human rights obligations

---

[192] Asylum Information Database, 'Greece: Appeal Rules Amended after Rebuttal of Turkey's Safety' (*AIDA*, 16 June 2016) <http://www.asylumineurope.org/news/01-07-2016/greece-appeal-rules-amended-after-rebuttal-turkeys-safety> accessed 14 August 2020.

[193] European Commission, 'Annex to the Sixth Report on the Progress made in the implementation of the EU–Turkey Statement', COM(2017) 323 final, Brussels, 13 June 2017, 4.

[194] Several NGOs documented numerous incidents of self-harm, suicide attempts, aggression, anxiety, and depression. See, for example, Human Rights Watch, 'EU/Greece: Asylum Seekers' Silent Mental Health Crisis' (*hrw.org*, 12 July 2017) <http://www.hrw.org/news/2017/07/12/eu/greece-asylum-seekers-silent-mental-health-crisis> accessed 14 August 2020.

[195] I Eliassen and S Malichudis, 'Europe's Refugee Regime Pushes External Borders to the Limit' (*Investigate Europe*, 19 February 2020) <http://www.investigate-europe.eu/en/2020/europes-new-refugee-regime-pushing-external-borders-to-the-limit/> accessed 14 August 2020.

[196] Human Rights Watch, 'Greece: A Year of Suffering for Asylum Seekers' (*hrw.org*, 15 March 2017) <http://www.hrw.org/news/2017/03/15/greece-year-suffering-asylum-seekers> accessed 14 August 2020.

because of Turkey's long-standing *refoulement* record, as well as the dire living conditions for asylum-seekers in the country.

Recently, the EU–Turkey statement experienced a major setback, resulting from the decision of Turkish President Erdogan to reopen Turkey's borders with Greece on 27 February 2020. This action was prompted by a small military defeat in the context of the ongoing Syrian conflict, causing fear that hundreds of thousands of new Syrian refugees would cross the border into Turkey. Underlying factors and growing Turkish dissatisfaction, however, may explain the sudden move of President Erdogan rather better. Turkey wanted to force the EU to keep up its end of the bargain. Under the 2016 statement, apart from the deal on the exchange of refugees, the EU was also obliged to take steps towards visa liberalization, a customs union upgrade, and accelerated negotiations over Turkish accession to the EU. Not much has been done to fulfil these 'promises'. On a tactical level, Turkey demands EU support for its military endeavours in Syria and Libya. Following the announcement of the border opening, thousands of refugees have tried to reach Greek territory, where they have been met with (severe) violence of Greek security forces pushing them back.[197] So far, these forceful expulsions and clear human rights violations in the border areas have not been condemned by the EU. On 9 March 2020, shortly after President Erdogan's decision to disregard Turkey's obligations under the EU–Turkey statement, a meeting was convened between him and the presidents of the European Council and the Commission, in order to overcome their differences with regard to migration, security, and stability in the region. It was decided to have the High Representative and the Turkish Minister for Foreign affairs re-evaluate the statement and clarify the interpretation relating to its implementation. This has bought the Union some time to clear the air and to restore dialogue with Turkey.[198]

---

[197] Human Rights Watch, 'Greece: Violence Against Asylum Seekers at Border: Detained, Assaulted, Stripped, Summarily Deported' (*hrw.org*, 17 March 2020) <http://www.hrw.org/news/2020/03/17/greece-violence-against-asylum-seekers-border> accessed 14 August 2020; B Mandiraci, 'Sharing the Burden' (n 140).

[198] Remarks by President Charles Michel after the meeting with President of Turkey Recep Tayyip Erdoğan in Brussels, Press Release, 9 March 2020, available at <http://www.consilium.europa.eu/en/press/press-releases/2020/03/09/remarks-by-president-charles-michel-after-the-meeting-with-president-of-turkey-recep-tayyip-erdogan/> accessed 14 August 2020.

9

Human Rights in EU External Action

9.1 Introduction

This chapter introduces the central aspects of human rights in EU external policies and representation. As such, it focuses on the second prong of the EU's relationship with human rights—their external promotion (as opposed to their internal protection). The chapter discusses the basic Treaty and policy framework governing the external promotion of human rights (and other values) by the EU, the tools the EU employs in this regard, and specific areas of external action, other than trade and development which are discussed separately in Chapters 10 and 11. Altogether, the elements discussed in this chapter, when seen in light of the EU's internal system of fundamental rights protection, are what makes the EU a global human rights actor.[1]

Note that the toolkit (see Figure 9.1) does not contain the Common Foreign and Security Policy (CFSP) which, albeit of a general nature, can—and by virtue of Article 22 of the Treaty on European Union (TEU) should—also contribute to the achievement of the EU's principled foreign policy objectives, including the promotion of human rights. Due to the specific features of the CFSP, its framework, tools, and EU action thereunder are discussed separately.

9.2 Horizontal Principles and Objectives

The general principles and objectives of EU external action are unsurprisingly enshrined in the EU Treaties (see Figure 9.1). The most important provisions in this regard are Articles 3(5) and 21 TEU, although Article 49 TEU (enlargement) and Article 8 TEU (neighbourhood) in conjunction with Article 2 TEU (EU values) are also of relevance for the respective policy domains. This is made explicit by Article 205 pf the Treaty on the Functioning of the European Union (TFEU) which relates to core EU external competences (trade, development, and humanitarian aid, but not the CFSP), as well as the specific provisions governing these competences (trade: Article 207(1) TFEU; development: 208(1) and 209(2) TFEU; financial assistance: 212(1) TFEU; humanitarian aid: 214(1) TFEU). The standard formula used in the TFEU when referring to foreign policy principles and objectives is that a given EU competence 'shall be carried out within the framework of the principles and objectives of its external action'.

When it comes to the specific objective of promoting human rights, the policy is elaborated in the EU Strategic Framework on Human Rights and Democracy which constitutes the central reference point in EU human rights policy. It is complemented and implemented

---

[1] T King, 'The European Union as a Human Rights Actor' in M O'Flaherty (ed), *Human Rights Diplomacy: Contemporary Perspectives* (Martinus Nijhoff 2011) 77.

The European Union and Human Rights. Jan Wouters and Michal Ovádek, Oxford University Press (2021). © Jan Wouters and Michal Ovádek. DOI: 10.1093/oso/9780198814177.003.0009

Figure 9.1 Principles and tools of EU external human rights engagement

by more specific policy documents (notably the EU Action Plan on Human Rights and Democracy) and instruments, discussed in the following section on the external human rights 'toolkit'.

A. Articles 3(5) and 21 TEU

The general principled philosophy of EU external action is enshrined in Article 21 TEU. This provision is meant to permeate all foreign policy conducted by the EU, including under the heading of the CFSP (Article 23 TEU). According to Article 22 TEU, the European Council is to identify strategic interests and objectives of the EU on the basis of Article 21 TEU. Moreover, Article 3(5) TEU partially restates some of the principles of Article 21 TEU; with respect to human rights it specifically mentions the protection of the rights of the child.

Consolidated version of the Treaty on European Union [2012] OJ C326/13

Article 3

5. In its relations with the wider world, the Union shall uphold and promote its values and interests and contribute to the protection of its citizens. It shall contribute to peace, security, the sustainable development of the Earth, solidarity and mutual respect among peoples, free and fair trade, eradication of poverty and **the protection of human rights, in particular the rights of the child**, as well as to the strict observance and the development of international law, including respect for the principles of the United Nations Charter.

Article 21

1. **The Union's action on the international scene shall be guided by the principles which have inspired its own creation**, development and enlargement, and which it seeks to advance in the wider world: democracy, the rule of law, **the universality and indivisibility of human rights and fundamental freedoms, respect for human dignity**, the principles of equality and solidarity, and respect for the principles of the United Nations Charter and international law.

   The Union shall seek to develop relations and build partnerships with third countries, and international, regional or global organisations which share the principles referred to in the first subparagraph. It shall promote multilateral solutions to common problems, in particular in the framework of the United Nations.

2. The Union shall define and pursue common policies and actions, and shall work for a high degree of cooperation in all fields of international relations, in order to:

   (a) safeguard its values, fundamental interests, security, independence and integrity;

   (b) **consolidate and support democracy, the rule of law, human rights and the principles of international law;**

   (c) preserve peace, prevent conflicts and strengthen international security, in accordance with the purposes and principles of the United Nations Charter, with the principles of the Helsinki Final Act and with the aims of the Charter of Paris, including those relating to external borders;

   (d) foster the sustainable economic, social and environmental development of developing countries, with the primary aim of eradicating poverty;

   (e) encourage the integration of all countries into the world economy, including through the progressive abolition of restrictions on international trade;

   (f) help develop international measures to preserve and improve the quality of the environment and the sustainable management of global natural resources, in order to ensure sustainable development;

   (g) assist populations, countries and regions confronting natural or man-made disasters; and

   (h) promote an international system based on stronger multilateral cooperation and good global governance.

3. **The Union shall respect the principles and pursue the objectives set out in paragraphs 1 and 2 in the development and implementation of the different areas of the Union's external action covered by this Title and by Part Five of the Treaty on the Functioning of the European Union, and of the external aspects of its other policies.**

The Union shall ensure consistency between the different areas of its external action and between these and its other policies. The Council and the Commission, assisted by the High Representative of the Union for Foreign Affairs and Security Policy, shall ensure that consistency and shall cooperate to that effect.

Article 21 TEU and Article 3(5) TEU commit the EU to pursue a foreign policy based on particular principles and objectives—a foreign policy with 'ethical dimensions'[2]—with

---

[2] U Khaliq, *Ethical Dimensions of the Foreign Policy of the European Union: A Legal Appraisal* (Cambridge University Press 2008).

human rights promotion and protection chiefly among them. The language of principles does not, however, create a self-standing legal basis on which EU external action can be based. Rather, these provisions create an obligation on the EU to act consistently with the principles whenever it acts externally on the basis of other provisions. As the last part of Article 21(3) TEU shows, the obligation applies not only to areas of external competence proper but also to 'external aspects' of other, including internal, policies. Tension exists between saying that Article 21 TEU does not supply a new legal basis for EU external action while at the same time asserting that it imposes a legal obligation on the EU to act in a certain way—the line between acting to honour the latter obligation and acting beyond the scope of existing competences can be very fine at times. In such boundary cases, assessing whether a line has been crossed will come down to normative choices, including that between more or less 'Europe' in external relations.

A similar tension can be observed in the implementation of Charter obligations by the Member States: on the one hand, the Charter obviously creates obligations incumbent on the Member States while on the other, the application of the Charter is restricted to the material scope of EU law. As the scope of EU law itself is subject to interpretation, the question of how far a human rights obligation in a given case can reach is not easy to settle a priori. What makes the external provisions additionally contested, however, is the presence not only of principles but also objectives of EU action. The objectives in Article 21 TEU and 3(5) TEU could therefore be interpreted by a willing court as legitimizing courses of action conducted on the basis of EU competences which would perhaps be seen *ultra vires* from a perspective confined strictly and only to the objectives of those competences themselves. Conversely, one has to recognize, in line with Alston and Weiler, that the EU must be considered the sole 'custodian of human rights' in areas of its exclusive competence, such as the common commercial policy,[3] whereas it must share this responsibility with Member States in areas of shared competence.

In any case, the obligatory character of the principles and objectives contained in Article 21 TEU and Article 3(5) TEU has been confirmed by the CJEU. In *ATAA*, the Court made clear that Article 3(5) TEU has the effect of binding the EU when adopting an act 'to observe international law in its entirety, including customary international law, which is binding upon the institutions of the European Union'.[4] In two recent cases, Article 21 TEU was cited in support of an expansive reading of the CJEU's circumscribed jurisdiction in the area of CFSP.[5] Elsewhere, the objectives of Article 21 TEU served to enlarge the span of EU policy in the field of development cooperation, prompting the Court to annul a Council Decision on the conclusion of an international agreement with Philippines for being based on the wrong legal basis.[6]

---

[3] P Alston and JHH Weiler, 'An "Ever Closer Union" in Need of a Human Rights Policy' (1998) 9 European Journal of International Law 658, 679.

[4] Judgment of 21 December 2011, *Air Transport Association of America and Others v Secretary of State for Energy and Climate Change*, C-366/10, ECLI:EU:C:2011:864, para 101. Customary international law includes aspects of international human rights law. See L Bartels, 'The EU's Human Rights Obligations in Relation to Policies with Extraterritorial Effects' (2014) 25 European Journal of International Law 1071, 1080–87.

[5] Judgment of 28 March 2017, *The Queen, ex parte PJSC Rosneft Oil Company v Her Majesty's Treasury and Others*, C-72/15, ECLI:EU:C:2017:236, para 72; Judgment of 19 July 2016, *H v Council and Others*, C-455/14 P, ECLI:EU:C:2016:569, para 41.

[6] See also *Rosneft* (n 5) para 88 where the CJEU states that thanks to, among others, Articles 3(5) and 21 TEU, CFSP has a 'wide scope of aims and objectives' and the Council has as a consequence 'a broad discretion' in designating persons and entities to be subject to restrictive measures.

Judgment of 11 June 2014, *Commission v Council*, C-377/12, ECLI:EU:C:2014:1903

36. According to Article 208(1) TFEU, European Union policy in the field of develop-ment cooperation is to be conducted within the framework of the principles and objectives—as resulting from Article 21 TEU—of the European Union's external action. The primary objective of that policy is the reduction and, in the long term, the eradication of poverty and the European Union must take account of the ob-jectives of development cooperation in the policies that it implements which are likely to affect developing countries. For implementation of that policy, **Article 209 TFEU**, upon which, inter alia, the contested decision is founded, **provides** in particular, in paragraph 2, **that the European Union may conclude with third countries and competent international organisations any agreement helping to achieve the objectives referred to in Article 21 TEU and Article 208 TFEU.**

37. It follows that **European Union policy in the field of development cooperation is not limited to measures directly aimed at the eradication of poverty, but also pursues the objectives referred to in Article 21(2) TEU,** such as the objective, set out in Article 21(2)(d), of fostering the sustainable economic, social and environ-mental development of developing countries, with the primary aim of eradicating poverty.

One of the pre-eminent experts on EU human rights obligations, Lorand Bartels, con-siders Article 21(1) TEU to oblige, albeit not explicitly, the EU to respect human rights both internally and externally. He wonders, however, how much further the principles and ob-jectives reach. A literal interpretation does not apparently yield many answers. The EU is bound to pursue the value-laden objectives, such as consolidation of human rights world-wide, guided by the principles, such as indivisibility and universality of human rights, but there is no specification of the means of achieving these already broad and relatively vague objectives. Such open-endedness leaves ample space for interpretation by the relevant actors and in the ultimate instance the CJEU, but it also makes more difficult to construct a case against the EU in case of concrete human rights violations occurring, as Articles 3(5) and 21 TEU establish only a general and programmatic responsibility of the EU with respect to human rights (and other values listed). This leads Bartels to the conclusion that while the EU is under an obligation to respect human rights which applies extraterritorially[7]—no small feat in itself—it is not obliged to protect or 'fulfil' human rights abroad proactively.[8] The author is also sceptical about the practical effects of the extraterritorial respect for human rights, namely their judicial enforceability, given constraints on legal standing, types of acts which can be challenged, and identification of sufficiently precise human rights obligations giving rise to liability.[9]

---

[7] Such an obligation also arises from the human rights clauses included in the EU's international agreements. See Section 9.3.F.

[8] Bartels finds that other sources of legal obligations, such as customary international law, do not add to the human rights obligations stemming from the EU Treaties and EU international agreements with other countries.

[9] L Bartels, 'The EU's Human Rights Obligations in Relation to Policies with Extraterritorial Effects' (2014) 25 European Journal of International Law 1071, 1091.

L Bartels, 'The EU's Human Rights Obligations in Relation to Policies with Extraterritorial Effects' (2014) 25 European Journal of International Law 1071

The Lisbon Treaty introduced into the Treaty on European Union (TEU) two provisions relevant to EU policies with extraterritorial effects. (...)

[Article 3(5) TEU] has three parts. It establishes EU objectives to 'promote' the EU's values and interests abroad, and to 'contribute to' the other norms mentioned. It establishes an obligation to achieve these objectives. And, according to the CJEU, it also establishes an obligation to act consistently with the norms mentioned, including international law and, by extension, international human rights obligations.

(...)

[Article 21(1) TEU] is similar to the obligation contained in Article 3(5) TEU. The difference is that Article 3(5) requires the EU to 'uphold' its values 'in its relations with the wider world' and to 'contribute' to a set of objectives, while Article 21(1) requires the EU to 'be guided by' a similar set of principles in its 'action on the international scene'. Both of these provisions impose constraints on EU external policies, albeit a softer constraint in the case of Article 21(1) TEU.

(...)

Article 21(3)(1) is significant in two ways. First, it extends the scope of application of the EU's external human rights obligations. Article 3(5) refers to the 'EU's relations with the wider world', and Article 21(1) to the EU's 'action on the international scene'. By contrast, Article 21(3)(1) refers not only to 'the development and implementation of the different areas of the Union's external action' but also—notably—to 'the development and implementation ... of the external aspects of [the EU's] other policies'. The principles set out in Article 21(3)(1) therefore apply not just to EU policies, nor even only to EU external policies, but also to the external aspects of the EU's internal policies. This is so, it might be added, even though Article 21 is located in a part of the EU Treaty devoted to external action. Secondly, Article 21(3)(1) is normatively stronger than Article 3(5) and Article 23(1). These require the EU to 'uphold', 'contribute to', and be 'guided by' the principles and objectives described therein. As the CJEU has affirmed, these phrases are not devoid of normative force. But insofar as it requires the EU to 'respect' the principles previously described, Article 21(3)(1) puts this beyond doubt.

It must be acknowledged that the principles listed in Article 21(1) do not, strictly speaking, include the principle of respect for human rights itself. Relevantly, this provision refers rather to the principle of respect for the universality and indivisibility of human rights and fundamental freedoms. But it makes no sense to oblige the EU to respect this principle without also obliging it to respect the human rights on which it is based. By necessary implication, then, it follows that the EU is obliged to respect human rights in its external and internal policies.

To say that the EU is required under EU law to ensure that its policies not have negative effects on human rights in third countries is itself a significant result. But do these provisions go further, and encompass the two other panels of the human rights triptych: the obligation to 'protect' the human rights of persons from the activities of other actors, and the obligation to 'fulfil' the human rights of those persons? In fact, the answer to these questions is much more muted. As mentioned, Article 3(5) TEU requires the EU to 'promote' human rights in its relations with the wider world and 'contribute to' the 'protection of human rights, in particular the rights of the child'. Article 21(2) TEU also states that the EU must act, unilaterally and in cooperation, in order to pursue the objectives of, inter alia, 'consolidat[ing] and support[ing] democracy, the rule of law, human rights and the principles of international law', and this requirement is reinforced by Article 21(3)(1) TEU. Certainly, this means that the EU must act in some way to pursue these objectives and achieve these ends. But these provisions do not require the EU to do this in any particular way. Thus, to give some examples, it cannot be said that the EU is required to act positively to protect persons located extraterritorially from the acts of EU businesses operating in other countries, or to even to provide development aid to developing countries in order to fulfil their human rights.

Although sharing in essence the view on the horizontal (or 'transversal') nature of Articles 3(5) and 21 TEU and their importance for the EU's foreign policy orientation, Vivian Kube paints a somewhat more optimistic picture of the EU's principled commitments in external relations. The author analysed the provisions in light of both human rights objectives forming part of EU competence (the 'can') and human rights obligations forming part of the EU's international responsibility (the 'must'). Kube posits that the EU subscribes to a progressive conception of human rights responsibility which, among others, transcends the logic of traditional international human rights instruments by going beyond the paradigm of effective control and territoriality of human rights protection. Moreover, the provisions are capable of also exerting 'softer' influence on the exercise of EU competences. For example, the spirit of Article 21 TEU has been invoked by the European Ombudsman to support a decision condemning the Commission for failing to conduct a human rights impact assessment prior to the conclusion of negotiations on the EU–Vietnam trade agreement.[10]

V Kube, 'The European Union's External Human Rights Commitment: What is the Legal Value of Article 21 TEU?', EUI Working Paper LAW 2016/10

(...) the human rights objective of external action of Art. 21 and 3(5) TEU expands the 'can' and the 'must' with respect to EU external action and its human rights relevance. It expands the 'can' in that the transversal nature of the human rights objective, as a general objective overarching all fields of external action, liberates EU policies that pursue human rights protection from the fragmentation of external policies, as it was the case pre-Lisbon. Although the human rights objective does not provide for a substantive competence and hence a legal base in itself, its all-encompassing status makes clear that it is relevant for all fields of EU external polices and shall be pursued with all instruments the EU has at its disposal. It clarifies the 'must' in that the clear linkage of human rights protection to external policies emphasizes the EU's commitment to human rights responsibility beyond territorial confines and thereby continuing the concept of fundamental rights applicability that is envisaged in the Charter. Abandoning the a priori linkage of human rights responsibility to territory and effective control is not necessarily a unique concept (as only a few international human rights instruments explicitly limit their applicability to territory and jurisprudence developed more flexible approaches) but it is unique in its

---

[10] European Ombudsman, Decision in case 1409/2014/MHZ on the European Commission's failure to carry out a prior human rights impact assessment of the EU–Vietnam free trade agreement, 26 February 2016.

clear acknowledgment and in its non-discriminatory scope of protection. Besides, it falls in line with the EU's mode of governance on the international scene: 'actor-ness' through legal instruments and norm promotion. Thereby the human rights objective puts the EU as a self-declared shaper of international norms at the forefront of human rights advancement by upholding a progressive concept of human rights responsibility that is able to more effectively and adequately take into account the impact of global economic regulation on the human rights situations of individuals far from home.

A further contribution to the debate on the scope of EU human rights responsibility derived from Articles 3(5) and 21 TEU has argued that for all their progressive outlook, the two provisions are insufficient to override the limits of EU competence which is above all subject to the principle of conferral, as already stated above. The author points to the continued absence of a human rights competence that would enable the EU to become a party to human rights treaties (ie without having to fish for a somewhat suitable legal basis for that purpose; see Chapter 5 as regards the UN CRPD) other than the ECHR. At the same time, the substantive confines of 'standard' EU competences (enshrined in the TFEU, previously known as 'Community law') can be circumvented by recourse to the CFSP. The institutional architecture of the CFSP, however, differs significantly from the rest of the EU (see below).

E Cannizzaro, 'The EU's Human Rights Obligations in Relation to Policies with Extraterritorial Effects: A Reply to Lorand Bartels' (2014) 24 European Journal of International Law 1093

The capacity to protect human rights worldwide, however, could be further impaired by the limits to EU action under the founding Treaties.

In spite of the broad set of objectives laid down by Articles 3(5) and 21, these two provisions do not confer new competences on the EU. As if to play down the innovative character of Article 3(5), Article 3(6) points out that '[t]he Union shall pursue its objectives by appropriate means commensurate with the competences which are conferred upon it in the Treaties'. In analogous terms, Article 21(3) indicates that the objectives of Article 21(1) and (2) will be pursued through 'the development and implementation of the different areas of the Union's external action covered by this Title and by Part Five of the Treaty on the Functioning of the European Union, and of the external aspects of its other policies'.

This limitation considerably curtails the set of means at the disposal of the Union to protect human rights beyond its boundaries. For example, the EU does not possess the competence to conclude human rights treaties and, therefore, to acquire the status of party to these treaties, which would confer on it the ability to require compliance by the other parties.

Nor can it be said that, in spite of the non-existence of a new competence, this objective can nonetheless be pursued by each of the policies that come within the external action of the Union. This conclusion would have required that the means of action which are conferred to the EU under the different areas of external action and under the external aspects of its other policies could be used unconditionally for the pursuit of political objectives.

In this perspective, the EU would be regarded as an entity empowered to use all its competence to attain its political objectives. Such a conclusion can be hardly drawn from the incoherent and fragmentary system of the EU's external relations. The combined reading of Articles 23 and 40 TUE seems to point to a different direction. Article 23 assigns the pursuit of the political objectives laid down by Article 21(1) and (2) to the primary competence of the CFSP. Article 40 TUE prevents the other EU substantive policies from autonomously pursuing the objectives of the CFSP.

The effect of these two provisions seems thus to confine the aspiration of the EU as a global champion of human rights to the narrows of the principle of conferral. Whereas the instruments of the CFSP can be used unconditionally to promote and to protect human rights, other instruments can be used only to the extent that they fall within the scope of the substantive competences assigned to the EU, to attain the specific objectives assigned to them. Should one assume that the extraterritorial protection of human rights pertains, primarily if not exclusively, to the CFSP, the somewhat disappointing conclusion should be drawn that Articles 3(5) and 21 TUE merely impose directives of foreign policy. To endow the Union with the means of actions necessary to play a different and more engaging role, a further development of the European constitutional framework seems to be indispensable.

B. EU Strategic Framework on Human Rights and Democracy

In 2012, the EU decided to adopt a so-called human rights package in order to strengthen, structure and make more visible the EU's commitment to human rights, particularly in external relations. The package consisted of a strategic framework on human rights and democracy; an EU action plan on human rights and democracy; and a decision appointing an EU Special Representative for Human Rights.

Council of the European Union, Human Rights and Democracy: EU Strategic Framework and Action Plan, 11855/12, 25 June 2012

Human rights throughout EU policy

The European Union is founded on a shared determination to promote peace and stability and to build a world founded on respect for human rights, democracy and the rule of law. These principles underpin all aspects of the internal and external policies of the European Union.

Human rights are universally applicable legal norms. Democracy is a universal aspiration. Throughout the world, women and men demand to live lives of liberty, dignity and security in open and democratic societies underpinned by human rights and the rule of law. Sustainable peace, development and prosperity are possible only when grounded upon respect for human rights, democracy and the rule of law.

(...)

Promoting the universality of human rights

The EU reaffirms its commitment to the promotion and protection of all human rights, whether civil and political, or economic, social and cultural. The EU calls on all States to implement the provisions of the Universal Declaration of Human Rights and to ratify and implement the key international human rights treaties, including core labour rights

conventions, as well as regional human rights instruments. The EU will speak out against any attempt to undermine respect for universality of human rights.
(...)

Pursuing coherent objectives

Article 21 of the Treaty on European Union has reaffirmed the EU's determination to promote human rights and democracy through all its external actions. The entry into legal force of the EU Charter of Fundamental Rights, and the prospect of the EU's acceptance of the jurisdiction of the European Court of Human Rights through its accession to the European Convention on Human Rights, underline the EU's commitment to human rights in all spheres. Within their own frontiers, the EU and its Member States are committed to be exemplary in ensuring respect for human rights. Outside their frontiers, promoting and speaking out on human rights and democracy is a joint responsibility of the EU and its Member States.

(...)

Human rights in all EU external policies

The EU will promote human rights in all areas of its external action without exception. In particular, it will integrate the promotion of human rights into trade, investment, technology and telecommunications, Internet, energy, environmental, corporate social responsibility and development policy as well as into Common Security and Defence Policy and the external dimensions of employment and social policy and the area of freedom, security and justice, including counter-terrorism policy. In the area of development cooperation, a human rights based approach will be used to ensure that the EU strengthens its efforts to assist partner countries in implementing their international human rights obligations.

Implementing EU priorities on human rights

The EU will continue to promote freedom of expression, opinion, assembly and association, both on-line and offline; democracy cannot exist without these rights. It will promote freedom of religion or belief and to fight discrimination in all its forms through combating discrimination on grounds of race, ethnicity, age, gender or sexual orientation and advocating for the rights of children, persons belonging to minorities, indigenous peoples, refugees, migrants and persons with disabilities. The EU will continue to campaign for the rights and empowerment of women in all contexts through fighting discriminatory legislation, gender-based violence and marginalisation.

The EU will intensify its efforts to promote economic, social and cultural rights; (...)

The death penalty and torture constitute serious violations of human rights and human dignity. (...)

The fair and impartial administration of justice is essential to safeguard human rights. The EU will continue to promote observance of international humanitarian law; it will fight vigorously against impunity for serious crimes of concern to the international community, including sexual violence committed in connection with armed conflict, not least through its commitment to the International Criminal Court.

Courageous individuals fighting for human rights worldwide frequently find themselves the target of oppression and coercion; the EU will intensify its political and financial support for human rights defenders and step up its efforts against all forms of reprisals. A vigorous and independent civil society is essential to the functioning of democracy and the implementation of human rights; effective engagement with civil society is a cornerstone of a successful human rights policy. The EU places great value on its regular dialogue with civil society both inside and outside the EU and is profoundly concerned at attempts in some countries to restrict the independence of civil society. As a leading donor to civil society, the EU will continue supporting human rights defenders under the European Instrument for Democracy and Human Rights and make funding operations more flexible and more accessible.

Working with bilateral partners

The EU will place human rights at the centre of its relations with all third countries, including its strategic partners. While firmly based on universal norms, the EU's policy on human rights will be carefully designed for the circumstances of each country, not least through the development of country human rights strategies. (…)

Working through multilateral institutions

The EU remains committed to a strong multilateral human rights system which can monitor impartially implementation of human rights norms and call all States to account. The EU will resist strenuously any attempts to call into question the universal application of human rights and will continue to speak out in the United Nations General Assembly, the UN Human Rights Council and the International Labour Organisation against human rights violations. (…)

The EU will continue its engagement with the invaluable human rights work of the Council of Europe and the OSCE. It will work in partnership with regional and other organisations (…) with a view to encouraging the consolidation of regional human rights mechanisms.

The EU working together

The European Parliament's democratic mandate gives it particular authority and expertise in the field of human rights. The Parliament already plays a leading role in the promotion of human rights, in particular through its resolutions. (…)

The Strategic Framework is a relatively short document (three pages) but it is densely packed with notions fleshing out the EU's commitment to human rights, frequently echoing the principles and objectives set out in Articles 3(5) and 21 TEU. In essence, the Strategic Framework is meant to function as an overarching policy anchor—a more policy-oriented restatement of the relevant Treaty provisions—for keeping human rights and democracy on the agenda (ideally in the centre) of EU external relations. This policy commitment is further made concrete through the EU Action Plan on Human Rights and Democracy, the first iteration of which was adopted together with the Strategic Framework and which should be updated every four years.[11] Of course, an important rationale behind producing these documents is the strengthening of the perception of the EU as a virtuous international actor, a 'normative' or 'civilizing' power.[12]

From the perspective of human rights, one of the most important principles underlined by the Strategic Framework is the EU's support to the ideas of universality and indivisibility of human rights which can also be found in Article 21(1) TEU. The Strategic Framework in

[11] Council of the European Union, 'Human Rights and Democracy: EU Strategic Framework and Action Plan', 11855/12, 25 June 2012.
[12] See Section 9.6.

particular accentuates that 'human rights are universally applicable legal norms' and that 'the EU will speak out against any attempt to undermine respect for universality of human rights'. This emphasis demonstrates that universality of human rights is at the heart of the EU's principle-oriented foreign policy; even though implementation might often lag behind the rhetoric,[13] highlighting universality is a strategic discursive move that helps justify parts of EU external action.

In addition, it is notable that although the EU sees a strong link between the ideas of human rights, democracy, and the rule of law,[14] human rights feature by far the most prominently in the Strategic Framework. On the contrary, the rule of law is scarcely referenced and is omitted even in conspicuously appropriate passages, such as in the context of the EU's commitment to the International Criminal Court. The human rights part of the Strategic Framework also mentions the need for engagement with civil society and human rights defenders as a core part of the EU's external human rights policy, along with the financing instruments the EU employs in this regard which are part of the EU's external human rights toolkit (see below).

Another objective of the Strategic Framework is boosting coherence of the EU's external human rights policy. The document in particular mentions what Carmen Gebhard termed 'external coherence' which 'relates to the way the EU presents itself to third parties or within a multilateral system' and which implies that 'any failure to coordinate positions within the EU (…) has a significant impact on the EU's ability to perform towards other major actors'.[15] The EU's external human rights posture is only credible if it manages proverbially to 'sweep around its own front door before it sweeps around others'.[16] This has become an increasing challenge in recent years, given that the internal fundamental rights and democracy situation in the EU includes both the EU institutions and its Member States. The EU is frequently accused of being democratically deficient, as it is difficult to hold EU elites accountable through elections in an EU-wide manner,[17] while some of the Member States have openly started to subvert common values with the EU ill-equipped to enforce them,[18] and all of that against the background of widespread human rights deficiencies in the treatment of incoming migrants and refugees occurring in recent times both at the EU's doorstep and inside the Union itself. The Strategic Framework pre-dates to some extent some of these momentous challenges but the fact remains that a robust policy commitment to human rights is more difficult for the EU to 'sell' abroad in 2020 than it was in 2012. And this still says nothing about the deterioration of the global human rights environment and indeed the undermining of the human rights paradigm itself, in concurrence with the rise and normalization of populist governments and rhetoric.[19] In a world where room for human rights and

---

[13] The rhetoric is also sometimes absent, as it notably was during the migrant and refugee crisis where highlighting the universality of human rights was an obvious counterpoint to the ill-treatment of thousands of migrating persons.

[14] See Ch 3.

[15] C Gebhard, 'Coherence' in C Hill and M Smith (eds), International Relations and the European Union (2nd edn, Oxford University Press 2011) 108–09.

[16] This is an argument that predates the 'polycrisis' engulfing the EU in recent years and touches upon all EU actors, including the CJEU. See G de Búrca, 'The European Court of Justice after Kadi' (2010) 51 Harvard International Law Journal 1, 3. M Ovádek, 'External Judicial Review and Fundamental Rights in the EU: A Place in the Sun for the Court of Justice' (2016) EU Diplomacy Papers 2/2016, 13 <http://www.coleurope.eu/system/files_force/research-paper/edp_2_2016_ovadek_0.pdf> accessed 14 August 2020.

[17] JHH Weiler, 'Epilogue: Living in a Glass House' in C Closa and D Kochenov, Reinforcing Rule of Law Oversight in the European Union (Cambridge University Press 2016).

[18] L Pech and KL Scheppele, 'Illiberalism Within: Rule of Law Backsliding in the EU' (2017) 19 Cambridge Yearbook of European Legal Studies 3.

[19] K Roth, 'The Dangerous Rise of Populism: Global Attacks on Human Rights Values' in Human Rights Watch, World Report 2017 (Events of 2016), 2017. This is unfortunately also the case within the EU itself, see for example: K

civil society has been shrinking,[20] the pursuit of the Strategic Framework's objectives may be all the more important but it is also that much more difficult.

The Strategic Framework is of course not the only policy document informing EU external relations. Among the most important recent policy statements there is the Global Strategy on Foreign and Security Policy,[21] and the new European Consensus for Development,[22] both of which affirm rhetorically that human rights inform EU external action in the various spheres. Although the Global Strategy mentions human rights 33 times in its 60 pages in a number of contexts, from building a rule-based system of global governance to addressing migration flows and internal mainstreaming across policy sectors, the discourse of human rights promotion in the world is not a centrepiece of the agenda; human rights are typically mentioned in addition to a range of other foreign policy objectives and the accompanying language is vague (unsurprisingly for a global strategic document). The European Consensus for Development commits the EU to integrating human rights into its development policies, including, for example, a commitment to the intersection of business and human rights.[23]

'Shared Vision, Common Action: A Stronger Europe. A Global Strategy for the European Union's Foreign And Security Policy', June 2016

(...) The EU is committed to a global order based on international law, which ensures human rights, sustainable development and lasting access to the global commons. This commitment translates into an aspiration to transform rather than to simply preserve the existing system. The EU will strive for a strong UN as the bedrock of the multilateral rules-based order, and develop globally coordinated responses with international and regional organisations, states and non-state actors.

(...) In a more contested world, the EU will be guided by a strong sense of responsibility. There is no magic wand to solve crises: there are no neat recipes to impose solutions elsewhere. However, responsible engagement can bring about positive change. We will therefore act promptly to prevent violent conflict, be able and ready to respond responsibly

---

Raj, 'How Nativist Populism Is Going Mainstream in Europe' (*hrw.org*, 21 February 2020) <http://www.hrw.org/news/2020/02/21/how-nativist-populism-going-mainstream-europe> accessed 14 August 2020.

[20] R Youngs and A Echagüe, 'Shrinking Space for Civil Society: The EU Response', European Parliament Study, April 2017; European Parliament, 'Report on addressing shrinking civil society space in developing countries', A8-0283/2017, 5 September 2017. Worryingly, the space for civil society has started to shrink also within the EU and in particular in the Member States openly challenging common EU values, especially in Hungary. See EU Agency for Fundamental Rights, *Challenges Facing Civil Society Organisations Working on Human Rights in the EU* (Publications Office of the European Union 2018). The European Commission has instituted an infringement action against Hungary in 2018, following the placing of restrictions on civil society organisations that receive funding from abroad. The action was recently upheld by the Grand Chamber of the CJEU, declaring the restrictions to be incompatible with Article 63 TFEU and Articles 7, 8, and 12 of the Charter of Fundamental rights: Judgment of 18 June 2020, *European Commission v Hungary (Transparency of associations)*, C-78/18, ECLI:EU:C:2020:476; see Ch 4.

[21] 'Shared Vision, Common Action: A Stronger Europe. A Global Strategy for the European Union's Foreign And Security Policy', June 2016.

[22] 'The New European Consensus on Development: "Our World, Our Dignity, Our Future" ', Joint Statement by the Council and the Representatives of the Governments of the Member States Meeting within the Council, the European Parliament and the European Commission, Brussels, 7 June 2017.

[23] See point 49 of the European Consensus on Development.

yet decisively to crises, facilitate locally owned agreements, and commit long-term. We will take responsibility foremost in Europe and its surrounding regions, while pursuing targeted engagement further afield. We will act globally to address the root causes of conflict and poverty, and to champion the indivisibility and universality of human rights.

(...) Repression suffocates outlets for discontent and marginalises communities. The EU will therefore promote human rights through dialogue and support, including in the most difficult cases. Through long-term engagement, we will persistently seek to advance human rights protection. We will pursue locally owned rights-based approaches to the reform of the justice, security and defence sectors, and support fragile states in building capacities, including cyber. (...)

The Mediterranean, Middle East and parts of sub-Saharan Africa are in turmoil, the outcome of which will likely only become clear decades from now. Solving conflicts and promoting development and human rights in the south is essential to addressing the threat of terrorism, the challenges of demography, migration and climate change, and to seizing the opportunity of shared prosperity.

(...) [the EU] will deepen dialogue with Iran and GCC countries on regional conflicts, human rights and counter-terrorism, seeking to prevent contagion of existing crises and foster the space for cooperation and diplomacy.

(...) The EU will also deepen trade and investment with China, seeking a level playing field, intellectual property rights protection, greater cooperation on high-end technology, dialogue on economic reform, human rights and climate action. (...) Across the Indo Pacific and East Asian regions, the EU will promote human rights and support democratic transitions such as in Myanmar/Burma.

(...) We will support the UN Human Rights Council and encourage the widest acceptance of the jurisdiction of the International Criminal Court and the International Court of Justice.

(...) We must become more joined-up across internal and external policies. The migration phenomenon, for example, requires a balanced and human rights-compliant policy mix addressing the management of the flows and the structural causes. This means overcoming the fragmentation of external policies relevant to migration. In particular, we will develop stronger links between humanitarian and development efforts through joint risk analysis, and multiannual programming and financing. We will also make different external policies and instruments migration-sensitive—from diplomacy and CSDP to development and climate—and ensure their coherence with internal ones regarding border management, homeland security, asylum, employment, culture and education.

(...) Long-term work on pre-emptive peace, resilience and human rights must be tied to crisis response through humanitarian aid, CSDP, sanctions and diplomacy.

Finally, we will systematically mainstream human rights and gender issues across policy sectors and institutions, as well as foster closer coordination regarding digital matters. Greater awareness and expertise on such issues is needed within the EEAS and the Commission.

9.3 The External Human Rights 'Toolkit'

In order to implement its principles and strategic objectives, the EU relies on a 'toolkit' consisting of a number of instruments targeting various aspects of external human rights promotion. In the following subsections we look at the EU Action Plan on Human Rights and Democracy, a more concrete and periodically updated sibling to the Strategic Framework; EU financing instruments, which offer tangible support and incentives abroad; EU Human Rights Guidelines; country strategies; human rights dialogues; and human rights clauses in international agreements. Tools falling under the CFSP, such as sanctions, are discussed separately in Section 9.4. Together, the EU's actions and the tools that it uses to promote and reaffirm its commitment to international human rights—despite inconsistencies and gaps between rhetoric and action—have been said to contribute to the development of human rights customary norms in international law.[24]

A. EU Action Plan on Human Rights and Democracy

In 2012, together with the Strategic Framework, the EU adopted an Action Plan setting out a list of actions that should be taken to reinforce the EU's commitment to human rights and democracy. The first Action Plan covered the period between 2012 and 2014 and a second Action Plan was set for 2015–2019. Currently, a new Action Plan is underway for the period 2020–2024.

Council of the European Union, Council Conclusions on the Action Plan on Human Rights and Democracy 2015–2019, 10897/15, 20 July 2015

2. Based on the Strategic Framework on Human Rights and Democracy and the 2012–2014 Action Plan, the European Union has made considerable progress in improving the impact and coherence of its actions on human rights and democracy. (…)

3. (…) The EU will put special emphasis on ownership by, and co-operation with, local institutions and mechanisms, including national human rights institutions, as well as civil society. The EU will promote the principles of non-discrimination, gender equality and women's empowerment. The EU will also ensure a comprehensive human rights approach to preventing and addressing conflicts and crises, and further mainstream human rights in the external aspects of EU policies in order to ensure better policy coherence, in particular in the fields of migration, trade and investment, development cooperation and counter terrorism.

4. The EU remains committed to implementing the entire human rights and democracy agenda as reflected in the 2012 Strategic Framework for Human Rights and Democracy, which continues to guide the Union's actions, and in the EU human rights guidelines, Council Conclusions and strategy papers. (…)

---

[24] JR Marín Aís, 'The Contribution of the EU to the Development of Customary Norms in the Field of Human Rights Protection' in P Eeckhout and M Lopez-Escudero (eds), *The European Union's External Action in Times of Crisis* (Hart Publishing 2016) 284–88.

EU Action Plan on Human Rights and Democracy

The purpose of this Action Plan is to continue implementing the EU Strategic Framework on Human Rights and Democracy, with sufficient flexibility so as to respond to new challenges as they arise. It builds upon the existing body of EU human rights and democracy support policies in the external action, notably EU guidelines, toolkits and other agreed positions, and the various external financing instruments, in particular the European Instrument for Democracy and Human Rights. This Action Plan covers relevant human rights aspects of the EU external action.

(...)

Objective	Action	Timeline	Responsibility
6. Strengthening co-operation with the UN and regional Human Rights and Democracy mechanisms	a. Strengthen human rights and democracy aspects in EU cooperation with the UN and regional organisations and mechanisms, in particular by pursuing synergies and common initiatives on key thematic issues and at important multilateral events.	Ongoing	EEAS, COM
	b. Promote dialogue and capacity building initiatives between regional human rights and democracy mechanisms.	Ongoing	EEAS, COM, MS
34. Improve public diplomacy and communication on human rights	a. Improve the accessibility and visibility of the EU's human rights policy by making more effective use of the internet and social media, including through an increased and more consolidated web presence.	By 2016	EEAS, COM, Council, MS
	b. Better communicate at country level to reach and engage with civil society and the public on country specific human rights priorities and activities.	By 2016	EEAS, COM, Council, MS

The Action Plan for 2015–2019 indicates the desired outcome of each planned action, the timing and which Union actors are responsible for their realisation. Altogether, there are 34 objectives (see two examples above), most of them further split into individual actions to be taken by the relevant responsible actors. The Action Plan builds on the commitments enumerated in the 2012–2014 Action Plan. As opposed to this previous Action Plan, it does not follow the structure of the Strategic Framework; instead, it is more autonomous and reflects the priorities and challenges of the EU as they developed since the adoption of the Strategic Framework in 2012.

It is obvious that the key challenge relating to both the Strategic Framework and the Action Plan is their implementation. Unfortunately, there is no established public mechanism for monitoring and evaluating progress on the individual actions or the overall objectives, with the exception of a mid-term review conducted for the first time, for the 2015–2019 Action Plan, in June 2017. This review, which as an instrument of self-evaluation cannot be seen as particularly objective, concluded that 'the EU has made good progress in implementing the Action Plan' and that 'it will be crucial to better communicate the EU human rights and democracy policy to citizens and partners through strong and effective public diplomacy'. The review contains little critical appraisal of the implementation of the Action Plan—it effectively only serves as a list of EU activities related to the Action Plan.

EU Action Plan on Human Rights and Democracy (2015-2019): Mid-Term Review June 2017, SWD(2017) 254 final, Brussels, 27 June 2017

However, more work is needed to fulfil some of these guiding principles, especially strengthening internal-external coherence; improving communication; and enhancing the EU's capacity to measure and evaluate the human rights impacts of its actions. In this regard, an improved and more systematic monitoring of actions will need to be performed periodically. The Action Plan was intended to focus on priorities where additional political momentum and enhanced commitment are needed. In practice, it comprehensively addresses almost all aspects of EU human rights and democracy policy. The EU has ambitious long-term aims, but the Action Plan could be most effective if fewer actions and commitments were prioritised more selectively.

The EU has made significant efforts on Chapter 1, boosting ownership of local actors. The EU operates the largest Human Rights Defenders support programme worldwide and has further expanded it since 2015. Financial co-operation has supported political parties and national parliaments. A strong engagement with local civil society, including via bilateral and multilateral diplomatic tools, financial tools, and public diplomacy, is key to address the shrinking space phenomenon.

Many actions under Chapter 2 on addressing human rights challenges, such as freedom of expression and freedom of religion or belief, are regular, recurrent and ongoing. Furthermore the EU upgraded several policies and adopted a more systematic and holistic approach. Work has started on developing an EU Toolkit on anti-discrimination, and on developing a more comprehensive approach to the death penalty and torture. The adoption of the revised Guidelines on children's rights was an important milestone. Continuing to discuss and evaluate the implementation of all other EU guidelines on human rights remains important to ensure their effective operationalisation and their continued relevance with evolving developments. Likewise, the EU will need to ensure that the [EU Gender Action Plan II] is effectively implemented. (...)

Since the previous Action Plan only covered the period until 31 December 2019, In March 2020 the Commission and the High Representative of the Union for Foreign Affairs and Security Policy proposed a new EU Action Plan on Human Rights and Democracy for the period of 2020–2024.[25] The renewed Plan is advanced in an Annex to their Joint Communication and has taken on a slightly different format than the previous one. It identifies five main lines of action: protecting and empowering individuals; building resilient, inclusive, and democratic societies; promoting a global system for human rights and democracy;

---

[25] European Commission and High Representative of the Union for Foreign Affairs and Security Policy, 'Joint Communication to the European Parliament and the Council, EU Action Plan on Human Rights and Democracy 2020–2024', JOIN(2020) 5 final, Brussels, 25 March 2020.

harnessing opportunities and addressing challenges posed by the use of new technologies; and delivering by working together. Those five overarching principles are further developed in more concrete objectives. Instead of providing a deadline for each of the actions and pointing to the responsible EU actors, the focus is on the policies and means of implementation for each line of action, such as human rights dialogues, United Nations Human Rights Council (UNHRC) and United Nations General Assembly (UNGA) Resolutions, direct support for human rights defenders, diplomacy and dialogue with civil society, the business sector, and other non-state actors. A new mid-term review of the implementation of the plan is affirmed as well. The new Draft Action Plan still needs to be endorsed by the Council.[26]

Joint Communication to the European Parliament and the Council, EU Action Plan on Human Rights and Democracy 2020–2024, JOIN(2020) 5 final, Brussels, 25 March 2020

(...) A lot has already been done. Since the adoption of the EU strategic framework on human rights and democracy in 2012, the first two EU action plans on human rights and democracy (2012–2014 and 2015–2019), the appointment of the first EU Special Representative for Human Rights (EUSR) in 2012 and the 2019 Council conclusions on democracy, the EU has become more coordinated, active, visible and effective in its engagement in and with third countries and more prominently engaged at multilateral level.

During the past years, the EU has acted more strategically and used its political weight and the human rights toolbox more effectively to address human rights violations and promote democratic, resilient and peaceful societies. It has contributed to achieving significant progress in countries and regions where human rights were under strain, through innovative engagement and investment in economic and social rights, and strong political and financial support to protect and empower human rights defenders, civil society and media actors. (...)

However, widespread challenges persist. Human rights and democracy are under severe stress in many countries across the world. Fundamental freedoms, like freedom of speech or assembly and media freedom also are under increasing threat. The impact of systemic efforts to undermine the rule of law, restrict civic and political space and weaken the multilateral rules-based order have been exacerbated by the retreat of some of the EU's traditional partners from the active promotion and defence of human rights and democratic values. (...)

The transition to the digital age brings immediate new opportunities and challenges. Digital technologies can advance human rights and democratisation by making public participation easier, increasing governmental accountability (...), awareness and access to education and information, facilitating economic and societal inclusion and access to quality public services. However, it can also support abusive, unlawful restrictions on movement and speech. Social media platforms are used to channel targeted disinformation and hate speech that often violate privacy and undermine democracy and human rights. (...)

---

[26] The Action Plan for 2015–2019 was largely taken over from the April 2015 Commission Communication, with only minor adjustments to be discerned in the Council's Conclusions.

The other key transition is driven by global environmental challenges such as environmental degradation, pollution and climate change. (...)

At the same time, conflicts have deepened and new dangers have emerged. Conflict and instability are threatening the livelihoods of millions across the globe, and the world is witnessing the highest levels of displaced persons on record. Investing in human rights, democracy and the rule of law is the best way to prevent societies from descending into crisis. (...)

This means early engagement to address human rights violations and support democracy, including through mediation and the prevention of electoral violence. A renewed focus on human rights and democracy will foster state and societal resilience. Security is better served when civil and political as well as economic, social and cultural rights are guaranteed. There is no sustainable security without human rights for all. Ensuring accountability and fighting impunity is central to that.

B. Financing instruments

A key tool of EU human rights promotion abroad, as well as of EU foreign policy more generally, is financing instruments. The EU does not, strictly speaking, have its own army or security personnel but it does have money which predisposes it conducts 'foreign policy through the purse'. Financing instruments are, in economic terms budgetary lines and credit capacity reserved for a particular purpose which are in legal terms enshrined in EU law (normally EU Regulations) with strategic rules on their use. As of 2020, there were 13 financial instruments dedicated to EU external action, 12 of which part of the EU budget (see Figure 9.2),[27] each with a different financial capacity: the European Development Fund (EDF), the Development Cooperation Instrument (DCI), the European Neighbourhood Instrument (ENI), the Instrument for Pre-accession Assistance (IPA II), the Instrument contributing to Stability and Peace (IcSP), the European Instrument for Democracy and Human Rights (EIDHR), the Partnership Instrument (PI), the Instrument for Nuclear Safety Cooperation (INSC), the Instrument for Greenland, the Macro-Financial Assistance programme (MFA), the External Lending Mandate (ELM), the Guarantee Fund for External Actions (GFEA), and the European Fund for Sustainable Development (EFSD). General rules and conditions for the provision of external financial assistance by most of these instruments are governed horizontally by the additional Regulation 236/2014.[28]

Generally, EU financial assistance can take the form of (i) grants; (ii) procurement contracts for services; supplies or works; (iii) general or sector budget support; (iv) contributions to trust funds set up by the Commission; or (v) financial instruments such as loans, guarantees,

---

[27] The European Development Fund is funded by EU Member States but it was up to now not included in the EU's Multiannual Financial Framework. However, it will be integrated into the general budget from 2021 onwards. See European Council, 'Special meeting—Conclusions', Brussels, 21 July 2020, para 3.

[28] Regulation (EU) No 236/2014 of the European Parliament and of the Council laying down common rules and procedures for the implementation of the Union's instruments for financing external action [2014] OJ L77/85.

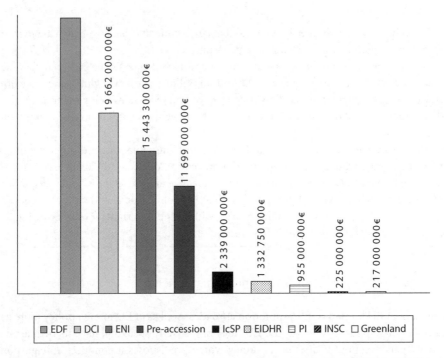

Figure 9.2 Budgets of EU external financing instruments for the period 2014–2020[29]

equity or quasi-equity, investments or participations, and risk-sharing instruments.[30] The last type of financing should occur under the lead of the European Investment Bank or a multilateral or bilateral European financial institution (such as development banks). There are also specific forms of financing available for the various financing instruments. Most peculiarly to human rights, under the EIDHR, the EU can make direct awards, if necessary without the need for co-funding, of low-value grants to human rights defenders; grants in 'most difficult conditions' where the publication of a call for proposals would be inappropriate; and grants to the Office of the UN High Commissioner for Human Rights and to the European Inter-University Centre for Human Rights and Democratisation.[31]

The current EIDHR for 2014–2020[32] builds on two predecessors[33] and has five core objectives: (i) support to at risk human rights defenders; (ii) support to thematic priorities of the EU on human rights, such as abolition of death penalty and prevention of torture; (iii) support to democracy and (iv) election observation missions (EOMs); and (v) support to targeted key actors and processes, such as international and regional human rights instruments and mechanisms, including civil society participation and cooperation with

---

[29] The budget of EDF in the period 2014–2020 was set at EUR 30.5 billion. It is the most capacious instrument by some distance and it serves to finance development and related actions in certain African, Caribbean, and Pacific (ACP) states. The relationship between the EU and ACP countries has origins in the colonial past of a number of EU Member States.

[30] Article 4(1) of Regulation 236/2014.

[31] Ibid, Article 6(1)(c).

[32] Regulation (EU) No 235/2014 of the European Parliament and of the Council establishing a financing instrument for democracy and human rights worldwide [2014] OJ L77/85.

[33] Regulation (EC) No 1889/2006 of the European Parliament and of the Council on establishing a financing instrument for the promotion of democracy and human rights worldwide [2006] OJ L386/1; Council Regulation (EC) No 975/1999 laying down the requirements for the implementation of development cooperation operations which contribute to the general objective of developing and consolidating democracy and the rule of law and to that of respecting human rights and fundamental freedoms [1999] OJ L120/1.

the international and regional bodies. The financial assistance must take into account the principles of non-discrimination on any ground, gender mainstreaming, participation, empowerment, accountability, openness, and transparency, but also the urgency of human rights situations around the world.[34] The precariousness and sensitivity of supporting human rights defenders and civil society in countries is reflected by the fact that the EIDHR allows for 'assistance to be provided independently of the consent of the governments and public authorities of the third countries concerned'.[35] At the same time, the drafters of the EIDHR Regulation recognized that 'the task of building and sustaining a culture of human rights and of supporting the emergence of an independent civil society (...) is essentially a continuous challenge which belongs first and foremost to the people of the country concerned'.[36]

Regulation (EU) No 235/2014 of the European Parliament and of the Council establishing a financing instrument for democracy and human rights worldwide [2014] OJ L77/85

Article 2

Scope

1. Union assistance shall focus on the following:
   (a) **support to and enhancement**, in line with the overall democratic cycle approach, **of participatory and representative democracy**, including parliamentary democracy, and the processes of democratisation, mainly through civil society organisations at the local, national and international levels (...)
   (b) **promotion and protection of human rights and fundamental freedoms**, as proclaimed in the UN Universal Declaration of Human Rights and other international and regional instruments in the area of civil, political, economic, social and cultural rights, mainly through civil society organisations (...)
   (c) **strengthening of the international framework** for the protection of human rights, justice, gender equality, the rule of law and democracy, and for the promotion of international humanitarian law (...)
   (d) building confidence in, and enhancing the reliability and transparency of, democratic electoral processes and institutions, at all stages of the electoral cycle (...)

It goes without saying that the EIDHR is meant to work in synergy with the overall principles of EU external action, the Strategic Framework and Action Plan on Human Rights and Democracy, other foreign policy tools such as political dialogue and diplomatic demarches, and crisis-related Union assistance provided under the IcSP.[37] At the same time, the EIDHR should also provide added value on top of what the EU does through other actions and financing instruments, given that human rights concerns should be mainstreamed across all EU policies. In particular, the fact that the EIDHR is capable of providing support independently of governmental approval makes it well-placed to support (even persecuted) human

---

[34] Article 2 of Regulation (EU) No 235/2014 (EIDHR 2014–2020).
[35] Ibid, recital 1 of the preamble.
[36] Ibid, recital 12 of the preamble.
[37] Ibid, recitals 7 and 14 of the preamble.

rights defenders, civil society, migrants, refugees, or internally displaced people who might otherwise be at the fringes of or even fighting incumbent governments' interests.[38]

The specific nature of the EIDHR is underscored by a comparison of the budgets of the various external financing instruments—the EIDHR does not belong to the 'big league' of EU instruments. Having said that, in light of the horizontal and cross-cutting character of human rights in EU policies, assistance provided under all instruments can, and often does, actively contribute to human rights objectives. Even when this is not the case, at the very least the funding cannot be used for purposes incompatible with human rights. It should be said, however, that typically all of the EU's largest external financing instruments have a visible human rights component as part of their rationale. For the main development instruments, including the EDF, this is present in the programming in the guise of the Rights-based Approach (RBA).[39] For the European Neighbourhood and Pre-accession instruments, albeit they also offer *de facto* development assistance, advancement of human rights (and the rest of EU values) is part of EU financing objectives at least since the pronouncement of the Copenhagen criteria (see below) which expressly linked EU membership with respect for human rights. Although the European Neighbourhood Policy (ENP) eschews the promise of EU membership—which is a powerful incentive for domestic reforms—the premise underlying EU funding through the ENI is still primarily that of conditionality: both the ENI and Pre-accession Instrument incentivize countries in the EU's neighbourhood to adopt EU values and laws (with the latter not always adding up to the former), one with the promise of EU membership (as of now concerning essentially countries in the Western Balkans) and one without. Despite EU enlargement grinding to a halt in recent years, the Pre-accession Instrument continues to represent a sizeable portion of the external action budget, financing the development of Western Balkan countries and their approximation to EU values and laws. Some of the various financing instruments can work in parallel in a given country or region, such as the EIDHR and ENI in the EU's eastern and southern neighbourhood.

Critical theory scholars who analysed the EIDHR and the financial assistance provided thereunder have found out that the instrument does not promote all visions of democracy and human rights equally, despite the EIDHR not being explicitly wedded to any particular ideological conception.[40] The civil society organizations and NGOs which stand to benefit the most from the EIDHR are typically internationally oriented and professionalized organizations whose output can be readily measured by donor evaluations. Therefore, despite EU statements pledging support to local actors and solutions, the most grassroots organizations are more likely to miss out on EIDHR funding.

M Kurki, 'Governmentality and EU Democracy Promotion: the European Instrument for Democracy and Human Rights and the Construction of Democratic Civil Societies' (2011) 5 International Political Sociology 349

The EU promotes an active and productive civil society. However, it also promotes rights-based CSOs and ones that will take on the responsibility to keep the state in check. At the

---

[38] Ibid, recital 16 of the preamble.
[39] See Ch 11.
[40] M Kurki, 'Governmentality and EU democracy promotion: the European Instrument for Democracy and Human Rights and the construction of democratic civil societies' (2011) 5 International Political Sociology 349,

same time, it promotes a civil society that will take on the functions of the state, when needed, and a civil society within which homo oeconomicus can productively function. (…) the EIDHR promotes a civil society of this kind, not by 'letting it be' but by actively bringing it about—interventions are necessary for the creation of the right kind of 'freedoms.' It encourages civil society organizations to realize themselves as entrepreneurial actors competing for funding and 'pitching' themselves as rational and progressive actors for change. At the same time, the project management tools of the EIDHR ensure that organizations and individuals within them regulate themselves to act in ways that are decentered, yet precise, action-centered, cost-effective, and objectively measurable. In so doing, the EIDHR seeks to manage the publics of the target states, pushing them in the direction of the right kind of freedoms and democracy-enhancing activities (activity centered, entrepreneurial and effective, state-challenging) and away from the wrong kind of (say aid dependent, politicized, or structural-reform oriented) civil society activities.

Although the EIDHR takes no sides in the ideological debate about what kind of democracy should be promoted, it seems that implicitly its objectives, CfPs [Call for Proposals], and management structures create an environment where a specific model is encouraged. Even if lip-service may be paid to social democracy or participatory democracy, or to political pluralism, dispositions that seem to contradict the core elements of these models (which emphasize democratic control of markets, strong regulating state, solidarity-enhancing and democratically functioning civil society of voluntary actors) seem to nevertheless be implied. This, arguably, creates some limits to the scope of democratic alternatives that are funded and assisted by the European Union. Not all organizations stand in quite the same stead to receive EU funding as Commission staff reluctantly do acknowledge. (…) things can be difficult for radical democratic organizations with 'overly' ambitious structural or nonactivity-based objectives; local organizations without an international framework or reach; non-competitive organizations or organizations without ability (or will) to compete for external funding; non-activity-based (and hence measurement-evasive) organizations; anti-European organizations, or non-professionalized non-managerially inclined organizations.

Currently, the Multiannual Financial Framework (MFF), the general EU seven-year budget, is being prepared for the 2021–2027 period. Many of the enumerated financing instruments will expire simultaneously with the current MFF. In this context, a major reform of the financing of EU external action is envisaged in order to make the budgeting more simple, flexible, and effective. Thereto, the European Commission proposed to merge the majority of the current stand-alone instruments into a single one, which will become the 'Neighbourhood, Development and International Cooperation Instrument' (NDICI).[41] The NDICI will also encompass the current EDF that was previously kept outside the EU general budget. Because of the specific procedure for nuclear-related activities under the Euratom Treaty, the INSC will be kept outside the new instrument. Furthermore, the current

362; H Mühlenhoff, 'Funding Democracy, Funding Social Services? The European Instrument for Democracy and Human Rights in the Context of Competing Narratives in Turkey' (2014) 16 Journal of Balkan and Near Eastern Studies 102.

[41] European Commission, 'Proposal for a Regulation of the European Parliament and of the Council establishing the Neighbourhood, Development and International Cooperation Instrument', COM(2018) 460 final, Brussels, 14 June 2018. For a commentary of the proposal see L Debuysere and S Blockmans, 'A Jumbo Financial Instrument for EU External Action?', Commentary Bertelsmann Stiftung and CEPS, 19 February 2019.

Greenland Instrument will be succeeded by a new 'Association of the Overseas Countries and Territories (including Greenland) with the European Union', which will also encompass funds for other overseas territories currently resorting under the EDF.[42] Finally, the Instrument for Pre-accession Assistance will remain separate in its third iteration (IPA III).[43] In July 2020, the outlines of the new MFF, including the coming into existence of NDICI, were approved by the European Council.[44] The regular EU budget will be reinforced by a fund for the European recovery from the Covid-19 crisis, Next Generation EU (NGEU).[45] The European Commission proposed to put EUR 10.5 billion[46] of the NGEU budget into the NDICI, to be used to tackle the negative consequences of the health crisis in partner countries.[47] This proposal was however not accepted by the European Council which, in its marathon session of 17–21 July 2020, allocated EUR 70.8 billion of the general MFF budget to NDICI.[48]

C. EU Human Rights Guidelines

EU Human Rights Guidelines represent another tool for promoting and mainstreaming human rights externally. These Guidelines are in essence legally non-binding documents, adopted by EU Member States in the Foreign Affairs Council (therefore intergovernmental), through which the EU sets out its view of a particular human rights issue. The Guidelines are at once addressed to EU institutions, bodies, and the Member States—in order to facilitate the mainstreaming and coherence of human rights in EU external action—and a statement to the international community that a particular human rights issue is important to the EU. The Guidelines also contain the EU's 'explanation' of the international human rights framework governing a given issue which is intended to be useful for both EU bodies and Member States, on the one hand, and foreign governments and civil society, on the other (sometimes facilitated by translations).[49] The EU has so far adopted 13 Human Rights Guidelines, some of which have also been revised. The Guidelines often cross-reference each other, not least because the EU maintains its commitment to the universality and indivisibility of human rights which also means that the application of one set of Guidelines cannot exclude others.

[42] European Commission, "Proposal for a Council Decision on the Association of the Overseas Countries and Territories with the European Union including relations between the European Union on the one hand, and Greenland and the Kingdom of Denmark on the other ('Overseas Association Decision'), COM(2018) 461 final, Brussels, 14 June 2018.

[43] European Commission, 'Proposal for a Regulation of the European Parliament and of the Council establishing the Instrument for Pre-accession Assistance (IPA III)', COM(2018) 465 final, Brussels, 14 June 2018.

[44] European Council, Special meeting—Conclusions, Brussels, 21 July 2020, 10, 55.

[45] Ibid, 2–9.

[46] This is counted in 2018 prices and amounts to EUR 11,448,070 million in current prices.

[47] European Commission, 'Amended Proposal for a [...] Regulation of the European Parliament and of the Council establishing the Neighbourhood, Development and International Cooperation Instrument, [...]' COM(2020) 459 final, Brussels, 29 May 2020.

[48] European Council, "Special meeting—Conclusions, Brussels, 21 July 2020, para 120; see also <http://www.consilium.europa.eu/en/infographics/recovery-plan-mff-2021-2027/> accessed 14 August 2020.

[49] One of the standard textbooks on EU foreign policy calls EU Human Rights Guidelines 'the backbone of a more targeted EU human rights diplomacy within CFSP'. See S Keukeleire and T Delreux, *The Foreign Policy of the European Union* (Palgrave Macmillan 2014) 136.

Table 9.1 Adopted EU Human Rights Guidelines (adapted from Wouters and Hermez 2016[50]).

EU Human Rights Guidelines	Date of Adoption	Date of Revision
Guidelines to EU policy towards third countries on the death penalty	29 June 1998	12 April 2013
Guidelines to EU policy towards third countries on torture and other cruel, inhuman or degrading treatment or punishment	9 April 2001	18 April 2008 20 March 2012 16 September 2019
EU Guidelines on human rights dialogues with third countries	13 December 2001	19 January 2009
EU Guidelines on children and armed conflict	4 December 2003	5 June 2008
Ensuring protection – European Union Guidelines on human rights defenders	2 June 2004	8 December 2008
European Union Guidelines on promoting compliance with international humanitarian law (IHL)	5 December 2005	1 December 2009
EU Guidelines on the promotion and protection of the rights of the child	10 December 2007	6 March 2017
EU Guidelines on violence against women and girls and combating all forms of discrimination against them	8 December 2008	NA
EU Guidelines on the promotion and protection of freedom of religion or belief	24 June 2013	NA
Guidelines to promote and protect the enjoyment of all human rights by lesbian, gay, bisexual, transgender and intersex (LGBTI) persons	24 June 2013	NA
EU Human Rights Guidelines on freedom of expression online and offline	12 May 2014	NA
EU Human Rights Guidelines on non-discrimination in external action	18 March 2019	NA
EU Human Rights Guidelines on Safe Drinking Water and Sanitation	17 June 2019	NA

The drafting of Guidelines is a joint endeavour between the European External Action Service (EEAS) and the Member States with varying involvement of the civil society.[51] Implicitly, Guidelines therefore also foster internal (and chiefly intergovernmental) consensus within the EU regarding the selected human rights issues, as Member States debate and ultimately have to agree on the text of the Guidelines. With the exception of the Guidelines on international humanitarian law,[52] all Guidelines have up to now been negotiated in the Council Working Party on Human Rights (COHOM). COHOM is also responsible for monitoring the implementation of the Guidelines and for periodically reviewing them, if necessary.[53] Following adoption, Guidelines are distributed to all EU Delegations for use in their

---

[50] J Wouters and M Hermez, 'EU Guidelines on Human Rights as a Foreign Policy Instrument: An Assessment' in S Poli (ed), *Human Rights in EU Foreign Affairs*, CLEER Papers 5/2015, 63–81.

[51] European Parliament, 'Resolution of 12 March 2015 on the Annual report on human rights and democracy in the world 2013 and the EU policy on the matter', P8_TA(2015)0076, para 45.

[52] P Wrange, 'The EU Guidelines on Promoting Compliance with International Humanitarian Law' (2010) 78 Nordic Journal of International Law 541.

[53] According to Wouters and Hermez, monitoring takes place twice per year, while review every three years. Not all Guidelines have been readopted following review, however. The 2017 revised EU Guidelines for the Promotion and Protection of the Rights of the Child, state that the Guidelines shall be reviewed 'regularly'. Wouters and Hermez (n 50) 69.

work, as they are meant to be practical and operational, for instance in cases when EU officials and personnel must respond to human rights violations in a third country. The EU Special Representative for Human Rights is also tasked with contributing to the implementation of the Guidelines,[54] as was the Special Envoy for the promotion of freedom of religion or belief outside the EU with respect to the Guidelines on Freedom of Religion or Belief.

EU Guidelines for the Promotion and Protection of the Rights of the Child (revised 2017)

The rights of the child are human rights. They are indivisible, universal and inalienable. The Treaty on European Union (Lisbon Treaty), which came into force in 2009, includes an explicit commitment to promote the protection of the rights of the child in EU internal and external action (refer to Annex 1 for an overview of EU Legal Instruments and Policy). With these Guidelines, the European Union reaffirms its commitment to comprehensively protect and promote the rights of the child in its external human rights policy, in line with the provisions of the UN Convention on the Rights of the Child and its Optional Protocols and other relevant international standards and treaties.

(…)

Since the adoption of the Guidelines in 2007, there have been numerous developments in relation to the rights of the child globally as well as in the evolution of EU policy on children in the EU external action, thus making the present revision of the Guidelines necessary. The year 2015 alone resulted in the adoption of a number of major international agreements, of which the 2030 Agenda for Sustainable Development, which commits to providing children and youth with a nurturing environment for the full realisation of their rights and capabilities, and the Financing for Development agreement (Addis Ababa Action Agenda) are particularly relevant.

(…)

The purpose of these [Guidelines] is to recall international standards on the rights of the child and to provide practical guidance to officials of EU institutions and EU Member States in order to (i) strengthen their role in promoting and protecting the rights of all children in EU external action by encouraging and supporting the strengthening of partner countries' own systems, and (ii) further strengthen their cooperation with international and civil society organisations.

(…)

The EU policy on the rights of the child is strongly guided by the UNCRC. All EU Member States are party to the UNCRC, the most widely ratified human rights treaty in history, currently ratified by 196 States parties. It is the most comprehensive human rights treaty and legal instrument for the promotion and protection of the entire complement of rights relevant to children: economic, social, cultural, civil and political. Adopted in 1989, this Convention outlines universal standards for the care, treatment, survival, development, protection and participation of all children. It was the first international instrument to explicitly recognise children as social actors and active holders of right.

(…)

---

[54] Article 3 of Council Decision (CFSP) 2019/346 appointing the European Union Special Representative for Human Rights [2019] OJ L62/12.

The EU should support and encourage partner countries to:

- Accede, ratify and adhere to and/or implement and enforce the relevant international or regional instruments and standards for the promotion and protection of the rights of the child, particularly the UNCRC and its 3 Optional Protocols, ILO Conventions 138 and 182.
- Review and withdraw reservations that the country has made with regard to the UNCRC and its three Optional Protocols
- Support the enactment and review of national legislation and related administrative guidance to ensure its compatibility with relevant international norms and standards on the rights of the child, in particular the UNCRC and its Optional Protocols. The review needs to consider the Convention holistically, as well as article by article, recognizing the interdependence and indivisibility of human rights.
- Review and revise relevant legislation pertaining to the functioning of the justice system and children's access to justice (...)

The revised EU Guidelines for the Promotion and Protection of the Rights of the Child are illustrative of the standard content of EU Human Rights Guidelines. The first part of the document recalls the principles of EU action on rights of the child which are an amalgam of international human rights law—in this case the UN Convention on the Rights of the Child (UNCRC) and its four horizontal principles of non-discrimination, best interests of the child, right to life, survival and development, and respect for the views of children—and EU policies and frameworks, such as the rights-based approach.[55] In the second part, the Guidelines set out EU priorities in the area: from advancing the implementation of the UNCRC and the 2030 Agenda for Sustainable Development to promoting gender equality between boys and girls. Third, the EU lists the external relations tools which can be utilized in support of the Guidelines: political dialogues, human rights dialogues, statements and démarches, EU Human Rights and Democracy Country Strategies, and bilateral and multilateral cooperation and trade instruments. The final part of the document is perhaps the most important: it concerns 'operational guidelines' on what the EU should be doing externally to contribute to the objectives of promoting and protecting the rights of the child in third countries. The operational guidelines are divided according to the system-strengthening approach which builds on the 'General Measures of Implementation' identified by the UN Committee on the Rights of the Child (the treaty-monitoring body of the UNCRC).[56] The different target areas of EU action are legislation and policy (encouraging alignment of national legislation with international obligations); national strategies and action plans (rooted in the UNCRC); bilateral and multilateral cooperation (raising rights of the child in international fora and dialogues); mobilizing financial resources (both in third countries and in the EU for specific projects and programmes); coordination mechanisms (enhancing coherence and complementarity between actions and actors); human resources and capacity building (providing training for EU officials on children's rights and supporting third countries to commit and develop human resources in this area); data, evidence, and

---

[55] See Ch 11 for more information about the rights-based approach.
[56] UN Committee on the Rights of the Child, 'General Comment No 5' (27 November 2003) UN Doc CRC/GC/2003/5.

knowledge (encouraging the collection of disaggregated data and development of rights-based indicators); and oversight and accountability (supporting government and private sector accountability).

Although on the whole the Guidelines follow and indeed, where relevant, copy from general EU human rights policy (documents such as the Strategic Framework), they add substance to the existing formulations of EU commitments. Together with fostering EU consensus and coherence on selected international human rights issues, as well as raising the profile of these issues on the international plane, it is undisputable that EU Human Rights Guidelines offer at least some added value to the EU's external action toolkit. The principal challenge therefore lies—and this holds for virtually all EU policy output—in implementing the Guidelines in practice, as gaps in knowledge, training, and dissemination persist.[57]

J Wouters and M Hermez, 'EU Guidelines on Human Rights as a Foreign Policy Instrument: An Assessment' in S Poli (ed), *Human Rights in EU Foreign Affairs*, CLEER Papers 5/2015

The implementation of the Guidelines faces a number of difficulties and challenges. For example, the European Parliament has indicated that the implementation of the Guidelines on torture remains insufficient and at odds with EU statements and commitments to address torture as a matter of priority, and called for an 'effective and results-oriented' implementation. (...)

A first challenge concerns the knowledge of the Guidelines by the officials on the ground. (...) when studying the implementation of the Guidelines on HRD, Bennett found that the recommendations laid down in the Guidelines had not been systematically implemented by all Member States and that implementation was inconsistent. Knowledge of the Guidelines varies greatly from diplomatic mission to mission, depending on the diplomats on the ground and their background knowledge: not all of them are human rights specialists. (...) Diplomatic missions often charge juniors in embassies with dealing with the Guidelines and do not always bring the Guidelines to the attention of other members of the mission. Consequently, 'guidance notes' on the Guidelines are now being circulated, offering a brief explanation of best practices regarding their implementation. Lastly, the Guidelines suffer from the gap that exists between 'headquarters' and field missions. Some diplomats prefer focusing on their primary task—fostering bilateral relations—and tend to attach less attention to the Guidelines so as not to hamper bilateral ties. In this regard, frustrations have been noted on the lack of coherent planning for the implementation of the Guidelines, with human rights too often being side-lined by other EU policy priorities. (...)

In our view, special attention ought to go to a more rigorous, systematic and effective training of officials in the field, both in EU Delegations and in Member State diplomatic missions. This idea was endorsed by the European Parliament, when it urged the EEAS and the Member States to engage in continued training and awareness-raising among EEAS and EU Delegation staff, and among Member State diplomats, so as to make sure

---

[57] See also Council of the European Union, 'Mainstreaming Human Rights across CFSP and other EU Policies', 10076/06, 7 June 2006; K Bennett, 'European Union Guidelines on Human Rights Defenders: A Review of Policy and Practice towards Effective Implementation' (2015) 19 International Journal of Human Rights 908.

that the Guidelines have the intended effect in shaping actual policies on the ground. This indeed poses a serious challenge: a study by Bennett on the implementation of the Guidelines on HRD revealed that the training available to diplomats on human rights does not consistently include an effective implementation of the Guidelines and that, even where EU Member States provide mandatory human rights training, some diplomats remain left out or are personally not committed. (…)

D. EU Human Rights and Democracy Country Strategies

As a way of bridging the distance between EU human rights policy developed in Brussels and its implementation in third countries by Union Delegations and Member States, the EU recently started to develop EU Human Rights and Democracy Country Strategies. These Strategies 'are prepared to a to a large extent at the local level by EU delegations and based on an analysis of the human rights situation in a given country' with a varying level of involvement of civil society and the partner country.[58] The local character of the Country Strategies boosts ownership of the relevant EU Delegations and Missions over their implementation, contrary to the implementation of the Human Rights Guidelines which normally come as instructions from the EU headquarters at Rond-point Robert Schuman in Brussels.[59] The Country Strategies and Guidelines should, nonetheless, complement each other.

The EU Human Rights and Democracy Country Strategies set out both long- and short-term objectives and also contain more specific activities—often financed under the EIDHR—envisaged as concrete steps towards realizing the objectives. As the implementation of the Country Strategies depends hugely on the willingness of the country concerned to undertake reforms and carry out activities, the elaboration and implementation of Country Strategies is very much a diplomatic endeavour on the part of the EU. The result may therefore be considerable flexibility and accommodation between the demands of human rights principles and local political context, especially as human rights issues tend almost always to constitute sensitive topics in international relations.

The underlying cooperative relationship between the EU and third countries accompanying EU Human Rights and Democracy Country Strategies is also at the heart of a chief aspect and controversy surrounding the Country Strategies: they are not made public. Kept secret, Country Strategies cannot be monitored and evaluated by external actors—chiefly civil society organizations—which makes it more difficult objectively to assess progress on human rights in a given country and conversely, easier for the EU and/or the partner country to manipulate the message about the state of human rights in the country. Moreover, the undisclosed nature of these Strategies runs contrary to the principle of transparency which is otherwise present in both internal EU administration and the management of projects.[60] The retort of the EU is that the non-disclosure of the Country Strategies is the only way of eliciting commitment to a human rights agenda from third countries. Country Strategies are sometimes accompanied by a press release which may give a very general and brief outline of the main priorities of the Country Strategy.

[58] Council of the European Union, *EU Annual Report on Human Rights and Democracy in the World in 2015* (Publications Office of the European Union 2016).

[59] Wouters and Hermez, 'EU Guidelines on Human Rights as a Foreign Policy Instrument' (n 50) 78.

[60] On the issue of publicity of instruments of human rights promotion, see JH Matláry, *Intervention for Human Rights in Europe* (Palgrave 2002) 51.

'EU Launches "2016–2020 Human Rights and Democracy Country Strategy" for Papua New Guinea', Press release, Port Moresby, 9 September 2016

The European Union (EU) and two of its Member States, France and United Kingdom, have recently endorsed a five-year '2016–2020 Country Strategy on Human Rights and Democracy for Papua New Guinea'. The main activities to drive the strategy will be financed under the European Instrument for Human Rights and Democracy (EIDHR), other relevant financing instruments, and through targeted public diplomacy.

The strategy identifies three priority areas which the European Union, jointly with France and United Kingdom, will pursue in PNG. These are to:

- Promote a Human Rights culture in Papua New Guinea society,
- Support the ratification and implementation of Human Rights international conventions and instruments, and
- Strengthen good governance, democracy and rule of law.

The strategy targets to promote activities in two separate ways. It aims to build on former and ongoing projects, in particular initiatives to prevent violence against women, through awareness raising, targeting leadership and decision makers and empowering survivors. It will also promote activities that support Human Rights Defenders, provide technical assistance to counter People Trafficking or assist with the development of the Public Finance Management Road Map. Moreover, the strategy will also explore issues such as empowering women, raising awareness of LGBTI rights, advocacy of death penalty abolition, international treaties compliance, establishment of a Human Rights Institution and support to the Referendum on Bougainville.

The implementation of this strategy has already started through the commitment of over PGK 3 million, to three PNG based organisations supporting the 2016 Call for Proposals under the European Instrument for Human Rights and Democracy (EIDHR). The selected projects will address issues of people trafficking, building the institutional capacity of women's organisation and its network, and promote children's rights and juvenile justice.

E. Human rights dialogues

Human rights dialogues are an instrument of EU external policy through which the EU attempts to exert pressure, support, or gather information about human rights in third countries with the ultimate objective of promoting human rights abroad. At the same time, human rights dialogues also contribute to the mainstreaming of human rights in EU external action—they are a way of keeping human rights on the agenda in relations with third countries. Despite their name, human rights dialogues may include, if appropriate, issues relating to the rule of law and democracy, not least due to the possible difficulty of separating the three principles.[61] As of 2020, the EU has been holding human rights dialogues in some form with over 40 countries around the world. The term 'human rights dialogues' comprises a relatively considerable range of international consultations held at various levels and fora.

---

[61] See Ch 3.

EU Guidelines on human rights dialogues with third countries (revised 2009)

2.1. dialogues or discussions of a rather general nature based on regional or bilateral treaties, agreements or conventions or strategic partnerships dealing systematically with the issue of human rights. These include in particular:

   2.1.1. relations with candidate countries;

   2.1.2. the Cotonou Agreement with the ACP States;

   2.1.3. relations between the EU and Latin America;

   2.1.4. the Barcelona process (Mediterranean countries) and the neighbourhood policy (countries of the Caucasus in particular);

   2.1.5. political dialogue with Asian countries in the context of ASEAN and ASEM;

   2.1.6. relations with the Western Balkans;

   2.1.7. bilateral relations in the framework of association and cooperation agreements.

2.2. dialogues focusing exclusively on human rights. At present there are several regular, institutionalised dialogues devoted solely to human rights between the European Union and a third country or regional organisation (e.g. dialogue with China, consultations with Russia, dialogue with the five States of Central Asia and dialogue with the African Union). These are highly structured dialogues and consultations held at the level of human rights experts from the capitals. At one time the European Union also maintained a human rights dialogue with the Islamic Republic of Iran. Others are held at the level of heads of mission (e.g. India, Pakistan and Vietnam). The fact that such dialogue exists does not have to mean that the human rights issue is not also discussed at other levels of the political dialogue. In addition, in the context of various cooperation or association agreements with third countries, there are specific sub-committees or groups dealing with the human rights issue. This is the case in particular with various countries on the southern shores of the Mediterranean such as Morocco, Tunisia, Lebanon, Jordan, Egypt, Israel and the Palestinian Authority.

2.3. ad hoc dialogues extending to CFSP-related topics such as that of human rights. The EU currently maintains such dialogues, for example with Sudan, at the level of heads of mission on the spot.

2.4. dialogues in the context of special relations with certain third countries, on the basis of broadly converging views. With the United States, Canada, New Zealand, Japan and the associated countries, for example, these mostly take the form of six-monthly meetings of experts, with the Troika representing the EU, before the Human Rights Council and the annual United Nations General Assembly. Provision is also made for consultations with the African Union prior to the meetings of the Human Rights Council and the Third Committee of the UN General Assembly. The main objective of these dialogues is to discuss issues of common interest and the possibilities for cooperation within multilateral human rights bodies.

In addition to dialogues at EU level, a number of Member States also maintain dialogues with various third countries at national level.

The core aspects of human rights-specific dialogues are set out in the EU Guidelines on human rights dialogues with third countries which were adopted in 2001 and updated in 2009. Human rights dialogues can be open on the initiative of the EU or a third country, although in reality it is almost always the EU that initiates this process. The decision to open a human rights dialogue is preceded by multiple steps, the first of which is a preliminary assessment of the human rights situation in the country concerned; the question of whether such a preliminary assessment is made in the first place is decided by the COHOM which also conducts the actual assessment, in coordination with other Council Working Parties, such as the Working Party on Development Cooperation (CODEV). The preliminary assessment of the human rights situation looks at

> developments in the human rights situation, the extent to which the government is willing to improve the situation, the degree of commitment shown by the government in respect of international human rights conventions, the government's readiness to cooperate with United Nations human rights procedures and mechanisms as well as the government's attitude towards civil society.[62]

The preliminary assessment is based primarily on

> reports by heads of mission, reports by the UN and other international or regional organisations, reports by the European Parliament and by the various non-governmental organisations working in the field of human rights, and Commission strategy papers for the countries concerned.[63]

Practical aims and added value of a human rights dialogue must be defined and considered prior to the decision to open one. Also before the launch of a dialogue, exploratory talks are held with the third country concerned with the aim of defining the objectives of a future human rights dialogue and to identify the ways in which that country could increase its human rights commitments. The results of these exploratory talks then feed back into the preliminary assessment prepared earlier, as well as into the overall decision on whether to continue with a more structured dialogue.[64] Ultimately, the decision on launching a human rights dialogue rests with the Council of the EU, following a discussion in COHOM and consultation with other appropriate Council Working Parties (chiefly CODEV). If for any reason the COHOM decides not to pursue a human rights dialogue with a given country, it will consider whether there is scope for strengthening the human rights dimension of regular political dialogues.[65] The decision to open a human rights dialogue, as well as the dialogue itself, is, despite being 'regulated' by the basic framework of the EU Guidelines on human rights dialogues, subject to 'pragmatism and flexibility' which reflects its diplomatic nature as well as the limits of the EU's principled foreign policy.

---

[62] EU Guidelines on human rights dialogues with third countries (revised 2009) 7.
[63] Ibid.
[64] Ibid, 8.
[65] Ibid, 9.

EU Guidelines on human rights dialogues with third countries (revised 2009)

4. Objectives of human rights dialogues

The objectives of human rights dialogues will vary from one country to another and will be defined on a case-by-case basis. These objectives may include:

(a) discussing questions of mutual interest and enhancing cooperation on human rights inter alia, in multinational fora such as the United Nations;

(b) registering the concern felt by the EU at the human rights situation in the country concerned, information gathering and endeavouring to improve the human rights situation in that country.

Moreover, human rights dialogues can identify at an early stage problems likely to lead to conflict in the future.

5. Issues covered in human rights dialogues

The issues to be discussed during human rights dialogues will be determined on a case-by-case basis. However, the European Union is committed to dealing with those priority issues which should be included on the agenda for every dialogue. These include the signing, ratification and implementation of international human rights instruments, cooperation with international human rights procedures and mechanisms, combating the death penalty, combating torture, combating all forms of discrimination, children's rights, and in particular those of children in armed conflicts, women's rights, freedom of expression, the role of civil society and the protection of human rights defenders, international cooperation in the field of justice, in particular with the International Criminal Court, promotion of the processes of democratisation and good governance, the rule of law and the prevention of conflict. The dialogues aimed at enhancing human rights cooperation could also include—according to the circumstances—some of the priority issues referred to above, (in particular the implementation of the main international human rights instruments ratified by the other party), as well as preparing and following up the work of the Human Rights Council in Geneva, of the Third Committee of the UN General Assembly in New York and of international and/or regional conferences. They are held on a reciprocal basis, which enables the third country to raise the human rights situation in the European Union.

COHOM, which brings together EU Member State representatives but is chaired by the EEAS,[66] is also responsible for following up the human rights dialogues, assessing them, and setting the core agenda of the dialogues. The managerial capacity in the EU for dialogues resides predominantly within the EEAS with a subsidiary role for the Council Secretariat and other EU bodies capable of providing input (such as the Commission and EU Delegations). The EEAS furthermore usually leads the EU representation in the human

---

[66] See Ch 2.

rights dialogues and conducts the talks with the chief representative of the third country.[67] The level of representation in the human rights dialogues varies but normally it involves relevant higher level EEAS/government officials. Regularly present in human rights dialogues, at least as observers, are also representatives of (interested) Member States and officials from the local Union Delegation or Mission. Overall, although the establishment of the EEAS along with the changes introduced by the Treaty of Lisbon have instilled in part a common EU element into the conduct of human rights dialogues, the instrument continues to be principally intergovernmental which means that the individual interests of 27 Member States have an important influence on EU human rights dialogues. These interests—such as trade—are not always or necessarily geared towards maximizing pressure on countries violating human rights.

In principle, the EU strives to involve civil society in human rights dialogues. Although there are no hard and fast rules, civil society organizations can be involved in the preparation of the preliminary assessment, in the dialogue itself, or in parallel consultations during a formal dialogue, and in the evaluation of the dialogue.[68] However, on account of the 'pragmatism and flexibility' which must be involved, civil society—or select, unwanted organizations—can just as well be excluded from human rights dialogues or crucial aspects of them. The issue of who participates in human rights dialogues is compounded by the overall lack of transparency; human rights dialogues and the content of the discussions is not made public, similarly to EU Human Rights and Democracy Country Strategies. Similar issues therefore plague the effectiveness of the dialogues: in the absence of publicity, there is no credible monitoring and evaluation of progress of the dialogue. The EU would counter that secrecy is the only possible way of having human rights dialogues with some countries, wary as they are of even the slightest encroachment on their sovereignty. The occasional publication of press releases does not satisfactorily remedy the opacity of human rights dialogues. Press releases tend to be general and vague on the content and sometimes even misleading.[69]

Most observers are not swayed by the EU's arguments about the need for human rights dialogues to be confidential and for good reasons—the EU is not really able to point to the dialogues being effective in the absence of public oversight.[70] Leading human rights NGOs have at times criticized the very idea of human rights dialogues: in 2011, Human Rights Watch wrote in its report that 'the quest for dialogue and cooperation is simply not a universal substitute for public pressure as a tool to promote human rights', with the EU singled out in particular as a serial offender enabling the proliferation of dialogue at the expense of pressure and action.[71] There have been repeated calls for the suspension of one of the most well-known and long-standing (ongoing since 1995) human rights dialogues between the

---

[67] One round of a human rights dialogue should take at least a full day.
[68] EU Guidelines on human rights dialogues with third countries (revised 2009) 11.
[69] B Majtényi, L Sosa, and A Timmer, 'Human rights concepts in EU Human Rights Dialogues' (2016) FRAME Deliverable 3.5, 8–9 <http://www.fp7-frame.eu/wp-content/uploads/2016/11/Deliverable-3.5.pdf> accessed 14 August 2020. Kinzelbach, for example, found that the atmosphere of one EU–China human rights dialogue described as 'frank' in an EU press release in its aftermath was in reality closer to 'frosty and aggressive': K Kinzelbach, *The EU's Human Rights Dialogue with China: Quiet Diplomacy and its Limits* (Routledge 2015) 180.
[70] Ibid.
[71] Human Rights Watch, *World Report 2011 (Events of 2010)*, 2011, 20.

EU and China in light of its ineffectiveness and the fact that it serves as an excuse not to engage with China—the EU's second biggest trading partner—more seriously on the issue of
human rights.[72] The most damning critique in this regard, however, came from academia.
Katrin Kinzelbach carried out what is one of the most important studies on EU human rights
policy about the 'quiet diplomacy' of the EU–China human rights dialogue. On the basis of
unparalleled information on the dialogue obtained through interviews and access to confidential documents, Kinzelbach concluded that the EU–China human rights dialogue is
completely ineffective due to underlying positions and perceptions of the parties;[73] even if
the human rights situation in China were to improve, it is unlikely it would be in any way attributable to the human rights dialogue with the EU.[74]

**K Kinzelbach, *The EU's Human Rights Dialogue with China: Quiet
Diplomacy and its Limits* (Routledge 2015)**

When the EU–China Human Rights Dialogue was first initiated in 1995, the Chinese
[Ministry of Foreign Affairs] used it to prevent another draft resolution at the UN Human
Rights Commission. International actors tailored threats and incentives around this aspiration, thereby manipulating the cost-benefit calculations made by Chinese leaders
on such issues as signing international human rights covenants, granting access to UN
human rights experts and releasing a few fairly well-known political prisoners. (...) In
the structured Human Rights Dialogue, the EU's representatives regularly voiced their
concerns, but they never negotiated specific concessions with the Chinese delegation.
Rather, the various EU representatives sought to convince their Chinese counterparts
of the benefit of human rights compliance and (...) of the positive effect that gestures
of goodwill could have on China's image abroad. Over the whole period discussed in
this book, from 1995 to 2010, the EU's quiet diplomacy vis-à-vis China remained anchored in repeated discussions—mainly but not only among mid-level officials—about
international principles and reputation. EU decision-makers at all levels ignored the fact
that social vulnerability was not indefinitely going to remain a key concern for Chinese
decision-makers, both because public memory of the Tiananmen massacre faded over
time and because rapid economic growth as well as the rise of China as a global power
provided new sources of legitimacy for the party state.

(...)

The EU's engagement in the Human Rights Dialogue (...) turned from fairly optimistic
in 1995 to entirely ceremonial in 2010. The position that the Council of the European
Union had still announced in 2000, namely that Dialogue was 'an acceptable option only
if enough progress is achieved and reflected on the ground' (...) disappeared from public

---

[72] Human Rights Watch, 'EU: Suspend China Human Rights Dialogue' (*hrw.org*, 19 June 2017); Open letter by
human rights NGOs concerning the EU–China summit, Brussels, 22 May 2017 <http://www.hrw.org/sites/de-
fault/files/supporting_resources/160522_eu_china_letter.pdf> accessed 14 August 2020.

[73] Kinzelbach calls the EU–China human rights dialogue 'impotent'. See Kinzelbach (n 69) 200.

[74] The position of human rights dialogues with the other rising Asian power, India, does not seem to be much
better. According to one observer, 'India will continue to be engaged with the EU on human rights. The human
rights dialogue will be held, but not always annually. Their proceedings are not made public and have 'a formulaic
appearance'. The Indian side does not take them 'too seriously' (...). Thus, human rights will continue to be ranked
rather low in New Delhi's policy agenda and interaction with the EU'. See RK Jain, 'India, the European Union and
Human Rights' (2017) 73 India Quarterly 411, 421.

statements as the Dialogue became more and more disappointing and even perfunctory. In 2012 one European Dialogue participant told me on condition of anonymity:

I am not aware that the EU has demanded results. Our Human Rights Dialogue with China is not about results, it is just a venue for us to voice concerns. Nobody in the EU expects concrete results from this process. If public statements on the Dialogue mention results anywhere, then that's just public relations-speak.

(...)

Based on the findings of this study, it can be predicted with a high level of certainty that the intended human rights promotion and protection in China, should it indeed materialize in the medium to long-term future, will not be causally linked to the EU–China Human Rights Dialogue.

F. Human rights clauses in international agreements

Since 1992, the EU has included a human rights clause in all its international agreements with third countries.[75] A human rights clause is nowadays part of EU international agreements with approximately 130 states worldwide.[76] The clause is a legally binding provision in international agreements with a standard form which aims to safeguard and bolster the EU's commitment to human rights in legal relations with third countries.[77] Most EU human rights clauses comprise two parts: an essential elements clause and a non-execution clause.

L Bartels, 'The EU's Human Rights Obligations in Relation to Policies with Extraterritorial Effects' (2014) 25 European Journal of International Law 1071

There are human rights clauses in treaties between the EU and over 120 other states. Their wording varies somewhat, but in their standard form they have two parts. The first is an 'essential elements' clause stating that:

Respect for democratic principles and human rights, as laid down in the Universal Declaration of Human Rights and other relevant international human rights instruments, as well as for the principle of the rule of law, underpins the internal and international policies of both Parties and constitutes an essential element of this Agreement.

The second is a 'non-execution' clause providing that either party may adopt 'appropriate measures' if the other fails to comply with its obligations under the agreement.

---

[75] D Horng, 'The Human Rights Clause in the European Union's External Trade and Development Agreements' (2003) 9 European Law Journal 677. The inclusion of human rights clauses in all treaties became an official policy in 1995. See European Commission, 'Communication on the inclusion of respect for democratic principles and human rights in agreements between the community and third countries', COM(95) 216 final, Brussels, 23 May 1995, 7–8.

[76] In the absence of a human rights clause, the EU relied in the case of an agreement with Syria on its preamble to partially suspend the operation of the agreement due to violations of the principles of the UN Charter. See Council Decision 2011/523/EU partially suspending the application of the Cooperation Agreement between the European Economic Community and the Syrian Arab Republic [2011] OJ L228/19.

[77] The most comprehensive treatment of the subject remains L Bartels, *Human Rights Conditionality in the EU's International Agreements* (Oxford University Press 2005).

These include the essential elements of the agreement. There are also typically other provisions elaborating on such 'appropriate measures'.

The legal effect of essential elements clauses is not entirely certain, but the conventional view is that they contain obligations binding on the parties. The scope of these clauses is broad, applying to both the internal and international policies of the parties. Moreover, the reference to international policies implies that these clauses govern extraterritorial effects of at least 'international' policies. Given the difficulty of distinguishing between internal policies and international policies, there seems little merit in seeking to draw a distinction between the two. One can therefore conclude that, textually, these clauses apply to policies with extraterritorial effects.

This interpretation is also supported by practice. In 2002, the EU adopted 'appropriate measures' under the Cotonou Agreement in relation to Liberia for a variety of reasons, one of which was its assistance to the Front uni révolutionnaire (RUF) of Sierra Leone, which was accused of committing gross human rights violations in that country. This followed a UN Security Council Resolution, and follow up activity, concerning Liberia's material and financial support to the RUF in Sierra Leone. The EU thus seems to have accepted that the essential elements clause covers policies with effects in other countries, independently of any extraterritorial conduct. For present purposes, this is an important result. The EU's human rights clauses are bilateral, and therefore under these clauses the EU's policies must also respect human rights in other states.

Human rights clauses vary to some extent, as the EU does not impose them unilaterally— they are part of international agreements to which the other party must agree as well. For example, one of the varied aspects can be the human rights instrument serving as the reference point of human rights compliance. The Universal Declaration on Human Rights is the most frequent reference point but others, such as the ECHR and Helsinki Final Act of 1975 of the Conference on Security and Cooperation in Europe, have been used as well. The absence of a reference to a particular human rights instrument, as is the case, for example, in the Euro-Mediterranean Association Agreement with Israel,[78] increases the vagueness of the human rights clause which in turn reduces its potential effectiveness. Another point of variance is whether in addition to human rights the clause contains a reference to 'democratic principles' or other value.[79] Similarly, the thresholds for terminating an agreement on account of human rights violations can differ. For example, Article 28(7) of the EU–Canada Strategic Partnership Agreement circumscribes the possibility of termination to 'particularly serious and substantial violation of human rights or non-proliferation'.

[78] Euro-Mediterranean Agreement establishing an association between the European Communities and their Member States, of the one part, and the State of Israel, of the other part [2000] OJ L147/3, Article 2. Note, however, the Joint Declaration to Article 2 which states: 'The Parties reaffirm the importance they attach to the respect of human rights as set out in the UN Charter including the struggle against xenophobia, anti-Semitism and racism.'

[79] The rule of law, respect for the principles of international law and market economy have occasionally found their way –into the list of essential elements. See N Hachez, ' "Essential Elements" Clauses in EU Trade Agreements—Making Trade Work in a Way that Helps Human Rights?' (2015) 53 Cuadernos Europeos de Deusto 81, 96.

Strategic Partnership Agreement between the European Union and its Member States, of the one part, and Canada, of the other part [2016] OJ L329/45

Article 2

Upholding and advancing democratic principles, human rights and fundamental freedoms

1. Respect for democratic principles, human rights and fundamental freedoms, as laid down in the Universal Declaration of Human Rights and existing international human rights treaties and other legally binding instruments to which the Union or the Member States and Canada are party, underpins the Parties' respective national and international policies and constitutes an essential element of this Agreement.

2. The Parties shall endeavour to cooperate and uphold these rights and principles in their own policies and shall encourage other states to adhere to those international human rights treaties and legally binding instruments and to implement their own human rights obligations.

3. The Parties are committed to advancing democracy, including free and fair electoral processes in line with international standards. Each Party shall inform the other of its respective election observation missions and invite the other to participate as appropriate.

4. The Parties recognise the importance of the rule of law for the protection of human rights and for the effective functioning of governance institutions in a democratic state. This includes the existence of an independent justice system, equality before the law, the right to a fair trial and individuals' access to effective legal redress.

Article 28

Fulfilment of obligations

7. In addition, the Parties recognise that a particularly serious and substantial violation of human rights or non-proliferation, as defined in paragraph 3, could also serve as grounds for the termination of the EU-Canada Comprehensive Economic and Trade Agreement (CETA) in accordance with Article 30.9 of that Agreement.

In terms of public international law, human rights clauses are generally consistent with Article 60(3)(b) of the Vienna Convention on the Law of Treaties (VCLT) which provides for the possibility to terminate or suspend a treaty by one of the parties in case of a 'violation of a provision essential to the accomplishment of the object or purpose of the treaty', subject to notification of the measure in accordance being taken and the reasons therefor to the other parties pursuant to Article 65 VCLT.[80] Although under the VCLT the time between notification and suspension/termination should normally be at least three months,[81] EU international agreements typically do not provide for such a notification period. Nor do EU

---

[80] Vienna Convention on the Law of the Treaties (adopted 23 May 1969, entered into force 27 January 1980) 1155 UNTS 331. See also E Riedel and M Will, 'Human Rights Clauses in External Agreements of the EC' in P Alston (ed), *The EU and Human Rights* (Oxford University Press 1999) 729.

[81] Article 65(2) VCLT.

human rights clauses provide for conciliation in the United Nations should one of the parties object to the notified measures but it can be safely presumed that the EU would normally alert the other party to its concerns before invoking the human rights clause to suspend or terminate an agreement.[82] Indeed, consultations based on the demand that the human rights clause is respected have taken place on several occasions (see Table 10.1).

The presence of dialogue prior to any sanctions is consistent with the discretionary character of human rights clauses. Despite the multiple human rights commitments in its legal framework and public statements to such effect, the EU judiciary has held that the EU is under no obligation to invoke human rights clauses, as is clear from their wording, and that individuals cannot derive justiciable rights from the human rights clauses—the clauses only apply to relations between contracting parties to the agreement concerned.

Judgment of 6 September 2011, *Mugraby v Council and Commission*, T-292/09, ECLI:EU:T:2011:418

56. In the present case, the applicant essentially criticises the Council and the Commission for having failed to suspend the Association Agreement as provided for in Article 86 thereof.

57. The applicant also claims that the Council and the Commission gave rise on his part, by reason of the various public statements that the defendants have made in the context of the management of the European Union's external policy with respect to development, to legitimate expectations as regards their willingness to actually enforce the obligations relating to human rights contained in Article 2 of the Association Agreement.

58. It follows from the wording of the second paragraph of Article 86 of the Association Agreement that the parties to it are not obliged to terminate or suspend the agreement where one of them does not fulfil one of the obligations imposed on it by the agreement.

59. Specifically, it is clear from the wording of the second paragraph of Article 86 of the Association Agreement and, in particular, from the use of the expression '[i]f either Party considers that the other Party has failed to fulfil an obligation under this Agreement', that each party to the agreement is free to decide whether there may be an infringement of the clause relating to the respect for fundamental human rights laid down in Article 2 by the Republic of Lebanon and, if so, of the nature and seriousness of such infringement. It is also clear from the use of the word 'may' that, in the event of an infringement of the provisions of the agreement, each party to the agreement is free to adopt the measure it regards as being the most appropriate. It is true that the suspension of the Association Agreement is a measure that the Community, through its competent institutions, may adopt. However, it is not obliged to adopt such a measure, nor does that measure represent the only measure available to deal with an infringement of the obligations in the Association Agreement.

---

[82] Article 65(3) VCLT refers to Article 33 of the UN Charter which contains a list of methods of pacific dispute settlement.

60. The **Council and the Commission enjoy a wide margin of discretion in the man-agement of the external relations of the European Union** with respect to development in so far as that management involves complex political and economic assessments. However, the applicant has not established that the Council and the Commission have manifestly and gravely disregarded the limits of the broad discretion that they have with regard to a possible suspension of the Association Agreement.

61. Even assuming that those institutions have manifestly and gravely exceeded the limits of their discretion and have thereby infringed Article 86, that article does not, in any event, give rights to individuals.

68. (...) **Article 86 of the Association Agreement is not sufficiently clear and precise and is subject, in its implementation** or effects, to the adoption of subsequent measures by the competent Community institutions, thereby **excluding the possibility that it may directly govern the applicant's situation**.

The legal design and soundness of human rights clauses in EU international agreements is, despite several caveats, for the most part the less controversial aspect of the clauses, even though it has been argued that the process for their triggering could be more inclusive.[83] What most observers are concerned about is the implementation of human rights clauses. Perhaps unsurprisingly, the Council of the EU sees them primarily as political tools leading to dialogue, and therefore subject to the changing whims of international diplomacy.[84] As a result, human rights clauses might not be activated when the situation on the ground would objectively call for this,[85] or they might be applied selectively, so as not to endanger EU relations with economically important partners. At the same time, invoking the clauses might not necessarily bring about the desired result; on the contrary, it could lead to a further deterioration of human rights in the country concerned. Targeting is a potential issue as well, given that the suspension of an agreement would most likely harm consumers and producers in the third country, despite it being the government or particular non-state groups most often responsible for rights violations.

[83] Bartels has observed that '[t]here is no reason why the EU, with its commitment to promoting human rights in the world, should not follow best practice, and introduce into its trade agreements a mechanism whereby individuals, civil society and the other EU institutions are able to require the Commission (or the EEAS) to investigate whether third countries are complying with human rights conditions to which they have committed in the context of a free trade agreement or unilateral trade preferences. Of course, this does not mean that these actors would have any role in the formal decision to suspend the agreement.' See L Bartels, 'The European Parliament's Role in relation to Human Rights in Trade and Investment Agreements', European Parliament Study, February 2014, 19.

[84] See Council of the European Union, Common approaches on the use of political clauses, 10491/1/09, 2 June 2009.

[85] Horn, Mavroidis, and Sapir call EU trade agreements legally inflated and as a consequence unenforceable and mere vehicles for 'declaratory diplomacy': 'European [preferential trade agreements] are marred by considerable legal inflation. They ambitiously cover a wide range of topics, going much beyond the multilateral commitments entered into by the partners within the framework of the World Trade Organisation, but they are mostly unenforceable—if not entirely devoid of substance. The Union, in other words, seems to be using trade agreements to promote its views on how countries of the world should be run, and it is able to enlist its trade partners to do this, albeit in a noncommittal or semi-committal way. Trade policy therefore provides a vehicle for declaratory diplomacy.' See H Horn, P Mavroidis, and A Sapir, 'Beyond the WTO—An Anatomy of EU and US Preferential Trade Agreements', Bruegel Blueprint No 7/2009.

> **N Hachez, '"Essential Elements" Clauses in EU Trade Agreements—Making Trade Work in a Way that Helps Human Rights?' (2015) 53 Cuadernos Europeos de Deusto 81**
>
> Essential elements have thus sparsely been invoked, they have not always led to sanctions proper but rather to consultations, and the sanctions when applied did not involve the lifting of trade preferences but rather 'suspension of meetings and technical co-operation programmes'. Moreover, essential elements clauses were only triggered in situations where drastic changes had taken place in the country in question, such as a coup, flawed elections, or brutal occurrences of grave human rights violations. Therefore, conditionality is normally not activated when human rights violations routinely take place in a country, unless the situation gravely and suddenly deteriorates. This is difficult to reconcile with the Strategic Framework and Action's plan statement that 'when faced with violations of human rights, the EU will make use of the full range of instruments at its disposal, including sanctions or condemnation (...)'
>
> It must be concluded that, in general the conditionality policy lacks any proper 'operational mechanism' for implementation, monitoring of human rights situations and evaluation of the effectiveness of sanctions. All this is supposed to take place through local diplomatic missions which lack time and resources to conduct such ground work. (...)
>
> Indeed, essential elements clauses seem to be considered chiefly as 'political' clauses by the Council, and many observers have pointed out that, in comparison with the US approach, which takes a binding approach towards a small and clearly defined number of standards, the EU's essential policies clauses are 'aspirational' and aimed at fostering dialogue. In any event, another author has warned against the temptation to activate essential elements clauses for the sole purpose of showing some muscle and/or avoiding the accusation of double standards. Indeed, apparently trade and other sanctions are only effective in certain contexts, and are completely useless in others. Therefore, risking to apply sanctions just to see them fail would harm rather than bolster the credibility of the Union's conditionality policy. In this regard, one must be prepared to accept that the removal of trade benefits is perhaps not an argument that is convincing enough to induce change on its own. The example of the little effective GSP+ sanctions taken, for example, against Belarus or Myanmar may corroborate this hypothesis, and may explain why a violation of essential elements have never given rise to sanctions of that sort. (...)

It has been suggested that the more recent association agreements between the EU and countries of the Eastern Partnership (the eastern limb of ENP) go somewhat beyond the standard EU practice on human rights clauses. First, the essential elements clause in the EU–Ukraine association agreement includes in addition to human rights a reference to the principle of the rule of law, both of which are moreover meant to 'form the basis of the domestic and external policies of the Parties'.[86] The Eastern Partnership association agreements also include other principles, such as non-proliferation of nuclear weapons, as essential elements. Second, the human rights clauses in these agreements have, in addition to their negative, dissuasive dimension, a positive function. The clauses are linked to the achievement of the

---

[86] Article 2 of Association Agreement between the European Union and its Member States, of the one part, and Ukraine, of the other part [2014] OJ L161/3.

agreements' objectives and in relation to domestic reforms on issues such as fight against corruption.[87]

N Ghazaryan, 'A New Generation of Human Rights Clauses? The Case of Association Agreements in the Eastern Neighbourhood' (2015) 40 European Law Review 391

While reflecting the EU's previous practice on HRCs, the Eastern AAs demonstrate that this practice is not set in stone. The standard model contains amendments to its essential elements and non-execution clauses. The scope of the essential elements clause is widened by the inclusion of additional elements and international instruments in its normative framework. In the case of Ukraine, the provision is also reflective of the political circumstances surrounding the signing of the relevant agreement. The three agreements demonstrate a novel practice of significantly expanding the General Principles beyond the essential elements, albeit in a somewhat arbitrary fashion as the distinctions between the Ukrainian AA and the Moldovan and Georgian AAs clearly demonstrate. The normative underpinning of the essential element clause indicates the most stringent standard in the neighbourhood to date, which might be explained by the level of political and economic proximity promised by the agreements.

The non-execution clause follows the now-standard distinction between taking appropriate measures in the event of general breaches of treaties and possible treaty suspension in cases of special urgency—replaced here by 'exceptional circumstances'—for breaches of essential elements. In contrast to other treaty obligations, DCFTA [Deep and Comprehensive Free Trade Area] obligations can be suspended in exceptional circumstances. This new practice is at odds with the EU's previous record and is intended to deprive the parties of the ENP's main incentive, the DCFTA. However, the negative application of the HRC clause remains unlikely, taking into account the scarce application of these provisions in the past. Moreover, the negative application would run counter to the very rationale of engagement through the ENP. The predominantly positive conditionality of the ENP, as well as the general trend in EU political conditionality, reveal an alternative, positive role of the HRCs [Human Rights Councils]. The content of the agreements, including their objectives, the provisions on political dialogue and the specific articles on political reform all reaffirm the positive functionality of the HRCs. The essential element clause provides the normative framework for any positive engagement in the domain of political reform and therefore underpins all other instruments deployed by the EU. It is this positive function that should be regarded as the added value of these provisions, rather than the unlikely possibility of negative measures in the event of a breach.

---

[87] Article 4 of Association Agreement between the European Union and the European Atomic Energy Community and their Member States, of the one part, and Georgia, of the other part [2014] OJ L261/4; Article 4 of Association Agreement between the European Union and the European Atomic Energy Community and their Member States, of the one part, and the Republic of Moldova, of the other part [2014] OJ L260/4.

9.4 Common Foreign and Security Policy (CFSP)

Despite the potential gains in increased leverage on the world stage, the EU was not endowed with a proper foreign policy competence at the outset of the integration project due to national sovereign sensitivities involved in the subject. One of the decisive historical blows in this respect was the rejection of the European Defence Community, which aimed to achieve a degree of military integration, in the French National Assembly in 1954.[88] As a consequence, common foreign policy in the early EU framework was confined to external aspects of the EU's predominantly economic policies—chiefly the common commercial policy—and the maintenance of relations between European countries and their former colonies. Although these external policies continue to be of key importance to what the EU does—and they have in fact expanded in scope since the Community's inception—in a separate but concurrent development the EU Member States laid the foundations of a European foreign policy.

The origin of European foreign policy is usually traced back to the Davignon Report adopted in Luxembourg on 27 October 1970 which provided for regular meetings between the foreign ministers of the then EEC. The political consultations on foreign policy matters became known as the European Political Cooperation (EPC) and it was to be incrementally refined through subsequent informal agreements between Member States (see Chapter 1). The EPC was institutionalized in the Single European Act, the first major revision of Treaties, and it became formally part of one European Union as the Common Foreign and Security Policy (CFSP) together with the Community and the also newly formalized Justice and Home Affairs (JHA) with the Maastricht Treaty. Despite formally belonging under the EU umbrella, the three 'pillars', as they became known, differed considerably. Whereas the Community pillar entailed a real transfer of competences to supranational institutions (chiefly the Commission), the CFSP and to a lesser extent JHA continued to be, as before their institutionalization within the EU, intergovernmental. While JHA has been since completely subsumed within the 'Community dimension' of the EU—and the pillar structure formally abolished—the intergovernmental essence of the CFSP can still be witnessed today despite a number of developments which provide certain nuances to the supranational-intergovernmental distinction.[89]

A. The CFSP and CSDP framework

Symbolically, the difference between the CFSP, including the CSDP, and the 'rest' is immediately evident in the fact that the CFSP and CSDP are essentially the only policies[90] still found in the TEU rather than the TFEU.[91] Some scholars have referred to the legal separateness

---

[88] Instead, the Member States only managed to agree on the revision of the 1948 Treaty of Brussels which was the basis of a Western European defence alliance called, since the 1954 revision, the Western European Union (WEU). In practice, the North Atlantic Treaty Organization (NATO) was and continues to be, thanks to the presence of the United States, by far the most important military pact involving European states. The WEU tasks were progressively transferred to the EU, first as European Security and Defence Policy (ESDP), then, since the Treaty of Lisbon, as Common Security and Defence Policy (CSDP). The WEU was disbanded in 2011.

[89] See H Sjursen Democracy and Integration in European Foreign and Security Policy' (2011) 18 Journal of European Public Policy 1078.

[90] Also part of the TEU are, for example, provisions concerning accession to and exit from the EU. Therefore it can be said that the 'enlargement policy', too, is based in the TEU.

[91] This is a vestige of EU legal history introduced in the Single European Act where the provisions on the EPC were part of the Single European Act (SEA) itself which came on top of the existing Treaties establishing the European Communities (the Coal and Steel Community, the Economic Community, and the Atomic Energy

of the CFSP as 'ring-fencing'.[92] Nevertheless, as a measure of strengthening inter-policy coherence, the principles guiding EU external action in general (Article 21 TEU) are also applicable to the CFSP by virtue of Article 23 TEU. Articles 24–41 TEU subsequently contain
the crux of the rules governing the CFSP.[93] The rules on the CSDP are contained in Articles
42–46 TEU.

Consolidated version of the Treaty on European Union [2012] OJ C326/13

Article 24

1. The Union's competence in matters of common foreign and security policy shall
   **cover all areas of foreign policy and all questions relating to the Union's security,
   including the progressive framing of a common defence policy that might lead to
   a common defence.**

   The common foreign and security policy is subject to **specific rules and procedures.** It shall be defined and implemented by the **European Council and the Council
   acting unanimously,** except where the Treaties provide otherwise. The adoption of legislative acts shall be excluded. The common foreign and security policy shall be **put
   into effect by the High Representative of the Union for Foreign Affairs and Security
   Policy and by Member States,** in accordance with the Treaties. The specific role of the
   European Parliament and of the Commission in this area is defined by the Treaties.
   **The Court of Justice of the European Union shall not have jurisdiction with respect
   to these provisions,** with the exception of its jurisdiction to monitor compliance with
   Article 40 of this Treaty and to review the legality of certain decisions as provided
   for by the second paragraph of Article 275 of the Treaty on the Functioning of the
   European Union.

2. Within the framework of the principles and objectives of its external action, the
   Union shall conduct, define and implement a common foreign and security policy,
   based on the development of **mutual political solidarity among Member States,**
   the identification of questions of general interest and the achievement of an ever-
   increasing degree of convergence of Member States' actions.
3. The Member States shall support the Union's external and security policy actively
   and unreservedly in a **spirit of loyalty and mutual solidarity** and shall comply with
   the Union's action in this area.

Community) that were amended by the SEA. The SEA 'proper'—that is, not its amending provisions—then became the TEU from the Maastricht Treaty onwards.

[92] PJ Cardwell, 'On "Ring-fencing" the Common Foreign and Security Policy in the Legal Order of the European
Union' (2013) 64 Northern Ireland Legal Quarterly 443.
[93] A number of TFEU provisions are relevant to the CFSP. The most important of those are Articles 215 and 275
TFEU on restrictive measures and jurisdiction of the CJEU, respectively.

> The Member States shall work together to enhance and develop their mutual political solidarity. They shall refrain from any action which is contrary to the interests of the Union or likely to impair its effectiveness as a **cohesive force in international relations**.
> The Council and the High Representative shall ensure compliance with these principles.

The most important aspects of the CFSP, as they emerge from the Treaty legal framework, are the following. The decision-makers in chief are the European Council, which decides on the overall political and strategic orientation of the EU when it comes to foreign policy, and the Council, which is in charge of more operational decisions. As a rule, and contrary to the ordinary legislative procedure which is the standard decision-making process as regards non-CFSP matters, the European Council and the Council decide by unanimity with qualified majority voting being the exception in cases where the European Council has already set the overall direction, requested action, or where a decision is required to implement an already existing EU action or position.[94] Decisions and guidelines taken by the (European) Council bind the Member States which must furthermore ensure that their own national positions are in conformity with the EU ones and that they act in mutual solidarity. The CFSP provisions are replete with wording concerning Member States' convergence and conformity with the common actions taken under the CFSP due to fears that this traditionally national area of competence—and still only partially 'Unionized'—might not be effectively and coherently implemented by the Member States. On the basis of the same rationale, the position of the High Representative of the Union for Foreign Affairs and Security Policy (at the same time a Vice-President of the Commission) was created. The High Representative is charged with implementing Council decisions (with the help of the EEAS), chairing the meetings of the Foreign Affairs Council (combined with an agenda-setting capacity), and generally being the face of EU foreign policy by conducting political dialogues with third parties and representing EU positions in international fora. His concurrent affiliation to the Commission as a Vice-President is meant to further bridge the CFSP and other (external) policies of the EU and he should also consult the European Parliament (EP) on the main aspects and choices of the CFSP.[95] While the role of the EP in the CFSP is greatly diminished under the Treaties,[96] the CJEU has emphasized the importance of democratic scrutiny when it comes to the conclusion of international agreements, even when they relate exclusively to the CFSP.

---

[94] The full list of exceptions to the unanimity requirement is contained in Article 31(2) TEU. According to Article 31(3) TEU, the European Council may decide, by unanimity, to introduce qualified majority voting in other cases.

[95] Article 36 TEU.

[96] There is considerable discussion regarding the extent to which the CFSP is subject to parliamentary scrutiny. See M Riddervold and G Rosén, 'Trick and Treat: How the Commission and the European Parliament Exert Influence in EU Foreign and Security Policies' (2016) 38 Journal of European Integration 687; A Huff, 'Executive Privilege Reaffirmed? Parliamentary Scrutiny of the CFSP and CSDP' (2015) 38 West European Politics 396; T Raunio and W Wagner, 'Towards Parliamentarisation of Foreign and Security Policy?' (2017) 40 West European Politics 1.

Judgment of 24 June 2014, *Parliament v Council (Mauritius)*, C-658/11, ECLI:EU:C:2014:2025

83. Admittedly, as noted in paragraph 55 of the present judgment, **the role which the Treaty of Lisbon has conferred on the Parliament in relation to the CFSP remains limited.**

84. Nevertheless, it cannot be inferred from that fact that despite its exclusion from the procedure for negotiating and concluding an agreement relating exclusively to the CFSP, the Parliament has no right of scrutiny in respect of that EU policy.

85. On the contrary, it is precisely for that purpose that the information requirement laid down in Article 218(10) TFEU applies to any procedure for concluding an international agreement, including agreements relating exclusively to the CFSP.

86. If the Parliament is not immediately and fully informed at all stages of the procedure in accordance with Article 218(10) TFEU, including that preceding the conclusion of the agreement, it is not in a position **to exercise the right of scrutiny which the Treaties have conferred on it in relation to the CFSP** (...)

Furthermore, the jurisdiction of the CJEU is considerably circumscribed with respect to the CFSP.[97] As a general rule, the CJEU's jurisdiction over CFSP provisions and measures is excluded. There are two important exceptions: monitoring the separation between CFSP and the rest of EU competences and review of restrictive measures. On the first issue, Article 40 TEU stipulates that CFSP competences should not affect and, conversely, be affected by EU competences enshrined in the TFEU. Second, by way of derogation from the general prohibition on CJEU jurisdiction over CFSP measures, Article 275 TFEU furthermore enables the CJEU to review the legality of decisions providing for restrictive measures adopted in the framework of the CFSP.

The CJEU approaches the prohibition on its jurisdiction over CFSP matters, rather than as the general rule that the TEU wording implies it is, as an exception to more general principles of law, namely the rule of law and respect for fundamental rights (in particular effective judicial protection).[98] In other words, the CJEU sees the exclusion of its jurisdiction in the CFSP as a carve-out from its overarching jurisdiction over all Union law.[99] The CJEU stressed in *Opinion 2/13* that, despite the partial lack of jurisdiction, the CFSP is equally part of the EU as other areas of Union competence and therefore, consistent with its prior doctrine,[100] judicial review of CFSP acts, actions, and omissions cannot be entrusted exclusively to a non-EU body (in that case the ECtHR).[101] The Court also openly admitted, for example in the *Mauritius* case, that in view of its responsibilities under Article 19 TEU,[102] the CFSP

---

[97] See Articles 24(1) TEU and 275(1) TFEU.

[98] See more generally on the role of law in EU foreign policy P Müller and P Slominski, 'The Role of Law in EU Foreign Policy-making: Legal Integrity, Legal Spillover, and the EU Policy of Differentiation towards Israel' (2017) 55 Journal of Common Market Studies 871.

[99] With the abolition of the pillar structure—and seeing as both EU Treaties have equal value—the argument is that for all their peculiarity, even CFSP measures fall under the umbrellas of EU law and action.

[100] Opinion of 8 March 2011, *Unified Patent Litigation System*, 1/09, ECLI:EU:C:2011:123, paras 78, 80 and 89.

[101] Opinion of 18 December 2014, *EU accession to the ECHR*, 2/13, ECLI:EU:C:2014:2454, para 255.

[102] Article 19 TEU mentions in the relevant part that the CJEU shall 'ensure that in the interpretation and application of the Treaties the law is observed'.

limitation on jurisdiction should be interpreted narrowly. The CJEU came to the same conclusion elsewhere by reference to the principle of effective judicial protection (given expression to by Article 47 of the Charter).[103]

Judgment of 24 June 2014, *Parliament v Council (Mauritius)*, C-658/11, ECLI:EU:C:2014:2025

69. As regards, first of all, the question of the Court's jurisdiction to rule on the second
plea, it must be noted, as the Council submits, that it is apparent from the final sentence of the second subparagraph of Article 24(1) TEU and the first paragraph of
Article 275 TFEU that the Court does not, in principle, have jurisdiction with respect to the provisions relating to the CFSP or with respect to acts adopted on the
basis of those provisions.

70. Nevertheless, the final sentence of the second subparagraph of Article 24(1) TEU
and the first paragraph of Article 275 TFEU **introduce a derogation from the rule
of the general jurisdiction** which Article 19 TEU confers on the Court to ensure
that in the interpretation and application of the Treaties the law is observed, and
they must, therefore, be interpreted narrowly.

In the *Mauritius* judgment the CJEU also chipped away from the CFSP jurisdictional prohibition by pointing out that since the procedure for concluding international agreements
in the CFSP is not CFSP-specific, it is subject to CJEU review regardless of the fact that in
substance the agreement concerns the (excluded) CFSP.[104] In addition, the Court adopted
restrictive interpretations of the exclusion of jurisdiction, so as to allow the review of public
procurement and personnel matters relating to a CFSP mission.[105] The generally restrictive
interpretation of the jurisdictional exclusion is dovetailed by an occasionally generous interpretation of the CJEU's seemingly limited competence in the CFSP. For example, in *Rosneft*,
the Court ruled that despite the fact that Article 275 TFEU appears to circumscribe the possibility to review restrictive measures to annulment procedures under Article 263(3) TFEU,
a more liberal interpretation enabling the review of validity of sanctions in the course of
preliminary proceedings should be favoured.[106] The overall result of the CJEU's case law regarding its own competence is an 'extended jurisdiction' keen on ensuring that EU constitutional principles—the rule of law, fundamental rights, democratic oversight—are to some
extent part of the CFSP framework.[107]

---

[103] *Rosneft* (n 5) para 74. The CJEU held that '[w]hile, admittedly, Article 47 of the Charter cannot confer jurisdiction on the Court, where the Treaties exclude it, principle of effective judicial protection nonetheless implies
that the exclusion of the Court's jurisdiction in the field of the CFSP should be interpreted strictly'.

[104] Judgment of 24 June 2014, *Parliament v Council (Mauritius)*, C-658/11, ECLI:EU:C:2014:2025,
paras 71–73.

[105] Judgment of 12 November 2015, *Elitaliana v Eulex Kosovo*, C-439/13 P, ECLI:EU:C:2015:753; *H v Council
and Commission* (n 5).

[106] The judgment turned on the wording of Article 24(1): '(. . .) the last sentence of the second subparagraph
of Article 24(1) TEU refers to the second paragraph of Article 275 TFEU in order to determine not the type of procedure under which the Court may review the legality of certain decisions, but rather the type of decisions whose
legality may be reviewed by the Court, within any procedure that has as its aim such a review of legality'. See *Rosneft*
(n 5) para 70.

[107] C Eckes, 'Common Foreign and Security Policy: The Consequences of the Court's Extended Jurisdiction'
(2016) 22 European Law Journal 492.

The CFSP is special compared to other EU policies not only in the ways it excludes supranational institutions and decision-making but, on the contrary, also in a more pro-European sense: unlike in other areas of EU action, there are no substantive limits on the CFSP competence. CFSP action can therefore relate to any aspect of foreign and security policy, including human rights and democracy promotion or other normative objectives, as long as the measures being taken are one of those listed in Article 25 TEU and the relevant procedures are followed.[108] Moreover, the language of the Treaties concerning the CFSP introduces the notion of mutual political solidarity in a bid to curb frequently stark divisions in national foreign policy positions, the coordination of which remains central to the effectiveness of the CFSP. The concepts of solidarity and 'spirit of loyalty' (Article 24(3) TEU) resemble the principle of sincere cooperation (Article 4(3) TEU) but it is a point of debate whether they complement, supersede, or apply exclusively in the CFSP.[109] In any case, it has been recognized that there is at the very least 'a strengthened obligation to act in good faith'.[110]

The CSDP is an integral part of the CFSP.[111] The Treaty framework provides for the possibility of military cooperation and integration, including full-scale common defence. Member States make available to the EU civilian and military capabilities to enable it to carry out any agreed-upon missions which must take place outside the territory of the EU. Decisions are, of course, taken by unanimity and in general the Member States enjoy considerable discretion regarding the extent to which they wish to implement the CSDP. The EU and the Member States are assisted by the European Defence Agency (EDA) which fulfils a range of predominantly analytical and supporting tasks aimed at fostering European military integration and cooperation, stimulating research and development of capabilities, strengthening the European defence industry, and coordination with EU policies.[112] The importance of NATO as still the primary security framework for most European countries is also recognized in the Treaty.[113]

Consolidated version of the Treaty on European Union [2012] OJ C326/13

Article 42

1. The common security and defence policy shall be an integral part of the common foreign and security policy. It shall provide the Union with an operational capacity drawing on civilian and military assets. The Union may use them on **missions outside the Union** for **peace-keeping, conflict prevention and strengthening**

---

[108] Article 25 TEU states that the EU is to conduct the CFSP by defining general guidelines; adopting decisions defining actions and positions to be taken by the EU and implementing arrangements therefor; and 'strengthening systematic cooperation between Member States in the conduct of the policy'.

[109] P Koutrakos, 'Primary Law and Policy in EU External Relations – Moving Away from the Big Picture' (2008) 33 European Law Review 666, 670; G De Baere, *Constitutional Principles of EU External Relations* (Oxford University Press 2008) 262; C Hillion, 'A Powerless Court? The European Court of Justice and the CFSP' in M Cremona and A Thies (eds), *The European Court of Justice and External Relations Law: Constitutional Challenges* (Hart Publishing 2014).

[110] *Hellenic Republic v Commission* [2008] ECLI:EU:C:2008:270, Opinion of AG Mazák, para 83.

[111] See generally P Koutrakos, *The EU Common Security and Defence Policy* (Oxford University Press 2013).

[112] See Article 45 TEU and Council Decision (CFSP) 2015/1835 defining the statute, seat and operational rules of the European Defence Agency [2015] OJ L266/55.

[113] In recent years, the EU and NATO have started a discourse of cooperation. See, for example, the EU Global Strategy, which mentions cooperation with NATO in a number of areas, from European defence to cybersecurity and capacity development abroad.

international security in accordance with the principles of the United Nations Charter. The performance of these tasks shall be undertaken using **capabilities provided by the Member States.**

2. The common security and defence policy shall include the progressive framing of a common Union defence policy. **This will lead to a common defence, when the European Council,** acting unanimously, **so decides.** It shall in that case recommend to the Member States the adoption of such a decision in accordance with their respective constitutional requirements.

   The policy of the Union in accordance with this Section shall not prejudice the specific character of the security and defence policy of certain Member States and shall **respect the obligations of certain Member States, which see their common defence realised in the North Atlantic Treaty Organisation (NATO),** under the North Atlantic Treaty and be compatible with the common security and defence policy established within that framework.

3. (…) Those Member States which together establish **multinational forces** may also make them available to the common security and defence policy.

   Member States shall undertake progressively to improve their military capabilities. The Agency in the field of defence capabilities development, research, acquisition and armaments (hereinafter referred to as 'the **European Defence Agency**') shall identify operational requirements, shall promote measures to satisfy those requirements, shall contribute to identifying and, where appropriate, implementing any measure needed to strengthen the industrial and technological base of the defence sector, shall participate in defining a European capabilities and armaments policy, and shall assist the Council in evaluating the improvement of military capabilities.

4. **Decisions** relating to the common security and defence policy, including those initiating a mission as referred to in this Article, **shall be adopted by the Council acting unanimously on a proposal from the High Representative** of the Union for Foreign Affairs and Security Policy or an initiative from a Member State. The High Representative may propose the use of both national resources and Union instruments, together with the Commission where appropriate.

6. Those Member States whose military capabilities fulfil higher criteria and which have made more binding commitments to one another in this area with a view to the most demanding missions shall establish **permanent structured cooperation** within the Union framework. (…)

7. If a Member State is the victim of armed aggression on its territory, the other Member States shall have towards it an obligation of aid and assistance by all the means in their power, in accordance with Article 51 of the United Nations Charter. This shall not prejudice the specific character of the security and defence policy of certain Member States.

   Commitments and cooperation in this area shall be consistent with commitments under the North Atlantic Treaty Organisation, which, for those States which are members of it, remains the foundation of their collective defence and the forum for its implementation.

The CSDP is still a sensitive area and therefore it should not surprise that progress towards more European integration has been selective so far. For example, a number of Member

States have formed multinational EU battlegroups—relatively small military units intended for rapid reaction to crises—but they have never been deployed. For now, no serious plan exists which envisages the creation of a common European army. However, recent years have seen an intensification of EU defence cooperation and integration, most probably prompted by the impending exit of the UK—which had been a staunch opponent of deeper integration in this area—from the EU and heightened rhetoric in the US about European countries' relatively low level of contributions to NATO. The most important step so far taken was the triggering of permanent structured cooperation (PESCO) in December 2017 by 25 Member States.[114] PESCO provides the governance framework for a deeper military integration among the participating Member States which will take place through, for example, the harmonization of weapons systems and development of joint capabilities, commands, and centres. Commitments undertaken by Member States as part of PESCO have a binding character and are subject to evaluations and supervision in the Council with the involvement of the High Representative, the EDA, the EEAS, and the EU Military Committee (EUMC). As of November 2019, 47 PESCO projects have been launched in domains such as air systems, cybersecurity, maritime surveillance, and training facilities.

Council Decision (CFSP) 2017/2315 establishing permanent structured cooperation (PESCO) and determining the list of participating Member States [2017] OJ L331/57

Article 6

Supervision, assessment and reporting arrangements

1. **The Council,** within the framework of Article 46(6) TEU, **shall ensure the unity, consistency and effectiveness of PESCO. The High Representative shall also contribute to those objectives.**

2. The High Representative shall be fully involved in proceedings relating to PESCO, in accordance with Protocol No 10.

3. The High Representative shall present an annual report on PESCO to the Council. This report shall be based on the contributions by the EDA, in accordance with Article 7(3)(a), and by the EEAS, in accordance with Article 7(2)(a). The High Representative's report shall describe the status of PESCO implementation, including the fulfilment, by each participating Member State, of its commitments, in accordance with its National Implementation Plan.

   The EUMC shall provide the Political and Security Committee with military advice and recommendations regarding to the annual PESCO assessment process.

   On the basis of the annual report on PESCO presented by the High Representative, the Council shall review once a year whether the participating Member States continue to fulfil the more binding commitments referred to in Article 3.

4. Any decision concerning the suspension of the participation of a Member State shall be adopted in accordance with Article 46(4) TEU only after the Member State has been given a clearly defined timeframe for individual consultation and reaction measures.

---

[114] The two Member States so far not participating in PESCO are Denmark and Malta.

B. Sanctions and restrictive measures

Sanctions represent one of the cornerstones of EU foreign policy to the extent that some scholars see the entire CFSP as having become 'oriented' towards them when it comes to responding to crises abroad.[115] Sanctions can take various forms: they can be diplomatic in nature, such as when the EU interrupts diplomatic relations with a third country; more frequently they are economic or financial in nature, such as when the EU imposes an embargo or freezes assets of a legal or natural person; or they can concern other types of restrictions, such as a travel ban. There are additional ways of categorizing EU sanctions (Figure 9.3),[116] for example depending on whether the EU is merely implementing UN sanctions or it imposes them autonomously. It is not uncommon for various types of sanctions to be applied simultaneously to address a situation comprehensively. The question whether sanctions are an effective means of achieving foreign policy objectives is a matter of considerable dispute but beyond the scope of this work.[117]

To take a famous example, in the case of *Kadi* (see Chapter 5), the EU imposed economic sanctions against Mr Kadi, namely it froze his assets. The sanctions were targeted (against a particular individual); the term 'smart' sanctions is sometimes used instead of 'targeted', which tries to convey the message that the sanctions are directed against those responsible, thereby reducing the collateral damage to the wider society which could be affected if blunter sanctions were used instead. The EU sanctions represented an implementation of UN Security Council measures. Their motive was primarily preventative: the sanctions aimed to preclude Mr Kadi from using his assets to sponsor the Al-Qaeda and the Taliban.

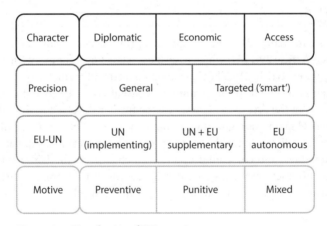

Character	Diplomatic	Economic	Access
Precision	General	Targeted ('smart')	
EU-UN	UN (implementing)	UN + EU supplementary	EU autonomous
Motive	Preventive	Punitive	Mixed

Figure 9.3 Typologies of EU sanctions

---

[115] PJ Cardwell, 'The Legalisation of European Union Foreign Policy and the Use of Sanctions' (2015) 17 Cambridge Yearbook of European Legal Studies 287, 288.

[116] Note that the official EU position would disagree with labelling any EU sanctions 'punitive'.

[117] See, for example, C Portela, 'The EU's Use of "Targeted" Sanctions: Evaluating Effectiveness' (2014) CEPS Working Document No 391, March 2014; A Vines, 'The Effectiveness of UN and EU Sanctions: Lessons for the Twenty-first Century' (2012) 88 (4) International Affairs 867; D Peksen and A Cooper Drury, 'Economic Sanctions and Political Repression: Assessing the Impact of Coercive Diplomacy on Political Freedoms' (2009) 10 Human Rights Review 393.

The most common sanctions imposed by the EU are those which follow the procedure under Article 215 TFEU. In the EU jargon, these are called restrictive measures. They are predominantly of an economic or financial nature and are most frequently targeted against an individual or a company. As of 2020, the EU has been applying a range of restrictive measures in relation to 34 different countries and/or the nationals thereof, in addition to various terrorist groups and organizations.[118]

Consolidated version of the Treaty on the Functioning of the European Union [2012] OJ C326/47

Article 215

1. Where a decision, adopted in accordance with Chapter 2 of Title V of the Treaty on European Union, provides for the **interruption or reduction**, in part or completely, **of economic and financial relations with one or more third countries**, the Council, **acting by a qualified majority** on a joint proposal from the High Representative of the Union for Foreign Affairs and Security Policy and the Commission, shall adopt the necessary measures. It shall inform the European Parliament thereof.

2. Where a decision adopted in accordance with Chapter 2 of Title V of the Treaty on European Union so provides, **the Council may adopt restrictive measures** under the procedure referred to in paragraph 1 **against natural or legal persons and groups or non-State entities.**

3. The acts referred to in this Article shall include necessary provisions on legal safeguards.

The procedure in Article 215 TFEU requires a prior decision being adopted on a CFSP legal basis (often Article 29 TEU) which as a rule is passed by unanimity. Therefore the fact that sanctions under Article 215 TFEU are adopted by qualified majority does not circumvent the obligation to obtain prior unanimous consent about the decision to impose restrictive measures in the first place. Powers can be further devolved to the Commission if, for example, the EU sanctions regime merely implements UN Security Council sanctions, in which case the Commission might be in charge of updating an annex stipulating the names of targeted individuals and companies in line with changes to the UN sanctions list. The implementation of sanctions entails considerable coordination among Member States, the authorities of which are essential in putting EU measures into effect.[119]

---

[118] See for an interactive map on EU sanctions: <http://www.sanctionsmap.eu/> accessed 14 August 2020.

[119] The EU maintains a best-practices document which aims to aid the effective implementation of restrictive measures. See Council of the European Union, 'Update of the EU Best Practices for the effective implementation of restrictive measures', 8519/18, 4 May 2018.

Council of the European Union, Guidelines on implementation and evaluation of restrictive measures (sanctions) in the framework of the EU Common Foreign and Security Policy - update, 5664/18, 4 May 2018

ANNEX I

Recommendations for working methods for EU autonomous sanctions

Restrictive measures against third countries, individuals or entities are an essential foreign policy tool of the EU in pursuing its objectives in accordance with the principles of the Common Foreign and Security Policy. In general terms, **restrictive measures are imposed to bring about a change in policy or activity** by the targeted country, part of a country, government, entities or individuals. They are preventive, non-punitive, instruments which should allow the EU to respond swiftly to political challenges and developments. **Sanctions should be used as part of an integrated and comprehensive policy approach involving political dialogue, complementary efforts and other instruments.** The EU and its Member States should actively and systematically communicate on EU sanctions, including with the targeted country and its population.

The measures should target the policies and the means to conduct them and those identified as responsible for the policies or actions that have prompted the EU decision to impose sanctions. **Such targeted measures should minimise adverse consequences for those not responsible for such policies and actions**, in particular the local civilian population or legitimate activities in or with the country concerned. The political objectives and criteria of the restrictive measures should be clearly defined in the legal acts. This would allow the EU to identify the conditions for amending or lifting the sanctions. The type of measures will vary depending on their objectives and their expected effectiveness in achieving these objectives under the particular circumstances, reflecting the EU's targeted and differentiated approach.

Restrictive measures must respect human rights and fundamental freedoms, in particular due process and the right to an effective remedy in full conformity with the jurisprudence of the EU Courts. The measures imposed must be proportionate to their objectives.

The uniform and consistent interpretation and effective implementation of the restrictive measures is essential to ensure their effectiveness in achieving the desired political objective.

The European External Action Service (EEAS) should have a key role in the preparation and review of sanctions regimes as well as in the communication and outreach activities accompanying the sanctions, in close cooperation with Member States, relevant EU delegations and the Commission.

The EU can, and does, impose restrictive measures as a way of responding to or preventing human rights violations anywhere in the world. In such cases, the choice of sanctions lies with the most targeted kind (Article 215(2) TFEU) which allows the EU to target only the persons, entities, or groups responsible without punishing the often already embattled population of the country where the violations occur. At the time of writing, restrictive measures in place concerning human rights abuses sanction individuals from, among others, Iran,[120] South Sudan,[121] Venezuela,[122] and Zimbabwe.[123] The following example concerning the situation in Iran following the suppression of demonstrations in 2011 is illustrative of EU restrictive measures imposed on individuals responsible for human rights violations in a third country.

Council Regulation (EU) No 359/2011 concerning restrictive measures directed against certain persons, entities and bodies in view of the situation in Iran [2011] OJ L100/1

(2) The **restrictive measures should target persons complicit in or responsible for directing or implementing grave human rights violations** in the repression of peaceful demonstrators, journalists, human rights defenders, students or other persons who speak up in defence of their legitimate rights, including freedom of expression, as well as persons complicit in or responsible for directing or implementing grave violations of the right to due process, torture, cruel, inhuman and degrading treatment, or the indiscriminate, excessive and increasing application of the death penalty, including public executions, stoning, hangings or executions of juvenile offenders in contravention of Iran's international human rights obligations.

Article 2

1. **All funds and economic resources belonging to, owned, held or controlled by the natural or legal persons, entities and bodies listed in Annex I shall be frozen.**
2. No funds or economic resources shall be made available, directly or indirectly, to or for the benefit of the natural or legal persons, entities or bodies listed in Annex I.
3. The participation, knowingly and intentionally, in activities the object or effect of which is, directly or indirectly, to circumvent the measures referred to in paragraphs 1 and 2 shall be prohibited.

Article 3

1. Annex I shall consist of a list of persons who, in accordance with Article 2(1) of Decision 2011/235/CFSP, **have been identified by the Council as being persons responsible for serious human rights violations in Iran**, and persons, entities or bodies associated with them.
   (...)

---

[120] Council Regulation (EU) No 359/2011 of 12 April 2011 concerning restrictive measures directed against certain persons, entities and bodies in view of the situation in Iran [2011] OJ L100/1, as amended to 2020 (latest Council Decision (CFSP) 2020/512 of 7 April 2020).

[121] Council Regulation (EU) 2015/735 of 7 May 2015 concerning restrictive measures in respect of the situation in South Sudan, and repealing Regulation (EU) No 748/2014 [2014] OJ L117/13, as amended to 2019 (latest Council Decision (CFSP) 2019/1211 of 15 July 2019).

[122] Council Regulation (EU) 2017/2063 of 13 November 2017 concerning restrictive measures in view of the situation in Venezuela [2017] OJ L295/60, as amended to 2019 (latest Council Decision (CFSP) 2019/1893 of 11 November 2019).

[123] Council Regulation (EC) No 314/2004 of 19 February 2004 concerning certain restrictive measures in respect of Zimbabwe [2004] OJ L55/1, as amended to 2020 (latest Council Regulation (EU) 2020/213 of 17 February 2020).

ANNEX I

20. | MOGHISSEH Mohammad (a.k.a. NASSERIAN) | Judge, Head of Tehran Revolutionary Court, branch 28. He has dealt with post-election cases. He issued long prison sentences during unfair trials for social, political activists and journalists and several death sentences for protesters and social and political activists. | Date of listing 12.4.2011

A different question is posed by the impact of EU sanctions on human rights, regardless of their purpose. First, there is the possibility that general economic sanctions, such as trade embargoes, harm the rights, in particular economic and social rights, of the general population of the country concerned. The EU should therefore conduct impact assessments to gain at least some understanding of the potential damage resulting from restrictive measures. Second, in the more frequent scenario when 'smart' sanctions are used, the question of human rights relates to the rights of the person or entity against whom restrictive measures are used. In this regard, the CJEU has developed a large body of case law specifying the various fundamental rights safeguards which must be in place for individuals affected by EU sanctions.[124] The judicial review focuses in particular on whether the decision to impose restrictive measures was sufficiently reasoned in the accompanying statement of reasons and whether there is sufficient evidence supporting the statement of reasons.[125] The fundamental rights importance of both criteria essentially rests in affording the defendant the possibility to state his case and thus have a fair trial. At the same time, the criteria enable the CJEU to exercise judicial control over EU executive actions which infringes upon the rights and freedoms of individuals.

It should also be pointed out that the practice of imposing sanctions without a prior authorization or listing by the UN Security Council, in other words autonomously or unilaterally, is far from uncontroversial from the perspective of international law.[126] In general, the EU to impose sanctions in accordance with a pre-existing UN mandate but in many cases it either adds supplementary sanctions to UN sanctions or imposes entirely autonomous restrictive measures. In some cases, the power balance preserved by the UN system prevents collective agreement on sanctions: when the EU and US imposed sanctions on Russia for annexing Crimea and violating Ukrainian sovereignty, the sanctions could not have been passed at the UN due to Russia being a permanent member of the Security Council with an unconditional veto power.

The UNHRC passed a resolution condemning the use of unilateral measures of the kind the EU regularly seeks to impose.[127] The resolution deems such measures contrary to international law and as violating the principle of sovereignty. It also highlighted that sanctions contribute to human rights violations in the countries targeted by them. The resolution, however, makes no mention of the fact that sanctions are often imposed in response to violations

---

[124] For an example of sanctions case law, see Ch 5 which discusses the Kadi saga.

[125] Another element under judicial control is designation criteria, meaning the criteria according to which sanctioned individuals are chosen. The CJEU admits a wide margin of discretion in relation to this element and it has never annulled restrictive measures on this ground. See Judgment of 28 November 2013, *Council v Manufacturing Support & Procurement Kala Naft Co*, C-348/12 P, ECLI:EU:C:2013:776, para 84; C Eckes, 'EU Restrictive Measures against Natural and Legal Persons: From Counterterrorist to Third Country Sanctions' (2014) 51 Common Market Law Review 869, 903.

[126] See, for example, R Mohamad, 'Unilateral Sanctions in International Law: A Quest for Legality' in A Marossi and M Bassett (eds), *Economic Sanctions under International Law* (TMC Asser Press 2015).

[127] Resolutions of the UN Human Rights Council are legally non-binding but are typically representative of the political stance and commitment of the majority in favour.

594 HUMAN RIGHTS IN EU EXTERNAL ACTION

of international law, including human rights. The resolution is illustrative of the division between developed and developing countries, the latter of which, together with great and regional powers wishing to curtail international criticism of their domestic affairs, champion the principle of state sovereignty and non-interference. Countries such as Russia had a direct and imminent self-interest in opposing unilateral sanctions due to the measures taken by the EU and US in relation to the crisis in Ukraine. On the contrary, the US and EU Member States, together with countries in the EU's neighbourhood and Japan, voted against the resolution. The resolution finally appointed a special rapporteur tasked with gathering information and studying the impact of sanctions on human rights.[128]

UNHRC Res 27/21 (26 September 2014) A/HRC/RES/27/21

Human rights and unilateral coercive measures

The Human Rights Council

1. *Calls upon* all States to stop adopting, maintaining or implementing unilateral coercive measures not in accordance with international law, international humanitarian law, the Charter of the United Nations and the norms and principles governing peaceful relations among States, in particular those of a coercive nature with extraterritorial effects, which create obstacles to trade relations among States, thus impeding the full realization of the rights set forth in the Universal Declaration of Human Rights and other international human rights instruments, in particular the right of individuals and peoples to development

8. *Recalls* that, according to the Declaration on Principles of International Law concerning Friendly Relations and Cooperation among States in accordance with the Charter of the United Nations, and to the relevant principles and provisions contained in the Charter of Economic Rights and Duties of States, proclaimed by the General Assembly in its resolution 3281 (XXIX) of 12 December 1974, in particular article 32 thereof, no State may use or encourage the use of economic, political or any other type of measure to coerce another State in order to obtain from it the subordination of the exercise of its sovereign rights and to secure from it advantages of any kind;

[Adopted by a recorded vote of 31 to 14, with 2 abstentions. The voting was as follows:

In favour:
Algeria, Argentina, Benin, Botswana, Brazil, Burkina Faso, Chile, China, Congo, Côte d'Ivoire, Cuba, Ethiopia, Gabon, India, Indonesia, Kenya, Kuwait, Maldives, Mexico, Morocco, Namibia, Pakistan, Peru, Philippines, Russian Federation, Saudi Arabia, Sierra Leone, South Africa, United Arab Emirates, Venezuela (Bolivarian Republic of), Viet Nam

Against:
Austria, Czech Republic, Estonia, France, Germany, Ireland, Italy, Japan, Montenegro, Republic of Korea, Romania, the former Yugoslav Republic of Macedonia, United Kingdom of Great Britain and Northern Ireland, United States of America

---

[128] See para 22 of UNHRC Res 27/21 (26 September 2014) A/HRC/RES/27/21.

Abstaining:
Costa Rica, Kazakhstan]

C. EU external representation and the Human Rights Council

Consolidated version of the Treaty on European Union [2012] OJ C326/13

Article 34

1. **Member States shall coordinate their action in international organisations and at international conferences. They shall uphold the Union's positions in such forums.** The High Representative of the Union for Foreign Affairs and Security Policy shall organise this coordination.

   In international organisations and at international conferences where not all the Member States participate, **those which do take part shall uphold the Union's positions.**

2. In accordance with Article 24(3), Member States represented in international organisations or international conferences where not all the Member States participate shall keep the other Member States and the High Representative informed of any matter of common interest.

Member States which are also members of the United Nations Security Council will concert and keep the other Member States and the High Representative fully informed. Member States which are members of the Security Council will, in the execution of their functions, defend the positions and the interests of the Union, without prejudice to their responsibilities under the provisions of the United Nations Charter.

When the Union has defined a position on a subject which is on the United Nations Security Council agenda, those Member States which sit on the Security Council shall request that the High Representative be invited to present the Union's position.

Due to the peculiar nature of the EU as neither state nor international organization, it often does not fit neatly into the traditional Westphalian international system. As a result, the EU cannot accede to a plethora of treaties and represent its interests as a single actor in many international fora.[129] Even where the EU is able to accede to treaties, the question of who will represent it frequently elicits convoluted answers in light of the EU's concurrent membership alongside its Member States. As elsewhere in the CFSP, coherence and coordination of EU and national positions is a key concern for the EU when it comes to external representation. The unity and coherence of EU external representation has been greatly facilitated by the latest Treaty change which strengthened the role of the High Representative and provided for the creation of the EEAS, including Union

---

[129] See the discussion of international human rights law in Ch 5. The EU has had to settle for observer status in a number of UN bodies. The only UN body where it has member status is the Food and Agricultural Organization (FAO).

Delegations. Positions to be held by the EU in international fora must, nevertheless, be first agreed in the Council.

J Wouters and AL Chané, 'Brussels Meets Westphalia: The EU and the UN' in P Eeckhout and M Lopez-Escudero (eds), *The European Union's External Action in Times of Crisis* (Hart Publishing 2016)

(...) Depending on the subject-matter and on the level of the meeting, the responsibility for the Union's external representation falls either upon the Commission, the President of the European Council, the HR/VP or the EEAS. (...) Whenever an issue falls within both an area of EU and of national competence, the responsible representative will be determined based on whether or not the 'thrust' or 'preponderance' of the issue lies within an area of EU competence.

The Commission represents the Union in all areas of EU competence that do not fall under the CFSP, with the President of the Commission assuming the role of EU representative at summit level. Concerning issues that fall under the CFSP, the tasks of external representation are divided between the HR/VP and the President of the European Council. The latter only plays a limited role in this context. (...)

Internal coordination of the Union's positions in UN fora serves a variety of purposes, all of which contribute to the larger goal of increasing the effectiveness and the impact of the external action of the EU. Primarily, coordination between the various EU Member States and EU institutions is necessary to ensure that all actors 'speak with one voice' and vote consistently. (...)

Generally, the process [of coordination] can be divided into the formulation of the general strategies in Brussels, and the fine-tuning of those positions on the ground in New York, Geneva, Rome (...) In Brussels, the Council of the EU develops the priorities and positions of the Union at the UN. It is assisted by the Political and Security Committee, which serves as the main contact point for the EU Delegation in New York with regard to CFSP and CSDP issues. Nevertheless, by far the largest part of the work is done in the Council's multiple working groups and committees, many of which have direct relevance for EU participation in the UN. (...) The Union's human rights policy at the UN—in particular at the UNGA's Third Committee and the Human Rights Council (HRC)—falls under the responsibility of the Working Party on Human Rights (COHOM) (...) Usually working parties meet no more than once per month, generally in a closed setting, convening delegates from the 28 Member States' capitals.

(...) An estimated 1300 coordination meetings are held in New York each year, another 1000 meetings in Geneva.

The EU's accession to the UN Convention on the Rights of Persons with Disabilities (UN CPRD) represents a rare instance of the Union becoming a party to an international human rights treaty.[130] The accession grants the EU access to the bodies established at the international level by the CRPD but in view of the concurrent membership of the Member States,[131] coordination of positions and decisions concerning voting and representation must

---

[130] See Ch 5 which discusses the EU relationship with the CRPD in more detail.
[131] The EU concluded the UN CRPD as a mixed agreement together with its Member States. This means that both the EU and the Member States are parties to the treaty.

be in place to avoid external disunity and confusion (as well as compliance with the requirements of the CRPD). A Code of Conduct has been agreed between the Member States and EU institutions regarding coordination and external representation relating to the CRPD and it is illustrative of the complexity accompanying the process. As the Code of Conduct has been drawn up before the EEAS became operational, the reader must substitute references to the Presidency for the EEAS. The document details how the EU strives to coordinate and formulate unified positions in practice to become more effective on the international stage. The international position of the EU and/or its Member States can, for example, be amplified when it is voiced multiple times by both the EU and the Member States.[132]

Code of Conduct 2010/C 340/08 between the Council, the Member States and the Commission setting out internal arrangements for the implementation by and representation of the European Union relating to the United Nations Convention on the Rights of Persons with Disabilities [2010] OJ C340/11

3. On matters falling within the **competence of the Member States**, the Member States will aim at elaborating **coordinated positions** whenever it is deemed appropriate.
4. On matters falling within the **Union's exclusive competence**, the Union will aim at elaborating **Union positions** (...)
5. On matters falling within **shared competence** and on matters where the Union coordinates, supports and/or supplements the actions of the Member States, **the Union and the Member States** will aim at elaborating **common positions** (...)

ESTABLISHING OF POSITIONS

6. All positions of the Union and its Member States referred to in paragraphs 3, 4 and 5 will be duly coordinated:
    (a) In matters referred to in paragraph 3 (...) [c]**oordinated positions will be expressed by the Presidency or if necessary by a Member State as appointed by the Presidency or by the Commission with the agreement of all Member States present.**
    (b) In matters referred to in paragraph 4, coordination meetings of the Commission and the Member States within the competent Council Working Group will be convened at the Presidency's own initiative or at the request of the Commission or a Member State before and during each meeting referred to in paragraph 1, with possible reference to the Disability High Level Group in its area of competence. These coordination meetings may consist of an electronic coordination in urgent cases.

Union positions will be expressed by the Commission.
    (c) In matters referred to in paragraph 5 (...) [t]**he Commission and the Member States in coordination meetings within the competent Council Working Group will decide who will deliver any statement to be made on behalf of the Union and its Member States in cases where the respective competences are inextricably linked.**

---

[132] E da Conceição-Heldt and S Meunier (eds), *Speaking With a Single Voice: The EU as an Effective Actor in Global Governance?* (Routledge 2015).

Common positions will be presented by the Commission when the preponderance of the matter concerned lies within the competence of the Union, and by the Presidency or a Member State when the preponderance of the matter concerned lies within the competence of the Member States.

For the purposes of establishing positions regarding points (a), (b) and (c), the following arrangements will apply:

> (i) in Brussels, within the competent Council Working Group, as early as possible ahead of the start of the meetings referred to in paragraph 1.

On receipt of the agenda of the meetings referred to in paragraph 1, the Commission will send to the Council Secretariat for circulation to the Member States an indication of the agenda items on which it is intended that statements are made and whether these statements should be made by the Commission and/or the Presidency.

The Council Secretariat will circulate those draft statements received from the Presidency (in relation to paragraph 3) and from the Commission (in relation to paragraphs 4 and 5) for circulation to the Member States and the Commission at least one week before the coordination meeting. The Council Secretariat will ensure that the draft statements are transmitted to the competent Council Working Group promptly;

> (ii) without prejudice to local arrangements for Union coordination, on-the-spot (in New York or Geneva (2)), particularly at the beginning and, if necessary, at the end of the meetings referred to in paragraph 1, with further coordination meetings being called whenever necessary throughout the series of meetings.

In cases where no position can be reached including for reasons relating to disagreement on the repartition of competences between the Union and its Member States, the matter will be referred without undue delay to the competent Council Working Group and/or, when applicable, other Council bodies. **If no agreement can be reached in these bodies, the matter will be referred to the Permanent Representatives Committee (Coreper).** However, in cases where meetings of the competent working group and, when applicable, of the relevant other Council bodies cannot be convened in time, the matter will be directly referred to Coreper, which will decide on the position on the basis of the voting rules laid down in the relevant EU Treaty dealing with the subject matter under consideration; (...)

SPEAKING IN CASES OF AGREED COORDINATED, UNION OR COMMON POSITIONS

> 7. Without prejudice to the speaking arrangements referred to in paragraph 6, a **Member State or the Commission may take the floor, after due coordination to support and/or develop the coordinated position, the Union position or the common position.**

VOTING IN CASES OF AGREED COORDINATED, UNION OR COMMON POSITIONS

> 8. (a) Subject to paragraph 6, and in accordance with Article 44.4 of the Convention, **the Commission, on behalf of the Union, will exercise the Union's voting rights on the basis of Union or common positions reached in the coordination**

process on matters referred to in paragraph 4, and in paragraph 5 when the preponderance of the matter concerned lies within the competence of the Union. It may be agreed that **in cases where the Union is not represented, the Member States will exercise their voting rights** on those matters, on the basis of Union and/or common positions.

(b) Subject to paragraph 6, and in accordance with Article 44.4 of the Convention, the Member States will exercise their voting rights on matters referred to in paragraph 3, and in paragraph 5 when the preponderance of the matter concerned lies within the competence of the Member States on the basis of coordinated or common positions reached in the coordination process.

(c) This paragraph does not apply to the right of Member States to vote pursuant to Article 34 of the Convention.

SPEAKING AND VOTING IN CASES OF NO COORDINATED, UNION OR COMMON POSITIONS

9. **Where no agreement between the Commission and the Member States is reached in accordance with paragraph 6, Member States may speak and vote on matters falling clearly within their competence on condition that the position is coherent with Union policies and in conformity with Union law. The Commission may speak and vote on matters falling clearly within the Union's competence to the extent necessary to defend the Union acquis.**

NOMINATIONS

10. Without prejudice to the right of Member States to nominate candidates for experts in accordance with Article 34.5 of the Convention and the right to vote in accordance with Article 34.5 of the Convention, **the Union may nominate a candidate on the basis of a Commission proposal to be agreed upon by consensus by the Member States** within the competent Council Working Group for an expert to the Committee on the Rights of Persons with Disabilities, on behalf of the Union. This procedure shall apply also to re-nomination of Union candidates.

The Union nominee shall be a citizen of the Union, holding the nationality of one of the Member States pursuant to paragraph 1 of Article 20 of the TFEU.

One of the most important global fora concerning human rights is the UN HRC, which was formed in 2006, replacing the UN Commission on Human Rights. It consists at any one time of 47 states elected in the UN General Assembly while respecting equitable geographical distribution which accords 7 seats to Western and 6 seats to Eastern European countries. EU Member States are therefore never in a position to dominate the HRC.[133] Wouters, Chané, Odermatt, and Ramopoulos discuss the status of the EU in the HRC.[134] The authors

[133] The rest of the seats are allocated in the following way: 13 seats for African states, 13 for Asia-Pacific, and 8 for Latin American and Caribbean states.

[134] See also J Wouters and K Meuwissen, 'The European Union at the UN Human Rights Council: Multilateral Human Rights Protection Coming of Age?' (2014) European Journal of Human Rights 135; G Macaj and A Koops, 'Inconvenient Multilateralism: The Challenges of the EU as a Player in the United Nations Human Rights Council' in JE Wetzel (ed), *The EU as a 'Global Player' in Human Rights?* (Routledge 2012).

explain how the ambitions of the EU with regards to external representation at the HRC, and more broadly the UN, had to be curtailed in the face of the sovereign realities of international relations (in particular visible at the UN). The EU's hybrid nature does not quite fit and states are reluctant to see supranational bodies taking over traditional diplomatic tasks of states. As a result, the EU has to make do for now with an observer status at the HRC which does not befit its importance or ambition to lead on human rights globally. In this regard, the authors also argue that the existence of the UN General Assembly Resolution 65/276 concerning the participation of the EU in the work of the UN is unlikely to extend the EU's enhanced status in the General Assembly to the HRC.

J Wouters and others, 'Improving the European Union's Status in the United Nations and the UN System: An Objective Without a Strategy?' in C Kaddous (ed), *The European Union in International Organisations and Global Governance: Recent Developments* (Hart Publishing 2015)

(…) Written with a view to eventual EC membership of UN bodies, the Commission's 2003 Communication 'The European Union and the United Nations: The Choice of Multilateralism' boldly demanded that the EC 'should be given the possibility to participate fully in the work of UN bodies where matters of Community competence are concerned, and Member States should contribute effectively towards this', and stated—referring to EC membership of the FAO and the Codex Alimentarius—that '[t]his option should also be pursued for other relevant organisations that belong to the UN system'. More than 10 years later, the Barroso–Ashton Strategy is far less ambitious. It avoids a clear commitment to any fixed negotiation goal and merely refers to the 'improvement of the EU status and its alignment with the objectives of the EU Treaties'. For the time being, full participation of the EU in the UN framework as a member organisation seems to have been abandoned as the final aim, giving way to a strategy of piecemeal steps towards modest upgrades wherever these appear to be legally and politically feasible.

One of the ways forward recommended by the Barroso–Ashton Strategy is the application of Resolution 65/276 in UNGA subsidiary organs. In particular, the Strategy recommends to focus, among others, on the HRC and to avoid 'reopening the resolution, under which [subsidiary bodies] are not explicitly covered'. The HRC, which in 2006 replaced the UN Commission on Human Rights, is a body of 47 elected UN Member States, tasked with the promotion of human rights and fundamental freedoms. It addresses cases of human rights violations, provides recommendations, and monitors the fulfilment of each state's human rights obligations through the universal periodic review (UPR). As one of the foremost global human rights fora it is of significant importance for the Union's external action.

(…) In mid-2012 the EU (…) adopted a 'Strategic Framework and Action Plan on Human Rights and Democracy' in which it 'underlines the leading role of the UN Human Rights Council in addressing urgent cases of human rights violations' and pledges to 'contribute vigorously to the effective functioning of the Council'. More specifically, items 9(a) and 23(b) of the Action Plan single out the HRC as a forum for the EU to promote economic, social and cultural rights and the freedom of religion or belief. Furthermore, the promotion of human rights, democracy and the rule of law ranked consistently as one of the EU's priorities during UNGA sessions. The EU was a strong supporter for the establishment of the HRC since the idea first emerged in the 2004 sessions of the Commission on Human Rights, quickly endorsing the initiative for its establishment. 'Welcom[ing] the presentation of a proposal reflecting the primacy of human rights by the creation of a Human Rights Council', the EU actively lobbied for the realisation of its vision of the Council, which foresaw not only the creation of a standing body, possibly with the rank of a main organ of the UN, but whose membership should also be elected by a two-thirds majority of the UNGA and be smaller in numbers, admitting only those states which demonstrated genuine interest in the promotion of human rights.

Although the EU eventually had to compromise on many of its positions, it commented favourably on the final outcome and welcomed the HRC as an improvement over the Commission on Human Rights. The Union has remained an active supporter of the HRC ever since, participating extensively in the 2009–2011 review process, supporting special procedures and the Office of the High Commissioner for Human Rights, and proposing or supporting resolutions, in particular focusing on the freedom of religion or belief, the rights of the child, freedom of expression and country situations. Despite several recent successes, the Union's impact at the HRC has often been described as marginal due to its inability, at least until recently, to forge cross-regional coalitions. This was caused by a lack of credibility in light of the Union's persistent 'double-standards problem', but also by its inflexible negotiation practice, defensive stance and insufficient outreach.

Effective EU participation is among others hindered by its legal status in the HRC. Full membership is only open to UN Member States. The Union has observer status, meaning that it cannot vote or sponsor resolutions, and while it has the right to make interventions, it may not do so in the speaking slots for states. The EU thus remains dependent on the representation by a Member State, in particular by the rotating Council Presidency. Even after the entry into force of the Lisbon Treaty, the Union's participation in the HRC is clogged by cumbersome internal coordination processes, which often focus on burden sharing rather than on substantive issues. This heavy focus on the internal process often leaves insufficient time and resources to gather support for EU positions and to build successful coalitions. The necessary internal coordination also reduces the Union's flexibility during negotiations and with regard to new and unforeseen developments. Nevertheless, caution should be exercised to regard a status upgrade as a panacea that will solve all of the above-mentioned issues. On the contrary, the Union must avoid contributing to the persistent bloc dynamics in the Council. In parallel with efforts to improve its status in the Council, it should fully seize the possibilities offered by EU Member States participating in the Council, which can support the Union's message and bring invaluable expertise and third country networks.

While there appear to be no plans to eventually aim for full EU membership of the HRC, the Barroso–Ashton Strategy considers the extension of Resolution 65/276 and thereby to grant the EU enhanced participation rights. This would permit the Union to participate in the work of the HRC 'in its own right', thus aligning its external representation with the requirements of Article 221 TFEU. However, the question remains whether it is legally and politically feasible to extend the application of Resolution 65/276 to the HRC. Adoption of the Resolution in the UNGA alone was not sufficient to modify the procedures of the HRC, given that the competence to decide on the granting of observer status and the modalities of participation rests with the HRC. (...)

Enhanced participation rights for the Union would be within reach, if, first, Resolution 65/276 was part of the rules of procedure established for the UNGA committees and if, second, the UNGA and the HRC did not decide against its application. (...) Given that Resolution 65/276 contains 'modalities ... for the participation of the representatives of the European Union, in its capacity as observer, in the sessions and work of the General Assembly and its committees', it can be regarded as forming part of the rules of procedure referred to in Rule 7(a) of the HRC's rules of procedure and would therefore find application in the HRC.

Second, however, the question remains as to whether the UNGA or the HRC 'subsequently [decided] otherwise'. (...) it was clearly not the intention of the drafters to modify the EU's status in the UN framework in general (...). Instead, Resolution 65/276 limits its application to the 'sessions and work of the General Assembly and its committees and working groups, in international meetings and conferences convened under the auspices of the Assembly and in United Nations conferences'. While this list is not explicitly declared to be exhaustive, it reveals a conscious inclusion of several subsidiary organs, namely committees and working groups, while other subsidiary bodies, such as boards, commissions, councils and panels, were omitted. It could therefore be argued that Resolution 65/276 implies a decision by the UNGA against its application in the HRC (...)

Independent of the legal aspects, the political feasibility of a status upgrade remains doubtful. Significant resistance, both externally and internally, against an enhanced EU status at the HRC has caused the current cautious approach of the Union. States, including the EU Member States, continue to regard human rights as a state prerogative and hesitate to accept 'that actors at the level of the EU ... take over the role of state actors'. The extension of Resolution 65/276 to the HRC therefore remains a rather distant possibility, which seems also reflected in the fact that it has completely disappeared in the 2013 information note on the implementation of the Barroso–Ashton Strategy.

The EU's difficulties at the HRC go far beyond its limited formal status as an observer. Research has shown that although the EU is able to reach common positions and 'speak with one voice', the time and effort expended on internal coordination is then lacking for building coalitions with other states and debating the substance of human rights protection.[135] Despite improvements in the previous decade which have increased effectiveness of coordination and introduced human rights strategy into EU foreign policy—notably through the creation of the EEAS and adoption of the Strategic Framework and Action Plans on human rights and democracy—the EU's influence at the HRC continues to be disappointing.[136] The EU is trying to pursue too many objectives at the HRC but without sufficient prioritization it is unable to rally the necessary support at the HRC for most of them. In addition, the EU's position is not helped by what is perceived by some states as hypocrisy and double standards when the EU and its Member States fail to live up to human rights domestically (such as on migration or religious discrimination) and by the political polarization of the HRC which undermines the institution as a whole.

---

[135] KE Smith, 'Speaking with One Voice? European Union Coordination on Human Rights Issues at the United Nations' (2006) 44 Journal of Common Market Studies 113; KE Smith, 'The European Union at the Human Rights Council: Speaking with One Voice but Having Little Influence' (2010) 17 Journal of European Public Policy 224.

[136] Although EU and Member State activity has increased in recent years. See KE Smith, 'EU Member States at the UN: A Case of Europeanization Arrested?' (2017) 55 Journal of Common Market Studies 628.

KE Smith, 'The European Union at the Human Rights Council: Speaking with One Voice but Having Little Influence' (2010) 17 Journal of European Public Policy 224

(…) while the EU member states are more united and can agree to issue more statements and make more interventions in the HRC as compared with the CHR [Commission on Human Rights], they are struggling to influence its agenda and outcomes. Internal effectiveness is not leading to greater external effectiveness. This may be seen in the number of times they have been outvoted in the roll-call votes. Of the 70 roll-call votes in the first 12 regular sessions of the HRC, EU member states have been in the minority on 55 occasions (78.5 per cent) (…) Perhaps most alarmingly for the EU's ability to influence a wide variety of states, it is usually joined by only a small number of other HRC members such as Canada, Japan, South Korea, Switzerland and Ukraine. Not even Latin American countries' democracies such as Argentina, Brazil or Mexico often vote with the EU.

There are several reasons why the EU is so isolated. There is a clear rich North vs. poor South polarization in the Human Rights Council (and UN system more generally). The EU faces several strong voices from the South, such as Egypt (which often speaks on behalf of the Africa Group), Pakistan (which often speaks for the [Organization of the Islamic Conference]), China, South Africa and Cuba; but there is also opposition from countries such as Russia. (…)

(…) The EU's reaction to the more difficult external environment at the HRC has been to focus on keeping the institution of the HRC going, which means trying to build some sort of consensus within it—no matter how much of a lowest common denominator this results in. EU ambitions on human rights have been lowered (…) It is an approach that concentrates not on addressing actual human rights situations around the world, but on the survival of the HRC itself. (…)

The EU's experiences at the Human Rights Council illustrate that 'practising' multilateralism is difficult for it to do. The EU faces serious challenges to its preferences for multilateralism and for strengthening international human rights law: it has been unable to influence the debates and agenda when it is outnumbered, and is 'rhetorically trapped' by its own commitment to multilateralism and international human rights protection. (…) Attempts to increase the EU's internal effectiveness need to be better linked to an analysis of what the EU can do to be more effective externally: speaking with one voice does not automatically translate into international influence.

The fact that the EU has become accustomed to speaking with one voice at the HRC should not be taken for granted. The essentially intergovernmental decision-making, sensitivity of human rights, and diversity of interests and priorities within the Union are always capable of disrupting the cohesion of EU external representation. An episode from the summer of 2017 provided an apt reminder of the potential fragility of this cohesion: the EU was about to present at the HRC a regular statement condemning human rights violations in China but Greece decided to veto the statement in a highly uncommon move.[137] Decision-making in the Council of the EU is typically consensual even if there are underlying differences, so

---

[137] 'Greece Blocks EU Statement on China Human Rights at U.N.' (*Reuters*, 18 June 2017) <https://www.reuters.com/article/us-eu-un-rights/greece-blocks-eu-statement-on-china-human-rights-at-u-n-idUSKBN1990FP> accessed 14 August 2020.

for one Member State to veto a public statement represents a considerable show of disunity. Moreover, the Greek veto was immediately linked with an inflow of Chinese investment at an economically troubled time in Greece. This episode brought out clearly the often referenced tension in EU foreign policy between material interests and the promotion of values and principles stipulated in Articles 2, 3(5), and 21 TEU. As Smith remarked in her study about EU influence at the HRC, 'while [the EU] persistently declares that "values" are at the heart of its foreign policy, hard material interests often knock these into second place'.[138]

In any case, EU external representation does not only consist of diplomatic overtures and voting in various international fora. The EU communicates with publics and governments around the world through a plethora of means, from social media to confidential dialogues. Since the Treaty of Lisbon, much of EU foreign policy communication comes from or involves the High Representative and his or her supporting diplomatic corps, the EEAS, which constitutes in itself a significant development in view of the traditionally intergovernmental nature of the CFSP. One of the most important discursive tools of the EU in this regard have become CFSP Declarations which are public statements—as opposed to, for example, démarches which are confidential—about a particular policy issue or geographical area, conveying the commonly agreed view of the EU, typically in response to a given event.[139] Paul James Cardwell conducted important research into the content of CFSP Declarations in light of the EU's commitment to the values mentioned in Articles 2 and 21 TEU.[140] The author found that Declarations have a significant place among EU foreign policy instruments and represent a positive example of the oft-criticized EU internal ability to produce common and consistent positions. The targeting of Declarations, however, also reveals the unwillingness of the EU to use this tool against certain countries despite their opposition to prominent features of the EU's global human rights agenda, such as the campaign to abolish the death penalty.

PJ Cardwell, 'Values in the European Union's Foreign Policy: An Analysis and Assessment of CFSP Declarations' (2016) 21 European Foreign Affairs Review 601

Declarations therefore require the input, and the agreement, of the Member States before they can be issued. For some Declarations, this process is uncontroversial. But there are likely to be more intense negotiations when the issue in question relates to matters which lie close to the core of national interests of one or more Member State(s), or where there is no pre-existing policy. All this takes places in a fast-moving context, since Declarations are (generally) rapidly issued in response to world events. The COREU [EU communication network] network is the usual means by which secure information is passed between Member States and has contributed to the development of frequent contacts and information-sharing between national governments and the EU institutions. Where there is difficulty in gaining agreement between the Member States—either on whether a Declaration should be issued at all, or what it should say—the final text may be worded

---

[138] Smith, 'Speaking with One Voice but Having Little Influence' (n 135) 241.
[139] Interestingly, Declarations are not mentioned in the Treaties. They have developed through institutional practice in the EPC and CFSP.
[140] See also T Vončina, 'Speaking with One Voice: Statements and Declarations as an Instrument of the EU's Common Foreign and Security Policy' (2011) 16 European Foreign Affairs Review 169.

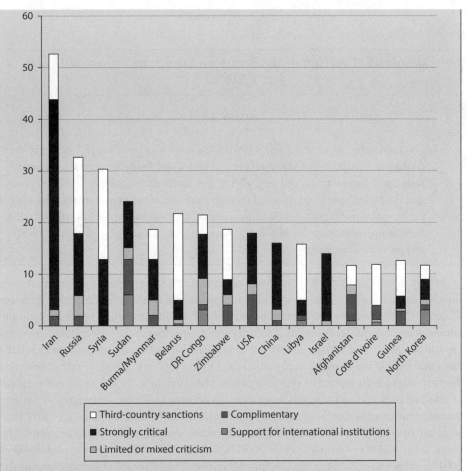

Figure 9.4 Most frequent third-country targets of declarations

in very general terms or may not appear at all. There is no guarantee therefore that a Declaration will necessarily be issued, even if the EU has done so before on a similar issue regarding another country.

This article examines the 708 Declarations which were issued by the High Representative (or Council, prior to the entry into force of the Treaty of Lisbon in 2011) over a nine-year period between 2007 and 2015. (...)

For some countries on the list, the subject matter is limited. For the United States, the Declarations only concern the use of the death penalty, with 'strongly critical' Declarations issued when it has been used (particularly in controversial circumstances) and 'complimentary' Declarations issued when a US state has abolished its use (such as Maryland in 2013). Declarations about Russia are almost exclusively related to criticism of its activities in neighbouring or breakaway states, and since 2011, the restrictive measures placed due to—according to the Declaration—'destabilizing' activities in Ukraine. On the other hand, Declarations addressed to Belarus, Syria, Iran, and Burma/Myanmar are almost exclusively of the 'strongly critical' type. This reveals that the approach to these countries has been repeated use of critical Declarations which combine with the imposition of restrictive measures.

D. CSDP missions

Consolidated version of the Treaty on European Union [2012] OJ C326/13

Article 43

1. The tasks referred to in Article 42(1), in the course of which the Union may use **civilian and military means,** shall include joint disarmament operations, humanitarian and rescue tasks, military advice and assistance tasks, conflict prevention and peace-keeping tasks, tasks of combat forces in crisis management, including peace-making and post-conflict stabilisation. All these tasks may contribute to the fight against terrorism, including by supporting third countries in combating terrorism in their territories.

As part of the CSDP, the EU is capable of deploying personnel and machinery of both the civilian and military kind in missions and operations worldwide. Currently, there are 17 active CSDP missions and operations, the bulk of which are civilian in nature, typically aiming to assist in the development of security sector capacities in the host country. Training, capacity-building, and various advisory interventions are called non-executive which indicates that the EU has merely a supportive role. On the contrary, executive operations conduct activities which replace or supplement core state functions such as peace enforcement or criminal prosecution and entail a significant interference with the sovereignty of the host country which means that they normally require a UN Security Council mandate. CSDP missions and operations can also have a dual executive/non-executive mandate. For example, the oldest active CSDP operation, EUFOR ALTHEA in Bosnia and Herzegovina established in 2004,[141] supports on the basis of a continually renewed[142] UN Security Council mandate the maintenance of a safe and secure environment in Bosnia and Herzegovina in accordance with the Dayton Agreement (executive part), as well as provides capacity building and training to the Bosnia's armed forces (non-executive part).[143] The furthest reaching executive mandate of any CSDP intervention has been conferred on EULEX Kosovo which is at the same time the largest civilian mission of the EU.[144] The mission assists in building up the rule of law in Kosovo by, among other things, supplying judges and prosecutors who conduct selected judicial proceedings and pursue criminal investigations either alone or together with Kosovar authorities. Despite the unique and deep nature of the EULEX intervention, its effectiveness has been called into question and bogged by corruption allegations. The mandate and resources of EULEX Kosovo have been progressively shrinking with the aim of transferring the executive powers to the local authorities. The mandate of the Joint Action has been extended several times and its future beyond the currently applicable end date, 14 June 2021,[145] is uncertain.

---

[141] Council Joint Action 2004/570/CFSP on the European Union military operation in Bosnia and Herzegovina [2004] OJ L252/10.

[142] See the latest UNSC Res 2496 (5 November 2019) S/RES/2496.

[143] EUFOR ALTHEA has replaced a preceding NATO force charged with maintaining peace in Bosnia and Herzegovina. The operation has also been significantly downsized and now includes around 600 personnel.

[144] Council Joint Action 2008/124/CFSP on the European Union Rule of Law Mission in Kosovo, EULEX KOSOVO [2008] OJ L42/92.

[145] Council Decision (CFSP) 2018/856 amending Joint Action 2008/124/CFSP on the European Union Rule of Law Mission in Kosovo (EULEX Kosovo) [2018] OJ L146/5.

From the perspective of human rights, the greater intrusiveness of the CSDP—and in particular CSDP military operations—increases commensurately the risk and gravity of human rights violations abroad for which the EU might be responsible. Worryingly, however, some commentators have observed that the present accountability framework for CSDP missions might not be adequate to provide a sufficient level of human rights protection if violations do occur. One part of the gaps in accountability mechanisms is the abovementioned circumscribed jurisdiction of the CJEU but the argument reaches further.

SØ Johansen, 'Accountability Mechanisms for Human Rights Violations by CSDP Missions: Available and Sufficient?' (2017) 66 International and Comparative Law Quarterly 181

When human rights are violated, there is a duty to provide accountability mechanisms—this is the essence of ECHR Article 13. The question at hand is thus whether CSDP missions, and thus the Union, are capable of violating human rights. To some, the idea that international organizations may be human rights violators seem backwards. There is a certain a normative bias in favour of international organizations. They are often perceived as inherently good; as promoters of human rights, and thus incapable of violating human rights. However, this perception is sometimes mistaken—as will be illustrated in the following when it comes to CSDP missions.

CSDP missions within both categories are capable of causing human rights violations, but the risk of violations varies between the categories, and between missions. One important factor explaining these variations in risk is the extent of which the missions make use of force. Military missions are normally expected to use force, either offensively or in self-defence, while civilian missions rarely use force. Another relevant factor is the issue of applicable law. While human rights law is generally applicable across both categories, military missions tasked with peacekeeping and peace enforcement may also involve the law of armed conflict. Whether the law of armed conflict is applicable to CSDP peacekeeping/peace enforcement missions cannot be answered in the abstract, but depends on an individual assessment of each situation. This assessment is both complex and difficult, and ultimately depends on the factual conduct of the EU forces on the ground.

(...)

NAVFOR Atalanta is a military CSDP mission launched in 2008, tasked with deterring, preventing and repressing acts of piracy off the Somali coast. Its mandate includes tasks such as keeping watch over the relevant areas, taking the necessary measures to protect vessels (including the use of force), as well as arresting, detaining and transferring captured pirates to States with jurisdiction to prosecute them. (...)

First, the human right to life may plausibly be violated in connection with a boarding and search of a (suspected) pirate vessel. Warships conducting the boarding are in principle allowed to use force, albeit subject to the rules governing law enforcement at sea. It is not unthinkable that force may be used in a manner that does not respect the strict requirements of necessity and proportionality that applies in this context. However, 'as the operational control rests with the Member State rather than with the EU Force Commander', it appears as if potential violations would not be attributable to the Union. Still, the Union might incur responsibility on the basis of its complicity (indirect responsibility). The concept of complicity has been recognized by the ILC in its Draft Articles on the Responsibility of International Organizations when they contribute to the violation by another State or international organization through aid, assistance, coercion, or direction and control. The provisions on aid and assistance seem to be particularly relevant, although their exact scope is uncertain. This uncertainty reflects the lack of judicial fora for cases alleging the responsibility of international organizations for human rights violations. Still, there are instances where the responsibility of international organizations has been touched upon by international courts, because the issue was incidental to a case against a State. The famous ECtHR case of Behrami and Saramati is a good example of this. In that case the attribution of the allegedly human rights violating conduct to the international organization (the UN) was essentially presupposed. The question for the ECtHR was essentially limited to whether the Member States that had contributed the troops that performed the conduct in question were (also) responsible.

Second, detention of pirates aboard a ship that is under the command of NAVFOR Atalanta would trigger the human right to liberty, as laid down in ECHR Article 5 and the corresponding CFR Article 6. Other provisions are also applicable, for example ECHR Article 3 and CFR Article 4, which prohibit degrading treatment or punishment. But, since it is the Commanding Officer of the vessel that decides whether to detain suspected pirates for the purpose of prosecuting them or to release them, breaches of human rights in connection with detention aboard would probably be attributed to the Member State to which the vessel belongs. The Union might nevertheless be held responsible for complicity, as explained just above.

A third potential scenario is one where a ship participating in NAVFOR Atalanta hands over a captured pirate to a State in violation of the principle of non-refoulement—which is inherent in ECHR Article 3 and CFR Article 4. Such transfers are facilitated by Transfer Agreements between the EU and States in region that are willing and able to prosecute suspected pirates. Those agreements are drafted with the CFP and the ECHR in mind, and provide for extensive diplomatic assurances and safeguards to protect the rights of suspected pirates that are transferred. However, there are some doubts whether all the transfer agreements are fully compatible with the CFR and the ECHR.

(...)

Human rights violations by CSDP missions seem to fall squarely within the category of violations over which the CJEU would lack jurisdiction. First, the Council decisions establishing such missions are not in themselves restrictive — it is their actual implementation that may cause human rights violations. It is therefore difficult to construe the human rights violating conduct of CSDP missions as 'restrictive measures' which would bring such cases within the ambit of the CJEU's jurisdiction. (...)

Another place to look for alternative accountability mechanisms is within the domestic court system of the Union's Member States. As the issue at hand is the Union's own responsibility—not that of a troop-contributing or otherwise cooperating Member State—there are several obstacles that may come in the way of effective accountability.

Domestic courts finding the Union responsible for a violation of the ECHR in connection with a CSDP mission will nonetheless have a hard time turning that responsibility into reality. Unless the Union voluntarily complies with the judgment, domestic courts lack powers of enforcement vis-à-vis the Union. This is because, although the Union under TFEU Article 274 may lack jurisdictional immunity, there is no similar exception for immunity against enforcement. According to TEU/TFEU Protocol No 7 on the privileges and immunities of the Union (TEU/TFEU Protocol No 7) Article 1, the Union's property and assets are [exempt] from 'any administrative or legal measure of constraint without the authorisation of the Court of Justice'. Given the CJEU's lack of jurisdiction on the merits of the cases under discussion, it cannot have the power to authorize enforcement of domestic judgments in the same area. Acknowledging such a power would be tantamount to the CJEU outsourcing the areas where it lacks jurisdiction to domestic courts, thus circumventing the restrictions put on the Court in the EU's constitutive treaties. It must not be forgotten that TFEU Article 275 sweepingly declares that the CJEU 'shall have no jurisdiction' over the CFSP.(...) Unless the judgments of domestic courts have sufficient 'bite', they cannot realistically prevent a violation, stop a continuing violation, or afford an appropriate remedy to those individuals whose rights have been violated.

With regard to CSDP missions, status agreements entered into between the Union and the host State may establish applicable accountability mechanisms. There are two types of such agreements: Status of Forces Agreements (SOFAs) for military missions and Status of Mission Agreements (SOMAs) for civilian missions. Since model texts have been drawn up for both types, the individual agreements made with each host State are materially similar. Both model texts have an identically worded article on claims for death, injury, damage and loss against the Union and its personnel.

However, also the claims procedure in the EU SOFAs/SOMAs seems to be tainted by insufficiency. Three aspects in particular deserve mention. First, the responsibility of the Union is excluded for damage or loss of property that is 'related to operational necessities' or 'caused by activities in connection with civil disturbances or protection of [the CSDP mission]'. Claims based on violations of the ECHR could be covered by this relatively broad waiver. Second, resort to binding arbitration is limited to claims exceeding EUR 40 000. Other claims are left to be resolved through diplomatic means, ie through negotiations. This filtering mechanism deprives those with ECHR claims of a low monetary value from having recourse to an accountability mechanism. Third, there is an inherent limitation in the fact that SOFAs/SOMAs are concluded with individual host States ad hoc. It is possible that human rights violations could occur outside the spatial scope of a SOFA/SOMA, eg in international waters, as is the case with the NAVFOR Atalanta mission. Taken together it seems as if the dispute resolution provisions in the Union's SOFAs/SOMAs are insufficient accountability mechanisms.

Each CSDP mission may, moreover, have accountability mechanisms that are specific to it. One example is the above-mentioned EULEX Kosovo, which has established a Human Rights Review Panel. It is tasked with reviewing [complaints] from individuals claiming to be the victim of human rights violations by EULEX Kosovo. Its mandate is, however, limited to examining whether a human rights violation occurred, and to making recommendations for remedial action (which cannot consist of financial recommendations) to the Head of Mission. In other words, the Human Rights Review Panel suffers from the same weaknesses of enforcement as the European Ombudsman. Thus, it too seems to be an insufficient accountability mechanism.

Human rights might often have been anathema to military staff but the EU is attempting to integrate them into the CSDP as part of its mainstreaming efforts.[146] Fostering human

---

[146] EU CIVCOM, 'Lessons and best practices of mainstreaming human rights and gender into CSDP military operations and civilian missions', 17138/10, 2010; European External Action Service, 'Report of the Baseline Study on the Integration of Human Rights and Gender into the EU's CSDP', EEAS(2016) 990, 10 November 2016.

rights as an integral part of any CSDP mission is predicated upon both civilian and military personnel taking part in CSDP missions receiving appropriate training in human rights.[147] Human rights and humanitarian law are also taken into account in the planning and decision-making processes in EU institutions where the relevant expertise resides with the legal services of each institution, among which the most important is the Council as far as the CSDP is concerned.[148] This is paramount in view of the fact that both the EU and the Member States may incur international responsibility for human rights violations, in addition to the internal fundamental rights obligations,[149] despite the deficient state of accountability mechanisms pointed out by Johansen.

A Sari and RA Wessel, 'International Responsibility for EU Military Operations: Finding the EU's Place in the Global Accountability Regime' in B Van Vooren, S Blockmans, and J Wouters (eds), *The EU's Role in Global Governance* (Oxford University Press 2013)

The EU certainly enjoys the competence to incorporate military assets into its institutional structure and the Council is competent to establish military operations as its subsidiary organs. However, none of the legal acts adopted in relation to EU military operations provide clear evidence of the Council's intention to confer the status of a subsidiary organ on them. Since this intention cannot be presumed, we were led to conclude that EU military operations are not de jure organs of the EU. However, they may still be classified as de facto organs, provided that the Union exercises the necessary degree of control over them. Although EU operations do not satisfy the high threshold of complete dependence demanded by the ICJ in its case-law, a strong argument can be made that they are subject to a particularly high degree of normative control by the EU and may be considered as its de facto organs on this basis. Accordingly (...) a presumption exists in favour of attributing the conduct of EU military operations to the EU on the grounds that they constitute de facto organs of the Union.

9.5 EU Enlargement and Neighbourhood Policy

The end of the Cold War in the early 1990s has brought with it an important challenge and opportunity for the EU. Europe was no longer physically divided by an 'iron curtain' and with the fall of the Soviet Union and communist governments the countries in Central and Eastern Europe (CEE) were no longer thrones of authoritarianism with a predetermined Soviet-oriented foreign policy. Human rights of course famously played a part in the

---

[147] ML Sanchez Barrueco, 'The Promotion and Protection of Human Rights During Common Security and Defence Policy Operations' in JE Wetzel (ed), *The EU as a 'Global Player' in Human Rights?* (Routledge 2012) 164.

[148] F Naert, 'The Application of Human Rights and International Humanitarian Law in Drafting EU Missions' Mandates and Rules of Engagement', Working Paper No 151, October 2011, KU Leuven Institute for International Law.

[149] See Ch 5. See also F Naert, 'The International Responsibility of the Union in the Context of Its CSDP Operations' in MD Evans and P Koutrakos (eds), *The International Responsibility of the European Union: European and International Perspectives* (Hart Publishing 2013); A Sari and RA Wessel, 'International Responsibility for EU Military Operations: Finding the EU's Place in the Global Accountability Regime' in B Van Vooren, S Blockmans, and J Wouters (eds), *The EU's Role in Global Governance* (Oxford University Press 2013).

downturn of communist authoritarianism following the adoption of the Helsinki Final Act of 1975 which became a vehicle for change, thanks in part to the diplomatic efforts of the Member States of the then European Community.[150]

The subsequently enacted and frequently refined enlargement policy of the EU has resulted in one of the most successful processes of democratization and human rights strengthening in the history.[151] The transition of CEE countries from communist to democratic rule was anything but straightforward and it was additionally accompanied by considerable economic hardship related to the transition from planned to market economies. During this time, the EU (and to a lesser extent, NATO) served as the guiding beacons for the (often overindulgent) hopes of many in the populations and governments in CEE countries. The EU's embrace of the CEE in the 1990s and its commitment to reuniting Europe (symbolized also by the reunification of Germany)[152] has in fact rhetorically entrapped the Member States into progressing with the Eastern enlargement even when their material interests may have advised against immediate and large-scale expansion.

F Schimmelfennig, 'The Community Trap: Liberal Norms, Rhetorical Action, and the Eastern Enlargement of the European Union' (2001) 55 International Organization 47

Both the Central and Eastern European states and the Western supporters of Eastern enlargement counted on the impact of rhetorical action in order to achieve their goal. The Central and Eastern European governments have based their claims to membership on the standard of legitimacy of the European international community: European identity and unity, liberal democracy, and multilateralism. They invoked the community's membership rules and took its ritualized pan-European liberal commitment at face value. They tried to demonstrate that these values and norms obliged the EU to admit them and that failing to do so would be an act of disloyalty to the ideational foundations of the European international community. They uncovered inconsistencies between the constitutive values and the past rhetoric and practice of the EC, on the one hand, and their current behavior toward the Central and Eastern European countries, on the other hand. In doing so, they have managed to 'mobilize' the institutionalized identity and to make enlargement an issue of credibility.

The most systematic and formal attempt to rhetorically commit the Community to Eastern enlargement can be found in the Commission's report, entitled 'Europe and the Challenge of Enlargement', to the Lisbon summit in June 1992. Prepared shortly after the signing of the first Europe Agreements, it marked the starting point of the Commission's attempt to turn the association 'equilibrium' into a concrete promise and preparation for enlargement. The Commission referred to the Community's vision of a pan-European liberal order as creating specific obligations in the current situation: 'The Community has

---

[150] R Davy, 'Helsinki Myths: Setting the Record Straight on the Final Act of the CSCE, 1975' (2009) 9 Cold War History 1.

[151] The success of the transition has in recent times become seen as less impressive in light of the democratic and human rights 'backsliding' in Hungary and Poland. See Ch 4.

[152] European Council, 'Presidency conclusions', Strasbourg, 8–9 December 1989.

never been a closed club, and cannot now refuse the historic challenge to assume its continental responsibilities and contribute to the development of a political and economic
order for the whole of Europe.' By stating that 'for the new democracies, Europe remains
a powerful idea, signifying the fundamental values and aspirations which their peoples
kept alive during long years of oppression,' the report obviously meant to shame those
members who betrayed 'Europe' out of their narrow self-interest.

(...) In the institutional environment of an international community, state actors can
strategically use community identity, values, and norms to justify and advance their self-
interest. However, strategic behavior is constrained by the constitutive ideas of the community and the actors' prior identification with them. Once caught in the community
trap, they can be forced to honor identity- and value-based commitments in order to protect their credibility and reputation as community members.

Following the 'mass' enlargement of 2004—when ten new Member States joined the EU—
the borders of the already enlarged EU significantly expanded. The EU acquired thousands
of kilometres of land borders with Croatia (which joined in 2013), Serbia, Romania (which
joined in 2007), Ukraine, and Belarus, as well as the Russian Kaliningrad enclave. While
Romania and Bulgaria were approaching accession and countries in the Western Balkans
and Turkey were broadly already included in the enlargement limb of EU external action—
the EU having unambiguously promised membership to these countries in 2003[153]—the
EU had no cohesive policy towards the other countries in Eastern Europe and the Southern
Caucasus. This was meant to change with the establishment of the ENP, first outlined by the
Commission in a 2003 communication entitled 'Wider Europe' which proposed that 'that
the EU should aim to develop a zone of prosperity and a friendly neighbourhood—a "ring of
friends"—with whom the EU enjoys close, peaceful and co-operative relations'. For reasons
related to divergent geopolitical interests of the Member States, the ENP also included countries of the Southern Mediterranean region with whom the EU had already cultivated relations for a longer period of time and as part of a number of overlapping frameworks (but
chiefly the Barcelona process).[154]

P Leino and R Petrov, 'Between "Common Values" and Competing
Universals—The Promotion of the EU's Common Values through the
European Neighbourhood Policy' (2009) 15 European Law Journal 654

Most of the EU neighbouring countries are transition countries, which are undergoing
the process of transformation from either colonial- or Soviet-style legal, political and economic traditions to Western standards of liberal democracy. The EU's common values are

[153] At the European Council summit in Thessaloniki in June 2003 the Member States adopted a text containing the following sentence: 'The European Council, recalling its conclusions in Copenhagen (December
2002) and Brussels (March 2003), reiterated its determination to fully and effectively support the European perspective of the Western Balkan countries, which will become an integral part of the EU, once they meet the established criteria.'
[154] PJ Cardwell, 'EuroMed, European Neighbourhood Policy and the Union for the Mediterranean:
Overlapping Policy Frames in the EU's Governance of the Mediterranean' (2011) 49 Journal of Common Market
Studies 219.

believed to provide an appropriate and credible model framework for domestic reforms in the neighbouring countries. The role of common values relates to the need to justify the required market reforms: it connects the EU policy towards its neighbouring countries to much greater goals, thus giving these reforms 'an aura of authority and legitimacy'. The market reform agenda, shared by the EU with many other Western actors, thus evidences the alliance between democracy and market economies. But, as Rittich has noted, at the same time, countries in transition are expected to adapt and subordinate their desires to the demands of a market economy, making their options highly restricted and coercive.

Like with the CEE candidate countries nearly 20 years before, the EU approach to the neighbouring countries can be criticised for reflecting largely an idealised and artificial vision of Western market economy, in which the EU represents the most advanced instantiation of the liberal democratic model. The neighbouring countries, on the other hand, are placed under an obligation to 'democratise' following an agenda set by the EU before they can be considered for true rapprochement with the EU. Consequently, as Kennedy has argued, such internationalisation of democratic rhetoric accompanies a domestic displacement of democratic policies, as 'politics is treated as having somehow already happened elsewhere'. In many ways, the ENP replicates the problematic arrangements surrounding the previous enlargements, causing the neighbouring countries to lose a level of independence at a crucial time in their democratic reform and economic restructuring programmes, while they receive even fewer tangible benefits in return than the applicant countries did before them.

The diffusion of human rights and democracy among the target countries of both the enlargement and the neighbourhood policy has, in the rhetoric of the EU, been one of the pillars of these policies. This is of course consistent with the overall objectives of EU policy as well as the requirements of EU membership which became prominent after the adoption of the so-called Copenhagen criteria. The main tool through which the EU seeks to achieve the dissemination of human rights has been conditionality which refers to the process of offering carrots (positive conditionality) or threatening with sticks (negative conditionality) in exchange for third countries taking steps to strengthen human rights protection domestically (typically signified by adopting laws in accordance with the EU's wishes).[155] In the context of enlargement policy, Grabbe identified five categories of mechanisms used by the EU to effect domestic changes in countries that are part of the accession process, the first of which is the most powerful conditionality tool: gate-keeping—access to negotiations and further stages in the accession process; benchmarking and monitoring; models—provision of legislative and institutional templates; money—aid and technical assistance; advice; and twinning.[156] From this typology it is clear that the fact that the main prize—EU membership—is not on offer in the ENP, which purposively avoids entrapping the EU by not giving ENP participating countries a membership perspective. This is bound to impede the effectiveness of conditionality in the ENP, regardless of the neighbourhood policy being otherwise largely modelled upon enlargement policy. Conditionality in both policies is, moreover,

[155] Human rights protection is of course but one, and usually not the main, goal of conditionality, but it is the main one of concern in the context of this book, along with the adjacent EU values (as they are often presented as a package).

[156] H Grabbe, 'How does Europeanization affect CEE governance? Conditionality, Diffusion and Diversity' (2001) 8 Journal of European Public Policy 1013, 1020.

overwhelmingly based on 'carrots' rather than 'sticks'. However, given that the number of carrots the EU can offer to partner countries is limited, the EU quickly discovered that it must ration their use. What happened in particular in enlargement policy is that carrots were cut into ever smaller slices—partly because the EU decided to slow down enlargement—which has translated into the accession process becoming longer, more demanding, and punctuated with countless veto points, allowing Member States to control the drip-feed of conditionality and, ultimately, EU enlargement tightly.

A. Copenhagen criteria and the accession process

Consolidated version of the Treaty on European Union [2012] OJ C326/13

Article 49

Any European State which respects the values referred to in Article 2 and is committed to promoting them may apply to become a member of the Union. The European Parliament and national Parliaments shall be notified of this application. The applicant State shall address its application to the Council, which shall act unanimously after consulting the Commission and after receiving the consent of the European Parliament, which shall act by a majority of its component members. The conditions of eligibility agreed upon by the European Council shall be taken into account.

The conditions of admission and the adjustments to the Treaties on which the Union is founded, which such admission entails, shall be the subject of an agreement between the Member States and the applicant State. This agreement shall be submitted for ratification by all the contracting States in accordance with their respective constitutional requirements.

The origins of EU enlargement (accession) policy can be traced to Article 237 of the Treaty of Rome (now in an amended form Article 49 TEU). The condition which has persisted in an unchanged form from the beginning is that the applicant country is a 'European State'. The geographical limits of this criterion have never been formally laid down by EU institutions and are ultimately, as most of the enlargement policy, subject to political decisions of EU Member States which hold the most power over the process. Nevertheless, when Morocco applied in 1987, its application was rejected on the grounds that it did not constitute a 'European State' for the purposes of what is now Article 49 TEU. It is not unreasonable to wonder, however, whether the EU would reach the same conclusion if Morocco was a rich rather than a lower-middle income country or a predominantly Christian one rather than Muslim. On the other hand, the fact that Turkey is a candidate country for EU membership shows that the stringency of the requirement to be a European State, but also factors other than geography or identity, are to a large extent politically and historically contingent.

In any case, the EU started to take more of an interest in the state of the countries applying for EU membership at the time of Spanish, Portuguese, and Greek accession. All three of these countries were emerging from authoritarian regimes and were moreover economically underdeveloped compared to the rest of the European Economic Community. It was the latter concern and the impact of a southern enlargement on the institutions and the common market which preoccupied the then members of the Community more,[157] although other considerations, such as security and the Cold War context, were also part of the equation. Greece avoided almost any kind of scrutiny, thanks to successful diplomatic efforts, and concluded negotiations earlier than Spain and Portugal which both faced some resistance in their accession process, albeit mainly on economic grounds.

The real breakthrough in the development of the EU enlargement policy came with the end of the Cold War and the desire to overcome East–West divisions in Europe. The opportunity was seen as an historical moment for Europe but one that nonetheless needed some ground rules, seeing as the newly liberated countries of Central and Eastern Europe just emerged from decades of totalitarian rule and centralized economic planning. The most well-known of the accession conditions laid down by the EU became the Copenhagen criteria adopted by the European Council at the Copenhagen summit in 1993. This is not to say that prior to this date there were no strings attached to EU membership in terms of values: adherence to liberal democracy was at least an implicit prerequisite and they were openly discussed as early as 1961 in the Birkelbach report, adopted unanimously in the Parliamentary Assembly.[158] But the Copenhagen criteria comprised an explicit and authoritative political statement which came, though perhaps not unexpectedly, at a crucial moment of European history.

European Council, Presidency conclusions, Copenhagen, 21–22 June 1993

The European Council welcomed the courageous efforts undertaken by the associated countries to modernize their economies, which have been weakened by 40 years of central planning, and to ensure a rapid transition to a market economy. The Community and its Member States pledge their support to this reform process. Peace and security in Europe depend on the success of those efforts.

The European Council today agreed that the associated countries in Central and Eastern Europe that so desire shall become members of the European Union. Accession will take place as soon as an associated country is able to assume the obligations of membership by **satisfying the economic and political conditions required**.

Membership requires that the candidate country has achieved **stability of institutions guaranteeing democracy, the rule of law, human rights and respect for and protection of minorities**, the existence of a functioning market economy as well as the capacity to cope with competitive pressure and market forces within the Union. Membership presupposes the candidate's ability to take on the obligations of membership including adherence to the aims of political, economic and monetary union.

The Union's capacity to absorb new members, while maintaining the momentum of European integration, is also an important consideration in the general interest of both the Union and the candidate countries.

---

[157] European Commission, 'General Considerations on the Problems of Enlargement', COM(78) 120 final, Luxembourg, 20 April 1978; L Tsoukalis, *The European Community and its Mediterranean Enlargement* (George Allen and Unwin 1981) 136.

[158] Parliamentary Assembly, 'Rapport fait au nom de la commission politique de l'Assemblée parlementaire européenne sur les aspects politiques et institutionnels de l'adhésion ou de l'association à la Communauté par M. Willi Birkelbach', 19 December 1961. The report was adopted unanimously (the Assembly was the predecessor of the European Parliament).

> The European Council will continue to follow closely progress in each associated country towards fulfilling the conditions of accession to the Union and draw the appropriate conclusions.

The criteria marked the beginning of the point when the Union, in particular the Commission, started to evaluate candidate countries on how well they comply with EU values and suggest reforms to ameliorate the situation. It needs to be stressed again, however, that regardless of the reports the Commission drew up during the accession processes—which themselves were affected by political considerations—it is the Member States which ultimately decide on whether an applicant country could move forward in the process. For example, in July 1997 the Commission condemned the situation in Slovakia, citing the 'lack of rootedness' and instability of its political institutions and shortcomings in the functioning of democracy.[159] Yet, all it took was one election, albeit a momentous one in which the quasi-authoritarian Mečiar was replaced by a liberal democratic government, for Member States to open accession negotiations with Slovakia less than three years after the Commission found fundamental flaws in the functioning of the country's institutions. For all the positive reforms which took place in that period, it is impossible for any country to develop key political and legal institutions in two and a half years, much less a culture with an internalized sentiment towards shared EU values. However, the calculation for decision-makers is much more complex than whether EU values have been internalized in a candidate countries. At the end of the twentieth century, the EU had to consider a range of questions when deciding on the fate of enlargement and this is without even tackling the national self-interest of existing members and internal capacity of the EU (one of the other Copenhagen criteria): for how long will populations in applicant countries sustain support for EU integration without a concrete date for membership? Would it last long enough (but how long?) for these countries to develop the necessary institutions and culture? Would such institutions and culture develop at all in the absence of progress towards membership? Should EU-oriented governments be rewarded by accession progress to stave off other political forces in the country? These are just a few questions purporting to show the difficulty of making enlargement decisions and that the support for EU values cannot be entirely, and this was the case especially for the Eastern enlargement, extricated from other factors and the broader political context. With the benefit of hindsight, the current situation in Hungary and Poland shows that insistence on EU values should have probably played a more important role in the Eastern enlargement.[160]

Another landmark in the development of the enlargement policy came at the Helsinki summit in 1999. Signalling that conditionality in the accession process was to become more targeted and the process more segmented and gradual, the European Council introduced the hitherto non-existent status of 'candidate country' and made the opening of accession negotiations explicitly conditional on human rights protection which as a consequence excluded Turkey from immediate talks.[161] Turkey had been harbouring EU membership hopes for a long time and it looked on with trepidation as CEE countries edged ahead in the enlargement process.[162] The EU and the Member States, keen on preserving a strong relationship with Turkey for reasons ranging from security to economics, were not ready to quash Turkey's

---

[159] G Pridham, 'The European Union's Democratic Conditionality and Domestic Politics in Slovakia: the Mečiar and Dzurinda Governments Compared' (2002) 54 Europe-Asia Studies 203, 224.

[160] D Kochenov, *EU Enlargement and the Failure of Conditionality: Pre-accession Conditionality in the Fields of Democracy and the Rule of Law* (Kluwer Law International 2008).

[161] European Council, 'Presidency conclusions', Helsinki, 10–11 December 1999, para 4.

[162] Turkey was one of the first countries to sign an association agreement with the European Economic Community which in 1995 culminated in the formation of a customs union with the EU.

membership hopes.[163] The membership perspective also conferred on the EU leverage with respect to Turkey, as evidenced by the customs union agreed between the two parties in 1995. The agreement gives Turkey no representation in the decision-making on external tariffs on industrial goods and the negotiation of preferential trade agreements.[164] Part of the reason why Turkey agreed to such a one-sided arrangement was that it represented a step towards EU membership. As the prospect of accession has become increasingly untenable at least in the short to medium term on account of Turkey's slide towards authoritarianism and violations of the rule of law and human rights, the idea of a more equal customs union had been considered in the Commission.[165] More recently, however, the Council has decided that under the prevailing circumstances, including repeated Turkish infringements of the ban on import duties under the guise of the exception of Article 16 of Decision No 1/95, 'no further work towards the modernisation of the EU–Turkey Customs Union could be foreseen'.[166] In addition, Turkey has recently tried to make use of the leverage it gained over the EU due to the latter's desire to stem the flow of migrants and refugees arriving to Greece.[167]

Following the 'big bang' enlargement of 2004, an 'enlargement fatigue' infiltrated the EU.[168] As a result, the enlargement policy was tightened and higher demands placed on candidate or potential candidate countries if they wished to make progress up the accession ladder. Only three accessions were completed since 2004: Romania and Bulgaria joined in 2007 and Croatia in 2013, the latter with the unofficial title of state best prepared ever to join the EU due to the protracted nature of the accession process. Five countries currently have the status of candidates, two are potential candidates (see Table 9.2).[169] The EU has opened accession negotiations with all five candidate countries, although the negotiations with Turkey are currently on a road to nowhere. The repressive measures taken by Turkish President Erdoğan after a failed coup d'état attempt in 2016 caused the EU to temporarily suspend the accession negotiations; no new chapters have been opened or closed since.[170]

At the beginning of the accession process is an application from a third country wishing to join the EU and thinking it can comply with the basic criteria set out in Article 49 TEU which now incorporate a reference to the EU's values listed in Article 2 TEU.[171] The application is submitted to the rotating Council Presidency which decides on forwarding the application to the Commission. The Commission is responsible for drafting an opinion on

---

[163] The Helsinki European Council conclusions boldly stated in paragraph 12 that 'Turkey is a candidate State destined to join the Union on the basis of the same criteria as applied to the other candidate States.' Although this promise resembles the one given to the Western Balkans countries, the EU regards it with a lot more flexibility.

[164] Decision No 1/95 of the EC–Turkey Association Council of 22 December 1995 on implementing the final phase of the Customs Union [1996] OJ L35/1.

[165] European Commission, 'Impact assessment accompanying the Recommendation for a Council Decision authorising the opening of negotiations with Turkey on an Agreement on the extension of the scope of the bilateral preferential trade relationship and on the modernisation of the Customs Union', COM(2016) 830 final, Brussels, 21 December 2016.

[166] See European Commission, 'Turkey 2019 Report accompanying the document Communication from the Commission to the European Parliament, the Council, the European Economic and Social Committee and the Committee of the Regions: 2019 Communication on EU Enlargement Policy', SWD(2019) 220 final, Brussels, 29 May 2019, 97–98 and 105.

[167] See Ch 8.

[168] A Szołucha, 'The EU and Enlargement Fatigue: Why has the European Union not Been Able to Counter Enlargement Fatigue?' (2010) 6 Journal of Contemporary European Research 107.

[169] Potential candidates are countries which have been promised membership at some stage but are not yet ready in the eyes of the EU to qualify for candidate status.

[170] See Council of the European Union, 'Council Conclusions on Enlargement and Stabilisation and Association Process', 10555/18, 26 June 2018, paras 30–35.

[171] Prior to the application, the EU would have already established comprehensive contractual relations with the country, involving numerous rights and obligations in various policy fields (most importantly economic integration) and typically taking the form of an association agreement.

Table 9.2 Countries currently part of the EU enlargement policy and their status

Countries	Association agreement	Candidate status	Accession negotiations	Negotiations chapters
Albania	In force since 1 April 2009	Candidate since 27 June 2014	Open since 25 March 2020	Yet to be decided
Bosnia and Herzegovina	In force since 1 June 2015	Potential candidate	Not open	None open
North Macedonia	In force since 1 April 2004	Candidate since 16 December 2005	Open since 25 March 2020	Yet to be decided
Kosovo	In force since 1 April 2016	Potential candidate	Not open	None open
Montenegro	In force since 1 May 2010	Candidate since 17 December 2010	Open since 29 June 2012	32 chapters open, 3 provisionally closed
Serbia	In force since 1 September 2013	Candidate since 1 March 2012	Open since 21 January 2014	18 chapters open, 2 provisionally closed
Turkey	In force since 1 December 1964	Candidate since 11 December 1999	Open since 3 October 2005	16 chapters open, 1 provisionally closed

the merits of the country's application, a process which begins with an extremely comprehensive questionnaire including thousands of questions about the country's readiness to become a member of the EU in light of the Copenhagen criteria and the EU's acquis.[172] Once the Commission is satisfied with the answers provided, it drafts the opinion evaluating the membership application against all the relevant criteria, including 35 policy chapters.[173] The opinion, which may be accompanied by recommendations on required progress, is then submitted to the Council which decides on whether and under what conditions the country can receive candidate status.

Questionnaire, Information requested by the European Commission to the Council of Ministers of Bosnia and Herzegovina for the preparation of the Opinion on the application of Bosnia and Herzegovina for membership of the European Union, December 2016

14. Please describe which institutions are defined as independent under the Constitution at all levels of governance. How are their constitutional guarantees of independence ensured?
292. Please provide succinct information on the country's constitutional order, legislation or other rules governing the area of fundamental rights, and their compatibility with the relevant international conventions.

---

[172] In the recent case of Bosnia and Herzegovina's application, the initial questionnaire consisted of 3,242 questions, 516 of which related to political (Copenhagen) criteria, 74 to economic (Copenhagen) criteria, and 2,652 to compliance with the EU acquis. Later, an additional 655 follow-up questions were posed.

[173] The delivery of the Commission's opinion can easily take more than a year and it is not based only on the questionnaire but also on a plethora of other inputs, among others from civil society and international organizations. In the case of Bosnia and Herzegovina, it took over three years counting from its application for membership: European Commission, 'Communication from the Commission to the European Parliament and the Council on Bosnia and Herzegovina's application for membership of the European Union', COM(2019) 261 final, 29 May 2019.

293. Provide a list of all human rights instruments and related protocols ratified by Bosnia and Herzegovina along with the date of signature and ratification. Include details of any reservations which have been made to those treaties and any declarations recognising the right of individuals to petition committees established by the conventions. In addition, please specify what legislation and provisions have been adopted to ensure compliance with the obligations stemming from these conventions. How are these implemented and monitored? Please indicate which department(s) is (are) in charge of following up on reporting to international monitoring bodies established under the different conventions ratified.

294. What is the rank of these conventions in the domestic legal system, including the constitution? Have Bosnia and Herzegovina introduced the direct applicability of international conventions in domestic law in all cases and at all levels?

295. What steps have been taken to cooperate with UN bodies dealing with human rights issues, including visits by UN special mechanisms (such as special rapporteurs), reporting to Treaty bodies and responding to Treaty body recommendations?

296. What are the competences of the Ombudsman in the field of human rights, the rights of women, rights of children, rights of persons with disabilities and protection of minorities? Does the Ombudsman have investigation power? Does the Ombudsman's mandate also extend for certain aspects to the private sector? How is the financing of the Ombudsman Institution regulated?

448. Please provide statistical information, if available, on the situation of minorities as compared with the majority population in respect of: housing; education (participation in primary, secondary and tertiary education); health services, employment and unemployment rates; infant mortality and life expectancy.

The conferral of the candidate status does not mean that negotiations start immediately. The opening of negotiations requires another unanimous decision of the Council and the EU may impose additional conditions when a country wishes to move from candidate status to open negotiations. Crossing this particular hurdle/veto point has in the past proven particularly difficult for North Macedonia, which had been a candidate country for more than a decade without progressing to accession negotiations. The reason has been, not uniquely in enlargement policy, overtly political: Greece was blocking Macedonia (including from NATO) due to a dispute over the name of the country. The dispute was only resolved when the previously named 'former Yugoslav Republic of Macedonia' agreed to change its name to 'Republic of North Macedonia'. After this decision took effect, the opening of accession negotiations indeed supervened in March 2020.

Commission Opinion on Serbia's application for membership of the European Union, COM(2011) 668 final, Brussels, 12 October 2011

Human rights are generally respected in Serbia. The Ombudsman and the Commissioner for access to information and data protection are playing an increasingly effective role in the oversight of the administration. The legal framework to combat discrimination has been substantially improved and mechanisms have been set up to oversee its implementation, which is at an early stage. The authorities have also been paying growing attention to safeguarding the respect of the freedom of assembly and freedom of association and the role of civil society. The newly adopted media strategy aims at substantially clarifying the legal and market environment in which media outlets are operating. More comprehensive and proactive action is expected from the relevant institutions in cases of threats and violence against journalists and media, emanating notably from radical groups. The current prison conditions are a matter of serious concern. A long awaited law on restitution as well as a new law on public property were adopted. Transparent and non discriminatory implementation of both laws has to be ensured and further measures taken to fully establish legal clarity over property rights. The Commission will monitor the implementation and application of these laws. (...) Further serious efforts, including financial resources, are needed in order to improve the status and socio-economic conditions of the Roma, who continue to be the most vulnerable and marginalised minority, as illustrated by the high number of illegal settlements.

Once formal negotiations are open, the candidate country starts to adopt swathes of existing EU law across the 35 different policy chapters (summarily called EU acquis). It can easily be the case that countries, wishing to display their readiness or for trade-related reasons, are already aligned with EU law in some areas, in which case the negotiating chapter can be provisionally closed without any domestic changes.[174] However, the candidate countries are not only required to transpose EU legislation into their domestic legal orders, they are also asked to embark on often wide-ranging reforms of the justice system, political and economic institutions, and others, in order to comply with the Copenhagen criteria. This is an important point in the context of the discussion on the internal-external coherence (the lack thereof), as the EU does not have similar leverage once candidate countries become members of the Union.[175] Moreover, it should be stressed that the adoption of the EU acquis does not automatically translate into compliance with the Copenhagen/political criteria/EU values. The acquis is of a predominantly technical character and it exists in areas of EU competence; the EU, however, has only limited internal competence when it comes to EU values. Even fundamental rights at the EU level are tied to the exercise of EU competence or implementation of EU law by the Member States.[176]

The opening of negotiations does not mean that all policy chapters become open at the same time. On the contrary, chapters are open at a rate decided unanimously by the Council on the recommendation by the Commission which, once again, allows the EU Member States to halt the accession process at any given moment. One of the innovations which have occurred in enlargement policy is that the usually most difficult chapters—chapters 23 and 24 on fundamental rights, justice, freedom, and security—are negotiated first. This underlines the importance the EU attaches to the preparedness of candidates in critical areas; country-specific issues, such as Serbia's relations with Kosovo,[177] can also be accorded similar priority treatment.[178]

---

[174] Normally this happens only with respect to chapters of lesser importance for the EU, such as those concerning science and research, where the EU anyway has a more limited presence.

[175] See Ch 4.

[176] See Ch 4 as regards the scope of applicability of the Charter.

[177] Note, however, that also some EU Member States have not formally recognized Kosovo as an independent country. This is also the reason why, uniquely, the association agreement between Kosovo and the EU is not a mixed agreement involving the legal participation of the Member States. The EU is the sole contracting party (along with Euratom) on its side of the agreement. See Stabilisation and Association Agreement between the European Union and the European Atomic Energy Community, of the one part, and Kosovo, of the other part [2016] OJ L71/3.

[178] The EU has recently re-emphasized the importance of good neighbourly relations as a pre-condition of EU membership. See European Commission, 'A credible enlargement perspective for and enhanced EU engagement with the Western Balkans', COM(2018) 65 final, Strasbourg, 6 February 2018.

In any case, negotiations under each chapter involve a number of steps. First, the Commission conducts a 'screening' exercise, with the involvement of the candidate country, in which it determines the level of the candidate's alignment with EU standards. The subsequent screening report translates into a recommendation for the Council regarding whether the chapter should be open or whether first certain conditions need to be met. These conditions are called 'opening benchmarks'. Second, the candidate country as well as the EU have to put forward their views of what should be done in the given policy field. The EU position will contain 'closing benchmarks'—the requirements which must be fulfilled for a chapter to be closed.[179] The EU position for some chapters, notably 23 and 24, can furthermore stipulate interim benchmarks. The Commission monitors the entire enlargement process and issues regular reports thereon.

European Commission, Montenegro 2016 Report, SWD(2016) 360 final, Brussels, 9 November 2016

Montenegro completed several legislative reforms to further align with the EU and international human rights standards and ensure that adequate mechanisms are in place to protect vulnerable groups from discrimination. Implementation of the legislation remains weak. Amendments to the overall legislative framework, to ensure a coherent sanctioning policy for human rights violations, have not been adopted yet. Institutional capacity needs to increase further. The Roma minority remains the most vulnerable and most discriminated-against community in various areas of life. Last year's recommendations have been partially implemented.

Shortcomings particularly affect the following areas:

- Human rights institutions, including the Ombudsman and the Ministry of Human Rights and Minorities, need to be strengthened further and their knowledge of international and European human rights law and standards increased. The Ministry's capacity to handle and supervise the spending of funds for minorities and religious communities remains limited;
- Implementation of the anti-discrimination framework needs to be more effective, and awareness by the general public needs to increase; lack of a uniform approach and low levels of penalties for human rights violations continues to create legal uncertainty;
- Impunity is still an issue of concern in connection with abuses in prisons and by the police. Judges and law enforcement officials' knowledge of European standards and case-law should be improved. Legislative measures to increase police accountability should be considered.

The accession process concludes with the signing and ratification of the accession treaty once all chapters have been negotiated, implemented, and closed. The accession treaty, in addition to bringing the candidate country into the EU formally, may stipulate transitional arrangements, including the suspension of certain benefits of EU membership for a limited period of time.[180] The treaty comes into force only after it is approved by the Commission, the Council, and the European Parliament, and signed and ratified by all EU Member States,

---

[179] Chapters are closed only provisionally until the entire accession process is completed.
[180] For example, a number of EU Member States imposed multi-year limitations on free movement of persons from CEE countries following their accession to the EU.

on the one hand, and the candidate country, on the other, in line with their constitutional requirements.

An example of a unique transitional provision, inserted in the accession treaty of Bulgaria and Romania, has been the possibility to continue monitoring certain areas of domestic activity. The mechanism for cooperation and verification (CVM) allows the Commission to monitor Bulgaria's and Romania's progress in developing the rule of law and fighting against corruption, two areas identified as problematic during the accession process. The CVM is unique not only because it has only been employed in the case of the two countries but also because there is no similar competence under the EU Treaties.[181] The CVM is therefore an example of mitigating the discord between external monitoring and conditionality and the internal absence thereof. The Commission draws up annual reports on the countries' accomplishments in light of benchmarks established prior to their accession, holds a dialogue on how progress can be achieved, and supports any positive measures through internal EU financing instruments and technical assistance.

Commission Decision of 13 December 2006 establishing a mechanism for cooperation and verification of progress in Bulgaria to address specific benchmarks in the areas of judicial reform and the fight against corruption and organised crime [2006] OJ L354/58

Article 1

Bulgaria shall, by 31 March of each year, and for the first time by 31 March 2007, **report to the Commission on the progress made** in addressing each of the benchmarks provided for in the Annex.

The Commission may, at any time, provide technical assistance through different activities or gather and exchange information on the benchmarks. In addition, the Commission may, at any time, organise expert missions to Bulgaria for this purpose. The Bulgarian authorities shall give the necessary support in this context.

ANNEX

Benchmarks to be addressed by Bulgaria, referred to in Article 1:

1. Adopt constitutional amendments removing any ambiguity regarding the **independence and accountability of the judicial system.**
2. Ensure a more transparent and efficient judicial process by adopting and implementing a new judicial system act and the new civil procedure code. Report on the impact of these new laws and of the penal and administrative procedure codes, notably on the pre-trial phase.
3. Continue the reform of the judiciary in order to enhance professionalism, accountability and efficiency. Evaluate the impact of this reform and publish the results annually.

---

[181] At the very least, the possibility of monitoring compliance with EU values post-accession has been disputed. See Ch 4.

4. Conduct and report on professional, non-partisan investigations into allegations of **high-level corruption**. Report on internal inspections of public institutions and on the publication of assets of high-level officials.
5. Take further measures to prevent and fight corruption, in particular at the borders and within local government.
6. Implement a strategy to fight organised crime, focussing on serious crime, money laundering as well as on the systematic confiscation of assets of criminals. Report on new and ongoing investigations, indictments and convictions in these areas.

The CVM explicitly links compliance with EU values, in particular the rule of law, with the fight against corruption and crime. This is an area which is likely to require further action from the EU, as deficiencies in the rule of law, democracy, and fundamental rights protection have been linked to corruption.[182] In the wake of liberal democratic backsliding in Poland and Hungary, and in light of persistent problems with institution-building in the Western Balkans, Vachudova has called for the CVM to become a regular feature of the enlargement policy. However, this would not represent a sufficient remedy in itself for the absence of an internal mechanism to evaluate existing Member States' compliance with Article 2 TEU values, as the CVM cannot be inserted retroactively into the accession treaties of, for example, Hungary and Poland.

MA Vachudova, 'Why Improve EU Rule of Law Oversight? The Two-Headed Problem of Defending Liberal Democracy and Fighting Corruption' in C Closa and D Kochenov (eds), *Reinforcing Rule of Law Oversight in the European Union* (Cambridge University Press 2016)

EU enlargement has been a remarkable tool for fostering domestic change which has included strengthening the Rule of Law and improving democratic institutions. Indeed, I have argued that enlargement has been the most successful democracy promotion policy ever implemented by an external actor (...)

(...) Aneta Spendzharova and I concluded that [the CVM] has been a controversial and modest but nevertheless successful instance of innovation by the EU as it has extended the EU's active leverage into the post-accession period. The Romanian and Bulgarian governments have both responded to specific demands in the CVM reports, strongly suggesting that in the absence of the CVM there would have been less reform. The detailed monitoring and assessment in the CVM reports, coupled with political pressure and concrete sanctions, can deliver substantial results. Given the huge problems besetting the Rule of Law, judicial quality and the fight against corruption in the Western Balkans states, the EU would do well to set up a CVM structure for each acceding state. This could always be dismantled rapidly if it were found to be unneeded. Some have observed a significant deterioration in the comportment of public officials in the areas of

---

[182] MA Vachudova, 'Why Improve EU Rule of Law Oversight? The Two-Headed Problem of Defending Liberal Democracy and Fighting Corruption' in C Closa and D Kochenov (eds), *Reinforcing Rule of Law Oversight in the European Union* (Cambridge University Press 2016).

accountability, transparency and combating corruption after their country joined the EU. A CVM structure would help deter backsliding.

EU pressure can be powerful when it is twinned with domestic incentives related to winning elections holding power. Civil society groups play an essential role in highlighting corruption and the need for judicial reform. The EU needs to rethink the civil society funding which is funnelled through government institutions, since this undermines the readiness of civil society groups to highlight corruption. EU leverage tied to the CVM process is also more effective in motivating governments if the EU threatens to withhold something that voters really want. The decision by some EU members in late 2010 and 2011 to block Romania's and Bulgaria's Schengen entry as a sanction for not meeting CVM benchmarks, did help trigger reform in both countries, since Schengen membership is valued by citizens.

Conditionality and material incentives do not comprise the only perspective on how and why EU transfers its rules and values to candidate countries. Constructivist theories would highlight how candidate countries become socialized in European discourses and models of behaviour—how they become 'Europeanized'.[183] The desire to join the foremost 'European club' can make actors—state officials and society at large—adapt their values and behaviour to correspond to their aspirations. In a typology developed by Schimmelfenig and Sedelmaier,[184] the materially incentivized conditionality of the EU is called the 'external incentives model' which is a process of rule transfer driven by the EU and resting on the 'logic of consequences' (a candidate country does something due to the positive or negative consequences attached to that behaviour). On the contrary, the constructivist approach is called the 'social learning model' which follows the 'logic of appropriateness' (a candidate country does something because it is the appropriate or 'right' behaviour) and under which the EU would argue for the normative legitimacy of its values and rules when 'pitching' them to the candidate countries. Where the process of rule transfer is driven by candidate countries, the model is 'lesson-drawing', as countries seek European solutions to domestic problems. Research has shown that the 'external incentives model' is the best explanatory framework of EU conditionality and rule transfers to the candidate countries.[185] However, a case study of LGBT rights promotion in Poland is just one example showing how both the external incentives model and arguments about legitimacy can also feed backlashes against EU human rights promotion,[186] in particular where this concerns politically sensitive topics.

[183] T Risse, 'Social Constructivism and European Integration' in A Wiener and T Diez (eds), *European Integration Theory* (Oxford University Press 2004).
[184] F Schimmelfennig and U Sedelmeier (eds), *The Europeanization of Central and Eastern Europe* (Cornell University Press 2005) 8–10.
[185] F Schimmelfennig and U Sedelmeier, 'Governance by Conditionality: EU Rule Transfer to the Candidate Countries of Central and Eastern Europe' (2004) 11 Journal of European Public Policy 661; F Schimmelfennig, 'EU Political Accession Conditionality after the 2004 Enlargement: Consistency and Effectiveness' (2008) 15 Journal of European Public Policy 918.
[186] Although the author argues that the backlash had an unintended positive effect on the activation of the LGBT rights community in Poland and ultimately yielded some gains. However, that assessment was made before the current conservative nationalist government started to undermine EU values, chiefly the rule of law but not only, in Poland. A major drawback for LGBT rights came with the institution of so-called LGBT-free zones in late 2019. Although both the European Parliament and the European Commission strongly condemned these declarations, the EU has not been able to counter effectively the government's anti-LGBT rhetoric, and the blatant discrimination and homophobia in Polish society. See European Parliament, 'Resolution on public discrimination and hate speech against LGBTI people, including LGBTI free zones', P9_TA(2019)0101, 18 December 2019.

C O'Dwyer, 'Does the EU Help or Hinder Gay-Rights Movements in Post-Communist Europe? The Case of Poland' (2012) 28 East European Politics 332

The year 1998 marked the moment that EU integration changed the political opportunity structure for gay-rights activists in Poland. (…) accession became a much more concrete policy process with specifically articulated rules, monitoring of progress, and admonitions about failures to reform, including failures regarding the LGBT minority. Building on earlier warnings, the European Parliament called on Poland to remove anti-gay provisions from its penal code in 2000. As the European Commission screened Polish law, it determined that the Polish Constitution's protections were neither explicit nor strong enough, and it mandated changes to the labour code specifically. Though the parliament strongly resisted adding sexual orientation as an anti-discrimination provision to the labour code, it bowed to the Commission's pressure in the end.

The EU's use of conditionality with regard to the Constitution and labour code fundamentally reshaped the framing of gay rights in Polish politics. In place of the narrative about personal failing, HIV/AIDS, and Christian charity, the issue now was framed as a question of national identity. Homosexuality mapped very easily onto a broader debate about Polish identity—national, religious, and as a part of Europe—that polarised the political spectrum in the early 2000s, a debate between the so-called Poland A and Poland B. Poland A was shorthand for the upwardly mobile, educated, usually urban Poles who took a more secular and cosmopolitan view of national identity. Poland B referred to the provincial, older, less-educated, churchgoing Poles who identified national identity with Catholicism. The EU became a mobilising tool for both sides. Gay-rights advocates claimed the legitimacy of EU norms; their political opponents from Poland B used the EU as a foil, painting it as a threat to traditional Polish values. As political discourse took on an increasingly nationalist tone, the EU's use of conditionality provoked defiant responses from Polish politicians on the right. (…)

Poland's entry into the EU on 1 May 2004 radically altered the political opportunity structure yet again, as the European Commission lost the legal leverage of conditionality. In interviews conducted in Warsaw in summer 2007, public officials noted that gay rights were now a domestic affair. Infractions against EU law could be brought before the courts, but as a post hoc and reactive approach, this constitutes weaker monitoring than during the accession phase. Public criticism of anti-gay policies, usually by the European Parliament, became the main, though not very effectual, source of leverage.

B. European Neighbourhood Policy (ENP)

The ENP was designed according to the enlargement policy template. However, it crucially misses the key incentive underlying candidate countries' domestic adaptation demanded by the EU, namely EU membership. Fundamentally, the EU's declarations concerning its objectives in the neighbourhood countries are not very different from those on enlargement and general foreign policy; the EU seeks to promote stability, democracy, the rule of law, and human rights. However, the geopolitical and security environment in which the ENP takes place is vastly different from the enlargement policy: from the near-failed state of Libya and war involving mass atrocities in Syria in the south to the ongoing conflict in Ukraine in the east, what promised to be a 'ring of friends' in 2003 looks more like a 'ring of fire' 17 years later.[187] The instability inevitably impacts the EU's ability to successfully promote human rights in the participating ENP countries and creates policy headaches for the EU, even though in theory the EU subscribes to the view that security and democracy are mutually reinforcing.[188]

M Nilsson and D Silander, 'Democracy and Security in the EU's Eastern Neighborhood? Assessing the ENP in Georgia, Moldova, and Ukraine' (2016) 12 Democracy and Security 44

The ENP stressed the importance of a democracy–security nexus. Indeed, the EU Commission argued that the ENP was about creating a 'ring of countries, sharing the EU's fundamental values and objectives . . .' and to promote 'milieu goals.' By building partnerships with neighboring states that included the promotion of democracy to each targeted state, neighboring Europe would become stable and prosperous, thus securing the EU's eastern and southern borders. (. . .)

First, one of the core objectives of the ENP was to promote democracy in the neighborhood. However, from the mid-2000s until today, Georgia, Moldova, and Ukraine have not seen democratic progress, and remaining partner states are authoritarian in nature. Although it may be argued that the neighboring states would be worse off democratically without EU democracy promotion, this study sets out very limited, if any, democratic improvements in these states. Second, in the three above-mentioned partner states, the EU's failure to promote democratization has not only led to unsolved security challenges in all three states, but it has also increased security challenges with Russia. While the EU has failed to address the frozen and hot conflicts with breakaway regions in partner states, the simultaneous push for ENP has also led to worsened security relations with Russia and the pro-Russian breakaway regions. In Moldova, there seems to be no immediate solution to the conflict between the breakaway region of Transnistria and the government of Moldova; indeed, Transnistria could very well be the next region to be annexed by Russia. In Georgia, after the war with Russia, South Ossetia and Abkhazia have become frozen conflicts and, recently, in 2014–2015, signed association agreements with Russia. The most recent conflict is Ukraine, where Crimea has already been annexed by Russia, and where the eastern part of the country is in a civil war with the government in Kiev. Due to Russia's support of eastern Ukraine, there is a strong possibility that these regions may ultimately become part of Russia. To conclude, the EU has failed to accomplish its Kantian vision of security through democracy in the neighborhoods surrounding it. While the

---

[187] H Haukkala, 'The EU's Regional Normative Hegemony Encounters Hard Realities: The Revised European Neighbourhood Policy and the Ring of Fire' in D Bouris and T Schumacher (eds), *The Revised European Neighbourhood Policy* (Palgrave Macmillan 2017).

[188] In the assessment of Börzel and van Hüllen, the goals of democracy and stability are frequently incompatible: 'it is the ENP's substantive inconsistency in seeking to promote effective and democratic governance that undermines the EU's external effectiveness. While the ENP conceives of the two objectives as complementary, the democratization of (semi-)authoritarian countries entails the risk of their destabilization at least in the short run. As a result, promoting effective and democratic governance become conflicting objectives. The lower the level of political liberalization and the higher the instability of a country, the more ineffective the EU is in asserting a democratic reform agenda in the ENP Action Plans, clearly favouring stability over change.' See TA Börzel and V van Hüllen, 'One Voice, One Message, but Conflicting Goals: Cohesiveness and Consistency in the European Neighbourhood Policy' (2014) 21 Journal of European Public Policy 1033.

eastern neighborhood has seen very limited democratic progress, the security situation is even worse today than before the ENP was launched. For that reason, one could also question the EU's ability to be a Kantian normative power in its neighborhood.

The geographical scope of the ENP is enormous. It comprises Algeria, Morocco, Egypt, Israel, Jordan, Lebanon, Libya, Palestine, Syria, Tunisia in the south, and Armenia, Azerbaijan, Belarus, Georgia, Moldova, and Ukraine in the east.[189] As the ENP is a relatively loose policy framework for the promotion of stability and EU values in the European neighbourhood,[190] the EU engages with the participating countries through various channels and with varying intensity. The EU maintains bilateral relations with all the partner countries which are typically based on a legal-contractual relationship in the form of an association agreement.[191] Regional engagements take place chiefly through the Eastern Partnership, which includes all the eastern neighbourhood countries, and the Union for the Mediterranean in the south, which has over time emerged as the EU's preferred forum in the Mediterranean region,[192] supplanting the Barcelona Process.

The ENP is a policy in flux. After its unveiling in 2003/4, the Commission suggested strengthening it in 2006, and revising it in response to the Arab Spring to offer more incentives in 2011, and revising it again in 2015 in response to perceived failures and developments on the ground to make it more flexible and partnership-like. The differences between the various versions of the policy, however, tend to be overemphasized. For example, differentiation—the practice of having regard to countries' individual situation rather than imposing a uniform blueprint—has been, at least in theory, part of the ENP from the beginning and it was underlined already in the first reevaluation of the policy in 2006, despite it being heralded as one of the hallmarks of the latest 2015 revision. In any case, the Commission policy papers also inadvertently reveal the progressive erosion of optimism regarding what can be achieved under the ENP.

European Commission, European Neighbourhood Policy Strategy paper, COM(2004) 373 final, Brussels, 12 May 2004

The objective of the ENP is to share the benefits of the EU's 2004 enlargement with neighbouring countries in strengthening stability, security and well-being for all concerned.

---

[189] Although geographically the countries of the Western Balkans are also in the EU's neighbourhood, they are part of the enlargement policy and not the ENP. Russia does not participate in the ENP; its framework with the EU is instead based on so-called common spaces, a relatively unambitious forum for dialogue and cooperation. However, due to the dire state of international relations, little cooperation in fact takes place between the two.

[190] S Lavenex, 'A Governance Perspective on the European Neighbourhood Policy: Integration beyond Conditionality?' (2008) 15 Journal of European Public Policy 938, 939.

[191] With the exception of Belarus, Armenia, Azerbaijan, Libya, and Syria, all ENP partner countries have signed a more or less deep association agreement with the EU at some stage in the past 20 years. The other countries have signed a less ambitious partnership/cooperation agreement with the EU, although in the case of Armenia this has been updated and enhanced in 2017, coming closer to an association agreement. The deepest and most comprehensive agreement is in place between the EU and Ukraine. The obsolete cooperation agreement with Syria, dating back to 1977, is partially suspended due to the ongoing war and associated infringements of international law and human rights perpetrated by the Syrian government.

[192] European Commission and High Representative of the Union for Foreign Affairs and Security Policy, 'Review of the European Neighbourhood Policy', JOIN(2015) 50 final, Brussels, 18 November 2015.

It is designed to **prevent the emergence of new dividing lines** between the enlarged EU and its neighbours and to offer them the chance to **participate in various EU activities**, through **greater political, security, economic and cultural co-operation.**

The **method** proposed is, together with partner countries, to **define a set of priorities, whose fulfilment will bring them closer to the European Union.** These priorities will be incorporated in jointly agreed Action Plans, covering a number of key areas for specific action: **political dialogue and reform**; trade and measures preparing partners for gradually obtaining a stake in the EU's Internal Market; justice and home affairs; energy, transport, information society, environment and research and innovation; and social policy and people-to-people contacts.

The **privileged relationship with neighbours will build on mutual commitment to common values principally within the fields of the rule of law, good governance, the respect for human rights, including minority rights, the promotion of good neighbourly relations, and the principles of market economy and sustainable development.** Commitments will also be sought to certain essential aspects of the EU's external action, including, in particular, the fight against terrorism and the proliferation of weapons of mass destruction, as well as abidance by international law and efforts to achieve conflict resolution.

The **Action Plans will draw on a common set of principles but will be differentiated, reflecting the existing state of relations with each country,** its needs and capacities, as well as common interests. The level of ambition of the EU's relationships with its neighbours will take into account the extent to which these values are effectively shared.

European Commission, Strengthening the European neighbourhood policy, COM(2006) 726 final, Brussels, 4 December 2006

Development and reform in our partner countries is primarily in their own interest, and it is their sovereign responsibility. But it is also in the interest of the EU to support partners in these efforts. (…) **The more progress a partner country makes in implementing reforms, the deeper the relationship can become, and the more support the EU should provide.**

Thus far, the **ENP has been largely bilateral**, between the EU and each partner country. **This is essential due to the large differences between partners in terms of their political and economic situations, needs and aspirations. Such differentiation needs to remain at the heart of the policy.**

Nevertheless, there are a number of **cross-cutting themes where the EU and its ENP partners, both South and East, share common interests** and concerns and which could usefully be addressed in a multilateral context. In areas such as energy, transport, the environment, rural development, information society, research cooperation, public health, financial services, border management, migration or maritime affairs, problems are often not merely bilateral in nature and could benefit from common debate, action and cooperation between the EU and all or most ENP partners. These areas are important for durable growth, prosperity, stability and security. (…)

To support our neighbours in pursuing demanding and costly reform agendas, **we must be able to present a more attractive offer on our side.** We can do more in relation to economic and commercial issues, to visa-facilitation and migration management to people-to-people contacts and contacts among administrators and regulators. More on political cooperation and regional cooperation, and more on financial cooperation.

European Commission and High Representative of the Union for Foreign Affairs and Security Policy, A new response to a changing Neighbourhood, COM(2011) 303 final, Brussels, 25 May 2011

The overthrow of long-standing repressive regimes in Egypt and Tunisia; the ongoing military conflict in Libya, the recent violent crackdown in Syria, continued repression in Belarus and the lingering protracted conflicts in the region, including in the Middle East, require us to look afresh at the EU's relationship with our neighbours.

A new approach is needed to strengthen the partnership between the EU and the countries and societies of the neighbourhood: to build and consolidate healthy democracies, pursue sustainable economic growth and manage cross-border links.

The new approach (...) aims to:

(1) **provide greater support to partners engaged in building deep democracy**—the kind that lasts because the right to vote is accompanied by rights to exercise free speech, form competing political parties, receive impartial justice from independent judges, security from accountable police and army forces, access to a competent and non-corrupt civil service—and other civil and human rights that many Europeans take for granted, such as the freedom of thought, conscience and religion;

(2) **support inclusive economic development**—so that EU neighbours can trade, invest and grow in a sustainable way, reducing social and regional inequalities, creating jobs for their workers and higher standards of living for their people;

(3) **strengthen the two regional dimensions of the European Neighbourhood Policy**, covering respectively the Eastern Partnership and the Southern Mediterranean, so that we can work out consistent regional initiatives in areas such as trade, energy, transport or migration and mobility complementing and strengthening our bilateral co-operation;

The partnership will develop with each neighbour on the basis of its needs, capacities and reform objectives. Some partners may want to move further in their integration effort, which will entail a greater degree of alignment with EU policies and rules leading progressively to economic integration in the EU Internal Market. The EU does not seek to impose a model or a ready-made recipe for political reform, but **it will insist that each partner country's reform process reflect a clear commitment to universal values that form the basis of our renewed approach.** (...)

The EU will uphold its policy of curtailing relations with governments engaged in violations of human rights and democracy standards, including by making use of targeted sanctions and other policy measures. **Where it takes such measures, it will not only uphold but strengthen further its support to civil society.** In applying this more differentiated approach, the EU will keep channels of dialogue open with governments, civil society and other stakeholders. (...)

A functioning democracy, respect for human rights and the rule of law are fundamental pillars of the EU partnership with its neighbours. There is no set model or a
ready-made recipe for political reform. While reforms take place differently from one
country to another, several elements are common to **building deep and sustainable democracy** and require a strong and lasting commitment on the part of governments. They
include:

- free and fair elections;
- freedom of association, expression and assembly and a free press and media;
- the rule of law administered by an independent judiciary and right to a fair trial;
- fighting against corruption;
- security and law enforcement sector reform (including the police) and the establishment of democratic control over armed and security forces.

Reform based on these elements will not only strengthen democracy but help to create
the conditions for sustainable and inclusive economic growth, stimulating trade and investment. They are the main benchmarks against which the EU will assess progress and
adapt levels of support.
(...)
While ENP Action Plans remain the framework for our general cooperation, **the EU
will suggest to partners that they focus on a limited number of short and medium-term
priorities, incorporating more precise benchmarks and a clearer sequencing of actions.**
The EU will adapt the priorities for its financial assistance accordingly. (...)

European Commission and High Representative of the Union for Foreign Affairs and Security Policy, Review of the European Neighbourhood Policy, JOIN(2015) 50 final, Brussels, 18 November 2015

(...) conflict, rising extremism and terrorism, human rights violations and other challenges to international law, and economic upheaval have resulted in major refugee flows.
These have left their marks across North Africa and the Middle East, with the aftermath
of the Arab Uprisings and the rise of ISIL/Da'esh. In the East, an increasingly assertive
Russian foreign policy has resulted in the violation of Ukrainian sovereignty, independence and territorial integrity. Protracted conflicts continue to hamper development in the
region.

In the meantime, the EU's own interdependence with its neighbours has been placed
in sharp focus. **Growing numbers of refugees are arriving at the European Union's borders** hoping to find a safer future. Energy crises have underlined the EU's need to work
with neighbours on energy security, including diversification of energy sources, routes
and suppliers. There have been acts of terror affecting the EU and the neighbourhood,
most recently the heinous terrorist attacks in Paris on 13th November.

**Differentiation and greater mutual ownership will be the hallmark of the new ENP,
recognising that not all partners aspire to EU rules and standards,** and reflecting the
wishes of each country concerning the nature and focus of its partnership with the EU.

The EU cannot alone solve the many challenges of the region, and there are limits to its leverage, but the new ENP will play its part in helping to create the conditions for positive development.

The public consultation has demonstrated that while the offer of a closer relationship with the EU for those countries which have undertaken governance reforms has encouraged change in some countries, **current practice and policy has been regarded by other partners as too prescriptive, and as not sufficiently reflecting their respective aspirations.** The consultation has further indicated that ownership by both partners and EU Member States needs to be stepped up; that cooperation should be given a tighter, more relevant focus; and that greater flexibility must be sought to enable the EU and its partners to respond to ever changing needs and circumstances.

More effective ways will be sought to promote democratic, accountable and good governance, as well as to promote justice reform, **where there is a shared commitment to the rule of law, and fundamental rights.** Open markets and growth, inclusive economic development, and in particular the prospects for youth, is highlighted as a key to stabilising societies in the neighbourhood. There will be greater attention to the energy security and climate action both of the EU and of the partners themselves.

There will be a new focus on stepping up work with our partners on security sector reform, conflict prevention, counter-terrorism and anti-radicalisation policies, in full compliance with international human rights law. More than ever after the November 13th terrorist attacks in Paris, intensified cooperation with our neighbours is needed in these areas. Safe and legal mobility and tackling irregular migration, human trafficking and smuggling are also priorities.

The new ENP will seek to deploy the available instruments and resources in a more coherent and flexible manner. Additionally, it will be important to seek a **deeper involvement of EU Member States** in re-energising work with our neighbours. Equally, the aim will be a deeper engagement with civil society and social partners.

On a regional level, the Eastern Partnership will be further strengthened in line with commitments at the Riga Summit in 2015. The Union for the Mediterranean can play an enhanced role in supporting cooperation between southern neighbours. The new ENP will now seek to involve other regional actors, beyond the neighbourhood, where appropriate, in addressing regional challenges.

Importantly, the latest ENP review subtly questions the premise that the policy is based on the shared commitment to EU values. However, the anchoring of the neighbourhood cooperation in EU values is not merely a policy choice subject of a given EU administration; rather it is constitutionally fixed by Article 8 TEU, similarly to how Article 2 TEU determines the value-foundation of the EU and Article 21 TEU lists general foreign policy principles of the EU.

Consolidated version of the Treaty on European Union [2012] OJ C326/13

Article 8

1. The Union shall develop **a special relationship with neighbouring countries,** aiming to establish an area of prosperity and good neighbourliness, **founded on**

the values of the Union and characterised by close and peaceful relations based on cooperation.

2. For the purposes of paragraph 1, the Union may conclude specific agreements with the countries concerned. These agreements may contain reciprocal rights and obligations as well as the possibility of undertaking activities jointly. Their implementation shall be the subject of periodic consultation.

The ENP is translated into more operational steps through the adoption of bilateral action plans (APs), association agendas, and, more recently (and replacing APs), partnership priorities. These documents set out reform priorities for a period between three to five years and they are more or less tailored to the needs and capacities of the partner countries. At the same time, regional policy choices, such as the four priorities adopted at the 2015 Eastern Partnership summit in Riga[193] and the five objectives 'beyond 2020' set out in the new Eastern Partnership framework,[194] should instil a degree of regional coherence into the bilateral relations. In any case, following the adoption of the 2015 ENP review, the newly adopted partnership priorities with a number of ENP countries, agreed together rather than imposed by the EU as was the case with some APs in the past, exhibit a lower level of ambition for reform, reflecting the fact that EU is coming to grips with the limitations of the reform potential of the ENP, as well as renewed emphasis on stability, security, and related issues such as migration.

Partnership Priorities between the European Union and Armenia, 21 February 2018

The Partnership Priorities seek to strengthen the relationship between the EU and Armenia and pursue the promotion of universal values and stability, resilience, security and prosperity built on democracy, human rights, rule of law and sustainable economic growth and openness. They are in line with the priorities set out by the Republic of Armenia and the EU, including those set out in the European Neighbourhood Policy (ENP) Review. The Partnership Priorities follow the principles of co-ownership and differentiation and stem from the four priorities jointly agreed at the 2015 Eastern Partnership (EaP) Riga Summit, which were confirmed by both sides at the EU–Eastern Partnership Foreign Affairs Ministerial Meeting in May 2016 as the guiding framework for future work. Finally, the Partnership Priorities are also in accordance with the 2030 Sustainable Development Goals and the 2015 Paris Agreement on climate change and their commitment to issues of economic, environmental and social sustainability and climate change.

---

[193] The summit established four broad priority areas for cooperation under the ENP: strengthening institutions and good governance; enhancing mobility and contacts between people; developing market opportunities; and strengthening energy security and improving energy and transport interconnections.

[194] Resilient, sustainable, and integrated economies; accountable institutions, the rule of law and security; environmental and climate resilience; resilient digital transformation; and resilient, fair, and inclusive societies. See European Commission and High Representative of the Union for Foreign Affairs and Security Policy, 'Joint Communication to the European Parliament, the European Council, the Council, the European Economic and Social Committee and the Committee of the Regions, Eastern Partnership policy beyond 2020, Reinforcing Resilience—An Eastern Partnership that delivers for all', JOIN(2020) 7 final, Brussels, 18 March 2020.

The EU and Armenia share common interests and values, notably in view of Armenia's engagement in economic and political reforms as well as regional cooperation, including in the framework of the Eastern Partnership. The new comprehensive agreement will renew and shape the legal basis for bilateral relations and the momentum should be seized to reinforce EU–Armenia relations, also through agreeing Partnership Priorities. This new overarching framework and the priority areas of cooperation will build on the mutual interest in enhancing our engagement taking into account EU's and Armenia's other international commitments.

The Partnership Priorities build on past fruitful cooperation including in the context of the implementation of the ENP Action Plan, which they will replace. These Partnership Priorities should shape the agenda for regular political dialogue meetings and sectoral dialogues as defined in the new Agreement, which will also be the framework for implementation and monitoring of the Priorities.

The future EU–Armenia financial cooperation and programming, notably the next Single Support Framework for Armenia for 2017–2020, will be based on these Partnership Priorities.

The case of Armenia illustrates the partial reconfiguration of the ENP. The partnership priorities adopted in 2018 run to barely 11 pages and contain few concrete points which could be directly implemented and monitored. In other words, the document sets out in vague terms the general orientation of EU–Armenian relations, in addition to reflecting certain mainstreaming priorities of current EU foreign policy agenda such as combating climate change and implementing the UN sustainable development goals. By contrast, the previous EU–Armenia AP, adopted in 2006 and extended in 2011, was 40 pages long and contained countless action points which were predominantly aimed at improving the governance and economic situation in Armenia, including human rights protection. However, as observed by the Commission in a regular country report in 2014, Armenia 'made limited progress in implementing the ENP Action Plan'. It must be also noted that the entire EU–Armenia relationship required reconsideration following Armenia's last minute decision to pull out of signing an association agreement with the EU in 2013 and instead join the Eurasian Economic Union. The country recently signed with the EU a 'Comprehensive and Enhanced Partnership Agreement' instead of the association agreement.[195]

In the absence of a membership perspective, providing financial support to ENP countries is of even higher importance from the perspective of conditionality than in the case of the pre-accession process. As a result, the concrete financing instruments also offer some room for expressing more concrete demands in relation to domestic reforms supported by EU money. To continue with the example of Armenia, the EU committed EUR 12 million in 2014 under the ENI instrument to support human rights protection in the country. The action specified a number of objectives concerning domestic adjustments which should lead to improved human rights protection. Although such actions cannot guarantee results on the ground, the fact that EU financing entails various safeguard procedures (reporting, evaluation, audits) ensures at least a certain degree of concreteness in the realization of the otherwise vague goal of enhancing human rights.

---

[195] Comprehensive and enhanced Partnership Agreement between the European Union and the European Atomic Energy Community and their Member States, of the one part, and the Republic of Armenia, of the other part [2018] OJ L23/4.

ANNEX 2 of the Commission Implementing Decision on the Annual Action Programme 2014 in favour of Armenia to be financed from the general budget of the European Union

---

Action Document for Support to Human Rights Protection
in Armenia

3.2. Expected results

1. **Improved protection of human rights through enacting and implementing relevant legislation** in the areas of right to free and fair elections, torture prevention, antidiscrimination (including minorities, people with disabilities and other vulnerable groups) and gender equality and child protection:
   i. Enhanced electoral system in line with CoE and OSCE Office for Democratic Institutions and Human Rights (ODIHR) recommendations;
   ii. Progress in torture prevention through legal, investigative and enforcement reforms;
   iii. Greater protection of persons belonging to minorities, people with disabilities and other vulnerable groups against discrimination;
   iv. Effective gender equality mechanisms and protection of victims of domestic/gender-based violence and abuse;
   v. Improved child protection system including deinstitutionalisation of children;
2. **Enhanced coordination and cooperation in the area of human rights and increased capacity** of relevant stakeholders:
   i. Effective coordination role and capacity of the Ministry of Justice for the implementation and annual revision of the Human Rights Action Plan and international human rights commitments;
   ii. Effective monitoring mechanisms and monitoring capacity of the Interagency Commission for the implementation of the provisions of the Human Rights Action Plan. (…)

It can be said more generally that the amounts committed by the EU to an ENP country are an indication of the level of ambition and perceived importance by the EU of the bilateral relationship. Countries displaying the highest appetite for European integration—at least in the form of being part of EU external governance[196]—typically receive the most EU funding. This is also consonant with the 'more for more' approach expounded in a number of the ENP policy documents, notably the 2011 post-Arab Spring review. However, as with enlargement policy, the relationship between financial aid and commitment to EU values and integration is not linear, as numerous politically contingent strategic considerations influence the EU's decision on when, where, and how much to provide in financial support. Moreover, the ENI financing instrument is not specific to supporting the promotion of human rights or EU values more generally; its remit is geographically limited, but essentially any action contributing to one of the EU's ENP objectives, which should be complementary to overarching external action objectives and principles, is eligible under the instrument. Typical actions

---

[196] S Lavenex and F Schimmelfenig, 'EU Democracy Promotion in the Neighbourhood: From Leverage to Governance?' (2011) 18 Democratization 885.

supported under ENI as part of the annual action programme financing relate to building up the capacity of state institutions, improving the rule of law/justice sector reform, support for democratic reforms including improvements in the media and with regard to freedom of speech, human rights initiatives relating to particular groups (such as women's rights), and anti-corruption. The grants awarded by the EU are often managed by international organizations (such as UN agencies), large international NGOs and development agencies of EU Member States. Although some EU institutions and Member States consider the bilateral and regional support under ENI to be of a different nature and higher strategic importance than other external action financing, as of 2021 it will as be included under the overarching financial instrument for external action (NDICI).[197]

Table 9.3 Available funding for 2016 annual action programmes per country under ENI, in million EUR[198]

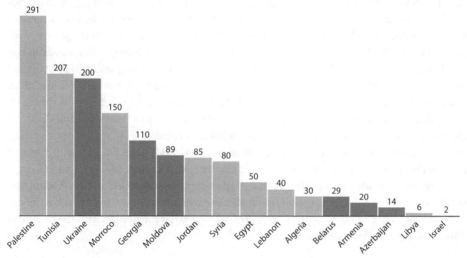

Controlling for the regular contribution to Palestine, Table 9.3 reveals that the five most rewarded countries in 2016 were those which expressed a desire to integrate and cooperate closely with the EU. In the case of Tunisia and Ukraine, the EU is still trying to maintain the momentum generated by recent revolutions which set these countries on a liberal-democratic path, something that had already happened—but continues to be monitored and rewarded by the EU—in Georgia in 2003. Similarly, Moldova, despite facing widespread poverty and numerous other challenges including a frozen conflict, is a democracy having

[197] European Council, 'Special meeting—Conclusions', Brussels, 21 July 2020, para 120.
[198] In the case of Palestine, the ENI contribution includes essential support for the functioning of the Palestinian (quasi-)state and the provision of essential services to the amount of EUR 252 million, awarded to the Palestinian Authority and the UN Relief and Works Agency (UNRWA) for Palestine refugees. The funding for Ukraine in 2016 was carried out by three special measures directed towards fighting corruption, improving the rule of law and comprehensive reform of public administration. The EUR 80 million provided as a special measure to Syria was devoted to helping the Syrian population cope with the crisis; it does not involve the Syrian government with which the EU suspended cooperation in 2011 and which remains under EU sanctions.

declared its desire to implement the necessary reforms which would bring it closer to the EU despite Russian pressure aiming to dissuade the country from pursuing such a course.[199] The relatively high level of funding for Morocco is less related to the democratic situation in the country, given that Morocco—despite recent reforms—is not a full democracy and it significantly curtails certain civil and political rights which could undermine the ruling monarchy.[200] It is more generally the case in the southern dimension of the ENP that in recent years the number one priority of the EU in the region has become migration, more specifically decreasing migration flows to Europe and 'addressing root causes of irregular migration'.[201] Even if indirectly and only in part, EU funding for Mediterranean ENP countries should be seen in light of the efforts to stem migratory pressures and refugee flows from Africa and the Middle East.[202]

In addition to funds, there is only a handful of material 'carrots' the EU is able to offer as part of ENP conditionality to its partner countries. An important one is market access and, more generally, trade integration. All of the association agreements signed between the EU and ENP countries have a trade liberalization component. As a result, ENP countries are able to benefit from reduced or zero tariffs when exporting to the EU. The attractiveness of this 'carrot' is, however, diminished in many cases as the ENP countries are, with the exception of Israel, developing and do not typically produce high-value goods in demand within the EU, in addition to having to face more advanced competition within the EU single market. Moreover, some ENP countries are already eligible for the EU's Generalised Scheme of Preferences+ (GSP(+)) scheme which might reduce their incentive to abide by EU conditions simply in order to sign a trade agreement with the EU that would produce few additional benefits.[203] As a result, the EU has decided in some cases to waive conditionality for granting market access in certain aspects of trade in goods—the DCFTA with Ukraine is one such example. The DCFTAs signed bilaterally with Ukraine, Moldova, and Georgia represent the most advanced trade agreements in existence between EU and ENP countries. Nevertheless, these agreements are more innovative when it comes to technical barriers to trade and sanitary and phytosanitary measures, where partial integration with the EU single market takes place, facilitating trade.

---

[199] Moldova, along with Ukraine and Georgia, signed an association agreement with the EU in 2014. Russia applied a range of coercive measures, from trade restrictions (such as on Moldovan wine) to military invasion in Ukraine, against all three countries for seeking integration with the EU which represents a challenge to its traditional hegemony in the region.

[200] Moreover, Morocco violates international law by infringing on the territorial integrity of Western Sahara, an issue which has affected international agreements concluded with the EU. See Judgment of 21 December 2016, *Council of the European Union v Front populaire pour la libération de la saguia-el-hamra et du rio de oro (Front Polisario)*, C-104/16 P, ECLI:EU:C:2016:973.

[201] European Commission and High Representative of the Union for Foreign Affairs and Security Policy, ''Review of the European Neighbourhood Policy, JOIN(2015) 50 final, Brussels, 18 November 2015, 15. See Ch 8.

[202] The ENI is, of course, not the primary source of migration-related funding. The EU has set up trust funds and refugee compacts which dispense billions of euros to African and Middle Eastern countries either affected by migratory and refugee flows (such as Jordan in connection to the Syrian War), act as transit countries en route to Europe (such as Libya) or are source countries for either migrants or refugees (such as Eritrea or Syria for refugees and Nigeria or Senegal for migrants).

[203] See Ch 10.

> ## G Van der Loo, *The EU-Ukraine Association Agreement and Deep and Comprehensive Free Trade Area: A New Legal Instrument for EU Integration without Membership* (Brill Nijhoff 2016)
>
> The first two DCFTA chapters (i.e. Market Access for Goods and Trade Remedies) establish the 'traditional' part of the DCFTA liberalisation, i.e. market access for trade in goods. This section is not innovative compared to other FTAs concluded by the EU, neither does it contain elements of an EU integration agreement. Market access conditionality is absent in these chapters since the liberalisation will be granted to Ukraine irrespective of its approximation to EU *acquis*. (…) Nevertheless, the scope of this liberalisation is exceptionally 'comprehensive' as most products are covered by the DCFTA. (…) Notable exceptions to the liberalisation are, on the part of the EU, the number of [tariff rate quotas] which will still be applied on several important Ukrainian agricultural export products and, on the part of Ukraine, the specific arrangements in the car sector. (…) The Moldova and Georgia DCFTAs are largely comparable to the Ukraine DCFTA; however, they include a 'negative list' for tariff reduction and less exceptions (sic) or sector-specific transitional mechanisms. In sum, these two DCFTA chapters significantly liberalise EU–Ukrainian trade relations; however, they do not lead to Ukraine's integration into (sections of) the EU Internal Market on the basis of legislative approximation and market access conditionality.

Other EU international agreements with the ENP countries can provide further sought-after rewards provided that conditions are met. The EU can make travelling easier by signing a visa facilitation agreement with an ENP country which the domestic population in the partner country and therefore also the governments want.[204] Similarly, transport connections can be significantly enhanced through the conclusion of aviation agreements which provide for liberalization of air transport services and harmonization of relevant legislation.[205] In terms of process, the EU attempts to support public sector capacity in partner countries through so-called twinning whereby civil servants from EU Member States are seconded to beneficiary administrations. Twinning, as much of the ENP, has origins in the enlargement policy, but its effectiveness is questioned in the ENP context.[206]

Overall, however, the menu of material incentives in the ENP is rather short and not sufficiently enticing for many partners to confer significant leverage on the EU. Above and beyond the lack of membership perspective, the EU has been accused of using the alternative incentives of the ENP in an inconsistent manner due to competing foreign policy objectives. Although this is in particular the case for the promotion of democracy, the close relationship between democracy, human rights, and the rule of law means that when stability and security in the neighbourhood was identified as a prevailing objective, the EU found it difficult to promote any of these values. Börzel and Lebanidze find that the probability that the

---

[204] See, for example, Agreement between the European Union and the Republic of Azerbaijan on the facilitation of the issuance of visas [2014] OJ L128/49.

[205] See, for example, Common Aviation Area Agreement between the European Union and its Member States, of the one part, and Georgia, of the other part [2012] OJ L321/1; Euro-Mediterranean Aviation Agreement between the European Union and its Member States, of the one part and the government of the State of Israel, of the other part [2013] OJ L208/3.

[206] S Roch, 'Between Arbitrary Outcomes and Impeded Process: The Performance of EU Twinning Projects in the EU's Eastern neighbourhood' (2017) 33 East European Politics 72.

EU will pursue democratic (and presumably human rights, although see the contribution of Kahn-Nisser below) conditionality is higher 'if it does not have to choose between democratisation and stability and if it can empower pro-democratic reform coalitions'.

T Börzel and B Lebanidze, ' "The Transformative Power of Europe" Beyond Enlargement: The EU's Performance in Promoting Democracy in its Neighbourhood' (2017) 33 East European Politics 17

In Morocco (…) the main priorities of the EU have been 'migration, anti-terrorism co-operation, regional conflicts [and] trade'. In order not to endanger the stability of the incumbent regime, the EU democracy promotion agenda and the ENP Action Plan for Morocco were rather modelled on 'careful liberalization' and on 'selective political reforms in carefully chosen areas'. As a manifestation of EU's stability-driven agenda, the EU's ambassador to Morocco conceded that the EU did not negotiate in the area of human rights since it was 'a sovereign issue dealt with by the Moroccan government'. In light of Arab Spring unrests Morocco was considered as an 'oasis of stability'.

(…)

Overall, we can identify three groups of states in the European neighbourhood, which differ from each other both in terms of consistency and effectiveness of EU democratic conditionality (…) The biggest group is comprised of all Southern neighbours, with the exception of Tunisia, and of Azerbaijan and Armenia in the East. In these countries, domestic conditions for consistency and effectiveness of EU democratic conditionality have been unfavourable. The EU faces a democratisation-stability dilemma. In the southern neighbourhood, migration control and terrorism have been the main concerns of the EU. In Azerbaijan, energy interests had utmost priority, and in Armenia the freezing of the Nagorny–Karabakh conflict and restoring diplomatic relations with neighbouring Turkey. Thus, it is not surprising that EU has never invoked democratic conditionality in the first place. But even if it had, the absence of pro-democratic reform coalitions would have rendered democratic conditionality ineffective.

The second group identified in the paper consists only of Belarus, where the EU applied democratic conditionality but not consistently. To be fair, the case of Europe's last dictatorship is overdetermined given the role of Russia in boosting Lukashenko's regime (…).

The third group is formed by Georgia, Moldova, Tunisia, and Ukraine, the four ENP countries where the EU applied democratic conditionality consistently and effectively. They have been sufficiently stable and featured pro-democratic reform coalitions the EU could empower.

(…)

Finally, much of the EU's democratic conditionality in the ENP states has been ex post in nature. Unlike punitive ex ante conditionality, ex-post conditionality draws on the provision or withdrawal of support as a reaction to (non-)compliance with democratic norms. In contrast to its clearly defined enlargement criteria, the EU's neighbourhood conditionality has often been vague and ill-defined. Hence, it is more difficult to isolate its causal effect.

A further important aspect of conditionality which was witnessed in the context of EU relations with Ukraine is that even if material incentives in exchange for enhancing human rights protection or achieving other value-laden objectives are only offered to the government representatives of a given country, the conditionality may function as a tool for societal mobilization. Domestic interest groups and civil society may exert pressure on governments on the basis of EU demands for reform when such actors can perceive the EU's policy towards their country (ie when the policy is conducted in the open). If the EU were to apply conditionality concerning the signing of an association agreement (for example) in secret,[207] the relevant domestic societal actors and networks would lack a credible international reference point—which in a number of societies is positively amplified by the normative attraction of 'Europe'—around which they can mobilize.

O Burlyuk and N Shapovalova, ' "Veni, Vidi, … Vici?" EU Performance and Two Faces of Conditionality towards Ukraine' (2017) 33 East European Politics 36

Perdidi or vici? At first sight, it is perdidi: the EU did not manage to get Yanukovych to fulfil its conditions and, in fact, the latter decided to withdraw his consent to sign the AA with the EU, giving preference to Russia's offer. However, paradoxically, the EU has achieved its objectives eventually: it has signed the AA with Ukraine and ensured that the country does not fall into authoritarianism. Moreover, the EU managed to save its face by not signing an agreement with 'a dictator', proving itself a consistent normative actor. Geopolitically, the Union succeeded in locking Ukraine away from choice in favour of Russia. In fact, it is vici, though it is difficult to put the merit on the EU. As an interviewed EU official put it, 'the EU overestimated its attractiveness to the Ukrainian government and underestimated its attractiveness to the people'. Although the decision of Yanukovych not to sign the AA and Euromaidan protests were a total surprise for the EU, sometimes what looks as unpredictability is simply the result of a failure to see the wider picture. It has been the main objective of this article to show this 'wider picture', in which conditionality may work according to a different logic. While the EU conditionality failed in bargaining with the Yanukovych regime, it has succeeded in mobilising and empowering domestic players—the society at large, opposition and civic groups—against the veto players.

Seeing the lack of membership perspective as a critical component of any leverage in the neighbourhood, some authors have suggested that external governance may pose a more successful model of EU values promotion than conditionality. External governance 'refers to institutionalized relationships with non-member (and non-candidate) countries such as the ENP countries, in which the partner countries commit themselves to approximate their domestic policies and legislation to the EU *acquis*'.[208] The institutionalization of relations typically takes the form of association and other EU international agreements which create the formal links and basis for cooperation between the EU and a third country and facilitate

---

[207] It is worth recalling that some of the dedicated human rights instruments, notably human rights dialogues, are conducted behind closed doors.

[208] S Lavenex and F Schimmelfenig, 'EU Democracy Promotion in the Neighbourhood' (n 196) 896.

rule transfer. As the argument goes, because principles conducive to liberal democratic governance—accountability, participation, and transparency—are embedded in EU legislation which is transposed to domestic legal orders of partner countries, democratic governance is able to spread in other systems.[209] However, such accommodation of the EU acquis—even if successful on a large scale—is not in itself sufficient to bring about liberal democratic change; deep political reforms and societal internalization of liberal-democratic values are necessary to make transitions sustainable. In the enlargement policy, the Copenhagen criteria were originally charged with ensuring that EU values are part and parcel of the transition package, not merely the transposition of the EU acquis. Even then, the current democratic and rule of law backsliding in some Member States has revealed the insufficiency of the implementation of the Copenhagen criteria. The limits of the external governance model must therefore also be seen in this light.

Finally, it is necessary to question the relationship between human rights promotion and democratization, both of which constitute objectives of EU external action and the ENP in particular. Although most scholarship, included that presented above, focuses on the role of the EU in democratization of the neighbourhood and views human rights (if at all) as merely implicated in this process, the research of Sara Kahn-Nisser shows that this orthodoxy may not in fact stand up to empirical scrutiny. Kahn-Nisser argues that the effectiveness of human rights and democracy promotion (called 'liberalization' and democratization respectively in the article) rests on different variables; they are 'similar but separate processes' and accordingly may require separate instruments to be achieved. The author finds that 'the most effective human rights promotion instrument is economic pressure whereas democratization is more influenced by emulation processes than by economic pressure'.

S Kahn-Nisser, 'Linkage Leverage Democratization and Liberalization: Is Promoting Democracy the Same as Promoting Human Rights?' (2018) 39 Policy Studies 90

Interestingly, leverage seems to be most important in combination with the EU policy model—as the interaction between the EU's human rights policy model and trade dependence is significant within the general study population. However, the interaction between trade leverage and the EU policy model does not have a significant impact on democratization processes. This may be attributable to the EU's more impressive record as an institution in the area of human rights as compared with its infamous democratic deficit. The EU's human rights record possibly increases the legitimacy of its demand that partners liberalize their human rights regime. The democratic deficit may undermine its ability to demand democratization. (. . .)

Financial leverage in the form of aid levels is significantly associated with subsequent liberalization only among non-democracies. This may be because the effectiveness of financial leverage depends upon the issue which triggered the sanctions being more important to the sender than to the receiver. This condition is not fulfilled in the case of democratization because regime survival is at stake. This is the reason why changes in financial assistance are not associated with democratization. Among democracies, liberalization is more likely to lead to a change of governments than among non-democracies.

---

[209] Ibid.

This is why non-democracies are more inclined to react positively to reductions in aid and liberalize their human rights policies; the level of threat to regime survival is lower. (...)

(...) democratization and human rights promotion are two distinct policy goals. From a theoretical point of view, the achievement of one of the goals does not necessarily contribute, and is not necessarily associated with the achievement of the other. From an empirical point of view (...) each of the goals requires different types of instruments. Both promotion of democratization and promotion of liberalization are served by a positive example on the part of the EU. A positive EU model increases the legitimacy of EU pressure, sends a message regarding the importance the EU attributes to democracy and human rights, and increases the reputational utility of democratizing and liberalizing. However, economic pressure is effective only in promoting human rights and not in promoting democracy. The difference between the two policy goals provides further support to the well-established claim that the instruments of international pressure should be tailor-fitted to the specific goal, to the power relations between sender and receiver, and to the balance between reputational and material costs and benefits calculations of the target country. (...)

9.6 Normative Power Europe? External Perceptions of the EU

The mantra about the EU exuding a normative appeal through its principled positions on issues such as the abolition of the death penalty has exerted a considerable grip on EU scholarship since the publication of the seminal paper on 'normative power Europe' (NPE) in 2002.[210] The belief that the EU is or should act as a normative power on the world stage has similarly seeped into official EU discourse and strengthened EU resolve to interlace its foreign policy with normative principles, such as the promotion of human rights, the rule of law, and democracy.

However, the research on NPE does not answer a crucial question concerning external perceptions of the EU: do foreign actors actually buy into the EU's self-portrayal as a virtuous power? Literature mapping external perceptions of the EU, as shrewdly summarized by Larsen,[211] gives a rather sobering assessment of the normative narrative. Most actors are sceptical of the EU's stated normative motives and instead perceive the Union's economic power as its most defining feature.[212] Rather than with NPE, such observations are more consistent with the theoretical framework of 'market power Europe' which focuses on the EU's ability to derive leverage from its size as one of the biggest and richest markets in the world, access to which represents a prized asset when it comes to negotiating trade agreements and regulatory standards.[213]

---

[210] I Manners, 'Normative Power Europe' (2002) 40 Journal of Common Market Studies 235. See also Ch 3.

[211] H Larsen, 'The EU as a Normative Power and the Research on External Perceptions: The Missing Link' (2014) 52 Journal of Common Market Studies 896.

[212] N Chaban and others, 'Images of the EU beyond Its Borders: Issue-Specific and Regional Perceptions of European Union Power and Leadership' (2013) 51 Journal of Common Market Studies 433, 443; S Lucarelli, 'The European Union in the Eyes of Others: Towards Filling a Gap in the Literature' (2007) 12 European Foreign Affairs Review 249, 269; S Lucarelli and L Fioramonti (eds), *External perceptions of the European Union as a Global Actor* (Routledge 2010) 222.

[213] C Damro, 'Market Power Europe' (2012) 19 Journal of European Public Policy 682.

H Larsen, 'The EU as a Normative Power and the Research on External Perceptions: The Missing Link' (2014) 52 Journal of Common Market Studies 896

Going through the different regions of the world, the normative dimension is characterized as 'completely absent' in interviews in the Pacific while it is 'somewhat visible' in Africa and southeast Asia together with the environmental and developmental dimensions (...). In quantitative terms, the EU was characterized as a normative power the most by political elites interviewed in the Philippines (approximately 20 per cent of those interviewed), whereas no interviewees in the Pacific categorized the EU as a normative power.

In the Garnet studies, the EU is not viewed as a normative power in Brazil, China, India, Russia or South Africa. The Union is not conceived as a normative power in the United States, where it is often viewed in terms of its Member States rather than as a unit. For Australian elites, the image of the EU as a normative power does not feature clearly. The Australian elite shows little understanding of how the EU projects a view of itself as a guardian of global governance and trade norms; the image of an economic power is dominant. The image of an economic power is also dominant in New Zealand, although the EU is seen as an important partner (but not a role model) in many political areas, and its historical, political and cultural links to New Zealand are given weight. In Canada, the view of the EU as an economic actor is also dominant. Even if there are examples of the EU's measures in, for instance, human rights being mentioned in favourable terms in the Canadian parliament, this dimension is not strong. Generally speaking, there are few signs of the EU being seen as a normative power in the western world.

(...)

There are some important geographical exceptions to the conclusion that the EU is not predominantly seen as a normative power. Such perceptions are much more prominent in the EU's eastern and southern neigbourhoods. According to Bengtson and Elgström, Ukraine, Georgia, Armenia, Azerbaijan and Moldova (but not Belarus) 'readily recognize both the great power status of the EU and the attractiveness of its normative agenda. [...] the civilizing mission of the EU is perceived in positive [...] terms as a contribution to desirable transformation'. Among the general public in these countries, values such as human rights, democracy and freedom of speech are frequently associated with Brussels. The EU is seen as having contributed to developing democracy in these countries and human rights are viewed as an important area of co-operation; however, in line with the general picture, trade and economic development remain the areas where the most important role for the EU is envisaged.

For Mexican elites, too, the EU is seen as a point of reference and a fundamental actor in the defence of human rights, democracy and multilateral institutions. 'The Mexican elite accepts the "moral" leadership of the EU on the international stage. [...] for Mexican political leaders the EU and Latin America have practically the same importance'. In South Africa, 'the EU was sometimes credited with a critical role in the consolidation of democracy and peacekeeping as well as raising standards of health and social development'. Singaporean and Filipino elites recognized the EU's leading role in promoting human rights and democracy, presenting a 'better version of democracy'. Perceptions of the EU as a normative power are thus more prominent in the countries neighbouring the EU and in a few individual countries around the world.

Quite importantly, the general absence of images of the EU as a normative power takes three very different forms. One variant is that the EU is not understood as having a special role in the normative field as it is not normatively different or superior, but is a political partner. The NPE label is sometimes met with puzzlement. This is the view that is found in the western world. A second variant is that the EU is seen as promoting certain legitimate norms. However, the EU's promotion of these norms is not viewed as credible as it is interpreted as a cover for attempts to exercise neo-colonial political control. The neo-colonial reading of the EU's actions, whatever their declared intentions, means that no space is opened up for seeing the EU as a unit connoting universal norms; the Union is almost seen as a negative normative power! For example, in an analysis of interviews with 11 diplomats at the UN (nine non-western), Brantner shows that the EU's leadership role in human rights is recognized. However, its overall impact is limited by the general reading through a 'neo-colonial lens'. Third World diplomats do not believe that neo-colonial aims are altered just by EU Member States acting together, even if their motives are not quite as suspicious as those of the United States.

The EU focus on human rights is frequently seen as a way of settling political scores—to regain neo-colonial control. As a diplomat from Singapore said during a UN debate about the death penalty: 'The EU wanted everybody to think the way they did. When their values "shift", our values must also "shift"' (...). The EU was also accused of double standards: the Union singles out countries for condemnation in cases where the price of attack is not high. In Iran, liberals see the EU's normative agenda as driven by its own economic agenda rather than by the promotion of democracy.

The sustainable growth element of normative power also clashes with what is seen as the EU's de facto actions in the economic field. Issues such as free trade, non-tariff barriers and agricultural subsidies produce an image of the EU as an actor that perpetuates neo-colonial domination. At the same time, we can also find nuances in the neo-colonial interpretation in the form of the understanding that the EU can be of help in the promotion of certain norms. The African Union (AU) officially shares the EU's concern for human rights, but asserts that the Africans have to solve things themselves.

The third variant is that the EU does not promote legitimate universal values. The Union's promotion of certain norms is understood as an expression of Eurocentrism and clashes with the views of other parts of the world. The EU is attempting to further its own norms in common with most other international actors. The Chinese and Russian elites share this view and thus are negatively disposed towards the EU's critical approach to human rights issues and democracy, seeing it as interference in internal political affairs. The view of sovereignty as taking precedence over human rights is also one that has gained ground in the UN for the last ten years. The position of the Organization of Islamic Conferences that defamation of religion is a threat to human rights, put forward in the UN Human Rights Commission for the last 10–15 years, is also an expression of how the EU's basic view of human rights is not universally accepted.

In summary, an image of the EU as a normative power can be found in its neighbourhood and in individual countries around the world, but, in general terms, the perception of the EU as an economic power is the dominant image. The general absence of an image of the EU as a normative power comes in three forms. The first presents the EU as a partner with no special normative status. The second sees the EU as a self-declared promoter of legitimate norms, but views this as an attempt by the EU and its former colonial powers to reintroduce neo-colonial control. A third sees the EU as a power that attempts to further its own norms rather than universal norms. In the three readings, the EU does not have a special status through its norms which might give it influence. To the extent that there is a component of EU normative power connotations that is widely accepted, it is the 'peace' element. The EU's status as a mediator or reconciler is viewed in less ambivalent, and more positive, terms than the rest of Manners' nine norms. It should be added that the research on external perceptions focusing on public opinion and the media corroborates this picture in general terms.

Far from representing a beacon of human rights aspirations in the world, the EU is more often perceived as an economic powerhouse, or worse, a neo-colonial power disguised behind a rhetoric of values. It is instructive that one of the few places where the EU's normative appeal is traceable in local perceptions is the eastern and southern neighbourhood, regions with which the EU engages more intensively than elsewhere, and where conditionality has been applied systematically as a foreign policy tool to effectuate concrete domestic transformations. Although external perceptions are obviously not objective assessments of the EU—Russia and China with their plainly realist brand of foreign policy, for example, would always criticize the EU for promoting values regardless of their intrinsic merit—views of the EU from abroad are helpful for understanding from where the EU derives its international power.[214] The answer more often turns out to be economic than normative power.

In the documented case of India, the assessment of EU human rights policy from abroad reveals a considerable mismatch between the European narrative about EU external action and the way EU human rights activity has been perceived in the 'target' country. Various actors deemed the EU to be Eurocentric, arrogant, incoherent, and ignorant of India's history and approach to human rights. This has caused some friction in the overall EU–India relations.[215]

RK Jain, 'India, the European Union and Human Rights' (2017) 73 India Quarterly 411

India has been critical of the incoherence in the EU's domestic and external human rights policy. For instance, whereas the EU calls upon third countries to accede to certain UN human rights instruments to which not all EU member states are themselves party, for example, the Optional Protocol to the UN Convention against Torture. Developing countries are also unhappy that while the EU repeatedly emphasises the universality of human rights standards, no EU member state has acceded to the UN Convention on the Rights of All Migrant Workers even though the United Nations considers this a core human rights convention (...)

To most stakeholders in India, the EU's understanding of the social milieu in India and the problems of the 5000 years old Indian society appears to be 'incomplete and even superficial'. On many of these issues, the EU's 'policies and prescriptions at times, are far too intrusive and even penal in nature, thus rendering them counterproductive'. What the EU needs to do is to adopt 'a more pragmatic and helpful approach' (...)

---

214 Larsen, 'The EU as a Normative Power and the Research on External Perceptions' (n 211) 910.
215 See also PP Chaudhuri, 'Mars, Venus and Rama: US, Europe and Indian Views on the Kashmir Problem' in RK Jain (ed), *India, Europe and South Asia* (Radiant 2007); PP Chaudhuri, 'India, Europe and the Rise of China' in RK Jain (ed), *India and the European Union in a Changing World* (Aakar Books 2014).

The EU's espousal of issues like human rights and the so-called social issues appear to lack a clear understanding of countries like India. The EU, a former Indian Ambassador to the EU stated, does not seem 'to appreciate the nature and significance of India's pluralistic multireligious and cultural secular democratic polity' (...). All these issues are 'deep-rooted and will take time to be resolved' (...). Indian society, another former Indian Ambassador to the EU, pointed out is 'vastly different' from European societies. This leads to 'vastly different approaches in addressing human rights issues; the Europeans respect how India is trying to cope with the problem and address the issue, but they don't quite understand our social milieu and situation' (...). The Europeans simply have no idea of the political skills that are needed and how difficult it is to resolve India's social problems.

The EU's 'staunchly upright stance' on human rights presents problems in its relationship with India. The EU will therefore need to develop 'a new approach, less confrontational and more constructive, and not judge each case within a vacuum' (...). In the ultimate analysis, the responsibility for initiating and implementing the multitude of structural, economic, social and political reforms necessary to improve human rights implementation must be taken by Indians themselves. External players can only play a supportive role and their capacities to bring about fundamental change are necessarily limited.

10

Human Rights in EU Trade Policy

10.1 Introduction

Ever since the entry into force of the Treaty of Lisbon in 2009, the EU has made the promotion of human rights an integral part of its trade relations with third countries. It has done so by requiring all external trade, cooperation, partnership, and association agreements, including unilateral preference regimes, to incorporate a variety of human rights commitments. While the first EU commitments to developing a sophisticated policy framework for human rights promotion through trade date back to the mid-1990s, the impact and credibility of the Union's efforts in this regard have for long been called into question, particularly—though not exclusively—because economic and political interests often collide with human rights concerns. This divergence between rhetoric and practice is partly the result of a set of broader coherency issues within EU foreign policy-making, which go beyond the scope of this chapter, but are also rooted in a more fundamental discussion on the nexus between free trade and respect for human rights.[1] After briefly sketching the general nexus between human rights and trade, this chapter first outlines the gradual integration of human rights priorities into EU trade policy. It then provides a critical analysis of the various ways in which these commitments and strategic priorities have been implemented through unilateral preference regimes as well as through regional and bilateral trade agreements, and includes an early assessment of the Union's use of sustainability impact assessments for trade negotiations. Finally, the chapter concludes with some critical remarks on the EU's promotion of human rights in trade.

10.2 The Nexus between Human Rights and Trade

Two schools of thought can be more or less discerned when it comes to the nexus between human rights and free trade. On the one hand, there are those who see human rights and free trade as conflicting objectives since they differ in scope and approach. International trade regimes, they would argue, aim to provide free movement of goods, services, and capital (and sometimes persons), and focus therefore primarily on providing equal opportunities to trading nations, without taking into account or catering for the (effects on the) well-being of individual human beings, which is the primary concern of human rights regimes. Even though economic interests are not necessarily opposed to human rights, and trade liberalization directly benefits select individuals and groups (the 'winners'), which also normally translates into an aggregate growth of economic welfare, free trade agreements (FTAs) invariably create a vulnerable situation for human rights, because the inherently economic rationale of trade is at best neutral and at worst detrimental to human rights.[2] Further,

---

[1] For an analysis of coherence issues affecting EU human rights policy, both internally as well as vis-à-vis third countries, see T Lewis and others, 'Coherence of Human Rights Policymaking in EU Institutions and Other EU Agencies and Bodies' (2014) FRAME Deliverable 8.1 <www.fp7-frame.eu/wp-content/uploads/2016/08/06-Deliverable-8.1.pdf> accessed 14 August 2020.

[2] I Abadir, 'International Trade and Human Rights: An Unfinished Debate' (2013) 14 German Law Journal 321.

The European Union and Human Rights. Jan Wouters and Michal Ovádek, Oxford University Press (2021). © Jan Wouters and Michal Ovádek. DOI: 10.1093/oso/9780198814177.003.0010

according to this reasoning, free trade regimes are argued to restrict a state's capacities to protect human rights, in the sense that (i) they limit a country's prerogative to condition market access on human rights performance; and (ii) they limit the policy space for governments to strengthen different types of labour market regulations, particularly in developing countries. On the contrary, trade liberalization can induce a regulatory race to the bottom to attract capital and foreign direct investment (FDI). Some empirical findings in the research seem to corroborate these arguments about the detrimental effects of free trade on human rights. A World Bank study covering the period 1985–2002, for instance, forewarned in this regard that 'most regions exhibit no sustained improvement over time in average labour rights performance, [on the contrary] most appear worse off in 2002 than in 1985'.[3]

At the other end of the spectrum, there are those who argue that free trade and human rights are mutually beneficial, in the sense that the growth of one contributes to the positive evolution of the other. Global trade liberalization, they argue, generates economic growth, employment, and higher standards of living; in short, social circumstances which are believed to be conducive to human rights and democratization.[4] Certain empirical findings to back this rationale point to a positive correlation between FDI flows and human rights, although recent research highlights the importance of absorption capacity in receiving states in this regard and suggests that in order to contribute to human rights, FDI policies should always be accompanied by policies aimed at supporting human development.[5] Similarly, others have argued that trade can have positive spill-over effects on human rights, since it allows for an exchange of ideas, technologies, and cultural norms and values; it therefore makes people in countries with fewer rights and freedoms aware of the conditions elsewhere, potentially incentivizing them to demand similar standards at home. Isolated countries may, on this view, be more prone to human rights violations.[6]

While experts disagree on the overall effect of trade liberalization on human rights, it is clear that the relation is tense and complex. Trade can be harmful or beneficial to human rights, depending on the circumstances, which is why international human rights bodies such as the UN Committee on Economic, Social, and Cultural Rights (ECOSOC) have increasingly reminded governments of their duties to comply with extraterritorial human rights obligations when concluding international trade and investment agreements.[7] This implies that in addition to their domestic adherence to human rights, states should ensure that the unilateral or bilateral trade regimes they enact do not harm the human rights of the people affected outside their domestic jurisdiction and that they monitor and regulate the behaviour of their companies and investors abroad. International trade actors are increasingly starting to address these obligations by applying human rights impact assessments of their

---

[3] M Levi and others, 'Aligning Rights and Interests: Why, When and How to Uphold Labor Standards' (2012) Background Paper for the World Development Report 2013, 7.

[4] Abadir (n 2) 332.

[5] J Michie, 'Foreign Direct Investment and "Human Capital Enhancement" in Developing Countries' (2002) 6 Competition and Change 363. On the need for cooperation between FDI and human development policies see V Kheng, S Sun, and S Anwar, 'Foreign Direct Investment and Human Capital in Developing Countries: A Panel Data Approach' (2017) 50 Economic Change and Restructuring 341.

[6] F van Hees, *Protection v. Protectionism: The Use of Human Rights Arguments in the Debate for and against the Liberalization of Trade* (Åbo 2004).

[7] See, for example, UN Committee on Economic, Social and Cultural Rights, 'General Comment No 12: The right to adequate food' (12 May 1999) UN Doc E/C.12/1999/5, paras 19 and 36; UN Committee on Economic, Social and Cultural Rights, 'General Comment No 14: The right to the highest attainable standard of health' (11 August 2000) UN Doc E/C.12/2000/4, para 39; UN Committee on Economic, Social and Cultural Rights, 'General Comment No 15: The right to water' (20 January 2003) UN Doc E/C.12/2002/11, paras 31 and 35–6. However, there are also more sceptical voices when it comes to extraterritorial human rights obligations. See, for example, L Bartels, 'The EU's Human Rights Obligations in Relation to Policies with Extraterritorial Effects' (2014) 25 European Journal of International Law 1071.

trade agreements and by adopting various codes of conduct for businesses on human rights. Moreover, concerned with rampant human rights violations across the globe, powerful trade actors like the US, Canada, and the EU have increasingly integrated human rights provisions in their trade agreements, more often than not conditioning market access and trade preferences on a partner country's performance in the area of human rights.[8]

It is against this backdrop, and partly in reaction to the disappointingly slow reform of the global trade system under the Doha Development Round, that the EU has progressively presented itself as a normative commercial actor. Indeed, the EU's *de facto* partial abandoning of multilateralism in international trade has cleared the way for the introduction of more normative 'beyond trade' considerations, including human rights promotion.[9]

10.3 Human Rights in EU Trade Policy since the Treaty of Lisbon

Human rights provisions have been part of the EU's trade agreements since the mid-1990s, as part of the gradual politicization of the partnership agreements between the EU and the Group of African, Caribbean, and Pacific Countries (ACP) and the establishment of new relations with countries formerly in the Soviet sphere of influence. While EU–ACP cooperation agreements have always been primarily geared towards development cooperation, they also include a trade component which is equally subject to the provisions and clauses of the overarching political agreement. The evolution of integrating human rights clauses in EU trade agreements therefore runs quite similarly to the progress in development cooperation (see Chapter 11) and will be discussed in further detail in Section 10.4.C.

Consolidated version of the Treaty on the Functioning of the European Union [2012] OJ C326/47

Article 207
1. The common commercial policy shall be based on uniform principles, particularly with regard to changes in tariff rates, the conclusion of tariff and trade agreements relating to trade in goods and services, and the commercial aspects of intellectual property, foreign direct investment, the achievement of uniformity in measures of liberalisation, export policy and measures to protect trade such as those to be taken in the event of dumping or subsidies. **The common commercial policy shall be conducted in the context of the principles and objectives of the Union's external action.**

While conditionality still features prominently in the EU's approach to human rights promotion through trade, subsequent policy innovations in the wake of the Treaty of Lisbon have induced a more proactive approach to human rights promotion, notably by requiring EU trade agreements to maintain a do-no-harm approach when it comes to the human rights implications of increased trade liberalization, and by ensuring that EU FTAs do not

---

[8] L Beke and others, 'Report on the Integration of Human Rights in EU Development and Trade Policies' (2014) FRAME Deliverable 9.1, 19–22 <www.fp7-frame.eu/wp-content/uploads/2016/08/07-Deliverable-9.1.pdf> accessed 14 August 2020.
[9] J Wouters and others (eds), *Global Governance Through Trade: EU Policies and Approaches* (Edward Elgar Publishing 2015).

unduly restrict the policy-making of its trade partners.[10] The legal basis for this more comprehensive approach is to be found in Article 207 TFEU read in conjunction with Article 21 TEU (analysed in Chapter 9), which made it an explicit and legal requirement for all relevant EU institutions and bodies to ensure that EU trade policy became a positive force for human rights. The last sentence of Article 207 TFEU recognized, for the first time, the intrinsic links between EU external policies and international trade ('common commercial policy'), and, following this logic, subjects EU trade policy to the commitments under Article 21 TEU (which chiefly contains the principles and objectives of EU external action), effectively requiring EU trade policy to contribute to human rights worldwide.[11]

Beyond direct human rights commitments under the provisions mentioned above, the Treaty of Lisbon has further enhanced the scope for trade to be a catalyst for human rights by strengthening the role of the European Parliament (EP) in concluding trade agreements. Indeed, some have argued that, given the latter's commitment to the protection of human rights, its democratic legitimacy, and formal independence from the Commission and the Member States, the EP constitutes an important institutional agent for human rights promotion in EU trade policy deliberations.[12] Essentially, the Lisbon Treaty enhanced the EP's role in trade policy in three ways. First, the EP has acquired veto power in that its consent is required for the conclusion of most international agreements.[13] The EP cannot, however, propose amendments to standing proposals. It can either entirely approve or reject the proposed agreement. With regard to human rights concerns, the EP has used this 'hard power of consent' on a number of occasions, for instance when it refused to consent to the EU–Morocco fisheries partnership because the agreement did not address the plight of people living in Western Sahara.[14]

Second, the EP was given the right to be informed at all stages of trade negotiation. Whereas earlier the EP was officially absent from this process, the European Commission is now legally obliged to report regularly on the progress of negotiations not only to the Council's Trade Policy Committee but also to the EP.[15] In combination with its veto power, the EP has managed to put this 'soft power of information' to good use, for example by requiring third countries to address human rights concerns as a precondition for the EP's consent. During the EU–Colombia negotiations, for instance, the EP requested the Colombian government 'to ensure the establishment of a transparent and binding road map on human, environmental and labour rights'.[16] Finally, Article 207(2) TFEU stipulates that 'acting by means of regulations in accordance with the ordinary legislative procedure', the EP and Council together have the competence to 'adopt the measures defining the framework for implementing the common commercial policy'.[17] This means that all general trade legislation, including unilateral trade preference reforms and their potential human rights implications, is enacted jointly by the EP and the Council acting as co-legislators.[18]

[10] S Bilal and I Ramdoo, 'A Comparative Analysis between the Caribbean and African EPAs' (2016) ECDPM Discussion Paper No 198.

[11] Recall, in particular, Article 21(1) and (2)(b) TEU. See also R Bendini, 'In-depth Analysis: The European Union's trade policy, five years after the Lisbon Treaty', European Parliament Study, March 2014, 9.

[12] S Velluti, 'The Promotion and Integration of Human Rights in EU External Trade Relations' (2016) 32 Utrecht Journal of International and European Law 41, 47.

[13] See Article 218(6)(a) TFEU.

[14] European Parliament, 'Legislative Resolution on the draft Council decision on the conclusion of a Protocol between the European Union and the Kingdom of Morocco setting out the fishing opportunities and financial compensation provided for in the Fisheries Partnership Agreement between the European Community and the Kingdom of Morocco', P7_TA(2011)0569, 14 December 2011.

[15] Article 207(3) TFEU.

[16] European Parliament, 'Resolution on the EU trade agreement with Colombia and Peru', P7_TA (2012)0249, 13 June 2012, para 15.

[17] Article 207(2) TFEU.

[18] Beke and others, 'Report on the Integration of Human Rights in EU Development and Trade Policies' (n 8) 26–27.

In the aftermath of the Lisbon Treaty, a series of policy documents were adopted to place human rights considerations into the mainstream across the different strands of EU external action. As one of the most visible manifestations of EU international relations, trade in particular was identified as an area in need of better coherence with the EU's human rights commitments, requiring it to 'work in a way that helps rather than hinders human rights concerns'.[19] In order to do so, an EU Strategic Framework and two subsequent corresponding Action Plans for Human Rights and Democracy were adopted, respectively covering the periods 2012–2014 and 2015–2019, which identified a series of human rights related 'action points' for the Union's trade policy to follow up.[20]

Council Conclusions on the Action Plan on Human Rights and Democracy 2015–2019, Doc No. 10897/15, 20 July 2015

Objective	Action	Timeline	Responsibility
25. Trade / investment policy	a. Provide support for and strengthen effective implementation, enforcement and monitoring of GSP+ beneficiaries' commitments (relevant HR treaties and ILO conventions), including through projects with key international bodies and civil society, including social partners.	Ongoing	EEAS, COM
	b. Continue to develop a robust and methodologically sound approach to the analysis of human rights impacts of trade and investment agreements, in ex-ante impact assessments, sustainability impact assessments and ex-post evaluations; explore ways to extend the existing quantitative analysis in assessing the impact of trade and investment initiatives on human rights.	By 2017	EEAS, COM, Council, MS
	c. EU Member States to strive to include in new or revised Bilateral Investment Treaties (BITs) that they negotiate in the future with third countries provisions related to the respect and fulfilment of human rights, including provisions on Corporate Social Responsibility, in line with those inserted in agreements negotiated at EU level.	Ongoing	MS
	d. Aim at systematically including in EU trade and investment agreements the respect of internationally recognised principles and guidelines on Corporate Social Responsibility, such as those contained in the OECD Guidelines for Multinational Enterprises, the UN Global Compact, the UN Guiding principles on business and human rights (UNGPs), the ILO Tripartite Declaration of Principles concerning Multinational Enterprises and Social Policy, and ISO 26000.	Ongoing	COM
	e. Regularly review the Regulation on trade in goods that can be used for capital punishment or torture (1236/2005), and the Dual Use goods Regulation (428/2009) to mitigate the potential risks associated with the uncontrolled export of ICT products that could be used in a manner that leads to human rights violations.	Ongoing	EEAS, COM

[19] European Commission and the High Representative of the European Union for Foreign Affairs and Security Policy, 'Human rights and Democracy at the heart of EU External Action—Towards a more effective approach', COM(2011) 866 final, Brussels, 12 December 2011, 12.

[20] European Commission and the High Representative of the European Union for Foreign Affairs and Security Policy, 'Action Plan on Human rights and Democracy (2015–2019), keeping human rights at the heart of the EU agenda', JOIN(2015) 16 final, Brussels, 28 April 2015, 23–24.

In correspondence with the 2015–2019 Action Plan for Human Rights and Democracy, the Directorate-General for Trade (hereinafter DG Trade) confirmed in its 2015 'Trade for All' communication that the EU's new approach 'involves using trade agreements and trade preference programmes as levers to promote, around the world, values like sustainable development, human rights, fair and ethical trade and the fight against corruption'.[21] DG Trade also identified consumer awareness as an additional aspect in ensuring that trade benefits, rather than hampers, human rights. EU trade policy should therefore 'reinforc[e] corporate social responsibility initiatives and due diligence across the production chain' with a focus on the respect of human rights and the social—including labour rights—and environmental aspects of value chains.[22] Further, according to the communication, human rights violations that may be found in global supply chains requiring particular attention include 'the worst forms of child labour, forced prison labour, forced labour as a result of trafficking in human beings and land grabbing'.[23]

In the recently proposed EU Action Plan on Human Rights and Democracy for the period 2020–2024 trade related actions are no longer bundled together but instead can be found scattered among the five overarching objectives.[24] The Generalized Scheme of Preferences (see below) is reconfirmed to be one of the main instruments at the EU's disposal to achieve its human rights objectives in the context of external action. Among the action points related to trade are the call to '[s]trengthen the implementation of human rights provisions in EU trade policy, including through the GSP and by promoting labour rights in the context of FTAs [and to u]se the full potential of monitoring mechanisms and further promote transparency, awareness and engagement with stakeholders' and to '[s]trive to eradicate torture globally through prevention, prohibition, accountability and redress for victims, including by promoting the Global Alliance for Torture-Free Trade'.[25]

Despite these commendable commitments, and regardless of the various soft and hard law measures put in place since the Lisbon Treaty, DG Trade up to now still does not have a unified strategy outlining just how it will systematically take into account human rights considerations across the different areas of trade policy-making. Given the acknowledged need for a 'coherent, transparent, predictable, feasible and effective' coordination of the Union's human rights and trade objectives, the lack of such a strategy arguably raises questions about the willingness behind the stated ambitions.[26] It is worth reiterating in this regard, however, that the EU's human rights provisions in trade agreements are but one tool in the Union's toolbox for human rights promotion abroad. Indeed, trade, in and of itself, is arguably an insufficient and/or too blunt an instrument to address human rights concerns in third countries. As such, the functioning and effectiveness of EU trade policy measures for human rights depends considerably on the extent to which these are applied in coordination with

---

[21] European Commission, 'Trade for all—Towards a more responsible trade and investment policy', COM(2015) 497 final, Brussels, 14 October 2015, 5.

[22] Ibid, 18 and 20.

[23] Ibid, 25.

[24] These are: protecting and empowering individuals; building resilient, inclusive, and democratic societies; promoting a global system for human rights and democracy; harnessing opportunities and addressing challenges posed by the use of new technologies; delivering by working together. See Ch 9.

[25] See Points I.A and III.C, European Commission and High Representative of the Union for Foreign Affairs and Security Policy, 'Annex to the Joint Communication to the European Parliament and the Council, EU Action Plan on Human Rights and Democracy 2020–2024', JOIN(2020) 5 final, Brussels, 25 March 2020.

[26] Beke and others, 'Report on the Integration of Human Rights in EU Development and Trade Policies' (n 8) 30.

other EU foreign policy instruments.[27] When assessing the impact of the EU's trade policy on human rights, the EU's overall relations with the country at hand should thus be taken into account, including any political framework or development cooperation agreements.

European Commission, Human Rights and Sustainable Development in the EU–Vietnam Relations with specific regard to the EU–Vietnam Free Trade Agreement, SWD(2016) 21 final, Brussels, 26 January 2016

Human rights considerations in trade policy initiatives should be seen as one component of a wider approach encompassing a broad range of policies and actions to address directly or indirectly human rights, that is, inter alia: political dialogues, co-operation at multilateral and bilateral levels, development aid and support. The external dimension of domestic policies in areas such as environment, employment, social affairs, health, good governance, the rule of law, education, migration, data protection, digital and audio-visual, as well as voluntary corporate social responsibility practices by the private sector, can also contribute to support human rights.

10.4 EU Trade Policy Instruments for Human Rights

Throughout the years of EU integration, a number of trade instruments and response mechanisms have been developed, which condition EU market access and preferential treatment—albeit to varying degrees—upon a partner country's respect for human rights. The following sections analyse these instruments, which can be grouped by whether they are unilateral (non-reciprocal) or agreed together with other parties. By recourse to unilateral or non-reciprocal trade regimes the EU either grants preferential market access to developing countries, notably the Generalized Scheme of Preferences (GSP and GSP+), in return for observing international human rights standards or by applying export control systems on certain goods related to human rights violations. On a bilateral or multilateral basis, the EU incorporates various human rights and sustainability provisions in international trade agreements.

A. Generalized Scheme of Preferences (GSP)

Established in 1971, the Generalized Scheme of Preferences (GSP) is not only one of the EU's main trade instruments for human rights promotion, particularly vis-à-vis developing countries, it is also the oldest. It should be noted, however, that the adoption of GSP-related acts was contested on legal grounds until 1987, as the Council of the EU consistently argued that such measures do not fall within the area of the common commercial policy.[28] GSP schemes were essentially designed to contribute to the economic development of developing countries by lowering the threshold for them to export to more prosperous markets. The EU GSP scheme was the first of its kind, although its general principles had been adopted at the 1968 UN Conference on Trade and Development (UNCTAD) in New Delhi.

---

[27] European Commission, Human Rights and Sustainable Development in the EU–Vietnam Relations with specific regard to the EU–Vietnam Free Trade Agreement, SWD(2016) 21 final, Brussels, 26 January 2016, 2–3.
[28] This argument was finally rejected in 1987 by the CJEU. See Judgment of 26 March 1987, *Commission of the European Communities v Council of the European Communities*, 45/86, ECLI:EU:C:1987:163.

> ### Second Session of the UNCTAD II, 31 January–29 March 1968, New Delhi
>
> ---
>
> ### *Resolution 21*
> [T]he objectives of the generalized, non-reciprocal, non-discriminatory system of preferences in favour of the developing countries, including special measures in favour of the least advanced among the developing countries, should be: (a) to increase their export earnings; (b) to promote their industrialization; and (c) to accelerate their rates of economic growth.

As of 1979, GSP systems were made compatible with the rules of the World Trade Organization (WTO), notably through the adoption of the 'enabling clause' which exempted GSPs from the most-favoured-nation (MFN) principle prevalent under the General Agreement on Tariffs and Trade (GATT).[29] The exemption provided the required legal basis at the international level for the GSP to be rolled out on a permanent basis, beyond the ten years initially intended. Thirteen different GSP schemes have been notified to the UNCTAD since then, all of which have granted reduced or zero tariff rates on a selection of products originating from developing countries. Least Developed Countries (LDCs), moreover, benefit from additional tariff cuts and a wider product coverage.

Since 1991, the EU has awarded additional preferences to eligible countries who manage to comply with a number of stated conditions regarding human rights. Initially, this type of positive conditionality was applied to incentivize a number of Latin American countries to enhance their commitment to combatting drug trafficking. Since 1995, the GSP Regulation introduced negative conditionality, meaning trade preferences could be suspended based on cases of forced labour. Subsequent revisions of the GSP Regulation increasingly incorporated references to International Labour Organization (ILO) Conventions and, later still, a variety of standards and commitments concerning the different dimensions of sustainable development and good governance, including climate change and anti-corruption measures. Because a GSP is a non-reciprocal trading regime, unilaterally established by the preference-giving trade actor, there is no leeway for third parties to negotiate any of the terms of the arrangement. It therefore gives, at least in theory, powerful trading hubs like the EU ample leverage to condition their preferential treatment upon a variety of normative considerations. The EU and the US are, nonetheless, the only two trading blocs who have explicitly linked their GSP schemes to human rights standards so far.[30]

In 2004, the WTO Appellate Body found that the EU GSP special 'drug arrangement' for countries combatting drug trafficking to be in breach of the Enabling Clause under which the GSP is normally exempted from the obligation of reciprocal MFN treatment.[31] A 2005 reform of the GSP addressed these discrimination concerns by establishing a differentiated, three-tier, approach consisting of a so-called general arrangement (standard GSP), a 'special incentive arrangement' (GSP+), and a special arrangement for LDCs called 'Everything But

---

[29] Under WTO rules, members cannot normally discriminate between their trading partners, granting one a special favour, such as lowering customs duties, requires doing so for all other WTO members as well.

[30] C Portela, *European Union Sanctions and Foreign Policy: When and Why Do They Work?* (Routledge 2010).

[31] See also K Moss, 'The Consequences of the WTO Appellate Body Decision in EC-Tariff Preferences for the African Growth Opportunity Act and Sub-Saharan Africa' (2006) 38 International Law and Politics 665.

Arms' (EBA). A sliding scale of trade preferences was thereby created, linking market access to a partner country's development status and its commitments to human rights and good governance.[32] The latest 2012 reform of the GSP Regulation—in force since January 2014— further modified access conditions to the different schemes, in particular for GSP and GSP+.

Regulation (EU) No 978/2012 of the European Parliament and of the Council applying a scheme of generalised tariff preferences and repealing Council Regulation (EC) No 732/2008 [2012] OJ L303/1

Article 1

1. The scheme of generalised tariff preferences (the 'scheme') shall apply in accordance with this Regulation.
2. This Regulation provides for the following tariff preferences under the scheme:
    (a) a general arrangement;
    (b) a special incentive arrangement for sustainable development and good governance (GSP+); and
    (c) a special arrangement for the least-developed countries (Everything But Arms (EBA)).

Article 9

1. A GSP beneficiary country may benefit from the tariff preferences provided under the **special incentive arrangement for sustainable development and good governance** referred to in point (b) of Article 1(2) if:
    (a) it is considered to be vulnerable due to a lack of diversification and insufficient integration within the international trading system, as defined in Annex VII;
    (b) **it has ratified all the conventions** listed in Annex VIII (the 'relevant conventions') and **the most recent available conclusions of the monitoring bodies** under those conventions (the 'relevant monitoring bodies') **do not identify a serious failure** to effectively implement any of those conventions;
    (c) in relation to any of the relevant conventions, it has not formulated a reservation which is prohibited by any of those conventions or which is for the purposes of this Article considered to be incompatible with the object and purpose of that convention.
    (d) it gives a binding undertaking to maintain ratification of the relevant conventions and to ensure the effective implementation thereof;
    (e) it **accepts without reservation the reporting requirements imposed by each convention** and gives a binding undertaking to accept regular monitoring and review of its implementation record in accordance with the provisions of the relevant conventions; and
    (f) it gives a **binding undertaking to participate in and cooperate with the monitoring procedure** referred to in Article 13.

The general GSP arrangement grants customs duty reductions on around 66 per cent of all EU tariff lines to developing countries classified by the World Bank as low income or

---

[32] L Bartels, 'The WTO Legality of the EU's GSP+ Arrangement' (2007) 10 Journal of International Economic Law 869.

lower-middle income economies, but which are not on the list of LDCs consolidated by the UN Committee for Development Policy, a subsidiary body of the UN Economic and Social Council. Tariff reductions depend on several factors, including whether the product at hand is considered 'sensitive', in the sense that it could harm or outcompete the internal EU production of that product. So-called product graduation can lead some countries to lose their preferential treatment on a certain product line, notably when their domestic industry is perceived to be sufficiently competitive.[33] The GSP+ regime constitutes 'a special incentive arrangement' which provides duty-free access to developing countries on roughly the same 66 per cent of all tariff lines as the standard GSP. The developing countries must, however, in addition to fulfilling the general GSP eligibility criteria, also comply with a number of vulnerability and sustainable development criteria. Unlike for standard GSP or EBA treatment, countries are not automatically added or removed from a list but need to apply individually to benefit from the preferences under the GSP+ scheme. Applications depend, among other things, on whether a country has ratified and is effectively implementing and complying with the monitoring requirements, 'without reservations', of some 27 international conventions concerning human and labour rights, good governance, and environmental protection. GSP+ beneficiaries are further obliged to cooperate with the European Commission by providing any necessary information required to assess their compliance with those international obligations.[34] The EBA initiative grants full duty-free and quota-free market access to LDCs, on all product lines, except arms and ammunition.

The 2012 reform of the GSP Regulation refocused GSP preferences on those countries most in need, in particular low and lower-middle income countries and LDCs. In recent years, many countries also graduated out of the scheme due to reaching upper middle-income economy status. As a result, the number of GSP beneficiaries decreased from 178 before the 2012 reform to 71 as of late 2019, 15 of which enjoy standard GSP status, 8 belong to the GSP+ scheme, while 48 LDCs qualify for EBA. Trade-wise, the total volume of imports to the EU under the three GSP schemes combined amounted to EUR 68.9 billion in 2018, growing steadily in recent years despite the falling number of beneficiaries. Of the total imports under the overall GSP system, 46.9 per cent was traded under the standard GSP regime, while GSP+ and EBA accounted for 13.8 per cent and 39.3 per cent respectively.[35] Unsurprisingly, the importance of the GSP in terms of absolute trade value remains limited. For some GSP countries, however (eg Bangladesh, Pakistan, and Sri Lanka), the share of their exports under the GSP's preferential access arrangements (mostly concerning garments) constitutes a significant part of their total exports worldwide, which explains some of the leverage the EU has arguably been able to harness in terms of human rights promotion through the GSP.[36]

While qualifying for EBA and GSP relies on purely economic criteria, as evaluated by UN bodies, all three GSP schemes incorporate an element of negative conditionality. Their respective preference arrangements can be withdrawn for any or all products in case of 'serious and systematic violation' of the principles laid down in the 15 core UN human rights and ILO labour rights conventions listed in Part A of Annex VIII of the GSP Regulation.[37]

---

[33] Article 8 of the 2012 GSP Regulation.

[34] Ibid, Article 13(2).

[35] European Commission and High Representative of the Union for Foreign Affairs and Security Policy, Joint Report to the European Parliament and the Council on the Generalised Scheme of Preferences covering the period 2018–2019, JOIN(2020) 3 final, Brussels, 10 February 2020.

[36] L Zamfir, 'Human Rights in EU Trade Policy: Unilateral Measures', Briefing Note European Parliamentary Research Service, January 2017, 2.

[37] Article 19 of the 2012 GSP Regulation.

Regulation (EU) No 978/2012 of the European Parliament and of the Council applying a scheme of generalised tariff preferences and repealing Council Regulation (EC) No 732/2008 [2012] OJ L303/1

ANNEX VIII

PART A
Core human and labour rights UN/ILO Conventions

1. Convention on the Prevention and Punishment of the Crime of Genocide (1948)
2. International Convention on the Elimination of All Forms of Racial Discrimination (1965)
3. International Covenant on Civil and Political Rights (1966)
4. International Covenant on Economic Social and Cultural Rights (1966)
5. Convention on the Elimination of All Forms of Discrimination Against Women (1979)
6. Convention Against Torture and other Cruel, Inhuman or Degrading Treatment or Punishment (1984)
7. Convention on the Rights of the Child (1989)
8. Convention concerning Forced or Compulsory Labour, No 29 (1930)
9. Convention concerning Freedom of Association and Protection of the Right to Organise, No 87 (1948)
10. Convention concerning the Application of the Principles of the Right to Organise and to Bargain Collectively, No 98 (1949)
11. Convention concerning Equal Remuneration of Men and Women Workers for Work of Equal Value, No 100 (1951)
12. Convention concerning the Abolition of Forced Labour, No 105 (1957)
13. Convention concerning Discrimination in Respect of Employment and Occupation, No 111 (1958)
14. Convention concerning Minimum Age for Admission to Employment, No 138 (1973)
15. Convention concerning the Prohibition and Immediate Action for the Elimination of the Worst Forms of Child Labour, No 182 (1999)

PART B

Conventions related to the environment and to governance principles

16. Convention on International Trade in Endangered Species of Wild Fauna and Flora (1973)
17. Montreal Protocol on Substances that Deplete the Ozone Layer (1987)
18. Basel Convention on the Control of Transboundary Movements of Hazardous Wastes and Their Disposal (1989)
19. Convention on Biological Diversity (1992)
20. The United Nations Framework Convention on Climate Change (1992)
21. Cartagena Protocol on Biosafety (2000)
22. Stockholm Convention on persistent Organic Pollutants (2001)

23. Kyoto Protocol to the United Nations Framework Convention on Climate Change (1998)
24. United Nations Single Convention on Narcotic Drugs (1961)
25. United Nations Convention on Psychotropic Substances (1971)
26. United Nations Convention against Illicit Traffic in Narcotic Drugs and Psychotropic Substances (1988)
27. United Nations Convention against Corruption (2004)

Qualifying for GSP+, however, requires complying with a larger set of normative conditions, thus constituting an element of positive conditionality. In short, GSP+ offers an incentive-based approach to encourage eligible developing countries to subscribe to a series of international standards and their respective monitoring frameworks, including environmental and good governance treaties (listed in part B of Annex VIII). Moreover, it is worth noting that when candidate countries go through the trouble of applying for GSP+ status, it means they have a clear interest—albeit one that is predominantly economic—in the scheme, which in turn implies, at least at a theoretical level, a greater willingness for domestic reforms, and greater EU leverage to help push for those reforms. GSP+, as a result, holds more potential for unilateral trade preferences to contribute positively to the human rights performance of partner countries.[38]

Compliance with the specified international treaties, moreover, provides the required justification for extra-preferential treatment under WTO rules, and therefore the Commission has to monitor it continuously. To do so, the Commission has developed score cards for each GSP+ country, which are used to measure the latter's compliance with the abovementioned 27 commitments. The score cards are centred around the shortcomings or challenges identified in evaluation reports of the relevant treaty-monitoring bodies. Entry assessments at the application stage provide a first snapshot of the domestic situation in this regard and scorecards then build on that analysis to identify any further outstanding issues that need to be addressed over the course of the GSP+ regime. As a result, the priorities identified in the scorecards will differ from one country to another. Current schemes are in place until the end of 2023, covering a period of ten years. The ongoing monitoring relies on information from regular updates by the relevant treaty-monitoring bodies, but also from thirds parties such as local experts and civil society.

Regulation (EU) No 978/2012 of the European Parliament and of the Council applying a scheme of generalised tariff preferences and repealing Council Regulation (EC) No 732/2008 [2012] OJ L303/1

Article 14
By 1 January 2016, and **every two years** thereafter, **the Commission shall present to the European Parliament and to the Council a report** on the status of ratification of the relevant conventions, the compliance of the GSP+ beneficiary countries with any reporting obligations under those conventions and the status of the effective implementation thereof.

---

[38] Zamfir, 'Human Rights in EU Trade Policy' (n 36) 8.

That report shall include: (a) the conclusions or recommendations of relevant monitoring bodies in respect of each GSP+ beneficiary country; and (b) the Commission's conclusions on whether each GSP+ beneficiary country respects its binding undertakings to comply with reporting obligations, to cooperate with relevant monitoring bodies in accordance with the relevant conventions and to ensure the effective implementation thereof. The report may include any information the Commission considers appropriate.

In drawing its conclusions concerning effective implementation of the relevant conventions, the Commission shall assess the **conclusions and recommendations of the relevant monitoring bodies**, as well as, without prejudice to other sources, information submitted by third parties, including **civil society**, **social partners**, the European Parliament or the Council.

Once a country is awarded GSP+ status, the Commission and the European Union External Action Service (EEAS) establish a dialogue with the relevant authorities of the beneficiary country to discuss their compliance in light of the issues identified in the scorecards. Such a dialogue between the two parties should from then on take place on a regular basis, at least once a year, as beneficiaries are expected to show progress on their commitments over time. Beyond the scorecards, the regular dialogues may also incorporate other sources of information, including input submitted by different types of stakeholders, the EP, and the Council. Based on the GSP+ dialogue and the scorecards, the Commission is required under the GSP Regulation to present a status report to the Council and the EP every two years. This includes a detailed assessment of each beneficiary's performance on the 27 conventions. Reports have thus far been issued in January 2016, January 2018, and February 2020.

European Commission, Report on the Generalised Scheme of Preferences covering the period 2016–2017, COM(2018) 36 final, Brussels, 19 January 2018

Kyrgyzstan, which joined GSP+ in January 2016, features for the first time in this report. Sri Lanka rejoined GSP+ in May 2017, the monitoring period therefore covers less than six months. In Armenia, the monitoring mission proved to be a valuable way to involve local civil society. In the absence of recent reports to the UN and ILO, the monitoring mission to Cabo Verde was crucial to collect the information needed for EU's assessment. The monitoring mission to the Philippines was an opportunity for the EU to express its concerns on recent human rights developments, while also recognizing progress on labour rights and socio-economic policies. In Paraguay and Bolivia, the issue of child labour was openly discussed with the participation of all relevant stakeholders, including the ILO and UNICEF. Georgia features for the last time as it has phased out of the GSP+ due to its DCFTA with the EU.

Overall, the GSP+ monitoring provided a structured approach and a solid basis for the assessment of each GSP+ beneficiary, building on the findings of UN and ILO monitoring bodies and on information provided by third parties, including civil society, social partners, the European Parliament and the Council. GSP+ monitoring is fully integrated into the EU's bilateral framework and dialogues, including the Human Rights Dialogues. In particular, GSP+ has supported countries like Pakistan, Sri Lanka, Mongolia and Bolivia to intensify their engagement in the EU Human Rights Dialogues.

At the same time, the Human Rights Dialogues provided a platform to discuss GSP+ related human rights issues. GSP+ has improved synergies and led to a mutually re-inforcing leverage of the two tools. Whilst GSP is an important enabling tool to address human rights and labour concerns in beneficiary countries, the EU is committed to use all relevant policies and instruments to support them in achieving their sustainable de-velopment and good governance goals. Given the nature of such issues and the need for structural and lasting solutions, GSP engagement requires a steady long-term commit-ment by both the EU and beneficiary countries.

When the monitoring framework described above identifies a violation of the GSP+ conditions, the Commission can, in the event of 'reasonable doubt', initiate a procedure for the temporary withdrawal of any and all preferences. Notably, when a violation or irregu-larity is established, the Commission has to specify a period of no longer than six months during which it shall 'assess all relevant information', including observations submitted by the beneficiary country under examination, to determine further course of action. Within three months after the expiry of the observation period, the Commission has to determine whether or not to temporarily withdraw the tariff preferences provided under the GSP+ scheme.

Regulation (EU) No 978/2012 of the European Parliament and of the Council applying a scheme of generalised tariff preferences and repealing Council Regulation (EC) No 732/2008 [2012] OJ L303/1

Article 19

1. The preferential arrangements referred to in Article 1(2) may be **withdrawn tem-porarily,** in respect of **all or of certain products originating in a beneficiary country,** for any of the following reasons:

   (a) serious and systematic violation of principles laid down in the conventions listed in Part A of Annex VIII;
   (b) export of goods made by prison labour;
   (c) serious shortcomings in customs controls on the export or transit of drugs (il-licit substances or precursors), or failure to comply with international conven-tions on anti-terrorism and money laundering;
   (d) serious and systematic unfair trading practices including those affecting the supply of raw materials, which have an adverse effect on the Union industry and which have not been addressed by the beneficiary country. For those un-fair trading practices, which are prohibited or actionable under the WTO Agreements, the application of this Article shall be based on a previous deter-mination to that effect by the competent WTO body;

> (e) serious and systematic infringement of the objectives adopted by Regional
> Fishery Organisations or any international arrangements to which the Union is
> a party concerning the conservation and management of fishery resources.

The summary of the GSP mechanism above describes a gradual process with sufficient opportunities for the country under scrutiny to address, and possibly remedy, the alleged violations. The Commission, however, retains ample discretion in deciding whether or not to trigger the procedure for temporary withdrawal of preferences, as well as in assessing when withdrawal is warranted. The GSP's withdrawal procedures have long been associated with a sense of opacity and a lack of objectivity and legal certainty. While the 2012 reform of the GSP Regulation arguably made the rules governing the change of status (including sanctions) more objective—*inter alia* to enhance the scheme's overall stability and predictability—a number of concerns regarding both the legitimacy and effectiveness of the GSP regime remain valid in view of how policy has translated into practice. Indeed, the use of GSP human rights conditionality has been the subject of long-standing criticism since its inception, although some have coined it a 'springboard for the promotion of human rights'.[39]

First, conditionality has rarely been enforced. GSP preferences have so far only been suspended four times, notably for Myanmar, Belarus, Sri Lanka, and Cambodia. In 1997, the GSP preferences of Myanmar/Burma were suspended on grounds of forced labour allegations until in July 2013 the EU, for the first time ever, decided to reinstate the preferences. The decision to reapply GSP preferences to Myanmar only came after a process of political and economic reforms began in 2011 and was further boosted by a favourable ILO decision that same year.[40] Belarus' GSP preferences were withdrawn in 2007 after violations of the ILO Conventions on freedom of association and collective bargaining were established. Belarus has since graduated to upper-middle income status and thus no longer qualifies for GSP treatment. Since 2010 however, the EU imposed unilateral import quotas covering the country's textile and clothing products—a punitive policy only possible because Belarus is not a WTO member.[41] In 2010, the Commission withdrew its GSP+ preferences from Sri Lanka because of massive and systematic human rights violations committed during the end of the civil war in 2008 and 2009. Sri Lanka reapplied for GSP+ status and in May 2017 this request was granted. In February 2020, the European Commission has decided to withdraw an important portion of Cambodia's trade preferences under the EBA scheme. Following long-voiced concerns over serious and systematic violations of several core human rights and labour rights conventions,[42] regular import tariffs are reintroduced for low added-value garment products, footwear, travel goods, and sugar.[43] It is the first time a partial withdrawal of trade preferences was enacted.

---

[39] Beke and others, 'Report on the Integration of Human Rights in EU Development and Trade Policies' (n 8) 35.
[40] L Beke and N Hachez, 'The EU GSP: A Preference for Human Rights and Good Governance? The Case of Myanmar', Leuven Centre for Global Governance Studies Working Paper No 155, March 2015, 18–20.
[41] Zamfir, 'Human Rights in EU Trade Policy' (n 36) 5.
[42] Namely violations of the International Covenant on Civil and Political Rights, the Convention concerning Freedom of Association and Protection of the Right to Organise, the Convention concerning the Application of the Principles of the Right to Organise and to Bargain Collectively and the International Covenant on Economic Social and Cultural Rights.
[43] European Commission, 'Delegated Regulation (EU) amending Annexes II and IV to Regulation (EU) No 978/2012 as regards the temporary withdrawal of the arrangements referred to in Article 1(2) of Regulation (EU) No 978/2012 in respect of certain products originating in the Kingdom of Cambodia', C(2020) 673 final, 12 February 2020.

In addition to the four occasions where GSP/EBA conditionality was enforced and resulted in temporary suspensions from the scheme, investigations were launched on three other occasions by the EU to assess allegations of human rights violations: against Pakistan in 1997 following allegations of child labour; against El Salvador in 2008 based on concerns regarding freedom of association; and against Bolivia in 2012 for insufficiently implementing the UN Single Convention on Narcotic Drugs. Four suspensions and three investigations arguably seems like a 'meagre catch' in view of the many other 'missed' occasions over the years.[44] With regard to the GSP scheme's biggest beneficiaries, Bangladesh and Pakistan, the EU's use of conditionality has proven to be challenging and complex given the trade-offs involved.[45] This relates to broader questions regarding the effectiveness of trade sanctions and negative conditionality in general, since punitive trade measures may have significant economic effects that go well beyond the targeted elite or sector.[46]

Second, a variety of observers have accused the EU of applying double standards in deciding whether or not to investigate and/or sanction GSP beneficiaries. This well-known critique regarding similar violations leading to different responses by the EU concerns both the countries at hand and the human rights concerned. With regard to the latter, some have argued that labour rights violations have been more likely to lead to suspensions than violations of civil or political rights. However, while four out of seven of the withdrawal procedures launched so far mainly or only concerned labour rights violations, the sample remains small and multiple examples of other serious labour violations went unpunished. This immediately highlights the different treatment of similar violations across different countries. Here, the EU has been accused of using punitive trade measures only if and when it was deemed strategically opportune to do so, raising questions about a 'dichotomy between norms and interests'.[47] It should be noted that since the 2012 review of the GSP Regulation, the Commission can issue withdrawal decisions on its own through delegated acts, without the political horse-trading usually involved in Council decisions.[48] Nevertheless, this has so far not led to greater stringency in assessing GSP beneficiaries, despite some observers identifying 'coherence by accident' between Common Foreign and Security Policy (CFSP) and GSP sanctions.[49]

Third, there seems to be an enforcement gap when it comes to GSP+ beneficiary countries' compliance on the ground with the international conventions they have ratified. While the prospect of GSP+ beneficiary status indeed appears to have positively incentivized countries such as Bolivia, Colombia, Venezuela, Mongolia, and El Salvador to ratify a number of ILO conventions, the domestic monitoring and enforcement of those conventions is

[44] Beke and Hachez, 'The EU GSP: A Preference for Human Rights and Good Governance?' (n 40) 6.

[45] Zamfir, 'Human Rights in EU Trade Policy' (n 36) 6–8. See also cases 1056/2018/JN and 1369/2019/JN on the European Commission's actions regarding the respect for fundamental labour rights in Bangladesh in the context of the EU's Generalised Scheme of Preferences before the European Ombudsman. The complainants believed that the Commission should have started a process of withdrawal of trade preferences, the Ombudsman decided that the decision not to do so remains within the wide margin of discretion awarded to the Commission in this regard.

[46] J Vandenberghe, 'On Carrots and Sticks: The Social Dimension of EC Trade Policy' (2008) 13 European Foreign Affairs Review 561, 577. See also Ch 9.

[47] J Orbie and L Tortell, 'The New GSP+ Beneficiaries: Ticking the Box or Truly Consistent with ILO Findings?' (2009) 14 European Foreign Affairs Review 663, 679; E Fierro, *European Union's Approach to Human Rights Conditionality in Practice* (Martinus Nijhoff 2003) 378; M Carbone and J Orbie, 'Beyond Economic Partnership Agreements: the European Union and the Trade–Development Nexus' (2009) 20 Contemporary Politics 1, 5.

[48] Beke and Hachez, 'The EU GSP: A Preference for Human Rights and Good Governance?' (n 40) 24.

[49] C Portela and J Orbie, 'Sanctions under the EU Generalised System of Preferences and Foreign Policy: Coherence by Accident?' in M Carbone and J Orbie (eds), *The Trade–Development Nexus in the European Union: Differentiation, Coherence and Norms* (Routledge 2015).

insufficient.[50] Commitments on paper have thus not been met in practice due to a lack of enforcement on the ground, a problem more generally associated with (lack of) implementation of international law and in particular international human rights treaties.[51]

In sum, the rather sporadic and inconsistent enforcement of the GSP's conditionality provisions has led many to question the scheme's overall effectiveness in terms of human rights promotion. The most glaring aspect is the perceived imbalance between, on the one hand, the EU's readiness to grant positive conditionality preferences to ratifying countries and, on the other hand, a reluctance to use negative conditionality in case of violations committed by those beneficiaries. It should be reiterated again, however, that the problems the GSP schemes aim to tackle are complex and country-specific, and that the effectiveness and use of GSP conditionality arguably depends on its coordination with other human rights and foreign policy instruments. Moreover, the enforcement of GSP obligations is closely linked to the enforcement of international law in the beneficiary countries, and in this light, it is unrealistic to expect the EU GSP mechanisms to improve the enforcement of international law worldwide radically.

B. Unilateral trade control measures

Within the margins of WTO rules, the EU can impose certain unilateral trade restrictions to protect human rights. Such restrictions limit the import and export of certain goods, either based on their potentially harmful effects on human rights or due to their country of origin. As such, roughly two types of unilateral trade control measures can be distinguished, depending on whether (i) the EU restricts the trade in goods with specific countries, as part of a wider set of sanctions under the CFSP, or (ii) issue-specific measures, which restrict the trade in certain goods that can have clear human rights-related implications.

Under the CFSP framework, the EU can adopt country-specific trade restrictions, either by implementing binding resolutions from the UN Security Council or based on an autonomous EU decision.[52] The latter manner of issuing trade sanctions outside of the UN framework has been considerably simplified by the Lisbon Treaty, which provided a new legal basis for a single-step mechanism allowing the EU to interrupt or reduce, in part or completely, any economic and financial relations with one or more third countries.[53] This is only possible, however, if the decision to do so is made in conformity with the overall objective of the Union's CFSP; in other words, based on the general provisions of the EU's external action, laid down in Article 21 TEU, which includes the advancement of 'the universality and indivisibility of human rights and fundamental freedoms'. As of 2020, 34 countries were subjected to restrictive measures by the EU. For most cases, this includes embargos on arms and related materials, a ban on exports of equipment for internal repression, and the freezing of funds and economic resources of specific persons, entities, or bodies. It is worth noting in this regard that the embargoed goods in question often correspond to those targeted by the EU's issue-specific trade measures.[54]

---

[50] Orbie and Tortell, 'The New GSP+ Beneficiaries' (n 47) 672.
[51] E Posner, *The Twilight of Human Rights Law* (Oxford University Press 2014).
[52] See Ch 9.
[53] Art 215(1) TFEU.
[54] For a more detailed discussion of EU country-specific measures, see Beke and others, 'Report on the Integration of Human Rights in EU Development and Trade Policies' (n 8) 36–38.

Since 2005, the EU has adopted an increasing number of issue-specific measures to mitigate risks of human rights abuses. Import and export restrictions have been issued for a variety of goods, ranging from instruments of torture and military equipment to goods whose production has been associated with human rights violations. With regard to trade in military and other harmful products, well-known examples include, among others, the 2005 Regulation on export restrictions for goods that can be used for 'capital punishment, torture or other cruel, inhuman or degrading treatment or punishment',[55] the 2008 Council Common Position on 'rules governing the control of exports of military technology and equipment',[56] and the 2009 Regulation on trade in dual-use goods. The latter relates to 'items, including software and technology, which can be used for both civil and military purposes', as well as 'all goods which can be used for both non-explosive uses and assisting in any way in the manufacture of nuclear weapons or other nuclear explosive devices'.[57]

In addition to goods that can be used to commit human rights violations, the EU has increasingly also used trade control instruments for goods produced in circumstances that have been related to human rights abuses. The most vulnerable sector in this regard is that of extractive industries and natural resources. Examples of EU trade restrictions in this area include the 2002 Regulation to implement the UN Kimberly Process Certification Scheme (KPCS), which aims to curb the international trade in so-called blood diamonds produced in, and often a cause of, circumstances of civil war, genocide, and violent human rights abuses. By subscribing to the KPCS, the EU obliges traders to provide certificates of origin for their goods and EU traders cannot trade with countries who have not signed up to the Certification Scheme.[58] Furthermore, the EU agreed in 2017 on a Regulation concerning trade in conflict minerals which obliges large importers of natural mineral resources to observe due diligence across the value chain.[59] The Regulation obliges EU importers to implement management system, risk mitigation, third-party audit, and disclosure obligations.

Regulation (EU) 2017/821 of the European Parliament and of the Council laying down supply chain due diligence obligations for Union importers of tin, tantalum and tungsten, their ores, and gold originating from conflict-affected and high-risk areas [2017] OJ L130/1

(1) Although they hold great potential for development, natural mineral resources can, in conflict-affected or high-risk areas, be a cause of dispute where their revenues

---

[55] Council Regulation (EC) No 1236/2005 concerning trade in certain goods which could be used for capital punishment, torture or other cruel, inhuman or degrading treatment or punishment [2005] OJ L200/1; now superseded by Regulation (EU) 2019/125 of the European Parliament and of the Council concerning trade in certain goods which could be used for capital punishment, torture or other cruel, inhuman or degrading treatment or punishment [2019] OJ L30/1.

[56] Council Common Position 2008/944/CFSP defining common rules governing control of exports of military technology and equipment [2008] OJ L335/99.

[57] Council Regulation (EC) No 428/2009 setting up a Community regime for the control of exports, transfer, brokering and transit of dual-use items [2009] OJ L134/1.

[58] Council Regulation (EC) No 2368/2002 of 20 December 2002 implementing the Kimberley Process certification scheme for the international trade in rough diamonds [2002] OJ L358/28.

[59] Regulation (EU) 2017/821 of the European Parliament and of the Council laying down supply chain due diligence obligations for Union importers of tin, tantalum and tungsten, their ores, and gold originating from conflict-affected and high-risk areas [2017] OJ L130/1.

fuel the outbreak or continuation of violent conflict, undermining endeavours towards development, good governance and the rule of law. In those areas, **breaking the nexus between conflict and illegal exploitation of minerals is a critical element in guaranteeing peace, development and stability**.

(2) The challenge posed by the desire to **prevent the financing of armed groups and security forces in resource-rich areas** has been taken up by governments and international organisations together with economic operators and civil society organisations, including women's organisations that are to the forefront of drawing attention to the exploitative conditions imposed by these groups and forces, as well as to rape and violence used to control local populations.

(3) **Human rights abuses are common in resource-rich conflict-affected and high-risk areas** and may include child labour, sexual violence, the disappearance of people, forced resettlement and the destruction of ritually or culturally significant sites.

(...)

Article 4

Management system obligations

Union importers of minerals or metals shall:

(a) **adopt**, and clearly communicate to suppliers and the public up-to-date information on, **their supply chain policy** for the minerals and metals potentially originating from conflict-affected and high-risk areas;

(b) incorporate in their supply chain policy s**tandards against which supply chain due diligence is to be conducted** consistent with the standards set out in the model supply chain policy in Annex II to the OECD Due Diligence Guidance;

(c) structure their respective internal management systems to support supply chain due diligence by **assigning responsibility to senior management**, in cases where the Union importer is not a natural person, to oversee the supply chain due diligence process as well as maintain records of those systems for a minimum of five years;

(d) strengthen their engagement with suppliers by incorporating their supply chain policy into contracts and agreements with suppliers consistent with Annex II to the OECD Due Diligence Guidance;

(e) establish a grievance mechanism as an early-warning risk-awareness system or provide such mechanism through collaborative arrangements with other economic operators or organisations, or by facilitating recourse to an external expert or body, such as an ombudsman;

Article 5

Risk management obligations

1. Union importers of minerals shall:

(a) **identify and assess the risks of adverse impacts in their mineral supply chain** on the basis of the information provided pursuant to Article 4 against the

> standards of their supply chain policy, consistent with Annex II to, and the due
> diligence recommendations set out in, the OECD Due Diligence Guidance;
> (b) implement a **strategy to respond to the identified risks** designed so as to pre-
> vent or mitigate adverse impacts (…)

Moreover, in order to 'provide civil society in resource-rich countries with the information needed to hold governments to account for any income made through the exploitation
of natural resources', the Commission has also promoted the adoption of the Extractive
Industries Transparency Initiative (EITI), particularly in developing countries. Established
at the 2002 World Summit on Sustainable Development in Johannesburg, the EITI constitutes a voluntary multi-stakeholder platform with the objective of fostering more transparency in the extractives sector by disclosing information about the payments from extractive
companies to resource-rich governments. While the EITI is voluntary, the US, through its
2010 Dodd–Frank Wall Street Reform Consumer Protection Act, and the EU, through its
Accounting and Transparency Directives, introduced binding disclosure requirements for
extractive companies based in the US and the EU respectively.[60] Adopted by the Commission
in 2013, the Accounting Directive introduced obligations regarding so-called country by
country reporting (CBCR), to companies listed and large non-listed extractive and logging
companies registered in the European Economic Area (EEA). The Directive requires them
to report, per country and project, on all their payments to governments.[61] Moreover, the
Accounting Directive advocates that resource-rich countries to take part in the EITI process
and, in order to ensure a level playing field among companies operating on the EU market, a
revision of the 2004 Transparency Directive introduced the same disclosure requirements to
all companies listed on EU regulated markets, even when they are not registered in the EEA
and/or are incorporated in a non-EU country.[62]

Finally, for the logging sector in particular, the EU in 2003 adopted the Forest Law
Enforcement, Governance and Trade (FLEGT) Action Plan. The Action Plan at the time constituted the EU's response to the failure of previous attempts at tackling global deforestation
and the related human rights concerns through binding international agreements and unilateral trade restrictions, as well as to the limited adoption of private certification schemes
in developing countries.[63] FLEGT has therefore been designed to tackle illegal timber and
the associated trade by using a combination of demand- and supply-side measures, focusing
respectively on the banning of illegal timber from the EU market, and supporting forest governance reforms and law enforcement in timber-producing countries. FLEGT established
an innovative, two-pronged, mutually reinforcing implementation design based on the

---

[60] Beke and others, 'Report on the Integration of Human Rights in EU Development and Trade Policies' (n
8) 46–47.

[61] Directive 2013/34/EU of the European Parliament and of the Council on the annual financial statements, consolidated financial statements and related reports of certain types of undertakings, amending Directive 2006/43/
EC of the European Parliament and of the Council and repealing Council Directives 78/660/EEC and 83/349/EEC
[2013] OJ L182/19.

[62] Directive 2013/50/EU of the European Parliament and of the Council amending Directive 2004/109/EC of
the European Parliament and of the Council on the harmonisation of transparency requirements in relation to
information about issuers whose securities are admitted to trading on a regulated market, Directive 2003/71/EC
of the European Parliament and of the Council on the prospectus to be published when securities are offered to
the public or admitted to trading and Commission Directive 2007/14/EC laying down detailed rules for the implementation of certain provisions of Directive 2004/109/EC [2013] OJ L294/13.

[63] B Cashore and others, 'Can Non-state Governance "Ratchet Up" Global Environmental Standards? Lessons
from the Forest Sector' (2007) 16 Review of European Community and International Environmental Law 158.

negotiation of Voluntary Partnership Agreements (VPAs) between the EU and timber producing countries. VPAs are bilateral trade agreements which frame the legal, institutional, and governance reforms required to ensure that all timber exports from VPA countries to the EU can be certified as legal. Each VPA therefore centres around a legality definition which constitutes a comprehensive understanding of what can and cannot be regarded as 'legal timber' under national law, which includes references to international treaty commitments and domestic forestry law, as well as labour rights and worker health and safety regulations and the rights of indigenous communities.

The other 'leg' of the FLEGT Action Plan implementation framework is the EU Timber Regulation,[64] adopted in 2010 and in force since March 2013. The aim of the Timber Regulation is to curb the EU's imports and consumption of illegally harvested timber by demanding either FLEGT certification or elaborate due diligence procedures from operators placing wood and wood products on the common market. For VPA countries with a functioning timber legality assurance system in place, the Timber Regulation rolls out 'green lane' access for FLEGT-licensed timber and timber products as well as for products protected under the Convention on International Trade in Endangered Species of Wild Fauna and Flora (CITES).[65] In addition to creating a general market incentive to curb illegal logging, the Timber Regulation explicitly complements and promotes VPAs by banning any timber from VPA countries that is not licensed by FLEGT, while providing preferential access to the EU market. The Timber Regulation therefore grants a significant market advantage to FLEGT-licensed timber compared to non-licensed timber since it imposes considerable additional costs on firms from non-VPA countries. This direct link between the Action Plans demand-side measures, implemented through the Timber Regulation, and the supply side, through the VPAs, is considered to be a strong incentive for timber-producing countries to take part in the FLEGT regime.[66]

C. Human rights clauses in EU trade agreements

EU bilateral and regional trade agreements have included so-called human rights clauses since the early 1990s, making the application of the agreement conditional upon a party's respect for human rights and democratic principles. As an 'essential element' of the agreement, the violation of the human rights clause allows the other party to take 'appropriate measures', including the suspension of the agreement.[67]

Human rights were incorporated for the first time in an EU trade and cooperation agreement under Article 5 of the 1989 Lomé IV Convention with the Group of African, Caribbean, and Pacific Countries (ACP). Article 5, however, simply reiterated the notion that development, as the Convention's primary objective, entailed the 'respect of and promotion of all human rights', but did not provide any legal tools to condition the agreement those principles

---

[64] Regulation (EU) No 995/2010 of the European Parliament and of the Council laying down the obligations of operators who place timber and timber products on the market [2010] OJ L295/23.

[65] In force since 1975, CITES is an intergovernmental agreement aimed at ensuring that international trade in tropical wild animals and plant species does not endanger their survival. As such, any imports or exports of animal and plant species covered by CITES should be authorized through a licensing system. Parties to the Convention are expected to identify both management and scientific authorities which should monitor and advise the licensing system.

[66] TERREA, S-FOR-S, TOPPERSPECTIVE, 'Evaluation of the EU FLEGT Action Plan (Forest Law Enforcement Governance and Trade) 2004–2014', Final Report Volume 1 (Main Report), 27 April 2016, 54.

[67] See Ch 9 for a general explanation of human rights clauses in EU international agreements.

effectively. The development of a more practical human rights clause, which could enable the suspension of an agreement in case of grave human rights violations, had nonetheless been a key objective of the EU by then for over a decade; to be precise, since 1977, when the EU tried to suspend its foreign aid to the Idi Amin regime in Uganda, only to realize the agreement in force did not allow for such suspension. While the Ugandan case was solved informally, repeated efforts on behalf of the EU to include more effective human rights language in the subsequent Conventions with the ACP went unsuccessful. Other countries however, proved more receptive to the EU's normative endeavours and in 1990, the Argentina–EU Cooperation Agreement became the first ever trade agreement to incorporate a functioning, enforceable human rights clause—included at the behest of Argentina itself.[68]

The fall of the Berlin Wall and the subsequent need to consolidate democracy in Central and Eastern European States, as well as similar perspectives of democratization across large tracts of Africa and Latin America in the early 1990s created further momentum in the West for a more 'political' approach to trade and development cooperation. In March 1991, the Commission adopted a 'Communication on Human rights, Democracy and Development Co-operation', soon followed by a Council resolution in November 1991, giving the Commission a specific mandate to include human rights clauses in agreements with third countries. Less than a year later, the European Council declared that democratic principles constituted an essential part of any agreement between the EU and the members of the then Conference on Security and Cooperation in Europe (today transformed into the Organization for Security and Co-operation in Europe (OSCE)). As such, EU agreements concluded after 1992 with the Baltic States and Albania contained a so-called Baltic clause which allowed for the immediate suspension of the agreement in case of serious violations of any essential provisions, including human rights.[69] Given its rigid formulation, the Baltic clause was soon abandoned in favour of a more flexible approach introduced under the EU–Bulgaria Agreement. The 'Bulgarian clause' proposed a wider scope of options beyond immediate suspension, including political dialogue and, if need be, 'appropriate measures'. The Bulgarian clause is now known as the 'non-execution clause' and constitutes an inherent aspect of the human rights clause's functioning, notably because it allows one contracting party to take action against the other in case the latter fails to comply with its obligations under the agreement.[70]

In 1995—the same year in which the revised Lomé IV Convention (also known as Lomé IV bis) introduced the first proper human rights conditionality clause in an EU–ACP agreement—the Commission issued a Communication 'on the inclusion of respect for human rights in agreements between the Community and third countries'.[71] The Council subsequently, by taking note of the Communication on 29 May, adopted the policy to include systematically enforceable human rights clauses in all future EU cooperation and trade agreements. The Council's resolution further emphasized the need to favour a positive, dialogue-centred approach to human rights, and that suspensions or other punitive measures under the clause should only be evoked as a last resort. While the 1995 Council

---

[68] L Bartels, *Human Rights Conditionality in the EU's International Agreements* (Oxford University Press 2005) 8–11.

[69] European Parliament, Working document on the Human Rights and Democracy Clause in European Union agreements, Committee on Foreign Affairs (AFET), 23 August 2005, 4.

[70] N Hachez, ' "Essential Elements" Clauses in EU Trade Agreements—Making Trade Work in a Way That Helps Human Rights?' (2015) 53 Cuadernos Europeos de Deusto 81, 89–91.

[71] Commission of the European Communities, 'Communication from the Commission on the inclusion of respect for human rights in agreements between the community and third countries', COM(95) 216 final, Brussels, 23 May 1995.

resolution mandated the systematic inclusion of human rights clauses, all EU trade agreements since 1992 had already included one. As a result, roughly over 120 EU trade agreements with countries all over the world now contain such clauses, typically located at the very beginning of the agreement.

With regard to their content, essential elements or human rights clauses have evolved somewhat over time in the way they are formulated, though in essence they all refer to the democratic principles and fundamental human rights underpinning the agreement at hand and, in combination with the non-execution clause, condition the agreement upon the parties' compliance with them. A good example of the standard formulation is Article 1 of the 2012 EU–Central America Association Agreement, accompanied by a non-execution clause (Article 355 of the Agreement).

Agreement establishing an Association between the European Union and its Member States, on the one hand, and Central America on the other [2012] OJ L346/3

Article 1

1. Respect for democratic principles and **fundamental human rights**, as laid down in the Universal Declaration of Human Rights, and for the rule of law, underpins the internal and international policies of both Parties and **constitutes an essential element of this Agreement.**

Article 355

2. If a Party considers that another Party has failed to fulfil an obligation under this Agreement, it may have **recourse to appropriate measures**. Before doing so, except in cases of special urgency, it shall submit to the Association Council within thirty days all relevant information required for a thorough examination of the situation with a view to seeking a solution acceptable to the Parties. In selecting which measures to adopt, priority shall be given to those which are least disruptive to the implementation of this Agreement. Such measures shall be notified immediately to the Association Committee and shall be the subject of consultations in the Committee if a Party so requests.

3. The Parties agree that the term 'cases of special urgency' in paragraph 2 means a case of material breach of this Agreement by one of the Parties. The Parties further agree that the term 'appropriate measures' referred to in paragraph 2 means measures taken in accordance with international law. It is understood that **suspension would be a measure of last resort.**

4. A material breach of this Agreement consists in:
   (a) repudiation of this Agreement not sanctioned by general rules of international law;
   (b) **violation of the essential elements of this Agreement.**

The non-execution clause above illustrates that certain conditions are to be taken into account when 'appropriate measures' are being adopted. First, priority must be given to 'proportionate' measures, which least disrupt the implementation of the agreement. Second, measures have to be taken in accordance with international law and, third, the suspension of the agreement is to be considered only in last resort. In addition, some clauses add that as soon as the cause of disruption disappears, so too should any punitive measures, while others add that 'cases of special urgency' can bypass any consultative procedures. Procedurally, it is worth noting that while none of the human rights clauses in EU trade agreements so far have been accompanied by a dedicated monitoring mechanism,[72] any issues arising under the essential elements clause can, and often must, be discussed within one of the organs established under the agreement.[73] The most obvious one in this regard is the primary bilateral organ for political dialogue, often called the Association Council or Joint Council. Indeed, under most non-execution clauses it is mandatory, except in 'cases of special urgency', to notify the Association or Joint Council of any appropriate measures, while consultations must be held and information should be provided to allow for a thorough examination of the situation at hand and how to address it in a mutually satisfactory manner. Such consultation procedures are particularly elaborate under Articles 96 and 97 of the Cotonou Partnership Agreement with the ACP Group.[74]

One of the main lines of criticism of EU human rights clauses in FTAs has to do with their implementation, or rather the lack thereof. Over the past 25 years, human rights clauses have been invoked only on a handful of occasions and only with respect to developing countries part of the ACP Group. However, there has never been any punitive action under a human rights clause, other than through the respective cooperation agreements between the EU and the ACP Group,[75] and human rights abuses, in and by themselves, have never constituted sufficient reason to give rise to 'appropriate measures' under non-execution clauses. Table 10.1, compiled by Døhlie Saltnes,[76] provides an overview of the countries that have been consulted under the essential elements clause, and why, up to 2013. The Commission's and High Representative's Evaluation of the Cotonou Partnership Agreement of 2016 adds thereto only one more instance of Art 96 consultation procedures, namely with regard to flawed elections in Burundi in 2015.[77]

The pattern and frequency of use of human rights clauses has led to twofold criticism. First, the EU has been accused of not enforcing human rights conditionality often enough, regularly letting human rights violations by trade partners go unpunished. The EP has remarked in this regard that 'failure to take appropriate or restrictive measures in the event of a situation marked by persistent human rights violations seriously undermines the Union's human rights strategy, sanctions policy and credibility'.[78] Other observers have pointed out in this regard that, in particular in comparison to the US approach which takes a more targeted and binding approach to human and labour rights commitments, the EU's essential elements clauses are to be seen as aspirational, testimonies of a joint commitment and basis to foster dialogue and joint engagement.[79] Others, however, have highlighted the limited effectiveness of punitive, reactionary measures, favouring the incremental, non-adversary

---

[72] In some agreements, however, subcommittees on human rights and democratic principles have been established on an ad hoc basis, the first of these being the EU–Morocco Association Agreement. See Decision No 1/2003 of the EU–Morocco Association Council setting up subcommittees of the Association Committee [2003] OJ L79/14.

[73] Bartels, *Human Rights Conditionality* (n 68) 11.

[74] These procedures are discussed in Ch 11.

[75] Lomé IV bis for the period 1995–1999 and the Cotonou Agreement for the period 2000–2020.

[76] J Døhlie Saltnes, 'The EU's Human Rights Policy: Unpacking the Literature on the EU's Implementation of Aid Conditionality' (2013) Arena Working Paper 2/2013, 7, Table 1.

[77] European Commission and High Representative of the Union for Foreign Affairs and Security Policy, 'Evaluation of the Cotonou Partnership Agreement', SWD(2016) 250 final, Brussels, 15 July 2016, 38–39.

[78] European Parliament, 'Resolution on the evaluation of EU sanctions as part of the EU's actions and policies in the area of human rights', P6_TA(2008)0405, 4 September 2008.

[79] Ibid.

approach maintained by the EU. Indeed, punitive trade measures are only effective in specific contexts and may backfire in others.[80]

Second, the seemingly selective way of applying the human rights clauses has raised more accusations of double standards. Only developing countries in a highly dependent relation with the EU under the Cotonou Agreement have so far been subjected to an activation of the clauses, while other, stronger trading partners remained out of reach. Moreover, as Table 10.1

Table 10.1 Consultations under the 'essential elements' clause, by country and reason for triggering

	Coup d'état	Flawed Elections	Human Rights	Rule of Law
2011 Guinea-Bissau			x	X
2010 Niger	x			
2009 Niger		x		
2009 Madagascar	x			
2009 Guinea	x			
2008 Mauritania	x			
2007 Fiji	x			
2005 Mauritania	X			
2004 Guinea		x		
2004 Togo		x	x	
2003 Guinea-Bissau	X			
2003 Central African Republic	X			
2001 Zimbabwe		x	x	x
2001 Liberia		x	x	x
2001 Côte d'Ivoire		x		
2000 Fiji	X			
2000 Haiti		x		
2000 Côte d'Ivoire	X			
1999 Guinea-Bissau	X			
1999 Comros	X			
1999 Niger	X			
1998 Togo		x		
1996 Niger	X			

---

[80] Hachez, '"Essential Elements" Clauses in EU Trade Agreements' (n 70) 102.

shows, conditionality has only been activated in reaction to severe and sudden deteriorations of the political situation in a partner country, involving political coups or other violations of democratic principles, which are not always accompanied by human rights abuses. More low-profile, yet systematic, abuses have paradoxically thus not been a matter of concern under the human rights clause, which again puts in doubt the tool's lack of (inclusive) monitoring capacity. Furthermore, it has been argued that—when human rights abuses are concerned—there is a disproportionate focus on civil and political rights at the expense of socio-economic rights.[81]

Finally, existing research has empirically identified how contestation concerning the integration of human rights conditionality into the EU's FTA can lead to the EU making concessions. Mckenzie and Meissner examined the negotiations of the EU–Singapore FTA (EUSFTA) and found that clashing commercial interests with the promotion of human rights resulted in the EU adopting incoherent positions. The case study is an important reminder that the mainstreaming of the EU's human rights agenda into bilateral trade relations is not necessarily welcomed with open arms by the negotiating partners, who might be capable of exploiting the accompanying contestation and internal divisions.

L Mckenzie and K Meissner, 'Human Rights Conditionality in European Union Trade Negotiations: the Case of the EU–Singapore FTA' (2017) 55 Journal of Common Market Studies 832

The EU's values of human rights—and practice of linking these values to FTAs through conditionality—were contested in negotiations with Singapore. Instead of leading to conflict between the EU and Singapore throughout the negotiations, or creating tension between EU decision-makers promoting incompatible sets of interests, the EU made a concession on conditionality. This concession occurred through a side letter that recognizes Singapore's human rights practices at the time of signing the agreement. This limited the EU's capability to use conditionality as an instrument for dialogue on issues such as Singapore's use of the death penalty and corporal punishment.

This concession was made possible because EU decision-makers such as the EP, which typically challenge the commercial orientation of players including the [Trade Policy Committee] and DG Trade, were not active in these negotiations. EP and EEAS passivity in this case—a product of the overarching orientation of the EU towards a prioritization of the trade agenda in relations with Southeast Asian states and of the EUSFTA's low salience—resulted in a weak (or conservative) position on values promotion. Concession-making is a necessary part of any trade negotiation. The conservative position on conditionality in this case, however, is problematic in that it undermines the EU's stated foreign policy position which is to: i) continue the link between its political agreement and trade policy through conditionality, and ii) to take a clear and active position on the promotion of human rights in relations with Southeast Asian states (...). In the EU's current negotiation of new generation FTAs, its foreign policy and trade agenda are in tension as instruments such as conditionality can—instead of improving

---

[81] AC Prickartz and I Staudinger, 'Policy vs Practice: The Use, Implementation and Enforcement of Human Rights Clauses in the European Union's International Trade Agreements' (2019) 3(1) Europe and the World: A Law Review 1, 20–22.

capability and visibility of EU foreign policy—force the EU to trade off foreign policy for the commercial agenda.

(…) The EU's concessions on human rights conditionality in the EUSFTA differs remarkably from the FTA negotiations with Colombia, Peru or Canada, for example, where the EU stood by its insistence on conditionality, and from the negotiations with the Mercado Común del Sur or the Republic of Korea, where the negotiation of values was not problematic. This variation in the EU's approach to advancing values throughout its FTA negotiations requires explanation. (…)

D. Sustainable development chapters in EU trade agreements

Beginning with the 2008 EU–Cariforum Economic Partnership Agreement (EPA), EU bilateral trade agreements have also started to incorporate so-called sustainable development chapters containing references to international labour and environmental standards. These chapters commit the contracting parties to respect labour and environmental standards and flow from the EU's constitutional framework requiring that the EU's external policies 'foster sustainable, economic, social and environmental development of developing countries, with the primary aim of eradicating poverty'.[82]

Sustainable development chapters are currently part of the 2008 EU–Cariforum EPA, the 2010 EU–Korea Agreement, the 2012 EU–Central America Association Agreement, the 2013 EU–Peru/Colombia/Ecuador Trade Agreement, the 2014 EU–Moldova, EU–Ukraine and EU–Georgia Association Agreements, the 2015 EU–Singapore FTA, the 2016 EU–Vietnam FTA, the 2016 EU–South African Development Community EPA, the 2017 Comprehensive Economic and Trade Agreement (CETA) with Canada, the 2018 EU–Mexico Trade Agreement (not yet ratified), the 2019 EU–Japan EPA, and the 2019 EU–Mercosur Trade Agreement (not yet ratified). All future EU trade agreements are also currently envisaged to include sustainability chapters.

Core elements of sustainable development chapters (adapted from Beke et al 2014)[83]

In terms of the commitments and operational provisions they contain, all recent trade agreements in force seem to revolve around a common core composed of several elements (not always in the same order):

- A reference to the following instruments:

  ○ The Rio Declaration on Environment (Colombia/Peru) and Development and Agenda 21 on Environment and Development of 1992 (Central America, South Korea, Colombia/Peru)

---

[82] Article 21 TEU.
[83] Beke and others, 'Report on the Integration of Human Rights in EU Development and Trade Policies' (n 8) 74.

- ○ The Johannesburg Plan of Implementation on Sustainable Development of 2002 (Central America, South Korea)
  - ○ The 2006 Ministerial Declaration of the UN Economic and Social Council on Full Employment and Decent Work (Central America, South Korea, Cariforum)
  - ○ The Cotonou Agreement (Cariforum)
  - ○ The Millennium Development Goals (Colombia/Peru).

- A reaffirmation by the parties of their general commitment to promote trade in a way that fosters sustainable development (Central America, South Korea).
- A reaffirmation that countries have the freedom to define their own level of social and environmental protection, and that social and environmental standards should not be used for protectionist purposes, although parties should strive to ensure high social and environmental standards (Central America, South Korea, Cariforum, Colombia/Peru).
- A commitment to strive towards high levels of social and environmental protection by:
  - ○ Implementing ILO Conventions and other multilateral instruments applicable to the parties (Central America, South Korea, Cariforum)
  - ○ Respecting, promoting and realizing in their laws and practice the core labour standards and associated ILO Conventions proclaimed in the ILO Declaration of Fundamental Principles and Rights at Work of 1998, namely:
    - ▪ the freedom of association and the effective recognition of the right to collective bargaining;
    - ▪ the elimination of all forms of forced or compulsory labour;
    - ▪ the effective abolition of child labour;
    - ▪ the elimination of discrimination in respect of employment and occupation. (Central America, South Korea, Cariforum, Colombia/Peru).
  - ○ Implementing a list of multilateral environmental agreements (Central America, Colombia/Peru).
- A commitment to cooperate to develop trade schemes and trade practices favouring sustainable development, notably in respect of particular themes such as forestry, fisheries, climate change (Central America, Colombia/Peru), fair trade and corporate social responsibility (South Korea, Colombia/Peru), biological diversity (Colombia/Peru), migrant workers (Colombia/Peru).
- A commitment not to lower or fail to apply social and environmental standards with a view to encouraging trade or attracting investment (Central America, South Korea, Cariforum, Colombia/Peru).

Sustainable development chapters contain labour and environmental standards, each entailing two types of obligations. First, they set out minimum obligations relating to the implementation of multilateral commitments. As such, they seemingly add little to the human rights clause in terms of substance. For instance, the ILO core labour standards provided under the sustainability chapter are already binding on the parties through their membership of the ILO, while other human rights are covered under the standard human rights clause. As far as environmental standards are concerned, the obligations under the chapter amount to no more than a reaffirmation of those obligations under the respective multilateral agreements signed and ratified by the contracting parties. The Commission has, however, stressed the importance of reiterating these references to international standards as a way of strengthening existing multilateral governance structures, rather than creating a bilateral set of rules on labour and environmental protection.[84] The second type of obligation requires the parties to refrain from reducing their current levels of social and environmental protection, while encouraging them to raise those levels as long as this is not done for protectionist purposes. This obligation is therefore part a potentially effective guarantee against regulatory decline, part a 'best endeavours provision'.[85]

Given their limited added value as 'hard law', the main innovation of sustainability chapters is to be found in the monitoring mechanisms they provide for, which human rights clauses generally lack. Sustainable development chapters generally establish dedicated institutional and civil society bodies which are meant to meet on a regular basis to discuss the ongoing implementation of sustainability commitments. Arguably the most important bodies are the bilateral institutions established for government-to-government interactions and civil society organizations (CSOs). First, bilateral (sub-)committees are set up specifically to address sustainable development issues on an intergovernmental basis. The breadth of the mandates of these committees vary to some extent. The Trade and Development Committee established under the EU–Cariforum EPA, for instance, can discuss any sustainable development issue, and is not limited to discussing only those matters directly linked to the implementation of the chapter.[86] Likewise, the Sub-committee on Trade and Sustainable Development under the EU–Colombia/Peru/Ecuador agreement is mandated to oversee the implementation of the chapter, including cooperation activities that contribute to its implementation, as well as to discuss matters of common interest related to the sustainability chapter.[87] The Trade and Sustainable Development Board in the EU–Central America agreement, however, is only mandated to oversee the implementation of the sustainable development chapter.[88]

Second, besides intergovernmental bilateral meetings, sustainable development chapters also provide for a forum for civil society involvement, including so-called Domestic Advisory Groups (DAG). DAGs and similar bodies serve as fora in which each party is bound to consult domestic labour and environment or sustainable development committees or groups. Stipulations regarding the constitution and consultation procedures for these groups are to be in accordance with national law but should guarantee a balanced representation of relevant interests. Furthermore, so-called Joint Forums bring together the DAG members of the different countries involved to discuss issues of common concern during meetings organized in parallel to the (annual) government-to-government meetings. It should be mentioned that the composition of DAGs and, more specifically, the selection procedures behind them, have been criticized for lacking transparency. Accusations have been made in this regard about governments favouring representatives that are, in some way or another, linked to the government, effectively excluding critical voices.[89]

---

[84] European Commission, Trade and Sustainable Development (TSD) chapters in EU Free Trade Agreements (FTAs), Non-paper of the Commission services, 11 July 2017, 4.

[85] L Bartels, 'Human Rights and Sustainable Development Obligations in EU Free Trade Agreements' (2013) 40 Legal Issues of Economic Integration 309.

[86] Article 230(3)(a) of Economic Partnership Agreement between the CARIFORUM States, of the one part, and the European Community and its Member States, of the other part [2008] OJ L289/3.

[87] Article 280(4) of Trade Agreement between the European Union and its Member States, of the one part, and Colombia and Peru, of the other part [2012] OJ L354/3.

[88] Article 294(3) of Agreement establishing an Association between the European Union and its Member States, on the one hand, and Central America on the other [2012] OJ L346/3.

[89] J Orbie and others, 'Promoting Sustainable Development or Legitimising Free Trade? Civil Society Mechanisms in EU Trade Agreements' (2016) 1 Third World Thematics: A TWQ Journal 529.

Beyond monitoring and dialogue, none of the sustainability chapters create binding enforcement mechanisms, nor can violations arising from the sustainable development obligations be addressed through the normal dispute-settlement procedures covering the rest of the trade agreement.[90] Sustainability chapters thus have their own dispute-settlement mechanism which differs from the general dispute-settlement procedures by foreseeing a role for civil society but, crucially, without the possibility to enforce sanctions. In case of a dispute under a sustainability chapter, one party can request the other to join a bilateral consultation, and, if deemed necessary, ask for a (sub-)committee to convene and consider the matter. If a bilateral consultation does not resolve the matter in a mutually satisfactory way, the complaining party can forward its grievances to a so-called Group of Experts. Such a Group is then mandated to assess and provide a report on whether or not one of the parties indeed failed to comply with the obligations contained in the chapter, as well as formulate non-binding recommendations to resolve the matter.[91]

Given the lack of proper enforcement mechanisms and the limited added value beyond more detailed labour and environmental standards, the EU's promotional approach of sustainable development chapters has been criticized as being too soft, particularly in comparison to similar provisions under US or Canadian trade agreements.[92] The question arises again, however, whether stricter mechanisms that are more oriented towards imposing sanctions automatically translate into better protection of social and environmental standards. Ultimately, the test for the EU's preference for long-term, dialogue-based engagement should be whether the sustainability chapters actually make a difference in the enhancement of labour and human rights standards in partner countries.

Sustainable development chapters have only been implemented for a relatively short period. The implementation of their provisions and monitoring mechanisms is therefore still unfamiliar and experimental for both the EU and its partners. Focus thus far has been on putting the relevant institutions and mechanisms in place. The structures established so far have facilitated a number of focused bilateral dialogues on matters ranging from non-discrimination in the workplace (EU–South Korea), freedom of association and collective bargaining (EU–Central America), and the protection of endangered species under the Convention on International Trade in Endangered Species of Wild Fauna and Flora (EU–Colombia). Thus far, only one case has been brought under a sustainable development chapter dispute-settlement mechanism. It concerns the breach of labour commitments by Korea under Chapter 13 of the EU–Korea FTA causing the EU to request the establishment of a Panel of Experts in July 2019.[93] The Panel has since been established and the first hearing is scheduled to take place in the near future.

Despite these initial promising signs, various stakeholders have voiced a number of concerns regarding the effectiveness of the chapters in practice, in particular with regard to addressing alleged violations and long-standing under-implementation of some of the international standards mandated as part of the commitment to sustainability. The limited research conducted so far on the application of the sustainability chapters at country level

---

[90] Except under the EU-CARIFORUM EPA where the normal dispute settlement procedures apply (although suspension of concessions is not possible). See Article 213(2) of the EU-CARIFORUM EPA.

[91] See for instance Articles 282–285 of the EU–Colombia/Peru Trade Agreement.

[92] K Lukas and A Steinkellner, 'Social Standards in Sustainability Chapters of Bilateral Free Trade Agreements' (2010) Ludwig Boltzmann Institute of Human Rights, 10–12.

[93] European Union, Republic of Korea—Compliance with obligations under Chapter 13 of the EU–Korea Free Trade Agreement, Request for the establishment of a Panel of Experts, Brussels, 4 July 2019, Ares(2019)4194229.

676 HUMAN RIGHTS IN EU TRADE POLICY

has found that, according to stakeholders, the lack of proper monitoring and enforcement mechanisms, in combination with rather broad references to international standards, favours a rather formalistic promotion of certain rights and standards, but does little to push domestic governments to actually enhance those rights and standards in their respective jurisdictions.

A Marx, B Lein, and N Brando, 'The Protection of Labour Rights in Trade Agreements: The Case of the EU–Colombia Agreement' (2016) 50 Journal of World Trade 587

With regard to the functioning of the monitoring and enforcement mechanism provided under the Agreement, there seems to be a lack of close monitoring and follow up on the implementation and enforcement of labour provisions—particularly since labour rights as such are not part of the EU's Human Rights Strategy with Colombia. This contrasts with the approach applied in the US–Colombia trade agreement. First, the US uses relatively high-level quarterly visits to discuss progress with their Colombian counterparts. Secondly, while sanctioning and hard conditionality are by no means ideal instruments to foster increasing recognition of labour rights protection, experience from the US–Colombia Agreement shows that, from time to time, they offer a necessary tool 'to get their [the Colombian government, ed.] attention'. Hence, a binding bilateral dispute-settlement mechanism, like the one provided under Title XII of the EU–Colombia Agreement could include the provisions under the Sustainability Chapter—effectively elevating labour and environmental provisions to the level of those provisions constituting, or consistent with, the adequate application and interpretation of the Agreement. At the level of the EU Delegation in Colombia, the follow up of the sustainability chapter could be strengthened. To do so, the EU Human Rights Focal Point could collaborate more closely with the Trade and Development sections at the Delegation. Again the US approach offers a noteworthy example in this respect. Since late April 2015, an attaché of the US Department of Labour has been seconded to the US embassy to Bogotá, whose sole responsibility it is to monitor the implementation of the [Labour Action Plan].

Concerning CSO engagement, we identify three critical concerns. First of all, there seems to be an overall lack of accountability of both Colombian government agencies and of the EU towards the domestic and transnational CSO mechanisms. Essentially, it is unclear how DG Trade on the EU side and the respective ministries on the Colombian side are supposed to deal with inputs from civil society under the Trade Agreement's current stipulations. Article 280(7) simply states that 'the Sub-Committee shall be open to receive and consider inputs, comments or views from the public on matters related to this Title'. With regard to the Domestic Mechanisms, Article 281 then adds in an equally broad manner that 'procedures for the constitution and consultation of such committees or groups [...], shall be in accordance with domestic law'. (...)

Secondly, there is a perceived lack of the formal coordination, information sharing and allocated resources required to allow these CSO mechanisms to effectively fulfil their mandates. While annual meetings are useful, the Parties should enable them, in every way, to set up a more regular dialogue in order to construct an agenda based on issues of mutual concern well ahead of their physical meetings. Similarly, it was considered vital for the usefulness of the CSO mechanisms that the Parties disclose any relevant information in order to allow for a meaningful debate, among the DAGs as well as vis-à-vis the Subcommittee. Finally, when it comes to assessing the impact of the Agreement there seems to be a lack of clarity about what this entails concretely. (…) While DG Trade releases annual implementation reports to brief the Council and the EP on the progress made against the different chapters of the Agreement, little is known about the impact of the trade agreement, let alone its impact on the labour situation. In March 2014, a delegation of the EP's INTA visited Peru and Colombia to assess the process of implementation of the Trade Agreement, focusing in particular on the commitments toward sustainable development. During their visit, the INTA members reportedly observed that 'while the purely trade provisions seemed to have been implemented correctly, further progress on the commitments […] in terms of labour rights and social dialogue was needed'. (…)

A vast majority of the stakeholders consulted in Brussels and Bogotá considered the EU labour rights language in the agreement to be too broad to be meaningful. Labour provisions were not formulated in a Specific Measurable Achievable Relevant and Time-bound (SMART) way, which hampers their monitoring, progress tracking and benchmarking. The perceived lack of an adequate monitoring and enforcement framework further adds to the shared notion among stakeholders that the EU's approach constitutes little more than 'window dressing', or even, as one correspondent called it, 'a box-ticking exercise' on treaty obligations. While not all interviewees voiced such radical criticism, most agreed that, since the labour provisions under the agreement are ratified by both parties under international conventions, their reference in the Sustainability Chapter adds little in terms of hard law. This is particularly relevant since Colombia has in fact developed a full-fledged legal-institutional framework for labour protection, but suffers from a significant compliance gap when it comes to enforcing this regulatory system in practice.

In addition, the analysis raises questions about the usefulness of a rigidly formalistic and top-down annual monitoring mechanism designed to monitor compliance with international labour standards which are de jure already in place. We found some evidence that the provisions on social dialogue are potentially important for monitoring and enforcement but that they need additional support to play a more significant role. The absence of a binding enforcement mechanism, and the lack of adequate engagement with CSOs, hampers the Agreement's overall contribution when it comes to following up on, and contributing to, a better de facto compliance with labour provisions.

10.5 Assessing the Human Rights Impact of EU Trade Agreements

EU trade agreements are subject to two types of ex-ante impact assessments and both, to some extent, incorporate human rights concerns. First, the Commission has since 2001 developed a comprehensive system of so-called Integrated Impact Assessments (IIAs) to assess the potential economic, social, and environmental impacts of any 'significant' policy proposal, including the opening of trade negotiations. With regard to trade policy, IIAs are conducted whenever a new agreement is in the pipeline, and it should contribute to deciding whether or not a Council mandate to start trade negotiations should be issued to the Commission.

The treatment of human rights issues under IIAs for trade initiatives has been anything but comprehensive in the past, however, and in 2015 the Commission's Directorate-General for Trade released a set of 'Guidelines on the analysis of human rights impacts in impact assessments for trade-related policy initiatives'.[94] Second, specific to trade policy, so-called sustainability impact assessments (SIAs) have to be conducted by independent experts during the early stages of major ongoing bilateral and plurilateral negotiations. General IIAs are conducted before SIAs, and their findings often identify issues requiring further assessment under the latter. In order to avoid overlap, this section focuses on SIAs, while IIAs are dealt with in Chapter 11 on human rights in EU development policy.[95]

While Commission services started using SIAs from 1999 onwards, it was only six years later, in 2006, that DG Trade issued a first 'Handbook for Trade Sustainability Impact Assessment'. The Handbook provided some much-needed methodological guidance to define and harmonize SIA practices and clarified how SIAs fit into the bigger picture of EU trade policy-making. Although the Handbook provided guidance on how and why to incorporate the three dimensions of sustainable development into EU trade policy decisions, it kept silent about human rights issues, which were implicitly deemed part of the social dimension of sustainability.[96] The absence of any human rights language in the 2006 handbook is striking, considering that Commission guidelines for the general IIA system required any ex-ante IA to check policy proposals for their compliance with the EU Charter of Fundamental Rights, which applies to both internal and external actions.[97]

S Velluti, 'The Promotion and Integration of Human Rights in EU External Trade Relations' (2016) 32 Utrecht Journal of International and European Law 41

(...) trade SIAs have been increasingly subject to criticism as they have failed to provide a proper assessment of how a given trade agreement will impact on human rights. In particular, it is argued that they do not adequately consider the real problems that developing countries (particularly LDCs) have. This is mainly because not all sectors are assessed as illustrated by the SIAs carried out in relation to the EU–ACP EPAs, which have not fully taken into account the impact that market integration has on small-scale farmers. Many NGOs have paid particular attention to the vulnerability of small-scale farmers due to their inability to deal with external shocks combined with a lack of infrastructure as well as abuses of human rights by both State and non-State actors. It has to be added that trade SIAs involve highly complex studies concerning a wide spectrum of sectors, stakeholders and economic, social and political variables that, as some IAs recognise, are very difficult to disaggregate and measure. To some extent, therefore, trade SIAs have inherent limitations which explains why they can only provide a limited perspective on a given trade agreement and its potential impact.

---

[94] European Commission, Guidelines on the analysis of human rights impacts in impact assessments for trade-related policy initiatives, 2 July 2015.
[95] See also N Hachez and B Lein, 'Assessing EU Human Rights Impact Assessments' in W Benedek and others (eds), *European Yearbook on Human Rights 2016*, 243–56.
[96] Ibid, 250.
[97] European Commission, 'Impact Assessment Guidelines', SEC(2005) 791/3, 15 June 2005, 28.

As of 2012, consultancy tenders for SIAs systematically contained a reference to human rights and the Charter, effectively requiring the experts conducting SIAs to take into consideration any potential human rights implications of the trade initiative under scrutiny. SIAs conducted before 2012 did not contain any specific analysis of potential human rights impacts and where human rights came up incidentally they concerned exclusively social rights, with impacts mostly perceived to be positive. From 2012 onwards, SIA reports have included dedicated sections on human rights effects, though still only as part of the social impacts section, generally leaving any potential trade effects on civil and political rights untouched. While the analysis of human rights impacts has become more credible since 2012, the findings generated do not differ all that much in scope and focus.[98] Moreover, the systematic integration of human rights in the terms of references for consultants did not amount to proper methodological guidance about conducting human rights impact assessments, with crucial methodological decisions being left to the consultants' discretion.

DG Trade put impact on human rights on equal footing with other impacts in the most recent SIA Handbook, released in 2016.[99] The new Handbook contains specific, if limited, guidance on how to assess human rights impacts in the context of all 'major' trade initiatives. This description arguably gives the Commission a relatively high level of discretion in terms of determining when (not) to subject ongoing trade negotiations to an SIA. In line with the 2015 Guidelines, the Handbook suggest a non-ideological approach to human rights impact assessments, in the sense that the human rights analysis as part of an SIA should not 'pass judgement on the actual human rights situation in a country, nor (...) decide whether the country is eligible for the conclusion of trade negotiations'.[100] Rather, it is meant to 'bring to the attention of policy-makers the potential impacts of the different options under consideration and thus, to support sound policy-making. An impact assessment should verify the existence of a problem, identify its underlying causes, [assess] whether EU action is needed, and analyse the advantages and disadvantages of available solutions.'

While perhaps an understandable approach to policy-making, the Commission's explicit neglect of a trading partner's domestic human rights track record can be perceived as problematic. Not using SIAs to prevent the Union from going into business with systematic human rights abusers goes against the spirit of the EU's Treaty commitments, as well as, concretely, its trade approach vis-à-vis developing countries, as exemplified by the GSP mechanism.[101] When it comes to the empirical assessment of potential trade effects, however, the Handbook does suggest a 'normative approach', as consultants should frame their findings with reference to the EU and international human rights framework as defined by the Charter and the core UN treaties and conventions, including ILO conventions on labour rights. Furthermore, consultants are advised to keep in mind the interdependent and interrelated nature of human rights, as any given trade measure is likely to cause multiple human rights impacts.

The Handbook further identifies stakeholder consultations as 'a particularly important source of information', departing from the belief that inclusive participation contributes to an efficient identification of human rights impacts and the groups of people most prone to

---

[98]   N Brando and others, 'The Impact of EU Trade and Development Policies on Human Rights' (2015), FRAME Deliverable 9.2, 95–97 <www.fp7-frame.eu/wp-content/uploads/2016/08/Deliverable-9.2.pdf> accessed 14 August 2020.

[99]   European Commission, *Handbook for Trade Sustainability Impact Assessment* (2nd edn, European Commission April 2016) 5.

[100]   Ibid, 21.

[101]   Hachez and Lein, 'Assessing EU Human Rights Impact Assessments' (n 95) 251.

bearing the burden thereof. To facilitate productive stakeholder involvement throughout the SIA,

> [c]onsultants are given a wide mandate to conduct far-reaching consultations with all rele-
> vant stakeholders including women and vulnerable groups (e.g. low income, children,
> people with disabilities, ethnic minorities, indigenous peoples and unskilled workers) in
> the EU and the partner country(ies).

This 'wide mandate' is a welcome addition to the SIA's guidance material, in particular in the context of human rights analyses, but future SIAs will have to show whether this will indeed change the prevailing practice of less inclusive stakeholder involvement.[102]

Once an SIA is complete, DG Trade issues a so-called position paper to state where it agrees and disagrees with the SIA's findings. The position paper is also where the Commission makes suggestions for future action, essentially to clarify how it will address the concerns identified in the SIA during the remainder of the trade negotiations. Position papers are public documents and are circulated to Member States, the EP, and EU Delegations as part of the policy process. Moreover, a committee incorporating representatives of all relevant Commission services is to be established to ensure that SIA recommendations are adequately monitored and, where necessary, implemented. While the findings generated from SIAs are obviously meant to be taken into account in the decision-making processes, they do not constitute a binding obligation. Past research of position papers has shown in this regard that the Commission's policy-making is not always well aligned with SIAs and sometimes even contradicts or ignores its suggestions outright, often by pointing to perceived additional positive impacts.[103]

Finally, it should be mentioned that the European Ombudsman has also weighed in on the issue of impact assessments of trade agreements. The Ombudsman found the Commission guilty of maladministration in 2016 after the Commission refused to conduct an ex-ante human rights impact assessment of the EU–Vietnam FTA, as recommended by the Ombudsman. The Commission pointed out, among others, that an SIA had already been conducted and therefore a dedicated human rights IA was not necessary. The European Ombudsman disagreed with that conclusion. After years of delays and while Vietnam's human rights situation remains a matter of 'concern', the Parliament and Council have in the beginning of 2020 both approved the conclusion of the ambitious EU–Vietnam FTA. The prior human rights impact assessment as called for by the Ombudsman and the EP has never been carried out.[104]

---

[102] Brando and others, 'The Impact of EU Trade and Development Policies on Human Rights' (n 98) 9.
[103] FIDH, 'Building Trade's Consistency With Human Rights—15 Recommendations to the EU on Impact Assessments', 3 March 2015, 17–18.
[104] See European Parliament, 'Resolution on the draft Council decision on the conclusion of the Free Trade Agreement between the European Union and the Socialist Republic of Viet Nam', P9_TA(2020)0027, 12 February 2020, para 40.

European Ombudsman, Decision in case 1409/2014/MHZ on the European Commission's failure to carry out a prior human rights impact assessment of the EU–Vietnam free trade agreement, 26 February 2016

9. Having examined the arguments and opinions put forward by the parties, the Ombudsman made the finding that **the Commission's refusal to carry out a human rights impact assessment for the FTA with Vietnam constitutes maladministration.** On 26 March 2015, the Ombudsman made a recommendation to the Commission that it carry out, without further delay, a human rights impact assessment in the matter.

10. In her analysis leading to her recommendation, the Ombudsman pointed out that good administration means, in the first place, observance of and respect for fundamental rights. In fact, where fundamental rights are not respected, there cannot be good administration. Accordingly, **EU institutions and bodies must always consider the compliance of their actions with fundamental rights and the possible impact of their actions on fundamental rights.** This applies also with respect to administrative activities in the context of international treaty negotiations. The EU Administration should not only ensure that the envisaged agreements comply with existing human rights obligations, and do not lower the existing standards of human rights protection, but should also aim at furthering the cause of human rights in the partner countries.

11. The Ombudsman noted that the principles set out in Article 21(1) TEU and Article 21(2) TEU apply also in the area of the common commercial policy. Although the Ombudsman agreed with the Commission that **there appears to be no express and specific legally binding requirement to carry out a human rights impact assessment concerning the relevant free trade agreement,** she took the view that it would be in conformity with the spirit of the legal provisions mentioned above to carry out a human rights impact assessment. **Since the 2009 sustainability impact assessment concerning ASEAN covers only certain aspects of the impact on social rights, it is not a proper substitute for a human rights impact assessment.**

24. In the Ombudsman's view, the Commission should do its utmost to assure EU citizens that it has thoroughly analysed the measures negotiated in the Free Trade Agreement in order to prevent or mitigate its negative impact on human rights in Vietnam. Indeed, the Commission is well aware of the specific human rights situation in Vietnam and in this context of the importance of assessing the impact of the Free Trade Agreement on human rights. The most certain way of doing so efficiently is to carry out a human rights impact assessment **in the preparation phase of the Free Trade Agreement and not after the Free Trade Agreement enters into force,** which the Commission says it will do. By their nature, negotiations aim at accommodating parties' objectives until a final agreement is reached. **For the human rights impact assessment to have a significant effect, it should be carried out before the agreement is concluded** if the trade which the agreement brings about is intended to have a positive impact on the human rights situation in a given country.

11

Human Rights in EU Development Policy

11.1 Introduction

The promotion of human rights has been a priority consideration in the Union's policy for development cooperation ever since the Lomé Conventions (1990–2000) introduced the first human rights clauses in EU partnership agreements. Since the early 1990s, and in particular after the 1992 Maastricht Treaty created a stand-alone EU development competence, human rights have been incorporated as a vital element of socio-economic development. The place of human rights in development policy was solidified at the constitutional level with the entry into force of the Lisbon Treaty which made the promotion of human rights in all EU external action a legal obligation. As a result, different institutional mechanisms, thematic guidelines, and dedicated instruments and strategies have been put in place to consolidate a comprehensive operational framework aimed at ensuring that EU development programs advance human rights worldwide coherently and consistently.

Unlike, for instance, trade, EU development policy is a shared competence, which means that both the EU and its Member States are entitled to act within this domain, as long as national actions do not undermine EU laws and positions. The sharing of competences, however, makes it more difficult for the EU to live up to the commitment of coherent and consistent promotion of human rights. In any case, substantial amount of coordination between the EU and the Member States is required in order to deliver coherence in development policy. At the same time, some see the sharing of the development competence as a doubling of efforts and, indeed, the EU with its Member States is the largest development aid donor in the world and arguably also wields the most leverage to promote human rights in developing countries. In spite of this potential, the role of the EU as a normative leader in development cooperation remains subject to a multitude of long-standing criticisms and various evaluations of EU human rights policy point to a series of mixed results and missed opportunities. While many of the Union's shortcomings in this regard stem from organizational challenges common to working within a multilateral bureaucracy, others are rooted in a deeper, more conceptual, divergence between the objectives and rationales of human rights and development.

11.2 Human Rights and Development

Since the early 1990s, an increasing convergence between development and human rights has brought the two communities of practice closer together and progress has been made in forging conceptual, institutional, and operational connections between the two areas. Disparities endure, however, and donors, including the EU, continue to grapple with what exactly it entails to integrate the promotion of human rights into their strategic mandates and day-to-day operations. Human rights promotion through development policy therefore

The European Union and Human Rights. Jan Wouters and Michal Ovádek, Oxford University Press (2021). © Jan Wouters and Michal Ovádek. DOI: 10.1093/oso/9780198814177.003.0011

often remains limited to the level of principles, values, and goals, whereas a real, long-term 'institutional exchange' between the two communities is yet to materialize.[1]

A. Different communities, diverging conceptions

For long, international development assistance and the much older field of human rights protection operated in isolation from one another. On the one side, human rights promotion was considered to be the domain of legal experts and high-profile advocacy campaigns focused on exposing the most brutal violations of human integrity.[2] Development assistance, on the other hand, was guided by a 'temptation of the technical', an ostensibly non-political approach focused on resource-intensive technical solutions to poverty and deprivation. From the 1980s onwards, human rights increasingly became part of a broader governance and democracy support agenda but were still considered to be 'too political' to be mixed up with development efforts under Cold War circumstances. While often working side-by-side in the same countries, the relationship between the human rights and the aid community was therefore often characterised by ambivalence or even wariness, as both sides tended to be sceptical of the other's values, goals, and methods.[3]

With the fall of the Berlin Wall, and the apparent triumph of market economics and liberal democracy it symbolized, Western donors began opening up to a more comprehensive understanding of development and increasingly linked political and economic reform. This new context urged practitioners and organizations from both sides to start building bridges with one another, both institutionally and in terms of substance.[4] The 1993 Vienna World Conference on Human rights affirmed that '[d]emocracy, development and respect for human rights and fundamental freedoms are interdependent and mutually reinforcing' and that 'the international community should support the strengthening and promoting of democracy, development and respect for human rights and fundamental freedoms in the entire world'.[5] Following suit, large international human rights non-governmental organizations (NGOs) progressively started broadening their scope beyond civil and political rights, while new rights-based NGOs emerged, focusing specifically on economic, social, and cultural rights.[6]

On the development side, human rights considerations were made part of the so-called governance turn of aid during the second half of the 1990s. Essentially, the 'victory of democracy' in post-Cold War Europe urged Western donors to reassess the role of the state in development. This responded to an increasing awareness among scholars and practitioners about the mediating effects of domestic politics and institutions on foreign aid efforts.[7] Donors came to recognize that certain types of institutional dynamics, such as patronage,

---

[1] R Archer, 'Linking Rights and Development: Some Critical Challenges' in S Hickey and D Mitlin (eds), *Rights-based Approaches to Development: Exploring the Potential and Pitfalls* (Kumarian Press 2009) 21.

[2] D D'Hollander, A Marx, and J Wouters, 'Integrating Human Rights into EU Development Cooperation Policy: Achievements and Challenges', Leuven Centre for Global Governance Studies Working Paper No 134, April 2014, 27–28.

[3] T Carothers, 'Democracy Support and Development Aid: The Elusive Synthesis' (2010) 21 Journal of Democracy 12.

[4] Ibid.

[5] World Conference on Human Rights, Vienna Declaration and Programme of Action, 25 June 1993.

[6] D'Hollander, Marx, and Wouters, 'The Impact of EU Trade and Development Policies on Human Rights' (n 2) 28.

[7] N Molenaers, S Dellepiane, and J Faust, 'Political Conditionality and Foreign Aid' (2015) 75 Journal of World Development 3.

corruption, as well as authoritarianism, were effectively undermining donor-driven socio-economic reforms for inclusive development.[8] Later research also showed how non-political or 'blind' foreign aid was often more of a curse than a blessing, as it entrenched harmful institutional dynamics and helped consolidate authoritarian rule in certain partner countries.[9] It is in this context that donors started issuing foreign policy statements on human rights in the mid-1990s, which were later complemented by agency-specific documents or guidelines on human rights and development. The latter often emphasized the positive contributions financial or technical assistance and bilateral dialogue could make to human rights promotion in partner countries.[10] Multilateral organizations, such as the UN, also developed their own human rights policy frameworks and in 2007, the Organisation for Economic Co-operation and Development's Development Assistance Committee (OECD's DAC) identified ten principles for promoting and integrating human rights in development policy, arguing that respect for human rights is seen as an objective in its own right but also as a critical factor for the longer-term sustainability of development activities.[11]

OECD Development Assistance Committee, 'Action-oriented policy paper on human rights and development', February 2007

The DAC has identified 10 principles intended to serve as basic orientations in key areas and activities where harmonised donor action is of particular importance:

1. Build a shared understanding of the links between human rights obligations and development priorities through dialogue.
2. Identify areas of support to partner governments on human rights.
3. Safeguard human rights in processes of state-building.
4. Support the demand side of human rights.
5. Promote non-discrimination as a basis for more inclusive and stable societies.
6. Consider human rights in decisions on alignment and aid instruments.
7. Consider mutual reinforcement between human rights and aid effectiveness principles.
8. Do no harm.
9. Take a harmonised and graduated approach to deteriorating human rights situations.
10. Ensure that the scaling-up of aid is conducive to human rights.

The above statement by the DAC points to a double rationale for donor agencies to work on human rights as part of their development strategies. One departs from the intrinsic value of human rights as such, while the other follows an instrumental rationale. However, acting

---

[8] D Acemoglu, S Johnson, and J Robinson, 'Reversal of Fortune: Geography and Institutions in the Making of the Modern World Income Distribution' (2002) 117 Quarterly Journal of Economics 1231.

[9] S Djankov, J Montalvo, and M Reynal-Querol, 'The Curse of Aid' (2008) 13 Journal Economic Growth 169.

[10] OECD and World Bank, *Integrating Human Rights into Development: Donor Approaches, Experiences, and Challenges* (2nd edn, OECD and World Bank 2013) 3–4.

[11] OECD Development Assistance Committee, 'Action-oriented Policy Paper on Human Rights and Development', February 2007, 6.

on both rationales can at times lead to conflicted policy as they differ considerably in how they value and implement human rights.

First, intrinsic reasoning for human rights promotion is rooted in moral or ethical norms, which are more or less reflected in international human rights law designed in the aftermath of the Second World War, which aspires to be universal and comprehensive. Through this lens, it is taken for granted that the duty to respect, protect, and promote human rights is inherently part of international activities such as development assistance. The moral considerations—or even obligations—underlying this legal framework further emphasize the positive association between human rights, human dignity, and poverty reduction. The intrinsic perspective therefore also entails that human rights, alongside good governance, the rule of law, and democracy, are part of the qualitative constituents of development. While proponents of the intrinsic rationale might believe that advancing human rights will also automatically contribute to social and economic development, this is secondary to the core objective of human rights promotion *as such*.[12] The intrinsic conception of human rights promotion translates into donors taking a more political approach to development, focusing on interventions that strengthen the institutional framework in beneficiary countries in areas such as law enforcement, media freedom, judiciary, advocacy, or even political party competition.[13]

Second, an instrumental rationale for human rights promotion through development departs from the notion that human rights considerations can improve processes and outcomes in development assistance. Proponents of the instrumental rationale thus believe in human rights support, based on the conviction that human rights principles of accountability, responsiveness, and participation contribute to more equitable socio-economic development overall. The instrumental approach therefore looks beyond strengthening institutions and political procedures to substantive outcomes such as equality, justice, and social welfare. Historically speaking, proponents of the instrumental rationale have tended to treat economic and social rights on a more equal footing with political and civil rights compared to the adherents of the intrinsic rationale.[14] Moreover, while valued in their own right for the political principles they enshrine, human rights are conceived as a means to an end (development). This implies that when a developing country is making significant socioeconomic progress in spite of a questionable human rights record, supporters of the instrumental rationale might tend to be more forgiving of such shortcomings.

While the added value of human rights promotion for development outcomes still engenders scepticism in parts of the development community—despite being part of the aid agenda for over two decades—many donors often tie their political work, such as on democracy support or governance reform, to the human rights framework. As observed by the OECD, '[t]he intrinsic value of human rights offers development actors an explicit normative and analytical framework, grounded in a consensual global legal regime of international human rights treaties'.[15] Rooted in universal legal principles, human rights (language) appeals to donors because it tends to be less prone to popular charges against external interventionism. However, the ease of 'rhetorical repackaging' of developmental and governance issues in more operational human rights principles, such as inclusion, non-discrimination, participation, and accountability, has led some to question to what extent the superficial use

---

[12] OECD and World Bank, *Integrating Human Rights into Development* (n 10) 8–10.
[13] T Carothers, 'Democracy Assistance: Political vs. Developmental' (2009) 20 Journal of Democracy 5, 7.
[14] Ibid, 8–9.
[15] OECD and World Bank, *Integrating Human Rights into Development* (n 10) 11.

of human rights language has contributed to the full integration of human rights obligations and principles in today's development policies.[16]

This distinction describes the differences between the intrinsic and the instrumental rationale in a rather black-and-white manner. In practice, however, the two narratives can be mutually reinforcing, and aid agencies generally use elements of both depending on the country context, organizational culture, and mandate. Nevertheless, the diverging perceptions about the interrelationship between human rights support and socio-economic development contributed to the evolution of different approaches of integrating human rights considerations into development policy, although they are frequently used in combination with each other.

Historically, two broad categories of instruments used by donors to integrate human rights into development cooperation can be distinguished: conditionality-based instruments and targeted assistance. First, the use of conditionality in development entails examining the human rights track record of a partner country to determine whether, what type, and how much funding it can access. In other words, donors aim to use financial leverage to influence—through incentives and disincentives—a partner government's performance and behaviour. Second, targeted aid and reform projects aim to address human rights and governance issues and support vulnerable groups or individuals directly. More recently, donors have introduced human rights as a concern that cuts across the various stages and focus areas of international development, notably by mainstreaming particular human rights concerns throughout their strategies and/or by using a human rights-based approach to the planning, implementing, and evaluating of development programmes.

B. Human rights-based conditionality in development cooperation

In the 1990s, conditionality mechanisms were generally of the punitive kind, defined by one author as 'the use of pressure, by the donor government, in terms of threatening to terminate aid, or actually terminating or reducing it, if conditions are not met by the recipient'.[17] Since the 2000s, however, conditionality instruments have significantly changed in terms of scope and objectives, and are now better described as 'the allocation and use of financial resources to sanction or reward recipients in order to promote democratic governance and human rights'.[18] Conditionality mechanisms now can be negative (sanction) or positive (reward) and can be applied ex-ante or ex-post, depending on whether human rights are used as a precondition or as an objective of development assistance. They can be proactive or reactive, and may be more or less 'hands-on', depending on the degree of interference in the domestic affairs of the beneficiary country.[19]

The use of conditionality approaches in foreign aid has been the subject of long-standing academic debates, mainly revolving about the consistency and impact of their use. With regard to the use of ex-ante selection criteria for aid allocation, human rights are identified as one of the preconditions for aid allocation by most Western donors. Little is known, however, about how human rights are interpreted in this regard, and what their relative weight

---

[16] Ibid, 72.

[17] O Stokke (ed), *Aid and Political Conditionality* (Frank Cass 1995) 12.

[18] Molenaers, Dellepiane, and Faust, 'Political Conditionality and Foreign Aid' (n 7) 2.

[19] S Koch, 'A Typology of Political Conditionality Beyond Aid: Conceptual Horizons Based on Lessons from the European Union' (2015) 75 Journal of World Development 97.

is within the allocation keys. Generally speaking, donors base their allocation decision on a needs assessment and the population size, proximity (both literally and symbolically, such as with regard to former colonies), and governance context of a prospective beneficiary— respect for human rights forming part of the latter component.[20] Despite calls for a shift towards a more focused, coordinated, and development-oriented approach to country selection and aid allocation, donors continue to use rather opaque selection procedures, which allow for a high degree of discretionary (and political) decision-making.[21] Interestingly, selectivity bias differs between bilateral and multilateral donors. According to Dollar and Levin, donors in bilateral relationships tend to rely primarily on political considerations in aid allocation, whereas multilaterals tend to give a stronger weight to macroeconomic governance.[22] When it comes to the selection of aid modalities, even less is known, and comparatively little research has focused on the determinants aid modalities.[23]

More research has been done on the use and effectiveness of ex-post, negative conditionality. It was found that the implementation of negative conditionality policies has been highly inconsistent in practice, largely due to the prioritisation of economic and commercial interests over normative concerns such as human rights or democracy promotion.[24] More recent research shows that while economic interests remain important in this regard, the inconsistent application of aid sanctions, criticized as 'double standards', is now mainly due to a prioritization of national security interests and geostrategic considerations. This reflects a broader shift to 'securitization of aid', 'where development assistance is subordinated to, and used instrumentally to promote, the security interests of the major powers'.[25] Regardless of this shift towards security interests, Crawford and Kacarska also found that most aid suspensions in the post-2000 era have continued to target low-income, aid-dependent countries in sub-Saharan Africa, generally in direct response to a military coup (rather than, for instance, a continuous deterioration of human rights). Conversely, the non-implementation of aid sanctions in cases of human rights violations or democratic regression is most evident in the Middle East and North Africa and, to a lesser extent, Central Asia.[26] When it comes to the effectiveness of aid sanctions large-scale studies found that economic sanctions (in the form of aid suspension or termination) tend to have significant unintended negative effects on the citizens of target countries.[27] Moreover, the leverage of aid sanctions on political reform

---

[20] P Clist, '25 Years of Aid Allocation Practice: Whither Selectivity?' (2011) 39 Journal of World Development 1724.

[21] European Centre for Development Policy Management, 'Differentiation in ACP-EU Cooperation Implications of the EU's Agenda for Change for the 11th EDF and Beyond', ECDPM Discussion Paper No 134, October 2012.

[22] D Dollar and V Levin, 'The Increasing Selectivity of Foreign Aid 1984–2002' (2006) 34 World Development 2034.

[23] M Winters and G Martinez, 'The Role of Governance in Determining Foreign Aid Flow Composition' (2012) 66 Journal of World Development 516; Molenaers, Dellepiane, and Faust, 'Political Conditionality and Foreign Aid' (n 7) 5.

[24] S Brown, 'Foreign Aid and Democracy Promotion: Lessons from Africa' (2005) 17 The European Journal of Development Research 179; K Del Biondo, 'EU Aid Conditionality in ACP Countries: Explaining Inconsistency in EU Sanctions Practice' (2011) 7 Journal of Contemporary European Research 380; K Del Biondo, 'Norms, Self-Interest and Effectiveness: Explaining Double Standards in EU Reactions to Violations of Democratic Principles in Sub-Saharan Africa' (2012) 25 Afrika Focus 109.

[25] G Crawford and S Kacarska, 'Aid Sanctions and Political Conditionality: Continuity and Change' (2017) 22 Journal of International Relations and Development 184, 205. See also M Furness and S Gänzle, 'The European Union's Development Policy: A Balancing Act between "A More Comprehensive Approach" and Creeping Securitization' in S Brown and J Grävingholt (eds), *The Securitization of Foreign Aid* (Palgrave Macmillan 2016).

[26] Crawford and Kacarska, 'Aid Sanctions and Political Conditionality' (n 25).

[27] D Drezner, 'Sanctions Sometimes Smart: Targeted Sanctions in Theory and Practice' (2011) 13 International Studies Review 96.

largely depends on the domestic institutional context; democracies tend to be more vulnerable to foreign aid sanctions than their autocratic peers.[28]

Because aid conditionality uses international financial assistance as a lever for progress or reform, it assumes a relationship of dependency between donor and beneficiary. Fundamental shifts in foreign policy and international relations, therefore, can have significant implications for the conditionality logic. The economic growth witnessed in many developing countries and the rise of less normative non-OECD donors with ambitious foreign policy initiatives, in particular China, are liable to limit the traction of traditional (Western) aid conditionality vis-à-vis developing countries.[29] Declining dependence on Western donors arising from the emergence of alternative donors offering aid without 'strings attached' pushes these traditional actors to find leverage across a variety of different policy areas, beyond financial aid. Whereas conditionality in general will remain an important mechanism for human rights promotion, the source of leverage will no longer be exclusively tied to the size of financial assistance, instead requiring a coherent strategy entailing incentives and sanctions across various policy areas such as trade, investment, energy, migration, and others.[30]

C. Programme support and financial instruments for human rights and good governance

Beyond allocating aid selectively to countries which perform better on human rights and governance, donors have integrated human rights promotion into their policies by targeting some of their resources and expertise directly at programmes aimed at promoting specific rights or addressing structural governance issues that impede the effective protection of those rights.

Despite the increasing use of truly integrative approaches to human rights support (described in Section 11.2.D), human rights and democratic governance projects remain the most visible core business of most donors' human rights strategies. The gradual expansion of this type of targeted support for human rights and democratic governance has developed into a self-standing development sector, often linked to a corresponding financial instrument to coordinate funding earmarked for human rights. According to the OECD, some 15.7 per cent of the total sector-allocatable Official Development Assistance (ODA) was allocated to 'support governance and peace' in 2014, making this the sector with the largest percentage of (sector-allocatable) ODA.[31] By comparison, sectors such as transport and storage (10.8 per cent), education (10.5 per cent), health (8.6 per cent), or water and sanitation (5.8 per cent) received significantly less, with the rest (59 per cent) going to 'other sectors'. More detailed figures illustrate that 83 per cent of the ODA for governance and peace was allocated to the sub-category of 'government and civil society', including 5.2 per cent (worth USD 900 million) for human rights specifically. Compared to other sector allocations, there

---

[28] RA Brooks, 'Sanctions and Regime Type: What Works, and When?' (2002) 11 Security Studies 1; Molenaers, Dellepiane, and Faust, 'Political Conditionality and Foreign Aid' (n 7) 5.

[29] C Hackenesch, 'Competing for Development: The European Union and China in Ethiopia', Discussion Paper 3/2011, Centre for Chinese Studies Stellenbosch University, November 2011.

[30] Koch, 'A Typology of Political Conditionality Beyond Aid' (n 19) 97.

[31] Sector-allocatable ODA refers to the share of total ODA which can be attributed to a specific sector. ODA not subject to such sector allocation includes, for example, general budget support, debt relief, humanitarian aid, and transactions within the donor country. In 2012, sector-allocatable ODA constituted 72 per cent of the total ODA.

is also a difference in terms of the aid vehicles used to deliver 'governance and peace' support. Essentially, the 'governance and peace' sector receives higher shares of its donor support through NGOs and civil society (25 per cent) and multilateral agencies (18 per cent) than the overall ODA sector-allocatable assistance, of which only 14 per cent goes through NGOs and civil society and 13 per cent through multilateral organizations.[32]

Long conceived as part of the democratic governance agenda, human rights support through development programmes has been around since the early 1990s and takes a wide variety of forms, including public sector reforms at different levels of governance, the promotion of dialogue between state and civil society, capacitating and protecting human rights defenders (HRDs) and national human rights institutions (NHRIs), strengthening the judicial infrastructure, training members of the parliament and opposition groups, supporting independent media outlets, and providing human rights education to civil servants.[33] Due to their framing as governance interventions, most programme support and financial instruments for human rights promotion have focused almost exclusively on civil and political rights, while less work has been done to strengthen human rights in areas of socio-economic development such as public financial management, health, education, food security, or access to public services. Indeed, human rights projects often aim to promote specific rights (eg freedom of speech, right to a fair trial) or empower certain vulnerable groups (typically women, children, ethnic, or religious minorities and people with disabilities). Human rights support therefore usually goes to international, national, or local civil society organizations or NGOs in order to build capacity and mobilize drivers of social change. Given the inevitably political nature of human rights and governance reform, donor support to domestic civil society or political actors, including the protection of HRDs, is often of a very sensitive nature, requiring discretion and an in-depth understanding of the local context. Individual human rights projects thus include, among other elements, research into, and mappings of, dominant actors and pervasive institutional dynamics and power relationships.

D. Human rights mainstreaming and the human rights-based approach to development

Mainstreaming human rights and applying a human rights-based approach (HRBA) to development are two different approaches aimed at generating a more systematic integration of human rights considerations into development interventions. Both stem from a sense of discontent with the traditional notion of human rights as a mere sub-component of democratic governance promotion. As noted above, the traditional isolation of human rights within the governance theme led to a separation between human rights and democracy support projects and the more 'traditional' technical development programmes in non-governance sectors such as food security, rural development, infrastructure, health, or education. This 'ghetto-ization' of human rights not only deprived the traditional development sectors of a human rights lens, it also institutionalized the perception that human rights considerations are beyond the responsibility of any non-specialized unit within the aid agency.[34]

---

[32] OECD Development Assistance Committee, 'Development Assistance Flows for Governance and Peace 2014', Backgrounder, 2014, 4–10.

[33] D'Hollander, Marx, and Wouters, 'The Impact of EU Trade and Development Policies on Human Rights' (n 2) 45.

[34] F Petrucci and others, 'Thematic Evaluation of the European Commission Support to Respect of Human Rights and Fundamental Freedoms (including Solidarity with Victims of Repression)', Final report, December 2011, 70.

Both mainstreaming and the HRBA thus depart from the idea that human rights are not the prerogative of one unit or sector but rather should be incorporated into the work of all staff and across all sectors. While both approaches aim to foster an institutional culture in which human rights principles are understood in a more comprehensive and systemic manner, across divisions and subject areas, it is worth pointing out that mainstreaming and HRBAs differ considerably in terms of scope and implications for an agency's day-to-day work.[35] That said, it should be noted that, given their interrelated nature, the difference is partly conceptual. In practice, mainstreaming policies often evolve into an HRBA and many donors do not explicitly differentiate between the two.

Mainstreaming incorporates all efforts by donors to integrate human rights in all projects and programmes, as well as screening and evaluating their interventions for potential human rights implications. The latter is often linked to an explicit 'do-no-harm' policy, which aims to identify and mitigate any negative human rights impacts.[36] Mainstreaming builds on, and expands, the mainstreaming agendas of other cross-cutting issues such as gender and environmental protection. In practice, mainstreaming policies are often translated into sector-specific guidelines or a series of organizational measures, for example using human rights focal points, to ensure that different thematic units take into account certain human rights considerations. By providing such practical, sector-specific guidance, donors aim to develop the organizational capacity and awareness to effectively mainstream (a selection of) cross-cutting human rights priorities. Somewhat counterintuitively perhaps, mainstreaming policies often concentrate and prioritize particular sub-themes or vulnerable groups, such as women's or children's rights, which all thematic departments are then to take into account and address in their areas of work.[37]

An HRBA is aimed at integrating human rights considerations 'horizontally' into all aspects of the design, implementation, monitoring, and evaluation of its development policies and programmes. HRBAs to development have been developed by donors and NGOs since the late 1990s, though some ambiguity remains about what precisely it entails for donor agencies and their work, and translating a HRBA policy into practice remains challenging and varies across different donors. The standard definition of an HRBA to development dates back to 2003, when the UN Agencies of the UN Development Group (UNDG) endorsed a 'Common Understanding', outlining three core principles for a HRBA to development.

UN Development Group, 'Statement of Common Understanding on Human Rights-Based Approaches to Development Cooperation and Programming', 7 May 2003

1. All development initiatives should **further the realisation of human rights** as laid down in the Universal Declaration on Human rights (UDHR) and other international human rights instruments;

---

[35] OECD and World Bank, *Integrating Human Rights into Development* (n 10) 27.
[36] Ibid.
[37] D'Hollander, Marx, and Wouters, 'The Impact of EU Trade and Development Policies on Human Rights' (n 2) 48–49; L Beke and others, 'Report on the Integration of Human Rights in EU Development and Trade Policies' (2014) FRAME Deliverable 9.1, 93–94 <http://www.fp7-frame.eu/wp-content/uploads/2016/08/07-Deliverable-9.1.pdf> accessed 14 August 2020.

2. **Human rights standards and principles** derived from the UDHR and other international human rights instruments **should guide all development programming** in all sectors and in all phases of the programming process; and
3. Development cooperation should contribute to the **development of the capacities** of 'duty-bearers' to meet their obligations and/or of 'rights-holders' to claim their rights.

The Common Understanding reflects, and in a way bridges, the long-standing dichotomy in human rights support through development. HRBA reasoning combines an intrinsic and an instrumental rationale. Notably, the intrinsic rationale dictates that donors and their agencies have the moral and legal duty to respect, protect, and promote human rights as stipulated under the UDHR, including in and with the partner countries where they operate. Indeed, the HRBA explicitly puts the realization of human rights as a primary goal of development assistance and requires development assistance to be guided by human rights principles and instruments. The instrumental rationale sees the HRBA as a way to improve the impact and effectiveness of development interventions by strengthening the capacities of duty-bearers (usually governments) to meet their human rights obligations and of rights-holders to claim their rights.

Applying a human rights lens to development problems bears considerable consequences for the day-to-day operations of an aid agency since it affects all different stages of the programming cycle, including problem analysis, project planning, implementation, monitoring, and evaluation methods. Given its far-reaching implications, and in particular its political reading of development problems, it should come as no surprise that the implementation of a HRBA to development remains challenging. Moreover, since HRBAs focus on long-term, sustainable changes to power and dependency dynamics, their results are often hard to quantify, particularly in the short to medium term—a characteristic which tends to clash with the results-based management policies of most mainstream donors these days.[38]

11.3 Human Rights in EU Development Cooperation

The EU as an international actor has progressively integrated human rights considerations into the various strands of its foreign relations, in particular trade and development. This occurred progressively but since the Treaty of Lisbon the commitment to human rights in external policies is unmistakeable.[39] Before mainstreaming human rights into development, however, the EU had to first be endowed with a proper development policy, despite its relations with the Group of African, Caribbean, and Pacific Countries (ACP) belonging to some of its earliest external engagements.

---

[38] N Brando and others, 'The Impact of EU Trade and Development Policies on Human Rights' (2015) FRAME Deliverable 9.2, 51–52 <http://www.fp7-frame.eu/wp-content/uploads/2016/08/Deliverable-9.2.pdf> accessed 14 August 2020.
[39] See Ch 9.

A. Evolution of the legal and policy framework

The gradual integration of human rights and democratic governance into the Union's development policy reflects not only the above-mentioned general 'governance turn' of foreign aid during the 1990s but also the evolution within the Union's main partnership vehicle with developing countries at the time, the successive agreements with the ACP Group. While the first two Lomé Conventions, covering the period from 1975 to 1985, refrained from addressing political issues—focusing exclusively on socioeconomic development—Lomé III (1985–1990) created a first opening to discuss human rights, in particular in relation to the struggle against apartheid. In wordings which reflected the sensitive nature of the subject, the then European Economic Community and the ACP Group adopted a joint declaration reaffirming that '[e]very individual has the right, in his own country or in a host country, to respect for his dignity and protection by the law'. The same declaration also reiterated that the parties would 'fight all forms of discrimination and to work for the eradication of apartheid'.[40] Resistance to mingling human rights and politics with development cooperation was still widespread, however, as many ACP countries had opposed a stronger declaration on human rights issues, despite a growing insistence on the side of the Community (particularly championed by the European Parliament).[41]

As a result of this increasing momentum to further integrate human rights and democratic governance in development, the Commission issued a Communication on 'Human rights, Democracy and Development Cooperation Policy' in 1991, outlining its approach to the human rights and development nexus. Referring to the declarations made in the Lomé IV Convention, it was argued that, depending on the circumstances, 'active promotion of human rights or a negative response to serious and systematic violations' could be warranted, 'wherever possible', although preference would be given to a 'positive approach of support and encouragement'. The Communication also stressed the need to 'promote frank and trusting dialogue on human rights with developing countries', and to 'keep the channels for dialogue open as far as possible, even in difficult situations'.[42]

It was in this context that the 1992 Maastricht Treaty introduced three major turning points for EU development policy. First, Title XVII of the Treaty finally gave the Union's development policy a specific legal basis, ensuring its permanence beyond 'an accident of history' resulting from a colonial past. Second, the new Treaty provisions further stipulated that, beyond socio-economic development, market integration, and poverty reduction, EU development cooperation should contribute to the general objectives of developing and consolidating democracy and the rule of law. Third, the Maastricht Treaty formalized the European Political Cooperation as Common Foreign and Security Policy (CFSP) with the mandate to, among others, 'develop and consolidate democracy and the rule of law, and respect for human rights and fundamental freedoms' (Article J.1). While development policy became a Community policy (first pillar), and therefore escaped the intergovernmental cooperation methods of the CFSP (second pillar), the new Treaty required that development

---

[40] Lomé III Convention, Annex I, Joint Declaration on Article 4. Note that declarations are not binding under international law. The declaration was incorporated (in an amended form) into the body of the Convention only with the subsequent Lomé IV.

[41] Petrucci and others, 'Thematic Evaluation of the European Commission Support to Respect of Human Rights and Fundamental Freedoms' (n 34) 11.

[42] European Commission, 'Human Rights, Democracy and Development Cooperation Policy, Commission Communication to the Council and Parliament', SEC(91) final, 25 March 1991, 6.

policy be consistent with, and appropriately linked to, CFSP objectives, arguably putting an end to the EU's proclaimed political neutrality in development relations.[43]

After its mid-term review in 1994–1995, the Lomé IV Convention—commonly referred to as Lomé IV bis (1995–2000)—took on a far more political approach than any of its predecessors, an evident result of the Maastricht momentum.[44] Essentially, the revision considerably strengthened the human rights wording by explicitly identifying the principles of human rights, democracy, the rule of law, and 'the sound management of public affairs' as 'essential elements' of the Convention. Failing to comply with the latter would allow any party, if bilateral consultations could not satisfactorily rectify the issue, to take 'appropriate measures' against the other, including the suspension of the agreement.[45]

In 2000, Lomé IV (bis) was replaced by the Cotonou Partnership Agreement (CPA or Cotonou from here on), starting a new era of EU–ACP cooperation, this time set to cover a period of 20 years (2000–2020). Cotonou signalled a significant overhaul of EU–ACP relations by giving the relationship a stronger political foundation centred around a deeper and wider political dialogue and a partnership of equals, based on mutual obligations, including respect for human rights. With regard to political dialogue, Article 8 of the CPA calls for a flexible approach 'in the appropriate format, and at the appropriate level including national, regional, continental or all-ACP level'.[46] This flexibility further includes the choice of items for discussion and pre-empts the need for specific terms of reference regarding the choice of venue, composition of the parties, and frequency of the dialogues. In practice, understanding the potential merits of this type of flexibility has not been self-evident, and in most ACP countries the political dialogue under Article 8 is a rigidly institutionalized and procedural annual meeting of limited duration, usually between high-level EU officials from Brussels and the relevant EU Delegation on the one side, and government officials or ministerial administrators on the other.[47]

In terms of content the dialogue can cover 'all the aims and objectives laid down in the Agreement', including a regular assessment of compliance with essential elements. As per Article 9, these comprise respect for human rights, democratic principles, and the rule of law.[48] At the time of drafting, ACP countries were concerned that political dialogue provisions, particularly in relation to human rights and democratic governance, would be mainly used in a reactive manner, when major violations or disagreements would arise, rather than as a constructive tool to discuss issues of mutual interest or concern in a deliberative manner. In order to address these concerns, the 2005 review of the Agreement provided a more nuanced linkage between political dialogue provisions (Article 8) and the

---

[43] D Frisch, 'The European Union's Development Policy: A Personal View of 50 Years of International Cooperation', ECDPM Policy Management Report, 2008, 22.

[44] Ibid, 26.

[45] K Arts, *Integrating Human Rights into Development Cooperation: The Case of the Lomé Convention* (Kluwer 1998) 196–200.

[46] Partnership agreement between the members of the African, Caribbean and Pacific Group of States of the one part, and the European Community and its Member States, of the other part, signed in Cotonou on 23 June 2000 [2000] OJ L317/3, Article 8.

[47] L Stathopoulos, 'Political Dialogue under Article 8 Reflects the Normal State of Affairs in Relations between the Community and the ACP States', The Courier ACP-EU No 200, September–October 2003, 18–20, 28; J Bossuyt, C Rocca, and B Lein, 'Political Dialogue on Human Rights under Article 8 of the Cotonou Agreement', European Parliament Study, March 2014, 31.

[48] While the EU wanted to include good governance as an essential element whose violation would lead to 'appropriate measures', the ACP partners opposed this and, after lengthy discussions, good governance was accepted as a 'fundamental element', not subject to any suspension clause. See Frisch, 'The European Union's Development Policy' (n 43).

conditionality framework outlined in Articles 96 and 97. To de-penalize the conception of political dialogue, the 2005 revision added provisions for an 'intensified political dialogue' which was supposed to ensure that all options for dialogue are explored before entering into the consultation procedures under the punitive framework of Articles 96 and 97. Intensive political dialogue therefore provides an opportunity to the parties to jointly agree on a set of benchmarks or targets for the country under scrutiny. If those targets are met satisfactorily, dialogue can continue under Article 8. If not, then the country at hand becomes subject to the consultation procedures under Articles 96 and 97. This dialogue-based way of dealing with concerns or violations has become typical of the EU's approach to crisis management and extends well beyond the realm of development policy.[49]

Shortly after the CPAs first revision, in 2006, the European Council, Parliament, and the Commission issued the first 'European Consensus on Development Cooperation', outlining a shared understanding of how the EU and its Member States were to contribute to inter-national development. With regard to human rights, the Consensus argued that progress in the protection of human rights, good governance, and democratization were fundamental prerequisites for poverty reduction and sustainable development. Moreover, conceived as a cross-cutting issue, human rights were to be mainstreamed in all of the Community's development activities. Human rights, alongside gender equality, democracy, good governance, children's rights, indigenous peoples' rights, environmental sustainability, and combatting HIV/AIDS, were therefore to be seen as both objectives in themselves as well as 'vital factors in strengthening the impact and sustainability of cooperation'.[50]

The most recent amendment of the EU's constitutional framework (the EU Treaties), brought about by the Lisbon Treaty, has continued the emphasis on integrating human rights in EU external relations.[51] Article 21 TEU, which lists the guiding principles for the EU's foreign policy, is a horizontal provision affecting also development cooperation. This is underlined multiple times in the TFEU: generally in Article 205 TFEU and, specifically to development, Articles 208 and 209(2) TFEU. The development provisions, however, specify that their primary objective is the reduction and eventual eradication of poverty. Moreover, development objectives are to be mainstreamed across EU policies which are likely to affect developing countries. Development cooperation is therefore both the subject of human rights mainstreaming and the object of mainstreaming of other policies. Articles 208–211 TFEU also enshrine the competences of the EU in development cooperation. These are de-cisively shared with the Member States. It should be mentioned though that the conclusion of the Cotonou Agreement is based on Article 217 TFEU (competence to conclude associ-ation agreement) which must therefore be seen as a *de facto* complementary power for the purposes of development cooperation.

---

[49] Bossuyt, Rocca, and Lein, 'Political Dialogue on Human Rights under Article 8 of the Cotonou Agreement' (n 47) 12–14.

[50] Joint declaration by the Council and the representatives of the governments of the Member States meeting within the Council, the European Parliament and the Commission on the development policy of the European Union entitled 'The European Consensus' [2006] OJ C46/40.

[51] See Ch 9.

Consolidated version of the Treaty on the Functioning of the European Union [2012] OJ C326/47

Article 208

1. Union policy in the field of development cooperation shall be conducted **within the framework of the principles and objectives of the Union's external action.** The Union's development cooperation policy and that of the Member States **complement and reinforce each other.**

Union development cooperation policy shall have as its **primary objective the reduction and, in the long term, the eradication of poverty. The Union shall take account of the objectives of development cooperation in the policies that it implements which are likely to affect developing countries.**

2. The Union and the Member States shall **comply with the commitments and take account of the objectives they have approved in the context of the United Nations** and other competent international organisations.

Article 209

1. The European Parliament and the Council, acting in accordance with the ordinary legislative procedure, shall adopt the **measures necessary for the implementation of development cooperation policy,** which may relate to multiannual cooperation programmes with developing countries or programmes with a thematic approach.
2. The Union may **conclude with third countries and competent international organisations any agreement** helping to achieve the objectives referred to in Article 21 of the Treaty on European Union and in Article 208 of this Treaty.
   The first subparagraph shall be without prejudice to Member States' competence to negotiate in international bodies and to conclude agreements.
3. The European Investment Bank shall contribute, under the terms laid down in its Statute, to the implementation of the measures referred to in paragraph 1.

Article 210

1. In order to **promote the complementarity and efficiency of their action, the Union and the Member States shall coordinate their policies on development cooperation** and shall consult each other on their aid programmes, including in international organisations and during international conferences. They may undertake joint action. Member States shall contribute if necessary to the implementation of Union aid programmes.

In the wake of the Lisbon revision, the EU continued to introduce operational and strategic reforms to live up to the now-strengthened human rights commitments. The 2011 Thematic Evaluation of EU human rights support noted that human rights had traditionally been conceptualized as the prerogative of a dedicated stream of work (eg on democratic governance), which operated in parallel with other thematic or geographic units. This so-called ghetto-ization of human rights was deemed to have had four implications reducing the effectiveness of EU human rights promotion. First, while Commission staff could see the value of human rights, they had difficulties integrating human rights considerations or principles in their day-to-day development work. Second, human rights dialogues with third countries were perceived to be largely disconnected from other trade, development, or foreign policy processes vis-à-vis the same country or region. Third, dedicated human rights units would receive ample responsibilities but lacked the political backing or resources required to make them operational. Fourth, with regard to the Commission's financial instruments, the evaluation found that, by relying exclusively on dedicated thematic instruments, the potential leverage of geographic instruments or other incentive mechanisms within the broader framework of EU external action (including trade) would remain untapped.

As discussed in Chapter 9, the most important human rights policy development during the Lisbon era has been the adoption of the Strategic Framework on Human Rights and Democracy and a corresponding Action Plan to put it into practice. For development policy in particular, the Strategic Framework notes that 'a human rights based approach will be used to ensure that the EU strengthens its efforts to assist partner countries in implementing their international human rights obligations'.[52] More broadly, concerning the EU's overall relations with third countries, the Strategic Framework supported the creation of country human rights strategies, signalling a move toward more country-specific approaches, away from one-size-fits-all blueprints.[53] The second Action Plan (2015–2019) again reiterated the commitment to implement a rights based approach to development 'into all EU development instruments and activities', in order to ensure an effective use and best interplay of all relevant EU policies, tools, and financing instruments, and to foster a more comprehensive and active approach to support economic, social, and cultural rights in the EU's external policy 'including in its programming of external assistance'. Such an interlinked nature of the EU's development policy is underpinned by judicial decisions interpreting the notion of development cooperation broadly when it comes to agreements with third countries which typically cover more than just one dimension of international relations. In a case concerning the Framework Agreement on Partnership and Cooperation between the European Union and the Republic of the Philippines, the Court of Justice of the European Union (CJEU) found that the inclusion of provisions on transport, environment, and migration was linked to the objective of fostering development cooperation.

Judgment of 11 June 2014, *European Commission v Council of the European Union*, C-377/12, ECLI:EU:C:2014:1903

36. According to Article 208(1) TFEU, European Union policy in the field of development cooperation is to be conducted within the framework of the principles and objectives—as resulting from Article 21 TEU—of the European Union's external action. The primary objective of that policy is the reduction and, in the long term, the eradication of poverty and the European Union must take account of the objectives of development cooperation in the policies that it implements which are likely to affect developing countries. For implementation of that policy, Article 209 TFEU, upon which, inter alia, the contested decision is founded, provides in particular, in paragraph 2, that the European Union may conclude with third countries

---

[52] Council of the European Union, 'Human Rights and Democracy: EU Strategic Framework and Action Plan', 11855/12, 25 June 2012.
[53] Ibid.

and competent international organisations any agreement helping to achieve the objectives referred to in Article 21 TEU and Article 208 TFEU.

37. It follows that **European Union policy in the field of development cooperation is not limited to measures directly aimed at the eradication of poverty, but also pursues the objectives referred to in Article 21(2) TEU,** such as the objective, set out in Article 21(2)(d), of fostering the sustainable economic, social and environmental development of developing countries, with the primary aim of eradicating poverty.

51. The **Framework Agreement itself displays a link between,** on the one hand, the cooperation that it aims to establish regarding **migration, transport and the environment** and, on the other, the objectives of **development cooperation.**

In light of the Lisbon Treaty changes and the adoption of the UN Sustainable Development Goals (SDGs) in 2015, EU Member States agreed on a New European Consensus on Development in June 2017[54] which effectively replaced the 2006 Consensus. The evolution from 'a strengthened approach to mainstreaming' in the previous Consensus towards a 'rights-based approach to development cooperation' can clearly be discerned from the recent document.[55] The SDGs are prominently featured throughout the New Consensus and the emphasis is put on the principle of leaving no-one behind.

B. Aid sanctions and political conditionality

Sanctioning aid recipients on account of severe human rights violations arguably constitutes the EU's most visible and long-standing approach to integrating human rights considerations in development policy. While the use of political conditionality has expanded and diversified over the years—now covering policies such as (pre-)accession and trade—sanctioning and conditionality specific to development cooperation stems primarily from two sources: the mechanism outlined in Article 96 of the Cotonou Agreement and the 'strings' attached to financial support from the EU budget.

The EU's use of aid sanctions goes back as far as 1977, when the then European Economic Community saw the need to suspend its aid allocations for the first time, albeit without a proper legal basis, in reaction to atrocities committed by the Idi Amin Dada regime in Uganda. Nevertheless, it was not until 1995, when the Lomé IV bis Convention entered into force, that the EU systematically included conditionality clauses, the so-called essential elements provisions, in most of its cooperation or association agreements. The most prominent example of this development is the Cotonou Agreement between the EU and the ACP Group. As already mentioned, Article 9 of the Cotonou Agreement identifies human rights, democratic principles, and the rule of law as essential elements underpinning the treaty. In case one of the parties considers that one or more of these essential elements have been violated, a three-step process can be initiated, as described under Article 96.[56]

---

[54] Joint statement by the Council and the representatives of the governments of the Member States meeting within the Council, the European Parliament and the Commission, New European Consensus on Development, 'Our World, Our Dignity, Our future' [2017] OJ C210/1.

[55] Ibid, para 16. See above for the differences and similarities between the two approaches.

[56] A separate, rarely used provision relating to serious cases of corruption is outlined in Article 97 of the Cotonou Agreement.

Partnership agreement between the members of the African, Caribbean and Pacific Group of States of the one part, and the European Community and its Member States, of the other part, signed in Cotonou on 23 June 2000 [2000] OJ L317/3 (as amended as of June 2018)

Article 96

Essential elements: consultation procedure and appropriate measures as regards human rights, democratic principles and the rule of law

1. Within the meaning of this Article, the term 'Party' refers to the Community and the Member States of the European Union, of the one part, and each ACP State, of the other part.

   1a. Both Parties agree to **exhaust all possible options for dialogue under Article 8**, except in cases of special urgency, prior to commencement of the consultations referred to in paragraph 2(a) of this Article.

2. (a) If, despite the political dialogue on the essential elements as provided for under Article 8 and paragraph 1a of this Article, a Party considers that the other Party fails to fulfil an obligation stemming from respect for human rights, democratic principles and the rule of law referred to in Article 9(2), it shall, except in cases of special urgency, **supply the other Party and the Council of Ministers with the relevant information required for a thorough examination of the situation** with a view to seeking a solution acceptable to the Parties. To this end, it shall invite the other Party to **hold consultations** that focus on the measures taken or to be taken by the Party concerned to remedy the situation in accordance with Annex VII.

The consultations shall be conducted at the level and in the form considered most appropriate for finding a solution.

The consultations shall begin no later than 30 days after the invitation and shall continue for a period established by mutual agreement, depending on the nature and gravity of the violation. **In no case shall the dialogue under the consultations procedure last longer than 120 days.**

If the consultations do not lead to a solution acceptable to both Parties, if consultation is refused or in cases of special urgency, appropriate measures may be taken. These measures shall be revoked as soon as the reasons for taking them no longer prevail.

(b) The term 'cases of special urgency' shall refer to **exceptional cases of particularly serious and flagrant violation of one of the essential elements** referred to in paragraph 2 of Article 9, that require an immediate reaction.

The Party resorting to the special urgency procedure shall inform the other Party and the Council of Ministers separately of the fact unless it does not have time to do so.

(c) The 'appropriate measures' referred to in this Article are measures taken in accordance with **international law, and proportional to the violation.** In the selection of these measures, **priority must be given to those which least disrupt** the application of this agreement. It is understood that suspension would be a measure of last resort.

If measures are taken in cases of special urgency, they shall be immediately notified to the other Party and the Council of Ministers. At the request of the Party concerned, consultations may then be called in order to examine the situation thoroughly and, if possible, find solutions. These consultations shall be conducted according to the arrangements set out in the second and third subparagraphs of paragraph (a).

First, except in situations of special urgency, Article 96 requires the country under scrutiny to provide the other party, as well as the ACP Council of Ministers, all the relevant information to examine the situation. Second, 'consultations' are organized to discuss the measures taken or to be taken by the party concerned to remedy the situation at hand. If, however, these consultations—which should take no longer than 120 days—do not lead to a satisfactory solution to both parties, or if consultations were to be refused, 'appropriate measures' are warranted, including, as a measure of last resort, the suspension of the agreement, which would typically also entail the suspension of development aid granted under it.

In practice, the EU's use of the essential elements clauses under Cotonou is broadly considered to be both inconsistent and ineffective in terms of addressing systemic human rights concerns. With regard to the former, negative aid conditionality has only been applied to poor and strategically less important ACP countries. Moreover, punitive action has exclusively been taken in cases of coup d'état or election fraud. Indeed, a self-standing violation of human rights in and by itself—let alone a systemic deterioration—has never constituted sufficient cause for aid sanctions.[57] Furthermore, similar violations have sometimes received significantly different responses from the EU, evoking criticism about the use of 'double standards'. The reasons behind these inconsistencies are roughly twofold. On the one hand, diverging strategic interests and/or historical ties have led EU Member States to prioritize or protect their sphere of influence with less regard for normative concerns. Second, triggering Article 96 consultations is perceived to be a rather confrontational approach compared to silent diplomacy (or doing nothing). As such, the costs of imposing sanctions must be weighed against the potential benefits, which are often meagre. Expectations about the relative effectiveness of punitive measures have to be taken into account, including the domestic position of the government of the country concerned and in particular the EU's overall leverage over it.[58] Finally, the effectiveness of aid suspensions under Article 96 is believed to be heavily context-specific, and in practice, the results in terms of providing lasting solutions or reversing violations are mixed at best. Zimelis identified several reasons for this lack of effectiveness, including the (lack of) aid dependency and overall leverage of the EU, as well as the nature of the regime at hand.[59] Other determinants of the perceived effectiveness of EU aid sanctions include, *inter alia*, an optimal mix of carrot and stick measures, coherence among the EU's different foreign policies (notably trade), as well as coherence between the EU's and Member States' action, involvement of powerful regional and continental actors

---

[57] C Portela, *European Union Sanctions and Foreign Policy: When and Why Do They Work?* (Routledge 2010) 142–43.

[58] See also Section 10.4.C Human rights clauses in EU trade agreements. Del Biondo, 'EU Aid Conditionality' (n 24); Del Biondo, 'Norms, Self-Interest and Effectiveness' (n 24).

[59] A Zimelis, 'Conditionality and the EU-ACP Partnership: A misguided Approach to Development?' (2011) 46 Australian Journal of Political Science 389, 402–03.

(including competing donors such as China), continuous political dialogue during and after Article 96 procedures, and a clear identification of the required steps to be taken to redress the situation.[60]

K Del Biondo, 'EU Aid Conditionality in ACP Countries: Explaining Inconsistency in EU Sanctions Practice' (2011) 7 Journal of Contemporary European Research 380

EU negative conditionality is often criticised for its lack of consistency. This article has investigated whether this inconsistency could also be identified in the case of the EU's relations with the group of African, Caribbean and Pacific (ACP) countries. Since the EU uses negative conditionality mainly to punish countries for negative evolutions in the electoral process, the article looked into five countries with questionable electoral records: Ethiopia, Rwanda, Nigeria, Kenya and Chad. Although the EU seems to agree that the elections that took place in the period between 2001-2010 in these countries did not meet international standards, it preferred to use political dialogue instead of punitive conditionality. (...) Security interests seemed to be most important in the economic-ally little important Sub-Saharan African region. More specifically, countries like Nigeria, Ethiopia and Kenya are key partners of the West in the fight against terrorism and in maintaining peace in their respective regions by means of diplomacy and peacekeeping troops. In Rwanda, the democratisation-stability dilemma might play a role, meaning that the EU chooses not to meddle in a country's internal affairs as long as it remains stable. Political-historic interests related to the colonial history of one of the EU Member States play a very large role in Chad and, to a much lesser degree, in Rwanda, but are less important in Kenya and Nigeria, where colonial relations have not impeded diplomatic rifts resulting from discussions about democratisation. Economic interests are a minor explanatory factor in the economically little important Sub-Saharan African region, but do play a role in Nigeria, which is an important oil producer. Apart from traditional ex-planations relating to the EU's interests (...) the EU might face a dilemma in countries that might not be democratic, but are nevertheless developing economically and socially. This thesis is illustrated with the case studies Ethiopia and Rwanda, where high economic growth, substantial progress regarding the Millennium Development Goals and rela-tively good technocratic governance stand in sharp contrast with negative evolutions in the democratic sphere.

In addition to *ex-post* negative conditionality attached to the Cotonou and other agree-ments—and arguably as a result of the latter's limited effectiveness—the EU has since re-cently also started to use its policy framework for budget support as a platform to address governance and human rights issues in partner countries. In 2011 the Commission issued a communication on the 'Future Approach to EU Budget Support to Third Countries'.[61] The

---

[60] IOB, 'The Netherlands and the European Development Fund—Principles and Practices Evaluation of Dutch involvement in EU development cooperation (1998–2012)', Ministry of Foreign Affairs of the Netherlands, 2013, 214.
[61] European Commission, 'The Future Approach to EU Budget Support to Third Countries', COM(2011) 638 final, Brussels, 13 October 2011.

new policy signalled a shift away from the previous technocratic approach, often criticized for its ambivalence to democratic governance conditions in recipient countries, towards a more contractual approach, effectively tying EU budget support more strictly to fundamental values of human rights, democracy and the rule of law. The new policy therefore allows the EU to differentiate its budget support mechanisms, depending on the prevailing political, economic, and social context in the recipient's country, and requires close coordination between the Commission, the European Union External Action Service, and the Member States to maximize effectiveness and leverage.[62] In order to reflect both the new spirit and differentiation of the EU's budget support mechanisms, the new policy identified three different categories of EU budget support contracts, allowing the EU to tailor its support to different country contexts.

First, 'Good Governance and Development Contracts' (GGDC) are general budget support measures allocated directly to the recipient's national budget. They are reserved exclusively for countries where the EU has 'trust and confidence' that state funds will be spent in a manner that respects and contributes to human rights and other fundamental values. Implicitly, therefore, the EU recognizes the partner's country track record on respecting key values when it grants GGDCs. Their aim is to foster domestic accountability and strengthen national control mechanisms, including through supporting public sector reforms, sound financial management, and domestic revenue mobilization. In order to qualify for a GGDC, the partner country concerned needs to pass a political risk assessment which takes into account its commitment to fundamental values such as human rights and democratic governance. Subsequent continuous monitoring throughout implementation allows for a swift response in case of 'slippage, policy reversals and deterioration'.[63]

Second, Sector Reform Contracts (SRC) are used in countries where the conditions do not permit the use of GGDCs. Allocations are therefore tied to a particular sector, based on the partner government's sector strategy, and aim to enhance that government's capacity to deliver specific sectoral objectives, address constraints, or improve service delivery (in particular for the poor). SRCs therefore remain a useful tool for human rights promotion since they can be used as a vector to improve governance and human rights in a given sector. The threshold to qualify for SRCs is less demanding than for GGDCs and assessments of preconditions must carefully balance political considerations against 'the need to serve and protect the population'. Particular care is needed where SRCs are granted for reform agendas concerning sensitive areas, such as the police and judiciary, which strongly affect human rights, the rule of law or democracy.

Third, State Building Contracts (SBC) are designed to help fragile partner countries perform vital state functions and deliver basic services to their populations. Here, a partner government's commitments to fundamental values are 'aspects to be considered, inter alia' in light of the overall policy and security situation, the financial risks, and the potential costs of non-intervention. Essentially, before engaging with fragile or conflict-affected states, the EU takes a forward-looking approach, balancing the developmental costs of inaction against the inherent risks of getting involved.[64]

[62] Ibid, 3; J Faust and others, 'The Future of EU Budget Support: Political Conditions, Differentiation and Coordination', European Think Tanks Group, 2012.
[63] European Commission Directorate-General for Development and Cooperation, 'EuropeAid, Budget Support Guidelines: Programming, Design and Management, A Modern Approach to Budget Support, Tools and Methods Series Working Document', 2012, 27; European Commission, 'The Future Approach' (n 61) 4.
[64] European Commission, 'Budget Support Guidelines' (n 63) 28.

When it comes to determining eligibility for one or the other type of budget support, the Commission applies a case-by-case, dynamic approach using a mix of both internal and external mechanisms and scorecards. The Commission's risk management framework for budget support operations looks at political risks, including risks to human rights, the rule of law, and democracy, macroeconomic risks, developmental risks, public finance management, and corruption. When a country situation deteriorates significantly, and all efforts to address the concern in a mutually satisfactory manner have failed, budget support allocations can be delayed, reduced, reallocated to other aid modalities, or suspended altogether as a measure of last resort.

The 2012 budget support guidelines that followed the 2011 Commission policy Communication have been updated in 2017. The three types of supporting contracts have been renamed, but their scope of application remains largely the same: GGDCs are now called Sustainable Development Goals Contracts, SRCs are now called Sector Reform Performance Contracts, and SBCs are now called State and Resilience Building Contracts. The new guidelines include the EU Enlargement Policy and take into account more recent developments and documents such as the SDGs, the Addis Ababa Action Agenda on Financing for Development, and the 2017 New European Consensus on Development.[65]

C. EU mainstreaming policy

Targeted support for human rights, despite its intrinsic value and necessity, has been criticized for creating the harmful notion that human rights are the exclusive preserve of governance support, separating it from the more 'traditional' aid branches of socio-economic development in non-governance sectors. As such, human rights mainstreaming policies and a rights-based approach have been developed to ensure that human rights considerations are adequately taken into account across the different strands and stages of EU external policy, including development cooperation. The human rights principles, objectives, and tools created for this purpose are discussed at length in Chapter 9; suffice to say that they apply fully to EU development policy. A short comment can be added as regards the use of impact assessments in the development department of the Commission: research on the incorporation of human rights in impact assessment reports published by Directorate-General of International Cooperation and Development (DEVCO) between 2011 and June 2015 identified a variety of ways in which different types of human rights language, generalized or specific, featured in these impact assessments. None of them, however, seemed to have looked into the potential human rights-related issues that may arise from the proposed development policy or regulation.[66]

D. The EU's rights-based approach to development

Similarly to mainstreaming, a human rights-based approach (HRBA) aims to take human rights considerations out of their silo and reposition them from a specialized sub-theme of donors' governance work to the front and centre of the development policy cycle. As

---

[65] European Commission DG International Cooperation and Development, 'DG European Neighbourhood Policy and Enlargement Negotiations, Budget Support Guidelines', September 2017.
[66] Brando and others, 'The Impact of EU Trade and Development Policies on Human Rights' (n 38) 73.

has been the case among most donors, the EU's recent commitments to applying a rights-based approach to development were originally closely linked to its mainstreaming objectives. A first such commitment is to be found in the 2011 Joint Communication on putting 'Human rights and Democracy at the heart of EU external action' which identified HRBA as a working method for mainstreaming human rights and democracy promotion across development policy.[67] The Council subsequently called for EU governance support to feature more prominently in all partnerships and identified a 'Rights-based Approach' (RBA) as one of the means to do so.[68] Beyond policy documents, Article 3(8) of the Regulation establishing the 2014–2020 Development Cooperation Instrument (DCI), commits the EU to promoting RBA when dispensing aid under the DCI. The provision echoes the language of the UN Development Group Common Understanding discussed above.

Regulation (EU) No 233/2014 of the European Parliament and of the Council establishing a financing instrument for development cooperation for the period 2014-2020 [2014] OJ L77/44

Article 3

General principles

8. The Union shall promote effective cooperation with partner countries and regions in line with international best practice. It shall align its support with their national or regional development strategies, reform policies and procedures wherever possible, and support democratic ownership, as well as domestic and mutual accountability. To that end, **it shall promote**:

   (b) **a rights-based approach encompassing all human rights, whether civil and political or economic, social and cultural**, in order to integrate human rights principles in the implementation of this Regulation, to assist partner countries in implementing their international human rights obligations and to **support the right holders**, with a focus on poor and vulnerable groups, **in claiming their rights;**

In order for these commitments to translate into day-to-day practice of EU development cooperation, and in direct follow-up to one of the actions listed in the 2012 Action Plan on Human Rights and Democracy, the Commission issued a 'toolbox' in April 2014 to help Commission staff with 'integrating human rights principles into EU operational activities for development, covering arrangements both at HQ and in the field for the synchronisation of human rights and development activities'.[69] The toolbox describes the EU's understanding

---

[67] European Commission and the High Representative for Foreign Affairs and Security Policy, 'Human Rights at the Heart of EU External Action—Towards a More Effective Approach', COM(2011) 886 final, Brussels, 12 December 2011.

[68] While the UN and most bilateral donors speak of a 'human' rights-based approach, the EU refers to a 'rights-based approach'. Yet, this disappearance of the 'h' should not be understood as a downgrade; on the contrary, it goes beyond the internationally recognized 'human' rights in order to include specific EU commitments to the advancement of other types of rights, including intellectual property rights, basic economic and social delivery rights, as well as sexual and reproductive health and rights.

[69] European Commission, 'Tool-box: A Rights-Based Approach, Encompassing All Human Rights for EU Development Cooperation, Staff Working Document', SWD(2014) 152 final, Brussels, 30 May 2014, 10.

of what an RBA to development implies. Essentially, the RBA as outlined under the toolbox aims to place the human rights dimension into the mainstream in all sectors of EU aid interventions, beyond the traditional spheres of governance and rule of law, into the traditionally more technical areas such as health care, education, food security, energy, and infrastructure. This does not imply a revision of priority areas in favour of governance-related sectors. The RBA offers 'a qualitative methodology to advance the analysis, design and implementation of development programme and projects to better reach target-groups and to strengthen their access to basic services in all sectors of intervention'.

The RBA also redefines development in the sense that it puts forward the accomplishment of human rights as an essential condition and a key catalyst to achieve any development objective, effectively adding human rights fulfilment as a fundamental aspect of the needs analysis to poverty alleviation.[70] In doing so, the RBA ensures that development interventions do not only address symptoms but effectively touch upon the incentive and power structures that form the root causes of governance problems. In addition, the rights narrative alters the understanding of development cooperation from voluntary cooperation to a legal rationale where 'duty bearers' are to uphold certain international treaty standards vis-à-vis 'rights holders'.

Previous donor experiences with HRBA have pointed to several challenges in implementing it. In the context of the EU's RBA, three particularly important concerns have been identified. First, it is questionable how much scope there is for the EU to work more politically in development, as mandated by the RBA. Essentially, the EU's RBA is supposed not only to treat the symptoms of development problems but also to address the power relations and incentive structures that constitute the root causes of development challenges. Applying an RBA throughout the policy and programming cycle of a development intervention implies taking a normative and political stance, notably because it requires analysing inequalities, unjust power relations, discriminatory practices, and, more importantly, the incentive structures that maintain them. Donors, including the EU, find it often difficult to address politics in development cooperation consistently, despite understanding that most development problems are political rather than technical, and that solutions therefore need to be 'locally owned' and necessitate working with and among forces that drive or impede better development outcomes. Making development more political inherently raises questions about the acceptability of foreign intervention in domestic politics and it makes development more susceptible to clashes with other foreign policy interests in the given region or country.

A second concern revolves around the overall institutional support and guidance required to apply a human rights perspective systematically and consistently across different programming stages and organizational units and mechanisms. In order for high-level policy commitments to 'trickle down' and become operational reality throughout the policy and programming cycle, the RBA needs clear and dedicated support from the leadership within the institution and an enabling corporate environment to guide, monitor, and manage its implementation. Based on a discourse analysis of 50 country strategies (2014–2020) under

---

[70] See para 3 of Council of the European Union, 'Council conclusions on a rights-based approach to development cooperation, encompassing all human rights', Brussels, 19 May 2014 (that welcomes the Commission's toolbox in para 2 and resembles what the OECD DAC has previously stated): 'The Council underlines that respect for and protection and fulfilment of human rights is a prerequisite for achieving sustainable development. A rights-based approach to development cooperation can significantly contribute to the realisation of human rights. This approach is premised on human rights principles and standards being both a means for and a goal of effective development cooperation.'

the EU's two main financing instruments for development (EDF and DCI), Lassen and others found that integration of RBA principles overall was limited and inconsistent in programming documents and appears to be even weaker 'downstream' at the level of sector programmes and results-based monitoring frameworks. Moreover, the study found that the incorporation of human rights considerations into sector programmes appears to be strongly biased towards governance topics such as democratization and justice, while it is weakest in economic sectors such as energy, infrastructure, and agriculture; the result is an overall neglect of economic, social, and cultural rights.[71]

A third and final consideration revolves around DG DEVCO's institutional culture and its readiness to comply with the objectives and principles of RBA in monitoring and evaluation. With regard to the latter, the UN Development Group Common Understanding recommends that development interventions should be geared towards assessing both the results of an intervention and the process by which it occurs. Such a focus on processes, rather than merely outputs, should help verify whether marginalized and vulnerable groups have been involved and participated in the development. Since human rights improvements may only be visible in the long term, making sure that the process of a development intervention is human rights-friendly is seen as a good way to evaluate the long-term effectiveness and sustainability of the intervention.[72] However, the evaluation stage of an aid intervention is where tension between the RBA's normative narrative and the traditional, output-based way of development programming, becomes most apparent: donors are often seen as preferring 'what is measurable' rather than 'what matters'.[73] A process-oriented, inclusive approach to evaluation makes it more complex and time-consuming and would require a fundamental overhaul in DG DEVCO's evaluation culture. Time and resource constraints have, moreover, become increasingly stringent and the prevailing logic of 'value for money' has led to evaluation models with a narrow focus on spending and tracing financial flows. Implementing the policy commitment to the RBA properly would therefore be likely to require a change in the Commission's bureaucratic culture.

---

[71] EM Lassen and others, 'Report on In-depth Studies of Selected Factors which Enable or Hinder the Protection of Human Rights in the Context of Globalisation' (2015) FRAME Deliverable 2.2, 95–112 <www.fp7-frame.eu/wp-content/uploads/2017/03/Deliverable-2.2.pdf> accessed 14 August 2020.

[72] UN HABITAT, 'HRBA Monitoring and Evaluation', Briefing Note, 9 December 2014.

[73] Brando and others, 'The Impact of EU Trade and Development Policies on Human Rights' (n 38) 51.

Index

Tables and figures are indicated by *t* and *f* following the page number, and footnotes by n. Case names are cited where the cases are discussed in detail. For a complete list of citations *see* the Table of Cases.